# Table of Contents

## 1

### Introducing Hardware . . . . . . . . . . . . .1

## 2

### Introducing Operating Systems . . . . . . .31

## 3

### PC Repair Fundamentals . . . . . . . . . . . .79

# CompTIA A+ 2006
# In Depth

## Jean Andrews, Ph.D.

THOMSON

COURSE TECHNOLOGY

Professional ■ Technical ■ Reference

Australia • Canada • Mexico • Singapore • Spain • United Kingdom • United States

**CompTIA A+ 2006 In Depth**
is published by Thomson Course
Technology PTR

**Executive Editor:**
Steve Helba

**Managing Editor:**
Larry Main

**Acquisitions Editors:**
Nick Lombardi, Megan Belanger

**Senior Product Manager:**
Michelle Ruelos Cannistraci

**Developmental Editor:**
Jill Batistick

**Marketing Manager:**
Mark Hughes

**Editorial Assistant:**
Jessica Reed

**Copy Editor:**
Karen Annett

**Proofreaders:**
Christine Clark, Karen A. Gill

**Manufacturing Coordinator:**
Justin Palmeiro

**Content Project Managers:**
Danielle Chouhan, Karen A. Gill

**Quality Assurance:**
Jeff Schwartz

**Cover Design:**
Mike Tanamachi

**Interior Design:**
Betsy Young

**Compositor:**
William Hartman

## 18

## PCs on the Internet . . . . . . . . . . . . . .881

## 19

## Securing Your PC and LAN . . . . . . . . .953

## 20

## Notebooks, Tablet PCs, and PDAs . . . .1013

# CompTIA A+ Essentials 2006 Examination Objectives

## DOMAIN 1 PERSONAL COMPUTER COMPONENTS

### 1.1 Identify the fundamental principles of using personal computers

| OBJECTIVES | CHAPTERS |
|---|---|
| Identify the names, purposes, and characteristics of storage devices | |
| ◢ FDD | 1, 8 |
| ◢ HDD | 1, 8 |
| ◢ CD/DVD/RW (e.g., drive speeds, media types) | 1, 10 |
| ◢ Removable storage (e.g., tape drive, solid state such as thumb drives, flash and SD cards, USB, external CD-RW, and hard drive) | 8, 9, 10 |
| Identify the names, purposes, and characteristics of motherboards | |
| ◢ Form Factor (e.g., ATX/BTX, microATX/NLX) | 4, 6 |
| ◢ Components | |
|   ◢ Integrated I/Os (e.g., sound, video, USB, serial, IEEE 1394/ FireWire, parallel, NIC, modem) | 1, 6, 9, 10 |
|   ◢ Memory slots (e.g., RIMM, DIMM) | 1, 6, 7, 20 |
|   ◢ Processor sockets | 5, 6 |
|   ◢ External cache memory | 1, 5 |
|   ◢ Bus architecture | 1, 5, 6, 9 |
|   ◢ Bus slots (e.g., PCI, AGP, PCIE, AMR, CNR) | 1, 6, 9 |
|   ◢ EIDE/PATA | 1, 8 |
|   ◢ SATA | 1, 8 |
|   ◢ SCSI Technology | 8 |
| ◢ Chipsets | 1, 5, 6 |
| ◢ BIOS/CMOS/Firmware | 1, 2, 3, 6, 11, 19 |
| ◢ Riser card/daughter board | 4, 6 |
| Identify the names, purposes, and characteristics of power supplies; for example, AC adapter, ATX, proprietary, voltage | 4, 6 |
| Identify the names, purposes, and characteristics of processors/CPUs | |
| ◢ CPU chips (e.g., AMD, Intel) | 1, 5 |
| ◢ CPU technologies | |
|   ◢ Hyperthreading | 5, 10 |
|   ◢ Dual core | 5, 10 |
|   ◢ Throttling | 5, 6, 12 |
|   ◢ Micro code (MMX) | 5, 10 |
|   ◢ Overclocking | 5, 6 |
|   ◢ Cache | 5 |
|   ◢ VRM | 5 |
|   ◢ Speed (real vs. actual) | 5 |
|   ◢ 32 vs. 64 bit | 5 |

| | |
|---|---|
| Identify the names, purposes, and characteristics of memory | |
| ◢ Types of memory (e.g., DRAM, SRAM, SDRAM, DDR/DDR2, RAMBUS) | 1, 7, 20 |
| ◢ Operational characteristics | |
| ◢ Memory chips (8, 16, 32) | 7 |
| ◢ Parity vs. non-parity | 6, 7 |
| ◢ ECC vs. non-ECC | 7 |
| ◢ Single-sided vs. double-sided | 7 |
| Identify the names, purposes, and characteristics of display devices; for example, projectors, CRT, and LCD | |
| ◢ Connector types (e.g., VGA, DVI/HDMi, S-Video, Component/RGB) | 1, 9 |
| ◢ Settings (e.g., V-hold, refresh rate, resolution) | 9 |
| Identify the names, purposes, and characteristics of input devices; for example, mouse, keyboard, bar code reader, multimedia (e.g., Web and digital cameras, MIDI, microphones), biometric devices, touch screen | 1, 9, 19 |
| Identify the names, purposes, and characteristics of adapter cards | |
| ◢ Video, including PCI/PCI-E and AGP | 9 |
| ◢ Multimedia | 10 |
| ◢ I/O (SCSI, serial, USB, parallel) | 9 |
| ◢ Communications, including network and modem | 9, 17 |
| Identify the names, purposes, and characteristics of ports and cables; for example, USB 1.1 and 2.0, parallel, serial, IEEE 1394/FireWire, RJ-45 and RJ-11, PS2/MINI-DIN, centronics (e.g., mini, 36), multimedia (e.g., 1/8 connector, MIDI, COAX, SPDIF) | 1, 6, 9, 10 |
| Identify the names, purposes, and characteristics of cooling systems; for example, heat sinks, CPU and case fans, liquid cooling systems, thermal compound | 4, 5 |

**1.2 Install, configure, optimize, and upgrade personal computer components**

| OBJECTIVES | CHAPTERS |
|---|---|
| Add, remove, and configure internal and external storage devices | |
| ◢ Drive preparation of internal storage devices, including format/file systems and imaging technology | 8, 10, 12, 20 |
| Install display devices | 2, 9, 20 |
| Add, remove, and configure basic input and multimedia devices | 3, 9, 10, 20 |

**1.3 Identify tools, diagnostic procedures, and troubleshooting techniques for personal computer components**

| OBJECTIVES | CHAPTERS |
|---|---|
| Recognize the basic aspects of troubleshooting theory; for example, | |
| ◢ Perform backups before making changes | 3, 8, 12, 13, 14, 20, 22 |
| ◢ Assess a problem systematically, and divide large problems into smaller components to be analyzed individually | 3, 8, 9, 13, 14, 21, 22 |
| ◢ Verify even the obvious, determine whether the problem is something simple, and make no assumptions | 3, 8, 9, 14, 21, 22 |

| | |
|---|---|
| ◢ Research ideas and establish priorities | 3, 8, 9, 14, 21, 22 |
| ◢ Document findings, actions and outcomes | 3, 9, 13, 21, 22 |

| Identify and apply basic diagnostic procedures and troubleshooting techniques; for example, | |
|---|---|
| ◢ Identify the problem, including questioning user and identifying user changes to computer | 3, 8, 9, 13, 14, 20, 21, 22 |
| ◢ Analyze the problem, including potential causes, and make an initial determination of software and/or hardware problem | 3, 8, 9, 13, 14, 20, 21, 22 |
| ◢ Test related components, including inspection, connections, hardware/software configurations, Device Manager, and consult vendor documentation | 3, 8, 9, 12 13, 14, 20, 21, 22 |
| ◢ Evaluate results and take additional steps if needed, such as consultation, use of alternate resources, manuals | 3, 8, 9, 13, 14, 20, 21, 22 |
| ◢ Document activities and outcomes | 3, 9, 13, 20, 21, 22 |

| | |
|---|---|
| Recognize and isolate issues with display, power, basic input devices, storage, memory, thermal, POST errors (e.g., BIOS, hardware) | 3, 4, 5, 6, 7, 8, 9, 20, 21 |

| Apply basic troubleshooting techniques to check for problems (e.g., thermal issues, error codes, power, connections including cables and/or pins, compatibility, functionality, software/drivers) with components; for example, | |
|---|---|
| ◢ Motherboards | 3, 5, 6, 20 |
| ◢ Power supply | 3, 4, 6, 20 |
| ◢ Processor/CPUs | 3, 5, 6 |
| ◢ Memory | 3, 7, 20 |
| ◢ Display devices | 2, 3, 9, 20 |
| ◢ Input devices | 3, 9, 20 |
| ◢ Adapter cards | 3, 9, 17 |

| | |
|---|---|
| Recognize the names, purposes, characteristics, and appropriate application of tools; for example, BIOS, self-test, hard drive self-test, and software diagnostic test | 1, 3, 6, 7, 8, 9, 20, 21 |

**1.4**  **Perform preventive maintenance on personal computer components**

| OBJECTIVES | CHAPTERS |
|---|---|
| Identify and apply basic aspects of preventive maintenance theory; for example, | |
| ◢ Visual/audio inspection | 3, 9, 20, 21 |
| ◢ Driver/firmware updates | 6, 9, 19, 20, 21 |
| ◢ Scheduling preventive maintenance | 3, 19, 20, 21 |
| ◢ Use of appropriate repair tools and cleaning materials | 3, 9, 10, 20, 21 |
| ◢ Ensuring proper environment | 3, 9, 20, 21 |
| Identify and apply common preventive maintenance techniques for devices, such as input devices and batteries | 3, 9, 20, 21 |

## DOMAIN 2 LAPTOPS AND PORTABLE DEVICES

2.1    Identify the fundamental principles of using laptops and portable devices

| OBJECTIVES | CHAPTERS |
|---|---|
| Identify names, purposes, and characteristics of laptop-specific: | |
| ◢ Form factors, such as memory and hard drives | 7, 20 |
| ◢ Peripherals (e.g., docking station, port replicator, and media/accessory bay) | 20 |
| ◢ Expansion slots (e.g., PCMCIA I, II, and III card and express bus) | 20 |
| ◢ Ports (e.g., mini PCI slot) | 20 |
| ◢ Communication connections (e.g., Bluetooth, infrared, cellular WAN, Ethernet) | 9, 17, 20 |
| ◢ Power and electrical input devices (e.g., auto-switching and fixed-input power supplies, batteries) | 20 |
| ◢ LCD technologies (e.g., active and passive matrix, resolution such as XGA, SXGA+ , UXGA, WUXGA, contrast radio, native resolution) | 9 |
| ◢ Input devices (e.g., stylus/digitizer, function (Fn) keys, and pointing devices such as touch pad, point stick/track point) | 9 |
| Identify and distinguish between mobile and desktop motherboards and processors, including throttling, power management, and WiFi | 17, 20 |

2.2    Install, configure, optimize, and upgrade laptops and portable devices

| OBJECTIVES | CHAPTERS |
|---|---|
| Configure power management | |
| ◢ Identify the features of BIOS-ACPI | 4, 20 |
| ◢ Identify the difference between suspend, hibernate, and standby | 4, 20 |
| Demonstrate safe removal of laptop-specific hardware, such as peripherals, hot-swappable devices, and non-hot-swappable devices | 9, 20 |

2.3    Identify tools, basic diagnostic procedures, and troubleshooting techniques for laptops and portable devices

| OBJECTIVES | CHAPTERS |
|---|---|
| Use procedures and techniques to diagnose power conditions, video, keyboard, pointer, and wireless card issues; for example, | 20 |
| ◢ Verify AC power (e.g., LEDs, swap AC adapter) | 20 |
| ◢ Verify DC power | 20 |
| ◢ Remove unneeded peripherals | 20 |
| ◢ Plug in external monitor | 9, 20 |
| ◢ Toggle Fn keys | 9, 20 |
| ◢ Check LCD cutoff switch | 9, 20 |
| ◢ Verify backlight functionality and pixilation | 9, 20 |
| ◢ Stylus issues (e.g., digitizer problems) | 9, 20 |
| ◢ Unique laptop keypad issues | 9, 20 |
| ◢ Antenna wires | 17, 20 |

2.4    Perform preventive maintenance on laptops and portable devices

| OBJECTIVES | CHAPTERS |
| --- | --- |
| Identify and apply common preventive maintenance techniques for laptops and portable devices; for example, cooling devices, hardware and video cleaning materials, operating environments including temperature and air quality, storage, transportation, and shipping | 3, 20 |

## DOMAIN 3  OPERATING SYSTEMS—UNLESS OTHERWISE NOTED, OPERATING SYSTEMS REFERRED TO WITHIN INCLUDE MICROSOFT WINDOWS 2000, XP PROFESSIONAL, XP HOME, AND MEDIA CENTER

3.1    Identify the fundamentals of using operating systems

| OBJECTIVES | CHAPTERS |
| --- | --- |
| Identify differences between operating systems (e.g., Mac, Windows, Linux) and describe operating system revision levels, including GUI, system requirements, application and hardware compatibility | 2 |
| Identify names, purposes, and characteristics of the primary operating system components, including registry, virtual memory, and file system | 2, 11, 12, 13 |
| Describe features of operating system interfaces; for example, | |
| ▲ Windows Explorer | 2, 13 |
| ▲ My Computer | 2, 13 |
| ▲ Control Panel | 2, 13 |
| ▲ Command Prompt | 2, 13 |
| ▲ My Network Places | 17, 21 |
| ▲ Taskbar/systray | 2, 13, 21 |
| ▲ Start menu | 2, 11, 21 |
| Identify the names, locations, purposes, and characteristics of operating system files; for example, | |
| ▲ Boot.ini | 14 |
| ▲ Ntldr | 14 |
| ▲ Ntdetect.com | 14 |
| ▲ Ntbootdd.sys | 14 |
| ▲ Registry data files | 12, 14 |
| Identify concepts and procedures for creating, viewing, managing disks, directories, and files in operating systems; for example, | |
| ▲ Disks (e.g., active, primary, extended, and logical partitions) | 2, 11, 12 |
| ▲ File systems (e.g., FAT32, NTFS) | 2, 11, 12, 13 |
| ▲ Directory structures (e.g., create folders, navigate directory structures) | 2, 13 |
| ▲ Files (e.g., creation, extensions, attributes, permissions) | 2, 13, 14 |

3.2    Install, configure, optimize, and upgrade operating systems—references to upgrading from Windows 95 and NT may be made

| OBJECTIVES | CHAPTERS |
| --- | --- |
| Identify procedures for installing operating systems, including: | |
| ▲ Verification of hardware compatibility and minimum requirements | 11, 20 |
| ▲ Installation methods (e.g., boot media such as CD, floppy, or USB, network installation, drive imaging) | 11, 20 |

| | |
|---|---|
| ◢ Operating system installation options (e.g., attended/ unattended, file system type, network configuration) | 11 |
| ◢ Disk preparation order (e.g., start installation, partition and format drive) | 11, 12 |
| ◢ Device driver configuration (e.g., install and upload device drivers) | 9, 11, 12 |
| ◢ Verification of installation | 9, 11, 12 |
| Identify procedures for upgrading operating systems, including: | |
| ◢ Upgrade considerations (e.g., hardware, application, and/or network compatibility) | 11 |
| ◢ Implementation (e.g., back up data, install additional Windows components) | 11 |
| Install/add a device, including loading, adding device drivers, and required software, including: | 12 |
| ◢ Determine whether permissions are adequate for performing the task | 9, 12, 13 |
| ◢ Device driver installation (e.g., automated and/or manual search and installation of device drivers) | 9, 12, 20, 21 |
| ◢ Using unsigned drivers (e.g., driver signing) | 9, 12, 17 |
| ◢ Verify installation of the driver (e.g., Device Manager and functionality) | 9, 12, 21 |
| Identify procedures and utilities used to optimize operating systems, for example, virtual memory, hard drives, temporary files, service, startup, and applications | 12, 13, 14 |

3.3 **Identify tools, diagnostic procedures, and troubleshooting techniques for operating systems**

| OBJECTIVES | CHAPTERS |
|---|---|
| Identify basic boot sequences, methods, and utilities for recovering operating systems | |
| ◢ Boot methods (e.g., safe mode, recovery console, boot to restore point) | 14, 19, 20 |
| ◢ Automated System Recovery (ASR) (e.g., Emergency Repair Disk (ERD)) | 12, 14 |
| Identify and apply diagnostic procedures and troubleshooting techniques; for example, | |
| ◢ Identify the problem by questioning user and identifying user changes to computer | 12, 13, 14, 22 |
| ◢ Analyze problem, including potential causes and initial determination of software and/or hardware problem | 12, 13, 14, 19 |
| ◢ Test related components, including connections, hardware/ software configurations, Device Manager, and consulting vendor documentation | 12, 13, 14, 22 |
| ◢ Evaluate results and take additional steps if needed, such as consultation, alternate resources, and manuals | 12, 13, 14, 19, 22 |
| ◢ Document activities and outcomes | 12, 13, 14, 19, 22 |
| Recognize and resolve common operational issues, such as blue screen; system lock-up; input/output device; application install, start, or load; and Windows-specific printing problems (e.g., print spool stalled, incorrect/incompatible driver for printer) | 13, 14, 19, 21 |
| Explain common error messages and codes; for example, | |
| ◢ Boot (e.g., invalid boot disk, inaccessible boot drive, missing NTLDR) | 3, 8, 14 |

| | |
|---|---|
| ◢ Startup (e.g., device/service failed to start, device/program in registry not found) | 13, 14, 19 |
| ◢ Event Viewer | 12, 13, 19 |
| ◢ Registry | 12, 19 |
| ◢ Windows reporting | 12 |

| Identify the names, locations, purposes, and characteristics of operating system utilities; for example, | |
|---|---|
| ◢ Disk management tools (e.g., Defrag, Ntbackup, Chkdsk, Format) | 12, 13, 14, 17 |
| ◢ System management tools (e.g., Device and Task Manager, Msconfig.exe) | 12, 14 |
| ◢ File management tools (e.g., Windows Explorer, Attrib.exe) | 2, 13, 19 |

**3.4    Perform preventive maintenance on operating systems**

| OBJECTIVES | CHAPTERS |
|---|---|
| Describe common utilities for performing preventive maintenance on operating systems; for example, software and Windows updates (e.g., service packs), scheduled backups/restore, restore points | 11, 12, 13, 19 |

## DOMAIN 4  PRINTERS AND SCANNERS

**4.1    Identify the fundamental principles of using printers and scanners**

| OBJECTIVES | CHAPTERS |
|---|---|
| Identify differences between types of printer and scanner technologies (e.g., laser, ink-jet, thermal, solid ink, impact) | 21 |
| Identify names, purposes, and characteristics of printer and scanner components (e.g., memory, driver, firmware) and consumables (e.g., toner, ink cartridge, paper) | 21 |
| Identify the names, purposes, and characteristics of interfaces used by printers and scanners, including port and cable types; for example, | |
| ◢ Parallel | 1, 9, 21 |
| ◢ Network (e.g., NIC, print servers) | 17, 21 |
| ◢ USB | 1, 9, 21 |
| ◢ Serial | 9, 21 |
| ◢ IEEE 1394/FireWire | 9, 21 |
| ◢ Wireless (e.g., Bluetooth, 802.11, infrared) | 9, 21 |
| ◢ SCSI | 8, 21 |

**4.2    Identify basic concepts of installing, configuring, optimizing, and upgrading printers and scanners**

| OBJECTIVES | CHAPTERS |
|---|---|
| Install and configure printers/scanners | |
| ◢ Power and connect the device using the local or network port | 21 |
| ◢ Install and update the device driver and calibrate the device | 21 |
| ◢ Configure options and default settings | 21 |
| ◢ Print a test page | 21 |
| Optimize printer performance; for example, printer settings such as tray switching, print spool settings, device calibration, media types, and paper orientation | 21 |

4.3   Identify tools, diagnostic procedures, and troubleshooting techniques for printers and scanners

| OBJECTIVES | CHAPTERS |
|---|---|
| Gather information about printer/scanner problems | |
| ◢ Identify symptom | 21 |
| ◢ Review device error codes, computer error messages, and history (e.g., event log, user reports) | 21 |
| ◢ Print or scan a test page | 21 |
| ◢ Use appropriate generic or vendor-specific diagnostic tools, including Web-based utilities | 21 |
| Review and analyze collected data | |
| ◢ Establish probable causes | 21 |
| ◢ Review service documentation | 21 |
| ◢ Review knowledge base and define and isolate the problem (e.g., software vs. hardware, driver, connectivity, printer) | 21 |
| Identify solutions to identified printer/scanner problems | |
| ◢ Define specific cause and apply fix | 21 |
| ◢ Replace consumables as needed | 21 |
| ◢ Verify functionality and get user acceptance of problem fix | 21 |

## DOMAIN 5   NETWORKS

5.1   Identify the fundamental principles of networks

| OBJECTIVES | CHAPTERS |
|---|---|
| Describe basic networking concepts | |
| ◢ Addressing | 17, 18 |
| ◢ Bandwidth | 17, 18 |
| ◢ Status indicators | 17 |
| ◢ Protocols (e.g., TCP/IP, including IP, classful subnet, IPX/SPX, including NWLink, NetBEUI/NetBIOS) | 17, 18 |
| ◢ Full-duplex, half-duplex | 17 |
| ◢ Cabling (e.g., twisted pair, coaxial cable, fiber optic, RS-232) | 17 |
| ◢ Networking models, including peer-to-peer and client/server | 11, 17 |
| Identify names, purposes, and characteristics of the common network cables | |
| ◢ Plenum/PVC | 17 |
| ◢ UTP (e.g., CAT-3, CAT-5/5-e, CAT-6) | 17 |
| ◢ STP | 17 |
| ◢ Fiber (e.g., single- and multi-mode) | 17 |
| Identify names, purposes, and characteristics of network cables (e.g., RJ-45 and RJ-11, ST/SC/LC, USB, IEEE 1394/FireWire) | 9, 17 |
| Identify names, purposes, and characteristics (e.g., definition, speed, and connections) of technologies for establishing connectivity; for example, | |
| ◢ LAN/WAN | 17, 18 |
| ◢ ISDN | 17, 18 |
| ◢ Broadband (e.g., DSL, cable, satellite) | 17, 18 |
| ◢ Dial-up | 9, 17, 18 |
| ◢ Wireless (all 802.11) | 17, 18, 20 |
| ◢ Infrared | 9, 17, 18, 20 |

| | |
|---|---|
| ◢ Authentication technologies | 9, 18, 19 |
| ◢ Malicious software protection | 19 |
| ◢ Data access (basic local security policy) | 13, 19 |
| ◢ Backup procedures and access to backups | 13, 19 |
| ◢ Data migration | 13, 19 |
| ◢ Data/remnant removal | 13, 19 |

6.3    **Identify tools, diagnostic procedures, and troubleshooting techniques for security**

| OBJECTIVES | CHAPTERS |
|---|---|
| Diagnose and troubleshoot hardware, software, and data security issues; for example, | |
| ◢ BIOS | 6, 19, 20 |
| ◢ Smart cards, biometrics | 9, 19 |
| ◢ Authentication technologies | 18, 19 |
| ◢ Malicious software | 19 |
| ◢ File system (e.g., FAT32, NTFS) | 19 |
| ◢ Data access (e.g., basic local security policy) | 13, 19 |
| ◢ Backup | 13, 19, 20 |
| ◢ Data migration | 13, 19 |

6.4    **Perform preventive maintenance for computer security**

| OBJECTIVES | CHAPTERS |
|---|---|
| Implement software security preventive maintenance techniques, such as installing service packs and patches and training users about malicious software prevention technologies | 3, 19 |

## DOMAIN 7  SAFETY AND ENVIRONMENTAL ISSUES

7.1    **Describe the aspects and importance of safety and environmental issues**

| OBJECTIVES | CHAPTERS |
|---|---|
| Identify potential safety hazards and take preventive action | 3, 20 |
| Use Material Safety Data Sheets (MSDS) or equivalent documentation and appropriate equipment documentation | 3 |
| Use appropriate repair tools | 3, 20 |
| Describe methods to handle environmental and human (e.g., electrical, chemical, physical) accidents, including incident reporting | 3, 19 |

7.2    **Identify potential hazards and implement proper safety procedures, including ESD precautions and procedures, safe work environment, and equipment handling**    3, 20

7.3    **Identify proper disposal procedures for batteries, display devices, and chemical solvents and cans**    3

## DOMAIN 8  PROFESSIONALISM AND COMMUNICATION

8.1    **Use good communication skills, including listening and tact/discretion, when communication with customers and colleagues**    3, 22

| OBJECTIVES | CHAPTERS |
|---|---|
| Use clear, concise, and direct statements | 22 |
| Allow the customer to complete statements— avoid interrupting | 22 |

| Clarify customer statements—ask pertinent questions | 22 |
| Avoid using jargon, abbreviations, and acronyms | 22 |
| Listen to customers | 22 |

8.2 Use job-related professional behavior, including privacy, confidentiality, and respect for the customer and customers' property (e.g., telephone, computer)

| OBJECTIVES | CHAPTERS |
| --- | --- |
| Behavior | |
| ▲ Maintain a positive attitude and tone of voice | 22 |
| ▲ Avoid arguing with customers and/or becoming defensive | 22 |
| ▲ Do not minimize customers' problems | 22 |
| ▲ Avoid being judgmental and/or insulting or calling the customer names | 22 |
| ▲ Avoid distractions and/or interruptions when talking with customers | 22 |
| Property | |
| ▲ Telephone, laptop, desktop computer, printer, monitor, etc. | 22 |

# CompTIA A+ 220-602
# 2006 Examination Objectives

## DOMAIN 1 PERSONAL COMPUTER COMPONENTS

**1.1    Install, configure, optimize, and upgrade personal computer components**

| OBJECTIVES | CHAPTERS |
|---|---|
| Add, remove, and configure personal computer components, including selection and installation of appropriate components; for example, | |
| ◢ Storage devices | 8, 10 |
| ◢ Motherboards | 6 |
| ◢ Power supplies | 4 |
| ◢ Processors/CPUs | 5 |
| ◢ Memory | 7 |
| ◢ Display devices | 9 |
| ◢ Input devices (e.g., basic, specialty, and multimedia) | 9 |
| ◢ Adapter cards | 9, 10, 17 |
| ◢ Cooling systems | 4, 5 |

**1.2    Identify tools, diagnostic procedures, and troubleshooting techniques for personal computer components**

| OBJECTIVES | CHAPTERS |
|---|---|
| Identify and apply basic diagnostic procedures and troubleshooting techniques | 3, 6, 9, 17, 20, 21 |
| ◢ Isolate and identify the problem using visual and audible inspection of components and minimum configuration | 3, 6, 9, 10, 20, 21 |
| Recognize and isolate issues with peripherals, multimedia, specialty input devices, internal and external storage, and CPUs | 3, 5, 8, 9, 10, 20, 21 |
| Identify the steps used to troubleshoot components (e.g., check proper seating, installation, appropriate component, settings, and current driver); for example, | |
| ◢ Power supply | 3, 4, 20 |
| ◢ Processor/CPUs and motherboards | 3, 5, 6, 20 |
| ◢ Memory | 3, 7, 20 |
| ◢ Adapter cards | 3, 9, 10 |
| ◢ Display and input devices | 3, 9, 20 |
| Recognize names, purposes, characteristics, and appropriate application of tools; for example, | |
| ◢ Multimeter | 20 |
| ◢ Anti-static pad and wrist strap | 3, 20 |
| ◢ Specialty hardware/tools | 3, 20 |
| ◢ Loop-back plugs | 3 |
| ◢ Cleaning products (e.g., vacuum, cleaning pads) | 3, 9, 10, 20, 21 |

1.3    Perform preventive maintenance of personal computer components

| OBJECTIVES | CHAPTERS |
|---|---|
| Identify and apply common preventive maintenance techniques for personal computer components; for example, | |
| ◢ Display devices (e.g., cleaning, ventilation) | 3, 9, 20 |
| ◢ Power devices (e.g., appropriate source, such as power strip, surge protector, ventilation, and cooling) | 3, 4, 20 |
| ◢ Input devices (e.g., covers) | 3, 9 |
| ◢ Storage devices (e.g., software tools, such as Defrag, and cleaning of optics and tape heads) | 3, 10, 12, 13, 15 |
| ◢ Thermally sensitive devices, such as motherboards, CPUs, adapter cards, memory (e.g., cleaning, airflow) | 3, 4, 5, 6, 20 |

## DOMAIN 2  LAPTOPS AND PORTABLE DEVICES

2.1    Identify fundamental principles of using laptops and portable devices

| OBJECTIVES | CHAPTERS |
|---|---|
| Identify appropriate applications for laptop-specific communication connections, such as Bluetooth, infrared, cellular WAN, and Ethernet | 9, 17, 20 |
| Identify appropriate laptop-specific power and electrical input devices, and determine how amperage and voltage can affect performance | 20 |
| Identify the major components of the LCD, including inverter, screen, and video card | 9, 20 |

2.2    Install, configure, optimize, and upgrade laptops and portable devices

| OBJECTIVES | CHAPTERS |
|---|---|
| Removal of laptop-specific hardware, such as peripherals, hot-swappable and non-hot-swappable devices | 9, 20 |
| Describe how video sharing affects memory upgrades | 20 |

2.3    Use tools, diagnostic procedures, and troubleshooting techniques for laptops and portable devices

| OBJECTIVES | CHAPTERS |
|---|---|
| Use procedures and techniques to diagnose power conditions, video, keyboard, pointer, and wireless card issues; for example, | |
| ◢ Verify AC power (e.g., LEDs, swap AC adapter) | 20 |
| ◢ Verify DC power | 20 |
| ◢ Remove unneeded peripherals | 20 |
| ◢ Plug in external monitor | 9, 20 |
| ◢ Toggle Fn keys | 9, 20 |
| ◢ Check LCD cutoff switch | 9, 20 |
| ◢ Verify backlight functionality and pixilation | 9, 20 |
| ◢ Stylus issues (e.g., digitizer problems) | 9, 20 |
| ◢ Unique laptop keypad issues | 9, 20 |
| ◢ Antenna wires | 17, 20 |

## DOMAIN 3 OPERATING SYSTEMS—UNLESS OTHERWISE NOTED, OPERATING SYSTEMS REFERRED WITHIN INCLUDE MICROSOFT WINDOWS 2000, XP PROFESSIONAL, XP HOME, AND MEDIA CENTER

3.1    Identify the fundamental principles of operating systems

| OBJECTIVES | CHAPTERS |
| --- | --- |
| Use command-line functions and utilities to manage operating systems, including proper syntax and switches; for example, | |
| ◢ Cmd | 2, 11, 13 |
| ◢ Help | 13, 14 |
| ◢ Dir | 13, 14 |
| ◢ Attrib | 13, 14, 19 |
| ◢ Edit | 13 |
| ◢ Copy | 13, 14 |
| ◢ Xcopy | 13 |
| ◢ Format | 13, 14 |
| ◢ Ipconfig | 17, 18 |
| ◢ Ping | 17, 18 |
| ◢ MD/CD/RD | 13, 14, 19 |
| Identify concepts and procedures for creating, viewing, and managing disks, directories, and files on operating systems | |
| ◢ Disks (e.g., active, primary, extended, and logical partitions and file systems, including FAT32 and NTFS) | 2, 11, 12, 19 |
| ◢ Directory structures (e.g., create folders, navigate directory structures) | 2, 13 |
| ◢ Files (e.g., creation, attributes, permissions) | 2, 13, 14 |
| Locate and use operating system utilities and available switches; for example, | |
| ◢ Disk Management Tools (e.g., Defrag, Ntbackup, Chkdsk, Format) | 12, 13, 14, 17 |
| ◢ System management tools | |
| ◢ Device and Task Manager | 2, 12, 14, 19 |
| ◢ Msconfig.exe | 12, 14 |
| ◢ Regedit.exe | 12, 14, 19 |
| ◢ Regedt32.exe | 12 |
| ◢ Cmd | 13 |
| ◢ Event Viewer | 12, 14, 19 |
| ◢ System Restore | 12, 14 |
| ◢ Remote Desktop | 18 |
| ◢ File management tools (e.g., Windows Explorer, Attrib.exe) | 2, 13, 14, 17, 19 |

3.2    Install, configure, optimize, and upgrade operating systems—references to upgrading from Windows 95 and NT may be made

| OBJECTIVES | CHAPTERS |
| --- | --- |
| Identify procedures and utilities used to optimize operating systems; for example, | |
| ◢ Virtual memory | 12 |
| ◢ Hard drives (e.g., disk defragmentation) | 11, 13 |
| ◢ Temporary files | 13, 18 |
| ◢ Services | 12, 14 |

| | |
|---|---|
| ◢ Startup | 11, 14 |
| ◢ Application | 12, 14 |

**3.3  Identify tools, diagnostic procedures, and troubleshooting techniques for operating systems**

| OBJECTIVES | CHAPTERS |
|---|---|
| Demonstrate the ability to recover operating systems (e.g., boot methods, recovery console, ASR, ERD) | 12, 13, 14 |
| Recognize and resolve common operational problems; for example, | |
| ◢ Windows-specific printing problems (e.g., print spool stalled, incorrect/incompatible driver form print) | 21 |
| ◢ Auto-restart errors | 14 |
| ◢ Blue screen error | 14, 19 |
| ◢ System lock-up | 14, 19 |
| ◢ Device drivers failure (input/output devices) | 9, 12, 14, 21 |
| ◢ Application install, start, or load failure | 12, 14, 19 |
| Recognize and resolve common error messages and codes; for example, | |
| ◢ Boot (e.g., invalid boot disk, inaccessible boot drive, missing NTLDR) | 8, 14 |
| ◢ Startup (e.g., device/service has failed to start, device/program in registry not found) | 12, 13, 14 19 |
| ◢ Event Viewer | 12, 14, 19 |
| ◢ Registry | 12, 14, 19 |
| ◢ Windows reporting | 12 |
| Use diagnostic utilities and tools to resolve operational problems; for example, | |
| ◢ Bootable media | 14, 20 |
| ◢ Startup modes (e.g., safe mode, safe mode with command prompt, or networking, step-by-step/single step mode) | 14, 19 |
| ◢ Documentation resources (e.g., user/installation manuals, Internet/Web-based training materials) | 13, 14, 19, 20 |
| ◢ Task and Device Manager | 2, 9, 12, |
| ◢ Event Viewer | 12, 19 |
| ◢ Msconfig | 12, 14, 19 |
| ◢ Recover CD/Recovery partition | 3, 14, 20 |
| ◢ Remote Desktop Connection and Assistance | 13, 18 |
| ◢ System File Checker (SFC) | 12, 14 |

**3.4  Perform preventive maintenance for operating systems**

| OBJECTIVES | CHAPTERS |
|---|---|
| Demonstrate the ability to perform preventive maintenance on operating systems, including software and Windows updates (e.g., service packs), scheduled backups/restore, restore points | 11, 12, 13, 19 |

## DOMAIN 4  PRINTERS AND SCANNERS

**4.1  Identify the fundamental principles of using printers and scanners**

| OBJECTIVES | CHAPTERS |
|---|---|
| Describe processes used by printers and scanners, including laser, ink dispersion, thermal, solid ink, and impact printers and scanners | 21 |

4.2    Install, configure, optimize, and upgrade printers and scanners

| OBJECTIVES | CHAPTERS |
|---|---|
| Install and configure printers and scanners | |
| ◢ Power and connect the device using the local or network port | 21 |
| ◢ Install and update the device driver, and calibrate the device | 21 |
| ◢ Configure options and default settings | 21 |
| ◢ Install and configure print drivers (e.g., PCL, PostScript, GDI) | 21 |
| ◢ Validate compatibility with operating system and applications | 21 |
| ◢ Educate the user about basic functionality | 21 |
| Install and configure printer upgrades, including memory and firmware | 21 |
| Optimize scanner performance, including resolution, file format, and default settings | 21 |

4.3    Identify tools and diagnostic procedures to troubleshoot printers and scanners

| OBJECTIVES | CHAPTERS |
|---|---|
| Gather information about printer/scanner problems | 21 |
| Review and analyze collected data | 21 |
| Isolate and resolve identified printer/scanner problems, including defining the cause, applying the fix, and verifying the functionality | 21 |
| Identify appropriate tools used for troubleshooting and repairing printer/scanner problems | |
| ◢ Multimeter | 21 |
| ◢ Screwdrivers | 21 |
| ◢ Cleaning solutions | 21 |
| ◢ Extension magnet | 21 |
| ◢ Test patterns | 21 |

4.4    Perform preventive maintenance of printers and scanners

| OBJECTIVES | CHAPTERS |
|---|---|
| Perform scheduled maintenance according to vendor guidelines (e.g., install maintenance kits, reset page counts) | 21 |
| Ensure a suitable environment | 21 |
| Use recommended supplies | 3, 21 |

## DOMAIN 5  NETWORKS

5.1    Identify the fundamental principles of networks

| OBJECTIVES | CHAPTERS |
|---|---|
| Identify names, purposes, and characteristics of basic network protocols and terminologies; for example, | |
| ◢ ISP | 18 |
| ◢ TCP/IP (e.g., gateway, subnet mask, DNS, WINS, static and automatic address assignment) | 17, 18 |
| ◢ IPX/SPX (NWLink) | 17 |
| ◢ NetBEUI / NetBIOS | 17 |
| ◢ SMTP | 18 |
| ◢ IMAP | 18 |
| ◢ HTML | 18 |
| ◢ HTTP | 18 |
| ◢ HTTPS | 18 |

| | |
|---|---|
| ◢ SSL | 18 |
| ◢ Telnet | 18 |
| ◢ FTP | 18 |
| ◢ DNS | 17 |
| Identify names, purposes, and characteristics of technologies for establishing connectivity; for example, | |
| ◢ Dial-up networking | 9, 18 |
| ◢ Broadband (e.g., DSL, cable, satellite) | 17, 18 |
| ◢ ISDN networking | 17, 18 |
| ◢ Wireless (all 802.11) | 17, 18 |
| ◢ LAN/WAN | 17, 18 |
| ◢ Infrared | 9, 17 |
| ◢ Bluetooth | 17 |
| ◢ Cellular | 17 |
| ◢ VoIP | 17, 18 |

**5.2    Install, configure, optimize, and upgrade networks**

| OBJECTIVES | CHAPTERS |
|---|---|
| Install and configure browsers | |
| ◢ Enable/disable script support | 18, 19 |
| ◢ Configure proxy and security settings | 18, 19 |
| Establish network connectivity | |
| ◢ Install and configure network cards | 17 |
| ◢ Obtain a connection | 17, 20 |
| ◢ Configure client options (e.g., Microsoft, Novell) and network options (e.g., domain, workgroup, tree) | 17 |
| ◢ Configure network options | 17 |
| Demonstrate the ability to share network resources | |
| ◢ Models | 11, 17 |
| ◢ Configure permissions | 13, 17, 19 |
| ◢ Capacities/limitations for sharing for each operating system | 13, 17, 18, 19 |

**5.3    Identify tools and diagnostic procedures to troubleshoot network problems**

| OBJECTIVES | CHAPTERS |
|---|---|
| Identify names, purposes, and characteristics of tools; for example, | |
| ◢ Command-line tools (e.g., Ipconfig.exe, Ping.exe, Tracert.exe, Nslookup.exe) | 17, 18 |
| ◢ Cable testing device | 17 |
| Diagnose and troubleshoot basic network issues; for example, | |
| ◢ Driver/network interface | 17 |
| ◢ Protocol configuration | 17, 18 |
| ◢ TCP/IP (e.g., gateway, subnet mask, DNS, WINS, static and automatic address assignment) | 17, 18 |
| ◢ IPX/SPX (NWLink) | 17 |
| ◢ Permissions | 13, 19 |
| ◢ Firewall configuration | 18 |
| ◢ Electrical interference | 17, 18 |

| | |
|---|---|
| **5.4    Perform preventive maintenance of networks, including securing and protecting network cabling** | 17 |

## DOMAIN 6 SECURITY

6.1   Identify the fundamental principles of security

| OBJECTIVES | CHAPTERS |
|---|---|
| Identify the purposes and characteristics of access control; for example, | |
| ▲ Access to operating system (e.g., accounts such as user, admin, and guest, groups, permission actions, types and levels), components, restricted spaces | 13, 19 |
| Identify the purposes and characteristics of auditing and event logging | 19 |

6.2   Install, configure, upgrade, and optimize security

| OBJECTIVES | CHAPTERS |
|---|---|
| Install and configure software, wireless, and data security; for example, | |
| ▲ Authentication technologies | 9, 18, 19 |
| ▲ Software firewalls | 18, 19 |
| ▲ Auditing and event logging (enable/disable only) | 19 |
| ▲ Wireless client configuration | 17, 19 |
| ▲ Unused wireless connections | 17 |
| ▲ Data access (e.g., permissions, basic local security policy) | 13, 19 |
| ▲ File systems (converting from FAT32 to NTFS only) | 11, 19 |

6.3   Identify tools, diagnostic procedures, and troubleshooting techniques for security

| OBJECTIVES | CHAPTERS |
|---|---|
| Diagnose and troubleshoot software and data security issues; for example, | |
| ▲ Software firewall issues | 18, 19 |
| ▲ Wireless client configuration issues | 17 |
| ▲ Data access issues (e.g., permissions, security policies) | 13, 19 |
| ▲ Encryption and encryption technology issues | 17, 18, 19, 20 |

6.4   Perform preventive maintenance for security

| OBJECTIVES | CHAPTERS |
|---|---|
| Recognize social engineering and address social engineering situations | 19 |

## DOMAIN 7 SAFETY & ENVIRONMENTAL ISSUES

| | | |
|---|---|---|
| 7.1 | Identify potential hazards and proper safety procedures, including power supply, display devices, and environment (e.g., trip, liquid, situational, atmospheric hazards, and high-voltage and moving equipment) | 3, 20 |

## DOMAIN 8 PROFESSIONALISM AND COMMUNICATION

8.1   Use good communication skills, including listening and tact/discretion, when communicating with customers and colleagues

| OBJECTIVES | CHAPTERS |
| --- | --- |
| Use clear, concise, and direct statements | 22 |
| Allow the customer to complete statements—avoid interrupting | 22 |
| Clarify customer statements—ask pertinent questions | 22 |
| Avoid using jargon, abbreviations, and acronyms | 22 |
| Listen to customers | 22 |

8.2   Use job-related professional behavior, including notation of privacy, confidentiality, and respect for the customer and customer's property

| OBJECTIVES | CHAPTERS |
| --- | --- |
| Behavior | |
| ◢ Maintain a positive attitude and tone of voice | 22 |
| ◢ Avoid arguing with the customer and/or becoming defensive | 22 |
| ◢ Do not minimize the customer's problems | 22 |
| ◢ Avoid being judgmental and/or insulting or calling the customer names | 22 |
| ◢ Avoid distractions and/or interruptions when talking with the customer | 22 |
| Property | |
| ◢ Telephone, laptop, desktop computer, printer, monitor, etc. | 22 |

# CompTIA A+ 220-603
# 2006 Examination Objectives

## DOMAIN 1 PERSONAL COMPUTER COMPONENTS

1.1    Install, configure, optimize, and upgrade personal computer components

| OBJECTIVES | CHAPTERS |
|---|---|
| Add, remove, and configure display devices and adapter cards, including basic input and multimedia devices | 9, 10, 17 |

1.2    Identify tools, diagnostic procedures, and troubleshooting techniques for personal computer components

| OBJECTIVES | CHAPTERS |
|---|---|
| Identify and apply basic diagnostic procedures and troubleshooting techniques; for example, | 3, 6, 9, 20, 21 |
| ◢ Identify and analyze the problem/potential problem | 3, 4, 5, 6, 7, 8, 9, 10, 17, 20, 21 |
| ◢ Test related components and evaluate results | 3, 4, 5, 6, 7, 9, 10, 17, 20, 21 |
| ◢ Identify additional steps to be taken if/when necessary | 3, 4, 5, 6, 7, 9, 10, 17, 20 |
| ◢ Document activities and outcomes | 12, 13, 14, 19, 22 |
| Recognize and isolate issues with display, peripheral, multimedia, specialty input device, and storage | 3, 4, 5, 6, 7, 8, 9, 10, 17, 20, 21 |
| Apply steps in troubleshooting techniques to identify problems (e.g., physical environment, functionality, and software/driver settings) with components, including display, input devices, and adapter cards | 3, 4, 5, 6, 7, 9, 10,17, 20, 21 |

1.3    Perform preventive maintenance on personal computer components

| OBJECTIVES | CHAPTERS |
|---|---|
| Identify and apply common preventive maintenance techniques for storage devices; for example, | 3, 9, 20, 21 |
| ◢ Software tools (e.g., Defrag, Chkdsk) | 12, 13 |
| ◢ Cleaning (e.g., optics, tape heads) | 3, 9, 10, 20, 21 |

## DOMAIN 2  OPERATING SYSTEMS—UNLESS OTHERWISE NOTED, OPERATING SYSTEMS REFERRED TO WITHIN INCLUDE MICROSOFT WINDOWS 2000, XP PROFESSIONAL, XP HOME, AND MEDIA CENTER

2.1    Identify the fundamental principles of using operating systems

| OBJECTIVES | CHAPTERS |
|---|---|
| Use command-line functions and utilities to manage Windows 2000, XP Professional, and XP Home, including proper syntax and switches; for example, | |
| ◢ Cmd | 2, 13 |
| ◢ Help | 13, 14 |
| ◢ Dir | 13, 14 |
| ◢ Attrib | 13, 14, 19 |
| ◢ Edit | 13 |
| ◢ Copy | 13, 14 |

| | |
|---|---|
| ◢ Xcopy | 13 |
| ◢ Format | 13, 14 |
| ◢ Ipconfig | 17, 18 |
| ◢ Ping | 17, 18 |
| ◢ MD/CD/RD | 13, 14, 19 |

| | |
|---|---|
| Identify concepts and procedures for creating, viewing, managing disks, directories, and files in Windows 2000, XP Professional, and XP Home; for example, | |
| ◢ Disks (e.g., active, primary extended, and logical partitions) | 2, 11, 12, 19 |
| ◢ File systems (e.g., FAT32, NTFS) | 2, 11, 12, 19 |
| ◢ Directory structures (e.g., create folders, navigate directory structures) | 2, 13 |
| ◢ Files (e.g., creation, extensions, attributes, permissions) | 2, 13, 14 |
| Locate and use Windows 2000, XP Professional, and XP Home utilities and available switches | |
| ◢ Disk Management Tools (e.g., Defrag, Ntbackup, Chkdsk, Format) | 12, 13, 14, 17 |
| ◢ System Management Tools | |
| ◢ Device and Task Manager | 2, 12, 14, 19 |
| ◢ Msconfig.exe | 12, 14 |
| ◢ Regedit.exe | 12, 14, 19 |
| ◢ Regedt32.exe | 12 |
| ◢ Cmd | 13 |
| ◢ Event Viewer | 12, 13, 14, 19 |
| ◢ System Restore | 12, 14 |
| ◢ Remote Desktop | 18 |
| ◢ File Management Tools (e.g., Windows Explorer, Attrib.exe) | 2, 13, 14, 17, 19 |

**2.2   Install, configure, optimize, and upgrade operating systems**

| OBJECTIVES | CHAPTERS |
|---|---|
| Identify procedures and utilities used to optimize the performance of Windows 2000, XP Professional, and XP Home; for example, | |
| ◢ Virtual memory | 12 |
| ◢ Hard drives (i.e., disk defragmentation) | 11, 13 |
| ◢ Temporary files | 13, 18 |
| ◢ Services | 12, 14 |
| ◢ Startup | 11, 14 |
| ◢ Applications | 12, 14 |

**2.3   Identify tools, diagnostic procedures, and troubleshooting techniques for operating systems**

| OBJECTIVES | CHAPTERS |
|---|---|
| Recognize and resolve common operational problems; for example, | |
| ◢ Windows-specific printing problems (e.g., print spool stalled, incorrect/incompatible driver form print) | 21 |
| ◢ Auto-restart errors | 14 |
| ◢ Blue screen error | 14, 19 |

| | |
|---|---|
| ◢ System lock-up | 14, 19 |
| ◢ Device drivers failure (input/output devices) | 9, 12, 14, 21 |
| ◢ Application install, start, or load failure | 12, 14, 19 |
| Recognize and resolve common error messages and codes; for example, | |
| ◢ Boot (e.g., invalid boot disk, inaccessible boot device, missing NTLDR) | 8, 14 |
| ◢ Startup (e.g., device/service has failed to start, device/program references in registry not found) | 12, 13, 14, 19 |
| ◢ Event Viewer | 12, 14, 19 |
| ◢ Registry | 12, 14, 19 |
| ◢ Windows | 12 |
| Use diagnostic utilities and tools to resolve operational problems; for example, | |
| ◢ Bootable media | 14, 20 |
| ◢ Startup modes (e.g., safe mode, safe mode with command prompt or networking, step-by-step/single step mode) | 14, 19 |
| ◢ Documentation resources (e.g., user/installation manuals, Internet/Web-based training materials) | 13, 14, 19, 20 |
| ◢ Task and Device Manager | 2, 9, 12, 14, 19 |
| ◢ Event Viewer | 12, 19 |
| ◢ Msconfig | 12, 14, 19 |
| ◢ Recovery CD/Recovery partition | 3, 14, 20 |
| ◢ Remote Desktop Connection and Assistance | 13, 18 |
| ◢ System File Checker (SFC) | 12, 14 |

**2.4**   **Perform preventive maintenance for operating systems**

| OBJECTIVES | CHAPTERS |
|---|---|
| Perform preventive maintenance on Windows 2000, XP Professional, and XP Home, including software and Windows updates (e.g., service packs) | 11, 12, 13, 19 |

## DOMAIN 3  PRINTERS AND SCANNERS

**3.1**   **Identify the fundamental principles of using printers and scanners**

| OBJECTIVES | CHAPTERS |
|---|---|
| Describe processes used by printers and scanners, including laser, ink dispersion, impact, solid ink, and thermal printers | 21 |

**3.2**   **Install, configure, optimize, and upgrade printers and scanners**

| OBJECTIVES | CHAPTERS |
|---|---|
| Install and configure printers and scanners | |
| ◢ Power and connect the device using network or local port | 21 |
| ◢ Install/update the device driver and calibrate the device | 21 |
| ◢ Configure options and default settings | 21 |
| ◢ Install and configure print drivers (e.g., PCL, PostScript, and GDI) | 21 |
| ◢ Validate compatibility with OS and applications | 21 |
| ◢ Educate user about basic functionality | 21 |
| Optimize scanner performance; for example, resolution, file format, and default settings | 21 |

**3.3** Identify tools, diagnostic procedures, and troubleshooting techniques for printers and scanners

| OBJECTIVES | CHAPTERS |
|---|---|
| Gather information required to troubleshoot printer/scanner problems | 21 |
| Troubleshoot a print failure (e.g., lack of paper, clear queue, restart print spooler, recycle power on printer, inspect for jams, check for visual indicators) | 21 |

## DOMAIN 4 NETWORKS

**4.1** Identify the fundamental principles of networks

| OBJECTIVES | CHAPTERS |
|---|---|
| Identify names, purposes, and characteristics of the basic network protocols and terminologies; for example, | |
| ◢ ISP | 18 |
| ◢ TCP/IP (e.g., gateway, subnet mask, DNS, WINS, static and automatic address assignment) | 17, 18 |
| ◢ IPX/SPX (NWLink) | 17 |
| ◢ NetBEUI/NetBIOS | 17 |
| ◢ SMTP | 18 |
| ◢ IMAP | 18 |
| ◢ HTML | 18 |
| ◢ HTTP | 18 |
| ◢ HTTPS | 18 |
| ◢ SSL | 18 |
| ◢ Telnet | 18 |
| ◢ FTP | 18 |
| ◢ DNS | 17 |
| Identify names, purposes, and characteristics of technologies for establishing connectivity; for example, | |
| ◢ Dial-up networking | 9, 18 |
| ◢ Broadband (e.g., DSL, cable, satellite) | 17, 18 |
| ◢ ISDN networking | 17, 18 |
| ◢ Wireless | 17, 18 |
| ◢ LAN/WAN | 17, 18 |

**4.2** Install, configure, optimize, and upgrade networks

| OBJECTIVES | CHAPTERS |
|---|---|
| Establish network connectivity and share network resources | 13, 17, 18, 19, 20 |

**4.3** Identify tools, diagnostic procedures, and troubleshooting techniques for networks

| OBJECTIVES | CHAPTERS |
|---|---|
| Identify the names, purposes, and characteristics of command-line tools; for example, | |
| ◢ Ipconfig.exe | 17, 18 |
| ◢ Ping.exe | 17, 18 |
| ◢ Tracert.exe | 17, 18 |
| ◢ Nslookup.exe | 17, 18 |

Diagnose and troubleshoot basic network issues; for example,

| | |
|---|---|
| ▲ Driver/network interface | 17 |
| ▲ Protocol configuration | 17, 18 |
|   ▲ TCP/IP (e.g., gateway, subnet mask, DNS, WINS, static and automatic address assignment) | 17, 18 |
|   ▲ IPX/SPX (NWLink) | 17 |
| ▲ Permissions | 13, 19 |
| ▲ Firewall configuration | 18 |
| ▲ Electrical interference | 17, 18 |

## DOMAIN 5  SECURITY

### 5.1  Identify the fundamental principles of security

| OBJECTIVES | CHAPTERS |
|---|---|
| Identify the names, purposes, and characteristics of access control and permissions | |
| ▲ Accounts, including user, admin, and guest | 13, 19 |
| ▲ Groups | 13, 19 |
| ▲ Permission levels, types (e.g., file systems and shared), and actions (e.g., read, write, change, and execute) | 13, 19 |

### 5.2  Install, configure, optimize, and upgrade security

| OBJECTIVES | CHAPTERS |
|---|---|
| Install and configure hardware, software, wireless and data security; for example, | |
| ▲ Smart card readers | 19 |
| ▲ Key fobs | 19 |
| ▲ Biometric devices | 9, 19 |
| ▲ Authentication technologies | 9, 18, 19, 20 |
| ▲ Software firewalls | 3, 18, 19 |
| ▲ Auditing and event logging (enable/disable only) | 19 |
| ▲ Wireless client configuration | 17, 19 |
| ▲ Unused wireless connections | 17 |
| ▲ Data access (e.g., permissions, security policies) | 13, 19 |
| ▲ Encryption and encryption technologies | 17, 18, 19, 20 |

### 5.3  Identify tools, diagnostic procedures, and troubleshooting techniques for security issues

| OBJECTIVES | CHAPTERS |
|---|---|
| Diagnose and troubleshoot software and data security issues; for example, | |
| ▲ Software firewall issues | 18, 19 |
| ▲ Wireless client configuration issues | 17 |
| ▲ Data access issues (e.g., permissions, security policies) | 13, 19 |
| ▲ Encryption and encryption technologies issues | 17, 18, 19, 20 |

### 5.4  Perform preventive maintenance for security

| OBJECTIVES | CHAPTERS |
|---|---|
| Recognize social engineering and address social engineering situations | 19 |

## DOMAIN 6 PROFESSIONALISM AND COMMUNICATION

6.1    Use good communication skills, including listening and tact/discretion, when communicating with customers and colleagues

| OBJECTIVES | CHAPTERS |
| --- | --- |
| Use clear, concise, and direct statements | 22 |
| Allow the customer to complete statements—avoid interrupting | 22 |
| Clarify customer statements—ask pertinent questions | 22 |
| Avoid using jargon, abbreviations, and acronyms | 22 |
| Listen to customers | 22 |

6.2    Use job-related professional behavior, including notation of privacy, confidentiality, and respect for the customer and the customer's property

| | CHAPTERS |
| --- | --- |
| | 22 |

# CompTIA A+ 220-604
# 2006 Examination Objectives

## DOMAIN 1 PERSONAL COMPUTER COMPONENTS

1.1   Install, configure, optimize, and upgrade personal computer components

| OBJECTIVES | CHAPTERS |
|---|---|
| Add, remove, and configure internal storage devices, motherboards, power supplies, processor/CPUs, memory, and adapter cards, including: | |
| ◢ Drive preparation | 8, 10, 12, 20 |
| ◢ Jumper configuration | 8 |
| ◢ Storage device power and cabling | 8, 10 |
| ◢ Selection and installation of appropriate motherboard | 6 |
| ◢ BIOS setup and configuration | 6 |
| ◢ Selection and installation of appropriate CPU | 5 |
| ◢ Selection and installation of appropriate memory | 7 |
| ◢ Installation of adapter cards, including hardware and software/drivers | 9, 10, 17 |
| ◢ Configuration and optimization of adapter cards, including adjusting hardware settings and obtaining network card connection | 9, 10, 17 |
| Add, remove, and configure cooling systems | 4, 5 |

1.2   Identify tools, diagnostic procedures, and troubleshooting techniques for personal computer components

| OBJECTIVES | CHAPTERS |
|---|---|
| Identify and apply diagnostic procedures and troubleshooting techniques; for example, | 3, 6, 9, 10, 20, 21 |
| ◢ Identify and isolate the problem using visual and audible inspection of components and minimum configuration | 3, 6, 9, 10, 20, 21 |
| Identify the steps used to troubleshoot components (e.g., check proper seating, installation, appropriate component, settings, current driver); for example, | |
| ◢ Power supply | 3, 4, 20 |
| ◢ Processor/CPUs and motherboards | 3, 5, 6, 20 |
| ◢ Memory | 3, 7, 20 |
| ◢ Adapter cards | 3, 9, 10, 17, 20 |
| Recognize names, purposes, characteristics, and appropriate application of tools; for example, | |
| ◢ Multimeter | 20 |
| ◢ Anti-static pad and wrist strap | 3, 20 |
| ◢ Specialty hardware/tools | 3, 20 |
| ◢ Loop-back plugs | 3 |
| ◢ Cleaning products (e.g., vacuum, cleaning pads) | 3, 9, 10, 20, 21 |

1.3    Perform preventive maintenance of personal computer components

| OBJECTIVES | CHAPTERS |
|---|---|
| Identify and apply common preventive maintenance techniques; for example, | |
| ◢ Thermally sensitive devices (e.g., motherboards, CPUs, adapter cards, memory) | 3, 4, 5, 6, 20 |
| ◢ Cleaning | 3, 9, 10, 20, 21 |
| ◢ Airflow (e.g., slot covers, cable routing) | 3, 4, 5, 6, 20 |
| ◢ Adapter cards (e.g., driver/firmware updates) | 3, 9, 10, 17, 20 |

## DOMAIN 2  LAPTOPS AND PORTABLE DEVICES

2.1    Identify the fundamental principles of using laptops and portable devices

| OBJECTIVES | CHAPTERS |
|---|---|
| Identify appropriate applications for laptop-specific communication connections; for example, | |
| ◢ Bluetooth | 9, 17, 20 |
| ◢ Infrared devices | 9, 17, 20 |
| ◢ Cellular WAN | 9, 17, 20 |
| ◢ Ethernet | 9, 17, 20 |
| Identify appropriate laptop-specific power and electrical input devices; for example, | |
| ◢ Output performance requirements for amperage and voltage | 20 |
| Identify the major components of the LCD (e.g., inverter, screen, video card) | 9, 20 |

2.2    Install, configure, optimize, and upgrade laptops and portable devices

| OBJECTIVES | CHAPTERS |
|---|---|
| Demonstrate the safe removal of laptop-specific hardware, including peripherals, hot-swappable, and non-hot-swappable devices | 9, 20 |
| Identify the effect of video sharing on memory upgrades | 20 |

2.3    Identify tools, diagnostic procedures, and troubleshooting techniques for laptops and portable devices

| OBJECTIVES | CHAPTERS |
|---|---|
| Use procedures and techniques to diagnose power conditions, video issues, keyboard and pointer issues, and wireless card issues; for example, | |
| ◢ Verify AC power (e.g., LEDs, swap AC adapter) | 20 |
| ◢ Verify DC power | 20 |
| ◢ Remove unneeded peripherals | 20 |
| ◢ Plug in external monitor | 9, 20 |
| ◢ Toggle Fn keys | 9, 20 |
| ◢ Check LCD cutoff switch | 9, 20 |
| ◢ Verify backlight functionality and pixilation | 9, 20 |
| ◢ Stylus issues (e.g., digitizer problems) | 9, 20 |
| ◢ Unique laptop keypad issues | 9, 20 |
| ◢ Antenna wires | 17, 20 |

## DOMAIN 3  PRINTERS AND SCANNERS

3.1    Identify the fundamental principles of using printers and scanners

| OBJECTIVES | CHAPTERS |
| --- | --- |
| Describe the processes used by printers and scanners, including laser, ink-jet, thermal, solid ink, and impact printers | 21 |

3.2    Install, configure, optimize, and upgrade printers and scanners

| OBJECTIVES | CHAPTERS |
| --- | --- |
| Identify the steps used in the installation and configuration processes for printers and scanners; for example, | |
| ◢ Power and connect the device using the network or local port | 21 |
| ◢ Install and update the device driver | 21 |
| ◢ Calibrate the device | 21 |
| ◢ Configure the options and default settings | 21 |
| ◢ Print a test page | 21 |
| Install and configure printer/scanner upgrades, including memory and firmware | 21 |

3.3    Identify tools, diagnostic methods, and troubleshooting procedures for printers and scanners

| OBJECTIVES | CHAPTERS |
| --- | --- |
| Gather data about printer/scanner problems | 21 |
| Review and analyze data collected about printer/scanner problems | 21 |
| Implement solutions to solve identified printer/scanner problems | 21 |
| Identify appropriate tools used for troubleshooting and repairing printer/scanner problems | |
| ◢ Multimeter | 21 |
| ◢ Screwdrivers | 21 |
| ◢ Cleaning solutions | 21 |
| ◢ Extension magnet | 21 |
| ◢ Test patterns | 21 |

3.4    Perform preventive maintenance of printer and scanner problems

| OBJECTIVES | CHAPTERS |
| --- | --- |
| Perform scheduled maintenance according to vendor guidelines (e.g., install maintenance kits, reset page counts) | 21 |
| Ensure a suitable environment | 21 |
| Use recommended supplies | 3, 21 |

## DOMAIN 4  SECURITY

4.1    Identify the names, purposes, and characteristics of physical security devices and processes

| OBJECTIVES | CHAPTERS |
| --- | --- |
| Control access to PCs, servers, laptops, and restricted spaces | |
| ◢ Hardware | 19 |
| ◢ Operating systems | 13, 19 |

4.2    Install hardware security

| OBJECTIVES | CHAPTERS |
|---|---|
| Smart card readers | 19 |
| Key fobs | 19 |
| Biometric devices | 9, 18, 19, 20 |

## DOMAIN 5 SAFETY AND ENVIRONMENTAL ISSUES

5.1    Identify potential hazards and proper safety procedures, including power supply, display devices, and environment (e.g., trip, liquid, situational, atmospheric hazards, high-voltage, and moving equipment)

| | CHAPTERS |
|---|---|
| | 3, 19, 20 |

# Introduction CompTIA A+

*CompTIA A+ 2006 In Depth* was written to be the very best tool on the market today to prepare you to support personal computers. Updated to include the most current technologies with a new chapter on securing your PC and small network and new content on supporting Windows 2000/XP, this book takes you from the just-a-user level to the I-can-fix-this level for PC hardware and software matters. It achieves its goals with an unusually effective combination of tools that powerfully reinforce both concepts and hands-on, real-world experiences. It also provides thorough preparation for the new 2006 CompTIA A+ certification exams. Competency in using a computer is a prerequisite to using this book. No background knowledge of electronics is assumed. An appropriate prerequisite course for this book would be a general course in microcomputer applications.

This book includes:

- ▲ **End-of-chapter material**, including a chapter summary, key terms, and review questions
- ▲ **Step-by-step instructions** on installation, maintenance, optimization of system performance, and troubleshooting
- ▲ **Video clips** featuring Jean Andrews illustrating key points from the text to aid your understanding of the material
- ▲ **A wide array of photos, drawings, and screen shots** supporting the text, displaying in detail the exact hardware and software features you will need to understand to manage and maintain your PC

In addition, the carefully structured, clearly written text is accompanied by graphics that provide the visual input essential to learning.

Coverage is balanced. While focusing on new hardware and software, the text also covers the real work of PC repair, where some older technology remains in widespread use and still needs support. For example, the book covers all the PCI and PCI Express expansion slot technologies but also addresses using AGP and ISA expansion slots because many systems with AGP and ISA slots are still in use. Also included is thorough coverage of operating system and applications support. Because Windows XP is currently the preferred Windows OS, four chapters are devoted to supporting it and Windows 2000. In addition, two chapters are dedicated to DOS and Windows 9x, because these operating systems are still present in the workplace. The four Windows 2000/XP chapters precede the two DOS and Windows 9x chapters, although the six chapters are written so that you can choose to cover the two DOS and Windows 9x chapters before you study the four Windows 2000/XP chapters. Because occasionally a PC technician sees a Linux installation on the desktop, an appendix covers this OS. You'll also find an appendix on the Mac OS.

This book provides thorough preparation for CompTIA's A+ 2006 certification examinations and maps completely to these new exam objectives. This certification credential's popularity among employers is growing exponentially, and obtaining certification increases your ability to gain employment and improve your salary. To get more information on A+ certification and its sponsoring organization, the Computing Technology Industry Association, see their Web site at *www.comptia.org*.

## FEATURES

To ensure a successful learning experience, this book includes the following features:

- ▲ *Learning objectives.* Every chapter opens with a list of learning objectives that set the stage for you to absorb the lessons of the text.
- ▲ *Comprehensive step-by-step troubleshooting guidance.* Troubleshooting guidelines are included in almost every chapter. In addition, Chapter 3 gives insights into general approaches to troubleshooting that help apply the specifics detailed in each chapter for different hardware and software problems.
- ▲ *Step-by-step procedures.* The book is chock-full of step-by-step procedures covering subjects from hardware installation and maintenance to optimizing system performance.
- ▲ *Art program.* Numerous detailed photographs, three-dimensional art, and screen shots support the text, displaying hardware and software features exactly as you will see them in your work.
- ▲ *Applying Concepts.* These sections offer practical applications for the material being discussed. Whether outlining a task, developing a scenario, or providing pointers, the Applying Concepts sections give you a chance to apply what you've learned to a typical PC problem.

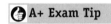

*Notes.* Note icons highlight additional helpful information related to the subject being discussed.

*A+ icons.* All the content that relates to CompTIA's A+ 2006 Essentials and 220-602 certification exams, whether it's a page or a sentence, is highlighted with an A+ icon. The icon notes the exam name and the objective number. This unique feature highlights the relevant content at a glance so that you can pay extra attention to the material.

*A+ Exam Tip boxes.* These boxes highlight additional insights and tips to remember if you are planning to take the CompTIA A+ exams.

*Caution icons.* These icons highlight critical safety information. Follow these instructions carefully to protect the PC and its data and to ensure your own safety.

*Video clips.* Short video passages reinforce concepts and techniques discussed in the text and offer insight into the life of a PC repair technician.

*End-of-chapter material.* Each chapter closes with the following features, which reinforce the material covered in the chapter:

*Chapter Summary.* This bulleted list of concise statements summarizes all major points of the chapter.

*Key Terms.* The content of each chapter is further reinforced by an end-of-chapter key-term list. The definitions of all terms are included at the end of the book in a full-length glossary.

*Review Questions.* You can test your understanding of each chapter with a comprehensive set of review questions. These questions check your understanding of fundamental concepts.

*CD Resource Pak.* The CD placed in the book includes video clips that feature Jean Andrews illustrating key concepts in the text and providing advice on the real world of PC repair. Other helpful tools on the CD include Frequently Asked Questions, Sample Reports, Troubleshooting Flowcharts, and an electronic Glossary.

# ACKNOWLEDGMENTS

Thank you to the wonderful people at Thomson Course Technology who continue to provide support, warm encouragement, patience, and guidance: Nick Lombardi, Michelle Ruelos Cannistraci, and Danielle Chouhan. You've truly helped make this edition fun! Thank you, Jill Batistick, Developmental Editor, for your careful attention to detail and your genuine friendship, and to Karen Annett, our excellent copy editor. Thank you, Susan Whalen and Serge Palladino, for your careful attention to the technical accuracy of this book. Thank you Abigail Reip for your research efforts.

Thank you to all the people who took the time to voluntarily send encouragement and suggestions for improvements to the previous editions. Your input and help is very much appreciated. Thanks also to the reviewers, listed next, who provided invaluable insights and showed a genuine interest in the book's success:

Paul J. Bartoszewicz, Hudson Valley Community College, Troy, NY

Steve Belville, Bryant & Stratton, Milwaukee, MI

Keith Conn, Cleveland Institute of Electronics, Cleveland, OH

Kevin Crawford, Community College of Rhode Island

Chuck Lund, Central Lakes College, Brainerd, MN

Erik Schmid, The Chubb Institute, Cherry Hill, NJ

Thank you to Joy Dark who was here with me making this book happen. I'm very grateful.

This book is dedicated to the covenant of God with man on earth.

Jean Andrews, Ph.D.

## PHOTO CREDITS

| | |
|---|---|
| Figure 10-36 | Courtesy of Plextor Corporation |
| Figure 10-40 | Courtesy of Quantum Corporation |
| Figure 10-43 | Courtesy of Maxell Corporation of America |
| Figure 10-44 | Courtesy of Quantum Corporation |
| Figure 10-45 | Courtesy of Hewlett-Packard Company |
| Figure 10-49 | Courtesy of Iomega |
| Figure 13-46 | Courtesy of Kaguru Solutions |
| Table 17-2a | Courtesy of Cables4Computer.com |
| Table 17-2b | Courtesy of Black Box Corporation |
| Table 17-2c | Courtesy of Tyco Electronics |
| Table 17-2d | Courtesy of Black Box Corporation |
| Figure 17-5a | Courtesy of Fiber Communications, Inc. (www.fiberc.com) |
| Figure 17-5b | Courtesy of Fiber Communications, Inc. (www.fiberc.com) |
| Figure 17-5c | Courtesy of Fiber Communications, Inc. (www.fiberc.com) |
| Figure 17-5d | Courtesy of Fiber Communications, Inc. (www.fiberc.com) |
| Figure 17-18 | Courtesy of Tekkeon, Inc. |
| Figure 17-23 | Courtesy of 3Com |
| Figure 17-24 | Courtesy of 3Com |
| Figure 17-75 | Courtesy of D-Link Corporation |
| Figure 19-5 | Courtesy of wesecure.com |
| Figure 19-42 | Courtesy of RSA Security |
| Figure 19-43 | Courtesy of IDenticard Systems |
| Figure 19-44 | Courtesy of Athena Smartcard Solutions Ltd. |
| Figure 19-45 | Courtesy of Aladdin |
| Figure 20-1 | Dougal Waters/Getty Images |
| Figure 20-8 | Courtesy of Kensington Technology Group |
| Figure 20-17 | Courtesy of IBM Corporation |
| Figure 20-18 | Courtesy of IBM Corporation |
| Figure 20-25 | Courtesy of AVerMedia Technologies, Inc. USA |
| Figure 20-26 | Courtesy of SanDisk Corporation |
| Figure 20-29 | Courtesy of Xterasys |
| Figure 20-30 | Courtesy of SIIG, Inc. |
| Figure 20-40 | Courtesy of Linksys |
| Table 20-3a | Courtesy of Kingston Technology |
| Table 20-3b | Courtesy of Crucial Technology |
| Table 20-3c | Courtesy of Crucial Technology |
| Table 20-3e | Courtesy of High Connection Density, Inc. |
| Figure 20-48 | Courtesy of LaCie |
| Figure 20-63 | © 2005 Dell Inc. All rights reserved |
| Figure 20-64 | © 2005 Dell Inc. All rights reserved |
| Figure 20-69 | Patrick Olear/Photo Edit Inc. |
| Figure 20-70 | Courtesy of Acer America Inc. |
| Figure 20-71 | Courtesy of Microsoft Corporation |
| Figure 20-71 | Courtesy of Garmin International |
| Figure 20-73 | Courtesy of Targus International |
| Figure 21-1 | Courtesy of Hewlett-Packard Company |
| Figure 21-6 | Courtesy of EPSON America, Inc. |
| Figure 21-9 | Courtesy of Xerox Corporation |
| Figure 21-11 | Courtesy of Visioneer |
| Figure 21-12 | Courtesy of NeatReceipts |

Most of the other photos are courtesy of Joy Dark and Jennifer Dark.

# PROTECT YOURSELF, YOUR HARDWARE, AND YOUR SOFTWARE

When you work on a computer, it is possible to harm both the computer and yourself. The most common accident that happens when attempting to fix a computer problem is erasing software or data. Experimenting without knowing what you are doing can cause damage. To prevent these sorts of accidents, as well as the physically dangerous ones, take a few safety precautions. The text that follows describes the potential sources of damage and danger and how to protect against them.

## POWER TO THE COMPUTER

To protect both yourself and the equipment when working inside a computer, turn off the power, unplug the computer, and always use a grounding bracelet, as described in Chapter 3. Consider the monitor and the power supply to be "black boxes." Never remove the cover or put your hands inside this equipment unless you know about the hazards of charged capacitors. Both the power supply and the monitor can hold a dangerous level of electricity even after they are turned off and disconnected from a power source.

## PROTECT AGAINST ESD

To protect the computer against electrostatic discharge (ESD), commonly known as static electricity, always ground yourself before touching electronic components, including the hard drive, motherboard, expansion cards, processors, and memory modules. You can ground yourself and the computer parts by using one or more of the following static control devices or methods:

- ◢ *Ground bracelet or static strap.* A ground bracelet is a strap you wear around your wrist. To protect components against ESD, the other end is attached to a grounded conductor, such as the computer case or a ground mat.
- ◢ *Ground mats.* Ground mats can come equipped with a cord to plug into a wall outlet to provide a grounded surface on which to work. Remember, if you lift the component off the mat, it is no longer grounded and is susceptible to ESD.
- ◢ *Static shielding bags.* New components come shipped in static shielding bags. Save the bags to store other devices that are not currently installed in a PC.

The best solution to protect against ESD is to use a ground bracelet together with a ground mat. Consider a ground bracelet to be essential equipment when working on a computer. However, if you find yourself in a situation without one, touch the computer case before you touch a component. When passing a chip to another person, touch the other person first so that ESD is discharged between you and the other person before you pass the chip. Leave components inside their protective bags until you're ready to use them. Work on hard floors, not carpet, or use antistatic spray on the carpets. Generally, don't work on a computer if you or the computer have just come inside from the cold.

When working inside older computers using the AT form factor, you can turn off the computer and leave the computer plugged in. However, for today's computers using the ATX or BTX form factor, it is best to unplug the computer from the wall outlet before you open the case.

There is an exception to the ground-yourself rule. Inside a monitor case, there is substantial danger posed by the electricity stored in capacitors. When working inside a monitor, you *don't* want to be grounded, as you would provide a conduit for the voltage to discharge through your body. In this situation, be careful *not* to ground yourself.

When handling motherboards and expansion cards, don't touch the chips on the boards. In addition, don't stack boards on top of each other, which could accidentally dislodge a chip. Hold cards by the edges, but don't touch the edge connections on the card.

Don't touch a chip with a magnetized screwdriver. When using a multimeter to measure electricity, be careful not to touch a chip with the probes. When changing DIP switches, don't use a graphite pencil, because graphite conducts electricity; a small screwdriver works well.

After you unpack a new device or software that has been wrapped in cellophane, remove the cellophane from the work area quickly. Don't allow anyone who is not properly grounded to touch components. Do not store expansion cards within one foot of a monitor, because the monitor can discharge as much as 29,000 volts of ESD onto the screen.

Hold an expansion card by the edges. Don't touch any of the soldered components on a card. If you need to put an electronic device down, place it on a grounded mat, inside a static shielding bag, or on a flat, hard surface. Keep components away from your hair and clothing.

## PROTECT HARD DRIVES AND DISKS

Always turn off a computer before moving it to protect the hard drive, which is always spinning when the computer is turned on (unless the drive has a sleep mode). Never jar a computer while the hard disk is running. Also, avoid placing a PC on the floor, where the user can accidentally kick it.

Follow the usual precautions to protect CD and DVD discs and floppy disks. Keep CDs and DVDs away from heat, direct sunlight, and extreme cold, and protect them from scratches. Protect floppy disks from magnetic fields. Don't open the floppy shuttle window or touch the surface of the disk inside the housing. Treat disks with care, and they'll generally last for years.

## COMPTIA AUTHORIZED CURRICULUM PROGRAM

The logo of the CompTIA Authorized Curriculum Program and the status of this or other training material as "Authorized" under the CompTIA Authorized Curriculum Program signifies that, in CompTIA's opinion, such training material covers the content of the CompTIA's related certification exam. CompTIA has not reviewed or approved the accuracy of the contents of this training material and specifically disclaims any warranties of merchantability or fitness for a particular purpose. CompTIA makes no guarantee concerning the success of persons using any such "Authorized" or other training material in order to prepare for any CompTIA certification exam.

The contents of this training material were created for the CompTIA A+ 2006 certification exams covering CompTIA certification objectives that were current as of August 9, 2006.

# STATE OF THE INFORMATION TECHNOLOGY (IT) FIELD

Most organizations today depend on computers and information technology to improve business processes, productivity, and efficiency. Opportunities to become global organizations and reach customers, businesses, and suppliers are a direct result of the widespread use of the Internet. Changing technology further influences how companies do business. This fundamental change in business practices has increased the need for skilled and certified IT workers across industries. This transformation has moved many IT workers out of traditional IT businesses and into various IT-dependent industries such as banking, government, insurance, and health care.

In 2004, the U.S. Department of Labor, Bureau of Labor Statistics, reported that there were 1.1 million computer and data processing services jobs within organizations and an additional 132,000 self-employed workers.

In any industry, the workforce is important to continuously drive business. Having correctly skilled workers in IT is a struggle with the ever-changing technologies. It has been estimated that technologies change approximately every 2 years. With such a quick product life cycle, IT workers must strive to keep up with these changes to continue to bring value to their employers.

## CERTIFICATIONS

Different levels of education are required for the many jobs in the IT industry. Additionally, the level of education and type of training required varies from employer to employer, but the need for qualified technicians remains constant. As technology changes and advances in the industry continue to rapidly evolve, many employers consistently look for employees who possess the skills necessary to implement these new technologies. Traditional degrees and diplomas do not identify the skills that a job applicant has. With the growth of the IT industry, companies increasingly rely on technical certifications to identify the skills that a particular job applicant possesses. Technical certifications are a way for employers to ensure the quality and skill qualifications of their computer professionals, and they can offer job seekers a competitive edge. According to Thomas Regional Industrial Market Trends, one of the 15 trends that will transform the workplace over the next decade is a severe labor and skill shortage, specifically in technical fields, which are struggling to locate skilled and educated workers.

There are two types of certifications: vendor neutral and vendor specific. Vendor-neutral certifications are those that test for the skills and knowledge required in specific industry job roles and do not subscribe to a specific vendor's technology solution. Vendor-neutral certifications include all of the Computing Technology Industry Association's (CompTIA) certifications, Project Management Institute's certifications, and Security Certified Program certifications. Vendor-specific certifications validate the skills and knowledge necessary to be successful by utilizing a specific vendor's technology solution. Some examples of vendor-specific certifications include those offered by Microsoft, IBM, Novell, and Cisco.

As employers struggle to fill open IT positions with qualified candidates, certifications are a means of validating the skill sets necessary to be successful within an organization. In most careers, salary and compensation are determined by experience and education, but in IT, the number and type of certifications that an employee earns also factor into salary and wage increases. The Department of Labor, Bureau of Labor Statistics, reported that the computer and data processing industry is expected to grow about 40% by the year 2014, compared to a 14% increase in the entire economy.

Certifications provide job applicants with more than just a competitive edge over their non-certified counterparts who apply for the same IT positions. Some institutions of higher education grant college credit to students who successfully pass certification exams, moving them further along in their degree programs. Certifications also give individuals who are interested in careers in the military the ability to move into higher positions more quickly. And many advanced certification programs accept and sometimes require entry-level certifications as part of their exams. For example, Cisco and Microsoft accept some CompTIA certifications as prerequisites for their certification programs.

## CAREER PLANNING

Finding a career that fits a person's personality, skill set, and lifestyle is challenging and fulfilling but can often be difficult. What are the steps individuals should take to find that dream career? Is IT interesting to you? Chances are that if you are reading this book, this question has been answered. What about IT do you like? The world of work in the IT industry is vast. Some questions to ask include the following: Are you a person who likes to work alone, or do you like to work in a group? Do you like speaking directly with customers, or do you prefer to stay behind the scenes? Is your lifestyle conducive to a lot of travel, or do you need to stay in one location? All of these factors influence your decision when faced with choosing the right job. Inventory assessments are a good first step toward learning more about your interests, work values, and abilities. There are a variety of Web sites that offer assistance with career planning and assessments.

The Computing Technology Industry Association (CompTIA) hosts an informational Web site called the TechCareer Compass (TCC) that defines careers in the IT industry. The TCC is located at *http://tcc.comptia.org*. This Web site was created by the industry and outlines over 100 industry jobs. Each defined job includes a job description, alternate job titles, critical work functions, activities and performance indicators, and skills and knowledge required by the job. In other words, it shows exactly what the job entails so that you can find one that best fits your interests and abilities. Additionally, the TCC maps over 750 technical certifications to the skills required by each specific job, allowing you to research and plan your certification training. The Web site also includes a resource section, which is updated regularly with articles and links to other career Web sites. The TechCareer Compass is the one-stop location for IT career information.

In addition to CompTIA's TechCareer Compass, there are many other Web sites that cover components of IT careers and career planning. Many of these sites can also be found in the TCC Resources section.

## CITATIONS

Bureau of Labor Statistics, U.S. Department of Labor. *Career Guide to Industries, 2006-07 Edition, Computer and Data Processing Services*. On the Internet at *www.bls.gov/oco/cg/cgs033.htm* (visited September 6, 2006).

Bureau of Labor Statistics, U.S. Department of Labor, *Occupational Outlook Handbook, 2006-07 Edition, Computer Support Specialists and System Administrators*. On the Internet at *www.bls.gov/oco/home.htm* (visited September 3, 2006).

Thomas Regional Industrial Market Trends. July 8, 2003 Newsletter: *15 Trends That Will Transform the Workforce*. On the Internet at *http://news.thomasnet.com/IMT/archives/2003/07/15_trends_that.html?t=archive* (visited September 3, 2006).

# WHAT'S NEW WITH COMPTIA A+ CERTIFICATION

In June 2006, CompTIA *(www.comptia.org)* published the objectives for the 2006 CompTIA A+ certification exams.

The format of the 2006 exams is new. Here are the key facts regarding these exams:

- ◢ Currently, there are four 2006 exams. Everyone must pass the CompTIA A+ Essentials exam. You must also pass one of three advanced exams, which are named the CompTIA A+ 220-602 exam, the CompTIA A+ 220-603 exam, and the CompTIA A+ 220-604 exam.
- ◢ All four exams cover the same content, which includes both hardware and software. The advanced exams cover the content in a greater depth than does the CompTIA A+ Essentials exam.
- ◢ The CompTIA A+ 220-602 exam is the most comprehensive of the three advanced exams. Basically, the CompTIA A+ 220-603 and CompTIA A+ 220-604 exams are subsets of the CompTIA A+ 220-602 exam.
- ◢ The type of CompTIA A+ certification you receive depends on which of the three advanced exams you pass, as diagrammed in Figure 1.

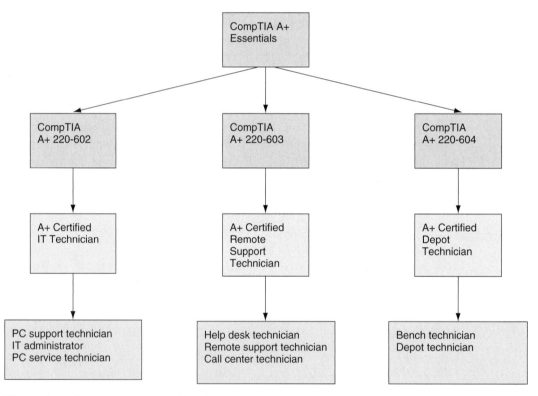

**Figure 1**  Paths to CompTIA A+ certification and job roles

▲ By passing the CompTIA A+ 220-602 and CompTIA A+ Essentials exams, you are awarded the CompTIA A+ Certification for IT Technician. This certification targets those who intend to work in a "mobile or corporate technical environment with a high level of face-to-face client interaction." Job roles include IT administrator, enterprise technician, field service technician, and PC support technician.

▲ By passing the CompTIA A+ 220-603 and CompTIA A+ Essentials exams, you are awarded the CompTIA A+ Certification for Remote Support Technician. This certification targets those who intend to work "in a remote-based work environment where client interaction, client training, operating system, and connectivity issues are emphasized." Job roles include help desk technician, remote support technician, and call center technician.

▲ By passing the CompTIA A+ 220-604 and CompTIA A+ Essentials exams, you are awarded the CompTIA A+ Certification for Depot Technician. This certification targets those who intend to work in settings where hardware is emphasized. Job roles include bench technician and depot technician.

Here is a breakdown of the domains covered on each of the four exams:

| Domain | CompTIA A+ Essentials | CompTIA A+ 220-602 | CompTIA A+ 220-603 | CompTIA A+ 220-604 |
|---|---|---|---|---|
| 1.0 Personal Computer Components | 21% | 18% | 15% | 45% |
| 2.0 Laptop and Portable Devices | 11% | 9% | 0 | 20% |
| 3.0 Operating Systems | 21% | 20% | 29% | 0 |
| 4.0 Printers and Scanners | 9% | 14% | 10% | 20% |
| 5.0 Networks | 12% | 11% | 11% | 0 |
| 6.0 Security | 11% | 8% | 15% | 5% |
| 7.0 Safety and Environmental Issues | 10% | 5% | 0 | 10% |
| 8.0 Communication and Professionalism | 5% | 15% | 20% | 0 |

# HOW TO BECOME COMPTIA CERTIFIED

This training material can help you prepare for and pass a related CompTIA certification exam or exams. In order to achieve CompTIA certification, you must register for and pass a CompTIA certification exam or exams. In order to become CompTIA certified, you must:

1. Select a certification exam provider. For more information, please visit *http://certification.comptia.org/default.aspx*.

2. Register for and schedule a time to take the CompTIA certification exam(s) at a convenient location.

3. Read and sign the Candidate Agreement, which will be presented at the time of the exam(s). The text of the Candidate Agreement can be found at *www.comptia.org/certification/general_information/candidate_agreement.aspx*.

4. Take and pass the CompTIA certification exam(s).

For more information about CompTIA's certifications, such as their industry acceptance, benefits, or program news, please visit *www.comptia.org/certification/default.asp*.

CompTIA is a not-for-profit information technology (IT) trade association. CompTIA's certifications are designed by subject matter experts from across the IT industry. Each CompTIA certification is vendor-neutral, covers multiple technologies, and requires demonstration of skills and knowledge widely sought after by the IT industry.

To contact CompTIA with any questions or comments, please call (1) (630) 678-8300 or email *questions@comptia.org*.

# CHAPTER 1

# Introducing Hardware

**In this chapter, you will learn:**

- That a computer requires both hardware and software to work
- About the many different hardware components inside of and connected to a computer

Like millions of other computer users, you have probably used your desktop or notebook computer to play games, surf the Web, write papers, or build spreadsheets. You can use all these applications without understanding exactly what goes on inside your computer case or notebook. But if you are curious to learn more about personal computers, and if you want to graduate from simply being the end user of your computer to becoming the master of your machine, then this book is for you. It is written for anyone who wants to understand what is happening inside the machine in order to install new hardware and software, diagnose and solve both hardware and software problems, and make decisions about purchasing new hardware and operating systems. The only assumption made here is that you are a computer user—that is, you can turn on your machine, load a software package, and use that software to accomplish a task. No experience in electronics is assumed.

In addition, this book prepares you to pass the A+ Essentials exam and any one of the advanced exams, which are the A+ 220-602, the A+ 220-603, or the A+ 220-604 exam, required by CompTIA (*www.comptia.org*) for A+ Certification. At the time this book went to print, the older 2003 A+ exams were still live; therefore, the book also includes the content on the 2003 A+ Core Hardware Service Technician exam and the A+ Operating System Technologies exam.

## HARDWARE NEEDS SOFTWARE TO WORK

In the world of computers, the term **hardware** refers to the computer's physical components, such as the monitor, keyboard, memory chips, and hard drive. The term **software** refers to the set of instructions that directs the hardware to accomplish a task. To perform a computing task, software uses hardware for four basic functions: input, processing, storage, and output (see Figure 1-1). Also, hardware components must communicate both data and instructions among themselves, which requires an electrical system to provide power, because these components are electrical. In this chapter, we introduce the hardware components of a computer system and help you see how they work. In Chapter 2, we introduce operating systems and how they work.

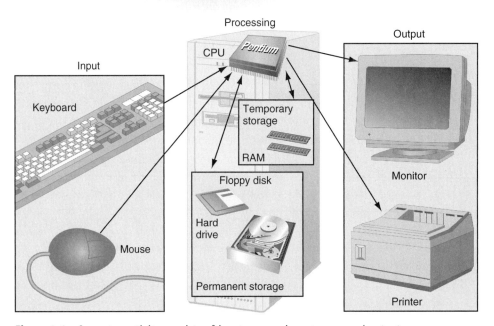

**Figure 1-1**   Computer activity consists of input, processing, storage, and output

A computer user must interact with a computer in a way that both the user and the software understand, such as with entries made by way of a keyboard or a mouse (see Figure 1-2). However, software must convert that instruction into a form that hardware can "understand." As incredible as it might sound, every communication between hardware and software, or between software and other software, is reduced to a simple yes or no, which is represented inside the computer by two simple states: on and off.

It was not always so. For almost half a century, people attempted to invent an electronic computational device that could store all 10 digits in our decimal number system and even some of our alphabet. Scientists were attempting to store a charge in a vacuum tube, which is similar to a light bulb. The charge would later be "read" to determine what had been stored there. Each digit in our number system, one through nine, was stored with increasing degrees of charge, similar to a light bulb varying in power from dim all the way up to bright. However, the degree of "dimness" or "brightness" was difficult to measure, and it would change because the voltage in the equipment could not be accurately regulated. For example, an eight would be stored with a partially bright charge, but later it would be read as a seven or nine as the voltage on the vacuum tube fluctuated slightly.

Then, in the 1940s, John Atanasoff came up with the brilliant idea to store and read only two values, on and off. Either there was a charge or there was not a charge, and this was easy to write and read, just as it's easy to determine if a light bulb is on or off.

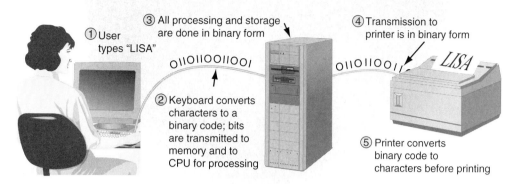

**Figure 1-2** All communication, storage, and processing of data inside a computer are in binary form until presented as output to the user

This technology of storing and reading only two states is called binary, and the number system that only uses two digits, 0 and 1, is called the **binary number system**. A 1 or 0 in this system is called a **bit**, or binary digit. Because of the way the number system is organized, grouping is often done in groups of eight bits, each of which is called a **byte**. (Guess what four bits are called? A nibble!)

In a computer, all counting and calculations use the binary number system. Counting in binary goes like this: 0, 1, 10, 11, 100, 101, and so forth. For example, in binary code the number 25 is 0001 1001 (see Figure 1-3). When text is stored in a computer, every letter or other character is first converted to a code using only zeros and ones. The most common coding method for text is ASCII (American Standard Code for Information Interchange). For example, the uppercase letter A in ASCII code is 0100 0001(see Figure 1-3).

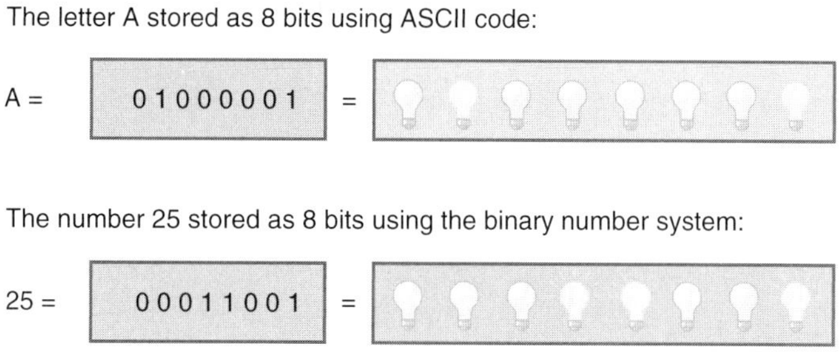

The letter A stored as 8 bits using ASCII code:

A = | 01000001 | = 🔆🔆🔆🔆🔆🔆🔆🔆

The number 25 stored as 8 bits using the binary number system:

25 = | 00011001 | = 🔆🔆🔆🔆🔆🔆🔆🔆

**Figure 1-3** All letters and numbers are stored in a computer as a series of bits, each represented in the computer as on or off

## PC HARDWARE COMPONENTS

In this section, we cover the major hardware components of a microcomputer system used for input, output, processing, storage, electrical supply, and communication. Most input and output devices are outside the computer case. Most processing and storage components are contained inside the case. The most important component in the case is the **central processing unit (CPU)**, also called the **processor** or **microprocessor**. As its name implies, this device is central to all processing done by the computer. Data received by input devices is read by the CPU, and output from the CPU is written to output devices. The CPU writes data and instructions in storage devices and performs calculations and other data processing. Whether inside or outside the case, and regardless of the function the device performs, each hardware input, output, or storage device requires these elements to operate:

▲ *A method for the CPU to communicate with the device.* The device must send data to and/or receive data from the CPU. The CPU might need to control the device by passing instructions to it, or the device might need to request service from the CPU.

▲ *Software to instruct and control the device.* A device is useless without software to control it. The software must know how to communicate with the device at the detailed level of that specific device, and the CPU must have access to this software in order to interact with the device. Each device responds to a specific set of instructions based on the device's functions. The software must have an instruction for each possible action you expect the device to accomplish.

▲ *Electricity to power the device.* Electronic devices require electricity to operate. Devices can receive power from the power supply inside the computer case, or they can have their own power supplied by a power cable connected to an electrical outlet.

In the next few pages, we take a sightseeing tour of computer hardware, first looking outside and then inside the case. I've tried to keep the terminology and concepts to a minimum in these sections, because in future chapters, everything is covered in much more detail.

## HARDWARE USED FOR INPUT AND OUTPUT

Most input/output devices are outside the computer case. These devices communicate with components inside the computer case through a wireless connection or through cables attached to the case at a connection called a **port**. Most computer ports are located on the back of the case (see Figure 1-4), but some cases have ports on the front for easy access.

For wireless connections, a wireless device communicates with the system using a radio wave or infrared port. The most popular input devices are a keyboard and a mouse, and the most popular output devices are a monitor and a printer.

**A+ Exam Tip**

The A+ Essentials exam expects you to know many computer terms, and lots of them are found in this chapter. Pay close attention to all key terms.

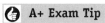
**Video**

Examining the Back of a PC

The **keyboard** is the primary input device of a computer (see Figure 1-5). The keyboards that are standard today are called enhanced keyboards and hold 104 keys. Ergonomic keyboards are curved to make them more comfortable for the hands and wrists. In addition, some keyboards come equipped with a mouse port used to attach a mouse to the keyboard, although it is more common for the mouse port to be on the computer case. Electricity to run the keyboard comes from inside the computer case and is provided by wires in the keyboard cable.

A **mouse** is a pointing device used to move a pointer on the screen and to make selections. The bottom of a mouse has a rotating ball or an optical sensor that tracks movement and controls the location of the pointer. The one, two, or three buttons on the top of the mouse serve different purposes for different software. For example, Windows XP uses the left mouse button to execute a command and the right mouse button to display related shortcut information.

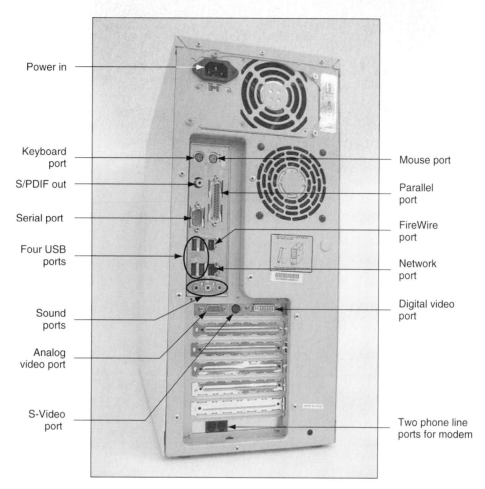

Power in
Keyboard port
S/PDIF out
Serial port
Four USB ports
Sound ports
Analog video port
S-Video port

Mouse port
Parallel port
FireWire port
Network port
Digital video port
Two phone line ports for modem

**Figure 1-4**  Input/output devices connect to the computer case by ports usually found on the back of the case

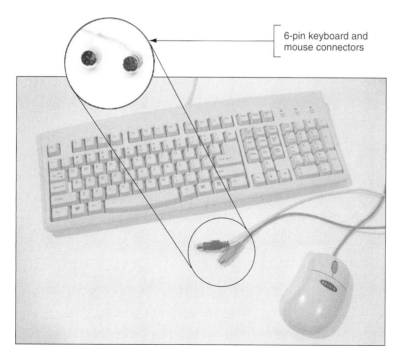

6-pin keyboard and mouse connectors

**Figure 1-5**  The keyboard and the mouse are the two most popular input devices

A+ ESS
1.1

The monitor and the printer are the two most popular output devices (see Figure 1-6). The **monitor** is the visual device that displays the primary output of the computer. Hardware manufacturers typically rate a monitor according to the diagonal size of its screen (in inches) and by the monitor's resolution, which is a function of the number of dots on the screen used for display.

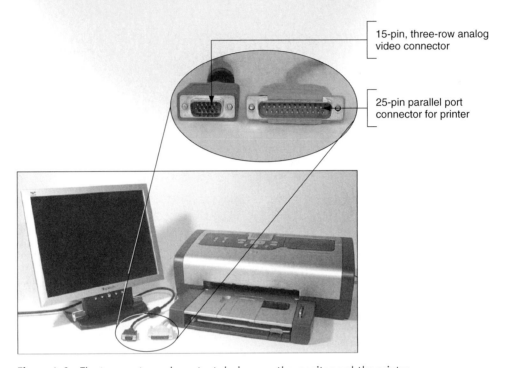

**Figure 1-6** The two most popular output devices are the monitor and the printer

A very important output device is the **printer**, which produces output on paper, often called **hard copy**. The most popular printers available today are ink-jet, laser, thermal, solid ink, and dot-matrix printers. The monitor and the printer need separate power supplies. Their electrical power cords connect to electrical outlets. Sometimes, the computer case provides an electrical outlet for the monitor's power cord, to eliminate the need for one more power outlet.

Figure 1-6 showed the most common connectors used for a monitor and a printer: a 15-pin analog video connector and a 25-pin parallel connector. Note that in addition, a digital monitor can use a digital video connector, and a printer sometimes uses a universal serial bus (USB) connector (see Figure 1-7).

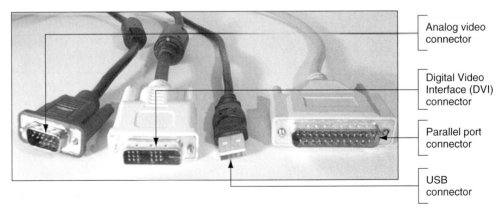

**Figure 1-7** Two video connectors and two connectors used by a printer

## HARDWARE INSIDE THE COMPUTER CASE

Most storage and all processing of data and instructions are done inside the computer case, so before we look at components used for storage and processing, let's look at what you see when you first open the computer case. Most computers contain these devices inside the case (see Figure 1-8):

- ◢ A motherboard containing the CPU, memory, and other components
- ◢ A floppy drive, hard drive, and CD drive used for permanent storage
- ◢ A power supply with power cords supplying electricity to all devices inside the case
- ◢ Circuit boards used by the CPU to communicate with devices inside and outside the case
- ◢ Cables connecting devices to circuit boards and the motherboard

**Figure 1-8** Inside the computer case

Some of the first things you'll notice when you look inside a computer case are circuit boards. A **circuit board** is a board that holds microchips, or integrated circuits (ICs), and the circuitry that connects these chips. Some circuit boards, called **expansion cards**, are installed in long narrow **expansion slots** on the motherboard. All circuit boards contain microchips, which are most often manufactured using (CMOS) **complementary metal-oxide semiconductor** technology. CMOS chips require less electricity and produce less heat than chips manufactured using earlier technologies such as TTL (transistor-transistor logic). The other major components inside the case look like small boxes, including the power supply, hard drive, CD drive, and floppy drive.

There are two types of cables inside the case: data cables, which connect devices to one another, and power cables or power cords, which supply power. Most often, you can distinguish between the two by the shape of the cable. Data cables are flat and wide, and power cords are round and small. There are some exceptions to this rule, so the best way to identify a cable is to trace its source and destination.

## THE MOTHERBOARD

The largest and most important circuit board in the computer is the **motherboard**, also called the **main board** or **system board** (see Figure 1-9), which contains the CPU, the component in which most processing takes place. The motherboard is the most complicated piece of equipment inside the case, and Chapter 6 covers it in detail. Because all devices must communicate with the CPU on the motherboard, all devices in a computer are installed directly on the motherboard, directly linked to it by a cable connected to a port on the motherboard, or indirectly linked to it by expansion cards. A device that is not installed directly on the motherboard is called a **peripheral device**. Some ports on the motherboard stick outside the case to accommodate external devices such as a keyboard, and some ports provide a connection for a device inside the case, such as a floppy disk drive.

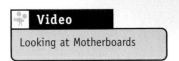
Video
Looking at Motherboards

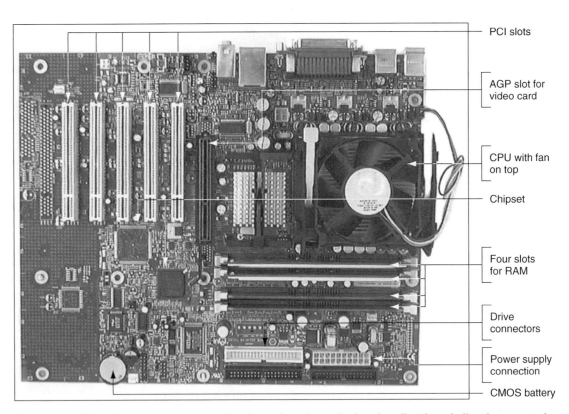

PCI slots

AGP slot for video card

CPU with fan on top

Chipset

Four slots for RAM

Drive connectors

Power supply connection

CMOS battery

**Figure 1-9** All hardware components are either located on the motherboard or directly or indirectly connected to it because they must all communicate with the CPU

Figure 1-10 shows the ports coming directly off a motherboard to the outside of the case: a keyboard port, a mouse port, a parallel port, two S/PDIF ports (for optical or coaxial cable), a FireWire port, a network port, four USB ports, six sound ports, and a wireless LAN antenna port. A **parallel port** transmits data in parallel and is most often used by a printer. A **S/PDIF (Sony-Philips Digital Interface) sound port** connects to an external home theater audio system, providing digital output and the best signal quality. A FireWire port (also called a 1394 port) is used for high-speed multimedia devices such as digital camcorders. A **universal serial bus (USB) port** can be used by many different input/output devices, such as keyboards, printers, scanners, and digital cameras.

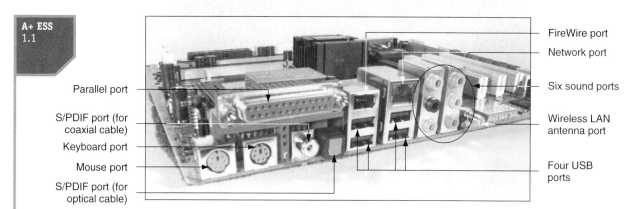

Parallel port

S/PDIF port (for coaxial cable)

Keyboard port

Mouse port

S/PDIF port (for optical cable)

FireWire port

Network port

Six sound ports

Wireless LAN antenna port

Four USB ports

**Figure 1-10**  A motherboard provides ports for common I/O devices

In addition to these ports, some older motherboards provide a **serial port** that transmits data serially (one bit follows the next); it is often used for an external modem or a serial mouse (a mouse that uses a serial port). A serial port looks like a parallel port but is not as wide. You will learn more about ports in Chapter 9.

Listed next are the major components found on all motherboards; some of them are labeled in Figure 1-9. In the sections that follow, we discuss these components in detail. Components used primarily for processing:

▲ Processor or CPU (central processing unit), the computer's most important chip
▲ Chipset that supports the processor by controlling many motherboard activities

Components used for temporary storage:

▲ RAM (random access memory) used to hold data and instructions as they are processed
▲ Cache memory to speed up memory access (optional, depending on the type of processor)

Components that allow the processor to communicate with other devices:

▲ Traces, or wires, on the motherboard used for communication
▲ Expansion slots to connect expansion cards to the motherboard
▲ The system clock that keeps communication in sync
▲ Connections for data cables to devices inside the case
▲ Ports for devices outside the case

Electrical system:

▲ Power supply connections to provide electricity to the motherboard and expansion cards

Programming and setup data stored on the motherboard:

▲ Flash ROM, a memory chip used to permanently store instructions that control basic hardware functions (explained in more detail later in the chapter)
▲ CMOS RAM and CMOS setup chip that holds configuration data

A+ ESS
1.1

## THE PROCESSOR AND THE CHIPSET

The processor or CPU is the chip inside the computer that performs most of the actual data processing (see Figure 1-11). The processor could not do its job without the assistance of the **chipset**, a group of microchips on the motherboard that control the flow of data and instructions to and from the processor, providing careful timing of activities (see Figure 1-12).

CPU fan

Motherboard

Heat sink

**Figure 1-11**   The processor is hidden underneath the fan and the heat sink, which keep it cool

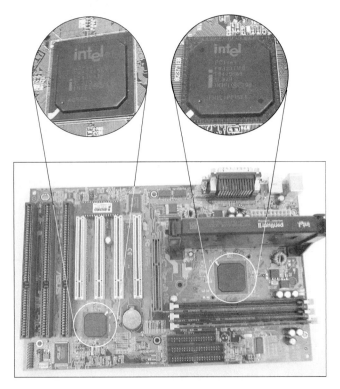

**Figure 1-12**   This motherboard uses two chips in its chipset (notice the bus lines coming from each chip used for communication)

In this book, we discuss various types of computers, but we focus on the most common personal computers (PCs), referred to as IBM-compatible. These are built around microprocessors and chipsets manufactured by Intel Corporation, AMD, VIA, SiS, Cyrix, and other manufacturers. The Macintosh family of computers, manufactured by Apple Computer, Inc., has been built around a family of microprocessors, the PowerPC by IBM, although Apple is currently moving toward Intel processors. You will learn more about processors and chipsets in Chapter 5.

## STORAGE DEVICES

In Figure 1-1, you saw two kinds of storage: temporary and permanent. The processor uses temporary storage, called **primary storage** or **memory**, to temporarily hold both data and instructions while it is processing them. Primary storage is much faster to access than permanent storage. However, when data and instructions are not being used, they must be kept in permanent storage, sometimes called **secondary storage**, such as a hard drive, CD, or floppy disk. Figure 1-13 shows an analogy to help you understand the concept of primary and secondary storage.

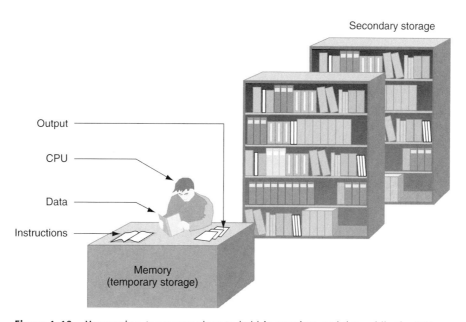

**Figure 1-13**   Memory is a temporary place to hold instructions and data while the CPU processes both

In our analogy, suppose you must do some research at the library. You go to the stacks, pull out several books, carry them over to a study table, and sit down with your notepad and pencil to take notes and do some calculations. When you're done, you leave with your notepad full of information and calculations, but you don't take the books with you. In this example, the stacks are permanent storage, and the books (data and instructions) are permanently kept there. The table is temporary storage, a place for you to keep data and instructions as you work with them. The notepad is your output from all that work, and you are the CPU, doing the work of reading the books and writing down information.

You kept a book on the table until you knew you were finished with it. As you worked, it would not make sense to go back and forth with a book, returning and retrieving it to and from the stacks. Similarly, the CPU uses primary storage, or memory, to temporarily hold data and instructions as long as it needs them for processing. Memory (your table) gives fast but temporary access, while secondary storage (the stacks) gives slow but permanent access.

## PRIMARY STORAGE

Primary storage is provided by devices called memory or **RAM (random access memory)**, located on the motherboard and on other circuit boards. RAM chips can be installed individually directly on the motherboard or in banks of several chips on a small board that plugs into the motherboard (see Figure 1-14). These small RAM boards are called memory modules. There are three general types of modules: a **DIMM (dual inline memory module)**, which is the most common type, a **RIMM** designed by Rambus, Inc., and an older, outdated type called a **SIMM (single inline memory module)**. Each type module comes in several sizes and features, and generally you must match the module size and type to that which the motherboard supports.

> **A+ Exam Tip**
>
> The A+ Essentials exam expects you to know about DIMMs and RIMMs.

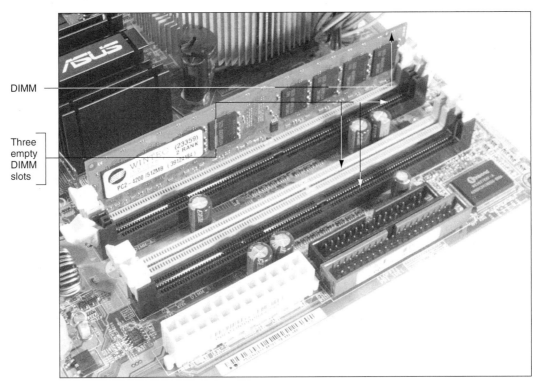

DIMM

Three
empty
DIMM
slots

**Figure 1-14**   A SIMM, DIMM, or RIMM holds RAM and is mounted directly on a motherboard

Whatever information is stored in RAM is lost when the computer is turned off, because RAM chips need a continuous supply of electrical power to hold data or software stored in them. This kind of memory is called **volatile** because it is temporary in nature. By contrast, another kind of memory holds its data permanently, even when the power is turned off. This type of memory is **nonvolatile** and is called **ROM (read-only memory)**. You will see examples of ROM chips later in the chapter and examples of RAM modules in Chapter 7.

**APPLYING CONCEPTS**      Using Windows XP, you can see what type of CPU you have and how much memory you have installed. Click **Start**, right-click **My Computer**, and then select **Properties** on the shortcut menu. Then click the

A+ ESS
1.1

**General** tab (see Figure 1-15). You can also see which version of Windows you are using. Using Windows 9x or Windows 2000, right-click the **My Computer** icon on your desktop, select **Properties** on the shortcut menu, and click the **General** tab.

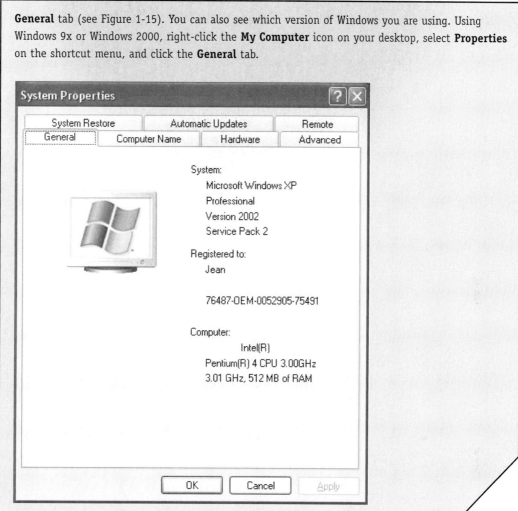

**Figure 1-15**   System Properties gives useful information about your computer and OS

## SECONDARY STORAGE

As you remember, the RAM on the motherboard is called primary storage. Primary storage temporarily holds both data and instructions as the CPU processes them. These data and instructions are also permanently stored on devices such as CDs, hard drives, and floppy disks, in locations that are remote from the CPU. Data and instructions cannot be processed by the CPU from this remote storage (called secondary storage) but must first be copied into primary storage (RAM) for processing. The most important difference between primary and secondary storage is that secondary

> **Notes**
>
> Don't forget that primary storage, or RAM, is temporary; as soon as you turn off the computer, any information there is lost. That's why you should always save your work frequently into secondary storage.

storage is permanent. When you turn off your computer, the information in secondary storage remains intact. The most popular secondary storage devices are hard disks, CDs, DVDs, USB flash drives, and floppy disks.

A **hard drive** is a sealed case containing platters or disks that rotate at a high speed (see Figure 1-16). As the platters rotate, an arm with a sensitive read/write head reaches across the platters, both writing new data to them and reading existing data from them.

**Figure 1-16**  Hard drive with sealed cover removed

### 🔴 A+ Exam Tip

The A+ Essentials exam expects you to know that a parallel ATA connector on a motherboard can support one or two EIDE devices, and a serial ATA connector can support only a single hard drive. The number and type connectors on the board determine the total number of drives the board can support.

### Notes

Confusion with industry standards can result when different manufacturers call a standard by a different name, which happens all too often with computer parts. The industry uses the terms ATA, IDE, and EIDE almost interchangeably even though technically they have different meanings. Used correctly, ATA refers to drive interface standards as published by ANSI. Used correctly, IDE refers to the technology used internally by a hard drive, and EIDE is commonly used by manufacturers to refer to the parallel ATA interface that CD drives, DVD drives, Zip drives, tape drives, and IDE hard drives can use to connect to a motherboard. The term IDE is most often used, when in fact EIDE is actually the more accurate name for the interface standards. To be consistent with manufacturer documentation, in this book, we loosely use the term IDE to mean IDE, EIDE, and parallel ATA. For instance, look closely at Figure 1-17 where the motherboard connectors are labeled Primary IDE and Secondary IDE, when technically they really should be labeled Primary EIDE and Secondary EIDE.

Most hard drives today use an internal technology called Integrated Drive Electronics (IDE). Most often, the interface between a hard drive and the motherboard is done according to an ATA (AT Attachment) standard as published by the American National Standards Institute (ANSI, see *www.ansi.org*).

The two major ATA standards for a drive interface are serial ATA (the newer standard) and parallel ATA (the older standard). Parallel ATA, sometimes called the EIDE (Enhanced IDE) standard or the IDE standard, allows for two connectors on a motherboard for two data cables (see Figure 1-17). Each IDE ribbon cable has a connection at the other end for an IDE device and a connection in the middle of the cable for a second IDE device. Using this interface, a

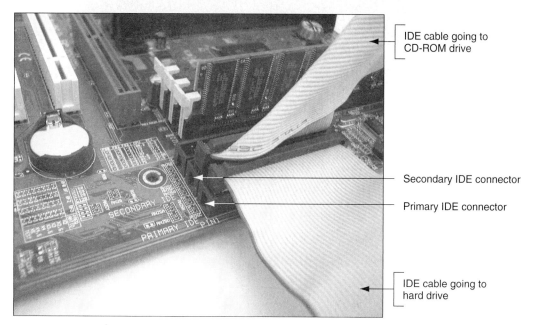

IDE cable going to
CD-ROM drive

Secondary IDE connector

Primary IDE connector

IDE cable going to
hard drive

**Figure 1-17** Using a parallel ATA interface, a motherboard has two IDE connectors, each of which can accommodate two devices; a hard drive usually connects to the motherboard using the primary IDE connector

motherboard can accommodate up to four IDE devices in one system. Hard drives, Zip drives, CD drives, DVD drives, and tape drives, among other devices, can use these four IDE connections, which are controlled by the chipset. A typical system has one hard drive connected to one IDE connector and a CD drive connected to the other (see Figure 1-18).

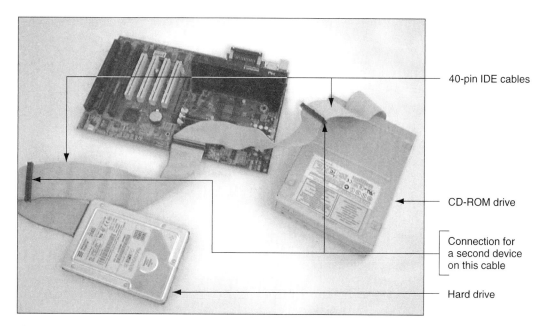

40-pin IDE cables

CD-ROM drive

Connection for
a second device
on this cable

Hard drive

**Figure 1-18** Two IDE devices connected to a motherboard using both IDE connections and two cables

The serial ATA standard allows for more than four drives installed in a system and applies only to hard drives and not to other drives. So, a motherboard that uses serial ATA for hard drives will also have parallel ATA connectors for other type drives. Figure 1-19 shows a serial ATA drive interface.

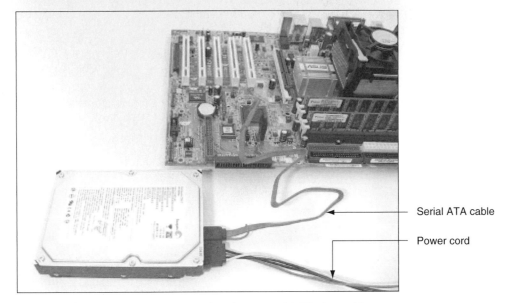

Serial ATA cable

Power cord

**Figure 1-19** A hard drive subsystem using the new serial ATA data cable

**Video**

Identifying Drives

Figure 1-20 shows the inside of a computer case with three IDE devices. The CD-ROM drive and the Zip drive share an IDE cable, and the hard drive uses the other cable.

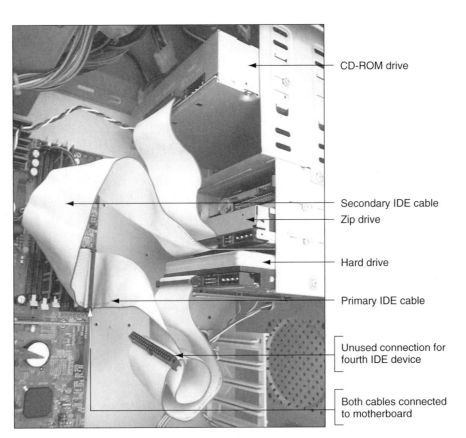

CD-ROM drive

Secondary IDE cable
Zip drive

Hard drive

Primary IDE cable

Unused connection for fourth IDE device

Both cables connected to motherboard

**Figure 1-20** This system has a CD-ROM and a Zip drive sharing the secondary IDE cable and a hard drive using the primary IDE cable

Both cables connect to the motherboard at the two IDE connections. (You will learn more about IDE, EIDE, and ATA in Chapter 8.)

A hard drive receives its power from the power supply by way of a power cord (see Figure 1-21). Looking back at Figure 1-20, you can see the power connections to the right of the cable connections on each drive. (The power cords are not connected to make it easier to see the data cable connections.) Chapter 8 covers how a hard drive works and how to install one.

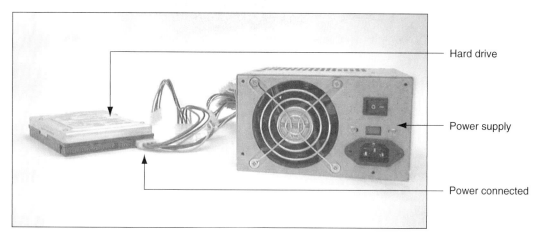

**Figure 1-21**   A hard drive receives power from the power supply by way of a power cord connected to the drive

Another secondary storage device sometimes found inside the case is a floppy drive that can hold 3.5-inch disks containing up to 1.44 MB of data. Most motherboards provide a connection for a floppy drive cable (see Figure 1-22).

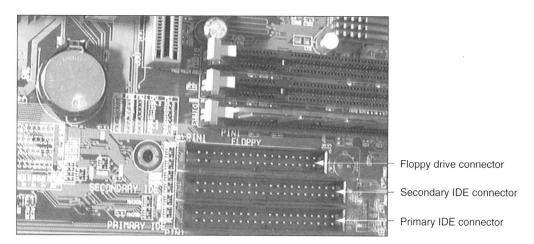

**Figure 1-22**   A motherboard usually provides a connection for a floppy drive cable

The floppy drive cable can accommodate one or two drives (see Figure 1-23). The drive at the end of the cable is drive A. If another drive were connected to the middle of the cable, it would be drive B in a computer system. Electricity to a floppy drive is provided by a power cord from the power supply that connects to a power port at the back of the drive.

Floppy drives are not as necessary as they once were because the industry is moving toward storage media that can hold more data, such as CDs, DVDs, and flash drives. For years, every PC and notebook computer had a floppy drive, but many newer notebook computers don't, and manufacturers often offer floppy drives on desktop systems as add-on options only.

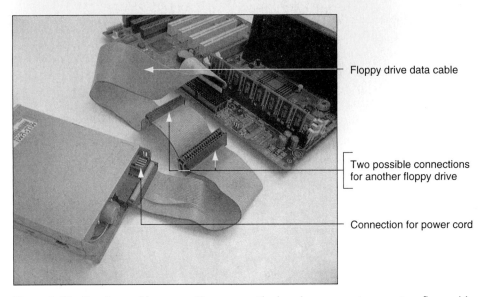

Floppy drive data cable

Two possible connections for another floppy drive

Connection for power cord

**Figure 1-23** One floppy drive connection on a motherboard can support one or two floppy drives

A CD-ROM (compact disc read-only memory) drive is considered standard equipment on most computer systems today because most software is distributed on CDs. Figure 1-24 shows the rear of a CD-ROM drive with the IDE data cable and power cord connected. Don't let the name of the CD-ROM drive confuse you. It's really not memory but secondary storage, because when you turn off the power, the data stored on a CD remains intact. Chapter 10 discusses different CD technologies and drives, some of which can both read and write data to the disc.

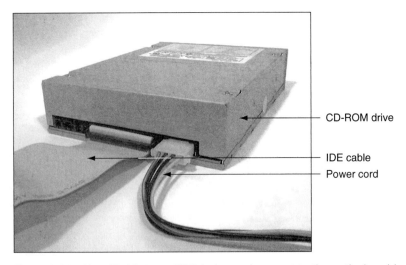

CD-ROM drive

IDE cable
Power cord

**Figure 1-24** Most CD drives are EIDE devices and connect to the motherboard by way of an IDE data cable

## MOTHERBOARD COMPONENTS USED FOR COMMUNICATION AMONG DEVICES

When you look carefully at a motherboard, you see many fine lines on both the top and the bottom of the board's surface (see Figure 1-25). These lines, sometimes called **traces**, are circuits or paths that enable data, instructions, and power to move from component to component on the board. This system of pathways used for communication and the protocol and methods used for transmission are collectively called the **bus**.

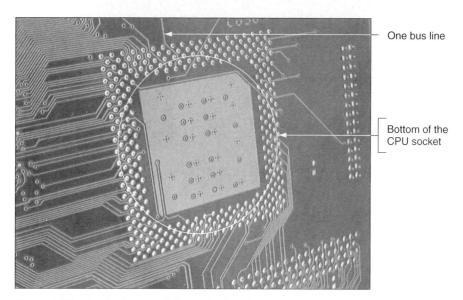

One bus line

Bottom of the
CPU socket

**Figure 1-25**  On the bottom of the motherboard, you can see bus lines terminating at the CPU socket

(A **protocol** is a set of rules and standards that any two entities use for communication.) The parts of the bus that we are most familiar with are the lines of the bus that are used for data, called the **data bus**.

Binary data is put on a line of a bus by placing voltage on that line. We can visualize that bits are "traveling" down the bus in parallel, but in reality, the voltage placed on each line is not "traveling," but rather is all over the line. When one component at one end of the line wants to write data to another component, the two components get in sync for the write operation. Then, the first component places voltage on several lines of the bus, and the other component immediately reads the voltage on these lines.

The CPU or other devices interpret the voltage, or lack of voltage, on each line on the bus as binary digits (0s or 1s). Some buses have data paths that are 8, 16, 32, 64, or 128 bits wide. For example, a bus that has eight wires, or lines, to transmit data is called an 8-bit bus. Figure 1-26 shows an 8-bit bus between the CPU and memory that is transmitting the letter A (binary 0100 0001). All bits of a byte are placed on their lines of the bus at the same time. Remember there are only two states inside a computer: on and off, which represent zero and one. On a bus, these two states are no voltage for a zero and voltage for a one. So, the bus in Figure 1-26 has voltage on two lines and no voltage on the other six lines, in order to pass the letter A on the bus.

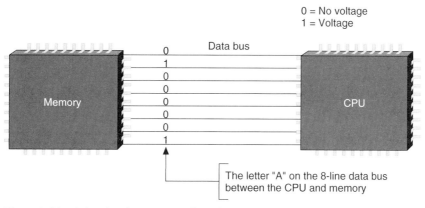

0 = No voltage
1 = Voltage

Data bus

Memory

0
1
0
0
0
0
0
1

CPU

The letter "A" on the 8-line data bus
between the CPU and memory

**Figure 1-26**  A data bus has traces or lines that carry voltage interpreted by the CPU and other devices as bits

This bus is only 8 bits wide, but most buses today are much wider: 16, 32, 64, or 128 bits wide. Also, most buses today use a ninth bit for error checking. Adding a check bit for each byte allows the component reading the data to verify that it is the same data written to the bus.

The width of a data bus is called the **data path size**. A motherboard can have more than one bus, each using a different protocol, speed, data path size, and so on. The main bus on the motherboard that communicates with the CPU, memory, and the chipset goes by several names: **system bus, front side bus (FSB)**, memory bus, **host bus**, local bus, or external bus. In our discussions, we'll use the term system bus or memory bus because they are more descriptive, but know that motherboard ads typically use the term front side bus. The data portion of most system buses on today's motherboards is 64 bits wide with or without additional lines for error checking.

One of the most interesting lines, or circuits, on a bus is the **system clock** or system timer, which is dedicated to timing the activities of the chips on the motherboard. A crystal on the motherboard (Figure 1-27), similar to that found in watches, generates the oscillation that produces the continuous pulses of the system clock. Traces carry these pulses over the motherboard to chips and expansion slots to ensure that all activities are synchronized.

Motherboard crystal generates the system clock

**Figure 1-27**   The system clock is a pulsating electrical signal sent out by this component that works much like a crystal in a wristwatch (one line, or circuit, on the motherboard bus is dedicated to carrying this pulse)

Remember that everything in a computer is binary, and this includes the activities themselves. Instead of continuously working to perform commands or move data, the CPU, bus, and other devices work in a binary fashion. Do something, stop, do something, stop, and so forth. Each device works on a clock cycle or beat of the clock. Some devices, such as the CPU, do two or more operations on one beat of the clock, and others do one operation for each beat. Some devices might even do something on every other beat, but all work according to beats or cycles. You can think of this as similar to children jumping rope. The system clock (child turning the rope) provides the beats or cycles, while devices (children jumping) work in a binary fashion (jump, don't jump). In the analogy, some children jump two or more times for each rope pass.

How fast does the clock beat? The beats, called the **clock speed**, are measured in **hertz (Hz)**, which is one cycle per second; **megahertz (MHz)**, which is one million cycles per second; and **gigahertz (GHz)**, which is one billion cycles per second. Common ratings for motherboard buses today are 1066 MHz, 800 MHz, 533 MHz, or 400 MHz, although you still see some motherboards rated at 200 MHz, 133 MHz, or slower. In other words, data or instructions can

A+ ESS
1.1

be put on the system bus at the rate of 800 million every second. A CPU operates from 166 MHz to almost 4 GHz. In other words, the CPU can put data or instructions on its internal bus at this much higher rate. Although we often refer to the speed of the CPU and the motherboard bus, talking about the frequency of these devices is more accurate, because the term "speed" implies a continuous flow, while the term "frequency" implies a digital or binary flow: on and off, on and off.

**Notes**

Motherboard buses are most often measured in frequencies such as 800 MHz, but sometimes you see a motherboard bus measured in performance such as the A8V motherboard by Asus built to support a high-end AMD processor (see *www.asus.com* and *www.amd.com*). This motherboard bus is rated at 2000 MT/s. One MT/s is one megatransfer per second or one million bytes per second transferred over the bus.

The lines of a bus, including data, instruction, and power lines, often extend to the expansion slots (see Figure 1-28). The size and shape of an expansion slot depend on the kind of bus it uses. Therefore, one way to determine the kind of bus you have is to examine the expansion slots on the motherboard.

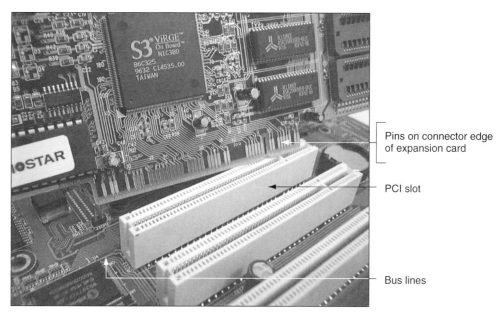

Pins on connector edge of expansion card

PCI slot

Bus lines

**Figure 1-28**  The lines of a bus terminate at an expansion slot where they connect to pins that connect to lines on the expansion card inserted in the slot

Figure 1-29 shows an older motherboard with three types of expansion slots, and Figure 1-30 shows a newer motherboard that also has three types of expansion slots. The types of slots shown on both boards include:

- ◢ PCI (Peripheral Component Interconnect) expansion slot used for input/output devices
- ◢ PCI Express slots that come in several lengths and are used by high-speed input/output devices
- ◢ AGP (Accelerated Graphics Port) expansion slot used for a video card
- ◢ ISA (Industry Standard Architecture) expansion slot is outdated and seldom seen today

Notice in Figures 1-29 and 1-30 the white PCI slots are used on both the older and newer boards. A motherboard will have one slot intended for use by a video card. The older board uses an AGP slot for that purpose, and the newer board uses a long PCI Express x16 slot for video.

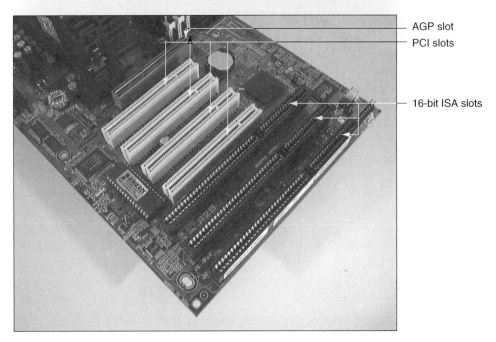

AGP slot
PCI slots
16-bit ISA slots

**Figure 1-29** PCI bus expansion slots are shorter than ISA slots and offset farther; the one AGP slot is set farther from the edge of the board

PCI Express currently comes in four different slot sizes; the longest size (PCI Express x16) and the shortest size (PCI Express x1) are shown in Figure 1-30.

With a little practice, you can identify expansion slots by their length, by the position of the breaks in the slots, and by the distance from the edge of the motherboard to a slot's position.

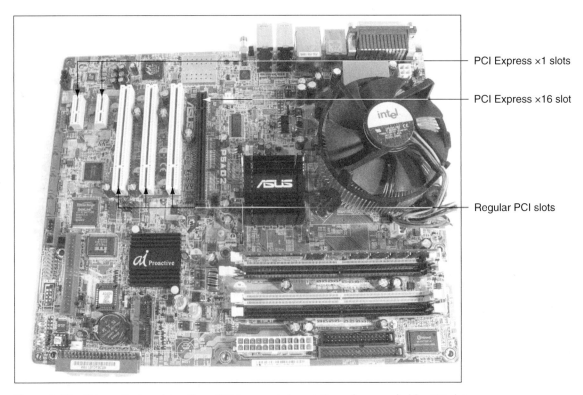

PCI Express ×1 slots
PCI Express ×16 slot
Regular PCI slots

**Figure 1-30** This motherboard has three PCI Express slots and three slower and older PCI slots

In Chapter 6, you'll learn that each expansion slot communicates with the CPU by way of its own bus. There can be a PCI Express bus, a PCI bus, an AGP bus, and, for older systems, an ISA bus, each running at different speeds and providing different features to accommodate the expansion cards that use these different slots. But all these buses connect to the main bus or system bus, which connects to the CPU.

## INTERFACE (EXPANSION) CARDS

Circuit boards other than the motherboard inside the computer are sometimes called circuit cards, adapter boards, expansion cards, interface cards, or simply **cards**, and are mounted in expansion slots on the motherboard (see Figure 1-31).

Modem card

PCI slot

Motherboard
Phone line ports

**Figure 1-31**   This circuit board is a modem card and is mounted in a PCI slot on the motherboard

Figure 1-32 shows the motherboard and expansion cards installed inside a computer case. By studying this figure carefully, you can see the video card installed in the one AGP slot, a sound card and a network card installed in two PCI slots (the other two PCI slots are not used), and a modem card installed in an ISA slot (two ISA slots are not used). Figure 1-32 also shows the ports these cards provide at the rear of the PC case.

**Video**

Identifying Expansion Cards

You can see a full view of a video card in Figure 1-33. These cards enable the CPU to connect to an external device or, in the case of the network card, to a network. The **video card** provides a port for the monitor. The sound card provides ports for speakers and microphones. The network card provides a port for a network cable to connect the PC to a network, and the modem card provides ports for phone lines. The technology to access these devices is embedded on the card itself, and the card also has the technology to communicate with the slot it is in, the motherboard, and the CPU.

The easiest way to determine the function of a particular expansion card (short of seeing its name written on the card, which doesn't happen very often) is to look at the end of the card that fits against the back of the computer case. A network card, for example, has a port designed to fit the network cable. An internal modem has one, or usually two, telephone jacks as its ports. You'll get lots of practice in this book identifying ports on expansion cards. However, as you examine the ports on the back of your PC, remember that sometimes the motherboard provides ports of its own.

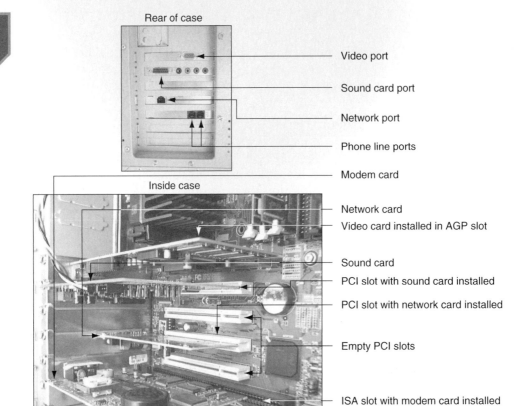

Rear of case

Video port

Sound card port

Network port

Phone line ports

Modem card

Inside case

Network card

Video card installed in AGP slot

Sound card

PCI slot with sound card installed

PCI slot with network card installed

Empty PCI slots

ISA slot with modem card installed

Modem card

Empty ISA slots

**Figure 1-32**    Four cards installed on a motherboard, providing ports for several devices

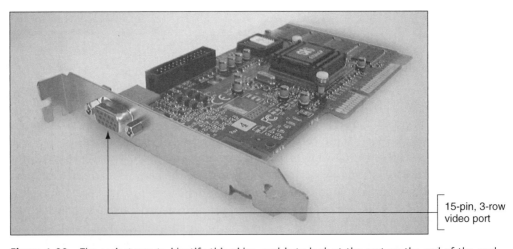

15-pin, 3-row
video port

**Figure 1-33**    The easiest way to identify this video card is to look at the port on the end of the card

## THE ELECTRICAL SYSTEM

The most important component of the computer's electrical system is the **power supply**, which is usually near the rear of the case (see Figure 1-34). This power supply does not actually generate electricity but converts and reduces it to a voltage that the computer can handle. A power supply receives 110–120 volts of AC power from a wall outlet and converts it to a much lower

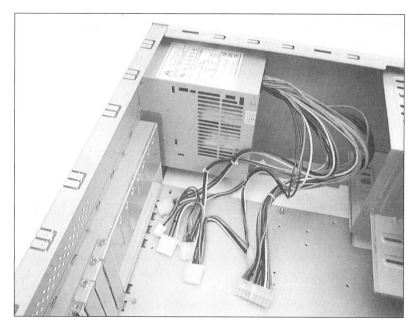

**Figure 1-34** Power supply with connections

DC voltage. Older power supplies had power cables that provided either 5 or 12 volts DC. Newer power supplies provide 3.3, 5, and 12 volts DC. In addition to providing power for the computer, the power supply runs a fan directly from the electrical output voltage to help cool the inside of the computer case. Temperatures over 185 degrees Fahrenheit (85 degrees Celsius) can cause components to fail. When a computer is running, this and other fans inside the case and the spinning of the hard drive and CD drive are the primary noisemakers.

Every motherboard has one or more connections to receive power from the power supply (see Figure 1-35). This power is used by the motherboard, the CPU, and other components that receive their power from ports and expansion slots coming off the motherboard. In addition, there might be other power connectors on the motherboard to power a small fan that cools the CPU or to power the CPU itself.

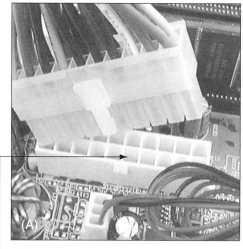
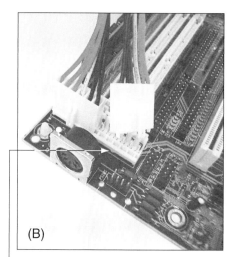

(A) — P1 power connector on a motherboard

(B) — Power connectors on a motherboard

**Figure 1-35** The motherboard receives its power from the power supply by way of one or more connections located near the edge of the board or near the processor

## INSTRUCTIONS STORED ON THE MOTHERBOARD AND OTHER BOARDS

Some very basic instructions are stored on the motherboard—just enough to start the computer, use some simple hardware devices such as a floppy disk and keyboard, and search for an operating system stored on a storage device such as a hard drive or CD. These data and instructions are stored on special ROM (read-only memory) chips on the board and are called the **BIOS (basic input/output system)**. Sometimes other circuit boards, such as a video card, also have ROM BIOS chips. In the case of ROM chips, the distinction between hardware and software becomes vague. Most of the time, it's easy to distinguish between hardware and software. For example, a floppy disk is hardware, but a file on the disk containing a set of instructions is software. This software file, sometimes called a **program**, might be stored on the disk today, but you can erase that file tomorrow and write a new one to the disk. In this case, it is clear that a floppy disk is a permanent physical entity, whereas the program is not. Sometimes, however, hardware and software are not so easy to distinguish. For instance, a ROM chip on a circuit board inside your computer has software instructions permanently etched into it during fabrication. This software is actually a part of the hardware and is not easily changed. In this case, hardware and software are closely tied together, and it's difficult to separate the two, either physically or logically. Software embedded into hardware is often referred to as **firmware** because of its hybrid nature. Figure 1-36 shows an embedded firmware chip on a motherboard that contains the ROM BIOS programs.

Coin battery

Firmware chip

**Figure 1-36**    This firmware chip contains flash ROM and CMOS RAM; CMOS RAM is powered by the coin battery located near the chip

The motherboard ROM BIOS serves three purposes: The BIOS that is sometimes used to manage simple devices is called **system BIOS**, the BIOS that is used to start the computer is called **startup BIOS**, and the BIOS that is used to change some settings on the motherboard is called **CMOS setup**.

These motherboard settings are stored in a small amount of RAM located on the firmware chip and called **CMOS RAM** or just CMOS. Settings stored in CMOS RAM include such things as the current date and time, which hard drives and floppy drives are present, and how the serial and parallel ports are configured. When the computer is first turned on, it looks to settings in CMOS RAM to find out what hardware it should expect to find. CMOS RAM is powered by a trickle of electricity from a small battery located on the motherboard or computer case, usually close to the firmware chip (refer back to Figure 1-36), so that when the computer is turned off, CMOS RAM still retains its data.

**A+ ESS 1.1**

1

Motherboard manufacturers often publish updates for the ROM BIOS on their mother-boards; if a board is giving you problems or you want to use a new feature just released, you might want to upgrade the BIOS. In the past, this meant buying new ROM chips and exchanging them on the motherboard. However, ROM chips on motherboards today can be reprogrammed. Called **flash ROM**, the software stored on these chips can be overwritten by new software that remains on the chip until it is overwritten. (You will learn how to do this in Chapter 6; the process is called flashing ROM.)

Important technologies the motherboard BIOS might support are Advanced Configuration and Power Interface (ACPI), Advanced Power Management (APM), and Plug and Play (PnP).

### ADVANCED CONFIGURATION AND POWER INTERFACE

Most motherboard BIOSs and operating systems support a power-saving feature using stan-dards developed by Intel, Microsoft, and Toshiba, called the **Advanced Configuration and Power Interface (ACPI)** standards. Using ACPI, a system can be powered up by an external device such as a keyboard. Windows 2000/XP and Windows 9x support ACPI. Microsoft calls an ACPI-compliant BIOS a "good" BIOS.

An older BIOS power management standard is **Advanced Power Management (APM)**, which is also supported by Windows 2000/XP and Windows 9x. APM is used only for power management on legacy notebook computers that don't support ACPI.

### PLUG AND PLAY

Another feature of both the BIOS and the OS is **Plug and Play (PnP)**, a standard designed to make the installation of new hardware devices easier. If the BIOS is a PnP BIOS, it will begin the process of configuring hardware devices in the system. It gathers information about the devices and then passes that information to the operating system. If the operat-ing system is also PnP-compliant, it will use that information to complete the hardware configuration.

ESCD (extended system configuration data) Plug and Play BIOS is an enhanced version of PnP. It creates a list of all the things you have done manually to the configuration that PnP does not do on its own. This ESCD list is written to the BIOS chip so that the next time you boot, the startup BIOS can faithfully relay that information to Windows. Windows 9x bene-fits from this information, but it is not important to Windows 2000/XP. The BIOS chip for ESCD BIOS is a special RAM chip called Permanent RAM, or PRAM, that can hold data written to it without the benefit of a battery, which the CMOS setup chip requires.

## >> CHAPTER SUMMARY

▲ A computer requires both hardware and software to work.

▲ The four basic functions of the microcomputer are input, output, processing, and storage of data.

▲ Data and instructions are stored in a computer in binary form, which uses only two states for data—on and off, or 1 and 0—which are called bits. Eight bits equal one byte.

▲ The four most popular input/output devices are the printer, monitor, mouse, and keyboard.

▲ The most important component inside the computer case is the motherboard, also called the main board or system board. It contains the most important microchip inside the case, the central processing unit (CPU), a microprocessor or processor, as well as access to other circuit boards and peripheral devices. All communications between the CPU and other devices must pass through the motherboard.

◢ A ROM BIOS or firmware microchip is a hybrid of hardware and software containing programming embedded into the chip.

◢ Most microchips are manufactured using CMOS (complementary metal-oxide semiconductor) technology.

◢ Each hardware device needs a method to communicate with the CPU, software to control it, and electricity to power it.

◢ Devices outside the computer case connect to the motherboard through ports on the case. Common ports are network, FireWire, sound, serial, parallel, USB, game, keyboard, and mouse ports.

◢ A circuit board inserted in an expansion slot on the motherboard can provide an interface between the motherboard and a peripheral device, or can itself be a peripheral. (An example is an internal modem.)

◢ The chipset on a motherboard controls most activities on the motherboard and includes several device controllers, including the USB controller, memory controller, IDE controller, and so forth.

◢ Primary storage, called memory or RAM, is temporary storage the CPU uses to hold data and instructions while it is processing both.

◢ RAM is stored on single chips, SIMMs, DIMMs, and RIMMs.

◢ Secondary storage is slower than primary storage, but it is permanent storage. Some examples of secondary storage devices are hard drives, CD drives, DVD drives, flash drives, Zip drives, and floppy drives.

◢ Most hard drives, CD drives, and DVD drives use an ATA interface standard commonly called EIDE (Enhanced Integrated Drive Electronics) technology, which can accommodate up to four EIDE or IDE devices on one system. Newer hard drives are the serial ATA interface standard.

◢ The system clock is used to synchronize activity on the motherboard. The clock sends continuous pulses over the bus that different components use to control the pace of activity.

◢ A motherboard can have several buses, including the system bus, the PCI Express bus, the PCI bus, the AGP bus, and the outdated ISA bus.

◢ The frequency of activity on a motherboard is measured in megahertz (MHz), or one million cycles per second. The processor operates at a much higher frequency than other components in the system, and its activity is measured in gigahertz (GHz), or one billion cycles per second.

◢ The power supply inside the computer case supplies electricity to components both inside and outside the case. Some components external to the case get power from their own electrical cables.

◢ ROM BIOS on a motherboard holds the basic software needed to start a PC and begin the process of loading an operating system. Most ROM chips are flash ROM, meaning that these programs can be updated without exchanging the chip.

◢ The CMOS setup program is part of ROM BIOS stored on the firmware chip. This program is used to change motherboard settings or configuration information. When power to the PC is turned off, a battery on the motherboard supplies power to CMOS RAM that holds these settings.

## >> *KEY TERMS*

For explanations of key terms, see the Glossary near the end of the book.

Advanced Configuration and
  Power Interface (ACPI)
Advanced Power Management
  (APM)
binary number system
BIOS (basic input/output system)
bit
bus
byte
cards
central processing unit (CPU)
chipset
circuit board
clock speed
CMOS (complementary metal-
  oxide semiconductor)
CMOS RAM
CMOS setup
data bus
data path size
DIMM (dual inline memory
  module)
expansion cards
expansion slots

firmware
flash ROM
front side bus (FSB)
gigahertz (GHz)
hard copy
hard drive
hardware
hertz (Hz)
host bus
keyboard
main board
megahertz (MHz)
memory
microprocessor
monitor
motherboard
mouse
nonvolatile
parallel port
peripheral device
Plug and Play (PnP)
port
power supply
primary storage

printer
processor
program
protocol
RAM (random access memory)
RIMM
ROM (read-only memory)
S/PDIF (Sony-Philips Digital
  Interface) sound port
secondary storage
serial port
SIMM (single inline memory
  module)
software
startup BIOS
system BIOS
system board
system bus
system clock
traces
USB (universal serial bus) port
video card
volatile

## >> *REVIEW QUESTIONS*

1. Which of the following is considered to be software?

   a. Monitor

   b. Memory chips

   c. Microsoft Word

   d. Mouse

2. The central processing unit is also called which of the following?

   a. Microprocessor

   b. CPA

   c. Software

   d. Monitor

3. Which of the following accurately reflects the purpose of secondary storage?

   a. Secondary storage is used for permanent storage.

   b. Secondary storage holds data during processing.

   c. Secondary storage holds instructions during processing.

   d. Secondary storage is located inside the case.

4. Which of the following is true about RAM?

   a. RAM stands for read-only memory.

   b. RAM is nonvolatile.

   c. RAM can be installed in banks of several chips on a small board that plugs into the motherboard.

   d. RAM refers to software that can be purchased and loaded onto a computer.

5. The system of pathways used for communication, and the protocol and methods used for transmission, are collectively called which of the following?

   a. RAM

   b. Bus

   c. Single inline memory module

   d. Cache memory

6. True or false? Software uses hardware to perform tasks related to input.

7. True or false? Circuit boards are used by the CPU for permanent storage.

8. True or false? Using a parallel ATA interface, a motherboard has two IDE connectors, each of which can accommodate four devices.

9. True or false? CD-ROM is considered to be primary storage.

10. True or false? The width of a data bus is called the data path size.

11. In the binary number system, a 1 or 0 is called a(n) _____.

12. Input/output devices communicate with components inside the computer case through a wireless connection or through cables attached to the case at a connection called a(n) _____.

13. The monitor is typically rated by hardware manufacturers according to the diagonal size of its screen and by the monitor's _____.

14. A device that is not installed directly on the motherboard is called a(n) _____.

15. The basic data and instructions used to start the computer are called _____.

## CHAPTER 2

# Introducing Operating Systems

In Chapter 1, you were introduced to the different hardware devices. In this chapter, you'll learn about the different operating systems, what they do, and how they work to control several of the more significant hardware devices. You'll also see how an OS provides the interface that users and applications need to command and use hardware devices. Finally, you'll learn to use several Windows tools and utilities that are useful to examine a system, change desktop settings, and view and manage some hardware devices.

As you work through this chapter, you'll learn that computer systems contain both hardware and software and that it's important for you as a computer technician to understand how they work together. Although the physical hardware is the visible part of a computer system, the software is the intelligence of the system that makes it possible for hardware components to work.

# OPERATING SYSTEMS PAST AND PRESENT

An **operating system (OS)** is software that controls a computer. It manages hardware, runs applications, provides an interface for users, and stores, retrieves, and manipulates files. In general, you can think of an operating system as the middleman between applications and hardware, between the user and hardware, and between the user and applications (see Figure 2-1).

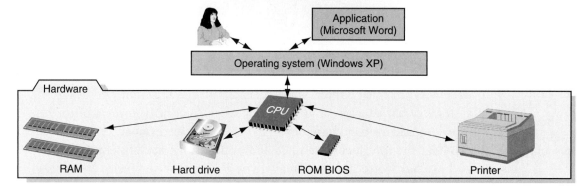

**Figure 2-1** Users and applications depend on the OS to relate to all applications and hardware components

Several applications might be installed on a computer to meet various user needs, but a computer really needs only one operating system. You need to be aware of the older and current operating systems described in the following sections of the chapter and how operating systems have evolved to support new hardware technologies and expanding user needs.

## DOS (DISK OPERATING SYSTEM)

DOS was the first OS among IBM computers and IBM-compatible computers. Figure 2-2 shows a computer screen using the DOS operating system. DOS is outdated as a viable option for a desktop computer operating system today. However, you need to know about it because it is sometimes still used in specialized systems that still use older applications

```
C:\>DIR \GAME

 Volume in drive C has no label
 Volume Serial Number is 0F52-09FC
 Directory of C:\GAME

 .            <DIR>       02-18-93    4:50a
 ..           <DIR>       02-18-93    4:50a
 CHESS        <DIR>       02-18-93    4:50a
 NUKE         <DIR>       02-18-93    4:51a
 PENTE        <DIR>       02-18-93    4:52a
 NETRIS       <DIR>       02-18-93    4:54a
 BEYOND       <DIR>       02-18-93    4:54a
        7 file(s)            0 bytes
                      9273344 bytes free

C:\>
```

**Figure 2-2** DOS provides a command-line prompt to receive user commands

and hardware that were created for DOS. For example, a microcomputer dedicated to controlling an in-house phone system might run DOS. Sometimes DOS is used on a floppy disk or CD that contains utilities to upgrade and diagnose problems with a hard drive or motherboard. That's because DOS can be used to boot and troubleshoot a computer when a more sophisticated OS is too cumbersome and has too much overhead.

DOS was the OS used by early versions of Windows, including Windows 3.1 and Windows 3.11 (collectively referred to as Windows 3.x). Windows 3.x had to use DOS because Windows 3.x didn't perform OS functions, but simply served as a user-friendly intermediate program between DOS, applications, and the user (see Figure 2-3). Windows 3.x is totally outdated and not covered in this book.

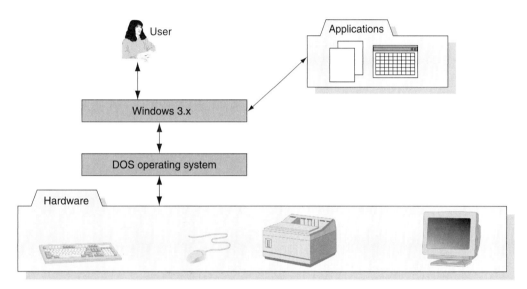

**Figure 2-3** Windows 3.x was layered between DOS and the user and applications to provide a graphics interface for the user and a multitasking environment for applications

Windows 9x/Me uses some DOS programs as part of the underlying OS (called a DOS core), and therefore has some DOS characteristics. When the Windows 9x/Me desktop fails, DOS can be used to troubleshoot the OS. DOS is covered as a troubleshooting OS in Chapter 15. Also, Windows 2000/XP offers a Recovery Console and a Command Prompt window where you use DOS-like commands. You'll learn about the Command Prompt window in Chapter 13 and the Recovery Console in Chapter 14.

## WINDOWS 9X/ME

Early OSs that used a DOS core are Windows 95, Windows 98, and Windows Me, collectively called Windows 9x/Me. These are true operating systems built on a DOS core that provide a user-friendly interface shown in Figure 2-4. Windows XP has largely replaced Windows 9x/Me, but you still occasionally see Windows 98 on a notebook or desktop computer for home use. (Many people chose not to upgrade from Windows 98 to Windows Me because they did not consider it a significant-enough upgrade to warrant the cost and hassle involved.)

Windows 9x/Me is a blend of low-end and high-end technologies. These operating systems fulfill the Microsoft commitment to be **backward-compatible** with older software and hardware while still taking advantage of newer technology. Windows 9x/Me is an OS that bridges two worlds (see Figure 2-5).

**Figure 2-4** Windows 98 SE desktop

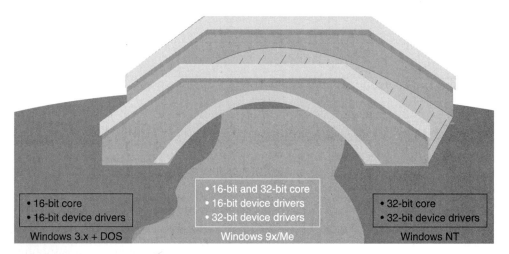

**Figure 2-5** Windows 9x/Me is the bridge from DOS to Windows NT

Table 2-1 lists the hardware requirements of Windows 9x/Me. Note that Table 2-1 gives the *recommended* minimum to run each version of Windows 9x/Me. You may find different values in other documentation, because these OSs might need more or less memory depending on whether you are installing on a new system or upgrading an older system, as well as which applications and OS features you choose to install. Also, sometimes Microsoft lists the minimum requirements to *install* an OS, which might be different from the requirements to *run* an OS. (Requirements in Table 2-1 are for running the OS.)

| Description | Windows 95 | Windows 98 | Windows Me |
|---|---|---|---|
| Processor | 486 or higher | Pentium | Pentium 150 MHz |
| RAM | 8 MB | 24 MB | 32 MB |
| Free hard drive space | 50 MB | 195 MB | 320 MB |

**Table 2-1** Recommended minimum hardware requirements for Windows 9x/Me

Keep these differences in mind when reviewing the lists of minimum hardware requirements for OSs throughout this chapter. Windows 9x/Me is covered in Chapter 16.

You cannot buy a new license for Windows 9x/Me, so the OS is considered a legacy OS. Microsoft no longer supports Windows 9x/Me. As a support technician, the only reason you would install an existing copy of Windows 9x/Me on a computer is in a situation where you are repairing a corrupted installation or replacing a hard drive.

> **Notes**
>
> Some instructors prefer to cover DOS and Windows 9x/Me before they cover Windows 2000/XP, and others prefer to start with Windows 2000/XP. To satisfy both approaches, know that Chapters 15 and 16 on DOS and Windows 9x/Me are written so that they can be covered first before you study the Windows 2000/XP chapters. On the other hand, Chapters 11 through 16 function well when covered sequentially.

## WINDOWS NT

Windows NT (New Technology) came in two versions: Windows NT Workstation for workstations, and Windows NT Server to control a network. Windows NT corrected many problems with Windows 9x/Me because it completely rewrote the OS core, totally eliminating the DOS core, and introduced many new problems of its own that were later solved by Windows 2000 and Windows XP.

The minimum hardware requirements for Windows NT on an IBM-compatible PC are listed below for informational purposes only. Because it's such a problem-riddled OS, don't install it unless you absolutely have no other option. For more information about Windows NT, see Appendix G.

- ▲ Pentium-compatible processor or higher
- ▲ 16 MB of RAM (32 MB is recommended)
- ▲ 125 MB of hard disk space

**A+ ESS
3.1**

## WINDOWS 2000

Windows 2000 is an upgrade of Windows NT, and also came in several versions, some designed for the desktop and others designed for high-end servers. Windows 2000 Professional was popular as an OS for the corporate desktop. Windows 2000 Server, Advanced Server, and Datacenter Server are network server OSs. Windows 2000 offered several improvements over Windows NT, including a more stable environment, support for Plug and Play, Device Manager, Recovery Console, Active Directory, better network support, and features specifically targeting notebook computers. The Windows 2000 Professional desktop is shown in Figure 2-6.

Hardware and software must qualify for all the Windows 2000 operating systems. To see if your hardware and applications qualify, check the Windows Marketplace Tested Products List at *testedproducts.windowsmarketplace.com* (see Figure 2-7). Alternately, for hardware, you can check the HCL at *www.microsoft.com/whdc/hcl/search.mspx*.

The recommended system requirements for Windows 2000 Professional are:

- ▲ 133 MHz Pentium-compatible processor
- ▲ 2 GB hard drive with at least 650 MB free space
- ▲ 64 MB RAM

Windows 2000 is considered a dying OS. You cannot buy a new license for it, and, except for providing security patches, Microsoft no longer supports the OS. Windows 2000 Professional and Windows XP are covered together in Chapters 11, 12, 13, and 14. Server OSs are not covered in this book.

**Figure 2-6** The Windows 2000 Professional desktop

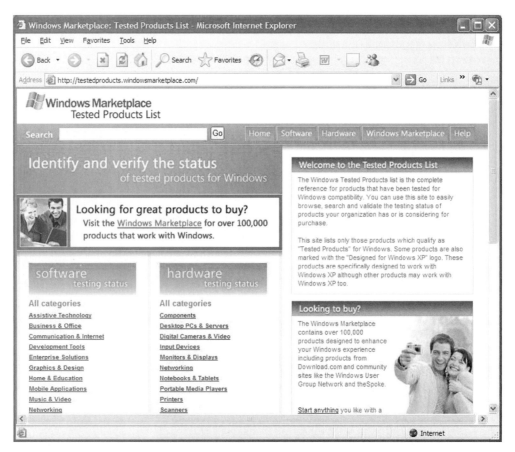

**Figure 2-7** Windows Marketplace Tested Products List

A+ ESS
3.1

# WINDOWS XP

Windows XP is an upgrade of Windows 2000 and attempts to integrate Windows 9x/Me and 2000, while providing added support for multimedia and networking technologies. The two main versions are Windows XP Home Edition and Windows XP Professional, though other less significant editions include Windows XP Media Center Edition, Windows XP Tablet PC Edition, and Windows XP Professional x64 Edition. This book focuses on Windows XP Professional and Windows XP Home Edition.

The Windows XP desktop (see Figure 2-8) has a different look from the desktops for earlier Windows. Windows XP has the ability for two users to log on simultaneously, both with their own applications open. Windows Messenger and Windows Media Player are inherent parts of Windows XP. And XP includes several advanced security features, including Windows Firewall.

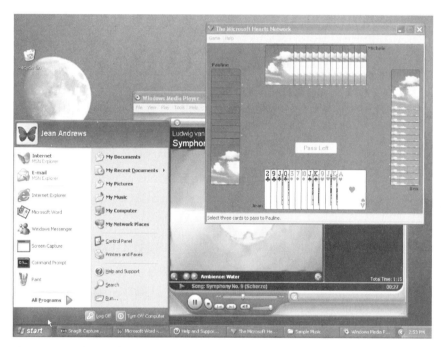

**Figure 2-8**   The Windows XP desktop and Start menu

The minimum requirements for Windows XP Professional are:

▲ A minimum of 64 MB of RAM, with 128 MB recommended
▲ At least 1.5 GB of free hard drive space, with 2 GB recommended
▲ A CPU that runs at least 233 MHz, with a 300-MHz CPU recommended. Windows XP can support two processors.

Windows XP is replacing all previous versions of Windows in the home market and for the corporate desktop.

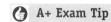
**Notes**

To know the Windows XP version, the CPU speed, and the amount of RAM installed on your computer, click the **Start** button on the Windows XP desktop and right-click **My Computer**. Select **Properties** on the shortcut menu and select the **General** tab.

**A+ Exam Tip**

The A+ Essentials exam expects you to know the system requirements for Windows 2000 Professional and Windows XP.

At the time this book went to print, when you buy a new Windows computer, Windows XP is installed. When deciding to upgrade to Windows XP, the only reasons you would not upgrade are to avoid the time and expense of the upgrade or when you have compatibility issues with older hardware and software. Windows XP is covered in Chapters 11, 12, 13, and 14 along with Windows 2000 Professional.

## WINDOWS VISTA

Windows Vista, code-named Longhorn, is the next generation of Windows operating systems by Microsoft. Windows Vista has a new graphical interface, a revamped engine, and a new interface between it and applications. At the time this book went to print, Microsoft had announced that it intended to release desktop and server versions of Windows Vista for multiple-license business users in November 2006 and for the consumer in January 2007.

## WINDOWS SERVER 2003

Windows Server 2003 is a suite of Microsoft operating systems including Windows Small Business Server 2003, Storage Server 2003, Server 2003 Web Edition, Server 2003 Standard Edition, Server 2003 Enterprise Edition, and Server 2003 Datacenter Edition. None of these operating systems are intended to be used for a personal computer, and they are not covered in this book.

## UNIX

Unix is a popular OS used to control networks and to support applications used on the Internet. There are several versions of Unix, which are called flavors or distributions. Unix is not covered in this book.

## LINUX

A variation of Unix that has recently gained popularity is Linux, an OS created by Linus Torvalds when he was a student at the University of Helsinki in Finland. Basic versions of this OS are available for free, and all the underlying programming instructions (called source code) are also freely distributed. Like Unix, Linux is distributed by several different companies, whose versions of Linux are sometimes called **distributions**. Popular distributions of Linux include SuSE (*www.novell.com/linux/suse*), RedHat (*redhat.com*), and TurboLinux (*www.turbolinux.com*). Linux can be used both as a server platform and a desktop platform, but its greatest popularity has come in the server market.

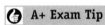
**A+ Exam Tip**

The A+ Essentials exam expects you to know when it is appropriate to use the Linux and Mac OS.

Network services such as a Web server or e-mail server often are provided by a computer running the Linux operating system. Linux is well-suited to support various types of server applications. Because Linux is very reliable and does not require a lot of computing power, it is sometimes used as a desktop OS, although it is not as popular for this purpose because it is not easy to install or use and few Linux applications are available. Linux is an excellent training tool for learning Unix.

Here are tips about the requirements to use the Linux OS:

▲ You don't have to install Linux on a hard drive in order to run it. You can download Linux from the Internet and burn it to a CD or DVD and boot from the disc to run Linux. You can also buy books on Linux that include the Linux OS on CD.

▲ You can download some distributions of Linux for free, but in most cases, you must pay for technical support.

▲ The minimum and recommended system requirements for Linux vary from one distribution to another. Expect to need at least a Pentium III or AMD Athlon processor with 256 MB of RAM. If you install the OS on your hard drive, you'll need at least 4 GB of free space.

Because many users prefer a Windows-style desktop, several applications have been written to provide a GUI shell for Unix and Linux. These shells are called X Windows. A typical X Windows screen is shown in Figure 2-9.

You can find out more about Linux by reading Appendix E.

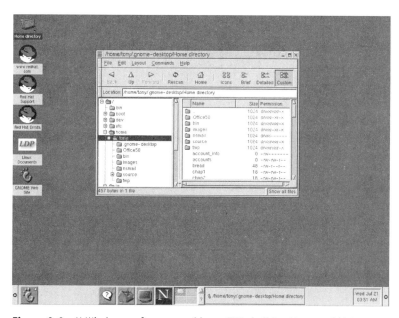

**Figure 2-9** X Windows software provides a GUI shell for Linux and Unix users

## OS/2

OS/2, developed by IBM and Microsoft, is less common for home desktop PCs, but is used in certain types of networks. Microsoft developed Windows NT using some of the core components of OS/2 and intended it to replace OS/2. OS/2 is not covered in this book.

## MAC OS

Currently, the Mac OS is available only on Macintosh computers by Apple Corporation (*www.apple.com*). The Mac and the Mac OS were first introduced in 1984. Several versions of the Macintosh OS have been written since 1984, the latest being Mac OS X (ten), which offers easy access to the Internet and allows any Macintosh computer to become a Web server for a small network.

Until recently, all Macintosh computers were built using a processor by PowerPC. Now, some Macs use processors by Intel, which means that it is now possible for Mac OS X to work on other Intel-based computers. It remains to be seen

> **Notes**
>
> Recently, Apple released Boot Camp software, which makes it possible to install Windows on a Mac computer as a dual boot with Mac OS X. A dual boot makes it possible to boot a computer into one of two installed OSs.

if Apple will make versions of the Mac OS X available for purchase and use on computers other than the Macintosh. Speculation says that if Apple chooses this route, Mac OS X will compete with Windows for the desktop OS market for IBM-compatible computers.

Because it is easy to use, the Mac OS has been popular in educational environments, from elementary school through the university level. It also provides excellent support for graphics and multimedia applications and is popular in the professional desktop publishing and graphics markets. Because IBM-compatible PCs have a larger share of the computer market, applications compatible with the Mac OS are not as readily available. Mac OS X requires at least 128 MB of RAM and 1.5 GB of hard drive space.

The Mac OS X interface is significantly different from that of the Mac OS 9, including two new features called the dock and the toolbar, as shown in Figure 2-10. When a Mac is turned on, a program called the Finder is automatically launched. This is the program that provides the desktop, which functions as the GUI for the Mac OS. Generally, under normal Mac OS operation, you cannot quit the Finder program.

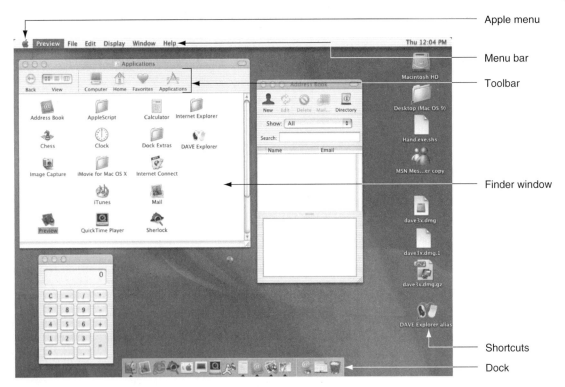

**Figure 2-10** The Mac OS X desktop is intuitive and easy to use

The Mac OS X tries to make installing hardware as smooth as possible without much user interaction by providing superior Plug and Play capabilities, so that new hardware devices can be added easily and are automatically recognized by the OS. Another important difference between Mac OS X and earlier versions is that Mac OS X provides better support for multitasking and is thus less likely to freeze when several applications are running simultaneously.

You can learn more about the Mac OS by reading Appendix F.

> **Notes**
>
> Although the initial cost of setting up a Macintosh system is generally higher than for a comparable IBM-compatible system, the cost of support and maintenance is generally lower for the Mac.

## WHAT AN OPERATING SYSTEM DOES

**A+ ESS
3.1**

Although there are important differences among them, OSs share the following four main functions:

📝 **Notes**

All Windows operating systems are produced by Microsoft (*www.microsoft.com*). Different flavors of Unix and Linux are produced by various manufacturers. You can learn more about Unix and Linux at *www.unix.org* and *www.linux.org*. For more information about the Mac OS, see *www.apple.com*, and for information about OS/2, see *www.ibm.com*.

▲ Providing a user interface

    ▲ Performing housekeeping procedures requested by the user, often concerning secondary storage devices, such as formatting new disks, deleting files, copying files, and changing the system date

    ▲ Providing a way for the user to manage the desktop, hardware, applications, and data

▲ Managing files

    ▲ Managing files on hard drives, DVD drives, CD drives, floppy drives, and other drives

    ▲ Creating, storing, retrieving, deleting, and moving files

▲ Managing applications

    ▲ Installing and uninstalling applications

    ▲ Running applications and managing the interface to the hardware on behalf of an application

▲ Managing hardware

    ▲ Managing the BIOS (programs permanently stored on hardware devices)

    ▲ Managing memory, which is a temporary place to store data and instructions as they are being processed

    ▲ Diagnosing problems with software and hardware

    ▲ Interfacing between hardware and software (that is, interpreting application software needs to the hardware and interpreting hardware needs to application software)

    ▲ Before we look more closely at each of these four main functions, let's turn our attention to the core components common to every operating system.

### OPERATING SYSTEM COMPONENTS

Every operating system has two main internal components: the shell and the kernel (see Figure 2-11). A **shell** is the portion of the OS that relates to the user and to applications. The shell provides a way for the user to do such things as select music to burn to a CD, install an application, or change the wallpaper on the Windows desktop. The shell does this using various interface tools such as Windows Explorer, the Control Panel, or My Computer, which can have command, menu, or icon-driven interfaces for the user. For applications, the shell provides commands and procedures that applications can call on to do such things as print a spreadsheet, read from a database, or display a photograph onscreen.

The core, or **kernel,** of the OS is responsible for interacting with hardware. It has more power to communicate with hardware devices than the shell has. Therefore, applications operating under the OS cannot get to hardware devices without the shell passing those requests to the kernel. This module approach that says, "You do your job and I'll do mine,

A+ ESS
3.1

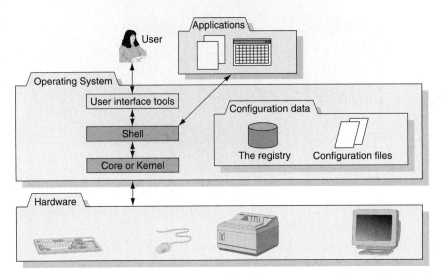

**Figure 2-11**    Inside an operating system, different components perform various functions

and we won't mess with each other's work" provides for a more stable system. If you think of an OS as a restaurant, the shell is like the hosts and waiters that serve customers, and the kernel is like the chefs and kitchen staff. Hosts and waiters are responsible for customer interaction but aren't allowed in the kitchen where the food is prepared.

An operating system needs a place to keep hardware and software configuration information, user preferences, and application settings that are used when the OS is first loaded and are accessed as needed by hardware, applications, and users. This information can be kept in databases or text files. Windows uses a database called the **registry** for most of this information. In addition, Windows keeps some data in text files called **initialization files**, which often have an .ini or .inf file extension. For example, an application might store in a text file or in the registry the settings preferred by the last user, such as background color, fonts, and text size. When the application is launched, the first thing it does is read the registry or text file and then loads the user's preferred settings.

Now let's look at a more detailed explanation of each of the four functions of an OS.

## AN OS PROVIDES A USER INTERFACE

A+
220-602
3.1

When you first turn on a PC, the operating system is loaded. After the OS is in control, it provides an interface on the computer screen (called the desktop) and waits for the user to do something (point, click, double-click, or type). The user is clicking a menu, typing a command, or double-clicking an icon using an interface that is command-driven, menu-driven, or icon-driven.

### COMMAND-DRIVEN INTERFACES

With a command-driven interface, you type commands to tell the OS to perform operations. Computer technicians who are good typists and are very familiar with DOS-like commands often prefer this kind of OS interface. For example, to type a command using Windows XP, click the **Start** button on the Windows taskbar and then click **Run**. The Run dialog box appears where you can type a command such as DEFRAG C:, which is the command to arrange data on your hard drive for better performance. You can also enter the command **Cmd** in the Run dialog box to get a Command Prompt window such as the one in Figure 2-12. From this window, you can enter commands such as Defrag C:. You will learn more about this and other commands in Chapters 13 and 15.

2

```
C:\WINDOWS\system32\cmd.exe - defrag C:                              _ □ x
Microsoft Windows XP [Version 5.1.2600]
(C) Copyright 1985-2001 Microsoft Corp.

C:\Documents and Settings\Jean Andrews>dir
 Volume in drive C has no label.
 Volume Serial Number is DCB8-611B

 Directory of C:\Documents and Settings\Jean Andrews

03/15/2006  07:43 PM    <DIR>          .
03/15/2006  07:43 PM    <DIR>          ..
03/31/2006  02:01 PM    <DIR>          Desktop
03/23/2006  02:40 PM    <DIR>          Favorites
12/05/2005  12:07 PM    <DIR>          My Documents
04/11/2006  02:38 PM         4,980,736 ntuser.dat
09/30/2004  04:04 PM    <DIR>          Start Menu
07/30/2005  02:05 PM    <DIR>          WINDOWS
               1 File(s)      4,980,736 bytes
               7 Dir(s)  46,515,404,800 bytes free

C:\Documents and Settings\Jean Andrews>defrag C:
Windows Disk Defragmenter
Copyright (c) 2001 Microsoft Corp. and Executive Software International, Inc.
```

**Figure 2-12**   Enter command lines in a Command Prompt window

## ICON-DRIVEN AND MENU-DRIVEN INTERFACES

Most Windows interface tools use a combination of menus and icons. An example is
Windows Explorer in Windows XP. From the drop-down menus, you can format disks,
rename files, copy and delete files, and perform many other operations to manage files and
storage devices (see Figure 2-13). You can also see in the figure many yellow file folder icons
representing Windows folders.

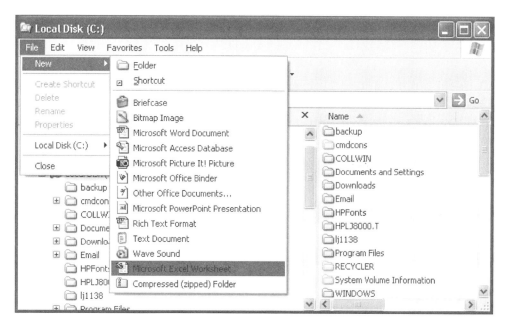

**Figure 2-13**   A menu-driven interface: Windows Explorer in Windows XP

With an icon-driven interface, sometimes called a **graphical user interface (GUI)**, you
perform operations by clicking icons (or pictures) on the screen. When an OS is first
executed, the initial screen that appears, together with its menus, commands, and icons, is
called the **desktop**.

A+ ESS
3.1

A+
220-602
3.1

# AN OS MANAGES FILES AND FOLDERS

An operating system is responsible for storing files and folders on a secondary storage device, such as a DVD, CD, flash drive, or hard drive, using an organizational method called the **file system.**

For hard drives, Windows uses either the FAT or the NTFS file system. The FAT file system is named after the **file allocation table (FAT)**, a table on a hard drive or floppy disk that tracks how space on a disk is used to store files. The latest version of FAT, FAT32, is a more efficient method of organization for large hard drives than FAT16 (the earlier version). The **New Technology file system (NTFS)** is supported by Windows NT/2000/XP and is designed to provide greater security and to support more storage capacity than the FAT file system.

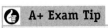

**A+ Exam Tip**

The A+ Essentials exam expects you to know all the key terms in this section.

A hard drive or floppy disk is composed of **tracks**, which are concentric circles (one circle inside the next) on the disk surface, shown in Figure 2-14. Each track is divided into several segments, each called a **sector**. Each sector can hold 512 bytes of data. A **cluster**, the smallest unit of space on a disk for storing a file, is made up of one or more sectors. A file system, either FAT or NTFS, tracks how these clusters are used for each file stored on the disk.

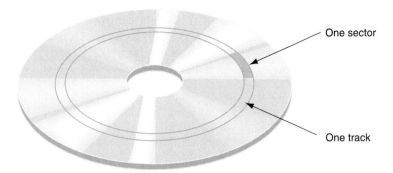

One sector

One track

**Figure 2-14**   A hard drive or floppy disk is divided into tracks and sectors; several sectors make one cluster

## FILES AND DIRECTORIES

Regardless of the file system used, every OS manages a hard drive by using directories (Windows calls these folders), subdirectories, and files. A **directory table** is a list of subdirectories and files. When a physical hard drive is first installed, it can be divided into one or more logical drives such as drive C and drive D. These logical drives are sometimes called volumes. When each logical drive is formatted, a single directory table is placed on the drive called the **root directory**. For a logical drive, such as drive C, the root directory is written as C:\. (Logical drives are discussed in more detail in the next section of the chapter.)

As shown in Figure 2-15, this root directory can hold files or other directories, which can have names such as C:\Tools. These directories, called **subdirectories, child directories,** or **folders,** can, in turn, have other directories listed in them. Any directory can have files and other subdirectories listed in it; for example, Figure 2-15 shows C:\wp\data\myfile.txt. In this path to the file, Myfile.txt, the C: identifies the logical drive. If a directory is on a floppy disk, then either A: or B: identifies it. If a directory is on a logical drive on a hard drive or on a CD, flash drive, or DVD, a letter such as C:, D:, or F: identifies it.

When you refer to a drive and directories that are pointing to the location of a file, as in C:\wp\data\myfile.txt, the drive and directories are called the **path** to the file (see Figure 2-16). When naming a file, the first part of the name before the period is called

A+ ESS
3.1

A+
220-602
3.1

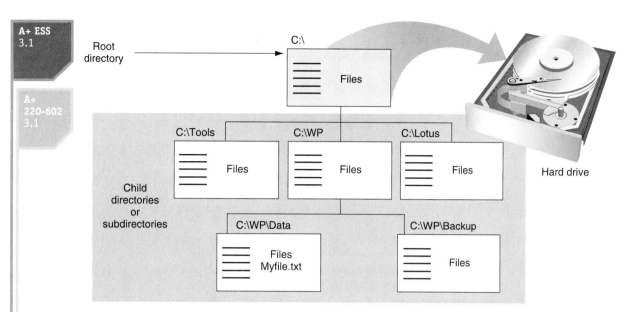

**Figure 2-15** A hard drive is organized into directories and subdirectories that contain files

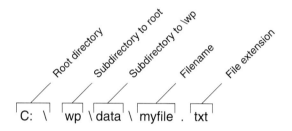

**Figure 2-16** The complete path to a file includes the logical drive letter, directories, filename, and file extension; the colon, backslashes, and period are required to separate items in the path

the **filename** (myfile), and the part after the period is called the **file extension** (txt), which, for Windows and DOS, always has three characters or fewer. The file extension identifies the file type, such as .doc for Microsoft Word document files or .xls for Microsoft Excel spreadsheet files.

## PARTITIONS AND LOGICAL DRIVES ON A HARD DRIVE

A hard drive is organized into one or more **partitions**. A partition can be a primary partition or an extended partition (see Figure 2-17). A primary partition can have only one logical drive, and an extended partition can have one or more logical drives. For example, a hard drive can have one primary partition with one logical drive in it called drive C, and one extended partition with two logical drives most likely called drive D and drive E.

Each **logical drive**, sometimes called a **volume**, is formatted using its own file system. For example, if a hard drive is divided into two logical drives, drive C might be formatted using the FAT32 file system and drive D might use the NTFS file system. Each logical drive has its own root directory and subdirectories.

Partitions can be created on a hard drive when the drive is first installed, when an OS is first installed, or after an existing partition becomes corrupted. When an OS is first installed, the installation process partitions and formats the drive if necessary. After Windows 2000/XP is installed, you can use the Disk Management tool to view partitions,

A+ ESS
3.1

A+
220-602
3.1

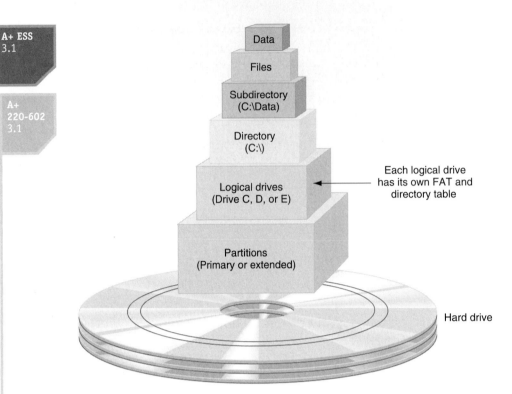

**Figure 2-17**    A hard drive is divided and organized at several levels

create new ones, and format logical drives. To open the Disk Management utility, use one of these methods:

▲ For Windows XP, click **Start, Control Panel.** (For Windows 2000, click **Start, Settings, Control Panel.**) Open the **Administrative Tools** applet. The Computer Management window opens. Click **Disk Management.** The Disk Management window opens.

▲ Click **Start, Run** and enter **Diskmgmt.msc** in the Run dialog box. Press **Enter.**

The Disk Management window in Figure 2-18 shows one hard drive that contains three primary partitions, which are formatted as drives C, E, and F. Drive C is using the NTFS file system and drives E and F are using the FAT32 file system. This drive has no extended partitions.

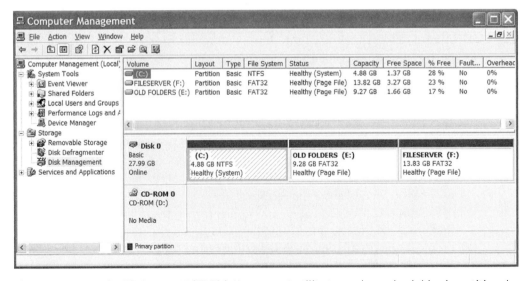

**Figure 2-18**    Use the Windows 2000/XP Disk Management utility to see how a hard drive is partitioned

A+ ESS
3.1

A+
220-602
3.1

You will learn more about how to manage partitions and logical drives using Disk Management in Chapter 11.

For Windows 9x/Me, the Fdisk command is used to create partitions, and the Format command is used to format logical drives. Chapter 15 covers how to use the Fdisk and Format commands. Table 2-2 lists the three file systems for Windows and DOS operating systems.

| | DOS | Windows 95 | Windows 98 | Windows NT | Windows 2000 | Windows XP |
|---|---|---|---|---|---|---|
| FAT16 | X | X | X | X | X | X |
| FAT32 | | X (for OSR2) | X | | X | X |
| NTFS | | | | X | X | X |

**Table 2-2**  Operating system support for file systems

**APPLYING|CONCEPTS**  When using Windows Explorer or My Computer, Windows does not distinguish between logical drives stored on the same hard drive or on different hard drives. For example, Figure 2-19 shows three drives, C, E, and F, that are logical drives on one physical hard drive shown earlier in Figure 2-18. If you right-click one drive, such as drive E in the figure, and select Properties on the shortcut menu, you can see the amount of space allotted to this logical drive and how much of it is currently used. Also note in the figure that drive E is formatted using the FAT32 file system.

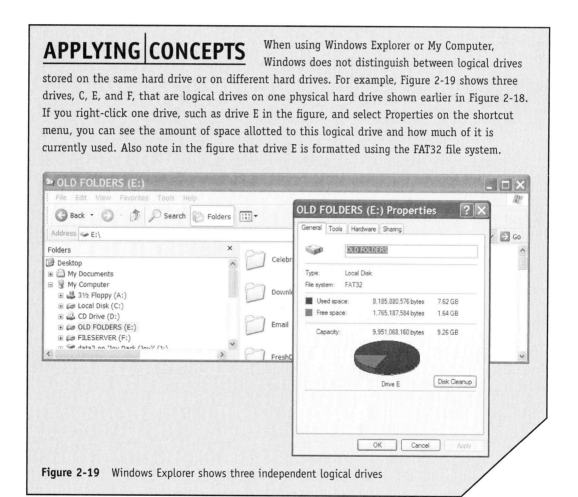

**Figure 2-19**  Windows Explorer shows three independent logical drives

## AN OS MANAGES APPLICATIONS

An operating system installs and runs all the other software on a PC. Software designed to perform a task for the user is called an application. An application, such as Microsoft Word, depends on an OS to provide access to hardware resources, to manage its data in memory and in secondary storage, and to perform many other background tasks.

A+
220-602
3.1

An application built to work with one OS, such as Windows 95, does not necessarily work with another, such as Windows XP, because of the different ways each OS manages an application. Windows 9x/Me was written to work with DOS or Windows 3.x applications, which was an early selling point for Windows 9x/Me, but Windows 2000/XP does not claim to support many legacy applications. So, when it's important that your application work correctly, make sure you use applications written specifically for your OS.

## INSTALLING APPLICATION SOFTWARE

The operating system is responsible for installing software using the installation program provided by the application. Application software is downloaded from the Internet or comes written on CDs, DVDs, or floppy disks. Usually it must be installed on a hard drive in order to run. During the installation, the install program creates folders on the hard drive and copies files to them. For Windows, it also makes entries in the Windows registry, and it can place icons on the desktop and add entries to the Start menu. Because the install program does all the work for you, installing a software package usually is very easy. Installing software is covered in later chapters.

A+ ESS
3.1

## LAUNCHING APPLICATION SOFTWARE USING THE WINDOWS DESKTOP

Before an application can be used, it must be started up, which is called running, loading, launching, or executing the application. Windows 2000/XP and Windows 9x/Me offer four ways to run software:

▲ *Use a shortcut icon.* Place a shortcut icon directly on the desktop for the applications you use often and want to get to quickly. A shortcut contains the command line that executes the application. To view this command line, right-click an application icon on the desktop to open a shortcut menu. On the shortcut menu, select **Properties**. The icon's Properties dialog box opens (see Figure 2-20). In this dialog box, you can view the complete command line that the icon represents. You will learn how to create shortcuts later in the chapter.

> **A+ Exam Tip**
>
> The A+ Essentials exam often expects you to know more than one way to do something. Knowing the four ways to load an application is a good example.

▲ *Use the Start menu.* Click the **Start** button, select **Programs** (or **All Programs** in Windows XP), and then select the program from the list of installed software.
▲ *Use the Run command.* Click the **Start** button, and then click **Run** to display the Run dialog box (see Figure 2-21). In this dialog box, enter a command line or click **Browse** to search for a program file to execute.
▲ *Use Windows Explorer or My Computer.* Execute a program or launch an application file by double-clicking the filename in Windows Explorer or My Computer.

## APPLYING | CONCEPTS

Practice the last three ways listed to load an application. Use Microsoft Paint as your sample application. The program file is Mspaint.exe. Execute the application by using the Start menu, using the Run dialog box, and using Windows Explorer.

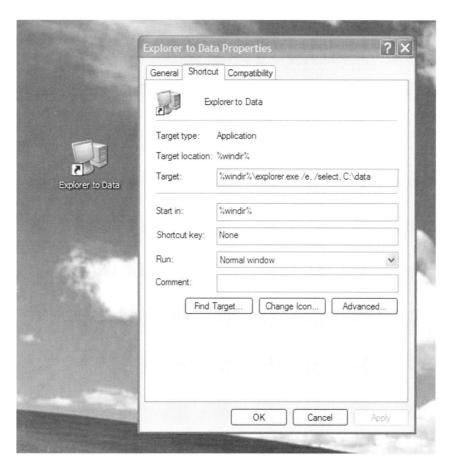

**Figure 2-20** The target for this shortcut is the C:\data folder, which will be displayed by Windows Explorer

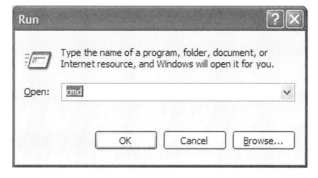

**Figure 2-21** The Windows Run dialog box allows you to enter DOS-like commands

## REAL (16-BIT), PROTECTED (32-BIT), AND LONG (64-BIT) OPERATING MODES

CPUs operate in three modes: 16-bit, 32-bit, or 64-bit modes, which are also called real mode, protected mode, and long mode, respectively. There are several differences between these three modes, but fundamentally, in 16-bit mode, or **real mode**, the CPU processes 16 bits of data at one time, in 32-bit mode, or **protected mode**, it processes 32 bits at a time, and in 64-bit mode, or **long mode**, it processes 64 bits at a time.

Early computers all used real mode, but no OS today uses this mode. In real mode, an application has complete access to all hardware resources. This sounds good on the surface, but this open-door policy can create problems when applications make conflicting or erroneous commands to hardware. On the other hand, in protected mode and long mode, the OS controls how an application can access hardware. This helps when more than one program is working at the same time, which is a type of **multitasking**, so that each program is protected from other programs making conflicting demands on hardware. In protected mode and long mode, the OS provides to each program a limited and controlled access to hardware resources. If a system has only a single CPU, then two programs cannot literally multitask. This is because a CPU can only do one thing at a time. The two programs only appear to multitask because, in protected mode or long mode, the OS allots CPU time to an application for a specified period. Then it preempts the processing to give the CPU to another application in a process called preemptive multitasking (see Figure 2-22). The end result is that the computer appears to be multitasking when it really is not. Windows 95 was the first version of Windows to provide preemptive multitasking.

**Figure 2-22** Using preemptive multitasking, more than one application appears to be using CPU resources

Some computers have more than one CPU either embedded in the same processor housing or installed as two separate processors on the same motherboard. For these systems, if the operating system is capable of it, it can feed tasks to each CPU working independently of each other in what is called true multiprocessing. Windows NT was the first Windows OS to support multiprocessing.

> **Notes**
>
> Real mode means that the software has "real" access to the hardware; protected mode means that more than one program can be running, and each one is "protected" from other programs accessing its hardware resources. Long mode processes twice as many bits at a time than protected mode.

DOS uses 16-bit mode; Windows 9x/Me and Windows NT/2000/XP all use 32-bit mode, although each OS is backward compatible with earlier modes. In other words, Windows 9x/Me and Windows NT/2000/XP can support an application that uses 16-bit mode. Windows XP Professional x64 Edition uses 64-bit mode, and is backward compatible with many applications that use 32-bit or 16-bit mode. Processors today are built to run in either 32-bit mode or 64-bit mode, but are backward compatible with 16-bit mode so that any PC can be booted up using DOS—a useful troubleshooting OS when more complex OSs fail.

All Pentium processors operate in 32-bit mode. Three high-end processors that operate in 64-bit mode are the Intel Itanium, the AMD Opteron, and the AMD Athlon 64. For these

A+ ESS
3.1

three processors, in order to use 64-bit mode, you need to install Windows XP Professional x64 Edition.

## 16-BIT, 32-BIT, AND 64-BIT SOFTWARE

Software written for Windows 3.x is called 16-bit Windows software. Data access is 16 bits at a time, and each program is written so that it should not infringe on the resources of other programs that might be running. Software programs written for Windows NT/2000/XP and Windows 9x/Me are called 32-bit programs, and software programs written for Windows XP Professional x64 Edition are called 64-bit programs.

Nearly all software written today is 32-bit or 64-bit (for the Itaniums, Opterons, and Athlon 64 processors), although 16-bit applications software still exists and might still work under any version of Windows. However, a 16-bit device driver won't work under Windows 2000/XP or Windows Me. The next section explains what a device driver is.

## AN OS MANAGES HARDWARE

An operating system is responsible for communicating with hardware, but the OS does not relate directly to the hardware. Rather, the OS uses device drivers or the BIOS to do the job. Figure 2-23 shows these relationships. Therefore, most software falls into three categories:

◢ Device drivers or the BIOS
◢ Operating system
◢ Application software

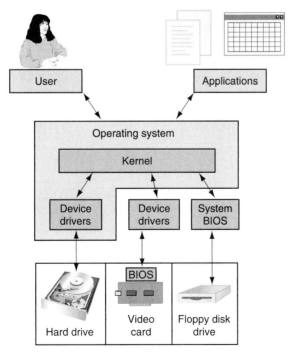

**Figure 2-23** An OS relates to hardware by way of BIOS and device drivers

## HOW AN OS USES DEVICE DRIVERS TO MANAGE DEVICES

**Device drivers** are small programs stored on the hard drive that tell the computer how to communicate with a specific hardware device such as a printer, network card, or modem. These drivers are installed on the hard drive when the OS is first installed or when new hardware is added to the system.

The OS provides some device drivers, and the manufacturer of the specific hardware device with which they are designed to interface provides others. In either case, device drivers are usually written for a particular OS and most likely need to be rewritten for use with another.

When you purchase a printer, DVD drive, Zip drive, digital camera, scanner, or other hardware device, bundled with the device might be a CD or set of floppy disks that contains the device drivers (see Figure 2-24). Sometimes, the device also comes bundled with a user manual and applications software that uses the device. You use the operating system to install the device drivers so it will have the necessary software to control the device. In most cases, you install the device and then install the device drivers. There are a few exceptions, such as a digital camera using a USB port to download pictures. Most often in this case, you install the software to drive the digital camera before you plug in the camera.

Gaming software

CD containing device drivers

Video card

User manual

**Figure 2-24** A device such as this video card comes packaged with its device drivers stored on a CD; alternatively, you can use device drivers built into the OS

> **Notes**
>
> Device drivers come from a number of sources. Some come with and are part of the operating system, some come with hardware devices when they are purchased, and some are provided for downloading over the Internet from a device manufacturer's Web site.

> **Notes**
>
> This book focuses on using 32-bit drivers because 16-bit drivers are not supported by Windows 2000/XP, and Windows XP Professional x64 Edition is not currently popular as a desktop OS.

There are three kinds of device drivers: 16-bit real-mode drivers, 32-bit protected-mode drivers, and 64-bit long-mode drivers. Windows 95 and Windows 98 support 16-bit and 32-bit drivers. Windows Me, Windows NT/2000, Windows XP Home Edition, and Windows XP Professional use only 32-bit drivers. Windows XP Professional x64 Edition only uses 64-bit drivers. Windows 9x/Me and Windows 2000/XP provide hundreds of 32-bit drivers for many different kinds of devices, and device manufacturers also provide their own 16-bit, 32-bit, and 64-bit drivers, which come bundled with the device or can be downloaded from the device manufacturer's Web site.

## Device Drivers Under Windows 2000/XP

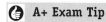

Before installing a new hardware device on a Windows 2000/XP system, check the Microsoft Windows Marketplace Web site to verify that the hardware has been tested by Microsoft, which assures you that the device driver provided by the manufacturer should not give you problems under Windows. To search the site, go to *http://testedproducts.windowsmarketplace.com.* (Hey, don't forget that the period at the end of the preceding sentence is *not* part of the URL.)

When 32-bit device drivers are installed, Windows 2000/XP and Windows 9x/Me record information about the drivers in the Windows registry. Each time Windows starts up, it reads these entries in the registry to know how to load the drivers needed at startup.

Sometimes, to address bugs, make improvements, or add features, manufacturers release device drivers that are more recent than those included with Windows or bundled with the device. Whenever possible, it is best to use the latest driver available for a device provided by the device manufacturer. You can usually download these updated drivers from the manufacturer's Web site. You will learn how to install, update, and troubleshoot drivers in later chapters.

> **🔔 A+ Exam Tip**
>
> The A+ Essentials exam expects you to know how to find and download a device driver.

---

# APPLYING CONCEPTS

Suppose you have just borrowed an HP Photosmart 7760 Deskjet printer from a friend, but you forgot to borrow the CD with the printer drivers on it. Instead of going back to your friend's apartment, you can go to the Hewlett-Packard Web site (*www.hp.com*), download the drivers to a folder on your PC, and install the driver under Windows. Figure 2-25 shows a Web page from the site listing downloadable drivers for ink-jet printers.

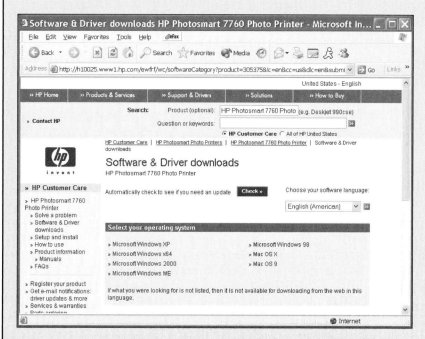

**Figure 2-25** Download the latest device drivers from a manufacturer's Web site

*A+ ESS 3.1*

### Device Drivers Under Windows 9x/Me

Windows 9x/Me comes with 32-bit drivers for hundreds of hardware devices. However, Windows does not provide drivers for all older devices, so a system might sometimes need to use an older 16-bit real-mode device driver. These 16-bit drivers are loaded by entries in the **Config.sys**, **Autoexec.bat**, and **System.ini** files, text files used to configure DOS and Windows 3.x that Windows 95 and Windows 98 support for backward compatibility. Windows Me does not support 16-bit drivers. In Chapter 16, you will learn how to install 32-bit drivers under Windows 9x/Me and 16-bit drivers under Windows 95/98.

## HOW AN OS USES SYSTEM BIOS TO MANAGE DEVICES

*A+ ESS 1.1*

Recall from Chapter 1 that the system BIOS (basic input/output system) on the motherboard is hard-coded or permanently coded into a computer chip called the firmware or ROM BIOS chip. The OS can communicate with simple devices, such as floppy drives or keyboards, through this system BIOS. In addition, system BIOS can be used to access the hard drive. An OS has a choice of using system BIOS or device drivers to access a device. Because device drivers are faster, the trend today is to use device drivers rather than the BIOS to manage devices.

When you think about it, you know that Windows does not load on a computer until after the monitor screen displays information, the keyboard can be used, and the computer has searched a floppy disk inserted into its drive, a CD, or the hard drive to find the OS to load. This means that the CPU knows how to communicate with these devices without the help of an OS. The CPU got the instructions needed for communication from system BIOS. However, after the OS is loaded, it might provide its own instructions to use for communication with a device or the OS can continue to use system BIOS for this job. As a rule of thumb, know that if the computer can use a device such as a monitor or keyboard before the OS is loaded, then system BIOS can control the device even though the OS might later use device drivers for the job. If the computer can't use a device, such as a mouse or a printer, until after an OS is loaded, then it must use device drivers to communicate. You have some control over how system BIOS recognizes and uses devices—changes are made using CMOS setup. How to use CMOS setup is discussed in Chapters 3 and 6.

## HOW AN OS MANAGES MEMORY

*A+ ESS 3.1*

Recall from Chapter 1 that memory or RAM is used to temporarily hold instructions and data to be processed by the CPU. The OS is responsible for moving data and instructions in and out of memory and for keeping up with what is stored where. During startup, the OS launches one or more utilities to manage memory, which survey the amount of memory present. The OS assigns addresses to each location of memory, and these addresses are sometimes displayed onscreen as hexadecimal numbers.

After memory addresses have been assigned to memory, they can be used for communication with all software layers. Device drivers, the OS, and application software are all working when a computer is running. During output operations, application software must pass information to the OS, which, in turn, passes that information to a device driver. The device drivers managing input devices must pass information to the OS, which passes it to the application software. These layers of software all identify the data they want to share by referring to the memory address of the data (see Figure 2-26).

> **Tip**
>
> The A+ Essentials exam expects you to know the purpose and characteristics of virtual memory.

In a 16-bit real mode environment, DOS allowed applications to have direct access to memory, and Windows 9x/Me offered a hybrid environment whereby applications could run in real mode (having direct access to memory) or in protected mode (the OS controls access to memory). Windows NT/2000/XP forces all programs to run in protected mode, and it controls how that software accesses memory.

Figure 2-26  Applications, the OS, and drivers pass data among them by communicating the address of memory holding the data

For example, in Figure 2-27, you can see that the 16-bit program running in real mode has direct access to RAM. But in protected mode, more than one program can run, and the programs must depend on the OS to access RAM. This arrangement also allows the OS some latitude in how it uses RAM. If the OS is low on RAM, it can store some data on the hard drive. This method of using the hard drive as though it were RAM is called **virtual memory**, and data stored in virtual memory is stored in a file on the hard drive called a **swap file** or **page file**. The Windows 2000/XP swap file is Pagefile.sys, and the Windows 9x/Me swap file is Win386.swp. The OS manages the entire process, and the applications know nothing about this substitution of hardware resources for RAM. How to manage the Windows swap files is covered in later chapters.

> **Notes**
>
> For more information on how an OS manages hardware resources, especially as this information applies to Windows 9x/Me, see Appendix A.

Real mode: One program has direct access to hardware

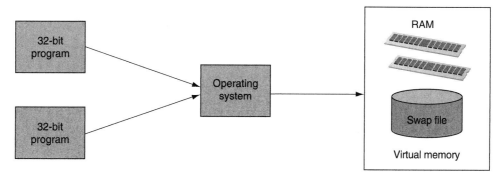

Protected mode: Multiple programs depend on the OS to access hardware

Figure 2-27  Protected mode allows more than one program to run, each protected from the other by the operating system

## OS TOOLS TO EXAMINE A SYSTEM

You have learned about many operating systems and OS components and functions in this chapter. When maintaining and troubleshooting a system, it is important for you to know how to use OS tools to examine and change the system. In this section, you'll learn how to use several of these tools, and others will be covered in future chapters.

> **A+ Exam Tip**
>
> The A+ Essentials exam expects you to be familiar with and know how to use the Windows 2000/XP desktop, My Computer, Windows Explorer, System Properties, Control Panel, Device Manager, and System Information. All these tools are discussed in this section. If the utility can be accessed by more than one method, you are expected to know all of the methods.

**A+ ESS 3.1**

### THE WINDOWS DESKTOP

The Windows desktop is the primary tool provided by the Windows shell. The Windows 2000/XP desktop can be customized and maintained to provide a user-friendly place to manage applications and often-used files. Figure 2-28 shows the Windows XP desktop after the user has clicked the Start button. Notice in the figure for Windows XP that the username for the person currently logged on is shown at the top of the Start menu.

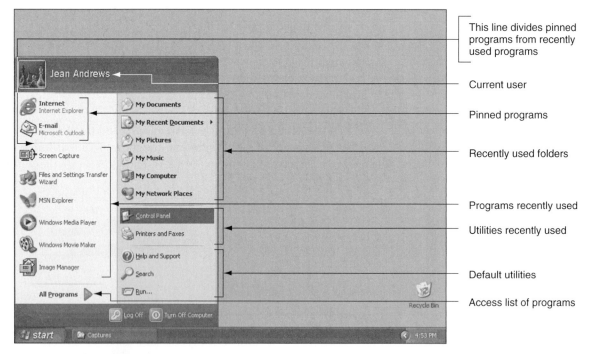

**Figure 2-28** The Windows XP desktop and Start menu

> **Notes**
>
> If you know how to move around in the Windows XP Start menu, you pretty much know how to move around in the Windows 2000 and Windows 9x/Me Start menus as well.

Applications at the top of the Start menu are said to be "pinned" to the menu—in other words, permanently listed there until you change them in a Start menu setting. Applications that are used often are listed below the pinned applications and can change from time to time. The programs in the white column on the left side of the Start menu are user-oriented applications, and the programs in the dark column on the right side of the menu are

A+ ESS
3.1

OS-oriented, and are most likely to be used by an administrator or technician responsible for the system.

When you point to **All Programs** in Figure 2-28, the list of currently installed software appears. Figure 2-29 shows the default entries that appear when you point to **Accessories** and then **System Tools**. You can use these tools to back up data, clean up a hard drive, schedule tasks, restore Windows settings, and do various other things when solving problems with Windows.

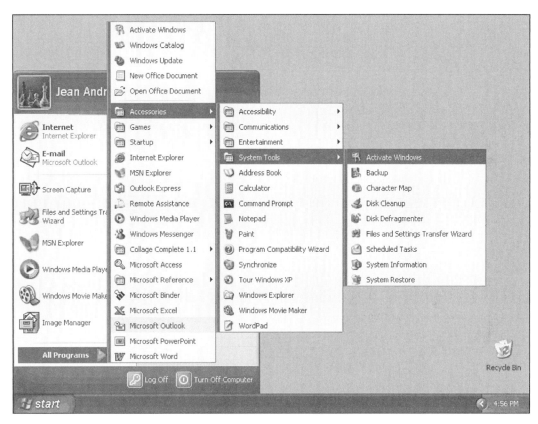

**Figure 2-29**   Click Start, All Programs to view the list of currently installed software

You can do several things to customize the Windows desktop. For example, you can make applications automatically load at startup, change the background on the desktop (called the wallpaper), create shortcuts to files and applications, control what goes in the taskbar, and make the environment more user-friendly. Let's now look at several tools to make the desktop look and work the way you want it to.

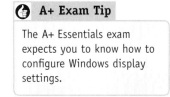

**A+ Exam Tip**

The A+ Essentials exam expects you to know how to configure Windows display settings.

A+ ESS
1.2
1.3

## DISPLAY PROPERTIES WINDOW

One tool useful for changing the way the desktop looks is the Display Properties window. To access this window, right-click anywhere on the desktop and select Properties from the shortcut menu, or you can open the Display applet in the Control Panel.

The left side of Figure 2-30 shows the Desktop tab of the Display Properties window for Windows XP; Figure 2-31 shows the Display Properties window for Windows 98.

**Figure 2-30**   The Windows XP Display Properties window lets you change settings for your desktop

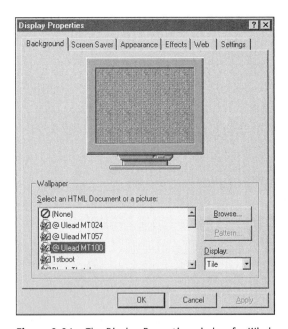

**Figure 2-31**   The Display Properties window for Windows 98

The Windows 98 window is similar to that of Windows 2000. Some things you can do from the Display Properties window are:

▲ Select a desktop wallpaper photo or a pattern, and pick a color scheme for the desktop.
▲ Select a screen saver and change its settings.
▲ Change power settings for the monitor.
▲ Change icon and shortcut settings.
▲ Change the color range, screen resolution, and screen refresh rate.
▲ Change drivers for the video card and monitor.
▲ Enable or display multiple monitors installed on the system.

**APPLYING|CONCEPTS** Changing the wallpaper (desktop background) is easy in Windows XP. All you have to do is click the **Desktop** tab, select the wallpaper, and click **Apply**. Any photographs you have stored in your Windows XP default folder for photographs (most likely, My Pictures) appear in the list for you to use as wallpaper. You can also use photographs you have stored in other folders as your wallpaper, but you will have to click the **Browse** button to go off and look for them. Another method to change your wallpaper is to use Windows Explorer. In Explorer, right-click the photograph's filename and select **Set as Desktop Background** from the shortcut menu.

When you first install Windows XP, only the Recycle Bin shows on the desktop by default. You can add other shortcuts by using the Display Properties window. In the window, click **Customize Desktop** to display the Desktop Items window, which is shown in Figure 2-30. You can check My Documents, My Computer, My Network Places, and Internet Explorer to add these icons to the desktop. Also notice on this window the option to have Windows clean up your desktop by moving any shortcuts that you have not used in the last 60 days to a separate folder.

**A+ ESS 3.1**

## THE TASKBAR AND SYSTEM TRAY

The **taskbar** is normally located at the bottom of the Windows desktop, displaying information about open programs and providing quick access to others (see Figure 2-32). The system tray is usually on the right side of the taskbar and displays open services. A **service** is a program that runs in the background to support or serve Windows or an application.

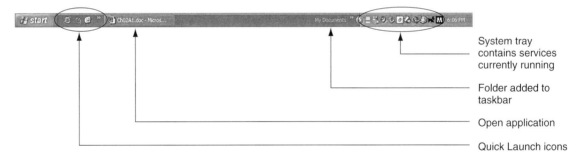

System tray contains services currently running

Folder added to taskbar

Open application

Quick Launch icons

**Figure 2-32** The Windows XP taskbar

You can control the taskbar, system tray, and Start menu from the Taskbar and Start Menu Properties window. To access this window, do the following:

▲ In Windows XP, right-click **Start** and select **Properties** from the shortcut menu. Another method is to right-click the taskbar and select Properties from the shortcut menu. A third method is to use the Control Panel. From the Control Panel, open the Taskbar Start Menu applet.

▲ In Windows 2000 or Windows 9x/Me, click **Start, Settings, Taskbar & Start Menu** or right-click the **taskbar** and select **Properties** from the shortcut menu.

For Windows XP, the window in Figure 2-33 opens. From it, you can add items to and remove items from the Start menu, control how the taskbar manages items in the system tray, and specify how the taskbar is displayed.

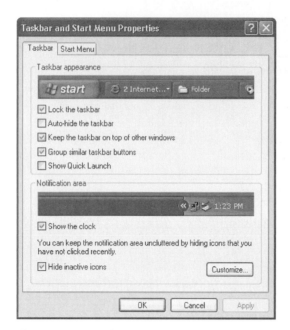

**Figure 2-33**   Use the Taskbar and Start Menu Properties window to control what appears in the Start menu and taskbar

Items displayed in the taskbar can be applications and services launched or not launched. An open application displays its title in the taskbar (see Figure 2-32). Quick Launch icons on the left are displayed in the taskbar so you can quickly find and launch them. To turn the Quick Launch display on or off, right-click the **taskbar**, select **Toolbars**, and then click **Quick Launch**. To add a new toolbar folder to the taskbar, right-click the **taskbar**, select **Toolbars**, and click **New Toolbar**. Then select the folder you want displayed in the taskbar, such as the My Documents folder in Figure 2-32.

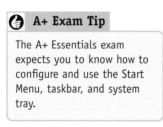

**A+ Exam Tip**

The A+ Essentials exam expects you to know how to configure and use the Start Menu, taskbar, and system tray.

The **system tray** is on the right side of the taskbar and displays icons for running services; these services include the volume control and network connectivity. Windows XP automatically hides these icons. To display them, click the left arrow on the right side of the taskbar. If you have a sluggish Windows system, one thing you can do is look at all the running services in the system tray and try to disable the services that are taking up system resources. How to do that is covered in later chapters.

For Windows 2000, the Taskbar and Start Menu Properties window is organized slightly differently than for Windows XP, but works about the same way. For Windows 9x/Me, the window is called the Taskbar Properties window, and is shown in Figure 2-34.

## SHORTCUTS

A **shortcut** on the desktop is an icon that points to a program you can execute, or to a file or folder. The user double-clicks the icon to load the software. Using Windows 2000/XP or Windows 9x/Me, you can create a shortcut in several ways:

- ▲ Select the file, folder, or program in Windows Explorer or in a My Computer window. From the **File** menu, select **Create Shortcut**.
- ▲ From the File menu in Explorer, click **New** and then click **Create Shortcut**.
- ▲ Right-click the file, folder, or program to which you want to create a shortcut, and select **Create Shortcut** from the menu.

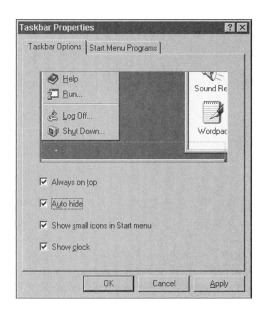

**Figure 2-34** Use the Windows 98 Taskbar Properties window to change taskbar and Start menu settings

◢ Drag the file, folder, or program to the desktop.
◢ Right-click the file, folder, or program and hold down the mouse button while dragging the item to the desktop. When you release it, a dialog box opens. Choose **Create Shortcut(s) Here.**
◢ Right-click the file, folder, or program and select **Create Shortcut** from the shortcut menu (see Figure 2-35).
◢ To edit a shortcut, right-click it and select **Properties** from the menu. To delete a shortcut, select **Delete** from this same menu.

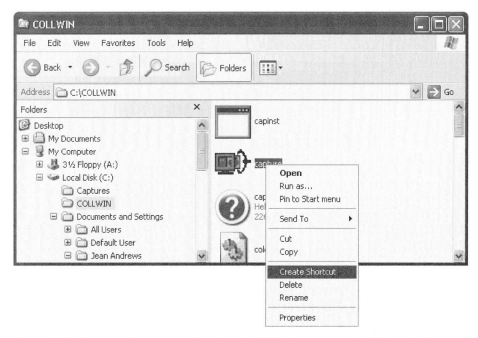

**Figure 2-35** Create a shortcut to a file using the file's shortcut menu in Windows Explorer

For Windows 9x/Me, another way to create a shortcut is to use the Taskbar Properties window (refer back to Figure 2-34). Click the **Start Menu Programs** tab. Then click the

**Add** button. The Create Shortcut Wizard appears, as shown in Figure 2-36. Enter the name of the program to which you want to create a shortcut, or browse for the file on your computer. In this example, we are creating a desktop shortcut to the Notepad application. Click **Next**. On the next window, you must select where to place the shortcut. Select **Desktop** at the top of the folder list to create a desktop shortcut, and then click **Next**. Follow the directions in the wizard to complete the process.

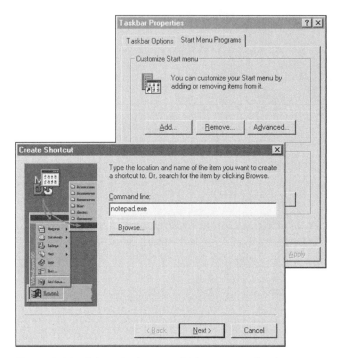

**Figure 2-36**   Select the item to which you want the shortcut to point

## MY COMPUTER AND WINDOWS EXPLORER

The two most useful tools to explore files and folders on your computer are My Computer and Windows Explorer. Under Windows 2000 and Windows 9x/Me, the tools work pretty much the same way. With Windows XP, they are really the same tools with different names.

To access My Computer, use one of these methods:

▲ For Windows XP, click **Start** and click **My Computer**.
▲ For Windows XP, open Windows Explorer and click **My Computer** in the left pane of the Explorer window.
▲ For Windows 2000 or Windows 9x/Me, double-click **My Computer** on the desktop.

Figure 2-37 shows the Windows XP My Computer window, and Figure 2-38 shows the My Computer folder as seen when using Windows 98 Explorer.

Windows Explorer can be opened in different ways, as follows:

▲ Right-click **My Computer** and select **Explore** from the menu.
▲ Right-click **Start** and select **Explore** from the menu.
▲ Open **My Computer** and then click the **View** menu, **Explorer Bar**, and **Folders**.
▲ For Windows 2000/XP, right-click either **My Network Places** or the **Recycle Bin** and select **Explore** from the menu.
▲ For Windows 9x/Me, click **Start**, **Programs**, and **Windows Explorer**.

A+ ESS
3.1

A+
220-602
3.1

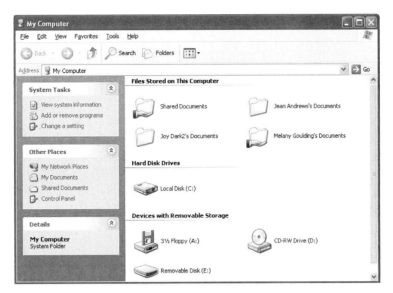

**Figure 2-37** Use Windows XP My Computer to manage system resources

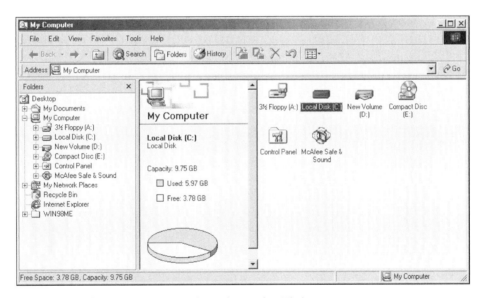

**Figure 2-38** The My Computer view in Explorer using Windows 98

◢ For Windows 9x/Me, right-click either the **Network Neighborhood** icon or the **Recycle Bin** icon and select **Explore** from the menu.

Let's now turn our attention to how to use My Computer or Explorer to manage files and folders and other system resources.

### USING SHORTCUT MENUS

The easiest way to manage drives, disks, folders, and files in Explorer or My Computer is to use the shortcut menus. To access a shortcut menu, right-click the icon representing the item you want to work with. Figure 2-39 shows the shortcut menu for the floppy drive as an example. Here are some tasks you can perform from a shortcut menu:

◢ Click **Explore** or **Open** to view the contents of the disk or folder. For Windows XP, contents of the disk or folder appear in a separate window. For Windows 9x/Me, if

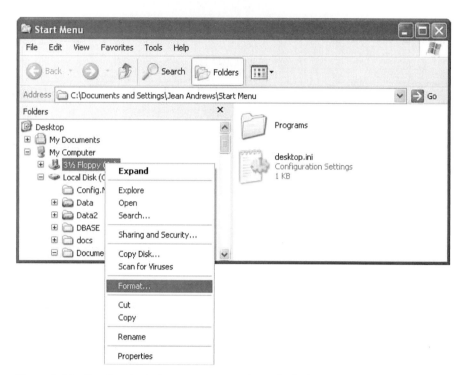

**Figure 2-39**   Use the shortcut menu to manage items in Explorer

you select **Explore**, the contents of the disk or folder appear in the same window, but when you select **Open**, they appear in a separate window.

▲ Click **Create Shortcut** to create a shortcut icon for the selected item.

▲ Select the **Properties** option to bring up a dialog box showing information about the selected item and allowing you to change settings for the item.

▲ If you have selected a disk or drive, click **Format** to format the disk or drive. This action erases everything on the disk or drive and/or prepares it for first use.

▲ To share a drive, folders, or files with other users on your network, click **Sharing and Security**. (For Windows 9x/Me, click **Sharing**.)

▲ For floppy drives, click **Copy Disk** to make a disk copy. The dialog box shown in Figure 2-40 opens, where the disk listed under "Copy from" is the source disk and the disk listed under "Copy to" is the target disk. Click **Start** to copy the disk.

▲ For Windows 9x/Me, click **Backup** to make a backup of a disk.

▲ When a file is selected, use additional options on the shortcut menu for files to do such things as editing, printing, and e-mailing the file and scanning the file for viruses.

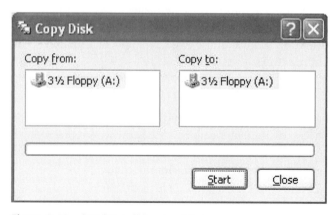

**Figure 2-40**   Copying a disk using Windows

**2**

A+ ESS
3.1

A+
220-602
3.1

◢ To create a file, for Windows 2000/XP, right-click in the unused white area in the right window of Explorer and select **New** from the shortcut menu. The menu lists applications you can use to create the file in the current folder (see Figure 2-41). For Windows 9x/Me, right-click a folder name and select **New** from the shortcut menu.

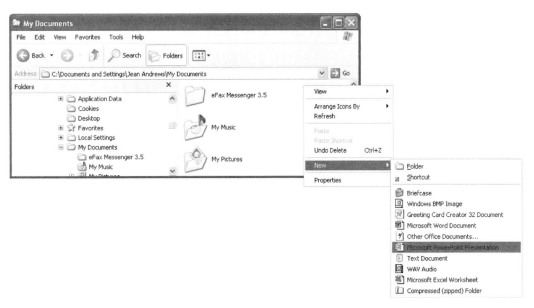

**Figure 2-41**    Create a new file using Windows Explorer

As you can see, some options on shortcut menus are the same for files, folders, drives, and disks; others are specific to particular items. The additional shortcut menu options may differ, depending on what programs you have installed to work with a particular item.

Now let's look in more detail at ways to use Windows Explorer to work with files and folders on your floppy disk or hard drive.

## CREATING A FOLDER

To create a folder, first select the folder you want to be the parent folder. (Remember that a parent folder is the folder that contains the child folder.) You select a folder by clicking the folder name. For example, to create a folder named Games under the folder named Download, first click the **Download** folder. Then click the **File** menu, select **New**, and select **Folder** from the submenu that appears. The new folder will be created under Download, but its name will be New Folder. The name New Folder is automatically selected and highlighted for you to type a new name. Type **Games** to change the folder name, as shown in Figure 2-42. You can create folders within folders within folders, but there is a limitation as to the maximum depth of folders under folders, which depends on the length of the folder names. In Chapter 13, you will learn that you can also create a folder using the MD or MKDIR command from a command prompt.

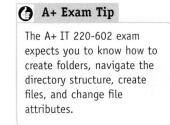

**A+ Exam Tip**

The A+ IT 220-602 exam expects you to know how to create folders, navigate the directory structure, create files, and change file attributes.

## DELETING A FOLDER

To delete a folder from Explorer, right-click the folder and select **Delete** from the shortcut menu. A confirmation dialog box asks if you are sure you want to delete the folder. If you click **Yes**, you send the folder and all its contents, including subfolders, to the Recycle Bin.

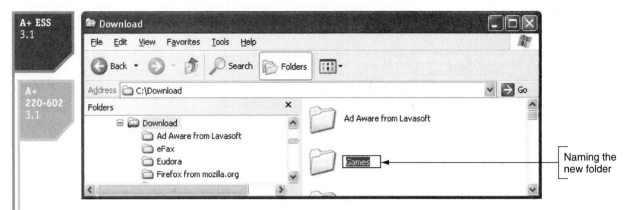

**Figure 2-42** Edit the new folder's name

Emptying the Recycle Bin will free up your disk space. Files and folders sent to the Recycle Bin are not *really* deleted until you empty the bin. To do that, right-click the **bin** and select **Empty Recycle Bin** from the shortcut menu. In Chapter 13, you will learn that you can also delete a folder using the RD or RMDIR command from a command prompt.

## CHANGING FILE ATTRIBUTES

Using Explorer or My Computer, you can view and change the properties assigned to a file; these properties are called the file attributes. Using these attributes, you can do such things as hide a file, make it a read-only file, or flag a file to be backed up. From Explorer or My Computer, right-click a file and select **Properties** from the shortcut menu. The Properties window shown in Figure 2-43 opens.

From the Properties window, you can change the read-only, hidden, and archive attributes of the file. The archive attribute is used to determine if a file has changed since the last backup. To change its value, click **Advanced** in the Properties window. In Chapter 13, you will learn that you

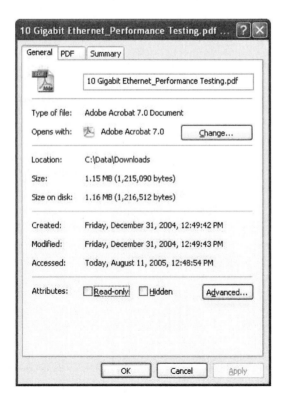

**Figure 2-43** Properties of a file in Windows

can also change these attributes of a file or folder using the Attrib command from a command prompt. There is one other attribute of a file, called the system attribute, that says a file belongs to the OS. This attribute can be changed with the Attrib command, but not by using Explorer.

### CHANGING FOLDER OPTIONS

You can also view and change options assigned to folders, which can control how users view the files in the folder and what they can do with these files.

Windows identifies file types primarily by the file extension. In Windows Explorer, by default, Windows has an annoying habit of hiding the extensions of files if it knows which application to use to open or execute the file. For example, just after installation, it hides .exe, .com, .sys, and .txt file extensions, but it does not hide .doc, .ppt, or .xls files until the software to open these files has been installed. Also, Windows really doesn't want you to see its own system files, so it hides these files from view until you force it to show them.

To view hidden files and file extensions, do the following:

1. Select the folder where system files are located.

2. Click **Tools** and then click **Folder Options**. The Folder Options window opens (see Figure 2-44).

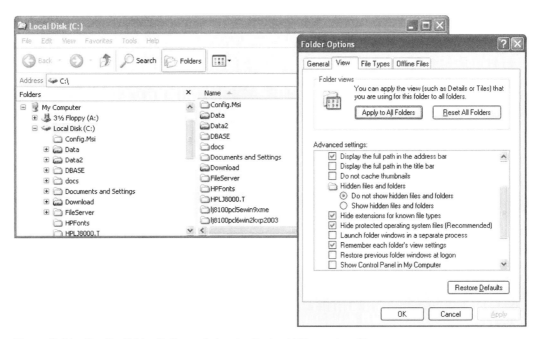

**Figure 2-44**  Use the Folder Options window to display hidden system files

3. Click the **View** tab. Select **Show hidden files and folders**. Uncheck **Hide extensions for known file types**. Uncheck **Hide protected operating system files**. Windows complains it doesn't want to show you these files. Click **Yes** to confirm that you really want to see them.

4. Click **Apply**. Click **OK** to close the Folder Options window.

## SYSTEM PROPERTIES

In Chapter 1, you saw how System Properties can be used to view the processor and memory installed. Recall that to open the System Properties window, right-click **My Computer** and select **Properties**. Another way to open the window is to click the **System** applet in the Control Panel.

Here is a list of things you can do with System Properties:

▲ On the General tab, view information about the system, including the installed OS, the amount of RAM installed, and registration information.

▲ For Windows XP, on the Computer Name tab, change the name of the computer on the network. For Windows 2000, this is done on the Network Identification tab.

▲ On the Hardware tab, access Device Manager and create new hardware profiles.

▲ On the Advanced tab, control computer performance and decide how system failures will be handled.

▲ For Windows XP, on the System Restore tab, turn this feature on or off. System Restore is covered in Chapter 12, and is not available for Windows 2000.

▲ For Windows XP, on the Automatic Updates tab, control how Windows Updates will work (see Figure 2-45). Automatic Updates is not available for Windows 2000.

▲ For Windows XP, on the Remote tab, manage how outside users can control your computer.

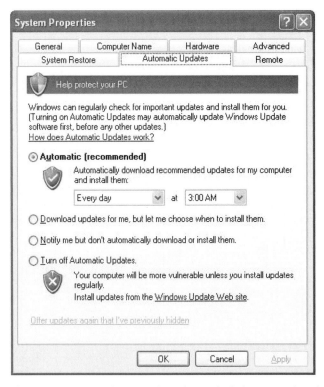

**Figure 2-45**  Control Automatic Updates of Windows XP using the System Properties window

A+ ESS
3.1

## CONTROL PANEL

The Control Panel is a window containing several small utility programs called applets that are used to manage hardware, software, users, and the system. For Windows XP, to access the Control Panel, click **Start** and then click **Control Panel**. For Windows 2000 and Windows 9x/Me, to open the Control Panel, click **Start, Settings,** and **Control Panel**.

Figure 2-46 shows the Windows XP Control Panel in Category View. Select a category to see the applets in that category, or click **Switch to Classic View** to see the applets when you first open the Control Panel, as they are displayed in earlier versions of Windows.

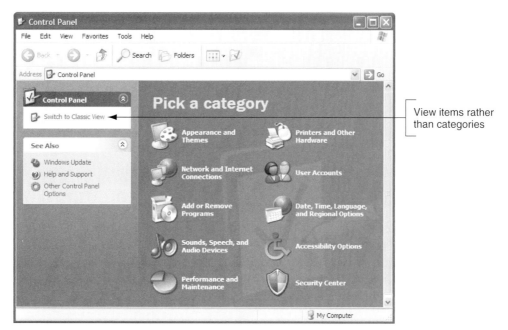

Figure 2-46 The Windows XP Control Panel is organized by category, although you can easily switch to Classic View

Besides accessing the several applets in the Control Panel from the Control Panel window, each applet can be accessed directly. You will learn how to do this as you learn to use these applets later in the book. For all the applets, if you know the name of the applet program file, you can launch the applet by using the Run dialog box. For example, to open the Mouse Properties applet, type **Main.cpl** in the Run dialog box, and then press **Enter**.

> **A+ Exam Tip**
>
> The A+ Essentials exam expects you to be familiar with the Control Panel and its applets.

## DEVICE MANAGER

Device Manager is your primary Windows tool when solving problems with hardware. It gives a graphical view of hardware devices configured under Windows and the resources and drivers they use. Using Device Manager, you can make changes, update drivers, and uninstall device drivers. For instance, when a device driver is being installed, Windows might inform you of a resource conflict, or the device simply might not work. You can use Device Manager as a useful fact-finding tool for resolving the problem. You can also use Device Manager to print a report of system configuration.

Here is how to access Device Manager under Windows 2000/XP and Windows 9x/Me. (Windows NT does not have a Device Manager.)

> **Notes**
>
> Use the Windows Search utility to search for all files that end with the file extension .cpl to see a list of Control Panel applets. Not all applets displayed in the Search Results window will be currently installed in the Control Panel.

- ◢ *Using Windows XP*. Click **Start**, right-click **My Computer**, and then select **Properties** on the shortcut menu. The System Properties dialog box appears. Click the **Hardware** tab and then click **Device Manager**. Or you can enter **Devmgmt.msc** in the Run dialog box.
- ◢ *Using Windows 2000*. Right-click the **My Computer** icon on the desktop, select **Properties** on the shortcut menu, click the **Hardware** tab, and then click the **Device Manager** button. You can also enter **Devmgmt.msc** in the Run dialog box.

**A+**
**220-602**
**3.1**
**3.3**

▲ *Using Windows 9x/Me.* Right-click the **My Computer** icon on the desktop, select **Properties** on the shortcut menu, and then click the **Device Manager** tab.

Device Manager for Windows XP is shown in Figure 2-47. Click a plus sign to expand the view of an item, and click a minus sign to collapse the view. Also notice the three-forked symbol near the bottom of the window representing a USB device.

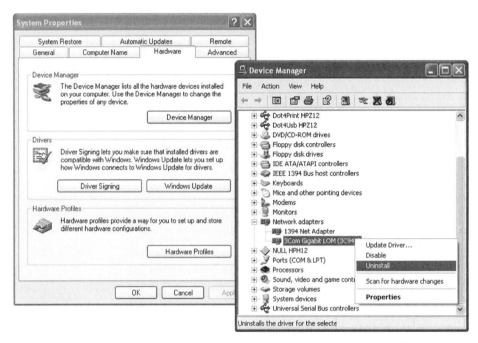

**Figure 2-47**    Windows XP Device Manager gives information about devices and allows you to uninstall a device

One thing you can do if you have a problem with an installed device is to use Device Manager to uninstall the device. Right-click the device and click **Uninstall** on the shortcut menu also showing in Figure 2-47. Then reboot and reinstall the device, looking for problems during the installation that point to the source of the problem. Sometimes reinstalling a device is all that is needed to solve the problem.

To find out more information about a device, right-click the device and select Properties on the shortcut menu. You can see the Properties dialog box for a network card in Figure 2-48. Many times, the source of a problem shows up in this window.

Figure 2-49 shows Device Manager under Windows 98 reporting a problem with a device using an exclamation point. Notice the open diamond symbol indicating the device is a SCSI device. (SCSI is discussed in Chapter 8.) In Device Manager, symbols that indicate a device's status are:

▲ A red X through the device name indicates a disabled device.
▲ An exclamation point on a yellow background indicates a problem with the device. (The device might still be functioning, but not in the way that Windows likes.)
▲ A blue I on a white field indicates that automatic settings were not used and resources have been manually assigned. It does not indicate a problem with the device.
▲ For Windows Me, a green question mark indicates a compatible driver is installed (not the driver designed for the device), which means the device might not be fully functional.

**Figure 2-48** The Properties window for a device helps you solve problems with the device

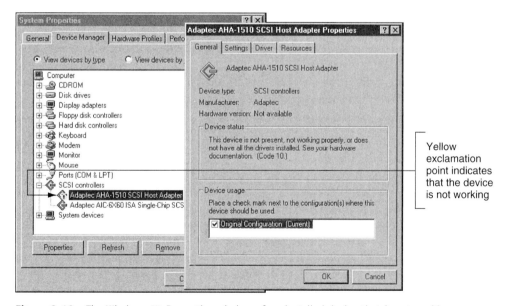

Yellow
exclamation
point indicates
that the device
is not working

**Figure 2-49** The Windows 98 Properties window of an installed device that is not working

When a device is giving problems, check the Properties dialog box of that device for information. The Device Properties dialog box that opens can give you helpful information about solving problems with the device. From this window, you can update the driver for a device, enable or disable a device, and uninstall a device. How to do all this is covered in later chapters.

Using Device Manager, you can get a printed report of system information, which can be useful to document the status of a system. To print the report using Windows XP, click the

A+
220-602
3.1
3.3

printer icon on the Device Manager toolbar. For Windows 2000, click **View** and then click **Print**. For Windows 9x/Me, click **Print**. There are three options for the report: System summary, Selected class or device, and All devices and system summary.

## SYSTEM INFORMATION

The System Information utility gives information similar to that given by Device Manager plus more. For example, it tells you the BIOS version you are using, the directory where the OS is installed, how system resources are used, information about drivers and their status, and much information about software installed on the system that is not included in Device Manager. This information is especially useful when talking with a technical support person on the phone who needs to know exactly what system and configuration is in front of you.

To run System Information using Windows 2000/XP or Windows 9x/Me, click **Start**, and then click **Run**. In the Run dialog box, enter **Msinfo32.exe**, and then click **OK**. The System Information dialog box opens (see Figure 2-50).

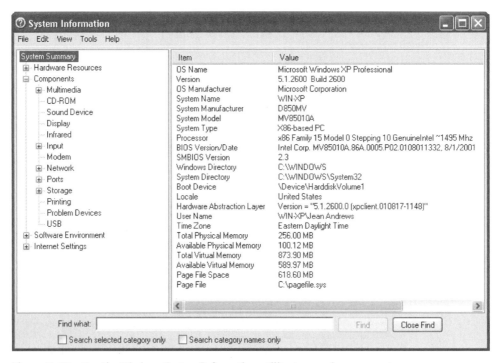

**Figure 2-50**   Use the Windows System Information utility to examine your system

System Information can be useful when strange error messages appear during startup. Use it to get a list of drivers that loaded successfully. If you have saved the System Information report when the system was starting successfully, comparing the two reports can help identify the problem device.

## WINDOWS HELP AND THE MICROSOFT WEB SITE

Windows Help might provide useful information when you try to resolve a problem. To access Windows XP Help, click **Start**, and then click **Help and Support**. For Windows 2000 and Windows 9x/Me, click **Start**, and then click **Help**.

In many cases, the Help information includes suggestions that can lead you to a solution. For example, suppose you were trying to connect to the Internet using a phone line, but can't make the call. You check the phone connection, the modem lights, and all the obvious things, but still can't get it to work. When you turn to the Help tool and search for help with a dial-up connection, the window in Figure 2-51 appears, which suggests you delete all dial-up networking connections and re-create them. Although doing this doesn't guarantee the solution, it's certainly worth trying.

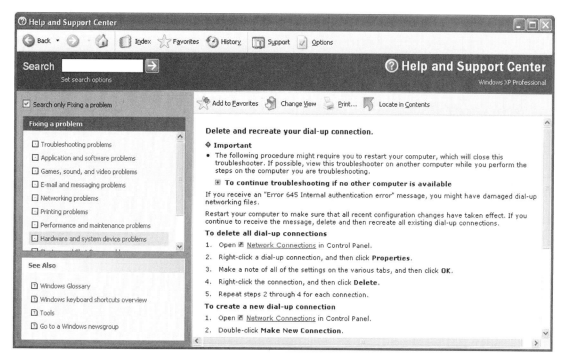

**Figure 2-51**  Troubleshooter making a suggestion to resolve a problem with using the modem to connect to the Internet

Also, the Microsoft Web site (*http://support.microsoft.com*), which is shown in Figure 2-52, has lots of information on troubleshooting. Search for the device, an error message, a Windows utility, a symptom, a software application, an update version number, or key words that lead you to articles about problem and solutions. You can also go to *www.microsoft.com* to browse for links on hardware and software compatibility. Other sources of help are application and device user and installation manuals, training materials, and the Web sites of application and device manufacturers. You can also use a search engine such as Google (*www.google.com*). Enter the error message, software application, symptom or Windows utility in the search box to search the Web for answers, suggestion, and comments.

> **Notes**
>
> If you are serious about learning to provide professional support for Windows, each OS has a resource kit, including support software and a huge reference book containing inside information about the OS. Check out *Microsoft Windows XP Professional Resource Kit* or *Microsoft Windows 2000 Professional Resource Kit*. Both are put out by Microsoft Press.

Beware, however, that you don't bump into a site that does more harm than good. Some sites are simply guessing, offering incomplete and possibly wrong solutions, and even offering a utility it claims will solve your problem but really contains only pop-up ads or spyware. Use only reputable sites you can trust. You'll learn about several of these excellent sites in this book.

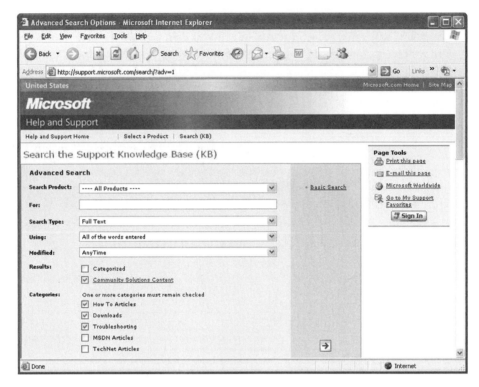

**Figure 2-52**    Microsoft Technical Support Web site

## KEYSTROKE SHORTCUTS IN THE OS

Table 2-3 lists a few handy keystrokes to use when working with Windows, including the function keys you can use during startup. You can also use the mouse to do some of these same things, but keystrokes are sometimes faster. Also, in some troubleshooting situations, the mouse is not usable. At those times, knowing these keystrokes can get you out of a jam.

| General Action | Keystrokes | Description |
| --- | --- | --- |
| While loading Windows | F8 | For Windows 2000/XP, to start in Safe Mode (covered in Chapter 14). |
| | Shift + F8 | For Windows 2000/XP, start with Step-by-step confirmation (covered in Chapter 14). |
| | F4 | For Windows 9x/Me, load previous version of DOS (covered in Chapter 16). |
| | F5 | For Windows 98/Me, start in Safe Mode (covered in Chapter 16). |
| | F8 or Ctrl | For Windows 98/Me, display startup menu (covered in Chapter 16). |
| Managing Windows and applications | Alt + Tab | Hold down the Alt key and press Tab to move from one loaded application to another. |
| | Ctrl + Tab and Ctrl + Shift + Tab | Move through tabbed pages in a dialog box. |
| | Alt + ESC | Hold down the Alt key and press Esc to cycle through items in the order they were opened. |

**Table 2-3**    Keystrokes that make working with Windows easier

| General Action | Keystrokes | Description |
|---|---|---|
| | F6 | In Windows 2000/XP, cycle through screen elements in a window or on the desktop. |
| | Win or Ctrl + Esc | Display Start menu. Use arrow keys to move over the menu. (The Win key is the one labeled with the Windows flag icon.) |
| | Win + E | Start Windows Explorer. |
| | Win + M | Minimize all windows. |
| | Win + Tab | Move through items on the taskbar. |
| | Win + R | Display the Run dialog box. |
| | Win + Break | Display the System Properties window. |
| | F5 | Refresh the contents of a window. |
| | Alt + F4 | Close the active application window, or, if no window is open, shut down Windows. |
| | Ctrl + F4 | Close the active document window. |
| | Alt + Spacebar | In Windows 2000/XP, display the System menu for the active window. To close this window, you can then use the arrow key to step down to Close. |
| | Alt + M | First put the focus on the Start menu (use Win or Ctrl + Esc) and then press Alt + M to minimize all windows and move the focus to the desktop. |
| | F10 or Alt | Activate the menu bar in the active program. |
| | F1 | Display help. |
| | Ctrl + Alt + Del | Display the Task List, which you can use to switch to another application, end a task, or shut down Windows. |
| | Application | When an item is selected, display its shortcut menu. (The Application key is labeled with a box and an arrow.) |
| Working with text anywhere in Windows | Ctrl + C | Shortcut to Copy. |
| | Ctrl + V | Shortcut for Paste. |
| | Ctrl + A | Shortcut for selecting all text. |
| | Ctrl + X | Shortcut for Cut. |
| | Ctrl + Z | Shortcut for Undo. |
| | Ctrl + Y | Shortcut for Repeat/Redo. |
| | Shift + arrow keys | Hold down the Shift key, and use the arrow keys to select text, character by character. |
| Managing files, folders, icons, and shortcuts | Ctrl + Shift while dragging a file | Create a shortcut. |
| | Ctrl while dragging a file | Copy a file. |
| | Shift + Delete | Delete a file without placing it in the Recycle Bin. |
| | F2 | Rename an item. |

Table 2-3  Keystrokes that make working with Windows easier (continued)

| General Action | Keystrokes | Description |
|---|---|---|
| | Alt + Enter | Display an item's Properties window. |
| Selecting items | Shift + click | To select multiple entries in a list (such as filenames in Explorer), click the first item, hold down the Shift key, and click the last item you want to select in the list. All items between the first and last are selected. |
| | Ctrl + click | To select several nonsequential items in a list, click the first item to select it. Hold down the Ctrl key and click other items anywhere in the list. All items you click are selected. |
| Using menus | Alt | Press the Alt key to activate the menu bar. |
| | Alt, letter | After the menu bar is activated, press a letter to select a menu option. The letter must be underlined in the menu. |
| | Alt, arrow keys, Enter | In a window, use the Alt key to make the menu bar active. Then use the arrow keys to move over the menu tree and highlight the correct option. Use the Enter key to select that option. |
| | Esc | Press Esc to exit a menu without making a selection. |
| Copying to the Clipboard | Print Screen | Copy the desktop to the Clipboard. |
| | Alt + Print Screen | Copy the active window to the Clipboard. |

**Table 2-3** Keystrokes that make working with Windows easier (continued)

## >> CHAPTER SUMMARY

▲ Operating systems used for desktop computers include DOS, Windows 9x/Me, Windows NT/2000/XP, Unix, a version of Unix called Linux, OS/2, and the Mac OS. The Windows Server 2003 operating systems are only used on servers. Windows Vista is the next Microsoft operating system.

▲ An operating system manages hardware; runs applications; provides an interface for users; and stores, retrieves, and manipulates files.

▲ Every OS is composed of two main internal components: a shell portion to interact with users, and applications and a kernel portion to interact with hardware.

▲ An OS provides an interface for the user that is command driven or icon and menu driven.

▲ An OS manages files and folders using a file system. Two Windows file systems are FAT and NTFS.

▲ A hard drive is organized into partitions that contain one or more logical drives or volumes.

▲ Three types of software are BIOS (firmware) and device drivers, operating systems (OSs), and application software. Sometimes, device drivers are considered part of the OS.

▲ Application software relates to the OS, which relates to BIOS and device drivers to control hardware.

▲ Most processors can operate in real or protected mode. In real mode, a CPU processes 16 bits at a time, and in protected mode, it processes 32 bits at a time. Some high-end processors operate in 64-bit mode (long mode).

▲ Device drivers are written using 16-bit, 32-bit, or 64-bit code. Most drivers today are 32-bit, protected-mode drivers that Windows loads from the registry.

▲ Windows Me and Windows NT/2000/XP use only 32-bit drivers, except for Windows XP Professional x64 Edition, which uses 64-bit drivers.

▲ Software manages memory by means of memory addresses that point to locations in RAM.

▲ Virtual memory uses hard drive space as memory to increase the total amount of memory available. In Windows, virtual memory is stored in the swap file. The Windows 9x/Me swap file is Win386.swp, and the Windows 2000/XP swap file is Pagefile.sys.

▲ From the Windows desktop, you can launch programs from the Start menu, a shortcut icon on the desktop, the Run dialog box, Windows Explorer, or My Computer.

▲ Windows utilities useful for maintaining and customizing a system, gathering information about the system and troubleshooting are the Display Properties window, the Taskbar and Start Menu Properties window, Windows Explorer, My Computer, System Properties, the Control Panel, Device Manager, and System Information.

▲ Use Windows Help and the Microsoft Web site to resolve problems and find useful information.

▲ A computer technician needs to know how to troubleshoot the OS using keystrokes when the mouse is not available.

## >> KEY TERMS

For explanations of key terms, see the Glossary near the end of the book.

| | | |
|---|---|---|
| child directory | kernel | root directory |
| cluster | logical drive | sector |
| CMOS setup | long mode | service |
| desktop | multitasking | shell |
| device driver | New Technology file system | shortcut |
| directory table | (NTFS) | startup BIOS |
| file allocation table (FAT) | operating system (OS) | subdirectory |
| file extension | partition | system BIOS |
| file system | path | system tray |
| filename | preemptive multitasking | taskbar |
| folder | protected mode | track |
| graphical user interface (GUI) | real mode | volume |
| initialization files | registry | |

## >> REVIEW QUESTIONS

1. Which of the following operating systems has been used in troubleshooting OS failures?

   a. Windows XP

   b. Windows Me

   c. Windows 3.1

   d. DOS

2. The Windows operating system uses which of the following to keep hardware and software configuration information, user preferences, and application settings that are used when the OS is first loaded?

   **a.** Kernel

   **b.** Registry

   **c.** Shell

   **d.** Hard drive

3. The file extension identifies which of the following?

   **a.** File type

   **b.** Subdirectory to the root directory

   **c.** Folder

   **d.** Root directory

4. CPUs operate in how many different modes?

   **a.** 1

   **b.** 2

   **c.** 3

   **d.** 4

5. Which of the following is the primary Windows tool that can be used when solving problems with hardware?

   **a.** System properties

   **b.** Windows Explorer

   **c.** File attributes

   **d.** Device Manager

6. True or false? An operating system (OS) is software that controls a computer.

7. True or false? The minimum requirements to install an OS are always the same as the requirements to run an OS.

8. True or false? A cluster is made up of only one sector.

9. True or false? There is only one way to load an application.

10. True or false? A primary partition can have only one logical drive.

11. Different versions of Unix or Linux are sometimes called _____.

12. Applications that have been written to provide a GUI shell for Unix and Linux are called

    _____.

13. A CPU operating in _____ mode means more than one program can be running, and each program is protected from other programs accessing its hardware resources.

14. _____ are small programs stored on the hard drive that tell the computer how to communicate with a specific hardware device such as a printer, network card, or modem.

15. The method of using the hard drive as though it were RAM is called

    _____.

## CHAPTER 3

# PC Repair Fundamentals

In the previous two chapters, you have been introduced to hardware and operating systems. In this chapter, you will learn about your job as a PC support technician and the tools and techniques you'll use. The best support technicians are good at preventing a problem from happening in the first place, so in this chapter, you'll learn how to develop a preventive maintenance plan and use it. You'll also learn how to work inside a computer case and about what happens when you first turn on a PC.

Next in the chapter, you'll learn about some common-sense guidelines to solving computer problems. You'll learn how to interview the user, how to isolate a problem into one that either happens before or after the boot, and how to troubleshoot and solve a problem with a failed boot. This chapter is the first of several chapters that take you one step at a time into diagnosing and solving PC problems.

This chapter lays a strong foundation for troubleshooting that we will build on in later chapters. Much of what is covered in this chapter is introductory in nature; in later chapters, we'll dig into the many details of troubleshooting each subsystem introduced in this chapter.

# PC SUPPORT TECHNICIAN TOOLS

A+ ESS
1.4
7.1

A+
220-602
1.2

Several hardware and software tools can help you maintain a computer and diagnose and repair computer problems. The tools you choose depend on the amount of money you can spend and the level of PC support you expect to provide.

Essential tools for PC troubleshooting are listed here, and several of them are shown in Figure 3-1. You can purchase some of these tools in a PC toolkit, although most PC tool kits contain items you really can do without.

**Figure 3-1** PC support technician tools

Here is a list of essential tools:

▲ Ground bracelet, ground mat, or ground gloves to use when working inside the computer case. How to use them is covered later in the chapter.
▲ Flat-head screwdriver.
▲ Phillips-head or cross-head screwdriver.
▲ Torx screwdriver set, particularly size T15.
▲ Tweezers, preferably insulated ones, for picking pieces of paper out of printers or dropped screws out of tight places.
▲ Extractor, a spring-loaded device that looks like a hypodermic needle. (When you push down on the top, three wire prongs come out that can be used to pick up a screw that has fallen into a place where hands and fingers can't reach.)
▲ Recovery CD, DVD, or floppy disk for any OS you might work on. (You might need several, depending on the OSs you support.)

The following tools might not be essential, but they are very convenient:

▲ Cans of compressed air or anti-static vacuum cleaner to clean dust from inside a computer case
▲ Cleaning solutions and pads such as contact cleaner, monitor wipes, cleaning solutions for CDs, DVDs, and tapes and drives
▲ Multimeter to check the power supply output (see Appendix B)
▲ Needle-nose pliers for removing jumpers and for holding objects in place while you screw them in (especially those pesky nuts on cable connectors)
▲ Cable ties to tie cables up and out of the way inside a computer case
▲ Flashlight to see inside the PC case

3

◢ AC outlet ground tester
◢ Network cable tester
◢ Loop-back plugs to test ports
◢ Small cups or bags to help keep screws organized as you work
◢ Antistatic bags (a type of Farady Cage) to store unused parts
◢ Chip extractor to remove chips (to pry up the chip; a simple screwdriver is usually more effective, however)
◢ Pen and paper for taking notes
◢ Diagnostic cards
◢ Utility software, virus detection software, and diagnostic software on floppy disks or CD

Keep your tools in a toolbox designated for PC troubleshooting. If you put disks and hardware tools in the same box, be sure to keep the disks inside a hard plastic case to protect them from scratches and dents. In addition, make sure the diagnostic and utility software you use is recommended for the hardware and software you are troubleshooting.

Now let's turn our attention to the details of several support technician tools, including recovery CDs, loop-back plugs, cleaning pads and solutions, and POST diagnostic cards.

## RECOVERY CDs

A recovery CD can be used to boot a system and repair or reinstall the Windows operating system. This recovery CD should be the Windows Setup CD that was used to originally install Windows. However, in a pinch, you can use another Windows Setup CD as long as it is for the version of Windows you are using.

If you have a notebook computer or a brand-name computer such as a Dell, IBM, or Gateway, use the recovery CD provided by the manufacturer instead of a regular Windows Setup CD. This recovery CD, as shown in Figure 3-2, has drivers specific to your system, and the Windows build that is on the recovery CD might be different from the one provided by an off-the-shelf Windows Setup CD. For example, a Windows XP Home Edition installation on a notebook computer might have been built with all kinds of changes made to it by the notebook manufacturer. These changes will make it different from a Windows XP Home Edition installation that was sourced from a package bought in a retail store. When you purchase a

**Figure 3-2** Windows Setup CD and Windows Recovery CDs for a notebook computer

brand-name computer, the recovery CD is sometimes included in the package. If it is not included, you can order it from the manufacturer. To order it, go to the manufacturer's Web site support section and find the recovery CD specific to your desktop or notebook computer.

For some brand-name computers, the hard drive contains a hidden recovery partition that can be used to reinstall Windows. Sometimes this hidden partition contains a utility that can be used to create a recovery CD. However, know that the CD must have already been created if it is to be there to help you in the event the entire hard drive fails. To access the utilities on the hidden partition, press a key during startup. Which key to press is displayed on the screen early in the boot before the OS is loaded. For example, one Gateway computer displays the message "Press F11 to start recovery." When you press F11, a menu is displayed giving you the opportunity to reinstall Windows from setup files kept in the hidden partition.

## LOOP-BACK PLUGS

A **loop-back plug** is used to test a serial, parallel, USB, network, or other port. To use one to test a port, you plug in the loop-back plug and then run the software that comes with the plug to test the port. Figure 3-3 shows loop-back plugs that come with CheckIt diagnostic software from SmithMicro Software (*www.smithmicro.com*).

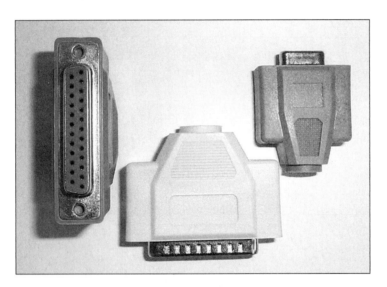

**Figure 3-3** Loop-back plugs used to test serial and parallel ports

## CLEANING PADS AND SOLUTIONS

As a PC technician, you'll find yourself collecting different cleaning solutions and cleaning pads to clean a variety of devices, including the mouse and keyboard, CDs and DVDs and their drives, tapes and tape drives, and CRT and LCD monitors. Figure 3-4 shows a few of these products. The contact cleaner in the figure is used to clean the contacts on expansion cards, which might solve a problem with a faulty connection. You'll learn how and when to use these products later in this chapter and in other chapters in the book.

Most of these cleaning solutions contain flammable and poisonous materials. Take care when using them that they don't get on your skin or in your eyes. To find out what to do if you accidentally get exposed to a dangerous solution, look on the instructions printed on the can or check out the material safety data sheet (see Figure 3-5). A **material safety data sheet (MSDS)** explains how to properly handle substances such as chemical solvents.

A+ ESS
1.4
6.1
7.1

A+
220-602
1.2
1.3
7.1

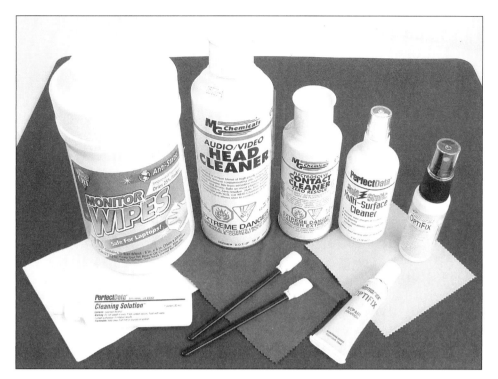

**Figure 3-4** Cleaning solutions and pads

**Figure 3-5** Each chemical you use should have available a material safety data sheet

An MSDS includes information such as physical data, toxicity, health effects, first aid, storage, shipping, disposal, and spill procedures. It comes packaged with the chemical, or you can order one from the manufacturer, or find one on the Internet (see *www.ilpi.com/msds*).

If you have an accident with these or other dangerous products, your company or organization might require you to report the accident to your company and/or fill out an accident report. Check with your organization to find out how to handle reporting these types of incidents.

## POST DIAGNOSTIC CARDS

Although not an essential tool, a POST **diagnostic card** can be of great help to discover and report computer errors and conflicts at POST. If you have a problem that prevents the PC from booting that you suspect is related to hardware, you can install the diagnostic card in an expansion slot on the motherboard and then attempt to boot. The card monitors the boot process and reports errors, usually as coded numbers on a small LED panel on the card. You then look up the number in the documentation that accompanies the card to get more information about the error and its source.

Examples of these cards are listed below. The Post Code Master card is shown in Figure 3-6.

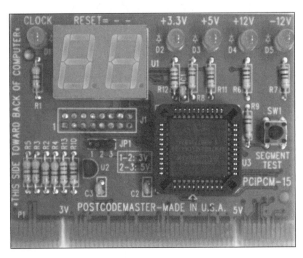

**Figure 3-6**   Post Code Master diagnostic card by MSD, Inc.

- ◢ PCI Error Testing/Debug Card by Winic Corporation (*www.winic.com*)
- ◢ POSTcard V3 by Unicore Software, Inc. (*www.unicore.com*)
- ◢ Post Code Master by MSD, Inc. (*www.postcodemaster.com*)

Before purchasing these or any other diagnostic tools or software, read the documentation about what they can and cannot do, and, if possible, read some product reviews. The Internet is a good source of information.

## *PERSONAL COMPUTER PREVENTIVE MAINTENANCE*

Much in this chapter is about troubleshooting, but it is much better to know how to take some steps to prevent certain computer problems from occurring in the first place. The more preventive maintenance work you do initially, the fewer problems you are likely to have later, and the less troubleshooting and repair you will have to do.

If you are responsible for the PCs in an organization, make and implement a preventive maintenance plan to help prevent failures and reduce repair costs and downtime. In addition, you need a disaster recovery plan to manage failures when they occur. PC failures are caused by many different environmental and human factors, including heat, dust, magnetism, power supply problems, static electricity, human error (such as spilled liquids or an accidental change of setup and software configurations), and viruses. The goals of preventive maintenance are to reduce the likelihood that the events that cause PC failures will occur and to lessen the damage if they do.

A+ ESS
1.4
2.4

A+
220-602
7.1

This section focuses on several preventive maintenance tasks including what to do when a computer becomes your permanent responsibility, how to create a preventive maintenance plan, how to deal with dust, how to prepare a computer for shipping, and how to dispose of used equipment.

# WHEN A PC IS YOUR PERMANENT RESPONSIBILITY

When you are the person responsible for a PC, either as the user or as the ongoing support person for the PC and the user, you need to prepare for future troubleshooting situations. This section describes tasks and procedures for doing this.

## KEEP GOOD BACKUPS OF DATA AND SYSTEM FILES

Suppose the hard drive on your computer stopped working. It's totally dead and everything on it is lost. How would that affect you? What would be lost and what would that cost you in time, stress, and money? You need to keep good backups of data, including your data files, e-mail address list, and e-mail attachments. You also need backups of Windows system files including the registry. How to back up Windows system files is covered in Chapter 12 and how to keep good backups of user data is covered in Chapter 13.

> **Notes**
>
> In most situations, you don't need to back up installed applications. If the application gets corrupted, you can install it again using the setup CDs. It's extremely important that you have the original setup CDs handy when a hard drive fails—without these CDs, you won't be able to reinstall the software. If you like, you can also make one backup copy of a setup CD. According to copyright laws, you have the right to make a backup of the installation CD or floppy disks in case the CD or disks fail. You can keep your copy in a safe place in the event that something happens to the original. Users that you support also need to understand that you cannot reinstall software installed on their systems if the software has been pirated and the CDs are no longer available.

## DOCUMENT ALL SETUP CHANGES, PROBLEMS, AND SOLUTIONS

When you first set up a new computer, start a record book about this computer, using either a file on disk or a notebook dedicated to this machine. In this notebook or file, record any changes in setup data as well as any problems you experience or maintenance that you do on this computer. Be diligent in keeping this notebook up to date, because it will be invaluable in diagnosing problems and upgrading equipment. Keep a printed or handwritten record of all changes to setup data for this machine, and store the record with the hardware and software documentation. This record needs to include changes to BIOS and jumper settings on the motherboard, which you'll learn how to do later in the chapter.

If you are not the primary user of the computer, you might want to keep the hardware documentation separate from the computer itself. Label the documentation so that you can easily identify that it belongs to this computer. Some support people tape a large envelope inside the computer case, containing

> **Notes**
>
> You can also keep a record of all troubleshooting you do on a computer in a word-processing document that lists all the problems you have encountered and the solutions you used. This will help you save time in troubleshooting problems you have encountered before. Store the document file on a flash drive or floppy disk that you keep with the computer's documentation. You might want to make a new printout each time the document changes.

important documentation and records specific to that computer. On the other hand, if you're also responsible for software reference manuals, know that these manuals need to be kept in a location that is convenient for users.

## PROTECT THE SYSTEM AGAINST VIRUSES AND OTHER ATTACKS

In today's world, most people have Internet access and the Internet is full of viruses, worms, and other malicious software looking for a way into your system. To protect your system, use the following tips:

### Always Use a Firewall

A firewall is hardware or software that prevents hackers or malicious software from getting into your computer without your knowledge. For Windows XP, you can use Windows Firewall. (Windows 2000 and Windows 9x/Me do not offer a firewall. For these OSs, you need to use third-party software.) Within Windows XP, you can change firewall settings by clicking **Start** and right-clicking **My Network Places**. Then, select **Properties** from the shortcut menu. The Network Connections window opens, as shown in Figure 3-7.

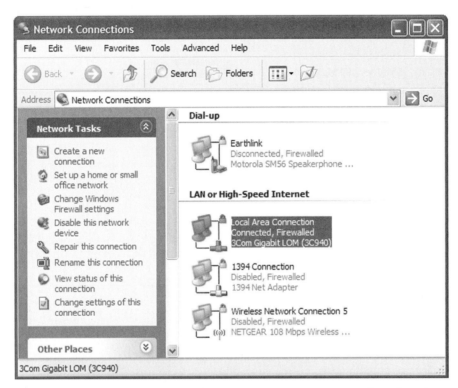

**Figure 3-7**  Use the Windows XP Network Connections window to change firewall settings

Select your network connection (in the figure, the Local Area Connection is selected), and click **Change Windows Firewall settings**. The Windows Firewall window opens, as shown in Figure 3-8. Make sure **On (recommended)** is selected and click **OK** to apply the change. You'll learn more about this and other firewalls in Chapter 19.

### Install and Run Antivirus Software

Install and run antivirus (AV) software and keep it current. Configure the AV software so that it automatically downloads updates to the software and runs in the background. To be effective, AV software must be kept current and must be turned on. Set the AV

A+ ESS
1.4
2.4
6.1
6.3

A+
220-602
7.1

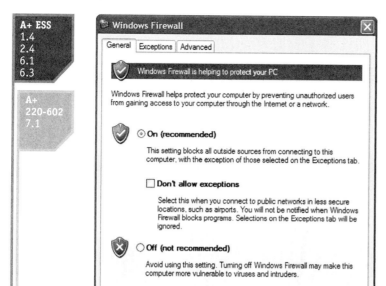

**Figure 3-8** Turn on Windows Firewall to protect your system

software to automatically scan e-mail attachments (see Figure 3-9). You'll find a list of AV software in Chapter 19 and more information about how to use it effectively to protect your system.

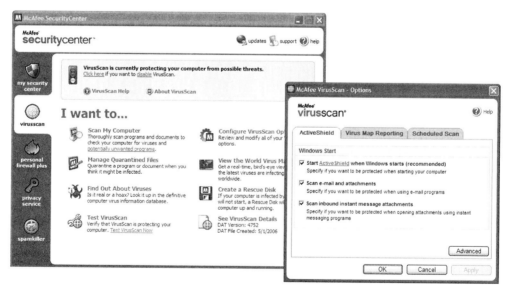

**Figure 3-9** Configure antivirus software to scan e-mail and instant message attachments and to download updates automatically

## Keep Windows Updates Current

Microsoft is continually releasing new patches, fixes, and updates for Windows XP, and, to a limited degree, for Windows 2000. For these OSs, you need to keep your installation of Windows current with all the latest updates. Many of these updates are to fix bugs in the system and to plug up security leaks.

Windows XP offers a way to automatically download and install updates. To verify that Windows XP is automatically maintaining updates when connected to the Internet, click **Start**, right-click **My Computer**, and select **Properties** from the shortcut menu. The System Properties dialog box opens. Click **Automatic Updates**, as shown in Figure 3-10. For best results, select **Automatic (recommended)** and choose the day and time to download and install updates. Click **OK** to apply your changes.

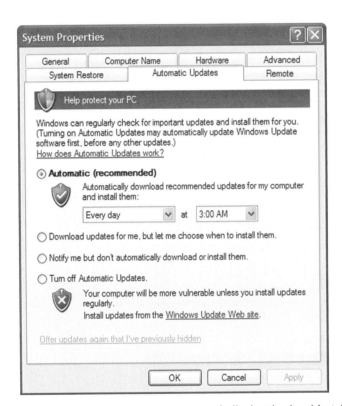

**Figure 3-10**   Set Windows XP to automatically download and install updates

Windows 2000 does not offer automatic updates. For this OS, you need to periodically go to the Microsoft Web site (*update.microsoft.com*) and manually download and install updates. Currently, Microsoft only updates Windows 2000 to solve problems with security. There are no more updates for Windows 9x/Me. You'll learn more about Windows 2000/XP updates in Chapter 11.

## PHYSICALLY PROTECT YOUR EQUIPMENT

There are some things you can do to physically protect your computer equipment. Here is my list of do's and don'ts. You can probably add your own tips to the list:

▴ *Don't move or jar your computer when it's turned on.* Before you move the computer case even a foot or so, power it down. Don't put the computer case under your desk where it might get bumped or kicked. Although modern hard drives are sealed and much less resistant to vibration than earlier models, it's still possible to crash a drive by banging into it while it's reading or writing data.

▴ *Don't smoke around your computer.* Tar from cigarettes can accumulate on fans, causing them to jam and the system to overheat. For older hard drives that are not adequately sealed, smoke particles can get inside and crash a drive.

◢ *Don't leave the PC turned off for weeks or months at a time.* Once my daughter left her PC turned off for an entire summer. At the beginning of the new school term, the PC would not boot. We discovered that the boot record at the beginning of the hard drive had become corrupted. PCs, like old cars, can give problems after long spans of inactivity.

◢ *Don't block air vents on the front and rear of the computer case or on the monitor.* Proper air circulation is essential to keeping a system cool. Also, for optimum airflow, put covers on expansion slot openings on the rear of the case and put faceplates over empty bays on the front of the case (see Figure 3-11).

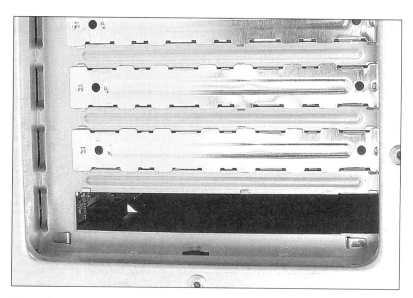

**Figure 3-11** For optimum airflow, don't leave empty expansion slots and bays uncovered

◢ *Use keyboard covers for dirty environments.* You can purchase plastic keyboard covers to protect the keyboard in a dirty or extremely dusty environment.

◢ *High humidity can be dangerous for hard drives.* I once worked in a basement with PCs, and hard drives failed much too often. After we installed dehumidifiers, the hard drives became more reliable.

◢ *In CMOS setup, disable the ability to write to the boot sector of the hard drive.* This alone can keep boot viruses at bay. However, before you upgrade your OS, such as when you upgrade Windows XP to Windows Vista, be sure to enable writing to the boot sector, which the OS setup will want to do. How to make changes to BIOS settings using the CMOS setup utility is covered later in the chapter.

◢ *If your data is really private, keep it under lock and key.* You can use all kinds of security methods to encrypt, password protect, and hide data, but if it really is that important, one obvious thing you can do is store the data on a removable storage device such as a flash drive and, when you're not using the data, put the flash drive in a fire-proof safe. And, of course, keep two copies. Sounds simple, but it works.

◢ *Protect your CDs, DVDs, and other storage media.* To protect discs, keep them away from direct sunlight, heat, and extreme cold. Don't allow the bottom of a CD or DVD to be scratched. Don't open the shuttle window on a floppy disk or touch the disk's surface. Keep floppy disks and hard drives away from magnetic fields. In Chapter 10, you'll learn how to clean CDs and DVDs.

◢ *Keep magnets away from your computer.* Don't work inside the computer case with magnetized screwdrivers and or sit magnets on top of the computer case.

A+ ESS
1.4
2.4
7.1
7.2

A+
220-602
1.3
7.1

▲ *Don't unpack and turn on a computer that has just come in from the cold.* If your new laptop has just arrived and sat on your doorstep in freezing weather, don't bring it in and immediately unpack it and turn it on. Wait until a computer has had time to reach room temperature to prevent damage from condensation and static electricity. In addition, when unpacking hardware or software, to help protect against static electricity, remove the packing tape and cellophane from the work area as soon as possible.

A+ ESS
1.4
2.4

A+
220-602
1.3
4.4
7.1

## CREATING A PREVENTIVE MAINTENANCE PLAN

It is important to develop an overall preventive maintenance plan. If your company has established written guidelines for PC preventive maintenance, read them and follow the procedures necessary to make them work. If your company has no established plan, make your own.

A preventive maintenance plan tends to evolve from a history or pattern of malfunctions within an organization. For example, dusty environments can mean more maintenance, whereas a clean environment can mean less maintenance. Table 3-1 lists some guidelines for developing a preventive maintenance plan that may work for you.

The general idea of preventive maintenance is to do what you can to make a PC last longer and cause as little trouble as possible. You may also be responsible for ensuring that data is secure and backed up, that software copyrights are not violated, and that users are supported. As with any plan, when designing your preventive maintenance plan, first define your overall goals, and then design the plan accordingly. The guidelines listed in Table 3-1 primarily address the problems that prevent a PC from lasting long and from performing well.

> **⚡ A+ Exam Tip**
>
> The A+ IT 220-602 exam expects you to know how to keep computers and monitors well ventilated and clean and to use protective covers for input devices such as the keyboard.

> **⚡ A+ Exam Tip**
>
> The A+ Essentials exam expects you to know how to clean internal and external components and use appropriate cleaning materials as part of a regular preventive maintenance plan.

| Component | Maintenance | How Often |
|---|---|---|
| Inside the case | ▲ Make sure air vents are clear.<br><br>▲ Use compressed air to blow the dust out of the case, or use a vacuum to clean vents, power supply, and fan.<br><br>▲ Ensure that chips and expansion cards are firmly seated. | Yearly |
| CMOS setup | ▲ Keep a written record of any changes you make to CMOS setup, or you can back up CMOS using third-party software such as Norton Utilities by Symantec (*www.symantec.com*). | Whenever changes are made to CMOS setup |
| Floppy drive | ▲ Clean the floppy drive only when the drive does not work. | When the drive does not work |
| Hard drive | ▲ Perform regular backups (covered in Chapter 13). | At least weekly |
|  | ▲ Delete temporary files and empty the Recycle Bin (covered in Chapter 13). | Monthly |

**Table 3-1** Guidelines for developing a PC preventive maintenance plan

**3**

A+ ESS
1.4
2.4

A+
220-602
1.3
4.4
7.1

| Component | Maintenance | How Often |
|---|---|---|
| | ▲ Defragment the drive and scan the drive for errors (covered in Chapter 13). | Monthly |
| | ▲ Using third-party utility software such as Norton Utilities, back up the partition table to floppy disk. | Whenever changes are made |
| Keyboard | ▲ Clean the keyboard (covered in Chapter 9). | Monthly |
| Mouse | ▲ Clean the mouse rollers and ball (covered in Chapter 9). | Monthly |
| Monitor | ▲ Clean the screen with a soft cloth. | At least monthly |
| Printers | ▲ Clean out the dust and bits of paper, using compressed air and a vacuum. Small pieces of paper can be removed with tweezers, preferably insulated ones.<br><br>▲ Clean the paper and ribbon paths with a soft, lint-free cloth.<br><br>▲ Don't re-ink ribbons or use recharged toner cartridges.<br><br>▲ If the printer uses an ozone filter, replace it as recommended by the manufacturer.<br><br>▲ Replace other components as recommended by the manufacturer. You can purchase maintenance kits from the printer manufacturer, which include a scheduled maintenance plan for the printer. | At least monthly or as recommended by the manufacturer |
| UPS/Surge Suppressors | ▲ Run weak battery test.<br>▲ Run diagnostic test. | As recommended by manufacturer |
| Software | ▲ If directed by your employer, check that only authorized software is present. | At least monthly |
| Written records | ▲ Keep a record of all software, including version numbers and the OS installed on the PC.<br><br>▲ Keep a record of all hardware components installed, including hardware settings.<br><br>▲ Record when and what preventive maintenance is performed.<br><br>▲ Record any repairs done to the PC. | Whenever changes are made |

**Table 3-1**  Guidelines for developing a PC preventive maintenance plan (continued)

## DEALING WITH DUST

A+
220-602
1.3
7.1

Dust is not good for a PC because it insulates PC parts like a blanket, which can cause them to overheat. Dust inside fans can jam fans; fans not working can cause a system to over-heat (see Figure 3-12). Therefore, ridding the PC of dust is an important part of preventive maintenance. Some PC technicians don't like to use a vacuum inside a PC because they're concerned that the vacuum might produce ESD. However, inside the PC case, it's safe to use a special antistatic vacuum designed to be used around sensitive equipment. If you don't have one of these vacuums, you can use compressed air to blow the dust out of the chassis, power supply, and fans. The dust will get all over everything; you can then use a regular vacuum to clean up the mess. While you're cleaning up dust, you can also blow or vacuum out the keyboard.

**Figure 3-12** This dust-jammed fan caused a system to overheat

# PREPARING A COMPUTER FOR SHIPPING

When shipping a desktop or notebook computer, remember that rough handling can cause damage, as can exposure to water, heat, and cold. The computer can also be misplaced, lost, or stolen. When you are preparing a computer for shipping, take extra precautions to protect it and its data. Follow these general guidelines when preparing to ship a computer:

- Back up the hard drive onto a tape cartridge or other backup medium separate from your computer. If you don't have access to a medium that can back up the entire drive, at the least, back up important Windows system files and all data to another media. Whatever you do, don't ship a computer that has the only copy of important data on the hard drive, or data that should be secured from unauthorized access. How to back up system files is covered in Chapter 12, and how to back up data is covered in Chapter 13.
- Remove any removable disks, tape cartridges, or CDs from the drives. Make sure that the tapes or disks holding the backup data are secured and protected during transit. Consider shipping them separately.
- Turn off power to the computer and all other devices.
- Disconnect power cords from the electrical outlet and the devices. Disconnect all external devices from the computer. For notebook computers, remove the battery.
- If you think someone might have trouble later identifying which cord or cable belongs to which device or connection, label the cable connections with white tape or white labels.
- Coil all external cords and secure them with plastic ties or rubber bands.
- Pack the computer, monitor, and all devices in their original shipping cartons or similar boxes with enough packing material to protect them. Each device needs to be wrapped or secured separately so devices will not bump against each other.
- Purchase insurance on the shipment. Postal insurance is not expensive and can save you a lot of money if materials are damaged in transit.

A+ ESS
6.1
7.3

A+
220-602
7.1

## DISPOSING OF USED EQUIPMENT

As a PC technician, it will often be your responsibility to dispose of used equipment and consumables, including batteries, printer toner cartridges, hard drives, and monitors. Table 3-2 lists such items and how to dispose of them. Manufacturer documentation and local environmental regulators can also provide disposal instructions or guidance.

| Part | How to Dispose |
|------|----------------|
| Alkaline batteries including AAA, AA, A, C, D, and 9 volt | Dispose of these batteries in the regular trash. First check to see if there are recycling facilities in your area. |
| Button batteries used in digital cameras, Flash Path, and other small equipment; battery packs used in notebooks | These batteries can contain silver oxide, mercury, lithium, or cadmium and are considered hazardous waste. Dispose of them by returning them to the original dealer or by taking them to a recycling center. To recycle, pack them separately from other items. If you don't have a recycling center nearby, contact your county for local regulations for disposal. |
| Laser printer toner cartridges | Return these to the manufacturer or dealer to be recycled. |
| Ink-jet printer cartridges<br><br>Computer cases, power supplies, and other computer parts<br><br>Monitors<br><br>Chemical solvents and cans | Check with local county or environmental officials for laws and regulations in your area for proper disposal of these items. The county might have a recycling center that will receive them. Discharge a monitor before disposing of it.. |
| Storage media such as hard drives, CDs, and DVDs | Do physical damage to the device so it is not possible for sensitive data to be stolen. Then the device can be put in the trash. |

**Table 3-2**  Computer parts and how to dispose of them

Monitors and power supplies can contain a charge even after the devices are unplugged. Most CRT monitors today are designed to discharge if allowed to sit unplugged for 60 minutes or more. To manually discharge a monitor, a high-voltage probe is used with the monitor case opened. Ask a technician trained to fix monitors to do this for you.

Don't throw out a hard drive that might have personal or corporate data on it unless you know the data can't be stolen off the drive. To assure yourself there's no way someone is going to read from the drive, you can take a hammer and nail and punch the drive housing, forcing the nail straight through to the other side so that all drive disks are damaged. To dispose of CDs, floppy disks, DVDs and other storage media, do similar damage, such as breaking a CD in half.

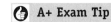
**A+ Exam Tip**

The A+ Essentials exam expects you to know how to follow environmental guidelines to dispose of batteries, CRTs, chemical solvents, and cans. If you're not certain how to dispose of a product, see its MSDS document.

A+ ESS
7.2

## *HOW TO WORK INSIDE A COMPUTER CASE*

A+
220-602
1.2
7.1

In this section, you'll learn how to take a computer apart and put it back together. When working inside a computer, note that you can damage both the computer and yourself. Here are some important safety precautions that will help keep you and your equipment safe as you go through the process of taking it apart and putting it back together:

▲ Make notes as you work so that you can backtrack later if necessary. (When you're first learning to take a computer apart, it's really easy to forget where everything fits when it's time to put it back together. Also, in troubleshooting, you want to avoid repeating or overlooking things to try.)

▲ To stay organized and not lose small parts, keep screws and spacers orderly and in one place, such as a cup or tray.

▲ Don't stack boards on top of each other: You could accidentally dislodge a chip this way.

▲ When handling motherboards and expansion cards, don't touch the chips on the boards. Hold expansion cards by the edges. Don't touch any soldered components on a card, and don't touch chips or edge connectors unless it's absolutely necessary. All this helps prevent damage from static electricity.

▲ To protect the chip, don't touch it with a magnetized screwdriver.

▲ Don't use a graphite pencil to change **DIP (dual inline package) switch** settings, because graphite is a conductor of electricity, and the graphite can lodge in the switch.

▲ In a classroom environment, after you have reassembled everything, have your instructor check your work before you put the cover back on and power up.

▲ To protect both yourself and the equipment when working inside a computer, turn off the power, unplug the computer, and always use a ground bracelet (which you will learn more about later).

▲ Never ever touch the inside of a computer that is turned on.

▲ Consider the monitor and the power supply to be "black boxes." Never remove the cover or put your hands inside this equipment unless you know about the hazards of charged capacitors and have been trained to deal with them. Both the power supply and the monitor can hold a dangerous level of electricity even after you turn them off and disconnect them from a power source. The power supply and monitor contain enough power to kill you, even when they are unplugged.

▲ When unpacking hardware or software, to help protect against static electricity, remove the packing tape and cellophane from the work area as soon as possible.

▲ To protect against static electricity, keep components away from your hair and clothing.

The last two bullets in this list are about static electricity. This topic is so important that it warrants its own subsection. That section comes up next; afterward, you'll read about how to take a computer apart and put it back together.

## STATIC ELECTRICITY

Suppose you come indoors on a cold day, pick up a comb, and touch your hair. Sparks fly! What happened? Static electricity caused the sparks. **Electrostatic discharge (ESD)**, commonly known as **static electricity**, is an electrical charge at rest. When you came indoors, this charge built up on your hair and had no place to go. An ungrounded conductor (such as wire that is not touching another wire) or a nonconductive surface (such as your hair) holds a charge until the charge is released. When two objects with dissimilar electrical charges touch, electricity passes between them until the dissimilar charges become equal.

To see static charges equalizing, turn off the lights in a room, scuff your feet on the carpet, and touch another person. Occasionally, you can see and feel the charge in your fingers. If you can feel the charge, you discharged at least 1,500 volts of static electricity. If you hear the discharge, you released at least 6,000 volts. If you see the discharge, you released at least

A+ ESS
7.2

A+
220-602
1.2
7.1

8,000 volts of ESD. A charge of only 10 volts can damage electronic components! You can touch a chip on an expansion card or motherboard, damage the chip with ESD, and never feel, hear, or see the discharge.

ESD can cause two types of damage in an electronic component: catastrophic failure and upset failure. A catastrophic failure destroys the component beyond use. An upset failure damages the component so that it does not perform well, even though it may still function to some degree. Upset failures are more difficult to detect because they are not as easily observed. Both types of failures permanently affect the device.

To protect the computer against ESD, always ground yourself before touching electronic components, including the hard drive, motherboard, expansion cards, processors, and memory modules. You can ground yourself and the computer parts by using one or more of the following static control devices or methods:

 **A+ Exam Tip**

The A+ Essentials exam emphasizes that you should know how to protect computer equipment as you work on it.

 **Caution**

A monitor can also damage components with ESD. Do not place or store expansion cards on top of or next to a monitor, which can discharge as much as 29,000 volts onto the screen.

◢ *Ground bracelet.* A **ground bracelet**, also called an antistatic strap or ESD bracelet, is a strap you wear around your wrist. One end attaches to a grounded conductor such as the computer case or a ground mat, or plugs into a wall outlet. (Only the ground prong makes a connection!) The bracelet also contains a resistor that prevents electricity from harming you. Figure 3-13 shows a ground bracelet.

**Figure 3-13** A ground bracelet, which protects computer components from ESD, can clip to the side of the computer case and eliminate ESD between you and the case

▲ *Ground mats.* Ground mats dissipate ESD and are commonly used by bench technicians (also called depot technicians) who assemble and repair computers at their work-
benches or in an assembly line. Ground mats have a connector in one corner that you
can use to connect the mat to ground (see Figure 3-14). If you lift a component off the
mat, it is no longer grounded and is susceptible to ESD, so it's important to use a
ground bracelet with a ground mat.

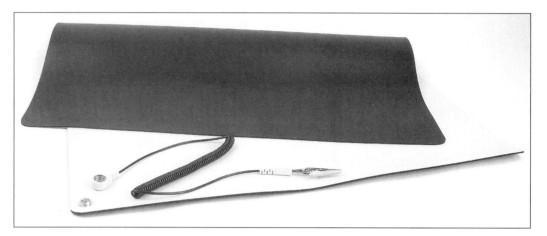

**Figure 3-14** A ground mat dissipates ESD and should be connected to ground

▲ *Static shielding bags.* New components come shipped in static shielding bags, also
called antistatic bags. These bags are a type of Faraday Cage, named after Michael
Faraday, who built the first cage in 1836. A Faraday Cage is any device that protects
against an electromagnetic field. Save the bags to store other devices that are not currently installed in a PC. As you work on a computer, know that a device is not protected from ESD if you place it on top of the bag; the protection is inside the bag (see
Figure 3-15).

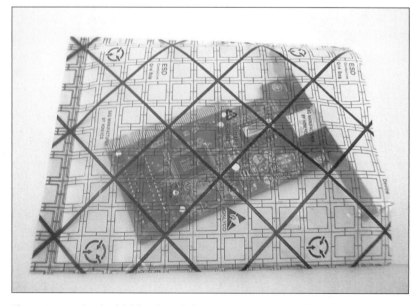

**Figure 3-15** Static shielding bags help protect components from ESD

A+ ESS
7.2

A+
220-602
1.2
7.1

▲ *Antistatic gloves*. You can purchase antistatic gloves designed to prevent an ESD discharge between you and a device as you pick it up and handle it (see Figure 3-16). The gloves can be substituted for an antistatic bracelet and are good for moving, packing, or unpacking sensitive equipment. However, they tend to get in the way when working inside computer cases.

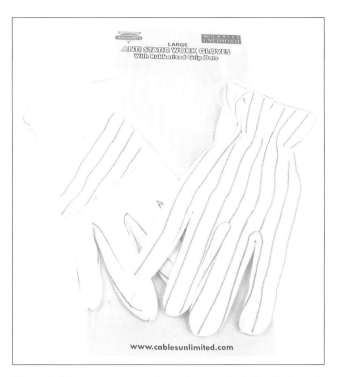

**Figure 3-16** Use antistatic gloves to prevent static discharge between you and the equipment you are handling

The best way to guard against ESD is to use a ground bracelet together with a ground mat. Consider a ground bracelet essential equipment when working on a computer. However, if you are in a situation in which you must work without one, touch the computer case or the power supply before you touch a component. When passing a circuit board, memory module, or other sensitive component to another person, ground yourself and then touch the other person before you pass the component. Leave components inside their protective bags until you are ready to use them. Work on hard floors, not carpet, or use antistatic spray on the carpets. Generally, don't work on a computer if you or the computer has just come in from the cold, because there is more danger of ESD when the atmosphere is cold and dry.

There are exceptions to the rule of always being grounded when you work with PCs. You *don't* want to be grounded when working inside a monitor, inside a power supply, or inside high-voltage equipment such as a laser printer. These devices maintain high electrical charges, even

**Notes**

When working inside the older AT cases, it was safe enough to leave the power cord plugged into the power outlet if the power switch was turned off. Leaving the power cord plugged in helped to ground the case. However, with newer ATX and BTX cases, residual power is still on even when the power switch on the rear of the case is turned off. Some motherboards even have a small light inside the case to remind you of this fact and to warn you that power is still getting to the system. For this reason, when working on newer ATX and BTX systems, be certain to unplug the power cord before working inside these cases.

when the power is turned off. Inside a monitor case, the electricity stored in capacitors can be dangerous. When working inside a monitor, laser printer, or power supply, you don't want to be grounded, because you would provide a conduit for the voltage to discharge through your body. In this situation, be careful not to ground yourself. *Don't* wear a ground bracelet when working inside these devices, because you don't want to be the ground for these charges!

## STEPS TO TAKE APART A COMPUTER

A PC technician needs to be comfortable with taking apart a computer and putting it back together. In most situations, the essential tools you'll need for the job are a ground bracelet, a Phillips-head screwdriver, a flat-head screwdriver, paper, and pen. As you work inside a computer, be sure to use a ground bracelet, the safety precautions in the chapter, and the guidelines in the following list:

1. If you are starting with a working computer, enter CMOS setup and write down any customized settings you have made so that, in the event you must return CMOS to its default settings, you can restore the customized settings. Back up any important data on the hard drive.

2. Power down the system and unplug it. Unplug the monitor, mouse, keyboard, and any other peripherals or cables attached and move them out of your way.

3. Put the computer on a table with plenty of room. Have a plastic bag or cup handy to hold screws. When you reassemble the PC, you will need to insert the same screws in the same holes. This is especially important with the hard drive, because screws that are too long can puncture the hard drive housing.

4. Sometimes I think figuring out how to open a computer case is the most difficult part of disassembling. To remove the cover of your PC, do the following:

   ◢ Many newer cases require you to remove the faceplate on the front of the case first. Other cases require you to remove a side panel first, and really older cases require you to first remove the entire sides and top as a single unit. Study your case for the correct approach.

   ◢ If you find screws on the rear of the case along the edges such as those in Figure 3-17, start with removing these screws.

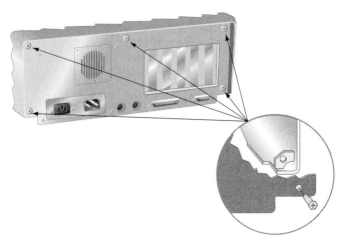

**Figure 3-17**　Locate the screws that hold the cover in place

◢ For a desktop case or tower case, locate and remove the screws on the back of the case. For a desktop case, like the one in Figure 3-17, look for the screws in each corner and one in the top. Be careful not to unscrew any screws besides these. The other screws probably are holding the power supply in place (see Figure 3-18).

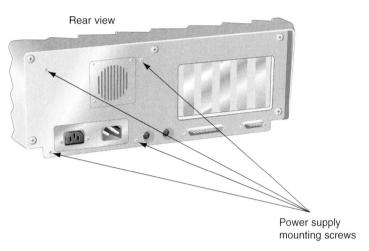

Rear view

Power supply
mounting screws

**Figure 3-18** Power supply mounting screws

◢ After you remove the cover screws, slide the cover forward and up to remove it from the case, as shown in Figure 3-19.

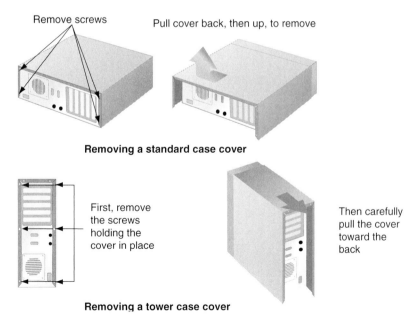

Remove screws

Pull cover back, then up, to remove

**Removing a standard case cover**

First, remove
the screws
holding the
cover in place

Then carefully
pull the cover
toward the
back

**Removing a tower case cover**

**Figure 3-19** Removing the cover

◢ Older tower cases also have the screws on the back. Look for screws in all four corners and down the sides (see Figure 3-19). Remove the screws and then slide the cover back slightly before lifting it up

**Video**

Opening a Computer Case

**A+ ESS**
**1.2**

to remove it. Some tower cases have panels on either side of the case, held in place with screws on the back of the case (see Figure 3-20). Remove the screws and slide each panel toward the rear, then lift it off the case.

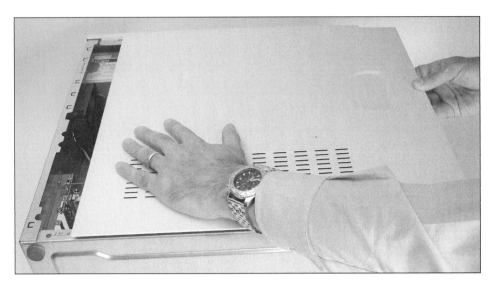

**Figure 3-20** Slide a side panel to the rear and then lift it off the case

▲ Newer cases require you to pop the front panel off the case before removing the side panels. Look for a lever on the bottom of the panel and hinges at the top. Squeeze the lever to release the front panel and lift it off the case (see Figure 3-21). Then remove a single screw (see Figure 3-22) and slide the side panel to the front and then off the case. Also, know that some case panels don't use screws; these side panels simply pop up and out with a little prying and pulling.

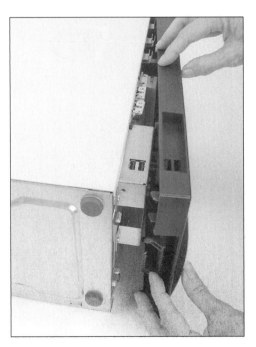

**Figure 3-21** Newer computer cases require you to remove the front panel before removing the side panels

A+ ESS
1.2

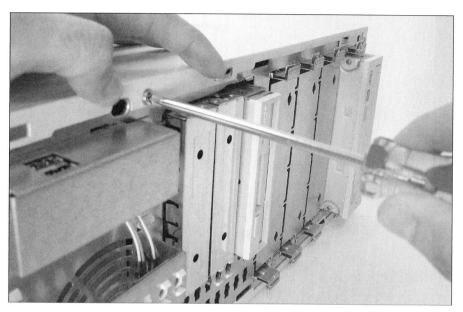

**Figure 3-22** One screw holds the side panel in place

5. If you're working on a tower case, lay it on its side so the motherboard is on the bottom. If you plan to remove several components, draw a diagram of all cable connections, DIP switch settings, and jumper settings. You might need the cable connection diagram to help you reassemble. If you want, use a felt-tip marker to make a mark across components, to indicate a cable connection, board placement, motherboard orientation, speaker connection, brackets, and so on, so that you can simply line up the marks when you reassemble.

6. Drives are connected to the motherboard with ribbon cables or thinner serial ATA cables. Before removing any ribbon cables, look for a red color or stripe down one side of each cable. This edge color marks this side of the cable as pin 1. Look on the board or drive that the cable is attached to. You should see that pin 1 or pin 2 is clearly marked, as shown in Figure 3-23. However, some boards mark pin 34 or pin 40. For these boards, pin 1 is on the other side of the connector. Also know that some boards and drives don't mark the pins, but rather have a notch in the connector so that a notched ribbon cable can only be inserted in one direction (see Figure 3-24).

**Figure 3-23** Pin 1 for this IDE connection is clearly marked

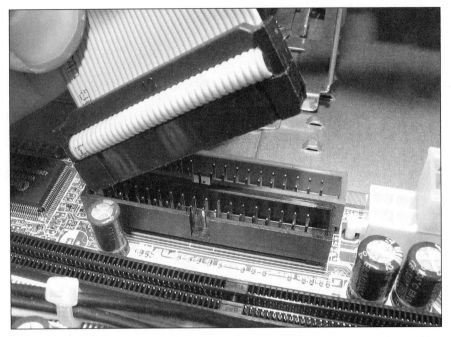

**Figure 3-24** The notch on the side of this floppy drive connector allows the floppy drive cable to connect in only one direction

Verify that the edge color is aligned with pin 1. Serial ATA cables can only connect to serial ATA connectors in one direction (see Figure 3-25).

**Figure 3-25** A serial ATA cable connects to a serial ATA connector in only one direction

7. A system might have up to three types of ribbon cables. A floppy drive cable has 34 pins and a twist in the cable. IDE cables have 40 pins. A CD or DVD drive can use the 40-conductor IDE cable, but most hard drives today use the higher quality 80-conductor IDE cable. See Figure 3-26 for a comparison of these three cables.

**3**

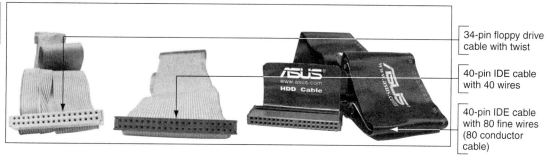

34-pin floppy drive cable with twist

40-pin IDE cable with 40 wires

40-pin IDE cable with 80 fine wires (80 conductor cable)

**Figure 3-26**  A system might have up to three types of ribbon cables

Remove the cables to all drives. Remove the power supply cords from the drives. Notice as you disconnect the power cord, the Molex connector is shaped so it only connects in one direction (see Figure 3-27).

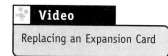

▶ **Video**

Replacing an Expansion Card

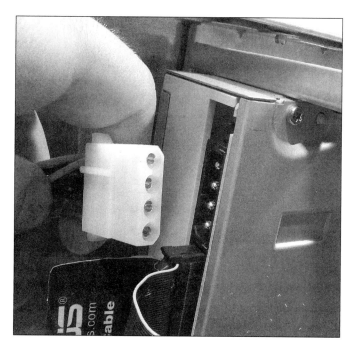

**Figure 3-27**  Molex power connector to a drive orients in only one direction

8. Do the following to remove the expansion cards:

▲ Remove any wire or cable connected to the card.

▲ Remove the screw holding the card to the case (see Figure 3-28).

▲ Grasp the card with both hands and remove it by lifting straight up. If you have trouble removing it from the expansion slot, you can *very slightly* rock the card from end to end (*not* side to side). Rocking the card from side to side might spread the slot opening and weaken the connection.

✎ **Notes**

Some video cards use a latch that helps to hold the card securely in the slot. To remove these cards, use one finger to hold the latch back from the slot, as shown in Figure 3-29, as you pull the card up and out of the slot.

**Figure 3-28**   Remove the screw holding an expansion card to the case

**Figure 3-29**   Hold the retention mechanism back as you remove a video card from its expansion slot

▲ As you remove the card, don't put your fingers on the edge connectors or touch a chip, and don't stack the cards on top of one another. Lay each card aside on a flat surface.

9. Depending on the system, you might need to remove the motherboard next or remove the drives next. My choice is to first remove the motherboard. It and the processor are the most expensive and easily damaged parts in the system. I like to get them out of harm's way before working with the drives. However, in some cases, you must remove

A+ ESS
1.2

the drives or the power supply before you can get to the motherboard. Study your situation and decide which to do first. To remove the motherboard, do the following:

◢ Unplug the power supply lines to the motherboard. You'll find a main power line, and maybe one auxiliary power line from the power supply to the motherboard. There might also be an audio wire from the CD drive to the motherboard. Disconnect it from the motherboard.

> **✎ Notes**
>
> Older AT power supplies and motherboards use two main power lines that plug in side-by-side on the motherboard and are labeled P8 and P9. You will want to be certain that you don't switch these two lines when reconnecting them, because this would cause the wrong voltage to flow in the circuits on the motherboard and could destroy the board. Fortunately, most connections today only allow you to place the lines in the correct order, which is always black leads on P8 next to black leads on P9. For these older boards, remember, "black to black."

◢ The next step is to disconnect wires leading from the front of the computer case to the motherboard. If you don't have the motherboard manual handy, be very careful to diagram how these wires connect because they are never labeled well on a motherboard. Make a careful diagram and then disconnect the wires. Figure 3-30 shows five leads and the pins on the motherboard that receive these leads. The pins are color-coded and cryptically labeled on the board. You'll learn more about matching these wires to their connectors in Chapter 6.

**Figure 3-30**  Five leads from the front panel connect to two rows of pins on the motherboard

◢ You're now ready to remove the screws that hold the motherboard to the case. For an older motherboard, instead of screws you'll see spacers that keep the board from resting directly on the bottom of the computer case. Carefully pop off these spacers and/or remove the screws (up to nine) that hold the board to the case (see Figure 3-31) and

**Figure 3-31** Remove up to nine screws that hold the motherboard to the case

then remove the board. Set it aside in a safe place. Figure 3-32 shows a motherboard sitting to the side of these spacers. One spacer is in place and the other is lying beside its case holes. Also notice in the photo the two holes in the motherboard where screws are used to connect the board to the spacers.

**Figure 3-32** This motherboard connects to a case using screws and spacers that keep the board from touching the case

▲ The motherboard should now be free. You can carefully remove it from the case, as shown in Figure 3-33.

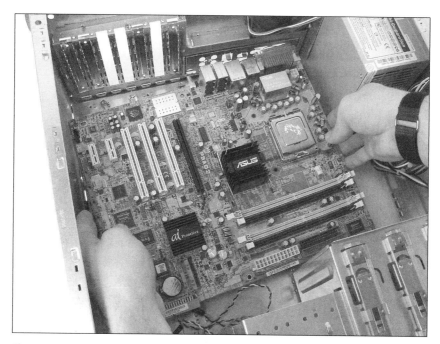

**Figure 3-33** Remove the motherboard from the case

10. To remove the power supply from the case, look for screws that attach the power supply to the computer case, as shown in Figure 3-34. Be careful not to remove

> ⚡ **Caution**
>
> Some processors have heavy cooling assemblies installed on top of them. For these systems, it is best to remove the cooler before you take the motherboard out of the case because the motherboard is not designed to support this heavy cooler when the motherboard is not securely seated in the case. How to remove this cooler is covered in Chapter 5.

**Figure 3-34** Removing the power supply mounting screws

any screws that hold the power supply housing together. You do not want to take the housing apart. After you have removed the screws, the power supply still might not be free. Sometimes, it is attached to the case on the underside by recessed slots. Turn the case over and look on the bottom for these slots. If they are present, determine in which direction you need to slide the power supply to free it from the case.

11. Remove each drive next, handling the drives with care. Here are some tips:

⬥ Some drives have one or two screws on each side of the drive attaching the drive to the drive bay. After you remove the screws, the drive slides to the front or to the rear and then out of the case.

⬥ Sometimes, there is a catch underneath the drive that you must lift up as you slide the drive forward.

⬥ Some drive bays have a clipping mechanism to hold the drive in the bay. First release the clip and then pull the drive forward and out of the bay (see Figure 3-35). Handle the drives with care.

**Figure 3-35** To remove this CD drive, first pull the clip forward to release the drive from the bay

⬥ Some cases have a removable bay for small drives (see Figure 3-36). These bays can hold narrow drives such as hard drives, floppy drives, and Zip drives. The bay is removed first and then the drives are removed from the bay. To remove the bay, first remove the screws or release the clip holding the bay in place and then slide the bay out of the case. The drives are usually installed in the bay with two screws on each side of each drive. Remove the screws and then the drives (see Figure 3-37).

Video

Replacing a Power Supply

## STEPS TO PUT A COMPUTER BACK TOGETHER

To reassemble a computer, reverse the process of disassembling. Do the following:

1. Install the power supply, drives, motherboard, and cards in the case. When installing drives, know that for some systems, it's easier to connect data cables to the drives and then slide the drives into the bay.

A+ ESS
1.2

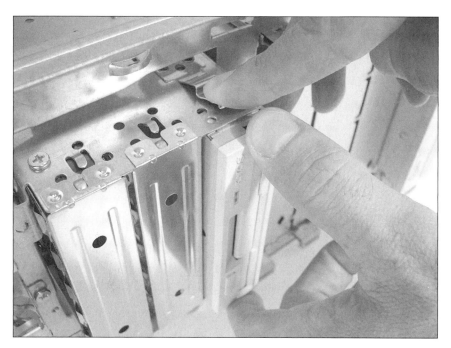

**Figure 3-36**  Push down on the clip and then slide the removable bay forward and out of the case

**Figure 3-37**  Drives in this removable bay are held in place with screws on each side of the bay

2. Connect all data and power cables. Before you replace the cover, take a few minutes to double-check each connection to make sure it is correct and snug.

3. Plug in the keyboard, monitor, and mouse.

4. In a classroom environment, have the instructor check your work before you power up.

5. Turn on the power and check that the PC is working properly. If the PC does not work, most likely the problem is a loose connection. Just turn off the power and go

**A+ ESS 1.2**

back and check each cable connection and each expansion card. You probably have not solidly seated a card in the slot. After you have double-checked, try again.

## UNDERSTANDING THE BOOT PROCESS

**A+ ESS 1.3**

Another skill you need as a PC support technician is to know how to fix a problem with booting the PC. The first steps in learning that skill are to know how to boot a PC and to understand what happens when you first turn on a PC and it begins the process of loading an operating system. That's the subject of this section of the chapter.

### BOOTING A COMPUTER

The term **booting** comes from the phrase "lifting yourself up by your bootstraps" and refers to the computer bringing itself up to a working state without the user having to do anything but press the on button. This boot can be a "hard boot" or a "soft boot." A **hard boot**, or **cold boot**, involves turning on the power with the on/off switch. A **soft boot**, or **warm boot**, involves using the operating system to reboot. For Windows XP, one way to soft boot is to click **Start**, click **Turn Off Computer**, and then click **Restart** (see Figure 3-38). For Windows NT/2000 and Windows 9x/Me, click **Start**, click **Shut Down**, and then select **Restart** and click **OK**. For DOS, pressing the keys **Ctrl**, **Alt**, and **Del** (or Delete) at the same time performs a soft boot. (You will often see this key combination written as **Ctrl+Alt+Del**.)

**Figure 3-38** Windows XP Turn off computer dialog box

### CHOOSING BETWEEN A HARD BOOT AND A SOFT BOOT

A hard boot is more stressful on your machine than a soft boot because of the initial power surge through the equipment that occurs when you press the power switch. Thus, whenever possible, use a soft boot. Also, a soft boot is faster because the initial steps of a hard boot don't happen.

To save time, you should always use the soft boot to restart unless soft booting doesn't work. If you cannot soft boot, look for power or reset buttons on the front or rear of the case. My newest computer has three power switches: a power button and a reset button on the front of the case and a power switch on the rear of the case (see Figure 3-39). The power button in front is a "soft" power button, causing a normal Windows shutdown and restart, and the reset button is a "hard" power switch, abruptly turning off power and then restarting. The switch on the rear of the case simply turns off the power abruptly and is a "hard" power button. Know, however, that some systems only have a single power switch on the front of the case.

A+ ESS
1.3

Soft power button
does a normal
Windows shutdown

Hard power switch
on rear of case

Hard power button
abruptly reboots

**Figure 3-39** This computer case has two power buttons on the front and one power switch on the rear of the case

## THE STARTUP BIOS CONTROLS THE BEGINNING OF THE BOOT

The **startup BIOS** is programming contained on the firmware chip on the motherboard that is responsible for getting a system up and going and finding an OS to load. A successful boot depends on the hardware, the BIOS, and the operating system all performing without errors. If errors occur, they might or might not stall or lock up the boot. Errors are communicated as beeps or as messages onscreen. Some of these error messages and beep codes are listed in Table 3-4 at the end of this chapter.

The functions performed during the boot can be divided into four parts, as shown in the following numbered list. The first two items in the list are covered in detail in this section. (The last two steps depend on the OS being used and are covered in later chapters.)

**Video**

Beep Codes

1. *The startup BIOS runs the POST and assigns system resources.* The **POST** (**power-on self test**) is a series of tests performed by the startup BIOS to determine if it can communicate correctly with essential hardware components required for a successful boot. The startup BIOS surveys hardware resources and needs, and assigns system resources to meet those needs (see Figure 3-40). The startup BIOS begins the startup process by reading configuration information stored primarily in CMOS RAM, and then comparing that information to the hardware—the processor, video slot, PCI slots, hard drive, and so on. (Recall that CMOS RAM is a small amount of memory on the motherboard that holds information about installed hardware.)

2. *The startup BIOS program searches for and loads an OS.* Most often the OS is loaded from logical drive C on the hard drive. Configuration information stored in CMOS RAM tells startup BIOS where to look for the OS. Most new BIOSs support loading the OS from the hard drive, a floppy disk, a CD, a DVD, or a USB device. The BIOS turns to the specified device, reads the beginning files of the OS, copies them into memory, and then turns control over to the OS. This part of the loading process works the same for any operating system; only the OS files being loaded change.

**Notes**

The four system resources on a motherboard that the OS and processor use to interact with hardware are IRQ lines, I/O addresses, memory addresses, and DMA channels, all defined in Table 3-3. Older systems using DOS and Windows 9x/Me required a technician to make decisions about managing these resources when installing hardware devices, but newer systems generally manage these resources without our involvement. For an explanation of how each resource works, see Appendix A.

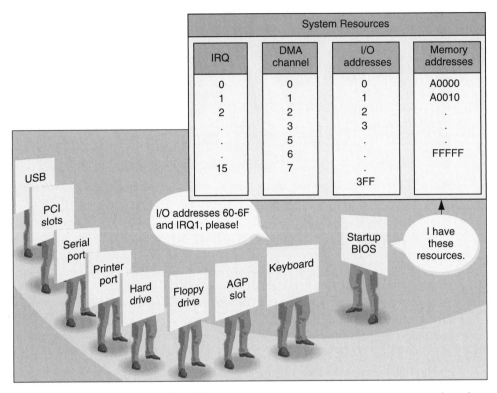

**Figure 3-40** Boot Step 1: The ROM BIOS startup program surveys hardware resources and needs and assigns system resources to satisfy those needs

| System Resource | Definition |
|---|---|
| IRQ numbers | A line of a motherboard bus that a hardware device or expansion slot can use to signal the CPU that the device needs attention. Some lines have a higher priority for attention than others. Each IRQ line is assigned a number (0 to 15) to identify it. |
| I/O addresses | Numbers assigned to hardware devices that software uses to send a command to a device. Each device "listens" for these numbers and responds to the ones assigned to it. I/O addresses are communicated on the address bus. |
| Memory addresses | Numbers assigned to physical memory located either in RAM or ROM chips. Software can access this memory by using these addresses. Memory addresses are communicated on the address bus. |
| DMA channels | A number designating a channel on which the device can pass data to memory without involving the CPU. Think of a DMA channel as a shortcut for data moving to and from the device and memory. |

**Table 3-3** System resources used by software and hardware

3. *The OS configures the system and completes its own loading.* The OS checks some of the same settings and devices that startup BIOS checked, such as available memory and whether that memory is reliable. Then the OS loads the core components necessary to access the files and folders on the hard drive and to use memory, the expansion buses on the motherboard, and the cards installed in these expansion slots. The OS also loads the software to control installed devices, such as the mouse, the video card,

the DVD drive, or the scanner. These devices generally have device drivers stored on the hard drive. The Windows desktop is then loaded.

4. *Application software is loaded and executed.* Sometimes an OS is configured to automatically launch application software as part of the boot. After this, the user is in control. When the user tells the OS to execute an application, the OS first must find the application software on the hard drive, CD, or other secondary storage device, copy the software into memory, and then turn control over to it. Finally, the user can command the application software, which makes requests to the OS, which, in turn, uses the system resources, system BIOS, and device drivers to interface with and control the hardware.

## POST AND ASSIGNMENT OF SYSTEM RESOURCES

When you turn on the power to a PC, the processor begins the boot by initializing itself and then turning to startup BIOS for instructions. The startup BIOS first performs POST. The following list contains the key steps in this process:

1. When the power is first turned on, the system clock begins to generate clock pulses.

2. The processor begins working and initializes itself (resetting its internal values).

3. The processor turns to memory address FFFF0h, which is the memory address always assigned to the first instruction in the ROM BIOS startup program.

4. This instruction directs the processor to run POST.

5. POST first checks the BIOS program operating it and then tests CMOS RAM.

6. A test determines that there has been no battery failure.

7. Hardware interrupts are disabled. (This means that pressing a key on the keyboard or using another input device at this point does not affect anything.)

8. Tests are run on the processor, and it is initialized further.

9. A check determines if this is a cold boot. If so, the first 16 KB of RAM is tested.

10. Hardware devices installed on the computer are inventoried and compared to configuration information.

11. The video card is tested and configured. During POST, before the processor has checked the video system, beeps sometimes communicate errors. Short and long beeps indicate an error; the coding for the beeps depends on the BIOS. After POST checks and verifies the video controller card (note that POST does not check to see if a monitor is present or working), POST can use video to display its progress.

12. POST checks RAM by writing and reading data. The monitor displays a running count of RAM during this phase.

13. Next, the keyboard is checked, and if you press and hold any keys at this point, an error occurs with some BIOSs. Secondary storage—including floppy disk drives and hard drives—ports, and other hardware devices are tested and configured. The hardware that POST finds is checked against the data stored in the CMOS chip, jumpers, and/or DIP switches to determine if they agree. IRQ, I/O addresses, and DMA assignments are made; the OS completes this process later. Some hardware devices have BIOSs of their own that request resources from startup BIOS, which attempts to assign these system resources as requested.

14. Some devices are set up to go into "sleep mode" to conserve electricity.

**15.** The DMA and interrupt controllers are checked.

**16.** CMOS setup is run if requested.

**17.** BIOS begins its search for an OS.

## STARTUP BIOS FINDS AND LOADS THE OS

After POST and the first pass at assignment of resources are complete, the next step is to load an OS. The startup BIOS looks to CMOS setup to find out which device is set to be the boot device. Most often the OS is loaded from logical drive C on the hard drive. The minimum information required on the hard drive to load an OS is shown in the following list. You can see some of these items labeled in Figure 3-41.

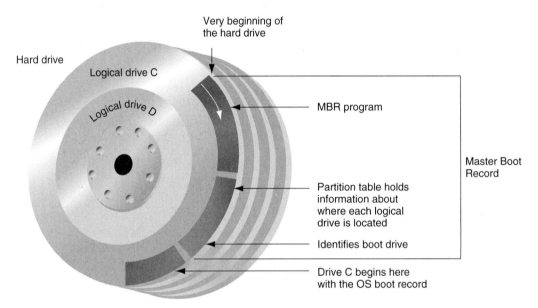

**Figure 3-41** For a successful boot, a hard drive must contain a healthy Master Boot Record (MBR) and a healthy OS boot record

▲ Even though a hard drive is a circular affair, it must begin somewhere. On the outer-most track, one sector (512 bytes) is designated the "beginning" of the hard drive. This sector, called the **Master Boot Record (MBR)**, contains two items. The first item is the master boot program, which is needed to locate the beginning of the OS on the drive.

▲ The second item in the MBR is a table, called the **partition table**, which contains a map to the partitions on the hard drive. This table tells BIOS how many partitions the drive has and how each partition is divided into one or more logical drives, which par-tition contains the drive to be used for booting (called the **active partition**), and where each logical drive begins and ends. Chapter 11 covers partitions and logical drives in more detail.

▲ At the beginning of the boot drive (usually drive C) is the OS **boot record**, which loads the first program file of the OS. (A **program file** contains a list of instructions stored in a file.) For Windows NT/2000/XP, that program is **Ntldr**, and for Windows 9x/Me, that program is **Io.sys**.

▲ The boot loader program for the OS (Ntldr or Io.sys) begins the process of loading the OS into memory. For Windows NT/2000/XP, Ntbootdd.sys is optional and used next (if the hard drive uses SCSI technology, which is discussed in Chapter 8), followed by

**3**

Boot.ini. For Windows 9x/Me, **Msdos.sys** is required next, followed by **Command.com**. These two files, plus Io.sys, are the core components of the real-mode portion of Windows 9x/Me. In addition to the files introduced here, Windows NT/2000/XP requires several more startup files, which you will learn about in Chapter 14.

> **Notes**
>
> Program files can be a part of the OS or applications and have a .com, .sys, .bat, or .exe file extension. Ntldr is an exception to that rule because it has no file extension.

## CHANGING THE BOOT SEQUENCE

The BIOS looks to CMOS RAM settings to find out which secondary storage device should have the OS (see Figure 3-42). CMOS might contain the setting for BIOS to look first to drive C, and, if it finds no OS there, then try drive A, or the setting might be first A then C. The order of drives that the BIOS follows when looking for an OS is called the boot sequence. You can change the boot sequence on your PC by using CMOS setup unless another technician responsible for the system has password protected it.

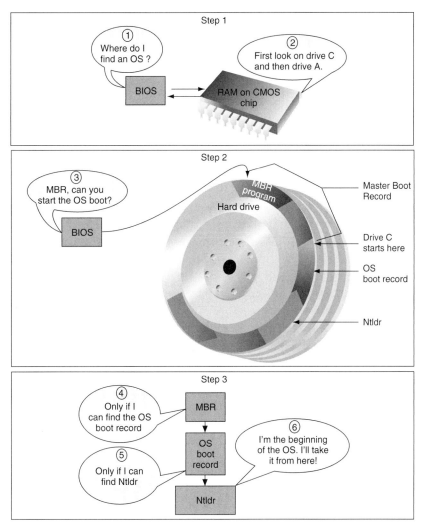

**Figure 3-42** Numbered steps show how BIOS searches for and begins to load an operating system (in this example, Windows NT/2000/XP is the OS)

A+ ESS
1.1
1.3

CMOS setup is accessed when you first turn on a computer. The keystrokes to enter CMOS setup are displayed somewhere on the screen during startup in a statement such as "Press the Del key to enter setup" or "Press F8 for setup." Different BIOSs use different keystrokes. The CMOS setup does not normally need to be changed except, for example, when there is a problem with hardware, a new floppy drive is installed, or a power-saving feature needs to be disabled or enabled. The CMOS setup can also hold one or two power-on passwords to help secure a system. Know that these passwords are not the same password that can be required by a Windows OS at startup. Figure 3-43 shows a CMOS setup screen that shows the boot sequence to be: (1) CD/DVD drive, (2) floppy drive, and (3) hard drive.

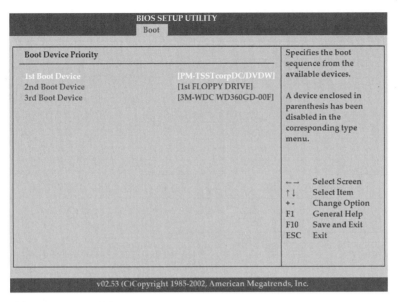

**Figure 3-43** CMOS Setup Boot menu

**APPLYING CONCEPTS** Reboot your PC and look for the message on the first or second display screen that tells you how to enter CMOS setup. Press that key. What version of BIOS are you using? Explore the CMOS setup menus until you find the boot sequence. What is the order of storage media that startup BIOS uses to find an OS? What keystrokes do you use to change that order? Exit setup without making any changes. The system should reboot to the Windows desktop.

## HOW TO TROUBLESHOOT A PC PROBLEM

A+ ESS
1.3

A+
220-602
1.2

When a computer doesn't work and you're responsible for fixing it, you should generally approach the problem first as an investigator and discoverer, always being careful not to compound the problem through your own actions. If the problem seems difficult, see it as an opportunity to learn something new. Ask questions until you understand the source of the problem. Once you understand it, you're almost done, because most likely the solution will be evident. Take the attitude that you can understand the problem and solve it, no matter how deeply you have to dig, and you probably will. In this section, you'll learn some fundamental rules useful when troubleshooting, and you'll also learn how to approach a troubleshooting problem, including how to interact with the user and how to handle an emergency.

A+ ESS
1.3

A+
220-602
1.2

## STEPS TO SOLVING A PC PROBLEM

Generally, when troubleshooting a PC problem (or any problem for that matter), you begin by asking a question and finding its answer (see Figure 3-44). Based on the answer, you then take appropriate action and evaluate the result. Always keep in mind that you don't want to make things worse, so you should use the least destructive solution. If you want to be an expert troubleshooter, there's one last, very important step: Document what you learned so you can carry it forward into the next troubleshooting situation.

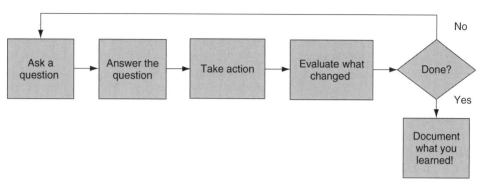

**Figure 3-44** General approach to troubleshooting

When facing a problem with a PC, follow this four-step process:

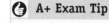 **A+ Exam Tip**

The A+ Essentials and IT 220-602 exams expect you to know about all the aspects of troubleshooting theory and strategy and how to apply the troubleshooting procedures and techniques described in this section.

1. Interview the user. You need to know what happened when the problem occurred, if valuable data is not backed up, and what you must do to reproduce the problem.

2. Take appropriate action to protect any valuable data on the computer that is not backed up. How to back up data is covered in Chapter 13.

3. Analyze the problem, make an initial determination of the problem, and begin testing, evaluating, and researching until the problem is solved.

4. If you think the problem is fixed, test the fix and the system. Make sure all is working before you stop. Then document activities, outcomes, and what you learned.

A+ ESS
1.3
8.1

## STEP 1: INTERVIEW THE USER

Begin by asking the user questions like these to learn as much as you can about the problem and its root cause:

▲ Please describe the problem. What error messages, unusual displays, or failures did you see? (Possible answer: I see this blue screen with a funny looking message on it that makes no sense to me.)

▲ When did the problem start? (Possible answer: When I first booted after loading this neat little screen saver I downloaded from the Web.)

▲ What was the situation when the problem occurred? (Possible answers: I was trying to start up my PC. I was opening a document in MS Word. I was researching a project on the Internet.)

▲ What programs or software were you using? (Possible answer: I was using Internet Explorer.)

▲ Did you move your computer system recently? (Possible answer: Well, yes. Yesterday I moved the computer case across the room.)

▲ Has there been a recent thunderstorm or electrical problem? (Possible answer: Yes, last night. Then when I tried to turn on my PC this morning, nothing happened.)

▲ Have you made any hardware, software, or configuration changes? (Possible answer: No, but I think my sister might have.)

▲ Has someone else used your computer recently? (Possible answer: Sure, my son uses it all the time.)

▲ Is there some valuable data on your system that is not backed up that I should know about before I start working on the problem? (Possible answer: Yes! Yes! My term paper! It's not backed up! You gotta get me that!)

▲ Can you show me how to reproduce the problem? (Possible answers: Yes, let me show you what to do.)

> **👍 A+ Exam Tip**
>
> The A+ Essentials exam expects you to know how to interact with a user and know what questions to ask given a troubleshooting scenario.

> **👍 A+ Exam Tip**
>
> The A+ Essentials exam expects you to know the importance of making backups before you make changes to a system.

A good PC support technician knows how to interact with a user so that the user gains confidence in your skills and does not feel talked down to or belittled. In Chapter 22, you'll learn more about these communication skills.

## STEP 2: BACK UP DATA

After you have talked with the user, be sure to back up any important data that is not currently backed up before you begin work on the PC. If valuable data is at stake and you have not yet backed it up, don't do anything to jeopardize it. Back it up as soon as possible. If you must take a risk with the data, let it be the user's decision to do so, not yours.

If the PC is working well enough to boot to the Windows desktop, you can use Windows Explorer to copy data to a flash drive, floppy disk, or other storage media. Chapter 13 covers backups in more detail. If you are about to change Windows configuration or install hardware or software, back up Windows system files as appropriate. How to do that is covered in Chapter 12.

## STEP 3: SOLVE THE PROBLEM

You are now ready to solve the problem. It's impossible to give a step-by-step plan that will solve any PC problem; therefore, in this section, you'll learn about the fundamental principles that you can apply to solve any computer problem. Then, later in this chapter and in other chapters in the book, you'll learn the step-by-step procedures you can use to solve problems with each major subsystem and component in a computer. In this section, you'll learn about several troubleshooting principles. The first is to establish your priorities.

### Establish Your Priorities

This rule can help make for a satisfied customer. Decide what your first priority is. For example, it might be to recover lost data, or to get the PC back up and running as soon as possible. Ask the user or customer for advice when practical.

## Know Your Starting Point

Find out what works and doesn't work before you take anything apart or try some possible fix. Suppose, for example, you decide the power supply is bad and exchange it. After you make the exchange, you discover the CD-ROM drive doesn't work. You don't know if you broke the drive while working on the system or it was already broken before you started. As much as possible, find out what works or doesn't work before you attempt a fix. For example, you can reboot the computer and read a file from CD or use an application to print a file on the network.

To help you solve the problem, gather as much information as you can about the problem by examining the computer. Find out the answers to these questions:

▲ What operating system is installed?
▲ What physical components are installed? What processor, expansion cards, drives, and peripheral devices are installed? Is the PC connected to a network?
▲ What is the nature of the problem? Does the problem occur before or after the boot? Does an error message appear? Does the system hang at certain times? Start from a cold boot, and do whatever you must do to cause the problem to occur. What specific steps did you take to duplicate the problem?
▲ Can you duplicate the problem? Does the problem occur every time you do the above steps, or is the problem intermittent? Intermittent problems are generally more difficult to solve than problems that occur consistently.

## Approach the Problem Systematically

When trying to solve the problem, start at the beginning and walk through the situation in a thorough, careful way. This one rule is invaluable. Remember it and apply it every time. If you don't find the explanation to the problem after one systematic walkthrough, then repeat the entire process. Check and double-check to find the step you overlooked the first time. Most problems with computers are simple, such as a loose cable or circuit board. Computers are logical through and through. Whatever the problem, it's also very logical. First, try to reproduce the problem, and then try to figure out whether it is a hardware or software problem. Determine if the problem occurs during or after the boot.

## MAKE NO ASSUMPTIONS

This rule is the hardest to follow, because there is a tendency to trust anything in writing and assume that people are telling you exactly what happened. But documentation is sometimes wrong, and people don't always describe events as they occurred, so do your own investigating. For example, if the user tells you that the system boots up with no error messages, but that the software still doesn't work, boot for yourself. You never know what the user might have overlooked.

## Analyze the Problem and Make an Initial Determination

Given what you've learned by interviewing the user, examining the computer, and duplicating the problem, consider what might be the source of the problem, which might or might not be obvious at this point. For example, if a user complains that his Word documents are getting corrupted, possible sources of the problem might be that the user does not know how to save documents properly, the software or the OS might be corrupted, the PC might have a virus, or the hard drive might be intermittently failing. Then, based on what you have initially discovered, decide if the problem is caused by software, hardware, or the user.

## Check Simple Things First

Most problems are so simple that we overlook them because we expect the problem to be difficult. Don't let the complexity of computers fool you. Most problems are easy to fix.

Really, they are! To save time, check the simple things first such as whether a power switch is not turned on or a cable is loose. Here are some practical examples of applying this principle:

▲ When a Word document gets corrupted, the most obvious or simplest source of the problem is that the user is not saving documents properly. Eliminate that possibility as the source of the problem before you look at the software or the hard drive.

▲ When a CD-ROM drive doesn't work, the problem might be that the CD is scratched or cracked. Check that first.

▲ If the video does not work, the problem might be with the monitor or the video card. When faced with the decision of which one to exchange first, choose the easy route: Exchange the monitor before the video card.

### Beware of User Error

Remember that many problems stem from user error. Watch what the user is doing and ask questions.

### Divide and Conquer

This rule is the most powerful. Isolate the problem. In the overall system, remove one hardware or software component after another, until the problem is isolated to a small part of the whole system. As you divide a large problem into smaller components, you can analyze each component separately. You can use one or more of the following to help you divide and conquer on your own system:

▲ In Windows, stop all non-essential services running in the background to eliminate them as the problem.

▲ Boot from a bootable CD or floppy disk to eliminate the OS and startup files on the hard drive as the problem.

▲ Remove any unnecessary hardware devices, such as a scanner card, internal modem, CD drive, and even the hard drive. Once down to the essentials, start exchanging components you know are good for those you suspect are bad, until the problem goes away. You don't need to physically remove the CD drive or hard drive from the bays inside the case. Simply disconnect the data cable and the power cable. Remember that the problem might be a resource conflict. If the network card worked well until the CD drive was reconnected and now neither works, try the CD drive without the network card. If the CD drive works, you most likely have a resource conflict.

### Trade Known Good for Suspected Bad

When diagnosing hardware problems, this method works well if you can draw from a group of parts that you know work correctly. Suppose the monitor does not work; it appears dead. The parts of the video subsystem are the video card, the power cord to the monitor, the cord from the monitor to the PC case, and the monitor itself. Also, don't forget that the video card is inserted into an expansion slot on the motherboard, and the monitor depends on electrical power. Suspect each of these five components to be bad; try them one at a time. Trade the monitor for one that you know works. Trade the power cord, trade the cord to the PC video port, move the video card to a new slot, and trade the video card. When you're trading a good component for a suspected bad one, work methodically by eliminating one component at a time. Don't trade the video card and the monitor and then turn on the PC to determine if they work. It's possible that both the card and the monitor are bad, but assume that only one component is bad before you consider whether multiple components need trading.

In this situation, suppose you keep trading components in the video subsystem until you have no more variations. Next, take the entire subsystem—video card, cords, and monitor—to a PC that you know works, and plug each of them in. If they work, you have isolated the problem to the PC, not the video. Now turn your attention back to the PC: the motherboard, the software settings within the OS, the video driver, and other devices. Knowing that the video subsystem works on the good PC gives you a valuable tool. Compare the video driver on the good PC to the one on the bad PC. Make certain the CMOS settings, software settings, and other settings are the same.

### Trade Suspected Bad for Known Good

An alternate approach works well in certain situations. If you have a working PC that is configured similarly to the one you are troubleshooting (a common situation in many corporate or educational environments), rather than trading good for suspected bad, you can trade suspected bad for good. Take each component that you suspect is bad and install it in the working PC. If the component works on the good PC, then you have eliminated it as a suspect. If the working PC breaks down, then you have probably identified the bad component.

### Become a Researcher

Following this rule is the most fun. When a computer problem arises that you can't easily solve, be as tenacious as a bulldog. Read, make phone calls, ask questions, then read more, make more calls, and ask more questions. Take advantage of every available resource, including online help, the Internet, documentation, technical support, and books such as this one. Learn to use a good search engine on the Web, such as *www.google.com*. What you learn will be yours to take to the next problem. This is the real joy of computer troubleshooting. If you're good at it, you're always learning something new.

### Write Things Down

Keep good notes as you're working. They'll help you think more clearly. Draw diagrams. Make lists. Clearly and precisely write down what you're learning. Later, when the entire problem gets "cold," these notes will be invaluable.

### Keep Your Cool and Don't Rush

In an emergency, protect the data and software by carefully considering your options before acting and by taking practical precautions to protect software and OS files. When a computer stops working, if unsaved data is still in memory or if data or software on the hard drive has not been backed up, look and think carefully before you leap! A wrong move can be costly. The best advice is not to hurry. Carefully plan your moves. Read the documentation if you're not sure what to do, and don't hesitate to ask for help. Don't simply try something, hoping it will work, unless you've run out of more intelligent alternatives!

### Don't Assume the Worst

When it's an emergency and your only copy of data is on a hard drive that is not working, don't assume that the data is lost. Much can be done to recover data. If you want to recover lost data on a hard drive, don't write anything to the drive; you might write on top of lost data, eliminating all chances of recovery.

### Reboot and Start Over

This is an important rule. Fresh starts are good for us and uncover events or steps that we might have overlooked. Take a break; get away from the problem. Begin again.

## STEP 4: VERIFY THE FIX AND DOCUMENT THE SOLUTION

If you think you have solved the problem, reboot the system and make sure everything is working before you stop. Ask the user to verify all is working. Then document what happened so you can take what you learned into the next troubleshooting situation. Write down the initial symptoms, the source of the problem, and what you did to fix it.

---

**APPLYING | CONCEPTS** Intermittent problems can make troubleshooting challenging. The trick in diagnosing problems that come and go is to look for patterns or clues as to when the problems occur. If you or the user can't reproduce the problem at will, ask the user to keep a log of when the problems occur and exactly what messages appear. Tell the user that intermittent problems are the hardest to solve and might take some time, but that you won't give up. Show the user how to get a printed screen of the error messages when they appear. Here's one method to print a screen shot:

1. Press the **Print Screen** key to copy the displayed screen to the Windows Clipboard.

2. Launch the Paint software accessory program and paste the contents of the Clipboard into the document. You might need to use the Zoom Out command on the document first. You can then print the document with the displayed screen, using Paint. You can also paste the contents of the Clipboard into a document created by a word-processing application such as Word.

---

## *TROUBLESHOOTING A FAILED BOOT*

It's really hard to learn to troubleshoot a PC in one fell swoop, so we're going to ease into it slowly. This section is your first introduction to troubleshooting, and we'll only cover simple problems, which, in this case, prevent the computer from booting correctly and don't involve loading the Windows desktop. Solutions in this section are limited to things that you can do that are quite simple.

### MY COMPUTER WON'T BOOT

It's been a long day; you've worked late, and now you sit down in front of your home PC to have a little relaxing fun surfing the Web, chatting with friends in foreign places, and updating your blog. You turn on your PC, and this big problem smacks you in the face; you just want to cry. Been there? I have.

What do you do first? First thing to remember is don't panic. Most PC problems are simple and can be simply solved, but you do need a game plan. That's what Figure 3-45 gives you. As we work our way through it, you're eliminating one major computer subsystem after another until you zero in on the problem. After you've discovered the problem, many times the solution is obvious.

Does the PC boot properly? If not, then ask, "Is the screen blank?" If it is blank and you cannot hear any spinning fans or drives and see no lights, then assume the problem has to do with the power system and begin troubleshooting there. If the screen is blank

A+ ESS
1.3
3.3

A+
220-602
1.2

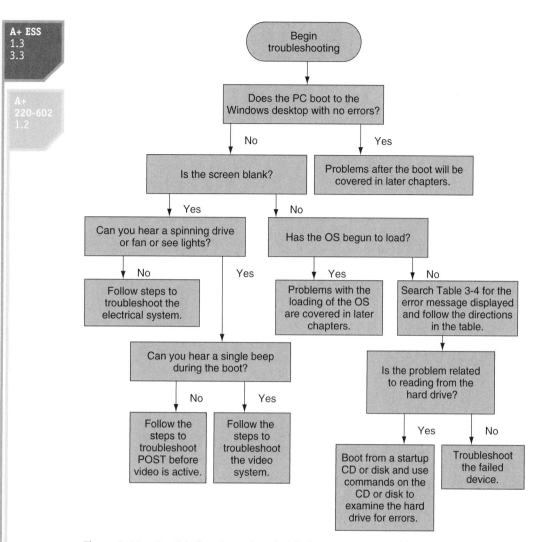

**Figure 3-45** Use this flowchart when first facing a computer problem

and you heard a single beep, then the BIOS has signaled that POST completed successfully and you can assume the problem must be with the video system. Thus, you should then begin troubleshooting video. If you see

> **A+ Exam Tip**
>
> The A+ Essentials and IT 220-602 exams expect you to be able to recognize and isolate problems during the boot caused by video, power, overheating, the keyboard, the hard drive, and memory. You also need to know how to deal with an error at POST.

an error message onscreen, but Windows has not started to load, then use the error message to help you identify the problem.

## TROUBLESHOOTING MAJOR SUBSYSTEMS USED FOR BOOTING

The remainder of this section is divided into the major categories of troubleshooting steps laid out in Figure 3-45. We'll look at problems with the electrical subsystem, problems with essential hardware devices such as the motherboard, memory, and the processor, problems with video, and problems with reading from the hard drive.

A+ ESS
1.3
3.3

A+
220-602
1.2

> **Notes**
>
> Because we're still early in the book, we have not covered problems that occur when a new component, operating system, or application has just been installed or some other major modification to the system has just been made. In such cases, you would assume that the problem was related to these changes. These types of problems are covered in later chapters.

## TROUBLESHOOTING THE ELECTRICAL SYSTEM

Without opening the computer case, the following list contains some questions you can ask and things you can do to solve a problem with the electrical system. The rule of thumb is "try the simple things first." In the next chapter, you will learn much more about the electrical system and more things you can try.

- ▲ Are there any burnt parts or odors? (Definitely not a good sign!) Read Chapter 4 before you do anything else!
- ▲ Is the power cord plugged in? If it is plugged into a power stripe or surge suppressor, is the device turned on and also plugged in?
- ▲ Is the power outlet controlled by a wall switch? If so, is the switch turned on?
- ▲ Is the circuit breaker blown? Is the house circuit overloaded?
- ▲ Are all switches on the system turned on? Computer? Monitor?
- ▲ Is there a possibility the system has overheated? If so, wait awhile and try again. If the system comes on, but later turns itself off, you might need additional cooling fans inside the unit. Where and how to install them is covered in the next chapter.

The next thing to do is to open the case and begin checking electrical components inside the case, which is covered in the next chapter.

## TROUBLESHOOTING POST BEFORE VIDEO IS ACTIVE

If the electrical system is working, one of the first things startup BIOS does is check the essential hardware components on the motherboard it must have to boot. If it sees a problem with a device it checks before it has access to video, BIOS communicates that problem as a beep code.

If you observe that power is getting to the system (you see lights and hear fans or beeps) but the screen is blank, turn off the system and turn it back on and carefully listen to any beep codes. Each BIOS manufacturer has its own beep codes, but Table 3-4 lists the more common meanings. For specific beep codes for your motherboard, see the Web site of the motherboard or BIOS manufacturer. Look in the motherboard documentation for the name of the BIOS manufacturer. If you can't find the name, then know that in Chapter 6 you'll learn how to identify the BIOS and motherboard.

Here is a list of the Web sites for the most common BIOS manufacturers:

- ▲ AMI BIOS: *www.ami.com*
- ▲ Award BIOS and Phoenix BIOS: *www.phoenix.com*
- ▲ Compaq or HP: *thenew.hp.com*
- ▲ Dell: *www.dell.com*
- ▲ IBM: *www.ibm.com*
- ▲ Gateway: *www.gateway.com*

If no beeps are heard, even after you reboot a couple of times, then assume the problem is with the processor, the BIOS, or the motherboard. All these problems are covered in Chapters 5 and 6.

A+ ESS
1.3
3.3

A+
220-602
1.2

| Beeps During POST | Description |
|---|---|
| One beep followed by three, four, or five beeps | Motherboard problems, possibly with DMA, CMOS setup chip, timer, or system bus. Most likely the motherboard will need replacing. How to do this is covered in Chapter 6. |
| Two beeps | The POST numeric code is displayed on the monitor. See the list of numeric codes later in this section. |
| Two beeps followed by three, four, or five beeps | First 64K of RAM has errors. The solution is to replace RAM, which is covered in Chapter 7. |
| Three beeps followed by three, four, or five beeps | Keyboard controller failed or video controller failed. Most likely these are embedded components on the motherboard. How to deal with these motherboard problems is covered in Chapter 6. |
| Four beeps followed by two, three, or four beeps | Problem with serial or parallel ports, system timer, or time of day, which probably means the motherboard must be replaced. |
| Continuous beeps | Problem with power supply. The power supply might need replacing; see Chapter 4. |

**Table 3-4** Beep codes and their meanings

## TROUBLESHOOTING VIDEO

If you hear one beep during the boot and you see a blank screen, then BIOS has successfully completed POST, which includes a test of the video card. You can then assume the problem must be with the monitor or the monitor cable. Ask these questions and try these things:

1. Is the monitor electrical cable plugged in?

2. Is the monitor turned on? Try pushing the power button on the front of the monitor. It should turn yellow or green, indicating the monitor has power.

3. Is the monitor cable plugged into the video port at the back of the PC and the connector on the rear of the monitor?

4. Try a different monitor and a different monitor cable that you know are working.

More things to do and try concerning the video system are covered in Chapter 9.

## TROUBLESHOOTING ERROR MESSAGES DURING THE BOOT

If video and the electrical systems are working, then most boot problems show up as an error message displayed onscreen. These error messages can have several sources:

▲ After video is active, a hardware device such as the keyboard, hard drive, or CD drive failed POST.

▲ After POST, when startup BIOS turned to the hard drive to find an OS, it could not read from the drive. Recall that it must be able to read the Master Boot Record containing the master boot program and partition table, the OS boot record, and the first OS boot program (Ntldr or Io.sys).

▲ After Ntldr or Io.sys are in control, they could not find the OS files they use to load the OS.

Now let's look at some possible error messages listed in Table 3-5, along with their meanings. For other error messages, look in your motherboard or computer documentation or use a good search engine to search for the error message on the Internet.

| Error Message | Meaning of the Error Message |
|---|---|
| Numeric codes during POST | Sometimes numeric codes are used to communicate errors at POST. Some examples for IBM XT/AT error codes include: |
| Code in the 100 range | Motherboard errors. Troubleshooting the motherboard is covered in Chapter 6. |
| Code in the 200 range | RAM errors. Troubleshooting RAM is covered in Chapter 7. |
| Code in the 300 range | Keyboard errors. Verify the keyboard is plugged in or try a known good keyboard. |
| Code in the 500 range | Video controller errors. The video card might need replacing. This is covered in Chapter 9. |
| Code in the 600 or 7300 range | Floppy drive errors. Verify CMOS setup has the floppy drive configured correctly. |
| Code in the 900 range | Parallel port errors |
| Code in the 1300 range | Game controller or joystick errors |
| Code in the 1700 range | Hard drive errors |
| Code in the 6000 range | SCSI device or network card errors |
| Configuration/CMOS error | Setup information does not agree with the actual hardware the computer found during boot. May be caused by a bad or weak battery or by changing hardware without changing setup. Check setup for errors. |
| Hard drive not found Fixed disk error | The BIOS cannot locate the hard drive, or the controller card is not responding. How to solve hard drive problems is covered in Chapter 8. |
| Invalid drive specification | The BIOS is unable to find a hard drive or a floppy drive that setup tells it to expect. Look for errors in CMOS setup. In Chapter 14, you'll learn to use the Diskpart command in the Windows 2000/XP Recovery Console to check the hard drive partition table. For a Windows 9x/Me system, use the Fdisk command on the Windows 9x/Me startup disk to check the partition table. Fdisk is covered in Chapter 15. |
| No boot device available | The hard drive is not formatted, or the format is corrupted, and there is no disk in drive A. Use Diskpart or Fdisk to examine the partition table on the hard drive. |
| Invalid partition table Error loading operating system Missing operating system Missing NTLDR Invalid boot disk Inaccessible boot device | The Master Boot program at the beginning of the hard drive displays these messages when it cannot find the active partition on the hard drive or the boot record on that partition. Use Diskpart or Fdisk to examine the drive for errors. |
| Error in Config.sys line xx | In a Windows 9x/Me environment, an entry in Config.sys is incorrect or is referencing a 16-bit program that is missing or corrupted. |
| Nonsystem disk or disk error Bad or missing Command.com No operating system found Can't find NTLDR | The disk in drive A is not bootable. Remove the disk in drive A and boot from the hard drive. If you still get the error, use Diskpart or Fdisk to examine the partition table on the hard drive. If you can access drive C, look for missing system files on the drive. For Windows 9x or DOS, use the Sys command to restore system files. |

**Table 3-5** Error messages and their meanings

**3**

A+ ESS
1.3
3.3

A+
220-602
1.2

| Error Message | Meaning of the Error Message |
|---|---|
| Not ready reading drive A: Abort, Retry, Fail? General failure reading drive A:; Abort, Retry, Fail? | The disk in drive A is missing, is not formatted, or is corrupted. Try another disk or remove the disk to boot from the hard drive. |
| Missing operating system, error loading operating system | The MBR is unable to locate or read the OS boot sector on the active partition, or there is a translation problem on large drives. Boot from a bootable floppy or CD and examine the hard drive file system for corruption. |
| Device or service has failed to start An error message about a reference to a device or service in the registry | These errors occur late in the boot when the OS is loading services and device drivers. How to handle these errors is covered in Chapter 14. |
| While Windows 2000/XP is loading, an unknown error message on a blue background displays and the system halts. | These errors are called stop errors or blue screen errors and are usually caused by viruses, errors in the file system, a corrupted hard drive, a corrupted system file, or a hardware problem. How to handle blue screen errors is covered in Chapter 14. |

**Table 3-5** Error messages and their meanings (continued)

Notice in the table that several problems pertain to BIOS not being able to read from the hard drive, and the suggested next step is to try booting from another media, which can be either a CD or floppy disk.

Each OS provides one or more methods and media to use if booting from the hard drive fails. Windows XP uses the setup CD or a floppy disk for this purpose, Windows 2000 uses the setup CD or a set of four rescue disks, and Windows 9x/Me uses a single rescue disk. In later chapters you'll learn to use all these methods for each OS.

## >> CHAPTER SUMMARY

◢ Tools used by a PC support technician might include screwdrivers, tweezers, recovery CDs, cans of compressed air, cleaning solutions, needle-nose pliers, multimeter, cable ties, flashlight, AC outlet ground tester, loop-back plugs, POST diagnostic cards, and utility software.

◢ To protect against ESD, a support technician can use a ground bracelet, ground mat, antistatic bags, and antistatic gloves.

◢ The goals of preventive maintenance are to make PCs last longer and work better, protect data and software, and reduce repair costs.

◢ When a PC is your permanent responsibility, keep good backups of data and system files, document all setup changes, problems, and solutions, and take precautions to protect the system against viruses and other attacks.

◢ To protect a system against attack, use a firewall, install and run antivirus software, and keep Windows updates current.

◢ A PC preventive maintenance plan includes blowing dust from the inside of the computer case, keeping a record of setup data, backing up the hard drive, and cleaning the mouse, monitor, and keyboard.

◢ Protecting software and hardware documentation is an important preventive maintenance chore.

◢ Never ship a PC when the only copy of important data is on its hard drive.

◢ CMOS setup holds most of the motherboard configuration information. In addition, some motherboards use jumpers or DIP switches for a few settings.

◢ The boot process can be divided into four parts: POST, loading the OS, the OS initializing itself, and loading and executing an application.

◢ The startup BIOS is in control when the boot process begins. Then the startup BIOS turns control over to the OS.

◢ During the boot, the ROM BIOS startup program performs a power-on self test (POST) and assigns system resources to devices. It then searches secondary storage for an OS.

◢ When the OS loads from a hard drive, the BIOS first executes the Master Boot Record (MBR) program, which turns to the partition table to find the OS boot record. The program in the OS boot record attempts to find a boot loader program for the OS, which for Windows NT/2000/XP is Ntldr. For Windows 9x/Me, the program is Io.sys.

◢ When troubleshooting a failed boot, the subsystems to check are the electrical system, the major components on the motherboard and other hardware required to boot, the video system, and errors that occur when BIOS tries to read from the hard drive.

## >> KEY TERMS

For explanations of key terms, see the Glossary near the end of the book.

| | | |
|---|---|---|
| boot record | hard boot | partition table |
| booting | Io.sys | POST (power-on self test) |
| cold boot | loop-back plug | program file |
| Command.com | Master Boot Record (MBR) | soft boot |
| diagnostic card | material safety data sheet | startup BIOS |
| DIP (dual inline package) switch | (MSDS) | static electricity |
| electrostatic discharge (ESD) | Msdos.sys | warm boot |
| ground bracelet | Ntldr | |

## >> REVIEW QUESTIONS

1. Which of the following steps can be used to protect your system against viruses, worms, and other malicious software?

   a. Keep Windows updates current.

   b. Minimize the time spent using the Web.

   c. Reload application software (such as Microsoft Word) frequently.

   d. Use multiple firewalls at the same time.

2. Which of the following steps can be used to manually discharge a monitor?

   a. Vacuum the dust.

   b. Use a monitor cleaner on the screen.

   c. Unplug the monitor.

   d. Use a high-voltage probe with the monitor case opened.

3. Which of the following best describes an upset failure caused by ESD?

   a. Upset failures are easy to detect.

   b. The failure destroys the component beyond use.

   c. The damaged component may continue to function, but it does not perform well.

   d. An upset failure prevents the computer from booting.

4. Which memory address is always assigned to the first instruction in the ROM BIOS start-up program?

   a. 000000

   b. 000001

   c. FFFF0h

   d. FFFFFF

5. Which of the following is the first question to answer in troubleshooting a PC problem?

   a. Is the problem related to reading from the hard drive?

   b. Does the PC boot to the Windows desktop with no errors?

   c. Is the screen blank?

   d. Can you hear a single beep during the boot?

6. True or false? A loop-back plug is used to test a serial, parallel, USB, network, or other port.

7. True or false? A preventive maintenance plan tends to evolve from a history or pattern of malfunctions within an organization.

8. True or false? Batteries containing silver oxide, mercury, or lithium can be disposed of in the regular trash.

9. True or false? Even when the power supply and monitor are unplugged, they contain enough power to kill you.

10. True or false? The MBR (Master Boot Record) contains the master boot program and the partition table.

11. A material safety data sheet (MSDS) explains how to properly handle _____.

12. The best way to guard against ESD is to use a(n) _____ together with a ground mat.

**13.** A hard boot, or _____, involves turning on the power with the on/off switch.

**14.** A warm boot involves using the _____ to reboot.

**15.** The POST, or _____, is a series of tests performed by the startup BIOS to determine if it can communicate correctly with essential hardware components required for a successful boot.

# Form Factors and Power Supplies

This chapter focuses on the power supply, which provides power to all other components inside the computer case. Several types of power supplies are available. The form factor of the computer case and motherboard drive which type of power supply can be installed in a system. Therefore, we begin the chapter discussing the form factors of computer cases, motherboards, and power supplies. To troubleshoot problems with the power system of a PC, you need a basic understanding of electricity. You'll learn about the measurements of electricity and the form in which it comes to you as house current. The chapter then covers how to protect a computer system from damage caused by electrical problems. Next, we discuss Energy Star devices that save energy. Finally, we talk about ways to detect and correct problems with the PC's electrical system, including how to change a defective power supply.

## COMPUTER CASE, MOTHERBOARD, AND POWER SUPPLY FORM FACTORS

This chapter is all about a computer's electrical system and power supply, such as the one shown in Figure 4-1. However, because motherboards, power supplies, and computer cases are often sold together and must be compatible with each other, we begin by looking at these three components as an interconnecting system. When you put together a new system, or replace components in an existing system, the form factors of the motherboard, power supply, and case must all match. The **form factor** describes the size, shape, and major features of a hardware component.

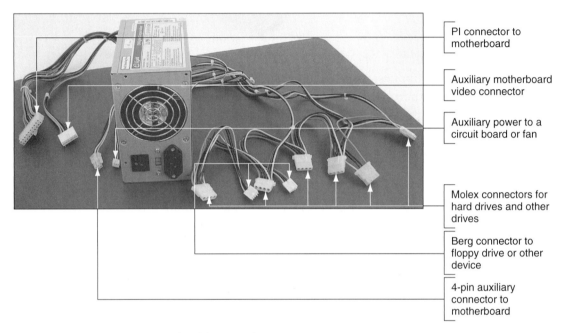

PI connector to motherboard

Auxiliary motherboard video connector

Auxiliary power to a circuit board or fan

Molex connectors for hard drives and other drives

Berg connector to floppy drive or other device

4-pin auxiliary connector to motherboard

**Figure 4-1**   Computer power supply with connections

When you are deciding which form factor to use, the motherboard drives the decision because it determines what the system can do. After you've decided to use a certain form factor for the motherboard, you must use the same form factor for the case and power supply. Using a matching form factor for the motherboard, power supply, and case assures you that:

> **Notes**
>
> A computer case is also known as a chassis.

- ◢ The motherboard fits in the case.
- ◢ The power supply cords to the motherboard provide the correct voltage, and the connectors match the connections on the board.
- ◢ The holes in the motherboard align with the holes in the case for anchoring the board to the case.
- ◢ Holes in the case align with ports coming off the motherboard.
- ◢ For some form factors, wires for switches and lights on the front of the case match up with connections on the motherboard.

When selecting a computer case, motherboard, and power supply, choose a design that fits its intended use. You might need a high-end tower system, a rack-mounted server, or a low-profile desktop. First decide which form factor you will use, which will apply to the case, motherboard, and power supply. Each type of form factor is discussed next, followed by a discussion of the different sizes and shapes of computer cases.

## TYPES OF FORM FACTORS

**A+ ESS 1.1**

Different form factors apply to power supplies, cases, and motherboards: the BTX, ATX, LPX, NLX, backplane systems, and the outdated AT form factor. Each of these form factors has several variations. The most common form factors used on personal computers today are the ATX, MicroATX, BTX, and NLX. The most popular form factor is the ATX, but the latest is the BTX. These form factors and other less common and up-and-coming form factors are discussed next.

> **A+ Exam Tip**
>
> The A+ Essentials exam expects you to recognize and know the more important features of the ATX, BTX, MicroATX, and NLX motherboards.

### AT FORM FACTOR

Of historical significance is the **AT** form factor, sometimes called **full AT**, that measure 12" × 13.8". These boards are no longer produced and you seldom see them around. The form factor uses the full-size AT cases that the original IBM AT (Advanced Technology) personal computer used in the 1980s. A smaller, more convenient version of AT called the Baby AT came later.

> **Video**
>
> Identifying Form Factors

AT motherboards were difficult to install, service, and upgrade. Another problem with the AT form factor is that the CPU was placed on the motherboard in front of the expansion slots; long cards might not fit in these slots because they will bump into the CPU. You can visualize this problem by looking at the AT motherboard in Figure 4-2.

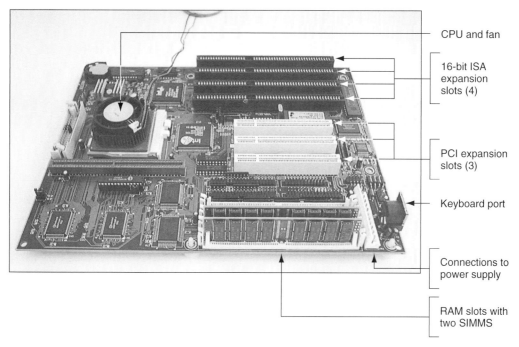

**Figure 4-2** The CPU on the AT motherboard sits in front of the expansion slots

**A+ ESS**
**1.1**

Power supplies for AT systems supply +5, –5, +12, and –12 volts to the motherboard and other components. The AT board uses two power connections, the **P8 connector** and the **P9 connector** (see Figure 4-3).

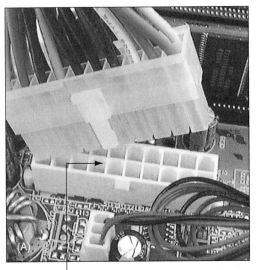
— P1 on an ATX motherboard

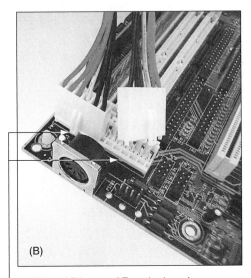
— P8 and P9 on an AT motherboard

**Figure 4-3**   ATX uses a single P1 power connector (A), but AT-type motherboards use P8 and P9 power connectors (B)

## BABY AT FORM FACTOR

The **Baby AT** form factor provided more flexibility than full AT. Baby AT was the industry standard form factor from about 1993 to 1997. Power supplies designed for the Baby AT form factor blow air out of the computer case, rather than pull air into it as does the AT case fan. At 13" × 8.7", Baby AT motherboards are smaller than full AT motherboards and fit in many types of cases, including newer ATX cases designed to provide backward compatibility.

The design of Baby AT motherboards did not resolve the problem with the position of the CPU in relation to expansion slots. In addition, because of the motherboard's configuration and orientation within the case, drives and other devices are not positioned close to their connections on the motherboard. This means that cables might have to reach across the motherboard and not be long enough or might get in the way of good airflow. Baby AT motherboards are no longer produced, but occasionally you still see one in use.

## ATX FORM FACTOR

ATX is the most commonly used form factor today. It is an open, nonproprietary industry specification originally developed by Intel in 1995. ATX improved upon AT by making adding and removing components easier, providing greater support for I/O devices and processor technology, and lowering costs.

With ATX, components on the motherboard are arranged so that they don't interfere with each other and for better position inside the case. In addition, the position of the power supply and drives inside the case makes connecting them to the motherboard easier and makes it possible to reduce cable lengths, which can help reduce the potential for EMI and corrupted data. EMI (electromagnetic interference) is explained later in the chapter. Connecting the switches and lights on the front of the case to components inside the case requires fewer wires, making installation simpler and reducing the potential for mistakes.

An ATX motherboard measures 12"× 9.6", so it's smaller than a full AT motherboard. On an ATX motherboard, the CPU and memory slots are rotated 90 degrees from the position on the AT motherboard. Instead of sitting in front of the expansion slots, the CPU and memory slots sit beside them, preventing interference with full-length expansion cards (see Figure 4-4). ATX is an evolution of the Baby AT form factor and blows air out of the case, as did Baby AT.

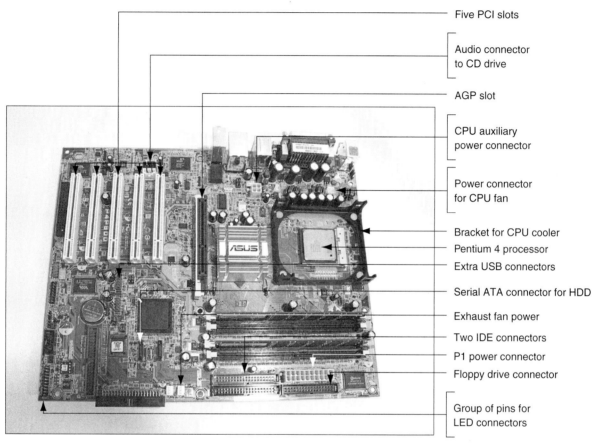

Five PCI slots

Audio connector to CD drive

AGP slot

CPU auxiliary power connector

Power connector for CPU fan

Bracket for CPU cooler
Pentium 4 processor
Extra USB connectors

Serial ATA connector for HDD

Exhaust fan power

Two IDE connectors

P1 power connector

Floppy drive connector

Group of pins for LED connectors

**Figure 4-4** The CPU on an ATX motherboard sits opposite the expansion slots and does not block the room needed for long expansion cards

The first ATX power supplies and motherboards use a single power connector called the **P1 connector** that includes, in addition to the voltages provided by AT, a +3.3-volt circuit for a low-voltage CPU (refer to Figure 4-3). The first ATX P1 connector has 20 pins.

The electrical requirements for motherboards change over time as new technologies make additional demands for power. When processors began to require more power, the ATX Version 2.1 specifications added a 4-pin auxiliary connector near the processor socket to provide an additional 12 V of power (see Figure 4-5). A power supply that provides this 4-pin 12-volt power cord is called an **ATX12V power supply**.

Later, when PCI Express slots were added to motherboards, more power was required and a new ATX specification (ATX Version 2.2) allowed for a 24-pin P1 connector. The extra 4 pins on the P1 connector provide 12V, 5V, and 3.3V pins and with this newer connector, the 4-pin auxiliary connector is no longer needed. Motherboards that support PCI Express and have the 24-pin P1 connector are sometimes called Enhanced ATX boards. Figure 4-6 shows a 20-pin P1 power cord from the power supply and a 24-pin P1 connector on a motherboard.

**Figure 4-5**  The 4-pin 12V auxiliary power connector on a motherboard

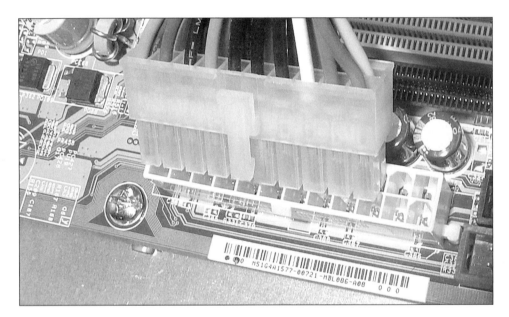

**Figure 4-6**  A 20-pin power cord ready to be plugged into a 24-pin P1 connector on an ATX motherboard

> **Notes**
>
> For more information about all the form factors discussed in this chapter, check out the form factor Web site sponsored by Intel at *www.formfactors.org*.

Figure 4-7 shows the power connectors used by a motherboard, floppy drive, and parallel ATA and serial ATA drives as defined in the ATX specifications.

Another feature of an ATX motherboard not found on AT boards is a **soft switch,** sometimes called the **soft power** feature. Using this feature, an OS, such as Windows 2000/XP or Windows 98, can turn off the power to a system after the shutdown procedure is done. In addition, CMOS can be configured to cause a keystroke or network activity to power up the system (wake on LAN). If a case has a soft switch and the installed operating system supports the feature, when a user presses the power switch on the front of the case while the computer is on, the OS goes through a normal shutdown procedure before powering off. There are several variations of ATX. The **Mini-ATX**, a smaller ATX motherboard (11.2" × 8.2"), can be used with ATX cases and power supplies. **FlexATX** allows for maximum flexibility in the design of system cases and boards and therefore can be a good choice for custom systems. FlexATX is used in slimline and all-in-one cases.

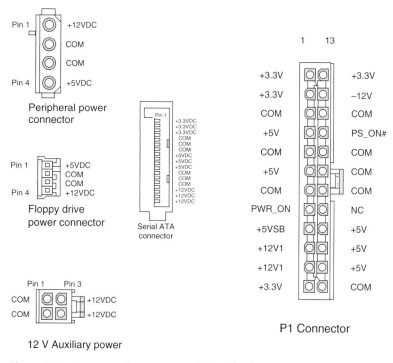

**Figure 4-7**  Power supply connectors defined by the ATX specifications

## MICROATX FORM FACTOR

The **MicroATX** form factor is a major variation of ATX and addresses some technologies that have emerged since the original development of ATX. MicroATX reduces the total cost of a system by reducing the number of I/O slots on the motherboard, reducing the power supplied to the board, and allowing for a smaller case size. MicroATX motherboards can be used in an ATX 2.1 computer case with minor modifications.

ATX is still the most popular motherboard form factor, and it remains to be seen if ATX will be replaced by BTX, the latest form factor.

## BTX FORM FACTOR

The **BTX (Balanced Technology Extended)** form factor was designed by Intel for flexibility and can be used by everything from large tower systems to those ultrasmall systems that sit under a monitor. BTX was designed to take full advantage of serial ATA, USB 2.0, and PCI Express technologies. The BTX form factor design focuses on reducing heat with better airflow and improved fans and coolers. It also gives better structural support for the motherboard than does ATX. BTX motherboards use a 24-pin power connector that has the same pinout arrangement as the ATX 24-pin P1 connector and can also use one or more auxiliary power connectors for the processor, fans, and lighting inside the case (for really cool-looking systems). Because the 24-pin connectors are the same, a BTX motherboard can use an ATX power supply.

In the case configuration shown in Figure 4-8, notice how the processor is sitting immediately in front of the intake fan installed on the front of the case. This intake fan together with the exhaust fan on the rear of the case produce a strong wind tunnel effect over the

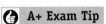

A+ ESS
1.1

processor, making it unnecessary to have a fan on top of the processor itself. Also notice in Figure 4-8 that memory modules and expansion cards fit into the slots parallel to airflow rather than blocking airflow as they sometimes do with ATX and AT form factors. Airflow in a BTX system is also designed to flow underneath the BTX motherboard.

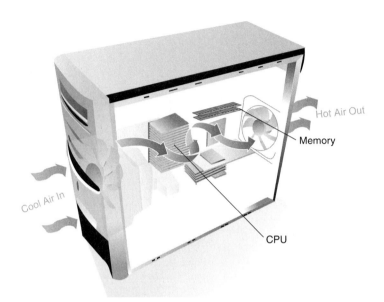

**Figure 4-8** Improved airflow in a BTX case and motherboard makes it unnecessary to have a fan on top of the processor

## LPX AND MINI-LPX FORM FACTORS

**LPX** and **Mini-LPX** form factors were originally developed by Western Digital for low-end personal computer motherboards and are used with low-profile cases. In these systems, the motherboard has only one expansion slot, in which a **riser card** (also called a **bus riser** or **daughter card**), is mounted. Expansion cards are mounted on the riser card, and the card also contains connectors for the floppy and hard drives. Difficult to upgrade, they cannot handle the size and operating temperature of today's faster processors. In addition, a manufacturer often makes proprietary changes to the standard LPX motherboard design, forcing you to use only the manufacturer's power supply. LPX and Mini-LPX use small cases called low-profile cases and slimline cases.

## NLX FORM FACTOR

The **NLX** form factor for low-end personal computer motherboards was developed by Intel in 1998 to improve on the older LPX form factor. The riser card (sometimes called a daughter board or daughter card) on an NLX motherboard is on the edge of the board, which differs from the LPX motherboard that has the riser card near the center of the board. The NLX form factor allowed for larger DIMM modules, support for AGP, and the ability to remove the motherboard without using tools. The NLX standard applies only to motherboards; NLX motherboards are designed to use ATX power supplies. An example of an NLX system is shown in Figure 4-9.

> 🖱 **A+ Exam Tip**
>
> The A+ Essentials exam expects you to know the purpose of the riser card or daughter board used with the NLX form factor.

**4**

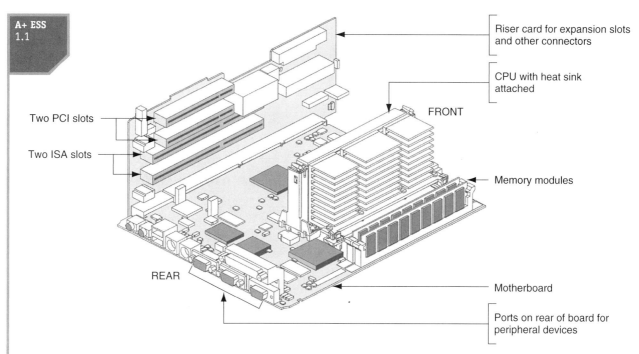

Riser card for expansion slots and other connectors

CPU with heat sink attached

FRONT

Two PCI slots

Two ISA slots

Memory modules

REAR

Motherboard

Ports on rear of board for peripheral devices

**Figure 4-9**  The NLX form factor uses a riser card that connects to the motherboard; the riser card provides expansion slots for the expansion cards

## BACKPLANE SYSTEMS

**Backplane systems** do not use a true motherboard; instead, they use backplanes such as the one shown in Figure 4-10. A backplane is a board that normally sits against the back of a proprietary case with slots on it for other cards. **Active backplanes** contain no circuits other

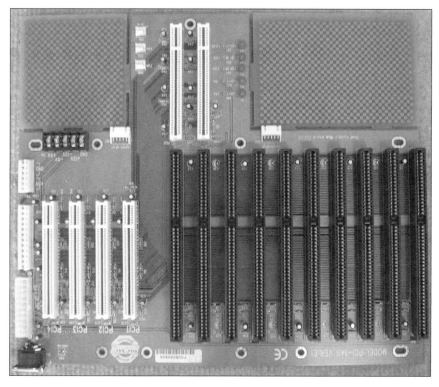

**Figure 4-10**  A 16-slot passive backplane board by Acqutek (*www.acqu.com*)

than bus connectors and some buffer and driver circuits. **Passive backplanes** contain no circuitry at all; the circuits are all on a mothercard, also called a CPU card. The mothercard is a circuit board that plugs into the backplane and contains a processor (see Figure 4-11). These systems are generally not used in personal computers. Passive backplanes are sometimes used for industrial rack-mounted systems and high-end file servers. A rack-mounted system is not designed for personal use, and often several of these systems are mounted in cases stacked on a rack for easy access by technicians.

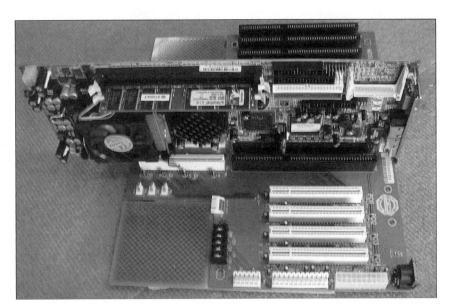

**Figure 4-11** This CPU card by Acqutek (*www.acqu.com*) plugs into a passive backplane board and contains socket 478 with a Pentium 4 processor installed

## TYPES OF CASES

Several types and sizes of cases are on the market for each form factor. The computer case, sometimes called the chassis, houses the power supply, motherboard, expansion cards, and drives. The case has lights and switches on the front panel that can be used to control and monitor the PC. Generally, the larger the case, the larger the power supply and the more amps it carries. These large cases allow for the extra space and power needed for a larger number of devices, such as multiple hard drives needed in a server.

Cases for personal computers and notebooks fall into three major categories: desktop cases, tower cases, and notebook cases. The following sections discuss each in turn.

### DESKTOP CASES

The classic case with four drive bays and around six expansion slots that sits on your desktop doing double duty as a monitor stand is called a **desktop case**. The motherboard sits on the bottom of a desktop case, and the power supply is near the back. Because of the space a desktop case takes, it has fallen out of favor in recent years and is being replaced by smaller and more space-efficient cases.

For low-end desktop systems, **compact cases**, sometimes called **low-profile cases** or **slimline cases**, follow either the NLX, LPX, or Mini-LPX form factor. Likely to have fewer drive bays, they generally still provide for some expansion. You can see the rear of a compact case in Figure 4-12. An LPX motherboard that uses this case has a riser card for expansion cards, which is why the expansion card slots in the figure run parallel to the motherboard sitting on the bottom of the case.

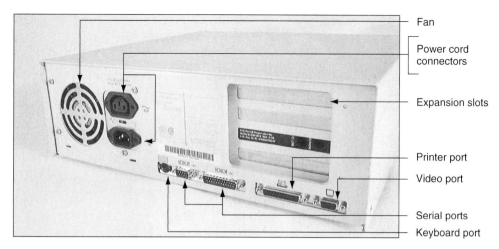

**Figure 4-12** Because the expansion slots are running parallel to the motherboard on the bottom of this desktop case, you know that a riser card is being used

## TOWER CASES

A **tower case** can be as high as two feet and has room for several drives. Often used for servers, this type of case is also good for PC users who anticipate upgrading, because tower cases provide maximum space for working inside a computer and moving components around. Figure 4-13 shows examples of each of the three main tower sizes, as well as two desktop cases.

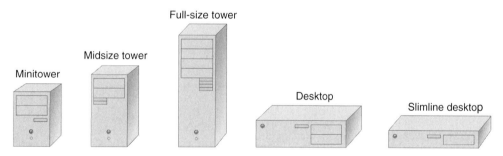

**Figure 4-13** Tower and desktop cases

The variations in cases are as follows:

◢ Midsize towers, also called miditowers, are the most popular. They are midrange in size and generally have around six expansion slots and four drive bays, providing moderate potential for expansion. They are used for ATX, Mini-ATX, and BTX systems.

◢ The minitower, also called a microtower, is the smallest type of tower case and does not provide room for expansion.

◢ Full-size towers are used for high-end personal computers and servers. They are usually built to accommodate ATX, Mini-ATX, and BTX systems (see Figure 4-14).

◢ Desktop cases are losing popularity because they take up too much space on our desks unless you place your monitor on top of it. If you have a desktop case, don't place it on its end because the CD or DVD drive will not work properly. Desktop cases are built to accommodate all form factors for personal computers.

◢ Slimline desktop cases are gaining in popularity for low-end personal computers because they come in cool colors and do double duty as a monitor stand.

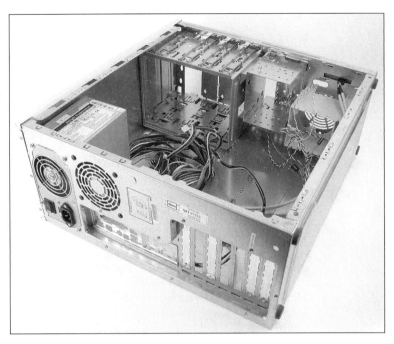

**Figure 4-14**  Full-size tower case for an ATX motherboard

## NOTEBOOK CASES

**Notebook cases** are used for portable computers that have all the components of a desktop computer. The cost and power of notebook systems vary widely. As with other small systems, notebooks can present difficulties in expansion. The smallest notebook cases are called subnotebooks. Notebook designs are often highly proprietary, but are generally designed to conserve space, allow portability, use less power, and produce less heat. The case fan in a notebook usually attaches to a thermometer and runs only when temperature needs to be lowered. In addition, the transformer and rectifier functions of the power supply are often moved to an AC adapter on the power cable.

Table 4-1 lists a few case and power supply vendors.

| Manufacturer | Web Site |
|---|---|
| Asus | www.asus.com |
| Axxion Group Corporation | www.axxion.com |
| Enlight Corporation | www.enlightcorp.com |
| Maxpoint Computers | www.enermaxusa.com |
| MGE Company | www.mgecompany.com |
| PC Power and Cooling | www.pcpowerandcooling.com |
| PCI Case Group | www.pcicase.co.uk |
| Sunus Suntek | www.suntekgroup.com |

**Table 4-1**  Manufacturers of cases and power supplies for personal computers

Toward our goal of learning about power supplies and the electrical current they provide, let's turn our attention to understanding how electricity is measured and about some of its properties.

# MEASURES AND PROPERTIES OF ELECTRICITY

In our modern world, we take electricity for granted, and we miss it terribly when it's cut off. Nearly everyone depends on it, but few really understand it. But to become a successful PC technician (that is, no fried motherboards, smoking monitors, or frizzed hair), you need to understand electricity, know how to use it, how it's measured, and how to protect computer equipment from its damaging power. So let's start with the basics. To most people, volts, ohms, watts, and amps are vague terms that simply mean electricity. All these terms can be used to measure some characteristic of electricity, as listed in Table 4-2.

> **Notes**
>
> To learn more about how volts, amps, ohms, and watts measure the four properties of electricity, see Appendix B.

| Unit | Definition | Computer Example |
|---|---|---|
| Volt (for example, 110 V) | A measure of electrical "pressure" differential. Volts are measured by finding the potential difference between the pressures on either side of an electrical device in a circuit. The symbol for volts is V. | An AT power supply provides four separate voltages: +12 V, -12 V, +5 V, and -5 V. An ATX power supply provides these voltages and +3.3 V as well. The BTX power supply provides +12 V, -12 V, +5 V, and +3.3 V. |
| Amp or ampere (for example, 1.5 A) | A measure of electrical current. Amps are measured by placing an ammeter in the flow of current. The symbol for Amps is A. | A 17-inch monitor requires less than 2 A to operate. A small laser printer uses about 2 A. A CD-ROM drive uses about 1 A. |
| Ohm (for example, 20 Ω) | A measure of resistance to electricity. Devices are rated according to how much resistance they offer to electrical current. The ohm rating of a resistor or other electrical device is often written somewhere on the device. The symbol for ohm is Ω. | Current can flow in typical computer cables and wires with a resistance of near zero Ω (ohm). |
| Watt (for example, 20 W) | A measure of electrical power. Whereas volts and amps are measured to determine their value, watts are calculated by multiplying volts by amps. Watts measure the total electrical power needed to operate a device. The symbol for watts is W. | A computer power supply is rated at 200 to 600 W. |

**Table 4-2**  Measures of electricity

Now let's look at how electricity gets from one place to another and how it is used in house circuits and computers.

## AC AND DC

Electricity can be either AC, alternating current, or DC, direct current. **Alternating current (AC)** goes back and forth, or oscillates, rather than traveling in only one direction. House current in the United States oscillates 60 times in one second (60 hertz). Voltage in the system is constantly alternating from positive to negative, which causes the electricity to flow first in one direction and then in the other. Voltage alternates from +110 V to -110 V. AC is the most economical way to transmit electricity to our homes and workplaces. By decreasing current and increasing voltage, we can force alternating current to travel great distances. When alternating current reaches its destination, it is made more suitable for driving our electrical devices by decreasing voltage and increasing current.

**Direct current (DC)** travels in only one direction and is the type of current that most electronic devices require, including computers. A **rectifier** is a device that converts alternating current to direct current. A **transformer** is a device that changes the ratio of current to voltage. Large transformers reduce the high voltage on power lines coming to your neighborhood to a lower voltage before the current enters your home. The transformer does not change the amount of power in this closed system; if it decreases voltage, it increases current. The overall power stays constant, but the ratio of voltage to current changes is illustrated in Figure 4-15.

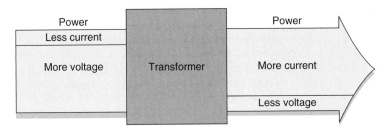

**Figure 4-15** A transformer keeps power constant but changes the ratio of current to voltage

A computer power supply changes and conditions the house electrical current in several ways, functioning as both a transformer and a rectifier. It steps down the voltage from the 110-volt house current to 3.3, 5, and 12 volts, or to 5 and 12 volts, and changes incoming alternating current to direct current, which the computer and its peripherals require. The monitor, however, receives the full 110 volts of AC voltage, converting that current to DC.

Direct current flows in only one direction. Think of electrical current like a current of water that flows from a state of high pressure to a state of low pressure or rest. Electrical current flows from a high pressure state (called hot) to a state of rest (called ground or neutral). For a PC, a line may be either +5 or –5 volts in one circuit, or +12 or –12 volts in another circuit. The positive or negative value is determined by how the circuit is oriented, either on one side of the power output or the other. Several circuits coming from the power supply accommodate different devices with different power requirements.

## HOT, NEUTRAL, AND GROUND

When AC comes from the power source at the power station to your house, it travels on a hot line and completes the circuit from your house back to the power source on a neutral line, as shown in Figure 4-16.

When the two lines reach your house and enter an electrical device, such as a lamp, electricity flows through the device to complete the circuit between the hot line and the neutral line. The device contains resistors and other electrical components that control the flow of electricity between the hot and neutral lines. In a controlled environment, the hot source then seeks and finds a state of rest by returning to the power station on the neutral line.

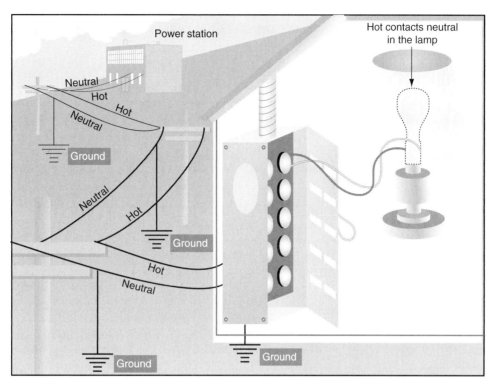

**Figure 4-16** Normally, electricity flows from hot to neutral to make a closed circuit in the controlled environment of an electrical device such as a lamp

A short circuit, or a short, occurs when uncontrolled electricity flows from the hot line to the neutral line or from the hot line to ground. Electricity naturally finds the easiest route to a state of rest. Normally that path is through some device that controls the current flow and then back through the neutral line. If an easier path (one with less resistance) is available, the electricity follows that path. This can cause a short, a sudden increase in flow that can also create a sudden increase in temperature—enough to start a fire and injure both people and equipment. Never put yourself in a position where you are the path of least resistance between the hot line and ground!

A fuse is a component included in a circuit and designed to prevent too much current from flowing through the circuit. A fuse is commonly a wire inside a protective case, which is rated in amps. If too much current begins to flow, the wire gets hot and eventually melts, breaking the circuit, as an open switch would, and stopping the current flow. Many devices have fuses, which can be easily replaced when damaged.

To prevent uncontrolled electricity from continuing to flow indefinitely, which can happen because of a short, the neutral line is grounded. Grounding a line means that the line is connected directly to the earth, so that, in the event of a short, the electricity flows into the earth and not back to the power station. Grounding serves as an escape route for out-of-control electricity. The earth is at no particular state of charge and so is always capable of accepting a flow of current.

The neutral line to your house is grounded many times along its way (in fact, at each electrical pole) and is also grounded at the breaker box where the electricity enters your house. You can look at a three-prong plug and see the three lines: hot, neutral, and ground (see Figure 4-17).

> ⚡ **Caution**
>
> Beware of the different uses of black wire. In PCs and in DC circuits, black is used for ground, but in home wiring and in AC circuits, black is used for hot!

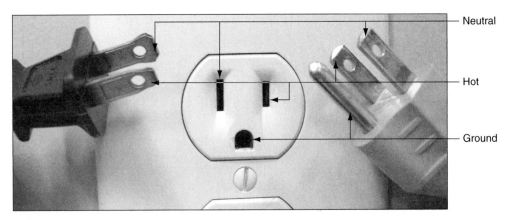

**Figure 4-17**   A polarized plug showing hot and neutral, and a three-prong plug showing hot, neutral, and ground

> **Notes**
>
> House AC voltage in the United States is about 110 V, but know that in other countries, this is not always the case. In many countries, the standard is 220 V. Outlet styles also vary from one country to the next.

Generally, electricians use green or bare wire for the ground wire, white for neutral, and black for hot in home wiring for 110-volt circuits. In a 220-volt circuit, black and red are hot, white is neutral, and green or bare is ground. To verify that a wall outlet is wired correctly, use a simple receptacle tester, as shown in Figure 4-18. Even though you might have a three-prong outlet in your home, the ground plug might not be properly grounded. To know for sure, always test the outlet with a receptacle tester.

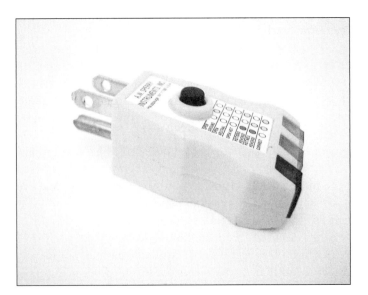

**Figure 4-18**   Use a receptacle tester to verify that hot, neutral, and ground are wired correctly

## SOME COMMON ELECTRONIC COMPONENTS

It's important you understand what basic electronic components make up a PC and how they work. Basic electronic components in a PC include transistors, capacitors, diodes, ground, and resistors (each of which we will discuss in detail in a moment). Figure 4-19 shows the symbols for these components.

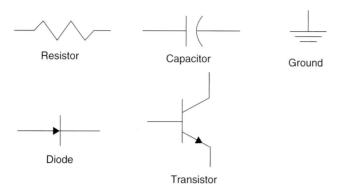

Figure 4-19   Symbols for some electronic components and for ground

To understand how these components are constructed, it helps to know that all the materials used to make the components fall into one of these three categories:

> **⚡ Caution**
>
> It's very important that PC components be properly grounded. Never connect a PC to an outlet or use an extension cord that doesn't have the third ground plug. The third line can prevent a short from causing extreme damage. In addition, the bond between the neutral and ground helps eliminate electrical noise (stray electrical signals) within the PC sometimes caused by other electrical equipment sitting very close to the computer.

- ◢ *Conductors*. Material, such as gold or copper, that easily conducts electricity
- ◢ *Insulators*. Material, such as glass or ceramic, that resists the flow of electricity
- ◢ *Semiconductors*. Material, such as silicon, whose ability to conduct electricity, when a charge is applied, falls between that of a conductor and an insulator

## TRANSISTOR

A **transistor** is an electronic device that can serve as a gate or switch for an electrical signal and can amplify the flow of electricity. Invented in 1947, the transistor is made of three layers of semiconductor material.

A charge (either positive or negative, depending on the transistor's design) placed on the center layer can cause the two outer layers of the transistor to complete a circuit to create an "on" state. An opposite charge placed on the center layer can make the reverse happen, causing the transistor to create an "off" state. Manipulating these charges to the transistor allows it to hold a logic state of either on or off. The on state represents binary 1 and the off state represents binary 0 when used to hold data in a computer.

When the transistor maintains this state, it requires almost no electrical power. Because the initial charge sent to the transistor is not as great as the resulting current that the transistor creates, a transistor sometimes is used as a small amplifier. For instance, transistors are used to amplify the tiny dots or pixels on an LCD monitor screen used to create a sharper image. The transistor is also used as the basic building block of an integrated circuit (IC), which is used to build a microchip.

## CAPACITOR

A **capacitor** is an electronic device that can hold an electrical charge for a period of time and can smooth the uneven flow of electricity through a circuit. Capacitors inside a PC power supply create the even flow of current the PC needs. Capacitors maintain their charge long after current is no longer present, which is why the inside of a power supply can be dangerous even when it is unplugged. You can see many capacitors on mother-boards, video cards, and other circuit boards (see Figure 4-20).

Crosshatch on top of capacitor

**Figure 4-20**   Capacitors on a motherboard or other circuit board often have embedded crossed lines on top

### DIODE

A **diode** is a semiconductor device that allows electricity to flow in only one direction. (A transistor contains two diodes.) One to four diodes used in various configurations can be used to convert AC to DC. Singularly or collectively, depending on the configuration, these diodes are called a rectifier.

### RESISTOR

A **resistor** is an electronic device that limits the amount of current that can flow through it. In a circuit, a resistor is used to protect a circuit from overload or to control the current. Resistors are color-coded to indicate the degree of resistance measured in ohms.

## PROTECTING YOUR COMPUTER SYSTEM

Now that you have learned some basic information about how electricity is measured and managed, let's look at ways to protect your computer system from the danger of electricity. Electricity can be a dangerous enemy to your computer when it comes in the form of static electricity, electromagnetic interference, and power surges. In the following sections, you'll learn about these dangers and what you can do to protect your computer against them.

## STATIC ELECTRICITY

In the previous chapter, you learned that static electricity (also called ESD) is a dangerous enemy when you're working inside a computer case. If you touch a sensitive computer component when there is a static charge on your body different from the static charge on the component, there is a resulting discharge as your body and the component reach equal charges. This sudden discharge can damage the component even when it is so slight you don't feel the spark. ESD is especially a problem in dry and cold climates. Recall from Chapter 3 to protect components against ESD, use a ground bracelet or ESD gloves. If you don't have this equipment available, be careful to touch the computer case before you touch a component so any charge between you and the case is dissipated before you touch a component.

Also remember from Chapter 3 to unplug the power cord from the computer case before working inside the case. Even when the power switch on the rear of the case is turned off, residual power is still on and can damage a system or give you a shock if you touch a live wire. Some motherboards even have a small light inside the case to remind you of this fact and to warn you that power is still getting to the system. For this reason, be certain to unplug the power cord before working inside it.

> **A+ Exam Tip**
>
> The A+ Essentials exam emphasizes that you should know how to protect computer equipment as you work on it.

## EMI (ELECTROMAGNETIC INTERFERENCE)

Another phenomenon that can cause electrical problems with computers is **electromagnetic interference (EMI)**. EMI is caused by the magnetic field produced as a side effect when electricity flows. EMI in the radio frequency range, which is called radio frequency interference (RFI), can cause problems with radio and TV reception. Data in data cables that cross an electromagnetic field can become corrupted, causing crosstalk. Crosstalk can be partially controlled by using data cables covered with a protective material; these cables are called shielded cables. Power supplies are also shielded to prevent them from emitting EMI.

If mysterious, intermittent errors persist on a PC, one thing to suspect is EMI. Try moving the PC to a new location. If the problem continues, try moving it to a location that uses an entirely different electric circuit. A simple way to detect EMI is to use an inexpensive AM radio. Turn the tuning dial away from a station and all the way down into a low-frequency range. With the radio on, you can hear the static that EMI produces. Try putting the radio next to several electronic devices to detect the EMI they emit.

If EMI in the electrical circuits coming to the PC causes a significant problem, you can use a line conditioner to filter the electrical noise that causes the EMI. Line conditioners are discussed later in the chapter.

> **Notes**
>
> PCs can emit EMI to other nearby PCs, which is one reason a computer needs to be inside a case. To help cut down on EMI between PCs, always install face plates in empty drive bays or slot covers over empty expansion slots.

> **Video**
>
> Testing for EMI

> **Notes**
>
> After you remove the source of EMI, the problem it is causing goes away. In contrast, the problems caused by ESD permanently damage a component.

## SURGE PROTECTION AND BATTERY BACKUP

A+
220-602
1.3

The power supplies in most computers can operate over a wide range of electrical voltage input; however, operating the computer under these conditions for extended periods of time can shorten not only the power supply's life, but also the computer's. Also, electrical storms can end a computer's life quite suddenly. To prevent such things from happening, consider installing a device to filter AC input.

A wide range of devices on the market condition the AC input to computers and their peripherals to eliminate highs and lows and provide backup power when the AC fails. These devices, installed between the house current and the computer, fall into three general categories: surge suppressors, power conditioners, and uninterruptible power supplies (UPSs). All these devices should have the UL (Underwriters Laboratory) logo, which says that the laboratory, a provider of product safety certification, has tested the device. The UL standard that applies to surge suppressors is UL 1449, first published in 1985 and revised in 1998.

## SURGE SUPPRESSORS

A **surge suppressor**, also called a **surge protector**, protects equipment against sudden changes in power level, such as spikes from lightning strikes. The device, such as the one shown in Figure 4-21, typically provides a row of power outlets, an on/off switch, and a protection light that indicates the device is protecting equipment from overvoltages (also called transient voltages) on AC power lines and telephone lines. Surge suppressors can come as power strips (note that not all power strips have surge protection), wall-mounted units that plug into AC outlets, or consoles designed to sit beneath the monitor on a desktop. Some provide RJ-11 telephone jacks to protect modems and fax machines from spikes.

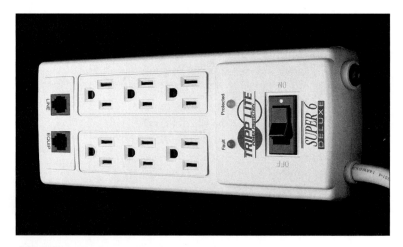

**Figure 4-21** This surge suppressor has six electrical outlets, two phone jacks, and a power protection light

A surge suppressor might be a shunt type that absorbs the surge, a series type that blocks the surge from flowing, or a combination of the two. A suppressor is rated in joules, which is a measure of work or energy. One **joule** (pronounced "jewel") is the work or energy required to produce one watt of power in one second, and a suppressor is rated as to the amount of joules it can expend before it no longer can work to protect the circuit from the power surge. Suppressors are commonly rated from 250 joules to several thousand joules— the higher the better.

Some suppressors are also rated by **clamping voltage** (also called let-through voltage), which is the voltage point at which a suppressor begins to absorb or block voltage. Normally, house current is rated at 120 V, so you would think the clamping voltage should be close to this number such as around 130 V. However, the clamping voltage value is best not set this low. House current regularly spikes past 200 V, and a PC power supply is

A+
220-602
1.3

designed to handle these types of quick spikes. If the surge suppressor kicks in to work on these spikes, not only is it unnecessary, but the suppressor is likely to wear out prematurely. A clamping voltage of 330 V or higher is appropriate.

The circuitry inside the suppressor that handles a surge can burn out if a surge is too high or lasts too long. In this case, most suppressors continue to work just like a normal extension cord, providing no surge protection. Because of this fact, it's important a surge suppressor has a light indicator that says the suppressor part of the device is still working. Otherwise, you might not have protection, but not know it.

A **data line protector** serves the same function for your telephone line to your modem that a surge suppressor does for the electrical lines. Telephone lines carry a small current of electricity and need protection against spikes, just as electrical lines do.

> **Notes**
>
> Whenever a power outage occurs, unless you have a reliable power conditioner or UPS installed, unplug all power cords to the PC, printers, monitors, and the like. Sometimes when the power returns, sudden spikes are accompanied by another brief outage. You don't want to subject your equipment to these surges. When buying a surge suppressor, look for those that guarantee against damage from lightning and that reimburse for equipment destroyed while the surge suppressor is in use.

When shopping for a surge protector, look for these features:

- ◢ Joules rating (more than 600 joules) and the time it takes for the protection to start working (less than 2 nanoseconds is good)
- ◢ Warranty for connected equipment and UL seal of approval
- ◢ A light that indicates the surge protection is working and phone line protection
- ◢ Let-through voltage rating and line noise filtering

When you plug in a surge protector, know that if the protector is not grounded using a three-prong outlet, the protector cannot do its job. One more thing to consider: You can purchase a whole-house surge protection system that is installed by an electrician at your breaker box. It's more expensive, but your entire house or office building is protected.

## POWER CONDITIONERS

In addition to providing protection against spikes, **power conditioners** also regulate, or condition, the power, providing continuous voltage during brownouts. These voltage regulators, sometimes called **line conditioners**, can come as small desktop units. They provide a degree of protection against **swells** or **spikes** (temporary voltage surges) and raise the voltage when it drops during **brownouts** or **sags** (temporary voltage reductions). Power conditioners are measured by the load they support in watts, volt-amperes (VA), or kilovolt-amperes (kVA).

To determine the VA required to support your system, multiply the amperage of each component by 120 volts and then add up the VA for all components. For example, a 17-inch monitor has "1.9 A" written on its back, which means 1.9 amps. Multiply that value by 120 volts, and you see that the monitor requires 228 VA or 228 watts. A Pentium PC with a 17-inch monitor and tape backup system requires about 500 VA or 500 watts of support.

Power conditioners are a good investment if the AC in your community suffers excessive spikes and brownouts. However, a device rated under 1 kVA will probably provide corrections only for brownouts, not for spikes. Line conditioners, like surge suppressors, provide no protection against a total blackout (complete loss of power).

## UNINTERRUPTIBLE POWER SUPPLY

A+
220-602
1.3

Unlike a power conditioner, the **uninterruptible power supply** (UPS) provides backup power in the event that the AC fails completely. The UPS also provides some filtering of the AC. A UPS offers these benefits:

▲ Conditions the line to account for both brownouts and spikes
▲ Provides backup power during a blackout
▲ Protects against very high spikes that could damage equipment

A UPS device that is suitably priced for personal computer systems is designed as a standby device (battery-powered circuit is used when AC input fails), an inline device (battery-powered circuit is used continually), or a **line-interactive** device (which combines features of the first two). Several variations of these three types of UPS devices are on the market at widely varying prices.

A common UPS device is a rather heavy box that plugs into an AC outlet and provides one or more outlets for the computer and its peripherals (see Figure 4-22). It has an on/off switch, requires no maintenance, and is very simple to install.

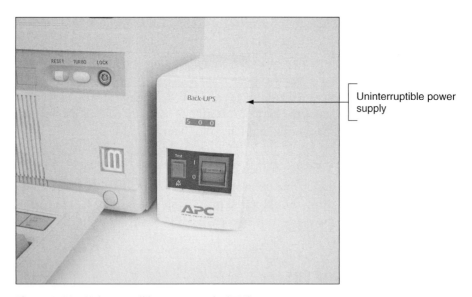

Uninterruptible power supply

**Figure 4-22** Uninterruptible power supply (UPS)

### The Smart UPS

When you look through ads of UPS devices, some of them are labeled as a smart UPS. A **smart UPS** (also called an **intelligent UPS**) can be controlled by software from a computer. For example, from the front panel of some UPSs you can check for a weak battery, but with a smart UPS, you can perform the same function from utility software installed on your computer. To accommodate this feature, a UPS must have a serial port or USB connection to the PC and a microprocessor on board.

Some activities this utility software and a smart UPS can do include the following:

▲ Diagnose the UPS.
▲ Check for a weak battery.
▲ Monitor the quality of electricity received.
▲ Monitor the percentage of load the UPS is carrying during a blackout.

**4**

A+
220-602
1.3

▲ Automatically schedule the weak-battery test or UPS diagnostic test.

▲ Send an alarm to workstations on a network to prepare for a shutdown.

▲ Close down all servers protected by the UPS during a blackout.

▲ Provide pager notification to a facilities manager if the power goes out.

▲ After a shutdown, allow for startup from a remote location over phone lines.

## What to Consider When Buying a UPS

When you purchase a UPS, do not buy a UPS that runs at full capacity. This is especially important for an inline UPS because this type of UPS is constantly recharging the battery. If this battery charger is operating at full capacity, it is producing a lot of heat, which can reduce the battery's life. The UPS rating should exceed your total VA or wattage output by at least 25 percent.

You should also be aware of the degree of line conditioning that the UPS provides. Consider the warranty and service policies as well as the guarantee the UPS manufacturer gives for the equipment that the UPS protects. For example, one standby UPS by Tripp Lite that costs less than $90 claims to support up to 750 VA or 450 watts power requirements for up to 35 minutes during a complete power failure. This smart UPS has a USB connector to a computer, and carries a guarantee on connected equipment of $100,000. Table 4-3 lists some UPS manufacturers.

| Manufacturer | Web Site |
|---|---|
| American Power Conversion Corp. (APC) | www.apcc.com |
| Circuit Components, Inc. | www.surgecontrol.com |
| CyberPower | www.cyberpowersystems.com |
| MGE UPS Systems | www.mgeups.com |
| Tripp Lite | www.tripplite.com |
| Belkin Corporation | www.belkin.com |
| Eaton Corporation | www.powerware.com |
| Liebert Corporation | www.liebert.com |
| Para Systems, Inc. | www.minuteman-ups.com |
| Toshiba International Corp. | www.tic.toshiba.com |

**Table 4-3** UPS manufacturers

## ENERGY STAR SYSTEMS (THE GREEN STAR)

A+ ESS
2.2

As you build or maintain a computer, one very important power consideration is energy efficiency and conservation. Toward that end, you should know that **Energy Star** systems and peripherals have the U.S. Green Star, indicating that they satisfy certain energy-conserving standards of the U.S. Environmental Protection Agency (EPA). Devices that can carry the Green Star are computers, monitors, printers, copiers, and fax machines.

Energy Star standards are designed to decrease overall

**Notes**

Office equipment is among the fastest growing source of electricity consumption in industrialized nations. Much of this electricity is wasted because people often leave computers and other equipment on overnight. Because Energy Star devices go into sleep mode when they are unused, they create overall energy savings of about 50 percent.

electricity consumption in the United States to protect and preserve natural resources. These standards, sometimes called the **Green Standards**, generally mean that the computer or the device has a standby program that switches the device to sleep mode when it is not in use. In addition, during **sleep mode**, the device must use no more than 30 watts of power.

## POWER-MANAGEMENT METHODS AND FEATURES

Computer systems implement Energy Star standards in several ways. All these methods of power management are intended to conserve energy. Some of the more significant ones are listed below:

▲ Advanced Configuration and Power Interface (ACPI), used with Windows 2000/XP and Windows 98/Me and supported by the system BIOS, is a set of standards so that BIOS can communicate with the OS about what hardware is present and what energy-saving features are present and how they can be used.
▲ The older Advanced Power Management (APM) specifications championed by Intel and Microsoft were used by older notebook computers and allow BIOS to control power management.
▲ AT Attachment (ATA) for hard drives and other type drives allows drives to stop spinning when not in use.
▲ Display Power Management Signaling (DPMS) standards for monitors and video cards

**Notes**

To see if your system is ACPI-compliant, open Device Manager and then open the Computer item in the list of devices (see Figure 4-23). Look for ACPI in the detail line.

ACPI is the current standard used by most desktop and notebook computers. Using this standard, there are four modes, S1 through S4, used to indicate different levels of power-saving functions. They are listed below from the least to the greatest energy-saving level:

▲ In S1 mode, the hard drive and monitor is turned off and everything else runs normally. Some manufacturers call this mode the sleep mode or standby mode.

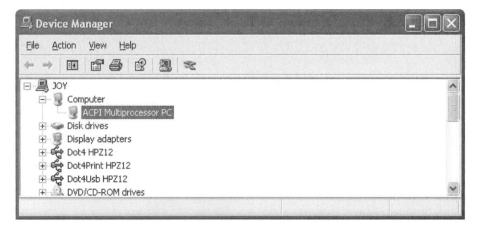

**Figure 4-23**  Use Device Manager to quickly see if a system is ACPI-compliant

▲ In S2 mode, the hard drive, monitor, and processor are turned off. This mode is also called standby or sleep mode.
▲ In S3 mode, everything is shut down except RAM and enough of the system to respond to a wake-up call such as pressing the keyboard or moving the mouse.

This mode is sometimes called sleep mode, suspend mode, standby mode, or suspend to RAM.

▲ S4 mode is called hibernation. In hibernation, everything in RAM is copied to a file on the hard drive and then the system shuts down. Later, when a power button is pressed, the system does not have to go through the slow boot process, but can quickly read contents of the hibernation file and restore the system to its state before S4 mode was enabled.

Some ACPI power-management features can be controlled from Windows and others can be controlled from BIOS. In many situations, Windows and BIOS share the control of a power-management feature, which can often cause conflicts and confusion. The trend is to manage power using Windows. For example, hibernation settings can be controlled from Windows, but hibernation in BIOS must be enabled before it will work. To manage power features in Windows, go to the Control Panel and open the Power Options applet. The Power Options Properties window opens. How to use this window is covered in Chapter 20.

To control power using the BIOS, go to CMOS setup and access the Power menu. Options on this menu depend on the BIOS. For example, in Figure 4-24, you see the Power screen for an Asus Pentium 4 motherboard BIOS (*www.asus.com*). The options on the left of the screen allow you to control the power-management features, and the right side of the screen gives not-too-helpful information about these options.

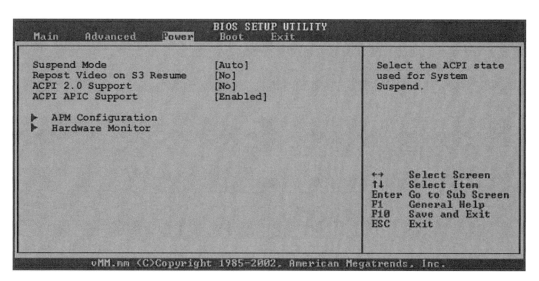

**Figure 4-24**  A power management BIOS setup screen showing power-management features

The following list describes each option shown in Figure 4-24:

▲ *Suspend Mode.* Choices are S1 Only, S3 Only, or Auto. Auto is the default choice, which can send everything except memory to sleep incrementally depending on how long the system remains inactive.

▲ *Repost Video on S3 Resume.* Choices are Yes or No. The default is No. For Windows 9x/Me, set it to Yes so that VGA BIOS POST is run after video comes out of an S3 sleep state.

▲ *ACPI 2.0 Support.* Choices are Yes or No. The default is No. ACPI stores information that it needs to pass on to the OS in a series of tables. The master table is the Root System Description Table (RSDT). Originally, this table was designed to use 32-bit addresses. By saying Yes to this choice, you can use additional 64-bit tables if you have a 64-bit processor such as the Itanium.

▲ *ACPI APIC Support.* Choices are Enabled or Disabled. The default choice is Enabled, which means the APIC (Advanced Programmable Interrupt Controller) information is included in ACPI information. This controller can sometimes solve problems with devices not coming out of a sleep state correctly.

▲ *APM Configuration.* When you select this choice, you are taken to a submenu where you can configure the legacy APM configuration. Normally, you wouldn't want to.

▲ *Hardware Monitor.* When you select this choice, you can configure how you want to monitor and (to some degree) control hardware devices, including the CPU temperature, fan speeds, and voltage output from the motherboard.

## ENERGY STAR MONITORS

Most computers and monitors sold today are Energy Star–compliant; you know they are compliant because they display the green Energy Star logo onscreen when the PC is booting. Most monitors that follow the Energy Star standards adhere to the **Display Power Management Signaling (DPMS)** specifications developed by Video Electronics Standards Association (VESA), which allow for the video card and monitor to go into sleep mode simultaneously.

> **Notes**
>
> For a monitor's power-saving feature to function, the video card or computer must also support this function.

To view and change energy settings of an Energy Star monitor using Windows 2000/XP, right-click the desktop and select Properties. The Display Properties dialog box opens. Click the Screen Saver tab. If your monitor is Energy Star–compliant, you will see the Energy Star logo at the bottom. When you click the Power button, the Power Options Properties dialog box opens, and you can change your power options (see Figure 4-25). Your power options might differ depending on the power-management features your BIOS supports.

> **Notes**
>
> For a Windows 9x/Me system, problems might occur if the system BIOS is turning off the monitor because of power-management settings, and Windows is also turning off the monitor. If the system hangs when you try to get the monitor going again, try disabling one or the other setting. It is best to use the OS or BIOS for power management, but not both.

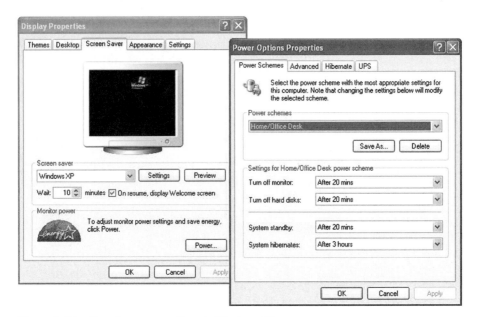

**Figure 4-25**   Changing power options in Windows XP

## TROUBLESHOOTING THE ELECTRICAL SYSTEM

Electrical problems can occur before or after the boot and can be consistent or intermittent. Many times PC repair technicians don't recognize the cause of a problem to be electrical because of the intermittent nature of some electrical problems. In these situations, the hard drive, memory, the OS, or even user error might be suspected as the source of the problem and then systematically eliminated before the electrical system is suspected. This section will help you to be aware of symptoms of electrical problems so that you can zero in on the source of an electrical problem as quickly as possible.

---

**APPLYING|CONCEPTS** Your friend Sharon calls to ask your help with a computer problem. Her system has been working fine for over a year, but now strange things are happening. Sometimes, the system powers down while she is working for no apparent reason, and sometimes Windows locks up. As you read this section, look for clues as to what the problem might be. Also, as you read, think of questions to ask your friend that will help you.

---

Possible symptoms of a problem with the electrical system are:

◢ The PC appears "dead"—no lights, no spinning drive or fan.
◢ The PC sometimes halts during booting. After several tries, it boots successfully.
◢ Error codes or beeps occur during booting, but they come and go.
◢ You smell burnt parts or odors. (Definitely not a good sign!)

Check the simple things first. Most PC problems have simple solutions. Try these things:

◢ Is everything connected and turned on? Are any cable connections loose? Is the computer plugged in?
◢ Are all the switches turned on? Computer? Monitor? Surge protector? Uninterruptible power supply? Separate circuit breaker? Is the wall outlet (or surge protector) in working condition?
◢ If the fan is not running, turn off the computer, open the case, and check the connections to the power supply. Are they secure? Are all cards securely seated?
◢ If you smell burnt parts, turn off the system and carefully search for the source of the problem. Look for shorts and frayed and burnt wires. Disassemble the parts until you find the one that is damaged.

As you read through the rest of this section on troubleshooting, you'll see other possible solutions to electrical problems during the boot such as loose internal connections.

### PROBLEMS WITH EXTERNAL POWER

A brownout (reduced current) of the house current might cause symptoms of electrical power problems. If you suspect the house current could be low, check other devices that are using the same circuit. A copy machine, laser printer, or other heavy equipment might be drawing too much power. Remove the other devices from the same house circuit.

A line conditioner might solve the problem of intermittent errors caused by noise in the power line to the PC. Try installing a line conditioner to monitor and condition voltage to the PC.

## PROBLEMS WITH LOOSE INTERNAL CONNECTIONS

A+ ESS
1.3

A+
220-602
1.1
1.2

Loose connections inside the computer case can cause a system to appear dead or reboot itself. For most of the ATX and BTX power supplies, a wire runs from the power switch on the front of the case to the motherboard. This wire must be connected to the pins on the motherboard and the switch turned on before power comes up. Check that the wire is connected correctly to the motherboard. Figure 4-26 shows a wire, which is labeled "REMOTE SW," connected to pins on the motherboard labeled "PWR.SW." If you are not sure of the correct connection on the motherboard, see the motherboard documentation. While inside the case, check all power connections from the power supply to the motherboard and drives. Also, some cases require the case's front panel be in place before the power-on button will work.

> **Notes**
>
> Remember from earlier in the chapter that strong magnetic or electrical interference can affect how a power system functions. Sometimes an old monitor emits too much static and EMI (electromagnetic interference) and brings a whole system down. When you troubleshoot power problems, remember to check for sources of electrical or magnetic interference such as an old monitor or electric fan sitting near the computer case.

Remote SW

**Figure 4-26**   For an ATX or BTX power supply, the remote switch wire must be connected to the motherboard before power will come on

## PROBLEMS THAT COME AND GO

If a system boots successfully to the Windows desktop, you still might have a power system problem. Some problems are intermittent, that is, they come and go. Here are some symptoms that might indicate an intermittent problem with the electrical system after the boot:

▲ The computer stops or hangs for no reason. Sometimes it might even reboot itself.
▲ Memory errors appear intermittently.
▲ Data is written incorrectly to the hard drive.
▲ The keyboard stops working at odd times.
▲ The motherboard fails or is damaged.
▲ The power supply overheats and becomes hot to the touch.
▲ The power supply fan becomes very noisy or stops.

A+ ESS
1.1
1.3

A+
220-602
1.1
1.2

Generally, intermittent problems (those that come and go) are more difficult to solve than a dead system. There can be many causes of intermittent problems, such as an inadequate power supply, overheating, and devices and components damaged by ESD. Each of these sources of intermittent problems is covered in this section.

## PROBLEMS WITH AN INADEQUATE POWER SUPPLY

If you have just installed a new device such as a second hard drive or a DVD drive and are concerned that the power supply is not adequate, you might test it after you finish the installation.

Make all the devices in your system work at the same time. For instance, you can make both the new drive and the floppy drive work at the same time by copying files from one to the other. If the new drive and the floppy drive each work independently, but data errors occur when both work at the same time, suspect a shortage of electrical power.

If you prefer a more technical approach, you can estimate how much total wattage your system needs by calculating the watts required for each device and adding them together. (Calculate watts by multiplying volts in the circuit by amps required for each device.) However, in most cases, the computer's power supply is more than adequate if you add only one or two new devices.

Power supplies for microcomputers range from 200 watts for a small desktop computer system to 600 watts for a tower floor model that uses many multimedia or other power-hungry devices. If you suspect your power supply is inadequate for newly installed devices, upgrade to one with a higher wattage rating.

## PROBLEMS WITH THE POWER SUPPLY, BOARDS, OR DRIVES

The power supply might be faulty or not be adequate for power needs, or components drawing power might be bad. These problems can cause the system to hang, reboot, give intermittent errors, or not boot at all. Expansion boards or drives might be defective and drawing too much power. Remove all nonessential expansion cards (modem, sound card, mouse) one at a time. This verifies that they are not drawing too much power and pulling the system down.

A system with a standard power supply of about 250 watts that has multiple hard drives, multiple CD drives, and several expansion cards is most likely operating above the rated capacity of the power supply, which can cause the system to unexpectedly reboot or give intermittent, otherwise unexplained errors. Upgrade the power supply as needed to accommodate an overloaded power system.

If these suggestions don't correct the problem, check the power supply by exchanging it for one you know is good.

You can use a multimeter to measure the voltage output of a power supply and determine if it is supplying correct voltages, but know that a power supply that gives correct voltages when you measure it might still be the source of problems, because power problems can be intermittent. See Appendix B to learn more about how to use a multimeter to measure voltage output from a power supply.

Video
Using a Multimeter

## PROBLEMS WITH THE POWER SUPPLY FAN

An improperly working fan sometimes causes power supply problems. Usually just before a fan stops working, it hums or whines, especially when the PC is first turned on. If this has just happened, replace the fan if you are trained to service the power supply. If not, replace the entire power supply. If you replace the power supply or fan and the fan still does not

A+ ESS
1.1
1.3

A+
220-602
1.1
1.2

work, the problem might not be the fan. A short somewhere else in the system drawing too much power might cause the problem. Don't operate the PC if the fan does not work. Computers without cooling fans can quickly overheat and damage chips.

To troubleshoot a nonfunctional fan, which might be a symptom of another problem and not a problem of the fan itself, follow these steps:

1. Turn off the power and remove all power cord connections to all components, including the connections to the motherboard, and all power cords to drives. Turn the power back on. If the fan works, the problem is with one of the systems you disconnected, not with the power supply or its fan.

2. Turn off the power and reconnect the power cords to the drives. If the fan comes on, you can eliminate the drives as the problem. If the fan does not come on, try one drive after another until you identify the drive with the short.

3. If the drives are not the problem, suspect the motherboard subsystem. With the power off, reconnect all power cords to the drives.

4. Turn off the power and remove the power to the motherboard by disconnecting P1 or P8 and P9. Turn the power back on.

5. If the fan works, the problem is probably not the power supply but a short in one of the components powered by the power cords to the motherboard. The power to the motherboard also powers expansion cards.

6. Remove all expansion cards and reconnect plugs to the motherboard.

7. If the fan still works, the problem is one of the expansion cards. If the fan does not work, the problem is the motherboard or something still connected to it.

## POWER PROBLEMS WITH THE MOTHERBOARD

A+
220-602
1.1
1.2
1.3

The motherboard, like all other components inside the computer case, should be grounded to the chassis. Look for a metal screw that grounds the board to the computer case. However, a short might be the problem with the electrical system if some component on the board makes improper contact with the chassis. This short can seriously damage the motherboard. Check for missing standoffs (small plastic or metal spacers that hold the motherboard a short distance away from the chassis). A missing standoff most often causes these improper connections. Also check for extra standoffs not used by the motherboard that might be touching a wire on the bottom of the board and causing a short.

> **⚡ Caution**
>
> Never replace a damaged motherboard with a good one without first testing or replacing the power supply. You don't want to subject another good board to possible damage.

Shorts in the circuits on the motherboard might also cause problems. Look for damage on the bottom of the motherboard. These circuits are coated with plastic, and quite often damage is difficult to spot. Also look for burned-out capacitors that are spotted brown or corroded.

Frayed wires on cable connections can also cause shorts. Disconnect hard drive cables connected directly to the motherboard. Power up with P1 or P8 and P9 connected but all cables disconnected from the motherboard. If the fan works, the problem is with one of the systems you disconnected.

## PROBLEMS WITH OVERHEATING

An overheated system can cause intermittent problems or cause the system to reboot or refuse to boot. In fact, the temperature inside the case should never exceed 100 degrees F (38 degrees C).

A+ ESS
1.1
1.3

A+
220-602
1.1
1.2
1.3

Here are some simple things you can do to solve an over-heating problem:

**A+ Exam Tip**

The A+ Essentials and IT 220-602 exams expect you to recognize that a given symptom is possibly power or heat related.

▲ Verify the cooler is connected properly to the processor. If it doesn't fit well, the system might not boot and certainly the processor will overheat.

▲ Use compressed air or an antistatic vacuum to remove dust from the power supply, the vents over the entire computer, and the processor heat sink. Excessive dust insulates components and causes them to overheat. Use an ESD-safe service vacuum or a can of compressed air—both can be purchased from electronic tools suppliers.

▲ Check airflow inside the case. Are all fans running? Are cables in the way of airflow? You might need to replace a fan or tie up cables so they don't obstruct airflow. A case is generally designed for optimal airflow when slot openings on the front and rear of the case are covered. To improve airflow, replace missing faceplates over empty drive bays and replace missing slot covers over empty expansion slots.

▲ After you close the case, leave your system off for a few hours. When you power up the computer again, let it run for 10 minutes, go into CMOS setup, check the temperature readings, and reboot. Next, let your system run until it shuts down. Power it up again and check the temperature in setup again. A significant difference in this reading and the first one you took after running the computer for 10 minutes indicates an overheating problem.

▲ Use tie wraps to secure cables and cords so that they don't block airflow across the processor.

If you try the preceding list of things to do and still have an overheating problem, it's time to move on to more drastic solutions. The problem might be caused by poor air circulation inside the case. The power supply fan in ATX cases blows air out of the case, pulling outside air from the vents in the front of the case across the processor to help keep it cool. Another exhaust fan is usually installed on the back of the case to help the power supply fan pull air through the case (see Figure 4-27).

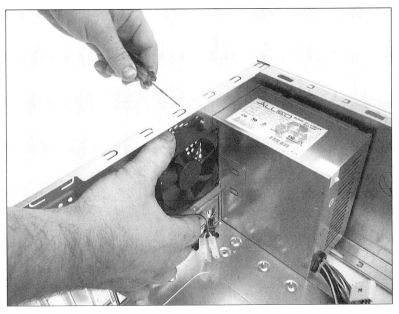

**Figure 4-27** Install one exhaust fan on the rear of the case to help pull air through the case

A+ ESS
1.1
1.3

A+
220-602
1.1
1.2
1.3

In addition, most processors require a cooler with a fan installed on top of the processor. Figure 4-28 shows a good arrangement of vents and fans for proper airflow and a poor arrangement.

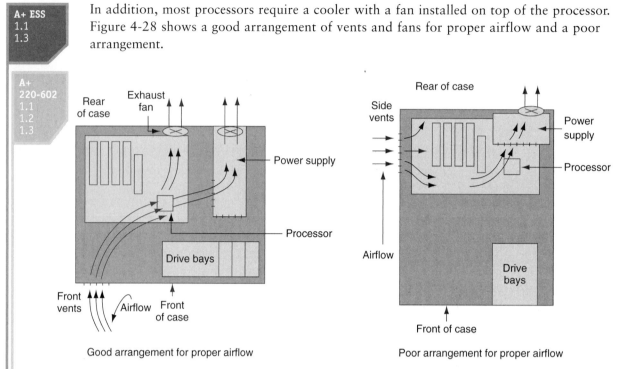

**Good arrangement for proper airflow**          **Poor arrangement for proper airflow**

**Figure 4-28** Vents and fans need to be arranged for best airflow

For better ventilation, use a power supply that has vents on the bottom and front of the power supply. Note in Figure 4-28 airflow is coming into the bottom of the power supply because of these bottom vents. The power supply in Figure 4-27 has vents only on the front and not on the bottom. Compare that to the power supply in Figure 4-29, which has vents on both the front and bottom.

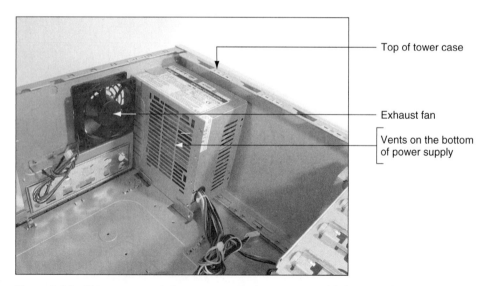

**Figure 4-29** This power supply has vents on the bottom to provide better airflow inside the case

An intake fan on the front of the case might help pull air into the case. Intel recommends you use a front intake fan for high-end systems, but AMD says a front fan for ATX systems is not necessary. Check with the processor manufacturer for specific instructions as to the

A+ ESS
1.1
1.3

A+
220-602
1.1
1.2
1.3

placement of fans and what type of fan and heat sink to use. You will see some examples of processor fans in Chapter 5.

When all else fails, you can try the following to solve stubborn overheating problems:

- Check that your system vents and at least one exhaust fan are in the right position so that air flows across the processor without expansion cards or ribbon cables obstructing the flow.
- Check with the processor manufacturer Web site that you are using the right size processor fan and heat sink and the right thermal compound recommended for the specific processor.
- Check that your power supply has vents on the bottom.
- An AGP video card generates a lot of heat. Make sure that you leave the PCI slot next to the AGP slot open to better ventilate the AGP card. Also, you can purchase a fan that installs in the empty expansion slot next to the video card to help keep it cool.
- Install hard drives in large bays using a bay kit to make the small drive fit in the large bay, thus improving airflow around the drive.
- Monitor the temperature inside the case using a temperature sensor that sounds an alarm when a high temperature is reached or uses software to alert you of a problem.

Be careful when trying to solve an overheating problem. Excessive heat itself may damage the CPU and the motherboard, and the hard reboots necessary when your system hangs may damage the hard drive. If you suspect damaged components, try substituting comparable components that you know are good.

## APPLYING | CONCEPTS

Back to Sharon's computer problem. Here are some questions that will help you identify the source of the problem:

- Have you added new devices to your system? (These new devices might be drawing too much power from an overworked power supply.)
- Have you moved your computer recently? (It might be sitting beside a heat vent or electrical equipment.)
- Does the system power down or hang after you have been working for some time?
- Are case vents free so that air can flow? (The case might be close to a curtain covering the vents.)

Intermittent problems like the one Sharon described are often heat related. If the system only hangs but does not power off, the problem might be caused by faulty memory or bad software, but because it actually powers down, you can assume the problem is related to power or heat.

If Sharon tells you that the system powers down after she's been working for several hours, you can probably assume overheating. Check that first. If that's not the problem, the next thing to do is replace the power supply.

## REPLACING THE POWER SUPPLY

The easiest way to fix a power supply you suspect is faulty is to replace it. A power supply is considered a **field replaceable unit (FRU)** for a PC support technician. When selecting a replacement power supply, be sure the new power supply uses the correct form factor, is adequately

 **A+ Exam Tip**

The A+ IT 220-602 exam expects you to know how to select and install a power supply.

> ⚡ **Caution**
>
> Remember from Chapter 3 that you need to consider the monitor and the power supply to be "black boxes." Never remove the cover or put your hands inside this equipment unless you know about the hazards of charged capacitors and have been trained to deal with them. Both the power supply and the monitor can hold a dangerous level of electricity even after you turn them off and disconnect them from a power source. The power supply and monitor contain enough power to kill you, even when they are unplugged.

rated for power in watts, and has all the power connectors needed by your system. To determine if the power supply really is the problem, turn off the PC, open the computer case, and set the new power supply on top of the old one. Disconnect the old power supply's cords and plug the PC devices into the new power supply. Turn on the PC and verify that the new power supply solves your problem before installing it.

Follow these steps to replace a power supply:

1. Turn off the power to the computer.

2. Remove all external cables from the computer case including the power cable.

3. Remove the computer case cover.

4. Inside the case, disconnect all power cords from the power supply to other devices.

5. Determine which components must be removed before the power supply can be safely removed from the case. You might need to remove the hard drive, several cards, or the CD drive. In some cases, you may even need to remove the motherboard.

6. Remove all the components necessary to get to the power supply. Remember to protect the components from static electricity as you work.

7. Unscrew the screws on the back of the computer case that hold the power supply to the case.

8. Look on the bottom or back of the case for slots that hold the power supply in position. Often the power supply must be shifted in one direction to free it from the slots.

9. Remove the power supply.

10. Place the new power supply in position, sliding it into the slots the old power supply used.

11. Replace the power supply screws.

12. Replace all other components.

13. Before replacing the case cover, connect the power cords, turn on the PC, and verify that all is working.

14. Turn off the PC, replace the cover, and connect all external cables.

15. Turn on the PC and verify all is working.

## >> CHAPTER SUMMARY

◢ A form factor is a set of specifications for the size and configuration of hardware components, such as cases, power supplies, and motherboards.

◢ The most common form factor today is ATX. There is an ATX variation called Mini-ATX. ATX superseded the earlier AT and Baby AT form factors. BTX is the lastest form factor.

▲ Other form factors include LPX and NLX, in which expansion cards are mounted on a riser card that plugs into the motherboard.

▲ Case types include desktop, low-profile or slimline desktops, minitower, miditower, full-size tower, and notebook. The most popular case type in use today is the miditower.

▲ Electrical voltage is a measure of the potential difference in an electrical system.

▲ Electrical current is measured in amps, and electrical resistance is measured in ohms.

▲ Wattage is a measure of electrical power. Wattage is calculated by multiplying volts by amps in a system.

▲ Microcomputers require direct current (DC), which is converted from alternating current (AC) by the PC's power supply inside the computer case.

▲ A PC power supply is actually a transformer and rectifier, rather than a supplier of power.

▲ Materials used to make electrical components include conductors, insulators, and semiconductors.

▲ A transistor is a gate or switch for an electrical signal, a capacitor holds an electrical charge, a diode allows electricity to flow in one direction, and a resistor limits electrical current.

▲ To protect a computer system against ESD, use a ground bracelet, ground mat, and static shielding bags.

▲ Protect a computer system against EMI by covering expansion slots (which also reduces dust inside the case and improves airflow), by not placing the system close to or on the same circuit as high-powered electrical equipment, and by using line conditioners.

▲ Devices that control the electricity to a computer include surge suppressors, line conditioners, and UPSs.

▲ A surge suppressor protects a computer against damaging spikes in electrical voltage.

▲ Line conditioners level the AC to reduce brownouts and spikes.

▲ A UPS provides enough power to perform an orderly shutdown during a blackout.

▲ There are two kinds of UPSs: the true UPS (called the inline UPS) and the standby UPS.

▲ The inline UPS is more expensive because it provides continuous power. The standby UPS must switch from one circuit to another when a blackout begins.

▲ Utility software at a remote computer or a computer connected to the UPS through a USB or serial cable can control and manage a smart UPS.

▲ Data line protectors are small surge suppressors designed to protect modems from spikes on telephone lines.

▲ A faulty power supply can cause memory errors, data errors, system hangs, or reboots; it can damage a motherboard or other components.

▲ To reduce energy consumption, the U.S. Environmental Protection Agency has established Energy Star standards for electronic devices.

▲ Devices that are Energy Star–compliant go into sleep mode, in which they use less than 30 watts of power.

▲ PCs that are Energy Star–compliant often have CMOS settings that affect the Energy Star options available on the PC.

▲ When troubleshooting the electrical system, consider the problem might be caused by loose connections, bad components drawing too much power, the power supply, or overheating.

## >> KEY TERMS

For explanations of key terms, see the Glossary near the end of the book.

| | | |
|---|---|---|
| active backplane | electromagnetic interference | passive backplanes |
| alternating current (AC) | (EMI) | power conditioners |
| amp | Energy Star | rectifier |
| ampere | field replaceable unit (FRU) | resistor |
| AT | FlexATX | riser card |
| ATX | form factor | sags |
| ATX12V power supply | full AT | sleep mode |
| Baby AT | Green Standards | slimline case |
| backplane system | intelligent UPS | smart UPS |
| brownouts | joule | soft power |
| BTX (Balanced Technology | line conditioner | soft switch |
| Extended) | line-interactive | spikes |
| bus riser | low-profile case | surge protector |
| capacitor | LPX | surge suppressor |
| clamping voltage | MicroATX | swells |
| compact case | Mini-ATX | tower case |
| data line protector | Mini-LPX | transformer |
| daughter card | NLX | transistor |
| desktop case | notebook case | uninterruptible power supply |
| diode | ohm | (UPS) |
| direct current (DC) | P1 connector | volt |
| Display Power Management | P8 connector | watt |
| Signaling (DPMS) | P9 connector | |

## >> REVIEW QUESTIONS

1. Which of the following drives the decision on which form factor to use?

   a. Motherboard

   b. CD-ROM

   c. Peripheral devices

   d. CPU

2. Which of the following is the latest form factor?

   a. NLX

   b. ATX

   c. BTX

   d. Baby AT

3. Which of the following is a reason that a riser card is used with the NLX form factor?

   a. Fewer cables are needed.

   b. It reduces heat with better airflow.

   c. It allows for a smaller case.

   d. It can remove the motherboard without using tools.

4. Which one of the following electronic devices holds an electrical charge for a period of time and smooths the uneven flow of electricity through a circuit?

   a. Transistor

   b. Capacitor

   c. Diode

   d. Resistor

5. Which one of the following electronic devices protects equipment against sudden changes in power level?

   a. Joule meter

   b. Electromagnetic Interference suppressor

   c. Advanced Configuration and Power Interface (ACPI)

   d. Surge protector

6. True or false? The form factor describes the size, shape, and major features of a hardware component.

7. True or false? Using a soft switch, an OS such as Windows XP can turn off the power to a system after the shutdown procedure is done.

8. True or false? BTX motherboards cannot use an ATX power supply.

9. True or false? Black wire is used for ground in PCs and in DC circuits, as well as in home wiring and in AC circuits.

10. True or false? A power supply is considered a field replaceable unit.

11. A computer case is also known as a(n) _____.

12. Motherboards that support PCI Express and have the 24-pin P1 connector are sometimes called _____ boards.

13. There are two types of backplanes: _____ and _____.

14. The smallest notebook cases are called _____.

15. When replacing a damaged motherboard with a good one, first test the _____.

# Processors and Chipsets

In the previous chapter, you learned about the different form factors used for motherboards. In this chapter, you'll learn about the most important components on the motherboard, the processor, and the chipset. You'll learn how a processor works and about the many different types and brands of processors and chipsets and how to make wise purchasing decisions. A processor must be kept cool, so this chapter covers the various cooling systems used for processors. Although the chipset is embedded on a motherboard, the processor is considered a field replaceable unit. And so you'll learn how to install and upgrade a processor.

# PROCESSORS

A+ ESS
1.1

A+
220-602
1.1

The processor installed on a motherboard and the chipset embedded on the board primarily determine the power and features of the system (see Figure 5-1). In this chapter, you'll learn about processors and chipsets and in the next chapter you'll learn about motherboards.

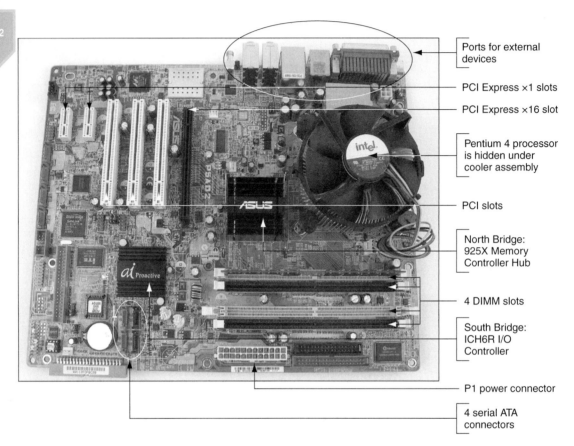

Ports for external devices

PCI Express ×1 slots

PCI Express ×16 slot

Pentium 4 processor is hidden under cooler assembly

PCI slots

North Bridge: 925X Memory Controller Hub

4 DIMM slots

South Bridge: ICH6R I/O Controller

P1 power connector

4 serial ATA connectors

**Figure 5-1** This Asus P5AD2 motherboard uses an Intel 925X chipset with a North Bridge and a South Bridge, and the motherboard has a Pentium 4 processor installed

Most IBM and IBM-compatible computers manufactured today use processors made by Intel (*www.intel.com*) or AMD (*www.amd.com*), or to a lesser degree by Cyrix, which is currently owned by VIA Technologies (*www.via.com.tw*). Processors are rated based on several factors that affect performance and the motherboards that can support them. These factors are listed here:

▲ The system bus speeds the processor supports. Today's front-side buses run at 1066, 800, 533, or 400 MHz. System buses and motherboards are covered in the next chapter.

▲ Processor core frequency measured in gigahertz, such as 3.2 GHz.

▲ Word size, either 32 bits or 64 bits, which is the number of bits a processor can process at one time.

▲ Data path for most computers today, which is 64 bits or 128 bits and is the number of bits a processor can receive at one time.

▲ Multiprocessing ability, which is the ability of a system to do more than one thing at a time. This is accomplished by several means, including two processing units installed on the same die (used by Pentium processors), a motherboard using two processor sockets (supported by Xeon processors), and two processors installed in the same processor housing (called dual-core processing).

◢ The amount of memory included with the processor. Today's processors all have some memory on the processor chip (called a die). Some processors have memory off the die but inside the processor housing, and some processors have memory embedded on the motherboard.

◢ Efficiency and special functionality of programming code. Examples of technologies used by a processor to improve efficiency of executing programming code are Intel's Hyper-Threading and AMD's HyperTransport.

◢ The type of RAM, motherboard, and chipset the processor supports. RAM comes in a variety of modules, speeds, and features, which are all discussed in Chapter 7. The processor must work with the chipset that is embedded on the motherboard. Chipsets are discussed later in this chapter. The processor and the chipset determine what type and how much RAM you can use in the system. And each processor is designed to fit a particular socket or slot on a motherboard.

## HOW A PROCESSOR WORKS

A processor contains three basic components: an input/output (I/O) unit, a control unit, and one or more arithmetic logic units (ALUs), as shown in Figure 5-2. The I/O unit manages data and instructions entering and leaving the processor. The control unit manages all activities inside the processor itself. The ALU does all comparisons and calculations.

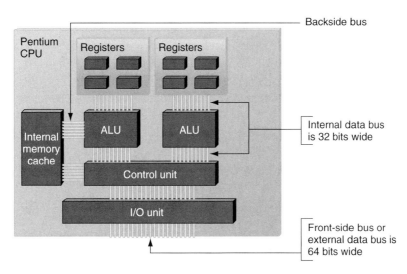

**Figure 5-2** Since the Pentium processor was first released in 1993, the standard has been for a processor to have two arithmetic logic units so that it can process two instructions at once

Registers are small holding areas on the processor chip that work much as RAM does outside the processor. Registers hold counters, data, instructions, and addresses that the ALU is currently processing. In addition to registers, the processor has its own internal memory cache that holds data and instructions waiting to be processed by the ALU. Also notice in Figure 5-2 the existence of the external bus, where data, instructions, addresses, and control signals are sent into and out of the processor. The data portion of the external bus is 64 bits wide. This bus is sometimes called the **front-side bus** (FSB) because it connects to the front side of the processor that faces the outside world. Inside the processor housing, data, instructions, addresses, and control signals travel on the **internal bus**. The data portion of that bus, called the internal data bus, is 32 bits wide. In Figure 5-2, you can see this internal data bus connects to each of the ALUs. The portion of the internal bus that connects the processor to the internal memory cache is called the **back-side bus (BSB)**. The processor's internal bus operates at a much higher frequency than the external bus (system bus).

Let's now turn our attention to the details of several characteristics of processors, including system bus speed, processor speed, data path size, multiprocessing abilities, memory cache, and instruction sets.

## SYSTEM BUS FREQUENCY OR SPEED

Recall that **bus frequency** is the frequency or speed at which data is placed on a bus. Remember also that a motherboard has several buses. Each bus runs at a certain frequency, some faster than others.

Although the motherboard has several buses, only the fastest bus connects directly to the processor. This bus has many names. It's called the front-side bus, the external bus, the **motherboard bus**, or the **system bus**. In the past, the more popular term was system bus, although the current trend is to call it the front-side bus; you see it written in computer ads as the FSB. In this book, we'll call it the system bus or the front-side bus.

Common speeds for the system bus are 1066 MHz, 800 MHz, 533 MHz, 400 MHz, 200 MHz, 133 MHz, and 100 MHz, although the bus can operate at several other speeds, depending on the processor and how the motherboard is configured.

> **Notes**
>
> When you read that Intel supports a motherboard speed of 533 MHz or 800 MHz, the speed refers to the system bus speed. Other slower buses connect to the system bus, which serves as the go-between for other buses and the processor.

## PROCESSOR FREQUENCY OR SPEED

**Processor frequency** is the speed at which the processor operates internally. The first processor used in an IBM PC was the 8088, which worked at about 4.77 MHz, or 4,770,000 clock beats per second. An average speed for a new processor today is about 3.2 GHz, or 3,200,000,000 beats per second. In less than one second, this processor "beats" more times than a human heart beats in a lifetime!

If the processor operates at 3.2 GHz internally but 800 MHz externally, the processor frequency is 3.2 GHz, and the system bus frequency is 800 MHz. In this case, the processor operates at four times the system bus frequency. This factor is called the **multiplier**. If you multiply the system bus frequency by the multiplier, you get the processor frequency:

$$\text{System bus frequency} \times \text{multiplier} = \text{processor frequency}$$

On some motherboards, you must know the value of the multiplier in order to configure the frequency of the processor and system bus. On other motherboards, the frequencies are automatically set by CMOS setup without your intervention. Older boards used jumpers on the motherboard or CMOS setup to set the system bus frequency and multiplier, which then determine the processor frequency. For these older boards, common multipliers were 1.5, 2, 2.5, 3, 3.5, and 4. You must know the documented processor speed in order to set the correct system bus frequency and multiplier, so that the processor runs at the speed for which it is designed.

Newer boards automatically detect the processor speed and adjust the system bus speed accordingly. Your only responsibility is to make sure you install a processor that runs at a speed the motherboard can support.

> **Notes**
>
> Processor frequencies or speeds are rated at the factory and included with the processor documentation. However, sometimes the actual speed of the processor might be slightly higher or lower than the advertised speed.

### Overclocking

For newer motherboards and processors, you can override the default frequencies by changing a setting in CMOS setup. For example, one CMOS setup screen allows you to set the processor frequency at 5%, 10%, 15%, 20%, or 30% higher than the default frequency. Running a motherboard or processor at a higher speed than the manufacturer suggests is called **overclocking** and is not recommended because the speed is not guaranteed to be stable. Also, know that running a processor at a higher-than-recommended speed can result in overheating, which can damage the processor.

## Throttling

Most motherboards and processors offer some protection against overheating so that, if the system overheats, it will throttle down or shut down to prevent the processor from being damaged permanently. If you plan to overclock a system, check CMOS setup for the option to enable automatic throttling. Turn it on so that the processor frequency will automatically decrease if overheating occurs. Also, some processors will throttle back when they begin to overheat in order to protect themselves from damage.

## DATA PATH SIZE AND WORD SIZE

The data path, sometimes called the external data path size, is that portion of the system bus that transports data into the processor. The **data path** in Figure 5-2 is 64 bits wide. The **word size**, sometimes called the internal data path size, is the largest number of bits the processor can process in one operation. Word size of today's processors is 32 bits (4 bytes) or 64 bits (8 bytes). The word size need not be as large as the data path size; some processors can receive more bits than they can process at one time, as in the case of the Pentium in Figure 5-2.

Recall from Chapter 2 that earlier processors always operated in real mode, using a 16-bit word size and data path on the system bus. Later, protected mode was introduced, which uses a 32-bit word size. Most applications written today use 32-bit protected mode, because the most popular processors today for desktop and notebook computers are the Pentiums, which use a 32-bit word size. But this is expected to soon change because Intel and AMD both have 64-bit processors that are currently used in the server market, and AMD has 64-bit processors for the desktop and notebook market.

> **Notes**
>
> To take full advantage of a 64-bit processor, such as the Intel Itanium or the AMD Athlon, software developers must recompile their applications to use 64-bit processing and write operating systems that use 64-bit data transfers. Microsoft provides a 64-bit version of Windows XP that works with the 64-bit processors.

## MULTIPROCESSING, MULTIPLE PROCESSORS, AND DUAL-CORE PROCESSING

CPU designers have come up with several creative ways of doing more than one thing at a time to improve performance. Three methods are popular: multiprocessing, dual processors, and dual-core processing. Multiprocessing is accomplished when a processor contains more than one ALU. Older processors had only a single ALU. Pentiums, and those processors coming after them, have at least two ALUs. With two ALUs, processors can process two instructions at once and, therefore, are true multiprocessing processors.

Because Pentiums have two ALUs, the front-side data bus is 64 bits wide, and the back-side data bus is only 32 bits wide. Because each ALU processes only 32 bits at a time, the industry calls the Pentium a 32-bit processor even though it uses a 64-bit bus externally.

> **Notes**
>
> Recall that Intel has 64-bit processors, called Itaniums, that have a 128-bit front-side bus, and AMD has the Opteron, the Athlon 64, and the Turion 64, all of which are 64-bit processors.

A second method of improving performance is installing more than one processor on a motherboard, creating a **multiprocessor platform**. A motherboard must be designed to support more than one processor by providing more than one processor socket. For example, some motherboards designed for servers have two processor sockets on the board for a dual-processor configuration. The processors installed on these boards must be rated to work in a multiprocessor platform. Some Xeon processors are designed to be used this way. You can install a single Xeon processor in one of the processor sockets, but for improved performance, a second Xeon can be installed in the second socket. In computer ads, a Xeon processor rated to run on a multiprocessor platform is listed as a Xeon MP processor (MP stands for multiprocessor).

The latest advancement in multiple processing is **dual-core processing**. Using this technology, the processor housing contains two processors that operate at the same frequency, but independently of each other. They share the front-side bus, but have independent internal caches. Figure 5-3 shows how dual-core processing is implemented by AMD, which is similar to Intel's configuration used by the Pentium D and Celeron D processors (D stands for dual-core). (For Pentium and Celeron dual-core processors, each of the two processors in the processor housing still use two ALUs.)

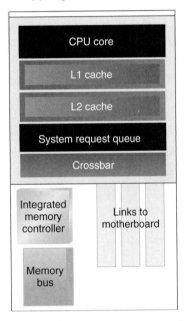 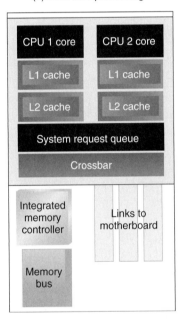

**Figure 5-3**  AMD dual-core processing using two Opteron processors in the single processor housing

## MEMORY CACHE

A **memory cache** is a small amount of RAM (referred to as **static RAM [SRAM]**) that is much faster than the rest of RAM, which is called dynamic RAM (DRAM). SRAM is faster than DRAM because SRAM does not need refreshing and can hold its data as long as power is available. (DRAM loses data rapidly and must be refreshed often.) The processor can process instructions and data faster if they are temporarily stored in SRAM cache. The cache size a processor can support is a measure of its performance, especially during memory-intensive calculations.

To take advantage of the little SRAM available, when the processor requests data or programming code, the memory controller anticipates what the processor will request next and copies that data or programming code to SRAM (see Figure 5-4). Then, if the controller guessed correctly, it can satisfy the processor request from SRAM without accessing the slower DRAM. Under normal conditions, the controller guesses right more than 90 percent of the time and caching is an effective way of speeding up memory access.

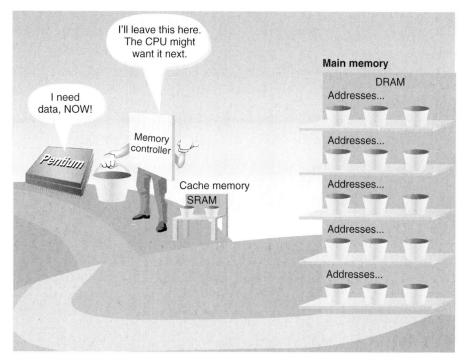

**Figure 5-4** Cache memory (SRAM) is used to temporarily hold data in expectation of what the processor will request next

In the past, SRAM was contained on the motherboards, and upgrading SRAM could be accomplished by adding SRAM to slots on the board. SRAM on a motherboard was contained in individual chips or on a memory module called a cache on a stick (COAST). Figure 5-5 shows an older motherboard supporting the Classic Pentium with 256 K of SRAM installed on the board in two single chips. A COAST slot is available to hold an additional 256 K.

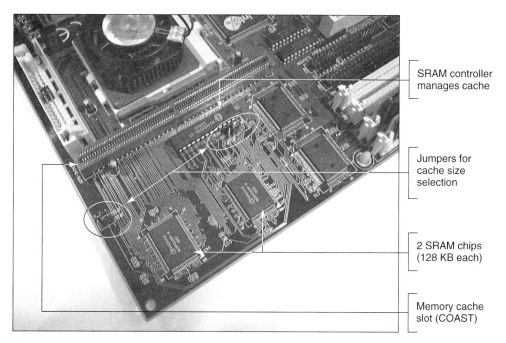

**Figure 5-5** SRAM on this older motherboard is stored in individual chips, and the board also has a COAST slot

Historically, SRAM used these different technologies: burst SRAM, pipelined SRAM, pipelined burst SRAM, and synchronous and asynchronous SRAM.

> **Notes**
>
> When making purchasing decisions about processors, consider that the more L1 or L2 cache the processor contains, generally the better the processor performs.

Most present-day motherboards don't contain SRAM—rather most SRAM is contained inside the processor housing as an embedded function of the processor itself. Processors have a memory cache inside the processor housing on a small circuit board beside the processor chip and also on the processor chip itself. In documentation, the chip is sometimes called a die. A memory cache on the processor chip is called an **internal cache**, a **primary cache**, or a **Level 1 (L1) cache**. A cache outside the processor microchip is called an **external cache**, a secondary cache, or a **Level 2 (L2) cache**.

Some processors use a type of Level 1 cache called **Execution Trace Cache**. For example, the Pentium 4 has 8 K of Level 1 cache used for data and an additional 12 K of Execution Trace Cache containing a list of operations that have been decoded and are waiting to be executed. Many times, a processor decides to follow one branch of operations in a program of instructions rather than another branch. Only branches of operations that the processor has determined will be executed are stored in the Execution Trace Cache, making the execution process faster.

> **Notes**
>
> When SRAM was contained on the motherboard, there was usually room to upgrade SRAM to improve performance. Because SRAM is now inside the processor housing, for today's systems, upgrading SRAM is not normally an option.

L2 caches are usually 128 K, 256 K, 512 K, 1 MB, or 2 MB in size. In the past, all L2 cache was contained on the motherboard, but beginning with the Pentium Pro, some L2 cache has been included inside the processor housing. Figure 5-6 shows two methods in which Intel implements L2 cache inside the processor housing. Using one method, a Pentium has L2 cache stored on a separate microchip within the processor housing, which is called **discrete L2 cache** or **On-Package L2 cache**. The back-side bus servicing this cache runs at half the speed of the processor, which is why Intel advertises this cache as "half speed On-Package L2 cache." Using another method, some Pentiums contain L2 cache directly on the same die as the processor core, making it difficult to distinguish between L1 and L2 cache;

> 👍 **A+ Exam Tip**
>
> The A+ Essentials exam expects you to know the purpose and characteristics of external cache memory.

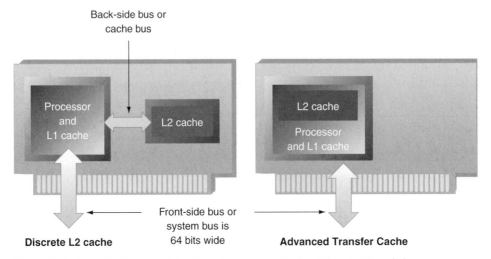

**Figure 5-6** Some Pentiums contain L2 cache on separate dies (discrete L2 cache), and some contain L2 cache on the same die (Advanced Transfer Cache)

this is called **Advanced Transfer Cache (ATC)**. ATC makes it possible for the Pentium to fit on a smaller and less expensive form factor. The ATC bus is 256 bits wide and runs at the same speed as the processor.

If there is L2 cache in the processor housing and additional cache on the motherboard, the cache on the motherboard is called **Level 3 (L3) cache**. In addition, some advanced processors manufactured by AMD have L1, L2, and L3 cache inside the processor housing. In this case, the L3 cache is further removed from the processor than the L2 cache, even though both are inside the processor housing. Table 5-1 summarizes the locations for memory caches.

| Memory Cache | Location |
|---|---|
| L1 cache | On the processor die. All processors today have L1 cache. |
| L2 cache | Inside the processor housing of newer processors, but not as close to the processor as L1 cache. The first processor to contain L2 was the Intel Pentium Pro. |
| L2 cache | On the motherboard of older systems. |
| L3 cache | Inside the processor housing, farther away from the processor than the L2 cache. The Intel Itanium housing contains L3 cache. |
| L3 cache | On the motherboard when there is L2 cache in the processor housing. L3 is used with some AMD processors. |

**Table 5-1**  The locations of memory caches in a system

## INSTRUCTION SET AND MICROCODE

Groups of instructions that accomplish fundamental operations, such as comparing or adding two numbers, are permanently built into the processor chip. Less efficient processors require more steps to perform these simple instructions than do more efficient processors.

These instructions are called **microcode** and the groups of instructions are collectively called the instruction set. Earlier processors use an instruction set called **reduced instruction set computing (RISC)**, and many later processors use a more complex instruction set called **complex instruction set computing (CISC)**.

The Intel Itaniums use a new instruction set called **explicitly parallel instruction computing (EPIC)**. With EPIC, the processor receives a bundle of commands at one time. The bundle also contains instructions for how the processor can execute two commands at the same time (in parallel), using the processor's multiprocessing abilities.

Intel has made several improvements to its instruction sets with multimedia applications in mind. These applications typically perform many repetitive operations, using the same command for a long stream of data. For these applications, MMX (Multimedia Extensions) is used by the Pentium MMX and Pentium II; SSE (Streaming SIMD Extension) is used by the Pentium III; and SSE2, SSE3, and Hyper-Threading for the Pentium 4. SIMD, which stands for "single instruction, multiple data," is a process that allows the CPU to receive a single instruction and then execute it on multiple pieces of data rather than receiving the same instruction each time each piece of data is received.

The Pentium 4 can use MMX, SSE, SSE2, SSE3, and Hyper-Threading. MMX and SSE help with repetitive looping, which happens a lot when the CPU is managing audio and graphics data. SSE also improves on 3D graphics.

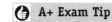 **A+ Exam Tip**

The A+ Essentials exam expects you to be familiar with the characteristics of the different processors. Know the purposes and characteristics of Hyper-Threading, dual-core processing, throttling, and overclocking.

> **Notes**
>
> Some instruction sets are tailored for specific functions, such as the Xeons' and Pentiums' Hyper-Threading Technology designed to improve multitasking performance whereby two threads of a process run in parallel.

AMD, a favorite CPU manufacturer for gamers and hobbyists, uses 3DNow!, a processor instruction set designed to improve performance with 3D graphics and other multimedia data. In addition, AMD uses HyperTransport! to increase bandwidth and PowerNow! to improve a processor's performance and lower power requirements.

## THE INTEL PROCESSORS

Early CPUs by Intel were identified by model numbers: 8088, 8086, 80286, 386, and 486. The model numbers were written with or without the 80 prefix and were sometimes preceded with an *i*, as in 80486, 486, or i486. After the 486, Intel introduced the Pentium processor, and several Intel processors that followed included Pentium in their names. Pentiums are sometimes identified simply with a *P*, as in P4 for Pentium 4.

More recently, Intel began using three-digit processor numbers to aid in identifying its processors. The Pentium processors use *5xx* to *8xx* (for example, Pentium Extreme Edition 840); the Celeron processors use *3xx* (for example, Celeron D Processor 340); and the Pentium M processors use *7xx* (for example, the Pentium M Processor 735). The numbering system along with the processor family name uniquely identify the processor, making it easier to compare processor benefits and features when making purchasing decisions. Generally, the higher the last two digits of the processor number within the processor family, the better the processor, considering the processor speed, system bus speed, architectural features, and cache size.

### OVERVIEW OF THE PENTIUM FAMILY OF PROCESSORS

A Pentium has two ALUs, so it can perform two calculations at once; it is, therefore, a true multiprocessor. Pentiums have a 64-bit external path size and two 32-bit internal paths, one for each ALU. Each ALU uses a 32-bit word size. Because the Celeron and the older Xeon processors have a 32-bit word size and 64-bit path size, they are also included in this discussion as belonging to the Pentium family. However, recent Xeon processors use a 64-bit word size, so they technically don't belong to the Pentium family, but are still included in our discussion.

Table 5-2 lists the eight types of Pentium processors: Classic Pentium, Pentium MMX, Pentium Pro, Pentium II, Xeon, Celeron, Pentium III, and Pentium 4. Within each type, there are several variations of processors. Earlier variations of the Pentium II processor included the Celeron and Xeon. At first, Intel produced a family of processors called the Pentium Xeon, but now the Xeon is considered by Intel to be a separate group of processors. The Xeon processors are intended to be used in high-end workstations and servers.

> **Notes**
>
> The Pentium 4 processors use full-speed Advanced Transfer Cache. The Pentium III processors use either ATC or half-speed On-Package cache. The Pentium II processors use half-speed On-Package cache.

### OLDER PENTIUMS NO LONGER SOLD BY INTEL

You need to be familiar with the older Pentiums that are no longer sold by Intel because many are still in use. The first Pentium to be manufactured by Intel was the Classic Pentium. Occasionally, you see a 166-MHz Classic Pentium system still supported in a corporation setting because it works just fine and runs a legacy application.

A+ ESS
1.1

| Processor | Processor Speeds (MHz or GHz) | System Bus Speeds (MHz) | Description |
|---|---|---|---|
| Classic Pentium | 60 to 200 MHz | 60, 66 | 16K L1 cache |
| Pentium MMX | 133 to 300 MHz | 66 | 32K L1 cache |
| Pentium Pro | 150 to 200 MHz | 60, 66 | 16K L1 and 256K, 512K, or 1 MB L2 cache |
| Pentium II | 233 to 450 MHz | 66, 100 | 32K L1 and 256K or 512K L2 cache |
| Pentium II Xeon | 400 or 450 MHz | 100 | 32K or 512K, 1MB, or 2MB L2 cache |
| Pentium III | 450 MHz to 1.33 GHz | 100, 133 | 32K L1 and 512K unified, nonblocking L2 cache or 256K L2 Advanced Transfer Cache |
| Pentium III Xeon | 600 MHz to 1 GHz | 100 or 133 | 32K L1 and 256K, 1 MB, or 2 MB L2 Advanced Transfer Cache |
| Celeron | 850 MHz to 2.9 GHz | 400, 533 | 32K Execution Trace Cache (ETC) and 128K or 256K Advanced Transfer L2 cache. Uses FC-PGA2 package. Installs in an mPGA478 socket. |
| Pentium 4 | 1.4 GHz to 3.06 GHz | 400, 533 | ETC L1 and 256K, 512K, or 1 MB L2 Advanced Transfer Cache, uses FC-PGA4, mPGA478, FC-PGA2, PPGA INT3, or PPGA INT2 packages, and DDR, Dual Channel DDR, or RDRAM memory. Installs in a 423-pin or 478-pin socket. |
| Xeon | 1.8 GHz to 3.2 GHz | 400, 533, 800 | ETC L1 and 512K to 2 MB L2 cache and none, 1MB, or 2 MB L3 cache. Uses Quad Channel DDR or DDR2 RAM. Can use dual-core processing. Uses FC-mPGA or int-microPGA package in a 603-pin or 604-pin socket. Newer Xeons are 64-bit processors. |
| Xeon MP | 1.4 GHz to 3.66 GHz | 400, 667 | ETC L1 and 256K, 512K, or 1 MB L2 cache and 512K to 8 MB L3 cache. Can use dual-core processing. Uses Quad Channel DDR or DDR2 RAM or Dual Channel DDR RAM. Uses FC-mPGA4 or int-microPGA package in a 603-pin or 604-pin socket. Some are 64-bit processors. |
| Celeron D 320 to 351 | 2.4 GHz to 3.2 GHz | 533 | ETC L1 and 256K L2 cache. Uses an FC-LGA, FC-PGA478, FC-PGA4, or FC-LGA4 package. Installs in an LGA775 land socket or mPGA478 pin socket. |
| Pentium 4 with HT Technology, 520 to 670 | 2.4 GHz to 3.8 GHz | 800 | ETC L1 and 512K to 2 MB L2 cache. Uses an FC-PGA2, FC-PGA4, or FC-LGA package, and installs in an LGA775 land socket. Uses DDR, Dual Channel DDR, or Dual Channel DDR2 RAM. |
| Pentium D, 820, 830, 840, 920, 930, 940, 950 | 2.8 GHz to 3.4 GHz | 800 | 2 MB or 4MB L2 cache. Dual-core processor uses an FC-LGA package and installs in an LGA775 socket. Uses Dual Channel DDR2 RAM. |

Table 5-2   The Intel desktop Pentium and Xeon family of processors

A+ ESS
1.1

| Processor | Processor Speeds (MHz or GHz) | System Bus Speeds (MHz) | Description |
|---|---|---|---|
| Pentium Extreme Edition, 840, 955 | 3.2 GHz to 3.46 GHz | 800, 1066 | 2 MB or 4 MB L2 cache. Dual-core processor uses an FC-LGA package and 955x or 975x chipset. Uses Dual Channel DDR2 RAM and installs in a LGA775 socket. |
| Pentium 4 Extreme Edition with HT | 3.2 GHz to 3.73 GHz | 800, 1066 | ETC L1 and 512K or 2 MB L2 and 2 MB L3 cache. Uses an FC-LGA, mPGA478, or FC-PGA2 package. Installs in a 775-land or 478-pin socket. Uses Dual Channel DDR and Dual Channel DDR2 RAM. |

**Table 5-2** The Intel desktop Pentium and Xeon family of processors (continued)

The Pentium MMX (Multimedia Extension) targeted the home game and multimedia market, and the Pentium Pro and Pentium II targeted the computing-intensive workstation and server market. The Pentium II was the first processor to use a slot (slot 1) instead of a socket to connect to the motherboard (processor sockets and slots are covered later in the chapter). Intel patented slot 1, thus attempting to force its competitors to stay with the slower socket technology as they developed equivalent processors.

The Pentium III (see Figure 5-7) uses either a slot or a socket and runs with the 100-MHz or 133-MHz system bus with a processor speed up to 1.33 GHz. The Pentium III introduced Intel's performance enhancement called SSE, for Streaming SIMD Extensions. (SIMD stands for single instruction, multiple data, and is a method MMX uses to speed up multimedia processing.) SSE is an instruction set designed to provide better multimedia processing than MMX.

**Figure 5-7** This Pentium III is contained in a SECC cartridge that stands on its end in slot 1 on a motherboard

The Pentium III Xeon is a high-end Pentium III processor that runs on the 100-MHz system bus. It was designed for midrange servers and high-end workstations. It uses a 330-pin slot called the SC330 (slot connector 330), sometimes called slot 2, and is contained within a cartridge called a Single Edge Contact Cartridge (SECC).

## CELERON

The Celeron processor is a low-end Pentium processor that targets the low-end PC multimedia and home market segments. Celerons use a 478-pin socket or a 775-land socket. You'll see examples of these sockets later in the chapter. Celerons use Level 2 cache within the processor housing and work well with the most common Windows applications. The more recent Celeron D processor uses dual-core processing.

## PENTIUM 4

The Pentium 4 processor (see Figure 5-8) currently runs at up to 3.8 GHz and has undergone several improvements since it was introduced. The earlier Pentium 4 processors use a 423-pin or 478-pin socket, and later Pentium 4 processors use Socket 775.

**Figure 5-8**  The Pentiums are sometimes sold boxed with a cooler assembly

The first Pentium 4 processors increased performance for multimedia applications such as digital video, as well as for new Web technologies, using a processor architecture Intel calls NetBurst. Later Pentium 4 processors use Hyper-Threading Technology. The motherboard and the operating system must both support HT Technology for it to be effective. Windows XP supports HT Technology, but Windows 2000 and Windows 9x/Me do not.

One of the latest Intel releases in the Pentium family is the Pentium 4 Extreme Edition with HT Technology, which is designed for high performance and can run on a 1066 MHz front-side bus. Dual-core processing is used by the Pentium D and Pentium 4

> **Notes**
>
> When first setting up a system using a Pentium 4 with HT Technology and Windows XP, check CMOS setup to verify that the motherboard support for HT Technology is enabled. If you use a Pentium 4 with HT Technology and an operating system other than Windows XP, use CMOS setup to disable HT Technology to avoid an unstable system. Remember that you can access CMOS setup by pressing a key at startup.

Extreme Edition. The latest Pentium processors all use the latest memory module type, DDR2. DDR2 is covered in Chapter 7.

## MOBILE PENTIUM PROCESSORS

Processors currently sold by Intel designed for mobility are the Pentium M, Mobile Pentium 4 with Hyper-Threading Technology, Mobile Pentium 4, Mobile Pentium 4 Processor-M, Celeron M, and Mobile Celeron. A Pentium M processor is the processor component of the Intel Centrino technology, which is an integrated component that includes the processor, chipset, and wireless LAN all bundled together for a notebook system. The Pentium M processor runs at up to 2.26 GHz, using a 533- or 400-MHz system bus. The Mobile Pentium 4 processor runs at up to 3.46 GHz, using a 533-MHz system bus. Both processors support low-voltage technologies designed to produce less heat, run on less power, and be housed in smaller and lighter notebooks.

## XEON PROCESSORS

Originally, the Xeon (pronounced "Zee-on") processors were 32-bit Pentium processors, but more recently, Intel is producing 64-bit Xeon processors that are no longer considered part of the Pentium family of processors. Xeons use Hyper-Threading Technology and dual-core processing and are designed to be used on servers and high-end workstations in a corporate environment. The Xeon can be used with dual-processor motherboards, and the Xeon MP (multiprocessing) can be used in a server that contains more than two processors. The 64-bit Xeon processors are more powerful than the Pentiums, but are not as robust as the Itaniums.

## THE ITANIUMS

Intel's first 64-bit processors for microcomputers are the Itaniums. The newest version of the Itanium, the Itanium 2, is shown in Figure 5-9. When installed, the processor fits inside a protective package called the PAC 611. Itaniums provide backward compatibility with older 32-bit applications, although the older applications are not able to take full advantage of the Itanium's capabilities. The Itaniums don't use Hyper-Threading, but do use EPIC, a newer instruction set than CISC used by the Pentium family of processors.

Table 5-3 shows the specifications for the two Itanium processors. The Itanium uses an L1 cache on the processor die and L2 and L3 caches on the processor board. The L2 cache is closer to the processor than the L3 cache. Even though the system bus speeds seem slow, know that the data path is 128 bits, which makes for a high-performance bus.

**Figure 5-9** The Itanium 2

## AMD PROCESSORS

Processors by Advanced Micro Devices, Inc., or AMD (*www.amd.com*), are popular in the game and hobbyist markets, and are generally less expensive than comparable Intel processors. Whereas Intel has chosen to stick with 32-bit Pentium

A+ ESS
1.1

| Processor | Current Processor Speeds | L1 Cache | L2 Cache | L3 Cache | System Bus Speed |
|-----------|--------------------------|----------|----------|----------|------------------|
| Itanium | 733 and 800 MHz | 32K | 96K | 2 MB or 4 MB | 266 MHz |
| Itanium 2 | 900 MHz to 1.66 GHz | 32K | 256K | 1.5 MB to 9 MB | 400 or 533 MHz |

**Table 5-3** The Intel Itanium processors

processors for the desktop and notebook market, AMD has concentrated on the 64-bit desktop and mobile processor market since it was first to market with the first 64-bit processor for the desktop, the Athlon 64. Older and newer AMD processors are discussed next.

## OLDER AMD PROCESSORS

Table 5-4 lists AMD desktop processors (*www.amd.com*) no longer sold by AMD. However, you need to be aware of them because many are still in use. AMD processors use different sockets and slots than do Intel processors, so the motherboard must be designed for one manufacturer's processor or the other, but not both. Many motherboard manufacturers offer two comparable motherboards—one for an Intel processor and one for an AMD processor. Earlier AMD processors used a 321-pin socket called Super Socket 7, which supports an AGP video slot and 100-MHz system bus. The AMD Athlon can use a 242-pin slot called Slot A, which looks like the Intel slot 1 and has 242 pins. Also, the AMD Athlon and the AMD Duron use a 462-pin socket called Socket A.

| Processor | Latest Clock Speeds (MHz or GHz) | Compares to | System Bus Speed (MHz) | Package Type | Socket or Slot |
|-----------|----------------------------------|-------------|------------------------|--------------|----------------|
| AMD-K6-2 | 166 to 500 MHz | Pentium II, Celeron | 66, 95, 100 | CPGA | Socket 7 or Super Socket 7 |
| AMD-K6-III | 350 to 450 MHz | Pentium II | 100 | CPGA | Super Socket 7 |
| Duron | 1 GHz to 1.3 GHz | Celeron | 200 | CPGA or OPGA | Socket A |
| Athlon | Up to 1.9 GHz | Pentium III | 200 | Card | Slot A |
| Athlon Model 4 | Up to 1.4 GHz | Pentium III | 266 | CPGA | Socket A |

**Table 5-4** Older AMD processors

## CURRENT AMD PROCESSORS

AMD processors currently sold by AMD are listed next:

◢ Processors designed for desktops include the Athlon 64 X2 Dual-Core (uses 939-pin socket), the Athlon 64 FX (uses a 939-pin or 940-pin socket), the Athlon 64 (uses a 754-pin or 939-pin socket), the Athlon XP (uses Socket A), and the 32-bit Sempron processor. The Sempron is comparable to the Celeron and uses Socket A or a 754-pin socket.

▲ Two processors designed for high-end workstations or servers are the Athlon MP, which uses Socket A, and the Opteron, which uses dual-core processing and Socket 940.

▲ Processors designed for notebooks include the Turion 64 Mobile, Mobile Athlon 64, Athlon 64 for Notebooks, Mobile Athlon XP-M, and Mobile Sempron.

AMD claims that the Athlon 64 X2 Dual-Core processor (see Figure 5-10) outperforms other AMD processors by about 30% because of its dual-core processing feature.

**Figure 5-10**  AMD Athlon 64 X2 Dual-Core processor

## VIA AND CYRIX PROCESSORS

Table 5-5 shows the performance ratings of older VIA and Cyrix processors. When VIA (*www.via.com.tw*) purchased Cyrix, it introduced a new processor, the VIA C3, which is similar to, but faster than, the Cyrix III processor (see Figure 5-11). The Cyrix and VIA processors use the same sockets as earlier Pentium processors. The VIA C3 also comes in a small EBGA package and even smaller nanoBGA package intended for use in personal electronic devices.

| Processor | Latest Clock Speeds (MHz) | Compares to | System Bus Speed (MHz) | Socket or Slot |
|-----------|---------------------------|-------------|------------------------|----------------|
| Cyrix M II | 300, 333, 350 | Pentium II, Celeron | 66, 75, 83, 95, 100 | Socket 7 |
| Cyrix III | 433 to 533 | Celeron, Pentium III | 66, 100, 133 | Socket 370 |
| VIA C3 | Up to 1.4 GHz | Celeron | 100, 133, 200 | Socket 370 |

**Table 5-5**  VIA and Cyrix processors

VIA is now concentrating on developing processors for personal electronics and the embedded device market. Current VIA processors include the following:

▲ The VIA C7 processor uses the nanoBGA2 package and is designed for personal electronic devices, home theater equipment, and desktop computers.

▲ The VIA C7-M uses the nanoBGA2 package and is designed for ultrasmall notebook computers.

**Figure 5-11** VIA C3 processor

## PROCESSOR PACKAGES

In the computer industry, the processor's housing is called the processor package. A processor package can be thin and lay flat in a socket such as the Pentium package shown in Figure 5-8, or the package can be a thicker cartridge type package such as the one shown in Figure 5-7. The cartridge package can have edge connectors similar to an expansion card and stand up on its end in a slot or it can lay flat in a socket. There are many variations of both kinds of packages used for desktop PCs and high-end workstations. In this section, you'll learn about these flat and thin packages and cartridge packages.

## FLAT AND THIN PROCESSOR PACKAGES

Most processor packages are flat and thin and can be square or rectangular. The package lays flat in a socket on the motherboard. The connectors on the bottom of the package can be pins or lands. You can see lands embedded on the bottom of the processor in Figure 5-11. Compare these lands to the pins on the bottom of the processor shown in Figure 5-12. The lands are the newer and preferred method of contact because pins can sometimes be bent when installing the processor. The processor package must fit the socket it is intended for.

Flat and thin processor packages used by Intel are listed next:

**Figure 5-12** This Intel Celeron processor is housed in the PPGA form factor, which has pins on the underside that insert into Socket 370

▲ *PPGA (Plastic Pin Grid Array)*. The processor is housed in a square box designed to fit flat into Socket 370 (see Figure 5-12). Pins are on the underside of the flat housing, and heat sinks or fans can be attached to the top of the housing by using a thermal plate or heat spreader. The early Celeron processors used this package with 370 pins.

◢ *PPGA INT2 and PPGA INT3.* These packages are used by Pentium 4s and have 423 pins.

◢ *PGA (Pin Grid Array).* Pins on the bottom of this package are staggered and can be inserted only one way into the socket. It is used by the Xeon with 603 pins. When used by the Pentium 4, it has 423 pins and is called the PGA 423 package.

◢ *int-microPGA 603.* This package has 603 pins and is used by the Xeon processors. It uses a zero-insertion force (ZIF) socket.

◢ *FC-mPGA and FC-mPGA4.* This package has 604 pins and is used by the Xeon processors.

◢ *OOI or OLGA (Organic Land Grid Array).* Used by some Pentium 4s, this 423-pin package is similar to the PGA package but is designed to dissipate heat faster.

◢ *FC-PGA (Flip Chip Pin Grid Array).* This package looks like the PPGA package and uses 370 pins in Socket 370. It is called a flip chip package because the processor is turned upside down so that the CPU die itself is on top of the processor housing, making it possible to apply a thermal solution directly to the die. Pins on the bottom of the package are staggered. Some Pentium III and Celeron processors use this package.

◢ *FC-PGA2 (Flip Chip Pin Grid Array 2).* This package is similar to the FC-PGA package, but has an integrated heat sink. When used by a Pentium III or Celeron processor, it has 370 pins. When used by the Pentium 4, it has 478 pins.

◢ *mPGA 478.* This package has 478 pins and is used by the Celeron and Pentium 4.

◢ *FC-LGA775 (Flip-Chip Land Grid Array), FC-LGA, or FC-LGA4.* This is the newest Pentium package used by the Pentium 4s and Celerons. It uses 775 lands rather than pins.

AMD has its own processor packages different from Intel. These flat and thin packages are listed next:

◢ *CPGA (Ceramic Pin Grid Array).* This is a flat package with pins on the underside used by several AMD processors, including the Duron, AMD-K6-2, and AMD-K6-III. Number of pins varies among processors.

◢ *OPGA (Organic Pin Grid Array).* This package is used by the AMD Athlon MP and Athlon XP and some models of the AMD Duron.

◢ *μPGA (Micro Pin Grid Array).* This package is used by the AMD 64-bit processors, including the AMD Opteron, Athlon 64 X2 Dual Core, Athlon 64, and Athlon 64 FX.

## CARTRIDGE PROCESSOR PACKAGES

Cartridge processor packages can stand up on their end and install in a slot on the motherboard or lay flat in a socket. Figure 5-13 shows a Pentium II with a heat sink and fan attached to it. In the figure, slot 1 on the motherboard has the arms of the slot in the upright position ready to receive the processor.

The following cartridge packages used by Intel stand on their end in a slot:

◢ *SECC (Single Edge Contact Cartridge).* The processor housing stands up on its end and inserts in a slot on the motherboard. The processor is completely covered with a black plastic housing, and a heat sink and fan are attached to the housing. You can't see the circuit board or edge connector in a SECC package. The Pentium II and Pentium III use a SECC package in slot 1 with 242 contacts. The Pentium II Xeon and Pentium III Xeon use a SECC with 330 contacts. You can see the SECC in Figure 5-7.

◢ *SECC2 (Single Edge Contact Cartridge, version 2).* This is similar to the SECC, but it does not have the heat sink thermal plate. Also, the edge connector on the processor

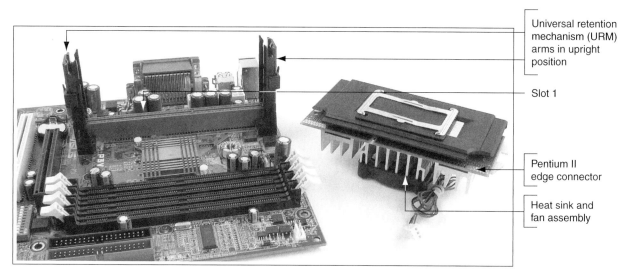

**Figure 5-13** Pentium II with heat sink and fan attached goes in slot 1 on this motherboard

circuit board is visible at the bottom of the housing. The Pentium II and Pentium III use the SECC2 package with 242 contacts.

▲ *SEP (Single Edge Processor)*. This package is similar to the SECC package, but the black plastic housing does not completely cover the processor, making the circuit board visible at the bottom of the housing. The first Celeron processors used the SEP package in slot 1. It has 242 contacts.

A cartridge package for a processor that lays flat in a socket on the motherboard is called a flat cartridge package. There is only one entry in this category:

▲ *PAC (Pin Array Cartridge)*. The Itaniums use this flat cartridge, which is about the size of an index card (see Figure 5-14). The Itanium uses the PAC418 socket, which has 418 pins, and the Itanium2 uses the PAC611 socket, which has 611 pins.

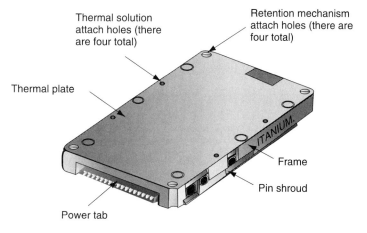

**Figure 5-14** 418-pin PAC processor package used by the Itanium

Every Intel processor has a specification number called a spec number printed somewhere on the processor. If you can find and read the number (sometimes difficult), you can use the Intel Web site (*processorfinder.intel.com*) to identify the exact processor. For example, suppose you read SL7KM on the processor. Figure 5-15 shows the results of searching the Intel site for this processor information.

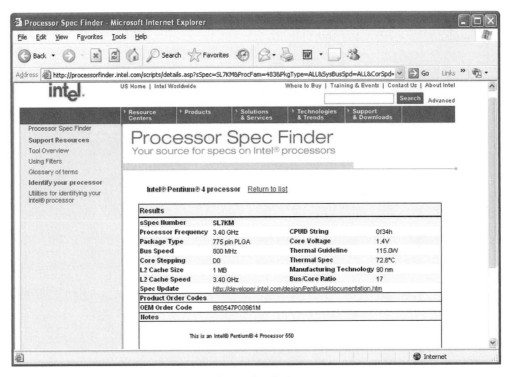

**Figure 5-15** Processor Spec Finder using the Intel Web site

A+ ESS
1.1

## PROCESSOR SOCKETS AND SLOTS

A processor connects to the motherboard by way of a socket (shown in Figure 5-1 with processor installed) or a slot (shown in Figure 5-13). The type of socket or slot supplied by the motherboard for the processor must match that required by the processor. Most processors today come in more than one package, so it is important to match the processor package to the motherboard that has the right socket or slot. Table 5-6 lists several types of sockets and slots used by Intel, AMD, and VIA processors. Early processors from different manufacturers used the same sockets, but later processors require proprietary sockets and slots.

### TYPES OF SOCKETS

Earlier Pentiums used a **pin grid array (PGA)** socket, with pins aligned in uniform rows around the socket. Later sockets use a **staggered pin grid array (SPGA)**, with pins staggered

| Connector Name | Used by Processor | Description |
| --- | --- | --- |
| Socket 4 | Classic Pentium 60/66 | 273 pins, 21 x 21 PGA grid supplies 5 V |
| Socket 5 | Classic Pentium 75/90/100/120/133 | 320 pins, 37 x 37 SPGA grid supplies 3.3 V |
| Socket 7 | Pentium MMX, Fast Classic Pentium, AMD K5, AMD K5, Cyrix M | 321 pins, 37 x 37 SPGA grid supplies 2.5 V to 3.3 V |
| Super Socket 7 | AMD K5-2, AMD K5-III | 321 pins, 37 x 37 SPGA grid supplies 2.5 V to 3.3 V |
| Socket 8 | Pentium Pro | 387 pins 24 x 26 SPGA grid supplies 3.3 V |

**Table 5-6** Processor sockets and slots for desktop computers

| Connector Name | Used by Processor | Description |
|---|---|---|
| Socket 370 or PGA370 Socket | Pentium III FC-PGA, Celeron PPGA, Cyrix III | 370 pins in a 37 x 37 SPGA grid supplies 1.5 V or 2 V |
| Slot 1 or SC242 | Pentium II, Pentium III | 242 pins in 2 rows, rectangular shape supplies 2.8 V and 3.3 V |
| Slot A | AMD Athlon | 242 pins in 2 rows, rectangular shape supplies 1.3 V to 2.05 V |
| Socket A or Socket 462 | AMD Athlon and Duron | 462 pins, SPGA grid, rectangular shape supplies 1.5 V to 1.85 V |
| Slot 2 or SC330 | Pentium II Xeon, Pentium III Xeon | 330 pins in 2 rows, rectangular shape supplies 1.5 V to 3.5 V |
| Socket 423 | Pentium 4 | 423 pins, 39 x 39 SPGA grid supplies 1.7 V and 1.75 V |
| Socket 478 | Pentium 4, Celeron | 478 pins in a dense micro PGA (mPGA) supplies 1.7 V and 1.75 V |
| Socket PAC418 | Itanium | 418 pins supplies 3.3 V |
| Socket PAC611 | Itanium 2 | 611 pins supplies 3.3 V |
| Socket 603 and 604 | Xeon, Xeon DP, and Xeon MP | 603 pins or 604 pins supply 1.5 and 1.7 V |
| Sockets 754, 939, and 940 | Athlon 64, Sempron, Opteron, and Athlon 64 FX | 754, 939, or 940 pins; Socket 754 is the most current socket |
| Socket LGA775 | Pentium 4, Celeron | 775 lands, not pins, and supplies 1.5 to 1.6 V |

**Table 5-6** Processor sockets and slots for desktop computers (continued)

over the socket to squeeze more pins into a small space. The latest Intel socket uses a **land grid array (LGA)** that uses lands rather than pins. This socket is called the LGA775 socket. It has 775 lands and is shown with the socket lever and top open in Figure 5-16.

PGA, SPGA, and LGA sockets are all square or nearly square. Earlier processor sockets, called **dual inline package (DIP)** sockets, were rectangular with two rows of pins down each side. DIP and some PGA sockets, called **low insertion force (LIF) sockets,** were somewhat troublesome to install because it was difficult to apply even force when inserting the processor in the socket. Current processor sockets, called **zero insertion force (ZIF) sockets,** have a small lever on the side that lifts the processor up and out of the socket. Push the lever down and the processor moves into its pin or land connectors with equal force over the entire housing. With this method, you can more easily remove and replace the processor if necessary.

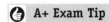

**A+ Exam Tip**

The A+ Essentials exam expects you to be familiar with the processor sockets in use today.

## TYPES OF SLOTS

Slots were used a few years back with some cartridge packages by Intel and AMD, but all processors sold today use sockets. Slot 1, Slot A, and slot 2 are all designed to accommodate processors using SEP or SECC housings that stand on end much like an expansion card. Clips on each side of the slot secure the processor in the slot. You can attach a heat sink or cooling fan to the side of the processor case.

Plastic cover
protects the
socket when
it's not in use

**Figure 5-16** Socket LGA775 is the latest Intel socket

Note that some motherboards with a slot 1 can accommodate processors that use flat packages, such as the Celeron housed in a PPGA package, by using a riser processor card (see Figure 5-17). The riser card inserts into slot 1, and the Celeron processor inserts into Socket 370 on the riser card. This feature, sometimes called a slocket, allows you to upgrade an older Pentium II system to the faster Celeron. Always consult the motherboard documentation to learn which processors the board can support.

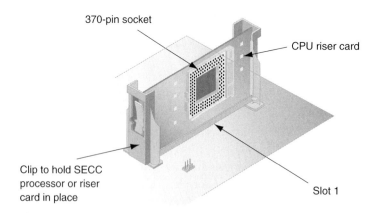

370-pin socket

CPU riser card

Clip to hold SECC
processor or riser
card in place

Slot 1

**Figure 5-17** A riser card can be used to install a Celeron processor into a motherboard with slot 1

Later in the chapter, you'll learn to install a processor on the motherboard, using both a socket and a slot. We now turn our attention to the chipset.

## THE CHIPSET

Recall from Chapter 1 that a chipset is a set of chips on the motherboard that collectively controls the memory cache, external buses, and some peripherals. Intel makes the most popular chipsets; Table 5-7 lists the currently available Intel chipsets.

**5**

| Common Name | Model Number | Processors Supported | System Bus Speed Supported | Memory Supported |
|---|---|---|---|---|
| "E" chipset family | E8870 | Up to four Itanium 2 processors | 400 MHz | DDR |
| | E8500 | Up to four Xeon MP processors | 667 MHz | DDR 266/333 or DDR2 400 |
| | E7525, E7520 | Dual 64-bit Xeon, Xeon | 800 MHz | DDR 333 and Dual Channel DDR2-400, DDR 266 |
| | E7505, E7501, E7500 | Dual Xeon processors | 400 MHz or 533 MHz | Dual Channel DDR 266 |
| | E7320 | Dual 64-bit Xeon, Xeon | 800 MHz | Dual Channel DDR2-400 and Dual Channel DDR 266 |
| | E7230 | Pentium 4 with HT, Pentium D | 1066 MHz or 800 MHz | Unbuffered Dual-Channel DDR2-667, 533, 400 |
| | E7221, E7210 | Pentium 4, Pentium 4 with HT | 800 MHz or 533 MHz | Unbuffered Dual-Channel DDR2-533, DDR2-400, DDR-400, DDR333/266 |
| | E7205 | Pentium 4, Pentium 4 with HT | 533 MHz or 400 MHz | Dual-Channel DDR 266 |
| i900 Express Series | 955X | Pentium Extreme Edition, Pentium D, Pentium 4 Extreme Edition with HT, Pentium 4 with HT | 1066 MHz or 800 MHz | Dual-Channel DDR2 |
| | 945G, 945P | Pentium D, Pentium 4 with HT, and all other System Bus Pentium processors | 1066 MHz, 800 MHz, or 533 MHz | Dual-Channel DDR2 |
| | 925XE | Pentium 4 | 1066 MHz or 800 MHz | Dual-Channel DDR2 533/400 |
| | 925X | Pentium 4, Pentium 4 Extreme Edition | 800 MHz | Dual-Channel DDR2 533/400 |
| | 915P, 915G, 915GV | Pentium 4 | 800 MHz, 533 MHz | Dual-Channel DDR2 533/400, DDR 400/333 |
| | 915GL, 915PL | Pentium 4 or Celeron D | 800 MHz or 533 MHz | Dual-Channel DDR 400/333, DDR 400/333 |

**Table 5-7** Intel chipsets

A+ ESS
1.1

| Common Name | Model Number | Processors Supported | System Bus Speed Supported | Memory Supported |
|---|---|---|---|---|
| | 910GL | Pentium 4, Celeron, Celeron D | 533 MHz | Dual-Channel DDR 400/333 |
| i800 Series | 875P | Pentium 4 | 800 MHz or 533 MHz | Dual-Channel DDR 400/ 333/266 |
| | 865G, 865PE, or 865GV, 865P, 848P | Pentium 4, Celeron, or Celeron D | 800 MHz, 533 MHz, or 400 MHz | Dual-Channel DDR 400/333/ 266 or DDR 400/333/266 |
| | 860 | Dual Xeon DP processors | 400 MHz | PC800/600 RDRAM |
| | 850E, 850 | Pentium 4 | 533 MHz or 400 MHz | PC1066/800/ 600 RDRAM |
| | 845, 845E, 845G, 845GL, 845PE, 845GE, 845GV | Pentium 4 or Celeron | 533 MHz or 400 MHz | DDR 333/266/ 200, PC133 SDRAM |
| | 840 | Dual Pentium III or Pentium III Xeon | 133 MHz or 100 MHz | PC800/600 RDRAM |
| | 820, 820E | Dual Pentium III or Pentium II | 133 MHz or 100 MHz | PC800/700/600 RDRAM |
| | 815, 815E, 815EP, or 815P, 815EG, 815G | Celeron or Pentium III | 133 MHz, 100 MHz, or 66 MHz | PC133/100/66 SDRAM |
| | 810E2, 810E, 810 | Celeron or Pentium III | 133 MHz, 100 MHz, or 66 MHz | PC100/66 SDRAM |

**Table 5-7** Intel chipsets (continued)

The types of memory listed in the table that are supported by these chipsets are explained in detail in Chapter 7.

Beginning with the Intel i800 series of chipsets, the interconnection between buses is done using a hub interface architecture, in which all I/O buses connect to a hub, which connects to the system bus. This hub is called the hub interface, and the architecture is called Accelerated Hub Architecture (see Figure 5-18). The fast end of the hub, which contains the graphics and memory controller, connects to the system bus and is called the hub's **North Bridge**. The slower end of the hub, called the **South Bridge**, contains the I/O controller hub. All I/O devices, except display and memory, connect to the hub by using the slower South Bridge. On a motherboard, when you see two major chips for the chipset, one is controlling the North Bridge and the other is controlling the South Bridge (refer to Figure 5-1).

Table 5-8 lists manufacturers of chipsets. Currently, Intel dominates the chipset market for several reasons: It knows more about its own Intel processors than other manufacturers do, and it produces the chipsets most compatible with the Pentium family of processors. Intel's investment in research and development also led to the creation of the PCI bus, the universal serial bus, the AGP, and more recently, the Accelerated Hub Architecture.

A+ ESS
1.1

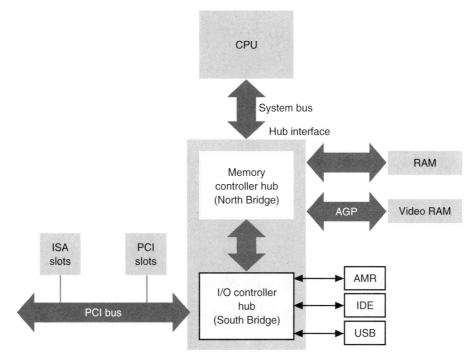

**Figure 5-18** Using Intel 800 series Accelerated Hub Architecture, a hub interface is used to connect slower I/O buses to the system bus

| Company | URL |
|---|---|
| ALi, Inc. | *www.ali.com.tw* |
| AMD | *www.amd.com* |
| Intel Corporation | *www.intel.com* |
| NVIDIA Corporation | *www.nvidia.com* |
| Silicon Integrated Systems Corp. (known as SiS) | *www.sis.com* |
| QuickLogic Corporation | *www.quicklogic.com* |
| Texas Instruments | *www.ti.com* |
| VIA Technologies, Inc. | *www.via.com.tw* |

**Table 5-8** Chipset manufacturers

Chipsets generate heat, but not as much heat as a processor generates. Most chipsets today have a heat sink installed on top that is appropriate to keep the chipset cool. These heat sinks are considered part of the motherboard and you should never have to replace or install one. However, when you install a processor, you must also install whatever cooler is necessary to keep the processor cool. We now turn our attention to heat sinks and cooling fans used for processors.

## HEAT SINKS AND COOLING FANS

A+
220-602
1.3

Because a processor generates so much heat, computer systems use a cooling assembly to keep temperatures below the Intel maximum limit of 185 degrees Fahrenheit/85 degrees Celsius (see Figure 5-19).

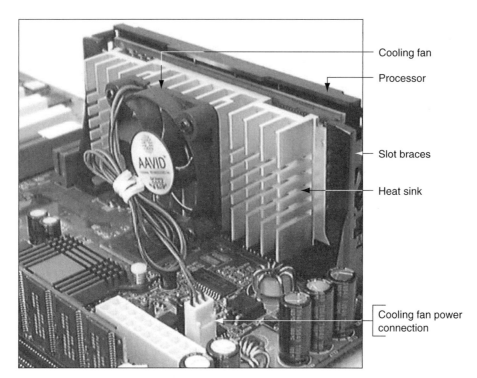

Figure 5-19 A processor cooling fan mounts on the top or side of the processor housing and is powered by an electrical connection to the motherboard

Good processor cooling fans maintain a temperature of 90–110 degrees F (32–43 degrees C). At one time, processor cooling fans were optional equipment used to prevent system errors and to prolong the life of the processor. Today's power-intensive processors installed on ATX motherboards require one or more cooling fans to maintain a temperature that will not damage the processor. High-end systems can have as many as seven or eight fans mounted inside the computer case. Using the BTX form factor, fewer fans are required and the processor might only have a heat sink sitting on top of it. Ball-bearing cooling fans last longer than other kinds.

The cooling fan usually fits on top of the processor with a wire or plastic clip. Sometimes a creamlike thermal compound is placed between the fan and the processor. This compound eliminates air pockets between the heat sink and processor, helping to draw heat off the processor. The thermal compound transmits heat better than air and makes an airtight connection between the fan and the processor. The fan is equipped with a power connector that connects to one of the power cables coming from the power supply or to a connector on the motherboard.

A processor might use a heat sink in addition to a cooling fan. A **heat sink** is a clip-on device that mounts on top of the processor; fingers or fins at its base pull the heat away from the processor. Today most cooling fans designed to mount on the processor housing also have a heat sink attached, as shown in Figure 5-19. The combination heat sink and cooling fan is sometimes called a **cooler**. A cooler is made of aluminum or copper. Copper is more expensive, but does a better job. For example, the Volcano 11+ by Thermaltake (*www.thermaltake.com*) is a copper cooler that can be set to run continuously or you can use a temperature-controlled fan speed (see Figure 5-20). The temperature sensor connects to the heat sink.

Heat sinks sometimes mount on top of other chips to keep them cool. For example, in Figure 5-21 you can see a heat sink mounted on top of a chipset sitting behind the Pentium 4 processor. Also notice in Figure 5-21 the frame to hold the cooler for the Pentium 4.

**Figure 5-20** Volcano 11+ by Thermaltake is a copper PC cooler

CPU

Frame to hold cooler

Socket 478

**Figure 5-21** A Pentium 4 installed in Socket 478

When purchasing a cooler, one factor to consider is the weight of the cooler; don't exceed Intel or AMD recommendations for the weight the processor can handle. Other factors to consider are the noise level and ease of installation of the cooler and the guarantee made by the cooler manufacturer.

## APPLYING|CONCEPTS

Before installing a cooling fan, read the directions carefully. Clips that hold the fan and heat sink to the processor frame or housing are sometimes difficult to install, and you must be very careful to use the right amount of thermal compound. If you use too much compound, it can slide off the housing and damage circuits on the motherboard.

When processors and coolers are purchased boxed together, the cooler might have thermal compound already stuck to the bottom (see Figure 5-22). For these installations, you install the processor and then install the cooler on top, causing the thermal compound to make contact with the processor.

**A+ ESS**
**1.1**

**A+**
**220-602**
**1.3**

Keeping a system cool is important; if the system overheats, components can be damaged. In addition to using a cooling fan, you can also install an alarm that sounds if a system overheats. Because the fan is a mechanical device, it is more likely to fail than the electronic devices inside the case. To protect the expensive processor, you can purchase a temperature sensor for a few dollars. The sensor plugs into a power connection coming from the power supply and mounts on the side of the case or the inside of a faceplate. The sensor sounds an alarm when the inside of the case becomes too hot.

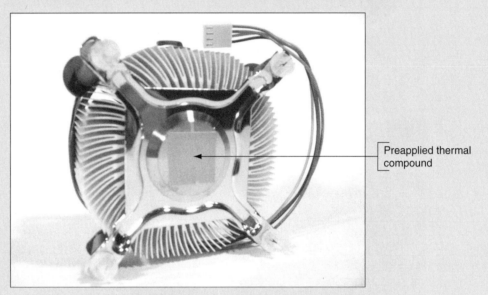

Preapplied thermal compound

**Figure 5-22**   Thermal compound is already stuck to the bottom of this cooler that was purchased boxed with the processor

In addition to using fans and heat sinks to keep a processor cool, there are more exotic options such as refrigeration, peltiers, and water coolers. These solutions are described in the following list; for the most part, they are used by hobbyists attempting to overclock a processor to the max. These cooling systems might include a PCI card that has a power supply, temperature sensor, and processor to control the cooler.

▲ A peltier is a heat sink carrying an electrical charge that causes it to act as an electrical thermal transfer device. The peltier's top surface can be as hot as 500 degrees F while the bottom surface next to the processor can be as cool as 45 degrees. The major disadvantage of a peltier is that this drastic difference in temperature can cause condensation inside the case when the PC is turned off.

▲ Refrigeration can also be used to cool a processor. These units contain a small refrigerator compressor that sits inside the case and can reduce temperatures to below zero.

▲ The most popular method of cooling overclocked processors is a water cooler unit. A small water pump sits inside the computer case, and tubes move distilled water up and over the processor to keep it cool.

Some manufacturers of these types of cooling systems are AquaStealth (*www.aquastealth.com*), asetek (*www.vapochill.com*), Thermaltake (*www.thermaltake.com*), and Frozenprocessor (*www.frozencpu.com*). Remember, overclocking is not a recommended best practice.

# INSTALLING A PROCESSOR

A+
220-602
1.1

A PC repair technician is sometimes called on to assemble a PC from parts, exchange a processor that is faulty, add a second processor to a dual-processor system, or upgrade an existing processor to improve performance. When selecting a processor to install in a particular motherboard, select a processor the board supports. Check the motherboard documentation for a list of processors that can be installed. You'll need to take into account the socket or slot the processor uses, its core frequency, the system bus speeds the processor supports, and features that will affect its performance. These features include multiprocessing abilities and features that affect efficiency of operation, such as Hyper-Threading by Intel or HyperTransport by AMD. After you have selected the processor, study its installation guide to find out what type of cooler to install, or you can purchase the cooler and processor boxed together. You'll also need some thermal compound if it is not included in the boxed processor and cooler. One important thing to consider when installing a processor is the voltage requirements of the processor, so we begin there.

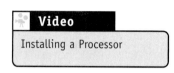

Video

Installing a Processor

You're now ready to install the processor in a socket or slot. Both of these types of installations are covered in this section.

A+ ESS
1.1

## VOLTAGE TO THE PROCESSOR

Earlier processors received all their electrical power from the traces or wires on the system bus that carry power. But many newer processors require additional power. For this reason, some motherboards include a new power connector, called the ATX12V (see Figure 5-23). For example, the Pentium 4 receives voltage from the +12-volt power line to the motherboard, rather than the lower-voltage lines that previous Pentiums used. Always read the motherboard and processor documentation to know how to use these auxiliary power connections.

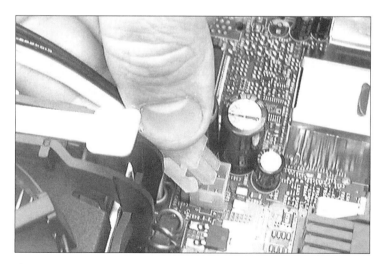

**Figure 5-23**  Auxiliary 4-pin power cord from the power supply connects to the ATX12V connector on the motherboard to provide power to the Pentium 4

For today's processors, when a processor is installed in a socket it is designed to use, the motherboard regulates the voltage to this socket that is needed by the processor. There is nothing more for you to do to regulate the voltage other than connect up the auxiliary power line. However, this is not the case with older processors because several older processors with different voltage requirements could use the same socket. You can see this for yourself by looking back at Table 5-5. Several older processors had different voltage requirements, yet used the same socket.

For example, the Celeron processor that uses 2.00 volts can be installed in Socket 370, but the Pentium III FC-PGA that uses either 1.60 or 1.65 volts can also be installed in Socket 370. A motherboard might have a Socket 370 built to support only the Celeron and another motherboard might have a Socket 370 built to support only the Pentium III FC-PGA. If you install a Pentium III FC-PGA in a socket designed only for the Celeron, the processor might physically fit in the socket, but the overvoltage can damage the Pentium III. For older processors, because sockets are more universal than for newer processors, its very important to use only a processor and processor package that the motherboard documentation claims the board can support.

Also be aware that some processors require one voltage for external operations and another for internal operations. Those that require two different voltages are called **dual-voltage processors**. Other processors are **single-voltage processors**.

## CPU VOLTAGE REGULATOR

Some older motherboards could accommodate more than one type of processor in a socket if you configure the voltage requirements of the processor during installation. For example, a motherboard might require that you set jumpers to configure the voltage to the processor. The motherboard might use a **voltage regulator module (VRM)** installed on the board to control the amount of voltage to the processor. A VRM can be embedded in the motherboard or can be added later when you upgrade the processor.

 **A+ Exam Tip**

The A+ Essentials exam expects you to understand the purpose of a VRM.

**APPLYING|CONCEPTS** As an example of having to configure the voltage requirements of an older processor, suppose you want to upgrade a Classic Pentium to the Pentium MMX on a motherboard that supports either processor. The Classic Pentium used only a single voltage (2.8 volts), but the Pentium MMX uses a core voltage of 2.8 volts and an I/O voltage of 3.3 volts. If you upgrade a system from the Classic Pentium to the Pentium MMX, you can use the motherboard's embedded VRM to regulate the 2.8 volts and install another VRM to regulate the 3.3 volts.

Figure 5-24 shows sample documentation of jumper settings to use for various processor voltage selections on an older motherboard. Notice that the two jumpers called JP16, located near Socket 7 on the board, select the voltage. For single voltage, on a Pentium, Cyrix 6 x 86, or AMD K5, both jumpers are open. Dual voltage, used by the Pentium MMX, Cyrix M2, and AMD K6, is selected by opening or closing the two jumpers according to the diagram. Follow the recommendations for your processor when selecting the voltages from documentation.

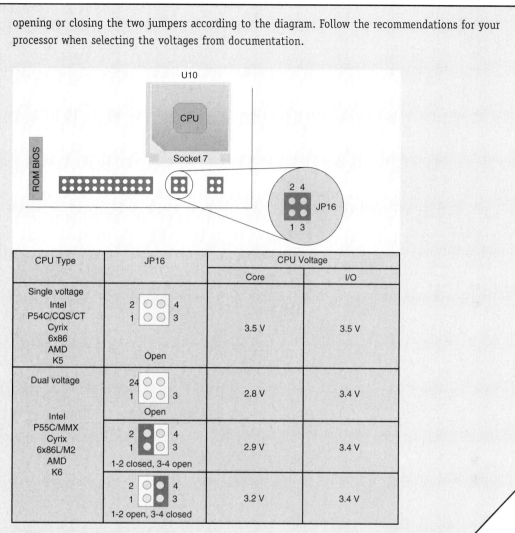

| CPU Type | JP16 | CPU Voltage | |
|---|---|---|---|
| | | Core | I/O |
| Single voltage<br>Intel<br>P54C/CQS/CT<br>Cyrix<br>6x86<br>AMD<br>K5 | 2 ○○ 4<br>1 ○○ 3<br><br>Open | 3.5 V | 3.5 V |
| Dual voltage | 24 ○○<br>1 ○○ 3<br>Open | 2.8 V | 3.4 V |
| Intel<br>P55C/MMX<br>Cyrix<br>6x86L/M2<br>AMD<br>K6 | 2 ●○ 4<br>1 ●○ 3<br>1-2 closed, 3-4 open | 2.9 V | 3.4 V |
| | 2 ○● 4<br>1 ○● 3<br>1-2 open, 3-4 closed | 3.2 V | 3.4 V |

**Figure 5-24** For older motherboards, a processor voltage regulator can be configured using jumpers on the motherboard to apply the correct voltage to the processor

When assembling a system from parts, sometimes it works best to install the processor and cooler on the motherboard before the board goes in the case. But for very heavy cooler assemblies, to protect the motherboard, first install the motherboard in the case and then install the processor and cooler. For the best order of installation, see the motherboard documentation. Also, for older motherboards, jumpers are sometimes set on the board to set the frequency or speed of the processor and system bus. How to set these jumpers and how to install motherboards are covered in the next chapter.

We'll look at three examples of installing a processor: a Pentium II installed in slot 1, a Pentium 4 installed in Socket 478, and a Pentium 4 installed in Socket 775.

## INSTALLING A PENTIUM II IN SLOT 1

When installing a processor, be careful to protect the processor and the motherboard against ESD as you work. Wear an antistatic bracelet and use other precautions you learned about in Chapter 3. For slot 1, used by the Pentium II, the motherboard uses a universal retention

A+
220-602
1.1

mechanism (URM), which is preinstalled on the board. Follow these steps to install the fan on the side of the processor first, and then install the processor on the motherboard:

1. Unfold the URM arms. Flip both arms up until they lock into position (refer to Figure 5-13).

2. Examine the heat sink, fan assembly, and processor to see how the cooling assembly brace lines up with holes in the side of the SECC (see Figure 5-25).

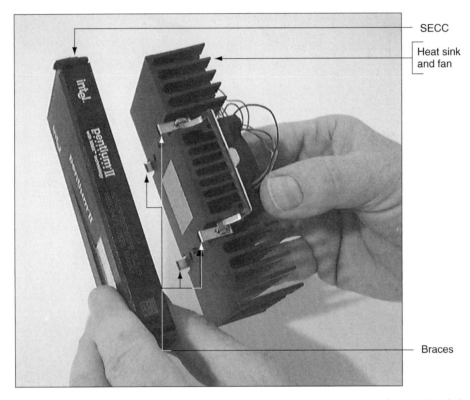

SECC

Heat sink and fan

Braces

**Figure 5-25**   The braces on the heat sink and fan assembly align with holes in the side of the SECC

3. Place the heat sink on the side of the SECC. The two should fit tightly together, with absolutely no space between them.

4. After you fit the heat sink and SECC together, place the SECC on a table and push the clamp on the fan down and into place to secure the cooling assembly to the SECC (see Figure 5-26).

5. Insert the cooling assembly and SECC into the supporting arms (see Figure 5-27). The SECC should fit snugly into slot 1, similar to the way an expansion card settles into an expansion slot. The arms should snap into position when the SECC is fully seated. Be certain you have a good fit.

6. Lock the SECC into position by pulling the SECC locks outward until they lock into the supporting arm lock holes.

A+
220-602
1.1

**Figure 5-26**  Push the clamp on the fan down until it locks in place, locking the heat sink and fan to the SECC

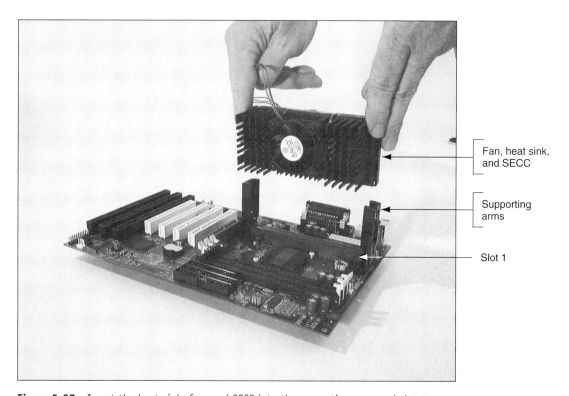

**Figure 5-27**  Insert the heat sink, fan, and SECC into the supporting arms and slot 1

7. Connect the power cord coming from the fan to the power connection on the mother-board (see Figure 5-28). Look for the power connection near slot 1. If you have trouble finding it, see the motherboard documentation.

A+
220-602
1.1

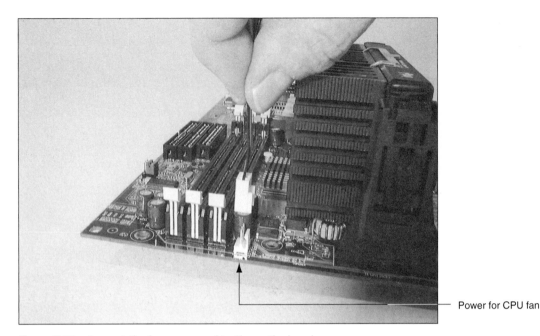

**Figure 5-28**   Connect the fan power cord to the motherboard

## INSTALLING A PENTIUM 4 IN SOCKET 478

If you look back at Figure 5-21, you can see the Pentium 4 installed in Socket 478 on a motherboard. Notice the frame or retention mechanism used to hold the cooler in place. This frame might come separately from the board or be preinstalled. If necessary, follow the directions that come with the motherboard to install the frame. Follow these steps to install the processor and cooler:

1. Lift the ZIF socket lever, as shown in Figure 5-29.

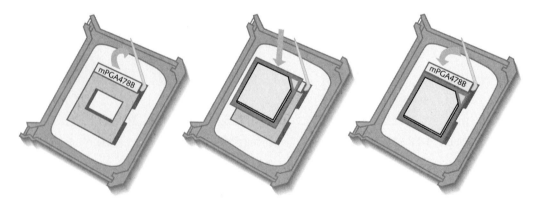

**Figure 5-29**   Install the processor in the mPGA478B socket

2. Place the processor on the socket so that the corner marked with a triangle is aligned with the connection of the lever to the socket. After the processor is in place, lower the lever to insert the processor firmly into the socket. As you work, be very careful not to force the processor in at an offset or disoriented position.

3. Before installing the processor cooling assembly over the processor, place a small amount of thermal compound on top of the processor. This greaselike substance helps

**5**

A+
220-602
1.1

transfer heat from the processor to the heat sink. Do not use too much; if you do, it may squish out the sides and interfere with other components.

4. Carefully examine the clip assembly that surrounds the fan and heat sink. Line up the clip assembly with the retention mechanism already installed on the motherboard, and press lightly on all four corners to attach it (see Figure 5-30).

**Figure 5-30** Carefully push the cooler assembly clips into the retention mechanism on the motherboard until they snap into position

5. After the cooling assembly is in place, push down the two clip levers on top of the processor fan (see Figure 5-31). Different coolers use different types of clipping mechanisms, so follow the directions that come with the cooler. Sometimes the clipping mechanism is difficult to clip onto the processor, and the plastic levers and housing are flimsy, so work carefully.

**Figure 5-31** The clip levers attach the cooling assembly to the retention mechanism around the processor

6. Connect the power cord from the processor fan to the power connection on the motherboard next to the cooler (see Figure 5-32).

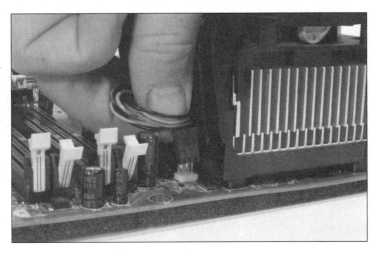

**Figure 5-32** Connect the processor fan power cord to the motherboard power connector

## INSTALLING A PENTIUM 4 IN SOCKET 775

The Pentium 4 we're installing in Socket 775 is shown in Figure 5-8 along with the cooler assembly. Because this cooler is so heavy, it is best to install it after the motherboard is securely seated in the case. Socket 775 has a lever and a socket cover. Figure 5-33 shows the socket with the lever and cover open, together with the processor (laying upside down) and the cooler.

👍 **Tip**

The A+ IT 220-602 exam expects you to know how to install a processor.

**Figure 5-33** Pentium 4, cooler, and open socket 775

A+
220-602
1.1

Do the following to install the processor and cooler using socket 775:

1. Push down on the lever and gently push it away from the socket to lift it (see Figure 5-34).

**Figure 5-34**   Release the lever from the socket

2. Lift the socket cover (see Figure 5-35).

**Figure 5-35**   Lift the socket cover

3. Orient the processor so that the notches on the two edges of the processor line up with the two notches on the socket (see Figure 5-36). Gently place the processor in the socket.

A+
220-602
1.1

**Figure 5-36** Place the processor in the socket orienting the notches on two sides

4. Close the socket cover. Push down on the lever and gently return it to its locked position (see Figure 5-37).

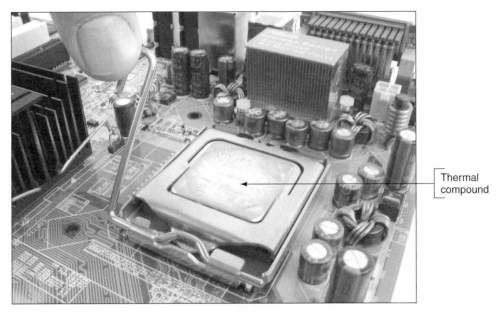

**Figure 5-37** Force is applied to the processor when the lever is pushed into position

Figure 5-38 shows how the cooler is aligned over the processor so that all four spacers fit into the four holes on the motherboard and the fan power cord connects to the power connector on the motherboard. First install the motherboard in the case (how to do this is covered in the next chapter). Then place the cooler over the four holes and push down on each fastener until you hear it pop into the hole (see Figure 5-39). (Later, if you need to remove the cooler, use a flathead screwdriver to turn each fastener counterclockwise to release it from the hole.)

A+
220-602
1.1

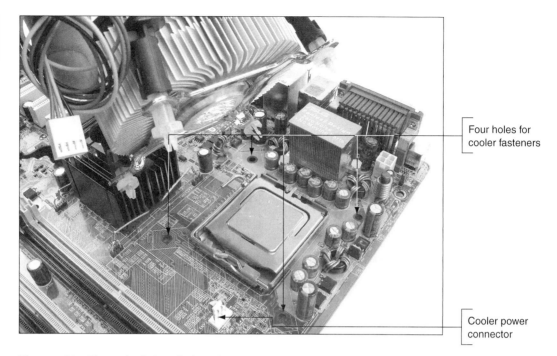

Four holes for
cooler fasteners

Cooler power
connector

**Figure 5-38**   The cooler is installed on the motherboard using four holes in the motherboard

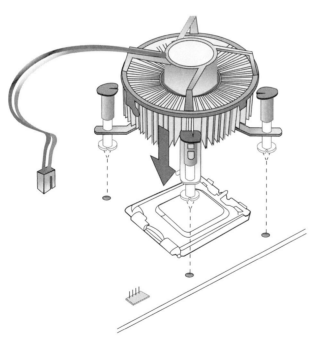

**Figure 5-39**   Four spacers on the cooler pop into each hole on the motherboard

A+ ESS
1.3

5. Connect the power cord from the cooler fan to the motherboard power connector near the processor, as shown in Figure 5-40.

A+
220-602
1.2

After the processor and cooler are installed, you can plug back up the system, turn it on, and verify all is working. If the power comes on (you hear the fan spinning and see lights), but the system fails to work, most likely the processor is not seated solidly in the socket or slot. Turn everything off and recheck your installation. If the system comes up and begins the boot process but suddenly turns off before the boot is complete, most likely the processor is

A+ ESS
1.3

A+
220-602
1.2

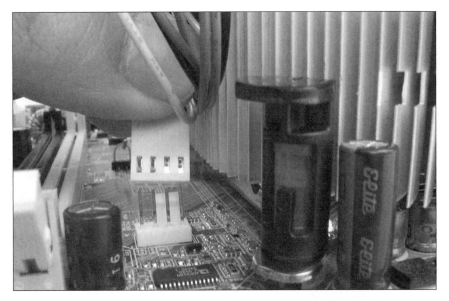

**Figure 5-40**   Connect the cooler fan power cord to the motherboard connector

**Notes**

Notice in Figure 5-37 that the processor has thermal compound already on it. If the compound seems light or has hardened, you can remove this compound using a soft cloth and add more thermal compound to the bottom of the cooler. Figure 5-41 shows new thermal compound added to the bottom of the cooler. Be careful to not apply too much compound that might ooze off onto the processor connectors.

overheating because the cooler is not installed correctly. Turn everything off and verify the cooler is securely seated and connected. After the system is up and running, you can check the CPU and motherboard temperatures by entering CMOS setup. Then, under the Power menu, look for a Hardware

Monitor window similar to the one shown in Figure 5-42. Other troubleshooting tips for processors are covered at the end of the next chapter.

**Figure 5-41**   When reinstalling a processor and cooler, you can add new thermal compound
to the bottom of the cooler

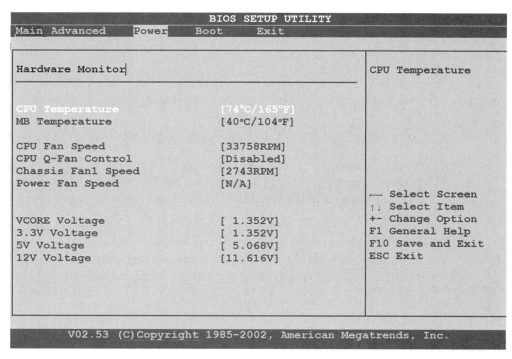

Figure 5-42 The CPU and motherboard temperature is monitored by CMOS setup

## >> CHAPTER SUMMARY

◢ The most important component on the motherboard is the processor, or central processing unit. The processor is rated according to its speed, efficiency of programming code, word size, data path size, size of internal cache, multiprocessing abilities, and special functions.

◢ Processor performance can be improved by using multiprocessing, multiple processors installed in a system, and dual-core processing.

◢ SRAM (static RAM) is fast and is used as a memory cache, which speeds overall computer performance by temporarily holding data and programming that the CPU may use in the near future.

◢ L1 cache is contained on the processor microchip, and L2 and L3 cache are external to this microchip. L2 and L3 can be on the motherboard or in the processor housing. If a processor has L2 cache, cache on the motherboard is called L3 cache.

◢ Older motherboards sometimes provided an extra COAST slot to upgrade SRAM, but most systems today come with an optimum amount of SRAM inside the CPU housing or on the motherboard.

◢ The Intel Pentium processor family includes the Classic Pentium, Pentium MMX, Pentium Pro, Pentium II, Celeron, Xeon, Pentium III, and Pentium 4.

◢ The Itanium, Intel's 64-bit processor family, has L1, L2, and L3 cache.

◢ AMD is Intel's chief competitor for the processor market. AMD produces the Athlon 64 X2 Dual-Core, Athlon 64 FX, Duron, Athlon, Athlon MP, Athlon XP, Opteron, Sempron, Turion, and Athlon 64 processors.

◢ Newer processors require extra cooling, which you can accomplish by installing a processor heat sink and cooling fan on top of or near the processor.

◢ Processor packages can be flat and thin or of the cartridge variety. Flat and thin packages are installed in sockets that use either pins or lands. Cartridges can be installed on their end in a slot or flat in a socket.

◢ Some processor sockets and slots are Socket 7, Socket 370, Socket 423, Socket 478, slot 1, Slot A, slot 2, Socket 603, Socket 775, Socket 754, Socket 939, and Socket 940. A slot looks like an expansion slot.

◢ A chipset is a group of chips on the motherboard that supports the processor. Intel is the most popular manufacturer of chipsets.

◢ A modern chipset uses a hub with two ends. The fast end of the hub is called the North Bridge and connects to the system bus, RAM, and processor. The slow end of the hub, called the South Bridge, connects to slower I/O buses.

◢ Because some legacy processors require one voltage for internal core operations and another voltage for external I/O operations, when upgrading a processor, you might have to upgrade or add a voltage regulator module to control these voltages.

◢ When installing a processor, for lighter cooler assemblies, install the processor and cooler on the motherboard and then install the motherboard in the case. When the cooling assembly is heavy and bulky, it is best to install it after the motherboard is securely seated in the case.

## >> KEY TERMS

For explanations of key terms, see the Glossary near the end of the book.

Advanced Transfer Cache (ATC)
back-side bus (BSB)
bus frequency
complex instruction set computing
  (CISC)
cooler
data path
discrete L2 cache
dual inline package (DIP)
dual-core processing
dual-voltage processors
Execution Trace Cache
explicitly parallel instruction
  computing (EPIC)
external cache

front-side bus (FSB)
heat sink
internal bus
internal cache
land grid array (LGA)
Level 1 (L1) cache
Level 2 (L2) cache
Level 3 (L3) cache
low insertion force (LIF) sockets
memory cache
microcode
motherboard bus
multiplier
multiprocessor platform
North Bridge

On-Package L2 cache
overclocking
pin grid array (PGA)
primary cache
processor frequency
reduced instruction set computing
  (RISC)
single-voltage processors
South Bridge
staggered pin grid array (SPGA)
static RAM (SRAM)
system bus
voltage regulator module (VRM)
word size
zero insertion force (ZIF) sockets

## >> REVIEW QUESTIONS

1. Which of the following terms refers to the largest number of bits the processor can process in one operation?

   **a.** Data path

   **b.** Overclocking

   **c.** Word size

   **d.** Throttle

2. Which of the following is the memory cache on the processor chip?

   a. Level 2 cache

   b. Primary cache

   c. Secondary cache

   d. DRAM

3. Which of the following best describes a PGA socket?

   a. The pins are staggered over the socket.

   b. The socket uses lands.

   c. It's a cartridge package for a processor that lays flat.

   d. The pins are aligned in uniform rows around the socket.

4. All I/O devices, except display and memory, connect to the hub by using which of the following?

   a. South Bridge

   b. PCI bus

   c. Accelerated Hub Architecture

   d. North Bridge

5. A cooler is a combination of a cooling fan and which of the following?

   a. Riser card

   b. Heat sink

   c. Resistor

   d. Housing

6. True or false? Multiprocessing is accomplished when a processor contains more than one ALU.

7. True or false? SIMD stands for "single instruction, multiple data."

8. True or false? Running a motherboard or processor at a lower speed than the manufacturer suggests is called overclocking.

9. True or false? AMD processors are popular in the game and hobbyist markets.

10. True or false? The front-side bus connects the processor to the internal memory cache.

11. The speed at which the processor operates internally is called _____.

12. The method for improving performance that is based on the processor housing containing two processors that operate at the same frequency but independently of each other is called _____ processing.

13. If there is L2 cache in the processor housing and additional cache on the motherboard, the cache on the motherboard is called _____ cache.

14. The processor's housing is called the _____.

15. The three basic components of a processor are _____, _____, and _____.

# Motherboards

In the previous chapter, we looked at the two most important components on the motherboard: the processor and chipset. In this chapter, we turn our attention to the motherboard itself. You'll learn about the buses and expansion slots on the motherboard and how to configure these and other components on the board. The motherboard is considered a field replaceable unit. So, in this chapter, you'll learn to troubleshoot problems with the motherboard and how to install and replace one.

## SELECTING A MOTHERBOARD

When selecting a motherboard, the first consideration is the form factor of the board. A motherboard form factor determines the size of the board and its features that make it compatible with power supplies, cases, processors, and expansion cards. The most popular motherboard form factor is the ATX. ATX motherboards have been around for a long time and have seen many improvements. A recent ATX motherboard designed for a Pentium 4 or Celeron processor is shown in Figure 6-1,

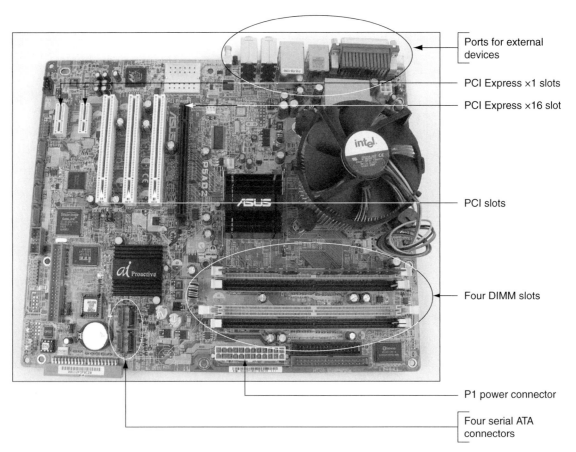

Ports for external devices

PCI Express ×1 slots

PCI Express ×16 slot

PCI slots

Four DIMM slots

P1 power connector

Four serial ATA connectors

**Figure 6-1**    An ATX motherboard with PCI Express and Socket 775

and an older ATX motherboard designed for a Pentium III is shown in Figure 6-2. An older motherboard form factor is the AT (see Figure 6-3).

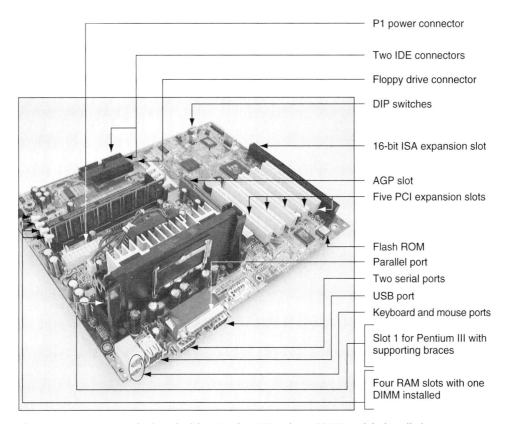

P1 power connector

Two IDE connectors

Floppy drive connector

DIP switches

16-bit ISA expansion slot

AGP slot
Five PCI expansion slots

Flash ROM
Parallel port
Two serial ports
USB port
Keyboard and mouse ports

Slot 1 for Pentium III with supporting braces

Four RAM slots with one DIMM installed

**Figure 6-2** An ATX motherboard with a Pentium III and one DIMM module installed

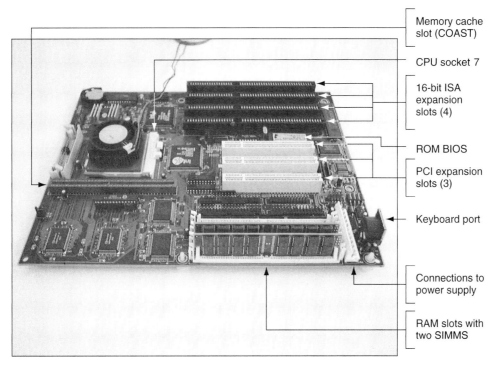

Memory cache slot (COAST)

CPU socket 7

16-bit ISA expansion slots (4)

ROM BIOS

PCI expansion slots (3)

Keyboard port

Connections to power supply

RAM slots with two SIMMS

**Figure 6-3** An older AT motherboard with memory cache and socket 7 for the Intel Classic Pentium processor. The processor with a fan on top is installed, as well as two SIMM memory modules.

The latest motherboard form factor is the BTX. Figure 6-4 shows a BTX motherboard, and Figure 6-5 shows a BTX case with a BTX motherboard installed. This BTX case has fans on the front and rear to force air over the processor heat sink. Notice in the figure the green encasement that directs airflow over the heat sink. Also notice the vents on the front case panel to help with airflow.

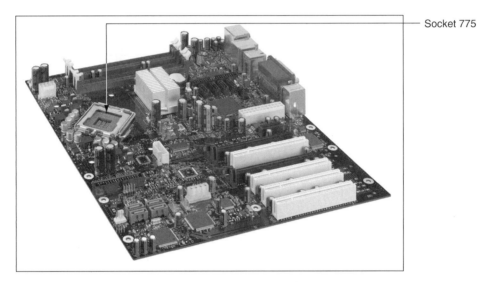

Socket 775

**Figure 6-4** A BTX motherboard with an LGA 775 land socket

Front panel

Air vents

Rear exhaust fan

Heat sink over processor

Encasement to direct airflow over heat sink

Front intake fan is behind this grid

**Figure 6-5** A BTX system is designed for optimum airflow

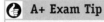 **A+ Exam Tip**

The A+ Essentials exam expects you to know about the ATX, BTX, microATX, and NLX form factors.

Each form factor has several sizes, which are listed in Table 6-1.

Because the motherboard determines so many of your computer's features, selecting the motherboard is a very important decision when you purchase a computer or assemble one from parts. Depending on which

| Type of Motherboard | Description |
| --- | --- |
| ATX | ▲ Developed by Intel for Pentium systems |
| | ▲ Includes a power-on switch that can be software-enabled and extra power connections for extra fans and processor voltage needs |
| | ▲ Uses a single 20-pin P1 power connector with optional 4-pin auxiliary power connector |
| | ▲ Measures 30.5 cm x 24.4 cm (12 inches x 9.6 inches) |
| Enhanced ATX | ▲ Improved ATX, specified in ATX version 2.2 |
| | ▲ Uses a 24-pin P1 power connector |
| | ▲ Supports PCI Express |
| MiniATX | ▲ An ATX board with a more compact design |
| | ▲ Measures 28.4 cm x 20.8 cm (11.2 inches x 8.2 inches) |
| MicroATX | ▲ A smaller ATX design intended to reduce overall system cost |
| | ▲ Measures 24.4 cm x 24.4 cm (9.6 inches x 9.6 inches) |
| | ▲ A smaller power supply and an ATX 2.1 case can be used |
| FlexATA | ▲ Smaller variation of microATX |
| | ▲ Measures 22.9 cm x 19.1 cm (9.0 inches x 7.5 inches) |
| | ▲ Uses same mounting holes as microATX |
| BTX | ▲ Has up to seven expansion slots |
| | ▲ Can be up to 325.12 mm wide |
| | ▲ Layouts of BTX motherboards include a tower, desktop, and small form factor layout |
| | ▲ BTX boards have a 24-pin power connector and can use an ATX 2.2 power supply with a 4-pin auxiliary connector |
| MicroBTX | ▲ Has up to four expansion slots |
| | ▲ Can be up to 264.16 mm wide |
| NanoBTX | ▲ Has up to two expansion slots |
| | ▲ Can be up to 223.52 mm wide |
| PicoBTX | ▲ None or one expansion slot |
| | ▲ Can be up to 203.20 mm wide |
| NLX | ▲ Improvement over earlier LPX design |
| | ▲ Uses a riser card (daughter board) near the edge of the board |
| | ▲ Sizes include 8.0 inches x 10.0 inches up to 9.0 inches x 13.6 inches |
| AT | ▲ Oldest type of motherboard, still used in some systems |
| | ▲ Uses P8 and P9 power connections |
| | ▲ Measures 30.5 cm x 33 cm (12 inches x 13 inches) |
| Baby AT | ▲ Smaller version of AT and is compatible with ATX cases |
| | ▲ Uses P8 and P9 power connections |
| | ▲ Measures 33 cm x 22 cm (12 inches x 8.7 inches) |

**Table 6-1**  Types of motherboards

A+ ESS
1.1

applications and peripheral devices you plan to use with the computer, you can take one of three approaches to selecting a motherboard. The first approach is to select the board that provides the most room for expansion, so you can upgrade and exchange components and add devices easily. A second approach is to select the board that best suits the needs of the computer's current configuration, knowing that when you need to upgrade, you will likely switch to new technology and a new motherboard. The third approach is to select a motherboard that meets your present needs with moderate room for expansion.

Ask the following questions when selecting a motherboard:

- What form factor does the motherboard use?
- Does the motherboard support the number and type of processor you plan to use (for example, Socket LGA 775 for the Intel Pentium 4 up to 3.3 GHz)?
- What are the supported frequencies of the system bus (for example, 1066/800/ 533 MHz)?
- What chipset does the board use?
- What type of memory does the board support (DDR or DDR2), and how much memory can the board hold?
- What type and how many expansion slots are on the board (for example, PCI, PCI Express, and AGP)?
- What hard drive controllers and connectors are on the board (for example, IDE, serial ATA, RAID, and SCSI)?
- What are the embedded devices on the board and what internal slots or connections does the board have? (For example, the board might provide a network port, wireless antenna port, FireWire port, two or more USB ports, modem port, and so forth.)
- What type of BIOS does the motherboard use?
- Does the board fit the case you plan to use?
- What is the warranty on the board?
- How extensive and user-friendly is the documentation?
- How much support does the manufacturer supply for the board?

Sometimes a motherboard contains a component more commonly offered as a separate device. A component on the board is called an embedded component or an on-board component. One example is support for video. The video port might be on the motherboard or might require a video card. The cost of a motherboard with an embedded component is usually less than the combined cost of a motherboard with no embedded component and an expansion card. If you plan to expand, be cautious about choosing a proprietary board that has many embedded components. Often such boards do not easily accept add-on devices from other manufacturers. For example, if you plan to add a more powerful video card, you might not want to choose a motherboard that contains an embedded video controller. Even though you can often use a jumper or CMOS setup to disable the proprietary video controller, there is little advantage to paying the extra money for it.

Table 6-2 lists some manufacturers of motherboards and their Web addresses.

**Tip**

If you have an embedded component, make sure you can disable it so you can use another external component if needed.

**Notes**

A motherboard is configured through jumpers or DIP switches on the board or through CMOS setup. Embedded components are almost always configured through CMOS setup.

| Manufacturer | Web Address |
|---|---|
| Abit | *www.abit.com.tw* |
| American Megatrends, Inc. (AMI) | *www.megatrends.com* or *www.ami.com* |
| ASUS | *www.asus.com* |
| BIOSTAR Group | *www.biostar.com.tw* |
| Dell | *www.dell.com* |
| First International Computer of America, Inc. | *www.fica.com* |
| Gateway | *www.gateway.com* |
| Gigabyte Technology Co., Ltd. | *us.giga-byte.com* |
| IBM | *www.ibm.com* |
| Intel Corporation | *www.intel.com* |
| Iwill Corporation | *www.iwill.net* |
| MicroStar International | *www.msicomputer.com* |
| Motherboards.com | *www.motherboards.com* |
| Supermicro Computer, Inc. | *www.supermicro.com* |
| Tyan Computer Corporation | *www.tyan.com* |

**Table 6-2** Major manufacturers of motherboards

## CONFIGURING AND SUPPORTING A MOTHERBOARD

The components on the motherboard that you must know how to configure and support are the expansion slots and other internal and external connectors. In this section, you'll learn about the expansion slots and the buses that support them, and then you'll learn how to configure these expansion slots and other components and connectors on the board. In later chapters, you'll learn more about the other connectors on the board, including memory module slots, and the various drive, USB, FireWire, serial, and parallel connectors.

### BUSES AND EXPANSION SLOTS

As cities grow, so do their transportation systems. Small villages have only simple, two-lane roads, but large cities have one-way streets, four-lane roads, and major freeways, each with their own set of traffic laws, including minimum and maximum speeds, access methods, and protocols. As microcomputer systems have evolved, so too have their "transportation" systems. The earliest PC had only a single simple bus. Today's PCs have four or five buses, each with different speeds, access methods, and protocols. As you have seen in previous chapters, backward compatibility dictates that older buses be supported on a motherboard, even when faster, better buses exist. All this makes for a maze of buses on a motherboard.

### WHAT A BUS DOES

Look on the bottom of the motherboard, and you see a maze of circuits that make up a bus. These embedded wires carry four kinds of cargo:

▲ *Electrical power.* Chips on the motherboard require power to function. These chips tap into a bus's power lines and draw what they need.

A+ ESS
1.1

▲ *Control signals.* Some wires on a bus carry control signals that coordinate all the activity.

▲ *Memory addresses.* Components pass memory addresses to one another, telling each other where to access data or instructions. The number of wires that make up the memory address lines of the bus determines how many bits can be used for a memory address. The number of wires thus limits the amount of memory the bus can address.

▲ *Data.* Data passes over a bus in a group of wires, just as memory addresses do. The number of lines in the bus used to pass data determines how much data can be passed in parallel at one time. The number of lines depends on the type of processor and determines the number of bits in the data path. (Remember that a data path is the part of the bus on which the data is placed; it can be 8, 16, 32, 64, or more bits wide.)

## BUS EVOLUTION

Just as a city's road system improves to increase the speed and number of lanes of traffic, buses have evolved around similar issues, data path and speed. Cars on a freeway generally travel at a continuous speed, but traffic on a computer's processor or bus is digital (on and off), rather than analog (continuous). The system clock keeps the beat for components. If a component on the motherboard works by the beat, or clock cycle, then it is synchronized, or in sync, with the processor. For example, the back-side bus of the Pentium works at half the speed of the processor. This means that the processor does something on each clock cycle, but the back-side bus is doing something on every other clock cycle.

Some components don't attempt to keep in sync with the processor, even to work at one-half or one-third of clock cycles. These components work asynchronously with the processor. They might work at a rate determined by the system clock or by another crystal on or off the motherboard. Either way, the frequency is much slower than the processor's and not in sync with it. If the processor requests something from one of these devices and the device is not ready, the device issues a **wait state**, which is a command to the processor to wait for slower devices to catch up.

The first expansion slots on early PCs were **Industry Standard Architecture (ISA) slots.** These slots had an 8-bit data path and ran at 4.77 MHz. Later, the 16-bit ISA slots were added that ran at 8.33 MHz. The 16-bit slots were backward-compatible with 8-bit cards; an 8-bit card used only a portion of the 16-bit slot. These 16-bit ISA slots are still in use on some older motherboards. In later chapters, you will learn how to support these legacy slots and cards.

Table 6-3 lists the various buses, in order of throughput speed from fastest to slowest. The evolution of buses includes earlier proprietary designs and the outdated ISA, EISA, MCA, and VESA buses. In Figure 6-6, you can see the shape of each of these bus connectors. Current buses include the USB bus, the IEEE 1394 (FireWire) bus, the original PCI bus, the AGP bus (for video only), the PCI-X, and the newer PCI Express bus. The USB, FireWire, and AGP buses are discussed in Chapter 9.

Looking at the second column of Table 6-3, you can see that a bus is called an expansion bus, local bus, local I/O bus, or local video bus. A bus that does not run in sync with the system clock is called an expansion bus and always connects to the slow end of the chipset, the South Bridge. Most buses today are local buses, meaning they run in sync with the system clock. If a local bus connects to the slower I/O controller hub or South Bridge of the chipset, it is called a local I/O bus. Because the video card needs to run at a faster rate than other expansion cards, this one slot always connects to the faster end of the chipset, the North Bridge. This video slot can be either an AGP slot or a PCI Express x16 slot, and the bus is called a local video bus. Several PCI buses are covered next.

| Bus | Bus Type | Data Path in Bits | Address Lines | Bus Speed in MHz | Throughput |
|---|---|---|---|---|---|
| System bus | Local | 64 | 32 | Up to 1600 | Up to 3.2 GB/sec |
| **Newer Bus Standards** | | | | | |
| PCI Express x16 | Local video and local I/O | Up to 16 lanes | Up to 16 lanes | 2.5 GHz to 40 GHz | Up to 4 GB/sec |
| PCI-X | Local I/O | 64 | 32 | 66, 133, 266, 533, 1066 | Up to 8.5 GB/sec |
| AGP | Local video | 32 | NA | 66, 75, 100 . . . | Up to 528 MB/sec |
| PCI | Local I/O | 32 or 64 | 32 | 33, 66 | 133, 266, or 532 MB/sec |
| FireWire | Local I/O or expansion | 1 | Serial | NA | Up to 3.2 Gb/sec (gigabits) |
| USB | Expansion | 1 | Serial | 3 | 12 to 480 Mbps (megabits) |
| **Older Bus Standards** | | | | | |
| VESA or VL Bus | Local video or expansion | 32 | 32 | Up to 33 | Up to 250 MB/sec |
| MCA | Expansion | 32 | 32 | 12 | Up to 40 MB/sec |
| EISA | Expansion | 32 | 32 | 12 | Up to 32 MB/sec |
| 16-bit ISA | Expansion | 16 | 24 | 8.33 | 8 MB/sec |
| 8-bit ISA | Expansion | 8 | 20 | 4.77 | 1 MB/sec |

**Table 6-3** Buses listed by throughput

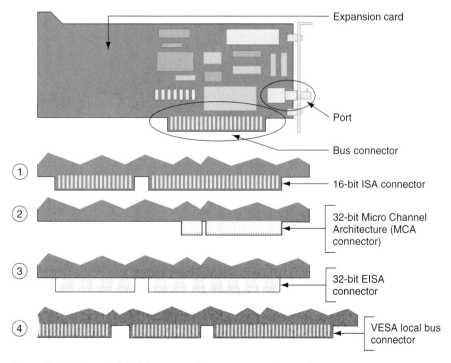

**Figure 6-6** Four outdated bus connections on expansion cards

## THE PCI BUSES

The original PCI bus was introduced by Intel in 1991, intended to replace the 16-bit ISA bus. For many years, most motherboards had both ISA and PCI slots. You can see an example of one of these boards in Chapter 1, Figure 1-12, which has three black 16-bit ISA slots, four white PCI slots, and an early version of an AGP slot. PCI has been improved several times; there are currently three major categories and within each category, several variations of PCI. In the following sections, we discuss each category in turn.

### Conventional PCI

The first PCI bus had a 32-bit data path, supplied 5 V of power to an expansion card, and operated at 33 MHz. It was the first bus that allowed expansion cards to run in sync with the CPU. PCI Version 2.x introduced the 64-bit, 3.3-V PCI slot, doubling data throughput of the bus. Because a card can be damaged if installed in the wrong voltage slot, a notch in a PCI slot distinguishes between a 5-V slot and a 3.3-V slot. A Universal PCI card can use either a 3.3-V or 5-V slot and contains both notches (see Figure 6-7).

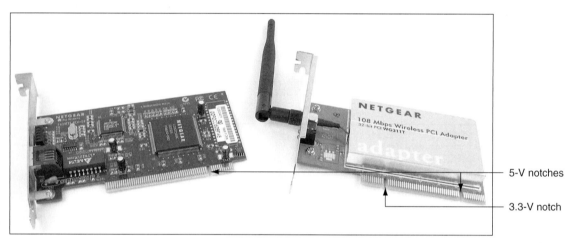

5-V notches

3.3-V notch

**Figure 6-7** A 32-bit, 5-V PCI network card and a 32-bit, universal PCI wireless card show the difference in PCI notches set to distinguish voltages in a PCI slot

Conventional PCI now has four types of slots and six possible PCI card configurations to use these slots (see Figure 6-8).

### PCI-X

The next evolution of PCI is PCI-X, which has had three major revisions; the latest is PCI-X 3.0. All PCI-X revisions are backward-compatible with conventional PCI cards and slots, except 5-V PCI cards are no longer supported. PCI-X is focused on technologies that increase bandwidth and data integrity and target the server market, and PCI-X revisions are generally keeping up with system bus speeds. Motherboards that use PCI-X tend to have several different PCI slots with some 32-bit or 64-bit slots running at different speeds.

### PCI Express

PCI Express (PCIe) uses an altogether different architectural design than conventional PCI and PCI-X and is not backward compatible with either. PCI Express is intended to ultimately replace both these buses as well as the AGP bus, although it is expected PCI Express will coexist with these buses for some time to come (see Figure 6-9). Whereas PCI uses a 32-bit or 64-bit parallel bus, PCI Express uses a serial bus, which is faster than a parallel bus because it transmits data in packets similar to how an Ethernet network, USB, and FireWire transmit data.

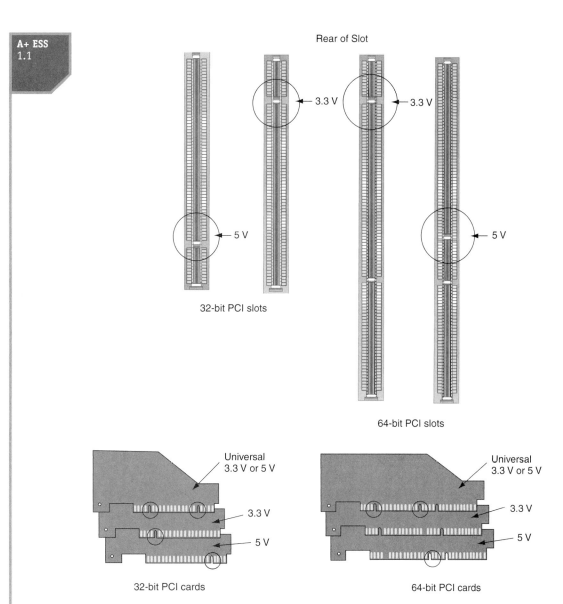

Rear of Slot

3.3 V

3.3 V

5 V

5 V

32-bit PCI slots

64-bit PCI slots

Universal
3.3 V or 5 V

3.3 V

5 V

Universal
3.3 V or 5 V

3.3 V

5 V

32-bit PCI cards

64-bit PCI cards

**Figure 6-8** With PCI Version 2.x, there are four possible types of expansion slots and six differently configured PCI expansion cards to use these slots

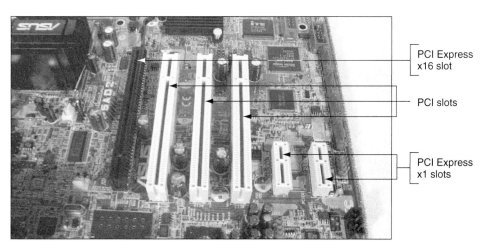

PCI Express
x16 slot

PCI slots

PCI Express
x1 slots

**Figure 6-9** Three PCI Express slots and three PCI slots on a motherboard

A+ ESS
1.1

Another difference in PCI Express is how it connects to the processor. Looking back in Chapter 5 at Figure 5-18, you can see that PCI cards all connect to the processor by way of a single PCI bus, which connects to the I/O controller hub or South Bridge. Compare this configuration to the one for PCI Express shown in Figure 6-10. With PCI Express, each PCI Express slot for a PCIe card has its own link or bus to the South Bridge, and one PCI Express slot has a direct link to the faster memory controller hub or North Bridge. This last PCI Express slot is intended to be used for a PCIe video card, thus replacing the slower AGP video slot. A motherboard will have either an AGP slot for the video card or a PCI Express x16 slot, but not both.

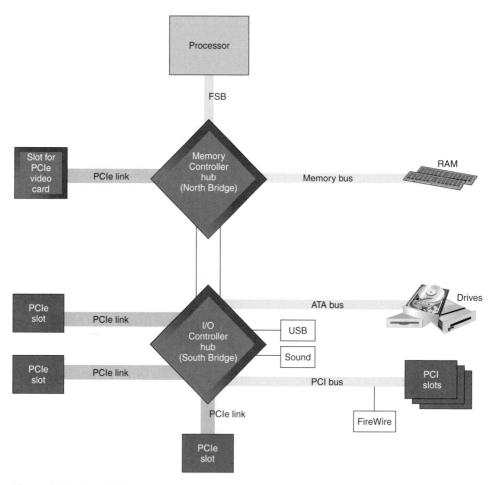

**Figure 6-10** How PCI Express connects to the chipset and processor

PCI Express currently comes in four different slot sizes called PCI Express x1 (pronounced "by one"), x4, x8, and x16 (see Figure 6-11). PCI Express x16 is the fastest and is used for the video card slot. A PCI Express x1 slot contains a single lane for data, which is actually four wires. One pair of wires is used to send data and the other pair receives data, one bit at a time. The x16 slot contains 16 lanes, each lane timed independently of other lanes. A shorter PCI Express card (such as a x1 card) can be installed in a longer PCI Express slot (such as a x4 slot).

## ON-BOARD PORTS, CONNECTORS, AND RISER SLOTS

In addition to expansion slots, a motherboard might also have several on-board ports, internal connectors, and riser slots.

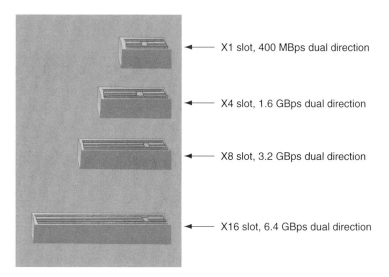

← X1 slot, 400 MBps dual direction

← X4 slot, 1.6 GBps dual direction

← X8 slot, 3.2 GBps dual direction

← X16 slot, 6.4 GBps dual direction

**Figure 6-11**  Current PCI Express slots

Ports coming directly off the motherboard are called **on-board ports** or integrated components. Almost all motherboards have a keyboard port, mouse port, parallel printer port, and one or more USB ports, and an older motherboard might have a serial port. In addition, the board might have a video port, sound ports, network port, modem port, 1394 (FireWire) port, and a port for a wireless antenna.

A motherboard might have several internal connectors, including parallel ATA connectors (also called EIDE connectors), a floppy drive connector, serial ATA connectors, SCSI connectors, or a 1394 connector.

To reduce the total cost of a computer system, some older motherboards might have a small expansion slot, about the length of a PCI Express x1 slot, called an **audio/modem riser (AMR)** slot (see Figure 6-12) or a **communication and networking riser (CNR)** slot.

▶ **Video**

PCI Express and On-Board Wireless

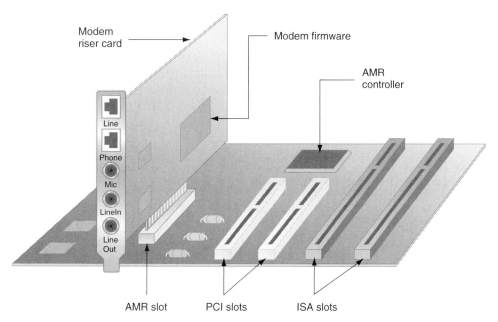

Modem riser card →

Modem firmware

AMR controller

Line

Phone

Mic

LineIn

Line Out

AMR slot        PCI slots        ISA slots

**Figure 6-12**  An audio/modem riser slot can accommodate an inexpensive modem riser card

These small slots accommodate small, inexpensive expansion cards called **riser cards**, such as a modem riser card, audio riser card, or network riser card. Part of a riser card's audio, modem, or networking logic is on the card, and part is on a controller on the motherboard.

### ⓐ A+ Exam Tip

The A+ Essentials exam expects you to be familiar with an AMR slot, CNR slot, and riser card, also called a daughter board.

Some motherboards come with connector modules that provide additional ports off the rear of the case. For example, Figure 6-13 shows three modules that came bundled with one motherboard. To use the ports on a module, you connect its cable to a connector on the motherboard and install the module in the place of a faceplate at the rear of the case.

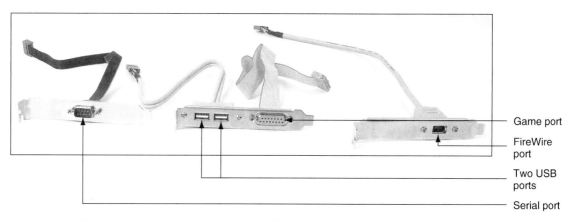

Game port

FireWire port

Two USB ports

Serial port

**Figure 6-13**   These modules provide additional ports off the rear of a computer case

### ✎ Notes

You don't have to replace an entire motherboard if one port fails. Most ports on a motherboard can be disabled through CMOS setup. On older motherboards, look for jumpers or DIP switches to disable a port. Then use an expansion card for the port instead.

## HARDWARE CONFIGURATION

You can configure the motherboard in three different ways: DIP switches, jumpers, and CMOS RAM. Storing configuration information by physically setting DIP switches or jumpers on the motherboard or peripheral devices is inconvenient, because it often requires you to open the computer case to make a change. A more convenient method is to hold configuration information in CMOS RAM. A program in BIOS, called CMOS setup, can then be used to easily make changes to the setup values stored in CMOS RAM.

In this section, you will learn more about each method of storing configuration information. We'll also look at some examples of CMOS setup screens.

### SETUP DATA STORED BY DIP SWITCHES

Many older motherboards and expansion cards and a few newer ones store setup data using a **dual inline package (DIP) switch**, as shown in Figure 6-14. A DIP switch has an ON position and an OFF position. ON represents binary 1 and OFF represents binary 0. If you add or remove equipment, you can communicate that to the computer by changing a DIP switch setting. When you change a DIP switch setting, use a pointed instrument such as a ballpoint pen to push the switch. Don't use a graphite pencil because graphite conducts electricity. In addition, pieces of graphite dropped into the switch can damage it.

**Figure 6-14** DIP switches are sometimes used to store setup data on motherboards

## SETUP DATA STORED BY JUMPERS

A motherboard can also retain setup or installation information in different settings of jumpers on the board. **Jumpers** are considered open or closed based on whether a jumper cover is present on two small posts or metal pins that stick up off the motherboard (see Figure 6-15). A group of jumpers is sometimes used to tell the system at what speed the CPU is running, or to turn a power-saving feature on or off.

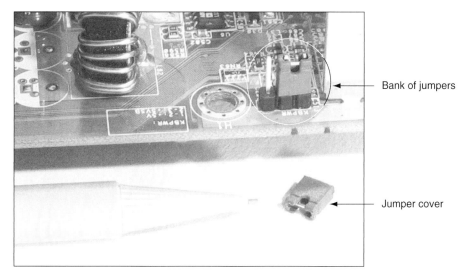

Bank of jumpers

Jumper cover

**Figure 6-15** Setup information about the motherboard can be stored by setting a jumper on (closed) or off (open). A jumper is closed if the cover is in place, connecting the two pins that make up the jumper; a jumper is open if the cover is not in place.

Most motherboards use at least one set of jumpers, such as the set in Figure 6-16. Look at the jumper cover in Figure 6-16b that is "parked," meaning it is hanging on a single pin for safekeeping but is not being used to turn a jumper setting on.

A typical setting that uses jumpers is enabling or disabling keyboard power-up. (With this feature enabled, you can press a key to power up the system.)

A+ ESS
1.1

a                          b                          c

**Figure 6-16**   A 6-pin jumper group on a circuit board (a) has no jumpers set to on, (b) has a cover parked on one pin, and (c) is configured with one jumper setting turned on

You change the jumper setting by removing the computer case, finding the correct jumper, and then either placing a metal cover over the jumper or removing the cover already there. Figure 6-17 shows a diagram of a motherboard with the keyboard power-up jumper. For older motherboards, typical uses of jumpers were to indicate the presence of cache memory or to communicate the type and speed of the CPU present.

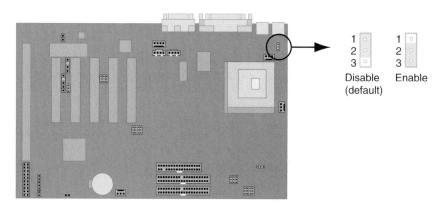

**Figure 6-17**   The keyboard power-up jumper allows you to use your keyboard to power up the computer

## SETUP DATA STORED IN CMOS RAM

Computers today store most configuration information in CMOS RAM, also called the real-time clock/nonvolatile RAM (RTC/NVRAM) chip, which retains the data even when the computer is turned off. (There are actually many CMOS chips on a motherboard, used for various purposes.) On older computers (mostly IBM 286 PCs built in the 1980s), changes are made to the CMOS setup data using a setup program stored on a floppy disk. You booted from the disk to launch the setup program, which allowed you to make changes to CMOS RAM stored on the motherboard. One major disadvantage of this method, besides the chance that you might lose or misplace the disk, is that the floppy disk drive must be working before you can change the setup. An advantage of this method is that you cannot unintentionally change the setup. If you have an older computer and you do not have the floppy disk with the setup program, check the Web site of the motherboard manufacturer or the BIOS manufacturer for a replacement disk.

> **Notes**
>
> Even though a computer has many CMOS chips, the term "CMOS chip" has come to mean the one chip on the mother-board that holds the configuration or setup information. If you hear someone ask: "What does CMOS say?" or "Let's change CMOS," the person is talking about the configuration or setup information stored on this one CMOS chip.

## Changing CMOS Using the Setup Program

The CMOS setup does not normally need to be changed except, for example, when there is a problem with hardware, a new floppy drive is installed, or a power-saving feature needs to be disabled or enabled. The CMOS setup can also hold one or two power-on passwords to help secure a system. Know that these passwords are not the same password that can be required by a Windows OS at startup.

On newer computers, you usually change the data stored in CMOS by accessing the setup program stored in ROM BIOS. You access the program by pressing a key or combination of keys during the boot process. The exact way to enter setup varies from one motherboard manufacturer to another. Table 6-4 lists the keystrokes needed to access CMOS setup for some common BIOS types.

| BIOS | Key to Press During POST to Access Setup |
|---|---|
| AMI BIOS | Del |
| Award BIOS | Del |
| Older Phoenix BIOS | Ctrl+Alt+Esc or Ctrl+Alt+s |
| Newer Phoenix BIOS | F2 or F1 |
| Dell computers using Phoenix BIOS | Ctrl+Alt+Enter |
| Older Compaq computers such as the Deskpro 286 or 386 | Place the diagnostics disk in the disk drive, reboot your system, and choose Computer Setup from the menu |
| Newer Compaq computers such as the ProLinea, Deskpro, Deskpro XL, Deskpro XE, or Presario | Press the F10 key while the cursor is in the upper-right corner of the screen, which happens just after the two beeps during booting* |
| All other older computers | Use a setup program on the disk that came with the PC |

*For Compaq computers, the CMOS setup program is stored on the hard drive in a small, non-DOS partition of about 3 MB. If this partition becomes corrupted, you must run setup from a bootable CD or floppy disk that comes with the system. If you cannot run setup by pressing F10 at startup, suspect a damaged partition or a virus taking up space in conventional memory.

**Table 6-4**  How to access CMOS setup

For the exact method you need to use to enter setup, see the documentation for your motherboard. A message such as the following usually appears on the screen near the beginning of the boot:

```
Press DEL to change Setup
```

or

```
Press F8 for Setup
```

When you press the appropriate key or keys, a setup screen appears with menus and Help features that are often very user-friendly. Although the exact menus depend on the maker and version of components you are working with, the sample screens that follow will help you become familiar with the general contents of CMOS setup screens. Figure 6-18 shows a main menu for setup. On this menu, you can change the system date and time, the keyboard language, and other system features.

Recall the discussion of power management from Chapter 4. The power menu in CMOS setup allows you to configure automatic power-saving features for your system, such as suspend mode. Figure 6-19 shows a sample power menu.

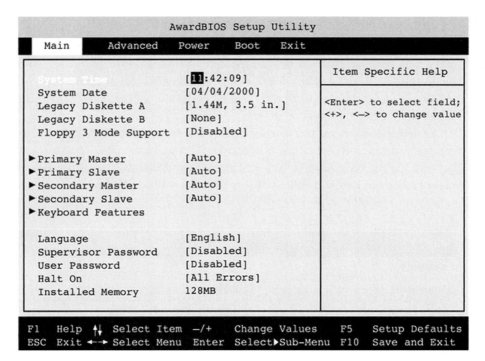

**Figure 6-18**   CMOS Setup Main menu

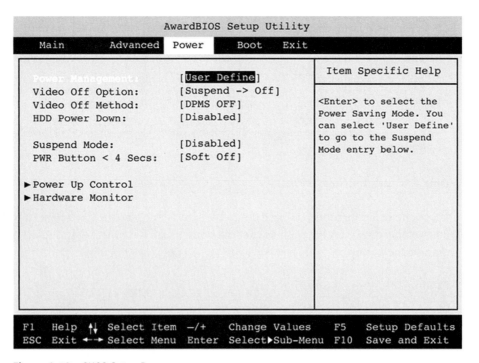

**Figure 6-19**   CMOS Setup Power menu

Figure 6-20 shows a sample Boot menu in CMOS setup. Here, you can set the order in which the system tries to boot from certain devices (called the boot sequence). Most likely when you first install a hard drive or an operating system, you will want to have the BIOS attempt to first boot from a CD and, if no CD is present, turn to the hard drive. After the OS is installed, to prevent accidental boots from a CD or other media, change CMOS setup to boot first from the hard drive. You will learn more about this in the installation procedures at the end of this chapter, as well as in later chapters.

A+ ESS
1.1

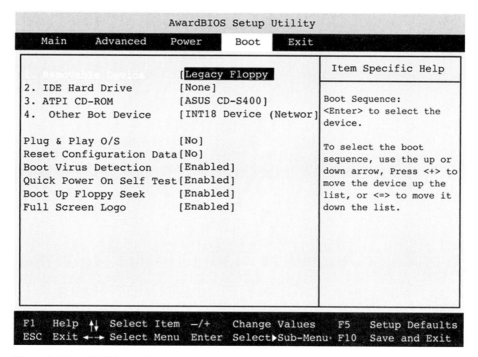

Figure 6-20  CMOS Setup Boot menu

Depending on the specific BIOS you are working with, an Advanced menu in the setup program or on other menus might contain other configuration options. When you finish, an exit screen such as the one shown in Figure 6-21 gives you various options, such as saving or discarding changes and then exiting the program, restoring default settings, or saving changes and remaining in the program.

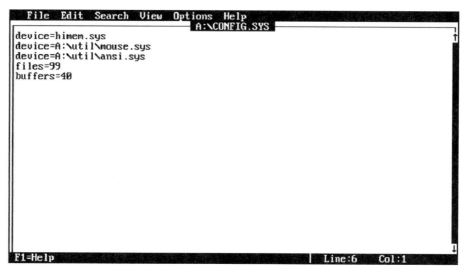

Figure 6-21  CMOS Setup Exit menu

## Changing CMOS Setup for Brand-Name Computers

Many brand-name computer manufacturers, such as IBM, Dell, and Gateway, use their own custom-designed setup screens. These screens differ from the ones just shown. For example, Figure 6-22 shows the IBM BIOS Setup main menu for an IBM Thinkpad notebook computer. Under the Config option on the screen, you can configure the network port,

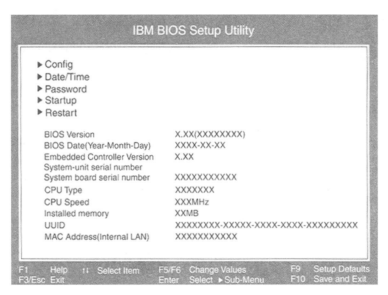

**Figure 6-22**   CMOS setup main menu for an IBM computer

serial port, parallel port, PCI bus, USB port, floppy drive, keyboard, display settings, power settings, power alarm, and memory settings.

Compare this CMOS main menu to the one shown in Figure 6-23 for a Gateway desktop computer. For all these different brand-name computers, what you can configure is similar, but the setup screens are likely to be organized differently.

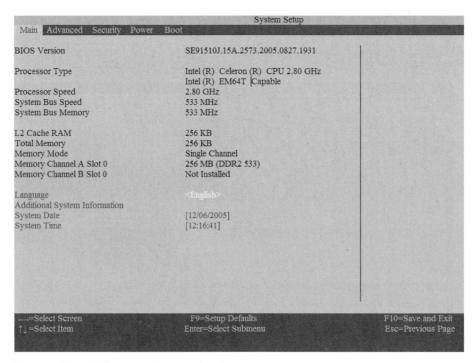

**Figure 6-23**   CMOS setup main menu for a Gateway computer

### Battery Power to CMOS RAM

A small trickle of electricity from a nearby battery enables CMOS RAM to hold configuration data even while the main power to the computer is off. If the battery is disconnected or fails, setup information is lost. An indication that the battery is getting weak is that the system date and time are incorrect after the PC has been turned off and turned back on.

A+ ESS
1.1

Several types of CMOS batteries are available:

▲ A 3.6-V lithium battery with a four-pin connector; connects with a Velcro strip
▲ A 4.5-V alkaline battery with a four-pin connector; connects with a Velcro strip
▲ A 3.6-V barrel-style battery with a two-pin connector; soldered on
▲ A 3-V lithium coin-cell battery

Figure 6-24 shows the coin cell, the most common type of CMOS battery.

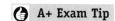
Coin cell battery

**Figure 6-24**   The coin cell is the most common type of CMOS battery

A+ ESS
1.1
6.3

## Setting Startup Passwords in CMOS

Access to a computer can be controlled using a **startup password**, sometimes called a **user password** or **power-on password**. If the password has been enabled and set in CMOS setup, the startup BIOS asks for the password during the boot just before the BIOS begins searching for an OS. If the password is entered incorrectly, the boot process terminates. The password is stored in CMOS RAM and is changed by accessing the setup screen. (This password is not the same as the OS password.) Many computers also provide a jumper near the chip holding CMOS RAM; when the jumper is set to on, the computer "forgets" any changes made to default settings stored in CMOS. By jumping these pins, you can disable a forgotten password.

> 🔔 **A+ Exam Tip**
>
> The A+ IT 220-602 exam expects you to be able to configure a motherboard. You need to know how and when to use CMOS setup to make appropriate changes. And to help secure a computer, you need to know how to set startup passwords.

## Lists of CMOS Settings

Motherboard manuals should contain a list of all CMOS settings, an explanation of their meanings, and their recommended values. When you purchase a motherboard or a computer, be sure the manual is included. If you don't have the manual, you can sometimes go to the motherboard manufacturer's Web site and download the information you need to understand the specific CMOS settings of your computer. Table 6-5 lists some CMOS settings. Several of these are discussed in future chapters.

> 📝 **Notes**
>
> In documentation, a.k.a. stands for "also known as."

| Category | Setting | Description |
|---|---|---|
| Standard | Date and time | Sets the system date and time (called the CMOS setup real-time clock). |
| | Keyboard | Tells the system if the keyboard is installed or not; useful if the computer is used as a print or file server and you don't want someone changing settings. |
| | Hard disk type | Records the size and mapping of the drive or sets to automatically detect the HDD (discussed in Chapter 8). |
| | Floppy disk type | Sets the floppy disk type; choices are usually $3^1/_2$-inch and $5^1/_4$-inch. |
| BIOS Features Menu | Quick boot | Enable/disable. Enable to cause POST to skip some tests and speed up booting. Disable this feature when installing or testing a motherboard to get a thorough POST. |
| | Above 1 MB memory test | Disables POST check of this memory to speed up booting; the OS checks this memory anyway. |
| | Memory parity error check | For older motherboards, enables parity checking to ensure that memory is correct. |
| | System boot sequence | Establishes the drive the system turns to first to look for an OS; normally the hard drive (drive C) and then CD or floppy drive (drive A). |
| | External cache memory | Enables L2 cache. A frequent error in setup is to have cache but not use it because it's disabled here. Used on older motherboards that have on-board cache memory. |
| | Password checking option | Establishes a startup password. Use this only if you need to prevent someone untrustworthy from using your PC. Sometimes there are two passwords, each with different levels of security. |
| | Video ROM Shadow C000, 16K | For DOS and Windows 9x, shadowing video ROM is recommended because ROM runs slower than RAM. |
| | System ROM Shadow F000, 64K | Enabling shadow system ROM is recommended. |
| | IDE multiblock mode | Enables a hard drive to read or write several sectors at a time; depends on the kind of hard drive you have. |
| | Plug and Play (PnP) | Enable/disable. Enable for Windows 9x, which uses PnP data from BIOS. Disable for Windows 2000/XP, which does all the PnP configuration. |
| | Boot sector virus protection | Gives a warning when something is being written to the boot sector of the hard drive. Can be a nuisance if your software is designed to write to the boot sector regularly. When installing or upgrading an operating system, disable this protection so the OS install process can alter the boot sector without interruption. |
| Advanced Chipset Setup | AT cycle wait state | Sets the number of wait states the processor must endure while it interfaces with a device on the ISA or EISA bus. Increase this if an old and slow ISA card is not working well. |

Table 6-5  CMOS settings and their purpose

| Category | Setting | Description |
| --- | --- | --- |
| | AGP capability | Switches between AGP 1x, AGP 2x, AGP 4x, and AGP 8x versions to accommodate different AGP video cards. |
| | AGP aperture size | Adjusts the amount of system memory AGP can address. |
| | AGP voltage | Sets AGP operating voltage according to video card requirements. |
| | VGA BIOS sequence | Determines the order in which PCI/AGP is initialized; important mainly with dual monitors. |
| | Processor serial number | Allows processor ID# to be switched off for privacy (Pentium III only). |
| | Serial port | Sets beginning I/O address and IRQ; sometimes you can enable/disable the port. |
| | Parallel port mode | ECP or EPP (differences are discussed in Chapter 9). |
| | Infrared | Enable/disable (sometimes enabling infrared disables the second serial port, which uses the same resources). |
| Power Management Menu | Power management | Disables or enables all power management features; these features are designed to conserve electricity. |
| | Video off method | Sets which way video to the monitor will be suspended. |
| | HDD power down | Disables or enables the feature to shut down the hard drive after a period of inactivity. |
| | Wake on LAN | Allows your PC to be booted from another computer on the same network; it requires an ATX or BTX power supply that supports the feature. |
| | Wake on keyboard | Allows you to power up your PC by pressing a certain key combination. |
| Hard Drive Settings | IDE HDD autodetect | Detects HDDs installed on either IDE channel; allows you to specify Normal, Large, or LBA mode, but Autodetect is recommended. |
| | Serial ATA | Configure to IDE or RAID. |
| | SMART monitoring | Monitors the HDD for failure. |
| Hardware Device Settings | Processor operating speed | Sets the appropriate speed for your processor; used for throttling and overclocking. |
| | External clock | Sets the system bus speed. |
| | I/O voltage | Sets the appropriate I/O voltage for the processor. |
| | Core voltage | Sets the appropriate core voltage for the processor. |

*Note*: The titles, locations, and inclusion or exclusion of BIOS categories and settings depend on the manufacturer, BIOS version, or both. For instance, Plug and Play might be a group of settings sharing a category with other settings in one version of BIOS, whereas Plug and Play might be its own category in another BIOS version.

**Table 6-5**  CMOS settings and their purpose (continued)

A+ ESS
1.1
6.3

## PROTECTING DOCUMENTATION AND CONFIGURATION SETTINGS

If the battery goes bad or is disconnected, you can lose the settings saved in CMOS RAM. If you are using default settings, reboot with a good battery and instruct setup to restore the default settings. Setup has to autodetect the hard drive present, and you need to set the date and time, but you can easily recover from the problem. However, if you have customized some CMOS settings, you need to restore them. The most reliable way to restore settings is to keep a written record of all the changes you make to CMOS.

If you are permanently responsible for a computer, you should consider keeping a written record of what you have done to maintain it. Use a small notebook or similar document to record CMOS settings that are not the default settings, hardware and software installed, network settings, and similar information. Suppose someone decides to tinker with a PC for which you are responsible, changes a jumper on the motherboard, and cannot remember which jumper she changed. The computer no longer works, and the documentation for the board is now invaluable. Lost or misplaced documentation greatly complicates the otherwise simple job of reading the settings for each jumper and checking them on the board. Keep the documentation well labeled in a safe place. If you have several computers to maintain, you might consider a filing system for each computer.

---

## APPLYING│CONCEPTS    *Saving and Restoring CMOS Settings Using Third-Party Utility Software*

If you lose CMOS settings, another way to restore them is to use a backup of the settings that you have previously saved on a floppy disk. One third-party utility that allows you to save CMOS settings is Norton Utilities by Symantec (*www.symantec.com*). Sometimes the support CD that comes with a motherboard has a utility on it to save CMOS settings to a floppy disk.

You can also download a shareware utility to record CMOS settings. One example follows, but know that the files might change with new releases of the software.

1. Access the Internet and use a search engine to find a site offering Cmos.zip. Two current locations are: *www.programmersheaven.com/zone24/cat31/4174.htm* and *www.computerhope.com/downlod.htm*.

2. Select and download Cmos.zip. You can then exit the Internet.

3. Unzip the compressed file and print the contents of the documentation file.

4. Double-click the **Cmos.exe** file you unzipped. The program shows the current contents of CMOS memory in a DOS box.

5. Enter **S** (for Save) at the command line. Enter the drive letter of your floppy drive and a filename to save the current CMOS settings to floppy disk. A sample path and filename might be **A:MYCMOS**.

6. Enter **Q** to quit the program.

### Notes

When you want to retrieve the contents of the file from the floppy disk, run the Cmos.exe program again, and enter L (for Load) at the command line, specifying the name of the file you saved on the floppy disk.

A+ ESS
1.1
1.4

A+
220-602
1.1

Another method is to carefully tape a cardboard folder to the inside top or side of the computer case and safely tuck the hardware documentation there. This works well if you are responsible for several computers spread over a wide area.

Regardless of the method you use, it's important that you keep your written record up to date and stored with the hardware documentation in a safe place. Leaving it in the care of users who might not realize its value is probably not a good idea. The notebook and documentation will be invaluable as you solve future problems with this PC.

## FLASHING ROM BIOS

Recall that ROM BIOS includes the CMOS setup program, the startup BIOS that manages the startup process, and the system BIOS that manages basic I/O functions of the system.

**APPLYING CONCEPTS**   When flashing ROM, the first step is to accurately identify the BIOS version currently installed. You can identify your motherboard and BIOS in several different ways:

▲ Look on the CMOS setup main screen for the BIOS manufacturer and version number.
▲ Look on the motherboard for the brand and model imprinted on the board (see Figure 6-25). If you download the BIOS upgrade from the motherboard manufacturer Web site, this information might be all you need to select the correct BIOS upgrade.

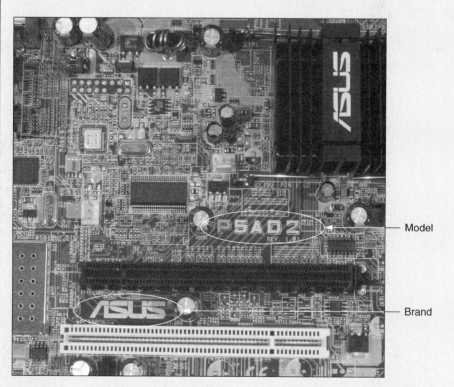

**Figure 6-25** The motherboard brand and model are imprinted somewhere on the board

▲ Use third-party software (such as BIOS Agent at *www.unicore.com*) or an OS utility (such as Windows System Information) to determine the BIOS information.
▲ Stop the boot process and look for the BIOS information reported early in the boot process.

A+ ESS
1.1
1.4

A+
220-602
1.1

To stop the boot process early so you can read the BIOS information, first try the following:

1. Turn off the system power and then turn it back on.

2. While memory is counting on the screen, hold down the Pause/Break key to stop the startup process.

3. Look for the long string of numbers in the lower-left corner of your screen that identifies the motherboard.

4. Look for the BIOS manufacturer and version number somewhere near the top of the screen.

If the above list doesn't work, try turning off the PC, unplugging the keyboard, and then turning on the PC. For older systems, the resulting keyboard error stops the boot process.

To flash ROM, carefully read the motherboard documentation, as different motherboards use different methods. If you can't find the documentation, check the motherboard manufacturer's Web site, and check the directions that came with the upgrade software. Generally, you perform these tasks:

1. Download the BIOS upgrade from the motherboard manufacturer Web site. If you can't find an upgrade on this site, try the BIOS manufacturer Web site or a third-party site. Most often you are instructed to save this upgrade to a bootable floppy disk.

2. Set a jumper on the motherboard, or change a setting in CMOS setup to tell BIOS to expect an upgrade.

3. Boot from the floppy disk and follow the menu options to upgrade BIOS. If the menu gives you the option to save the old BIOS to disk, do so in case you need to revert to the old BIOS.

4. Set the jumper back to its original setting, reboot the system, and verify that all is working.

 **Notes**

> After flashing BIOS, if the motherboard gives problems, you need to consider that the chipset drivers might also need updating. To update the chipset drivers, go to the Web site of the motherboard manufacturer and download the chipset driver files for the OS you are using. Then follow the manufacturer's instructions to perform the update.

Makers of BIOS code are likely to change BIOS frequently because providing the upgrade on the Internet is so easy for them. You can get upgraded BIOS code from manufacturers' Web sites or disks, or from third-party BIOS resellers' Web sites or disks. Generally, however, follow the principle that "if it's not broke, don't fix it"; update your BIOS only if you're having a problem with your motherboard or there's a new BIOS feature you want to use.

**Caution**

> Be *very careful* that you upgrade BIOS with the correct upgrade and that you follow the manufacturer's instructions correctly. Upgrading with the wrong file could make your system BIOS useless. If you're not sure that you're using the correct upgrade, *don't guess*. Check with the technical support for your BIOS before moving forward. Before you call technical support, have the information that identifies your BIOS and motherboard available.

A+ ESS
1.1
1.4

A+
220-602
1.1

All these programs are considered firmware and are stored on a chip on the motherboard, called the ROM BIOS chip or firmware chip. If a motherboard becomes unstable (such as when the system hangs at odd times), some functions are lost (such as a USB port stops working), or you want to incorporate some new feature or component on the board (such as when you upgrade the processor), you might need to upgrade the programming stored on the ROM BIOS chip. The process of upgrading or refreshing the ROM BIOS chip is called flashing ROM.

Figure 6-26 shows a sample Web site for flash ROM BIOS upgrades for Intel motherboards. If you can't find an upgrade on your motherboard or BIOS manufacturer Web site, try the BIOS Upgrades Web site by eSupport.com, Inc. at *www.esupport.com*. Table 6-6 lists BIOS manufacturers. A list of motherboard manufacturers is given in Table 6-2 earlier in the chapter.

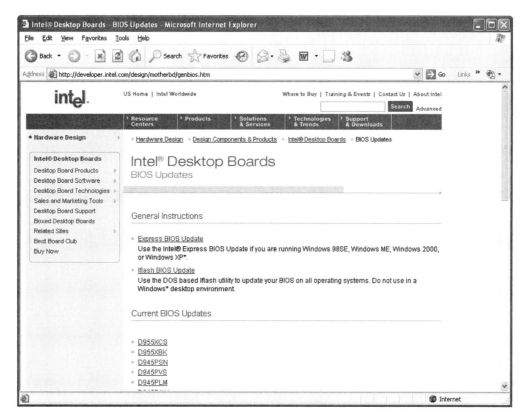

**Figure 6-26** Intel displays a list of motherboard model numbers that have a Flash BIOS upgrade available

| Company | URL |
|---|---|
| American Megatrends, Inc. (AMI) | *www.megatrends.com* or *www.ami.com* |
| Compaq and Hewlett-Packard | *thenew.hp.com* |
| Dell | *www.dell.com* |
| eSupport.com (BIOS upgrades) | *www.esupport.com* |
| Gateway | *www.gateway.com* |
| IBM | *www.ibm.com/support* |
| Phoenix Technologies (First BIOS, Phoenix, and Award) | *www.phoenix.com* |
| Wim's BIOS | *www.wimsbios.com* |

**Table 6-6** BIOS manufacturers

## MOTHERBOARD DRIVERS

A motherboard comes bundled with a CD that contains drivers for all the onboard components. Most likely Windows can use its own internal drivers for these components, but if you have trouble with an onboard component or want to use a feature that is not working, use the motherboard CD to install the manufacturer drivers into Windows. Also, the motherboard manufacturer updates motherboard drivers from time to time. For an unstable motherboard, you can try downloading and installing updated chipset drivers and other drivers for onboard components.

The motherboard CD might also contain useful utilities such as a utility that you can install under Windows to monitor the CPU temperature and alert you if overheating occurs.

## *REPLACING A MOTHERBOARD*

When you replace a motherboard, you pretty much have to disassemble an entire computer, install the new motherboard, and reassemble the system. The following list is meant to be a general overview of the process and is not meant to include the details of all possible installation scenarios, which can vary according to the components and OS you are using. The general process for replacing a motherboard is as follows:

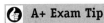

**A+ Exam Tip**

The A+ IT 220-602 exam expects you to know how to select and install a motherboard.

1. *Verify that you have selected the right motherboard to install in the system.* The new motherboard should have the same form factor as the case, support the RAM modules and processor you want to install on it, and have other internal and external connectors you need for your system.

2. *Determine proper configuration settings for the motherboard.* Especially important are any jumpers, DIP switches, or CMOS settings specifically for the processor, and RAM speeds and timing. Read the motherboard manual from cover to cover. You can also check the manufacturer Web site for answers to any questions you might have.

3. *Remove components so you can reach the old motherboard.* Turn off the system and disconnect all cables and cords. Open the case cover and remove all internal cables and cords connected to the motherboard. Remove all expansion cards. To safely remove the old motherboard, you might have to remove drives.

4. *Set any jumpers or switches on the new motherboard.* This is much easier to do before you put the board in the case.

5. *Install the processor and processor cooler.* The processor comes already installed on some motherboards, in which case you just need to install the cooler. You might need to add thermal compound. Also, if you are working with a heavy cooling assembly, some manufacturers suggest you install the motherboard in the case before installing the cooler. Follow motherboard and processor installation instructions. Processor instructions take precedent over motherboard instructions.

6. *Install RAM into the appropriate slots on the motherboard.*

7. *Install the motherboard.* Place the motherboard into the case and, using spacers or screws, securely fasten the board to the case.

**6**

A+
220-602
1.1

8. *Attach cabling that goes from the case switches to the motherboard, and from the power supply and drives to the motherboard.* Pay attention to how cables are labeled and to any information in the documentation about where to attach them. Position and tie cables neatly together to make sure they don't obstruct the fans and the airflow.

9. *Install the video card on the motherboard.* Usually this card goes into the AGP slot or PCI Express x16 slot.

10. *Plug the computer into a power source, and attach the monitor and keyboard.* Note that you do not attach the mouse now, for the initial setup. Although the mouse generally does not cause problems during setup, initially install only the things you absolutely need.

11. *Boot the system and enter CMOS setup.* As you learned earlier in the chapter, you can do this using several methods, depending on what type of system you have.

12. *Make sure settings are set to the default.* If the motherboard comes new from the manufacturer, it will already be at default settings. If you are salvaging a motherboard from another system, you might need to reset settings to the default. Generally a jumper or switch sets all CMOS settings to default settings. You will need to do the following while you are in CMOS:

   ▲ Check the time and date.
   ▲ Check the floppy drive type.
   ▲ Make sure abbreviated POST is disabled. While you're installing a motherboard, you generally want it to do as many tests as possible. After you know the system is working, you can choose to abbreviate POST.
   ▲ Set the boot order to the hard drive, then a CD, if you will be booting the OS from the hard drive.
   ▲ Make sure "autodetect hard disk" is set so that the system automatically looks for drives.
   ▲ Leave everything else at their defaults unless you know that particular settings should be otherwise.
   ▲ Save and exit.

13. *Observe POST and verify that no errors occur.*

14. *Check for conflicts with system resources.* For Windows, use Device Manager to verify that the OS recognizes all devices and that no conflicts are reported.

15. *Install the motherboard drives.* If your motherboard comes with a CD that contains some motherboard drivers, install them now.

16. *Install any other expansion cards and drives.* Install each device and its drivers, one device at a time, rebooting and checking for conflicts after each installation.

17. *Verify that everything is operating properly, and make any final OS and CMOS adjustments, such as power management settings.*

Now let's look at the details of installing the motherboard into the computer case.

> **Notes**
>
> Whenever you install or uninstall software or hardware, keep a notebook with details about the components you are working on, configuration settings, manufacturer specifications, and other relevant information. This helps if you need to backtrack later, and can also help you document and troubleshoot your computer system. Keep all hardware documentation for this system together with the notebook in an envelope in a safe place.

**Caution**

As with any installation, remember the importance of using a ground strap (ground bracelet) to ground yourself when working inside a computer case to protect components against ESD.

**Video**

Preparing a Motherboard for Installation

# PREPARING THE MOTHERBOARD TO GO INTO THE CASE

Before you begin preparing the motherboard, read the manual that comes with it from beginning to end. The steps listed in this section are general, and you will need to know information specific to your motherboard. Visually familiarize yourself with the configuration of the case and the motherboard.

## SETTING THE JUMPERS

The first step in preparing the motherboard to go in the case is to set the jumpers or DIP switches. When doing an installation, read the motherboard documentation carefully, looking for explanations of how jumpers and DIP switches on the board are used. This information differs from one motherboard to another. For older boards, a jumper group might control the system bus frequency and another group might control the CPU frequency multiplier. Set the jumpers and DIP switches according to the hardware you will be installing.

For example, Figure 6-27 shows the documentation for one motherboard that uses three jumpers to configure the BIOS; the jumper group is shown in Figure 6-28. Set the jumper group to the normal setting so that BIOS uses the current configuration for booting. Once set, the jumpers should be changed only if you are trying to recover when the power-up password is lost or flashing BIOS has failed. Figure 6-28 shows the jumper cap in the normal position.

| Jumper Position | Mode | Description |
|---|---|---|
| 1 □ ● ○ 3 | Normal (default) | The current BIOS configuration is used for booting. |
| 1 □ ● ○ 3 | Configure | After POST, the BIOS displays a menu in CMOS setup that can be used to clear the user and supervisor power-on passwords. |
| 1 □ ○ ○ 3 | Recovery | Recovery is used to recover from a failed BIOS update. Details can be found on the motherboard CD. |

**Figure 6-27** BIOS configuration jumper settings

Jumpers set for normal boot

**Figure 6-28** BIOS setup configuration jumpers

6

A+
220-602
1.1

## ADDING THE PROCESSOR, FAN, HEAT SINK, AND MEMORY MODULES

Now that you have set the jumpers on the motherboard, you are ready to add the processor itself. Check out Chapter 5 for information on how to install a processor and cooler assembly. You then need to install RAM in the memory slots. Chapter 7 covers how to buy and install RAM for a specific motherboard.

Video

Installing a Processor

## INSTALLING THE MOTHERBOARD IN THE CASE

Here are the general steps for installing the motherboard in the case:

1. Install the faceplate. The faceplate or I/O shield is a metal plate that comes with the computer case and fits over the ports to create a well-fitting enclosure for them. A case might have several faceplates designed for several types of motherboards. Select the correct one and discard the others (see Figure 6-29). Insert the faceplate in the hole at the back of the case (see Figure 6-30).

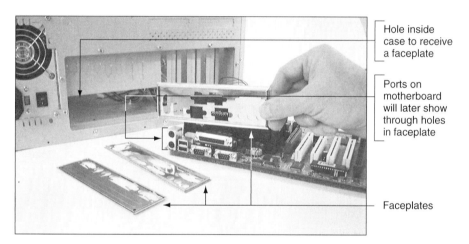

Figure 6-29   The computer case comes with several faceplates. Select the faceplate that fits over the ports that come off the motherboard. The other plates can be discarded.

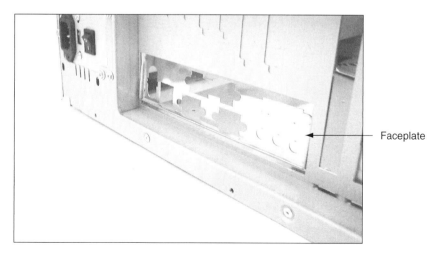

Figure 6-30   Install the faceplate in the hole at the rear of the computer case

A+
220-602
1.1

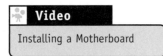

Installing a Motherboard

2. Install the standoffs. **Standoffs**, also called **spacers**, are round plastic or metal pegs that separate the motherboard from the case, so that components on the back of the motherboard do not touch the case. Make sure the locations of the standoffs match the screw holes on the motherboard (see Figure 6-31). If you need to remove a standoff to move it to a new slot, needle-nose pliers work well to unscrew or unplug the standoff. The case will have more holes than you need to support several types of motherboards.

Spacer installed

Spacer not installed

Hole in motherboard for screw to attach board to spacer

**Figure 6-31**    The spacers line up with the holes on the motherboard and keep it from touching the case

3. Place the motherboard inside the case (see Figure 6-32), and use screws to attach it to the case. Figure 6-33 shows how you must align the standoffs to the holes on the motherboard. The screws fit into the standoffs you installed earlier. There should be at least six standoff/screw sets, and there might be as many as nine. Use as many as there are holes in the motherboard.

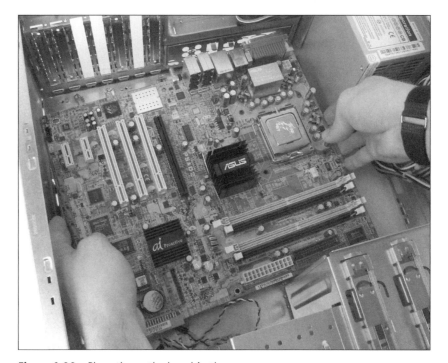

**Figure 6-32**    Place the motherboard in the case

**Figure 6-33** Use screws to attach the motherboard to the case via the spacers

4. Connect the power cord from the power supply to the P1 power connection on the motherboard. (If you are using an AT motherboard, you have two power connections, P8 and P9, which are connected using the black-to-black rule.) See Figure 6-34.

**Figure 6-34** The 20-pin connector supplies power to the motherboard

5. Connect the 4-pin auxiliary power cord coming from the power supply to the motherboard, as shown in Figure 6-35. This cord supplies the supplemental power required for a Pentium 4 processor.

A+
220-602
1.1

**Figure 6-35** The auxiliary 4-pin power cord provides power to the Pentium 4 processor

6. Connect the wire leads from the front panel of the case to the motherboard. These are the wires for the switches and lights on the front of the computer. Because your case and your motherboard might not have been made by the same manufacturer, you need to pay close attention to the source of the wires to determine where they connect on the motherboard. For example, Figure 6-36 shows a computer case that has five wires from the front panel that connect to the motherboard.

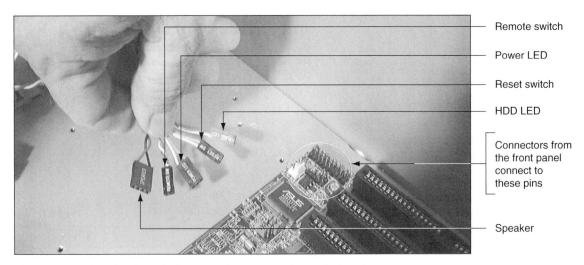

**Figure 6-36** Five wires from the front panel connect to the motherboard

The five wires showing in the figure are labeled as follows:

▲ *Remote switch*. Controls power to the motherboard; must be connected for the PC to power up
▲ *Power LED*. Light indicating that power is on
▲ *Reset switch*. Used to reboot the computer

▲ *HDD LED.* Controls a light on the front panel that lights up when any IDE device is in use. (LED stands for light-emitting diode; an LED is a light on the front panel.)

▲ *Speaker.* Controls the speaker.

7. To know which wire connects to which pins, see the motherboard documentation or look for cryptic labels imprinted on the motherboard near the banks of pins. Sometimes the motherboard documentation is not clear, but guessing is okay when connecting a wire to a connection. If it doesn't work, no harm is done.

> **📝 Notes**
>
> To help orient the connector on the motherboard pins, look for a small triangle embedded on the connector that marks one of the outside wires as pin 1 (see Figure 6-37). Look for pin 1 to be labeled on the motherboard as a small 1 embedded to either the right or the left of the group of pins. Also, sometimes the documentation marks pin 1 as a square pin in the diagram, rather than round like the other pins. The diagram in Figure 6-38 shows what you can expect from motherboard documentation where the leads connect to the pins in Panel 1.

**Figure 6-37** Look for the small triangle embedded on the wire lead connectors to orient the connector correctly to the motherboard connector pins

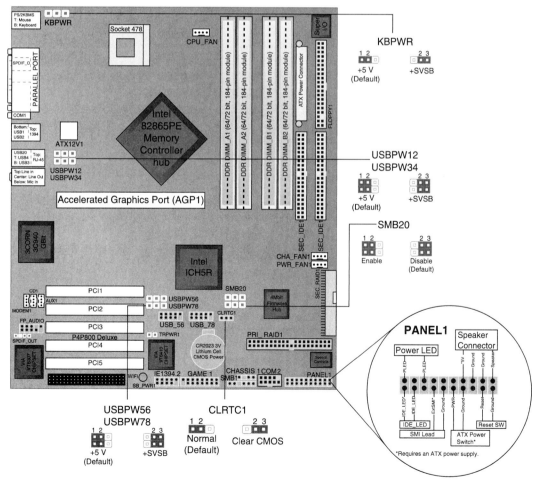

**Figure 6-38** Connector group for front-panel leads

8. Depending on your motherboard, there might be a cable to connect an internal USB connection to USB ports on the front of the case. Connect the cable, as shown in Figure 6-39.

Two USB ports on the front of the case

**Figure 6-39**    Connect the cable coming from the USB ports on the front of the case to one of the two USB connectors on the motherboard

## COMPLETING THE INSTALLATION

After you install the motherboard and connect all cables and cords, next you install the video card and plug in the keyboard and monitor. You are now ready to turn on the system and observe POST occurs with no errors. After the Windows desktop loads, insert the CD that came bundled with the motherboard and execute any setup program on the CD. Follow the steps onscreen to install any drivers, which might include drivers for onboard devices and ports such as video, network, audio, USB, RAID, or the chipset.

Look back at the general list of steps to replace a motherboard at the beginning of this section for the list of things to check and do to complete the installation and return the system to good working order.

## *TROUBLESHOOTING THE MOTHERBOARD AND PROCESSOR*

Items that can be exchanged without returning the motherboard to the factory are called field replaceable units (FRUs). On older AT motherboards, these FRU components were the processor, RAM, RAM cache, ROM BIOS chip, and CMOS battery. On newer motherboards, FRU components are the processor, RAM, and CMOS battery. Also, the motherboard itself is an FRU. As you troubleshoot the motherboard and discover that some component is not working, such as a network port, you might be able to disable that component in CMOS setup and install a card to take its place.

**A+ Exam Tip**

The A+ Essentials and IT 220-602 exams expect you to know how to troubleshoot problems with motherboards and processors.

When troubleshooting the motherboard, use whatever clues POST can give you. Recall that, before it checks video, POST reports any error messages as beep codes. When a PC boots, one beep indicates that all is well after POST. If you

hear more than one beep, look up the beep code in Chapter 3. Error messages on the screen indicate that video is working. If the beep code or error message is not in Chapter 3, try the Web site of the ROM BIOS or motherboard manufacturer for information. Figure 6-40 shows the Web site for AMI with explanations of beep codes produced by its startup BIOS.

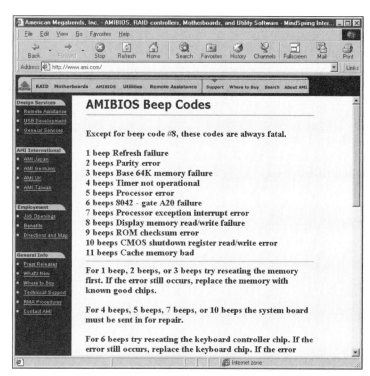

**Figure 6-40**  The ROM BIOS manufacturer's Web site is a good source of information about beep codes

Remember that you can try substituting good hardware components for those you suspect are bad. Be cautious here. A friend once had a computer that would not boot. He replaced the hard drive, with no change. He replaced the motherboard next. The computer booted up with no problem; he was delighted, until it failed again. Later he discovered that a faulty power supply had damaged his original motherboard. When he traded the bad one for a good one, the new motherboard also got zapped! If you suspect problems with the power supply, check the voltage coming from the power supply before putting in a new motherboard! (Instructions on troubleshooting the power supply are in Chapter 4.)

The following sections contain descriptions of some common problems and what to do about them.

## PROBLEMS WITH INSTALLATIONS

If you have just installed a new processor on a working motherboard and the system does not boot, do the following:

1. Open the case and check these things:

▲ Did you install thermal paste (thermal compound) between the processor and the heat sink?

▲ Is the cooler securely fastened to the frame on the motherboard? If the cooler and thermal paste are not installed correctly, the CPU can overheat during the boot, causing BIOS to immediately power down the system.

▲ Remove the processor from its socket and look for bent or damaged pins or lands on the socket and processor.

2. Reinstall the processor and try the boot again.

3. Reinstall the old processor, flash BIOS, and then try the new processor again.

If you have just installed a new motherboard that is not working, check the following:

- Have you installed the front cover on the case? Sometimes a system refuses to power up until this cover is in place.
- Is there a power switch on the back of the case that is not turned on?
- Study the documentation and verify all connections are correct. Most likely this is the problem. Remember the Power Switch lead from the front of the case must be connected to the panel on the motherboard.
- Verify the processor, thermal compound, and cooler are all installed correctly.
- Remove RAM and reinstall the modules.
- Verify a standoff that is not being used by the motherboard is not under the motherboard and causing a short.
- If the system can boot into Windows, install all motherboard drivers on the CD that came bundled with the board.
- Check the motherboard Web site for other things you can check or try.

## PROBLEMS WITH THE MOTHERBOARD AND PROCESSOR

Symptoms that a motherboard or processor is failing can appear as:

- The system begins to boot but then powers down.
- An error message displays during the boot. Investigate this message.
- The system becomes unstable, hangs, or freezes at odd times.
- Intermittent Windows or hard drive errors occur.
- Components on the motherboard or devices connected to it don't work.

The motherboard might have come bundled with a support CD. Look on it for drivers of board components that are not working. For example, if the USB ports are not working, try updating the USB drivers with those stored on the support CD. Load the CD and follow directions onscreen.

If this doesn't resolve the problem, try the following:

- A power-saving feature might be the source of the problem. Ask yourself, "Is the system in a doze or sleep mode?" Many "green," or environmentally friendly, systems can be programmed through CMOS to suspend the monitor or even the drive if the keyboard or processor has been inactive for a few minutes. Pressing any key usually causes operations to resume exactly where the user left off.
- If the fan is running, reseat or replace the processor, BIOS, or RAM. Try installing a DIMM in a different slot. A POST code diagnostic card is a great help at this point. These cards are discussed in Chapter 22.
- Sometimes a dead computer can be fixed by simply disassembling it and reseating cables, adapter cards, socketed chips, and SIMMs, DIMMs, or RIMMs. Bad connections and corrosion are common problems.
- Check jumpers, DIP switches, and CMOS settings.
- Look for physical damage on the motherboard. Look for frayed traces on the bottom of the board or brown or burnt capacitors on the board.
- Check CMOS for a temperature reading that indicates overheating.

A+ ESS
1.3

A+
220-602
1.2

▲ Flash BIOS.

▲ A dead or dying battery may cause problems. Sometimes, after a long holiday, a weak battery causes the CMOS to forget its configuration.

▲ Try using the CD that came with the motherboard, which most likely has diagnostic tests on it that might identify the problem with the motherboard.

▲ Reduce the system to essentials. Remove any unnecessary hardware, such as expansion cards, and then try to boot again.

▲ Exchange the processor.

▲ If an onboard component isn't working but the motherboard is stable, go into CMOS setup and disable the component. Then install a replacement component using a port or expansion slot.

▲ Exchange the motherboard, but before you do, measure the voltage output of the power supply or simply replace it, in case it is producing too much power and has damaged the board.

---

# APPLYING|CONCEPTS

Jessica complained to Wally, her PC support technician, that Windows was occasionally giving errors, data would get corrupted, or an application would not work as it should. At first Wally suspected Jessica might need a little more training in how to open and close an application or save a file, but he discovered user error was not the problem. He tried reinstalling the application software Jessica most often used, and even reinstalled Windows, but the problems persisted.

Then he began to suspect a hardware problem. Carefully examining the motherboard revealed the source of the problem: failing capacitors. Look carefully at Figure 6-41 and you can see five bad capacitors with bulging and discolored heads. (Know that sometimes a leaking capacitor can also show crusty corrosion at the base of the capacitor.) When Wally replaced the motherboard, the problems went away.

### Notes

Catastrophic errors (errors that cause the system to not boot or a device to not work) are much easier to resolve than intermittent errors (errors that come and go).

Bad capacitors

**Figure 6-41** These five bad capacitors have bulging and discolored heads

## >> CHAPTER SUMMARY

▲ The motherboard is the most complicated of all components inside the computer. It contains the processor and accompanying chipset, real-time clock, ROM BIOS, CMOS configuration chip, RAM, RAM cache, system bus, expansion slots, jumpers, ports, and power supply connections. The motherboard you select determines both the capabilities and limitations of your system.

▲ Some components can be built in to the motherboard, in which case they are called on-board components. Other components can be attached to the system in some other way, such as on an expansion card.

▲ A bus is a path on the motherboard that carries electrical power, control signals, memory addresses, and data to different components on the board.

▲ A bus can be 16, 32, 64, or more bits wide. The first ISA bus had an 8-bit data path. The second ISA slot had a 16-bit data path.

▲ Some outdated buses are the 16-bit ISA, 32-bit MCA and EISA buses, and VESA bus. Current buses are the PCI bus, AGP bus, and PCI Express. A local bus runs in sync with the system clock and is designed to allow fast devices quicker and more direct access to the processor than other buses. In addition, if the bus connects to the North Bridge of the chipset, it has more direct and faster access to the processor than if it attaches to the slower South Bridge. A bus slot used for a PCI Express x16 or AGP video card connects to the North Bridge.

▲ The most common method of configuring components on a motherboard is CMOS setup. Some motherboards also use jumpers or DIP switches to contain configuration settings.

▲ Jumpers on older motherboards can be used to set the motherboard speed and the processor frequency multiplier, which determines the processor speed. For newer boards, these settings are autodetected without the use of jumpers.

▲ ROM chips contain the programming code to manage POST and the system BIOS and to change CMOS settings. The setup or CMOS chip holds configuration information.

▲ Sometimes ROM BIOS programming stored on the firmware chip needs updating or refreshing. This process is called flashing BIOS.

▲ When installing a motherboard, first study the motherboard and set jumpers and DIP switches on the board. Sometimes the processor and cooler are best installed before installing the motherboard in the case. When the cooling assembly is heavy and bulky, it is best to install it after the motherboard is securely seated in the case.

## >> KEY TERMS

For explanations of key terms, see the Glossary near the end of the book.

audio/modem riser (AMR)
communication and networking
   riser (CNR)
dual inline package (DIP) switch
Industry Standard Architecture
   (ISA) slot

jumper
on-board ports
power-on password
riser card
spacers
standoffs

startup password
user password
wait state

## >> REVIEW QUESTIONS

1. The BTX form factor has up to how many expansion slots?

    a. 1

    b. 4

    c. 7

    d. 10

2. The PCI Express bus currently comes in how many different slot sizes?

    a. 1

    b. 2

    c. 3

    d. 4

3. Where is CMOS RAM typically located?

    a. On a RAM (RTC/NVRAM) chip

    b. On a floppy disk

    c. On a CD

    d. On external storage

4. Which of the following statements best describes how to access the setup program stored in ROM BIOS on newer computers?

    a. Use the Start menu from the desktop.

    b. Press a key or combination of keys during the boot process.

    c. Download a program from the manufacturer's Web site.

    d. Use a boot disk.

5. Which of the following best describes a start-up password?

    a. The password is different from the power-on password.

    b. The password is the same as the OS password.

    c. The password is changed by accessing the setup screen.

    d. Start-up passwords can never be disabled by using a jumper.

6. True or false? A board that has many embedded components easily accepts add-on devices from other manufacturers.

7. True or false? The number of wires that make up the memory address lines of the bus determines how many bits can be used for a memory address.

8. True or false? When one port fails, the entire motherboard must be replaced.

9. True or false? Standoffs are round plastic or metal pegs that separate the motherboard from the case, so that components on the back of the motherboard do not touch the case.

10. True or false? A jumper is closed if the cover is in place.

11. A component on the motherboard is called a(n) _____ or a(n) _____ component.

12. Embedded components are almost always configured through _____.

13. A device issues a(n) _____, which is a command to the processor to wait for slower devices to catch up.

14. The first expansion slots on early PCs were Industry Standard Architecture (ISA) slots which had a(n) _____ data path and ran at _____ MHz.

15. A bus that does not run in sync with the system clock is called a(n) _____ bus.

## CHAPTER 7

# Upgrading Memory

In earlier chapters, we talked about several important hardware components, how they work, and how to support them. In this chapter, we look at another component, memory, and examine the different memory technologies and how to upgrade memory. Memory technologies have evolved over the years. When you support an assortment of desktop and notebook computers, you'll be amazed at all the different variations of memory modules used in newer computers and older computers still in use. A simple problem of replacing a bad memory module can become a complex research project if you don't have a good grasp of current and past memory technologies. The first part of the chapter is devoted to studying all these technologies. Then we look at how to upgrade memory. Adding more memory to a system can sometimes greatly improve performance. Finally, you'll learn how to deal with problems with memory. In later chapters, you'll learn how to manage memory using Windows 2000/XP and Windows 9x/Me.

## RAM TECHNOLOGIES

A+ ESS
1.1

Recall that memory temporarily holds data and instructions as the CPU processes them and that computer memory is divided into two categories, ROM (read-only memory) and RAM (random access memory). ROM retains its data when the PCI is turned off, but RAM loses all its data. In Chapter 5, you learned about static RAM (SRAM) contained within the processor housing and sometimes embedded on the motherboard. In Chapter 6, you learned about ROM that is contained in the firmware chip on the motherboard where it holds the ROM BIOS. In this chapter, we focus on dynamic RAM (DRAM). Let's begin by summarizing what has already been covered in earlier chapters about SRAM and DRAM:

▲ In Chapter 1, you learned that most RAM is stored on the motherboard in modules called DIMMs, RIMMs, or SIMMs. An example of a DIMM is shown in Figure 7-1.

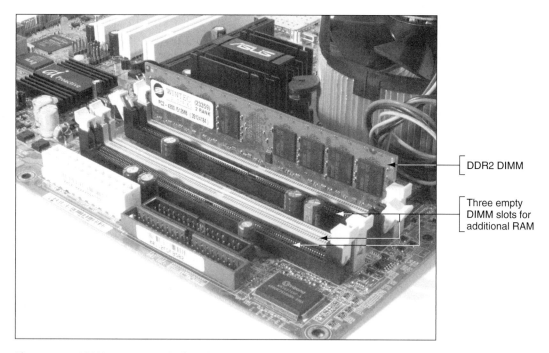

**Figure 7-1**  DRAM on most motherboards today is stored on DIMMs

▲ In Chapter 5, it was explained there can be two types of RAM: dynamic RAM (DRAM) and static RAM (SRAM). SRAM is faster than DRAM because SRAM does not lose its data as quickly as does DRAM and does not have to be refreshed as often.

▲ In Chapter 5, you learned that most processors today contain a memory cache inside the processor housing used to speed up memory access. This cache is made of SRAM because SRAM is faster than DRAM. Some motherboards have a small SRAM cache embedded on the motherboard separate from the cache inside the processor housing.

In earlier PCs, main memory was stored on the motherboard as single, socketed chips, but today DRAM is always stored in either DIMM, RIMM, or SIMM modules, which plug directly into the motherboard. The major differences among these modules are the width of the data path that each type of module accommodates and the way data moves from the system bus to the module. Figure 7-2 shows some examples of memory modules.

> ## Notes
>
> You might be interested in knowing why SRAM doesn't have to be refreshed the way DRAM does. SRAM and DRAM are both made of transistors, which are switches, and a transistor switch can stay in place as long as it has voltage available. However, DRAM transistor switches are charged by capacitors, which must be recharged, and SRAM transistors don't use capacitors. SRAM is more expensive than DRAM; therefore, most computers have a little SRAM and a lot of DRAM.

| Description of Module | Example |
| --- | --- |
| 240-pin DDR2 DIMM is currently the fastest memory. Can support dual channels or be installed as a single DIMM. Has one notch near the center of the edge connector. | 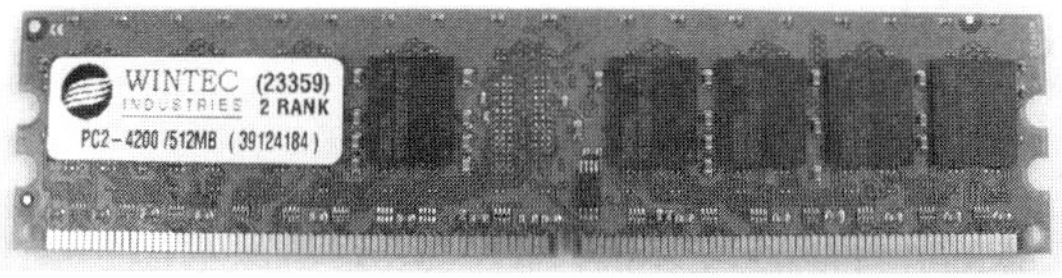 |
| 184-pin DDR DIMM can support dual channeling or be installed as single DIMMs. Has one offset notch. | 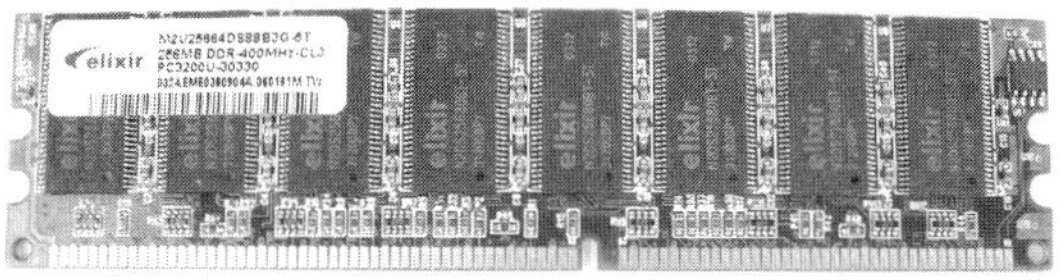 |
| 168-pin SDR DIMM has two notches that are positioned on the edge connector to indicate buffered, registered, unbuffered, and voltage requirements. |  |
| RIMM has 184 pins and two notches near the center of the edge connector. |  |
| 72-pin SIMM must be installed two modules to a bank of memory. |  |
| 30-pin SIMM must be installed four modules to a bank of memory. |  |

Figure 7-2  Types of memory modules

Older DRAM memory technologies operated asynchronously with the system bus, but newer DRAM memory types operate synchronously. To understand the difference between asynchronous and synchronous memory, consider this analogy: Children are jumping rope with a long rope, and one child on each end is turning the rope. A child who cannot keep in step with the turning rope can only run through on a single pass and must come back around to make another pass. A child who can keep in step with the rope can run into the center and jump awhile, until he is tired and runs out. Which child performs the most rope-jumping cycles in a given amount of time? The one who keeps in step with the rope. Similarly, synchronous memory retrieves data faster than asynchronous memory, because it keeps time with the system clock.

Table 7-1 summarizes DRAM technologies, old and new. How these DRAM technologies are used with SIMMs, DIMMs, and RIMMs is discussed in more detail in the following sections.

| Technology | Description | Used with |
|---|---|---|
| **Old Technologies** | | |
| Conventional | Used with earlier PCs but currently not available. | ▲ 30-pin SIMM |
| Fast page memory (FPM) | Improved access time over conventional memory. FPM is seldom seen today. | ▲ 30-pin or 72-pin SIMM<br>▲ 168-pin DIMM |
| Extended data out (EDO) | Refined version of FPM that speeds up access time. Might still see it on older motherboards. | ▲ 72-pin SIMM<br>▲ 168-pin DIMM |
| Burst EDO (BEDO) | Refined version of EDO that significantly improved access time over EDO. Seldom seen today because Intel chose not to support it. | ▲ 72-pin SIMM<br>▲ 168-pin DIMM |
| Synchronous DRAM (SDRAM) | SDRAM runs in sync with the system clock and is rated by clock speed, whereas earlier types of memory run independently of (and slower than) the system clock. | ▲ 66/100/133/150 MHz, 168-pin DIMM<br>▲ 66/100/133 MHz, 144-pin SO-DIMM |
| **Current Technologies** | | |
| DDR (Double-Data Rate) SDRAM | A faster version of SDRAM. | ▲ 184-pin DIMM, up to 500 MHz<br>▲ 200-pin SO-DIMM, up to 400 MHz |
| Rambus DRAM (RDRAM) | RDRAM is housed on a RIMM, uses a faster system bus (800 MHz or 1066 MHz), and can use a 16- or 32-bit data path. | ▲ 184-pin or 168-pin RIMM with 16-bit single channel<br>▲ 232-pin RIMM with 32-bit dual channel |
| DDR2 | Faster than DDR and uses less power. | ▲ 240-pin DIMM up to 2 GB size<br>▲ 214-pin SO-DIMM up to 1 GB size<br>▲ 244-pin Mini-DIMM |
| Dual Channeling | A technique whereby the memory controller interleaves access to DIMM pairs. | ▲ Used by DDR and DDR2 DIMMs |

**Table 7-1** DRAM memory technologies

A+ ESS
1.1

The goal of each new technology is increasing overall throughput while retaining accuracy. The older the motherboard, the older the memory technology it can use, so as a PC technician, you must be familiar with older technologies even though the boards sold today only use the latest memory technology.

> **Notes**
>
> Smaller versions of DIMMs and RIMMs, called SO-DIMMs and SO-RIMMs, are used in notebook computers. (SO stands for "small outline.") MicroDIMMs are used on subnotebook computers and are smaller than SO-DIMMs. You'll learn more about these memory modules and how to upgrade memory in notebooks in Chapter 20.

## SIMM TECHNOLOGIES

SIMMs have a 32-bit data path and are rated by speed, measured in nanoseconds (ns). Common SIMM speeds are 60, 70, or 80 ns. This speed is a measure of access time, which is the time it takes for the processor to access the data stored on a SIMM. The access time includes the time it takes for the processor to request the data, for the memory controller to locate the data on the SIMM and place the data on the memory bus, for the processor to read the data off the bus, and for the memory controller to **refresh** the memory chip on the SIMM. Note that an access time of 60 ns is faster than an access time of 70 ns. Therefore, the smaller the speed rating is, the faster the chip.

> **Notes**
>
> **EDO (extended data out)** was used on 72-pin SIMMs on motherboards rated at about 33 to 75 MHz. EDO was also used on earlier DIMMs and video memory and often provides on-board RAM on various expansion boards.

A+ ESS
1.1

## DIMM TECHNOLOGIES

Next came DIMM technologies, which have a 64-bit data path. (Some early DIMMs had a 128-bit data path, but they're now obsolete.) A DIMM (dual inline memory module) is called that because it has independent pins on opposite sides of the module. SIMMs have pins on both sides of the module, too, but with a SIMM, each pin pair is tied together into a single contact. A DIMM can have memory chips on one side (single-sided) or both sides (double-sided) of the module.

DIMMs are rated by speed and the amount of memory they hold. DIMMs have 168, 184, or 240 pins on the edge connector of the board and hold from 8 MB to 2 GB of RAM. The early DIMMs used EDO (168 pins) or **burst EDO (BEDO),** which is a refined version of EDO. BEDO was faster than EDO, but never gained a market share because Intel chose not to support it. BEDO and EDO DIMMs have two notches on the edge connector and run at constant speeds independent of the system bus speed.

> **A+ Exam Tip**
>
> The A+ Essentials exam expects you to know the purposes and characteristics of the following memory technologies: DRAM, SRAM, SDRAM, DDR, DDR2, and Rambus.

The first DIMM to run synchronized with the system clock is **synchronous DRAM (SDRAM),** which has two notches, and uses 168 pins. An early version of SDRAM is **SyncLink SDRAM (SLDRAM),** which was never embraced by the industry.

DIMMs have undergone several improvements. Next, we'll look at these DIMM technologies used to improve the performance and reliability of DIMMs. They include DDR, DDR2, buffered, registered, and dual channel DIMMs.

## DDR AND DDR2 DIMMS

Current DIMM technologies are DDR and DDR2. **Double Data Rate SDRAM (DDR SDRAM or SDRAM II)** is an improved version of SDRAM. When DDR first came out, it was called DDR SDRAM or SDRAM II. DDR runs twice as fast as regular SDRAM, has one notch, and uses 184 pins. Instead of processing data for each beat of the system clock, as regular SDRAM does, it processes data when the beat rises and again when it falls, doubling the data rate of memory. If a motherboard runs at 200 MHz, DDR memory runs at 400 MHz. A consortium of 20 major computer manufacturers supports DDR. It is an open standard, meaning that its users pay no royalties.

After DDR SDRAM was introduced, regular SDRAM became known as Single Data Rate SDRAM (SDR SDRAM). The latest SDRAM is **DDR2 SDRAM**, which is faster than DDR, uses less power, and has a 240-pin DIMM and a 64-bit data path.

## BUFFERED AND REGISTERED DIMMS

Buffers and registers hold data and amplify a signal just before the data is written to the module. Some DIMMs use buffers, some use registers, and some use neither. If a DIMM uses buffers, it's called a buffered DIMM; if it uses registers, it's called a registered DIMM. If a memory module doesn't support registers or buffers, it's always referred to as an unbuffered DIMM.

Older EDO and FPM modules used buffers, which did not degrade performance. SDRAM modules use registers, which do reduce performance somewhat but make it possible for the motherboard to support a larger number of modules. A fully buffered DIMM (FB-DIMM) uses an advanced buffering technique that makes it possible for servers to support a large number of DIMMs.

Notches on memory modules are positioned to identify the technologies that the module supports. In Figure 7-3, the position of the notch on the left identifies the module as registered (RFU), buffered, or unbuffered memory. The notch on the right identifies the voltage used by the module. The position of each notch not only helps identify the type of module, but also prevents the wrong kind of module from being used on a motherboard.

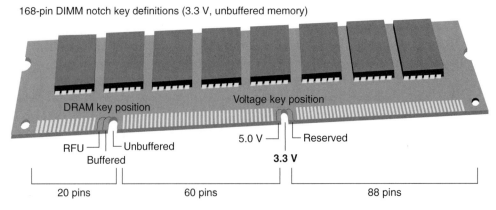

**Figure 7-3** The positions of two notches on a SDRAM DIMM identify the type of DIMM and the voltage requirement and also prevent the wrong type from being installed on the motherboard

## DUAL CHANNELING

To improve overall memory performance, a motherboard can use dual channels with either DDR or DDR2 DIMMs. With **dual channels**, the memory controller can communicate with two DIMMs at the same time, effectively doubling the speed of memory access.

A+ ESS
1.1

Figure 7-4 shows how dual channeling works on a motherboard with four DIMM slots. The board has two channels, Channel A and Channel B. Each channel can implement dual channeling. With dual channeling, the two DIMMs installed in the two slots labeled Channel A can be accessed at the same time. If two more DIMMs are installed in Channel B slots, they can be accessed at the same time. Two memory buses connect to DIMM slots, and each bus uses the normal 64-bit data path of the system bus, making an effective data path of 128 bits.

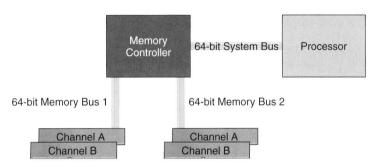

**Figure 7-4** Using dual channels, the memory controller can read from two DIMMs at the same time

For dual channeling to work, the pair of DIMMs in a channel must be equally matched in size, speed, and features, and it is recommended they come from the same manufacturer. Suppose two matching DIMMs are installed in Channel A slots. The memory controller reads from both DIMMs at the same time using the two 64-bit memory buses. The controller then places data on the 64-bit system bus to the processor, interleaving between the two buses of Channel A.

A motherboard using dual channeling configuration is shown in Figure 7-1. The two DIMM slots for Channel A are yellow, and the two Channel B slots are black. To accomplish dual channeling, matching DIMMs must be installed in the yellow slots, and, if either of the black slots are used, they, too, must have a matching pair of two DIMMs, although this pair does not have to match the first pair. That's because Channel A runs independently of Channel B. If the two DIMM slots of a channel are not populated with matching pairs of DIMMs, then the motherboard reverts to single channeling. You'll see an example of motherboard documentation using dual channeling later in the chapter.

## RIMM TECHNOLOGIES

**Direct Rambus DRAM** (sometimes called **RDRAM** or **Direct RDRAM** or simply Rambus) is named after Rambus, Inc., the company that developed it. RDRAM uses RIMM memory modules. A few years back, it was thought that RIMM memory modules might replace or at least compete with the DIMM market, but this has not been the case. RIMMs are expensive and now slower than current DIMMs. Thus, they are quickly becoming a legacy memory (no pun intended).

 **Tip**

RDRAM data can travel on a 16- or 32-bit data path. RDRAM works like a packeted network, not a traditional system bus, and can run at internal speeds of 800 MHz to 1600 MHz.

With RIMMs, each memory slot on the motherboard must be filled to maintain continuity throughout all slots. If a slot does not hold a RIMM, it must hold a placeholder module called a **C-RIMM (Continuity RIMM)** to ensure continuity throughout all slots. The C-RIMM contains no memory chips (see Figure 7-5).

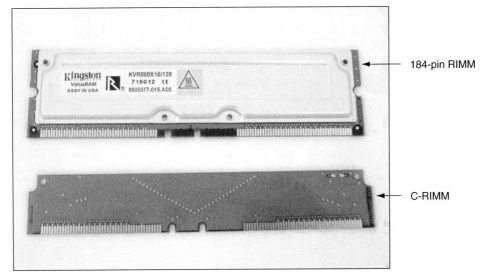

184-pin RIMM

C-RIMM

**Figure 7-5** A C-RIMM or RIMM must be installed in every RIMM slot on a motherboard

Concurrent RDRAM, an earlier version of Rambus memory, is not as fast as Direct RDRAM. Rambus designed the RDRAM technology but does not actually manufacture RIMMs: It licenses the technology to memory manufacturers. Because these manufacturers must pay licensing fees to use RDRAM, the industry did not embrace RIMMs and turned to improving and advancing DIMM technologies.

## ERROR CHECKING AND PARITY

In older machines, RAM existed as individual chips socketed to the motherboard in banks or rows of nine chips each. A **bank** is an area on the motherboard that holds the minimum number of memory chips or memory modules that must work together as a unit. Because the data path of earlier memory buses was eight bits, eight memory chips were required for the data path. Each bank held one byte by storing one bit in each chip, with the ninth chip holding a parity bit (see Figure 7-6). On older PCs, the parity chip was separated slightly from the other eight chips. **Parity** refers to an error-checking procedure in which either every byte has an even number of ones or every byte has an odd number of ones. The use of a parity bit means that every byte occupies nine rather than eight bits.

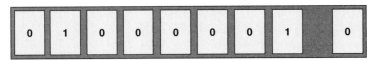

**Figure 7-6** Eight chips and a parity chip hold nine bits that represent the letter A in ASCII with even parity

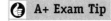

**A+ ESS
1.1**

Parity is a method of testing the integrity of the bits stored in RAM or some secondary medium, or testing the integrity of bits sent over a communications device. When data is written to RAM, the computer calculates how many ON bits (binary 1) are in the eight bits of a byte. If the computer uses odd parity, it makes the ninth or parity bit either a 1 or a 0, to make the number of ones in the nine bits odd. If it uses even parity, the computer makes the parity bit a 1 or a 0 to make the number of ones in the nine bits even.

Later, when the byte is read back, the computer checks the odd or even state. If the number of bits is not an odd number for odd parity or an even number for even parity, a **parity error** occurs. A parity error always causes the system to halt. On the screen, you see the error message "Parity Error 1" or "Parity Error 2" or a similar error message about parity. Parity Error 1 is a parity error on the motherboard; Parity Error 2 is a parity error on an expansion board.

Older DRAM memory used parity checking, but today's memory uses an altogether new method of error checking called **ECC (error-correcting code)** that can detect and correct an error in a single bit. Memory modules today are either ECC or non-ECC, and there are some improvements in ECC that ECC memory might use. The first ECC method can detect and correct an error in one bit of the byte. Newer ECC methods can detect an error in two bits but cannot correct these double-bit errors.

Some SDRAM, DDR, DDR2, and RIMM memory modules support ECC. DIMMs that support ECC have an odd number of chips on the module (the odd chip is the ECC chip), whereas a DIMM normally has only an even number of chips. A DIMM is normally a 64-bit module, but ECC makes it a 71- or 72-bit module; the extra 7 or 8 bits are used to verify the integrity of every 8 bits stored on the module and to correct any error, when possible. ECC memory costs more than non-ECC memory, but it is more reliable and is generally used on servers.

As with most other memory technologies discussed in this chapter, when buying memory to add to a motherboard, match the type of memory to the type the board supports. To see if your motherboard supports parity or ECC memory, look for the ability to enable or disable the feature in CMOS setup, or check the motherboard documentation.

> **A+ Exam Tip**
>
> The A+ Essentials exam expects you to know that parity memory uses 9 bits (8 bits for data and 1 bit for parity). You also need to be familiar with ECC and non-ECC memory technologies.

> **Notes**
>
> RAM chips that have become undependable and cannot hold data reliably can cause parity errors. Sometimes this happens when chips overheat or power falters.

> **Tip**
>
> Some older motherboards support parity memory, and some use only nonparity memory. If a SIMM has an odd number of chips, it is likely **parity memory**; an even number of chips usually indicates **nonparity memory**.

## CAS LATENCY AND RAS LATENCY

Two other memory features are **CAS Latency** (CAS stands for "column access strobe") and **RAS Latency** (RAS stands for "row access strobe"), which are two ways of measuring speed. Both features refer to the number of clock cycles it takes to write or read a column or row of data off a memory module. Times to read or write data are two or three clock cycles.

> **Notes**
>
> In memory ads, CAS Latency is sometimes written as CL, and RAS Latency might be written as RL.

> **Tip**
>
> When selecting memory, use the memory type that the motherboard manufacturer recommends.

CAS Latency is used more than RAS Latency. CL2 (CAS Latency 2) is a little faster than CL3 (CAS Latency 3). Ads for memory modules sometimes give the CAS Latency value within a series of timing numbers, such as 5-5-5-15. The first value is CAS Latency, which means the module is CL5. The second value is RAS Latency.

## TIN OR GOLD LEADS

On a motherboard, the connectors inside the memory slots are made of tin or gold, as are the edge connectors on the memory modules. It used to be that all memory sockets were made of gold, but now most are made of tin to reduce cost. You should match tin leads to tin connectors and gold leads to gold connectors to prevent a chemical reaction between the two metals, which can cause corrosion. Corrosion can create intermittent memory errors and even make the PC unable to boot.

## MEMORY SPEEDS

Several factors contribute to how fast memory runs, and speeds are measured in different ways. Measurements of speed include nanoseconds, MHz, PC rating, CAS Latency, and RAS Latency. Technologies that might affect speed include ECC, parity memory, dual channeling, and buffering. Recall that a SIMM's speed is measured in nanoseconds.

SDRAM, DDR, DDR2, and RIMM are measured in MHz. A DDR module is often described with its speed in the name, such as DDR266 for a DDR running at 266 MHz, or DDR333 for a DDR running at 333 MHz. Sometimes a DIMM or RIMM speed is measured in a PC rating. A PC rating is a measure of the total bandwidth of data moving between the module and the CPU. To understand PC ratings, let's take an example of a DDR DIMM module that runs at 266 MHz (DDR266). The module has a 64-bit (8 bytes) data path. Therefore, the transfer rate is 8 bytes multiplied by 266 MHz, which yields 2128 MB/second. This value equates to the PC rating of PC2100 for a DDR266 DIMM. For DDR2 memory, the PC rating is sometimes written as PC2. Current PC ratings are PC1600 (200 MHz), PC2100 (266 MHz), PC2700 (333 MHz), PC3200 (400 MHz), PC 4000 (500 MHz), PC 4200 (533 MHz), PC 5300 (667 MHz), and PC 6400 (800 MHz).

Factors to consider when looking at the overall speed of memory are listed below:

▲ *How much RAM is installed.* The more memory there is, the faster the system. Generally use as much memory in a system as it can support and you can afford.

▲ *The memory technology used.* DDR2 is faster than DDR, and DDR is faster than SDR SDRAM. Where required by the motherboard, buffered or registered memory can improve performance. For all these technologies, use what the board supports.

▲ *The speed of memory in ns, MHz, or PC rating.* Use the fastest memory the motherboard supports. If you install modules of different speeds in the same system, the system will run at the slowest speed or might become unstable. Know that most computer ads today give speeds in MHz or PC rating, but some ads give both values.

▲ *ECC/parity or non-ECC/nonparity.* Non-ECC or nonparity is faster and less expensive. Use what the board supports.

**A+ ESS**
**1.1**

▲ *CL or RL rating.* The lower the better. Use what the board supports, although most boards don't specify a particular CL rating.

▲ *Dual channeling.* To use this motherboard feature, install matching pairs of DIMMs from the same manufacturer in each pair of channel slots.

## HOW TO UPGRADE MEMORY

**A+**
**220-602**
**1.1**

To upgrade memory means to add more RAM to a computer. Adding more RAM might solve a problem with slow performance, applications refusing to load, or an unstable system. When Windows does not have adequate memory to perform an operation, it gives an "Insufficient memory" error.

When first purchased, many computers have empty slots on the motherboard, allowing you to add DIMMs or RIMMs to increase the amount of RAM, and sometimes memory goes bad and must be replaced. In this section, we talk about how to select, purchase, and install memory.

### HOW MUCH AND WHAT KIND OF MEMORY TO BUY

When you add more memory to your computer, ask yourself these questions:

▲ How much memory do I need?
▲ How much RAM is currently installed in my system?
▲ How many and what kind of memory modules are currently installed on my motherboard?
▲ How much and what kind of memory can I fit on my motherboard?
▲ How do I select and purchase the right memory for my upgrade?

All these questions are answered in the following sections.

### HOW MUCH MEMORY DO I NEED?

With the demands today's software places on memory, the answer is probably, "All you can get." The minimum requirement for Windows 2000/XP is 64 MB of RAM to install (not necessarily run) the OS. Windows 95 and Windows 98 require 16 MB to 32 MB of memory. But for adequate performance, install 128 MB into a Windows 9x/Me system and 256 MB or more into a Windows 2000/XP system. I have 512 MB of RAM installed on my Windows XP desktop PC, which gives me good performance.

---

**APPLYING | CONCEPTS**    **HOW MUCH MEMORY IS CURRENTLY INSTALLED?**

To determine how much memory your Windows system has, you can use the Properties window of My Computer or you can use the System Information window, which gives more useful information. To use System Information, in the Run dialog box, type **Msinfo32** and press **Enter**. The System Information window shown in Figure 7-7 reports the total and available amounts of physical and virtual memory. (Recall from Chapter 2 that virtual memory is space on the hard drive that the OS can use as overflow memory. You'll learn how to manage virtual memory in later chapters.)

A+
220-602
1.1

If the amounts of available physical and virtual memory are low and your system is sluggish, it's a good indication you need to upgrade memory.

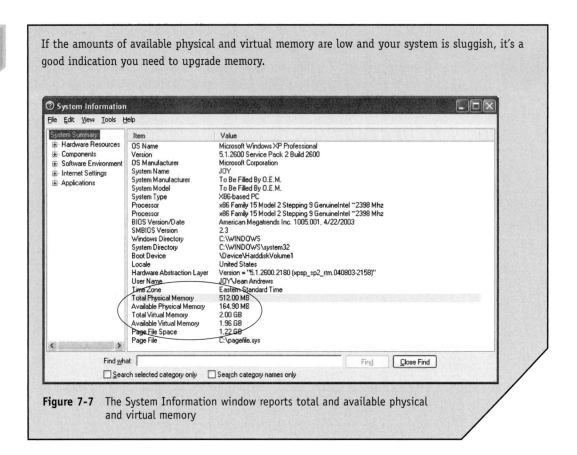

**Figure 7-7**   The System Information window reports total and available physical and virtual memory

## HOW MANY AND WHAT KIND OF MEMORY MODULES ARE CURRENTLY INSTALLED?

The next step to upgrading memory is to determine what type of memory the motherboard is currently using and how many memory slots are used. In this section, we also take into consideration you might be dealing with a motherboard that has no memory currently installed. If the board already has memory installed, you want to do your best to match the new memory with whatever is already installed. To learn what memory is already installed, do the following:

▲ Open the case and look at the memory slots. How many slots do you have? How many are filled? Remove each module from its slot and look on it for imprinted type, size, and speed. For example, a module might say "PC2-4200/512MB." The PC2 tells you the memory is DDR2, the 4200 is the PC rating and tells you the speed, and the 512MB is the size. This is not enough information to know exactly what memory to purchase, but it's a start.

▲ Examine the module for the physical size and position of the notches. Compare the notch positions to those in Figures 7-2 and 7-3.

▲ Read your motherboard documentation. If the documentation is not clear (and some are not) or you don't have the documentation, look on the motherboard for the imprinted manufacturer and model (see Figure 7-8). With this information, you can search a good memory Web site such as Kingston (*www.kingston.com*) or Crucial (*www.crucial.com*), which can tell you what memory this board supports.

▲ If you still have not identified the memory type, you can take the motherboard and the old memory modules to a good computer parts store and they should be able to match it for you.

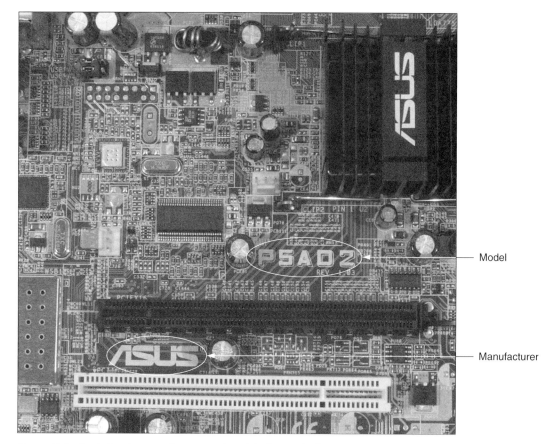

Figure 7-8 Look for the manufacturer and model of a motherboard imprinted somewhere on the board

## HOW MUCH AND WHAT KIND OF MEMORY CAN FIT ON MY MOTHERBOARD?

Now that you know what memory is already installed, you're ready to decide how much and what kind of memory modules you can add to the board. Keep in mind that if all memory slots are full, sometimes you can take out small-capacity modules and replace them with larger-capacity modules, but you can only use the type, size, and speed of modules that the board is designed to support. Also, if you must discard existing modules, the price of the upgrade increases.

**Video**

Selecting Memory

To know how much memory your motherboard can physically hold, read the documentation that comes with the board. Not all sizes of memory modules fit on any one computer. You need to use the right number of SIMMs, DIMMs, or RIMMs with the right amount of memory on each module to fit the memory banks on your motherboard. Next, let's look at what to consider when deciding how many and what kind of SIMMs, DIMMs, or RIMMs to add to a system.

### 30-Pin SIMMs

On older motherboards, 30-pin SIMMs are installed in groups of four. SIMMs in each group or bank must be the same type and size. See the motherboard documentation for the exact combination of SIMMs in each bank that the board can support.

### 72-Pin SIMMs

To accommodate a 64-bit system bus data path, 72-pin SIMMs have a 32-bit data path and are installed in groups or banks of two. Most older motherboards that use these SIMMs have one to three banks that can be filled with two, four, or six SIMMs. The two SIMMs in each bank must match in size and speed. See the motherboard documentation for the sizes and type of SIMMs the board supports.

### RIMM Modules

When you purchase a system using RIMMs, all RIMM slots will be filled with either RIMMs or C-RIMMs. When you upgrade, you replace one or more C-RIMMs with RIMMs. Match the new RIMMs with those already on the motherboard, following the recommendations of the motherboard documentation.

Let's look at one example of a RIMM configuration. The current system has 256 MB installed RAM. The motherboard is an Intel D850MV board, and it's shown in Figure 1-9 of Chapter 1. If you look carefully at that photo, you can see there are four RIMM slots. The first two slots are populated with RIMMs and the second two slots hold C-RIMMs. The label on one of the RIMMs is shown in Figure 7-9. Before we interpret this rather cryptic label, let's examine the motherboard documentation concerning upgrading RAM.

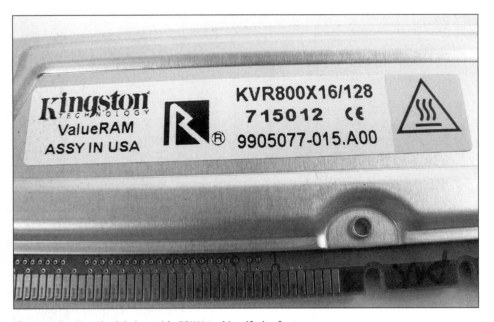

**Figure 7-9**   Use the label on this RIMM to identify its features

Table 7-2 shows the table found in the motherboard manual to be used to decide how to upgrade RAM. The column headings in the table are not as clear as they need to be, but I've written them as they are written in the motherboard documentation so you can learn to understand this kind of cryptic documentation. In the table, a chip on a RIMM module is called a component (sometimes it's also called a device). The first column tells us the amount of memory stored on one component (one chip). This value is called the density of the RIMM, which is 128 Mb (megabits) or 256 Mb (megabits). If you multiply the density times the number of components on a RIMM, you get the total amount of memory on one RIMM. The remaining columns in the table list the number of components per RIMM supported by this board, which are 4, 6, 8, 12, or 16 components per RIMM.

| Rambus Technology | Capacity with 4 DRAM Components per RIMM | Capacity with 6 DRAM Components per RIMM | Capacity with 8 DRAM Components per RIMM | Capacity with 12 DRAM Components per RIMM | Capacity with 16 DRAM Components per RIMM |
|---|---|---|---|---|---|
| 128/144 Mb | 64 MB | 96 MB | 128 MB | 192 MB | 256 MB |
| 256/288 Mb | 128 MB | 192 MB | 256 MB | 384 MB | 512 MB |

**Table 7-2** One motherboard's memory configurations using RIMMs

Let's look at one sample calculation from the table. Look in the first row of the first column and read the value 128 Mb. The second column shows the amount of memory for RIMMs with four devices. To get that amount, multiply 128 Mb by 4, which yields 512 Mb (megabits). Divide that number by 8 to convert the value to megabytes, which gives 64 MB of RAM on this RIMM.

One last item in the table needs explaining. This board supports ECC or non-ECC memory, so that's why there are two values in the first column. For example, in the first row the density is stated as 128/144 Mb. The second number, 144 Mb, applies to the ECC version of a non-ECC 128-Mb chip. In the second row, the 288-Mb RIMM is the ECC version of the 256-Mb RIMM. The extra bits are used for error correcting. A data path on a RIMM is 16 bits without ECC and 18 bits with ECC. The extra 2 bits are used for error correcting. For a 128 Mb component, an additional 16 Mb are required for error correcting.

This motherboard has two memory banks with two slots in each bank. The board requires that the RIMMs in a bank must match in size and density. As for speed, the board supports PC600 or PC800 RDRAM, which for a RIMM refers to the speeds of 600 MHz or 800 MHz. All RIMMs installed must run at the same speed. For ECC to work, all RIMMs installed must support ECC.

With this information in hand, let's look back at Figure 7-9 and interpret the label on this RIMM. The important information for us is "800X16/128." The value 128 is the size of the RIMM, 128 MB. The value 800 is the speed, 800 MHz. The value X16 tells us this RIMM is a non-ECC RIMM. (If it had been ECC compliant, the value would have been X18.)

Now we know exactly what kind of RIMM to buy for our upgrade. The RIMMs in the second bank don't have to match in size or density with the RIMMs in the first bank, but they do need to match in speed. To upgrade this system to 512 MB, we'll need to purchase two non-ECC, 800 MHz RIMMs that each contain 128 MB of RAM. It's also best to match the manufacturer and buy Kingston modules.

## DIMM Modules

Today's DIMMs have a 64-bit data path and can thus be installed as a single module rather than in pairs. Pentium motherboards that use single-sided DIMM modules use only one socket to a bank, because the DIMM module accommodates a data path of 64 bits. Single-sided DIMMs come in sizes of 8, 16, 32, 64, and 128 MB, and double-sided DIMMs come in sizes of 32, 64, 128, 256, and 512 MB, 1 GB, and 2 GB. Single-sided DIMMs contain one 64-bit bank, and double-sided DIMMs contain two 64-bit banks, one on each side of the DIMM. A DIMM slot can therefore hold two banks, one on each side of a double-sided DIMM.

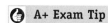

**A+ Exam Tip**

The A+ Essentials exam expects you to know how to upgrade a system using DIMMs or RIMMs. SIMMs are not covered on the exam.

Let's look at an example of a board that supports single-sided DIMMs. The Pentium motherboard uses 168-pin DIMM modules, and the documentation says to use unbuffered,

3.3-V, PC100 DIMM SDRAM modules. The PC100 means that the modules should be rated to work with a motherboard that runs at 100 MHz. You can choose to use ECC modules. If you choose not to, CMOS setup should show the feature disabled. Three DIMM sockets are on the board, and each socket represents one bank. Figure 7-10 shows the possible combinations of DIMMs that can be installed in these sockets.

| DIMM Location | 168-Pin DIMM | | Total Memory |
|---|---|---|---|
| Socket 1 (Rows 0 & 1) | SDRAM 8, 16, 32, 64, 128, 256 MB | ×1 | |
| Socket 2 (Rows 2 & 3) | SDRAM 8, 16, 32, 64, 128, 256 MB | ×1 | |
| Socket 3 (Rows 4 & 5) | SDRAM 8, 16, 32, 64, 128, 256 MB | ×1 | |
| | Total System Memory (Max 768 MB) | = | |

**Figure 7-10** This table is part of the motherboard documentation and is used to show possible DIMM sizes and calculate total memory on the motherboard

Let's look at another example of a DIMM installation. The motherboard is the Asus P4P800 shown in Chapter 5, Figure 5-30. The board allows you to use three different speeds of DDR DIMMs in one to four sockets on the board. The board supports dual channeling. Looking carefully at the photo in Figure 5-30, you can see two blue memory sockets and two black sockets. The two blue sockets use one channel and the two black sockets use a different channel. For dual channeling to work, matching DIMMs must be installed in the two blue sockets. If two DIMMs are installed in the two black sockets, they must match each other.

This board supports up to 4 GB of unbuffered 184-pin non-ECC memory running at PC3200, PC2700, or PC2100. The documentation says the system bus can run at 800 MHz, 533 MHz, or 400 MHz, depending on the speed of the processor installed. Therefore, the speed of the processor determines the system bus speed, which determines the speed of memory modules you can install.

Figure 7-11 outlines the possible configurations of these DIMM modules, showing that you can install one, two, or four DIMMs and which sockets should hold these DIMMs. To take advantage of dual channeling on this motherboard, you must populate the sockets according to Figure 7-11, so that identical DIMM pairs are working together in DIMM_A1 and DIMM_B1 sockets (the blue sockets), and another pair can work together in DIMM_A2 and DIMM_B2 sockets (the black sockets).

| | | Sockets | | | |
|---|---|---|---|---|---|
| Mode | | DIMM_A1 | DIMM_A2 | DIMM_B1 | DIMM_B2 |
| Single-channel | (1) | Populated | — | — | — |
| | (2) | — | Populated | — | — |
| | (3) | — | — | Populated | — |
| | (4) | — | — | — | Populated |
| Dual-channel* | (1) | Populated | — | Populated | — |
| | (2) | — | Populated | — | Populated |
| | (3) | Populated | Populated | Populated | Populated |

**Figure 7-11** Motherboard documentation shows that one, two, or four DIMMs can be installed

This motherboard has two installed DDR DIMMs. The label on one of these DIMMs is shown in Figure 7-12. The important items on this label are the size (256 MB), the speed (400 MHz or 3200 PC rating), and the CAS Latency (CL3). With this information and

A+ ESS
1.1

A+
220-602
1.1

knowledge about what the board can support, we are now ready to select and buy the memory for the upgrade. For example, if you decide to upgrade the system to 1 GB of memory, you would buy two DDR, 400 MHz, CL3 DIMMs that support dual channeling. For best results, you need to also match the manufacturer and buy Elixir memory.

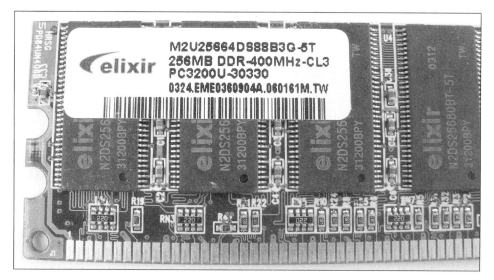

**Figure 7-12**    Use the label on this DIMM to identify its features

Let's look at two examples of boards that use a combination of single-sided and double-sided DIMMs. The Intel CC820 motherboard has two DIMM slots that can use two single-sided DIMMs, two double-sided DIMMs, or one single-sided and one double-sided DIMM. In the last case, the single-sided DIMM must be in the first slot. Figure 7-13 shows part of the board's documentation explaining how these DIMMs can be installed.

| Types of DIMMs to Be installed | Slot 0 | Slot 1 |
|---|---|---|
| One DIMM | DIMM | Empty |
| Two DIMMs - Same size, same number of sides (both single-sided or both double-sided) | Either DIMM | Either DIMM |
| Two DIMMs - Different sizes | Larger DIMM | Smaller DIMM |
| Two DIMMs - Same size, one is single-sided and one is double-sided | Single-sided DIMM | Double-sided DIMM |

**Figure 7-13**    The Intel CC820 motherboard can use a combination of single-sided and double-sided DIMMs

This next example is a little more complicated. The Abit ZM6 board has three DIMM slots, and the chipset can support up to four 64-bit banks. Using three slots to fill four banks is accomplished by installing a combination of single-sided and double-sided DIMMs. Figure 7-14 shows how this can be done, considering that a single-sided DIMM uses only one bank, but a double-sided DIMM uses two banks of the four available.

As you can see, the motherboard documentation is essential when selecting memory. If you can't find the motherboard manual, look on the motherboard manufacturer's Web site.

| Bank 1 | Bank 2 | Bank 3 | Bank 4 | Slots used |
|--------|--------|--------|--------|------------|
| Single-sided DIMM | | | | 1 |
| Double-sided DIMM | | | | 1 |
| Single-sided DIMM | Single-sided DIMM | | | 2 |
| Single-sided DIMM | Single-sided DIMM | Single-sided DIMM | | 3 |
| Double-sided DIMM | | Single-sided DIMM | | 2 |
| Double-sided DIMM | | Double-sided DIMM | | 2 |
| Double-sided DIMM | | Single-sided DIMM | Single-sided DIMM | 3 |

**Figure 7-14** How three DIMM slots can use four 64-bit memory banks supported by a motherboard chipset

## HOW DO I SELECT AND PURCHASE THE RIGHT MEMORY?

You're now ready to make the purchase. As you select your memory, you might find it difficult to find an exact match to SIMMs, DIMMs, or RIMMs already installed on the board. If necessary, here are some compromises you can make:

▲ When matching memory, for best results, also match the module manufacturer. But in a pinch, you can try using memory from two different manufacturers.

▲ Because SIMMs are so outdated, your choices will be slim. When buying SIMMs, you should match speed; although if you have to buy a different speed, know that all SIMMs installed will run at the speed of the slowest SIMM. Always put the slower SIMMs in the first bank.

Now let's look at how to select top-quality memory and how to use a Web site or other computer ad to search for the right memory.

### Buying High-Quality Memory

Before you buy, you need to be aware that chips embedded on a memory module can be high-grade, low-grade, remanufactured, or used. Poor-quality memory chips can cause frequent errors in Windows or cause the system to be unstable, so it pays to know the quality and type of memory you are buying.

Stamped on each chip of a RAM module is a chip ID that identifies the date the chip was manufactured. Look for the date in the YYWW format, where YY is the year the chip was made, and WW is the week of that year. For example, 0510 indicates a chip made in the tenth week of 2005. Date stamps on a chip that are older than one year indicate that the chip is probably used memory. If some chips are old, but some are new, the module is probably remanufactured. When buying memory modules, look for ones with dates on all chips that are relatively close together and less than one year old.

New chips have a protective coating that gives them a polished, reflective surface. If the chip's surface is dull or matted, or you can scratch off the markings with a fingernail or knife, suspect that the chip has been re-marked. **Re-marked chips** have been used, returned to the factory, marked again, and then resold. For best results, buy memory from a reputable source that sells only new components.

7

A+
220-602
1.1

## Using a Web Site to Research Your Purchase

When purchasing memory from a Web site such as Crucial Technology's site (*www.crucial.com*) or Kingston Technology's site (*www.kingston.com*), look for a search utility that will match memory modules to your motherboard (see Figure 7-15). These utilities are easy to use and help you confirm you have made the right decisions about type, size, and speed to buy. They can also help if motherboard documentation is inadequate, and you're not exactly sure what memory to buy.

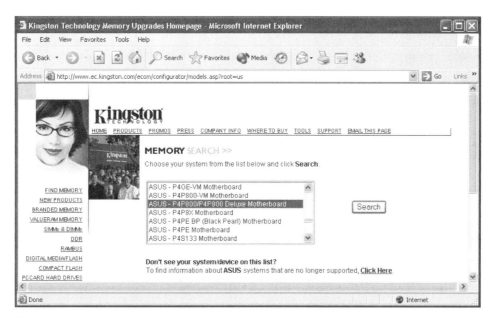

**Figure 7-15**  Web sites used to purchase memory, such as this Kingston site, often provide search utilities to help you select the right memory modules for your motherboard

Let's look at one example on the Crucial site. Suppose we're looking for DDR, 400 MHz, CL3, unbuffered DIMMs for a dual channeled motherboard. We want to install 256 MB of RAM, so we need two 128 MB modules. Figure 7-16 shows the Crucial Web site where I found that match. It's the last item in the list.

## Reading Ads About Memory Modules

Sometimes Web sites or printed material present memory ads as cryptic tables that can be difficult to read if you're not familiar with the shorthand used. This is especially true when you're buying older memory technologies for an old system. Figure 7-17 shows a typical memory module ad listing various types of DIMMs and RIMMs.

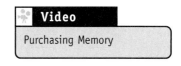

Let's take a closer look at this ad. For each memory module, the ad lists the amount of memory, density, speed, and price. For DIMMs, the ad lists the density of the module, which tells us the width of the data bus, whether the module supports error checking, and the size of the module. Here's how it works. The density is written as two numbers separated by an x, such as 16 x 64, and is read "16 by 64." Let's start with the second number, which is 64 or 72. If it's 64, then it's the width of the data bus in bits, grouped as eight bits to a byte. If the number is 72, then it's the width of the data bus plus an extra bit for each byte, used for error checking and correction (for ECC memory).

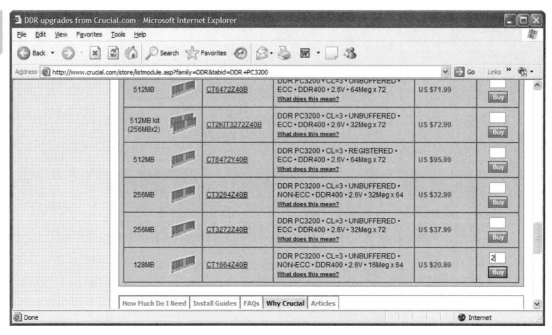

**Figure 7-16** Selecting memory off the Crucial Web site

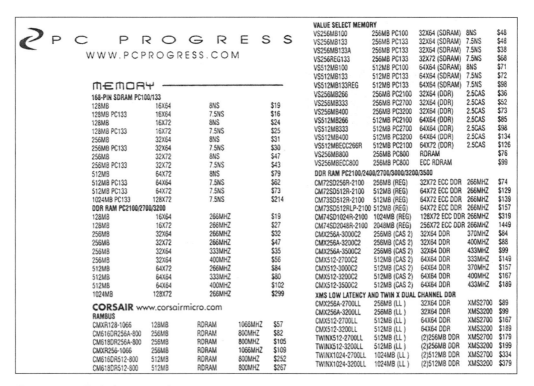

**Figure 7-17** Typical memory ad

When calculating the module's size, ignore the ninth bit and use only the value 64 to calculate. Convert this number to bytes by dividing it by 8, and then multiply that value (number of bytes) by the number on the left in the density listing, to determine the size of the module. For example, if the density is $16 \times 64$, the size of the module is $16 \times (64/8) = 16 \times 8 = 128$ MB.

A+
220-602
1.1

## INSTALLING MEMORY

When installing RAM modules, remember to protect the chips against static electricity, as you learned in Chapter 3. Follow these precautions:

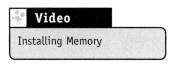

▲ Always use a ground bracelet as you work.
▲ Turn off the power, unplug the power cord, and remove the cover to the case.
▲ Handle memory modules with care.
▲ Don't stack cards or modules because you can loosen a chip.
▲ Usually modules pop into place easily and are secured by spring catches on both ends. Make sure that you look for the notches on one side or in the middle of the module that orient the module in the slot.

Let's now look at the details of installing a SIMM, a RIMM, and a DIMM.

### INSTALLING SIMMS

For most SIMMs, the module slides into the slot at an angle, as shown in Figure 7-18. (Check your documentation for any instructions specific to your modules.) As you install each SIMM, make sure each module is securely placed in its slot. Then turn on the PC and watch POST count the amount of memory during the boot process. If the memory count is not what you expect, power off the system, then carefully remove and reseat each module. To remove a module, release the latches on both sides of the module and gently rotate it out of the socket at a 45-degree angle.

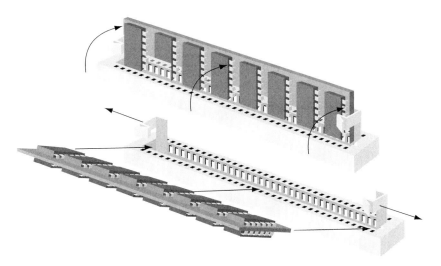

**Figure 7-18** Installing a SIMM module

### INSTALLING RIMMS

For RIMM modules, install the RIMMs beginning with bank 0, followed by bank 1. If a C-RIMM is already in the slot, remove the C-RIMM by pulling the supporting arms on the sides of the socket outward and pulling straight up on the C-RIMM. When installing the RIMM, notches on the edge of the RIMM module will help you orient it correctly in the socket. Insert the module straight down in the socket (see Figure 7-19). When it is fully inserted, the supporting arms should pop back into place.

RIMM supporting arms
in outward position

**Figure 7-19** Install RIMM modules in banks beginning with bank 0

## INSTALLING DIMMS

For DIMM modules, small latches on each side of the slot hold the module in place, as shown in Figure 7-20. To install a DIMM, first pull the supporting arms on the sides of the slot outward. Look on the DIMM edge connector for the notches, which help you orient the DIMM correctly over the slot, and insert the DIMM straight down into the slot. When the DIMM is fully inserted, the supporting arms should pop back into place. Figure 7-21 shows a DIMM being inserted into a slot on a motherboard.

Most often, placing memory on the motherboard is all that is necessary for installation. When the computer powers up, it counts the memory present without any further instruction and senses the features that the modules support, such as parity or ECC.

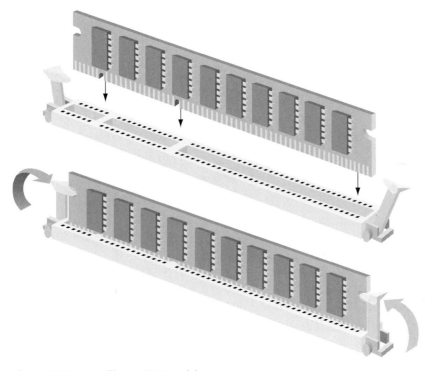

**Figure 7-20** Installing a DIMM module

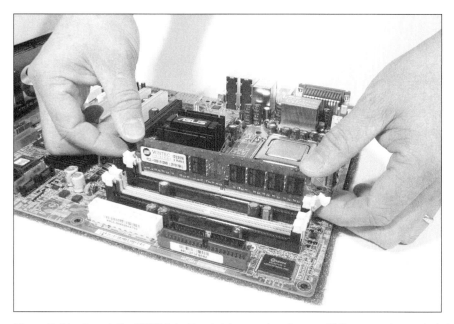

**Figure 7-21** Insert the DIMM into the slot by pressing down until the support arms lock into position

For some older computers, you must tell CMOS setup the amount of memory present. Read the motherboard documentation to determine what yours requires. If the new memory is not recognized, power down the system and reseat the module. Most likely it's not installed solidly in the slot.

## TROUBLESHOOTING MEMORY

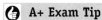

Issues with memory modules can cause a variety of problems, including boot failure; errors that cause the system to hang, freeze, or become unstable; and intermittent application errors. In Windows, memory errors can cause frequent **General Protection Fault (GPF)** errors. We now look at things that can go wrong with memory and what to do about them.

> **A+ Exam Tip**
>
> The A+ IT 220-602 exam expects you to know how to troubleshoot problems with memory.

### UPGRADE PROBLEMS

When upgrading memory, if the computer does not recognize new SIMMs, DIMMs, or RIMMs, or if memory error messages appear, do the following:

- Remove and reinstall the module. Make sure it sits in the socket at the same height as other modules, and clips on each side of the slot are in latched positions.
- Check that you have the right memory modules supported by your motherboard. Verify that CMOS setup recognizes the memory features correctly.
- Check that you have installed the right module size, as stated in the motherboard documentation. Verify each module that was already installed or newly installed.
- Remove the newly installed memory and check whether the error message disappears. Try the memory in different sockets. Try installing the new memory without the old installed. If the new memory works without the old, the problem is that the modules are not compatible.

- Clean the module edge connectors with a soft cloth or contact cleaner. Blow or vacuum dust from the memory sockets.
- Try flashing BIOS. Perhaps BIOS has problems with the new memory that a BIOS upgrade can solve.

## RECURRING PROBLEMS

Recurring errors during normal operations can mean unreliable memory. If the system locks up or you regularly receive error messages about illegal operations and General Protection Faults occur during normal operation, and you have not just upgraded memory, do the following:

- Run a current version of antivirus software to check for viruses.
- Run diagnostic software such as PC Technician (*www.windsortech.com*) to test memory.
- Are the memory modules properly seated? Remove and reinstall each one. For a DIMM module, try a different memory slot.
- Replace memory modules one at a time. For example, if the system only recognizes six out of eight megabytes of RAM, swap the last two SIMM modules. Did the amount of recognized RAM change? You might be able to solve the problem just by reseating the modules.
- Sometimes a problem can result from a bad socket or a broken trace (a fine-printed wire or circuit) on the motherboard. If so, you might have to replace the entire motherboard.
- The problem might be with the OS or applications. Download the latest patch for the software from the manufacturer's Web site. Make sure Windows has all the latest patches and service packs applied.
- If you have just installed new hardware, the hardware device might be causing an error, which the OS interprets as a memory error. Try uninstalling the new hardware.
- A Windows error that occurs randomly and generates an error message with "exception fault 0E at >>0137:BFF9z5d0" or similar text is probably a memory error. Test, reseat, or replace RAM.
- Excessive hard drive use and a sluggish system might indicate excessive paging. Check virtual memory settings.

**Notes**

Other than PC Technician, Memtest86 is a utility to test installed memory modules. Check the site *www.memtest86.com* to download this program.

A sluggish system that occasionally gives "Insufficient memory" errors probably needs more RAM. Try the following:

- Scan the system for viruses and other malicious software. Clean up and defrag the hard drive (how to do this is covered in Chapter 12).
- Using the System Properties window, find out how much RAM is installed and compare that to the recommended amounts. Consider adding more RAM.
- Verify that virtual memory settings are optimized for your system. (Virtual memory is covered in Chapter 12.)
- Don't open too many applications at the same time. Look for running background services that are not necessary and using up valuable memory resources.

## CHAPTER SUMMARY

- DRAM (dynamic RAM) is slower than SRAM because it needs constant refreshing.

- DRAM is stored on three kinds of modules: SIMM, DIMM, and RIMM modules.

- SIMM memory modules must be installed in pairs and are considered outdated technology for today's computers.

- DIMM technology has been improved several times and is currently the most popular type of memory.

- Direct Rambus DRAM, Double Data Rate SDRAM (DDR SDRAM), and DDR2 are the three current memory technologies.

- Synchronous DRAM (which moves in sync with the system bus) is a faster kind of memory than the less expensive asynchronous DRAM (which does not move in sync with the system bus) found on SIMMs.

- When upgrading memory, use the type, size, and speed the motherboard supports and match new modules to those already installed. Features to match include buffered, registered, unbuffered, single-sided, double-sided, CL rating, tin or gold connectors, support for dual channeling, ECC, non-ECC, parity, nonparity, speed in ns, MHz, or PC rating, DDR, DDR2, and size in MB or GB. Using memory made by the same manufacturer is recommended.

- When buying memory, beware of remanufactured and re-marked memory chips, because they have been either refurbished or re-marked before resale.

- When troubleshooting Windows memory errors, know the problems might be caused by a virus, Windows corruption, application corruption, failing hardware device, memory modules not seated properly, or failing memory modules.

## KEY TERMS

For explanations of key terms, see the Glossary near the end of the book.

bank
burst EDO (BEDO)
cache on a stick (COAST)
CAS Latency
C-RIMM (Continuity RIMM)
DDR2 SDRAM
Direct Rambus DRAM
Direct RDRAM
Double Data Rate SDRAM
  (DDR SDRAM)

dual channel
dynamic RAM (DRAM)
ECC (error-correcting code)
EDO (extended data out)
General Protection Fault (GPF)
nonparity memory
parity
parity error
parity memory
RAS Latency

RDRAM
refresh
re-marked chips
SDRAM II
synchronous DRAM (SDRAM)
SyncLink DRAM (SLDRAM)

## >> REVIEW QUESTIONS

1. How many bits are in the SIMMs data path?

   a. 16

   b. 32

   c. 64

   d. 128

2. Which of the following statements best describes DDR?

   a. DDR doubles the data rate of memory by processing data when the beat of the clock rises and again when it falls.

   b. DDR runs more slowly than regular SDRAM.

   c. DDR uses 168 pins.

   d. DDR improves on DDR2.

3. With dual channels, the memory controller can communicate with how many DIMMs at the same time?

   a. 1

   b. 2

   c. 3

   d. 4

4. Which of the following best describes odd parity?

   a. It makes the parity bit a 1 or a 0 to make the number of 1s in the 9 bits even.

   b. A parity error occurs only when there is an odd number of bits.

   c. It makes the ninth or parity bit either a 1 or a 0 to make the number of 1s in the 9 bits odd.

   d. Newer DRAM systems also use odd parity error checking.

5. Which of the following best describes the features CAS Latency and RAS Latency?

   a. Both features refer to the size of the memory module.

   b. RAS Latency is used more than CAS Latency.

   c. It takes four or five clock cycles to read or write data.

   d. Both features refer to the number of clock cycles it takes to write or read a column or row of data off a memory module.

6. True or false? In a DIMM (dual inline memory module), each pin pair is tied together into a single contact.

7. True or false? The smaller the speed rating is, the faster the chip.

8. True or false? Notches on memory modules are used to identify the technologies that the module supports.

9. True or false? For dual channeling to work, the pair of DIMMs in a channel must be equally matched in size, speed, and features.

10. True or false? Some memory slots on the motherboard can be empty.

11. If a memory module doesn't support registers or buffers, it's always referred to as a(n) _____ DIMM.

12. A(n) _____ is an area on the motherboard that holds the minimum number of memory chips or memory modules that must work together as a unit.

13. In older DRAM memory systems, a(n) _____ error always caused the system to halt.

14. Parity memory uses _____ bits.

15. Computer memory is divided into two categories: _____ and _____ .

# Hard Drives

The hard drive is the most important secondary storage device in a computer, and supporting hard drives is one of the more important tasks of a PC support technician. This chapter introduces the different kinds of hard drive technologies that have accounted for the continual upward increase in hard drive capacities and speeds over the past few years. The ways a computer interfaces with a hard drive have also changed several times over the years as both the computer and hard drives improve the technologies and techniques for communication. In this chapter, you will learn about past and present methods of communication between the computer and drive so that you can support both older and newer drives.

A hard drive is logically organized to hold data using methods similar to the ones used by floppy disks. We'll begin the chapter by discussing how data is organized on floppy disks and how to install a floppy disk. This information will help you understand the next sections of the chapter about hard drive organization and installation. Finally, you'll learn what to do when you have problems installing a drive and how to troubleshoot problems with hard drives after they are installed.

# LEARNING FROM FLOPPY DRIVES

Floppy drives are an older technology mostly replaced by CD drives and USB flash memory. However, you still see them around and you need to know how to support them. More important, knowing how floppy drives work and are installed can be a great foundation for learning to support hard drives. In the following sections, you'll learn how floppy drives work and how to install and troubleshoot them.

## HOW FLOPPY DRIVES WORK

Recall that memory is organized in two ways: physically (pertaining to hardware) and logically (pertaining to software). Similarly, data is stored physically and logically on a secondary storage device such as a floppy drive. Physical storage involves how data is written to and organized on the storage media, whereas logical storage involves how the OS and BIOS organize and view the stored data.

This section explains first how data is physically stored on a floppy disk and also how the OS logically views the data. Then you'll learn about what happens when a floppy disk is formatted for the first time. All the concepts learned here regarding physical and logical organization of data and how a disk is formatted also apply to hard drives.

### HOW DATA IS PHYSICALLY STORED ON A FLOPPY DISK

Years ago, a **floppy disk drive (FDD)** came in two sizes to accommodate either a $5\frac{1}{4}$-inch or $3\frac{1}{2}$-inch floppy disk. The $3\frac{1}{2}$-inch disks were formatted as high density (1.44 MB), extra-high density (2.88 MB), and double density (720K). The only floppy drives you see in use today are the $3\frac{1}{2}$-inch, high-density drives that hold 1.44 MB of data.

Figure 8-1 shows the floppy drive subsystem, which consists of the floppy drive, its cable, and its connections. The data cable connects to a 34-pin floppy drive connector on the motherboard.

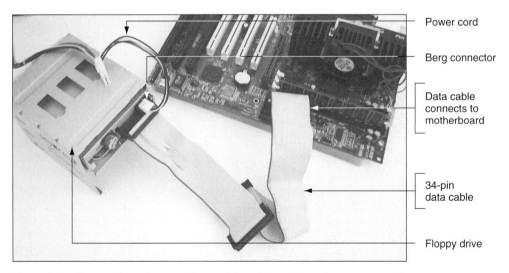

**Figure 8-1**   Floppy drive subsystem: floppy drive, data cable, and power connection

A floppy drive cable has 34 pins. Newer cables have a connector at each end and accommodate a single drive, but older cables, like the one in Figure 8-1, have an extra connector

A+ ESS
1.1

or two in the middle of the cable for a second floppy drive. For these systems, you can install two floppy drives on the same cable, and the drives will be identified by BIOS as drive A and drive B. Figure 8-2 shows an older floppy drive cable. Notice in the figure the twist in the cable. The drive that has the twist between it and the controller is drive A. The drive that does not have the twist between it and the controller is drive B. Also notice in the figure the edge color down one side of the cable, which identifies the pin-1 side of the 34-pin connector.

> **⚡ A+ Exam Tip**
>
> The A+ Essentials exam expects you to be familiar with a floppy disk drive (FDD).

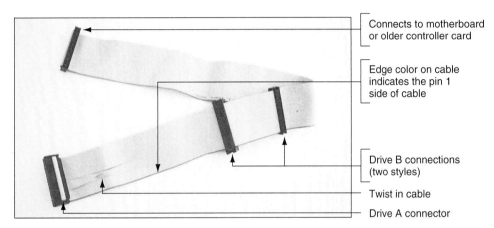

**Figure 8-2**  Twist in cable determines which drive will be drive A

Floppy drives receive power from the power supply by way of a power cord, as shown in Figure 8-3. The power cord plugs into the back of the drive. Recall that most hard drives use the larger Molex connector, but floppy drives use the smaller Berg connector. The Berg connector has a small plastic latch that snaps in place when you connect it to the drive.

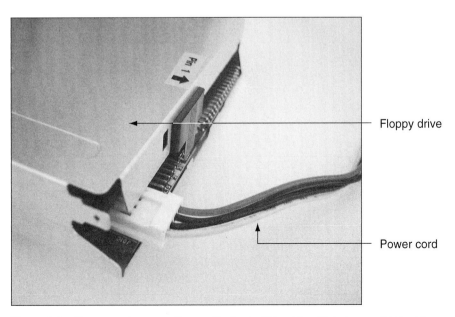

**Figure 8-3**  Power supply connection on the back of the drive (Note how well this drive manufacturer labeled pin 1 on the data connection.)

When floppy disks are first manufactured, the disks have nothing on them; they are blank sheets of magnetically coated plastic. Recall from Chapter 2 that disks are organized in tracks and sectors. Before data can be written to the disk, it must first be mapped in concentric circles called tracks, which are divided into segments called sectors (see Figure 8-4).

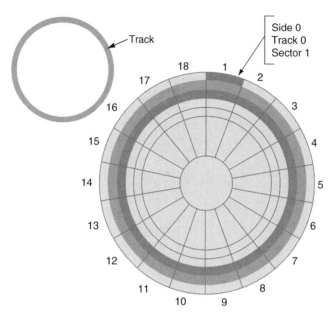

**Figure 8-4**   $3\frac{1}{2}$-inch, high-density floppy disk showing tracks and sectors

The process of marking tracks and sectors to prepare the disk to receive data is called **formatting** the disk; you do this using the Format command at a command prompt or the Windows Explorer shortcut menu, as you learned in Chapter 2. Figure 8-4 shows how a $3\frac{1}{2}$-inch, high-density floppy disk is formatted into tracks and sectors. There are 80 tracks, or circles, on the top side of the disk and 80 more tracks on the bottom. The tracks are numbered 0 through 79. Each side of the disk has 18 sectors, numbered 1 through 18. Although the circles, or tracks, on the outside of the disk are larger than the circles closer to the center, all tracks store the same amount of data. Data is written to the tracks as bits, either 0s or 1s. Each bit is a magnetized, rectangular spot on the disk. Between the tracks and spots are spaces that are not magnetized. This spacing prevents one spot from affecting the magnetism of a nearby spot. The difference between a 0 spot and a 1 spot is the orientation of the spot's magnetization on the disk surface.

Data is written to and read from the disk via a magnetic **read/write head** mechanism in the floppy drive (see Figure 8-5). Two heads are attached at the end of an actuator arm that freely moves over the surface of the disk. The arm has one read/write head above the disk and another below the disk. Moving in unison back and forth across the disk, the two heads lightly touch the surface of the disk, which spins at 360 rpm (revolutions per minute). (Note that the read/write heads of a hard drive never touch the surface.) Data is written first to the bottom and then to the top (label side) of the disk, beginning at the outermost circle and moving in. In Figure 8-5, the floppy disk is shown bottom-side-up so that you can see the round metal pad on which the disk spins.

8

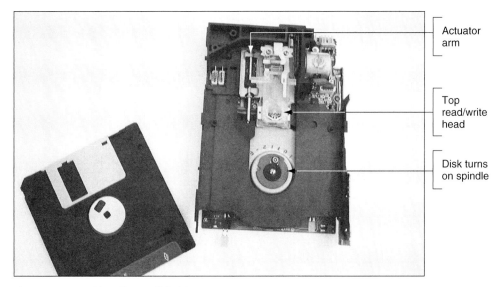

**Figure 8-5** Inside a floppy disk drive

## HOW DATA IS LOGICALLY STORED ON A FLOPPY DISK

Under Windows 2000/XP, a hard drive can use either the NTFS or FAT file system, but under all Windows operating systems, a floppy drive is always formatted using the FAT12 file system. Using the FAT file system, a **cluster**, sometimes called a **file allocation unit**, is a group of sectors that is the smallest unit on a disk that the OS uses to hold a file or a portion of a file. "Sector" refers to the way data is physically stored on a disk, whereas "cluster" describes how data is logically organized. The BIOS manages the disk as physical sectors, but the OS considers the disk only a long list of clusters that can each hold a fixed amount of data, as shown in Figure 8-6. The OS keeps that list of clusters in the file allocation table (FAT).

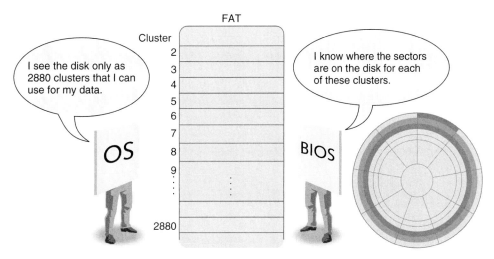

**Figure 8-6** Clusters, or file allocation units, are managed by the OS in the file allocation table, but BIOS manages these clusters as one or two physical sectors on the disk

The $3\frac{1}{2}$-inch, high-density floppy disk has 80 tracks × 18 sectors per track on each side, for a total of 1440 sectors on each side. The disk has only one sector per cluster, making 1440 × 2 sides, or 2880 clusters. Because each cluster holds 512 bytes (one sector) of data, a

### Notes

There is a discrepancy in the way the computer industry defines a megabyte. Sometimes 1 megabyte = 1,000 kilobytes; at other times, we use the relationship 1 megabyte = 1,024 kilobytes.

$3\frac{1}{2}$-inch, high-density floppy disk has $2880 \times 512 = 1,474,560$ bytes of data. Divide this number by 1024 to convert bytes to kilobytes and you will find out that the storage capacity of this disk is 1440 kilobytes. You can then divide 1440 by 1000 to convert kilobytes to megabytes, and the storage is 1.44 MB.

## HOW A FLOPPY DISK IS FORMATTED

Recall that before a floppy disk can be used, it must be formatted. Most floppy disks come already formatted, but occasionally you will need to format one. Whether you use the Format command or Windows Explorer to format a floppy disk, the following are created:

▲ *Tracks and sectors.* The tracks and sectors are created by writing tracks as a series of F6s in hex and, as necessary, writing the sector address mark to identify the beginning sector on a track

▲ *The boot record.* The first sector on the disk, called the **boot sector** or **boot record**, contains the information about the disk, including the total number of sectors, the number of sectors per cluster, the number of bits in each FAT entry, and the version of DOS or Windows used to format the disk. The boot record also includes the name of the program for which it searches to load an OS, either Io.sys or Ntldr. If one of these files is on the disk, this program searches for and loads the rest of the OS files needed on the disk to boot; then the disk is said to be bootable. The boot sector is always located at the beginning of the disk at track 0, sector 1 (bottom of the disk, outermost track). This uniform layout and content allows any version of DOS or Windows to read any floppy disk.

▲ *Two copies of the file allocation table (FAT).* Because the width of each entry in the FAT is 12 bits, the FAT on a floppy disk is called a 12-bit FAT, or **FAT12**. The FAT lists how each cluster (or file allocation unit) on the disk is currently used. A file is stored in one or more clusters that do not have to be contiguous on the disk. In the FAT, some clusters might be marked as bad (the 12 bits to mark a bad cluster are FF7h). An extra copy of the FAT immediately follows the first. If the first is damaged, sometimes you can recover your data and files by using the copy.

▲ *The root directory.* The root directory contains a fixed number of rows to accommodate a predetermined number of files and subdirectories. A $3\frac{1}{2}$-inch, high-density floppy disk has 224 entries in the root directory. Some important items in a directory are a list of filenames and their extensions, the time and date of creation or last update of each file, and the file attributes. These are on/off switches indicating the archive, system file, hidden file, and read-only file status of the file or directory.

The root directory and all subdirectories contain the same information about each file. Only the root directory has a limitation on the number of entries. Subdirectories can have as many entries as disk space allows. Because long filenames require more room in a directory than short filenames, assigning long filenames reduces the number of files that can be stored in the root directory.

**8**

## HOW TO INSTALL A FLOPPY DRIVE

Many computers today come with a hard drive and CD-ROM drive, but don't include a floppy drive, although the motherboard most likely has a 34-pin floppy drive connector. Most computer cases also have one or more empty bays for a $3\frac{1}{2}$-inch floppy drive, Zip drive, or second hard drive.

If you have no extra bay and want to add a floppy drive, you can attach an external drive that comes in its own case and has its own power supply. Most external drives today connect to the main system using a USB port, such as the one in Figure 8-7.

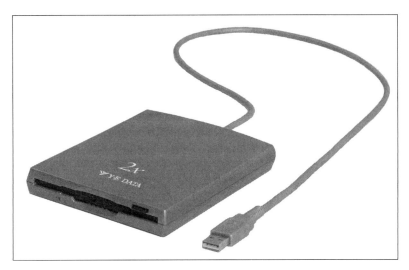

**Figure 8-7** An external floppy drive uses a USB connection

Floppy drives are now so inexpensive that repairing one is impractical. After you've determined that the drive itself has a problem, open the case, remove the drive, and replace it with a new one. This procedure takes no more than 30 minutes, assuming that you don't damage or loosen something in the process and create a new troubleshooting opportunity.

Here are the steps to add or replace a floppy drive. As described in Chapter 3, be sure to protect the computer against ESD as you work.

1. Turn off the computer, unplug the power cord, and remove the cover.

2. Unplug the power cable to the old floppy drive. Steady the drive with one hand while you dislodge the power cable with the other hand. Unplug the data cable from the old drive.

3. Unscrew and dismount the drive. Some drives have one or two screws on each side that attach the drive to the drive bay. After you remove the screws, the drive usually slides to the front and out of the case. Sometimes, you must lift a catch underneath the drive as you slide the drive forward. Sometimes, the drive is installed into a removable bay. For this type of case, first unscrew the screws securing the bay (most likely these screws are on the front of the case) and remove the bay. Then unscrew and remove the drive from the bay.

4. Slide the new drive into the bay. Screw the drive down with the same screws used on the old drive. Make sure the drive is anchored so that it cannot slide forward or backward, or up or down, even if a user turns the case on its side.

5. If you are adding (not replacing) a floppy drive, connect the floppy drive data cable to the motherboard. Align the edge color of the ribbon cable with pin 1 on the motherboard connectors. Some connectors only allow you to insert the cable in one direction. Be sure

A+
220-602
1.1

the end of the cable with the twist connects to the drive and the other end to the motherboard.

6. Connect the data cable and power cord to the drive. Make sure that the data cable's colored edge is connected to the pin 1 side of the connection, as shown in Figure 8-8. With some newer floppy drives, pin 1 is marked as an arrow on the drive housing (see Figure 8-9).

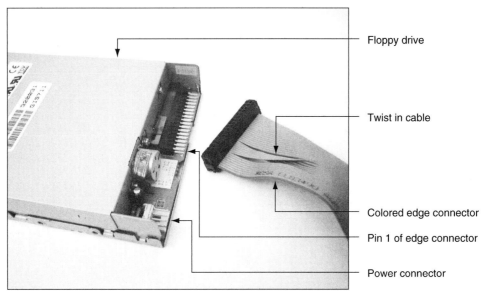

Floppy drive

Twist in cable

Colored edge connector

Pin 1 of edge connector

Power connector

**Figure 8-8** Connect colored edge of cable to pin 1

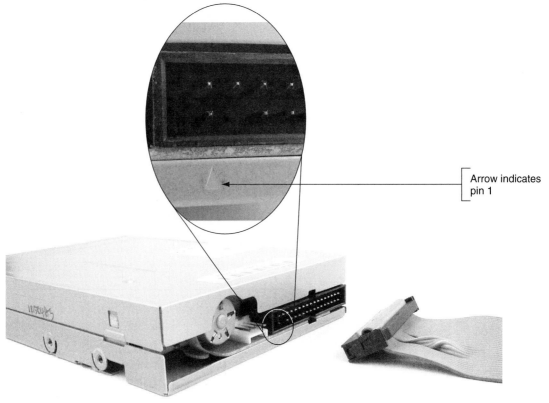

Arrow indicates pin 1

**Figure 8-9** Pin 1 is marked on this floppy drive with an arrow on the drive housing

A+
220-602
1.1

Most connections on floppy drives are oriented the same way, so this one probably has the same orientation as the old drive. The power cable goes into the power connection in only one direction. Be careful not to offset the connection by one pin.

7. Replace the cover, turn on the computer, and enter CMOS setup to verify the drive is recognized with no errors. If you are adding (not replacing) a floppy drive, you must inform CMOS setup by accessing setup and changing the drive type. Boot to the Windows desktop and test the drive by formatting a disk or copying data to a disk.

In the troubleshooting section at the end of this chapter, you'll learn about problems with floppy drives and what you can do about them. Now let's turn our attention to hard drives. We'll begin by discussing how a hard drive works.

> **Notes**
>
> Note that you can turn on the PC and test the drive before you replace the computer case cover. If the drive doesn't work, having the cover off makes it easier to turn off the computer, check connections, and try again. Just make certain that you don't touch anything inside the case while the computer is on. Leaving the computer on while you disconnect and reconnect a cable is very dangerous for the PC and will probably damage something—including you!

## HOW HARD DRIVES WORK

A+ ESS
1.1

A floppy disk has a single disk made of mylar inside the diskette plastic housing, but a hard drive has one, two, or more platters, or disks, that stack together and spin in unison inside a sealed metal housing that contains firmware to control reading and writing data to the drive and to communicate with the

> **Video**
>
> Inside a Hard Drive

motherboard. The top and bottom of each disk has a read/write head that moves across the disk surface as all the disks rotate on a spindle (see Figure 8-10). All the read/write heads are controlled by an actuator, which moves the read/write heads across the disk surfaces in unison. The disk surfaces are covered with a magnetic medium that can hold data as magnetized spots.

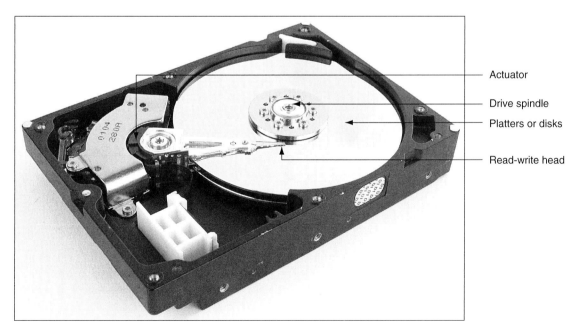

Actuator
Drive spindle
Platters or disks
Read-write head

**Figure 8-10** Inside a hard drive case

Figure 8-11 shows a close-up of the hard drive in Figure 8-10. You can see that this drive has two platters. Both sides of each platter are used to store data. However, on some hard drives, the top side of the first platter holds only the information that is used to track data and manage the disk. Each side, or surface, of one hard drive platter is called a **head**. (Don't confuse this with the read/write mechanism that moves across a platter, which is called a read/write head.) Thus, the drive in Figure 8-11 has four heads because there are two platters, each having two heads.

Read/write head

Read/write heads between the platters (another is underneath the bottom platter)

Two disks have four tracks (one on each head) that make one cylinder

**Figure 8-11**  A hard drive with two platters

Recall that a track is a circle on a disk surface that is divided into segments called sectors. All the tracks that are the same distance from the center of the platters on a hard drive together make up one cylinder. For example, the hard drive in Figure 8-10 has four heads. The four tracks on these heads that are equidistant from the center of the platters make one cylinder. Suppose a disk has 300 tracks per head; it would then have 300 cylinders. As with floppy disks, data is written to a hard drive beginning at the outermost track. The entire first cylinder is filled before the read/write heads move inward and begin filling the second cylinder.

The drive fits into a bay inside the computer case where it is securely attached with clips or braces and screws. This helps prevent the drive from being jarred while the disk is spinning and the heads are very close to the disk surface.

A hard drive requires a controller board filled with ROM programming to instruct the read/write heads how, where, and when to move across the platters and write and read data. For today's hard drives, the **hard drive controller** is firmware on a circuit board on or inside the drive housing and is an integral part of it. Figure 8-12 shows the bottom side of a hard drive, which has this circuit board exposed. Most modern drives protect the board inside the drive housing. The controller and drive are permanently attached to one another. Don't confuse this controller with the ATA controller, which is part of the motherboard chipset and controls the parallel and serial ATA connections on the motherboard. These two controllers work together to manage communication between the motherboard and the hard drive.

Track and sector markings are written to a hard drive before it leaves the factory in a process called low-level formatting. Let's look at how these markings are written, and then we'll look at options you have concerning low-level formatting.

A+ ESS
1.1

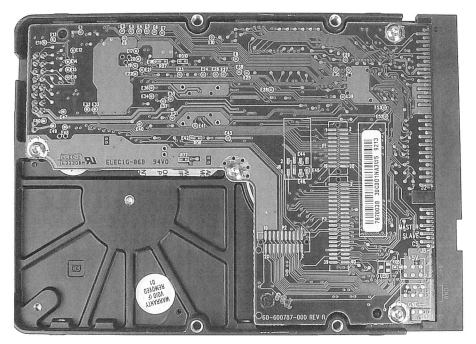

**Figure 8-12** Bottom of a hard drive shows the circuit board that contains the drive controller

## TRACKS AND SECTORS ON THE DRIVE

Older drives used a straightforward method of writing the tracks and sectors on the drive. They had either 17 or 26 sectors per track over the entire drive platter (see Figure 8-13). The centermost track determines the number of bytes that a track can hold and forces all other tracks to follow this restriction. Thus, the larger tracks near the outside of the platter end up containing the same number of bytes as the smaller tracks near the center of the platter. This arrangement makes formatting a drive and later accessing data simpler, but wastes drive space.

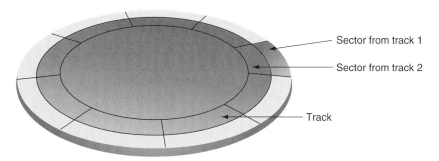

Sector from track 1

Sector from track 2

Track

**Figure 8-13** Floppy drives and older hard drives use a constant number of sectors per track

Today's drives eliminate this restriction. The number of sectors per track on a drive is not the same throughout the platter. In this new formatting system, called **zone bit recording** (see Figure 8-14), tracks near the center have the smallest number of sectors per track, and the number of sectors increases as the tracks grow larger. In other words, each track on an IDE drive is designed to have the optimum number of sectors appropriate to the size of the track. What makes this arrangement possible, however, is one fact that seldom changes: Every sector on the drive still has 512 bytes. Without this consistency, the OS needs a much more complex interface to the data on the drive.

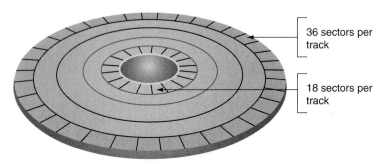

36 sectors per track

18 sectors per track

**Figure 8-14**   Zone bit recording can have more sectors per track as the tracks get larger

Because each track can have a different number of sectors, the OS cannot communicate with the hard drive controller (firmware on the hard drive) using sector and track coordinates, as it does with floppy disks and older hard drives. For current systems, the BIOS and the OS use a simple sequential numbering system called logical block addressing (LBA) to address all the sectors on the hard drive without regard to where these sectors are located.

## LOW-LEVEL FORMATTING

Recall that when the OS formats a floppy disk, it writes sector and track markings on the disk. With IDE drives, because the track and sector markings don't follow a simple pattern, track and sector markings are written on the hard drive at the factory. This process is called **low-level formatting**. The OS still executes the remainder of the format process (creating a boot sector, file system, and root directory), which is called **high-level formatting** or **operating system formatting**.

With older drives, because the track and sector markings were written in a simple way as a constant number of sectors per track, technicians performed the low-level format when they installed the drive. Technicians would use a utility program to do the job. System BIOS, the OS, or utility software such as Norton Utilities or SpinRite could perform the low-level format. Because sector and track markings eventually fade, a hard drive eventually gives lots of bad sector errors. In the old days, the solution was to back up all the data on the drive and perform a low-level format to get a clean start. If a drive were periodically low-level formatted, it would last for years and years.

For today's drives, the track and sector markings on the drive created at the factory are normally expected to last for the life of the drive. For this reason, today's drives are considered more disposable than yesterday's drives. When track and sector markings fade, as they eventually do, and the drive gives many "Bad Sector or Sector Not

> **Notes**
>
> As computer parts become less expensive and labor becomes more expensive, the trend to replace rather than fix is becoming the acceptable best practice in the PC industry.

Found" errors or becomes unusable, you salvage whatever data is still on the drive, throw the drive away, and buy a new one!

Manufacturers of today's hard drives advise to never do a low-level format. Using the wrong format program could permanently destroy the drive, unless the drive controller was smart enough to ignore the command. However, if you're about to throw out the drive anyway and you have the time to tinker, you might want to consider attempting a low-level format. Ask the manufacturer for a program to perform a low-level format of the drive. Note, however, that some manufacturers distribute these programs only to dealers, resellers, or certified service centers.

You should know another thing about low-level formatting. On the Web, you can download utilities from hard drive manufacturers and others that claim to be a low-level format utility but are actually a zero-fill utility. These programs work by checking each sector for errors (as does the Windows 2000/XP Chkdsk command) and filling each sector with zeroes. They're great for cleaning up a hard drive, but don't low-level format.

Now that you have an understanding of how data is physically written to a hard drive, let's turn our attention to how much data can be stored on the drive.

## CALCULATING DRIVE CAPACITY ON OLDER DRIVES

In the early 1990s, hard drives used a constant number of sectors per track and measuring drive capacity was straightforward. Let's learn how to do that before we see how it's done today. All sectors in a track held 512 bytes regardless of the track's radius. If you knew the number of tracks, heads, and sectors per track, you could calculate the storage capacity of a drive, because all tracks had the same number of sectors. Software and operating systems were written to interface with the system BIOS, which managed a hard drive by assuming that for each hard drive there was a fixed relationship among the number of sectors, tracks, heads, and cylinders.

If you knew how many heads, cylinders (tracks), and sectors a drive had, you could calculate the capacity of the drive. This information was usually written on the top of the drive housing, as shown in Figure 8-15. For another older drive, if the drive parameters are 855 cylinders, 7 heads, and 17 sectors/track, the drive capacity would have been calculated as 855 cylinders × 7 heads × 17 sectors/track × 512 bytes/sector, which gives 52,093,440 bytes. If you divided this value by 1,024 to convert to KB and then divided by 1,024 again to convert to MB, you would end up with a drive capacity of 49.68 MB.

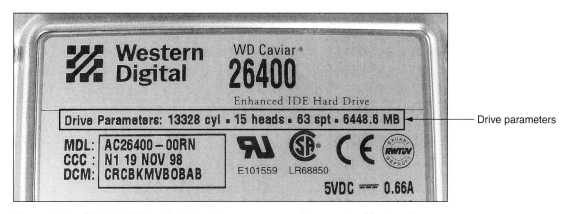

**Figure 8-15**  Older hard drives had the drive parameters written on the drive housing

### Notes

When installing a hard drive, it was once necessary to tell CMOS setup the drive capacity by telling it how many heads, cylinders, and sectors the drive had. Today, most startup BIOSs offer autodetection, so the BIOS detects the new drive and automatically selects the correct drive capacity and configuration.

### Notes

For today's drives, to know the capacity of the drive, look for it written on the drive label. As for the number of heads, cylinders, and sectors per track, only the hard drive controller knows and it's not telling.

### Notes

In technical documentation, you might see a hard drive abbreviated as HDD (hard disk drive). However, this chapter uses the term hard drive.

### Video

Examining Hard Drives

## DRIVE CAPACITY FOR TODAY'S DRIVES

After the drive is installed, you can use the operating system to report the capacity of a hard drive. Recall from Chapter 2 that for Windows NT/2000/XP and Windows 9x/Me, using Windows Explorer, right-click the drive letter and select **Properties** on the shortcut menu. Record the capacity of each logical drive on the hard drive, and then add them together to get the entire hard drive capacity, assuming all space on the hard drive is partitioned and formatted. For Windows 2000/XP, use Disk Management, and for Windows 9x, use Fdisk to report the capacity of an entire hard drive regardless of whether the drive is fully partitioned and formatted.

## HARD DRIVE INTERFACE STANDARDS

One technology about hard drives that you need to understand is the different ways a hard drive interfaces with the computer. Several interface standards exist for hard drives and other drives and devices to connect to connectors and ports on a motherboard, including the several ATA standards, SCSI, USB, FireWire (also called 1394), and Fibre Channel. All of these standards are discussed in this section. By far, the most popular standard is ATA, so we begin there.

## THE ATA INTERFACE STANDARDS

The ATA interface standards define how hard drives and other drives such as CD, DVD, tape, and Zip drives interface with a computer system. The standards define how the drive controller communicates with the BIOS, the chipset on the motherboard, and the OS. The standards also define the type of connectors used by the drive and the motherboard or expansion cards.

These ATA interface standards control data speeds and transfer methods and are developed by Technical Committee T13 (*www.t13.org*) and published by **ANSI (American National Standards Institute,** *www.ansi.org*.) Table 8-1 lists these standards. As these standards developed, different drive manufacturers called them different names, which can be confusing when reading documentation or advertisements.

When selecting a hard drive standard, you should select the fastest standard your motherboard supports. Keep in mind that the OS, the system BIOS on the motherboard, and the firmware on the drive must all support your selected standard. If one of these three does not support the selected standard, the other two will probably revert to a slower standard that all three can use, or the drive will not work at all. You'll learn how to handle these incompatibility issues later in the chapter.

| Standard (Can Have More Than One Name) | Speed | Description |
|---|---|---|
| ATA*<br>IDE/ATA | Speeds range from 2.1 MB/sec to 8.3 MB/sec | The first T13 and ANSI standard for IDE hard drives. Limited to no more than 528 MB. Supports PIO modes 0-2. |
| ATA-2*<br>ATAPI, Fast ATA,<br>Parallel ATA (PATA),<br>Enhanced IDE (EIDE) | Speeds up to 16.6 MB/sec | Broke the 528-MB barrier. Allows up to four IDE devices, defining the EIDE standard. Supports PIO modes 3-4 and DMA modes 1-2. |
| ATA-3* | Speeds up to 16.6 MB/sec (little speed increase) | Improved version of ATA-2 and introduced SMART. |
| ATA/ATAPI-4*<br>Ultra ATA, Fast ATA-2,<br>Ultra DMA Modes 0-2,<br>DMA/33 | Speeds up to 33.3 MB/sec | Defined Ultra DMA modes 0-2 and an 80-conductor cable to improve signal integrity. |
| ATA/ATAPI-5*<br>Ultra ATA/66,<br>Ultra DMA/66 | Speeds up to 66.6 MB/sec | Ultra DMA modes 3-4. |
| ATA/ATAPI-6*<br>Ultra ATA/100,<br>Ultra DMA/100 | Speeds up to 100 MB/sec | Requires the 80-conductor cable. Defined Ultra DMA mode 5, and supports drives larger than 137 GB. |
| ATA/ATAPI-7*<br>Ultra ATA/133,<br>Serial ATA (SATA),<br>SAS STP | Parallel transfer speeds up to 133 MB/sec<br>Serial transfer speeds up to 150 MB/sec | Can use the 80-conductor cable or serial ATA cable. Defines Ultra DMA mode 6, serial ATA (SATA), and Serial Attached SCSI (SAS) coexisting with SATA. |

ATA/ATAPI-8 is currently being drafted.

*Name assigned by the T13 Committee

**Table 8-1** Summary of ATA interface standards for storage devices

Let's now turn our attention to several ATA standards that affect the cabling method used and the transfer rates. These standards include parallel and serial data transmission, DMA and PIO transfer modes, and independent device timing. We begin by looking at the two data transmission standards, parallel or serial. These two standards account for the two types of cables ATA connections can use: parallel ATA cables or serial ATA cables.

## PARALLEL ATA OR EIDE CABLING

**Parallel ATA**, also called the **EIDE (Enhanced IDE)** standard or, more loosely, the IDE standard, allows for two connectors on a motherboard for two 40-pin data cables. These ribbon cables can accommodate one or two drives, as shown in Figure 8-16. All ATA standards since ATA-2 support this configuration. Parallel ATA or EIDE applies to other drives besides hard drives, including CD drives, Zip drives, tape drives, and so forth.

EIDE is named after **IDE (Integrated Device Electronics)** technology. Actually, IDE technology pertains to how the hard drive itself works, rather than to an interface standard. However, in the industry, IDE and EIDE are loosely used to talk about an interface standard. (That's not exactly correct, but it's what we do.) An EIDE drive such as a CD, DVD, tape, or

**A+ ESS**
**1.1**

Zip drive must follow the **ATAPI (Advanced Technology Attachment Packet Interface)** standard in order to connect to a system using an EIDE connector. Using this standard, up to four parallel ATA devices can connect to a motherboard using two data cables.

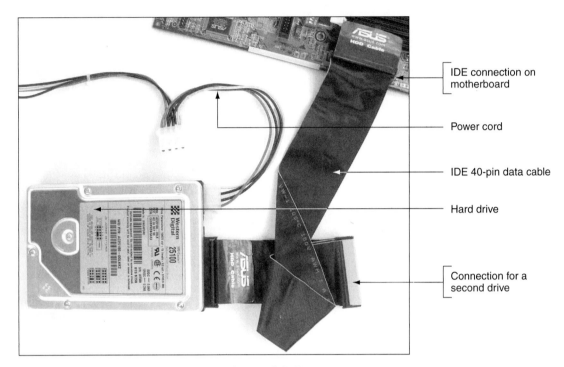

IDE connection on motherboard

Power cord

IDE 40-pin data cable

Hard drive

Connection for a second drive

**Figure 8-16** A PC's hard drive subsystem using parallel ATA

Under parallel ATA, two types of ribbon cables are used. The **80-conductor IDE cable** has 40 pins and 80 wires. Forty wires are used for communication and data, and an additional 40 ground wires reduce crosstalk on the cable. An older 40-conductor cable has 40 wires and 40 pins. An 80-conductor IDE cable is required by ATA/100 and above. Figure 8-17 shows a comparison between the two parallel cables. The 80-conductor cable is color-coded with the blue connector always connected to the motherboard. The connectors on each cable otherwise look the same, and you can use an 80-conductor cable in place of a 40-conductor cable in a system. The maximum length of both cables is 18 inches.

> **Notes**
>
> Acronyms sometimes change over time. Years ago, we all knew IDE to mean Integrated Drive Electronics. As the term began to apply to other devices than hard drives, we renamed the acronym to become Integrated Device Electronics.

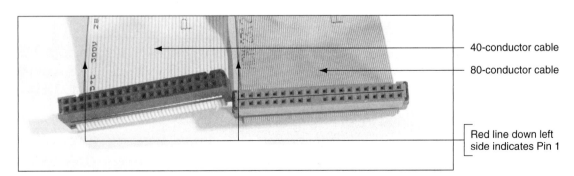

40-conductor cable

80-conductor cable

Red line down left side indicates Pin 1

**Figure 8-17** In comparing the 80-conductor cable to the 40-conductor cable, note they are about the same width, but the 80-conductor cable has many more and finer wires

A+ ESS
1.1

## SERIAL ATA CABLING

A consortium of manufacturers, called the Serial ATA International Organization (SATA-IO; see *www.sata-io.org*) and led by Intel, developed the **serial ATA (SATA)** standards. These standards use a serial data path rather than the traditional parallel data path. (Essentially, the difference between the two is that data is placed on a serial cable one bit following the next, but with parallel cabling, all data in a byte is placed on the cable at one time.) The T13 committee is clarifying and further defining serial ATA as it enhances the latest ATA/ATAPI-7 standard, which, as of this writing, is still a work in progress. Current transfer speed is 150 MB/sec, although standards are in the works that should up the speed to 300 or even 600 MB/sec.

Serial ATA drives use a **serial ATA cable**. Currently there are two types of serial ATA cables: an external serial ATA cable and an internal serial ATA cable.

The latest SATA standard allows for external drives (drives outside the case) and is called **external SATA (eSATA)**. eSATA is up to six times faster than USB or FireWire. External SATA drives use a special external shielded serial ATA cable up to 2 meters long.

An internal serial ATA cable can be up to 1 meter in length, has 7 pins, and is much narrower compared to the 40-pin parallel IDE cable (see Figure 8-18). Serial ATA is a little faster than parallel ATA/133, but is currently more expensive because it is a relatively new technology. Serial ATA has been introduced into the industry not so much to handle the speeds of current drives, but to position the industry for the high-performance large drives expected to soon be inexpensive enough to fit into the desktop hard drive market. Another advantage of serial ATA is the thin cables don't hinder airflow inside a case as much as the wide parallel ATA cables do. One additional advantage is that serial ATA supports hot-swapping, also called hot-plugging. With hot-swapping, you can connect and disconnect a drive while the system is running.

If you have a parallel ATA drive and a serial ATA connector on the motherboard or you have a serial ATA drive and a parallel ATA connector on the motherboard, you can purchase

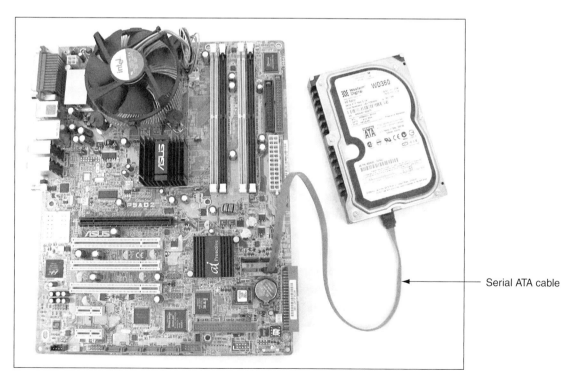

Serial ATA cable

**Figure 8-18** A hard drive subsystem using the new serial ATA data cable

an adapter to make the hard drive connector fit your motherboard connector. Figure 8-19 shows a converter. For a motherboard that does not have a serial ATA connector or does not have enough of them, you can purchase an expansion card to provide both internal and external serial ATA connectors for drives.

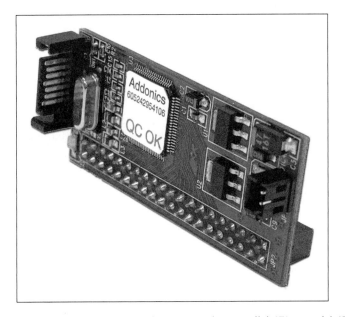

**Figure 8-19**   Sabrent IDE Ultra ATA-100/133 parallel ATA to serial ATA converter

When serial ATA was first introduced into the market, only hard drives used it, but now all kinds of drives are using serial ATA, including CD, DVD, and tape drives. However, because PATA drives are still so commonplace, a motherboard needs at least one 40-pin parallel ATA connector for one or two EIDE drives (see Figure 8-20).

Two serial
ATA connectors

Two RAID
connectors

Two regular
IDE connectors

**Figure 8-20**   This motherboard has a variety of ATA drive connectors

In Figure 8-20, the RAID (redundant array of independent disks) connectors are a hard drive interface method used with servers, which makes it possible to connect multiple hard drives together into a RAID array to improve performance and automatically recover from a failure. You'll learn more about RAID in Chapter 10.

## DMA OR PIO TRANSFER MODES

A hard drive uses one of two methods to transfer data between the hard drive and memory: **DMA (direct memory access) transfer mode** or **PIO (Programmed Input/Output) transfer mode**. DMA transfers data directly from the drive to memory without involving the CPU. PIO mode involves the CPU and is slower than DMA mode, which does not involve the CPU.

There are different modes for PIO and DMA due to the fact that both standards have evolved over the last few years. There are five PIO modes, from the slowest (PIO mode 0) to the fastest (PIO mode 4), and seven DMA modes from the slowest (DMA mode 0) to the fastest (DMA mode 6).

Most often, when installing a drive, the startup BIOS autodetects the drive and selects the fastest mode that the drive and the BIOS support. After installation, you can go into CMOS setup and verify that setup recognized the drive correctly.

## INDEPENDENT DEVICE TIMING

As you saw in Table 8-1, there are different hard drive standards, each running at different speeds. If two hard drives share the same parallel ATA cable but use different standards, both drives will run at the speed of the slower drive unless the motherboard chipset controlling the ATA connections supports a feature called Independent Device Timing. Most chipsets today support this feature and with it, the two drives can run at different speeds as long as the motherboard supports those speeds.

## BREAKING THE 137 GB BARRIER

In 2002, the ATA/ATAPI-6 standard, also called the ATA/100 standard, was published and led the way to break a significant barrier with hard drive interfaces. Up until these standards were published, a hard drive could not have more than 137 GB of data. This limitation was caused by the fact that the hard drive, the system BIOS, and the OS used 28 bits to communicate addresses to the data on the drive (see Figure 8-21). The largest address that 28 bits could hold was 1111 1111 1111 1111 1111 1111 1111 in binary, which converts to 268,435,455 in decimal. Each address represented the location of one 512-byte sector on the drive so that the drive could have no more than 268,435,455 sectors. Therefore, the addressable space on the drive was 268,435,455 times 512, which yields 137,438,952,960 bytes, or about 137 GB. Understand the barrier limitation of 137 GB was not in how much data could be written to the drive, but how much data could be addressed by the interface to the drive. The newer ATA/ATAPI-6 allows 48 bits for the address, increasing the addressable space on a hard drive up to 144 petabytes (144,000,000,000,000,000 bytes). It's estimated that this limitation won't affect us for at least 50 years.

For your system to support drives larger than 137 GB, the OS, the system BIOS, the ATA controller (sometimes called the IDE controller in documentation), and the hard drive must all support the standard. Before investing in a drive larger than 137 GB, verify that your motherboard and the OS support it. If your motherboard does not support these drives, first check with the BIOS manufacturer for a possible update and flash BIOS. If an updated BIOS is not available, you can purchase an expansion card to provide the hard drive connectors that support the size drive you want to use. Note that Windows 9x does not support drives larger than 137 GB unless third-party software provided by the hard drive manufacturer is used. Windows 2000/XP support drives larger than 137 GB if service packs are applied.

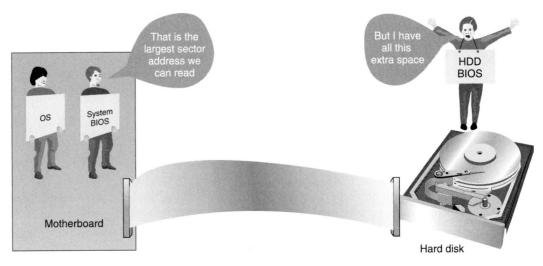

**Figure 8-21** The 137-GB barrier existed because of the size of the numbers used to address a sector

## CONFIGURING PARALLEL AND SERIAL ATA DRIVES IN A SYSTEM

Following the parallel ATA or EIDE standard, a motherboard can support up to four EIDE devices using either 80-conductor or 40-conductor cables. The motherboard offers two IDE connectors (see Figure 8-22). Each connector accommodates one IDE channel, and each channel can accommodate one or two IDE devices. One channel is called the primary channel and the other channel is called the secondary channel. Each IDE connector uses one 40-pin cable. The cable has two connectors on it: one connector in the middle of the cable and one at the far end for two EIDE devices. An EIDE device can be a hard drive, DVD drive, CD-ROM drive, Zip drive, or other type of drive. One device is configured to act as the master controlling the channel, and the other device on the channel is the slave. There are, therefore, four possible configurations for four EIDE devices in a system:

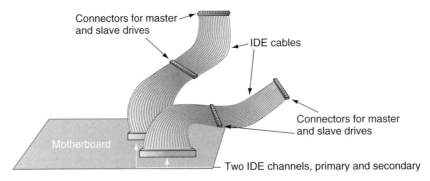

**Figure 8-22** A motherboard has two IDE channels; each can support a master and slave drive using a single EIDE cable

- ◢ Primary IDE channel, master device
- ◢ Primary IDE channel, slave device
- ◢ Secondary IDE channel, master device
- ◢ Secondary IDE channel, slave device

The master or slave designations are made by setting jumpers or DIP switches on the devices or by using a special cable-select data cable. Documentation can be tricky.

A+ ESS
1.1

Some hard drive documentation labels the master drive setting as the Drive 0 setting and the slave drive setting as Drive 1 setting rather than using the terms master and slave. The connectors on a parallel ATA 80-conductor cable

**Notes**

When installing a hard drive on the same channel with an ATAPI drive such as a CD-ROM drive, always make the hard drive, the master, and the ATAPI drive the slave. An even better solution is to install the hard drive on the primary channel and the CD drive and any other drive on the secondary channel.

are color-coded (see Figure 8-23). Use the blue end to connect to the motherboard; use the black end to connect to the drive. If you only have one drive connected to the cable, put it on the black connector at the end of the cable, not the gray connector in the middle.

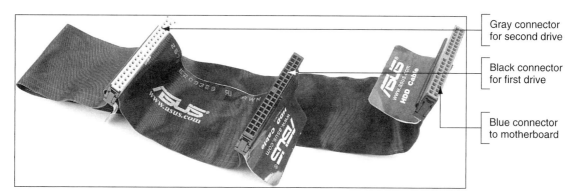

Gray connector for second drive

Black connector for first drive

Blue connector to motherboard

**Figure 8-23** 80-conductor cable connectors are color-coded

The motherboard might also be color-coded so that the primary channel connector is blue (see Figure 8-24). This color-coding is intended to ensure that the ATA/66/100/133 hard drive is installed on the primary IDE channel.

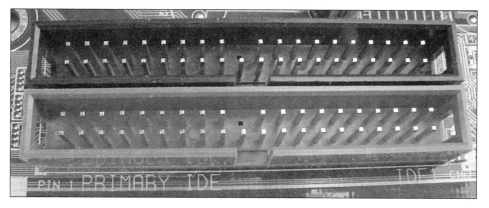

**Figure 8-24** The primary IDE channel connector is often color-coded as blue

If a motherboard supports serial ATA, most likely it has two or four serial ATA connectors and one or two parallel ATA connectors. A serial ATA cable can accommodate only a single drive, so you don't have to use jumpers to set master or slave assignments. According to one motherboard documentation, when installing serial ATA drives

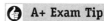 **A+ Exam Tip**

The A+ Essentials exam expects you to know how to configure PATA and SATA devices in a system.

using Windows 2000/XP, you can install up to six ATA devices in the system, including up to four parallel ATA devices and up to two serial ATA devices. Using Windows 9x/Me, you can install up to four devices using a combination of parallel ATA and serial ATA devices. You can have up to four parallel ATA devices and up to two serial ATA devices as long as the total number of devices in the Windows 9x/Me system does not exceed four.

In Figure 8-25, you can see the back of two hard drives; one uses a serial ATA interface and the other uses a parallel ATA interface. Notice the parallel ATA drive has a bank of jumpers and a 4-pin power connector. These jumpers are used to determine master or slave settings on the IDE channel. Because a serial data cable accommodates only a single drive, there is no need for jumpers on the drive for master or slave settings. However, a serial ATA drive might have jumpers used to set features such as the ability to power up from standby mode. Most likely, if jumpers are present on a serial ATA drive, the factory has set them as they should be and advises you not to change them.

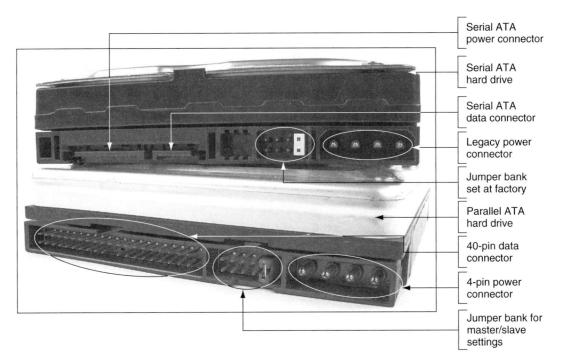

**Figure 8-25** Rear of a serial ATA drive and a parallel ATA drive

The power connector for a serial ATA drive is different from a regular EIDE device. To accommodate the special power connector, a serial ATA drive often comes with its own special power adapter or power cord (see Figure 8-26). Some serial ATA drives have two power connectors, as does the one in Figure 8-25. Choose between the serial ATA power connector (which is the preferred connector) or the legacy 4-pin connector, but never install two power cords to the drive at the same time because this could damage the drive. You will see examples of parallel and serial ATA installations later in the chapter.

## USING AN ATA CONTROLLER CARD

An ATA drive usually connects to the motherboard by way of a data cable from the drive to a parallel or serial ATA connection directly on the motherboard. However, you can use an ATA controller card to provide the ATA connectors when: (1) the motherboard IDE

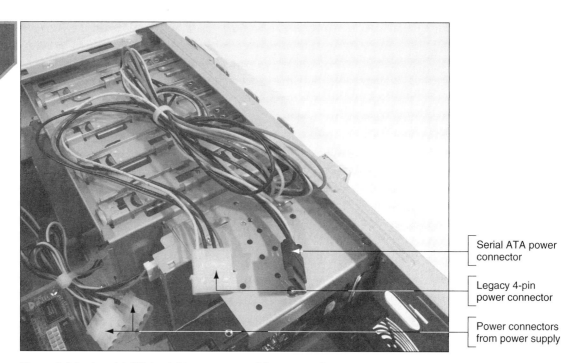

Serial ATA power
connector

Legacy 4-pin
power connector

Power connectors
from power supply

**Figure 8-26**  A serial ATA hard drive uses a special power cord to connect to a 4-pin power connector
coming from the power supply

connectors are not functioning; or (2) the motherboard does not support an ATA standard
you want to implement (such as a large-capacity drive). For example, suppose your older
motherboard supports ATA/100, but your hard drive uses ATA/133. You can purchase a
controller card such as the one by Belkin (*www.belkin.com*), shown in Figure 8-27. This
card uses a PCI slot, provides two 40-pin parallel IDE connections, and supports ATA/133
and previous ATA standards.

**Figure 8-27**  This Ultra ATA/133 controller card by Belkin uses a PCI slot and has two 40-pin IDE
connections that can accommodate up to four EIDE devices

Because a parallel ATA connector can accommodate one data cable for two drives, the card can support up to four drives. If you take into account the motherboard has two ATA/100 parallel ATA connectors that can support up to four drives, the entire system collectively can support up to eight parallel ATA drives when you use the card.

## SCSI TECHNOLOGY

Other than ATA, another interface standard for drives and other devices is SCSI, which provides better performance and greater expansion capabilities for many internal and external devices, including hard drives, CD-ROM drives, DVD drives, printers, and scanners. SCSI devices tend to be faster, more expensive, and more difficult to install than similar IDE devices. Because they are more expensive and more difficult to install, they are mostly used in corporate settings and are seldom seen in the small office or used on home PCs.

SCSI (pronounced "scuzzy") stands for **Small Computer System Interface** and is a standard for communication between a subsystem of peripheral devices and the system bus. The SCSI bus can support up to 7 or 15 devices, depending on the SCSI standard. The SCSI bus controller can be an expansion card called a host adapter or can be embedded on the motherboard. If it's embedded on the motherboard, the board will have one or more internal or external SCSI connectors.

### THE SCSI SUBSYSTEM

If a motherboard does not have an embedded SCSI controller, the gateway from the SCSI bus to the system bus is the host adapter, a card inserted into an expansion slot on the motherboard. The adapter card, called the **host adapter**, is responsible for managing all devices on the SCSI bus. A host adapter can support both internal and external SCSI devices, using one connector on the card for a ribbon cable or round cable to connect to internal devices, and an external port that supports external devices (see Figure 8-28).

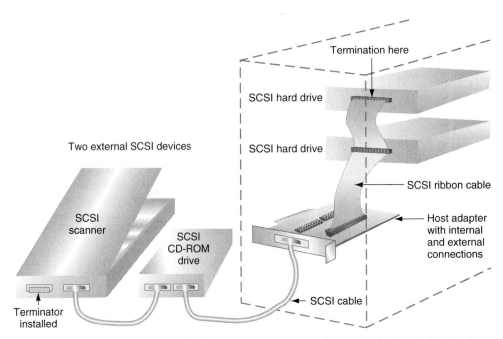

**Figure 8-28** Using a SCSI bus, a SCSI host adapter can support internal and external SCSI devices

A+ ESS
1.1
4.1

All the devices and the host adapter form a single daisy chain. In Figure 8-28, this daisy chain has two internal devices and two external devices, with the SCSI host adapter in the middle of the chain.

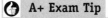

**A+ Exam Tip**

The A+ Essentials exam expects you to know that a motherboard might provide a SCSI controller and connector, or the SCSI host adapter can be a card installed in an expansion slot.

All devices go through the host adapter to communicate with the CPU or directly with each other without involving the CPU. Each device on the bus is assigned a number from 0 to 15 called the **SCSI ID**, by means of DIP switches, dials on the device, or software settings. The host adapter is generally assigned a number larger than all other devices, either 7 or 15. Cables connect the devices physically in a daisy chain, sometimes called a straight chain. The devices can be either internal or external, and the host adapter can be at either end of the chain or somewhere in the middle. The SCSI ID identifies the physical device, which can have several logical devices embedded in it. For example, a CD-ROM jukebox—a CD-ROM changer with trays for multiple CDs—might have seven trays. Each tray is considered a logical device and is assigned a **Logical Unit Number (LUN)** to iden-tify it, such as 1 through 7 or 0 through 6. The ID and LUN are written as two numbers separated by a colon. For instance, if the SCSI ID is 5, the fourth tray in the jukebox is device 5:4.

**Notes**

During installation, when setting IDs for internal devices, older devices required that you set jumpers on the device. These devices use a binary code to set IDs, with three pin pairs for narrow SCSI and four pin pairs for wide SCSI. Figure 8-29 shows the jumper settings for wide SCSI IDs.

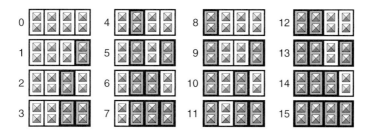

**Figure 8-29**  Wide SCSI ID binary jumper settings for internal devices

To reduce the amount of electrical "noise," or interference, on a SCSI cable, each end of the SCSI chain has a **terminating resistor**. The terminating resistor can be a hardware device plugged into the last device on each end of the chain (see Figure 8-30), or the chain can have software-controlled termination resistance, which makes installation simpler.

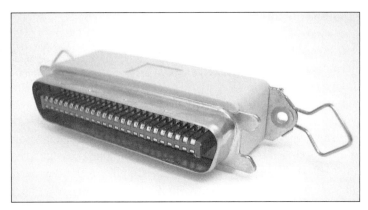

**Figure 8-30** External SCSI terminator

## VARIOUS SCSI STANDARDS

Just as with IDE/ATA standards, SCSI standards have improved over the years and use different names. SCSI standards are developed by the SCSI T10 Technical Committee (*www.t10.org*) and sent to ANSI, which publishes and maintains the official versions of the standards. The SCSI Trade Association, which promotes SCSI devices and standards, can also be accessed at *www.t10.org*. In addition to varying standards, SCSI also uses different types of cabling and different bus widths. Because there are so many variations with SCSI, when setting up a SCSI subsystem, it's important to pay careful attention to compatibility and make sure all devices, the host adapter, cables, and connectors can work together.

The three major versions of SCSI are SCSI-1, SCSI-2, and SCSI-3, commonly known as Regular SCSI, Fast SCSI, and Ultra SCSI. The latest SCSI standard, serial SCSI, also called serial attached SCSI (SAS), allows for more than 15 devices on a single SCSI chain, uses smaller, longer, round cables, and uses smaller hard drive form factors that can support larger capacities than earlier versions of SCSI. Serial SCSI is compatible with serial ATA drives in the same system, and claims to be more reliable and better performing than serial ATA. For more information on serial SCSI, see the SCSI Trade Association's Web site at *www.serialattachedscsi.com*.

## OTHER INTERFACE STANDARDS

Other than ATA and SCSI, some other technologies used by hard drives are USB, FireWire (IEEE 1394), and Fibre Channel, which can all be used by external hard drives. Let's now look at USB, IEEE 1394, and Fibre Channel interfaces.

### USB

USB (universal serial bus) is a popular way to connect many external peripheral devices to a system. The first USB standard, USB 1.0, is not fast enough to be used for a hard drive, but the latest standards, USB 1.1 and USB 2.0 (Hi-Speed USB) are fast enough. Most computers today have two or more USB ports, making USB an easy way to add a second external hard drive to a system. For example, Maxtor (*www.maxtor.com*) has a 120-GB external drive for

A+ ESS
1.1

under $200 that works with a USB 2.0 or USB 1.1 interface. Windows 98SE, Windows Me, and Windows 2000/XP support USB 1.1, and Windows XP supports USB 2.0 with a service pack applied. Before buying a USB hard drive, verify your OS and the motherboard USB connection support the same USB standard as the drive. Chapter 9 includes more information about USB.

### IEEE 1394 OR FIREWIRE

IEEE 1394, also known as FireWire (named by Apple Computers) and i.Link (named by Sony Corporation), uses serial transmission of data and is popular for multimedia and home entertainment applications. IEEE refers to the Institute of Electrical and Electronics Engineers, which published standard 1394, more commonly known as FireWire. For more information, see *www.ieee.org*. For example, SmartDisk, Inc.(*www.smartdisk.com*), a manufacturer of multimedia devices, makes a hard drive designed for home entertainment electronics that uses FireWire or USB for the external hard drive interface (see Figure 8-31).

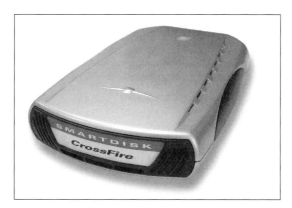

**Figure 8-31** This CrossFire hard drive holds 160 GB and uses a 1394a or USB 2.0 connection

A FireWire device connects to a PC through a FireWire external port or internal connector provided either directly on the motherboard or by way of a FireWire expansion card. For a computer system to use FireWire, the operating system must support it. Windows 98, Windows 2000, and Windows XP support FireWire, but Windows 95 and Windows NT do not. Chapter 9 includes more information about FireWire.

### FIBRE CHANNEL

Fibre Channel is another type of interface that can support hard drives. Fibre Channel is designed for use in high-end systems that have multiple hard drives. To be precise, Fibre Channel is a type of SCSI technology, but in the industry, it is considered a rival of SCSI for high-end server solutions. One advantage Fibre Channel has over SCSI is that you can connect up to 126 devices together on a single Fibre Channel bus, as compared to 16 SCSI devices connected together on the same bus. Fibre Channel is faster than SCSI when

**A+ ESS
1.1**

more than five hard drives are strung together to provide massive secondary storage, but it is too expensive and has too much overhead to be a good solution for the average desktop PC or workstation.

## SELECTING AND INSTALLING A HARD DRIVE

**A+
220-602
1.1**

This section of the chapter covers how to select a hard drive and then how to install it. You'll learn what to look for when selecting a drive and then how to install a drive in a system using either a parallel ATA drive and a serial ATA drive.

### HOW TO SELECT A HARD DRIVE

When making purchasing decisions, you need to match the HDD technologies to the OS and the motherboard in a system. In most cases, when installing a drive, you don't need to know which ATA standard a hard drive supports, because the startup BIOS uses autodetection. With **autodetection**, the BIOS detects the new drive and automatically selects the correct drive capacity and configuration, including the best possible standard supported by both the hard drive and the motherboard.

One exception is when you install a new drive that the startup BIOS is not designed to support. The BIOS will either not recognize the drive at all or will detect the drive and report in CMOS setup that the drive has a smaller capacity or fewer features than it actually does. In this situation, your older BIOS or hard drive controller card does not support the newer ATA standard the drive is using. The solution is to flash BIOS, replace the controller card, or replace the motherboard.

---

**APPLYING|CONCEPTS** When purchasing a hard drive, consider the following factors that affect performance, use, and price:

▲ *The capacity of the drive.* Today's hard drives for desktop systems are in the range of 20 GB to more than 500 GB. The more gigabytes, the higher the price.

▲ *The spindle speed.* Hard drives for desktop systems run at 5400, 7200, or 10,000 RPM. The most common are 5400 and 7200 RPM. 7200 RPM drives are faster, make more noise, put off more heat, and are more expensive than 5400 RPM drives.

▲ *The technology standard.* Most likely, the hard drive technology standard you'll want to select is Ultra ATA/100, Ultra ATA/133, or Serial ATA 150, although you might choose SCSI or FireWire. As always, be sure your motherboard supports the standard you choose.

▲ *The cache or buffer size.* Look for a 2-MB or 8-MB cache (also called a buffer). The more the better, though the cost goes up as the size increases.

▲ *The average seek time (time to fetch data).* Look for 13 to 8.5 ms (milliseconds). The lower the number, the higher the drive performance and cost.

When selecting a drive, match the drive to what your motherboard supports. To find out what drive the motherboard supports, you can check the motherboard documentation or the CMOS setup screen

A+
220-602
1.1

for information. For example, the CMOS setup screens for one motherboard give these options:

- LBA Mode can be enabled or disabled.
- Multisector transfers (block mode) can be set to Disabled, 2, 4, 8, or 16 sectors.
- PIO Mode can be set to Auto, 0, 1, 2, 3, or 4.
- Ultra DMA Mode can be set to Disabled, 0, 1, 2, 3, 4, or 5.
- Cable detected displays the type of cable (40-conductor or 80-conductor).

Remember, when you install the drive, you won't have to set these values, because autodetection should do that for you. However, reading about the values allows you to know what the board supports and what drive you can purchase. After all, there's no point in buying an expensive hard drive with features your system cannot support.

> **Notes**
>
> Some BIOSs support a method of data transfer that allows multiple data transfers each time software requests data. This method is called **block mode** and should be used if your hard drive and BIOS support it. However, if you are having problems with hard drive errors, you can try disabling block mode. You can use CMOS setup to make this change.

After you know what drive your system can support, you then can select a drive that is appropriate for the price range and intended use of your system. For example, Seagate has two lines of IDE hard drives: The Barracuda is less expensive and intended for the desktop market, and the Cheetah is more expensive and targets the server market. When purchasing a drive, you can compare price and features by searching the Web sites of the drive manufacturers, some of which are listed in Table 8-2. The same manufacturers usually produce ATA drives and SCSI drives.

| Manufacturer | Web Site |
|---|---|
| Fujitsu America, Inc. | www.fujitsu.com |
| IBM PC Company | www.ibm.com |
| Maxtor Corporation | www.maxtor.com |
| Quantum Corporation | www.quantum.com |
| Seagate Technology | www.seagate.com |
| Western Digital | www.wdc.com |

**Table 8-2**   Hard drive manufacturers

Now let's turn our attention to the step-by-step process of installing an ATA hard drive. We begin by looking at special concerns that arise when installing a hard drive in a system that has an older BIOS that doesn't support the newer drive.

## INSTALLATIONS USING LEGACY BIOS

Before installing a new hard drive, know the hard drive standards the BIOS on your motherboard supports. Here are the older standards that you might encounter with older motherboards:

- *CHS (cylinder, head, sector) mode or normal mode used for drives less than 528 MB.* System BIOS expects the hard drive controller to communicate the location of data on

A+
220-602
1.1

the drive using cylinder, head, and track coordinates. Using CHS mode, a drive can have no more than 1,024 cylinders, 16 heads, 63 sectors per track, and 512 bytes per sector. Therefore, the maximum amount of storage on a hard drive using CHS mode is 528 MB or 504 MB, depending on how the calculations are done (1K = 1,000 or 1K = 1,024). You'll probably never see one of the obsolete boards around, but, then again, you never know.

▲ *Large mode or ECHS mode used for drives between 504 MB and 8.4 GB.* System BIOS expects the hard drive controller to send cylinder, head, and track coordinates, but the BIOS communicates a different set of parameters to the OS and other software. This method is called translation, and system BIOS is said to be in large mode, or ECHS (extended CHS) mode.

▲ *33.8 GB limitation.* System BIOS on some systems does not recognize a drive larger than 33.8 GB, which can cause the system to lock up during POST, or to boot, but incorrectly report the size of the drive.

▲ *137 GB limitation.* System BIOS does not support the ATA/ATAPI-6 standard, which makes it unable to recognize drives larger than 137 GB.

If you want to install a drive in a system whose BIOS does not support it, you have the following choices:

▲ *Let the BIOS see the drive as a smaller drive.* For some systems, the BIOS assigns a drive capacity smaller than the actual capacity. You can use this method, although it wastes drive space. With other BIOSs, the system refuses to boot when it sees a drive it does not support.

▲ *Upgrade the BIOS.* The least expensive solution is to upgrade the BIOS. Be certain you use a BIOS upgrade compatible with your motherboard. It's also a good idea to update the chipset drivers at the same time you update the BIOS. You can download the BIOS upgrade and the chipset driver update from the motherboard manufacturer's Web site.

▲ *Replace the motherboard.* This is the most expensive solution.

▲ *Use software that interfaces between the older BIOS and the newer drive.* Most drive manufacturers provide software that performs the translation between an older BIOS and the newer drive. Examples of such translation or disk overlay software are Disk Manager by Ontrack Data International, Inc. (*www.ontrack.com*), SpeedStor by Storage Dimensions, EZ-Drive by Phoenix (*www.phoenix.com*), MaxBlast by Maxtor (*www.maxtor.com*), and DiscWizard by Seagate (*www.seagate.com*). You can find the software on a floppy disk with the drive or download it from the drive manufacturer's Web site. Boot from a floppy disk with the software installed, and follow directions onscreen. Before you decide to use this method, read the documentation on the hard drive manufacturer's Web site to understand how to handle problems that might later arise with the drive.

▲ *Use an ATA controller card to provide the ATA connector and firmware to substitute for motherboard BIOS.* You saw a photograph of one of these controller cards in Figure 8-27 earlier in the chapter.

## STEPS TO INSTALL A PARALLEL ATA HARD DRIVE

We'll first look at how to install a parallel ATA hard drive and then look at the differences between that installation and one using a serial ATA drive.

To install a parallel ATA drive, you need the drive, an 80-conductor or 40-conductor data cable, and perhaps a kit to make the drive fit into a much larger bay. If the motherboard

A+
220-602
1.1

does not provide an IDE connection, you also need an adapter card.

To install a parallel ATA hard drive, do the following:

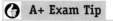

**A+ Exam Tip**

The A+ Essentials exam expects you to know how to install a device such as a hard drive. Given a list of steps for the installation, you should be able to order the steps correctly or identify an error in a step.

1. Prepare for the installation by preparing the existing computer system for a disassembly, reading the documentation, planning the drive configuration, and preparing your work area.

2. Set jumpers or DIP switches on the drive.

3. Physically install the drive inside the computer case, and attach the power cord and data cable.

4. Use CMOS setup to verify that autodetect correctly detected the drive.

5. If you are installing an OS on the drive, boot from the Windows setup CD. If the drive is not intended to hold an OS (it's a second drive in a two-drive system, for example), use the Windows 2000/XP Disk Management utility or the Windows 9x/Me Fdisk and Format commands to partition and format the drive.

**Video**

Installing a Hard Drive

Let's now look at each of the preceding steps in more detail.

## STEP 1: PREPARE FOR THE INSTALLATION

Prepare for the installation by knowing your starting point, reading the documentation, planning the drive configuration, and preparing your work area.

### Know Your Starting Point

As with installing any other devices, before you begin installing your hard drive, make sure you know where your starting point is. Do this by answering these questions: How is your system configured? Is everything working properly? Verify which of your system's devices are working before installing a new one. Later, if a device does not work, the information will help you isolate the problem. Remember from earlier chapters that keeping notes is a good idea whenever you install new hardware or software or make any other changes to your PC system. Write down what you know about the system that might be important later.

As always, just in case you lose setup information in the process, write down any varia-

**Notes**

When installing hardware and software, don't install too many things at once. If something goes wrong, you won't know what's causing the problem. Install one device, start the system, and confirm that the new device is working before installing another.

tions in setup from the default settings. Two good places to record CMOS settings are the notebook you keep about this computer and the manual for the motherboard.

### Read Documentation

Before you take anything apart, carefully read all the documentation for the drive and controller card, and the part of your PC documentation that covers hard drive installation. Look for problems you have not considered, such as differing ATA standards. Check your motherboard documentation to verify the BIOS accommodates

A+
220-602
1.1

the size and type of hard drive you want to install. If you are not sure which ATA standards your motherboard supports, you can look for different options on the CMOS setup screens.

## Plan the Drive Configuration

You must decide which IDE connector to use and if another drive will share the same IDE data cable with your new drive. Remember, when using parallel ATA, there are two IDE connectors on a motherboard, the primary and secondary IDE channels. Each channel can support up to two drives, a master and a slave, for a total of up to four EIDE drives in a system.

When possible, leave the hard drive as the single drive on one channel, so that it does not compete with another drive for access to the channel and possibly slow down performance. Use the primary channel before you use the secondary channel.

> **Notes**
>
> If you have three or fewer devices, allow the fastest hard drive to be your boot device and the only device on the primary channel.

Place the fastest devices on the primary channel and the slower devices on the secondary channel. This pairing helps keep a slow device from pulling down a faster device. As an example of this type of pairing, suppose you have a Zip drive, CD-ROM drive, and two hard drives. Because the two hard drives are faster than the Zip drive and CD-ROM drive, put the two hard drives on one channel and the Zip drive and CD-ROM drive on the other.

Make sure that you can visualize all the steps in the installation. If you have any questions, keep researching until you locate the answer. You can also call technical support or ask a knowledgeable friend for help. As you get your questions answered, you might discover that what you are installing will not work on your computer, but that is better than coping with hours of frustration and a disabled computer. You cannot always anticipate every problem, but at least you can know that you made your best effort to understand everything in advance. What you learn in thorough preparation pays off every time!

## Prepare Your Work Area and Take Precautions

The next step is to prepare a large, well-lit place to work. Set out your tools, documentation, new hardware, and notebook. Remember the basic rules concerning static electricity, which you learned in Chapter 3. Be sure to protect against ESD by wearing a ground bracelet during the installation. You need to also avoid working on carpet in the winter when there's a lot of static electricity.

Some added precautions for working with hard drives are as follows:

- Handle the drive carefully.
- Do not touch any exposed circuitry or chips.
- Prevent other people from touching exposed microchips on the drive.
- When you first take the drive out of the static-protective package, touch the package containing the drive to a screw holding an expansion card or cover, or to a metal part of the computer case, for at least two seconds. This drains the static electricity from the package and from your body.
- If you must set down the drive outside the static-protective package, place it component-side-up on a flat surface.
- Do not place the drive on the computer case cover or on a metal table.

So now you're ready to start work. Turn off the computer and unplug it. Unplug the monitor and move it to one side. Remove the computer case cover. Check that you have an available power cord from the power supply.

You need to decide which bay will hold which drive. To do that, examine the locations of the drive bays and the length of the data cables and power cords. Bays designed for hard drives do not have access to the outside of the case, unlike bays for Zip drives and other drives in which disks are inserted. Also, some bays are wider than others to accommodate wide drives such as CD-ROM drives and DVD drives (see Figure 8-32). Will the data cable reach the drives and the motherboard connector? If not, rearrange your plan for locating the drives in the bays, or purchase a custom-length data cable.

> **Notes**
>
> If there are not enough power cords from a power supply, you can purchase a Y connector that can add an additional power cord.

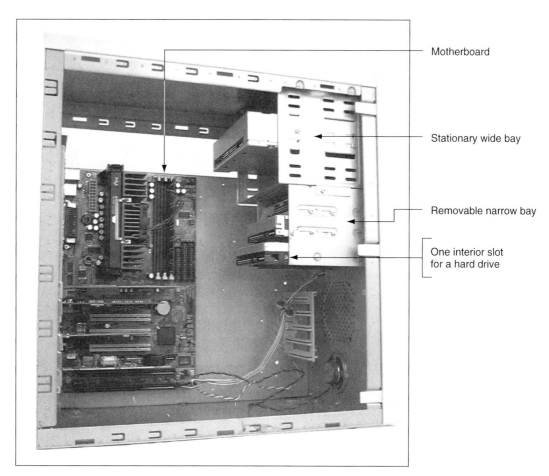

Motherboard

Stationary wide bay

Removable narrow bay

One interior slot for a hard drive

**Figure 8-32**  Plan for the location of drives within bays

## STEP 2: SET JUMPERS

You normally configure a hard drive by setting jumpers on the drive housing. Often, diagrams of the jumper settings are printed on the top of the hard drive housing (see Figure 8-33). If they are not, see the documentation or visit the Web site of the drive manufacturer. (Hands-On Project 8-5 lets you practice this.)

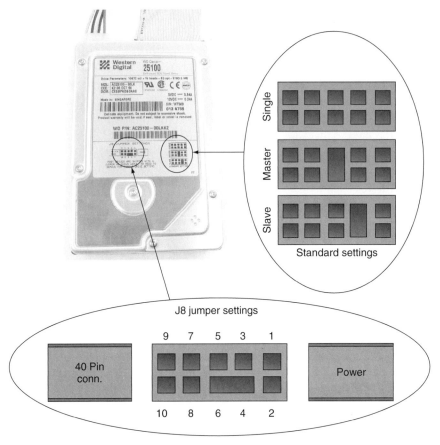

**Figure 8-33** A parallel ATA drive most likely will have diagrams of jumper settings for master and slave options printed on the drive housing

Table 8-3 lists the four choices for jumper settings, and Figure 8-34 shows a typical jumper arrangement for a drive that uses three of these settings. In Figures 8-33 and 8-34, note that a black square represents an empty pin and a black rectangle represents a pair of pins with jumper in place. Know that your hard drive might not have the first configuration as an option, but it should have a way of indicating if the drive will be the master device. The factory default setting is usually correct for the drive to be the single drive on a system. Before you change any settings, write down the original ones. If things go wrong, you can revert to the original settings and begin again. If a drive is the only drive on a channel, set it to single. For two drives on a controller, set one to master and the other to slave.

| Configuration | Description |
| --- | --- |
| **Single-drive configuration** | **This is the only hard drive on this EIDE channel. (This is the standard setting.)** |
| **Master-drive configuration** | **This is the first of two drives; it most likely is the boot device.** |
| **Slave-drive configuration** | **This is the second drive using this channel or data cable.** |
| **Cable-select configuration** | **The cable-select data cable determines which of the two drives is the master and which is the slave.** |

**Table 8-3** Jumper settings on a parallel ATA hard drive

## 8

A+
220-602
1.1

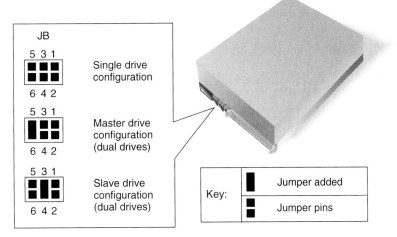

**Figure 8-34** Jumper settings on a hard drive and their meanings

Some hard drives have a cable-select configuration option. If you choose this configuration, you must use a cable-select data cable. When you use one of these cables, the drive nearest the motherboard is the master, and the drive farthest from the motherboard is the slave. You can recognize a cable-select cable by a small hole somewhere in the data cable.

> **Notes**
>
> Know that some hard drive manufacturers label the master setting as Drive 0 and the slave setting as Drive 1.

## STEP 3: MOUNT THE DRIVE IN THE BAY

Now that you've set the jumpers, your next step is to look at the drive bay that you will use for the drive. The bay can be stationary or removable. With a removable bay, you first remove the bay from the computer case and mount the drive in the bay. Then, you put the bay back into the computer case. In Figure 8-32, you can see a stationary, wide bay for large drives and a removable, narrow bay for small drives, including the hard drive.

In the following steps, you will see how the hard drive is installed in a computer case that has three other drives: a DVD drive, a Zip drive, and a floppy drive. Do the following to install the hard drive in the bay:

1. Remove the bay for the hard drive, and insert the hard drive in the bay. You can line up the drive in the bay with the front of the computer case (see Figure 8-35) to see how drives will line up in the bay. Put the hard drive in the bay flush with the front of the bay so it will butt up against the computer case once the bay is in position (see Figure 8-36). Line up other drives in the bay so they are flush with the front of the computer case. In Figure 8-36, a floppy drive and Zip drive are already in the bay.

2. You must be able to securely mount the drive in the bay; the drive should not move when it is screwed down. Line up the drive and bay screw holes, and make sure everything will fit. After checking the position of the drive and determining how screws are placed, install four screws (two on each side) to mount the drive in the bay.

> **Notes**
>
> Do not allow torque to stress the drive. For example, don't force a drive into a space that is too small for it. Also, placing two screws in diagonal positions across the drive can place pressure diagonally on the drive.

A+
220-602
1.1

**Figure 8-35**   Line up the floppy drive in the removable bay so it's flush with the front of the case

**Figure 8-36**   Position the hard drive flush with the end of the bay

3. Decide whether to connect the data cable to the drive before or after you insert the bay inside the computer case, depending on how accessible the connections are. In this example, the data cables are connected to the drives first and then the bay is installed inside the computer case. In the photograph in Figure 8-37, the data cables for all the drives in the bay are connected to the drives.

A+
220-602
1.1

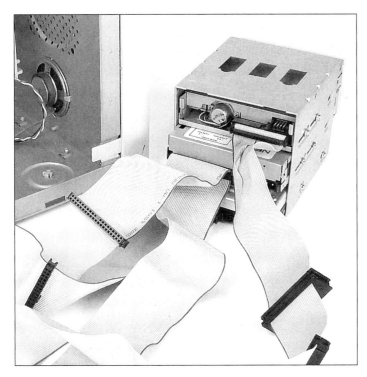

**Figure 8-37** Connect the cables to all three drives

4. The next step is to place the bay back into position and secure the bay with the bay screw or screws (see Figure 8-38). Note that some bays are secured with clips. For example, for the bay shown in Figure 8-39, when you slide the bay into the case, you will hear the clipping mechanism pop into place when the bay is all the way in.

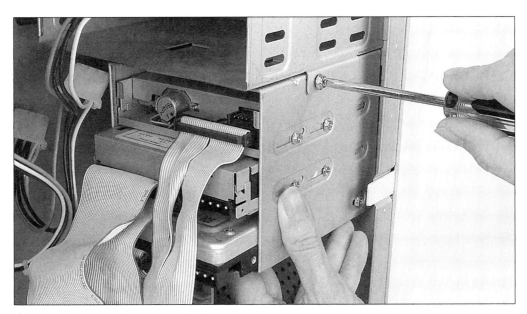

**Figure 8-38** Secure the bay with the bay screw

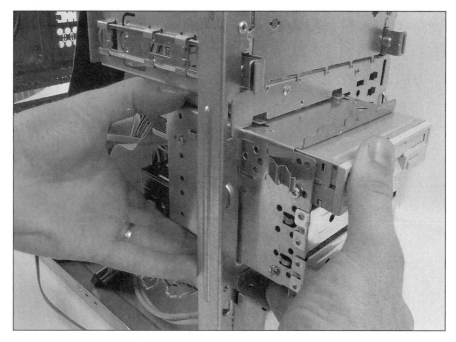

**Figure 8-39**  Slide the bay into the case as far as it will go

> **Notes**
>
> The previous steps to install a hard drive assume that you are using a removable bay. However, some computer cases use small, stationary bays like the one in Figure 8-40. For these installations, you need only slide the drive into the bay and secure it with four screws, two on each side of the bay.

5. You can now install a power connection to each drive (Figure 8-41). In Figure 8-41, the floppy drive uses the small Berg power connection, and the other drives use the large Molex ones. It doesn't matter which of the power cords you use, because they all produce the same voltage. Also, the cord only goes into the connection one way.

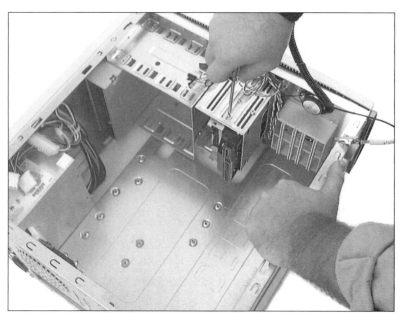

**Figure 8-40**  To install a drive in a stationary bay, slide the drive in the bay and secure it with four screws

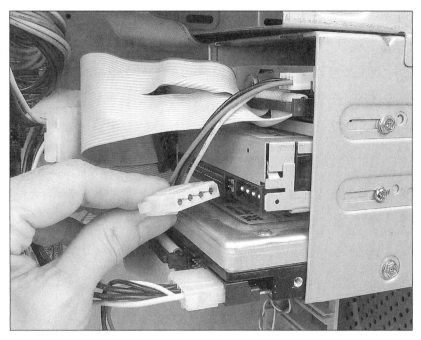

**Figure 8-41** Connect a power cord to each drive

6. Next, connect the data cable to the IDE connector on the motherboard (see Figure 8-42). Make certain pin 1 and the edge color on the cable align correctly at both ends of the cable. Normally, pin 1 is closest to the power connection on the drive.

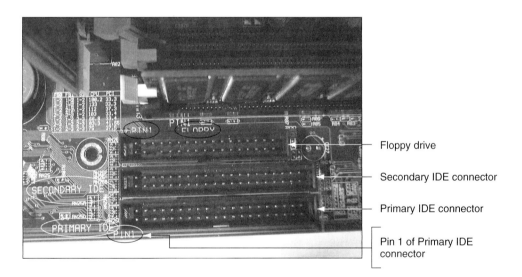

— Floppy drive

— Secondary IDE connector

— Primary IDE connector

— Pin 1 of Primary IDE connector

**Figure 8-42** Floppy drive and two IDE connectors on the motherboard

7. If you are mounting a hard drive in an external bay, install a bay cover in the front of the case. Internal bays do not need this cover (see Figure 8-43).

8. When using a motherboard connection, if the wire connecting the motherboard to the hard drive light on the front of the case was not connected when the motherboard was installed, connect it now. If you reverse the polarity of the LED wire, the light will not work. Your motherboard manual should tell you the location of the LED wires on the motherboard.

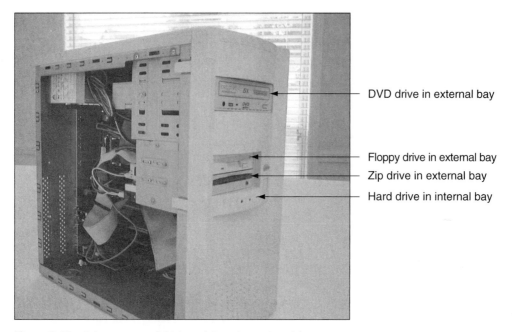

DVD drive in external bay

Floppy drive in external bay

Zip drive in external bay

Hard drive in internal bay

**Figure 8-43** A tower case might have internal or external bays

> **Caution**
>
> Be sure the screws are not too long. If they are, you can screw too far into the drive housing and damage the drive itself.

> **Notes**
>
> If the drive light does not work after you install a new drive, try reversing the LED wire on the motherboard pins.

9. Before you replace the case cover, plug in the monitor and turn on the computer. (On the other hand, some systems won't power up until the front panel is installed.) Verify that your system BIOS can find the drive before you replace the cover and that it recognizes the correct size of the drive. If you have problems, refer to the troubleshooting section at the end of this chapter.

## STEP 4: USE CMOS SETUP TO VERIFY HARD DRIVE SETTINGS

When you first boot up after installing a hard drive, go to CMOS setup and verify that the drive has been recognized and that the settings are correct. Let's look at typical CMOS setup screens for an Award BIOS used on a motherboard with two parallel ATA connectors. The CMOS setup screens to view and change hard drive parameters are shown in Figures 8-44 through 8-47. Figure 8-44 shows the choice for IDE HDD Auto Detection in the third item in the second column. If Auto Detection is not enabled, enable it, and then save and exit setup. Later, after you have rebooted with the new drive detected, you can return to setup, view the selections that it made, and make appropriate changes.

It's interesting to see how this Award BIOS is designed to support older hard drives using legacy standards. Notice in Figure 8-45 the column labeled *mode*, referring to how the BIOS relates to the drive. Choices are normal, large, LBA, and auto. Most likely, when auto is the choice, setup automatically selects LBA, the current standard.

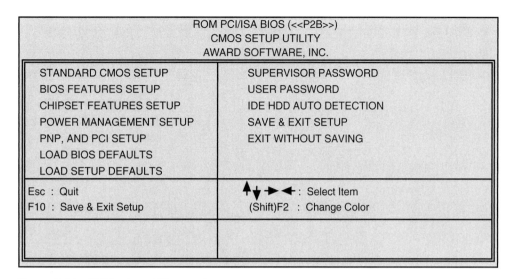

**Figure 8-44**  CMOS setup utility opening menu

```
                    ROM PCI/ISA BIOS (<<P2B>>)
                     CMOS SETUP UTILITY
                     AWARD SOFTWARE, INC.

  STANDARD CMOS SETUP              SUPERVISOR PASSWORD
  BIOS FEATURES SETUP             USER PASSWORD
  CHIPSET FEATURES SETUP          IDE HDD AUTO DETECTION
  POWER MANAGEMENT SETUP          SAVE & EXIT SETUP
  PNP, AND PCI SETUP              EXIT WITHOUT SAVING
  LOAD BIOS DEFAULTS
  LOAD SETUP DEFAULTS

  Esc : Quit                      ↑↓ → ◄ : Select Item
  F10 : Save & Exit Setup         (Shift)F2 : Change Color
```

```
                    ROM PCI/ISA BIOS (<<P2B>>)
                     STANDARD CMOS SETUP
                     AWARD SOFTWARE, INC.

  Date (mm:dd:yy) : Wed, Mar 25 1998
  Time (hh:mm:ss) :  9 :  5 :  2

  HARD DISKS        TYPE  SIZE  CYLS  HEAD  PRECOMP  LANDZ  SECTOR   MODE

  Primary Master  : Auto    0     0     0       0       0      0    NORMAL
  Primary Slave   : None    0     0     0       0       0      0    ----------
  Secondary Master: Auto    0     0     0       0       0      0    NORMAL
  Secondary Slave : None    0     0     0       0       0      0    ----------

  Drive A : 2.88M, 3.5 in.
  Drive B : 1.44M, 3.5 in.
  Floppy 3 Mode Support : Disabled           Base Memory     :     0K
                                             Extended Memory :     0K
                                             Other Memory    :   512K
  Video   : EGA/VGA
  Halt On : All Errors                       Total Memory    :   512K

  Esc: Quit          ↑↓ → ◄ : Select Item          PU/PD/+/- : Modify
  F1 : Help          (Shift)F2 : Change Color
```

**Figure 8-45**  Standard CMOS setup

In Figure 8-46 (starting with the tenth item in the second column), you can see the hard drive features that the chipset on this motherboard supports. They are Ultra DMA, PIO, and DMA modes. Leave all these settings at Auto, and let the BIOS make the choice according to its detection of the features your hard drive supports.

In Figure 8-47, the 12th item in the first column indicates that the BIOS on this motherboard supports block mode. From this screen, you can also select the boot sequence (see ninth item in first column). Choices for this BIOS are A, C; A, CD Rom, C; CD Rom, C, A; D, A; F, A; C only; Zip, C; and C, A. Also notice on this screen (eighth item in the first column) that this BIOS supports booting from a SCSI drive even when an IDE drive is present. Booting from the IDE drive is the default setting.

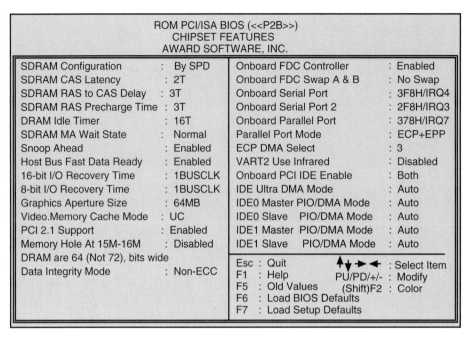

**Figure 8-46** CMOS setup for chipset features

```
                    ROM PCI/ISA BIOS (<<P2B>>)
                        CHIPSET FEATURES
                       AWARD SOFTWARE, INC.

  SDRAM Configuration        : By SPD    Onboard FDC Controller   : Enabled
  SDRAM CAS Latency          : 2T        Onboard FDC Swap A & B   : No Swap
  SDRAM RAS to CAS Delay     : 3T        Onboard Serial Port      : 3F8H/IRQ4
  SDRAM RAS Precharge Time   : 3T        Onboard Serial Port 2    : 2F8H/IRQ3
  DRAM Idle Timer            : 16T       Onboard Parallel Port    : 378H/IRQ7
  SDRAM MA Wait State        : Normal    Parallel Port Mode       : ECP+EPP
  Snoop Ahead                : Enabled   ECP DMA Select           : 3
  Host Bus Fast Data Ready   : Enabled   VART2 Use Infrared       : Disabled
  16-bit I/O Recovery Time   : 1BUSCLK   Onboard PCI IDE Enable   : Both
  8-bit I/O Recovery Time    : 1BUSCLK   IDE Ultra DMA Mode       : Auto
  Graphics Aperture Size     : 64MB      IDE0 Master PIO/DMA Mode : Auto
  Video.Memory Cache Mode    : UC        IDE0 Slave  PIO/DMA Mode : Auto
  PCI 2.1 Support            : Enabled   IDE1 Master PIO/DMA Mode : Auto
  Memory Hole At 15M-16M     : Disabled  IDE1 Slave  PIO/DMA Mode : Auto
  DRAM are 64 (Not 72), bits wide
  Data Integrity Mode        : Non-ECC   Esc : Quit              ↑↓→← : Select Item
                                         F1  : Help       PU/PD/+/- : Modify
                                         F5  : Old Values  (Shift)F2 : Color
                                         F6  : Load BIOS Defaults
                                         F7  : Load Setup Defaults
```

**Figure 8-47** CMOS setup for BIOS features

```
                    ROM PCI/ISA BIOS (<<P2B>>)
                        BIOS FEATURES SETUP
                       AWARD SOFTWARE, INC.

  CPU Internal Core Speed    : 350Mhz    Video  ROM BIOS Shadow  : Enabled
                                         C8000 - CBFFF  Shadow   : Disabled
  Boot Virus Detection       : Enabled   CC000 - CFFFF  Shadow   : Disabled
  CPU Level 1 Cache          : Enabled   D0000 - D3FFF  Shadow   : Disabled
  CPU Level 2 Cache          : Enabled   D4000 - D7FFF  Shadow   : Disabled
  CPU Level 2 Cache ECC Check: Disabled  D8000 - DBFFF  Shadow   : Disabled
  BIOS Update                : Enabled   DC000 - DFFFF  Shadow   : Disabled
  Quick Power On Self Test   : Enabled
  HDD Sequence SCSI/IDE First: IDE       Boot Up NumLock Status   : On
  Boot Sequence              : A,C       Typematic Rate Setting   : Disabled
  Boot Up Floppy Seek        : Disabled  Typematic Rate (Chars/Sec) : 6
  Floppy Disk Access Control : R/W       Typematic Delay (Msec)   : 250
  IDE HDD Block Mode Sectors : HDD MAX
  Security Option            : System
  PS/2 Mouse Function Control: Auto
  PCI/VGA Palette Snoop      : Disabled  Esc : Quit              ↑↓→← : Select Item
  OS/2 Onboard Memory > 64M  : Disabled  F1  : Help      PU/PD/+/- : Modify
                                         F5  : Old Values  (Shift)F2 : Color
                                         F6  : Load BIOS Defaults
                                         F7  : Load Setup Defaults
```

After you confirm that your drive is recognized, the size of the drive is detected correctly, and supported features are set to be automatically detected, reboot the system. Then the next thing to do is to use an operating system to prepare the drive for first use.

## STEP 5: USE WINDOWS SETUP TO PARTITION AND FORMAT A NEW DRIVE

If you are installing a new hard drive in a system that is to be used for a new Windows installation, after you have physically installed the drive, boot from the Windows setup CD and

A+ ESS
1.1

A+
220-602
1.1

follow the directions on the screen to install Windows on the new drive. The setup process partitions and formats the new drive before it begins the Windows installation. If you are installing a second hard drive in a system that already has Windows 2000/XP installed on the first hard drive, use Windows to partition and format the second drive. After physically installing the second hard drive, boot into Windows as usual. Then use Disk Management to partition and format the new drive. Disk Management is covered in Chapter 11. Also covered in Chapter 11 are how to make good decisions as to how many partitions to use on a hard drive and what file system to use for each partition. For Windows 9x/Me, to partition and format the drive, use the Fdisk and Format commands, which are covered in Chapter 15.

## SERIAL ATA HARD DRIVE INSTALLATIONS

Serial ATA hard drives are easier to install than parallel ATA drives because there are no jumpers to set on the drive and each serial ATA connector and cable is dedicated to a single drive. You install the drive in the bay the same as a parallel ATA drive. Next, connect a power cord to the drive. If your serial ATA drive has two power connectors, use only one.

Read the motherboard documentation to find out which serial ATA connectors on the board to use first. For example, the motherboard shown earlier in the chapter in Figure 8-18 has four serial ATA connectors and one parallel ATA connector. You can see a close-up of these four serial ATA connectors in Figure 8-48. The documentation says to use the two red connectors (labeled SATA1 and SATA2 on the board) before you use the black connectors (labeled SATA3 and SATA4). Connect the serial ATA data cable to the hard drive and to the red SATA1 connector. For both the drive and the motherboard, you can only plug the cable into the connector in one direction. Check all your connections and you're now ready to power up the system and verify the drive was recognized correctly.

**Figure 8-48**  This motherboard has four serial ATA connectors

Figures 8-49 and 8-50 show CMOS setup screens for this system when two hard drives are installed. A DVD drive is installed as the Primary IDE Master (using the parallel ATA connector) and the two serial ATA hard drives are installed as the Third IDE Master (using the first red serial ATA connector) and Fourth IDE Master (using the second red serial ATA connector).

A+
220-602
1.1

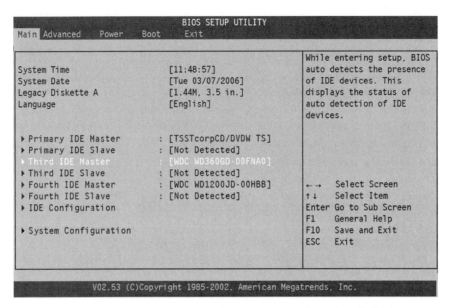

**Figure 8-49** American Megatrends, Inc. CMOS setup screen shows installed drives

To see how the first hard drive is configured, highlight it and press Enter. The screen in Figure 8-50 appears showing the size of the drive, the hard drive standards the BIOS supports, and that most of these standards are automatically detected. In comparing the older BIOS screen shown earlier in Figure 8-45 to this newer BIOS screen, notice that the older BIOS gives cylinder, head, and sector information so that you can manually calculate the size of an installed drive, but the newer BIOS only gives the detected size of a drive.

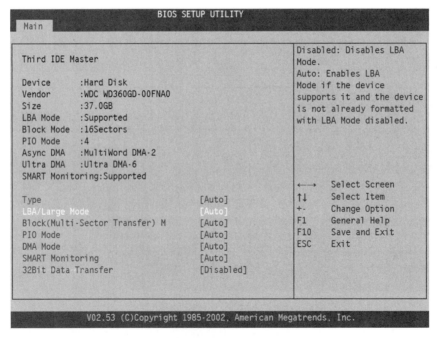

**Figure 8-50** CMOS setup screen showing the size of the drive and supported standards

After you have verified the drive is detected correctly, reboot the system and move on to the next step of installing an operating system.

**A+
220-602
1.1**

## INSTALLING A HARD DRIVE IN A WIDE BAY

If you are mounting a hard drive into a bay that is too large, a universal bay kit can help you securely fit the drive into the bay. These inexpensive kits should create a tailor-made fit. In Figure 8-51, you can see how the universal bay kit adapter works. The adapter spans the distance between the sides of the drive and the bay. Figure 8-52 shows the drive installed in a wide bay.

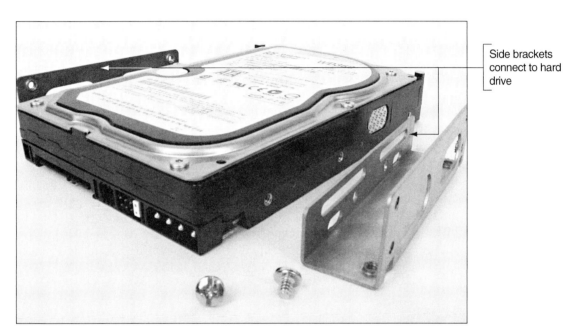

Side brackets connect to hard drive

**Figure 8-51** Use the universal bay kit to make the drive fit the bay

**Figure 8-52** Hard drive installed in a wide bay using a universal bay kit adapter

# TROUBLESHOOTING HARD DRIVES

A+
220-602
1.2

In this part of the chapter, you'll learn to troubleshoot problems with hard drives and floppy drives. The following sections cover problems with hard drive installations and problems that occur after the installation with hard drives and floppy drives. Problems with hardware also are covered. How to deal with problems caused by a corrupted Windows installation is covered in Chapters 14, 15, and 16.

## PROBLEMS WITH HARD DRIVE INSTALLATIONS

Sometimes, trouble crops up during an installation. Keeping a cool head, thinking things through carefully a second, third, and fourth time, and using all available resources will most likely get you out of any mess.

Installing a hard drive is not difficult unless you have an unusually complex situation. For example, your first hard drive installation should not involve the intricacies of installing a second SCSI drive in a system that has two SCSI host adapters. Nor should you install a second drive in a system that uses an IDE connection for one drive on the motherboard and an adapter card in an expansion slot for the other drive. If a complicated installation is necessary and you have never installed a hard drive, ask for expert help.

Here are some errors that cropped up during a few hard drive installations, their causes, and what was done about them. Everyone makes mistakes when learning something new, and you probably will too. You can then add your own experiences to this list.

- Shawn physically installed an IDE hard drive. He turned on the machine and accessed CMOS setup. The hard drive was not listed as an installed device. He checked and discovered that autodetection was not enabled. He enabled it and rebooted. Setup recognized the drive.
- When first turning on a previously working PC, John received the following error message: "Hard drive not found." He turned off the machine, checked all cables, and discovered that the data cable from the motherboard to the drive was loose. He reseated the cable and rebooted. POST found the drive.
- Lucia physically installed a new hard drive, replaced the cover on the computer case, and booted the PC with a bootable floppy disk in the drive. POST beeped three times and stopped. Recall that diagnostics during POST are often communicated by beeps if the tests take place before POST has checked video and made it available to display the messages. Three beeps on most computers signal a memory error. Lucia turned off the computer and checked the memory modules on the motherboard. A module positioned at the edge of the motherboard next to the cover had been bumped as she replaced the cover. She reseated the module and booted from a floppy disk again, this time with the cover still off. The error disappeared.
- Jason physically installed a new hard drive and turned on the computer. He received the following error: "No boot device available." He forgot to insert a bootable disk. He put the disk in the drive and rebooted the machine successfully.
- Stephen physically installed the hard drive, inserted a floppy disk in the disk drive, and rebooted. He received the following error message: "Configuration/CMOS error. Run setup." This error message is normal for an older BIOS that does not support autodetection. POST had found a hard drive it was not expecting. The next step is to run setup.

A+
220-602
1.2

◢ Larry physically installed the card and drive and tried to reboot from a floppy disk. Error message 601 appeared on the screen. Any error message in the 600 range refers to the floppy disk. Because the case cover was still off, he looked at the connections and discovered that the power cord to the floppy disk drive was not connected. (It had been disconnected earlier to expose the hard drive bay underneath.) Larry turned off the machine and plugged in the cable. The error disappeared.

◢ The hard drive did not physically fit into the bay. The screw holes did not line up. Juan got a bay kit, but it just didn't seem to work. He took a break, went to lunch, and came back to make a fresh start. Juan asked others to help view the brackets, holes, and screws from a fresh perspective. It didn't take long to discover the correct position for the brackets in the bay.

◢ Maria set the jumpers on a hard drive and physically installed the drive. She booted and received the following error message: "Hard drive not present." She rechecked all physical connections and found everything okay. After checking the jumper settings, she realized that she had set them as if this were the second drive of a two-drive system, when it was the only drive. She restored the jumpers to their original state. In this case, as in most cases, the jumpers were set at the factory to be correct when the drive is the only drive.

If CMOS setup does not recognize a newly installed hard drive, check the following:

◢ Does your system BIOS recognize large drives? Check CMOS setup.

◢ Has CMOS setup been correctly configured for autodetection?

◢ Are the jumpers on the drive set correctly?

◢ Have the power cord and data cable been properly connected? Verify that the parallel ATA data cable colored edge is connected to pin 1 on the edge connectors of both the motherboard and the drive.

◢ Check the Web site of the drive manufacturer for suggestions, if the above steps don't solve your problem. Look for diagnostic software that can be downloaded from the Web site and used to check the drive.

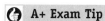 **A+ Exam Tip**

The A+ 220-602 exam might give you a symptom and expect you to select a probable source of a problem from a list of sources. These examples of what can go wrong can help you connect problem sources to symptoms.

 **Caution**

One last warning: When things are not going well, you can tense up and make mistakes more easily. Be certain to turn off the machine before doing anything inside! Not doing so can be a costly error. For example, a friend had been trying and retrying to boot for some time, and got frustrated and careless. He plugged the power cord into the drive without turning the PC off. The machine began to smoke and everything went dead. The next thing he learned was how to replace a power supply!

A+ ESS
1.3
3.3

# HOW TO APPROACH A HARD DRIVE PROBLEM AFTER THE INSTALLATION

After the hard drive is working, later problems can arise, such as corrupted data files, a corrupted Windows installation, or a hardware problem that causes the system to refuse to boot. In this section, you'll learn about some tools you can use to solve hard drive problems and how to approach the problem and prioritize what to do first. Then, in later sections, we'll look at some specific error messages and symptoms and how to deal with them.

## START WITH THE END USER

When an end user brings a problem to you, begin the troubleshooting process by interviewing the user. When you interview the user, you might want to include these questions:

- ◢ Can you describe the problem and show me how to reproduce it?
- ◢ Was the computer recently moved?
- ◢ Was any new hardware or software recently installed?
- ◢ Was any software recently reconfigured or upgraded?
- ◢ Did someone else use your computer recently?
- ◢ Does the computer have a history of similar problems?
- ◢ Is there important data on the drive that is not backed up?
- ◢ Can you show me how to reproduce the problem?

After you gather this basic information, you can prioritize what to do and begin diagnosing and addressing the hard drive problems.

## PRIORITIZE WHAT YOU HAVE LEARNED

If a hard drive is not functioning and data is not accessible, setting priorities helps focus your work. For most users, data is the first priority unless they have a recent backup. Software can also be a priority if it is not backed up. Reloading software from the original installation disks or CD can be time-consuming, especially if the configuration is complex or you have written software macros or scripts but did not back them up.

If a system won't boot from the hard drive and your first priority is to recover data on the drive, before you try to solve the hardware or Windows problem that prevents booting, you need to consider removing the drive and installing it as a second drive in a working system. If the partition table on the problem drive is intact, you might be able to copy data from the drive to the primary drive in the working system. Then turn your attention to solving the original problem.

If you have good backups of both data and software, hardware might be your priority. It could be expensive to replace, but downtime can be costly, too. The point is, when trouble arises, determine your main priority and start by focusing on that.

## BE AWARE OF AVAILABLE RESOURCES

Be aware of the resources available to help you resolve a problem:

- ◢ *Product documentation* often lists error messages and their meanings.
- ◢ *The Internet* can also help you diagnose hardware and software problems. Go to the Web site of the product manufacturer, and search for the FAQs (frequently asked questions) list or bulletin board. It's likely that others have encountered the same problem and posted the question and answer. If you search and cannot find your answer, you can post a new question.
- ◢ *Technical support* from the ROM BIOS, hardware, and software manufacturers can help you interpret an error message, or it can provide general support in diagnosing a problem. Most technical support is available during working hours by telephone. Check your documentation for telephone numbers. An experienced computer troubleshooter once said, "The people who solve computer problems do it by trying something and making phone calls, trying something else and making more phone calls, and so on, until the problem is solved."
- ◢ *Norton Utilities* by Symantec (*www.symantec.com*) offers several easy-to-use tools to prevent damage to a hard drive, recover data from a damaged hard drive, and

A+ ESS
1.3
3.3

A+
220-602
1.2

improve system performance. Many functions of these tools have been taken over and improved by utilities included with recent versions of Windows. The most commonly used Norton Utilities tools now are the recovery tools. Two examples are Norton Disk Doctor, which automatically repairs many hard drive and floppy disk problems, and UnErase Wizard, which allows you to retrieve accidentally deleted files. When using Norton Utilities, be certain you use the version of the software for the operating system you have installed. Using Norton with the wrong OS can do damage.

▲ *PartitionMagic* by Symantec (*www.symantec.com*) lets you manage partitions on a hard drive more quickly and easily than with Fdisk for Windows 9x/Me or Disk Management for Windows 2000/XP. You can create new partitions, change the size of partitions, and move partitions without losing data or moving the data to another hard drive while you work. You can switch file systems without disturbing your data, and you can hide and show partitions to secure your data.

> **Notes**
>
> Always check compatibility between utility software and the operating system with which you plan to use it. One place you can check for compatibility is the service and support section of the software manufacturer's Web site.

▲ *SpinRite* by Gibson Research (*www.grc.com*) is hard drive utility software that has been around for years. Still a DOS application without a sophisticated GUI interface, SpinRite has been updated to adjust to new drive technologies. It supports FAT32, NTFS, SCSI, Zip drives, and Jaz drives. You can boot your PC from a floppy disk and run SpinRite from a floppy, which means that it doesn't require much system overhead. Because it is written in a language closer to the binary code that the computer understands, it is more likely to detect underlying hard drive problems than software that uses Windows, which can stand as a masking layer between the software and the hard drive. SpinRite analyzes the entire hard drive surface, performing data recovery of corrupted files and file system information. Sometimes, SpinRite can recover data from a failing hard drive when other software fails.

▲ *GetDataBack* by Runtime Software (*www.runtime.org*) can recover data and program files even when Windows cannot recognize the drive. It can read FAT and NTFS file systems and can solve problems with a corrupted partition table, boot record, or root directory.

▲ *Hard drive manufacturer's diagnostic software* is available for download from the Web site of many hard drive manufacturers. For example, Maxtor's diagnostic software is PowerMax

> **Notes**
>
> Remember one last thing. After making a reasonable and diligent effort to resolve a problem, getting the problem fixed could become more important than resolving it yourself. There comes a time when you might need to turn the problem over to a more experienced technician.

(*www.maxtor.com*). Download the software and use it to create a bootable diagnostic floppy disk. You can then boot from the floppy and use it to examine a Maxtor hard drive for errors and, if necessary, low-level format the drive.

 **A+ Exam Tip**

> The A+ Essentials exam expects you to know about diagnostic software to test hard drives.

## HARD DRIVE HARDWARE PROBLEMS

In this section, we look at different problems with the hard drive that present themselves during the boot. These problems can be caused by the hard drive subsystem, by the partition table or file system on the drive, or by files required for the OS to boot. When trying to

A+ ESS
1.3
3.3

A+
220-602
1.2

solve a problem with the boot, you need to decide if the problem is caused by hardware or software. All the problems discussed in this section are caused by hardware. In Chapters 12, 13, and 14, you'll learn how to deal with slow response time for hard drives, problems that cause errors when loading the operating system, and problems with missing or corrupted data files. All these type errors are caused by software.

## PROBLEMS AT POST

Recall from Chapter 3 that the BIOS performs the POST at the beginning of the boot to verify that essential hardware devices are working. Hardware problems usually show up at POST, unless there is physical damage to an area of the hard drive that is not accessed during POST. Hardware problems often make the hard drive totally inaccessible. If BIOS cannot find a hard drive at POST, it displays an error message similar to this:

```
Hard drive not found

Fixed disk error

Invalid boot disk

Inaccessible boot device

Numeric error codes in the 1700s or 10400s
```

The reasons BIOS cannot access the drive can be caused by the drive, the data cable, the electrical system, the motherboard, the controller card (if one is present), or a loose connection. Here are some things to do and check:

- If BIOS displays numeric error codes during POST, check the Web site of the BIOS manufacturer for explanations of these numeric codes.
- Remove and reattach all drive cables. Check for correct pin 1 orientation.
- If you're using a controller card, remove and reseat it or place it in a different slot.
- Check the jumper settings on the drive.
- Inspect the drive for damage, such as bent pins on the connection for the cable.
- Determine if the hard drive is spinning by listening to it or lightly touching the metal drive (with power on).
- Check the cable for frayed edges or other damage.
- Check the installation manual for things you might have overlooked. Look for a section about system setup, and carefully follow all directions that apply.
- Be sure the power cable and drive data cable connections are good.
- Check CMOS setup for errors in the hard drive configuration. If you suspect an error, set CMOS to default settings, make sure autodetection is turned on, and reboot the system.
- Try booting from another media such as the Windows XP setup CD. If you can boot using another media, you have proven that the problem is isolated to the hard drive subsystem. The next thing to do is to use the Windows XP Recovery Console to try to access the drive. How to do that is covered in Chapter 14. Don't skip this step if you have valuable data on the drive. Sometimes the Recovery Console can be used to recover data even if the drive won't boot.

A+ ESS
1.3
3.3

A+
220-602
1.2

◢ Check the drive manufacturer Web site for diagnostic software. You might be able to download the software to floppy disk or CD, boot from the disk or CD, and run the software to diagnose the drive. For example, you can download Data Lifeguard Diagnostic for DOS from the Western Digital Web site (*www.westerndigital.com*), burn the software to CD, and boot from the CD (see Figure 8-53). Using the software, you can do a quick test to check the drive for physical problems or an extended test to repair any correctable problems. You can also write zeroes to every sector on the drive to get a fresh start with the drive. Other hard drive manufacturers have similar programs. For example, Seagate offers SeaTools (see Figure 8-54) that can be downloaded and used to create a bootable CD or floppy that can be used to test and analyze most ATA and SCSI drives by Seagate and other manufacturers.

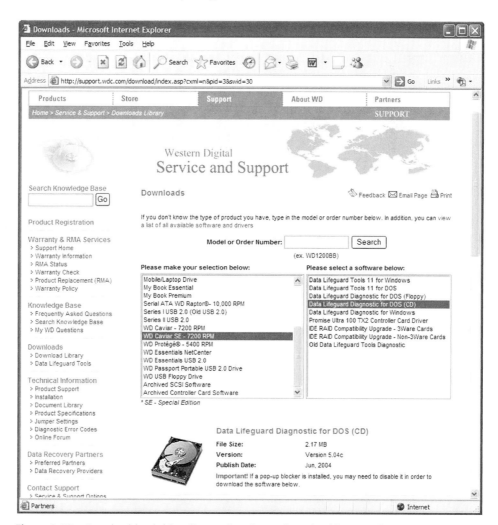

**Figure 8-53** Download hard drive diagnostic software from the drive manufacturer's Web site

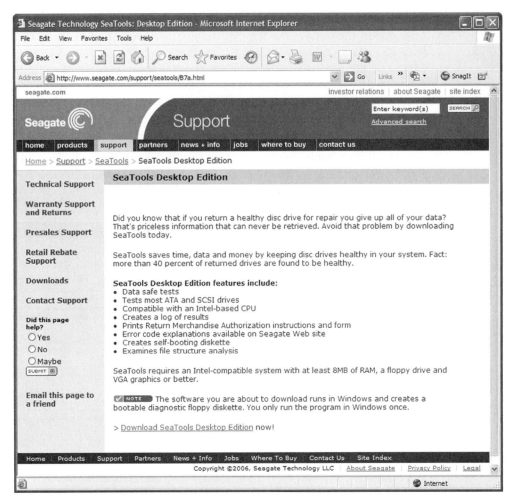

**Figure 8-54** Use SeaTools by Seagate to create a diagnostic CD or floppy to test and analyze hard drives

◢ If it is not convenient to create a boot CD with hard drive diagnostic software installed, you can move the drive to a working computer and install it as a second drive in the system. Then you can use the diagnostic software installed on the primary hard drive to test the problem drive. While you have the drive installed in a working computer, be sure to find out if you can copy data from it to the good drive so that you can recover any data not backed up. Note that for these temporary tests, you don't have to physically install the drive in the working system. Open the computer case. Carefully lay the drive on the case and connect a power cord and data cable (see Figure 8-55). Then turn on the PC. While you have the PC turned on, be *very careful* to not touch the drive or touch inside the case. Also, while a tower case is lying on its side like the one in Figure 8-55, don't use the CD or DVD drive.

> **Notes**
>
> For less than $40, you can purchase a USB to IDE converter such as the one in Figure 8-56 to connect a failing parallel ATA hard drive to a working computer using a USB port. Some converters have ports for parallel ATA connections, serial ATA connections, and connections for hard drives used in notebook computers. These converters are really handy when troubleshooting problems with hard drives.

A+ ESS
1.3
3.3

A+
220-602
1.2

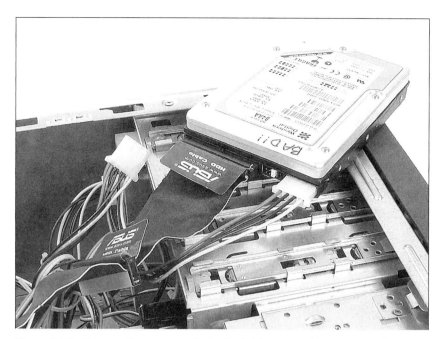

**Figure 8-55**  Temporarily connect a faulty hard drive to another system to diagnose the problem and try to recover data

◢ If the drive still does not boot, exchange the three field replaceable units—the data cable, the adapter card (optional), and the hard drive itself—for a hard drive subsystem. Do the following in order:

   ◢ Reconnect or swap the drive data cable.

   ◢ Reseat or exchange the drive adapter card, if one is present.

   ◢ Exchange the hard drive for a known good unit.

◢ If the hard drive refuses to work but its light stays on even after the system has fully booted, the problem might be a faulty controller on the hard drive or motherboard. Try replacing the hard drive. Next try an ATA controller card to substitute for the ATA connectors on the motherboard or replace the motherboard.

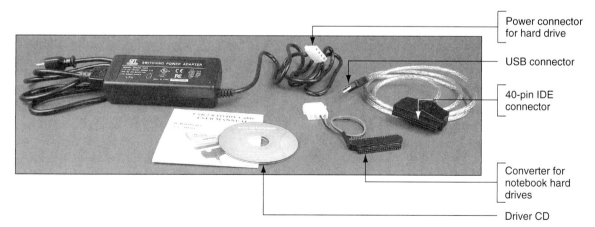

Power connector for hard drive

USB connector

40-pin IDE connector

Converter for notebook hard drives

Driver CD

**Figure 8-56**  Use a USB to IDE converter for diagnostic testing and to recover data from a failing hard drive

A+ ESS
1.3
3.3

A+
220-602
1.2

◄ Sometimes older drives refuse to spin at POST. Drives that have trouble spinning often whine at startup for several months before they finally refuse to spin altogether. If your drive whines loudly when you first turn on the computer, never turn off the computer. One of the worst things you can do for a drive that is having difficulty starting up is to leave the computer turned off for an extended period of time. Some drives, like old cars, refuse to start if they are unused for a long time.

A bad power supply or a bad motherboard also might cause a disk boot failure. If the problem is solved by exchanging one of the field replaceable units listed, you still must reinstall the old unit to verify that the problem was not caused by a bad connection.

## BUMPS ARE BAD!

The read/write heads at the ends of the read/write arms on a hard drive get extremely close to the platters but do not actually touch them. This minute clearance between the heads and platters makes hard drives susceptible to destruction. Should a computer be bumped or moved while the hard drive is operating, a head can easily bump against the platter and scratch the surface. Such an accident causes a "hard drive crash," often making the hard drive unusable.

If the head mechanism is damaged, the drive and its data are probably total losses. If the first tracks that contain the partition table, boot record, FAT (for that file system), or root directory are damaged, the drive could be inaccessible, although the data might be unharmed.

Here's a trick that might work for a hard drive whose head mechanism is intact but whose first few tracks are damaged. First, find a working hard drive that has the same partition table information as the bad drive. Take the computer case off, place the good drive on top of the bad drive housing, and connect a spare power cord and the ATA data cable to the good drive. Leave a power cord connected to the bad drive. Boot from a bootable CD or floppy disk. No error message should show at POST. Access the good drive by entering C: at the command prompt. The C prompt should show on the monitor screen.

Without turning off the power, gently remove the data cable from the good drive and place it on the bad drive. Do not disturb the power cords on either drive or touch chips on the drive logic boards. Immediately copy the data you need from the bad drive to another media, using the Copy command. If the area of the drive where the data is stored, the FAT or MFT, and the directory are not damaged, this method should work.

Here's another trick for an older hard drive having trouble spinning when first turned on. Remove the drive from the case, hold it firmly in both hands, and give the drive a quick and sudden twist that forces the platters to turn inside the drive housing. Reinstall the drive. It might take several tries to get the drive spinning. After the drive is working, immediately make a backup and plan to replace the drive soon.

## INVALID DRIVE OR DRIVE SPECIFICATION

If you get the error message "Invalid drive or drive specification," the system BIOS cannot read the partition table information. You'll need to boot from a recovery CD or bootable floppy disk to check the partition table using the Diskpart or Fdisk command. How to do that is covered in later chapters.

## BAD SECTOR ERRORS

Track and sector markings on a drive sometimes "fade" off the hard drive over time, which causes "bad sector" errors to crop up. These errors can also occur if an area of the drive has become damaged. Do not trust valuable data to a drive that has this kind of trouble. Plan to replace the drive soon. In the meantime, make frequent backups and leave the power on. You'll learn more about this and other software errors in Chapter 13.

## TROUBLESHOOTING FLOPPY DRIVES AND DISKS

A+ ESS
1.3
3.3

A+
220-602
1.2
3.3

Table 8-4 lists errors that occur during and after the boot with the floppy drive or disks.

| Problem or Error Message | What to Do About It |
|---|---|
| During the boot, numeric error messages in the 600 range or text error messages about the floppy drive appear onscreen | ◢ The floppy drive did not pass POST, which can be caused by problems with the drive, data cable, or motherboard. Check power and data cable connections.<br><br>◢ Try a different power cord.<br><br>◢ Check CMOS setup and reboot.<br><br>◢ Use a head-cleaning kit to clean the floppy drive heads.<br><br>◢ Replace the drive. |
| Cannot read from a floppy disk | ◢ The disk is not formatted. Try a different disk or try formatting this disk.<br><br>◢ The shuttle window on the floppy disk cannot open fully.<br><br>◢ The command just issued has a mistake or is the wrong command.<br><br>◢ The disk is inserted incorrectly.<br><br>◢ Something is lodged inside the disk's plastic housing. Check the shuttle window.<br><br>◢ Does the drive light come on? CMOS setup might be wrong, or the command you're using might be wrong. |
| Non-system disk or disk error. Replace and strike any key when ready.<br><br>No operating system found<br><br>Missing NTLDR<br><br>Invalid system disk<br><br>Invalid boot disk | ◢ You are trying to boot from a disk that is not bootable. Try a different disk or remove the disk and boot from the hard drive. |
| Not ready reading drive A:, Abort, Retry, Fail? | ◢ The disk in drive A is not readable. Try formatting the disk. |
| General failure reading drive A:, Abort, Retry, Fail? | ◢ The disk is badly corrupted or not yet formatted. |
| Track 0 bad, disk not usable | ◢ The disk is bad or you or trying to format it using the wrong parameters on the Format command. |
| Write-protect error writing drive A: | ◢ The disk is write-protected and the application is trying to write to it. Close the switch shown in Figure 8-57. |
| Bad sector or sector not found reading drive A, Abort, Retry, Ignore, Fail? | ◢ Sector markings are corrupted or fading. Press I to ignore that sector and move on. Don't trust this disk with important data. |

Table 8-4   Floppy drive and floppy disk errors that can occur during and after the boot

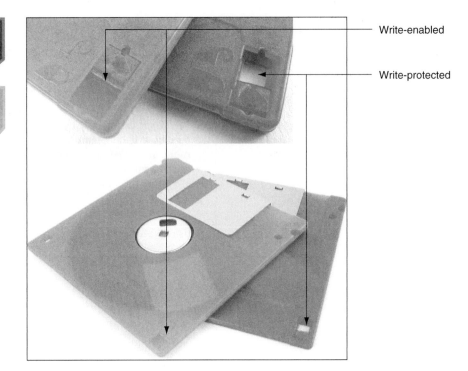

A+ ESS
1.3
3.3

A+
220-602
1.2
3.3

Write-enabled

Write-protected

**Figure 8-57** For you to write to a disk, the write-protect notch must be closed

## >> *CHAPTER SUMMARY*

▲ Today's floppy disks are $3\frac{1}{2}$-inch, high-density disks that hold 1.44 MB of data.

▲ A floppy drive data cable has 34 pins and can accommodate one or two floppy drives.

▲ Floppy disks are formatted into 80 tracks, each with 18 sectors of 512 bytes. Each cluster holds one sector. The boot record contains information about the organization of data on the disk and the name of the boot loader program (Ntldr or Io.sys) used to make the disk bootable.

▲ Most hard drives today use IDE technology, which has a complex method of organizing tracks and sectors on the disks.

▲ For current systems today, the BIOS and the OS use logical block addressing (LBA) to address all the sectors on a hard drive without regard to where these sectors are located.

▲ A hard drive is low-level formatted at the factory with tracks and sectors, and high-level formatted using an operating system. The high-level format creates a file system on the drive.

▲ Several ATA standards pertain to hard drives, including parallel ATA, EIDE, Fast ATA, Ultra ATA, Ultra ATA/66, Ultra ATA/100, Ultra ATA/133, and serial ATA.

▲ An EIDE device (also called a parallel ATA device) such as a hard drive or CD-ROM drive can be installed as a master drive, slave drive, or single drive on a system.

▲ The EIDE standards support two IDE connections on a motherboard, a primary and a secondary. Each connection can support up to two EIDE devices for a total of four devices on a system.

▲ Parallel ATA or EIDE standards apply to hard drives, CD-ROM drives, tape drives, Zip drives, and others.

◢ Serial ATA (SATA) supports a single serial ATA drive on a data cable connected to a serial ATA connector on a motherboard. External SATA (eSATA) can be used by an external drive.

◢ Most BIOSs today can autodetect the presence of a hard drive if the drive is designed to give this information to the BIOS.

◢ Installing a hard drive includes setting jumpers or DIP switches on the drive; physically installing the adapter card, cable, and drive; changing CMOS setup; and partitioning and formatting the drive.

◢ You can use an ATA controller card to provide additional ATA connectors in a system to add extra drives or to use newer standards the motherboard does not support.

◢ Drive interface standards include ATA, SCSI, USB, FireWire, and Fibre Channel.

◢ Protect the drive and the PC against static electricity during installation.

## >> KEY TERMS

For explanations of key terms, see the Glossary near the end of the book.

| | | |
|---|---|---|
| 80-conductor IDE cable | external SATA (eSATA) | parallel ATA |
| ANSI (American National Standards Institute) | FAT12 | PIO (Programmed Input/Output) transfer mode |
| ATAPI (Advanced Technology Attachment Packet Interface) | file allocation unit | read/write head |
| | floppy disk drive (FDD) | SCSI (Small Computer System |
| autodetection | hard drive controller | Interface) |
| block mode | head | SCSI ID |
| boot record | high-level formatting | serial ATA (SATA) |
| boot sector | host adapter | serial ATA cable |
| cluster | IDE (Integrated Device Electronics) | terminating resistor |
| DMA (direct memory access) transfer mode | Logical Unit Number (LUN) | zone bit recording |
| EIDE (Enhanced IDE) | low-level formatting | |
| | operating system formatting | |

## >> REVIEW QUESTIONS

1. Which of the following allows Windows to read any floppy disk?

   a. Each cluster holds 512 bytes of data.

   b. The boot sector is always located at the beginning of the disk at track 0, sector 1.

   c. The commonly used definition of a cluster. A cluster is a group of sectors that is the smallest unit on a disk that the OS uses to hold a file or a portion of a file.

   d. The use of a file allocation table.

2. A $3\frac{1}{2}$-inch, high-density floppy disk has how many entries in the root directory?

   a. 32

   b. 64

   c. 128

   d. 224

3. How many heads does a drive with two platters have?

   **a.** 1

   **b.** 2

   **c.** 3

   **d.** 4

4. The process of low-level formatting refers to which of the following?

   **a.** Using both sides of a platter to store data

   **b.** Storing data on the hard drive by filling the entire first cylinder before moving the read/write heads inward and filling the second cylinder

   **c.** Writing track and sector markings to a hard drive before it leaves the factory

   **d.** Storing firmware on a circuit board on or inside the drive housing

5. Which of the following terms refers to the new formatting system used on hard drives, the system in which tracks near the center have the smallest number of sectors per track, and the number of sectors increases as the tracks grow larger?

   **a.** Zone bit recording

   **b.** FAT12

   **c.** Low-level formatting

   **d.** High-level formatting

6. True or false? When a hard drive uses the PIO (Programmed Input/Output) transfer mode to transfer data from the hard drive to memory, the transfer involves the CPU.

7. True or false? Floppy drives are now so inexpensive that repairing one is impractical.

8. True or false? "SCSI" is a standard for communication between a subsystem of peripheral devices and the system bus.

9. True or false? The read/write heads at the ends of the read/write arms on a hard drive touch the surface of the platters lightly.

10. True or false? The larger tracks on the outside of a $3\frac{1}{2}$-inch, high-density floppy disk store more data than the tracks closer to the center.

11. A(n) _____ refers to the way data is physically stored on a disk, whereas a(n) _____ describes how data is logically organized.

12. All read/write heads are controlled by a(n) _____, which moves the read/write heads across the disk surfaces in unison.

13. All the tracks that are the same distance from the center of the platters on a hard drive together make up one _____.

14. To reduce the amount of electrical "noise," or interference, on a SCSI cable, each end of the SCSI chain has a(n) _____.

15. The process of marking tracks and sectors to prepare the disk to receive data is called _____ the disk.

# Installing and Supporting I/O Devices

This chapter is packed full of details about the many I/O devices a PC support technician must be familiar with and must know how to install and support. We begin with the easiest-to-support devices (the keyboard and mouse) and move on to the more complicated devices, including video, peripheral devices, and expansion cards. At the end of the chapter, you'll learn how to troubleshoot problems with I/O devices. This chapter builds the foundation for Chapter 10, in which you will learn about multimedia devices.

# BASIC PRINCIPLES TO SUPPORT I/O DEVICES

A+ ESS
1.1
3.2

A+
220-602
1.1

An I/O device can be either internal (installed inside the computer case) or external (installed outside the case). Internal devices include drives, such as hard drives, CD drives, DVD drives, Zip drives, and floppy drives. Internal devices can also be expansion cards inserted in expansion slots on the motherboard, such as a network card, modem card, video capture card, and video card. External devices include keyboards, monitors, mice, printers, scanners, digital cameras, and flash drives. You can connect an external device to the system using ports coming off the motherboard (serial, parallel, USB, IEEE 1394, and so forth), or a port can be provided by an expansion card.

In this chapter, you will learn a ton of information about these many I/O devices. However, for all these different devices, some basic principles apply to supporting each one of them. These principles are applied in numerous places throughout this chapter and are summarized here so you can get a first look at them. That being said, consider these fundamental principles and concepts used when supporting I/O devices:

▲ *Every I/O device is controlled by software.* When you install a new I/O device, such as a modem or printer, you must install both the device and the device drivers to control the device. These device drivers must be written for the OS you are using. Recall from earlier chapters that the exception to this principle is some simple devices, such as the floppy disk drive, that are controlled by the system BIOS or device drivers embedded in the OS. For the floppy drive, recall from Chapter 8 that when you install a floppy drive, you don't need to install a device driver; all you need to do is check CMOS setup to verify the drive is recognized.

▲ *When it comes to installing or supporting a device, the manufacturer knows best.* In this chapter, you will learn a lot of principles and procedures for installing and supporting a device, but when you're on the job installing a device or fixing a broken one, read the manufacturer documentation and follow those guidelines first. For example, for most installations, you install the device before you install the device driver. However, for some devices such as a digital camera and some modems, you install the device driver first. Check the device documentation to know which to do first.

▲ *Some devices need application software to use the device.* For example, after you install a scanner and its device drivers, you might also need to install Adobe Photoshop to use the scanner.

▲ *Problems with a device can sometimes be solved by updating the device drivers.* Device manufacturers often release updates to device drivers. Update the drivers to solve problems with the device or to add new features.

▲ *Learning about I/O devices is a moving target.* No matter how much information can be packed into this chapter, it won't be enough. I've done my best to make sure everything presented in this chapter is current, but I know that by the time this book is in print, some of the content will already be outdated. To stay abreast of all the latest technologies, an excellent source for information is the Internet. Use a good search engine to look up additional information about the I/O devices in this chapter and to learn about others.

We now turn our attention to the essential I/O devices for a PC: the keyboard, pointing devices, and video display.

## *WORKING WITH KEYBOARDS*

Keyboards have either a traditional straight design or a newer ergonomic design, as shown in Figure 9-1. The word ergonomic means "designed for safe and comfortable interaction between human beings and machines." The ergonomically safer keyboard is designed to keep your wrists high and straight. Some users find it comfortable, and others do not.

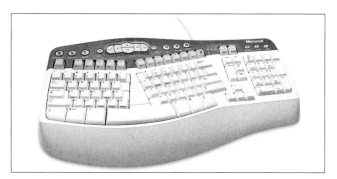

**Figure 9-1**  An ergonomic keyboard

Keyboards differ in the feel of the keys as you type. Some people prefer more resistance than others, and some like more sound as the keys make contact. A keyboard might have a raised bar or circle on the F and J keys to help your fingers find the home keys as you type. Another feature is the depth of the ledge at the top of the keyboard that holds pencils, and so on. Some keyboards have a mouse port on the back, and specialized keyboards have trackballs or magnetic scanners for scanning credit cards in retail stores.

A danger from using keyboards too much is a type of repetitive stress injury (RSI) known as carpal tunnel syndrome (CTS). CTS is caused by keeping the wrists in an unnatural position and having to execute the same motions (such as pressing keys on a keyboard) over prolonged periods of time. You can help prevent CTS by keeping your elbows at about the same level as the keyboard and keeping your wrists straight and higher than your fingers. I've found that a keyboard drawer that slides out from under a desk surface is much more comfortable because the keyboard is low enough for me to keep the correct position. If I'm working at a desk with no keyboard drawer, I sometimes type with the keyboard in my lap to relieve the pressure on my arms and shoulders. Figure 9-2 shows a typist learning the correct position for her hands and arms at the keyboard.

**Figure 9-2**  Keep wrists level, straight, and supported while at the keyboard

## HOW KEYBOARD KEYS WORK

Keyboards use one of two common technologies in the way the keys make contact: foil contact or metal contact. When you press a key on a foil-contact keyboard, two layers of foil make contact and close a circuit. A small spring just under the keycap raises the key again after it is released.

The more expensive and heavier metal-contact keyboards generally provide a different touch to the fingers than foil-contact keyboards. Made by IBM and AT&T, as well as other companies, the metal-contact keyboards add an extra feel of solid construction that is noticeable to most users, giving the keystroke a clear, definitive contact. When a key is pressed, two metal plates make contact, and again a spring raises the key when it is released.

## KEYBOARD CONNECTORS

Keyboards connect to a PC by one of four methods: a DIN connector (mostly outdated now), a PS/2 connector (sometimes called a mini-DIN), a USB port, or the more recently available wireless connection.

The DIN connector (DIN is an acronym of the German words meaning "German industry standard") is round and has five pins. The most common keyboard and mouse connector is the smaller round PS/2 connector, which has six pins (see Figure 9-3).

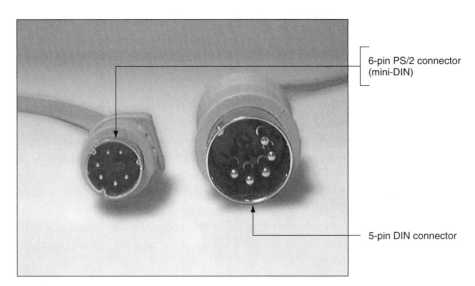

6-pin PS/2 connector (mini-DIN)

5-pin DIN connector

**Figure 9-3** Two common keyboard connectors are the PS/2 connector and the DIN connector

Table 9-1 shows the pinouts for the two connector types.

| Description | 5-Pin Connector (DIN) | 6-Pin Connector (PS/2) |
|---|---|---|
| Keyboard data | 2 | 1 |
| Not used | 3 | 2 |
| Ground | 4 | 3 |
| Current (+5 volts) | 5 | 4 |
| Keyboard clock | 1 | 5 |
| Not used | — | 6 |

**Table 9-1** Pinouts for keyboard connectors

A+ ESS
1.1

A+
220-602
1.1

If the keyboard you use has a different connector from the keyboard port of your computer, use a keyboard connector adapter, like the one shown in Figure 9-4, to convert DIN to PS/2 or PS/2 to DIN.

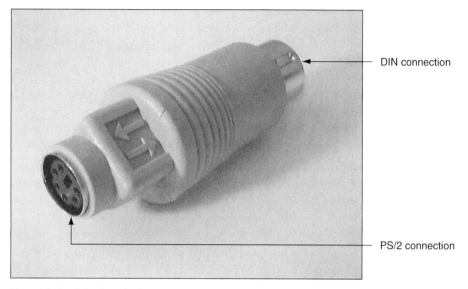

DIN connection

PS/2 connection

**Figure 9-4** A keyboard adapter

Also, some keyboards are cordless, using radio frequency (RF) or, for older cordless devices, using infrared to communicate with a sensor connected to the keyboard port. For example, a cordless keyboard and mouse made by Logitech (*www.logitech.com*) use a receiver that plugs into a normal keyboard port (see Figure 9-5).

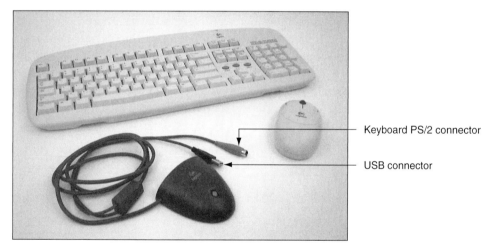

Keyboard PS/2 connector

USB connector

**Figure 9-5** This wireless keyboard and mouse by Logitech use a receiver that connects to either a USB or keyboard port

**Notes**

Most computer cases have two PS/2 connectors: one for the mouse and the other for the keyboard. Physically, the mouse or keyboard connector fits into either port, but the mouse connector only works in the mouse port, and the keyboard connector only works in the keyboard port. This can make for a frustrating experience when setting up a computer. To help tell the two ports apart, know that a green PS/2 port is probably the mouse port and a purple port is most likely the keyboard port.

## INSTALLING KEYBOARDS

Most often, installing a keyboard simply means plugging it in and turning on the PC. Because the system BIOS manages the keyboard, no keyboard drivers are necessary. The exception to this is a wireless keyboard that needs a driver to work. In this case, you must use a regular keyboard to install the software to use the wireless keyboard. Plug in the receiver, insert the CD or floppy disk, and run the setup program on the disk. You can then use the wireless keyboard.

## CLEANING THE KEYBOARD

Heavily used input devices such as the mouse and keyboard need to be regularly cleaned to keep them working well. Food, dirt, and dust can accumulate under the keys and cause keys not to work. Routinely, you can use a damp cloth to clean a keyboard surface. (Note that "damp" is not the same thing as "wet"!) You can also turn the keyboard upside down and lightly bump multiple keys with your flat palm, which will help loosen and remove debris.

> **Notes**
>
> For a list of keyboard manufacturers, see Table 9-2 later in this chapter, in a section titled, "Other Pointing Devices."

Use a can of compressed air to blow dust and debris out of the keyboard. If a few keys don't respond well to your touch, remove the caps on the bad keys with a chip extractor. Spray contact cleaner into the key well. Repeatedly depress the contact to clean it. Don't use rubbing alcohol to clean the key well, because it can leave a residue on the contact. If a keyboard is extremely dirty, you can clean all the keys using this method.

## *THE MOUSE AND OTHER POINTING DEVICES*

A pointing device allows you to move a pointer on the screen and perform tasks such as executing (clicking) a command button. Common pointing devices are the mouse, the trackball, and the touch pad (see Figure 9-6). IBM and Lenovo ThinkPad notebooks use a unique and popular pointing device embedded in the keyboard (see Figure 9-7). Some mice, such as the one shown in Figure 9-8, are wireless and come with keypads, which are useful for working with notebook computers. The wireless connection is made through a receiver that plugs into a USB port.

**Figure 9-6** The most common pointing devices: a mouse, a trackball, and a touch pad

**9**

**Figure 9-7** An IBM ThinkPad pointing device

**Figure 9-8** This wireless mouse and keypad use a USB wireless receiver

## MOUSE TECHNOLOGIES

Mouse technologies include the wheel mouse and the optical mouse. Inside a wheel mouse is a ball that moves freely as you drag the mouse on a surface. As shown in Figure 9-9, two or more rollers on the sides of the ball housing turn as the ball rolls against them. Each roller turns a wheel. The turning of the wheel is sensed by a small light beam as the wheel "chops" the light beam when it turns. The chops in the light beams are interpreted as mouse movement and sent to the CPU. One of two rollers tracks the x-axis (horizontal) movement of the mouse, and a second roller tracks the y-axis (vertical) movement.

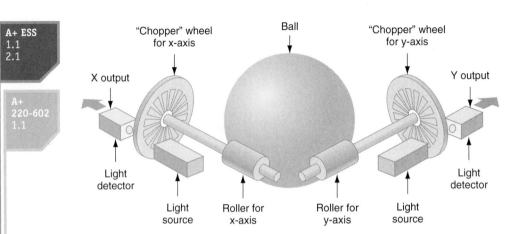

**Figure 9-9** How a wheel mouse works

> **Tip**
>
> Many applications allow you to customize mouse button functions.

An optical mouse replaces the ball in a standard mouse with a microchip, miniature red light or laser light, and camera. The light illuminates the work surface, the camera takes 1500 snapshots every second, and the microchip reports the tiniest changes to the PC. An optical mouse works on most opaque surfaces and doesn't require a mouse pad. The bottom of an optical mouse has a tiny hole for the camera rather than a ball, and the light glows as you work.

A mouse can have two or three buttons or a scroll wheel. Software must be programmed to use these buttons. Almost all applications use the left button, and Windows uses the right button to display shortcut menus. You can use the scroll wheel between the two buttons to move through large documents onscreen.

A mouse can connect to the computer by several methods:

▲ By using a dedicated, round PS/2 mouse port coming directly from the motherboard (the mouse is then called a **motherboard mouse** or **PS/2-compatible mouse**)

▲ By using a mouse bus card that provides a PS/2 mouse port (the mouse is then called a **bus mouse**)

▲ By using the serial port (the mouse is then called a **serial mouse**)

▲ By using a USB port

▲ By using a Y-connection with the keyboard so that both the keyboard and the mouse can share the same port

▲ By using a cordless technology whereby the mouse sends signals to a sensor on the PC or to an access point connected to the PC

Except for the cordless mouse, all of these methods produce the same results (that is, the mouse port type is transparent to the user). Therefore, the advantages and disadvantages of each connection type are based mainly on the resources they require. The motherboard mouse is most users' first choice because the port on the motherboard does not take any resources that other devices might need. If you are buying a new mouse that you plan to plug into the motherboard port, don't buy a bus mouse unless the motherboard documentation states that you can use a bus mouse. The motherboard port and the bus port are identical, but a bus mouse might not work on the motherboard port.

If you have a motherboard mouse port, use it. If it becomes damaged, you can switch to a serial port or USB port. The motherboard mouse port most likely uses IRQ 12. If you are not using a mouse on this port, the motherboard might release IRQ 12 so that other devices

A+ ESS
1.1
2.1

A+
220-602
1.1

can use it. Check the documentation for your motherboard to determine how the unused IRQ is managed.

The serial mouse requires a serial port and an IRQ for that port. Most people prefer a USB or bus mouse to a serial port mouse so that the serial port remains available for another device. A bus mouse can use a bus card if the motherboard does not have a mouse port.

## CLEANING A MOUSE

A+ ESS
1.4

A+
220-602
1.1
1.2

The rollers inside the wheel mouse housing collect dirt and dust and occasionally need cleaning. To clean a mouse, remove the cover of the mouse ball from the bottom of the mouse. The cover usually comes off with a simple press and shift or turn motion. Use compressed air to blow out dust. Clean the rollers with a cotton swab dipped in a very small amount of liquid soap. The sticky side of duct tape works well to clean the mouse ball.

You can purchase a cleaning kit for a mouse, trackball, and keyboard such as the one showing in Figure 9-10. However, using an expensive cleaning kit is not necessary for most maintenance needs.

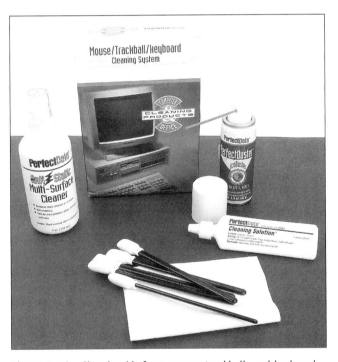

**Figure 9-10** Cleaning kit for a mouse, trackball, and keyboard

## TOUCH SCREENS

A+ ESS
1.1
2.1

A+
220-602
1.1

A **touch screen** is an input device that uses a monitor or LCD panel as the backdrop for input options. In other words, the touch screen is a grid that senses clicks and drags (similar to those created by a mouse) and sends these events to the computer by way of a serial or USB connection.

When someone is using a touch screen, the monitor displays user options and the user touches one of these options. The touch screen receives that touch in a way similar to how a mouse would receive a click. A touch screen can be embedded inside a monitor for a desktop system or an LCD panel in a notebook, or the touch screen can be installed on top of the monitor screen or LCD panel as an add-on device. As an add-on device, the touch screen has its own AC adapter to power it.

When installing a touch screen add-on device, follow the manufacturer's directions to attach the touch screen to the monitor or LCD panel, connect the USB or serial cable and the power cable, and then install the touch screen device drivers and management software. Then reboot the PC. You must then calibrate the touch screen to account for the monitor's resolution using the management software. If the resolution is later changed, the touch screen must be recalibrated. The screen can be cleaned with a damp cloth using a mild solution of alcohol and water.

## OTHER POINTING DEVICES

Other pointing devices are trackballs and touch pads. A trackball is really an upside-down wheel mouse. You move the ball on top to turn rollers that turn a wheel sensed by a light beam. A touch pad allows you to duplicate the mouse function, moving the pointer by applying light pressure with one finger somewhere on a pad that senses the x, y movement. Some touch pads let you double-click by tapping their surfaces. Buttons on the touch pad serve the same function as mouse buttons. Use touch pads or trackballs where surface space is limited, because they remain stationary when you use them. Touch pads are popular on notebook computers.

Table 9-2 lists some of the manufacturers of keyboards, pointing devices, touch screens, and fingerprint readers.

| Manufacturer | Web Site |
| --- | --- |
| BioStik | www.biostik.com |
| Mitsumi | www.mitsumi.com |
| Logitech | www.logitech.com |
| Microsoft | www.microsoft.com |
| Intel | www.intel.com |
| Belkin | www.belkin.com |
| Keytec, Inc. | www.magictouch.com |

**Table 9-2** Manufacturers of keyboards, pointing devices, and fingerprint readers

## *SPECIALTY INPUT DEVICES*

The keyboard and mouse are basic input devices that you need to know how to support. However, you also might be called on to support specialty devices such as a barcode reader, fingerprint reader, or other device. If you generally know how to support I/O devices, you will be able to figure out how to support a specialty device by carefully reading the documentation that comes with the device. This section helps you become familiar with some specialty devices, including barcode readers and biometric devices such as a fingerprint reader.

### BARCODE READERS

A barcode reader is used to scan barcodes on products to maintain inventory or at the point of sale (POS). Barcode readers come in a variety of shapes, sizes and features, including a pen wand (simplest and least expensive), slot scanners (to scan ID cards as they are slid through a slot), a CCD scanner (Charge-Couple Device scanner is a gun-type scanner often used at check-out counters), an image scanner (includes a small video camera), and a laser scanner (most expensive and best type).

A barcode reader can interface with a PC using several methods. Some readers use a wireless connection, a serial port, a USB port, or a keyboard port. If the reader uses a keyboard port, most likely it has a splitter (called a keyboard wedge) on it for the keyboard to use, and data read by the barcode reader is input into the system as though it were typed using the keyboard. Figure 9-11 shows a barcode reader by Symbol that is a laser scanner and can use a PC keyboard wedge or a USB port.

**Figure 9-11** Handheld or hands-free barcode scanner by Metrologic

When a barcode reader scans a barcode, it converts the code into numbers that are transferred to software on the computer. This software identifies two types of information from the numeric code: the company and the product. At point of sale, this information is then used to look up the price of the product in price tables accessed by the software.

## FINGERPRINT READERS AND OTHER BIOMETRIC DEVICES

A biometric device is an input device that inputs biological data about a person, which can be input data to identify a person's fingerprints, handprints, face, voice, eye, and handwritten signatures. Figure 9-12 shows one biometric input device that scans your iris. Iris scanning is one of the most accurate ways to identify a person using biological data. The biometric data collected is then used to authenticate that person using some type of access control system.

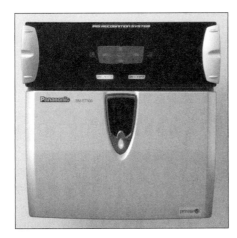

**Figure 9-12** An iris recognition camera by Panasonic (*www.panasonic.com/iris*)

Using a biometric device, a person presses his finger against a fingerprint reader or puts his face in front of a Web cam that has been programmed to scan facial features, and be authenticated into a computer or network using data that has previously been recorded

A+ ESS
1.1
6.1
6.2
6.3

A+
220-602
1.1
6.2

about this person. For desktop and notebook computer users, the most common biometric device is a fingerprint reader.

Although using biometric devices is gaining in popularity, the disadvantages of using these devices still outweigh the advantages. The most important disadvantage to using biometric devices is the danger of false negatives or false positives. For organizations with high security needs, security personnel must decide the fault tolerance limit of the input data. If you set the fault tolerance limit too low (to make sure only the person's data is the only data authenticated) then you run the risk that the person will not be authenticated (false negative). If you set the fault tolerance level too high (to make sure this person gets authenticated), you run the risk that someone with similar biometric data can get access (false positive). Biometric devices are still to be considered in the pioneering stage of development. For best security, use a combination of two authentication techniques such as a smart card and a password. You'll learn more about security authentication in Chapter 19.

For convenience, some people enjoy using a fingerprint reader to log onto their Windows desktop or a Web site rather than having to enter a password. These fingerprint readers are not to be considered as the only authentication to control access to sensitive data: for that, use a strong password. Fingerprint readers can look like a mouse and use a wireless or USB connection, such as the one shown in Figure 9-13. Or they can be embedded on the side of a keyboard or on the side of a flash drive. Some are embedded on cards that fit into PC Card slots for notebook computers. To use some fingerprint readers, you press your finger on the oval input surface, and for other readers, you slide your finger across a bar that scans your fingerprint as it goes by.

> **Notes**
>
> For more information about biometric devices and how they can be used, see the Web site of the International Biometric Industry Association at *www.ibia.org*.

> **A+ Exam Tip**
>
> The A+ Essentials exam expects you to know about these input devices: mouse, keyboard, barcode reader, Web camera, digital camera, microphone, biometric devices, and touch screen. All these devices are covered in this chapter or the next.

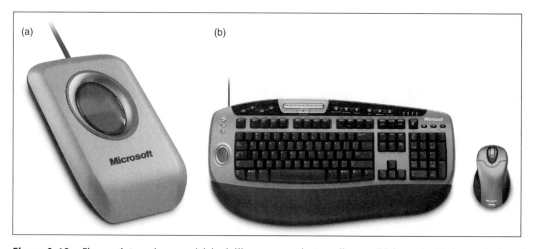

(a)                                    (b)

**Figure 9-13**    Fingerprint readers can (a) look like a mouse, but smaller, or (b) be embedded on a keyboard

A+ ESS
1.2
6.1
6.2
6.3

Most fingerprint readers that are not embedded in other devices use a USB connection. For most USB devices, you install the software before you plug in the device. For example, using the fingerprint reader by Microsoft, shown in Figure 9-13a, do the following:

1. Insert the setup CD in the optical drive. The installation program on the CD launches. You must accept the license agreement. Figure 9-14 shows one window of the installation

A+ ESS
1.2
6.1
6.2
6.3

A+
220-602
1.1
6.2

process where you are reminded that a fingerprint reader is not to be used when security is required.

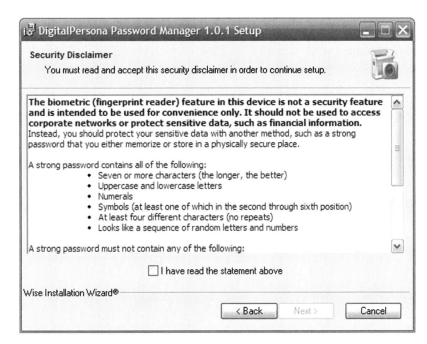

**Figure 9-14** The setup program for this fingerprint reader warns to not rely on the reader to protect sensitive data

2. During the installation process, you are told to plug in the reader so it can be enabled. Do so when you are prompted.

3. Next, the Fingerprint Registration Wizard launches so that you can record your fingerprint (called registering your fingerprint). Figure 9-15 shows one screen in the wizard where you select which finger it is you are about to record.

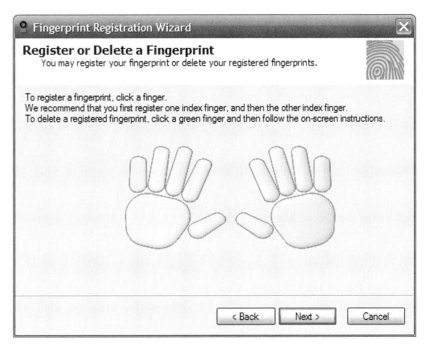

**Figure 9-15** To register a fingerprint, select the finger you want to record

4. Then on the next screen, which is shown in Figure 9-16, press the reader four times to verify your fingerprint. You can then record more fingerprints or close the wizard.

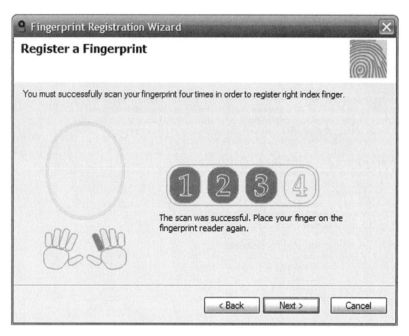

**Figure 9-16** A fingerprint is registered after it is recorded four times

5. To use your fingerprints in the place of passwords, when you are logging onto Windows or onto a Web site, press your finger to the fingerprint reader.

Fingerprint readers that are used a lot can get dirty and refuse to read. To clean a fingerprint reader, use the sticky side of duct tape or clear tape, or clean it with a mild solution of glass cleaner containing ammonia. Don't use an alcohol solution to clean fingerprint readers.

# MONITORS, PROJECTORS, AND VIDEO CARDS

The primary output device of a computer is the monitor. The two necessary components for video output are the monitor and the video card (also called the video controller, video adapter, and graphics adapter). Monitors work well for a single user or a small group of two or three users. For larger groups, a projector can connect to a second video port. Monitors, projectors, and video cards are all covered in this section.

## MONITORS

If you've shopped for a monitor recently, you're aware that the two main categories of monitors are the CRT monitor (takes up a lot of desk space and costs less) and the **LCD monitor** (frees your desk space, looks cool, and costs more). The older CRT (cathode-ray tube) technology was first used in television sets, and the newer LCD (liquid crystal display) technology was first used in notebook PCs. LCD monitors are also called **flat panel monitors** for the desktop.

A+ ESS
1.1
2.1

A+
220-602
1.1
2.1

Let's now look at how CRT and LCD monitors work, and then we'll look at how to select one. Installing two or more monitors on a single computer is really a great help for some users, so you'll also learn how to do that.

## HOW A CRT MONITOR WORKS

Many monitors use CRT technology, in which the filaments at the back of the cathode tube shoot a beam of electrons to the screen at the front of the tube, as illustrated in Figure 9-17. Plates on the top, bottom, and sides of the tube control the direction of the beam. The beam is directed by these plates to start at the top of the screen, move from left to right to make one line, and then move down to the next line, again moving from left to right. As the beam moves vertically down the screen, it builds the image. By turning the beam on and off and selecting the correct color combination, the grid in front of the filaments controls what goes on the screen when the beam hits that portion of the line or a single dot on the screen. When hit, special phosphors on the back of the monitor screen light up and produce colors. The grid controls which one of three electron guns fires, each gun targeting a different color (red, green, or blue) positioned on the back of the screen.

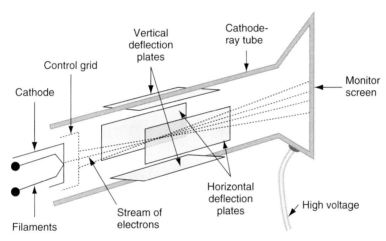

**Figure 9-17**   How a CRT monitor works

## HOW AN LCD MONITOR WORKS

An LCD monitor produces an image using a liquid crystal material made of large, easily polarized molecules. Figure 9-18 shows the layers of the LCD panel that together create the image. At the center of the layers is the liquid crystal material. Next to it is the layer responsible for providing color to the image. These two layers are sandwiched between two grids of electrodes. One grid of electrodes is aligned in columns, and the other electrodes are aligned in rows. The two layers of electrodes make up the electrode matrix. Each intersection of a row electrode and a column electrode forms one pixel on the LCD panel. Software can manipulate each pixel by activating the electrodes that form it. The image is formed by scanning the column and row electrodes, much as the electronic beam scans a CRT monitor screen.

A+ ESS
1.1
2.1

A+
220-602
1.1
2.1

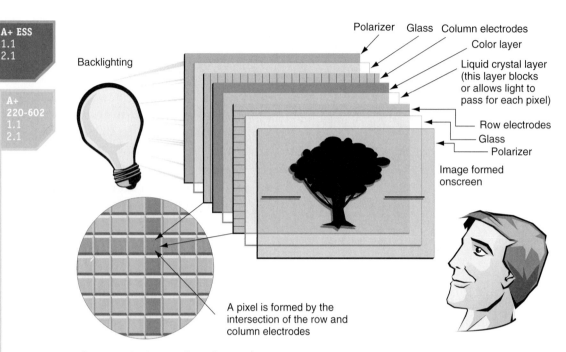

**Figure 9-18** Layers of an LCD panel

The polarizer layers outside the glass layers in Figure 9-18 are responsible for preventing light from passing through the pixels when the electrodes are not activated. When the electrodes are activated, light on the backside of the LCD panel can pass through one pixel on the screen, picking up color from the color layer as it passes through the pixel.

Expect an LCD monitor you purchase today to use a technology called **TFT (thin film transistor)**, which has almost completely replaced an older technology called **DSTN (dual-scan twisted nematic)**. Using TFT technology, a transistor that amplifies the signal is placed at every intersection in the grid, which further enhances the pixel quality. A DSTN display is less expensive than a TFT display and provides a lower-quality image. With DSTN, two columns of electrodes are activated at the same time. TFT display is sometimes called **active matrix display**, and DSTN display is sometimes called **passive matrix display**.

Many LCD monitors are built to receive either an analog signal or a digital signal from the video card and have two ports to accommodate either signal. If the signal is analog, it must be converted to digital before the monitor can process it. LCD monitors are designed to receive an analog signal so that you can use a regular video card that works with a CRT monitor, thus reducing the price of upgrading from a CRT to an LCD monitor. Figure 9-19 shows the back of an LCD monitor.

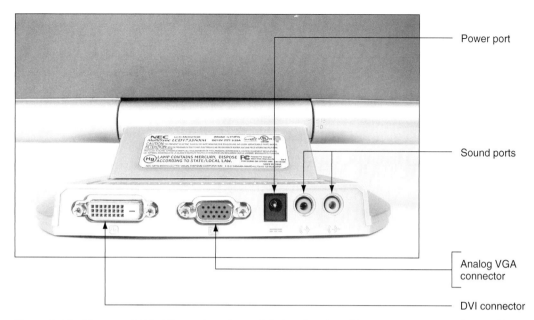

Power port

Sound ports

Analog VGA connector

DVI connector

**Figure 9-19** The rear of this LCD monitor shows digital and analog video ports to accommodate a video cable with either a 15-pin analog VGA connector or a digital DVI connector

## CHOOSING BETWEEN A CRT MONITOR AND AN LCD MONITOR

When choosing between a CRT monitor and an LCD monitor, consider that an LCD monitor takes up much less desk space than a CRT monitor, is lighter, requires less electricity to operate, and is more expensive. Of course, there are other features that you need to compare as well. Table 9-3 summarizes these features; several of the more important ones are discussed in the following subsections.

| Monitor Characteristic | CRT Monitor | LCD Monitor | Description |
|---|---|---|---|
| Screen size | X | X | Diagonal length of the screen surface. Common lengths are 14, 15, 17, 19, or 21 inches. |
| Refresh rate | X | | The number of times an electronic beam fills a video screen with lines from top to bottom in one second, or the number of frames it can build in one second. Common refresh rates are 60, 70, and 75 Hz. A monitor rated at 75 Hz can build 75 frames per second. (For comparison, a movie displays 24 frames per second.) |
| Interlaced | X | | The electronic beam draws every other line with each pass, which lessens the overall effect of a lower refresh rate. |
| Response time | | X | The time it takes for an LCD monitor to build one screen. The lower the better. A monitor with a 12-ms response time can build 83 frames per second, and a 16-ms monitor can build 63 frames per second. |

**Table 9-3** Important features of a monitor

A+ ESS
1.1
2.1

A+
220-602
1.1
2.1

| Monitor Characteristic | CRT Monitor | LCD Monitor | Description |
|---|---|---|---|
| Dot pitch | X | | The distance between adjacent dots on the screen. An example of a dot pitch is .28 mm. |
| Resolution | X | X | The number of spots or pixels on a screen that can be addressed by software. Values can range from 640 x 480 up to 1920 x 1200 for high-end monitors. |
| Pixel pitch | | X | Some LCD manufacturers call the monitor resolution the pixel pitch, and others call the distance between pixels the resolution. |
| Color quality | X | X | The number of bits used to store data about color for each pixel. Values are 8 bits, 16 bits, 24 bits, and 32 bits. Windows calls 24-bit and 32-bit color Truecolor. |
| Multiscan | X | | CRT monitors that offer a variety of refresh rates so they can support several video cards. |
| Connectors | X | X | The most popular connectors are the 15-pin VGA connector for analog video (RGB video) and the digital video (DVI) connector. Both connectors are shown in Figure 9-19. |
| Contrast ratio | | X | The contrast between true black and true white on the screen. The higher the contrast the better. 1000:1 is better than 700:1. |
| Viewing angle | | X | The angle of view when an LCD monitor becomes difficult to see. A viewing angle of 170 degrees is better than 140 degrees. |
| Display type | | X | For LCD monitors, TFT (active matrix) is better than DSTN (passive matrix). |
| Display type | X | | For CRT monitors, flat screen monitors are high-end monitors that use a flat screen to help prevent glare. |
| Backlighting | | X | For LCD monitors, some use better backlighting than others, which yields a brighter and clearer display. |

**Table 9-3**  Important features of a monitor (continued)

### Refresh Rate and Response Time

For CRT monitors, the **refresh rate,** or vertical scan rate, is the number of times in one second an electronic beam can fill the screen with lines from top to bottom. Refresh rates differ among monitors. The Video Electronics Standards Association (VESA) set a minimum refresh rate standard of 70 Hz, or 70 complete vertical refreshes per second, as one requirement of Super VGA monitors. (Many older VGA [Video Graphics Adapter] monitors are still in use, but most sold today meet the standards for Super VGA.) Slower refresh rates

A+ ESS
1.1
2.1

A+
220-602
1.1
2.1

make the image appear to flicker, whereas faster refresh rates make the image appear solid and stable. For LCD monitors, the response time is the time it takes for an LCD monitor to build all the pixels for one screen or frame, and is measured in ms (milliseconds). An LCD monitor with a response time of 16 ms yields about the same results as a CRT refresh rate of 60 Hz. LCD response times overall have been slightly less than CRT refresh rates.

> **Notes**
>
> The refresh rate and response time are set by using the Display applet in Control Panel.

> **Caution**
>
> If you spend many hours in front of a computer, use a good monitor with a high refresh rate or response time. The lower rates that cause monitor flicker can tire and damage your eyes. Because the refresh rates of CRT monitors are generally higher than the response times of LCD monitors, people who spend hours and hours in front of a monitor often prefer a CRT monitor. Also, when you first install a monitor, set the rate at the highest value the monitor can support.

### Interlaced or Noninterlaced

**Interlaced** CRT monitors draw a screen by making two passes. On the first pass, the electronic beam strikes only the even lines, and on the second pass, the beam strikes only the odd lines. The result is that a monitor can have a slow refresh rate with a less noticeable overall effect than there would be if the beam hit all lines for each pass. Interlaced monitors generally have slightly less flicker than **noninterlaced** monitors, which always draw the entire screen on each pass. Buy an interlaced monitor if you plan to spend long hours staring at the monitor. Your eyes will benefit.

### Dot Pitch

**Dot pitch** is the distance between the spots, or dots, on a CRT screen that the electronic beam hits. Remember that three beams build the screen, one for each of three colors (red, green, and blue). Each composite location on the screen is really made up of three dots and is called a **triad**. The distance between a color dot in one triad and the same color dot in the next triad is the dot pitch. The smaller the pitch is, the sharper the image. Dot pitches of .28 mm or .25 mm give the best results and cost more. Although less expensive monitors can have a dot pitch of .35 mm or .38 mm, they can still create a fuzzy image, even with the best video cards.

### Resolution and Pixel Pitch

For CRT monitors, **resolution** is a measure of how many spots on a CRT screen are addressable by software. Each addressable location is called a **pixel** (for picture element), which is composed of several triads. Because resolution depends on software, the video controller card must support the resolution, and the software you are using must make use of the monitor's resolution capabilities. The standard for most software packages is $800 \times 600$ pixels, although many monitors offer a resolution of $1024 \times 768$ pixels or higher. The resolution is set in Windows from the Display applet in the Control Panel and requires a driver specific for that resolution. Higher resolution usually requires more video RAM.

For LCD monitors, the number of pixels on the screen is sometimes called the resolution and sometimes called the pixel pitch. Whereas a CRT monitor is designed to use several resolutions, an LCD monitor uses only one resolution, called the native resolution, which is the actual (and fixed) number of pixels built into the monitor. When you change display settings to use a lower resolution than the monitor's native resolution, the LCD displayed area is reduced in size (creating a black area around the display) or video driver

A+ ESS
1.1
2.1

A+
220-602
1.1
2.1

 **A+ Exam Tip**

The A+ Essentials exam expects you to know about these resolutions used on LCD monitors: XGA, SXGA+, UXGA, and WUXGA. In addition, you need to be familiar with these terms: active and passive matrix, contrast ratio, and native resolution.

software builds each screen by mapping data using the chosen resolution onto the native resolution. This scaling process can slow down response time and/or cause an LCD monitor to appear fuzzy, which is why most serious gamers prefer CRT monitors to LCD monitors. For sharpest images when using an LCD monitor, use the highest resolution the monitor supports. If you do decide to use a different resolution than the native resolution, for the sharpest display, select a resolution that uses the same ratio of horizontal pixels to vertical pixels that the native resolution uses.

The different resolution standards are as follows:

▲ VGA (Video Graphics Array) supports up to 640 × 480, which is a 4:3 ratio between horizontal pixels and vertical pixels.
▲ SVGA (Super VGA) supports up to 800 × 600.
▲ XGA (eXtended Graphics Array) supports up to 1024 × 768.
▲ SXGA (Super XGA) supports up to 1280 x 1024 and was first to use a 5:4 ratio between horizontal pixels and vertical pixels.
▲ SXGA + is a variation of SXGA and uses a resolution of 1400 × 1050.
▲ WSXGA + (Wide SXGA + ) uses a resolution of 1680 × 1050.
▲ UXGA (Ultra XGA) supports up to 1600 × 1200.
▲ WUXGA (Wide UXGA) supports up to 1920 × 1200.

To convert the resolution to the number of pixels, multiply the horizontal pixels by vertical pixels. For example, SXGA supports up to 1280 × 1024 pixels or 1.3 million pixels.

**Notes**

There is some debate about the danger of monitors giving off ELF (extremely low frequency) emissions of electromagnetic fields. Standards to control ELF emissions are Sweden's MPR II standard and the TCO '95 standards. The TCO '95 standards also include guidelines for energy consumption, screen flicker, and luminance. Most monitors manufactured today comply with the MPR II standard, but very few comply with the more stringent TCO '95 or TCO '99 standards.

A+ ESS
1.2

A+
220-602
1.1

# APPLYING|CONCEPTS     INSTALLING DUAL MONITORS

To increase the size of your Windows desktop, you can install more than one monitor for a single computer. Setting up dual monitors gives you more space for your Windows desktop as well as some redundancy if one goes down.

The following dual-monitor installation process assumes that you are using Windows XP and that you already have a monitor installed. To install dual monitors, you can use two video cards, one for each monitor, or you can use a video card that provides two video ports.

To install a second monitor and a dual-monitor setup using two video cards:

1. Verify that the original video card works properly, determine whether it is PCI Express or AGP, and decide whether it is to be the primary monitor.

A+ ESS
1.2

A+
220-602
1.1

2. Verify that the new PCI video card is compatible with Windows XP.

3. Boot the PC and enter CMOS setup. If CMOS has the option to select the order that video cards are initialized, verify that the currently installed card is configured to initialize first. If it does not initialize first, then, when you install the second card, video might not work at all when you first boot with two cards.

4. Install a second video card in the PCI slot nearest to the AGP or PCI Express slot, and attach the second monitor.

5. Boot the system. Windows recognizes the new hardware and might prompt you for the location of the drivers. If Windows does not recognize you have new hardware to install, go to the Control Panel and select **Add Hardware** to manually install the drivers.

6. Now you are ready to configure the new monitor. Right-click the **desktop** and select **Display Properties** from the shortcut menu. The Display Properties dialog box shown in Figure 9-20 appears. Select the **Settings** tab.

**Figure 9-20**   You must choose to activate a second monitor before it will be used by Windows

7. Notice that there are two numbered blue boxes that represent your two monitors. When you click one of these blue boxes, the Display drop-down menu changes to show the selected monitor, and the Screen resolution and the Color quality display settings also follow the selected monitor. This lets you customize the settings for each monitor. If necessary, arrange the boxes so that they represent the physical arrangement of your monitors.

**Notes**

In Figure 9-20, if you arrange the two windows side by side, your extended desktop will extend left or right. If you arrange the two windows one on top of the other, your extended desktop will extend up and down.

A+ ESS
1.2

A+
220-602
1.1

8. On the Settings tab of the Display Properties dialog box, adjust your Screen resolution and the Color quality settings according to your preferences. Check **Extend my Windows desktop onto this monitor**. To save the settings, click **Apply**. Depending on the Advanced display settings in effect, you might be asked to restart your computer. The second monitor should initialize and show the extended desktop.

 **Notes**

Settings for each video adapter that you add to your system must be saved and applied individually. Windows 2000/XP supports up to 10 separate monitors on a single system, and Windows 9x/Me supports up to nine monitors.

9. Close the Display Properties dialog box. From the **Start** menu, open an application and verify that you can use the second monitor by dragging the application over to the second monitor's desktop.

After you add a second monitor to your system, you can move from one monitor to another simply by moving your mouse. Switching from one monitor to the other does not require any special keystroke or menu option.

A+ ESS
1.1

## USING A PROJECTOR

A monitor gives excellent performance when only two or three people are viewing, but you may want to use a projector in addition to a monitor when larger groups of people are watching. Projectors are great in the classroom, for sales presentations, or for watching the Super Bowl with your friends. The prices of projectors have dropped significantly in the past few years, making them more of an option for business and pleasure. One portable projector, shown in Figure 9-21, has a native resolution of XGA 1024 × 768, and can connect to a desktop or notebook computer by way of a 15-pin video port or S-Video port.

**Figure 9-21** Portable XGA projector by NEC

To use a projector, you'll need an extra video port. For desktop computers, you'll need to install a second video card or use a video card that has two video ports. Most notebook computers are designed to be used with projectors and provide the extra 15-pin video port. To use a projector, plug in the projector to the extra port and then turn it on. For a notebook computer, use a function key to activate the video port. For most notebooks, you can toggle the function key to: (1) use the LCD display and not use the port; (2) use both the LCD display and the port; or (3) use the port and don't use the LCD display. Also, when you first use the projector, it will show a mirrored image of exactly what you see on your LCD panel. If you want to make

A+
220-602
1.1

A+ ESS
1.1

the projector an extension of the desktop, you can use the Display properties window. On that window, click the **Settings** tab, select the projector in the list of display devices, and then select **Extend my Windows desktop onto this monitor**. The projector now works as a dual monitor.

### Notes

Many of us use PowerPoint by Microsoft for group presentations. If you configure your projector as a dual monitor, you can use PowerPoint to display a presentation to your audience on the projector at the same time you are using your LCD display to manage your computer. To do so, open PowerPoint in **Presenter View**, and then on the Slide Show menu, click **Set Up Show**. Next, under Multiple Monitors, check **Show Presenter View**. Then select the projector in the list, and click **Display slide show**.

## VIDEO CARDS

Recall that the video controller card is the interface between the monitor and the computer. These cards are sometimes called graphic adapters, video boards, graphics cards, or display cards. Sometimes the video controller with a video port is integrated into the motherboard. If you are buying a motherboard with an integrated video controller, make sure that you can disable the controller on the motherboard if it gives you trouble. You can then install a video card and bypass the controller and port on the motherboard.

### Video

Installing a Video Card

A video card can pass data to a monitor or other display device in four ways. Each method uses a different type of video port on a video card. These five ports are used to connect to the monitor or television cable. Figure 9-22 shows a video card that has three of the five ports.

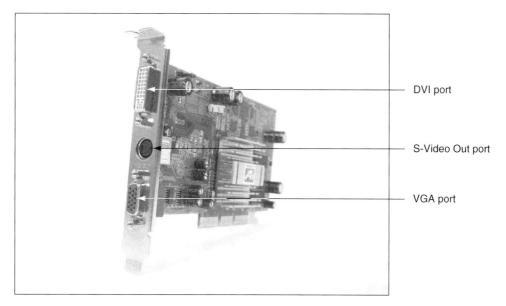

DVI port

S-Video Out port

VGA port

**Figure 9-22** This ATI Radeon video card has three ports for video out: DVI, S-Video, and the regular VGA port

The five methods of data transfer are as follows:

▲ *RGB video using a VGA port*. This is the standard analog video method of passing three separate signals for red, green, and blue, which most video cards and CRT monitors use. This method uses a regular 15-pin Super-VGA port (commonly called a VGA port).

▲ *DVI (Digital Visual Interface)*. This method is the digital interface standard used by digital monitors such as a digital LCD monitor and digital TVs (HDTV). For a video

A+ ESS
1.1

A+
220-602
1.1

card that only has a DVI port, you can purchase a VGA converter so you can connect a standard VGA video cable to use a regular analog monitor (see Figure 9-23).

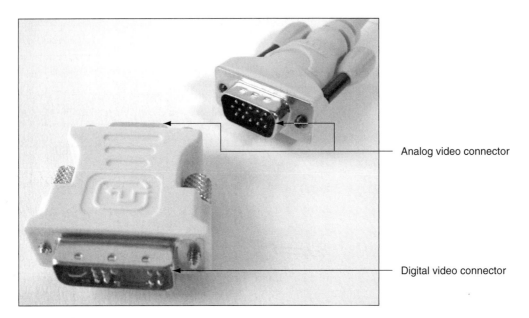

Analog video connector

Digital video connector

**Figure 9-23** Digital to analog video port converter

▲ *Composite video.* Using this method, the red, green, and blue (RGB) are mixed together in the same signal. This is the method used by television, and can be used by a video card that is designed to send output to a TV. This method uses a Composite Out port, which is round and is the same size as the S-Video Out port shown in Figure 9-22, but has only a single pin in the center of the port. Composite video does not produce as sharp an image as RGB video or S-Video.

▲ *S-Video (Super-Video).* This method sends two signals over the cable, one for color and the other for brightness, and is used by some high-end TVs and video equipment. It uses a 4-pin round port. The television and the video card must support this method and you must use a special S-Video cable like the one shown in Figure 9-24. This standard is not as good as RGB for monitors, but is better than Composite video when output to a television.

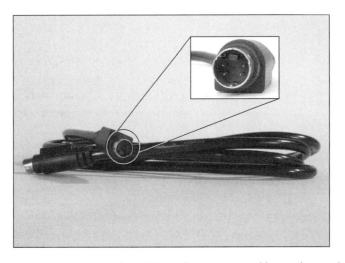

**Figure 9-24** An S-Video cable used to connect a video card to an S-Video port on a television

A+ ESS
1.1

A+
220-602
1.1

◢ *HDMI (High-Definition Multimedia Interface)*. HDMI is the latest digital audio and video interface standard. It is not widely available on video cards or motherboards, but is expected to ultimately replace DVI. HDMI is currently used on televisions and other home theatre equipment. To connect a PC to this equipment that uses HDMI, you can purchase a HDMI to DVI cable such as the one shown in Figure 9-25.

**Figure 9-25**  An HDMI to DVI cable can be used to connect a PC that has a DVI port to home theatre equipment that uses an HDMI port

The quality of a video subsystem is rated by how it affects overall system performance, video quality (including resolution and color), power-saving features, and ease of use and installation. Because the video controller on the video card is separate from the core system functions, manufacturers can use a variety of techniques to improve performance without being overly concerned about compatibility with functions on the motherboard. An example of this flexibility is the many ways memory is managed on a video controller. Two main features to look for in a video card are the bus it uses and the amount and type of video RAM it has or can support. Also know that a motherboard might have its own on-board video controller and video port, but that this video subsystem is probably very basic and lacks many of the features you'll read about in this section.

## THE BUSES USED BY VIDEO CARDS

Four buses have been used for video cards in the past 20 years or so. Listed in the order they were introduced, they are the VESA bus, the regular PCI bus, the AGP bus, and the newer PCI Express bus. The VESA and AGP buses were developed specifically for video cards, and the PCI buses are used for many types of cards, including a video card.

Video cards currently use the AGP bus or the PCI Express x16 bus. For most personal computer motherboards, if a second video card is installed for dual monitors, it uses a regular PCI slot. A motherboard will have a PCI Express x16 slot or an AGP slot, but not both. PCI Express x16 is much faster than AGP, but currently AGP is still the most popular slot for a video card.

AGP can share system memory with the CPU to do its calculations, and, therefore, does not always have to first copy data from system memory to video memory on the graphics card. This feature, known as direct memory execute (DIME), is probably the most powerful feature of AGP.

## Different AGP Standards

AGP has evolved over the years, and the different AGP standards can be confusing. AGP standards include three major releases (AGP 1.0, AGP 2.0, and AGP 3.0), one major change in the AGP slot length standard (AGP Pro), four different speeds (1x, 2x, 4x, and 8x) yielding four different throughputs, three different voltages (3.3 V, 1.5 V, and 0.8 V), and six different expansion slots (AGP 3.3 V, AGP 1.5 V, AGP Universal, AGP Pro 3.3 V, APG Pro 1.5 V, and AGP Pro Universal). To help you make sense of all this, Table 9-4 sorts it all out.

| Standard | Speeds (Cycles Per Clock Beat) | Maximum Throughput | Voltage | Slots Supported |
|---|---|---|---|---|
| AGP 1.0 | 1x | 266 MB/sec | 3.3 V | Slot keyed to 3.3 V |
| AGP 2.0 | 1x, 2x, or 4x | 533 MB/sec or 1.06 GB/sec | 3.3 V or 1.5 V | Slot keyed to 1.5 V<br><br>Slot keyed to 3.3 V<br><br>Universal slot (for either 1.5-V or 3.3-V cards) |
| AGP Pro | Applies to all speeds | NA | 3.3 V or 1.5 V | AGP Pro 3.3 V keyed<br><br>AGP Pro 1.5 V keyed<br><br>AGP Pro Universal (for either 1.5-V or 3.3-V cards) |
| AGP 3.0 | 4x or 8x | 2.12 GB/sec | 1.5 V and 0.8 V | Universal AGP 3.0 (4x/8x) slot<br><br>Slot keyed to 1.5 V<br><br>AGP Pro 1.5-V keyed slot |

**Table 9-4**   AGP standards summarized

As you can see from Table 9-4, there are several different AGP slots and matching card connectors that apply to the different standards. When matching video cards to AGP slots, be aware of these several variations. For instance, the first two slots in Figure 9-26 are used by cards that follow the AGP 1.0 or AGP 2.0 standards. These slots have key positions so that you cannot put an AGP 3.3-V card in an AGP 1.5-V slot or vice versa. The third slot is a universal slot that can accommodate 3.3-V or 1.5-V cards. All three slots are 2.9 inches wide and have 132 pins, although some pins are not used. Figure 9-27 shows a motherboard with an older AGP 3.3-V slot. Notice how the keyed 3.3-V break in the slot is near the back side of the motherboard where expansion cards are bracketed to the case.

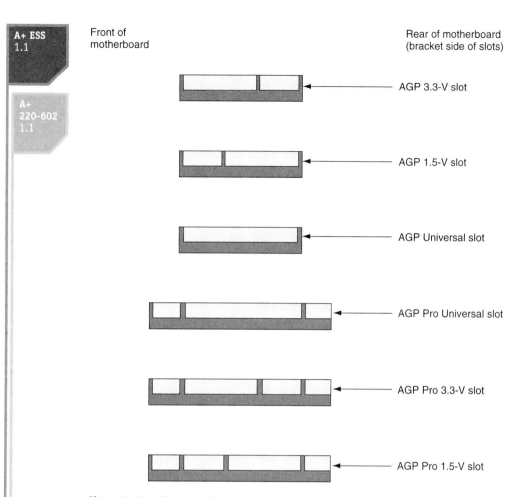

Front of
motherboard

Rear of motherboard
(bracket side of slots)

AGP 3.3-V slot

AGP 1.5-V slot

AGP Universal slot

AGP Pro Universal slot

AGP Pro 3.3-V slot

AGP Pro 1.5-V slot

**Figure 9-26**  Six types of AGP slots

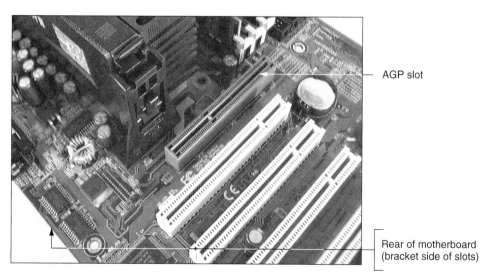

AGP slot

Rear of motherboard
(bracket side of slots)

**Figure 9-27**  This motherboard uses an AGP 3.3-V slot, which accommodates an
AGP 1.0 video card

Another AGP standard, called AGP Pro, has provisions for a longer slot. This 180-pin slot has extensions on both ends that contain an additional 20 pins on one end and 28 pins on the other end, to provide extra voltage for a high-end AGP video card that consumes more than 25 watts of power. These wider slots might be keyed to 3.3 V or 1.5 V or might be a Universal Pro slot that can hold either 3.3-V or 1.5-V cards. Also, when using an AGP Pro video card, leave the PCI slot next to it empty to improve ventilation and prevent overheating.

The latest AGP standard, AGP 3.0, runs at 8x or 4x speeds. APG 3.0 cards can be installed in an AGP 1.5-V slot, but signals are put on the data bus using 0.8 V. It's best to install an AGP 3.0 card in a slot that is designed to support AGP 3.0 cards. However, if you install an AGP 3.0 card in an older AGP 1.5-V slot, the card might or might not work, but the card will not be damaged.

> **Notes**
>
> If you're trying to buy an AGP video card to match a motherboard slot, you have to be really careful. When reading an AGP ad, it's hard to distinguish between AGP 3.3 V and AGP 3.0, but there's a big difference in these standards, and they are not interchangeable.

An AGP video card will be keyed to 1.5 V or 3.3 V or a universal AGP video card has both keys so that it can fit into either a 1.5-V keyed slot or a 3.3-V keyed slot. A universal AGP video card also fits into a universal AGP slot. If an AGP video card does not make use of the extra pins provided by the AGP Pro slot, it can still be inserted into the AGP Pro slot if it has a registration tab that fits into the end of the Pro slot near the center of the motherboard. Earlier in the chapter, Figure 9-22 showed a universal AGP video card with two notches on the edge connector and a registration tab that makes it possible to fit the card in an AGP Pro slot.

## PCI Express

Recall from Chapter 6 that PCI Express is the latest version of PCI. PCI Express x16 is about twice as fast as AGP x8 and will ultimately replace AGP. Motherboards that support PCI Express x16 for the video card have a PCI Express x16 bus dedicated to video apart from the PCI Express bus used by the other PCI Express slots on the board. Figure 9-28 shows a PCI Express video card. Notice the tab next to the card's connectors that fits into a retention mechanism on the motherboard to help stabilize the card.

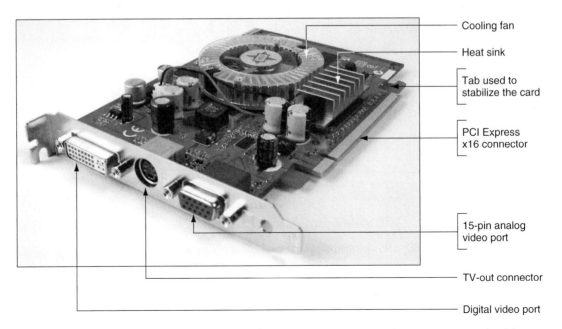

Cooling fan

Heat sink

Tab used to stabilize the card

PCI Express x16 connector

15-pin analog video port

TV-out connector

Digital video port

**Figure 9-28** This PCX 5750 graphics card by MSI Computer Corporation uses the PCI Express x16 local bus

A+ ESS
1.1

A+
220-602
1.1

## GRAPHICS ACCELERATORS

One of the more important advances made in video cards in recent years is the introduction of graphics accelerators. A **graphics accelerator** is a type of video card that has its own processor to boost performance. With the demands that graphics applications make in the multimedia environment, graphics accelerators have become not just enhancements, but common necessities, especially among the gaming crowd.

The processor on a graphics accelerator card is similar to a CPU but specifically designed to manage video and graphics. Some features included on a graphics accelerator are MPEG decoding, 3-D graphics, dual porting, color space conversion, interpolated scaling, EPA Green PC support, digital output to flat panel display monitors, and application support for popular, high-intensity graphics software such as Auto-CAD and Quark. All these features are designed to reduce the burden on the motherboard CPU and perform the video and graphics functions much faster than the motherboard CPU.

> **Notes**
>
> One problem high-end graphics cards have is overheating. One possible solution is a PCI fan card mounted next to the graphics card such as the one shown in Figure 9-29.

**Figure 9-29** A PCI fan card by Vantec can be used next to a high-end graphics card to help keep it cool

## VIDEO MEMORY

Older video cards had no memory, but today they need memory to handle the large volume of data generated by increased resolution and color. Video memory is stored on video cards as memory chips.

The amount of data a video card receives from the CPU for each frame (or screen) of data is determined by the screen resolution (measured in pixels), the number of colors (called color depth and measured in bits), and the enhancements to color information (called alpha blending). The more data required to generate a single screen of data, the more memory is required to hold that data. Memory on the video card that holds one frame of data before it is sent to the monitor is called a frame buffer.

Several factors affect the amount of memory required for the frame buffer, which can be as much as 8 MB. However, in addition to needing memory to hold each frame buffer, a graphics accelerator card might also need memory for other purposes. Software that builds 3-D graphics onscreen often uses textures and backgrounds, and sometimes a graphics card holds these backgrounds in memory to build future screens. Large amounts of video RAM keep the card from having to retrieve this data from the hard drive or system RAM multiple times.

In addition, to improve performance, the graphics card might use buffering, in which the card holds not just the frame being built, but the next few frames. Because of backgrounds and buffering, a high-end card might need as much as 512 MB of RAM. See the graphics card documentation for information about memory recommendations for maximum performance.

The following list describes the different types of video memory:

- ▲ **VRAM (video RAM)** is a type of dual-ported memory, which means that video memory can be accessed by both the input and output processes at the same time.
- ▲ **SGRAM (synchronous graphics RAM)** is similar to SDRAM and is discussed in Chapter 7. It is not dual-ported memory, but is faster than VRAM because it can synchronize itself with the CPU bus clock and uses other methods to increase overall performance for graphics-intensive processing.
- ▲ **WRAM (window RAM)** is dual ported and less expensive than VRAM. WRAM was named more for its ability to manage full-motion video than for its ability to speed up Microsoft Windows video processing. WRAM's increased speed is primarily due to its own internal bus on the chip, which has a data path that is 256 bits wide.
- ▲ **MultiBank DRAM (MDRAM)** is not dual ported, but is faster than VRAM or WRAM. It uses relatively small 32K blocks of memory that can be independently accessed.
- ▲ **3-D RAM** was designed specifically to improve performance when simulating 3-D graphics. This chip can calculate which pixel of a 3-D graphic to display, depending on whether the pixel is behind other pixels, and, therefore, out of sight in a 3-D graphic. If the pixel is not to be visible, the chip writes it back to memory for use later.
- ▲ **Direct RDRAM (DRDRAM)**, also discussed in Chapter 7, is used on video cards and game systems and is designed to work well with video streaming.
- ▲ **Graphics DDR (GDDR)**, **Graphics DDR2 (GDDR2)**, and **Graphics DDR3 (GDDR3)** are types of SDRAM specifically designed for video cards. Recall that DDR and DDR2 SDRAM are discussed in Chapter 7. DDR3 is an advanced version of DDR2. GDDR3 is considered the up-and-coming video memory that is expected to replace other types.

When upgrading memory on a video card, you must match the memory to the card. To do so, start by removing the card from the system and then installing the new memory chip. When you turn on the system, video memory counts up onscreen before system memory is counted. At this point, you can verify that the correct amount of video memory is installed.

> **Notes**
>
> When you match a monitor to a video card, a good rule of thumb is to match a low-end video card to a low-end monitor, a midrange video card to a midrange monitor, and a high-end video card to a high-end monitor, to get the best performance from both devices. However, you can compare the different features of the video card to those of the monitor, such as the resolutions and the refresh rates supported.

# APPLYING CONCEPTS  INSTALLING A VIDEO CARD

In general, when installing an expansion card, first read the documentation for the card and set any jumper switches or DIP switches on it. Like most cards today, the AGP 3.0 8x video card we are installing is Plug and Play–compatible and has no jumpers. The video card, shown in Figure 9-30, is a universal AGP card that is keyed for 3.3-V or 1.5-V slots and has a registration tab that allows it to also fit into an AGP Pro slot.

> **A+ Exam Tip**
>
> The A+ Essentials exam expects you to know how to install a video card.

A+ ESS
1.2

A+
220-602
1.1

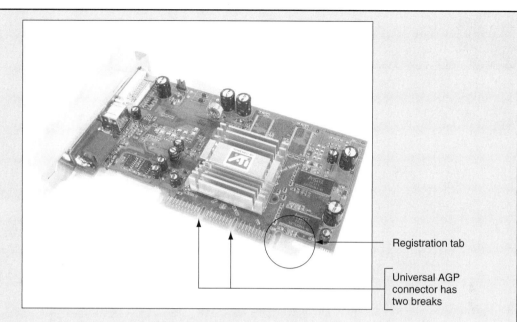

**Figure 9-30** AGP 3.0 8x universal video card

To install the video card, do the following:

1. An AGP slot might require a retention mechanism around it that helps hold the card securely in the slot. Some motherboards require that you install this retention mechanism on the slot before you install the card, as shown in Figure 9-31. Check your motherboard documentation for specific instructions.

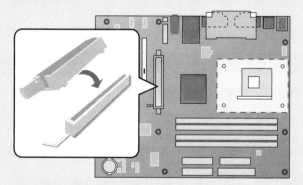

**Figure 9-31** Some motherboard installations require you to install a retention mechanism around the AGP slot before installing the video card

2. Remove the faceplate for the slot from the computer case, and slide back the retention mechanism on the slot. Insert the card in the slot and slide the retention mechanism back in position. The retention mechanism slides over the registration tab at the end of the AGP slot to secure the card in the slot. Use a single screw to secure the card to the computer case (see Figure 9-32).

**Figure 9-32**  Secure the video card to the case with a single screw

3.  Replace the computer case cover, plug in the video cable, and turn on the system. When Windows starts up, it will launch the Found New Hardware Wizard. Follow the onscreen instructions to install the drivers. Windows will most likely install its own generic video drivers.

4.  To take full advantage of the features of your video card, rather than using Windows generic drivers, you need to use the video card drivers provided by the manufacturer. To do that, right-click anywhere on the desktop and select **Properties** on the shortcut menu. The Display Properties window opens, as shown in Figure 9-33.

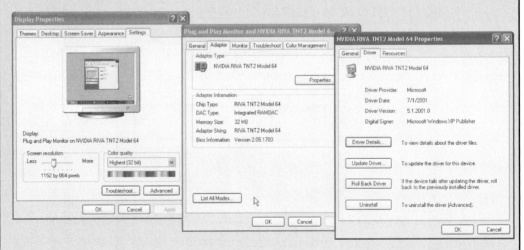

**Figure 9-33**  Updating the video card drivers in Windows XP

5. Select the **Settings** tab and click **Advanced**. On the next window, click the **Adapter** tab, also shown in Figure 9-33. The adapter's Properties window opens.

6. Insert the CD that came with the video card and click **Update Drivers**. Follow the onscreen directions to install the new drivers.

7. After the drivers are installed, use the Display Properties window to check the resolution and refresh rate for the monitor.

For more information about video cards, including graphics accelerators, see the Web sites of the manufacturers listed in Table 9-5.

| Manufacturer | Web Site |
| --- | --- |
| ASUSTeK Computer, Inc. | *www.asus.com* |
| ATI Technologies, Inc. | *www.ati.com* |
| Creative Technology, Ltd. | *www.creative.com* |
| Gainward Co., Ltd. | *www.gainward.com* |
| Hercules Computer Technology | *www.hercules.com* |
| Matrox Graphics, Inc. | *www.matrox.com* |
| MSI Computer Corporation | *www.msicomputer.com* |
| nVidia | *www.nvidia.com* |
| VisionTek | *www.visiontek.com* |

**Table 9-5**  Video card manufacturers

We now turn our attention to using standard ports for installing devices on a computer system. Then you will learn how to install expansion cards in expansion slots.

## USING PORTS AND EXPANSION SLOTS FOR ADD-ON DEVICES

Devices can plug into a port that comes directly off the motherboard, such as a serial, parallel, USB, FireWire (IEEE 1394), or network port. Or a port, such as serial ATA, video, or SCSI, can be provided by an expansion card. In this section, you'll learn how to use the serial, parallel, USB, and FireWire ports that come directly off a motherboard. Then you'll learn how to install expansion cards in expansion slots on the motherboard.

Figure 9-34 shows the ports on the rear of a computer case; some of them are provided by the motherboard and others are provided by an expansion card. When deciding what type of port a new device should use, the speed of the port is often a tiebreaker. Table 9-6 shows the speeds of various ports, from fastest to slowest.

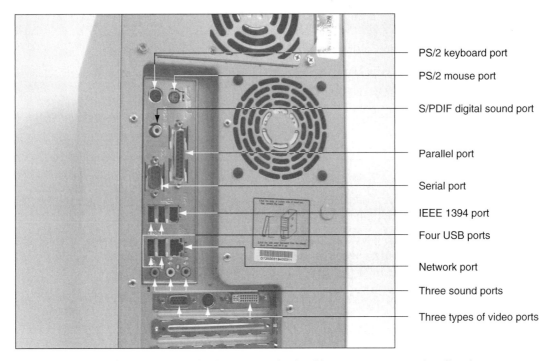

PS/2 keyboard port

PS/2 mouse port

S/PDIF digital sound port

Parallel port

Serial port

IEEE 1394 port

Four USB ports

Network port

Three sound ports

Three types of video ports

**Figure 9-34** Rear of computer case showing ports; only the video ports are not coming directly off the motherboard

| Port Type | Maximum Speed |
| --- | --- |
| 1394b (FireWire)* | 1.2 Gbps (gigabits per second) or 800 Mbps (megabits per second)** |
| Hi-Speed USB 2.0 | 480 Mbps |
| 1394a (FireWire) | 400 Mbps |
| Original USB | 12 Mbps |
| Parallel | 1.5 Mbps |
| Serial | 115.2 Kbps (kilobits per second) |

*IEEE 1394b has been designed to run at 3.2 Gbps, but products using this speed are not yet manufactured.

**FireWire 800 is the industry name for 1394b running at 800 Mbps.

**Table 9-6** Data transmission speeds for various port types

## USING SERIAL PORTS

Serial ports were originally intended for input and output devices such as a mouse or an external modem. Recall from Chapter 1 that a serial port transmits data in single bits, one bit following the next. You can identify these ports on the back of a PC case by (1) counting the pins and (2) determining whether the port is male or female. Serial ports have been mostly outdated by USB ports, and many new computers don't have a serial port.

Figure 9-35 shows two serial ports, one parallel port, and one game port for comparison. Serial ports are sometimes called DB9 and DB25 connectors. DB stands for data bus and refers to the number of pins on the connector. Serial ports are almost always male ports, and parallel ports are almost always female ports.

A+ ESS
1.1
4.1

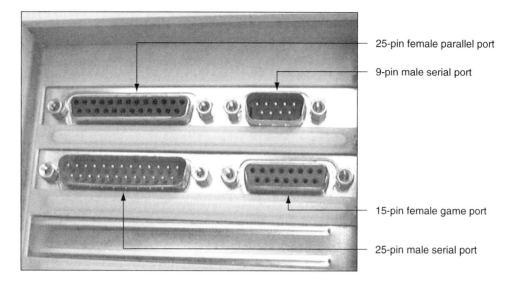

25-pin female parallel port

9-pin male serial port

15-pin female game port

25-pin male serial port

**Figure 9-35** Serial, parallel, and game ports

A serial port conforms to the interface standard called RS-232c (Reference Standard 232 revision c), which is why a serial port is sometimes called the RS-232 port. The maximum cable length for a serial cable according to RS-232 standards is 50 feet. This interface standard originally called for 25 pins, but because microcomputers use only nine of those pins, manufacturers often installed a modified 9-pin port. You almost never see a 25-pin serial port on today's PCs. However, if you ever see one on a very old PC, know that the 25-pin port uses only nine pins; the other pins are unused. You can buy an adapter to convert a 25-pin port to a 9-pin port, and vice versa, to accommodate a cable you already have.

Recall that an internal device or a port that an external device is using needs an IRQ to hail the attention of the CPU and the CPU needs a range of I/O addresses to communicate with the device or port. To simplify how computer and I/O device manufacturers assign these system resources to ports, the industry has designated two configurations for system resources that apply to serial ports and designated them as COM1 and COM2. Later, two more configurations were designated as COM3 and COM4. These COM assignments each represent a designated IRQ and an I/O address range, as shown in Table 9-7.

**Notes**

A **null modem cable** is an older type of cable that uses serial ports to connect two computers so they can communicate. A null modem cable looks and works like a serial cable except the read and write lines in the cable are reversed so that one computer writes data to a pin in the cable that is read by the other computer. Null modem cables were used before most computers had network ports. Today, use a crossover cable and network ports to connect two computers. You'll learn how to use crossover cables in Chapter 17.

A+ ESS
1.1
4.1

| Port | IRQ | I/O Address (in Hex) | Type |
|------|------|---------------------|------|
| COM1 | IRQ 4 | 03F8–03FF | Serial |
| COM2 | IRQ 3 | 02F8–02FF | Serial |
| COM3 | IRQ 4 | 03E8–03EF | Serial |
| COM4 | IRQ 3 | 02E8–02EF | Serial |
| LPT1 | IRQ 7 | 0378–037F | Parallel |
| LPT2 | IRQ 5 | 0278–027F | Parallel |

**Table 9-7** Default port assignments on many computers

Most serial and parallel ports today connect directly to the motherboard, and the COM and LPT assignments are made in CMOS setup. The ports can also be enabled and disabled in setup. Sometimes the setup screen shows the COM assignments, and sometimes you see the actual I/O address and IRQ assignments (see Figure 9-36). In addition, one or more serial, parallel, USB, or game ports can be provided by an **I/O controller card**. Older I/O controller cards used jumpers and DIP switches to configure the serial and parallel ports on the card.

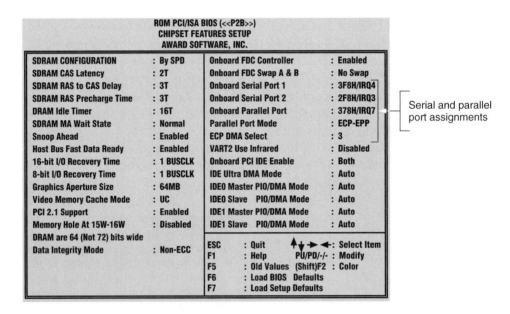

**Figure 9-36** CMOS Setup screen for chipset features

To verify that the port is working with no errors for any Windows OS, you can use Device Manager. To do so, click the **+** sign beside Ports to show the list of ports, click a communications port, such as COM1, and click Properties. You will then see the Properties dialog box shown in Figure 9-37, if you are using Windows XP (other Windows OSs look similar).

When a serial port is used by an external modem, you need to know that in documentation, the serial port is called the **DTE** (**Data Terminal Equipment**) and the modem is called the **DCE** (**Data Communications Equipment**). When supporting an external modem using a serial port, it's important to know that communication is controlled by both the modem and the serial port, and settings must be correct for both the device and the port. The settings that control serial-port communication are called **port settings**.

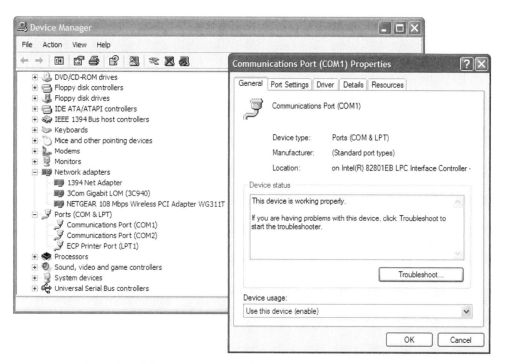

**Figure 9-37**   Properties of the COM1 serial port in Windows XP

To view the port setting for an external modem using a serial port, in Device Manager, right-click the serial port, labeled **Communications Port (COM1)**, and select **Properties**. The serial port's Properties dialog box opens. Select the **Port Settings** tab as shown in Figure 9-38. Note that the first drop-down list shows the bits per second of the port, which is currently set at 128,000 bps. Unless you have reason to do otherwise, verify that Bits per second is set to the highest value, Data bits is set to 8 (data is sent in 8-bit segments), Parity is set to None (no error checking by the port), Stop bits is set to 1 (bit used to control flow), and Flow control is set to Hardware (let the modem control data flow). Click **OK** when you're done.

**Figure 9-38**   Port settings for a Windows XP serial port used by an external modem

Serial ports are fast becoming outdated because they are being replaced by USB ports, which are easier to configure and use. Most computers now come with two or more USB ports, and might or might not have one serial port.

## INFRARED TRANSCEIVERS

An **infrared transceiver**, also called an **IrDA (Infrared Data Association) transceiver** or an **IR transceiver** provides an infrared port for wireless communication. Television remote controls communicate with the TV or set top box using infrared transmission. On desktop and notebook computers, infrared is used by wireless keyboards, mice, and printers. On notebooks, an infrared receiver is often used for communication between the notebook and a PDA (such as a Pocket PC or Blackberry) to transfer information. Also, an older PC might use an infrared device to connect to a network.

> ⓘ **A+ Exam Tip**
>
> The A+ Essentials exam expects you to know how an infrared transceiver might be used on a notebook computer.

For a motherboard that does not have built-in support for an infrared transceiver, an external transceiver can be plugged into a USB or serial port. If the transceiver is Plug and Play, you need only connect the device and turn on the PC. Windows automatically detects and installs the infrared driver, using the Add New Hardware Wizard. Figure 9-39 shows a remote control that can be used with multimedia applications installed on a notebook computer. The remote communicates with the notebook by way of an IR transceiver connected to a USB port.

**Figure 9-39** This remote control is an infrared device that uses an IR transceiver connected to a notebook by way of a USB port

An onboard infrared transceiver often uses the resources on a motherboard designated for a serial port. Sometimes an older motherboard provides a 5-pin connection for a proprietary IrDA-compliant infrared transceiver. In this case, the transceiver mounts on the outside of the case, and a wire goes through a small hole in the case to connect to the 5-pin connection. The motherboard manual will then instruct you to use CMOS setup to enable "UART2 Use

Infrared." **UART (universal asynchronous receiver-transmitter)** refers to the logic on the motherboard that controls the serial ports on the board, and is sometimes referred to as the UART 16550. When you enable "UART2 Use Infrared," the infrared transceiver uses system resources assigned to COM2. Because the infrared transceiver is now using these resources, the COM2 serial port does not have access to the resources and is disabled.

For legacy transceivers, install the transceiver using the Add New Hardware applet in the Control Panel, or run the device driver setup program. For serial port transceivers, the transceiver uses the resources of the serial port for communication and creates a virtual infrared serial port and a virtual infrared parallel port for infrared devices. During the installation, you are told what these virtual ports are and given the opportunity to change them. For example, if you physically connect the transceiver to COM2, the virtual ports will be COM4 for infrared serial devices and LPT3 for an infrared printer. The IRQ and I/O addresses for the infrared system are those that have been previously assigned to COM2. To activate the transceiver, you double-click the Infrared icon in the Control Panel. If the icon is not visible, press F5 to refresh the Control Panel.

Infrared wireless is becoming obsolete because of the line-of-sight issue: There must be an unobstructed "view" between the infrared device and the receiver. Short-range radio technology such as Bluetooth is becoming the most popular way to connect a wireless I/O device to a nearby computer, because with radio waves there is no line-of-sight issue.

> **Notes**
>
> Infrared standards are defined by the Infrared Data Association (IrDA). Their Web site is *www.irda.org*.

## USING PARALLEL PORTS

Parallel ports, commonly used by older printers, transmit data in parallel, eight bits at a time. Most parallel cables are only six feet (1.8 meters) long, though no established standard sets maximum cable length. However, to ensure data integrity, you should avoid using a parallel cable longer than 15 feet (4.5 meters). (In fact, Hewlett-Packard recommends that cables be no longer than 10 feet, or 3 meters.) If the data is transmitted in parallel over a very long cable, the data integrity is sometimes lost.

Parallel ports were originally intended to be used only for printers to receive data. However, some parallel ports are used for input/output devices, such as older tape drives and older external CD-ROM drives. Parallel ports that can handle communication in both directions are called bidirectional parallel ports. Also, today's printers and OSs expect the printer to be able to communicate with the OS such as when it needs to hail the OS that it is out of paper. These printers require bidirectional parallel ports.

### TYPES OF PARALLEL PORTS

Parallel ports fall into three categories: standard parallel port (SPP), **EPP (Enhanced Parallel Port)**, and **ECP (Extended Capabilities Port)**. The standard parallel port is sometimes called a normal parallel port or a Centronics port, named after the 36-pin Centronics connection used by printers (see Figure 9-40). A standard port allows data to flow in only one direction and is the slowest of the three types of parallel ports. In contrast to a standard port, EPP and ECP are both bidirectional. ECP was designed to increase speed over EPP by using a DMA channel; therefore, when using ECP mode you are using a DMA channel.

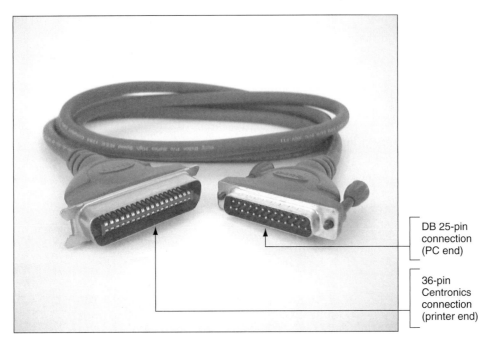

DB 25-pin
connection
(PC end)

36-pin
Centronics
connection
(printer end)

**Figure 9-40** A parallel cable has a DB25 connection at the PC end of the cable and a 36-pin Centronics connection at the printer end of the cable

Over the years, both hardware and software manufacturers have implemented several parallel port designs, all attempting to increase speed and performance. To help establish industry standards, a committee supported by the Institute of Electrical and Electronics Engineers (IEEE) was formed in the early 1990s and created the **IEEE 1284** standards for parallel ports. These standards require backward compatibility with previous parallel port technology. Both EPP and ECP are covered under the IEEE 1284 specifications.

There is little interest in developing better parallel ports. The interest isn't there because USB ports are faster and easier to configure. In fact, the evolution of parallel ports has pretty much come to a halt. Note, however, that although USB ports are replacing parallel ports, most computers still come with one parallel port.

**Notes**

When using EPP or ECP printers and parallel ports, be sure to use a printer cable that is IEEE 1284–compliant. Older, noncompliant cables will not work properly with these printers. To find out if a cable is compliant, look for the label somewhere on the cable. Also, note that a printer using a parallel port can use a 36-pin Centronics connector, or some newer printers use the smaller 36-pin Micro-Centronics or mini-Centronics connector.

## CONFIGURING PARALLEL PORTS

Before you configure a parallel port, you need to determine whether the port is using an I/O card or whether it is connecting off the motherboard. If the port is on an I/O card, look to the card documentation to learn how to assign system resources to the port. If the parallel port is coming directly off the motherboard, use CMOS setup to configure the port (look back at Figure 9-36). In CMOS setup, you can set the port's resources to use LPT1 or LPT2. On the other hand, for some BIOSs such as the one in Figure 9-36, you can assign an IRQ and I/O address range (see the fifth row in the second column).

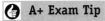 **A+ Exam Tip**

The A+Essentials exam expects you to be familiar with serial and parallel ports found on motherboards.

A+ ESS
1.1
4.1

Setup can have up to four different settings for parallel port modes. For the BIOS in Figure 9-36, choices for parallel port mode are Normal, EPP, ECP, and EPP + ECP (see the sixth row in the second column). If you select ECP or EPP + ECP, you must also make an ECP DMA selection. Choices for the DMA selection are DMA Channel 1 or 3.

> **Notes**
>
> If you have trouble using a motherboard port, such as a serial, parallel, USB, or 1394 port, check CMOS setup to make sure the port is enabled. If you have problems with resource conflicts, try disabling ECP mode for the parallel port. EPP mode gives good results and does not tie up a DMA channel.

A+ ESS
1.1
2.2
4.1
5.1

A+
220-602
2.2
3.3

## USING USB PORTS

USB ports are fast becoming the most popular ports for slower I/O devices such as printers and modems. USB is much faster than regular serial or parallel ports and uses higher-quality cabling. USB is also much easier to manage because it eliminates the need to resolve resource conflicts manually.

> **Notes**
>
> USB was originally created by a seven-member consortium, including Compaq, Digital Equipment, IBM, Intel, Microsoft, NEC, and Northern Telecom, and was designed to make the installation of slow peripheral devices as effortless as possible.

USB allows for **hot-swapping** and **hot-pluggable** devices. These two terms mean that a device can be plugged into a USB port while the computer is running, and the host controller will sense the device and configure it without your having to reboot the computer. Some I/O devices that use a USB connection are mice, joysticks, keyboards, printers, scanners, monitors, modems, digital cameras, fax machines, barcode readers, and digital telephones.

One to four USB ports are found on most new motherboards (see Figure 9-41). Older motherboards that have no USB ports or not enough USB ports can be upgraded by adding a PCI-to-USB controller card in a PCI slot to provide one or more USB ports. Sometimes a motherboard will have a USB port on the front of the case for easy access (see Figure 9-42).

> **Caution**
>
> Even though USB devices are hot-swappable, it's not always a good idea to plug or unplug a device while it is turned on. If you do so, especially when using a low-quality USB cable, you can fry the port or the device if wires in the USB connectors touch (creating a short) as you plug or unplug the connectors.

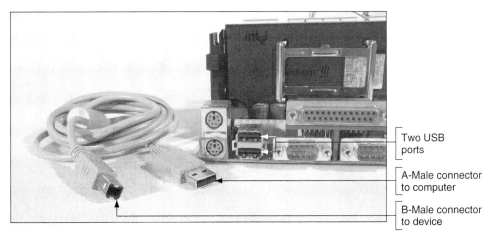

Two USB ports

A-Male connector to computer

B-Male connector to device

**Figure 9-41** A motherboard with two USB ports and a USB cable; note the rectangular shape of the connection as compared to the nearby serial and parallel D-shaped ports

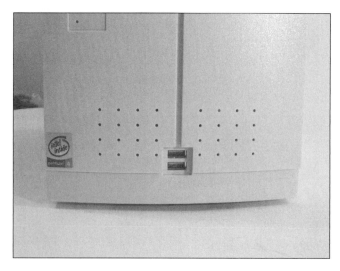

**Figure 9-42**    One or more USB ports on the front of a computer case make for easy access

## USB VERSIONS

USB Version 1.1 (sometimes called Basic Speed USB or Original USB) allows for two speeds, 1.5 Mbps and 12 Mbps, and works well for slow I/O devices. USB Version 2.0 (sometimes called Hi-Speed USB or USB2) allows for up to 480 Mbps, which is 40 times faster than Original USB. Hi-Speed USB is backward-compatible with slower USB devices. The USB Implementers Forum, Inc. (*www.usb.org*), the organization responsible for developing USB, has adopted the symbols shown in Figure 9-43 to indicate if the product is certified by the organization as compliant with Original USB or Hi-Speed USB.

**Figure 9-43**    Hi-Speed and Original USB logos appear on products certified by the USB forum

## USB HOST CONTROLLER

A USB **host controller**, which for most motherboards is included in the chipset, manages the USB bus. Sometimes a motherboard has two USB controllers; each is enabled and disabled in CMOS setup. As many as 127 USB devices can be daisy chained together using USB cables. In a daisy chain, one device provides a USB port for the next device. Figure 9-44 shows a keyboard and a mouse daisy chained together and connecting to a single USB port on an iMac computer. There can also be a standalone **hub** into which several devices can be plugged.

A+ ESS
1.1
2.2
4.1
5.1

A+
220-602
2.2
3.3

**Figure 9-44** A keyboard and a mouse using a USB port daisy chained together

A USB cable has four wires, two for power and two for communication. The two power wires (one carries voltage and the other is a ground) allow the host controller to provide power to a device. The connector on the host computer or hub end is called the A-Male connector, and the connector on the device end of the cable is called the B-Male connector. The A-Male connector is flat and wide, and the B-Male connector is square. (Look back at Figure 9-41 to see both these connectors.) In addition, because some devices such as a digital camera are so small, USB standards allow for mini-A connectors and mini-B connectors. You can see one of these mini-B connectors in Figure 9-45 used with a digital camera. The A-Male connector of this USB cable is regular size to connect to a computer's USB port.

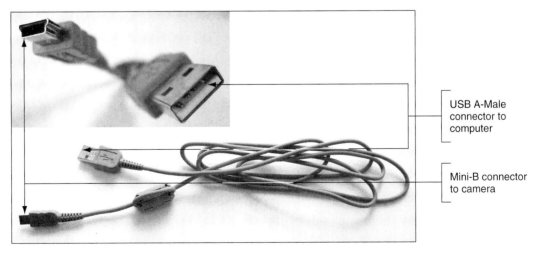

USB A-Male
connector to
computer

Mini-B connector
to camera

**Figure 9-45** The digital camera USB cable uses a mini-B connector and a regular size A-Male connector

A+ ESS
1.1
2.2
4.1
5.1

A+
220-602
2.2
3.3

USB cables for Original USB can be up to 3 meters (9 feet, 10 inches) and Hi-Speed USB cables can be up to 5 meters (16 feet, 5 inches). If you need to put a USB device farther from the PC than the cable is long, you can use a USB hub in the middle to effectively double the distance.

In USB technology, the host controller polls each device, asking if data is ready to be sent or requesting to send data to the device. The host controller manages communication to the CPU for all devices, using only a single IRQ (see Figure 9-46), I/O address range, and DMA channel to do so.

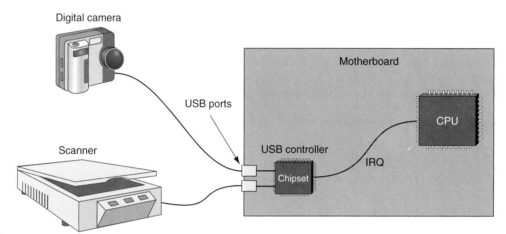

**Figure 9-46** The USB controller has a single IRQ line that it uses when any USB device needs attention

Windows 95 OSR 2.1 was the first Microsoft OS to support USB, although Windows 98 offers much improved USB support. Besides Windows 95 with the USB update and Windows 98, Windows 2000 and Windows XP support Original USB, but Windows NT does not. Windows XP, with service packs applied, supports Hi-Speed USB.

## PREPARING TO INSTALL A USB DEVICE

To install a USB device, you need:

- ◢ A motherboard or expansion card that provides a USB port
- ◢ An OS that supports USB
- ◢ A USB device
- ◢ A USB device driver

Recall that device drivers come from Windows or from the device manufacturer. Whenever possible, use drivers from the manufacturer. However, make sure you are using drivers written for the Windows OS you are using.

## INSTALLING A USB DEVICE

Some USB devices such as printers require that you plug in the device before installing the drivers, and some USB devices such as scanners require you to install the drivers before plugging in the device. For some devices, it doesn't matter which is installed first. Carefully read and follow the device documentation. For example, the documentation for one digital camera says that if you install the camera before installing the driver, the drivers will not install properly.

Follow these general steps to install a USB device such as a scanner, where the scanner is plugged in before installing the drivers:

1. Using Device Manager, verify that the USB host controller driver is installed under Windows. For example, Figure 9-47 shows Windows XP Device Manager displaying the Properties dialog box for a USB controller. Note in the figure the symbol for USB. Also notice the first entry in the Universal Serial Bus controllers list. An entry of "Standard Enhanced" means that this controller supports Hi-Speed USB. If the controller is not installed, install it from the Control Panel by double-clicking the **Add New Hardware** icon.

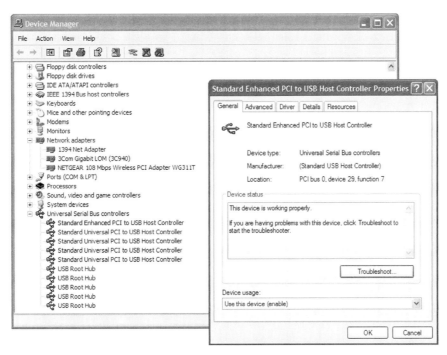

**Figure 9-47** Using Device Manager, verify that the USB controller is installed and working properly

If you have a problem installing the controller, verify that support for USB is enabled in setup. You also might check the motherboard documentation or the drivers CD that came with your motherboard for help when troubleshooting problems with the USB controller. For example, if none of the USB ports work, you can update the USB controller drivers. To do that, on the USB controller properties window, click the **Driver** tab and then click **Update Driver**. The Hardware Update Wizard launches, as shown in Figure 9-48. When given the opportunity, point to the drivers on CD that came with your motherboard or download new drivers from the motherboard manufacturer Web site.

2. Plug in the USB device. Within a few seconds, Windows should launch the Found New Hardware Wizard to install the device drivers. If the wizard does not launch automatically, go to the Control Panel and double-click the **Add New Hardware** icon. If you still have problems, try turning off the PC, plugging in the device, and rebooting. If that fails to install the drivers, look for and run the setup program on the CD or floppy disk that came with the device. After the drivers are installed, for most devices, you should see the device

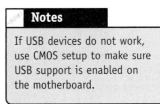

**Notes**

If USB devices do not work, use CMOS setup to make sure USB support is enabled on the motherboard.

**A+ ESS**
1.1
1.4
2.2
4.1
5.1

**A+**
220-602
2.2
3.3

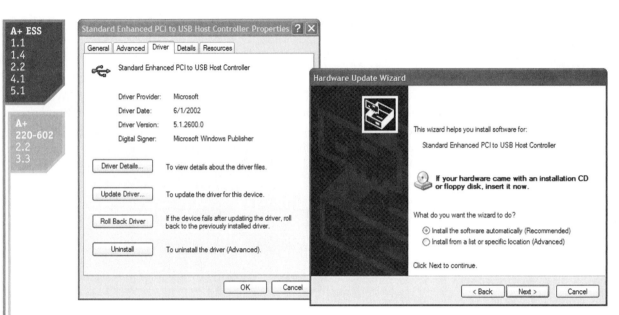

**Figure 9-48**    Updating drivers

listed in Device Manager. Verify that Windows sees the device with no conflicts and no errors.

3. Install the application software to use the device. For example, most scanners come with some software to scan and edit images. After you install the software, use it to scan an image.

---

**Notes**

Some motherboards provide extra ports that can be installed in faceplate openings off the back of the case. For example, Figure 9-49 shows a module that has a game port and two USB ports. To install the module, remove a faceplate and install the module in its place. Then connect the cable from the module to the connector on the motherboard.

---

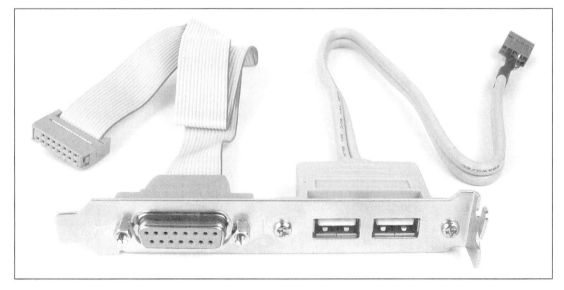

**Figure 9-49**    This connector provides two USB ports and one game port

A+ ESS
1.1
4.1
5.1

A+
220-602
2.2

# USING IEEE 1394 PORTS

**FireWire** and **i.Link** are common names for another peripheral bus officially named **IEEE 1394** (or sometimes simply called 1394). The name is derived from the name of the group that designed the bus. IEEE was primarily led by Apple Computer and Texas Instruments in the initial design.

FireWire is similar in design to USB, using serial transmission of data, but it is faster. In fact, FireWire supports data speeds as high as 3.2 Gbps (gigabits per second), which is much faster than USB. FireWire is likely to replace SCSI as a solution for high-volume, multimedia external devices such as digital camcorders, DVDs, and hard drives. SCSI is a very fast, but difficult-to-configure, peripheral bus.

FireWire devices are hot-pluggable and can be daisy chained together and managed by a host controller using a single set of system resources (an IRQ, an I/O address range, and a DMA channel). One host controller can support up to 63 FireWire devices.

The two standards for IEEE 1394 are IEEE 1394a and 1394b, although IEEE 1394c is on the drawing board. 1394a supports speeds up to 400 Mbps and is sometimes called FireWire 400. 1394a allows for cable lengths up to 4.5 meters (15 feet) and for up to 16 cables daisy chained together. 1394a supports two types of connectors and cables: a 4-pin connector that does not provide voltage to a device and a 6-pin connector that does (see Figure 9-50). The cable for a 6-pin port is wider than the 4-pin cable.

> **Notes**
>
> For interesting information about 1394, surf the 1394 Trade Association's Web site at *www.1394ta.org*.

> **Tip**
>
> Windows XP, Windows 2000, and Windows 98 all support FireWire. (Windows 95 and Windows NT do not.)

> **Tip**
>
> IEEE 1394a ports are common on newer, high-end motherboards and are expected to become standard ports on all new motherboards and to become as commonplace as USB ports are now.

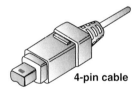

(Device requires AC adapter)

**4-pin cable**

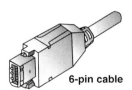

(Two pins are used for voltage and ground)

**6-pin cable**

**Figure 9-50** Two types of IEEE 1394a cable connectors; the 6-pin cable provides voltage to the device from the PC

The newer standard, 1394b, supports speeds up to 3.2 Gbps, but current devices on the market are running at only 800 Mbps, which is why 1394b is also called FireWire 800. 1394b can use cables up to 100 meters (328 feet), and uses a 9-pin connector. You can use a 1394 cable that has a 9-pin connector at one end and 4-pin or 6-pin connector at the other end to connect a 1394a device to a 1394b computer port, causing the port to run at the slower speed. Figure 9-51 shows a FireWire 800 adapter that provides three 1394 ports: two 1394b 9-pin ports and one 1394a 6-pin port.

A+ ESS
1.1
4.1
5.1

A+
220-602
2.2

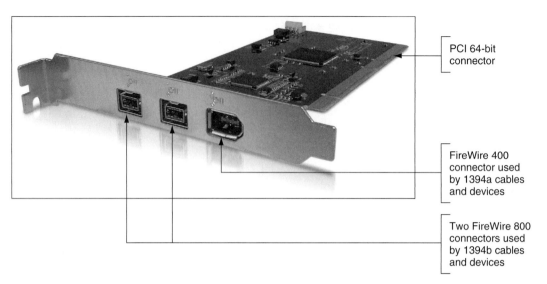

PCI 64-bit
connector

FireWire 400
connector used
by 1394a cables
and devices

Two FireWire 800
connectors used
by 1394b cables
and devices

**Figure 9-51** This 1394 adapter card supports both 1394a and 1394b and uses a 64-bit PCI bus connector

> **Notes**
>
> A variation of 1394 is **IEEE 1394.3**, which is designed for peer-to-peer data transmission. Using this standard, imaging devices such as scanners and digital cameras can send images and photos directly to printers without involving a computer.

IEEE 1394 uses **isochronous data transfer,** meaning that data is transferred continuously without breaks. This works well when transferring real-time data such as that received by television transmission. Because of the real-time data transfer and the fact that data can be transferred from one device to another without involving the CPU, IEEE 1394 is an ideal medium for data transfers between consumer electronics products, such as camcorders, VCRs, TVs, and digital cameras.

Figure 9-52 shows an example of how this data transfer might work. A person can record a home movie using a digital camcorder and download the data through a digital VCR to a 1394-compliant external hard drive. The 1394-compliant digital VCR can connect to and send data to the hard drive without involving the PC. The PC can later read the data off the hard drive and use it as input to video-editing application software. A user can edit the data

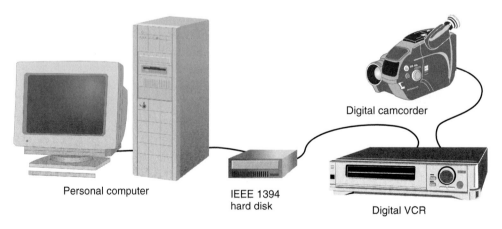

Digital camcorder

Personal computer

IEEE 1394
hard disk

Digital VCR

**Figure 9-52** IEEE 1394 can be used as the interface technology to connect consumer audio/visual equipment to a PC

9

A+ ESS
1.1
4.1
5.1

A+
220-602
2.2

and design a professional video presentation complete with captioning and special effects. Furthermore, if the digital camcorder is also 1394-compliant, it can download the data directly to the PC by way of a 1394 port on the PC. The PC can then save the data to a regular internal hard drive.

Windows 98, Windows 2000, and Windows XP support IEEE 1394 storage devices, printers, scanners, and other devices. Windows 98 Second Edition supports IEEE 1394 storage devices but not IEEE 1394 printers and scanners. For Windows 98 Second Edition, you can also download an update from the Microsoft Web site (*windowsupdate. microsoft.com*) to solve problems that occurred when devices were removed while the PC was still running.

To use a 1394 port with Windows, follow these steps:

1. You first need to verify that Windows recognizes that an IEEE 1394 controller is present on the motherboard. To do this, open **Device Manager** and look for the 1394 Bus Controller listed as an installed device. Click the **+** sign beside the controller in Device Manager to see the specific brand of 1394 controller that the board contains. If the controller is not installed or is not working, reinstall the driver. Then, in the Control Panel, double-click the **Add New Hardware** icon. If you have problems installing the driver, verify that 1394 support is enabled in setup.

2. Read the device documentation to decide if you install the drivers first or plug in the device first.

3. If you plug in the device first, plug it into the 1394 port. Then, install the device drivers for the 1394-compliant device. Without rebooting, you should be able to use the Add New Hardware icon in the Control Panel. For example, after you have installed the drivers for a camcorder, you should see the device listed in Device Manager under Sound, video, and game controllers. If you don't see the device listed, turn the device off and then on again.

4. If you need to install the drivers first, use the Add New Hardware icon in the Control Panel or follow the documentation instructions to run a setup program on CD. After the drivers are installed, plug the device into the 1394 port. The device should immediately be recognized by Windows.

5. Install the application software to use the device. A 1394-compliant camcorder is likely to come bundled with video-editing software, for example. Run the software to use the device.

**APPLYING|CONCEPTS** For motherboards that provide FireWire ports, the board might come with an internal connector for an internal FireWire hard drive. This connector can also be used for a module that provides additional FireWire ports off the back of the PC case. Figure 9-53 shows a motherboard with the pinouts of the FireWire

A+ ESS
1.1
4.1
5.1

A+
220-602
2.2

connector labeled. The module is also shown in the figure. To install this module, remove a face-plate and install the module in its place. Then connect the cable to the motherboard connector.

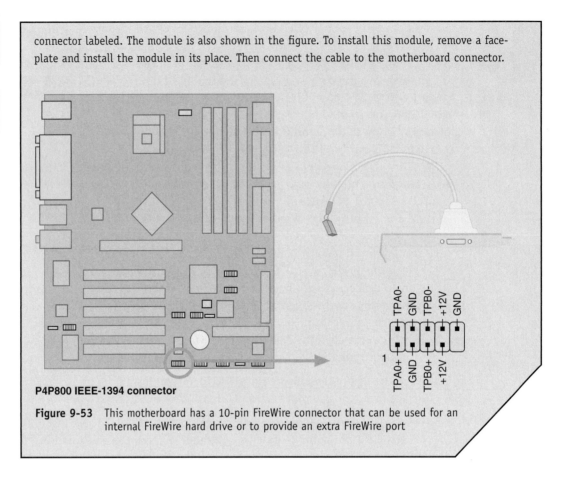

**P4P800 IEEE-1394 connector**

**Figure 9-53**   This motherboard has a 10-pin FireWire connector that can be used for an internal FireWire hard drive or to provide an extra FireWire port

A+ ESS
1.2
3.2

A+
220-602
1.1

## INSTALLING AND SUPPORTING EXPANSION CARDS

Most motherboards today have three or more regular PCI slots and one slot designed for a video card. The slot intended for the video card is an AGP slot or a PCI Express x16 (pronounced "by sixteen") slot. For example, the motherboard in Figure 9-54 has three regular PCI slots, one PCI Express x16 slot with a video card installed, and two PCI Express x1 slots. (See Figure 5-1 in Chapter 5 for a close-up of this same motherboard.)

You'll see all kinds of expansion cards on the market, such as video cards, modem cards, network cards, IEEE 1394 controllers, USB controllers, floppy drive controllers, hard drive controllers, wireless NICs, sound cards, and many more. Today, all these cards are Plug and Play (PnP), meaning you don't have to set jumpers or DIP switches on the card to use system resources and installations should be easy to do using the Windows Found New Hardware Wizard. To know how to support the older expansion cards that are not Plug and Play and use the legacy ISA expansion slots, see Appendix C.

In this section, you'll learn how to select an expansion card, install the card (a modem card in our example) in a PCI expansion slot, and support PCI cards. Recall that earlier in the chapter you learned about the specifics of installing a video card in an AGP slot.

### SELECTING PCI CARDS

When selecting a PCI card for your motherboard, recall from Chapter 6 that there are several PCI and PCI Express standards. For PCI cards, you must match the notches on the card to the keys in the PCI slot so that the voltage requirements of the card will match the voltage provided by the slot. Also, know that you can install a 32-bit PCI card into a longer 64-bit PCI slot. In this case, the extended end of the long PCI slot is unused.

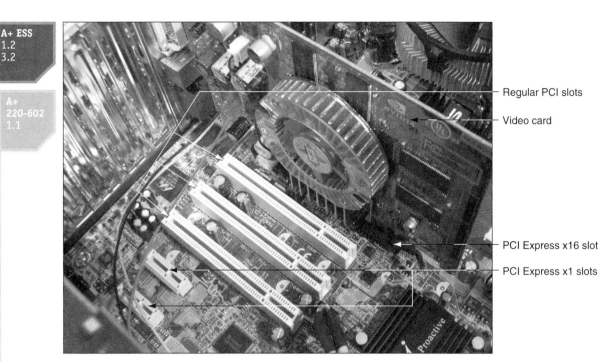

Figure 9-54 Asus P5AD2 motherboard with the MSI GeForce FX5750 video card installed in a PCI Express x16 slot

For motherboards that support the PCI-X standards, these PCI slots might support several different speeds. But know that when more than one PCI card is installed in PCI slots using the same PCI bus, the PCI bus runs at the speed of the slowest PCI card.

## INSTALLING AND CONFIGURING A PCI MODEM CARD

A **modem** is a device used by a PC to communicate over a phone line. A modem can be an external device (see Figure 9-55) connected to a USB or serial port, a modem card (see Figure 9-56) using either a PCI or PCI Express slot, or a smaller and less expensive modem riser card. Also, some motherboards have a modem port as an on-board component. On notebook computers, a modem is an embedded component on the motherboard or is a PC Card installed in a PC Card slot.

A modem provides one or two RJ-11 (registered jack 11) ports used by phone lines. Modems are rated by speed; the most common modem speed is 56.6 Kbps, although a few modems are

Figure 9-55 Zoom V.92 Mini Fax External Modem uses a USB connection

**Figure 9-56**   This 56K V.92 PCI modem card comes bundled with a phone cord and setup CD

still rated at 28.8 Kbps or 33.6 Kbps. Other than speed, other features supported by modems are the ability to compress data, provide error checking, and support video conferencing. The latest modem standard is **V.92**, which allows for quick connect (reduces handshake time), modem on hold (allows call waiting without breaking the connection to the ISP), and improved upload speeds for large files.

> **Notes**
>
> Because of the sampling rate (8,000 samples every second) used by phone companies when converting an analog signal to digital, and taking into account the overhead of data transmission (bits and bytes sent with the data that are used to control and define transmissions), the maximum transmission rate that a modem can attain over a regular phone line is about 56,000 bps or 56 Kbps. Although theoretically possible, most modem connections don't actually attain this speed. When connecting to an ISP using a dial-up connection, to achieve 56 Kbps, the ISP must use a digital connection to the phone company.

**APPLYING|CONCEPTS**   Bill was hurriedly setting up a computer for a friend. When he got to the modem, he installed it as he had installed many modems in the past. He put the modem card in the PCI slot and turned on the PC for Plug and Play to do its job. When the Found New Hardware Wizard launched, he installed the drivers, but the modem wouldn't work. He tried again and again to reinstall the modem, but still it didn't work. After four hours of trying to get the modem to work, he concluded the modem was bad. Then it hit him to read the instructions that came with the modem. He opened the booklet and in very large letters on the very first page it said, "The modem WILL NOT WORK if you install the card first and the software second." Bill took the card out and followed the instructions and within five minutes he was surfing the Net. Bill says that from that day forward he *always* reads *all* instructions first and leaves his ego at the door!

Follow these general steps to install a modem card:

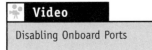

**Video**

Disabling Onboard Ports

▲ Read the modem documentation. The manufacturer's instructions to install the modem might be different from those listed here.

▲ If you are installing the modem card to replace an onboard modem port, enter CMOS setup and disable the onboard modem port.

A+ ESS
1.2
1.4
3.2
5.1

A+
220-602
1.1
5.1

▲ Protect the PC from ESD by using an antistatic bracelet and ground mat.

▲ Power down the PC and unplug it. Open the computer case, locate the slot you plan to use, and remove the faceplate from the slot. Sometimes a faceplate punches or snaps out, and sometimes you have to remove a faceplate screw to remove the faceplate.

▲ Insert the card in the expansion slot. Be careful to push the card directly into the slot, without rocking it from side to side. Rocking it from side to side can widen the expansion slot, making it more difficult to keep a good contact. If you have a problem getting the card into the slot, you can insert the end away from the side of the case in the slot first and gently rock the card from front to rear into the slot. The card should feel snug in the slot. You can almost feel it snap into place. If you find out later that the card does not work, most likely it is not seated securely in the slot. Check that first and then, if possible, try a different slot.

▲ Insert the screw that connects the card to the case (refer back to Figure 9-32). Be sure to use this screw; if it's not present, the card can creep out of the slot over time.

▲ Replace the case cover, power cord, and other peripherals. (If you want, you can leave the case cover off until you've tested the device, in case it doesn't work and you need to reseat it.)

▲ Plug the telephone line from the house into the line jack on the modem (see Figure 9-57). The second RJ-11 jack on the modem is for an optional telephone. It connects a phone so that you can more easily use this same phone jack for voice communication.

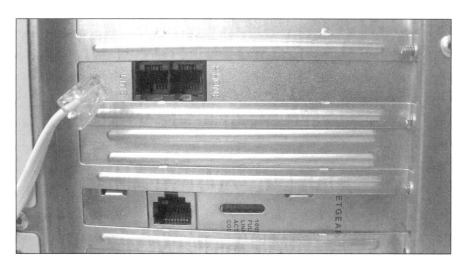

**Figure 9-57** An RJ-11 connection on a modem is the same as that used for a regular phone connection

Turn on your computer and follow these steps to configure the modem using Windows XP:

▲ Be aware that when Windows 2000/XP installs a new hardware device, if any interaction with the user is required during the installation, the user must be logged into the system with a user account that has administrative privileges.

▲ When you turn on the PC, Windows Plug and Play detects a new hardware device. In most cases, Windows XP will install its own drivers without giving you the opportunity to use manufacturer's drivers on CD. You might have to boot twice: once to allow Plug and Play to detect firmware on the modem card that runs the modem (called the UART which stands for universal asynchronous receiver-transmitter) and again to detect the modem. Also, if your modem has add-on features such as a Fax service, you might have to reboot again as this feature is installed. Follow onscreen directions until you reach the Windows desktop.

▲ In most cases, Windows XP installs a modem card without giving you the opportunity to use the modem manufacturer drivers on the modem setup CD. After Windows XP completes the installation, to install the drivers on CD, open **Device Manager**. Right-click the modem and select **Properties** from the shortcut menu. The modem Properties window opens. Click the **Driver** tab and then click **Update Driver**. When the Hardware Update Wizard launches and asks permission to connect to Windows Update Web site to search for updated drivers, select **No, not this time** and click **Next** (see Figure 9-58).

**Figure 9-58**    Use the Hardware Update Wizard to install the modem manufacturer drivers

▲ Insert the CD that came bundled with the modem. On the next wizard screen, select **Install from a list or specific location (Advanced)** and click **Next**.

▲ On the next screen shown in Figure 9-59, select **Search for the best driver in these locations**. Also select **Include this location in the search**, but don't select any other option on this screen. Click the **Browse** button and point to the location of the Windows XP drivers on the CD. Click **OK** and then click **Next**. Click **Finish** to complete the wizard and update the modem drivers. Reboot the system so the updated drivers will be loaded.

**Notes**

Keep in mind that during a hardware installation, if the drivers are not digitally signed by Microsoft, Windows will ask if you want to continue the installation using unsigned drivers. In this situation, choose to continue. Later, if the device doesn't work or gives problems, you can try to find Microsoft-certified drivers for the device.

▲ After the modem drivers are installed, verify the OS configured the modem correctly. Once again open **Device Manager** and the modem **Properties** window. Verify that Windows says the modem is working.

▲ If you want to use Windows to make calls without using other software, create a dial-up Networking Connection. Right-click **My Network Places** and select **Properties** on the shortcut menu. The Network Connections window opens (see Figure 9-60).

▲ Click **Create a new connection**. The New Connection Wizard launches. Click **Next**. The Network Connection Type dialog box opens (also shown in Figure 9-60). Select the type of connection and click **Next**. For example, if you want to connect to the Internet through your ISP, click **Connect to the Internet**. Complete the wizard.

A+ ESS
1.2
1.4
3.2
5.1

A+
220-602
1.1
5.1

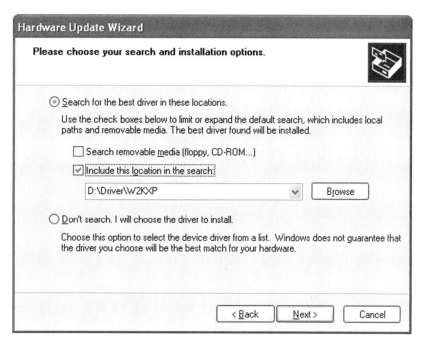

**Figure 9-59**  In the Hardware Update Wizard, point to the location of driver files on the modem setup CD

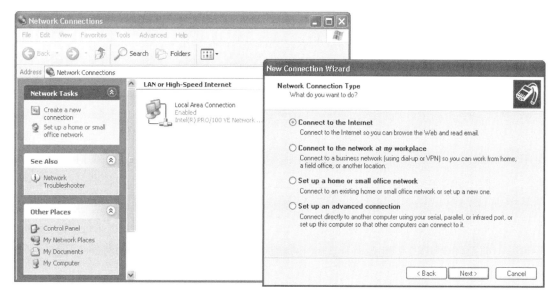

**Figure 9-60**  Create a Windows XP dial-up Network Connection

You need to know the phone number of your ISP, your user name, and password. Chapter 18 gives more information about connecting to an ISP and some troubleshooting guidelines when these connections give problems.

◢ For easy access, you can copy the Network Connection you just created from the Network Connections window to your desktop as a shortcut.

◢ Test the modem by making a dial-up connection to your ISP.

For Windows 2000 and Windows 9x/Me, installing and configuring the modem is the

> **Notes**
>
> Sometimes an installation disk has several directories, one for each operating system it supports. For example, for Windows 2000, look for a directory named \WIN2K or \W2KXP. The OS is looking for a directory that has a file with an .inf extension.

A+ ESS
1.2
1.4
3.2
5.1

A+
220-602
1.1
5.1

same as Windows XP except it will be easier to use manufacturer's drivers on the installation CD. For Windows 2000, to install the manufacturer drivers, after the Found New Hardware Wizard launches, when given the opportunity, select **CD-ROM drives** and **Specify a location** to point to the location of driver files on the modem installation CD (see Figure 9-61).

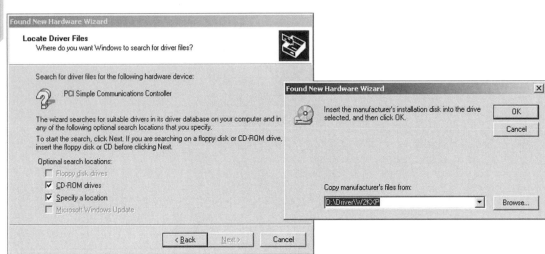

**Figure 9-61** Install a modem under Windows 2000 using the modem drivers on the manufacturer installation CD

After a modem is installed, if you have problems using the modem, try these things:

1. Verify the phone line is connected to a modem port. The phone line might be plugged into the network port by mistake.

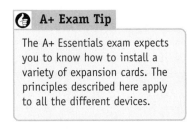

**A+ Exam Tip**

The A+ Essentials exam expects you to know how to install a variety of expansion cards. The principles described here apply to all the different devices.

2. Check the phone line. Can you make a call using a telephone? Do you need to dial a 9 or 8 to get an outside line?

3. Perform a diagnostic test on the modem. For Windows 2000/XP, open **Device Manager**, right-click the modem, and select **Properties** on the shortcut menu. The modem's Properties dialog box opens. Click the **Diagnostics** tab and then click the **Query Modem** button. See Figure 9-62. If the OS cannot communicate with the modem, nothing appears in the Command and Response box. However, if the OS receives responses from the modem, the dialog box appears. These commands, called AT commands, are used by software to communicate with a modem.

4. Try updating the modem drivers. To do that, right-click the modem in Device Manager and choose **Update Driver** from the shortcut menu. Follow directions onscreen. First try using the drivers that came with the modem on CD. If that doesn't work, try downloading new device drivers from the modem manufacturer's Web site.

5. Try uninstalling and reinstalling the modem. To uninstall the modem, right-click it in Device Manager and select **Uninstall** from the shortcut menu. To reinstall the modem, reboot to launch the Found New Hardware Wizard.

6. Read the modem's documentation for more things to do and try. Try moving the modem to a different PCI slot.

A+ ESS
1.2
1.4
3.2
5.1

A+
220-602
1.1
5.1

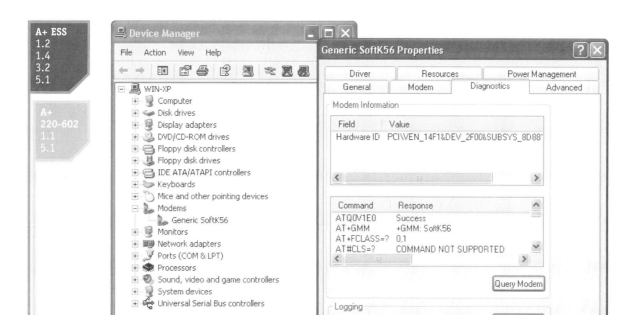

**Figure 9-62** Windows XP uses AT commands to perform a diagnostic test of a modem

---

> **Notes**
>
> Sometimes an external specialized device, such as a CAD/CAM device or security reader, comes bundled with an expansion card that provides a port for the device. When installing such devices, always read the documentation carefully before you begin. Also, motherboards sometimes offer special slots or connectors to be used for such things as IDE controllers, RAID controllers, USB controllers, temperature sensors, and internal audio input. Follow the motherboard documentation and the device documentation to install these devices.

## SUPPORTING MULTIPLE PCI CARDS

Know that the PCI controller, which is part of the motherboard chipset, manages the PCI bus, the expansion slots, and all the PCI cards. The startup BIOS assigns IRQs to the PCI bus controller during the boot process. A PCI card does not need exclusive use of an IRQ because the PCI controller uses interrupt levels to manage the interrupt needs of a card. The controller assigns each PCI expansion slot an interrupt level, named level A, B, C, D, and so forth. When a PCI card in one of these slots requests an interrupt, the interrupt level is passed to the PCI controller, which uses an IRQ to hail the CPU for attention.

However, if you use Device Manager to see the resources assigned to a PCI card, Device Manager reports an IRQ assigned to it. For example, in Figure 9-63, Device Manager is displaying the resources assigned to a PCI network card for Windows XP. Notice that the IRQ assigned to the card is IRQ 9. You need to realize that this IRQ can also be used by other devices on the PCI bus.

If two heavy-demand PCI devices end up sharing an IRQ, they might not work properly. If you suspect a shared IRQ is the source of a problem, try moving one of the devices to a different PCI slot, so that a device with a heavy demand (such as a 1394 adapter) is matched with a low-demand device (such as a modem).

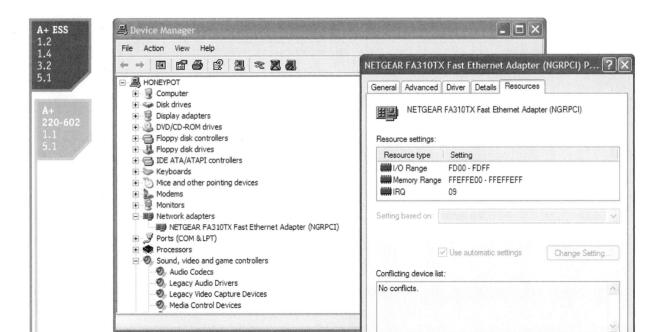

**Figure 9-63** Use Device Manager to determine which IRQ has been assigned to a PCI device

## TROUBLESHOOTING I/O DEVICES

Generally, when troubleshooting an I/O device, follow these steps:

1. For a new installation, suspect the drivers are not installed correctly, the device is not plugged in or set in the expansion slot correctly, or the application software does not work. Start at the beginning of the installation and redo and recheck each step.

2. For problems after an installation, ask the user what has just changed in the system. For example, if there has been a recent thunderstorm, the device might have been damaged by electricity. Maybe the user has just installed some software or changed Windows settings.

3. Analyze the situation and try to isolate the problem. For example, decide if the problem is most likely caused by hardware or software.

4. Check simple things first. Is the device getting power? Is it turned on? Is the data connection secure? Try rebooting the system to get a fresh start.

5. Try using Device Manager to uninstall the device. Then reboot and install the drivers again.

6. Exchange the device for a known good one or install the suspected device in a working system.

7. After the problem is fixed, document the symptoms, the source of the problem, and the solution so you have that to take into the next troubleshooting situation.

Let's now look at specific instructions for troubleshooting a keyboard, a mouse, and other I/O devices.

A+ ESS
1.3
1.4
2.3

A+
220-602
1.2
1.3
2.3

## TROUBLESHOOTING KEYBOARDS

Keyboards can give problems if they are not kept clean. If dirt, food, or drink are allowed to build up, one or more keys might stick or not work properly. Chips inside the keyboard can fail, and the keyboard cable or port connector can go bad. Because of its low cost, when a keyboard doesn't work, the solution is most often to replace it. However, you can try a few simple things to repair one, as described next.

### A FEW KEYS DON'T WORK

For keypads on regular keyboards or notebook computers, is the Num Lock key set correctly? For regular keyboards, if a few keys don't work, try turning the keyboard upside down and lightly bumping multiple keys with your flat palm to help loosen and remove debris. Next, you can remove the caps on the bad keys with a chip extractor. Spray contact cleaner into the key well. Repeatedly depress the contact to clean it. Don't use rubbing alcohol to clean the key well, because it can leave a residue on the contact. If this method of cleaning solves the problem, clean the adjacent keys as well.

### THE KEYBOARD DOES NOT WORK AT ALL

If the keyboard does not work at all, first check to see if the cable is plugged in. Maybe it's plugged into the mouse port by mistake. PC keyboard cables can become loose or disconnected. If the cable connection is good and the keyboard still does not work, swap it with another keyboard of the same type that you know is in good condition, to verify that the problem is in the keyboard, not the computer.

If the problem is in the keyboard, check the cable. If possible, swap the cable with a known good one, perhaps from an old discarded keyboard. Sometimes a wire in a PC keyboard cable becomes pinched or broken. Most cables can be easily detached from the keyboard by removing the few screws that hold the keyboard case together, then simply unplugging the cable. Be careful as you work; don't allow the keycaps to fall out! In Appendix B, you can learn how to use a multimeter to test a cable for continuity. You can use this method to verify that the cable is good.

> **⚡ Caution**
>
> Always power down a PC before plugging in a keyboard. The keyboard must be detected during the boot.

On the motherboard, the chipset and the ROM BIOS chip both affect keyboard functions. You might choose to flash BIOS to verify that system BIOS is not the source of the problem. Otherwise, the entire motherboard might have to be replaced, or you can try substituting a USB keyboard for the PS/2 keyboard.

### KEY CONTINUES TO REPEAT AFTER BEING RELEASED

This problem can be caused by a dirty contact. Some debris can have conductive properties, short the gap between the contacts, and cause the key to repeat. Try cleaning the key switch with contact cleaner.

Very high humidity and excess moisture sometimes short key switch contacts and cause keys to repeat because water is an electrical conductor. The problem usually resolves itself after the humidity level returns to normal. You can hasten the drying process by using a fan (not a hot hair dryer) to blow air at the keyboard.

### KEYS PRODUCE THE WRONG CHARACTERS

This problem is usually caused by a bad chip. PC keyboards actually have a processor mounted on the logic board inside the keyboard. Try swapping the keyboard for one you know is good. If the problem goes away, replace the original keyboard.

### MAJOR SPILLS ON THE KEYBOARD

When coffee or sugary drinks spill on the keyboard, they create a sticky mess. The best solution to stay up and running is to simply replace the keyboard. You can try to save the keyboard by thoroughly rinsing it in running water, perhaps from a bathroom shower. Make sure the keyboard dries thoroughly before you use it. Let it dry for two days on its own, or fewer if you set it out in the sun or in front of a fan. In some situations, such as a factory setting where dust and dirt are everywhere, consider using a clear, plastic keyboard cover.

## TROUBLESHOOTING A TOUCH SCREEN

If a touch screen does not work, here are some things you can try:

▲ Check that the touch screen cable is connected to the PC and Device Manager recognizes the device with no errors.
▲ Examine the screen for excessive scratches. Too many scratches might mean the screen needs replacing. Instruct the user to only use fingers or a stylus approved by the touch screen manufacturer on the screen. Also, check with the touch screen manufacturer to see if a screen protector is available.
▲ Examine the edges of the touch screen for crumbs or other particles that might have lodged between the touch screen grid and the monitor screen. You can use a clean and dry toothbrush to gently clean around the edges of the touch screen to dislodge these particles.
▲ If the touch screen is not accurate, recalibrate the screen. See the touch screen documentation for instructions. If the monitor screen resolution needs changing, follow instructions in the touch screen documentation to know how to do this.
▲ Try uninstalling and reinstalling the touch screen under Windows.

## TROUBLESHOOTING A MOUSE OR TOUCHPAD

If the mouse or touchpad on a notebook computer does not work or the pointer moves like crazy over the screen, do the following to troubleshoot the device:

▲ Check the mouse port connection. Is it secure? The mouse might be accidentally plugged into the keyboard port.
▲ Check for dust or dirt inside the mouse. Reboot the PC.
▲ In the Control Panel, open the **Mouse** applet and verify settings. (Note these settings apply to a mouse on any type computer as well as a touchpad on a notebook computer.) To update the mouse drivers, click the **Hardware** tab and then click **Properties**. On the mouse properties window, click the **Driver** tab and then click **Update Drivers**.
▲ Try a new mouse.
▲ Using Device Manager and the Add New Hardware icon in the Control Panel, first uninstall and then reinstall the mouse driver. Reboot the PC.
▲ Reboot the PC and select the logged option from the startup menu to create the Ntbtlog.txt file. Continue to boot and check the log for errors.
▲ For a notebook touchpad, was an external mouse connected to the notebook when it was first booted? Check CMOS setup to see if the touchpad was set to be disabled if a mouse is present at startup.

A+ ESS
1.3
2.3

A+
220-602
1.2
1.3
2.3

## TROUBLESHOOTING MONITORS AND VIDEO CARDS

For monitors as well as other devices, if you have problems, try doing the easy things first. For instance, try to make simple hardware and software adjustments. Many monitor problems are caused by poor cable connections or bad contrast/brightness adjustments.

> **Tip**
>
> A user very much appreciates a PC support technician who takes a little extra time to clean a system being serviced. When servicing a monitor, take the time to clean the screen with a soft dry cloth.

Typical monitor problems and how to troubleshoot them are described next.

### POWER LIGHT (LED) DOES NOT GO ON; NO PICTURE

For this problem, try the following:

- Is the monitor plugged in? Verify that the wall outlet works by plugging in a lamp, radio, or similar device. Is the monitor turned on? Look for a cutoff switch on the front and on the back.
- If the monitor power cord is plugged into a power strip or surge protector, verify that the power strip is turned on and working and that the monitor is also turned on. Look for an on/off switch on the front and back of the monitor. Some monitors have both.
- If the monitor power cord is plugged into the back of the computer, verify that the connection is tight and the computer is turned on.
- A blown fuse could be the problem. Some monitors have a fuse that is visible from the back of the monitor. It looks like a black knob that you can remove (no need to go inside the monitor cover). Remove the fuse and look for the broken wire indicating a bad fuse.
- The monitor might have a switch on the back for choosing between 110 volts and 220 volts. Check that the switch is in the right position.

> **Caution**
>
> A monitor retains a charge even after the power cord is unplugged. If you are trained to open a monitor case to replace a fuse, unplug the monitor and wait at least 60 minutes before opening the case so that capacitors have completely discharged.

> **Notes**
>
> When you turn on your PC, the first thing you see on the screen is the firmware on the video card identifying itself. You can use this information to search the Web, especially the manufacturer's Web site, for troubleshooting information about the card.

If none of these solutions solves the problem, the next step is to take the monitor to a service center.

### POWER LED IS ON, NO PICTURE ON POWER-UP

For this problem, try the following:

- Check the contrast adjustment. If there's no change, leave it at a middle setting.
- Check the brightness or backlight adjustment. If there's no change, leave it at a middle setting.

A+ ESS
1.3
2.3

A+
220-602
1.2
1.3
2.3

◢ Make sure the cable is connected securely to the computer.

◢ If the monitor-to-computer cable detaches from the monitor, exchange it for a cable you know is good, or check the cable for continuity.

◢ If this solves the problem, reattach the old cable to verify that the problem was not simply a bad connection.

◢ Confirm that the proper system configuration has been set up. Some older motherboards have a jumper or DIP switch you can use to select the monitor type.

◢ Test a monitor you know is good on the computer you suspect to be bad. Do this and the previous step to identify the problem. If you think the monitor is bad, make sure that it also fails to work on a good computer.

◢ Check the CMOS settings or software configuration on the computer. When using Windows 2000/XP or Windows 9x/Me, boot into Safe Mode. For Windows 2000/XP, press F8 and then choose Safe Mode from the menu, and for Windows 9x/Me press F5 during the boot. This allows the OS to select a generic display driver and low resolution. If this works, change the driver and resolution.

◢ Reseat the video card. For a PCI card, move the card to a different expansion slot. Clean the card's edge connectors, using a contact cleaner purchased from a computer supply store.

◢ If there are socketed chips on the video card, remove the card from the expansion slot and then use a screwdriver to press down firmly on each corner of each socketed chip on the card. Chips sometimes loosen because of thermal changes; this condition is called **chip creep**.

◢ Trade a good video card for the video card you suspect is bad. Test the video card you think is bad on a computer that works. Test a video card you know is good on the computer that you suspect is bad. Whenever possible, do both.

◢ If the video card has socketed chips that appear dirty or corroded, consider removing them and trying to clean the pins with contact cleaner. Normally, however, if the problem is a bad video card, the most cost-effective measure is to replace the card.

◢ Go into CMOS setup and disable the shadowing of video ROM.

◢ Test the RAM on the motherboard with diagnostic software.

◢ For a motherboard that is using an AGP or a PCI-Express video card, try using a PCI video card in a PCI slot.

◢ Trade the motherboard for one you know is good. Sometimes, though rarely, a peripheral chip on the motherboard of the computer can cause the problem.

◢ For notebook computers, is the LCD switch turned on? Function keys are sometimes used for this purpose.

◢ For notebook computers, try connecting a second monitor to the notebook and use the function key to toggle between the LCD panel and the second monitor. If the second monitor works, but the LCD panel does not work, the problem might be with the LCD panel hardware. How to solve problems with notebook computers is covered in Chapter 20.

## POWER IS ON, BUT MONITOR DISPLAYS THE WRONG CHARACTERS

For this problem, try the following:

◢ Wrong characters are usually not the result of a bad monitor but of a problem with the video card. Trade the video card for one you know is good.

◢ Exchange the motherboard. Sometimes a bad ROM or RAM chip on the motherboard displays the wrong characters on the monitor.

9

## MONITOR FLICKERS, HAS WAVY LINES, OR BOTH

For this problem, try the following:

▲ Monitor flicker can be caused by poor cable connections. Check that the cable connections are snug.

▲ Does the monitor have a degauss button to eliminate accumulated or stray magnetic fields? If so, press it.

▲ Check if something in the office is causing a high amount of electrical noise. For example, you might be able to stop a flicker by moving the office fan to a different outlet. Bad fluorescent lights or large speakers can also produce interference. Two monitors placed very close together can also cause problems.

▲ If the vertical scan frequency (the refresh rate at which the screen is drawn) is below 60 Hz, a screen flicker might appear. To change the refresh rate, right-click the desktop and select **Properties** from the shortcut menu. The Display Properties window opens. Click the **Settings** tab, and then click the **Advanced** button. The video hardware properties window opens. Click the **Monitor** tab (see Figure 9-64). For best results, make sure the option, **Hide modes that this monitor cannot display** is checked. Then select the highest screen refresh rate listed in the drop-down list.

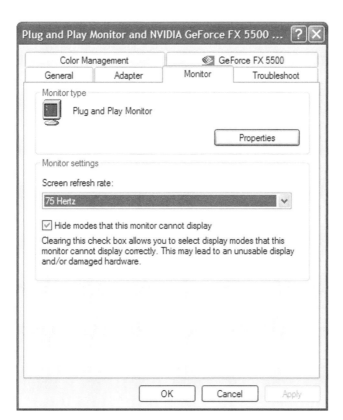

**Figure 9-64** To reduce monitor flicker, increase the screen refresh rate

▲ For older monitors that do not support a high enough refresh rate, your only cure might be to purchase a new monitor. Before making a purchase, verify that the new monitor will solve the problem.

▲ For older monitors, use the controls on the monitor to check vertical hold (V-hold), which can cause the display to scroll.

A+ ESS
1.3
2.3

A+
220-602
1.2
1.3
2.3

▲ Using other controls on the monitor, you can change brightness, contrast, and horizontal and vertical display positions on the screen.

▲ Open the Control Panel, click **Display**, and then click **Settings** to see if a high resolution (greater than 800 × 600) is selected. Consider these issues:

1. The video card might not support this resolution or color setting.

2. There might not be enough video RAM; see the video card documentation for the recommended amount.

3. The added (socketed) video RAM might be a different speed than the soldered memory.

## NO GRAPHICS DISPLAY OR THE SCREEN GOES BLANK WHEN LOADING CERTAIN PROGRAMS

For this problem, try the following:

▲ A special graphics or video accelerator card is not present or is defective.
▲ Software is not configured to do graphics, or the software does not recognize the installed graphics card.
▲ The video card does not support the resolution and/or color setting.
▲ There might not be enough video RAM; see the video card for the recommended amount.
▲ The added (socketed) video RAM might be a different speed than the soldered memory.
▲ The wrong adapter/display type is selected. Start Windows from Safe Mode to reset the display.

## SCREEN GOES BLANK 30 SECONDS OR ONE MINUTE AFTER THE KEYBOARD IS LEFT UNTOUCHED

A Green motherboard (one that follows energy-saving standards) used with an Energy Saver monitor can be configured to go into standby or doze mode after a period of inactivity. This might be the case if the monitor resumes after you press a key or move the mouse. Video might be set to doze after a period set as short as 20 seconds to as long as one hour. The power LED normally changes from green to orange to indicate doze mode. Monitors and video cards using these energy-saving features are addressed in Chapter 4.

> **Notes**
>
> Problems might occur if the motherboard power-saving features are turning off the monitor, and Windows screen saver is also turning off the monitor. If the system hangs when you try to get the monitor going again, try disabling one or the other. If this doesn't work, disable both.

You might be able to change the doze features by entering the CMOS menu and looking for an option such as Power Management. In addition, note that some monitors have a Power Save switch on the back. Make sure this is set as you want.

The screen saver feature of Windows can also set the monitor to turn off after so many minutes of inactivity. The number of minutes is set in the Display Properties window. Open the Control Panel, select Display, and then select Screen Saver.

## POOR COLOR DISPLAY

For this problem, try the following:

▲ Read the monitor documentation to learn how to use the color-adjusting buttons to fine-tune the color.
▲ Exchange video cards.

A+ ESS
1.3
2.3

A+
220-602
1.2
1.3
2.3

▲ Add more video RAM; see the video card for the recommended amount.

▲ Check if a fan, a large speaker (speakers have large magnets), or a nearby monitor could be causing interference.

▲ If the monitor displays blue and green, but no red, then the red electron gun might be bad. Replace the monitor. Same for missing blue or green colors.

▲ Odd-colored blotches on the screen might indicate a device such as a speaker or fan is sitting too close to the monitor and emitting EMI. Move any suspected device away from the monitor.

## PICTURE OUT OF FOCUS OR OUT OF ADJUSTMENT

For this problem, try the following:

▲ Check the adjustment knobs on the control panel on the outside of the monitor.

▲ Change the refresh rate. Sometimes this can make the picture appear more focused.

▲ You can also make adjustments inside the monitor that might solve the problem. If you have not been trained to work inside the monitor, take it to a service center.

> **Notes**
>
> For LCD monitors, you can improve how fonts are displayed on the screen. On the Display Properties window, click the **Appearance** tab and then click **Effects**. The Effects dialog box appears (see Figure 9-65). Check **Use the following method to smooth edges of screen fonts**. Then, from the drop-down list, select **ClearType**. Click **OK** twice to close both windows.

## CRACKLING SOUND

Dirt or dust inside the unit might be the cause. Someone at a computer monitor service center trained to work on the inside of the monitor can vacuum inside it. Recall from Chapter 4 that a monitor holds a dangerous charge of electricity and you should not open one unless trained to do so.

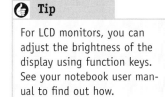

> **Tip**
>
> For LCD monitors, you can adjust the brightness of the display using function keys. See your notebook user manual to find out how.

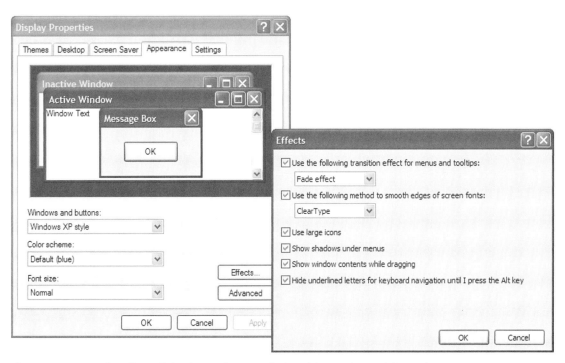

**Figure 9-65** Use the Effects dialog box to improve displayed fonts using an LCD monitor

A+ ESS
1.3
2.3

A+
220-602
1.2
1.3
2.3

## DISPLAY SETTINGS MAKE THE SCREEN UNREADABLE

When the display settings don't work, you can easily return to standard VGA settings, which include a resolution of 640 x 480. Do the following:

- For Windows 2000/XP or Windows 9x/Me, reboot the system and press the **F8** key after the first beep.
- When the Windows 2000/XP Advanced Options menu or the Windows 9x/Me startup menu appears, select **Safe Mode** to boot up with minimal configurations and standard VGA display mode. For Windows 2000/XP, you can also try Enable VGA Mode from the Advanced Options menu.

> **⚡ Caution**
>
> A CRT monitor screen is made of leaded glass, and a monitor contains capacitors that can hold a charge even after the monitor is unplugged. Therefore, it's important to dispose of a monitor correctly. For capacitors to fully discharge, it is not safe to remove the cover of a monitor until it has remained unplugged for at least one hour. To know how to dispose of a monitor, check with local county or environment officials for laws and regulations that apply to your area.

- Double-click the **Display** icon in the Control Panel, and reset it to the correct video configuration.

## >> CHAPTER SUMMARY

- Adding new devices to a computer requires installing hardware and software. Even if you know how to generally install an I/O device, always follow the specific instructions of the product manufacturer.

- Use Device Manager under Windows to determine what resources currently installed devices use.

- A keyboard can use a DIN, PS/2, USB, or wireless connection.

- Biometric input devices, such as a fingerprint reader or iris scanner, collect biological data and compare it to that recorded about the person to authenticate the person's access to a system.

- Features to consider when purchasing a monitor are the screen size, refresh rate, interlacing, response time, dot pitch or pixel pitch, resolution, multiscan ability, color quality, contrast ratio, viewing angle, display type (active or passive matrix), backlighting, and type of connector (analog or digital) used by the monitor.

- A video card is rated by the bus that it uses and the amount of video RAM on the card. Both features affect the overall speed and performance of the card.

- Some types of video memory are VRAM, SGRAM, WRAM, 3-D RAM, MDRAM, G-DDR, G-DDR2, G-DDR3, and DRDRAM.

- Most computers provide one or more USB ports, one parallel port, and perhaps an IEEE 1394 port or serial port to be used for a variety of devices.

- The PCI bus is presently the most popular local bus. The VESA local bus is an outdated standard designed by the Video Electronics Standards Association for video cards. For video cards, the VESA bus was replaced by PCI, which was then replaced by the AGP bus, and more recently by the PCI Express bus.

- Generally, expansion cards use PCI Express or PCI slots.

- UART logic on a motherboard chipset controls serial ports.

▲ Because data might become corrupted, parallel cables should not exceed 15 feet (4.5 meters) in length. HP recommends that the cables not exceed 10 feet (3 meters).

▲ Three types of parallel ports are standard, EPP, and ECP. The ECP type uses a DMA channel.

▲ Serial ports are sometimes configured as COM1, COM2, COM3, or COM4, and parallel ports can be configured as LPT1, LPT2, or LPT3.

▲ The USB bus only uses one set of system resources for all USB devices connected to it, and USB devices are hot-pluggable.

▲ The IEEE 1394 bus provides 4-pin, 6-pin, or 9-pin connectors, uses only one set of system resources, and is hot-pluggable.

▲ The PCI bus runs in sync with the CPU, and the PCI controller manages system resources for all PCI cards. Resources are assigned to PCI slots during startup.

## >> KEY TERMS

For explanations of key terms, see the Glossary near the end of the book.

| | | |
|---|---|---|
| 3-D RAM | hot-pluggable | passive matrix display |
| active matrix display | hot-swapping | pixel |
| bus mouse | hub | PS/2-compatible mouse |
| chip creep | i.Link | refresh rate |
| DCE (Data Communications Equipment) | I/O controller card | resolution |
| | IEEE 1284 | serial mouse |
| Direct RDRAM (DRDRAM) | IEEE 1394 | SGRAM (synchronous graphics RAM) |
| dot pitch | IEEE 1394.3 | |
| DSTN (dual-scan twisted nematic) | infrared transceiver | TFT (thin film transistor) |
| | interlaced | touch screen |
| DTE (Data Terminal Equipment) | IR transceiver | triad |
| ECP (Extended Capabilities Port) | IrDA (Infrared Data Association) transceiver | UART (universal asynchronous receiver-transmitter) |
| EPP (Enhanced Parallel Port) | | |
| FireWire | isochronous data transfer | USB host controller |
| flat panel monitor | LCD monitor | VRAM (video RAM) |
| graphics accelerator | motherboard mouse | WRAM (window RAM) |
| Graphics DDR (G-DDR) | MultiBank DRAM (MDRAM) | |
| Graphics DDR2 (G-DDR2) | noninterlaced | |
| Graphics DDR3 (G-DDR3) | null modem cable | |

## >> REVIEW QUESTIONS

1. Which of the following best describes how you get a wireless keyboard to work?

   a. Clean the keyboard before the first use.

   b. Use a regular keyboard to install the software to use the wireless keyboard.

   c. Turn any radios in the room off while you are installing the driver for the wireless keyboard.

   d. Install the driver for the mouse before you install the driver for the keyboard.

2. Which of the following best describes how an LCD monitor works?

   a. The image is produced using a liquid crystal material made of large, easily polarized molecules.

   b. One layer of electrodes makes up the electrode matrix.

   c. The grid controls which one of three electron guns fires, each gun targeting a different color (red, green, or blue) positioned on the back of the screen.

   d. The filaments at the back of the cathode tube shoot a beam of electrons to the screen at the front of the tube.

3. Which of the following statements best describes the refresh rate for CRT monitors?

   a. The refresh rate is also called the horizontal scan rate.

   b. Refresh rates do not typically differ among monitors.

   c. The refresh rate is the number of times in one second an electronic beam can fill the screen with lines.

   d. CRT screens draw a screen by making two passes.

4. Which of the following statements best describes a graphics accelerator and its purpose?

   a. One problem that high-end graphics cards have is overheating.

   b. Some features included on a graphics accelerator are MPEG decoding, 3-D graphics, and dual porting.

   c. The graphics accelerator does not have a processor to manage video and graphics.

   d. It is a type of video card that has its own processor to boost performance.

5. Which of the following statements best describes a standard parallel port?

   a. A standard parallel port allows data to flow in only one direction.

   b. A standard parallel port is the slowest of the three types of parallel ports.

   c. A parallel port is faster and easier to configure than USB ports.

   d. Setup can have up to four different settings for parallel port modes.

6. True or false? With the exception of the floppy drive, every I/O device is controlled by software.

7. True or false? When installing a touch screen add-on device, you must then calibrate the touch screen to account for the monitor's resolution using the management software.

8. True or false? An LCD monitor you purchase today will likely use a technology called TFT (thin film transistor).

9. True or false? Dot pitch is the total number of spots, or dots, on a CRT screen that the electronic beam hits.

10. True or false? An LCD monitor is designed to use several resolutions.

11. Keyboards use one of two common technologies in the way the keys make contact: _____ or _____.

12. Mouse technologies include the _____ and the _____ mouse.

**9**

13. Chips sometimes loosen because of thermal changes, a condition called
    _____.

14. TFT display used by LCD monitors is sometimes called a(n) _____
    display.

15. When a serial port is used by an external modem, the serial port is called the
    _____ and the modem is called _____.

# Multimedia Devices and Mass Storage

**T**he ability to create output in a vast array of media—audio, video, and animation, as well as text and graphics—has turned PCs into multimedia machines. The multimedia computer has much to offer, from videoconferencing for executives to tools for teaching the alphabet to four-year-olds. This chapter examines multimedia devices, what they can do, how they work, and how to support them. You will also learn about storage devices such as CDs, DVDs, removable drives, and tape drives, including installation and troubleshooting. These mass storage devices are used to hold multimedia data and, in some cases, to store backups.

# MULTIMEDIA ON A PC

The goal of multimedia technology is to use sights, sounds, and animation to make computer output look as much like real life as possible. Remember that computers store data digitally and ultimately as a stream of only two numbers: 0 and 1. In contrast, sights and sounds have an infinite number of variations and are analog in nature. The challenge for multimedia technology is to bridge these two worlds.

In this section, you'll first learn about the CPU technologies designed specifically for processing multimedia data and then we'll turn our attention to learning about some cool multimedia devices, including sound cards, digital cameras, MP3 players, TV tuners, and video capture cards.

## CPU TECHNOLOGIES FOR MULTIMEDIA

Intel and AMD clearly dominate the CPU market, and both companies have made strides toward better CPU technologies used for multimedia.

Three early CPU improvements Intel made to its processors with multimedia applications in mind are **MMX (Multimedia Extensions)**, used by the Pentium MMX and Pentium II; **SSE (Streaming SIMD Extension)**, used by the Pentium III; and SSE2, SSE3, and Hyper-Threading for the Pentium 4. **SIMD**, which stands for "single instruction, multiple data," is a process that allows the CPU to receive a single instruction and then execute it on multiple pieces of data rather than receiving the same instruction each time each piece of data is received.

An instruction set is the group of operations that a CPU knows how to perform. These operations are preprogrammed into the processor logic when the CPU is manufactured. SSE2 has a larger instruction set than SSE, and SSE3 improves on SSE2. The Pentium 4 can use MMX, SSE, SSE2, SSE3, and Hyper-Threading. MMX and SSE help with repetitive looping, which happens a lot when the CPU is managing audio and graphics data. SSE also improves on 3D graphics.

> **A+ Tip**
>
> The A+ Essentials exam expects you to be familiar with the characteristics of the different processors. Know the purposes of MMX, Hyper-Threading, and dual-core processing.

AMD is a favorite CPU manufacturer for gamers and hobbyists. For its processors, AMD uses 3DNow!, a processor instruction set designed to improve performance with 3D graphics and other multimedia data. In addition, AMD uses HyperTransport! to increase bandwidth and PowerNow! to improve a processor's performance and lower power requirements. AMD was first to market with 64-bit processors for the desktop, and AMD also uses dual-core processing.

## SOUND CARDS AND ONBOARD SOUND

A sound card (an expansion card with sound ports) or onboard sound (sound ports embedded on a motherboard) can record sound, save it in a file on your hard drive, and play it back. Some sound cards and onboard sound give you the ability to mix and edit sound, and even to edit the sound using standard music score notation. Sound cards or motherboards with onboard sound have output ports for external speakers and input ports for a microphone, CD or DVD player, or other digital sound equipment.

The number and type of sound ports on a motherboard or sound card depend on the sound standards the card or board supports. For good sound, you definitely need two or more external speakers and an amplifier. Most cards sold today support the audio compression method also used by HDTV (high-definition TV) called Dolby AC-3 sound compression. Other names

A+ ESS
1.1

A+
220-602
1.1

given to this standard are Dolby Digital Surround, Dolby Surround Sound, or, the most common name, Surround Sound. The **Surround Sound** standard supports up to eight separate sound channels of sound information for up to eight different speakers, each producing a different sound. The number of speakers depends on the version of Surround Sound the motherboard or card supports. These speakers are known as Front Left and Right, Front Center, Rear Left and Right, and Subwoofer. Surround Sound Version 7.1 added two rear speakers in addition to the ones just mentioned. Because each channel is digital, there is no background noise on the channel, and a sound engineer can place sound on any one of these speakers. The sound effects can be awesome! The latest version of Surround Sound is Version 10.1.

The motherboard shown in Figure 10-1 contains onboard sound. Device drivers and a user manual for sound come bundled with the motherboard on CD. The purposes of the eight sound ports are listed in Table 10-1 for 2-, 4-, 6-, and 8-channel sound. The two S/PDIF (Sony/Philips Digital Interconnect Format) ports are used to connect to external sound equipment such as a CD or DVD player.

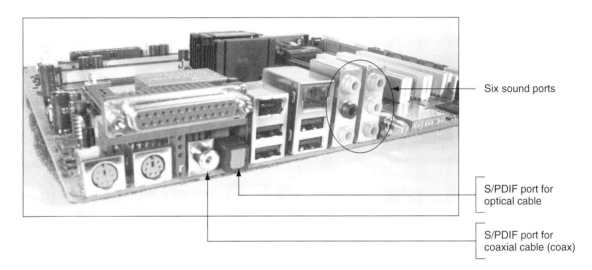

**Figure 10-1** This motherboard with onboard sound has eight sound ports

| Port | 2-Channel (Headset) | 4-Channel | 6-Channel | 8-Channel |
|------|---------------------|-----------|-----------|-----------|
| Light blue | Line in | Line in | Line in | Line in |
| Lime | Line out | Front speaker out | Front speaker out | Front speaker out |
| Pink | Mic in | Mic in | Mic in | Mic in |
| Gray | N/A | Rear speaker out | Rear speaker out | Rear speaker out |
| Black | N/A | N/A | N/A | Side speaker out |
| Yellow-orange | N/A | N/A | Center or subwoofer | Center or subwoofer |
| Gray half-oval | Optical S/PDIF out port connects an external audio output device using a fiber-optic S/PDIF cable | | | |
| Yellow | Coaxial S/PDIF out port connects an external audio output device using a coaxial S/PDIF cable | | | |

**Table 10-1** Sound ports on a motherboard

Also, sound cards might be Sound Blaster-compatible, meaning that they understand the commands sent to them that have been written for a Sound Blaster card, which is generally considered the standard for PC sound cards. In addition, some cards have internal input connectors to connect to a CD or DVD drive or TV Tuner card so that analog or digital sound goes directly from the device to the sound card, bypassing the CPU. Table 10-2 lists some sound card manufacturers.

| Manufacturer | Web Site |
| --- | --- |
| Aopen | www.aopen.com |
| Chaintech | www.chaintechusa.com |
| Creative | www.creative.com and www.soundblaster.com |
| Diamond Multimedia | www.diamondmm.com |
| Guillemot Corporation | www.hercules.com |
| PPA | www.ppa-usa.com |
| Sabrent | www.sabrent.com |
| SIIG | www.siig.com |
| Turtle Beach | www.tbeach.com |

**Table 10-2**   Sound card manufacturers

**Notes**

A good source for information about hardware devices (and software) is a site that offers product reviews and technical specifications and compares product prices and features. Check out these sites: CNET Networks (*www.cnet.com*), Price Watch (*www.pricewatch.com*), Tom's Hardware Guide (*www.tomshardware.com*), and Epinions, Inc. (*www.epinions.com*).

## SAMPLING AND DIGITIZING THE SOUND

Sound passes through three stages when it is computerized: first, the sound is digitized— that is, converted from analog to digital; next, the digital data is stored in a compressed data file; later, the sound is reproduced or synthesized (digital to analog or digital out).

Sound is converted from analog to digital storage by first sampling the sound and then digitizing it. When you record sound, the analog sound is converted to analog voltage by a microphone and passed to the sound card, where it is digitized. The sound is sampled at set intervals. Each sample taken is stored as a number. The number of bits used to store the sample is called the sample size and greatly affects the quality of the digitized sound. Common sample sizes are 8, 16, and 24 bits.

The **sampling rate** of a sound card, which is the number of samples taken of the analog signal over a period of time, is usually expressed as samples (cycles) per second, or **hertz (Hz)**. One thousand hertz (one kilohertz) is written as kHz. A low sampling rate provides a less-accurate representation of the sound than a high sampling rate. Our ears detect up to about 22,000 samples per second, or hertz. Studies show that in order to preserve the original sound, a digital sampling rate must be twice the frequency of the analog signal. Therefore, the sampling rate of music CDs is 44,100 Hz, or 44.1 kHz, although the sampling rates of high-end sound cards can be higher. When you record sound on a PC, the sampling rate is controlled by the recording software.

The larger the sample size is, the more accurate the sampling. If 8 bits are used to hold one number, the sample range can be from −128 to +127. This is because 1111 1111 in

A+ ESS
1.1

A+
220-602
1.1

binary (FF in hex) equals 255 in decimal, which, combined with zero, equals 256 values. Sound samples are considered both positive and negative numbers, so the range is –128 to +127 rather than 0 to 255. However, if 16 bits are used to hold the range of numbers, then the sample range increases dramatically, because 1111 1111 1111 1111 in binary (FFFF in hex) is 65,535 in decimal, meaning that the sample size can be –32,768 to +32,767, or a total of 65,536 values. High-fidelity music CDs use this 16-bit sample size. Samples can also be recorded on a single channel (mono) or on two channels (stereo). After the sound is recorded and digitized, many sound cards convert the digitized sound to **MP3** format, which takes up less space on a hard drive or other media than does raw digitized sound.

A+ ESS
1.2

## INSTALLING A SOUND CARD

Most sound cards come with device drivers as well as all the software needed for normal use, such as application software to play music CDs or record music. Later in this part of the chapter, you'll see how to install a sound card. The card that will be used is shown in Figure 10-2. It's a 24-bit Creative Labs Sound Blaster card that has a universal PCI connector and works under Windows NT/2000/XP, Windows 9x/Me, and DOS. The card comes with a user manual, drivers, and application software all on a CD.

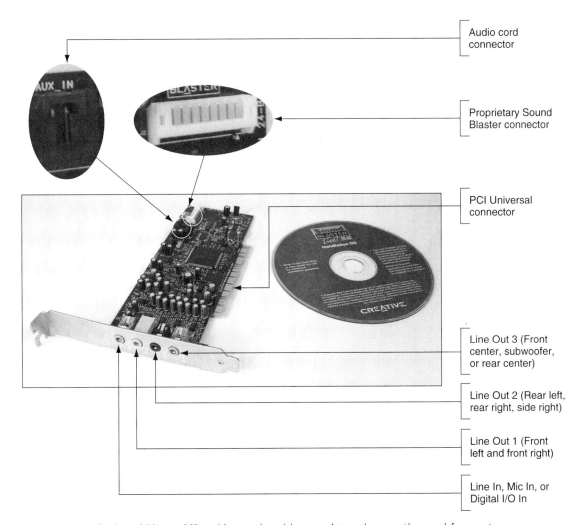

**Figure 10-2**  The Sound Blaster PCI 24-bit sound card has two internal connections and four ports

The Sound Blaster card shown in Figure 10-2 has several ports that are labeled in the figure. The sound-out ports can support analog speakers or amplifiers that are externally powered. Typical color codes for these ports are:

 **A+ Tip**

The A+ Essentials exam expects you to know the characteristics of adapter cards used in multimedia applications and how to install these cards. You need to know about a sound card, video card, TV tuner card, SCSI, FireWire (1394), and USB adapter cards. The detailed installation learned in this section applies to other adapters as well as a sound card.

▲ *Blue*. Line in for music synthesizers, a microphone, DVD player, CD player, or other external device producing sound. It can also be used with a Digital I/O Module available from Creative. (If a card has a separate port for a microphone other than the Line-in port, most likely the microphone port will be red.)

▲ *Green*. Line out (Front speakers out, usually center port on the card). Use this port for a single speaker.

▲ *Black*. Rear out and Side Right out (for a sound system that uses a 7.1 speaker system).

▲ *Orange (sometimes yellow on other sound cards)*. Front Center out, Subwoofer speaker, or Side Left (for a sound system that uses a 7.1 speaker system).

**Notes**

The trend for today's motherboards is to embed sound capability on the board. If this onboard sound is giving problems, try using Device Manager to uninstall the sound drivers and then use the setup CD that came bundled with the motherboard to reinstall the drivers. If you want to upgrade to better sound by using a sound card, you can use CMOS setup to disable the onboard sound and then install a sound card.

The sound card has two internal connections (connections to something inside the case). The AUX In connector is used to connect devices that provide audio into the card, including a CD drive, DVD drive, TV Tuner card, and MPEG decoder card. The second internal connector is a proprietary connector used for other Creative devices.

# APPLYING|CONCEPTS

Generally, the main steps to install a sound card are to install the card in an empty PCI slot on the motherboard and install the drivers on the CD that comes with the sound card. Also, on the CD you might find applications to install. Follow these steps to install a sound card:

1. Wear a ground bracelet to protect against ESD, as described in Chapter 3.

2. Turn off the PC, remove the cover, and locate an empty expansion slot for the card. Because this installation uses the connecting wire from the sound card to the CD drive (the wire comes with the sound card), place the sound card near enough to the CD drive so that the wire can reach between them.

3. Attach the wire to the sound card (see Figure 10-3) and to the CD drive or DVD drive.

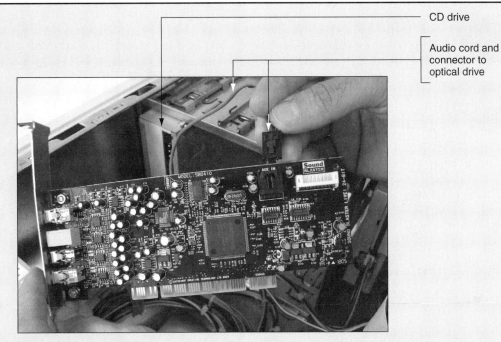

CD drive

Audio cord and connector to optical drive

**Figure 10-3** Connect the wire to the sound card that will make the direct audio connection from the CD drive

4. Remove the cover from the slot opening at the rear of the PC case, and place the card into the PCI slot, making sure that the card is seated firmly. Use the screw taken from the slot cover to secure the card to the back of the PC case.

5. Check again that both ends of the wire are still securely connected and that the wire is not hampering the CPU fan, and then replace the case cover.

**Notes**

Some high-end sound cards have a power connector to provide extra power to the card. For this type of card, connect a power cable with a miniature 4-pin connector to the card. Be careful! Know for certain the purpose of the connector is for power. Don't make the mistake of attaching a miniature power cord designed for a $3\frac{1}{2}$-inch disk drive coming from the power supply to the audio input connector on the sound card. The connections appear to fit, but you'll probably destroy the card by making this connection.

6. Plug in the speakers to the ports at the back of the sound card, and turn on the PC. The speakers might or might not require their own power source. Check the product documentation or manufacturer's Web site for more information.

**Notes**

In this installation, we connected the audio cord from the sound card to a CD drive. However, sometimes you might connect the audio cord to a DVD drive or TV Tuner card.

**Notes**

Some sound cards have a built-in amplifier. If this is the case and you are using a speaker system that includes an amplifier, disable the amplifier on the card either by setting a jumper on the card or by using the utility software that comes with the card. See the card's documentation for instructions.

**A+ ESS**
**1.2**

**A+**
**220-602**
**1.1**

## Installing the Sound Card Driver

After the card is installed, the device drivers must be installed. This installation uses Windows XP, but a Windows 2000 or Windows 9x/Me installation works about the same way (important differences are noted in the steps). That being said, follow these steps using Windows XP to install the sound card drivers:

1. After physically installing the card, turn on the system. When Windows XP starts, it detects that new audio hardware is present. A bubble message appears on the system tray (see Figure 10-4) and the Found New Hardware Wizard opens (see Figure 10-5).

**Figure 10-4**   Windows XP detects new hardware is present

**Figure 10-5**   The Windows XP Found New Hardware Wizard steps you through a hardware installation

2. To use the drivers on the CD that came with the sound card, select **Install from a list or specific location (Advanced)** and click **Next**. (For Windows 9x/Me, in the New Hardware Wizard window, select **Search for the Best Driver for Your Device (Recommended)** and click **Next**.)

> ✎ **Notes**
>
> When Windows 2000/XP is searching for drivers, it is looking for a driver information file that has an .inf extension.

3. The next window in the wizard opens (see Figure 10-6). Select **Search for the best driver in these locations**, and check **Search removable media**. Also check **Include this location in the**

A+ ESS
1.2

A+
220-602
1.1

**search** and verify the CD drive letter is showing. In Figure 10-6, that drive is D:\. Click **Next**. (For Windows 9x/Me, check **Specify a Location**. Click the **Browse** button and point to the driver path, such as **D:\Audio\English\Win98drv** for Windows 98 or **D:\Audio\English\Win2k** for Windows 2000. Click **Next**.)

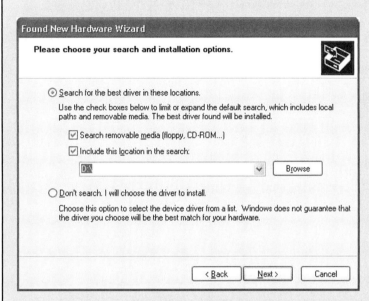

**Figure 10-6** The Found New Hardware Wizard asks for directions for locating driver files

4. Windows XP locates the driver files and loads them. On the final screen of the wizard shown in Figure 10-7, click **Finish**. You're now ready to test the sound card.

**Figure 10-7** The Found New Hardware Wizard has successfully finished the installation

5. To test the sound card, insert a music CD in the optical drive. Depending on how Windows XP is configured, the CD might automatically play, nothing will happen, or, if this is the

first time a music CD has been used with the system, the Audio CD window opens, as shown in Figure 10-8.

**Figure 10-8**   Windows XP asks what to do with the detected music CD

6. Select **Play Audio CD using Windows Media Player** and click **OK**. Windows Media Player launches to play the CD (see Figure 10-9).

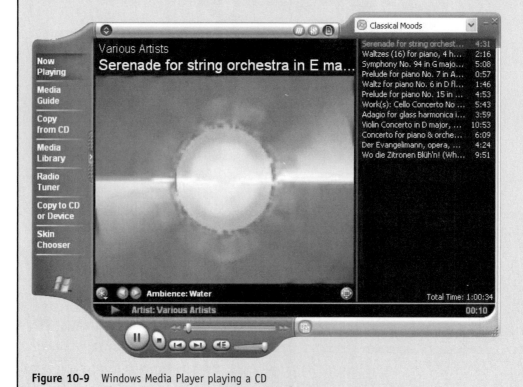

**Figure 10-9**   Windows Media Player playing a CD

A+ ESS
1.2

A+
220-602
1.1

7. The volume might need adjusting. You can adjust the volume by several methods and you might have to use more than one of them to get it right. Here are the ways:

▲ Windows Media Player has a volume control sliding bar, as shown at the bottom of Figure 10-9.

▲ To use the Windows XP volume control, click **Start, All Programs, Accessories, Entertainment, Volume Control.** The Volume Control window opens, as shown in Figure 10-10. Uncheck the **Mute** boxes and adjust the balance and volume.

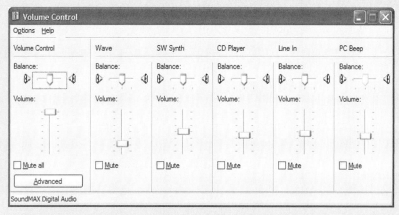

**Figure 10-10**   Windows XP Volume Control window controls volume

▲ You can also use a volume control icon on the taskbar. To create the icon, open the **Sounds and Audio Devices** applet in Control Panel. The Sounds and Audio Devices Properties window opens, as shown in Figure 10-11. Check **Place volume icon in the taskbar** and click **OK.** Adjust or mute the volume using this icon.

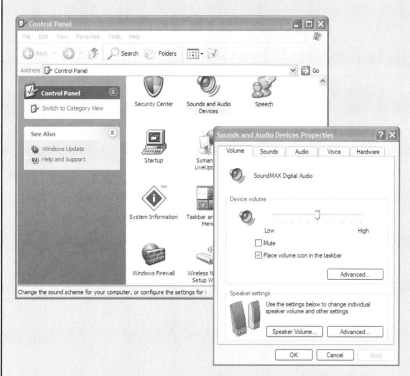

**Figure 10-11**   Use the Sounds and Audio Devices Properties window to place a volume control icon on the taskbar

A+ ESS
1.2

A+
220-602
1.1

◢ Many speakers and amplifiers have on/off switches and volume control buttons used to adjust the noise volume. Also, for notebook computers, look for buttons on the keyboard to adjust volume.

### Recording Sound

As a final test of your sound card, if you have a microphone available, do the following to record a sample sound:

1. Click **Start, All Programs, Accessories, Entertainment**, and **Sound Recorder**. The Sound Recorder opens, as shown in Figure 10-12.

**Figure 10-12** Record sounds using Windows Sound Recorder

2. Click the **Record** button (the red dot in the lower-right corner) to record, and click the Stop button (the black rectangle next to the red dot) when you're done. As a fun test of recording sound, create a welcome message in your own voice. Then, to save the message in a sound file, click **File, Save As**. When you save the sound to a file, Windows uses a Wave file format with the .wav file extension.

3. If you want, you can substitute this .wav file for one of the Windows sounds that plays when you open or close applications, shut down Windows, or perform many other Windows activities that can be accompanied by sound. To change the sounds for various Windows events, go to the Control Panel, open the **Sounds and Audio Devices applet**, and select the **Sounds** tab.

> **Notes**
>
> With most sound cards, the CD containing the sound card driver has application software for the special features offered by the card. Launch the sound card CD to install this software and also look for user manuals stored on the CD and diagnostic software to use if you have a problem with the sound card.

### Notes on Windows 2000/XP Installations

Here are a few additional tips you need to know about installing hardware using Windows 2000/XP:

◢ When installing a hardware device, the Windows XP Found New Hardware Wizard might proceed with the installation using Microsoft drivers without giving you the opportunity to select manufacturer drivers. To prevent this from happening, run the setup program on the manufacturer's CD that is bundled with the card before installing the card. Later, after the card is installed, Windows will use the manufacturer's installed drivers for the card.

▲ When Windows XP installs a device, it verifies that Microsoft has digitally signed the drivers. Depending on how the OS is configured, you might or might not be allowed to keep going if the drivers are not digitally signed. If the drivers have been written for Windows XP, even though they are not certified by Microsoft, they should still work in a Windows XP system.

▲ You must be signed onto Windows XP using an account that has administrative privileges in order to use the Found New Hardware Wizard and install a hardware device. How to set up an administrative account is covered in Chapter 13.

▲ After the installation, you can use Device Manager to verify there are no errors. Open Device Manager, select the device, right-click it, and select Properties on the shortcut menu. Troubleshooting problems with sound cards is covered later in the chapter.

## DIGITAL CAMERAS AND FLASH MEMORY DEVICES

Digital cameras are becoming more popular as quality improves and prices go down. Digital camera technology works much like scanner technology, except it is much faster. It essentially scans the field of image set by the picture taker and translates the light signals into digital values, which can be stored as a file and viewed, manipulated, and printed with software that interprets the stored values appropriately.

TWAIN is a standard format used by digital cameras and scanners for transferring images. You can transfer images from the camera to your computer's hard drive using a cable supplied with the camera. The cable might attach directly to the camera or connect to a cradle the camera sits in to recharge or upload images. The cable can use a USB, FireWire (IEEE 1394), serial, or parallel connection. Also, some cameras use an infrared or other wireless connection. Or, if your computer has a flash card reader and your camera uses a compatible flash card, you can remove the flash card from the camera, insert it in the reader, and upload the images.

Digital cameras can hold their images both in embedded memory that cannot be removed or exchanged and in removable flash memory devices. Both these types of memory retain data without a battery.

A storage device that uses memory chips to store data instead of spinning disks (such as those used by hard drives and CD drives) is called a **solid state device (SSD)**, also called a **solid state disk**. Examples of solid state devices are jump drives (also called key drives or thumb drives), flash memory cards, and solid state disks used as hard drives in notebook computers designed for the most rugged uses.

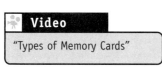
**Video**
"Types of Memory Cards"

Several types of flash memory cards on the market today are shown and described in Table 10-3. These cards might be used in digital cameras, cell phones, MP3 players, handheld computers, digital camcorders, and other portable devices.

| Flash Memory Device | Example |
|---|---|
| *Secure Digital (SD)* cards are the most popular flash memory cards, and currently hold up to 4 GB of data. | SanDisk 2.0GB SD |
| *Multimedia Cards (MMC)* look like SD cards, but the technology is different and they are not interchangeable. Generally, SD cards are faster than MMC cards. | SanDisk 64MB MultiMediaCard |

**Table 10-3**  Flash memory devices

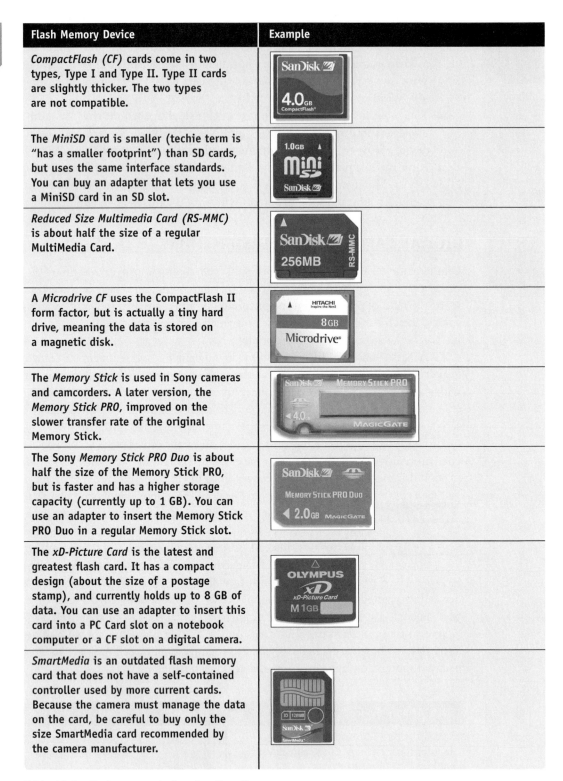

| A+ ESS 1.1 | Flash Memory Device | Example |
|---|---|---|
| | *CompactFlash (CF)* cards come in two types, Type I and Type II. Type II cards are slightly thicker. The two types are not compatible. | |
| | The *MiniSD* card is smaller (techie term is "has a smaller footprint") than SD cards, but uses the same interface standards. You can buy an adapter that lets you use a MiniSD card in an SD slot. | |
| | *Reduced Size Multimedia Card (RS-MMC)* is about half the size of a regular MultiMedia Card. | |
| | A *Microdrive CF* uses the CompactFlash II form factor, but is actually a tiny hard drive, meaning the data is stored on a magnetic disk. | |
| | The *Memory Stick* is used in Sony cameras and camcorders. A later version, the *Memory Stick PRO*, improved on the slower transfer rate of the original Memory Stick. | |
| | The Sony *Memory Stick PRO Duo* is about half the size of the Memory Stick PRO, but is faster and has a higher storage capacity (currently up to 1 GB). You can use an adapter to insert the Memory Stick PRO Duo in a regular Memory Stick slot. | |
| | The *xD-Picture Card* is the latest and greatest flash card. It has a compact design (about the size of a postage stamp), and currently holds up to 8 GB of data. You can use an adapter to insert this card into a PC Card slot on a notebook computer or a CF slot on a digital camera. | |
| | *SmartMedia* is an outdated flash memory card that does not have a self-contained controller used by more current cards. Because the camera must manage the data on the card, be careful to buy only the size SmartMedia card recommended by the camera manufacturer. | |

**Table 10-3**  Flash memory devices (continued)

Figure 10-13 shows a digital camera that uses an xD Picture Card and a USB cable for uploading images, and in Figure 10-14, you can see a Sony digital camera that has a Memory Stick PRO slot. An adapter allows a Memory Stick PRO Duo to use the slot. Another option for storage in a digital camera is a Mini CD-R/RW, which is installed in the digital camera and can also be moved to a computer and read by a regular CD drive.

**10**

**Figure 10-13** This digital camera uses an xD Picture Card and uploads images by way of a USB cable

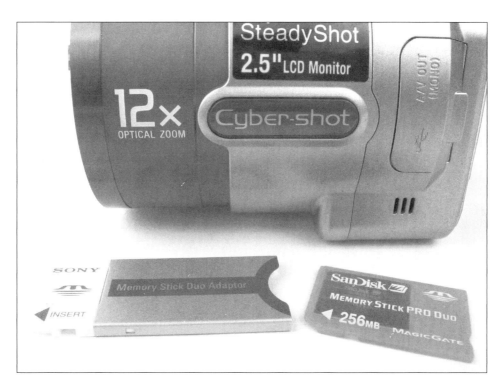

**Figure 10-14** This Sony digital camera has a Memory Stick PRO slot that can accommodate a Memory Stick PRO Duo with adapter; images upload by way of a USB cable

You can use a Web site such as *www.cdnet.com* or *www.compusa.com* to find and compare other digital cameras, storage media, and flash card readers. Select the camera first and then purchase the card storage device the camera supports. Some cameras might come bundled with the storage device.

To transfer images to your PC, to use the software that is bundled with your camera, first install the software. If the camera is designed to work with Windows XP, Windows XP can upload images from the camera without any additional software.

After the images are on the PC, use the camera's image-editing software, or another program such as Adobe PhotoShop, to view, touch up, and print the picture. The picture file, which is usually in **JPEG (Joint Photographic Experts Group)** format, can then be imported into documents. JPEG is a common compression standard for storing photos. Most JPEG files have a .jpg file extension. In addition, a high-end camera might support the uncompressed TIFF format. **TIFF (Tagged Image File Format)** files are larger, but retain more image information and give better results when printing photographs.

> **👍 A+ Tip**
>
> The A+ Essentials exam expects you to know how to install the software bundled with your digital camera before attaching the camera to your PC.

Most digital cameras have a video-out port that allows you to attach the camera to any TV, using a cable provided with the camera. You can then display pictures on TV or copy them to videotape. Table 10-4 lists manufacturers of digital cameras.

| Manufacturer | Web Site |
|---|---|
| Canon | *www.usa.canon.com* |
| Casio | *www.casio.com* |
| Epson | *www.epson.com* |
| Fujifilm | *www.fujifilm.com* |
| Hewlett-Packard | *www.photosmart.com* |
| Kodak | *www.kodak.com* |
| Minolta | *www.minolta.com* |
| Nikon | *www.nikonusa.com* |
| Olympus | *www.olympusamerica.com* |
| Sony | *www.sonystyle.com* |
| Toshiba | *www.toshiba.com* |

**Table 10-4** Digital camera manufacturers

## WEB CAMERAS AND MICROPHONES

>  **A+ Exam Tip**
>
> The A+ Essentials exam expects you to know the purposes and characteristics of digital cameras, Web cameras, and microphones.

A Web camera is a video camera that is used to capture digital video that can be used to feed live video on the Internet. The camera usually connects to a computer by way of a USB, FireWire, composite video, or S-video port. A Web cam refers to both a digital video camera and a Web site that provides a live or prerecorded video broadcast. One interesting Web site, Web Cam Central (*www.camcentral.com*), tracks

A+ ESS
1.1

other Web sites that have Web cams and provides some Web cams of its own. For example, one of the Web cams listed by Web Cam Central is the live Web cam at a marina in Cape Cod, Massachusetts (see Figure 10-15).

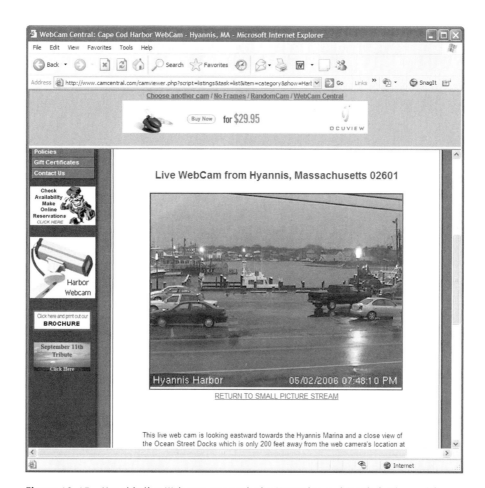

**Figure 10-15** Use this live Web cam to watch the Nantucket and Martha's Vineyard ferry boats come and go

Besides the larger Web cameras used to produce live video for Web cam sites, you can buy an inexpensive Web camera to use for personal chat sessions and video conferencing such as the one shown in Figure 10-16.

First, use the setup CD to install the software and then plug in the Web camera to a USB port. You can use the camera with or without the headset. If you want to include sound in your chat sessions, plug the two sound connectors into the speaker out and microphone in ports on your computer. These ports are embedded in notebook computers, as shown in Figure 10-16. For desktop computers, the ports are part of the sound card or they are onboard ports.

Next, use chat software such as MSN Messenger to create a live video session. For example, when you open MSN Messenger, if you or your chat friend has a Web camera installed, a small camera icon appears in the lower-left corner of your photo (see Figure 10-17). Click it to invite your friend to view your Web camera streaming video.

If you both have a speaker and microphone connected, you can also create a video conferencing session with video and voice. To begin a video conversation with sound, on the menu at the top of the MSN Messenger window, click **Voice**.

**Figure 10-16** This personal Web camera clips to the top of your notebook and comes packaged with an ear clip headset that includes a microphone and speaker

## MP3 PLAYERS

A popular audio compression method is MP3, a method that can reduce the size of a sound file as much as 1:24 without much loss of quality. An MP3 player is a device or software that plays MP3 files. MP3 players are small but can store a lot of information. Figure 10-18 shows a typical MP3 player.

### COMPRESSION METHODS USED WITH MP3 PLAYERS

One of the better-known multimedia data compression standards is MPEG, an international standard for data compression for motion pictures, video, and audio. Developed by the **Moving Pictures Experts Group (MPEG)**, it tracks movement from one frame to the next and stores only what changes, rather than compressing individual frames. MPEG compression can yield a compression ratio of 100:1 for full-motion video (30 frames per second, or 30 fps).

Use this icon to start a video session

**Figure 10-17** Instant Messenger session using a Web camera

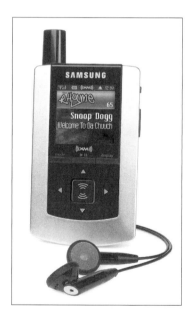

**Figure 10-18** The portable Samsung Helix XM2go is an XM Satellite Radio and MP3 player

Currently, several MPEG standards are available: MPEG-1, MPEG-2, and MPEG-4. MPEG-1 is used to compress audio on CD and is the basis for MP3. MPEG-2 is used to compress video films on DVD. MPEG-3 was never fully developed or used. MPEG-4 is used for video transmissions over the Internet.

MPEG compression is possible because it cuts out or drastically reduces sound that is not normally heard by the human ear. In the regular audio CD format (uncompressed), one minute of music takes up about 10 MB of storage. The same minute of music in MP3 format takes only about 1 MB of memory. This makes it possible to download music in minutes rather than hours. Sound files downloaded from the Internet are most often MP3 files. MP3 files have an .mp3 file extension. For more information about MPEG and MP3, see *www.mpeg.org*.

## HOW MP3 PLAYERS WORK

Most portable MP3 players today store MP3 files in onboard memory or hard drives, which can be expanded using an add-on flash memory card, such as SecureDigital, CompactFlash, or Memory Stick. MP3 files are downloaded from the PC to the MP3 player, in contrast to a digital camera, which transfers or uploads data to the PC.

You can purchase and download MP3 music files from Web sites such as EMusic (*www.emusic.com*) and MP3.com (*www.mp3.com*). After the files are downloaded to your PC, you can play them on your PC using MP3 player software such as Windows Media Player or MusicMatch Jukebox (see *www.musicmatch.com*), transfer them to a portable MP3 player, or convert them into an audio CD if your computer has a writable CD drive. There are also CD/MP3 players that can play CDs in either standard audio format or MP3-format. A CD can store 10 hours or more of music in MP3 format. You can also play the MP3 files directly from the Internet without first downloading them, which is called **streaming audio**. MP3 files are generally transferred to portable devices using a USB or FireWire cable.

Also, you can convert files from your regular music CDs into MP3 files (a process called ripping because the copyright owner of the music is considered to be ripped off), and play them on your computer or download them to an MP3 player. "Ripper" software copies the music file from the CD, and encoder software compresses the file into MP3 format. CD rippers, MP3 encoders, and MP3 player software can be downloaded from the Internet. For example, see the MusicMatch site at *www.musicmatch.com*.

Table 10-5 lists some manufacturers of MP3 players.

| Manufacturer | Web Site |
| --- | --- |
| Apple Computers | *www.apple.com* |
| Creative Labs | *www.creative.com* |
| Dell | *www.dell.com* |
| Intel | *www.intel.com* |
| MachSpeed | *www.machspeed.com* |
| Panasonic | *www.panasonic.com* |
| Pine Technology | *www.xfxforce.com* |
| Rio (was SONICblue) | *www.rioaudio.com* |
| Samsung | *www.samsungusa.com* |
| SanDisk | *www.sandisk.com* |
| Sony | *www.sonystyle.com* |

**Table 10-5** MP3 player manufacturers

A+ ESS
1.1

## MIDI DEVICES

MIDI (stands for "musical instrument digital interface" and pronounced "middy") is a set of standards that are used to represent music in digital form. Whereas MP3 is a method of storing a sound file in compressed format, MIDI is a method of digitally describing and storing every individual note played by each individual instrument used in making music. With MIDI files and MIDI software, you can choose to listen to only a single instrument being played or change one note played by that instrument. MIDI can be used to creatively produce synthesized music, mute one instrument or voice, and edit a song with your own voice or instrument. MIDI standards are used to connect electronic music equipment, such as keyboards and mixers, or to connect this equipment to a PC for input and output.

Most sound cards can play MIDI files, and most electronic instruments have MIDI ports. To mix and edit music using MIDI on your PC, you'll need MIDI editing software such as JAMMER Professional by SoundTrek (*www.soundtrek.com*).

> **⊕ A+ Exam Tip**
>
> The A+ Essentials exam expects you to know about MIDI input devices, ports, and cables.

A MIDI port is a 5-pin DIN port that looks like a keyboard port, only larger. Figure 10-19 shows MIDI ports on electronic drums. A MIDI port is either an input port or an output port, but not both. Normally, you would connect the MIDI output port to a mixer, but you can also use it to connect to a PC. If your PC does not have MIDI ports, you can use a MIDI-to-USB cable like the one in Figure 10-20. The two MIDI connectors on the cable are for input and output.

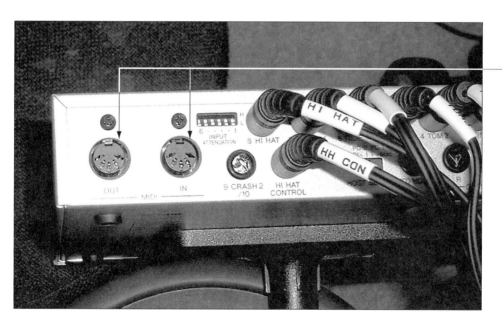

5-pin MIDI-out and MIDI-in ports

**Figure 10-19**   MIDI ports on an electronic drum set

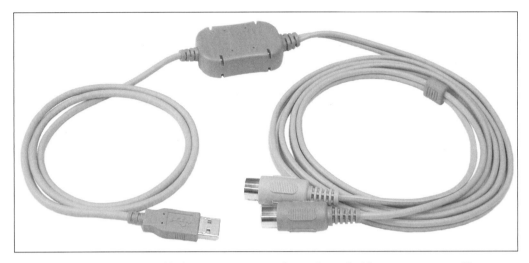

**Figure 10-20**    MIDI-to-USB cable lets you connect an electronic musical instrument to your PC

Some keyboards have a USB port to interface with a PC using MIDI data transmissions. For example, the keyboard shown in Figure 10-21 has a USB port and can output sound to a PC or receive standard MIDI files (SMF) to play.

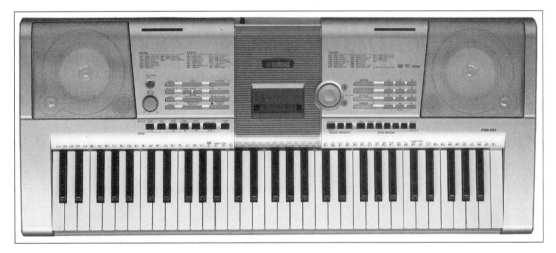

**Figure 10-21**    This keyboard by Yamaha has a USB port to be used as a MIDI interface

## TV TUNER AND VIDEO CAPTURE CARDS

A TV **tuner card** can turn your computer into a television. A port on the card receives input from a TV cable and lets you view television on your computer monitor. A **video capture card** lets you capture this video input and save it to a file on your hard drive. Some cards are a combination TV tuner card and video capture card, making it possible for you to receive television input and save that input to your hard drive. A high-end TV tuner/video capture card might also serve as your video card. And, too, some motherboards and notebook computers have onboard TV tuners and TV captures, such as the notebook shown in Figure 10-22.

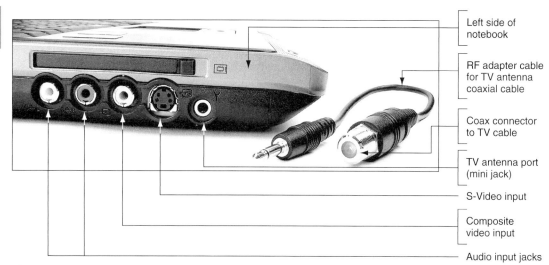

Left side of notebook

RF adapter cable for TV antenna coaxial cable

Coax connector to TV cable

TV antenna port (mini jack)

S-Video input

Composite video input

Audio input jacks

**Figure 10-22** This notebook computer has embedded TV tuner and video capture abilities

To use this notebook to watch TV and capture live TV, plug in a TV coaxial cable (also called "coax" for short) to the RF adapter that is included, which plugs into the antenna mini-jack. Other ports labeled in Figure 10-22 can be used to capture input from a camcorder or VCR or input data from other audio and video equipment that use these audio input, composite video, and S-video ports. Using a cable with a standard RCA cable harness (red, white, and yellow ports), such as the one in Figure 10-23, you can use this notebook to display and/or record data from a DVD player or game box. The cable in Figure 10-23 connects to an Xbox.

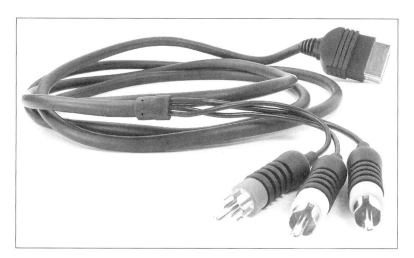

**Figure 10-23** Standard RCA cable harness connects to digital game box

**A+ ESS
1.1**

Captured video can be saved as motion clips or stills and then edited. With the right card and software, you can create your own video and animated CDs and DVDs. To help you select a video capture card, look for these features on the card, which follow the standards created by the NTSC (National Television Standards Committee) for the USA:

- The port and interface the camera uses with your PC, which might be a FireWire (IEEE 1394), S-video, or composite video port
- Data transfer rates, which affect price
- Capture resolution and color-depth capabilities
- Ability to transfer data back to a digital camcorder or VCR
- Stereo audio jacks
- Video-editing software bundled with the card

For a TV tuner card, look for these features:

- Ability to do instant replay and program scheduling
- Input ports for coaxial cable TV, TV antenna, video equipment, and game boxes
- TV or VCR port for output
- Remote control so you can flip TV channels from across the room

For a desktop system, expect a TV tuner or video capture card to fit into a PCI, PCI Express x16, or AGP slot. Some take the place of your regular video card and some install beside it. One example of a TV tuner and video capture card is the AVerTV PVR 150 Plus PCI card shown in Figure 10-24.

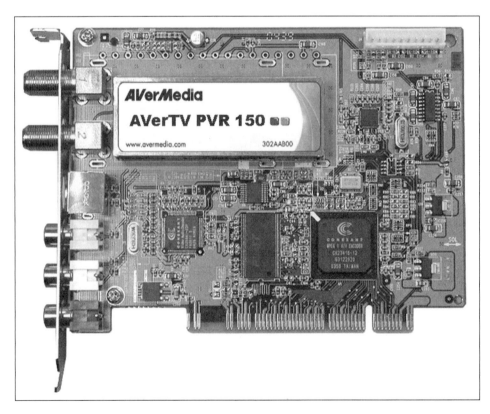

**Figure 10-24**  The AVerTV PVR 150 video capture and TV tuner card by AVerMedia uses a PCI slot and works alongside a regular video card

Also, an external device can be used as a TV tuner and to capture video and stills. For notebook computers, the device can use the PC Card slot, or it can use a USB port. One example is the WinTV-USB device by Hauppauge Computer Works shown in Figure 10-25. It connects to a USB port and comes with a cord to connect to the Line-in port of a sound card.

**Figure 10-25** Use this USB device to watch TV on your desktop or notebook computer and capture video and stills

Table 10-6 lists some manufacturers of TV tuner and video capture cards.

| Manufacturer | Web Site |
|---|---|
| ASUS | *www.asus.com* |
| ATI | *www.ati.com* |
| AVerMedia | *www.aver.com* |
| Creative Labs | *www.creative.com* |
| Hauppauge Computer Works | *www.hauppauge.com* |
| Matrox | *www.matrox.com* |
| Pinnacle Systems | *www.pinnaclesys.com* |
| Sabrent | *www.sabrent.com* |

**Table 10-6** Video capture card manufacturers

## *OPTICAL STORAGE TECHNOLOGY*

CDs and DVDs are popular storage media for multimedia data, and CDs are the most popular way of distributing software. Both DVD and CD technologies use patterns of tiny pits on the surface of a disc to represent bits, which a laser beam can then read. This is why they are called optical storage technologies. CD (compact disc) drives use the **CDFS (Compact Disc File System)** or the **UDF (Universal Disk Format) file system,** and DVD drives use the newer UDF file system.

Windows supports both file systems, which include several standards used for audio, photographs, video, and other data. Most CD drives support several CDFS formats, and most DVD drives support several UDF formats and the CDFS format for backward compatibility. In this section, you will learn about the major optical storage technologies, including their similarities and differences, their storage capacities, and variations within each type.

### USING CDs

Of the multimedia components discussed in this chapter, the most popular is the CD drive. CDs are used to distribute software, sound files, and other multimedia files. CD drives are read-only devices or read/writable.

During the manufacturing process, data can be written to a CD only once because the data is actually embedded in the surface of the disc. Figure 10-26 shows a CD surface laid out as one continuous spiral of sectors of equal length that hold equal amounts of data. If laid out in a straight line, this spiral would be 3.5 miles long. The surface of a CD stores data as pits and lands. **Lands** are raised areas or bumps, and **pits** are recessed areas on the surface; each represents either a 1 or a 0, respectively. The bits are read by the drive with a laser beam that distinguishes between a pit and a land by the amount of deflection or scattering that occurs when the light beam hits the surface.

**Figure 10-26** The spiral layout of sectors on a CD surface

During manufacturing, the plastic CD is imprinted with lands and pits (the process is called burning the CD) and then covered with a thin coat of aluminum (see Figure 10-27). An acrylic surface is added to protect the data, and finally a label is imprinted on the top of the CD.

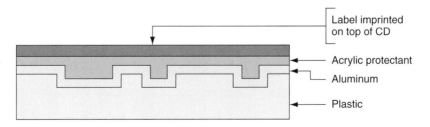

**Figure 10-27** A CD is constructed of plastic, aluminum, and acrylic

A+ ESS
1.1

A+
220-602
1.1

When a CD drive reads a CD, a small motor with an actuator arm moves the laser beam to the sector on the track it needs to read. If the disc were spinning at a constant speed, the speed near the center of the disc would be greater than the speed at the outer edge. However, the laser beam needs to read each sector at the same constant speed. To create this effect of constant speed as the disc turns, called **constant linear velocity (CLV)**, the CD drive uses a mechanism that slows down the disc when the laser beam is near the center of the disc, and speeds up the disc when the laser beam is near the outer edge. Thus, the beam is over a sector for the same amount of time, no matter where the sector is.

The transfer rate of the first CD drives was about 150 kilobytes per second of data (150 KBps), with the rpm (revolutions per minute) set to 200 when the laser was near the center of the disc and 500 at the outer edge. This transfer rate was about right for audio CDs. To show video and motion without a choppy effect, however, the speed of the drives was increased to double speed (150KBps × 2), quad speed (150KBps × 4), and so on. CD drives with speeds at 52x and 56x (52 and 56 times the audio speed) are not uncommon now. Audio CDs must still drop to the original speeds of 200 to 500 rpm and a transfer rate of 150 KBps. Some later CD drives use CLV technology in combination with **constant angular velocity (CAV)**. With CAV, the disc rotates at a constant speed, just as is done with hard drives.

> **Notes**
>
> When you choose a CD drive, look for the multisession feature, which means that the drive can read a disc that has been created in multiple sessions. To say a disc was created in **multisessions** means that data was written to the disc at different times rather than in a single long session.

>  **Tip**
>
> Some CD drives have power-saving features controlled by the device driver. For example, when the drive waits for a command for more than five minutes, it enters Power Save Mode, causing the spindle motor to stop. The restart is automatic when the drive receives a command.

## CD-ROM, CD-R, AND CD-RW

If a CD drive can only read a CD and not write to it, the drive is called a CD-ROM drive. Two types of CD drives that can record or write to a CD are **CD-R (CD-recordable)** drives and **CD-RW (CD-rewritable)** drives, the latter of which allow you to overwrite old data with new data. CD-RW drives have made CD-R drives outdated.

You can buy three different kinds of discs: a regular CD disc (purchased with data already burned on it), a CD-R disc (to write to once), or a CD-RW disc (to write and overwrite). CD-RW discs cost more than CD-R discs. You can tell the difference between a CD and a CD-R or CD-RW disc by the color of the bottom of the disc. CD-R and CD-RW discs are blue, black, or some other color, and CDs are silver. A CD-RW drive can burn either a CD-R or CD-RW disc, but for the drive to overwrite old data, you must use a more expensive CD-RW disc. One drawback of using CD-RW discs is that these discs cannot be read by some older CD-ROM drives or audio CD players.

> **Notes**
>
> CD-RW discs are useful in developing CDs for distribution. A developer can create a disc, test for errors, and rewrite to the disc without wasting many discs during development. After the disc is fully tested, CD-R discs can be burned for distribution. These discs cost less than CD-RW discs and are more likely to work with older CD drives.

# APPLYING | CONCEPTS

Windows XP can burn a CD without any extra software installed. It's very simple; first select all files you want to burn on the CD. To do that, right-click a file and select Send To from the shortcut menu, or you can drag and drop the file onto the CD-RW drive. Then select CD-RW drive (see Figure 10-28). After all files are selected, the next step is to burn the CD. Using My Computer, double-click the CD-RW drive. The files you have selected will appear in the right pane (see Figure 10-29). To burn the CD, click **Write these files to CD**.

If you plan to burn a lot of CDs or want to create music or video CDs, you might want to use software designed for that purpose to make your job easier. Some CD-RW drives come bundled with burn software. One example is Nero by Nero Inc. (*www.nero.com*).

When purchasing a CD-R/RW drive, know that some drives are multisession drives, and some are not. Also many CD-RW drives can also read a DVD. These drives are called combo drives, and are becoming popular as the prices of optical drives continue to drop.

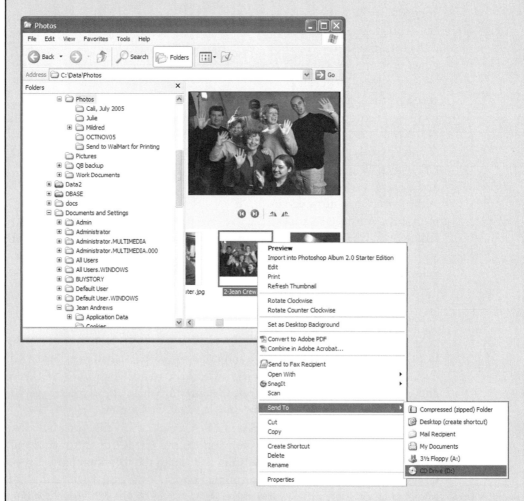

**Figure 10-28**   Using Windows XP, the first step to burn a CD is to select files for the CD

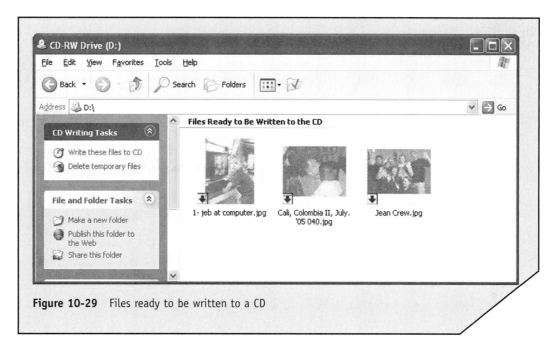

**Figure 10-29** Files ready to be written to a CD

## HOW AN OPTICAL DRIVE CAN INTERFACE WITH THE MOTHERBOARD

When you purchase a CD or DVD drive, consider how the drive will interface with the system. Optical drives can interface with the motherboard in several ways:

▲ Using a parallel ATA interface (also called an EIDE interface); the drive can share an EIDE connection and cable with another drive. However, know that if the other drive is a hard drive, hard drive performance might suffer. Parallel ATA is the most popular interface method for CD and DVD drives, and is also used by tape drives and Zip drives.

▲ Using a serial ATA interface (also called a SATA interface); the drive is the only drive on the serial ATA cable. Serial ATA optical drives are not yet commonplace, but are expected to eventually be more popular than parallel ATA drives.

▲ Using a SCSI interface with a SCSI host adapter.

▲ Using a portable drive and plugging into an external port on your PC, such as a USB port, FireWire port, or SCSI port.

## INSTALLING A CD DRIVE

Once installed, the CD or CD-RW drive becomes another drive on your system, such as drive D or E. After it is installed, you access it just like any other drive by typing D: or E: at the command prompt, or by accessing the drive through Windows Explorer or My Computer.

Currently, the most popular interface for an optical drive is parallel ATA, also called EIDE. Figure 10-30 shows the rear of an EIDE CD drive. Note the jumper bank that can be set to cable select, slave, or master. Recall from Chapter 8 that, for EIDE, there are four choices for drive installations: primary master, primary slave, secondary master, and secondary slave. If the drive will be the second drive installed on the cable, then set the drive to slave. If the drive is the only drive on

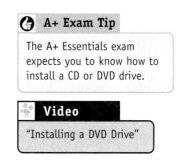

🔔 **A+ Exam Tip**

The A+ Essentials exam expects you to know how to install a CD or DVD drive.

**Video**

"Installing a DVD Drive"

A+ ESS
1.1
1.2

A+
220-602
1.1

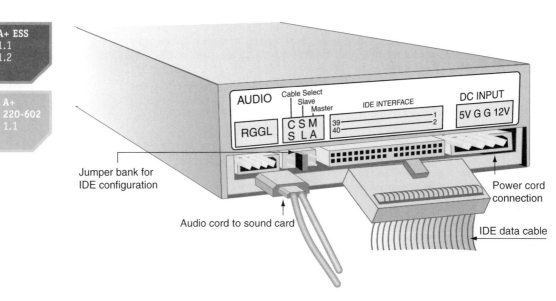

**Figure 10-30** Rear view of an EIDE CD drive

the cable, choose master, because single is not a choice. The cable select setting is used if a special EIDE cable-select cable determines which drive is master or slave. If the CD drive shares an IDE channel with a hard drive, make the hard drive the master and the CD drive the slave.

> **Notes**
>
> Computer standards can have confusing and often contradicting names. To be correct, the standard for the drive interface in Figure 10-30 is parallel ATA, but the industry loosely uses the term EIDE to describe the standard. And sometimes a manufacturer uses an incorrect term to describe its products. Look at Figure 10-30 where the manufacturer labeled its CD drive's interface as an IDE connection when it really meant an EIDE connection. You should also know that most motherboard manufacturers label their EIDE connections as IDE connections.

> **Notes**
>
> For ATA/100 hard drives and above, you use an 80-conductor IDE cable for the hard drive on one channel and a regular 40-conductor cable for the CD drive on the other channel.

When given the choice of putting the CD drive on the same cable with a hard drive or on its own cable, choose to use its own cable. A CD drive that shares a cable with a hard drive can slow down the hard drive's performance. Most systems today have two EIDE connections on the motherboard, probably labeled IDE1 and IDE2, so most likely you will be able to use IDE2 for the CD drive.

**APPLYING | CONCEPTS** Follow these general steps to install a CD or DVD drive, using safety precautions to protect the system against ESD:

1. A computer case has some wide bays for DVD and CD drives and some narrow ones for hard drives, Zip drives, and floppy drives. Open the case and decide which large bay to use for the drive. If you use the top bay, the drive will be up and out of the way of other components inside the case.

A+ ESS
1.1
1.2

A+
220-602
1.1

2. Older cases use screws to secure the drive to the sides of the bay, and some bays have a clipping mechanism to secure the drive. The bay in Figure 10-31 has a clipping mechanism. For this bay, using two fingers, squeeze the two clips on each side of the bay together to release them and pull them forward. Remove the faceplate from the front of the bay.

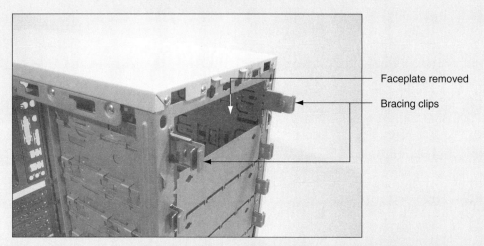

Faceplate removed

Bracing clips

**Figure 10-31**  To prepare a large bay for an optical drive, punch out the faceplate and pull the bracing clips forward

3. Slide the drive into the bay (see Figure 10-32). To see how far to push the drive into the bay, align it with the front of the case, as shown in Figure 10-33.

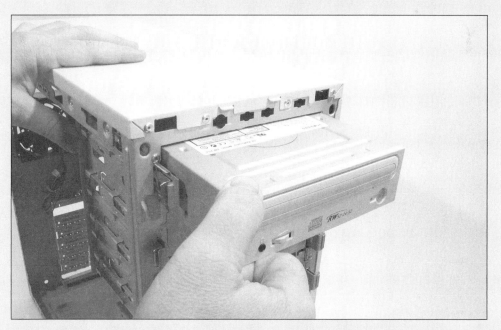

**Figure 10-32**  Slide the optical drive into the bay

A+ ESS
1.1
1.2

A+
220-602
1.1

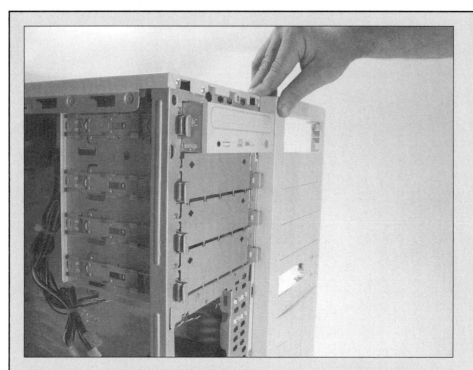

**Figure 10-33**    To judge how far to insert the optical drive in the bay, align it with the front of the case

4. To secure the drive, push the clips back into position. For bays that use screws, put two screws on each side of the drive, tightening the screws so the drive can't shift, but avoiding overtightening them. Use the screws that come with the drive; screws that are too long can damage the drive. If necessary, buy a mounting kit to extend the sides of the drive so that it fits into the bay and attaches securely.

5. Connect a power cord to the drive.

6. For EIDE drives, connect the 40-pin cable to the IDE motherboard connector and the drive, being careful to follow the pin 1 rule: Match the edge color on the cable to pin 1 on both the adapter card and the drive. Generally, the colored edge is closest to the power connector.

7. Attach one end of the audio cord to the drive and the other end to the sound card or, for onboard sound, to the motherboard. Figure 10-34 shows an audio cord connected to the motherboard.

**Figure 10-34**    The audio cable connected to the audio connector on the motherboard; the other end of the cable is connected to the optical drive

8. Some drives have a ground connection, with one end of the ground cable attaching to the computer case. Follow the directions included with the drive.

9. Check all connections and turn on the power. Press the eject button on the front of the drive. If it works, then you know power is getting to the drive. Put the case cover back on.

10. Turn on the PC. Windows launches the Found New Hardware Wizard. Windows supports EIDE CD drives using its own internal drivers without add-on drivers, so the installation of drivers requires little intervention on your part. If the Found New Hardware Wizard does not launch, go to the Control Panel and double-click the **Add Hardware** icon to launch the Add New Hardware Wizard. Click **Next** when you are prompted to begin installing the software for the new device. Complete the installation by following the directions of the Add New Hardware Wizard.

11. The drive is now ready to use. Press the eject button to open the drive shelf, and place a CD or DVD in the drive. Now access the disc using Windows Explorer.

### Notes

If you have a problem reading a CD, verify that you placed the CD in the tray label-side-up and that the format is compatible with your drive. If one CD doesn't work, try another—the first CD might be defective or scratched. When installing an optical drive that burns CDs or DVDs, after you have verified the drive can read a disc, if you are using Windows XP, you can burn a CD to verify that function. If burning software came bundled with the drive, now is the time to install it.

### Notes

A CD drive can be set so that when you insert a CD, software on the CD automatically executes, a feature called Autorun or Autoplay. To turn the feature on using Windows 9x/Me, open **Device Manager**, right-click the CD drive, and select **Properties**. In the Properties dialog box, select the **Settings** tab and then select **Auto insert notification**. For Windows XP, many options for managing content on CDs are available. To customize how Windows XP handles a CD, open **My Computer**, right-click the drive, and select **Properties** from the shortcut menu. The CD drive Properties dialog box opens; click the **Autoplay** tab (see Figure 10-35).

To prevent a CD from automatically playing when Autoplay is enabled, hold down the Shift key when inserting the CD.

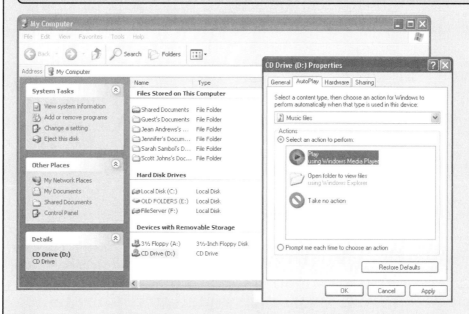

**Figure 10-35**  For Windows XP, use My Computer to tell the OS how to handle the Autoplay feature for your CD drive

A+ ESS
1.1

A+
220-602
1.1

## USING DVDs

For years, the multimedia industry struggled to come up with an inexpensive storage media that would conveniently hold a full-length movie. That goal was met by more than one technology, but the technology that has clearly taken the lead is **DVD** (**digital video disc** or **digital versatile disc**); see Figure 10-36. It takes up to seven CDs to store a full-length movie, but it only requires one DVD. A DVD can hold 8.5 GB of data, and if both the top and bottom surfaces are used, it can hold 17 GB of data, which is enough for more than eight hours of video storage. Recall that DVD uses the Universal Disk Format (UDF) file system.

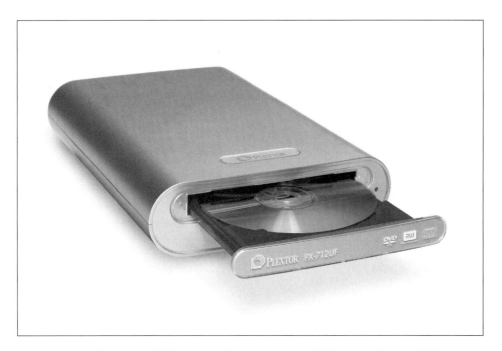

**Figure 10-36**    This external DVD drive by Plextor can use an IEEE 1394 or Hi-Speed USB connection and supports several speeds and read/write standards, including 8X DVD+R, 16X DVD+R/RW, 12X DVD-ROM, 16X CD-R write, 48X CD-RW rewrite, and 40X CD read

**Notes**

The discrepancy in the computer industry between one billion bytes (1,000,000,000 bytes) and 1 GB (1,073,741,824 bytes) exists because 1 KB equals 1,024 bytes. Even though documentation might say that a DVD holds 17 GB, in fact it holds 17 billion bytes, which is only 15.90 GB.

### DISTINGUISHING BETWEEN A DVD AND A CD

When you look at the surface of a CD and a DVD, it is difficult to distinguish between the two. They both have the same 5-inch diameter and 1.2-mm thickness, and the same shiny surface. However, a DVD can use both the top and bottom surface for data. If the top of the disc has no label, data is probably written on it, and it is most likely a DVD. Because a DVD uses a shorter wavelength laser, it can read smaller, more densely packed pits, which increases the disc's capacity. In addition, a second layer is added to the DVD, an opaque layer that also holds data and almost doubles the capacity of the disc. Compare the drawing of a CD in Figure 10-27, which has only a single layer of data on the bottom of the disc to the drawing of a DVD in Figure 10-37, in which the DVD has double layers on both the top and bottom.

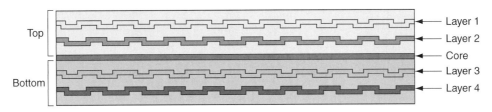

**Figure 10-37** A DVD can hold data in double layers on both the top and bottom of the disc yielding a maximum capacity of 17 GB

## STORAGE ON A DVD

The different amounts of data that can be stored on a DVD depend on these factors:

Single-sided, single-layer DVD can hold 4.7 GB of data

Single-sided, double-layer DVD can hold 8.5 GB of data

Double-sided, single-layer DVD can hold 9.4 GB of data

Double-sided, double-layer DVD can hold 17 GB of data

A DVD-ROM drive should be able to read a DVD that uses any one of the four methods of storing data.

Audio data is stored on a DVD in Dolby AC-3 compression or Surround Sound format discussed earlier in the chapter. For video data, DVD uses MPEG-2 video compression and requires MPEG-2 decoder software to decompress and decode the DVD compressed data. Current DVD drives use MPEG decoder software that comes bundled with the drive, and Windows XP has its own internal decoder software. For earlier DVD drives, this MPEG software was stored as firmware on an MPEG decoder card that came bundled with the DVD drive. The MPEG decoder card and the drive were installed at the same time.

## DVD STANDARDS

Besides DVD-ROM drives that read DVDs, some DVD drives can write to DVD discs. Table 10-7 describes the DVD standards used for reading and writing. All have similar but

| DVD Standard | Description |
|---|---|
| DVD-ROM | Read-only. A DVD-ROM drive can also read CDs. |
| DVD-R | DVD recordable. Uses a similar technology to CD-R drives. Holds about 4.7 GB of data. |
| DVD-R Dual Layer (DL) | DVD recordable in two layers. Doubles storage to 8.5 GB of data on one surface. |
| DVD-RW | Rewritable DVD. Also known as erasable, recordable device. Media can be read by most DVD-ROM drives. |
| DVD+R | DVD recordable is similar to and competes with DVD-R. Holds about 4.7 GB of data. |
| DVD+R Double Layer (DL) | DVD recordable in two layers. Doubles storage to 8.5 GB of data on one surface. |
| DVD+RW | Rewritable DVD. Uses DVD+R technology. |
| DVD-RAM | Recordable and erasable. DVD-RAM discs are sometimes stored in cartridges. The standard is supported by Toshiba, Hitachi, and Panasonic, who say future DVD-RAM discs will hold up to 50 GB of data. |

**Table 10-7** DVD standards

not identical features, so compatibility of standards is an issue. Most DVD drives support several competing standards. When buying a DVD drive, look for the standards it supports and also look for its ability to burn CDs.

To be sure your DVD burner is compatible with most discs, choose one that supports both DVD-R and DVD+R formats. For rewriteable formats, the best DVD burners support DVD-RW and DVD+RW. (DVD-RAM is not yet that common.) When selecting a DVD drive, also consider the write-once speeds and the rewriteable speeds. Current maximum speeds for write-once are 16X for DVD-R SL and DVD+R SL, 6X for DVD-R DL, and 8X for DVD+R DL. Current maximum speeds for rewritable burners are 6X for DVD-RW, 8X for DVD+RW, and 12X for DVD-RAM.

> **A+ Exam Tip**
>
> The A+ Essentials exam expects you to know about the drive speeds and media types of CD and DVD drives.

> **Notes**
>
> A DVD combo drive supports many formats and speeds. For example, the Plextor PX-716SA Dual Layer DVD Writer supports DVD+R, DVD-R, DVD+RW, DVD-RW, CD-R, and CD-RW. It has double layer capability, burns at 6X to 48X speeds, and uses a serial ATA interface to the motherboard.

Two new and competing DVD formats are HD-DVD (high-density DVD) and Blu-ray Disc, both using blue laser formats. HD-DVD can hold up to 30 GB of data, and Blu-ray can hold up to 50 GB of data. Each standard is backed by a strong consortium of industry leaders, and both groups claim to be the solution for the confusing and complex DVD standards that plague the current market. For more information about HD-DVD, see *www.dvdsite.org*, and for information about Blu-ray, see *www.blu-raydisc.com*.

## INSTALLING A DVD DRIVE

A DVD drive looks like a CD drive and is installed the same way. Instructions for installing an optical drive are given earlier in the chapter, and there's no need to repeat them here.

Figure 10-38 shows the front and rear of a DVD drive. Just as with a CD drive, you will need to connect the power cord, EIDE data cable, and audio cord to the drive. This DVD drive has two connectors for the audio cord. The 4-pin connector is used for analog sound and the 2-pin connector is used for digital sound. Most often you'll use the 4-pin analog connection to connect to a sound card or to the motherboard. The 2-pin connector is seldom used because Windows XP transfers digital sound from the drive to the sound card without the use of a direct cable connection.

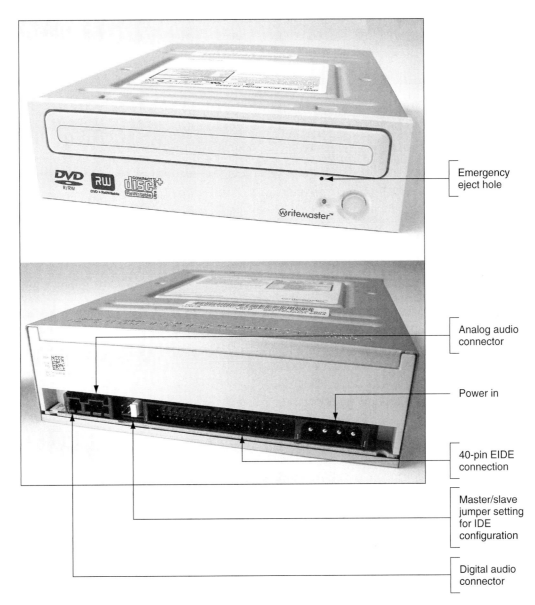

Emergency
eject hole

Analog audio
connector

Power in

40-pin EIDE
connection

Master/slave
jumper setting
for IDE
configuration

Digital audio
connector

**Figure 10-38** Front and rear of a DVD drive

## CARING FOR OPTICAL DRIVES AND DISCS

Most problems with CD and DVD discs are caused by dust, fingerprints, scratches, surface defects, or random electrical noise. Also, a CD or DVD drive will not properly read a CD or DVD when the drive is standing vertically, such as when someone turns a desktop PC case on its side to save desk space.

Use these precautions when handling CDs or DVDs:

▲ Hold the disc by the edge; do not touch the bright side of the disc where data is stored.

▲ To remove dust or fingerprints, use a clean, soft, dry cloth. Don't wipe the disc in a circular motion. Always wipe from the center of the disc out toward the edge.

▲ Don't paste paper on the surface of a CD. Don't paste any labels on the top of the CD, because this can imbalance the CD and cause the drive to vibrate. You can label a CD using a felt-tip pin. Don't label a DVD if both sides hold data.

A+ ESS
1.1
1.2
1.4

A+
220-602
1.1
1.2
1.3

▲ Don't subject a disc to heat or leave it in direct sunlight.

▲ Don't make the center hole larger.

▲ Don't bend a disc.

▲ Don't drop a disc or subject it to shock.

▲ If a disc gets stuck in the drive, use the emergency eject hole to remove it. Turn off the power to the PC first. Then insert an instrument such as a straightened paper clip into the hole to eject the tray manually.

▲ When closing a CD or DVD tray, don't push on the tray. Press the close button on the front of the drive.

▲ Don't use cleaners, alcohol, and the like on a disc unless you use a cleaning solution specifically designed for optical discs like the cleaning kit in Figure 10-39. Using this kit, you can spray the cleaning solution on a disc and then wipe it off with the soft purple cloth. To fix a scratch on a disc, use the repair solution made of aluminum oxide. Apply a small amount to the scratch and gently rub it with the yellow cloth. Then clean the disc using the cleaning solution.

> **📝 Notes**
>
> A CD, CD-R, CD-RW, or DVD is expected to hold its data for many years; however, you can prolong the life of a disc by protecting it from exposure to light.

Optical drive technologies are interesting to study. For the tech-hungry reader, I suggest you check out the animated explanation at the Web site of HowStuffWorks, Inc. (*www.howstuffworks.com*). Table 10-8 lists manufacturers of optical drives.

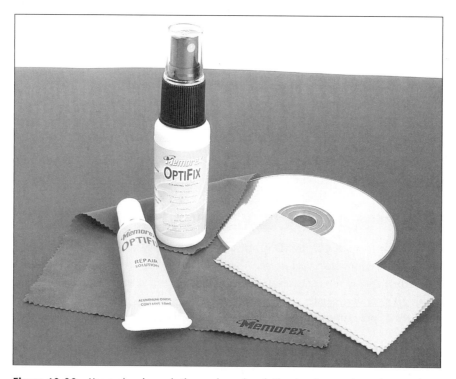

**Figure 10-39** Use a cleaning solution and repair solution to clean and repair scratches on optical discs

| Manufacturer | Web Site |
|---|---|
| Addonics | www.addonics.com |
| ASUS | www.asus.com |
| BenQ | www.benq.com |
| Creative Labs | www.creative.com |
| Hewlett-Packard | www.hp.com |
| IBM | www.ibm.com |
| Intel | www.intel.com |
| Panasonic | www.panasonic.com |
| Pioneer | www.pioneerelectronics.com |
| Plextor | www.plextor.com |
| Samsung | www.samsung.com |
| Sony Electronics | www.sonystyle.com |
| Toshiba | www.toshiba.com |

**Table 10-8** Optical drive manufacturers

## HARDWARE USED FOR BACKUPS AND FAULT TOLERANCE

A+ ESS
1.1

A+
220-602
1.1

How valuable is your data? How valuable is your software? In many cases, the most valuable component on the desktop is not the hardware or the software, but the data. Think about each computer you support. What would happen if the hard drive failed? You should create backups to prepare for that situation. Whether your hard drive contains a large database or just a few word-processing files, make backups. Never keep an important file on only one medium. Make a copy to a disc, file server, or tape backup. In addition, consider keeping some of your backups in an off-site location.

Your backup policy depends on what you are backing up and your organization's policies. If you use your PC to interface with a server, for example, and all data is stored on the server and not on the PC, then you will only back up software. (The person responsible for the server usually backs up the data. You might want to check with the responsible party in your organization to make sure this is being done.) If you keep original application CDs in a safe place, and if you have multiple copies of them, you might decide not to back up the applications. In this case, if a hard drive fails, your chore is to reload several software packages.

In a business environment, if you keep important data on your PC, the easiest way to maintain a backup is to back up the data to another computer on the network. In this situation, there's always the chance that data on both the PC and the other computer can become corrupted. However, if the other computer is a file server, most likely it has its own automated backup utility to back up to either tape or a larger mainframe computer. Before you back up to the server, check with the server administrator to make sure that space is available and company policy allows you to do this.

If you keep important data on your PC in your home or small office, you need to seriously consider a sophisticated backup method. Plan for the worst case! You might decide to install a second hard drive and back up the data to this drive, or you could use an external hard drive. Another solution is a good tape backup system or other removable media such as CDs or DVDs. If your computer is networked to other computers, you can back up to another computer on the network. Of all the backup methods, backing up to another computer on a LAN is probably the simplest.

If you travel a lot, keeping good backups of data on your notebook computer might be a problem. Several Internet companies have solved this backup-on-the-go problem by providing remote backup services over the Internet. In a hotel room or other remote location, connect to the Internet and back up your data to a Web site's file server. If data is lost, you can easily recover it by connecting to the Internet and logging on to your backup service Web site. Two online backup services are @ Backup (*www.backup.com*) and Remote Backup Systems (*www.remote-backup.com*). Also, some high-end notebooks have two hard drives installed; you can use one to back up the other.

> **Notes**
>
> For backing up large amounts of data to a file server or other media, invest in backup software such as Ghost by Symantec (*www.symantec.com*) or PC BackUp by StompSoft (*www.stompsoft.com*).

Regardless of the backup method you use, back up the data after about four to ten hours of data entry. For a small office, this might mean you should make backups every night.

This section first discusses using tape drives and then using removable drives for backups.

## TAPE DRIVES

Tape drives (see Figure 10-40) are an inexpensive way of backing up an entire hard drive or portions of it. Tape drives are more convenient and less expensive for backups than CDs, DVDs, or flash drives. Tapes currently have capacities of 20 to 800 GB compressed and come in several types and formats. Although tape drives don't require that you use special backup software to manage them, you might want to invest in specialized backup software to make backups as efficient and effortless as possible. Many tape drives come with bundled software, and Windows offers a Backup utility that can use tape drives. Several of the more common standards and types of tape drives and tapes are described in this section.

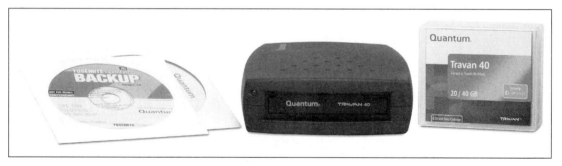

**Figure 10-40** This Quantum Travan 40 tape drive holds up to 40 GB of data; it comes with backup software, data cartridge, USB 2.0 cable, power supply, power cord, and documentation

The biggest disadvantage of using tape drives is that data is stored on tape by **sequential access**; to read data from anywhere on the tape, you must start at the beginning of the tape and read until you come to the sought-after data. Sequential access makes recovering files slow and inconvenient, which is why tapes are not used for general-purpose data storage.

Table 10-9 lists some manufacturers of tape drives.

| Manufacturer | Web Site |
|---|---|
| DLT | www.dlttape.com |
| Exabyte | www.exabyte.com |
| Hewlett Packard | www.hp.com |
| Imation | www.imation.com |
| Iomega | www.iomega.com |
| Quantum Corporation | www.quantum.com |
| Seagate | www.seagate.com |
| Sony | www.sony.com |

**Table 10-9**  Tape drive manufacturers

## HOW A TAPE DRIVE INTERFACES WITH A COMPUTER

A tape drive can be external or internal. An external tape drive costs more but can be used by more than one computer. A tape drive can interface with a computer in these ways:

- ▲ An external or internal drive can use a SCSI bus. This method works well if the tape drive and the hard drive are on the same SCSI bus, which contains a data pass-through just to the SCSI system.
- ▲ An external or internal drive can use a USB connection, its own proprietary controller card, or a parallel port.
- ▲ An internal drive can use the parallel ATA or serial ATA interface.

Currently, the most popular tape drive interfaces for internal drives are parallel ATA, SCSI, and serial ATA; for external drives, USB and SCSI are the most popular, and external serial ATA tape drives are expected to be available soon. Figure 10-41 shows the rear of a parallel ATA tape drive. You can see the connections for a power supply and a 40-pin IDE cable as well as jumpers to set the drive to master, slave, or cable select. This setup is similar for any EIDE device.

Jumper bank to set master, slave, or cable select

40-pin connection for IDE cable

Power supply connection

**Figure 10-41**   The rear of a parallel ATA (IDE ATAPI) tape drive

A+ ESS
1.1

A+
220-602
1.1

### Notes

When installing a parallel ATA tape drive, don't put the drive on the same IDE data cable as the hard drive, or it might hinder the hard drive's performance. A typical configuration is to install the hard drive as the sole device on the primary IDE channel and let a CD or DVD drive and tape drive share the second channel. Then, you can set the optical drive to master and the tape drive to slave on that channel.

## THE TAPES USED BY A TAPE DRIVE

Tape drives accommodate one of two kinds of tapes: full-sized **data cartridges** are $4 \times 6 \times \frac{5}{8}$ inches, and the smaller **minicartridges**, like the one in Figure 10-42, are $3\frac{1}{4} \times 2\frac{1}{2} \times \frac{3}{5}$ inches. Minicartridges are more popular because their drives can fit into a standard $3\frac{1}{2}$-inch drive bay of a PC case.

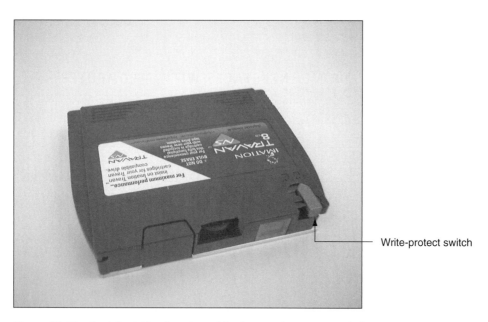

Write-protect switch

**Figure 10-42**  A minicartridge for a tape drive has a write-protect switch

The technology used by tape drives to write to tapes is similar to that used by floppy drives (see Chapter 8). A FAT at the beginning of the tape tracks the location of data and bad sectors on the tape. The tape must be formatted before data can be written to it. You can purchase factory-formatted tapes to save time.

When purchasing tapes, carefully match tapes to tape drives because several standards and sizes exist. One standard developed by 3M is Travan, which is backed by many leaders in the tape drive industry. There are different levels of Travan standards, called TR-1 through TR-8. Other tape standards include DDS, DAT, VXA-1, VXA-2, AIT-2, AIT-3, AIT-4, Super AIT, DLT (Digital Linear Tape), LTO, SDLT (Super DLT), SLR, and MLR QIC cartridges. Quarter-Inch Cartridge Drive Standards, Inc. (QIC at *www.qic.org*) is a trade association responsible for shaping many of these standards. One of the more current tape standards is the LTO Ultrium 3. For example, the Maxell LTO Ultrium 3 data tape cartridge can hold 400 GB of data or 800 GB of compressed data (see Figure 10-43). It can be used by the Quantum LTO-3 tape drive shown in Figure 10-44. DDS tapes and drives, a version of DAT, are also popular.

A+ ESS
1.1

A+
220-602
1.1

**Figure 10-43** This Maxell LTO Ultrium 3 data tape cartridge can hold up to 800 GB of compressed data

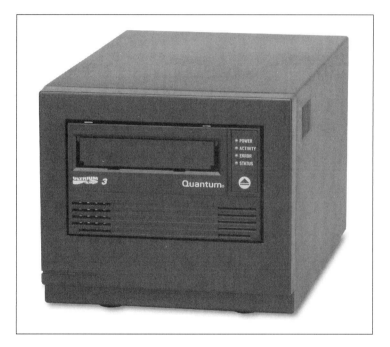

**Figure 10-44** Quantum Ultrium LTO-3 tape drive

Note that tape drives are likely to be able to read other formats than the formats they use for writing. For example, the Seagate Certance 40-GB tape drive writes to and reads 40-GB TR-6 tapes, and can read from 20-GB TR-5 tapes. Your best bet is to read the tape drive documentation to know what tapes the drive supports.

Here are some tips about how to care for and clean tapes and tape drives:

**Tip**

For an interesting photo gallery of tape media, see *www.BackupWorks.com*.

▲ Keep tapes away from magnetic fields.
▲ Don't expose tapes to heat, the sun, extreme cold, or sudden changes in temperature.

▲ Newer tape drives don't need cleaning as often as the older ones did. To know when and how to clean the tape drive heads, read the documentation that comes with the drive or check the Web site of the drive manufacturer. You might be told to use a cleaning tape in the drive (see Figure 10-45). Keep track of how often you use the cleaning tape, because they are only designed to work a certain number of times and then thrown away. (Look on the cleaning tape package to know how many times it can clean). Some drive heads can also be cleaned with a wet-type head-cleaning spray designed for magnetic tape such as the cleaner in Figure 10-46.

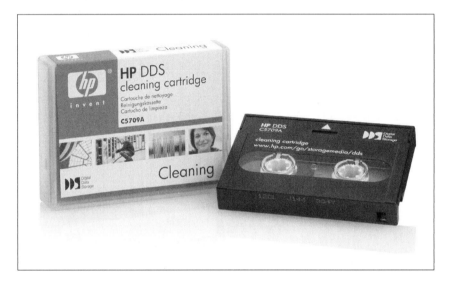

**Figure 10-45**   HP says this cleaning cartridge is good for 50 cleanings

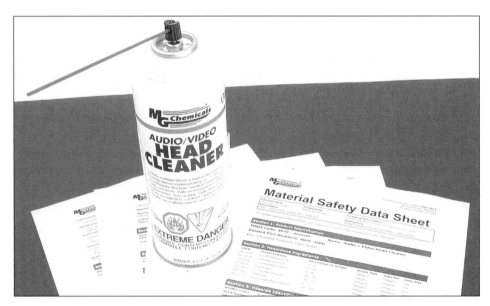

**Figure 10-46**   Head cleaner for magnetic tape by MG Chemicals

▲ Although you can manually clean individual tapes with head-cleaning spray, it's pretty time-consuming and probably not worth the effort. If a tape starts to give errors, buy a new one. If you are responsible for managing a lot of tapes, consider buying a magnetic tape cleaning machine that retensions, vacuums, inspects, and wipes tapes automatically. Do a google search on "magnetic tape cleaners" to turn up several cleaning devices with a wide variety of prices and features.

## REMOVABLE DRIVES

A removable drive can be either an external or internal drive. Using a removable drive provides several advantages:

▲ Increases the overall storage capacity of a system
▲ Makes it easy to move large files from one computer to another
▲ Serves as a convenient medium for making backups of hard drive data
▲ Makes it easy to secure important files (To keep important files secure, keep the removable drive locked in a safe when it is not being used.)

When purchasing a removable drive, consider how susceptible the drive is when dropped. The **drop height** is the height from which the manufacturer says you can drop the drive without making it unusable. Also consider how long the data will last on the drive. The **half-life** (sometimes called life expectancy or shelf life) of the disk is the time it takes for the magnetic strength of the medium to weaken by half. Magnetic media, including traditional hard drives and floppy disks, have a half-life of five to seven years, but writable optical media such as CD-Rs have a half-life of 30 years.

### TYPES OF REMOVABLE DRIVES

This section covers several of the newer and older removable drives on the market. One newer drive is the Microdrive CF introduced earlier in this chapter. The drive comes in several sizes up to 4 GB. It uses the CompactFlash II form factor, and you can purchase a PC Card adapter to make it convenient to use in a laptop computer (see Figure 10-47).

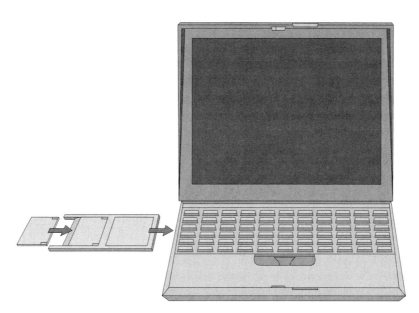

**Figure 10-47**  The Microdrive CF inserts into a PC Card adapter, which fits into a notebook PC Card slot

A less expensive and more convenient type of drive, ranging in size from 1 GB to 60 GB, is a flash drive that goes by many names, including a flash pen drive, jump drive, thumb drive, and key drive. These flash drives are a solid state device made of flash memory rather than a rotating disk. One popular example of a flash pen drive is the JumpDrive by Lexar Media (*www.card-media.co.uk*). The drive (see Figure 10-48) offers 64 MB to 4 GB of storage, conveniently fits on a keychain, and snaps into a USB port.

A+ ESS
1.1

A+
220-602
1.1

**Figure 10-48** This JumpDrive holds 128 MB of data and snaps into a USB port

Another removable drive is the Iomega HDD drive by Iomega (*www.iomega.com*). The drive (see Figure 10-49) is small enough to fit into your shirt pocket and uses a USB or 1394 connection. It comes bundled with Iomega Automatic Backup and Symantec Norton Ghost software, holds from 20 GB to 250 GB of data, and is a great backup solution for a PC hard drive. Iomega says it's rugged enough that you don't have to worry about dropping it.

**Figure 10-49** This 60-GB HDD portable hard drive by Iomega has a USB 2.0 and FireWire connection and is small enough to fit in your pocket

One type of older removable drive is the Iomega $3\frac{1}{2}$-inch Zip drive, which stores 100 MB, 250 MB, or 750 MB of data on each of its disks, and has a drop height of 8 feet (see Figure 10-50). An internal Zip drive uses an EIDE interface. The external Zip drive plugs into a USB, FireWire, parallel, or SCSI port. The drive and disk look like a traditional

**Figure 10-50** An internal Zip drive kit includes the IDE Zip drive, documentation, drivers on floppy disk, and one Zip disk

$3\frac{1}{2}$-inch floppy disk drive and disk, but the disk is slightly larger. Zip drives can't read standard $3\frac{1}{2}$-inch floppy disks.

Another removable drive is SuperDisk, originally developed by Imation, which stores 120 MB or 240 MB of data. The drives are currently made by other manufacturers, but Imation still makes the removable disks. SuperDisk 120-MB drives are backward-compatible with double-density (720K) and high-density (1.44 MB) floppy disks, and SuperDisk 240-MB drives are backward-compatible with SuperDisk 120-MB drives and both sizes of floppy disks.

The SuperDisk is really two disk drives in one. It can use the old technology to read from and write to regular floppy disks, and it can use laser technology to read and write 120-MB or 240-MB disks. SuperDisk is up to 27 times faster than regular floppy drives. SuperDisk drives can be purchased as external (USB or parallel port) or internal drives. As internal drives, they are installed using the 40-pin EIDE connection, and not using the 34-pin floppy drive connection.

SuperDisk and Zip drives are considered fading, out-of-date technologies. For removable data storage, it's best to purchase the newer flash drive devices.

## INSTALLING A REMOVABLE DRIVE

Installing an internal removable drive such as a Zip drive is similar to installing a hard drive. For an EIDE drive, set the drive to master or slave on an IDE channel. If the external or internal drive is a SCSI drive, the SCSI host adapter must already be installed and configured.

Do the following to install a removable drive:

1. Read the documentation about how to install the drive. Some USB or 1394 devices require you to install the software before plugging up the device. Other installations plug up the device and then install the software. The documentation will tell you the correct order to use. When using Windows XP, most likely no software is needed; just plug in the drive and Windows recognizes it immediately.

2. If software is needed and you install the software before you install the device, install the software now.

3. Identify the connectors. Many removable drives use either a USB port, a FireWire port, or a SCSI port for connection.

4. For a USB or FireWire device, connect the USB or FireWire cable to the USB or FireWire port. Go to Step 9.

5. For a SCSI device, with the SCSI host adapter installed, connect the SCSI cable to the drive and to the SCSI port on the host adapter.

6. For a SCSI drive, set the drive's SCSI ID. If the device is the last one on a SCSI chain, install a terminator on the device.

7. You might also need to set the host adapter to recognize an external device. See the documentation for the host adapter. (SCSI is covered in Chapter 8.)

8. Check all your connections and plug the AC power cord for the drive into a wall socket.

9. Turn on your PC. If you have not yet installed the software, do that now.

10. If you have problems, turn everything off and check all connections. Power up and try again. You can use Device Manager to uninstall the device drivers and get a fresh start.

A+ ESS
1.1

A+
220-602
1.1

# FAULT TOLERANCE, DYNAMIC VOLUMES, AND RAID

**Fault tolerance** is a computer's ability to respond to a fault or catastrophe, such as a hardware failure or power outage, so that data is not lost. If data is important enough to justify the cost, you can protect the data by continuously writing two copies of it, each to a different hard drive. This method is most often used on high-end, expensive file servers, but it is occasionally appropriate for a single-user workstation. In addition, sometimes you can improve performance by writing data to two or more hard drives so that a single drive is not excessively used.

Collectively, the methods used to improve performance and automatically recover from a failure are called **RAID** (**redundant array of inexpensive disks** or **redundant array of independent disks**). There are several levels of RAID, but here we discuss only the most commonly used levels. We first look at how an operating system supports fault tolerance and improves hard drive performance, and then at how these methods are implemented with RAID hardware.

## DYNAMIC VOLUMES UNDER WINDOWS

Windows 2000/XP implements fault tolerance by using a type of hard drive configuration called dynamic volumes or dynamic disks. Using this method of organizing hard drives, you can also write data across multiple hard drives to improve performance. In this part of the chapter, we first explain what basic disks and dynamic disks are and then look at different ways to implement fault tolerance under each OS.

> **A+ Exam Tip**
>
> The A+ Essentials exam expects you to know about adding, removing, and configuring hard drives that use imaging technologies.

### Basic Disks and Dynamic Disks

Windows 2000/XP offers two ways to configure a hard drive: as a basic disk or a dynamic disk. A **basic disk** is the same as the configuration used with DOS, Windows 9x/Me, and Windows NT. By default, Windows 2000/XP uses basic disk configuration. With basic disk configuration, you generally create partitions of a set size and then do not change them. If you want to change the size of a partition, you either have to reinstall Windows (if Windows is installed on that partition) or use special third-party software that allows you to change the size of a partition without losing your data. Within partitions, you create logical drives (sometimes called basic volumes) of set size.

**Dynamic disks** don't use partitions or logical drives; instead, they use **dynamic volumes**, which are called dynamic because you can change their size. Data to configure the disk is stored in a disk management database that resides in the last 1 MB of storage space at the end of a hard drive. DOS, Windows 9x/Me, and Windows NT cannot read dynamic disks. Dynamic disks are compatible only with Windows 2000 and Windows XP.

> 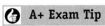 **Notes**
>
> Because a dynamic disk requires 1 MB of storage for the disk management database, if you are partitioning a basic disk and expect that one day you might want to convert it to a dynamic disk, leave 1 MB of space on the drive unpartitioned, to be used later for the disk management database.

### Ways to Use Windows Dynamic Disks

Dynamic disks can be used to improve performance or for fault tolerance. A dynamic volume is contained within a dynamic disk and is a logical volume similar to a logical drive in a basic disk. There are five types of dynamic volumes; the third type is used to improve performance and the last two types are used for fault tolerance:

▲ A **simple volume** corresponds to a primary partition on a basic disk and consists of disk space on a single physical disk.

**10**

◢ A **spanned volume** appears as a simple volume but can use space from two or more physical disks. It fills the space allotted on one physical disk before moving on to the next. This increases the amount of disk space available for a volume. However, if one physical disk on which data that is part of a spanned volume fails, all data in the volume is lost. Spanned volumes are sometimes called JBOD (just a bunch of drives).

◢ A **striped volume** (also called **RAID 0**) also can use space from two or more physical disks and increases the disk space available for a single volume. The difference between a spanned volume and a striped volume is that a striped volume writes to the physical disks evenly rather than filling allotted space on one and then moving on to the next. This increases disk performance as compared to access time with a spanned volume.

◢ A **mirrored volume** (also called **RAID 1** or drive imaging) duplicates data on another drive and is used for fault tolerance. Each drive has its own volume, and the two volumes are called mirrors. If one drive fails, the other continues to operate and data is not lost. A variation of mirroring is disk duplexing, which uses two controllers, one for each drive, thus providing more fault tolerance than mirroring. Mirrored volumes are supported only by server OSs (such as Windows Server 2003 and Windows 2000 Server).

◢ A **RAID-5 volume** is striped across three or more drives and uses parity checking, so that if one drive fails, the other drives can re-create the data stored on the failed drive. Data is not duplicated, and, therefore, RAID-5 makes better use of volume capacity. RAID-5 volumes increase performance and provide fault tolerance. RAID-5 volumes are only supported by server OSs (such as Windows Server 2003 and Windows 2000 Server).

Figure 10-51 shows the difference between basic disk and dynamic disk organization. A basic disk or a dynamic disk can use any file system supported by Windows 2000/XP (FAT16, FAT32, and NTFS). Note that Windows 2000 Professional and Windows XP do not support the types of dynamic disks that provide fault tolerance (mirrored volume and RAID-5), so the only reasons to use dynamic disks under these OSs are to improve disk performance and to increase the size of a single volume. Dynamic drives offer little advantage for a system with only a single hard drive, and they are not supported at all on laptop computers.

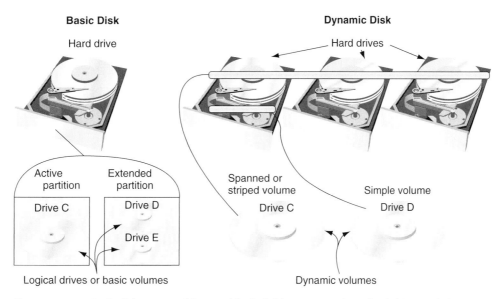

**Figure 10-51**  Basic disks use partitions and logical drives to organize a hard drive, and dynamic disks use dynamic volumes to organize multiple hard drives

**A+ ESS
1.2**

**A+
220-602
1.1**

> ### Notes
>
> After Windows 2000/XP is installed, you can use the Windows 2000/XP Disk Management utility to switch from basic to dynamic or dynamic to basic, and change the file system on either type of disk. For a striped volume using Windows 2000/XP, each hard drive in the array must have the same amount of free space available to the volume and must use the same file system (FAT16, FAT32, or NTFS).

Table 10-10 summarizes which methods are used by the various OSs. The table uses the same terms used in the documentation for each OS to describe the methods supported.

| Windows Version | Volume and RAID Types Supported |
| --- | --- |
| Windows 9x/Me | — |
| Windows NT Workstation | RAID 0 (striped) |
| Windows 2000 Professional | Simple, spanned, and striped (RAID 0) |
| Windows XP Professional | Simple, spanned, and striped (RAID 0) |
| Windows NT Server, Windows 2000 Server, and Windows Server 2003 | Simple, spanned, striped (RAID 0), mirrored (RAID 1), and RAID 5 |

**Table 10-10**   Types of volumes and RAID used in different versions of Windows

## HARDWARE RAID

Another way to implement RAID is to use hardware. In order to use hardware RAID, your hard drive controller or motherboard must support RAID. (The OS is not aware of a hardware RAID implementation.) A group of hard drives implementing RAID is called an **array**. Here are the different ways your motherboard or adapter can support a RAID array:

▲ *The motherboard IDE controller supports RAID.* Figure 10-52 shows a motherboard that has two regular IDE connectors, two serial ATA connectors that can be configured for RAID, and two parallel RAID connectors. This board supports spanning,

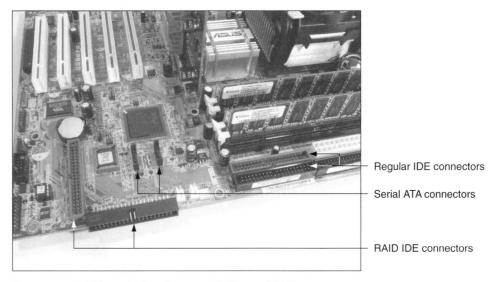

— Regular IDE connectors

— Serial ATA connectors

— RAID IDE connectors

**Figure 10-52**   This motherboard supports RAID 0 and RAID 1

A+ ESS
1.2

A+
220-602
1.1

RAID 0, RAID 1, and a combination of RAID 0 and RAID 1. First, you install the drives and then use CMOS setup to configure the RAID array.

▲ *Install a RAID-compliant IDE controller card and disable the IDE controller on your motherboard.* Use this option if your motherboard does not support RAID. Install the controller card and drives and then use the software bundled with the controller card to configure the RAID array.

▲ *The motherboard SCSI controller supports RAID or you install a SCSI host adapter that supports RAID.* SCSI was introduced in Chapter 8.

When installing a hardware RAID system, for best performance, all hard drives in an array must be identical in brand, size, speed, and other features. As with installing any hardware, first read the documentation that comes with the motherboard or RAID controller and follow those specific directions rather than the general guidelines given here. Generally, to set up a RAID array, first install the hard drives, connecting the data cables to the RAID connectors on the motherboard or controller. Next, if your motherboard is controlling the RAID array, enter CMOS setup and verify that the RAID drives were autodetected correctly and the correct RAID type is selected. When using serial ATA for your RAID drives, you'll need to configure the serial ATA ports to hold a RAID array, as shown in Figure 10-53.

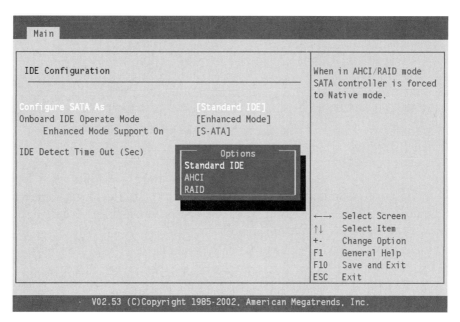

**Figure 10-53** Configure serial ATA ports on the motherboard to enable RAID

When using a RAID controller card, use the software that came bundled with the card to configure your RAID array. For some RAID controllers, whether on a card or on a motherboard, a RAID driver is installed from within Windows after Windows has been installed on one of the RAID drives. After everything is set up, the OS and applications see the RAID array as a single volume such as drive D. Later, if errors occur on one of the drives in the RAID array, the RAID drivers notify the OS and thereafter direct all data to the good drives.

For file servers using RAID 5 that must work continuously and hold important data, it might be practical to use hardware that allows for hard drive hot-swapping, which means you can remove one hard drive and insert another without powering down the computer. However, hard drives that can be hot-swapped cost significantly more than regular hard drives. RAID hard drive arrays are sometimes used as part of a storage area network (SAN). A SAN is a network that has the primary purpose of providing large amounts of data storage.

A+ ESS
1.2

A+
220-602
1.1

**Notes**

For best performance and reliability, use a hardware RAID implementation instead of software RAID. Using hardware RAID, the RAID controller duplicates the data so the OS is not involved. Also, for an OS implementation of RAID, the OS active partition cannot be part of the RAID array, so you must have a non-RAID drive in your system as well as the RAID array. If this drive fails, then the system goes down regardless of the health of the RAID array. Therefore, for the best fault tolerance, use hardware RAID.

# TROUBLESHOOTING MULTIMEDIA DEVICES

A+
220-602
1.2

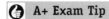 **A+ Exam Tip**

The A+ Essentials and A+ 220-602 exams expect you to be a good PC troubleshooter and present different troubleshooting scenarios for you to solve. This section is good preparation for that skill.

This section covers some troubleshooting guidelines for CD, CD-RW, DVD, DVD-RW, tape drives, and sound cards. As with other components you have learned about, remember not to touch chips on circuit boards or disk surfaces where data is stored, stack components on top of one another, or subject them to magnetic fields or ESD.

## PROBLEMS WITH CD, CD-RW, DVD, OR DVD-RW INSTALLATION

Use the following general guidelines when a CD, CD-RW, DVD, or DVD-RW drive installation causes problems. These guidelines are useful even if your computer does not recognize the drive (for example, no drive D is listed in Windows Explorer):

▲ Check the data cable and power cord connections to the drive. Is the stripe on the data cable correctly aligned to pin 1? (Look for an arrow or small 1 printed on the drive. For a best guess, pin 1 is usually next to the power connector.)

▲ For an EIDE drive, is the correct master/slave jumper set? For example, if both the hard drive and the CD or DVD drive are hooked to the same ribbon cable, one must be set to master and the other to slave. If the CD or DVD drive is the only drive connected to the cable, then it should be set to single or master.

▲ For an EIDE drive, is the IDE connection on the motherboard disabled in CMOS setup? If so, enable it.

▲ If you are using a SCSI drive, are the proper IDs set? Is the device terminated if it is the last item in the SCSI chain? Are the correct SCSI drivers installed?

▲ If you are booting from a Windows 9x/Me startup disk, check drivers, including entries in Config.sys and Autoexec.bat, and verify that Mscdex.exe is in the correct directory.

▲ Is another device using the same port settings? Check system resources listed in Device Manager. Is there an IRQ conflict with the IDE primary or secondary channel or the SCSI host the drive is using?

▲ Suspect a boot virus. This is a common problem. Run a virus scan program.

## PROBLEMS WHEN BURNING A CD

When trying to burn a CD, sometimes Windows refuses to perform the burn or the burned CD is not readable. Here are some things that might go wrong and what to do about them:

▲ A CD can hold about 700 MB of data. Be sure your total file sizes don't exceed this amount.

◢ The hard drive needs some temporary holding space for the write process. Make sure you have at least 1 GB of free space.

◢ If something interrupts the write process before the burning is done, you might end up with a bad CD. Disable any screen saver and close other programs before you begin.

◢ If several CDs give you problems, try a different brand of CDs.

◢ The burn process requires a constant flow of data to the CD. If you have a sluggish Windows system, a CD might not burn correctly. Try using a slower burn rate to adjust for a slow data transfer rate. To slow the burn rate, right-click the CD-RW drive and select **Properties** from the shortcut menu. Click the **Recording** tab (see Figure 10-54). Choose a slower write speed from the drop-down menu. Notice in the Recording tab window you can also point to a drive different from drive C to hold temporary files for burning. Use this option if drive C is full, and another drive has more available space.

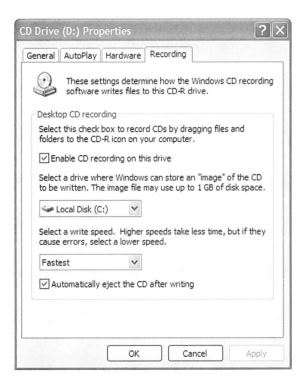

**Figure 10-54**  Slow down the CD-RW write speed to account for a slow Windows system

## TROUBLESHOOTING SOUND PROBLEMS

Problems with sound can be caused by a problem with the sound card itself, but you might also have problems with system settings, bad connections, or a number of other factors. Here are some questions you can try to answer to diagnose the problem:

◢ Are the speakers plugged into the correct line "Out" or the "Spkr" port of the sound card (the middle port or green port)? Most problems with sound are caused by not properly connecting the speaker cables to the correct speaker ports.

◢ Is the audio cord attached between the optical drive and the analog audio connector on the sound card?

◢ Are the speakers turned on?

A+
220-602
1.2

▲ Is the speaker volume turned up?

▲ Is the transformer for the speaker plugged into an electrical outlet on one end and into the speakers on the other end?

▲ Is the volume control for Windows turned up? Are the Mute check boxes unchecked? (To check for Windows XP, click Start, All Programs, Accessories, Entertainment, and Volume Control. To check for Windows 98, click Start, Programs, Accessories, Multimedia, and Volume Control.)

▲ Check Device Manager to verify the sound card is installed and shows no problems or conflicts.

▲ Does the sound card have a "diagnose" file on the install disk?

▲ Does the sound card have manufacturer configuration utility software installed? If so, open the utility and verify the sound card ports you are using are enabled and other settings are correct.

▲ Verify your speakers work. Try connecting them to a CD player.

## PROBLEMS INSTALLING A SOUND CARD

If you have just installed a sound card, and it doesn't produce sound, try these things:

▲ You might have the wrong drivers installed. Try downloading new or updated drivers. (Once I tried to install a sound card using drivers on the accompanying CD, but the CD bundled with the card was for the wrong card. Downloading new drivers from the sound card Web site solved the problem.)

▲ Using Device Manager, uninstall the sound card and then reinstall it using the Add New Hardware applet in the Control Panel.

▲ To check for a bad connection, turn off the computer, and then remove and reinstall the sound card.

▲ Replace the sound card with one you know is good.

## GAMES DON'T HAVE SOUND

If your sound card works except when playing a certain really cool game, try these things:

▲ Go to the sound card manufacturer Web site and download the latest drivers for the card. Using Device Manager, update the drivers or uninstall the card and then install it using the latest drivers.

▲ Try disabling all utilities you have running in the background such as a screen saver program or antivirus software. If this solves the problem, then enable first one and then the next until you find the utility causing the problem.

▲ Try reducing sound acceleration. To do that, in the Control Panel, open the **Sounds and Audio Devices** applet. On the Volume tab, Speaker settings, click **Advanced** (see Figure 10-55). The Advanced Audio Properties window opens. Click the **Performance** tab. Move the Hardware acceleration slide to the left one click. Try the game again. If it still doesn't make noise, move the slide one more click. You might have to move it all the way to the left.

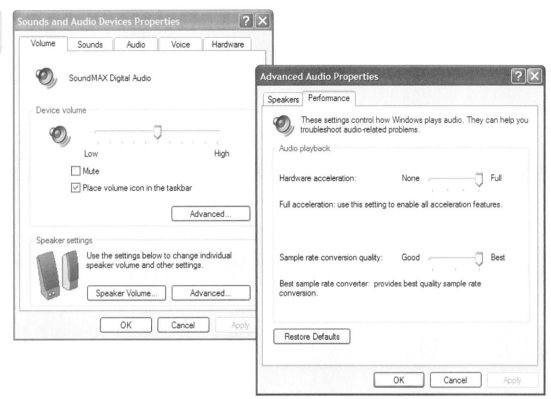

**Figure 10-55** Adjust sound hardware acceleration

## TROUBLESHOOTING TAPE DRIVES

The following list describes tape drive problems you might encounter and suggestions for dealing with them.

### A MINICARTRIDGE DOES NOT WORK

If your minicartridge is not working, consider the following:

- ◢ If you are trying to write data, verify that the minicartridge is write-enabled.
- ◢ Are you inserting the minicartridge correctly? Check the user guide.
- ◢ Check that you are using the correct type of minicartridge. See the user guide.
- ◢ Is the minicartridge formatted? The software performs the format, which can take an hour or more.
- ◢ Use the backup software to retension the tape. Some tape drives require this, and others do not. Retensioning fast-forwards and rewinds the tape to eliminate loose spots.
- ◢ Take the minicartridge out and reboot. Try the minicartridge again.
- ◢ Try using a new minicartridge. The old one might have worn out.
- ◢ The tape might be unspooled, a problem usually caused by dust inside the drive. Blow all dust out of the drive and use a new tape.
- ◢ As with floppy disks, if the tape was removed from the drive while the drive light was on, the data being written at that time might not be readable.

## DATA TRANSFER IS SLOW

If your data transfer is slow, consider the following:

▲ Change tape software settings for speed and data compression.
▲ If supported by the tape drive, try an accelerator card to improve speed.
▲ Try a new minicartridge.
▲ If the tape drive can do so, completely erase the tape and reformat it. Be sure that the tape drive can perform this procedure before you tell the software to do it.
▲ If you have installed an accelerator card, verify that the card is connected to the tape drive.
▲ Check that there is enough memory and hard drive space for the software to run.

## THE DRIVE DOES NOT WORK AFTER THE INSTALLATION

If your drive is not working, consider the following:

▲ Check that pin 1 is oriented correctly to the data cable at both ends.
▲ Use Device Manager to check for errors.

## THE DRIVE FAILS INTERMITTENTLY OR GIVES ERRORS

If your drive is not working all the time, consider the following:

▲ The tape might be worn out. Try a new tape.
▲ Clean the read/write head of the tape drive. See the tape drive user guide for directions.
▲ For an external tape drive, move the drive as far as you can from the monitor and computer case.
▲ Reformat the tape.
▲ Retension the tape.
▲ Verify that you are using the correct tape type and tape format.

## >> CHAPTER SUMMARY

▲ Multimedia PCs and devices are designed to create and reproduce lifelike presentations of sight and sound.

▲ MMX, SSE, SSE2, SSE3, and Hyper-Threading by Intel and 3DNow!, HyperTransport!, and PowerNow! by AMD improve the speed of processing graphics, video, and sound, using improved methods of handling high-volume repetition during I/O operations. Dual-core processing is also used by Intel and AMD.

▲ To take full advantage of MMX, SSE, or 3DNow! technology, software must be written to use its specific capabilities.

▲ All computer communication is digital. To be converted to digital from analog, sound and images are sampled, which means their data is measured at a series of representative points. More accurate sampling requires more space for data storage.

▲ Installing a sound card includes physically installing the card and then installing the sound card driver and sound application software.

▲ If only one speaker connection is used, connect it to the green sound port on the sound card, which is usually a middle port.

10

◢ Digital cameras use light sensors to detect light and convert it to a digital signal stored in an image file (usually JPEG format).

◢ MP3 is a version of MPEG compression used for audio files. Portable MP3 players store and play MP3 files downloaded from a PC, using internal memory and flash storage devices.

◢ A TV tuner card turns your PC or notebook into a television. A video capture card allows you to capture input from a camcorder or directly from TV. Combo cards have both abilities.

◢ CDs and DVDs are optical devices with data physically embedded into the surface of the disc. Laser beams are used to read data off the disc by measuring light reflection.

◢ The speed of CD and DVD drives slows down as the laser beam moves from the inside to the outside of the disc.

◢ Internal CD and DVD drives can have an EIDE, serial ATA, or SCSI interface, and external optical drives can use a USB port, 1394 port, or SCSI port.

◢ The most common interfaces for internal optical drives are parallel ATA and serial ATA.

◢ Data is only written to the shiny underside of a CD, which should be protected from damage. Data can be written to both sides of a DVD.

◢ A DVD can store a full-length movie and uses software or an accompanying decoder card to decode the MPEG-compressed video data and Surround Sound compressed audio.

◢ Tape drives are an inexpensive way to back up an entire hard drive or portions of it. Tape drives are more convenient for backups than removable disks.

◢ The most convenient backup media is another hard drive on the same or another computer. For traveling with a notebook, some Web sites provide online remote backup.

◢ Some examples of removable drives are Microdrive, JumpDrive, Iomega HDD, Zip drive, and SuperDisk.

◢ Five types of dynamic volumes used by Windows 2003/2000 Server are simple volume, spanned volume, striped volume (RAID 0), mirrored volume (RAID 1), and RAID 5.

◢ Windows XP supports spanned and striped (RAID 0) volumes.

◢ Hardware RAID is considered a better solution for fault tolerance than software RAID.

## >> KEY TERMS

For explanations of key terms, see the Glossary near the end of the book.

| | | |
|---|---|---|
| array | dynamic volume | multisession |
| basic disk | fault tolerance | pits |
| CDFS (Compact Disc File System) | half-life | RAID (redundant array of inexpensive disks or redundant array of independent disks) |
| CD-R (CD-recordable) | hertz (Hz) | |
| CD-RW (CD-rewritable) | JPEG (Joint Photographic Experts Group) | |
| constant angular velocity (CAV) | lands | RAID 0 |
| constant linear velocity (CLV) | minicartridge | RAID 1 |
| data cartridge | mirrored volume | RAID-5 volume |
| drop height | MMX (Multimedia Extensions) | sampling rate |
| DVD (digital video disc or digital versatile disc) | Moving Pictures Experts Group (MPEG) | sequential access |
| | | SIMD (single instruction, multiple data) |
| dynamic disk | MP3 | simple volume |

>> *REVIEW QUESTIONS*

1. How many separate sound channels of sound information can the Surround Sound standard support?

    a. 4

    b. 6

    c. 8

    d. 10

2. High-fidelity music CDs use how many bits in their sample size?

    a. 8

    b. 16

    c. 32

    d. 64

3. Which of the following sound card color codes is typically used for "line in" for external devices producing sound?

    a. Blue

    b. Green

    c. Black

    d. Orange

4. Which of the following formats might be used by a high-end camera to give better results when printing photographs?

    a. TIFF

    b. JPEG

    c. BMP

    d. GIF

5. Which of the following statements best describes the MIDI format?

    a. A method of storing a sound file in compressed format

    b. A common compression standard for storing photos

    c. A method for digitizing streaming video

    d. A method of digitally describing and storing every note played by each instrument used in making music

6. True or false? The sampling rate of a sound card is the number of samples taken of the analog signal over a period of time.

7. True or false? To prevent the Windows XP Found New Hardware Wizard from proceeding with the installation of a hardware device using Microsoft drivers, run the setup program on the manufacturer's CD that is bundled with the card before installing the card.

8. True or false? The surface of a CD stores data as pits and lands.

9. True or false? To create the effect of constant speed as the disc turns, the CD drive uses a mechanism that speeds up the disc when the laser beam is near the center of the disc and slows down the disc when the laser beam is near the outer edge.

10. True or false? When installing a parallel ATA tape drive, put the drive on the same IDE data cable as the hard drive to improve the hard drive's performance.

11. CD (compact disc) drives use the _____ or _____ file system.

12. A computer's ability to respond to a fault or catastrophe, such as a hardware failure or power outage, so that data is not lost is called _____.

13. A standard format used by digital cameras and scanners for transferring images is called _____.

14. A(n) _____ volume appears as a simple volume but can use space from two or more physical disks.

15. A storage device that uses memory chips to store data instead of spinning disks (such as those used by hard drives and CD drives) is called a(n) _____.

# CHAPTER 11

# Installing Windows 2000/XP

**W**indows 2000 and Windows XP share the same basic Windows architecture and have similar characteristics. Historically, Windows 2000 is the culmination of the evolution of Microsoft operating systems from the 16-bit DOS operating system to a true 32-bit, module-oriented operating system, complete with improved security, user-friendly Plug and Play installations, and other easy-to-use features. Windows XP includes additional support for multimedia, Plug and Play, and legacy software, making the final step for Microsoft to announce the merging of Windows 9x/Me and Windows NT operating systems into a single OS.

Windows XP is the current choice as a Windows OS for personal computers and it is the only Windows OS for which you can buy a license. (At the time this book went to print, Windows Vista was not yet available.) However, because many individual users and corporations still rely on Windows 2000, you need to know how to support it.

This chapter lays the foundation for understanding the architecture of Windows 2000/XP and then shows you how to plan a Windows XP and Windows 2000 Professional installation, the steps to perform the installations, and what to do after the OS is installed.

## Notes

Some instructors and readers might prefer to study DOS and Windows 9x/Me before you study Windows 2000/XP. This book is designed so that you can cover Chapters 15 and 16 on DOS and Windows 9x/Me before you cover Chapters 11, 12, 13, and 14 on Windows 2000/XP; you can also cover all six chapters sequentially. Also, if you are studying this book in preparation for the A+ exams, know that content in Chapters 15 and 16 is not covered on the exams and can be skipped.

## FEATURES AND ARCHITECTURE OF WINDOWS 2000/XP

In this section of the chapter, you'll learn about the features, versions, and architecture of Windows 2000/XP. First we'll look at the several Windows 2000/XP versions and when it is appropriate to use each. Then you'll learn about the operating modes used by Windows, its networking features, and how it handles hard drives and file systems on those drives. Finally, you'll learn about when it is appropriate to use Windows XP or Windows 2000.

### VERSIONS AND FEATURES OF WINDOWS XP AND 2000

Windows XP comes in several varieties: Windows XP Professional, Windows XP Home Edition, Windows XP Media Center Edition, Windows XP Tablet PC Edition, and Windows XP Professional x64 Edition (formally called Windows XP 64-Bit Edition).

Windows XP Home Edition and Windows XP Professional have these features, among others, that are not included with Windows 2000:

▲ A new user interface, shown in Figure 11-1. Notice how different it looks from the desktops of earlier Windows versions such as Windows 98 and Windows 2000.

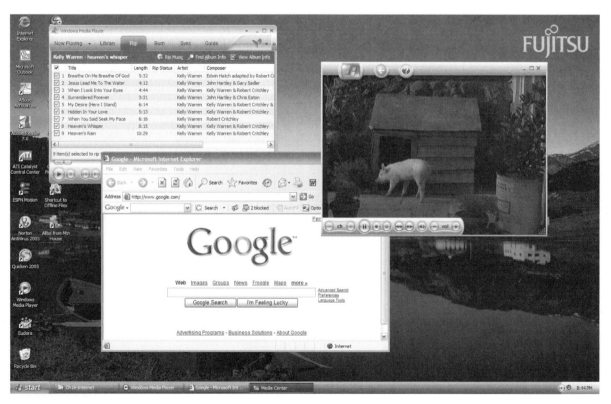

**Figure 11-1**   New user interface and sample windows

▲ The ability for two or more users to be logged on simultaneously. Each user has a separate profile, and Windows XP can switch between users, keeping a separate set of applications open for each user.

▲ Windows Media Player for Windows XP, a centralized application for working with digital media.

▲ Windows Messenger for instant messaging, conferencing, and application sharing.

▲ Windows Security Center was added with Windows XP Service Pack 2.

▲ The ability to burn a CD simply by dragging and dropping a folder or file onto the CD-R device icon (see Figure 11-2).

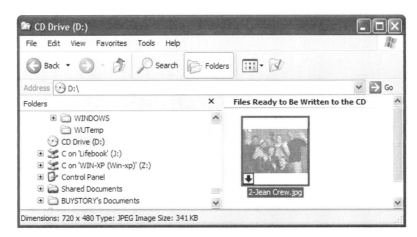

**Figure 11-2** Files can be dragged and dropped to the CD folder for later burning to CD

▲ A way for someone to assist a user at the computer by remotely controlling the computer, called Remote Assistance.

▲ An expanded Help feature.

▲ Advanced security features.

In addition to these features of Windows XP Home Edition, Windows XP Professional offers:

▲ A way for a user to control the computer from a remote location, called Remote Desktop

▲ A way for an administrator to manage user profiles from a server (roaming profiles)

▲ Additional security features

▲ Multilingual capabilities

▲ Support for new higher-performance processors

Windows XP Media Center Edition is an enhanced version of Windows XP Professional, and includes additional support for digital entertainment hardware such as video recording integrated with TV input. When you first launch Media Center (see Figure 11-3), it takes you through a wizard to configure how you will connect to TV (by satellite, cable, or set-top box) and if and how you want it to track TV listings available from your local cable company (see Figure 11-4). It's designed for the high-end PC home market and is only available when preinstalled on a high-end PC manufactured by a Microsoft partner. Windows XP Tablet PC Edition is also built on Windows XP Professional with additional support for tablet PCs. For more information about tablet PCs, see Chapter 20.

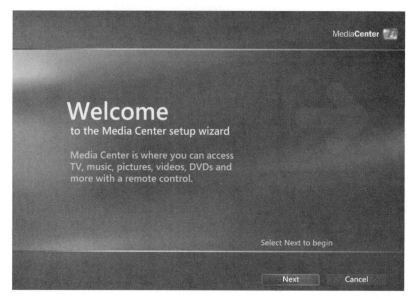

**Figure 11-3**   Set up Media Center so you can watch and record TV

**Figure 11-4**   Media Center is set to watch live TV, record TV, search your online
              TV guide, and play movies

There is also Windows XP Professional x64 Edition, which used to be called Windows XP
64-Bit Edition. This version of Windows XP uses 64-bit code and is designed to be used with
64-bit processors such as the AMD Athlon 64 or Opteron or the Intel Itanium. The OS is
used for high-end gaming computers using AMD processors, for servers, or for heavily technical workstations that run scientific and engineering applications and need greater amounts
of memory and higher performance than standard desktop PCs. For example, an aircraft
designer who uses software to simulate how various conditions affect aircraft materials might
use Windows XP Professional x64 Edition on a system that supports resource-intensive
simulation and animation applications.

Windows XP has several built-in features to manage audio and video, including support for
inputting images from digital cameras and scanners, a Windows Movie Maker for editing

video, and Windows Media Player, Version 8. (Windows Me has Media Player, Version 7.) With Media Player, you can play DVDs, CDs, and Internet radio. There's a jukebox for organizing audio files, including MP3 files used on music CDs. You can also burn your own music CDs using Media Player with a CD-R or CD-RW drive. To access the Media Player, click Start, All Programs, and Windows Media Player. Figure 11-5 shows the Media Player window.

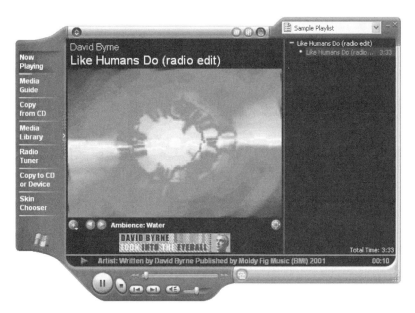

**Figure 11-5**  Windows Media Player

---

**Notes**

Windows Internet Explorer, Windows Media Player, a firewall, and other Microsoft products are tightly integrated with the Windows XP operating system. Some users see this as a disadvantage, and others see it as an advantage. Tight integration allows applications to interact easily with other applications and the OS, but makes it more difficult for third-party software to compete with Microsoft applications and more difficult to remove or reinstall an integrated component that is giving problems.

---

Windows 2000 includes four operating systems:

- *Windows 2000 Professional* was designed to replace both Windows 9x and Windows NT Workstation as a personal computer desktop or notebook OS. It is an improved version of Windows NT Workstation, using the same new technological approach to hardware and software, and has all the popular features of Windows 9x, including Plug and Play.
- *Windows 2000 Server* is the improved version of Windows NT Server and is designed as a network operating system for low-end servers.
- *Windows 2000 Advanced Server* is a network operating system that has the same features as Windows 2000 Server but is designed to run on more powerful servers.
- *Windows 2000 Datacenter Server* is a network operating system that is a step up from Windows 2000 Advanced Server. It is intended for use in large enterprise operations centers.

**A+ Exam Tip**

Microsoft offers several operating systems designed to run on servers, including Windows 2000 Server and Windows Server 2003. None of the server operating systems is covered on the A+ exams.

## WINDOWS 2000/XP ARCHITECTURE AND OPERATING MODES

Windows 2000/XP operates in two modes, user mode and kernel mode, which each take advantage of different CPU functions and abilities. (The Windows 2000/XP architecture was also used by Windows NT.) In Figure 11-6, you can see how OS components are separated into user mode and kernel mode components.

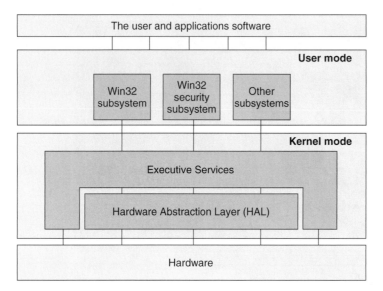

**Figure 11-6**  User mode and kernel mode in Windows 2000/XP and how they relate to users, application software, and hardware

### USER MODE

**User mode** is a processor mode in which programs have only limited access to system information and can access hardware only through other OS services. The OS has several **subsystems,** or OS modules, that use this mode and interface with the user and with applications. The Windows tools you use, such as Windows Explorer, run primarily in user mode. In Figure 11-6, note the Win32 subsystem, which is probably the most important user mode subsystem because it manages and provides an environment for all 32-bit programs, including the user interface (such as the one for Explorer). The Win32 security subsystem provides logon to the system and other security functions, including privileges for file access.

All applications relate to Windows 2000/XP by way of the Win32 subsystem, either directly or indirectly. Figure 11-7 shows how various programs that run under Windows 2000/XP interact with subsystems. For instance, each legacy DOS application resides in its own NTVDM. An **NTVDM (NT virtual DOS machine)** is a carefully controlled environment that Windows 2000/XP provides. In it, a DOS application can interface with only one subsystem and cannot relate to anything outside the system. All 16-bit Windows 3.x applications reside in a **Win16 on Win32 (WOW)** environment. Within the WOW, these 16-bit applications can communicate with one another and the WOW, but that's as far as their world goes. Figure 11-7 shows three 16-bit Windows 3.x applications residing in a WOW that resides in one NTVDM. Because each DOS application expects to run as the only application on a PC, each has its own NTVDM.

You can see in Figure 11-7 that 32-bit applications do not require an NTVDM and can relate to the Win32 subsystem directly, because they are written to run in protected mode. They can also use a single line of communication (called single-threading) with the Win32 subsystem or multiple lines for interfacing (called **multithreading**) with the Win32 subsystem, depending on what the process requests. A **thread** is a single task that the process requests from the kernel,

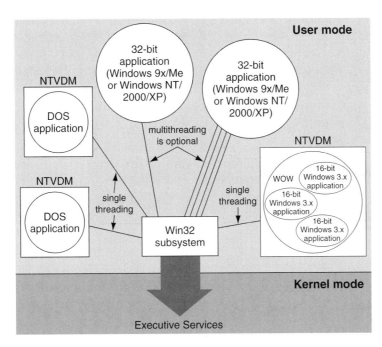

**Figure 11-7** Environment subsystems in Windows 2000/XP user mode include NTVDMs for DOS and Windows 3.x applications and optional multithreading for 32-bit applications

such as the task of printing a file. A **process** is a program or group of programs that is running, together with the system resources assigned to it, such as memory addresses, environmental variables, and other resources. Figure 11-8 shows how the Microsoft Word program (msword.exe) is launched as a running process together with its resources and running threads.

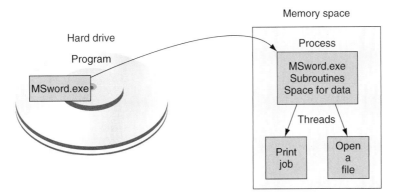

**Figure 11-8** A process is a running program and its resources

Sometimes a process is called an instance, such as when you say, "Open two instances of Internet Explorer." Technically, you are saying to open two Internet Explorer processes. An example of multithreading is Microsoft Word requesting that the subsystem read a large file from the hard drive and print a job at the same time. Single-threading happens when the application does not expect both processes to be performed at the same time but simply passes one request followed by another.

## KERNEL MODE

**Kernel mode** is the operating system mode in which programs have extensive access to system information and hardware. Kernel mode is used by two main components: the HAL and a group of components collectively called executive services. The **HAL (hardware abstraction layer)** is the layer between the OS and the hardware. The HAL is available in different versions, each designed to address the specifics of a particular CPU technology. **Executive services** interface between the subsystems in user mode and the HAL. Executive services components manage hardware resources by way of the HAL and device drivers. Windows 2000/XP was designed to port easily to different hardware platforms. Because only the components operating in kernel mode actually interact with hardware, they are the only parts that need to be changed when Windows 2000/XP moves from one hardware platform to another.

Applications in user mode have no access to hardware resources. In kernel mode, executive services have limited access to hardware resources, but the HAL primarily interacts with hardware. Limiting access to hardware mainly to the HAL increases OS integrity because more control is possible. With this isolation, an application cannot cause a system to hang by making illegal demands on hardware. Overall performance is increased because the HAL and executive services can operate independently of the slower, less efficient applications using them.

## NETWORKING FEATURES

A+ ESS
5.1

A+
220-602
5.2

A workstation running Windows 2000/XP can be configured to work as one node in a workgroup or one node on a domain. A **workgroup** is a logical group of computers and users that share resources (Figure 11-9), where administration, resources, and security on a workstation are controlled by that workstation. Each computer maintains a list of users and their rights on that particular PC. A Windows **domain** is a group of networked computers that share a centralized directory database of user account information and security for the entire group of computers (Figure 11-10). A workgroup uses a **peer-to-peer** networking model, and a domain uses a **client/server** networking model. Using the client/server model, the directory database is controlled by a Network Operating System (NOS). Popular NOSs are Windows Server 2003, Windows 2000 Server, Novell NetWare, Unix, Linux, and Mac OS. Windows 2000 for the desktop has network client software built in for Windows

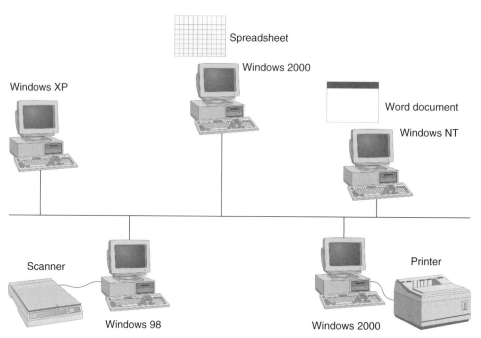

**Figure 11-9** A Windows workgroup is a peer-to-peer network where no single computer controls the network and each computer controls its own resources

11

A+ ESS
5.1

A+
220-602
5.2

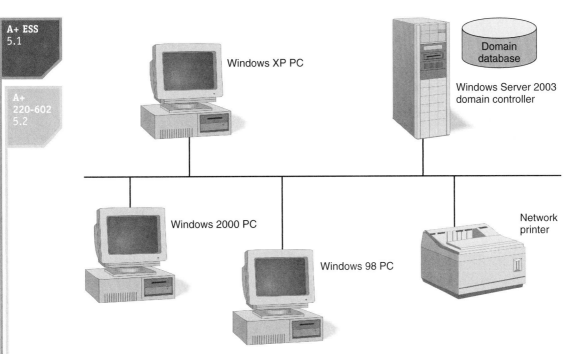

Windows XP PC

Domain
database

Windows Server 2003
domain controller

Windows 2000 PC

Windows 98 PC

Network
printer

**Figure 11-10**  A Windows domain is a client/server network where security on each PC
or other device is controlled by a centralized database on a domain controller

servers (Microsoft Client), Mac OS (AppleTalk Client), and Novell NetWare (Client for
NetWare). Windows XP supports Microsoft Client and Client for NetWare. Alternately,
for Novell NetWare, you can install Novell's version of its client software.

## WINDOWS DOMAINS

In a Windows 2000 Server or Windows Server 2003 domain, a network administrator
manages access to the network through a centralized database. In Figure 11-10, you see
the possible different components of a Windows domain. Every domain has a **domain
controller**, which stores and controls a database of (1) user accounts, (2) group accounts,
and (3) computer accounts. This database is called the directory database or the **security
accounts manager (SAM)** database.

Because the domain controller database is so important, Windows allows backup copies of the
database to exist on more than one computer in the domain. Under Windows NT, a network can
have a primary domain controller and one or more backup domain controllers. The **primary
domain controller (PDC)** holds the original directory database, and read-only copies are stored
on **backup domain controllers (BDCs)**. An administrator can update the database on the PDC
from any computer on the network, and the BDCs later get a copy of the updated database.

With Windows 2000 Server and Windows Server 2003, a network can have any number
of domain controllers, each keeping a copy of the directory that can be edited. An administrator can update the directory on any one of these domain controllers, which will then
communicate the change to the other domain controllers.

When Windows NT and Windows 2000/2003 domain controllers are on the same network, conflicts can result because of the differences in the way the domain controllers work
in each OS. For this reason, Windows 2000 runs in two modes: native mode and mixed
mode. **Native mode** is used when no Windows NT domain controllers are present, and **mixed
mode** is used when there is at least one Windows NT domain controller on the network.
Mixed mode is necessary when a large network is being upgraded from Windows NT to
Windows 2000/2003, and some servers have been upgraded but others have not. When you

install Windows 2000 Server or Windows Server 2003, the default mode is mixed mode. After the installation, an administrator can choose to migrate to native mode by using the Computer Management console, which you will learn about in the next chapter. Once you change a domain to native mode, you cannot change it back to mixed mode.

In addition to native mode and mixed mode, another networking feature new to Windows 2000 is **Active Directory**, a directory database and service that allows for a single administration point for all shared resources on a network. In Windows 2000 Server and Windows Server 2003, the security accounts manager (SAM) database is part of Active Directory. Active Directory can track file locations, databases, Web sites, users, services, and peripheral devices, including printers, scanners, and other hardware. It uses a locating method similar to that used by the Internet. Windows 2000 Server and Windows Server 2003 versions provide Active Directory, and Windows 2000 Professional and Windows XP act as Active Directory clients, or users, of the directory.

## WINDOWS 2000/XP LOGON

A+ ESS
5.1

A+
220-602
5.2

Regardless of whether Windows 2000/XP computers are networked or not, every Windows 2000/XP workstation has an **administrator account** by default. An administrator has rights and permissions to all computer software and hardware resources and is responsible for setting up other user accounts and assigning them privileges. During the Windows 2000/XP installation, you enter a password to the default administrator account. When the workstation is part of a Windows workgroup, you can log on as an administrator after the OS is installed and create local user accounts. If the workstation is part of a domain, a network administrator sets up global user accounts that apply to the entire domain, including giving access to the local workstations. Local user accounts, as well as other ways to secure a workstation, are covered in Chapter 13.

When Windows 2000/XP starts up, you must log on before you can use the OS. Windows XP displays a logon screen by default. For Windows 2000, you see the logon screen when you press Ctrl+Alt+Del. To log on, enter a user name and password, and click **OK**. Windows 2000/XP tracks which user is logged on to the system and grants rights and permissions according to the user's group or to specific permissions granted this user by the administrator. If you do not enter a valid account name and password, Windows 2000/XP does not allow you access to the system.

Using Windows XP, more than one user can be logged on at the same time. In Windows XP, if you are in a workgroup and want to log off or log on as another user, you can press **Ctl-Atl-Del** and the Log Off Windows dialog box appears (see Figure 11-11). If you belong to a domain, when you press Ctl-Atl-Del, the Windows Security dialog box appears. You can use this dialog box for logging on and off.

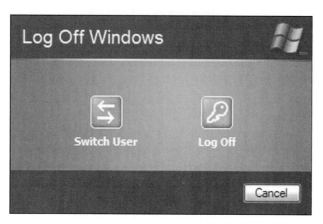

**Figure 11-11**   Switch users or log off in Windows XP

# HOW WINDOWS 2000/XP MANAGES HARD DRIVES

A hard drive is divided into 512-byte sectors. These sectors on a hard drive are organized into partitions and logical drives. An OS manages a logical drive with a file system, and the OS itself is installed on one of these logical drives. When Windows 2000/XP is installed on a new hard drive, four steps are involved in logically organizing the drive:

1. Cylinders on the drive are divided into partitions, and a partition table at the beginning of the drive records where each partition begins and ends on the drive.

2. Each partition is divided into one or more logical drives, which are named drive C, D, E, and so forth. Creating these first two levels is called partitioning the drive.

3. Each logical drive (also called a volume) is formatted with a file system, FAT16, FAT32, or NTFS. This step is called formatting a drive (logical drive, that is).

4. If the hard drive is to be the boot device in a system, the last step of preparing the drive is to install an operating system on logical drive C. This step is called installing an OS.

We next explain how partitions, logical drives, and file systems look and work, and how to make good decisions when choosing how many and how big each logical drive on a hard drive will be; this process is called "slicing" your drive.

## UNDERSTANDING PARTITIONS AND LOGICAL DRIVES

Recall that a hard drive can be organized into one or more partitions and that partitions contain logical drives. Figure 11-12 shows an example with the hard drive divided into two partitions.

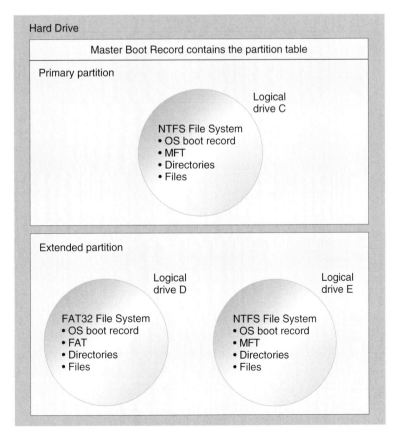

**Figure 11-12** A hard drive is divided into one or more partitions that contain logical drives

A+ ESS
3.1

A+
220-602
3.1

The first partition contains one logical drive (drive C), and the second partition is divided into two logical drives (D and E). The first sector at the beginning of a hard drive (512 bytes located on head 0, track 0, sector 1) is called the master boot sector or, more commonly, the Master Boot Record (MBR), which contains two items:

▲ The master boot program (446 bytes), which loads the OS boot program stored in the OS boot record. (The OS boot program begins the process of loading the OS.)
▲ The partition table, which contains the description, location, and size of each partition on the drive (up to four).

Table 11-1 lists the contents of the MBR. The first item is the master boot program and the last five items in Table 11-1 make up the partition table.

| Item | Bytes Used | Description |
| --- | --- | --- |
| 1 | 446 bytes | Master boot program that calls the OS boot program on the OS boot record |
| 2 | 16-byte total | Description of the first partition |
| | 1 byte | Is this the bootable partition? (Yes = 90h, No = 00h) |
| | 3 bytes | Beginning location of the partition |
| | 1 byte | System indicator; possible values are:<br><br>0 = Not a DOS partition<br><br>1 = DOS with a 12-bit FAT<br><br>4 = DOS with a 16-bit FAT<br><br>5 = Not the first partition<br><br>6 = Partition larger than 32 MB |
| | 3 bytes | Ending location of partition |
| | 4 bytes | First sector of the partition table relative to the beginning of the disk |
| | 4 bytes | Number of sectors in the partition |
| 3 | 16 bytes | Describes second partition, using same format as first partition |
| 4 | 16 bytes | Describes third partition, using same format as first partition |
| 5 | 16 bytes | Describes fourth partition, using same format as first partition |
| 6 | 2 bytes | Signature of the partition table, always AA55 |

**Table 11-1** Hard drive MBR containing the master boot program and the partition table

During POST, the master boot program stored at the beginning of the MBR executes and checks the integrity of the partition table itself. If the master boot program finds any corruption, it refuses to continue execution, and the disk is unusable. If the table entries are valid, the master boot program looks in the table to determine which partition is the active partition, which, in most cases, is the first partition on the drive. The **active partition** is the partition on the hard drive used to boot the OS. It most often contains only a single logical drive (drive C) and is usually the first partition on the drive. Windows 2000/XP calls the active partition the **system partition**.

A+ ESS
3.1

A+
220-602
3.1

The master boot program looks in the first sector of this active partition to find and execute the OS boot program. This first sector of the active partition is called the OS boot record, and, if the active partition is the first partition on the drive, this sector is physically the second sector on the drive, immediately following the MBR sector.

Using DOS or Windows 9x, a hard drive can have one or two partitions. Using Windows 2000/XP, a drive can have up to four partitions. A partition can be a **primary partition** (having only one logical drive in the partition, such as drive C, in which case it is sometimes called a logical partition) or an **extended partition** (having more than one logical drive, such as drive D and drive E). There can be only one extended partition on a drive. Therefore, with DOS and Windows 9x, the drive can have one primary and one extended partition. Under Windows 2000/XP, the drive can have four partitions, but only one of them can be an extended partition. The active partition is always a primary partition.

> **Notes**
>
> Suppose you try to boot your system and get the message, "Invalid drive specification." This error can be caused by a number of problems; a possibility is a **boot sector virus**. This type of virus attacks the MBR master boot program. To replace the MBR program with a fresh one, use the Windows 2000/XP Fixmbr command or the Windows 9x Fdisk /MBR command.

> **A+ Exam Tip**
>
> The A+ Essentials exam expects you to know the difference between these terms: active partition, primary partition, extended partition, and logical partition.

## WINDOWS 2000/XP BOOT PARTITION AND SYSTEM PARTITION

Windows 2000/XP assigns two different functions to hard drive partitions holding the OS (see Figure 11-13). The **system partition**, normally drive C, is the active partition of the hard drive. This is the partition that contains the OS boot record. Remember that the MBR program looks to this OS boot record for the boot program as the first step in turning the PC over to an OS. The other partition, called the **boot partition**, is the partition where the Windows 2000/XP operating system is stored.

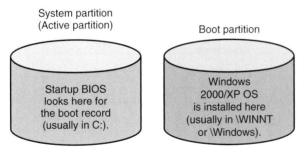

System partition
(Active partition)

Boot partition

Startup BIOS looks here for the boot record (usually in C:).

Windows 2000/XP OS is installed here (usually in \WINNT or \Windows).

**Figure 11-13**  Two types of Windows 2000/XP hard drive partitions

For most installations, the system partition and the boot partition are the same (drive C) and Windows is installed in C:\Windows (for Windows XP) or C:\Winnt (for Windows 2000). An example of when the system partition and the boot partition are different is when Windows XP is installed as a dual boot with Windows 2000. Figure 11-14 shows how

> **Notes**
>
> Don't be confused by the terminology here. It is really true that, according to Windows 2000/XP terminology, the Windows OS is on the boot partition, and the boot record is on the system partition, although that might seem backward. The PC boots from the system partition and loads the Windows 2000/XP operating system from the boot partition.

Windows XP is installed on drive E and Windows 2000 is installed on drive C. For Windows XP, the system partition is drive C and the boot partition is drive E. (For Windows 2000 on this computer, the system and boot partitions are both drive C.)

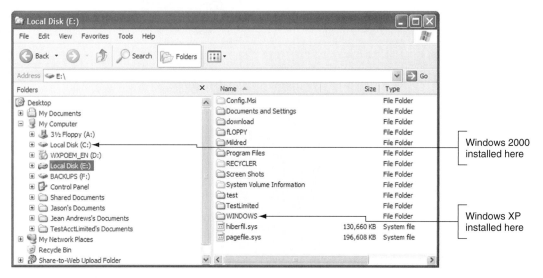

Windows 2000 installed here

Windows XP installed here

**Figure 11-14** Windows XP and Windows 2000 installed on the same system

> **Notes**
>
> To know what file system a logical drive is using, in Windows Explorer, right-click the drive and select **Properties** from the shortcut menu (see Figure 11-15).

## UNDERSTANDING FILE SYSTEMS

Each logical drive or volume must have a file system installed; the process is called formatting the drive. The file system is needed for the OS to track where on the drive it places files and folders.

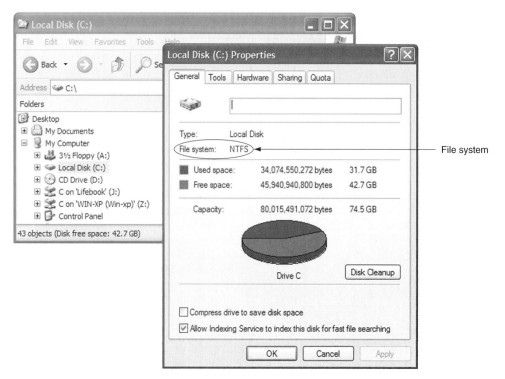

File system

**Figure 11-15** This drive C is using the NTFS file system

A+ ESS
3.1

A+
220-602
3.1

Recall that floppy disks use the FAT12 file system, which you learned about in Chapter 8. The only difference between FAT12 and FAT16 or FAT32 is the number of bits used for each entry in the FAT. The structure of the boot record, FAT, and root directory that makes up the FAT12 file system also applies to FAT16 and FAT32. Let's now look at how each file system is organized, the advantages of each file system, and what you need to know when slicing your drive.

### FAT16

DOS and all versions of Windows support the FAT16 file system, which uses 16 bits for each cluster entry in the FAT. Using FAT16, the smallest cluster size is four sectors. Because each sector is 512 bytes, a cluster that contains four sectors is 2,048 bytes. Because an OS writes a file to a drive using one or more clusters, the least amount of space it uses for one file is 2,048 bytes. If a file contains less than 2,048 bytes, the remaining bytes in the cluster are wasted. This wasted space is called **slack**. If a drive contains many small files, much space is wasted.

This problem could be partially solved if the cluster size were smaller than four sectors. However, just the opposite is true: The more sectors assigned to the logical drive, the more sectors per cluster. This is because the OS is limited by the number of bits in the FAT that it uses to number the clusters. For FAT16, the FAT table has 16 bits for each cluster number. Using 16 bits, the largest possible number is 65,535 (binary 1111 1111 1111 1111). Therefore, it is not possible to have more than 65,535 clusters when using FAT16. Consequently, the number of sectors assigned to each cluster must be large in order to accommodate a large logical drive.

### FAT32

Beginning with Windows 95 OSR2 (OS Release 2), Microsoft offered a FAT that contains 32 bits per FAT entry instead of the older 12-bit or 16-bit FAT entries. Only 28 bits are used to hold a cluster number; the remaining four bits are not used.

FAT32 is efficient for logical drives up to 16 GB. In this range, the cluster size is 8K. After that, the cluster size increases to about 16K for drives in the 16-GB to 32-GB range. Windows 2000/XP supports FAT32 only for drives up to 32 GB. For drives larger than 32 GB, the NTFS file system is used.

> **Notes**
>
> Using Windows tools, changing the size of a partition or logical drive or changing a file system on a drive erases everything on the logical drive. If you want to resize a drive or partition or change file systems without losing your data, you can use a third-party utility. One very good utility is Norton PartitionMagic by Symantec (*www.symantec.com*). Figure 11-16 shows a Norton PartitionMagic screen from which you can resize a partition without disturbing data. This software also examines a hard drive and tells you how much of the drive is used for slack space. Knowing this can help you decide if a file system change will yield more usable drive space.

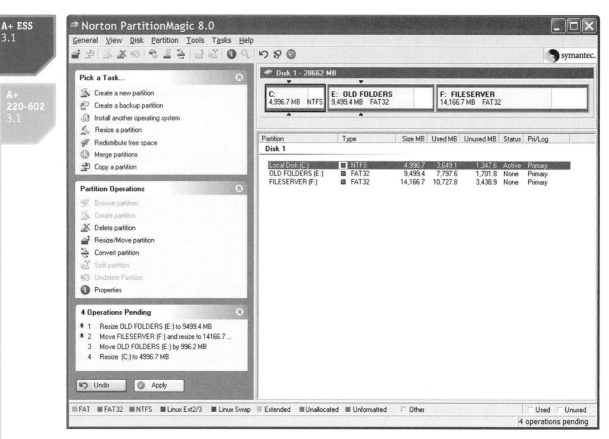

**Figure 11-16**    Use Norton PartitionMagic to create, resize, and merge partitions and redistribute free space on partitions

### NTFS

Windows 2000/XP supports **NTFS (New Technology file system)**. NTFS is designed to provide more security and be more efficient than the FAT file system. NTFS uses a database called the **master file table (MFT)** to hold information about files and directories and their locations on the hard drive. For Windows 2000/XP, in most situations, use NTFS, but use FAT32 if you have Windows 9x/Me installed on the drive as a second OS.

When a logical drive is formatted for NTFS, each cluster can range from 512 bytes on smaller disks to 4K on larger disks. Clusters are numbered sequentially by logical cluster numbers (LCN) from the beginning to the end of the drive. Each cluster number is stored in a 64-bit entry, compared to either 16 bits for FAT16 or 32 bits for FAT32.

The MFT tracks the contents of a logical drive by using one or more rows for each file or directory on the drive, and, if a data file is small, the entire file is contained in the MFT. As shown in Figure 11-17, the MFT information about each file is contained in one record, or row, including header information (abbreviated H in Microsoft documentation); standard information (SI) about the file, including date and time; filename (FN); data about the location of the file; and security information about the file, called the security descriptor (SD). Entries in the MFT are ordered alphabetically by filename to speed up a search for a file listed in the table.

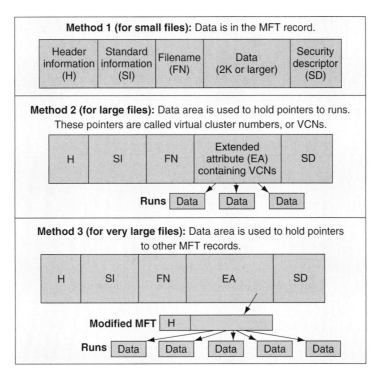

**Figure 11-17**   The NTFS file system uses a master file table to store files using three methods, depending on the file size

Also notice in Figure 11-17 that the data area in the MFT record is 2K for small logical drives but can be larger for larger logical drives. For small files (generally about 1500 bytes or less), if the data can fit into the 2K area, the file description and the file's data are fully contained within the MFT.

---
**Notes**

When upgrading from Windows 9x/Me to Windows 2000/XP, it is best to install NTFS at the same time you install the OS from the setup CD, though you can convert a FAT file system to NTFS after Windows 2000/XP is installed. To convert a FAT32 volume to an NTFS volume, first back up all important data on the drive and then use this command at a command prompt: **convert D: /FS:NTFS**, where D: is the drive to be converted. Keep in mind that the program requires some free space on the drive. If it doesn't find enough free space, the program terminates.

---

On the other hand, if the file is moderately large and the data does not fit into the MFT, the data area in the MFT becomes an extended attribute (EA) of the file, which only points to the location of the data. The data itself is moved outside the table to clusters called runs. The record in the MFT for this moderately large file contains pointers to these runs. Each data run, or cluster, assigned to the file is given a 64-bit virtual cluster number (VCN). The MFT maps the VCNs for the file onto the LCNs for the drive. This mapping is stored in the area of the MFT record that would have contained the data if the file had been small enough.

---
**Notes**

Windows NT Workstation 4.0 uses NTFS Version 4.0 (NTFS4) file system. Windows 2000/XP uses the latest version of NTFS, the one introduced by Windows NT Server 4.0, called the NTFS Version 5.0 (NTFS5) file system. The NTFS5 version includes numerous enhancements over previous versions but cannot be read by Windows NT Workstation 4.0 unless Windows NT 4.0 Service Pack 4 is applied.

In the third method shown in Figure 11-17, if the file is so large that the pointers to all the VCNs cannot be contained in one MFT record, then additional MFT records are used. The first MFT record is called the base file record and holds the location of the other MFT records for this file.

## ADVANTAGES OF NTFS AND FAT

When choosing between the NTFS file system and the FAT16 or FAT32 file system, consider the advantages that NTFS offers over FAT:

- ◢ NTFS is a recoverable file system. NTFS retains copies of its critical file system data and automatically recovers a failed file system. It uses this information the first time the disk is accessed after a file system failure.
- ◢ NTFS under Windows 2000/XP supports encryption (encoding files so they can't be deciphered by others) and disk quotas (limiting the hard drive space available to a user).
- ◢ NTFS supports compression (reducing the size of files and folders). FAT32 supports compression of an entire logical drive but not compression of individual files or folders.
- ◢ NTFS provides added security in the event you boot from floppy disks:

  - ◢ If you boot a PC using a DOS or Windows 9x boot disk, you can access the hard drive of a Windows 2000/XP system that uses the FAT file system, but you cannot access an NTFS file system.
  - ◢ If you boot a PC using the Windows 2000/XP Recovery Console, you can access the NTFS file system only if you provide an administrator password. In fact, if the administrator forgets his or her password to the OS, the hard drive is not accessible from the Recovery Console. When using Windows tools, the only recourse is to reload the OS.

> **Notes**
>
> Third-party utility software can sometimes help you recover a forgotten administrator password. For example, ERD Commander by Winternals (*www.winternals.com*) is a bootable operating system on CD that contains Locksmith, a utility that lets you reset a forgotten administrator password. Boot a Windows 2000/XP system from the ERD Commander CD to launch a Windows-like desktop from which you can use several recovery tools.

- ◢ NTFS supports mirroring or imaging drives, meaning that two copies of data can be kept on two different drives to protect against permanent data loss in case of a hard drive crash. This feature makes NTFS an important alternative for file servers.
- ◢ NTFS uses smaller cluster sizes than FAT16 or FAT32, making more efficient use of hard drive space when small files are stored.
- ◢ NTFS supports large-volume drives. NTFS uses 64-bit cluster numbers, whereas FAT16 uses 16-bit cluster numbers and FAT32 uses 32-bit cluster numbers. Because the number of bits assigned to hold each cluster number is so large, the cluster number itself can be large, and the table can accommodate very large drives with many clusters. Overall, NTFS is a more effective file system for drives larger than 1 GB, is more reliable, and offers more features.

The advantages of the FAT file system over NTFS include the following:

- ◢ The FAT file system has less overhead than the NTFS file system and, therefore, works best for hard drives that are less than 500 MB.

A+ ESS
3.1

A+
220-602
3.1

A+ ESS
3.1

A+
220-602
3.1

▲ The FAT file system is compatible with Windows 9x/Me and DOS operating systems. If you plan to use either DOS or Windows 9x/Me on the same hard drive as Windows 2000/XP, use the FAT file system so that DOS and Windows 9x/Me can access files used by Windows 2000/XP.

▲ Legacy applications designed for Windows 9x/Me, but installed on a Windows 2000/XP system, might not work with the NTFS file system. To support these applications, use the FAT file system.

After you have divided a hard drive into partitions and logical drives, each logical drive can be formatted using any file system the OS supports. For example, you can create two logical drives, drive C and drive D. Using Windows 2000/XP, drive C can be formatted using FAT32, and drive D can be formatted using NTFS.

## HOW MANY PARTITIONS DO YOU NEED?

When you configure a new hard drive or install Windows 2000/XP, you must decide how many partitions you use and the size of each partition. You can leave some space unused that you might want to hold until a new need arises such as installing another OS on the drive.

Your first step is to remember that the active or primary partition has only one logical drive C. You can have up to three more partitions (one can be an extended partition). Each primary partition has one logical drive, and within the extended partition, you can put several logical drives. You determine how many logical drives and what portion of the extended partition is allotted to each.

For most situations using Windows 2000/XP, you will only use one primary partition containing drive C and format it using the NTFS file system. However, here are reasons to use more partitions and more logical drives:

▲ You plan to install more than one OS on the hard drive, creating what is called a dual-boot system. For example, you might want to install Windows 98 on one partition and Windows XP on another so you can test software under both operating systems. For this situation, create two partitions.

▲ Some people prefer to use more than one logical drive to organize data on their hard drives. For example, you might want to create a second partition on the drive to be used exclusively to hold a backup of data from another computer on the network. Another example is when you want to install Windows and all your applications on one partition and your data on another. Having your data on a separate partition makes backing up easier.

>  **Caution**
>
> It's convenient to back up one partition (or logical drive) to another partition on a different hard drive. However, don't back up one partition (or logical drive) to another partition on the same hard drive, because when a hard drive fails, quite often all partitions on the drive are damaged and you will lose both your data and your backup.

▲ The larger the logical drive, the larger the cluster size, and the more slack or wasted space. For large drives, you might want to use two or more logical drives to optimize space by reducing the cluster size. In this situation, use as few logical drives as possible but still keep cluster size to a minimum.

▲ FAT16 and FAT32 have limitations on the size of a logical drive they support. For these file systems, you might have to use more than one logical drive to use all available space on the drive.

Table 11-2 gives the information you need to determine how to slice your drive. Notice that the largest logical drive possible using DOS or Windows 9x FAT16 is 2 GB. (This limitation is

rooted in the largest cluster number that can be stored in a 16-bit FAT entry.) For Windows 2000/XP, FAT16 logical drives can be no larger than 4 GB. However, you can see from the table that to make a drive that big, the cluster size must be huge. Also, the largest hard drive that FAT16 can support is 8.4 GB; if the drive is larger than that, you must use FAT32.

| File System | Size of Logical Drive | Sectors Per Cluster | Bytes Per Cluster |
|---|---|---|---|
| FAT16 | Up to 128 MB | 4 | 2,048 |
| | 128 to 256 MB | 8 | 4,096 |
| | 256 to 512 MB | 16 | 8,192 |
| | 512 MB to 1 GB | 32 | 16,384 |
| | 1 GB to 4 GB* | 64 | 32,768 |
| FAT32 | 512 MB to 8 GB | 8 | 4,096 |
| | 8 GB to 16 GB | 16 | 8,192 |
| | 16 GB to 32 GB | 32 | 16,384 |
| | More than 32 GB** | 64 | 32,768 |
| NTFS | Up to 512 MB | 1 | 512 |
| | 512 MB to 1 GB | 2 | 1,024 |
| | 1 GB to 2 GB | 4 | 2,048 |
| | More than 2 GB | 8 | 4,096 |

*For DOS and Windows 9x, the largest FAT16 is 2 GB. For Windows NT/2000/XP, the largest FAT16 is 4 GB.

**Windows 2000/XP does not support FAT32 for drives larger than 32 GB.

**Table 11-2**   Size of some logical drives compared to cluster size for FAT16, FAT32, and NTFS

When a logical drive is first created, a drive letter is assigned to each logical drive. For a primary partition, drive C is assigned to the one volume, and drives D, E, and so forth are assigned to volumes in the other partitions. However, if a second hard drive is installed in a system, the program takes this into account when assigning drive letters. If the second hard drive has a primary partition, the program assigns it to drive D, leaving drive letters E, F, G, H, and so forth for the volumes in the other partitions of both hard drives. For example, in a two-hard-drive system in which each hard drive has a primary partition, an extended partition, and three logical drives, the drive letters for the first hard drive are C, E, and F, and the drive letters for the second hard drive are D, G, and H.

If the second hard drive is not going to be the boot device, it does not have to have a primary partition. If you put only a single extended partition on that drive, then the program assigns the drive letters C, D, and E to the first drive and F, G, H, and so forth to the second drive.

## WHEN TO USE WINDOWS 2000 AND WINDOWS XP

If you're thinking of upgrading from Windows 2000 to Windows XP, know that Windows XP is generally more stable than Windows 2000. It was designed to avoid situations that occurred with Windows 2000, which caused drivers and applications to bring these systems down. Installing Windows XP should also be easier than installing Windows 2000. In addition, Windows XP has increased security, including a built-in Internet firewall designed to protect a home PC connected directly to the Internet by way of an always-on connection such as a cable modem or DSL. (Firewalls, cable modems, and DSL are covered in Chapters 18

11

and 19.) Also, many new hardware devices provide drivers only for Windows XP, and applications are written only for XP.

On the other hand, if you have a notebook computer, know that notebook computer manufacturers often create their own unique build for an operating system. If you are supporting an old notebook computer that was purchased with Windows 2000 on it, continue to use the notebook manufacturer's version of this OS. In general, it's best to not upgrade an OS on a notebook unless you want to use some feature the new OS offers.

For notebooks, follow the general rule, "If it ain't broke, don't fix it." If a notebook is working well with Windows 2000 installed and serving its purpose, leave it alone.

## PLAN THE WINDOWS 2000/XP INSTALLATION

This section explains what you need to do before you begin an installation of Windows XP or Windows 2000. Careful planning and preparation before you begin the installation will help make sure Windows 2000/XP installs successfully and all your hardware and applications work under the newly installed OS.

Generally, before installing Windows 2000/XP, do the following:

▲ For Windows XP, verify that the system meets the minimum and recommended requirements shown in Table 11-3. For Windows 2000, you must have at least 650 MB of free space on your hard drive, at least 64 MB of RAM, and a 133-MHz Pentium-compatible CPU or higher. You'll also need to verify that all installed hardware components and software are compatible with Windows XP or Windows 2000 and you have Windows XP or Windows 2000 drivers for hardware devices. Also make sure your hard drive is large enough to hold the OS, applications, and data.

| Component or Device | Minimum Requirement | Recommended Requirement |
|---|---|---|
| One or two CPUs | Pentium II 233 MHz or better | Pentium II 300 MHz or better |
| RAM | 64 MB | 128 MB up to 4 GB |
| Hard drive partition | 2 GB | More than 2 GB |
| Free space on the hard drive partition | 1.5 GB (bare bones) | 2 GB or more |
| CD-ROM drive or DVD-ROM drive | 12x | 12x or faster |
| Video | Super VGA (800 x 600) | Higher resolutions are nicer |
| Input devices | Keyboard and mouse or other pointing device | Keyboard and mouse or other pointing device |

**Table 11-3** Minimum and recommended requirements for Windows XP Professional

▲ Decide about Windows 2000/XP installation options. Your choices are a clean install (gives you a fresh start), an upgrade (picks up previous Windows settings and installed software), or dual boot (install Windows 2000/XP to work alongside the currently installed OS).

▲ Decide how you will partition your hard drive and what file system you will use.

▲ Decide how your computer will connect to a network, including whether the PC will be configured as a workstation in a workgroup or as part of a domain.

▲ Decide how the installation process will work. You can install the OS from the original Windows 2000/XP setup CD, from setup files stored on your hard drive, or

A+ ESS
3.2

A+
220-602
3.2

from across the network. In addition, you can perform an attended or unattended installation.

◢ Make a final checklist to verify that you have done all of the and are ready to begin the installation.

> **Notes**
>
> Remember that the requirements of an OS vary depending on which version you have installed and what applications and hardware you have installed with it. Also, occasionally Microsoft will adjust a minimum or recommended requirement.

## MINIMUM REQUIREMENTS AND HARDWARE COMPATIBILITY

Before you begin the Windows 2000/XP installation, ask yourself the following to verify your system qualifies and gather up what you'll need to get it going under Windows 2000/XP:

◢ *What CPU and how much RAM is installed?* Recall from earlier chapters that you can use the My Computer icon on the Windows desktop to determine the current CPU and available RAM (see Figure 11-18).

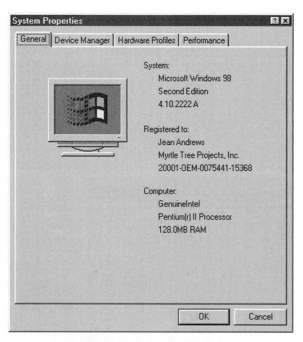

**Figure 11-18**   Windows 98 reports how much RAM is available, which is an important factor when deciding to upgrade to Windows 2000/XP

◢ *How much hard drive space is available?* To see how much hard drive space is available on a logical drive, open Windows Explorer, right-click the drive letter, and select **Properties** from the shortcut menu (see Figure 11-19). Part of the installation process for an upgrade is to clean up the hard drive, which might free some hard drive space. Even though Windows XP requires only 1.5 GB to install, you cannot achieve acceptable results unless you have at least 2.0 GB of free hard drive space on the volume that holds Windows XP. (Windows 2000 requires a minimum of 650 MB of free space to install.) However, for best results, use a hard drive partition with at least 10 GB of free space so your key applications can be installed on the same partition. For best results for users that have many applications, make the partition about 15 GB. To know how many and how large are the partitions on the drive, in Windows 9x/Me, use the Fdisk command and, in Windows 2000/XP, use the Disk Management utility from the Windows desktop. Figure 11-20 shows the

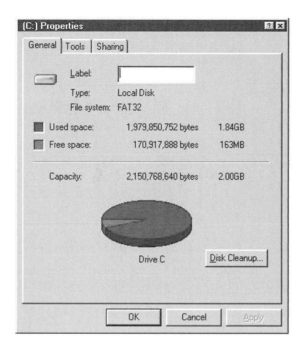

Figure 11-19  Make sure you have enough free hard drive space for Windows 2000/XP

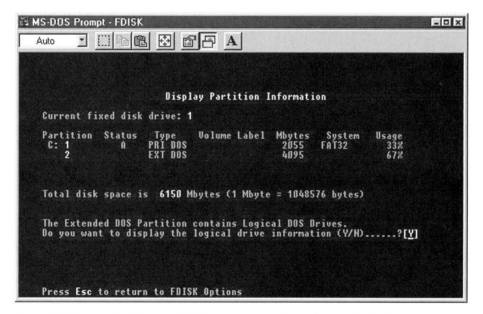

Figure 11-20  Use the Windows 98 Fdisk command to find out how a hard drive is partitioned

Fdisk utility displaying partition information for a Windows 98 hard drive. (You'll learn more about Fdisk in Chapter 15.) To install Windows 2000/XP on this drive, you'll most likely need to repartition the drive into one large partition.

▲ *Does my motherboard BIOS qualify?* Your motherboard BIOS should meet the **Advanced Configuration and Power Interface (ACPI)** standards developed by Intel, Microsoft, and Toshiba, which apply to system BIOS, the OS, and certain hardware devices and software to control when a device goes into an inactive state in order to conserve power. To take full advantage of Windows 2000/XP power management abilities, your system BIOS must be ACPI-compliant. If your BIOS is not ACPI-compliant and you install Windows, Windows does not install ACPI support but installs a legacy HAL that does not support ACPI. If you later flash your BIOS to make it ACPI-compliant, you have to reinstall

**A+ ESS**
1.1
3.2

**A+**
220-602
3.2

**A+ ESS**
3.2

Windows to include ACPI support. A BIOS made after January, 1999, is ACPI compliant, and most likely you'll never be called on to upgrade a system that old. However, to know if your BIOS is compliant, enter CMOS setup and look for ACPI information and features. If your BIOS is not compliant, maybe you can flash the BIOS with an upgrade. Chapter 6 discusses how to flash BIOS.

▲ *Will my software work under Windows 2000/XP?* For Windows XP, most software written for Windows 2000 or Windows 98/Me will work under Windows XP. However, there are several ways you can make sure. One way is to run the Readiness Analyzer. Use the following command from the Windows XP CD, substituting the drive letter of your CD-ROM drive for D in the command line, if necessary:

```
D:\I386\Winnt32 /checkupgradeonly
```

Depending on the release of Windows XP, your path might be different. The process takes about 10 minutes to run and displays a report that you can save and later print. The default name and path of the report is C:\Windows\compat.txt. The report is important if you have software you are not sure will work under Windows XP. If the analyzer reports that your software or hardware will not work under Windows XP, you might choose to upgrade the software or set up a dual boot with your old OS and Windows XP. (Dual-boot setup is covered later in the chapter.) For Windows 2000, to find out if your system qualifies, you can run the Check Upgrade Only mode on the Windows 2000 setup CD.

▲ *Will my hardware devices work under Windows 2000/XP?* If you can find Windows XP or Windows 2000 drivers for your device, then you can assume the device will install and work under Windows 2000/XP. To find the drivers, first look on the device's setup CD. If you don't find them there, go to the hardware manufacturer Web site and search for Windows XP drivers or Windows 2000 drivers for the device. If you find Windows XP or Windows 2000 drivers, then download them and you're good to go.

> **Notes**
>
> When upgrading to Windows 2000/XP, if the Windows 2000/XP Setup cannot find a critical driver such as the driver to control a hard drive, it cancels the upgrade.

If you plan to erase the hard drive as part of the installation, store these drivers on floppy disks, burn a CD, or put them on a network drive until you're ready to install them under Windows 2000/XP. If you cannot find an upgrade, sometimes a device will work if you substitute a Windows driver written for a similar device. Check the documentation for your device, looking for information about other devices it can emulate. It is especially important to know that you have Windows XP or Windows 2000 drivers for your network card or modem card before you install the OS, because you need the card to access the Internet to get upgrades.

> **Notes**
>
> Microsoft offers the Windows Marketplace of tested products page at *testedproducts.windowsmarketplace.com*. Click the Hardware tab to see a list of hardware device categories. Figure 11-21 shows the beginning of the list of qualifying modem cards. However, if you find your device listed, you still have to locate the Windows XP or Windows 2000 drivers. Also, just because a device is not listed doesn't mean it won't work under Windows 2000/XP.

▲ *What if I can't find the drivers?* If you are not sure you have the right Windows XP or Windows 2000 drivers for your hardware components, then install Windows 2000/XP as a dual boot with your current OS. Later, when you get the component working under Windows 2000/XP, you can uninstall the other OS.

A+ ESS
3.2

A+
220-602
3.2

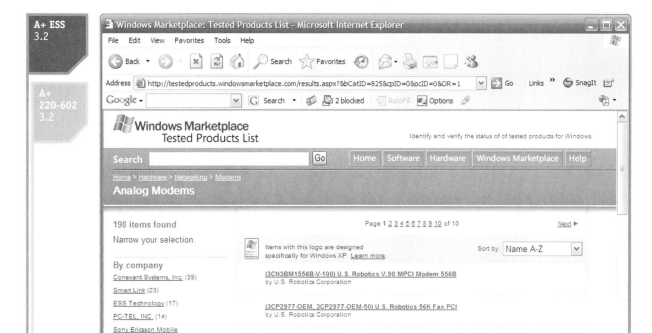

**Figure 11-21** Use the Microsoft Web site to verify that your computer, peripheral devices, and applications all qualify for Windows 2000/XP

## UPGRADE, CLEAN INSTALL, OR DUAL BOOT?

If you are installing Windows 2000/XP on a new hard drive, then you are doing a clean install. If Windows 9x/Me or Windows NT/2000 is already installed on the hard drive, then you have three choices:

- ◢ You can perform a clean install, overwriting the existing operating system and applications.
- ◢ You can perform an upgrade installation.
- ◢ You can install Windows 2000/XP in a second partition on the hard drive and create a dual-boot situation.

Each of these options has advantages and disadvantages.

### CLEAN INSTALL—ERASING EXISTING INSTALLATIONS

A clean install that overwrites the existing installation has some advantages; one advantage is that you get a fresh start. With an upgrade, problems with applications or the OS might follow you into the Windows 2000/XP load. If you erase everything (format the hard drive), then you are assured that the registry as well as all applications are as clean as possible. The disadvantage is that, after Windows 2000/XP is installed, you must reinstall application software on the hard drive and restore the data from backups. If you do a clean install, you can choose to format the hard drive first, or simply do a clean install on top of the existing installation. If you don't format the drive, the data will still be on the drive, but the previous operating system settings and applications will be lost.

If you decide to do a clean install, verify that you have all the application software CDs or floppy disks and software documentation. Back up all the data, and verify that the backups are good. Then, and only then, format the hard drive or begin the clean install without formatting the drive. If you don't format the hard drive, be sure to run a current version of antivirus software before you begin the installation.

## DECIDE BETWEEN AN UPGRADE OR CLEAN INSTALL

If you plan to set up a dual boot, then you will perform a clean install for Windows 2000/XP. If you already have an OS installed and you do not plan a dual boot, then you have a choice between an upgrade and a clean install.

> **Notes**
>
> You cannot upgrade a compressed Windows 9x drive. You must uncompress it before you can upgrade to Windows 2000/XP.

The advantages of upgrading are that all applications and data and most OS settings are carried forward into the new Windows 2000/XP environment, and the installation is faster. If you perform an upgrade, you must begin the installation while you are in the current OS (from the Windows desktop). If you are working from a remote location on the network, you cannot do an upgrade.

When deciding between a clean install and an upgrade, consider these issues regarding the currently installed OS and the about-to-be installed OS:

 **A+ Exam Tip**

The A+ Essentials exam expects you to know the upgrade paths available to Windows 2000/XP.

▲ You can use the less expensive upgrade version of Windows XP Professional to upgrade from Windows 98, Windows Me, Windows NT 4.0, and Windows 2000 to Windows XP Professional.

▲ You can use the less expensive upgrade version of Windows XP Home Edition to upgrade from Windows 98 or Windows Me to Windows XP Home Edition.

▲ If you currently have Windows 95 installed, you must do a clean install using the more expensive "For a New PC" version of Windows XP Professional or Windows XP Home Edition.

▲ If you have Windows 9x/Me installed, know that upgrading to Windows 2000/XP requires that you have Windows 2000/XP drivers for all your hardware and many times applications must also be reinstalled. Therefore, little time and effort is saved with upgrading over a clean install.

▲ Upgrading from Windows 2000 to Windows XP is usually more successful because drivers, applications and registry entries are more likely to carry forward into the new OS than when upgrading from Windows 9x/Me.

▲ All versions of Windows 9x/Me and Windows NT Workstation 3.51 and higher can be upgraded to Windows 2000.

▲ If you are upgrading from Windows NT using NTFS, Setup automatically upgrades to the Windows 2000/XP version of NTFS.

▲ If you are upgrading from Windows NT using FAT16 or Windows NT with third-party software installed that allows Windows NT to use FAT32, Setup asks you whether you want to upgrade to NTFS.

## CREATING A DUAL BOOT

The ability to boot from both Windows XP and Windows 2000 on the same machine or to boot Windows 2000/XP and another OS, such as DOS or Windows 98, is called a **dual boot**.

Don't create a dual boot unless you need two operating systems, such as when you need to verify that applications and hardware work under Windows 2000/XP before you delete the old OS. Windows 2000/XP does not support a second operating system on the same partition, so you must have at least two partitions on the hard drive.

Recall that Windows 2000/XP can support up to four partitions on a hard drive. All four can be primary partitions (which can have only one logical drive), or one of the partitions can be an extended partition (which can have several logical drives). For the first primary partition, the active partition, that drive is drive C. For a dual boot with Windows 2000/XP, one OS is installed in the active partition on drive C, and the other OS is installed on another partition's logical drive.

Because of the incompatibility problems between the Windows NT NTFS file system and the Windows 2000/XP NTFS file system, a dual boot between Windows NT and Windows 2000/XP is not recommended.

## HARD DRIVE PARTITIONS AND FILE SYSTEMS

For Windows XP, this OS needs at least a 2-GB partition for the installation (but use a larger partition if at all possible) and should have about 1.5 GB of free space on that partition. Windows 2000 needs a minimum of 650 MB, but use at least a 2-GB partition. You can install Windows 2000/XP on the same partition as another OS, but Windows 2000/XP overwrites the existing OS on that partition. If you do not have a free 2-GB partition for the installation, you must delete smaller partitions and repartition the drive. Deleting a partition erases all data on it, so be sure to create backups first. Follow these general directions to ensure that partitions on the hard drive are adequate to install Windows 2000/XP:

- For Windows 9x/Me, use Fdisk at the command prompt, and for Windows 2000, use Disk Management to determine what partitions are on the drive, how large they are, what logical drives are assigned to them, and how much free space on the drive is not yet partitioned.
- If existing partitions are too small, look at the free space on the drive. If there is enough free space that is not yet partitioned, use that free space to create a new partition that is at least 2 GB.
- If you cannot create a 2-GB or larger partition, back up your data, delete the smaller partitions, and create a 2-GB or larger active partition on the drive.
- If you have free space on the drive for other partitions, don't partition them at this time. First install Windows XP and then use Disk Management under Windows XP to partition the remaining free space on the drive.

Before you start the installation, decide which file system you will use. The file systems supported by Windows 2000/XP are FAT16, FAT32, and NTFS. Here are the general directions for selecting a file system:

- Use the NTFS file system if you are interested in file and folder security, file compression, control over how much disk space a user is allowed, or file encryption.
- Use the FAT32 file system if you are setting up a dual boot with Windows 9x/Me and each OS must access all partitions.
- Use the FAT16 file system if you are setting up a dual boot with MS-DOS or Windows NT and each OS must access all partitions.
- For a dual boot between Windows 2000 and Windows XP, you can use either the FAT32 or NTFS file system.

## WILL THE PC JOIN A WORKGROUP OR A DOMAIN?

If you are installing Windows 2000/XP on a network, you must decide how you will access the network. If you have fewer than 10 computers networked together, Microsoft recommends that you join these computers in a workgroup, in which each computer controls its own resources. In this case, each user account is set up on the local computer, independently from user accounts on other PCs. There is no centralized control of resources. For more than 10 computers, Microsoft recommends that you use a domain controller running a network operating system such as Windows Server 2003 to control network resources. (Windows 2000 or Windows XP Professional installed on a workstation can then be a client on this Windows network.) You will also want to use a domain controller if you want to administer and secure the network from a centralized location, or if several centralized resources on the network are shared by many users. How to manage workgroups is covered in Chapter 13, but managing a domain controller is beyond the scope of this book.

> **Notes**
>
> Windows XP Home Edition does not support joining a domain. If you plan to use a domain controller on your network, install Windows XP Professional.

You need to know how to configure the computer to access the network. You should know these things before you begin the installation:

- ◢ The computer name and workgroup name for a peer-to-peer network.
- ◢ The username, user password, computer name, and domain name for a domain network.
- ◢ For TCP/IP networks, how the IP address is assigned, either dynamically (gets its IP address from a DHCP server when it first connects to the network) or statically (IP address is permanently assigned to the workstation). If the network is using static IP addressing, you need the IP address for the workstation. (DHCP servers, which are used to assign IP addresses when a computer connects to a network, are covered in Chapters 17 and 18.)

## HOW WILL THE INSTALLATION PROCESS WORK?

If you are installing Windows 2000/XP on a networked PC, you have a choice where you'll store the Windows 2000/XP installation files. Without a network, you can install the OS from a CD in the computer's CD drive, but with a network, you can store the files on a file server on the network and perform the installation from the file server. If you will be doing multiple installations on the network, consider using a file server. Copy all the files from the \i386 folder on the Windows 2000/XP CD to a folder on the file server and then share that folder on the network. During the installation, when you are ready for the CD, point the setup program to the file server folder instead.

> **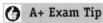 A+ Exam Tip**
>
> The A+ Essentials exam expects you to know about unattended installations and about the convenience of putting the Windows setup files in the \i386 directory on a file server. A server used in this way is called a **distribution server**.

A+ ESS
3.2

A+
220-602
3.2

> ### Notes
>
> For a Windows 2000/XP installation on a single computer, before the installation, you might want to copy the Windows 2000/XP installation files to the hard drive into a folder named \i386. You can do this if the hard drive is already formatted and you don't intend to format it during the installation. Having the installation files stored on the hard drive is handy later when you want to install additional Windows 2000/XP components.

If you are installing Windows 2000/XP on a desktop or notebook computer that does not have a CD drive, consider using an external CD drive that connects to a USB port. If you need to boot from the Windows 2000/XP setup CD, keep in mind that most computers allow you to boot from a USB device. If you can't boot from a USB device, you can boot from a floppy disk and start the Windows installation from a command prompt.

Windows 2000/XP offers a number of options for installation that can be automated so you don't need to sit at the computer responding to the questions that setup asks during installation. One method, called an **unattended installation**, is performed by storing the answers to installation questions in a text file or script that Windows 2000/XP calls an **answer file**. A sample answer file is stored on the Windows 2000/XP CD. If you must perform many installations on computers that have the same Windows 2000/XP setup, it might be worth your time to develop an answer file to perform unattended installations. You can perform unattended installations for both upgrades and clean installs. How to set up unattended installations is beyond the scope of this chapter.

> ### Notes
>
> To learn how to create an unattended installation of Windows XP, go to the Microsoft Support Web site (*support.microsoft.com*) and search for the Microsoft Knowledge Base article 314459. For unattended Windows 2000 installations, search for article 216258. You can also search the Web site for other articles on this subject.

Another option is **drive imaging**, sometimes called **disk cloning** or disk imaging, which replicates the drive to a new computer or to another drive on the same computer. All contents of the drive, including the OS, applications, and data, get duplicated to the new drive. To clone a drive after the installation, use the Sysprep.exe utility to remove configuration settings such as the computer name that uniquely identifies the PC. Then clone the entire hard drive to a new PC using third-party drive-imaging software. Examples of drive-imaging software are Drive Image and Norton Ghost by Symantec Corp (*www.symantec.com*) and ImageCast by Phoenix Technologies (*www.phoenix.com*).

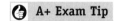 **A+ Exam Tip**

The A+ Essentials exam expects you to know about drive imaging.

Another option you must decide upon is how you will proceed through the installation process. When you first start a Windows Setup program, it will offer you choices for how you want to step through the installation. Choices might be Custom, Typical, Express, or others. You have more control over a Custom installation, but a Typical or Express installation is easier to do and should be used in most situations. You'll learn more about these options later in the chapter.

## FINAL CHECKLIST

Before you begin the installation, complete the final checklist shown in Table 11-4 to verify that you are ready.

A+ ESS
3.2

A+
220-602
3.2

| Things to Do | Further Information |
|---|---|
| Does the PC meet the minimum or recommended hardware requirement? | CPU:<br>RAM:<br>Hard drive partition size:<br>Free space on the partition: |
| Do you have in hand the Windows 2000/XP device drivers for your hardware devices? | List hardware and software that need to be upgraded: |
| Do you have the product key available? | Product key: |
| Have you decided how you will join a network? | Workgroup name:<br>Domain name:<br>Computer name: |
| Will you do an upgrade or clean install? | Current operating system:<br>Does the old OS qualify for an upgrade? |
| For a clean install, will you set up a dual boot? | List reasons for a dual boot:<br>For a dual boot<br>    Size of the second partition:<br>    Free space on the second partition:<br>    File system you plan to use: |
| Have you decided on a file system? | File system you plan to use: |
| Have you backed up important data on your hard drive? | Location of backup: |

**Table 11-4** Checklist to complete before installing Windows 2000/XP

**Notes**

The Product Key is written on the CD cover of the Windows XP setup CD or affixed to the back of the Windows XP documentation booklet, as shown in Figure 11-22. Technicians sometimes mount the Product Key sticker on the side of a computer. Try looking for it there (see Figure 11-23). For notebook computers, look for the Product Key sticker on the bottom of the notebook. If you have lost the Product Key and are moving this Windows XP installation from one PC to another, you can use a utility to find out the Product Key. On the PC that has the old Windows XP installation, download and run the key finder utility from Magical Jelly Bean Software at *www.magicaljellybean.com/keyfinder.shtml*.

Product Key sticker

**Figure 11-22** The Product Key is on a sticker on the back of the Windows XP documentation

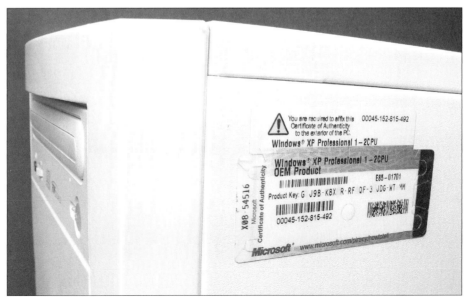

**Figure 11-23** The Product Key is sometimes placed on the side or front of a computer case

## STEPS TO INSTALL WINDOWS XP

**A+ ESS**
**3.2**

**A+**
**220-602**
**3.2**

This section explains the steps to install Windows XP as a clean install (with and without another OS already installed), as an upgrade, and in a dual-boot environment. Before we get into the step-by-step instructions, here are some general tips about installing XP:

▲ If you want to begin the installation by booting from the Windows CD in a CD drive or other media such as a USB device, verify that the boot sequence is first the CD drive or USB device, then the hard drive (see Figure 11-24).

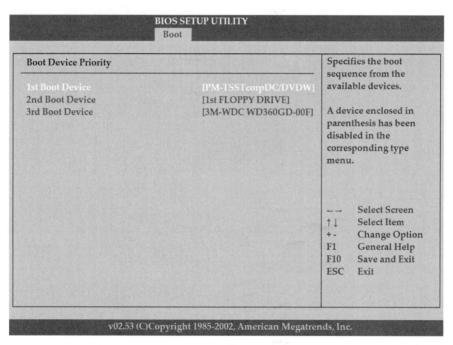

**Figure 11-24** Use CMOS setup to verify the boot sequence looks to the optical drive before it checks the hard drive for an operating system

▲ Also, because Windows 2000/XP prefers to handle its own Plug and Play hardware installations without the help of BIOS, Microsoft recommends that you disable the Plug and Play feature of your motherboard BIOS.

▲ Disable any virus protection setting that prevents the boot sector from being altered.

▲ You can use two programs to install Windows 2000/XP: Winnt.exe and Winnt32.exe. Winnt.exe is the 16-bit version of the setup program and Winnt32.exe is the 32-bit version. Both are located in the \i386 directory. You can use Winnt.exe for a clean install on a computer running MS-DOS, but not to perform an upgrade. Use Winnt32.exe for a clean install or an upgrade on a computer running Windows. Regardless of whether you use Winnt.exe or Winnt32.exe, the program executed is called Setup in Windows documentation. In addition, if you boot from the Windows 2000/XP CD, the Setup.exe program in the root directory of the CD is launched, which displays a setup menu.

▲ If the computer does not have a CD drive and you cannot boot from the hard drive, you can boot from an external CD drive attached to the PC by way of a USB port. Another option is to boot from a DOS bootable floppy disk; then run the Winnt.exe program and point to the setup files stored on the hard drive or another device.

**A+ ESS**
3.2

▲ For a notebook computer, connect the AC adapter and use this power source for the complete OS installation, updates, and installation of hardware and applications. You don't want the battery to fail you part way through a process.

**A+**
220-602
3.2

## WINDOWS XP CLEAN INSTALL WHEN AN OS IS NOT ALREADY INSTALLED

Follow these general directions to perform a clean install of Windows XP on a PC that does not already have an OS installed:

1. Boot from the Windows XP CD, which displays the menu shown in Figure 11-25. This menu might change slightly from one Windows XP release to another. Press **Enter** to select the first option. If your PC does not boot from a CD, go to a command prompt and enter the command **D:\i386\Winnt.exe**, substituting the drive letter of your CD-ROM drive for D, if necessary. (The path might vary depending on the release of Windows XP.) The End-User License agreement appears. Accept the agreement by pressing **F8**.

> **Notes**
>
> When installing Windows from across the network to a remote PC, you can only do a clean install. In this situation, run Winnt32.exe on the local Windows computer to perform a clean install on the remote PC.

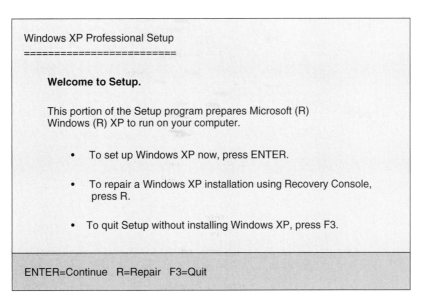

**Figure 11-25**  Windows XP Setup opening menu

2. Setup lists all partitions that it finds on the hard drive, the file system of each partition, and the size of the partition. It also lists any unpartitioned free space on the drive. From this screen, you can create and delete partitions and select the partition on which you want to install Windows XP. If you plan to have more than one partition on the drive, create only one partition at this time. The partition must be at least 2 GB in size and have 1.5 GB free. However, if you have the space, make it much larger so all applications can be installed on this partition—say about 10 GB. After the installation, you can use Disk Management to create the other partitions. Figure 11-26 shows an example of the list provided by Setup when the entire hard drive has not yet been partitioned.

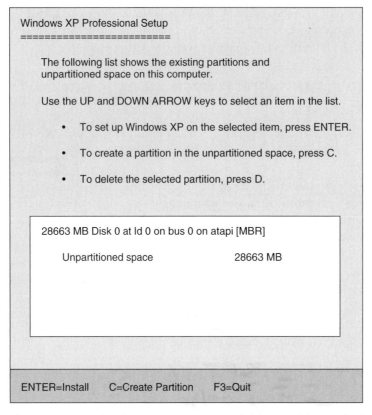

```
Windows XP Professional Setup
============================

    The following list shows the existing partitions and
    unpartitioned space on this computer.

    Use the UP and DOWN ARROW keys to select an item in the list.

      •   To set up Windows XP on the selected item, press ENTER.

      •   To create a partition in the unpartitioned space, press C.

      •   To delete the selected partition, press D.


    ┌──────────────────────────────────────────────────────────┐
    │  28663 MB Disk 0 at Id 0 on bus 0 on atapi [MBR]          │
    │                                                          │
    │     Unpartitioned space                    28663 MB      │
    │                                                          │
    │                                                          │
    └──────────────────────────────────────────────────────────┘


  ENTER=Install      C=Create Partition      F3=Quit
```

**Figure 11-26**  During Setup, you can create and delete partitions and select a partition
on which to install Windows XP

3. If you created a partition in Step 2, Setup asks which file system you want to use to format the partition, NTFS or FAT. If the partition is at least 2 GB in size, the FAT file system will be FAT32. Select a file system for the partition. The Setup program formats the drive, completes the text-based portion of setup, and loads the graphical interface for the rest of the installation. The PC then restarts.

4. Select your geographical location from the list provided. Windows XP will use it to decide how to display dates, times, numbers, and currency. Select your keyboard layout. Different keyboards can be used to accommodate special characters for other languages.

5. Enter your name, the name of your organization, and your product key.

6. Enter the computer name and the password for the Administrator account. This password is stored in the security database on this PC. If you are joining a domain, the computer name is the name assigned to this computer by the network administrator managing the domain controller.

7. Select the date, time, and time zone. The PC might reboot.

8. If you are connected to a network, you will be asked to choose how to configure your network settings. The Typical setting installs Client for Microsoft Networks, File and Printer Sharing, and TCP/IP using dynamically assigned IP addresses. The Custom setting allows you to configure the network differently. If you are not sure which to use, choose the Typical settings. You can change them later. How networks are configured is covered in Chapter 17.

> **Notes**
>
> It is *very* important that you remember the Administrator password. You cannot log on to the system without it.

**A+ ESS**
3.2

**A+**
220-602
3.2

9. Enter a workgroup or domain name. If you are joining a domain, the network administrator will have
given you specific directions on how to configure user
accounts on the domain.

## WINDOWS XP CLEAN INSTALL WHEN AN OS IS ALREADY INSTALLED

For a clean install on a PC that already has an OS installed,
follow these general directions:

1. Close any open applications. Close any boot management software or antivirus software that might be
   running in the background.

2. Insert the Windows XP CD in the CD drive. Autorun launches the opening window
   shown in Figure 11-27. Your screen might look different depending on the release of
   Windows XP you are using. (If the menu does not, you can start the installation by
   using this command in the Run dialog box: **D:\i386\winnt32.exe**, where you substitute the drive letter of your CD drive for D, if necessary.)

> **Notes**
>
> During a normal Windows XP installation, setup causes the system to reboot three times.

> 👉 **A+ Exam Tip**
>
> The A+ Essentials exam expects you to know how to do a Windows XP clean install and an upgrade to Windows XP.

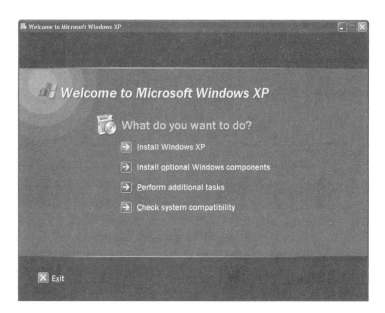

**Figure 11-27** Windows XP Setup menu

3. Select the option to **Install Windows XP**. On the next screen, under Installation Type,
   select **New Installation**. Read and accept the licensing agreement. The installation
   process works the same as in the preceding procedure, picking up with Step 2.

## UPGRADE TO WINDOWS XP

When performing an upgrade to Windows XP, follow these general directions:

1. Clean up the hard drive: erase unneeded or temporary files, empty the Recycle Bin,
   defragment the drive (use Windows 9x/Me or Windows 2000 Disk Defragmenter), and
   scan the drive for errors (use Windows 9x/Me ScanDisk or Windows 2000 Chkdsk).

2. If you have determined that you must upgrade hardware or software and that these upgrades are compatible with your old OS, perform the upgrades and verify that the hardware or software is working.

3. If you do not have the latest BIOS for your motherboard, flash your BIOS.

4. Back up important files.

5. Scan the hard drive for viruses using a current version of antivirus software.

6. If you have a compressed hard drive, uncompress the drive. The only exception is that if you are using Windows NT file compression on an NTFS drive, you do not need to uncompress it.

7. Uninstall any hardware or software that you know is not compatible with Windows XP and for which you have no available upgrade. Reboot the system.

8. You're now ready to do the upgrade. Insert the Windows XP Upgrade CD in the CD-ROM drive. The Autorun feature should launch the Setup program, with the menu shown in Figure 11-27. Select the option to **Install Windows XP**.

9. If the Setup menu does not appear, you can enter the Setup command in the Run dialog box. Use the command **D:\i386\winnt32.exe**, where you substitute the drive letter of your CD-ROM drive for D, if necessary. Also, the path on your setup CD might be different, depending on the OS release you are using.

10. On the next screen, under Installation Type, select **Upgrade**. The menu gives you two options:

   ◢ *Express Upgrade*. This upgrade uses existing Windows folders and all the existing settings it can.
   ◢ *Custom Upgrade*. This upgrade allows you to change the installation folder and the language options. Using this option, you can also change the file system to NTFS.

11. Select the type of upgrade, and accept the licensing agreement.

12. Select the partition on which to install Windows XP. If the drive is configured as FAT and you want to convert to NTFS, specify that now. Note that Windows XP has an uninstall utility that allows you to revert to Windows 98 if necessary. This uninstall tool does not work if you convert FAT to NTFS.

13. Setup does an analysis of the system and reports any compatibility problems. Stop the installation if the problems indicate that you will not be able to operate the system after the installation.

14. For an upgrade from Windows 98 or Windows Me to Windows XP, the Setup program converts whatever information it can in the registry to Windows XP. At the end of the installation, you are given the opportunity to join a domain. For Windows NT and Windows 2000 upgrades, almost all registry entries are carried forward into the new OS; the information about a domain is not requested because it is copied from the old OS into Windows XP.

## DUAL BOOT USING WINDOWS XP

You can configure Windows XP to set up a dual boot with another operating system. Start the installation as you would for a clean install on a PC with another operating system already installed. When given the opportunity, choose to install Windows XP on a different partition than the other OS. Windows XP recognizes that another OS is installed and sets up the startup menu to offer it as an option for booting. After the installation, when you boot with a dual boot, the **boot loader menu** automatically appears and asks you to select an operating system, as shown in Figure 11-28.

```
Please select the operating system to start:


    Microsoft Windows XP Professional
    Microsoft Windows 98

Use the up and down arrow keys to move the highlight to your choice.
Seconds until highlighted choice will be started automatically: xx
Press ENTER to choose.




For troubleshooting and advanced startup options for Windows, press F8.
```

**Figure 11-28** Menu displayed for a dual boot

The first active partition (drive C) must be set up with a file system that both operating systems understand. For example, for a dual boot with Windows 98, use the FAT32 file system. For a dual boot with Windows 2000, use either the FAT32 or the NTFS file system. You should install the other operating system first, and then you can install Windows XP in a different partition. When you install Windows XP on another partition, it places only the files necessary to boot in the first active partition, which it calls the system partition. This causes Windows XP to initiate the boot rather than the other OS. The rest of Windows XP is installed on a second partition, which Windows XP calls the boot partition. This is the same way that Windows NT and Windows 2000 manage a dual boot with an older OS.

> **Notes**
>
> When setting up a dual boot, always install the older operating system first.

Earlier Windows operating systems were not aware of applications installed under the other OS in a dual boot. For example, in a dual boot with Windows 98 and Windows 2000, an application had to be installed twice, once under Windows 98 and once under Windows 2000. However, Windows XP is able to use an application installed under the other OS in a dual boot. For example, if you set up a dual boot with Windows XP and Windows 98, an application installed under Windows 98 can be executed from Windows XP. This application might be listed under the Start menu of Windows XP. If it is not, you can use Windows XP Explorer to locate the program file. Double-click the application to run it from Windows XP. This makes implementing a dual boot easier because you don't have to install an application under both OSs.

## AFTER THE WINDOWS XP INSTALLATION

Immediately after you have installed Windows XP, there are several things to do to prepare the system for use and protect it against disaster. They include the following:

1. Activate Windows XP using Product activation (how to do that is coming up).

2. Verify you can access the network and the Internet. Then access the Internet and download and install all OS service packs, updates, and patches.

3. Verify that all hardware works and install additional devices, such as printers, as needed. (How to install hardware is covered in Chapter 12.)

4. Create user accounts for Windows XP. (Chapter 13 covers creating user accounts.)

**Notes**

After you have set up user accounts, new users might want to transfer their data and settings from their old PC to the new Windows XP PC. How to do all this is covered in Chapter 13.

5. Install additional Windows components. To install Windows components, open the Add or Remove Programs applet in the Control Panel. Click **Add/Remove Windows Components,** as shown in Figure 11-29. Then check a component you want to install and click **Next.** Follow the directions onscreen.

6. Install applications. (Don't attempt to install applications and components before you first download and install service packs and patches.)

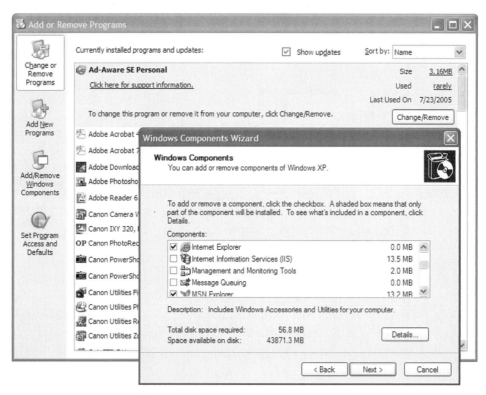

**Figure 11-29** Add or remove Windows components using the Add or Remove Programs applet

**⊘ A+ Exam Tip**

The A+ Essentials exam expects you to know that after the Windows installation you need to apply service patches and updates, verify user data, and install additional Windows components.

7. Verify that the system functions properly, and back up the system state. This backup of the system can later help you recover the OS in the event of system failure. (How to back up the system state is covered in Chapter 12.)

8. You also might want to uninstall some Windows XP components or at least curtail how they function. For example, when Windows XP starts, it loads Windows Messenger by default, which consumes system resources even if you are not using it. To stop Windows Messenger from loading at startup, click **Start, All Programs,** and **Windows Messenger.** If the .NET Passport Wizard launches, close the wizard.

A+ ESS
3.2

A+
220-602
3.2

Click **Tools** on the menu bar, and then click **Options**. The Options window opens, as shown in Figure 11-30. Click the **Preferences** tab and uncheck **Run this program when Windows starts**. Click **OK**.

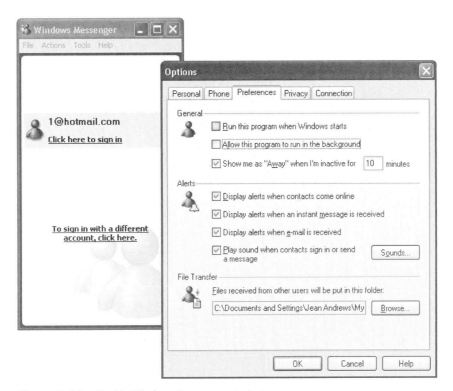

**Figure 11-30** Disable Windows Messenger at startup

## PRODUCT ACTIVATION

**Product activation** is a method used by Microsoft to prevent unlicensed use of its software so that you must purchase a Windows XP license for each installation of Windows XP. The license was introduced with Microsoft Office XP, and Microsoft says it will continue using product activation in all future Microsoft products. The first time you log on to the system after the installation, the Activate Windows dialog box appears with these three options (see Figure 11-31):

▲ Yes, let's activate Windows over the Internet now
▲ Yes, I want to telephone a customer service representative to activate Windows
▲ No, remind me to activate Windows every few days

If you choose to activate Windows over the Internet and are connected to the Internet at the time, the process is almost instant. Windows XP sends a numeric identifier to a Microsoft server, which sends a certificate activating the product on your PC. You have up to 30 days after installation to activate Windows XP; after that the system will not boot. If you install Windows XP from the same CD on a different computer and you attempt to activate Windows from the new PC, a dialog box appears telling you of the suspected violation of the license agreement. You can call a Microsoft operator and explain what caused the discrepancy. If your explanation is reasonable (for example, you uninstalled Windows XP from one PC and installed it on another), the operator can issue you a valid certificate. You can then type the certificate value into a dialog box to complete the boot process.

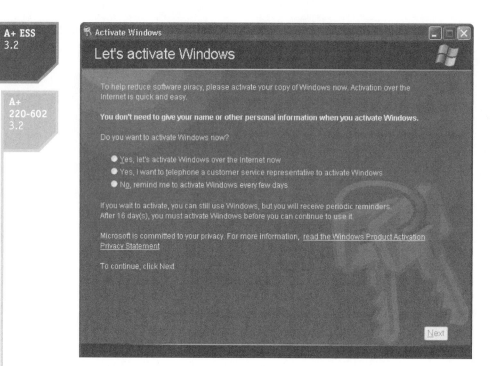

**Figure 11-31**   Product activation is a strategy used by Microsoft to prevent software piracy

## UPDATE WINDOWS

The Microsoft Web site offers patches, fixes, and updates for known problems and has an extensive knowledge base documenting problems and their solutions. It's important to keep these updates current on your system to fix known problems and plug up security holes to keep viruses and worms out.

> **Notes**
>
> If you don't have an Internet connection, you can download Windows updates to another computer and then transfer them to the computer you are working on. Also, you can order a CD from Microsoft for Windows XP Service Pack 2, which contains improved security features (among other things).

### HOW TO INSTALL UPDATES

To launch Windows Update, connect to the Internet and then click **Start**, point to **All Programs**, and click **Windows Update**. Or you can access Windows Update by going to the Microsoft site *windowsupdate.microsoft.com*. When you get to the site, click **Express Install (Recommended)** to begin the update process.

> **Notes**
>
> If you think you might later want to uninstall a critical update or service pack, select the option to Save uninstall information. Later, to uninstall the fix, again execute the downloaded file. When given the option, select "Uninstall a previously installed service pack."

The Windows Update process uses ActiveX controls to scan your system, find your device drivers and system files, and compare these files to the ones on the Windows Update server. If you do not already have Active Setup and the ActiveX controls installed on your computer, a prompt to install them appears when you access the site. After Windows Update scans your system and locates update packages and new versions of drivers and system files, it offers you the option of selecting files for download. Click **Download and Install Now,** and the window on the right side of Figure 11-32 appears so you can watch the progress.

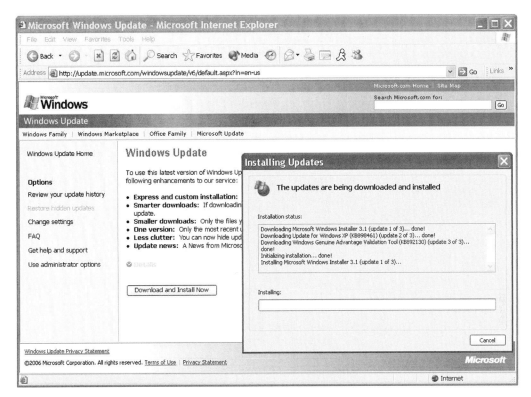

**Figure 11-32** Installing updates to Windows XP

If your Windows setup CD is old or the PC hasn't been updated in a while, Windows selects the updates in the order you can receive them and will not necessarily list all the updates you need on the first pass. After you have installed the updates listed, go back and start again until Windows Updates tells you there is nothing left to update. It might take two or more passes to get the PC entirely up to date.

## WINDOWS XP SERVICE PACK 2 (SP2)

So far, Microsoft has released two major service packs for Windows XP. The latest is Service Pack 2. Service Pack 2 offers some really great benefits, including Windows Firewall and Internet Explorer Pop-up Blocker. As you work your way through the Windows Update process, when the system is ready to receive Service Pack 2, you'll see it listed as the only update to download and install. It will take some time and a reboot to complete the process of installing Service Pack 2. You'll need at least 1.8 GB of free space on the drive for the installation. Alas, Figure 11-33 shows what will happen if the hard drive doesn't have enough free space for the SP2 installation.

A+ ESS
3.2
3.4

A+
220-602
3.2
3.4

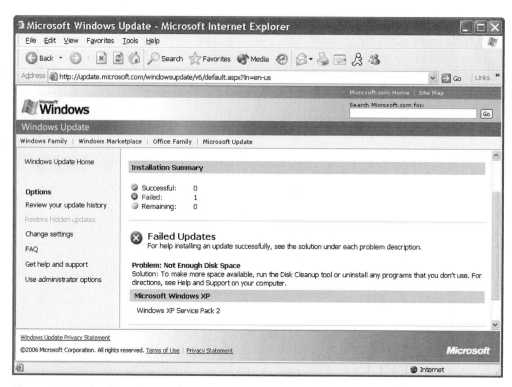

**Figure 11-33**    Service Pack 2 won't install because of lack of free space on the hard drive

## AUTOMATIC UPDATES

After you've gotten Windows XP current with all its updates, set the system so that it will stay current. To do that, click **Start**, right-click **My Computer**, and click **Properties**. In the System Properties window, click the **Automatic Updates** tab (see Figure 11-34).

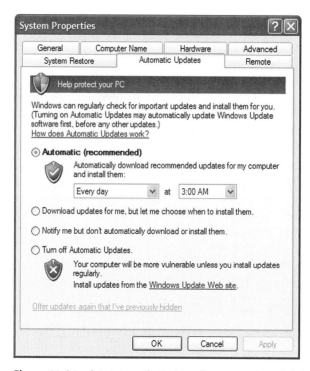

**Figure 11-34**    Set Automatic Updates for automatic and daily updating

A+ ESS
3.2
3.4

A+
220-602
3.2
3.4

You'll want to make these automatic update settings according to how the PC connects to the Internet and user habits. For an always-up broadband connection (such as cable modem or DSL), select **Automatic (recommended)** and choose to automatically download and install updates every day. If the PC doesn't have an always-up Internet connection (such as dial-up), you might want to select **Notify me but don't automatically download or install them.** This option works better if a user doesn't want to be bothered with a long and involved download when the PC first connects to the ISP using a slow dial-up connection. Discuss the options with the user. Make sure the user understands that if the update process is not fully automated, he or she needs to take the time to do the updates at least once a week.

## STEPS TO INSTALL WINDOWS 2000

A+ ESS
3.2

A+
220-602
3.2

In this section, you'll learn about the difference in the installation processes between Windows XP and Windows 2000. A clean install, upgrade, and dual-boot installation of Windows 2000 use the same installation programs as does Windows XP: the 16-bit Winnt.exe program, or the 32-bit Winnt32.exe installation program.

### CLEAN INSTALLATION

The Windows 2000 package comes with documentation and a CD. For United States distributions, the package includes a floppy disk to provide 128-bit data encryption. (This disk is not included in distributions to other countries because of laws that prohibit 128-bit data encryption software from leaving the United States.)

If your PC is capable of booting from a CD, then insert the CD and turn on the PC. The Welcome to Setup screen appears (see Figure 11-35). Press **Enter** to begin the installation.

> **Notes**
>
> If you are having problems with Windows Setup detecting your hard drive, the problem might be out-of-date BIOS. Try flashing BIOS and then attempting the Windows installation again. Chapter 6 gives more information about flashing BIOS.

> **A+ Tip**
>
> The A+ Essentials exam expects you. To know how to perform a clean install of Windows 2000 Professional.

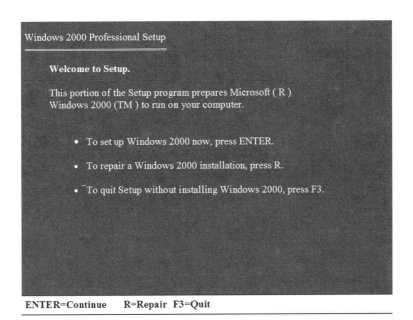

Figure 11-35 Windows 2000 setup screen after booting from the setup CD

A+ ESS
3.2

A+
220-602
3.2

On the next screen, press **F8** to accept the end-user license agreement (EULA). Then skip to Step 6 in the following list of steps. However, if your PC does not boot from a CD and you have a clean, empty hard drive, first create a set of Windows 2000 setup disks to boot the PC and to begin the installation. The remaining installation is done from the CD.

To make the four setup disks, follow these directions:

1. Using a working PC, format four floppy disks.

2. Place the Windows 2000 CD in the CD-ROM drive and a formatted floppy disk in the floppy disk drive. For Windows 9x/Me, click **Start**, then **Run**, and enter this command in the Run dialog box (substitute the letter of the CD-ROM drive for D: and the letter of the floppy drive for A:, if necessary):

   **D:\bootdisk\makeboot.exe A:**

3. Insert new disks in the drive as requested. Label the disks Windows 2000 Setup Disks 1, 2, 3, and 4.

4. Now begin the Windows 2000 installation. Boot the PC from the first setup disk created earlier. You will be asked to insert each of the four disks in turn and then asked to insert the Windows 2000 CD.

5. The Windows 2000 license agreement appears. Accept the agreement and the Welcome screen appears, as shown in Figure 11-36. Select **Install a new copy of Windows 2000** and click **Next**. On the next screen, accept the license agreement. The setup process is now identical to that of booting directly from the CD. Save the four setup floppy disks in case you have future problems with Windows 2000.

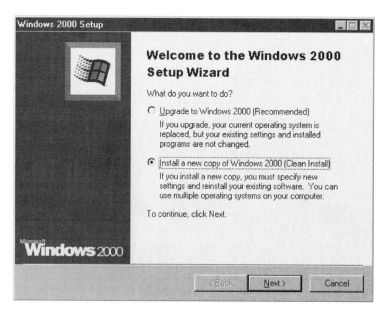

**Figure 11-36**   Using the Setup Wizard, you can do an upgrade, do a clean install, or create a dual boot

6. Windows 2000 searches the hard drive for partitions and asks which partition to use. If the partitions are not created, it creates them for you. You are asked to decide which file system to use. If the hard drive is already partitioned and contains a partition larger than 2 GB, and you select the FAT file system, then Windows 2000 automatically formats the drive using the FAT32 file system.

7. During installation, you are given the opportunity to change your keyboard settings for different languages, enter your name and company name, and enter the product key found on the CD case. You are also given the opportunity to enter date and time settings and an administrator password.

8. If Setup recognizes that you are connected to a network, it provides the Networking Settings window to configure the computer to access the network. If you select Typical settings, then Setup automatically configures the OS for your network. If the configuration is not correct after the installation, you can make changes.

9. At this point in the installation, you are asked to remove the Windows 2000 CD and click **Finish**. The computer then restarts. After Windows 2000 loads, it completes the process of connecting to the network. You are asked questions about the type of network. (For example, does the network use a domain or workgroup?) When the configuration is complete, verify that you have access to the network if there is one.

## CLEAN INSTALL WHEN THE HARD DRIVE HAS AN OPERATING SYSTEM INSTALLED

To do a clean install of Windows 2000, do the following:

1. Insert the Windows 2000 CD in the CD-ROM drive. If your PC detects the CD, a window opens with the message "This CD-ROM contains a newer version of Windows than the one you are presently using. Would you like to upgrade to Windows 2000?" Answer **No**. The Install Windows 2000 window appears (see Figure 11-37).

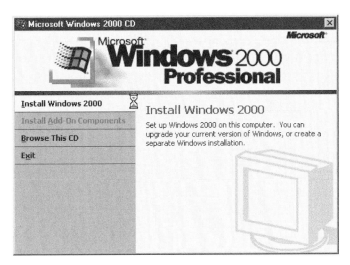

**Figure 11-37** Windows 2000 Setup window

2. Click **Install Windows 2000**. The Windows Setup Wizard opens, as shown in Figure 11-36. Select **Install a new copy of Windows 2000 (Clean Install)**. Windows displays the license agreement and asks you to accept it. Enter the product key from the back of the CD case, and you will be given the opportunity to select special options. After a reboot, the installation continues as described earlier.

3. When you insert the setup CD, if the setup menu does not automatically, start the installation by entering the command **D:\i386\ winnt32.exe** in the Run dialog box. Substitute the drive letter of the CD drive for D:, if necessary.

A+ ESS
3.2

A+
220-602
3.2

## UPGRADE INSTALLATION

To upgrade your operating system from Windows 9x/Me or Windows NT using the Windows 2000 CD, first prepare for the installation as described for a Windows XP upgrade earlier in the chapter. Then do the following:

1. Insert the Windows 2000 CD in the CD-ROM drive. If your system is set to detect the CD automatically, it runs the setup program and shows a message asking if you want to upgrade your computer to Windows 2000. Answer **Yes** and the installation begins. If Windows does not detect the CD, click **Start**, then **Run**, enter **D:\i386\winnt32.exe** in the Run dialog box, and then click **OK**. Substitute the drive letter of the CD-ROM drive for D:, if necessary. On the Welcome to Windows 2000 Setup Wizard window, select **Upgrade to Windows 2000 (Recommended)**. Follow the directions on the screen.

2. Windows 2000 Setup performs the upgrade in two major stages: the Report phase and the Setup phase. During the Report phase, Windows 2000 Setup scans the hardware, device drivers, current operating system, and applications for compatibility. In this phase, if Setup recognizes that the device driver or application will not work under Windows 2000, it gives you the opportunity to provide a new device driver or files that will update the application. Next, Setup generates a report of its findings. If its findings indicate that an unsuccessful installation is likely, you can abandon the installation. Then check with hardware and software manufacturers for fixes. In the Report phase, Setup also creates an answer file that it uses during the Setup phase, installs the Windows 2000 boot loader, and copies Windows 2000 installation files to the hard drive.

3. The PC reboots and the Setup phase begins, which has two parts: the Text mode and the GUI mode. In the Text mode, Setup installs a Windows 2000 base in the same folder that the old OS is in, usually C:\Windows for Windows 9x/Me and C:\WINNT for Windows NT. The target folder cannot be changed at this point. Setup then moves the Windows registry and profile information to %windir%\setup\temp, where %windir% is the path to the Windows folder, most likely C:\Windows\setup\temp.

4. The PC reboots again and the GUI mode of Setup begins. Setup reads information that it saved about the old Windows system and makes appropriate changes to the Windows 2000 registry. It then migrates application DLLs to Windows 2000 and reboots for the last time. The upgrade is complete.

> **Notes**
>
> During installation, Windows 2000 records information about the installation to a file called Setuplog.txt. This file is useful when troubleshooting any problems that occur during installation.

5. After the installation is complete, access the Internet and download all service packs, patches, and updates. To install updates, click **Start** and then click **Windows Update**. Make sure that Windows 2000 Service Pack 4 is installed. SP4 is the last service pack Microsoft made available for Windows 2000 before it stopped providing mainstream support for the OS. Also install any additional Windows components you need, hardware devices, and applications. You'll also need to set up user accounts. Verify that all applications and installed hardware devices work. After everything is done, make a backup of the system state to be used in the event of a system failure. How to back up the system state is covered in Chapter 12, and how to set up user accounts is covered in Chapter 13.

**11**

## >> CHAPTER SUMMARY

◢ There are presently five versions of Windows XP: Windows XP Home Edition, Windows XP Professional, Windows XP Media Center Edition, Windows XP Tablet PC Edition, and Windows XP Professional x64 Edition.

◢ Windows 2000 is actually a suite of operating systems: Windows 2000 Professional, Windows 2000 Server, Windows 2000 Advanced Server, and Windows 2000 Datacenter Server.

◢ The two architectural modes of Windows 2000/XP are user mode and kernel mode. Kernel mode is further divided into two components: executive services and the hardware abstraction layer (HAL).

◢ A process is a unique instance of a program running together with the program resources and other programs it may use. A thread is one task that the process requests from the kernel, such as the task of printing a file.

◢ An NTVDM provides a DOS-like environment for DOS and Windows 3.x applications.

◢ Windows 3.x 16-bit applications run in a WOW.

◢ A workgroup is a group of computers and users sharing resources. Each computer maintains a list of users and their rights on that particular PC. A domain is a group of networked computers that share a centralized directory database of user account information and security.

◢ Of all Windows 2000/XP accounts, the administrator account has the most privileges and rights. It can create user accounts and assign them rights.

◢ Windows 2000 can run in native mode and mixed mode. Native mode is used when all domain servers are Windows 2000 servers. Mixed mode is used when a domain has both Windows 2000 and Windows NT servers controlling the domain.

◢ Windows 2000/XP supports FAT16, FAT32, and NTFS. NTFS under Windows 2000/XP is not compatible with NTFS under Windows NT.

◢ For the FAT file system, the DOS or Windows operating system views a hard drive through a FAT (file allocation table), which lists clusters, and a directory, which lists files.

◢ For the NTFS file system, information about files and directories is stored in the master file table (MFT).

◢ A hard drive is divided into partitions, which might also be divided into logical drives, or volumes. A Master Boot Record (MBR) at the beginning of the hard drive contains a table of partition information. Each logical drive contains a file system, either FAT16, FAT32, or NTFS.

◢ Windows 2000/XP supports four partitions, one of which can be an extended partition. The active partition, which Windows 2000/XP calls the system partition, is used to boot the OS.

◢ Windows 2000/XP offers a clean install and an upgrade installation. A clean install overwrites all information from previous operating system installations on the hard drive.

◢ You can install Windows XP as a dual boot with Windows 2000, because they both use the same version of NTFS. To dual boot Windows 2000/XP with Windows 9x/Me or Windows NT, you must use FAT32 or FAT16. Always install the older OS first, and install Windows 2000/XP on a different partition than another OS.

◢ Hardware and software must be compatible with Windows 2000/XP. Check the Microsoft Web site to verify compatibility with Windows 2000/XP before beginning an installation. If you need to flash BIOS, do it before you begin the installation.

◢ Unlike earlier versions of Windows, Windows XP is aware of applications installed under another OS when it is installed as a dual boot.

◢ Microsoft uses product activation to prevent the use of its software products, including Windows XP, on more than one computer.

◢ After the installation, install any Windows updates or service packs and any additional Windows components. Install all hardware and applications and verify everything is working.

## >> KEY TERMS

For explanations of key terms, see the Glossary near the end of the book.

Active Directory
active partition
administrator account
Advanced Configuration and
    Power Interface (ACPI)
answer file
backup domain controllers
    (BDCs)
boot loader menu
boot partition
boot sector virus
client/server
disk cloning
distribution server
domain

domain controller
drive imaging
dual boot
executive services
extended partition
HAL (hardware abstraction layer)
kernel mode
master file table (MFT)
mixed mode
multithreading
native mode
NTFS (New Technology file
    system)
NTVDM (NT virtual DOS
    machine)

peer-to-peer
primary domain controller
    (PDC)
primary partition
product activation
security accounts manager
    (SAM)
slack
system partition
thread
unattended installation
Win16 on Win32 (WOW)
workgroup

## >> REVIEW QUESTIONS

1. Which of the following interfaces exists between the subsystems in user mode and the HAL (hardware abstraction layer)?

   **a.** Win32 (WOW)

   **b.** Executive services

   **c.** Mulithread

   **d.** Win32 (WOW)

2. When Windows 2000 runs in mixed mode, how many Windows NT domain controllers are present?

   **a.** 0.

   **b.** 1.

   **c.** 1 or more.

   **d.** The term "domain controller" is not related to mixed mode.

3. Windows 2000 includes how many operating systems?

   **a.** 1

   **b.** 2

   **c.** 3

   **d.** 4

4. Which of the following statements best describes why Windows XP can be installed as a dual boot with Windows 2000?

   **a.** Each logical drive or volume has a file system installed.

   **b.** There is minimal wasted space (or slack) for each operating system.

   **c.** A FAT32 volume can be easily converted to an NTFS volume.

   **d.** They both use the same version of NTFS.

5. Which of the following terms refers to the method used by Microsoft to prevent unlicensed use of its software that is based on purchasing a Windows XP license for each installation of Windows XP?

   **a.** Product activation

   **b.** Boot loader

   **c.** Disk cloning

   **d.** Unattended installation

6. True or false? Windows XP has the ability for two or more users to be logged on simultaneously, and for a user to control the computer from a remote location.

7. True or false? User mode is the operating system mode in which programs have extensive access to system information and hardware.

8. True or false? For most installations, the system partition and the boot partition are the same (drive C).

9. True or false? Using Windows tools, changing the size of a partition or logical drive or changing a file system on a drive erases everything on the logical drive.

10. True or false? A thread is a program or group of programs that is running, together with the system resources assigned to it, such as memory addresses, environmental variables, and other resources.

11. During installation, Windows 2000 records information about the installation to a file called _____.

12. A(n) _____ attacks the MBR master boot program.

13. A Windows _____ is a group of networked computers that share a centralized directory database of user account information and security for the entire group of computers.

14. A(n) _____ partition has more than one logical drive, such as drive D and drive E.

15. The database containing user accounts, group accounts, and computer accounts is called the _____.

# Maintaining Windows 2000/XP

In the previous chapter, you learned about the Windows 2000/XP architecture and how to install Windows 2000/XP. This chapter covers supporting and maintaining Windows 2000/XP, including installing and supporting hardware and applications, protecting and maintaining Windows system files, and optimizing the OS. As a support technician, because you might be called on to edit the Windows registry, you'll also learn about the registry and how to safely edit it manually. In the chapter, we use Windows XP as our primary OS, but, as you read, know that we'll point out any differences between Windows XP and Windows 2000 so that you can use this chapter to study both these operating systems. As you read, you might consider following the steps in the chapter first using a Windows XP system and then going through the chapter again using a Windows 2000 system.

# SUPPORTING HARDWARE AND APPLICATIONS

This section discusses how to install hardware with Windows 2000/XP. Because hard drives are installed differently than other devices, you'll learn about the special tools and methods used to install hard drives. Then we'll discuss what to do when you have a problem with a hardware device using Windows. Next, you'll learn how to install applications including special considerations for legacy applications. You'll also learn about some additional Windows tools to monitor and manage hardware and applications. By the time you finish this section of the chapter, you should know how to support hardware and applications using Windows 2000/XP.

## INSTALLING HARDWARE UNDER WINDOWS 2000/XP

**A+ ESS**
**3.2**
**3.3**

**A+**
**220-602**
**3.1**

Only administrators can install a hardware device if any type of user input is required. Any user can install a hardware device only if the following are true: the device drivers can be installed without user input, all files necessary for a complete installation are present, the drivers have been digitally signed (**digital signatures** are digital codes that can be used to authenticate the source of files), and there are no errors during installation. If one of these conditions is not met, someone logged onto the system with administrator privileges must do the installation. How to create a user account and assign administrative privileges to that account are covered in Chapter 13.

To install a hardware device, it's best to use the device drivers written specifically for the OS (Windows XP or Windows 2000). If your hardware device comes bundled with drivers for Windows 2000/XP on CD or floppy disk, use those drivers. If the drivers are not written for your specific OS (2000 or XP), go to the manufacturer's Web site to download the correct drivers. Look for a Download or Support link on the home page or search on the device. Figure 12-1 shows links on the Sound Blaster Web site (*www.soundblaster.com*).

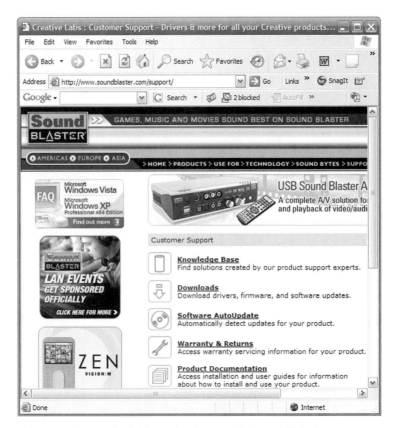

**Figure 12-1**   Download drivers from the manufacturer's Web site

If a driver is not available from the manufacturer, you can try these Web sites:

▲ *www.driverzone.com* by Barry Fanion
▲ *www.driverguide.com* by DriverGuide.com
▲ *www.helpdrivers.com* by Elsten Jerson
▲ *www.windrivers.com* by Jupitermedia Corporation
▲ *www.drivershq.com* by Drivers HeadQuarters
▲ *www.pcdrivers.com* by PCdrivers, Inc.

Here are general directions to install a hardware device using Windows 2000/XP:

1. If necessary, download the driver files to your hard drive. Don't forget which folder you put them in.

2. Read the instructions that come bundled with the device or that you downloaded from the Internet. It is especially important to find out if you need to install the device first or the drivers first. Always follow the specific instructions of a device manufacturer when installing a device (see Figure 12-2).

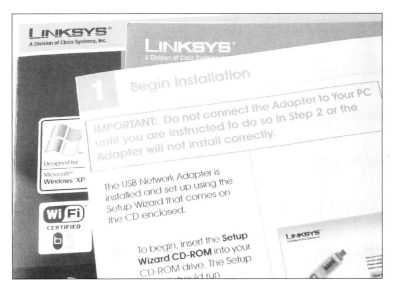

**Figure 12-2** This documentation makes it clear to install the software before installing the device

3. If instructions that come bundled with your device say to install the software before you install the device, first run the setup CD that came bundled with the device. Sometimes the device setup program will tell you when in the process to plug in the device.

Next, let's look at specific directions for installing a device under Windows XP and then under Windows 2000.

## STEPS TO INSTALL A HARDWARE DEVICE USING WINDOWS XP

Follow these steps to install a device using Windows XP:

1. If the installation begins by first installing the device, power down the computer and physically install the device. (For USB or FireWire devices, it is not necessary to power down the PC before you plug in the device.) After the device is installed and

**A+ ESS**
3.2
3.3

**A+**
220-602
3.1

Windows XP first starts, a bubble message appears on the system tray (see Figure 12-3) and the Found New Hardware Wizard opens (see Figure 12-4).

**Figure 12-3** Windows XP detects new hardware is present

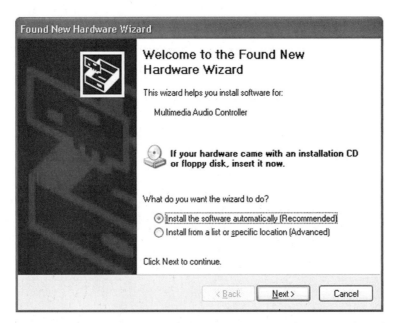

**Figure 12-4** The Windows XP Found New Hardware Wizard steps you through a hardware installation

> **Notes**
>
> When Windows 2000/XP is searching for drivers, it is looking for a driver information file that has an .inf extension.

**2.** So that you can use the drivers on CD that came with the device or your downloaded drivers, click **Install from a list or specific location (Advanced)**. If you want to use drivers that come bundled with Windows, click **Install the software automatically (Recommended)**. Click **Next** to continue.

**3.** The next window in the wizard appears (see Figure 12-5). Click **Search for the best driver in these locations**. If your drivers are on CD, check **Search removable media**. If your drivers are on your hard drive, check **Include this location in the search**. Then click **Browse** and locate the folder on the hard drive where you put the drivers. Click **Next**.

**4.** Windows XP locates the driver files and installs them. On the final screen of the wizard, click **Finish**.

12

A+ ESS
3.2
3.3

A+
220-602
3.1

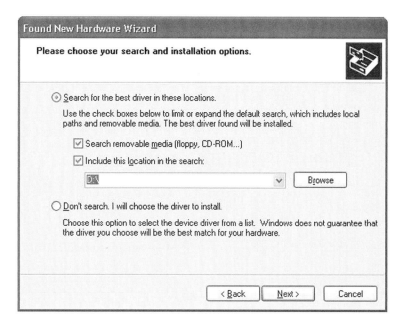

Figure 12-5  The Found New Hardware Wizard asks for directions to locate driver files

**5.** Go to Device Manager and make sure Windows recognizes the device with no errors. Figure 12-6 shows the properties window of a device that is working properly.

Figure 12-6  Device Manager reporting that the newly installed device is working properly

**6.** Now test the device to make sure it works. For example, if you have just installed a CD-RW drive, try burning a CD.

Sometimes Windows XP proceeds with a hardware installation using Microsoft drivers without displaying a dialog box that allows you to search for the driver files that

### Notes

When a new device is being installed, if Windows recognizes the drivers were not digitally signed by Microsoft, it displays a dialog box similar to that in Figure 12-7 (which, in this particular case, is for a Netgear wireless adapter). Now you have a decision to make. You can stop the installation and go to the manufacturer's Web site to try to find approved drivers, or you can continue with the installations. For most devices, it is safe to continue the installation using unsigned drivers. To do that, click **Continue Anyway.**

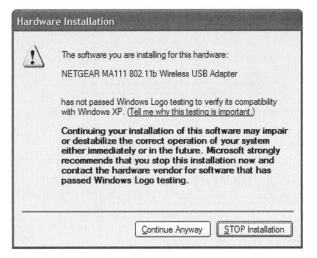

**Figure 12-7** Windows asks you for a decision about using unsigned drivers

you want to use for the installation. To prevent this from happening, run the setup program on the manufacturer's CD that is bundled with the device before installing the device. Later, after the device is installed, Windows will use the manufacturer's installed drivers for the device.

For example, Windows XP normally installs a modem using its own internal drivers. After you physically install the modem, when you first start up Windows, it simply tells you the modem is installed, giving you no options. If that happens to you, use Device Manager to uninstall the modem. Then use the modem setup CD to install the modem drivers. Next time you start Windows, it will detect the new modem and use the drivers that you have already installed. Another way to install manufacturer drivers is to first allow Windows XP to install its own drivers. Then, after the installation, use Device Manager to update these drivers to the manufacturer drivers. How to update drivers is covered later in this chapter.

## STEPS TO INSTALL A DEVICE USING WINDOWS 2000

To install a device using Windows 2000, do the following:

1. Follow specific manufacturer instructions to begin the installation by installing the setup CD or physically installing the device.

2. After you have installed the device, the Found New Hardware Wizard automatically launches (see Figure 12-8). Click **Next.**

A+ ESS
3.2
3.3

A+
220-602
3.1

**Figure 12-8** The Found New Hardware Wizard automatically launches as soon as Windows 2000 recognizes a new device is installed

3. In the next window, which is shown in Figure 12-9, click **Search for a suitable driver for my device (recommended)** and click **Next.** This choice lets you select a driver provided by Windows 2000 or use the device manufacturer drivers.

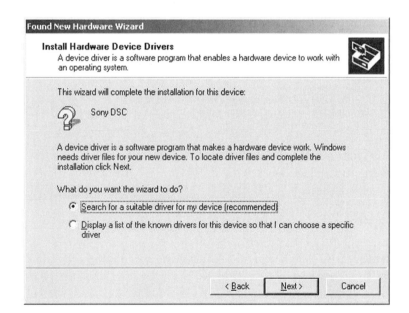

**Figure 12-9** Tell the Found New Hardware Wizard how to select a driver for the device

4. On the next window, click **Specify a location,** if necessary, and then click **Next.** In the following window, shown in Figure 12-10, click the **Browse** button and locate the driver files you want to use, either on CD or stored on your hard drive. Click **OK** to complete the installation.

A+ ESS
3.2
3.3

A+
220-602
3.1

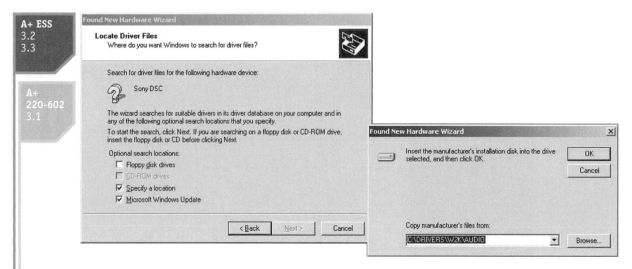

**Figure 12-10** Point to the location of driver files for a new device

If the Found New Hardware Wizard does not automatically launch or you have a problem with the wizard, you can use the Add/Remove Hardware applet in the Control Panel to install the device. After the device is installed, use Device Manager to verify the device is working properly and then test the device.

A+ ESS
1.2
3.1
3.2
3.3

## PREPARING A HARD DRIVE FOR FIRST USE

Some hardware devices, such as a hard drive or memory, require special tools to set them up and manage them. In this part of the chapter, you'll learn to set up a new hard drive. Later in the chapter, you'll learn about the Windows tools to manage memory, which can help optimize a Windows 2000/XP system.

### OS TOOLS TO PARTITION AND FORMAT A HARD DRIVE

Recall from the previous chapter that when Windows 2000/XP is first installed, it will create one or more partitions on a hard drive and install a file system (NTFS or FAT) on each logical drive in each partition. Creating partitions and logical drives and formatting logical drives can be done in the following ways:

▲ When installing Windows 2000/XP, the Windows setup process executed from the Windows setup CD creates partitions and logical drives, assigns letters to these drives, and formats them as you specify. During installation, you must use some or part of the hard drive to create the primary partition and format drive C. Partitioning and formatting the rest of the hard drive can wait until after Windows is installed.

▲ After Windows 2000/XP is installed, any partition or logical drive except the one on which Windows is installed can be created using Disk Management, available from the Windows desktop. You can use Windows Explorer, Disk Management, or the Format command to format each logical drive.

▲ Using Windows 2000/XP, the Diskpart command, which is part of the Recovery Console, can be used to partition a drive and create logical drives within these

A+ ESS
1.2
3.1
3.2
3.3

A+
220-602
3.1

partitions. In Windows XP, the Diskpart command is available at a command prompt as well. How to use the Recovery Console is covered in Chapter 14.

▲ You can also use third-party software such as PartitionMagic to partition a drive, create logical drives, and format them. This software can create, resize, move, split, or combine partitions and logical drives without erasing data. It can also convert one file system to another without losing data.

### Notes

Original equipment manufacturers (OEMs), such as Dell and IBM, routinely create a hidden partition on a hard drive where they store recovery routines and a backup of the OS. For example, a Lenovo ThinkPad notebook computer has a hidden partition on the hard drive. To recover from a system failure, you can press a key at startup to access software on this partition. It displays a menu from which you can choose to reinstall the OS back to its state at the time the ThinkPad was purchased. If these recovery partitions are hidden, you can use PartitionMagic, which is partition management software by Symantec (*www.symantec.com*), to display these hidden partitions.

## APPLYING|CONCEPTS

Windows Explorer or My Computer does not distinguish between logical drives stored on the same hard drive or on different hard drives. For example, Figure 12-11 shows three drives, C, D, and E, that are logical drives on one physical hard drive. If you right-click one drive, such as drive D in the figure, and select **Properties** on the shortcut menu, you can see the amount of space allotted to this logical drive and how much of it is currently used. Also note in the figure that drive D is formatted using the FAT32 file system. It is possible for one logical drive to be formatted with one file system and other logical drives on the same hard drive to be formatted with a different file system such as FAT16 or NTFS. To know what logical drives belong to what physical drives, use Disk Management.

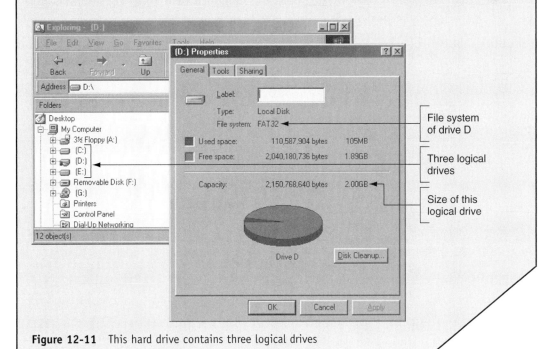

**Figure 12-11** This hard drive contains three logical drives

There are several reasons to partition and format a drive:

◢ When you first install a new hard drive, you must partition it to prepare it for use.
◢ If an existing hard drive is giving errors, you can repartition the drive and reformat each logical drive to begin fresh. Repartitioning destroys all data on the drive, so back up important data first.
◢ If you suspect a virus has attacked the drive, you can back up critical data and repartition to begin with a clean drive.
◢ If you want to wipe a hard drive clean and install a new OS, you can repartition a drive in preparation for formatting it with a new file system. If you do not want to change the size or number of partitions, you don't have to repartition the drive.

Now let's look at how to use the Disk Management window.

## DISK MANAGEMENT

**Disk Management** is a graphical, user-friendly utility that you can use to create partitions and format logical drives. Disk Management can also be used to create volumes on dynamic disks, and to convert a basic disk to a dynamic disk. Recall from Chapter 10 that Windows 2000/XP offers two ways to configure a hard drive: as a basic disk or a dynamic disk. A basic disk uses the same configuration used by Windows 9x/Me and DOS whereby a disk is divided into partitions, which are divided into logical drives. Dynamic disks don't use partitions or logical drives; instead they use dynamic volumes, which are called dynamic because you can change their size. Dynamic disks are mainly used when you want to implement RAID where files can be stored across more than one physical hard drive.

Here are two ways to access the Disk Management utility:

◢ In the Control Panel, open the **Administrative Tools** applet and double-click **Computer Management**. The Computer Management window opens (see Figure 12-12). Click **Disk Management**.
◢ Type **Diskmgmt.msc** in the Run dialog box and press **Enter**.

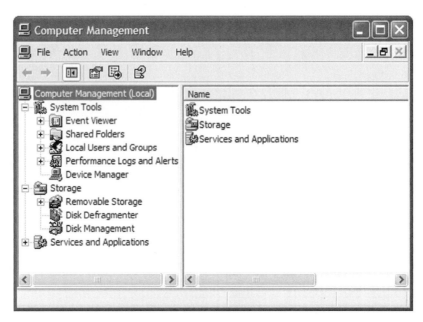

**Figure 12-12** Computer Management window

**12**

A+ ESS
1.2
3.1
3.2
3.3

A+
220-602
3.1

When Disk Management first loads, it examines the drive configuration for the system and displays all installed drives in a graphical format so you can see how each drive is allocated. For example, the Disk Management window shown in Figure 12-13 shows one hard drive installed that has a single drive C formatted with the NTFS file system. Compare this figure to Figure 12-14, which shows a system that has one hard drive installed that is sliced into three partitions. Notice in Figure 12-14 the color coding at the bottom of the window: dark blue for the primary partition (drive C), green for an extended partition (none in the figure), and light blue for logical drives (drive E and drive F).

> **A+ Exam Tip**
>
> The A+ Essentials exam expects you to be able to use the Disk Management window.

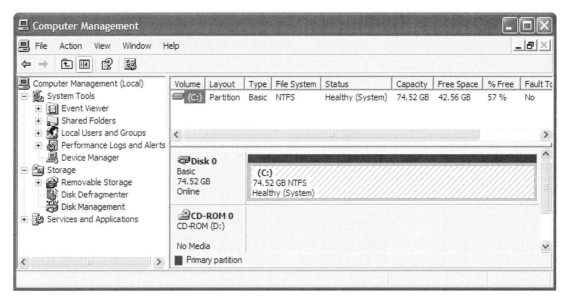

**Figure 12-13**  Disk Management shows installed drives, partitions, and file systems

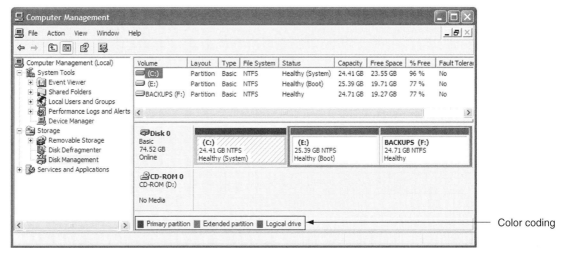

Color coding

**Figure 12-14**  This one hard drive has three partitions

You can now do the following to partition and format the new drive:

1. After you install a new second hard drive in the system and then access Disk Management, you'll see the new drive in the window. Right-click the new drive and select **New Partition** from the shortcut menu, as shown in Figure 12-15. The New Partition Wizard launches. Click **Next**.

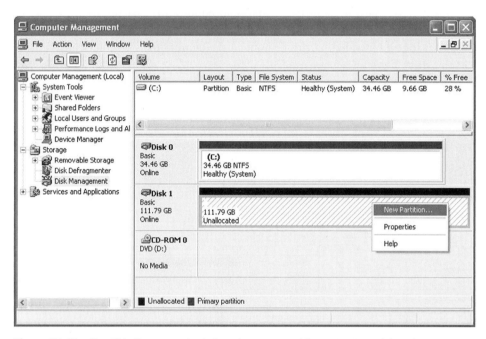

**Figure 12-15** The Disk Management window shows a new drive not yet partitioned

2. On the next screen, chose **Primary partition**, as shown in Figure 12-16, and click **Next**. Recall that a primary partition has only a single logical drive.

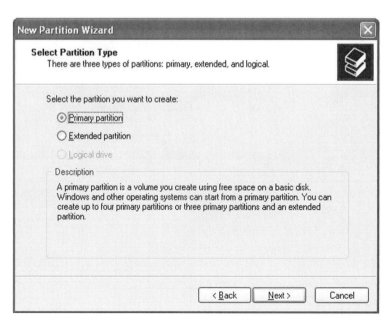

**Figure 12-16** The first partition on a hard drive should be the primary partition

A+ ESS
1.2
3.1
3.2
3.3

A+
220-602
3.1

3. On the next screen, you can decide to include all the available space on the drive in this one partition or leave some for other partitions. Enter the amount of available space for this partition and click **Next**. On the next screens, you must decide the drive letter to be assigned to the logical drive, the file system (**NTFS** is the best choice), and the volume name. When the wizard finishes partitioning and formatting the drive, it will look similar to the drive shown in Figure 12-17.

4. Make sure you can use the drive space by using Explorer to create a folder in the new partition and copy some files to it.

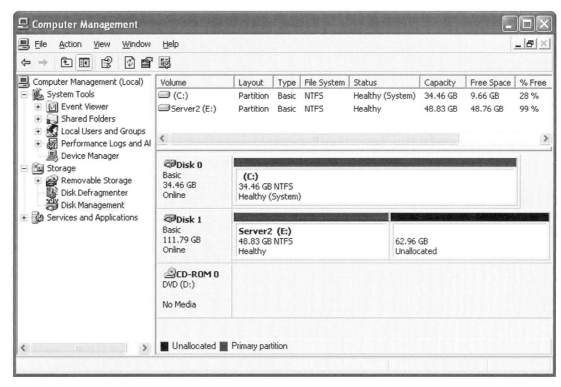

**Figure 12-17** One partition created and formatted on the new hard drive

A+ ESS
1.3
3.2
3.3

A+
220-602
3.1
3.2
3.3

## SOLVING HARDWARE PROBLEMS USING WINDOWS 2000/XP

As with all computer problems, begin solving the problem by questioning the user, identifying recent changes to the system, and making an initial determination of the software or hardware problem. After you've solved the problem, don't forget to document the initial symptoms, what actions you took, and the outcome. When a device won't work under Windows 2000/XP or gives errors, you can try these things to solve the problem:

▲ *Try a simple reboot*. Reboot the system; many times that alone solves your problem.

▲ *Check Device Manager*. Use Device Manager to search for useful information about problems with the device.

▲ *Uninstall the device using Device Manager*. Use Device Manager to uninstall the device. Then reboot and reinstall the drivers. To uninstall the device, right-click the device in Device Manager and select **Uninstall** from the shortcut menu (see Figure 12-18).

> **Notes**
>
> You must be logged on with administrator privileges to make changes from Device Manager.

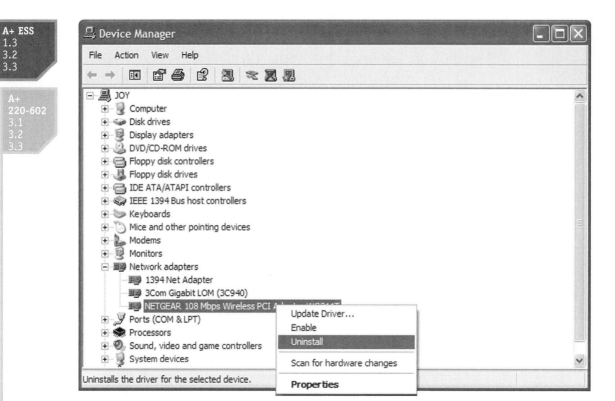

**Figure 12-18**  Use Device Manager to uninstall a device

▲ *Uninstall the device using utility software.* Some USB or FireWire devices and other devices don't show up in Device Manager. For these devices, you can use the Add or Remove Programs applet to uninstall the software for the device, which includes its device drivers.

▲ *Update device drivers.* For some situations, you can update the existing drivers. How to update drivers is coming up.

▲ *Roll back drivers.* If the problem began when you updated the drivers, roll back the drivers to the previous version. You can use Device Manager to do the rollback.

▲ *Check CMOS setup for errors.* Some devices, such as motherboard ports and expansion slots, hard drives, optical drives, floppy drives, and tape drives, are detected by the system BIOS and reported on the CMOS setup screens. On these screens, you can disable or enable some of these devices (see Figure 12-19). Know that, for ports and expansion slots, CMOS setup recognizes the port or slot, but not the device or expansion card using that slot. Any device that shows up in CMOS setup should also be listed in Device Manager. To access CMOS setup, press a key at startup before Windows loads. A message displays onscreen early in the startup process such as "Press F2 for setup" or "Press Del for BIOS setup."

▲ *Check Event Viewer for errors.* Use Event Viewer to check for hardware errors recorded in a Windows log that might help give you clues. How to use Event Viewer is covered later in the chapter.

▲ *Return to an earlier restore point.* For Windows XP, try using System Restore to return the system to an earlier point in time before the device installation. System Restore is also covered later in the chapter.

▲ *Verify device drivers.* If you suspect the drivers might be the source of the problem, you can verify the drivers are certified by Microsoft. How to do that is coming up.

▲ *Use utilities that come bundled with the device.* When you use the device setup CD to install the device drivers, many times the setup also installs utilities to manage the device.

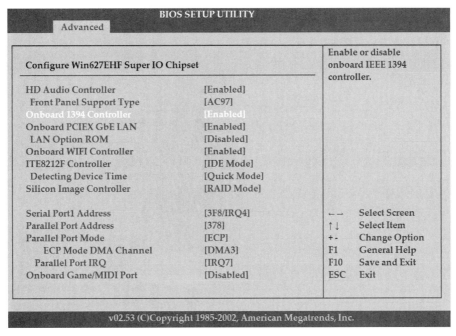

**Figure 12-19** In CMOS setup, you can disable and enable motherboard ports and other components

Look for such a utility listed under the Start, All Programs menu. When you have problems with a device, look for this utility and any diagnostic or testing software the utility might offer. For problems with hard drives, you can most likely download a diagnostic utility from the hard drive manufacturer Web site.

Now that you have a good feel for the general approach to solving hardware problems, let's look at how to update drivers, roll back drivers, and verify that a particular driver has been certified.

## UPDATING AND ROLLING BACK DRIVERS

Suppose you install a new application on your computer and the function keys on your keyboard don't work the way the application says they should. Or suppose you read that your sound card manufacturer has just released a driver update for your card and you want to try them out. Both of these situations are good reasons to try the Update Driver process. Here's how to use Device Manager to update the drivers for a device:

1. Locate drivers for your device and have the CD handy or download the driver files from the manufacturer's Web site to your hard drive.

2. Using Device Manger, right-click the device and select **Properties** from the shortcut menu. The Properties window for that device appears (see Figure 12-20).

3. Select the **Driver** tab and click **Update Driver**. The Hardware Update Wizard opens. On the first screen of the wizard, you are asked permission for Windows to look for drivers on the Windows Update Web site. If you are providing the drivers, select **No, not this time** and click **Next**. However, if you are trying to update drivers for a component that uses Windows drivers (such as a Microsoft keyboard, mouse, or fingerprint reader), then give permission. In this situation, the wizard goes to the Microsoft Web site, searches for updates to the driver, informs you if there is an update, and asks permission to install the update. Windows XP only suggests an update if the hardware

A+ ESS
1.3
3.2
3.3

A+
220-602
3.1
3.2
3.3

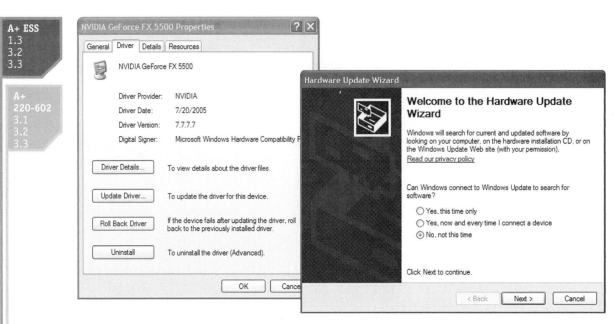

**Figure 12-20**    Use Device Manager to update drivers for a device

ID of the device exactly matches the hardware ID of the update. A hardware ID is a number the manufacturer assigns to a device that uniquely identifies the product.

4. If you are providing the drivers, on the next wizard screen, click **Install from a list or specific location** (**Advanced**). On the next screen, click **Search for the best driver in these locations** and then check **Include this location in the search** check box. You can then click **Browse** to locate the driver files. Remember, Windows is looking for an .inf file to identify the drivers. Continue to follow directions onscreen to complete the installation.

> **Notes**
>
> If you do not have an always-on connection to the Internet and you want Windows to search for driver updates on the Windows Update site, connect to the Internet before you launch the Update Device Driver Wizard.

> **Notes**
>
> By default, Device Manager hides legacy devices that are not Plug and Play. To view installed legacy devices, click the **View** menu of Device Manager, and check **Show hidden devices** (see Figure 12-21).

If you update a driver and the new driver does not perform as expected, you can revert to the old driver by using the Driver Rollback feature. To revert to a previous driver, open the Properties window for the device (see Figure 12-20), and click **Roll Back Driver**. If a previous driver is available, it will be installed. In many cases, when a driver is updated, Windows saves the old driver in case you want to revert to it. Keep in mind that Windows does not save printer drivers when they are updated and does not save drivers that are not functioning properly at the time of an update.

You can also copy an older driver from another PC or a backup medium to this PC for a rollback. Two files are needed: a .sys file and an .inf file. The .sys file is the actual driver, and the .inf file contains information about the driver. Put these files in the C:\Windows\system32\ reinstallbackups\ folder, and then perform the rollback.

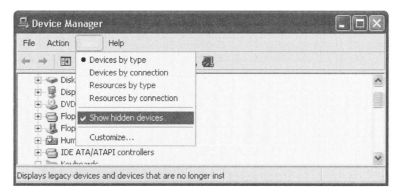

**Figure 12-21** By default, Windows XP does not display legacy devices in Device Manager; you show these hidden devices by using the View menu

## VERIFY THAT DRIVERS ARE CERTIFIED BY MICROSOFT

Windows 2000/XP supports the verification of digital signatures assigned to device drivers and application files, which certifies that the driver or other software has been tested and approved by Microsoft's Windows Hardware Quality Labs (WHQL) for Windows 2000 or Windows XP. If you suspect a problem with a driver, do one of the following to verify that it is digitally signed by Microsoft:

▲ *Use the File Signature Verification tool.* Type the **Sigverif.exe** command in the Run dialog box. This command displays information about digitally signed files, including device driver files and application files, and logs information to *systemroot*\Sigverif.txt (most likely *systemroot* is C:\).

▲ *Use the Driver Query tool.* To direct output to a file, including information about digital signatures, enter this command in the Run dialog box:

```
Driverquery/si > myfile.txt
```

▲ *Use Device Manager.* In a device's Properties dialog box, click the **Driver** tab and then click **Driver Details**. In the Driver File Details window under Digital Signer, look for Microsoft Windows XP Publisher (for Microsoft drivers) or Microsoft WHQL (for manufacturer drivers).

> 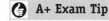 **A+ Exam Tip**
>
> The A+ Essentials exam expects you to be familiar with methods to verify that drivers and applications are signed.

As a Windows administrator, you might want to control what happens when you or someone else attempts to install a device that is not digitally signed. To do that, open the System Properties window and then click the **Hardware** tab (see Figure 12-22). Then click the **Driver Signing** button. The Driver Signing Options window opens, also shown in Figure 12-22. Select how you want Windows to handle unsigned driver installations and click **OK**.

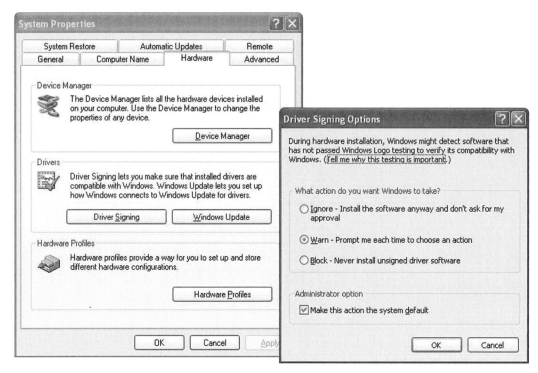

**Figure 12-22**    Tell Windows how you want it to handle installing an unsigned driver

> **Notes**
>
> Use the Driver Query tool to save information about your system to a file when the system is healthy. Later, if you have a problem with drivers, you can compare reports to help identify the problem driver.

## INSTALLING AND SUPPORTING APPLICATIONS

To install applications and other software under Windows 2000/XP, you can use the Add or Remove Programs applet in the Control Panel, or you can run the application's setup program from the Run dialog box. You can install software only if you have Administrator privileges. An installed program is normally made available to all users when they log on. If a program is not available to all users, try installing the program files in the C:\Documents and Settings\All Users folder.

From the Windows 2000/XP Add or Remove Programs window, shown in the background of Figure 12-23, you can change or remove presently installed programs; add new programs from a CD, a floppy disk, or from Microsoft over the Internet; and add or remove Windows components.

> **Notes**
>
> To uninstall software, select the software to uninstall, and then click the **Change/Remove** icon. If other users are logged on to the system, the Warning message in Figure 12-23 appears. Log everyone off and then uninstall the software.

> **Notes**
>
> The Windows 2000 Add/Remove Programs utility, shown in Figure 12-24, looks and works the same as the Windows XP utility. In the figure, note the expanded drop-down menu in the upper-right corner, which shows how you can sort the view of presently installed programs.

A+ ESS
3.2

A+
220-602
3.2
3.3

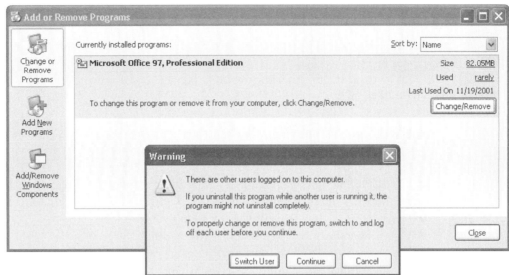

**Figure 12-23** To uninstall software using the Add or Remove Programs applet, only one user, an administrator, should be logged on to the system

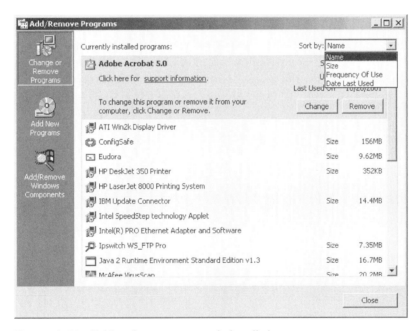

**Figure 12-24** Making changes to currently installed programs

## HOW TO INSTALL LEGACY SOFTWARE UNDER WINDOWS XP

Legacy applications written for DOS, Windows 9x/Me, or Windows NT might work under Windows 2000 or Windows XP, might not work at all, or might be sluggish. Legacy applications that don't work under Windows 2000 are more likely to work under

> **Notes**
>
> You can cause a program to launch automatically each time you start Windows by putting a shortcut to the program in the Startup menu folder for the user. For each user, this folder is C:\Documents and Settings\*Username*\Start Menu\Programs \Startup. If you want the software to start up automatically for all users, put the shortcut in this folder: C:\Documents and Settings\All Users\Start Menu\Programs \Startup.

A+ ESS
3.2

A+
220-602
3.2
3.3

Windows XP. Some legacy applications that you should not attempt to run under Windows XP are older versions of antivirus software, and maintenance and cleanup utilities. In these cases, it is best to upgrade your software to versions designed to work under Windows XP.

If a legacy application does not start up and run successfully after you have installed it, try the following:

◢ Check the Microsoft Web site for updates to Windows 2000/XP or the Microsoft application (*windowsupdate.microsoft.com*). You learned how to perform Windows updates in the previous chapter.

◢ Check the software manufacturer's Web site for updates or suggestions on how to run the software under Windows 2000/XP.

◢ Consider upgrading the software to a later version.

◢ Use the Windows XP Compatibility Mode utility.

The **Compatibility Mode utility** provides an application with the environment it expects from the operating system for which it was designed, including Windows 95, Windows 98, Windows Me, Windows NT, and Windows 2000. (Compatibility mode does not apply to DOS applications.) There is more than one way to use the utility, but the easiest way is to create a shortcut on the desktop to an installed application and then set the properties of the shortcut to use compatibility mode. After you create the shortcut to the application, right-click it and select **Properties** from the shortcut menu. The Properties window appears (see Figure 12-25). Select the **Compatibility** tab, check **Run this program in compatibility mode for,** and then select the operating system that you want Windows XP to emulate. Click **Apply** to apply the change. Run the software to find out whether the problem is solved.

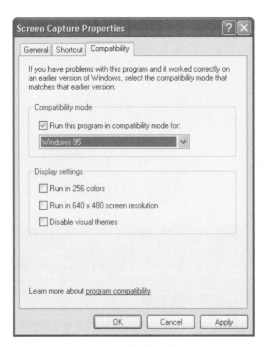

**Figure 12-25**   Setting Windows XP to run a legacy program in compatibility mode

If it is not solved, you can provide Microsoft with information that might help it fix the problem in some future Windows XP update. To provide the information, run the Program Compatibility Wizard. Click **Start, All Programs, Accessories,** and **Program Compatibility**

**Wizard.** Follow directions on the wizard screen to locate the program file. After you locate the program file, you are asked to test the application and then respond to the questions shown in Figure 12-26.

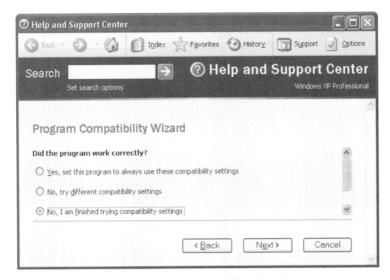

**Figure 12-26** Using the Program Compatibility Wizard

If you answer, **No, I am finished trying compatibility settings,** then the screen in Figure 12-27 appears. If you respond **Yes** to the question, "Would you like to send this information to Microsoft?", then the information needed to help Microsoft solve problems with the application is transmitted to the Microsoft Web site over the Internet.

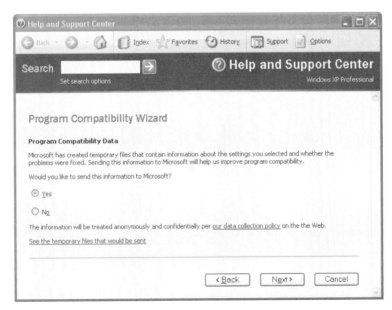

**Figure 12-27** If running a legacy program in compatibility mode does not solve the problem, you can send helpful information to Microsoft

## HOW TO SOLVE PROBLEMS WITH APPLICATIONS

When Windows XP encounters a problem with an application, it uses the Error Reporting service to collect information about the problem and display a message similar to the one shown in Figure 12-28. If you are connected to the Internet, you can click **Send Error Report** to get suggestions about the problem from Microsoft. Microsoft will also use the information you send to help with future Windows updates and patches.

**Figure 12-28**    A serious Windows error sometimes generates this Microsoft Windows dialog box

After the information is sent, a dialog box similar to the one in the foreground in Figure 12-29 appears. Click **More information** to see Microsoft's insights and suggestions about the problem. Your browser will open and display information from Microsoft. If the problem is caused by a Microsoft product such as Internet Explorer or Microsoft Office, sometimes the Web site will point you to a patch you can download to fix the problem. An example of this available patch is showing in the background in Figure 12-29.

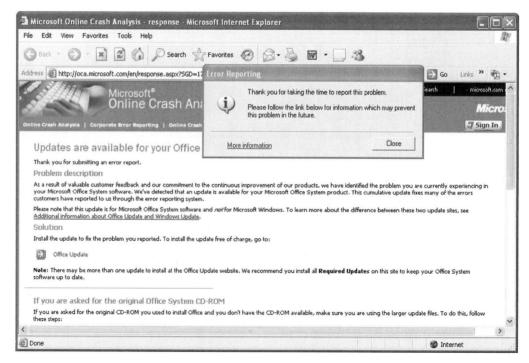

**Figure 12-29**    Click More information to see Microsoft's insights into a problem

Windows 2000 does not offer the Error Reporting service, but both Windows 2000 and Windows XP have Dr. Watson, a similar utility that automatically launches when an application problem occurs. It generates a report that you can then send to the software developers to help them solve the problem. By default, Dr. Watson stores the log file, Drwtsn32.log, in this folder for Windows XP: C:\Documents and Settings\All Users.WINNT\Application Data\Microsoft\DrWatson. For Windows 2000, the file is stored here: C:\Documents and Settings\All Users\Documents\DrWatson folder. To change the location of the file, use the Drwtsn32 command, which launches the Dr. Watson window shown in Figure 12-30.

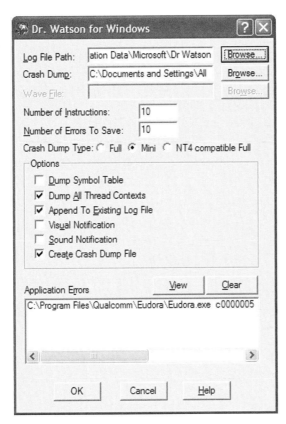

**Figure 12-30** Change settings for a Dr. Watson log file and crash dump

Here are some other useful tips for solving problems with applications:

◢ *Try a reboot.* Reboot the system and see if that doesn't solve the problem.

◢ *Suspect a virus is causing a problem.* Scan for viruses and check Task Manager to make sure some strange process is not interfering with your applications. How to use Task Manager to identify a bad process is covered later in the chapter.

◢ *Windows update might solve the problem.* When Microsoft is aware of application problems caused by Windows, it sometimes releases a patch to solve the problem. Make sure Windows updates are current.

◢ *You might be low on system resources.* Close all other applications. Check Task Manager to make sure you have unnecessary processes closed. If you must run more than one application at a time, you can increase the priority level for an application that is not getting its fair share of resources. To do that, on the **Processes** tab of Task Manager, right-click the application and click **Set Priority**.

A+ ESS
3.2
3.3

A+
220-602
3.2
3.3

Then increase the priority level. (Know that this works only for the current session.)

▲ *Download Updates or Patches for the Application.* Software manufacturers often publish updates or patches for their software to address known problems. You can go to the software Web site to download these updates and get information about known problems.

▲ *Uninstall and reinstall the application.* Sometimes an application gives problems because the installation gets corrupted. You can try uninstalling and reinstalling the application. However, in doing so you might lose any customized settings, macros, or scripts.

▲ *Run the application under a different user account.* The application might require that the user have privileges not assigned to the current account. Try running the application under an account with administrator privileges.

▲ *Install the application under a different account.* If an application will not install, the user account you are using might not have permission to install software. Install software using an account with administrative privileges.

▲ *Consider data corruption.* It might appear the application has a problem when the problem is really a corrupted data file. Try creating an entirely new data file. If that works, then suspect that previous errors might be caused by corrupted data. You might be able to recover part of a corrupted file by changing its file extension to .txt and importing it into the application as a text file.

▲ *Consider hard drive or file system problems.* Some older applications expect the file system used on the hard drive to be FAT32. If your drive is using the NTFS file system, problems might occur. Try installing the application and its data on a FAT32 partition.

▲ *Try restoring default settings.* Maybe a user has made one-too-many changes to the application settings. Try restoring all settings to their default values. This might solve a problem with missing toolbars and other functions.

A+ ESS
3.2

## TOOLS USEFUL TO MANAGE HARDWARE AND APPLICATIONS

Besides the Windows utilities you've already learned about so far in this chapter, you also need to be aware of several other tools useful to monitor hardware and software and solve problems when they occur. In this section, you'll learn about the Computer Management console, the Microsoft Management Console, Event Viewer, and the Windows 2000/XP Support Tools, including Dependency Walker.

### COMPUTER MANAGEMENT

Computer Management is a window that consolidates several Windows 2000/XP administrative tools that you can use to manage the local PC or other computers on the network. To use most of these tools, you must be logged on as an administrator, although you can view certain settings and configurations in Computer Management if you are logged on with lesser privileges.

To access Computer Management, open the **Control Panel**, open the **Administrative Tools** window, and then double-click the **Computer Management** icon. The Computer Management window opens (see Figure 12-31). Using this window, you can access Event Viewer, Device Manager, Disk Management, Disk Defragmenter (covered in Chapter 13), Services Console, and manage user groups (also covered in Chapter 13). You can also monitor problems with hardware, software, and security. Several tools available from the Computer Management window are covered in this chapter.

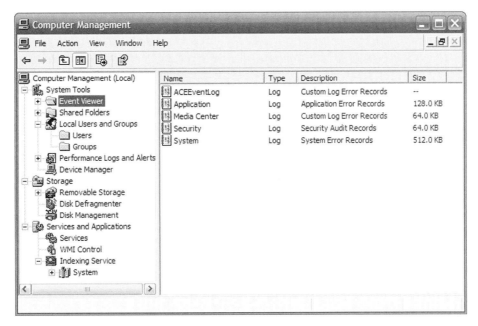

**Figure 12-31** Windows 2000/XP Computer Management combines several administrative tools into a single easy-to-access window

### Notes

By default, the Administrative Tools group is found in the Control Panel, but you can add the group to the All Programs menu. To do that for Windows XP, right-click the taskbar and select **Properties** from the shortcut menu. The Taskbar and Start Menu Properties window opens. Select the **Start Menu** tab and then click **Customize** (as shown on the left side of Figure 12-32). Click the **Advanced** tab, as shown on the right side of Figure 12-32. Scroll down through the list, select **Display on the All Programs Menu**, and click **OK**. Now, to use the Administrative Tools group, click **Start, All Programs**, and **Administrative Tools**. (To add the tool to the Start menu in Windows 2000, in the Taskbar and Start Menu Properties window, click the **Advanced** tab.)

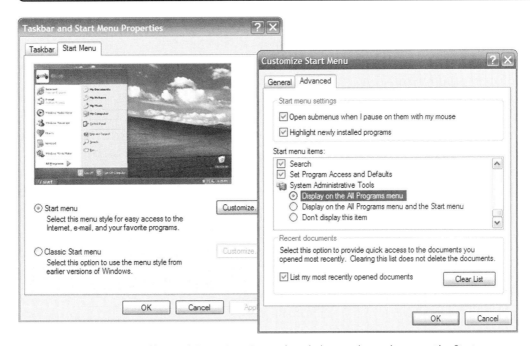

**Figure 12-32** Use the Taskbar and Start Menu Properties window to change items on the Start menu

A+ ESS
3.2

## MICROSOFT MANAGEMENT CONSOLE

Microsoft Management Console (MMC) is a Windows utility that can be used to build your own customized console windows. A **console** is a single window that contains one or more administrative tools such as Device Manager or Disk Management. In a console, these individual tools are called **snap-ins**. An example of a console is Computer Management, which has a filename of Compmgmt.msc. (Event Viewer and Disk Defragmenter are two snap-ins in that console.) A console is saved in a file with an .msc file extension, and a snap-in in a console can itself be a console. When you use MMC to build a console, you can use any of the snap-ins listed in Table 12-1. To use all the functions of MMC, you must be logged on with administrator privileges.

| Snap-in | Description |
|---|---|
| Active X Control | Enables you to add ActiveX controls to your system |
| Certificates | Provides certificate management at the user, service, or computer level |
| Component Services | Links to the Component Services management tool, which is located in the Control Panel |
| Computer Management | Links to the Computer Management tools in the Control Panel |
| Device Manager | Lets you see what hardware devices you have on your system and configure device properties |
| Disk Defragmenter | Links to the Disk Defragmenter utility (Defrag.exe) |
| Disk Management | Links to the Disk Management tool |
| Event Viewer | Links to the Event Viewer tool, which displays event logs for the system |
| Fax Service Management | Enables you to manage fax settings and devices |
| Folder | Enables you to add a folder to manage from MMC |
| Group Policy | Provides a tool to manage group policy settings |
| Indexing Service | Searches files and folders using specified parameters |
| IP Security Policy Management | Manages Internet communication security |
| Link to Web Address | Enables you to link to a specified Web site |
| Local Users and Groups | Provides a tool to manage settings for local users and groups |
| Performance Logs and Alerts | Gives you an interface from which to set up and manage logs of performance information and alerts about system performance |
| Removable Storage Management | Enables you to manage settings and configuration information for removable storage devices such as Zip drives and tape backup drives |
| Security Configuration and Analysis | Enables you to manage configuration of security settings for computers that use security template files |
| Services | Provides a centralized interface for starting, stopping, and configuring system services |
| Shared Folders | Provides information about shared folders, open files, and current sessions |
| System Information | Contains information about the system that you can use when troubleshooting |

**Table 12-1**  Some MMC snap-ins

**12**

You can use MMC to create a console that contains some popular utility tools. Follow these steps for Windows XP (differences for Windows 2000 are noted) to create one console:

1. Click **Start,** click **Run,** enter **MMC** in the Run dialog box, and then click **OK.** An empty console window appears, as shown in Figure 12-33.

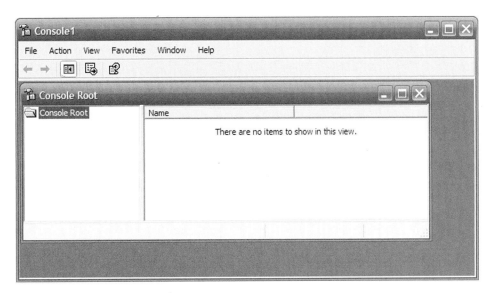

**Figure 12-33**   An empty console

2. Click **File** on the menu bar (in Windows 2000, click **Console**), and then click **Add/Remove Snap-in.** The Add/Remove Snap-in window opens, as shown on the left side of Figure 12-34. This window on the left is empty because no snap-ins have been added to the console.

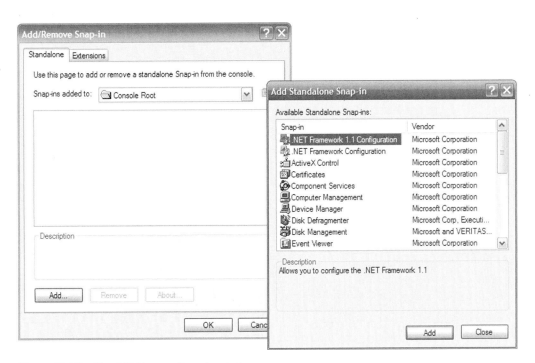

**Figure 12-34**   The Add/Remove Snap-in window

A+ ESS
3.2

3. Click **Add**. You see a list of snap-ins that can be added to a console, as shown on the right side of Figure 12-34. Select a snap-in and then click **Add**.

4. If parameters for the snap-in need defining, a dialog box opens that allows you to set up these parameters. The dialog box offers different selections, depending on the snap-in being added. When you have made your selections, click **Finish**. The new snap-in appears in the Add/Remove Snap-in window.

5. Repeat Steps 3 and 4 to add all the snap-ins that you want to the console. When you finish, click **Close** in the Add Standalone Snap-in window showing in Figure 12-34, then click **OK**.

6. The left side of Figure 12-35 shows a console with four snap-ins added. To save the console, click **File** on the menu bar (for Windows 2000, click **Console**), and then click **Save As**. The Save As dialog box opens, as shown on the right side of the figure.

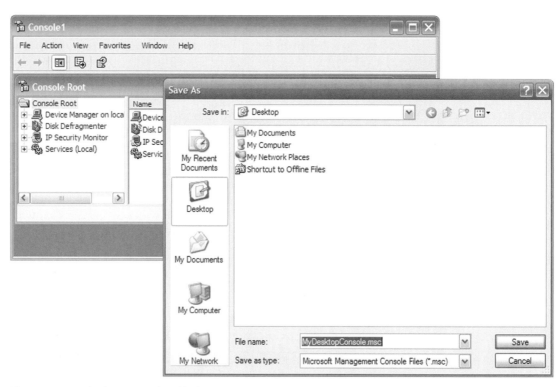

**Figure 12-35**  Saving a console with four snap-ins

7. The default location for the console file is C:\Documents and Settings\\*username*\\Start Menu\Programs\Administrative Tools. However, you can save the console to any location, such as the Windows desktop. However, if you save the file to its default location, the console will appear as an option under Administrative Tools on the Start menu. Select the location for the file, name the file, and click **Save**.

8. Close the console window.

A+ ESS
3.2
3.3

A+
220-602
3.1
3.3

**Notes**

After you create a console, you can copy the .msc file to any computer or place a shortcut to it on the desktop.

## EVENT VIEWER

Event Viewer is a Windows 2000/XP tool useful for troubleshooting problems with Windows, applications, and hardware. Of all these types of problems, it is most useful when troubleshooting problems with hardware.

**12**

A+ ESS
3.2
3.3

A+
220-602
3.1
3.3

Event Viewer displays logs of significant events such as a hardware or network failure, OS error messages, a device or service that has failed to start, or General Protection Faults.

Event Viewer (Eventvwr.msc) is a Computer Management console snap-in. You can open it by using the Computer Management window, by entering **Eventvwr.msc** in the Run dialog box, or by clicking **Start**, **All Programs** (for Windows 2000, **Programs**), **Administrative Tools**, **Event Viewer**. Either way, the window in Figure 12-36 opens.

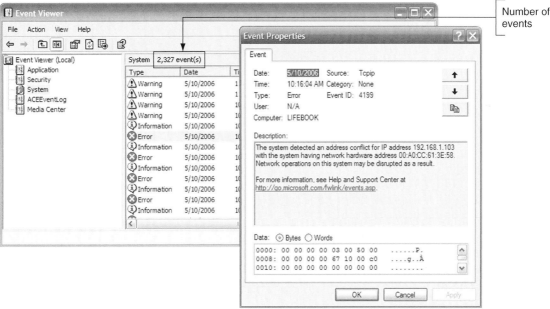

Number of events

**Figure 12-36** Use Event Viewer to see information about events with applications, security, and the system

Depending on the OS version and original equipment manufacturer (OEM) features, Event Viewer shows three or more logs. The first three logs in Figure 12-36 are standard to all systems. They are described next:

▲ *The application log* records application events. The events recorded depend on what the developer of the application set to trigger a log entry. One type of event recorded in this log is an Error Reporting event, which you learned about earlier in the chapter.

▲ *The security log* records events based on audit policies, which an administrator sets to monitor user activity such as successful or unsuccessful attempts to access a file or log on to the system. Only an administrator can view this log.

▲ *The system log* records events triggered by Windows components, such as a device driver failing to load during the boot process. Windows 2000/XP sets which events are recorded in this log. All users can access this log file.

The security log records security audit events. You'll learn more about these audit events in Chapter 19. The system and application logs can record three types of events:

▲ *Information* events are recorded when a driver, service, or application functions successfully.

▲ *Warning* events are recorded when something happens that may indicate a future problem but does not necessarily indicate that something is presently wrong with the system. For example, low disk space might trigger a warning event.

▲ *Error* events are recorded when something goes wrong with the system, such as a necessary component failing to load, data getting lost or becoming corrupted, or a system or application function ceasing to operate.

To view a log within Event Viewer, click the log that you want to view in the left pane. This generates a summary of events that appears in the right pane. Double-click a specific event to see details about it (refer back to Figure 12-36).

Notice in the figure that over 2,000 events are listed in the system log. That can be a lot of events to read! To save time, you might want to view only certain events and not the entire list to find what you're looking for. Fortunately, you can filter events so only certain ones are listed. To do that, right-click a log in the left pane and select **Properties** from the shortcut menu. The log's Properties window appears. Click the **Filter** tab (see Figure 12-37).

**Figure 12-37** Criteria to filter events in Event Viewer

To filter events, you can use several event characteristics to build these filters, which are listed in Table 12-2.

| Event Characteristics | Description |
|---|---|
| Event type | The type of event, such as information, error, or warning |
| Event source | The application, driver, or service that triggered the event |
| Category | The category that the event falls under, such as an attempt to log on to the system or access a program |
| Event ID | A number that identifies the event and makes tracking events easier for support personnel |

**Table 12-2** Event characteristics that can be used to filter events

12

| Event Characteristics | Description |
| --- | --- |
| User | The logon name for a user |
| Computer | The name of a computer on the system |
| From: To: | The range of events that you want to view. You can view the events from first to last event, or you can view all events that occurred on a specific date and in a specific time range. |

**Table 12-2** Event characteristics that can be used to filter events (continued)

Another way you can avoid a ballooning log file is to set a size limit and specify what happens when the log reaches this limit. If you right-click a log, select **Properties** on the shortcut menu, and click the **General** tab, you can set the maximum size of the log in megabytes (as well as view general information about the log). You can set the log to over-write events as needed, overwrite events that are more than a specified number of days old, or not overwrite events at all. Select this last option when system security is high and you do not want to lose any event information. If you select this option, the system simply stops recording events when the log file reaches the maximum size (see Figure 12-38).

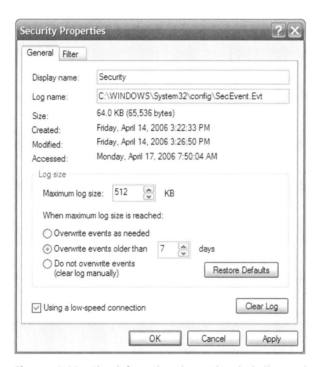

**Figure 12-38** View information about a log, including maximum size of the log file, in the System Log Properties dialog box

To allow the system to record events in the log after a log reaches maximum size, you have to review the events and clear the log manually, either by clicking the **Clear Log** button in the Properties dialog box or selecting **Clear All Events** from the Action menu. Before clearing the log, Event Viewer gives you a chance to save it.

Event Viewer can be useful when you suspect someone is attempting to illegally log onto a system and you want to view login attempts. But Event Viewer is most useful in solving intermittent hardware problems. For example, on our network we have a file server and

A+ ESS
3.2
3.3

A+
220-602
3.1
3.3

several people in the office update Microsoft Word documents stored on the server. For weeks people complained about these Word documents getting corrupted. We downloaded the latest patches for Windows and Microsoft Office and scanned for viruses thinking that the problem might be with Windows or the application. Then we suspected a corrupted template file for building the Word documents. But nothing we did solved our problem of corrupted Word documents. Then one day someone thought to check Event Viewer on the file server. The Event Viewer had faithfully been recording errors when writing to the hard drive. What we had suspected to be a software problem was, in fact, a failing hard drive, which was full of bad sectors. We replaced the drive and the problem went away.

A+ ESS
3.2

## WINDOWS 2000/XP SUPPORT TOOLS AND DEPENDENCY WALKER

Windows 2000/XP offers several support tools that you can install. They are located in the \Support\Tools folder on the Windows 2000/XP CD. To install them, you can run the Setup program located in that folder (see Figure 12-39). To start the Setup program, enter this command in the Run dialog box (but don't include the ending period): **D:\Support\Tools\Setup.exe.** If necessary, substitute the drive letter of your CD-ROM drive for D in the command line. In this folder, you can also find some documentation files about the support tools.

**Figure 12-39**    The \Support\Tools folder on the Windows XP CD

 **Notes**

A file with an .htm or .html file extension is a hypertext markup language (HTML) file. A **hypertext** file is a text file that contains hypertext tags to format the file and create hyperlinks to different points in the file or to other files. Hypertext files are used on the Web and are read and displayed using a Web browser such as Microsoft Internet Explorer or Netscape Navigator. To read a hypertext file using Windows Explorer, double-click the filename; your default browser will open the file.

One Support Tool utility is Dependency Walker (Depends.exe), which lists all the files used by an application. It can be useful when you've installed an application, but the application doesn't work correctly. Go to a computer that has the application installed correctly and use Dependency Walker to get a report of files used by the application. Then use Dependency Walker to get the same report on the computer with the problem. You can then compare the two reports, looking for DLL files that are missing on the bad installation, are not the correct size, or are incorrectly date-stamped. A DLL file is a Windows file with a .dll file extension that an application uses to relate to Windows. Dependency Walker can also be useful if an application is giving General Protection Fault errors. Compare a report of files the application uses on a good computer to files used on the computer giving errors.

To use Windows XP Dependency Walker, click **Start**, point to **All Programs** and **Windows Support Tools**, and then click **Command Prompt**. A Command Prompt window opens showing the current directory as C:\Program Files\Support Tools. To see a list of tools, type the command **Dir** and press **Enter**. To use Dependency Walker, type the command **Depends** and press **Enter**. The Dependency Walker window opens. When you click **File** and **Open** and then navigate to a program file and click **Open**, the Dependency Walker window displays a list of files on which this program is dependent. Figure 12-40 shows the dependencies for the Notepad.exe program.

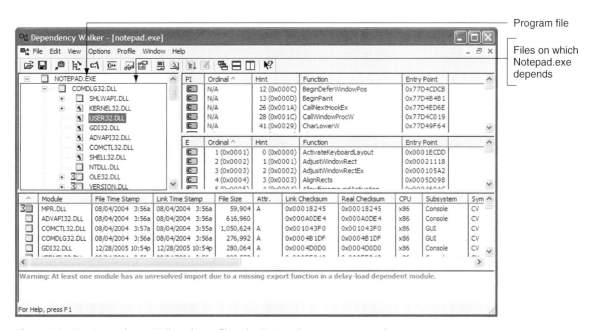

**Figure 12-40** Dependency Walker shows files the Notepad.exe program needs to run

To use Windows 2000 Dependency Walker, click **Start**, point to **Programs, Windows 2000 Support Tools**, and **Tools**, and then click **Dependency Walker**. Figure 12-41 shows a Dependency Walker window. Click **File** on the menu bar, click **Open**, and then select the main executable file for an application. In the figure, Apache.exe is selected. Apache is a popular Web server application. The window lists all supporting files that Apache.exe uses and how they depend on one another.

A+ ESS
3.2

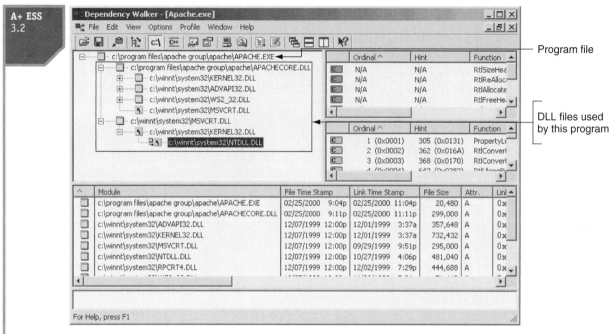

— Program file

— DLL files used
by this program

**Figure 12-41** You can use Dependency Walker to solve problems with applications

## PROTECTING AND MAINTAINING WINDOWS SYSTEM FILES

A+ ESS
1.3
3.4

A+
220-602
3.1
3.4

When you first become responsible for a Windows 2000/XP system, one of the first things you need to do is make sure procedures are set in place to keep Windows updated and to keep good backups of system files and user data. In the previous chapter, you learned how to set Windows XP to perform automatic updates and how to update Windows 2000. In this section, you'll learn several ways you can keep good backups of system files. In the next chapter, you'll learn how to back up user data.

Tools and methods offered by Windows 2000/XP to protect and back up critical system files are Windows File Protection, System Restore (Windows XP only), backing up the system state, and Automated System Recovery (Windows XP only). All these tools are covered in the following sections. You need to know how to make the necessary backups and then how to use these backups in the event a problem arises.

> **Notes**
>
> Recall that to update Windows XP, click **Start, All Programs, Windows Update**. For Windows 2000, click **Start, Windows Update**. Another way to update either OS is to open your browser and go to the *windowsupdate.microsoft.com* Web site to download and install updates.

Windows 2000/XP calls the files critical to a successful operating system load the **system state data**. This includes all files necessary to boot the OS, the Windows 2000/XP registry, and all system files in the *%SystemRoot%* folder, the folder in which Windows 2000/XP is installed.

> **Notes**
>
> Windows XP is most likely installed in C:\Windows. Windows 2000 is likely to be installed in C:\WINNT. Microsoft documentation sometimes calls the folder in which Windows is installed *\winnt_root* or *%SystemRoot%*. To help you become comfortable with both names, we use them both in this chapter.

**12**

# WINDOWS FILE PROTECTION

A+ ESS
1.3
3.4

A+
220-602
3.1
3.3
3.4

Windows 2000/XP provides a feature called Windows File Protection (WFP) to protect system files from being accidentally changed or deleted. When applications are installed, the installation program might attempt to overwrite a Windows system file with a version that the application knows it needs. Applications tend to use the same Windows system files, so if an application changes one of these shared system files, another application that depends on the file might give errors or the system might even become unstable. Also, users might attempt to accidentally delete an important Windows system file, or malicious software might attempt to overwrite a system file with an infected version. For all these reasons, Windows File Protection does not allow system files to be altered or deleted. System files protected have a .sys, .dll, .ttf, .fon, .ocs, or .exe file extension.

> **Notes**
>
> As Windows File Protection protects system files, it does allow legitimate updates to those files, when necessary.

Windows File Protection protects system files by keeping copies of good system files in the C:\Windows\system32\dllcache folder shown in Figure 12-42 (for Windows 2000, the folder is C:\WINNT\system32\dllcache). When WFP wants to validate a system file, it compares it to one in this folder and uses the one in the folder to replace a questionable system file. If it doesn't have a good system file in the Dllcache folder, it requests that you insert the Windows 2000/XP setup CD so it can get a fresh copy.

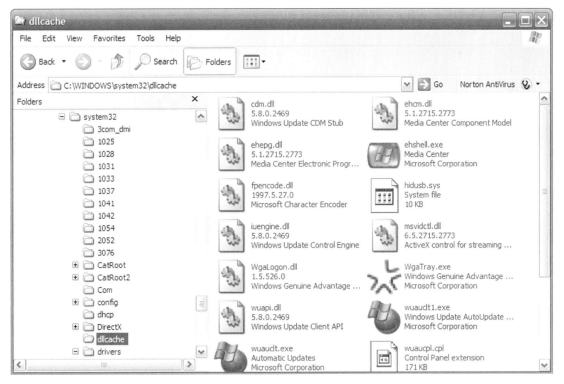

**Figure 12-42** Windows File Protection stores good copies of system files in the C:\Windows\system32\ dllcache folder

Windows File Protection works by using two processes. One is a background process that notifies WFP when a protected file is modified. WFP then checks the file signature to see whether it is the correct Microsoft version of the file. If the file version is not

A+ ESS
1.3
3.4

A+
220-602
3.1
3.3
3.4

correct, WFP looks in the Dllcache folder, which contains cached copies of system files, or asks that the Windows 2000/XP CD be inserted so that WFP can find the file and restore it from the CD. Replacing incorrect system files with correct ones from the Windows 2000/XP CD requires administrative permissions. If a non-administrator user is logged on when WFP activates, WFP does not prompt that user to insert the Windows 2000/XP CD, but waits until an administrator logs on to request the CD and replace the file.

> **Notes**
>
> If a file has been modified, is correctly signed as a Microsoft-approved version, and is not present in the Dllcache folder, WFP adds it to that folder to be used as the correct version on future scans.

When WFP restores a file, it shows the following message by default, replacing *file_name* with the name of the system file it restored:

```
A file replacement was attempted on the protected system file
file_name. To maintain system stability, the file has been restored
to the correct Microsoft version. If problems occur with your
application, please contact the application vendor for support.
```

If you see this message, carefully note what application was working at the time and what happened just before the message. Maybe an application is being installed, a virus is present, a corrupted application is performing an illegal operation, or a user has made a mistake. It is important to have as much information as possible to figure out which applications might need to be scanned for viruses or replaced altogether.

The other tool that WFP uses is the **System File Checker (SFC)**. (The program filename is Sfc.exe.) This tool can be used in several situations. If the administrator set the system to perform an unattended installation, the SFC checks all protected system files after Setup is completed to see whether they were modified during the installation. If any incorrect modifications have been made or if any important system files are unsigned, WFP retrieves a copy of the file from the Dllcache folder or requests it from the Windows 2000/XP CD.

An administrator can also use the SFC command to verify that the system is using correct versions of all protected system files, either as a preventative maintenance measure or when he or she suspects that system files have become corrupted or deleted. For example, if more than one application gives errors or Windows gives errors after the boot, you might suspect system files have been corrupted. To use System File Checker, you can type **sfc.exe** or **sfc** in a Command Prompt window or in the Run dialog box. When you type this command, you need to include one of the switches listed in Table 12-3. For example, to perform an immediate scan of protected system files, you would use this command line: **sfc /scannow**. Figure 12-43 shows the result of using this command and switch.

| Switch | Function |
|---|---|
| /cachesize=x | Sets the size of the file cache, in megabytes |
| /cancel | Discontinues scans of protected system files |
| /enable | Enables normal operation of WFP |
| /purgecache | Empties the file cache and immediately scans all protected system files, populating the Dllcache folder with confirmed correct versions of system files (may require insertion of the Windows 2000/XP CD as the source for correct versions) |

**Table 12-3**  Switches for the SFC utility

A+ ESS
1.3
3.4

A+
220-602
3.1
3.3
3.4

| Switch | Function |
|--------|----------|
| /quiet | Replaces incorrect versions of system files with correct ones without prompting the user |
| /scanboot | Performs a scan of protected system files every time the system boots |
| /scannow | Performs an immediate scan of protected system files |
| /scanonce | Performs a scan of protected system files the next time the system boots |
| /? | Displays a list of available switches for the sfc command |

**Table 12-3** Switches for the SFC utility (continued)

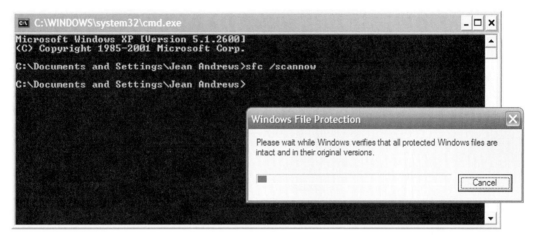

**Figure 12-43** Use the SFC utility to scan the system for corrupted system files

## WINDOWS XP SYSTEM RESTORE

A+
220-602
3.1
3.4

The **System Restore** utility is new to Windows XP. System Restore can be set to routinely make snapshots of critical Windows system files necessary to load the OS. When Windows XP is giving problems, you can use System Restore to restore the system state to its condition at the time a snapshot was taken.

The restore process does not affect user data on the hard drive but can affect installed software and hardware, user settings, and OS configuration settings. Also, the restore process cannot help you recover from a virus or worm infection unless the infection is launched at startup. The restoration is taken from a snapshot of the system state, called a **restore point**, that was created earlier. The system automatically creates a restore point before you install new software or hardware or make other changes to the system. You can also manually create a restore point at any time.

> **Notes**
>
> System Restore only works to recover from errors if the registry is somewhat intact because restore points replace certain keys in the registry but cannot completely rebuild a totally corrupted registry. On the other hand, restoring the system state from a previous backup completely restores the registry from the backup.

# APPLYING|CONCEPTS

By default, Windows XP System Restore is turned on when the OS is first installed. To be on the safe side, when you first become responsible for a system, do the following to verify that Windows XP System Restore is turned on:

1. Right-click **My Computer** and select **Properties** from the shortcut menu. The System Properties window opens.

2. Click the **System Restore** tab, as shown in Figure 12-44. Make sure **Turn off System Restore** is not checked. On this window, you can also see how much disk space is allotted to keeping restore points.

**Figure 12-44**   System Restore is turned on and off using the System Properties window

3. If you have made changes to this window, click **Apply**. Click **OK** to close the window.

   To manually create a restore point:

1. Click **Start, All Programs, Accessories, System Tools**, and **System Restore**. The System Restore window appears, as shown in Figure 12-45.

2. The System Restore window gives you two choices: Restore my computer to an earlier time and Create a restore point. Select **Create a restore point**, and then click **Next**.

3. Type a description of the restore point, such as **Just before I updated the video driver**. The system automatically assigns the current date and time to the restore point.

4. Click **Create** and then **Close**. The restore point is saved in the System Volume Information folder on drive C. (Users cannot access this folder.)

   If your system is giving you problems, for example, if errors occur after you have installed a hardware device, first try to use Driver Rollback to fix the problem so that as few changes as possible to the system are lost. If Driver Rollback does not work or is not appropriate, do the following to revert the system to the restore point:

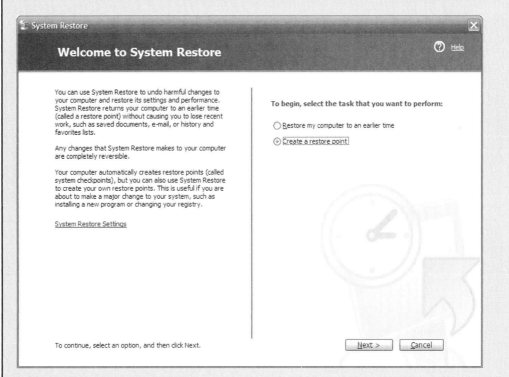

**Figure 12-45** Use System Restore to manually create a restore point before making major changes to the system

1. Click **Start, All Programs, Accessories, System Tools**, and **System Restore**.

2. If necessary, click **Restore my computer to an earlier time**, and then click **Next**. A window appears, as shown in Figure 12-46. Notice the two restore points in the figure, one created by the system and one created manually.

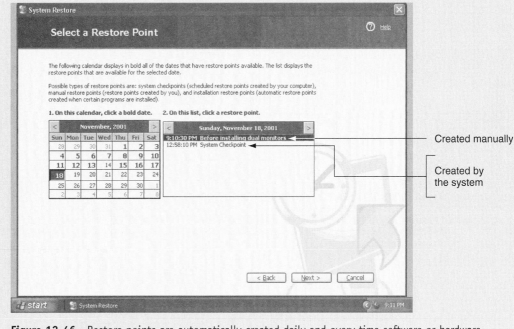

**Figure 12-46** Restore points are automatically created daily and every time software or hardware is installed

A+ ESS
1.3
3.4

A+
220-602
3.1
3.4

**3.** Select the date and time and the specific restore point. Click **Next** twice.

Windows XP reboots and restores the system state to the settings saved in the restore point. Changes to user data are not affected, but any installation or configuration changes made after the restore point are lost. I've noticed that antivirus software is often affected by using a restore point; so much so that I've had to reinstall the software, so use System Restore sparingly. In Chapter 14, you'll learn how to use System Restore and other tools to solve problems when Windows 2000/XP won't boot.

## BACK UP AND RESTORE THE SYSTEM STATE

Creating restore points can help in some situations, but an even better way to protect the system state is to make a backup of all system state files using the Windows 2000/XP Backup utility. How to back up and restore the system state is covered in this section. You will want to make a habit of always backing up the system state before you make major changes to a system so that you can undo your changes if need be. Backing up the system state also creates a backup of the registry, which will be useful when you need to manually edit the registry.

> **Notes**
>
> The Windows 2000/XP Backup utility is not normally installed in Windows XP Home Edition. For this OS, however, you can install it by double-clicking the Ntbackup.msi file in the D:\Valueadd\ MSFT\Ntbackup folder on the Windows XP setup CD.

### BACK UP THE SYSTEM STATE

When you back up the system state data, you cannot select which files you want to back up because Windows 2000/XP always backs up all of them. Here is the process for backing up the system state:

1. Click **Start**, point to **All Programs** (**Programs** in Windows 2000), **Accessories, System Tools,** and then click **Backup.** (Or you can enter **Ntbackup.exe** in the Run dialog box.) Depending on how the utility is configured, the Backup Utility window opens or the Backup or Restore Wizard launches (see Figure 12-47). If the wizard launches, click **Advanced Mode** to see the Backup Utility window.

2. On the Backup Utility window, click the **Backup** tab (see Figure 12-48).

3. Check the **System State** box in the list of items you can back up. Notice in Figure 12-48 that the system state includes the boot files and the registry. It also includes the COM+ (Component Object Model) Registration Database, which contains information about applications and includes files in the Windows folders.

4. Click **Browse** to point to where you want the backup saved. You can back up to any media, including a folder on the hard drive, Zip drive, tape drive, or network drive. For better protection, back up to another media than your hard drive, such as another hard drive on the network. Click **Start Backup** to begin the process. A dialog box appears. Click **Start Backup** again.

**Figure 12-47**  Backup or Restore Wizard

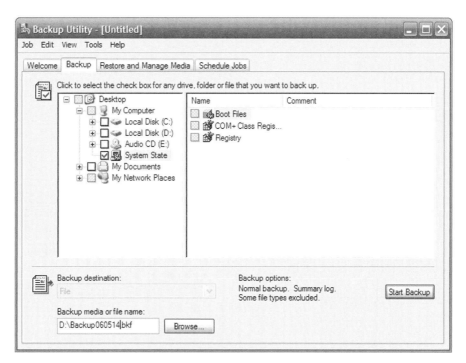

**Figure 12-48**  Back up the Windows 2000/XP registry and all critical system files

## RESTORE THE SYSTEM STATE

If Windows gives errors or the registry gets corrupted, you can restore the system to the state it was in when the last System State backup was made. To do that, launch the Windows

> **Notes**
>
> When you back up the system state, the registry is also backed up to the folder %SystemRoot%\repair\RegBack. If you later have a corrupted registry, you can copy files from this folder to the registry folder, which is %SystemRoot%\System32\Config.

A+ ESS
1.3
3.4

A+
220-602
3.1
3.4

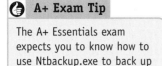

**A+ Exam Tip**

The A+ Essentials exam
expects you to know how to
use Ntbackup.exe to back up
the system state.

Backup tool by clicking **Start**, pointing to **All Programs**
(**Programs** in Windows 2000), **Accessories**, and **System Tools**,
and then clicking **Backup**. Or you can type **Ntbackup.exe** in
the Run dialog box and press **Enter**. Either way, the Backup
window opens showing the Backup tab. You then need to
click the **Restore and Manage Media** tab (**Restore** tab in
Windows 2000), which is shown in Figure 12-49.

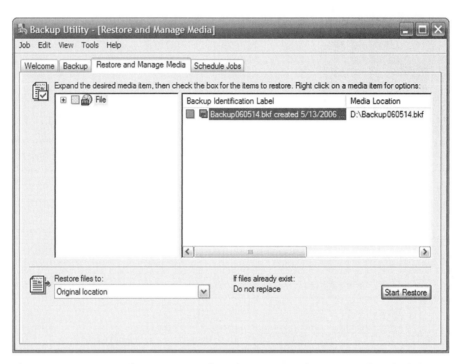

**Figure 12-49** Restore the system state from the Restore and Manage Media tab of the Backup dialog box

From the Restore and Manage Media tab, first select the backup you want to restore.
Then, in the list box in the lower-left corner, select the location to which the backup is to
be restored. Click the **Start**
Restore** button in the lower-
right corner to start the
process. Remember that you
can restore the system state as
a way of restoring the registry.

**Notes**

If you ever need to manually edit the Windows registry, it's
a good idea to make a backup of the registry first. The easiest
and safest way to do that is to back up the entire system
state. Later, if you need to undo your changes to the registry,
use the Backup utility to restore the system state.

The biggest limitation to using
the Backup utility to restore the
system state is that, in order to
use the utility, you must be able to boot to the Windows desktop. How to deal with problems
when you can't boot to the Windows desktop is covered in Chapter 14.

## WINDOWS XP AUTOMATED SYSTEM RECOVERY

A+ ESS
3.3
3.4

A+
220-602
3.3
3.4

You can use the Windows XP Automated System Recovery (ASR) tool to back up the
entire drive on which Windows is installed (most likely drive C). Later, if Windows gets
corrupted, you can recover the system from the last time you made an ASR backup. Keep
in mind, however, that everything on the drive since the ASR backup was made is lost,

A+ ESS
3.3
3.4

A+
220-602
3.3
3.4

including installed software and device drivers, user data, and any changes to the system configuration.

In this section, you will learn how to make the ASR backup, how to restore the system from the backup, and about best practices when using the ASR tool.

## CREATING THE ASR BACKUP AND ASR DISK

The ASR backup process creates two items: a full backup of the drive on which Windows is installed and an ASR floppy disk on which information that will help Windows use Automated System Recovery is stored. The ASR backup process places the location of the backup file on the floppy. The backup file will be just as large as the contents of the hard drive volume, so you will need a massive backup medium, such as another partition on a different hard drive, a tape drive, or a writeable CD-R or CD-RW drive.

**Caution**

Do not back up drive C to a folder on drive C. The ASR backup process allows you to do this, but restoring later from this backup does not work. In addition, when a hard drive partition fails, most likely other partitions on the drive will also be lost, and so will your backup if you've put it on one of these other partitions. Therefore, to better protect your installation, back up to a different hard drive or other media.

Follow these directions to create the backup and the ASR floppy disk:

**Notes**

To use Automated System Recovery in Windows XP Home Edition, the Backup utility must first be installed.

1. Click **Start, All Programs, Accessories, System Tools,** and **Backup.** The Backup or Restore Wizard appears (see Figure 12-50).

**Figure 12-50** Use the Backup or Restore Wizard to back up the hard drive partition after the Windows XP installation is complete

2. Click the **Advanced Mode** link. The Backup Utility window appears. On the Welcome tab, click **Automated System Recovery Wizard.** On the following screen, click **Next.**

3. The Backup Destination window appears. Select the location of the medium to receive the backup and insert a disk into the drive. This disk will become the ASR disk. Click **Next**.

4. Click **Finish**. The backup process shows its progress, as seen in Figure 12-51.

5. When the backup is finished, label the ASR disk with the name of the disk, the date it was created, and the computer's name, and put the disk in a safe place.

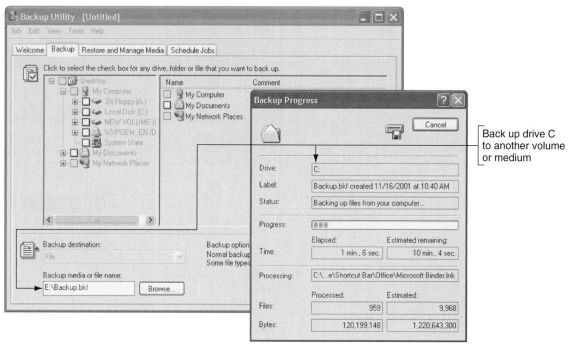

**Figure 12-51** The Backup utility can create a backup of drive C and an ASR disk to be used later for the Automated System Recovery utility

## RESTORING THE SYSTEM USING AN ASR BACKUP

To restore the logical drive to its state when the last ASR disk set was made, do the following:

1. Insert the Windows XP CD in the CD-ROM drive, and hard boot the PC.

2. You will see a message that says "Press any key to boot from CD." Press any key.

3. A blue screen appears with the message "Press F6 to load RAID or SCSI drivers." If your system uses RAID or SCSI, press **F6**. If your system does not use RAID or SCSI, ignore the message.

4. At the bottom of the blue screen, a message says, "Press F2 to run the Automated System Recovery process." Press **F2**.

5. The screen shown in Figure 12-52 appears, instructing you to insert the ASR floppy disk. Insert the disk and then press **Enter**.

Windows XP Setup then does the following:

1. Loads files it needs to run

2. Repartitions and reformats the drive (see Figure 12-53)

A+ ESS
3.3
3.4

A+
220-602
3.3
3.4

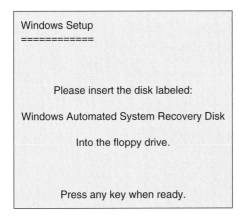

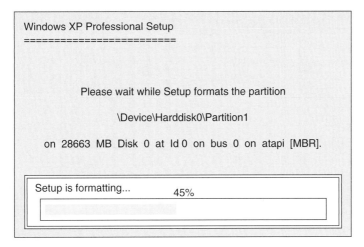

**Figure 12-52** Automatic System Recovery process must have the ASR floppy disk

**Figure 12-53** As part of the Automatic System Recovery process, Windows XP Setup repartitions and reformats the volume holding Windows XP

3. Installs Windows from the Windows XP CD

4. Launches the Automatic System Recovery Wizard to restore the Windows system state, applications, and data to what they were at the time of the last ASR backup

As the ASR recovery process progresses, it erases everything on the volume being restored and reformats the logical drive just before the Windows XP installation process begins.

## PLANNING AHEAD FOR AUTOMATED SYSTEM RECOVERY

As you have seen, Automated System Recovery is a drastic step in recovering a failed Windows XP startup. All software and hardware installations, user data, and user settings on the Windows XP volume made after the backup are lost. For this reason, it's a good idea to carefully plan how best to use Automated System Recovery. Here's one suggestion: When you install Windows XP, create a partition for Windows XP that will hold Windows XP and all installed software, but not the user data. Use a second partition on the drive for user data, say drive D. After you have installed all applications and devices, make an ASR backup of drive C to a different hard drive or other media. Then use Ntbackup to schedule daily or weekly backups of the user data on drive D. In the event of a total system failure, you can recover drive C from the ASR backup media and then recover the user data from your daily or weekly backups of that data.

A+ ESS
3.3
3.4

A+
220-602
3.3
3.4

A+ ESS
3.1

A+
220-602
3.1

To set your advance planning in place, partition the hard drive so that drive C is large enough for Windows and other software, but the bulk of the hard drive space is devoted to user data. Make drive C about 5 to 15 GB in size, which should be plenty of room for Windows and other software.

# THE WINDOWS 2000/XP REGISTRY

The Windows 2000/XP registry is a hierarchical database containing information about all the hardware, software, device drivers, network protocols, and user configuration needed by the OS and applications. Many components depend on this information, and the registry provides a secure and stable location for it. Table 12-4 lists ways in which some components use the registry.

| Component | Description |
| --- | --- |
| Setup programs for devices and applications and Windows Update programs | Setup programs can record configuration information in the registry and query the registry for information needed to install drivers and applications. They can also make an entry in the registry to cause a program to run the next time Windows starts, a technique often used to complete an installation process that requires a reboot. |
| User profiles maintained and used by the OS | Windows maintains a profile for each user that determines the user's environment. User profiles are kept in files, but, when a user logs on, the profile information is written to the registry, where changes are recorded, and then later written back to the user profile file. The OS uses this profile to control user settings and other configuration information specific to this user. |
| Files active when Ntldr is loading the OS | During the boot process, NTDetect.com surveys present hardware devices and records that information in the registry. Ntldr loads and initializes device drivers using information from the registry, including the order in which to load them. |
| Device drivers | Device drivers read and write configuration information from and to the registry each time they load. The drivers write hardware configuration information to the registry and read it to determine the proper way to load. |
| Hardware profiles | Windows can maintain more than one set of hardware configuration information (called a hardware profile) for one PC. The data is kept in the registry. An example of a computer that has more than one hardware profile is a notebook that has a docking station. Two hardware profiles describe the notebook, one docked and the other undocked. This information is kept in the registry. |
| Application programs | Many application programs read the registry for information about the location of files the program uses and various other parameters. |

**Table 12-4**   Components that use the Windows 2000/XP registry

Most users never see or care about the registry, its organization, or contents. However, as a PC support technician, you need to be familiar with the registry and know how to protect it from corruption. Occasionally, you might need to manually edit the registry to solve a problem that cannot be solved any other way. The following sections look at how the registry is organized, how to back up and recover the registry, and how you can manually edit the registry.

A+ ESS
3.1

A+
220-602
3.1

# HOW THE REGISTRY IS ORGANIZED

When studying how the registry is organized, keep in mind that there are two ways to look at this organization: physical and logical. To fully understand the nature of the registry, you need to be familiar with both.

## LOGICAL ORGANIZATION OF THE REGISTRY

Logically, the organization of the registry looks like an upside-down tree with six branches, called keys or subtrees (see Figure 12-54), which are categories of information stored in the registry. Each key is made up of several subkeys that may also have subkeys, and subkeys hold, or contain, values. Each value has a name and data assigned to it. Data in the registry is always stored in values, the lowest level of the tree.

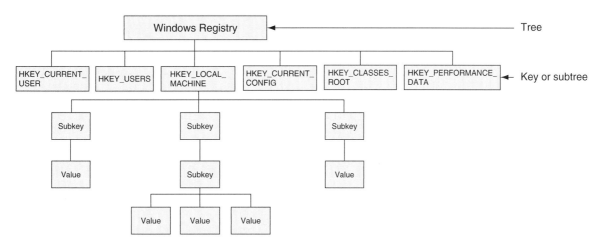

**Figure 12-54** The Windows 2000/XP registry is logically organized in an upside-down tree structure of keys, subkeys, and values

The six subtrees shown in Figure 12-54 are listed in Table 12-5 together with their primary functions. As the table shows, the HKEY_LOCAL_MACHINE subtree is the mainstay key of the registry.

| Subtree (Main Keys) | Primary Function |
|---|---|
| **HKEY_CLASSES_ROOT** | Contains information about software and the way software is configured. It contains one key for every file extension for which the OS has an associated application. |
| **HKEY_CURRENT_USER** | Contains information about the currently logged-on user. This key points to data stored in HKEY_USERS |
| **HKEY_LOCAL_MACHINE** | Contains all configuration data about the computer, including information about device drivers and devices used at startup. The information in this key does not change when different users log on. |
| **HKEY_USERS** | Contains information used to build the logon screen and the ID of the currently logged-on user. |

**Table 12-5** The six subtrees of the Windows 2000/XP registry

| Subtree (Main Keys) | Primary Function |
|---|---|
| HKEY_CURRENT_CONFIG | Contains information about the active hardware configuration, which is extracted from the data stored in the HKEY_LOCAL_MACHINE subkeys called SOFTWARE and SYSTEM |
| HKEY_PERFORMANCE_DATA | Does not contain data, but is used as a pass-through for performance data from Windows to programs that monitor performance. Because this key cannot be edited, it does not show up in the Registry Editor window. |

**Table 12-5** The six subtrees of the Windows 2000/XP registry (continued)

When you first open the Windows Registry Editor to view and edit the registry, you see a window similar to that in Figure 12-55. In the figure, there are five high levels showing, one for each key or subtree that can be edited. (The sixth key showing in Figure 12-54, the HKEY_PERFORMANCE_DATA key, does not appear in the editor because data isn't stored in this key. The key is used only as a pointer to performance data provided by Windows so that applications that monitor Windows performance can easily access this performance data.)

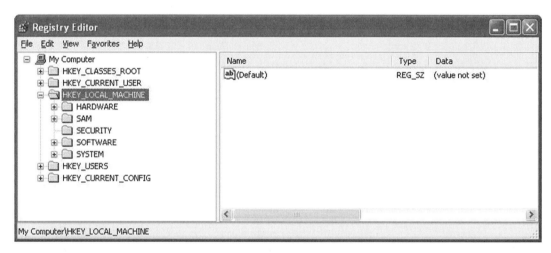

**Figure 12-55** Windows Registry Editor shows the five high-level subtrees in the Windows 2000/XP registry that can be edited

## PHYSICAL ORGANIZATION OF THE REGISTRY

The physical organization of the registry is quite different from the logical organization.

 **Tip**

Notice in Figure 12-55 that the HKEY_LOCAL_MACHINE subtree has been opened to show subkeys under it; several subkeys have their own subkeys. If you click a subkey that has values assigned to it, those values appear on the right side of the window. Later in this section, you will see how to edit values in the registry.

Physically, the registry is stored in five files called hives. Figure 12-56 shows the way the five subtrees that hold data are stored in hives. (Remember, one subtree does not hold data and does not use a hive.)

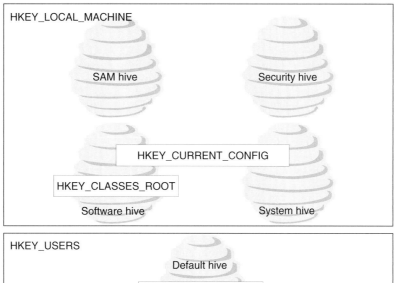

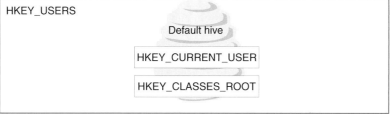

**Figure 12-56** The relationship between registry subtrees (keys) and hives

Here is the breakdown:

▲ HKEY_LOCAL_MACHINE (abbreviated HKLM) data is kept in four hives: the SAM hive, the Security hive, the Software hive, and the System hive. In addition, the HARDWARE subkey of the HKLM key is built when the registry is first loaded, based on data collected about the current hardware configuration.

▲ HKEY_USERS (abbreviated HKU) data is partly kept in the Default hive and partly gathered from these two files:

    ▲ \Documents and Settings\*username*\Ntuser.dat

    ▲ \Documents and Settings\*username*\Local Settings\Application Data\Microsoft\Windows\Usrclass.dat

▲ HKEY_CURRENT_CONFIG (abbreviated HKCC) data is gathered when the registry is first loaded into memory. Data is taken from the HKLM keys, which are kept in the Software hive and the System hive.

▲ HKEY_CLASSES_ROOT (abbreviated HKCR) data is gathered when the registry is built into memory. It gathers data from these locations:

    ▲ HKLM keys that contain system-wide data stored in the Software hive

    ▲ For the currently logged on user, data is taken from the HKCU keys, which gather current user data from the file \Documents and Settings\*username*\Local Settings\Application Data\Microsoft\Windows\Usrclass.dat.

▲ HKEY_CURRENT_USER (abbreviated HKCU) data is built at the time the registry is loaded into memory when a user logs on. Data is taken from HKEY_USERS data kept in the Default hive and data kept in the Ntuser.dat and Usrclass.dat files of the current user.

As you can see, only two main keys have associated hives, HKEY_LOCAL_MACHINE (four hives) and HKEY_USERS (the Default hive). Looking back at Figure 12-55, you can

> **Notes**
>
> Device Manager reads data from the combined HKLM\HARDWARE key to build the information it displays about hardware configurations. You can consider Device Manager to be an easy-to-view presentation of this HARDWARE key data.

> **Notes**
>
> Also important to understand is that the registry as we know it with its six subtrees doesn't really exist as such until it is built in memory. Because so much of what we call the registry depends on the current hardware configuration and the currently logged on user, the registry is a dynamic entity dynamically built from changing data.

see the five subkeys for HKEY_LOCAL_MACHINE. The HARDWARE subkey is built from hardware configuration at the time the registry is loaded into memory, but the other four subkeys come from the hives they are named after (Sam, Security, Software, and System).

From Figure 12-56, you can also see that some subtrees use data contained in other subtrees. For instance, the HKEY_CURRENT_USER data is a subset of the data in the HKEY_USERS subtree. HKEY_CURRENT_CONFIG uses data contained in the HKEY_LOCAL_MACHINE subtree. And HKEY_CLASSES_ROOT uses data from HKEY_LOCAL_MACHINE and HKEY_USERS. However, don't let this physical relationship cloud your view of the logical relationship among these subtrees. Although data is shared among the different subtrees, logically speaking, none of the five main subtrees is subordinate to any other.

The five registry hives are stored in the \%*SystemRoot%*\system32\config folder as a group of files. In a physical sense, each hive is a file. Each hive is backed up with a log file and a backup file, which are also stored in the \%*SystemRoot%*\system32\config folder.

## BACKING UP AND RECOVERING THE REGISTRY

Before you the edit the registry, it's very important you first make a backup so that if you make a mistake or your changes cause a problem, you can backtrack your changes. There are basically two ways to back up the registry: the safest way is to back up the entire system state including the registry, or you can back up only keys in the registry that you expect to change.

### BACKING UP THE SYSTEM STATE ALSO BACKS UP THE REGISTRY

Earlier in the chapter, you learned how to use the Windows 2000/XP Backup utility to back up the system state. When the system state is backed up, the Backup utility also puts a copy of the registry files in these locations:

▲ **C:\Windows\repair\**. Backups are placed here at the end of the Windows 2000 and Windows XP installations. Also, Windows XP places backups here whenever the system state is backed up using the Windows Backup utility.

▲ **C:\Windows\repair\RegBack\**. Windows 2000 places backups here whenever the system state is backed up using the Windows Backup utility.

Later, if you need to recover the registry or the entire system state, you can use the Ntbackup routine to restore the system state or you can copy the backed-up registry files into the C:\Windows\system32\config folder.

### BACKING UP INDIVIDUAL KEYS IN THE REGISTRY

A less time-consuming method of backing up the registry is to back up a particular key that you plan to edit. However, know that if the registry gets corrupted, having a backup of only a

A+ ESS
3.1

A+
220-602
3.1

particular key will most likely not help you much when trying a recovery. Also, don't use this technique to back up the entire registry or an entire tree within the registry. Use this method only to back up a subkey and all the subkeys within it. Before you edit a subkey, back it up first.

To back up a key along with its subkeys in the registry, follow these steps:

1. Open the registry editor. To do that, click **Start, Run**, type **Regedit** in the Run dialog box and then press **Enter**.

2. For Windows XP, select the key you want to back up and right-click it. Click **Export** in the shortcut menu, as shown in Figure 12-57. The Export Registry File dialog box appears, as shown in Figure 12-58.

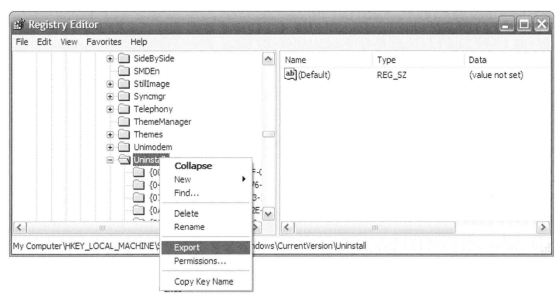

**Figure 12-57**   Using the Windows XP registry editor, you can back up a key and its subkeys using the Export command

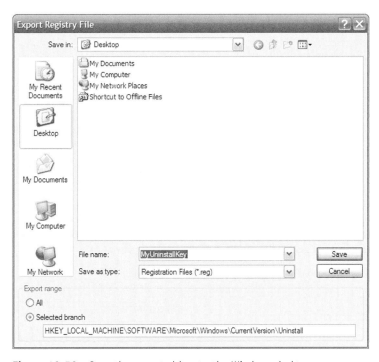

**Figure 12-58**   Save the exported key to the Windows desktop

3. Select the location to save the export file and name the file. A convenient place to store an export file while you edit the registry is the desktop. Click **Save** when done. The file saved will have a .reg file extension. (To export a registry key using Windows 2000, select the key, click **Registry** on the menu bar, and then click **Export Registry File.**)

4. You can now edit the key. Later, if you need to undo your changes, exit the registry editor and double-click the saved export file. The key and its subkeys saved in the export file will be restored. After you're done with an export file, delete it.

### Notes

Changes to the registry take effect immediately and are permanent. Therefore, before you edit the registry, you should use one of the two backup methods just discussed so that you can restore it if something goes wrong.

### A+ Exam Tip

The A+ Essentials exam expects you to know the difference between Windows 2000 Regedit.exe and Regedt32.exe, and when to use each. You should also know that Windows XP has only a single registry editor.

### Notes

With Windows XP, typing either Regedt32 or Regedit in the Run dialog box launches the Regedit.exe program.

## EDITING THE REGISTRY

When you make a change in the Control Panel, Device Manager, or many other places in Windows 2000/XP, the registry is modified automatically. This is the only way most users will ever change the registry. However, on rare occasions you might need to edit the registry manually, for example, when you uninstall an application and registry entries are not completely removed and these orphan entries are giving startup errors.

Windows XP has only a single registry editor, Regedit.exe. Windows 2000 offers two registry editors, each with a slightly different look and feel, and with some slight differences, as follows:

▲ Regedt32.exe is located in the \%*SystemRoot*%\system32 folder. It shows each key in a separate window. Under the Options menu, you have the option to work in read-only mode. Regedt32.exe has a Security menu that allows you to apply permissions to keys and subkeys to control which user accounts have access to these keys.

▲ Regedit.exe is located in the \%*SystemRoot*% folder and shows all keys in the same window. It has a look and feel similar to Explorer. Regedit.exe has the advantages that you can export the registry to a text file and use a more powerful search tool than the one in Regedt32.exe, but has the disadvantage that it cannot display registry values longer than 256 characters. Use Regedit.exe to export registry keys before you edit them.

Let's look at a sample situation in which you might need to edit the registry: changing the name of the Recycle Bin on the Windows XP desktop for a currently logged on user. To make the change, do the following:

1. To open Registry Editor, click **Start, Run,** and then type **Regedit** in the Run dialog box. Click **OK.** The Registry Editor window appears.

2. Locate the subkey that is listed after this paragraph. This subkey is the name of the Recycle Bin on the Windows desktop. You can click the plus sign (+) to the left of the yellow folder icon of each subkey to move down through the tree. As you click through the hierarchy to get to this key, note that if the currently selected subkey has a value, that value appears in the right pane of the window.

HKEY_CURRENT_USER\Software\Microsoft\Windows\CurrentVersion\Explorer\
CLSID\645FF040-5081-101B-9F08-00AA002F954E

3. For Windows XP, right-click the subkey and select **Export** from the shortcut menu (see Figure 12-59). Name the export file **RecycleKey.reg** and save the file to the Windows desktop. Click **Save**. For Windows 2000, select the key, click **Registry** on the menu bar, click **Export Registry File**, and save the file to the Windows desktop.

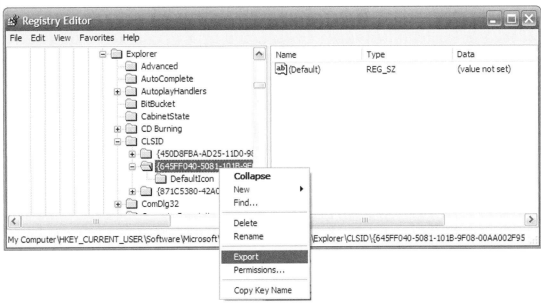

**Figure 12-59**  Export the key before you edit it

4. In Figure 12-60, notice in the right pane that "(value not set)" is listed under Data. This means that no value is set and the default value will be used. The default value for this name is Recycle Bin. Position the window on the screen so that you can see the Recycle Bin icon. In the right pane, double-click (**Default**), the name of the value. The Edit String dialog box appears, also shown in Figure 12-60. The Value data should be empty in the dialog box. If a value is present, you selected the wrong value. Check your work and try again. To help you find the right key, notice the current key is displayed at the bottom of the Registry Editor window.

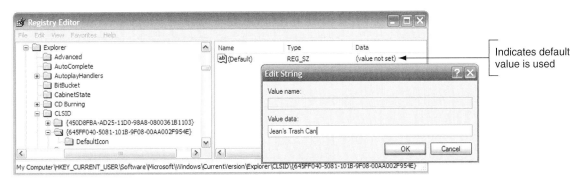

**Figure 12-60**  Editing a registry subkey value

5. Enter a new name for the Recycle Bin. For example, in Figure 12-60, the new name is "Jean's Trash Can." Click **OK**.

6. To see your change, right-click the desktop and select **Refresh** on the shortcut menu. The name of the Recycle Bin changes.

7. To restore the name to the default value, in the Registry Editor window, again double-click the name of the value. The Edit String dialog box appears. Delete your entry and click **OK**.

8. To verify the change is made, right-click the desktop and select **Refresh** on the shortcut menu. The Recycle Bin name should return to its default value.

9. To exit the Registry Editor window, click **File, Exit**.

10. It might be confusing to later find export keys on your desktop. To clean up after yourself, right-click the **RecycleKey.reg** icon on the Windows desktop and select **Delete** from the shortcut menu.

From these directions, you can see that changes made to the registry take effect immediately. Therefore, take extra care when editing the registry. If you make a mistake and don't know how to correct a problem you create, then you can restore the system state or double-click the exported key to recover. When you double-click an exported key, the registry is updated with the values stored in this key.

## OPTIMIZING THE WINDOWS 2000/XP ENVIRONMENT

Sluggish Windows systems are so frustrating, and as a PC support technician, you need to know how to configure the Windows 2000/XP environment for optimum performance and how to teach users to do the necessary routine maintenance to keep Windows running smoothly. Here is a summary of the tasks you need to do when you first become responsible for a Windows 2000/XP system:

▲ Put procedures in place to back up Windows system files after you have made major changes to a system such as installing software or hardware or adding a new user account. You can use the Backup Utility to back up just the system state, or, for Windows XP, you can use Automated System Recovery to back up the entire drive C. In some cases, it's appropriate to use both methods. Also make sure Windows XP System Restore is turned on.

▲ Set Windows XP so that it automatically downloads updates, and, for Windows 2000, put in place the necessary schedule and procedures to manually download these updates.

▲ Use a firewall and antivirus software to protect the system from attack. (Firewalls and antivirus software are covered in Chapter 19.)

▲ Create user accounts so that users can do their jobs and perform routine maintenance, but cannot make major changes to the system that you have not authorized. (How to set up user accounts is covered in Chapter 13.)

▲ Put procedures in place to keep current backups of user data. (How to do that is covered in Chapter 13.)

▲ Teach users how to routinely clean up the hard drive and how to verify that their data backups are current and the data recovery routines work (covered in Chapter 13).

▲ Check the Windows 2000/XP operating environment to be certain that unneeded software and services are not clogging up the works and that memory settings are optimized.

This last item in the bulleted list is the subject of this section of the chapter. We'll first look at some tools to manage software and then how to uninstall unwanted software. Finally, you'll learn how to optimize memory settings.

### Notes

When you first become responsible for a sluggish Windows 2000/XP system and you do all the tasks described in this and the next two chapters, but the system is still sluggish, you might want to consider that the problem is related to hardware. There might not be enough installed RAM or the processor might need upgrading. In general, upgrading an existing PC is recommended as long as the cost of the upgrade stays below half the cost of buying a new machine.

## TOOLS TO MANAGE SOFTWARE

In this section, we'll look at three tools to help you manage startup and running software: Windows 2000/XP Task Manager, the Windows XP System Configuration Utility (commonly called Msconfig), and the Services console.

### Notes

Viruses, adware, worms, and other malicious software can use Windows resources and pull a system down. Keep anti-virus software running in the background. If you see a marked decrease in Windows performance, scan the hard drive for viruses, worms, and adware. Chapter 19 gives more information on how to protect from malicious software.

### TASK MANAGER

Task Manager (Taskman.exe) lets you view the applications and processes running on your computer as well as performance information for the processor and memory. There are three ways you can access Task Manager:

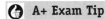

### A+ Exam Tip

The A+ Essentials exam expects you to know how to use Task Manager, Msconfig.exe, and the Services Console.

▲ Press **Ctrl+Alt+Delete**. Depending on your system, Task Manager appears or the Windows Security window opens. If the security window opens, click the **Task Manager** button.
▲ Right-click a blank area on the taskbar, and then select **Task Manager** on the shortcut menu.
▲ Press **Ctrl+Shift+Esc**.

Windows 2000 Task Manager has three tabs: Applications, Processes, and Performance. Windows XP Task Manager adds two additional tabs, Networking and Users. (The Users tab shows only when a system is set for Fast User Switching and lets you monitor other users logged onto the system.) On the Applications tab (see Figure 12-61), each application loaded can have one of two states: Running or Not Responding. If an application is listed as Not Responding, you can end it by selecting it and clicking the End Task button at the bottom of the window. You will lose any unsaved information in the application.

The second tab, the Processes tab, lists system services and other processes associated with applications, together with how much CPU time and memory the process uses. This information can help you determine which applications are slowing down your system. Figure 12-62 shows the list of processes for a Windows XP system immediately after the installation was completed with no applications installed. Figure 12-63 shows a similar window for Windows 2000.

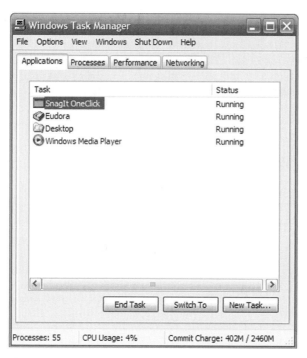

**Figure 12-61** The Applications tab in Task Manager shows the status of active applications

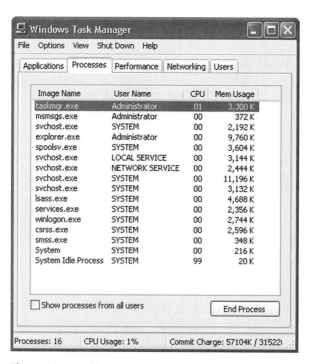

**Figure 12-62** This Processes tab of Task Manager shows Windows processes running in the background of a barebones Windows XP system

When you have a sluggish Windows system, close all open applications and open **Task Manager**. Check the **Applications** tab to make sure no applications are running. Then click the **Processes** tab. Compare the list in Figure 12-62 (for Windows XP) or Figure 12-63 (for Windows 2000) with the list of processes running on the sluggish system. Any extra processes you see might be caused by unwanted applications running in the background or malicious software running. If you see a process running that you are not familiar with, search the Microsoft web site (*support.microsoft.com*) to verify the process is legitimate.

A+ ESS
1.1
3.2
3.3

A+
220-602
3.1
3.2
3.3

If you don't find it there, do a general Google search on the process. If you find that the process is not legitimate, stop the process and immediately run antivirus software. Chapter 19 gives more information about ridding your system of malicious software.

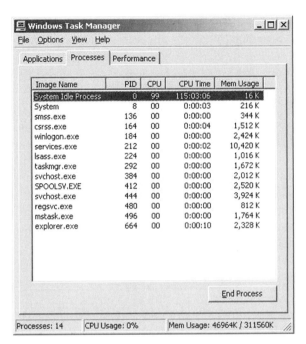

**Figure 12-63** Windows 2000 running processes immediately after a fresh installation of the OS

The third tab, the Performance tab, is shown in Figure 12-64. It provides details about how a program uses system resources. You can use these views to identify which applications and processes use the most CPU time.

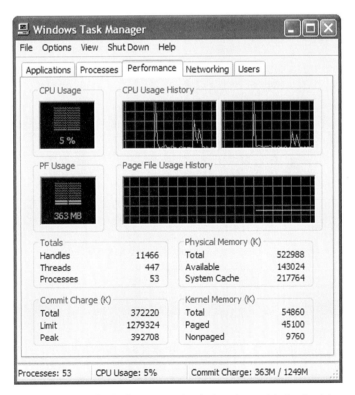

**Figure 12-64** The Performance tab window shows details about how system resources are being used

On the Performance tab, notice the four frames at the bottom of the window. These frames give the following information:

▲ The *Totals* frame indicates how much the system is currently being used by counting handles (indicates a device or file is being accessed), threads (unit of activity within a process), and processes (programs running). The information in these entries tells you how heavily the system is used.

▲ The *Physical Memory* frame lists Total (amount of RAM), Available (RAM not used), and System Cache (RAM in use). The information in these entries tells you if you need to upgrade RAM.

▲ The *Commit Charge* frame lists Total (current size of virtual memory, also called the page file or swap file), Limit (how much of the paging file can be allocated to applications before the size of the paging file must be increased), and Peak (maximum amount of virtual memory used in this session). The information in these entries tells you if you need to increase the size of the paging file.

▲ The *Kernel Memory* frame indicates how much RAM and virtual memory the OS uses. This frame lists Total (sum of RAM and virtual memory), Paged (how much of the paging file the OS uses), and Nonpaged (how much RAM the OS uses). The information in these entries tells you how much memory the OS is using. If usage is high, look for OS processes you can eliminate.

The fourth Windows XP tab, the Networking tab, lets you monitor network activity and bandwidth used. You can use it to see how heavily the network is being used by this computer (see Figure 12-65).

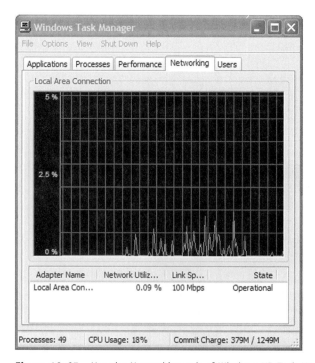

**Figure 12-65**　Use the Networking tab of Windows XP Task Manager to monitor network activity

Each application running on your computer is assigned a priority level, which determines its position in the queue for CPU resources. This priority level can be changed for applications that are already loaded by using Task Manager. If an application performs slowly,

**12**

increase its priority. You should only do this with very important applications, because giving an application higher priority than certain background system processes can sometimes interfere with the operating system.

To use Task Manger to change the priority level of an open application, do the following:

> **Notes**
>
> If your desktop locks up, you can use Task Manager to refresh it. To do so, press **Ctrl+Alt+Del** and then click **Task Manager**. Click the **Processes** tab. Select **Explorer.exe** (the process that provides the desktop) and then click **End Process**. Click **Yes**. Then click the **Applications** tab. Click **New Task**. Enter **Explorer.exe** in the Create New Task dialog box and click **OK**. Your desktop will be refreshed and any running programs will still be open.

> **Notes**
>
> Remember: Any changes you make to an application's priority level affect only the current session.

1. In Task Manager, click the **Applications** tab. Right-click the application and select **Go To Process** from the shortcut menu. The Processes tab is selected and the process that runs the application is selected.

2. Right-click the selected process. From the shortcut menu that appears, set the new priority. First try **AboveNormal**. If that doesn't give satisfactory performance, then try **High**.

---

# APPLYING CONCEPTS

Suppose a friend asks you to help her solve a problem with her Windows XP system that is moving very slowly. You open **Task Manager**, select the **Processes** tab, and see a window similar to that in Figure 12-66. Notice that the Ccapp.exe process is using 99% of CPU time. When you click the **Performance** tab, you see why the system is running so slowly (see Figure 12-67). This one process is consistently using most of the CPU resources.

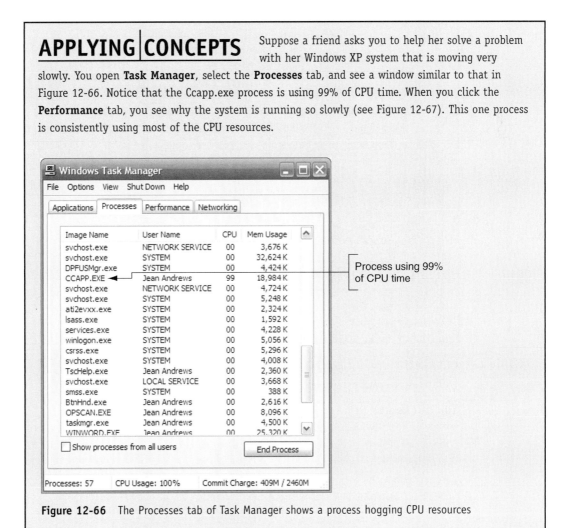

**Figure 12-66** The Processes tab of Task Manager shows a process hogging CPU resources

A+ ESS
1.1
3.2
3.3

A+
220-602
3.1
3.2
3.3

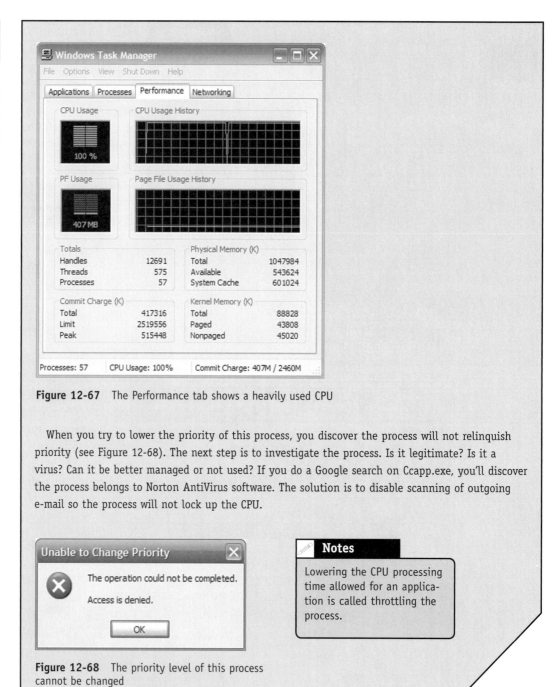

**Figure 12-67** The Performance tab shows a heavily used CPU

When you try to lower the priority of this process, you discover the process will not relinquish priority (see Figure 12-68). The next step is to investigate the process. Is it legitimate? Is it a virus? Can it be better managed or not used? If you do a Google search on Ccapp.exe, you'll discover the process belongs to Norton AntiVirus software. The solution is to disable scanning of outgoing e-mail so the process will not lock up the CPU.

**Notes**

Lowering the CPU processing time allowed for an application is called throttling the process.

**Figure 12-68** The priority level of this process cannot be changed

## SYSTEM CONFIGURATION UTILITY (MSCONFIG)

You can use the Windows XP System Configuration Utility (Msconfig.exe), which is commonly called "M-S-config," to find out what processes are launched at startup and to temporarily disable a process from loading. This utility is included with Windows XP and Windows 98/Me, but it is not included with Windows 2000. For Windows 2000, however, you can use a third-party utility similar to Msconfig to help you diagnose startup problems. One good utility is Autoruns from Sysinternals (*www.sysinternals.com*).

You can use Msconfig as a temporary fix to disable a program or service at startup, but it should not be considered a permanent fix. Once you've decided you want to make the change permanent, use other tools to permanently remove that process from Windows startup. To use Msconfig, enter **msconfig.exe** in the Run dialog box. The window in Figure 12-69 opens. On the General tab, you can decide to start Windows XP as a normal startup or a diagnostic startup with basic devices and services only. Or you can decide to use a selective startup where you control which services and programs to launch.

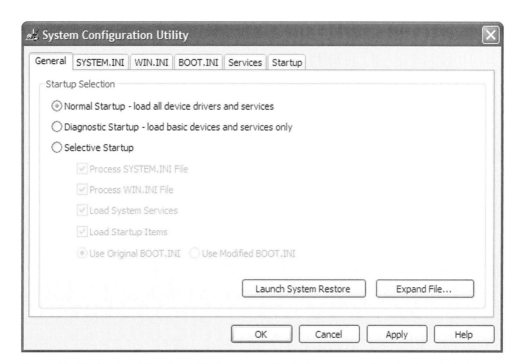

**Figure 12-69** Use the MSconfig utility to temporarily disable processes from loading at startup

Notice in Figure 12-69 these three tabs: SYSTEM.INI, WIN.INI, and BOOT.INI. Using these tabs, you can edit the contents of these three initialization files. Most likely you won't find much reason to do this because System.ini and Win.ini are used only to manage 16-bit drivers and applications. Boot.ini is also probably best left unchanged, unless you want to change the Windows boot parameters, which include which OS will boot (when two OSs are installed) or to which hard drive the system looks to find an OS.

The other two important tabs used to temporarily control the Windows startup process are the Services tab and the Startup tab. The Services tab contains a list of services automatically launched at startup, and the Startup tab contains a list of programs started by entries in the registry or in startup folders. On the Services tab, shown in Figure 12-70, when you check **Hide All Microsoft Services**, you can easily see the third-party services that you might want to disable. Click **Disable All** to disable all these services.

The Startup tab is showing in Figure 12-71. You can disable all programs listed or check and uncheck an item to control individual startup items. When you're done, click **Apply**, close the utility, and reboot your system. If this solves your problem, go back to Msconfig and enable

> **Notes**
>
> Msconfig reports only what it is programmed to look for when listing startup programs and services. It looks only in certain registry keys and startup folders, and sometimes Msconfig does not report a startup process. Therefore, don't consider its list of startup processes to be exhaustive.

A+ ESS
3.2
3.3

A+
220-602
3.1
3.2
3.3

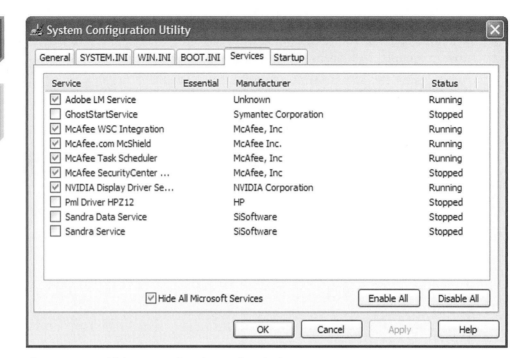

**Figure 12-70** Third-party services that are launched at startup

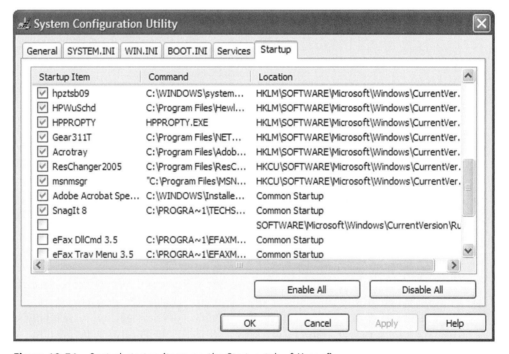

**Figure 12-71** Control startup items on the Startup tab of Msconfig

one program at a time until the problem reappears. You've then discovered the program that is your problem. You'll need to investigate this program. If you don't recognize it, try entering its name in an Internet search engine such as *www.google.com* for information about the program. If the program is a service, you can permanently stop it using the Services console, discussed next. Chapter 14 discusses more in-depth solutions to cleaning up startup processes.

**12**

## SERVICES CONSOLE

The Services console is used to control the Windows and third-party services installed on a Windows 2000/XP system. To launch the Services console, type **Services.msc** in the Run dialog box and press **Enter**. For Windows XP, click the **Extended** tab at the bottom of the window (see Figure 12-72). As you select each service, the box on the left describes the service. If the description is missing, most likely the service is a third-party service put there by an installed application. (The Windows 2000 Services console does not have the Extended tab and does not give descriptions of services.) To get more information about a service, right-click its name and select **Properties** from the shortcut menu. In the console, Startup Types are Automatic (starts when Windows loads), Manual (starts as needed), or Disabled (cannot be started).

> ### Notes
>
> For Windows XP, if you suspect a Windows system service is causing the problem, you can use Msconfig to disable the service. If this works, then replace the service file with a fresh copy from the Windows setup CD.

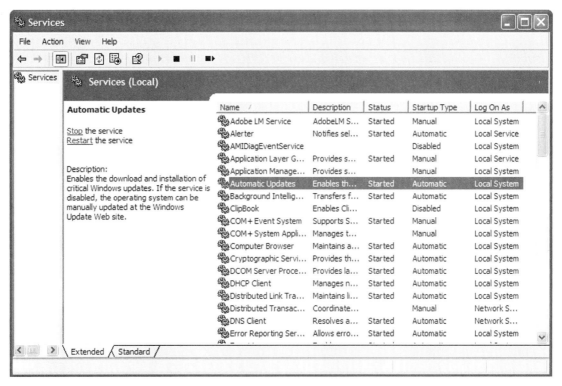

**Figure 12-72** The Services window is used to manage Windows services

Research each third-party service whose Startup Type is set to Automatic and decide if you need to disable the service or uninstall the software responsible for the service. For most Windows services, you can use the Control Panel or other Windows utilities to control a particular service. (For example, you can stop and start Automatic Updates from the System Properties window.) For third-party services, they can often be stopped by using the utility installed along with the service which you can access from the Start menu. However, you can also use the Services console to disable a service; in the console, use its Properties window (see Figure 12-73). In the Startup type dropdown list, select **Disabled** and then click **Apply**.

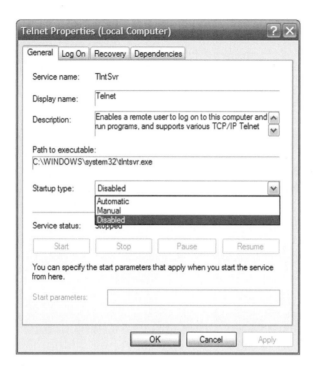

**Figure 12-73**    Use a service properties window to manage the service

## UNINSTALL UNWANTED SOFTWARE

As you search through a Windows system and find software that is no longer needed, rather than just disabling it, take the time to uninstall it. Doing so helps to keep your system clean and free of problems. For hardware devices, use Device Manager to uninstall the software or, for some devices such as a USB digital camera, use the Add or Remove Programs applet in the Control Panel or an uninstall routine in the Start menu. For applications, first try to uninstall the software using the Add or Remove Programs applet. If this method doesn't work, look for an uninstall utility in the Start menu. As a last resort, you can manually uninstall the software.

Now let's look at how to use the Add or Remove Programs applet in the Control Panel and uninstall routines. Then we'll turn our attention to how to manually remove software that won't go away by other means.

### ADD OR REMOVE PROGRAMS APPLET IN THE CONTROL PANEL

Using the Add or Remove Programs applet in the Control Panel, select the hardware device or application and click **Change/Remove** (see Figure 12-74). Then follow the directions onscreen.

> **Notes**
>
> Before uninstalling software, make sure it's not running in the background. Antivirus software can't be uninstalled if it's still running. You can use Task Manager to end all processes related to the software. Then remove the software.

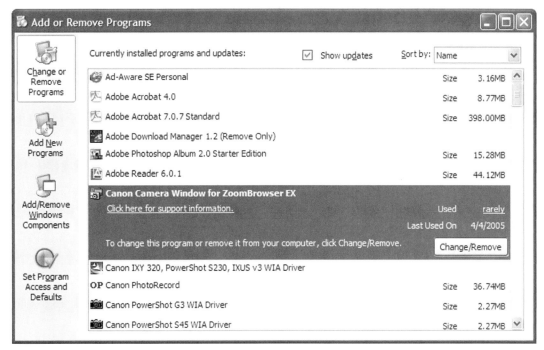

**Figure 12-74** Use the Add or Remove Programs applet to uninstall a few hardware devices and most applications

## UNINSTALL ROUTINE

If you don't find the software listed in the Add or Remove Programs windows or the uninstall routine there does not work, try to find an uninstall utility in the Start menu. For example, in Figure 12-75 you can see Uninstall WinPatrol as an option for this software installation. Click this option and follow the directions onscreen to uninstall the software.

Next, verify the software is no longer listed in the Add or Remove Programs window. If the software is still listed in the window, you can select it and then click **Remove**. Windows will tell you the software has already been uninstalled and ask if you want it removed from the list. When you say okay, the software will be removed from the list.

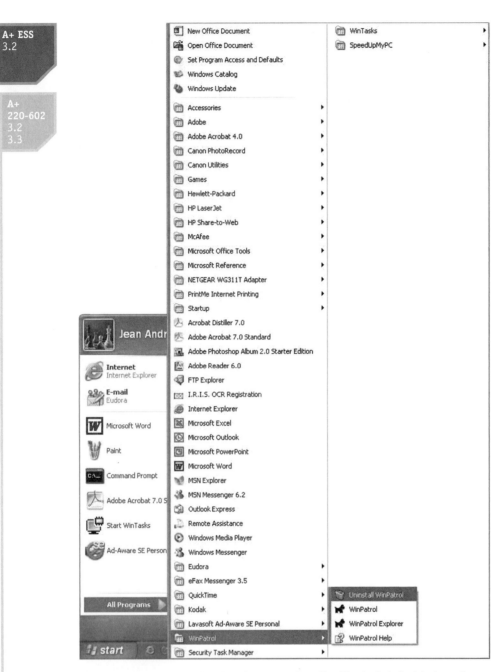

**Figure 12-75** Some applications have an uninstall utility included with the software

## DELETE PROGRAM FILES

Sometimes, you receive an error when you try to use Add or Remove Programs or an uninstall routine. When this happens, you can manually delete the program files and registry entries used by the software you want to uninstall. In our example, we'll manually uninstall the WinPatrol software by BillP Studios:

1. Most likely, the program files are stored in the C:\Program Files folder on the hard drive (see Figure 12-76). Using Windows Explorer, look for a folder in the Program Files folder that contains the software. In Figure 12-76, you can see the WinPatrol software under the BillP Studios folder. Keep in mind, however, that you might not

**Figure 12-76** Program folders are usually stored in the C:\Program Files folder

find the program files you're looking for in the C:\Program Files folder because when you install software, the software installation program normally asks you where to install the software. Therefore, the program files might be anywhere, and you might need to search a bit to find them.

2. Delete the WinPatrol folder and all its contents. You can also delete the BillP Studios folder.

## DELETE REGISTRY ENTRIES

Editing the registry can be dangerous, so do so only when you have no other choice. In other words, when you are in this position, proceed with caution! Here is how you delete registry entries that cause a program to be listed as installed software in the Add or Remove Programs window:

1. Click **Start**, click **Run**, and then type **regedit** in the Run dialog box. Click **OK** to open the Registry Editor.

2. Locate the key that follows this step. The key contains the entries used to create the list of installed software in the Add or Remove Programs window: HKEY_LOCAL_MACHINE\Software\Microsoft\Windows\CurrentVersion\Uninstall

3. Back up the Uninstall key to the Windows desktop so that you can backtrack if necessary. To do that for Windows XP, right-click the Uninstall key and select **Export** from the shortcut menu (see to Figure 12-77). For Windows 2000, click **Registry** on the menu bar, and then click **Export Registry File**.

4. In the Export Registry File dialog box, select the **Desktop**. Enter the filename as **Save Uninstall Key**, and click **Save**. You should see a new icon on your desktop named Save Uninstall Key.reg.

5. The Uninstall key is a daunting list of all the programs installed on your PC. When you expand the key, you'll see a long list of subkeys in the left pane, which appear to

**Figure 12-77** Back up the Uninstall key before you edit it

have meaningless names that won't help you find the program you're looking for. Select the first subkey in the Uninstall key and watch as its values and data are displayed in the right pane (see Figure 12-78). Step down through each key, watching the details in the right pane until you find the program you want to delete.

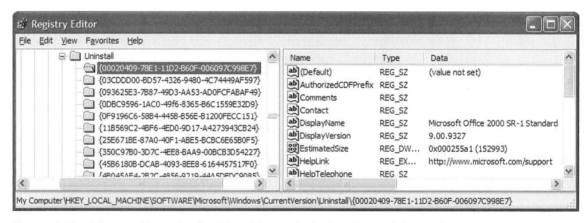

**Figure 12-78** Select a subkey under the Uninstall key to display its values and data in the right pane

6. To delete the key, right-click the key and select **Delete** from the shortcut menu (see Figure 12-79). When the Confirm Key Delete dialog box appears asking you to confirm the deletion, click **Yes**. Be sure to search through all the keys in this list because the software might have more than one key. Delete them all and exit the registry editor.

7. Open the Add or Remove Programs window and verify that the list of installed software is correct and the software you are uninstalling is no longer listed.

8. If the list of installed software is not correct, you can undo your changes to the registry by double-clicking the **Save Uninstall Key.reg** icon on your desktop to restore the Uninstall key.

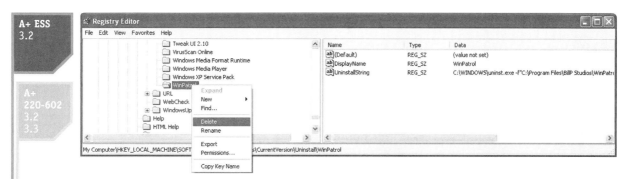

**Figure 12-79** Delete the registry key that lists the software in the Add or Remove Programs window

9. If the list in the Add or Remove Programs window is correct, clean up your Windows desktop by deleting the Save Uninstall Key.reg icon and file. Right-click the icon on your desktop and select **Delete** from the shortcut menu.

Restart the PC and watch for any startup errors about a missing program file. The software might have stored startup entries in the registry, in startup folders, or as a service that is no longer present and causing an error. If you see an error, use Msconfig to find out how the program is set to start. You'll then need to delete this startup entry by editing the registry, deleting a shortcut in a startup folder, or disabling a service using the Services console. You'll learn more about searching out and deleting startup entries in Chapter 14.

---

**Notes**

In addition to the support tools described in this part of the chapter, third-party diagnostic software can be of help. For example, ConfigSafe by imagineLAN, Inc. (*www.imaginelan.com*) is a utility that tracks configuration changes to Windows 9x/Me or Windows NT/2000/XP and can restore the system to a previously saved configuration. It comes preinstalled with some Windows 2000 installations. To use ConfigSafe to make a backup of the registry before installing a new device or application, click **Start, Programs**, and **ConfigSafe**. When the ConfigSafe window appears, select the **Camera** icon. Type a name for the snapshot of the registry and click **OK**. Later if you need to restore the registry, open the CongfigSafe window and follow the directions on the screen.

---

## MANAGING WINDOWS 2000/XP MEMORY

Under Windows 2000/XP, physical memory (RAM) and virtual memory (space on the hard drive) are both managed by the Virtual Memory Manager (VMM). The Virtual Memory Manager provides a set of memory addresses (called a memory space) to each application, as shown in Figure 12-80. When an application or device driver is launched, the first thing it does is request space in memory to keep its data. The application or device driver can only say, "I want memory." It cannot tell Windows which physical memory or which memory addresses it wants, or even the range of addresses it wants to fall within. The Virtual Memory Manager is the interface between the application or driver and the physical and virtual memory that the VMM controls.

Memory is allocated in 4K segments or pages. Applications and devices written for Windows 2000/XP only know how many pages they have. VMM takes care of the rest. It is free to store these pages in RAM or on the hard drive in the swap file named **Pagefile.sys**. When Windows 2000/XP is installed, it sets the swap file to 1.5 times the amount of installed RAM, sets the maximum size at 3 times the installed RAM, and puts the file, Pagefile.sys, as a hidden file in the root directory of the hard drive where Windows is installed. If necessary, you can change the location and sizes of the file.

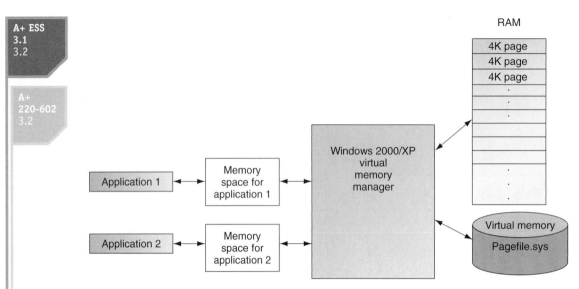

**Figure 12-80**    Windows 2000/XP memory management

Here are some guidelines to remember in managing memory and virtual memory:

▲ With Windows 2000/XP, there is little performance gain by setting the page file to a fixed size. (In contrast, with Windows 9x/Me, setting the page file to a fixed size can sometimes improve performance.)

▲ If you have plenty of memory (512 MB or more) and are short on hard drive space, you can limit the maximum size of the page file. In this situation, make the maximum size the same as the amount of RAM installed.

▲ If you're short on RAM (less than 512 MB) and have sufficient hard drive space, you can increase the maximum size of the page file up to 4096 MB (4 GB).

▲ If drive C has limited space, you can move the page file to another logical drive on the same physical drive or to another physical drive installed in the system.

▲ If you have two or more physical hard drives installed in your system, you can gain some performance by spreading the page file over several physical drives. However, if you have sliced a hard drive into two or more logical drives, don't spread the page file over these logical drives because this causes the hard drive controller to work harder locating the page file in different physical locations on the one drive.

▲ For Windows XP, memory is allocated between applications and file caching to the hard drive. By default, it allocates most of RAM to applications and less to file caching. This works best unless the system is being used as a file server, Web server, or in some other server application. Sometimes, for these server applications, you can improve performance by setting Windows to allocate more memory resources toward file caching. To do this, in the Performance Options window shown in the following steps, set Windows to run in System cache mode.

> **Notes**
>
> When deciding where to put the page file, don't put the file on a second hard drive that is slower than the Windows hard drive. Doing so can slow down performance.

Even though Windows allows you to completely eliminate virtual memory from your system, don't do it. You might have plenty of RAM, but some applications will still give out-of-memory errors when they don't have enough virtual memory. Also, some Windows procedures expect to find some virtual memory to use.

12

A+ ESS
3.1
3.2

A+
220-602
3.2

# APPLYING | CONCEPTS

To change memory settings and page file sizes in Windows 2000/XP, do the following:

1. Right-click **My Computer** and select **Properties** on the shortcut menu.

2. The System Properties dialog box opens. Click the **Advanced** tab.

3. For Windows XP, click **Settings** under Performance. For Windows 2000, click the **Performance Options** button.

4. The Performance Options dialog box opens. Click the **Advanced** tab (see Figure 12-81). Notice in this window how you can decide the priorities for processor scheduling, and for Windows XP, memory usage. Unless you're using this computer as a Web server or other server on the network, for Windows XP, select **Programs** for both Processor scheduling and Memory usage, and, for Windows 2000, select **Applications**.

**Figure 12-81** Setting performance options for Windows XP

5. Click the **Change** button.

6. The Virtual Memory dialog box opens (see Figure 12-82). In this dialog box, you can change the size of the paging file and select the drive for the file. If you select more than one drive, the file will be spread over these drives.

Upgrading memory can sometimes greatly improve Windows performance. If a system routinely runs memory-hungry applications such as video-editing software (for example, Adobe Creative Suite), drafting software (for example, Autodesk AutoCAD), or database

> **Notes**
>
> You can also access the Windows 2000/XP Performance Options dialog box from the Computer Management window. To do so, open the Computer Management window, right-click **Computer Management (Local)**, and select **Properties** on the shortcut menu.

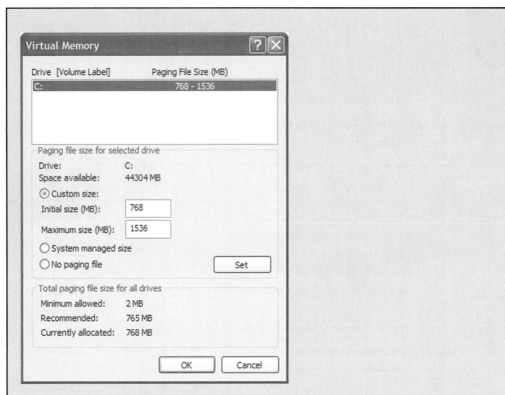

**Figure 12-82** Use the Virtual Memory dialog box to change paging file settings

management software (for example, Microsoft SQL Server), you need to install as much RAM in the system as it will hold. However, for normal use, to know if your system would benefit from an upgrade, open **Task Manager** and click the **Performance** tab. If the Total Physical Memory is less than the Total Commit Charge, Windows is having to use the page file excessively. Therefore, more RAM is needed. Figure 12-83 shows an example of a system that is in need of an upgrade.

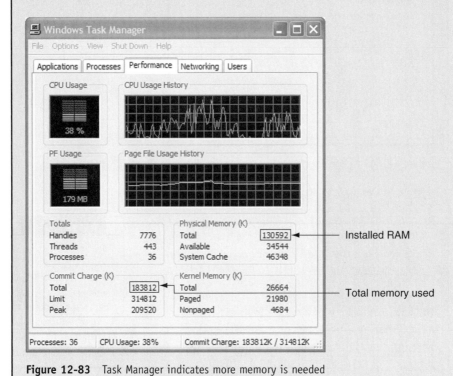

**Figure 12-83** Task Manager indicates more memory is needed

A+ ESS
3.1
3.2

A+
220-602
3.2

Compare this figure to Figure 12-64 earlier in the chapter. In the system shown in Figure 12-64, 1 GB of RAM is installed, and the Performance tab shows that this memory is more than sufficient.

In addition to the information in this chapter, other important sources of information about Windows 2000 are the Microsoft Web site at *support.microsoft.com* and the *Windows 2000 Professional Resource Kit* by Microsoft Press. The *Resource Kit* includes a CD that contains additional Windows 2000 utilities. These resources can further help you understand Windows 2000 and solve problems with the OS. Also remember that user manuals, the Web, training manuals, and product installation documentation are all excellent sources of information.

## >> CHAPTER SUMMARY

▲ Any user can install a hardware device if the device can be installed without user input, all files necessary for a complete installation are present, the drivers have been digitally signed, and there are no errors during installation.

▲ When a second hard drive is installed, Disk Management in Windows 2000/XP is used to prepare the disk for use. Diskpart can also be used from the Recovery Console.

▲ Windows XP offers processes to help find updates for a driver, roll back a driver if an update fails, and verify that a driver is certified by Microsoft. Generally, hardware devices are mostly managed by Windows 2000/XP Device Manager.

▲ You can install software in Windows 2000/XP only if you have Administrator privileges.

▲ Compatibility mode in Windows XP provides an application written for Windows 9x/Me or later with the environment for which it was designed.

▲ Windows XP uses the Error Reporting service to report application problems to Microsoft and perhaps suggest a fix.

▲ The Computer Management window is a console that includes several useful Windows utilities.

▲ Microsoft Management Console (MMC) can be used to create customized consoles to manage the OS.

▲ Event Viewer is used to view system, application, and security events.

▲ Windows 2000/XP Support Tools can be installed from the Windows 2000/XP CD and include several utilities to support hardware and applications.

▲ Windows File Protection (WFP) protects the system files against an application, a virus, or a user changing or deleting them. System File Checker is part of the WFP system.

▲ Windows XP System Restore maintains a list of restore points that can be used to restore the system state to a previous point in time before a problem occurred.

▲ Back up the Windows 2000/XP system state on a regular basis using the Backup utility. This backup includes system files, files to load the OS, and the registry. Back up the system state before editing the registry.

▲ Windows XP Automated System Recovery can be used to back up the entire drive C to prepare for a corrupted Windows installation.

◢ When solving problems with a sluggish Windows 2000/XP system, remove unwanted software, scan for viruses, clean up the hard drive, and consider the possibility you might need to upgrade memory or some other hardware component.

◢ The Windows registry should always be backed up before you edit it. Only edit it when other methods of solving a problem have failed.

◢ Task Manager and Msconfig (for Windows XP only) can be used to determine if a process is launched at startup that you can remove or disable to improve Windows performance.

◢ Task Manager is used to manage processes and measure performance, giving information about the processor, memory, the hard drive, and virtual memory.

◢ Virtual memory uses hard drive space as memory to increase the total amount of memory available. In Windows 2000/XP, virtual memory is stored in a swap file named Pagefile.sys.

◢ Virtual memory is managed in Windows 2000/XP from the System Properties dialog box.

## >> KEY TERMS

For explanations of key terms, see the Glossary near the end of the book.

| | | |
|---|---|---|
| console | hypertext | System Restore |
| digital signatures | restore point | system state data |
| Disk Management | snap-ins | |
| hardware profile | System File Checker (SFC) | |

## >> REVIEW QUESTIONS

1. During installation of a hardware device, Windows 2000/XP searches for a driver information file that has which of the following extensions?

   **a.** .ini

   **b.** .inf

   **c.** .dat

   **d.** .reg

2. When a new device is being installed, if Windows recognizes the drivers were not digitally signed by Microsoft, which of the following decisions do you have to make?

   **a.** Whether or not to physically install the modem

   **b.** Whether or not to test the device being installed

   **c.** Whether or not to continue with the installation using unsigned drivers

   **d.** Whether or not to install from a specific location

3. Which of the following terms refers to the snapshot of the system state that is used during a system restoration?

   **a.** Registry

   **b.** Console

   **c.** Event log

   **d.** Restore point

4. Which of the following features do you use to revert to the old driver if you update a driver and the new driver does not perform as expected?

   **a.** Plug and Play feature

   **b.** Device Driver Wizard

   **c.** Show hidden devices feature

   **d.** Driver Rollback feature

5. Which of the following utilities provides an application with the environment that it expects from the operating system for which it was designed?

   **a.** Compatibility Mode

   **b.** Dependency Walker

   **c.** Error Reporting Service

   **d.** Microsoft Management Console

6. True or false? During installation of a hardware device using Windows XP, if the installation begins by installing the device, you must power down the computer first and then physically install the device.

7. True or false? Any type of user can install a hardware device.

8. True or false? When installing Windows 2000/XP, you must use some or part of the hard drive to create the primary partition and format drive C.

9. True or false? The files critical to successfully loading Windows 2000/XP are called system state data.

10. True or false? Windows 2000 Regedit.exe and Regedt32.exe are just two different names used for the same registry editor.

11. Digital codes that can be used to authenticate the source of files are called
    _____.

12. Windows can maintain more than one set of hardware configuration information called a(n) _____.

13. Two tasks that can be accomplished using Disk Management are
    _____ and _____.

14. The _____ command in the Run dialog box displays information about digitally signed files, including device driver files and application files.

15. In a console, individual administrative tools such as Device Manager or Disk Management are called _____.

# Supporting Windows 2000/XP Users and Their Data

**In this chapter, you will learn:**

- How to set up and support Windows 2000/XP user accounts
- About some tools useful when supporting users and their data
- How to maintain a hard drive and keep good backups

**I**n the previous chapter, you learned how to support and maintain the Windows 2000/XP operating system. This chapter focuses on meeting user needs and supporting their data. In Windows 2000/XP, everything a user is allowed or not allowed to do is determined by the privileges assigned to the currently active user account. Therefore, the first step in learning how to support users is to learn how to set up and support a user account that meets the user's needs. Next, you'll learn about some Windows tools that can help you support users so that they can effectively do their jobs.

Last in the chapter, we'll focus on supporting the hard drive. The hard drive normally holds most user data and all user preferences and settings. Keeping the hard drive working well and keeping good backups are essential to maintaining the system and its data so that users don't have to be concerned about having to deal with a sluggish system or corrupted or lost data.

## *MANAGING USER ACCOUNTS*

Windows 2000/XP requires a user to log onto the system with a valid user account before he or she can use Windows. If you are responsible for managing these accounts, you need to know how to set up a user account and how to help the user transfer files and settings that belong to his or her account from one computer to another.

### UNDERSTANDING AND SETTING UP USER ACCOUNTS

In this section, you'll learn how to create and manage user accounts. If several users need access to a computer, to save time, you'll find it easier to manage user accounts and their profiles at the group level rather than individually. Let's first look at the different types of user accounts, the different groups to which a user account can belong, and how an account's user profile can be managed. Then you'll see how to create accounts and control how a user logs on and how to deal with a forgotten password.

> **Notes**
>
> Windows XP Professional supports a multilingual environment. For non-English speaking users, consider downloading and installing the Multilingual User Interface (MUI) components for Windows XP. To know more about these options, their benefits, and limitations, go to the Microsoft Web site and search on the TechNet article with the title "Comparing Windows XP Professional Multilingual Options."

### TYPES OF USER ACCOUNTS

A **user account** defines a user to Windows and records information about the user, including the user name, the password used to access the account, groups to which the account belongs, and the rights and permissions assigned to the account. Permissions assigned to a user account control what the user can and cannot do and access in Windows.

There are two types of user accounts in Windows 2000/XP:

▲ **Global user accounts**, sometimes called domain user accounts, are used at the domain level, created by an administrator using Windows 2000 Server or Windows Server 2003, and stored in the SAM (security accounts manager) database on a Windows domain controller. A user can log on to any computer on the networked domain using a global user account, and the information about a global user account's rights and permissions apply to each workstation in the domain. The centralized SAM database is part of Active Directory, which is a repository of information used to manage a Windows network that is itself managed by Windows 2000 Server or Windows Server 2003. When a user logs on, the domain controller on the network manages the user account logon (see Figure 13-1). How to set up and manage global user accounts in a Windows domain is not covered in this book.

▲ A **local user account** is created on a local computer and allows a user access to only that one computer. An administrator creates a local user account, assigns a user name and password to the account, and gives the account rights and permissions. As a general rule, a user account should have no more rights than a user needs to do his or her job. For example, an administrator who is responsible for setting up and maintaining user accounts in an office workgroup can set the permissions on a user account to deny the user the right to install a printer, install software, or do any other chores that change the PC software or hardware environment.

Local user accounts are set up and managed at each individual workstation. When Windows 2000/XP is first installed, it automatically creates two local accounts, called **built-in user accounts**, as follows:

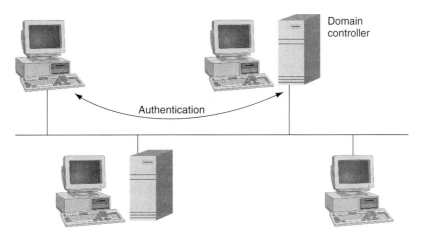

**Figure 13-1** On a domain, a user account login is managed by the domain controller

▲ *The built-in administrator account.* An administrator has rights and permissions to all computer software, data, and hardware resources. Under Windows 2000/XP, the administrator can create other user accounts and assign corresponding rights and permissions to individual accounts, to groups of selected accounts, or to all accounts that use the computer.

▲ *The built-in guest account.* The built-in guest account has very limited privileges and gives someone who does not have a user account access to a computer. The guest account is useful in a business environment where many people use a single computer for limited purposes and it is not practical for all of them to have unique user accounts. For example, a hotel might provide a computer in the lobby for its guests who would log onto Windows using the built-in guest account.

## USER GROUPS

A user group is a predefined set of permissions and rights assigned to user accounts, and is an efficient way for an administrator to manage multiple user accounts that require these same permissions and rights. When installed, Windows 2000/XP sets up several user groups, including the following:

▲ *Administrator.* An account that is a member of the Administrator group can install or uninstall devices and applications and can perform all administrative tasks. When Windows 2000/XP is first installed, one user account is created in this group and the account is called the Administrator.

▲ *Backup Operators.* An account that is a member of the Backup Operator group can back up and restore any files on the system regardless of their access privileges to these files.

▲ *Power Users.* A Power User account can read from and write to parts of the system other than their own local drive, install applications, and perform limited administrative tasks.

▲ *Limited Users group (also known as Limited account or Users account).* An account that is a member of the Limited Users group has read-write access only on its own folders, read-only access to most system folders, and no access to other users' data. Using a Limited account, a user cannot install applications or carry out any administrative responsibilities.

▲ *Guests group.* An account that is a member of the Guests group is intended to be used by people who use a workstation only once or occasionally and have limited access to files and resources. A guest account has permission to shut down a computer. When Windows 2000/XP is first installed, one Guest account is created.

A+ ESS
3.1
3.2
6.1
6.2
6.3

A+
220-602
3.1
5.2
5.3
6.1
6.2

A+ ESS
3.1
3.2
6.1
6.2
6.3

A+
220-602
3.1
5.2
5.3
6.1
6.2

With most Windows 2000/XP systems, an administrator can manage user accounts using only the administrator, limited account, and guest accounts. When an account is first created, the only available choices are administrator and limited. After the account is created, an administrator can assign an account to a group other than these two. Table 13-1 summarizes the permissions granted to the three account types: administrator, limited, and guest account.

| Action Permitted | Administrator Account | Limited Account | Guest Account |
|---|---|---|---|
| Create user accounts | Yes | | |
| Change system files | Yes | | |
| Read other user account files | Yes | | |
| Add or remove hardware | Yes | | |
| Change other user account passwords | Yes | | |
| Change your own user account password | Yes | Yes | |
| Install any software | Yes | | |
| Install most software | Yes | Yes | |
| Save documents | Yes | Yes | Yes |
| Use installed software | Yes | Yes | Yes |

**Table 13-1**   Actions permitted for three account types

## ACCESS CONTROL

One of the main reasons for using account types that limit certain activities is so that an administrator can control what data files a user can access. For example, suppose a group of users in the Accounting Department works together in a workgroup. Some of these users need access to all payroll data, but other users are only allowed access to accounts payable and accounts receivable. In order to provide for this type of access control, an administrator will decide which type of user account an employee needs.

Suppose Danielle needs to use the local network to access payroll data that is stored on Kelly's computer. In order to provide for that access, the administrator must set up a user account for Danielle on Kelly's computer. Figure 13-2 shows what happens if a user tries to use

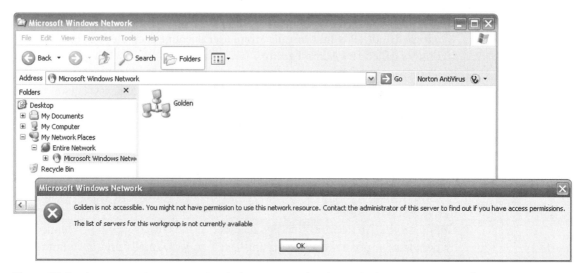

**Figure 13-2**   A user cannot access a networked computer unless he or she has an account on that computer

A+ ESS
3.1
3.2
6.1
6.2
6.3

A+
220-602
3.1
5.2
5.3
6.1
6.2

My Network Places to access a remote computer on the network without proper permissions. To keep this error from happening, an administrator needs to create an account on each individual computer in the workgroup that the user needs to access.

Also notice in Table 13-1 that a user account with limited or guest privileges cannot view the folders belonging to another account. Figure 13-3 shows the error displayed when a limited-account user attempted to view the files belonging to another user.

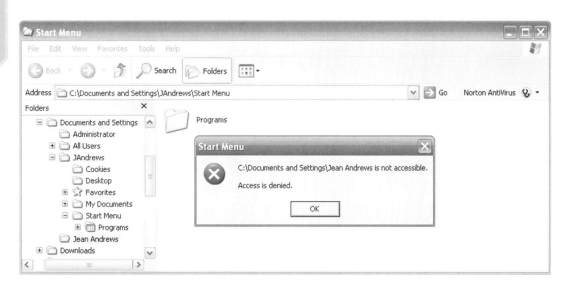

**Figure 13-3** This user does not have access to another user's folders

Even though a limited or guest account cannot normally access files belonging to another account, an administrator can make exceptions as needed. The Cacls (change access control lists) command can be used to view and change the access control for files and folders.

Suppose, for example, an administrator wants to give permission for a user account, JSmith, to have access to a file, Myfile.txt. Figure 13-4 shows the use of five Cacls commands that can be used. The first, third, and fifth commands display access information for the Myfile.txt file (Cacls Myfile.txt). The second command grants read-only access for the

**Figure 13-4** Use the Cacls command to change user permissions for files and folders

A+ ESS
3.1
3.2
6.1
6.2
6.3

A+
220-602
3.1
5.2
5.3
6.1
6.2

user JSmith. (In the command line, the /E parameter says to edit the list and the /G parameter says to grant permission to the following user. The :R parameter says the permission is read-only.) The fourth command revokes JSmith's access permission. In Chapter 19, you'll learn how you can take more control over which user account has access to which files and folders.

## USER PROFILES

After an administrator creates a local user account and the user logs on for the first time, the system creates a **user profile** for that user. A folder is created in the C:\Documents and Settings folder that is named the user account such as C:\Documents and Settings\JSmith. By default, the user profile and the user's data are stored in this folder and its subfolders. When the user changes settings to customize his or her computer and then logs off, the user profile is updated so that settings can be restored the next time the user logs on.

An administrator can manage user profiles by using one or more of the following:

▲ *Group profiles.* A profile that applies to a group of users is called a **group profile**. Group profiles are useful when the same settings apply to several users.

▲ *Roaming user profiles.* If the computer is networked to other computers in a Windows workgroup, the administrator must create a user account on each computer in the workgroup that this user needs to access. When the user logs on to each computer in the workgroup, he or she would have to reestablish the user profile at each computer, re-creating desktop settings and application settings for each computer unless the administrator implements a feature called roaming user profiles. With **roaming user profiles**, settings established by a user at one computer are stored in a file on a file server on the network and shared with all computers in the workgroup. When a user moves from one computer to another computer in the workgroup, the roaming profile follows the user so that he or she does not have to redo settings at each computer.

▲ *Mandatory user profiles.* Another type of profile used with workgroups is a **mandatory user profile**. This profile is a roaming user profile that applies to all users in a user group, and individual users cannot change that profile. It is used in situations where users perform only specific job-related tasks.

An administrator creates group, roaming, and mandatory profiles using the Computer Management console under the Administrative Tools applet in the Control Panel. To view all profiles stored on a Windows XP computer, use the System Properties window. Click **Start** and then right-click **My Computer**. Select **Properties** and then click the **Advanced** tab, as shown in Figure 13-5. Under User Profiles, click the **Settings** button. For a Windows 2000 computer, in the System Properties window, click the **User Profiles** tab.

## CREATING LOCAL USER ACCOUNTS

When setting up accounts for users, you need to be aware of these restrictions:

▲ User names for Windows 2000/XP logon can consist of up to 15 characters.
▲ Passwords can be up to 127 characters.
▲ User accounts can be set up with or without passwords. Passwords provide greater security. Where security is a concern, always set a password for the Administrator account.
▲ Passwords can be controlled by the administrator, but generally, users should be allowed to change their own passwords.

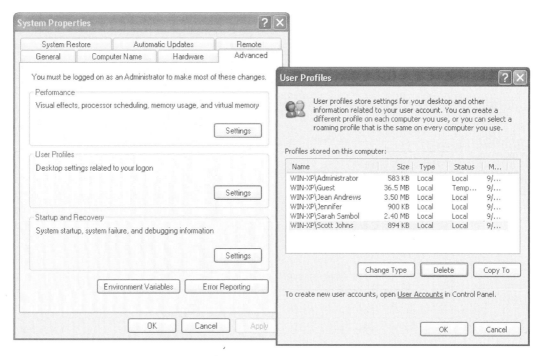

**Figure 13-5** View all user profiles stored on this PC using the System Properties window

Where security is a concern, follow these guidelines to make passwords as secure as possible:

▲ Do not use a password that is easy to guess, such as one consisting of real words, your telephone number, or the name of your pet.

▲ Use a password that is a combination of letters, numbers, and even nonalphanumeric characters.

▲ Use at least seven characters in a password.

> **Notes**
>
> In Chapter 19, you'll learn more about how to create the most secure passwords.

**APPLYING CONCEPTS**   As an administrator, you can create a user account using the Computer Management console or the User Accounts applet in the Control Panel. If the account is created in Computer Management, the account will automatically be added to the Limited group. If it is created using the Control Panel, the new account will be a member of the Administrator group.

To create a local user account using Computer Management, follow these steps:

1. Log on to the computer as an administrator.

2. Right-click **My Computer**. Select **Manage** on the shortcut menu. The Computer Management console window opens. (Note that you can also access Computer Management by way of the **Control Panel**, **Administrative Tools** applet.)

3. Expand **Local Users and Groups** by clicking the plus sign to its left. Right-click **Users** and then select **New User** on the shortcut menu. The New User window opens (see Figure 13-6). Enter the User name, enter the password twice, and check the boxes to decide how and when the password can be changed. You can also enter values for the Full name and Description to help identify the user. Click **Create**.

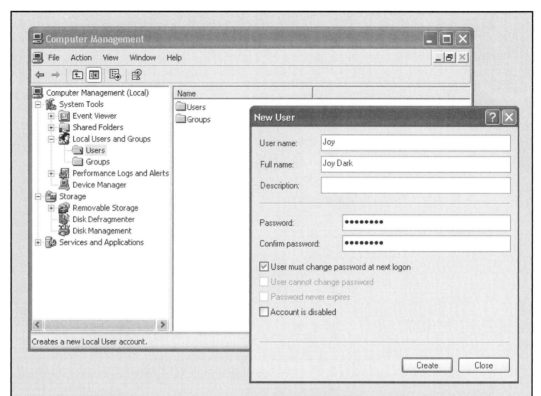

**Figure 13-6**    Create a user account using either Computer Management or the User Account applets in the Control Panel

4. The account is created with the default type Limited, which means the account cannot create, delete, or change other accounts; make system-wide changes; or install software. If you want to give the account Administrator privileges, then open the **Control Panel** and double-click the **User Accounts** applet.

5. The User Accounts window opens, listing all accounts. To make changes to an account, click **Change an account**, and then click the account you want to change.

6. In the next window, you can choose to change the name of the account, change the password, remove a password, change the picture icon associated with the account, change the account type, or delete the account. Click **Change the account type**.

7. In the next window, select **Computer administrator** and click **Change Account Type**. Click **Back** twice on the menu bar to return to the opening window.

When you set up a user account, the account can be put into the Administrator group or the Limited Group. However, if you want to put the account into another user group, you must use the Computer Management console, as follows:

1. In the Computer Management windows, under Local Users and Groups, click **Groups**. The list of groups appears in the right pane (see Figure 13-7).

2. Right-click the group you want to assign a user and select **Add to Group** from the shortcut menu. The group's Properties window appears. For example, in Figure 13-8, the Power Users Properties window is showing. Listed in this window are all users assigned to this group.

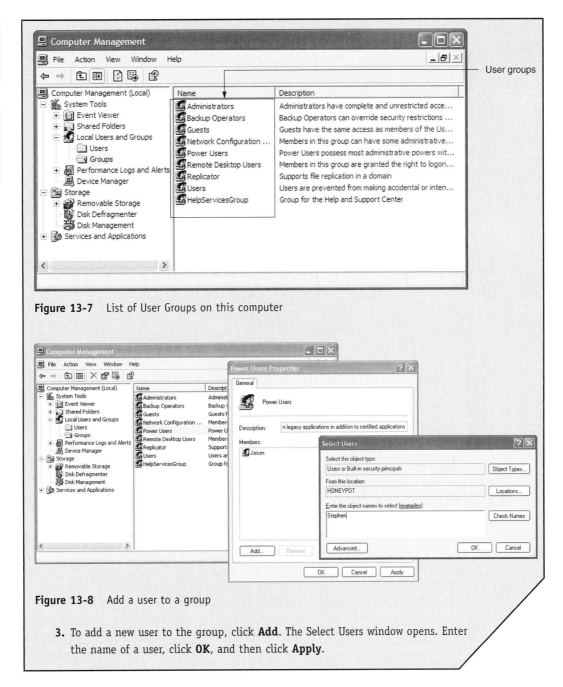

User groups

**Figure 13-7** List of User Groups on this computer

**Figure 13-8** Add a user to a group

3. To add a new user to the group, click **Add**. The Select Users window opens. Enter the name of a user, click **OK**, and then click **Apply**.

## CONTROLLING HOW A USER LOGS ON

With Windows 2000, there is only one way to log on to the system: pressing the Ctrl+Alt+Del keys to open the logon window. Also, with Windows 2000, one user must log off before another can log on. However, Windows XP allows more than one user to be logged on at the same time (called multiple logons), and, in a Windows XP workgroup, you have some options as to how logging on works:

▲ *Welcome screen.* The default option is a Welcome screen that appears when the PC is first booted or comes back from a sleep state. All users are listed on the Welcome screen along with a picture (which can be the user's photograph); a user clicks his or her user name and enters the password.

A+ ESS
3.1
3.2
6.1
6.2
6.3

A+
220-602
3.1
5.2
5.3
6.1
6.2

> **Notes**
>
> When Windows XP lists the user accounts on the Welcome screen, it does not show the built-in administrator account in the list. If you want to log onto the system using this account, press Ctrl-Alt-Del. The Log On to Windows dialog box appears. Under User name, type **administrator**, and enter the password. Click **OK** to log on.

▲ *Logon window.* Instead of the Welcome screen, the user must press **Ctrl+Alt+Del** to get to a logon window similar to Windows 2000.

▲ *Fast User Switching Enabled.* Fast User Switching enables more than one user to be logged on to the system.

If the option is enabled, when a user clicks Start and then clicks Log Off, the Log Off Windows dialog box opens, as shown in Figure 13-9. This dialog box gives three choices: Switch User, Log Off, and Cancel. Click **Switch User** and then select a new account from the list of user accounts. After you enter a password, the screen goes blank and then the desktop configured for the new user appears. Each user can have his or her own set of applications open at the same time. When users switch back and forth, Windows keeps separate instances of applications open for each user.

**Figure 13-9** Use the Log Off Windows dialog box to switch users in a multiple logon environment

▲ *Fast User Switching Disabled.* If this option is disabled, only one user can log on at a time. In the Log Off Windows dialog box, the Switch User option does not appear. Disable Fast User Switching when you want to conserve resources because performance is poor when several users leave applications open.

▲ *Automatic logon.* You can use automatic logon so that the Welcome screen does not appear and you are not required to select or enter a user account or enter its password. This method is like leaving your front door wide open when you leave home; it's not recommended because anyone can access your system.

To change the way a user logs on, open the Control Panel, and then open the **User Accounts** applet. Click **Change the way users log on or off**. The User Accounts window opens as shown in Figure 13-10. If you want to require users to press Ctl-Alt-Del to get a logon window, then uncheck **Use the Welcome screen**. If you want to allow only one user

> **Notes**
>
> For a computer that belongs to a domain, you can enable automatic logon by editing the registry. How to do that is covered in the Microsoft Knowledge Base Article 315231.

logged on at a time, then uncheck **Use Fast User Switching**. When you're done with your changes, click **Apply Options** to close the window.

To use automatic logon and bypass logging on altogether, for a standalone computer or one that is networked in a workgroup, enter **control userpasswords2** in the Run dialog box and press **Enter**. The User Accounts window shown in Figure 13-11 appears. Uncheck **Users must enter a user name and password to use this computer** and then click **Apply**.

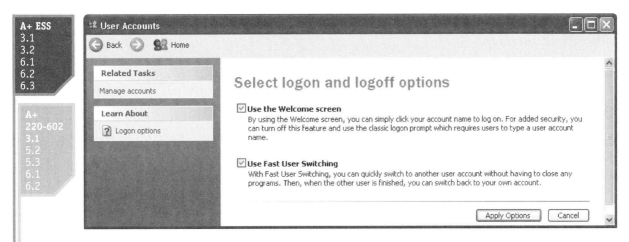

**Figure 13-10** Options to change the way users log on or off

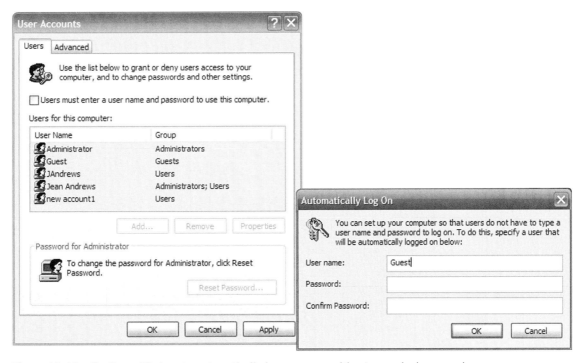

**Figure 13-11** Configure Windows to automatically log on a user without a required password

A dialog box appears asking that you enter the user account and password that you want to use to automatically log on. Enter the account and password, and click **OK** twice to close both windows. Later, if you want to log onto the computer using a different user account, hold down the **Shift** key while Windows is starting.

## FORGOTTEN PASSWORD

Sometimes a user forgets his or her password or the password is compromised. If this happens and you have Administrator privileges, you can reset the password.

Keep in mind, however, that resetting a password causes the OS to lock the user out from using encrypted email or files or from using Internet passwords stored on the computer. You can reset a password using the Computer Management console or the User Accounts applet. In the Computer Management console, right-click the user account and select **Set Password**

in the shortcut menu. A dialog box appears warning you of the danger of losing data when you reset a password. Click **Proceed** to close the box. The Set Password dialog box appears (see Figure 13-12). Enter the new password twice and click **OK**.

**Figure 13-12**  An administrator can reset a user account password

Because of the problem of losing encrypted data and Internet passwords when a user password is reset, each new user should create a **forgotten password floppy disk** for use in the event the user forgets the password. To create the disk, open the **User Accounts** applet in the Control Panel, click the account, and select **Prevent a forgotten password** under Related Tasks in the left pane of the window shown in Figure 13-13. Follow the wizard to create the disk. Explain to the user the importance of keeping the disk in a safe place in case it's needed later. If a user enters a wrong password at logon, he or she will be given the opportunity to use the disk.

> **Notes**
>
> The forgotten password floppy disk should be kept in a protected place so that others cannot use it to gain unauthorized access to the computer.

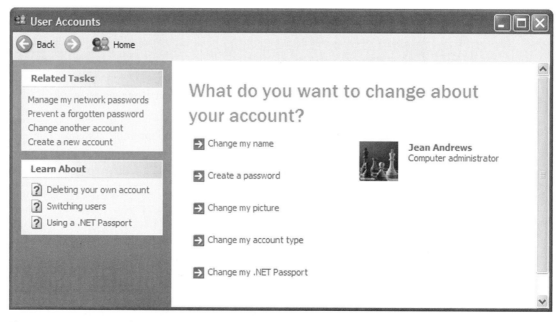

**Figure 13-13**  Create a forgotten password floppy disk

A+ ESS
3.1
3.2
6.1
6.2
6.3

A+
220-602
3.1
5.2
5.3
6.1
6.2

# TRANSFERRING USER FILES AND PREFERENCES TO A NEW PC

When you're setting up a new user on a Windows XP computer, the user might want to move user files and preferences from another PC to this new PC. There are two tools to do that: the Files and Settings Transfer Wizard and the User State Migration Tool (USMT). These tools can help make a smooth transition because a user who is moving from one PC to another does not have to manually copy files and reconfigure OS settings.

Both utilities transfer files in the Documents and Settings folder as well as user preferences. Settings transferred include settings for Display Properties, Internet Explorer, MS Messenger, Netmeeting, Microsoft Office, Outlook Express, Media Player, and others. The transfer tools work if the old computer's OS is Windows 95, Windows 98, Windows 98SE, Windows ME, Windows NT 4.0, Windows 2000, or Windows XP (32-bit). Both transfer tools are discussed in this section.

> **Notes**
>
> Before using either of these tools, install antivirus software on the destination computer in case transferring user files also transfers a virus. You don't want the new PC to get infected. Also, make sure to apply all service packs and updates to Windows XP on the new computer before you perform the transfer. These service packs solved some problems with the tools that we'll be discussing in this section.

## WINDOWS XP FILES AND SETTINGS TRANSFER WIZARD

The Windows XP **Files and Settings Transfer Wizard** is intended to be used by the user rather than the administrator. There is more than one way to use the wizard, but the steps listed below are the easiest method:

1. On the old computer, insert the Windows XP setup CD and open Windows Explorer. Locate on the CD the \Support\Tools folder and double-click the Files and Settings Transfer Wizard program, **Fastwiz.exe**. The wizard launches. Click **Next**.

2. On the next screen, you are asked if this is the new or old computer. Select **Old computer** and click **Next**.

3. The screen in Figure 13-14 appears, asking you to select a transfer method. Select **Other (for example, a removable drive or network drive)**. Click **Browse** and point to a

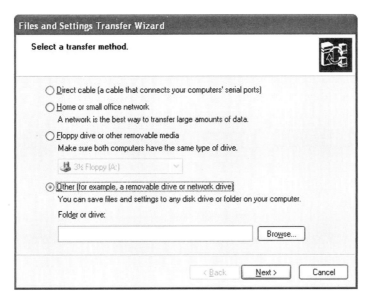

**Figure 13-14** The Files and Settings Transfer Wizard is asking where to save data to be transferred

location to save the files and settings. If both the old and new computers are on the same network, it's convenient to point to a folder on the new computer. Click **OK** and then click **Next**.

4. Follow the wizard instructions on the next screens to select the files and settings you want to transfer. Then the wizard saves all the files and settings to the location you have specified. Click **Finish** to close the wizard.

5. Now go to the new computer and log onto your user account that is to receive the files and settings. Click **Start, All Programs, Accessories, System Tools**, and **Files and Settings Transfer Wizard**. The wizard's Welcome window opens. When you click **Next**, the wizard asks if this is the New computer or Old computer. Select **New computer** and then click **Next**. Figure 13-15 shows the next screen. Select **I don't need the Wizard Disk. I have already collected my files and settings from my old computer** and click **Next**.

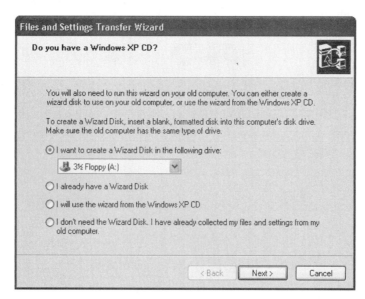

**Figure 13-15**  On the new computer, the Files and Settings Transfer Wizard can be used to point to the location of saved files and settings

6. Follow the wizard instructions onscreen to point to the location of the saved files and settings and close the wizard. You must log off and log back on in order for the changes to take effect.

7. Verify that all your data and settings are available on the new PC. If security is a concern, be sure to go back to the old PC and delete all folders in the user profile so that others can't access that data. A simple way to delete the user profile and all user data kept in the Documents and Settings folder is to use the User Accounts applet in the Control Panel to delete the user account on the old PC.

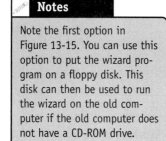

**Notes**

Note the first option in Figure 13-15. You can use this option to put the wizard program on a floppy disk. This disk can then be used to run the wizard on the old computer if the old computer does not have a CD-ROM drive.

## USER STATE MIGRATION TOOL (USMT)

The Files and Settings Transfer Wizard is intended to be used by users, and the User State Migration Tool (USMT) is designed to be used by administrators. The **User State Migration Tool (USMT)** is a command-line tool that works only when the new Windows XP system is a member of a Windows domain.

13

A+ ESS
3.1
3.2
6.1
6.2
6.3

A+
220-602
3.1
5.2
5.3
6.1
6.2

A+ ESS
3.1

A+
220-602
3.1

An administrator uses two commands at the command prompt of this tool: the **scanstate** command, which is used to copy the information from the old computer to a server or removable media, and the **loadstate** command, which is used to copy the information to the new computer. These two commands can be stored in batch files and executed automatically when installing Windows XP over a large number of computers in an enterprise. For details on how to use the command lines in a batch file, see the *Windows XP Resource Kit* by Microsoft Press.

# TOOLS FOR SUPPORTING USERS AND THEIR DATA

In this part of the chapter, you'll learn about some tools that can help you support users. The tools covered are the Command Prompt window and its commands, Task Scheduler, Group Policy, Start menu, and Remote Assistance.

## THE COMMAND PROMPT WINDOW

For all versions of Windows, you can open a Command Prompt window and use it to enter command lines to perform a variety of tasks, such as deleting a file or running the System File Checker utility. To open the window, click **Start**, click **Run**, and enter **Cmd** or **Cmd.exe** in the Run dialog box. When you're working in a Command Prompt window, to clear the window, type **Cls** and press **Enter**. To close the window, type **exit** and press **Enter**, as shown in Figure 13-16.

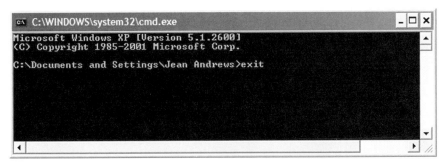

**Figure 13-16**  Use the exit command to close the Command Prompt window

Many of the commands you will learn about in this section can also be used from the Recovery Console. The Recovery Console is a command-line OS that you can load from the Windows 2000/XP setup CD to troubleshoot a system when the Windows desktop refuses to load. How to use the Recovery Console is covered in the next chapter.

> **Notes**
>
> As you work through the following list of commands, keep in mind that if you enter a command and want to terminate its execution before it is finished, you can press Ctrl+Break to do so.

 **A+ Exam Tip**

> The A+ Essentials exam expects you to know how to use the Cmd command to get a Command Prompt window.

### FILE NAMING CONVENTIONS

When using the Command Prompt window to create a file, keep in mind that filename and file extension characters can be the letters a through z, the numbers 0 through 9, and the following characters:

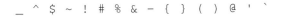

In a Command Prompt window, if a filename has spaces in it, it is sometimes necessary to enclose the filename in double quotes.

A+ ESS
3.1

A+
220-602
3.1

## WILDCARD CHARACTERS IN COMMAND LINES

 **A+ Exam Tip**

The A+ 220-602 exam expects you to know how to use the Help, Dir, Attrib, Edit, Copy, Xcopy, Format, MD, CD, RD, Defrag, and Chkdsk commands, which are all covered in this section.

As you work at the command prompt, you can use two **wildcard** characters in a filename to execute a command on a group of files, or in an abbreviated filename if you do not know the entire name. The question mark (?) is a wildcard for one character, and the asterisk (*) is a wildcard for one or more characters. For example, if you want to find all files in a directory that start with A and have a three-letter file extension, you would use the following command:

```
dir a*.???
```

## HELP

Use this command to get help about any command. Table 13-2 lists some sample applications of this command:

| Command | Result |
|---|---|
| Help Xcopy | Gets help about the Xcopy command |
| Help | Lists all commands |
| Help \|More | Lists information one screen at a time |

**Table 13-2** Sample Help commands

## DIR

Use this command to list files and directories. Table 13-3 lists some examples using additional parameters, wildcards, and a filename:

| Command | Result |
|---|---|
| DIR /P | Lists one screen at a time |
| DIR /W | Presents information using wide format, where details are omitted and files and folders are listed in columns on the screen |
| DIR *.txt | Lists all files with a .txt file extension |
| DIR Myfile.txt | Checks that a single file is present |

**Table 13-3** Sample Dir commands

## DEL OR ERASE

The Del or Erase command erases files or groups of files. If the command does not include drive and directory information, the OS uses the default drive and directory when executing the command. The default drive and directory, also called the current drive and directory, shows in the command prompt. Note that in the command lines in this section, the command prompt is not bolded, but the typed command is in bold.

To erase all files in the A:\DOCS directory, use the following command:

```
C:\> ERASE A:\DOCS\*.*
```

A+ ESS
3.1

A+
220-602
3.1

To erase all files in the current default directory, use the following command:

```
A:\DOCS> DEL *.*
```

To erase all files in the current directory that have no file extensions, use the following command:

```
A:\DOCS> DEL *.
```

To erase the file named Myfile.txt, use the following command:

```
A:\> DEL MYFILE.TXT
```

### COPY [*DRIVE:\PATH\]FILENAME [DRIVE:\PATH\]FILENAME*

The Copy command copies a single file or group of files. The original files are not altered. To copy a file from one drive to another, use a command similar to this one:

```
A:\> COPY C:\Data\Myfile.txt A:\mydata\Newfile.txt
```

The drive, path, and filename of the source file immediately follow the Copy command. The drive, path, and filename of the destination file follow the source filename. If you do not specify the filename of the destination file, the OS assigns the file's original name to this copy. If you omit the drive or path of the source or the destination, then the OS uses the current default drive and path.

To copy the file Myfile.txt from the root directory of drive C to drive A, use the following command:

```
C:\> COPY MYFILE.TXT A:
```

Because the command does not include a drive or path before the filename Myfile.txt, the OS assumes that the file is in the default drive and path. Also, because there is no destination filename specified, the file written to drive A will be named Myfile.txt.

To copy all files in the C:\DOCS directory to the floppy disk in drive A, use the following command:

```
C:\> COPY C:\DOCS\*.* A:
```

To make a backup file named System.bak of the System file in the \Windows\system32\config directory of the hard drive, use the following command:

```
C:\WINDOWS\system32\config> COPY SYSTEM SYSTEM.BAK
```

If you use the Copy command to duplicate multiple files, the files are assigned the names of the original files. When you duplicate multiple files, the destination portion of the command line cannot include a filename.

> **Notes**
>
> When trying to recover a corrupted file, you can sometimes use the Copy command to copy the file to new media, such as from the hard drive to a floppy disk. During the copying process, if the Copy command reports a bad or missing sector, choose the option to ignore that sector. The copying process then continues to the next sector. The corrupted sector will be lost, but others can likely be recovered. For Windows 2000/XP, the Recover command can be used to accomplish the same thing.

A+ ESS
3.1

A+
220-602
3.1

## RECOVER

Use the Recover command to attempt to recover a file when parts of the file are corrupted. To use it, you must specify the name of a single file in the command line, like so:

```
C:\Data> Recover Myfile.doc
```

## XCOPY /C /S /Y /D:

The Xcopy command is more powerful than the Copy command. It follows the same general command-source-destination format as the Copy command, but it offers several more options. For example, you can use the /S parameter with the Xcopy command to copy all files in the directory \DOCS, as well as all subdirectories under \DOCS and their files, to the disk in drive A, like so:

```
C:\> XCOPY C:\DOCS\*.* A: /S
```

To copy all files from the directory C:\DOCS created or modified on March 14, 2006, use the /D switch, as in the following command:

```
C:\> XCOPY C:\DOCS\*.* A: /D:03/14/06
```

Use the /Y parameter to overwrite existing files without prompting, and use the /C parameter to keep copying even when an error occurs.

## MKDIR [DRIVE:]PATH OR MD [DRIVE:]PATH

The Mkdir command (abbreviated MD, for "make directory") creates a subdirectory under a directory. To create a directory named \Game on drive C, you can use this command:

```
C:\> MD C:\Game
```

The backslash indicates that the directory is under the root directory. To create a directory named Chess under the \Game directory, you can use this command:

```
C:\> MKDIR C:\Game\Chess
```

Note that the OS requires that the parent directory Game already exist before it creates the child directory Chess.

Figure 13-17 shows the result of the Dir command on the directory \Game. (Remember that it makes no difference if you use uppercase or lowercase in a command line.) Note the two initial entries in the directory table, the . (dot) and the .. (dot, dot) entries. The Mkdir command creates these two entries when the OS initially sets up the directory. You cannot edit these entries with normal OS commands, and they must remain in the directory for the directory's lifetime. The . entry points to the subdirectory itself, and the .. entry points to the parent directory, in this case, the root directory.

## CHDIR [DRIVE:]PATH OR CD [DRIVE:]PATH OR CD..

The Chdir command (abbreviated CD, for "change directory") changes the current default directory. Using its easiest form, you simply state the drive and the entire path that you want to be current, like so:

```
A:\> CD C:\GAME\CHESS
```

13

A+ ESS
3.1

A+
220-602
3.1

```
C:\WINDOWS\system32\cmd.exe                                    _ □ ×

C:\GAME>dir
 Volume in drive C has no label.
 Volume Serial Number is DCB8-611B

 Directory of C:\GAME

05/16/2006  02:07 PM    <DIR>          .
05/16/2006  02:07 PM    <DIR>          ..
               0 File(s)              0 bytes
               2 Dir(s)  45,675,298,816 bytes free

C:\GAME>md CHESS

C:\GAME>dir
 Volume in drive C has no label.
 Volume Serial Number is DCB8-611B

 Directory of C:\GAME

05/16/2006  02:07 PM    <DIR>          .
05/16/2006  02:07 PM    <DIR>          ..
05/16/2006  02:07 PM    <DIR>          CHESS
               0 File(s)              0 bytes
               3 Dir(s)  45,675,298,816 bytes free

C:\GAME>
```

**Figure 13-17**   Results of the Dir command on the \Game directory

The command prompt now looks like this:

C:\GAME\CHESS>

To move from a child directory to its parent directory, use the .. variation of the command:

C:\GAME\CHESS> **CD..**

C:\GAME>

Remember that .. always means the parent directory. You can move from a parent directory to one of its child directories simply by stating the name of the child directory:

C:\GAME> **CD CHESS**

C:\GAME\CHESS>

Remember to not put a backslash in front of the child directory name; doing so tells the OS to go to a directory named Chess that is directly under the root directory.

## RMDIR *[DRIVE:]PATH* OR RD *[DRIVE:]PATH*

The Rmdir command (abbreviated RD, for "remove directory") removes a subdirectory. Before you can use the Rmdir command, three things must be true:

▲ The directory must contain no files.
▲ The directory must contain no subdirectories.
▲ The directory must not be the current directory.

The . and .. entries are present when a directory is ready for removal. For example, to remove the \Game directory in the preceding example, the Chess directory must first be removed, like so:

`C:\>` **`RMDIR C:\GAME\CHESS`**

Or, if the \GAME directory is the current directory, you can use this command:

`C:\GAME>` **`RD CHESS`**

After you remove the CHESS directory, you can remove the \GAME directory. However, it's not good to attempt to saw off a branch while you're sitting on it; therefore, you must first leave the \GAME directory like this:

`C:\GAME>` **`CD..`**

`C:\>` **`RD \GAME`**

## ATTRIB

The Attrib command displays or changes the read-only, archive, system, and hidden attributes assigned to files. To display the attributes of the file Myfile.txt, you can use this command:

`C:\>` **`ATTRIB MYFILE.TXT`**

To hide the file, you can use this command:

`C:\>` **`ATTRIB   +H MYFILE.TXT`**

To remove the hidden status of the file, you need to use this command:

`C:\>` **`ATTRIB -H MYFILE.TXT`**

To make the file a read-only system file, use this command:

`C:\>` **`ATTRIB   +R   +S MYFILE.TXT`**

When you put more than one parameter in the Attrib command, the order doesn't matter. This command works the same way as the one above:

`C:\>` **`ATTRIB   +S   +R MYFILE.TXT`**

To remove the read-only system status of the file, use this command:

`C:\>` **`ATTRIB -R -S MYFILE.TXT`**

The archive bit is used to determine if a file has changed since the last backup. To turn on the archive bit, use this command:

`C:\>` **`ATTRIB   +A MYFILE.TXT`**

**13**

A+ ESS
3.1
3.3

A+
220-602
3.1

A+ ESS
3.1

To turn off the archive bit, use this command:

`C:\> ` **`ATTRIB -A MYFILE.TXT`**

## CHKDSK *[DRIVE:]* /F /R

Using Windows 2000/XP, the Chkdsk command fixes file system errors and recovers data from bad sectors. Used without any parameters, the Chkdsk command only reports information about a drive and does not make any repairs. However, used with the /F parameter, Chkdsk fixes file system errors it finds. These errors include those in the FAT or MFT caused by clusters marked as being used but not belonging to a particular file (called lost allocation units) and clusters marked as belonging to more than one file (called cross-linked clusters). A lost cluster is one that has no FAT or MFT entry pointing to it, and a cross-linked cluster is one that has two or more FAT or MFT entries pointing to it. (In the sample commands following, we're not showing the command prompt because the default drive and directory are not important.) To check the hard drive for these types of errors and repair them, use this command:

**`CHKDSK C: /F`**

To redirect a report of the findings of the Chkdsk command to a file that you can later print, use this command:

**`CHKDSK C: >Myfile.txt`**

Use the /R parameter of the Chkdsk command to fix file system errors and also examine each sector of the drive for bad sectors, like so:

**`CHKDSK C: /R`**

If Chkdsk finds bad sectors, it attempts to recover the data; it cannot actually repair bad sectors. The Chkdsk command will not fix anything unless the drive is locked, which means the drive has no open files. If you attempt to use Chkdsk with the /F or /R parameter when files are open, Chkdsk tells you of the problem and asks permission to run the next time Windows is restarted.

For Windows 2000/XP, Chkdsk can be used in a Command Prompt window, in the Recovery Console, or from the Windows desktop. (How to use Chkdsk from the Windows 2000/XP desktop is covered later in the chapter along with an expanded explanation of what the utility does and how it works.)

## DEFRAG *[DRIVE:]*/S

The Defrag command examines a hard drive or disk for **fragmented files** (files written to a disk in noncontiguous clusters) and rewrites these files to the disk or drive in contiguous clusters. You use this command to optimize a hard drive's performance.

Use the /S:N parameter to sort the files on the disk in alphabetical order by filename, like so:

**`DEFRAG C: /S:N`**

Use the /S:D parameter to sort the files on the disk by date and time, as shown here:

**`DEFRAG C: /S:D`**

If Defrag discovers a drive does not need defragging, it gives that report and stops. The Defrag command works under Windows 9x/Me and Windows XP. It is not available from the Windows 2000/XP Recovery Console, and the command is not included with Windows 2000. You can also defrag a drive using the Disk Defragmenter utility from the Windows 2000/XP desktop. This utility is covered later in the chapter.

### EDIT [DRIVE:PATH]FILENAME

The Edit program (Edit.com) is a handy, "quick and dirty" way to create and edit text files while working at a command prompt. For example, to create a file named Mybatch.bat in the C:\Data folder, use this command (a discussion of .bat files is coming up):

`C:\> EDIT C:\Data\Mybatch.bat`

If the file does not already exist, Edit creates an empty file. Later, when you exit the Edit editor, changes you made are saved to the newly created file. Figure 13-18 shows the Mybatch.bat file being edited.

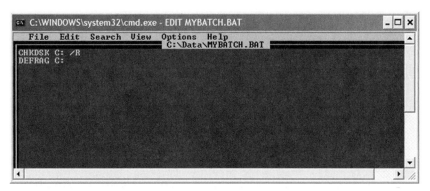

**Figure 13-18** Using the Edit editor to create and edit the Mybatch.bat file

After you have made changes in this window, you can exit the editor this way: Press the **Alt** key to activate the menus, select the **File** menu, and then choose **Exit**. When asked if you want to save your changes, respond **Yes** to exit the editor and save changes. (You can also use your mouse to point to menu options.)

A file with a .bat file extension is called a **batch file**. You can use a batch file to execute a group of commands from a command prompt. To execute the commands stored in the Mybatch.bat file, enter the command Mybatch.bat at a command prompt, as shown in Figure 13-19.

Notice in Figure 13-19 that the Chkdsk command could not run because the system is currently in use. Later in the chapter, you'll learn how to schedule a batch routine to run in the middle of the night when it is unlikely the system will be in use.

> **Notes**
>
> Do not use word-processing software, such as Word or WordPerfect, to edit a batch file unless you save the file as a text (ASCII) file. Word-processing applications use control characters in their document files; these characters keep the OS from interpreting commands in a batch file correctly.

```
C:\WINDOWS\system32\cmd.exe - mybatch.bat                    _ □ x

C:\Data>EDIT MYBATCH.BAT

C:\Data>mybatch.bat

C:\Data>CHKDSK C: /R
The type of the file system is NTFS.
Cannot lock current drive.

Chkdsk cannot run because the volume is in use by another
process.  Would you like to schedule this volume to be
checked the next time the system restarts? (Y/N) n

C:\Data>DEFRAG C:
Windows Disk Defragmenter
Copyright (c) 2001 Microsoft Corp. and Executive Software Interna

Analysis Report
    74.52 GB Total,  42.53 GB (57%) Free,  7% Fragmented (15% fil
>
_
```

**Figure 13-19**   Executing the batch file

## FORMAT *DRIVE:*/V:*LABEL*/Q /FS: *FILESYSTEM*

Recall that you can format a floppy disk using Windows Explorer and you can format a hard drive using Disk Management. In addition, you can use the Format command from a Command Prompt window and from the Windows 2000/XP Recovery Console. Table 13-4 lists various sample uses of the Format command.

| Command | Description |
|---|---|
| Format A: /V:mylabel | Allows you to enter a volume label only once when formatting several disks. The same volume label is used for all disks. A volume label appears at the top of the directory list to help you identify the disk. |
| Format A: /Q | Re-creates the root directory and FATs if you want to quickly format a previously formatted disk that is in good condition. /Q does not read or write to any other part of the disk. |
| Format D: /FS:NTFS | Formats drive D using the NTFS file system. |
| Format D: /FS:FAT32 | Formats drive D using the FAT32 file system. |

**Table 13-4**   Sample usages of the Format command

## TASK SCHEDULER

With the Windows 2000/XP Task Scheduler utility, you can schedule a batch routine, script, or program to run daily, weekly, monthly or at certain events such as startup. Scheduled tasks are stored in the C:\Windows\Tasks folder.

In the following steps, we'll schedule the Mybatch.bat file that you saw created earlier in the chapter to run at 11:59 p.m. every Monday. Recall that we created the Mybatch.bat file using the Edit command. You can also create a batch file using Notepad.

1. Click **Start**, **All Programs** (**Programs** for Windows 2000), point to **Accessories**, **System Tools**, and click **Scheduled Tasks**. The Scheduled Tasks window opens, as shown in Figure 13-20.

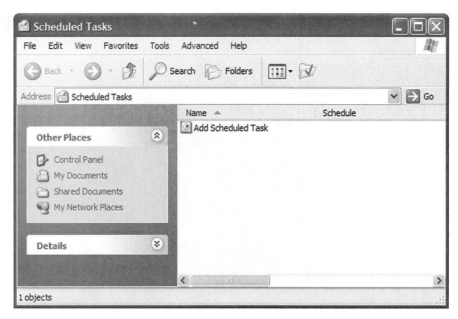

**Figure 13-20** Use the Scheduled Tasks window to add, delete, or change a scheduled task

2. Double-click **Add Scheduled Task**. The Scheduled Task Wizard opens. Click **Next**. To select the program to schedule, click **Browse** and find and click the program file. In our example, we're using the **Mybatch.bat** file in the \Data folder. Click **Open**.

3. Enter a name for the scheduled task and select how often to perform the task, as shown in Figure 13-21, and then click **Next**.

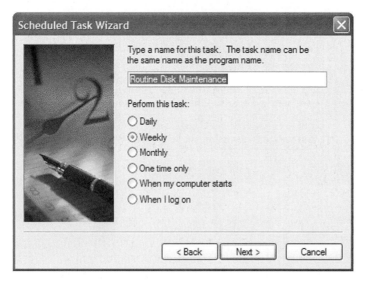

**Figure 13-21** Name the task and select when it will be performed

4. Enter the start time and select the day of the week for the task to execute. For example, enter **11:59 PM every Monday**. Click **Next**.

5. Enter your or another username and the password to this user account. The task will run under this account name. Click **Next**.

6. The wizard reports the scheduled task parameters. Click **Finish**.

A+ ESS
3.4

7. To change settings for a scheduled task, right-click the task and select **Properties** from the shortcut menu. The properties window opens with the name of the task in the title bar of the window, as shown in Figure 13-22. You can use this window to change the initial and advanced settings for a task.

**Figure 13-22**  Advanced settings for a scheduled task

Later, to get a listing of information about scheduled tasks that have already run, open the Scheduled Tasks utility. If the details of previously run tasks are not shown in the window, you can click **View**, **Details**, to display these details.

> **Notes**
>
> Notice in Figure 13-22 the power management options to not run the task when a notebook computer is running on batteries and also the option to power up a system to run the task. This feature requires a motherboard that supports the option for software to power up the PC and the feature is enabled in CMOS setup. To learn if your motherboard supports the feature, see CMOS setup or the motherboard documentation. If not, the PC must be turned on for the scheduler to work.

A+ ESS
6.1
6.2
6.3

A+
220-602
5.2
5.3
6.1
6.2
6.3

## GROUP POLICY

Another way to manage what users can do and how the system can be used is by applying settings from the **Group Policy** console (Gpedit.msc) under Windows XP Professional and Windows 2000 Professional.

Group Policy works by making entries in the registry, applying scripts to the Windows startup, shutdown, and logon processes, and affecting security settings. Group Policy is intended to be used on a domain where group polices are managed by Active Directory, although you can use it on a standalone computer or a computer in a workgroup. Group Policy can be applied to your computer, regardless of the currently logged-on user (called Computer Configuration in the Group Policy console) or can be applied to each

> **Notes**
>
> Windows XP Home Edition does not have the Group Policy console.

A+ ESS
6.1
6.2
6.3

A+
220-602
5.2
5.3
6.1
6.2
6.3

user who logs on (called User Configuration in the Group Policy console). Computer-based policies are applied just before the logon window is displayed, and user-based policies are applied after a user logs on. For a standalone computer or a computer in a workgroup, to control the computer for all users, use Computer Configuration instead of User Configuration to implement Group Policy settings.

To access the Group Policy console, enter **gpedit.msc** in the Run dialog box. Notice in the Group Policy window (see Figure 13-23) the two main groups of policies: Computer Configuration and User Configuration.

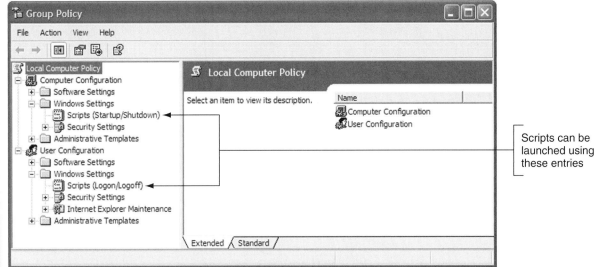

**Figure 13-23**   Using the Group Policy console, you can control many Windows events and settings, including the startup process

Also in Figure 13-23, you can see four ways a script can be launched using Group Policy: at startup, shutdown, when a user logs on, or when a user logs off. Because a script can launch a program, Group Policy can be used to launch a program. These scripts are stored in one of these four folders:

▲ C:\WINDOWS\System32\GroupPolicy\Machine\Scripts\Startup
▲ C:\WINDOWS\System32\GroupPolicy\Machine\Scripts\Shutdown
▲ C:\WINDOWS\System32\GroupPolicy\User\Scripts\Logon
▲ C:\WINDOWS\System32\GroupPolicy\User\Scripts\Logoff

It's important to know about these four folders because malicious software has been known to hide in them. When trying to solve a problem with startup or shutdown, one thing you can do is look in these four folders for any unwanted scripts or programs. You'll learn more about startup and shutdown problems in Chapter 14 and about ridding your system of malicious software in Chapter 19.

To see what Group Policies are currently applied to the system, you can enter the Windows 2000/XP command, **Gpresult.exe**, at a command prompt, or you can use the Windows XP Help and Support Center. To use the Help and Support center, click **Start, Help and Support**. On the right side of the window, click **Use Tools to view your computer information and diagnose problems**. Then, in the left pane, click **Advanced System Information**. Next click **View Group Policy settings applied**. Information is first collected and then the window in Figure 13-24 appears.

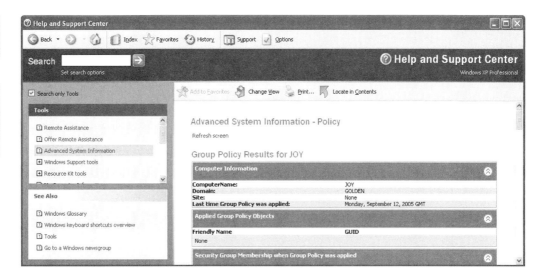

**Figure 13-24** Use the Help and Support Center to view Group Policies currently applied to your system and environment

To add or remove a Group Policy that is executed at startup, open the Group Policy console (Gpedit.msc) and do the following:

1. In the Group Policy window, under either Computer Configuration or User Configuration, open **Administrative Templates**, open **System**, and then open **Logon** (see Figure 13-25).

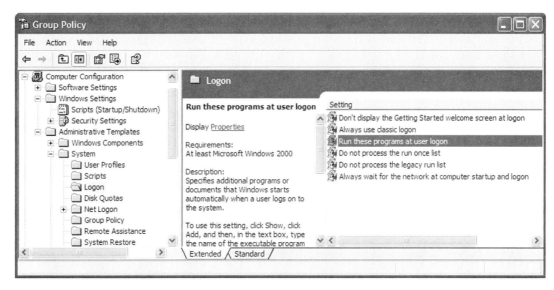

**Figure 13-25** Use Group Policy to launch a program or script at logon

2. In the right pane, double-click **Run these programs at user logon**, which opens the properties window shown on the left side of Figure 13-26. Select **Enabled** and then click **Show**. The Show Contents dialog box opens, which is shown on the right side of Figure 13-26.

3. To add a script or executable program to the list of items to run at logon, click **Add**. In the figure, a batch file has been added so that you can see a sample of a program that will launch at logon. To remove an item from the list, select it and click **Remove**. Click **OK** to close the dialog box and **Apply** to apply the changes. Click **OK** to close the Properties window.

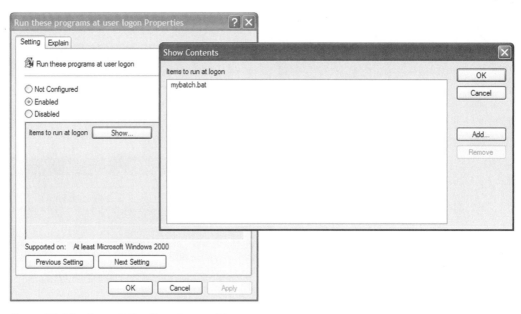

**Figure 13-26** Group Policy items to run at logon

4. To put into effect the changes you have made, reboot the system or enter the command **Gpupdate.exe** at the command prompt.

A+ ESS
3.1

## CONTROLLING THE START MENU

An administrator might want to control the programs that appear on the Start menu for all users. To control the Start menu and the Taskbar, right-click the **Start** button and select **Properties**. The Taskbar and Start Menu Properties window opens, as shown on the left side of Figure 13-27. Click **Customize** to change the items on the Start menu, as shown on the right side of the figure.

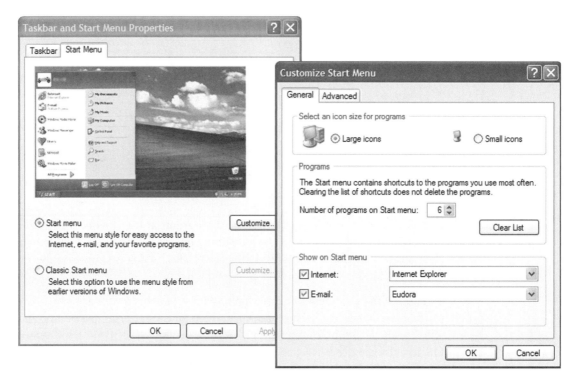

**Figure 13-27** Customize the taskbar and Start menu

A+ ESS
3.1

You can also control items that appear in the Windows XP All Programs menu or the Windows 2000 Programs menu. To do that, right-click the **Start** button and select **Open All Users** from the shortcut menu, as shown in Figure 13-28. The Start Menu folder opens as shown in Figure 13-29. Items in this folder appear at the top of the All Programs or Programs menu. Open the **Programs** folder to view and change items that appear in the lower part of the All Programs or Programs menu.

**Figure 13-28**  Shortcut menu available on the Start button

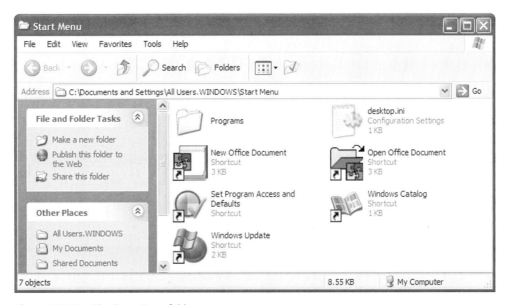

**Figure 13-29**  The Start Menu folder

A+
220-602
3.4

## WINDOWS XP REMOTE ASSISTANCE

Windows XP also offers two new features called Remote Desktop and Remote Assistance. **Remote Desktop** allows a user to connect to and use their Windows XP computer from anywhere on the Internet. You will learn to use Remote Desktop in Chapter 18. Using **Remote Assistance**, a user sitting at the PC can give a support technician at a remote location full access to the desktop. Let's first look at how you as a technician can use Remote Assistance, and then we'll look at what has to be in place before you can use it.

### HOW TO USE REMOTE ASSISTANCE

As a PC support technician, you might be called on to help a Windows XP user over the phone. If you've ever had to work with a novice user in this situation, you know how frustrating this can be. Remote Assistance can help both you and the user through this situation

A+
220-602
3.4

by allowing the user to give you remote control of his or her desktop. As you work, the user can watch the desktop as you solve the problem at hand. As the user watches, it's a good idea to explain what you are doing and why you are doing it so that the user can learn from the experience and be comfortable with what you are doing. As you use Remote Assistance, you can talk with the user over the phone or by a chat window that is part of Remote Assistance.

To use Remote Assistance, the user sends you an invitation to help, and then you accept the invitation and initiate the session. The user then agrees to allow you to connect and must also agree to give you control of his desktop. The user can also require you to enter a password to connect and can put a time limit on when the invitation will expire. In this section, we're assuming that Remote Assistance has already been set up for first use. How to set up Remote Assistance for first use is covered in the next section.

Have the user do the following to send you an invitation:

1. Click **Start, Help and Support**. The Help and Support Center opens (see Figure 13-30). Click **Invite a friend to connect to your computer with Remote Assistance**. On the next window, click **Invite someone to help you**.

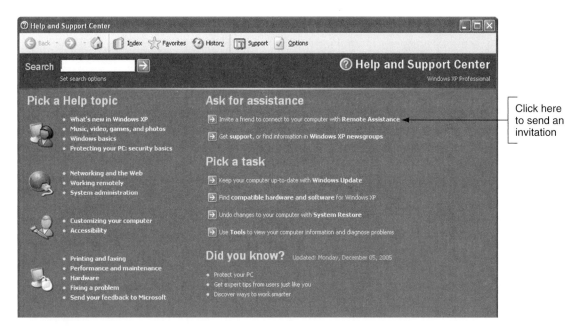

**Figure 13-30** The first step in using Remote Assistance is a user sends an invitation

2. In the next window, shown in Figure 13-31, the user must select how the invitation will be sent. The invitation is actually an encoded file named RcBuddy.MsRcIncident. The user can send the file to you in one of three ways: by using Windows Messenger, by using e-mail, or by saving the file to some location such as a floppy disk or shared folder on a file server. Either way, you must have the file in order to accept the invitation. For the e-mail invitation, the user enters your e-mail address and then clicks **Invite this person**. A box appears allowing the user to enter a text message. The user can enter any text message and then clicks **Continue**.

3. On the next screen, shown in Figure 13-32, the user can set a time limit on the invitation and enter a password that you must use in order to make the connection. The user can tell you the password over the phone. The user then clicks **Send Invitation**.

4. When you receive the e-mail, the invitation is an attached file.

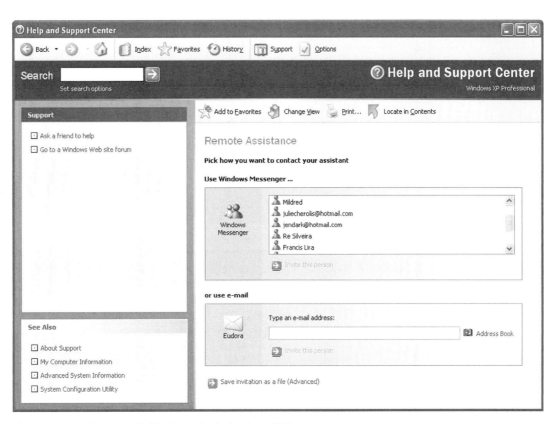

**Figure 13-31** The user decides how the invitation will be sent

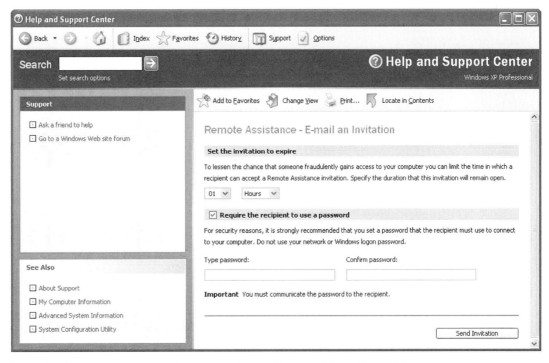

**Figure 13-32** The user can require a password and set a time limit on the invitation

**A+**
**220-602**
**3.4**

The next step is for you to accept the invitation and initiate the session, as follows:

1. Double-click the invitation file. If the user has required a password, a dialog box appears asking for it. Enter the password and click **Yes**.

2. The Remote Assistance window opens on your desktop, similar to the one shown in Figure 13-33. The left pane of the Remote Assistance window shows the chat session that you and the user share for communication. The right pane is the user's desktop just as the user sees it. To take control of the user's desktop, click **Take Control** on the menu.

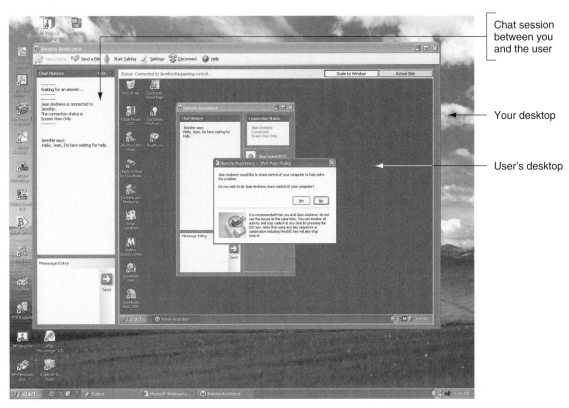

Chat session between you and the user

Your desktop

User's desktop

**Figure 13-33** The Remote Assistance window on the technician's desktop

3. A dialog box appears on the user's screen, as shown in Figure 13-34. When the user clicks **Yes**, you can control the desktop.

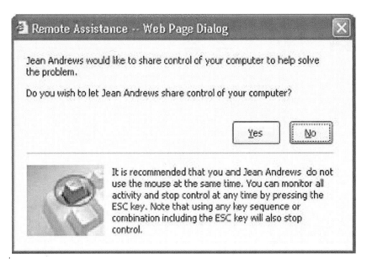

**Figure 13-34** The user must perform this final step of the invitation

A+
220-602
3.4

**4.** The user's desktop looks like the one in Figure 13-35. The Remote Assistance window is displayed with a white chat box on the left side that can be used for the two of you to chat.

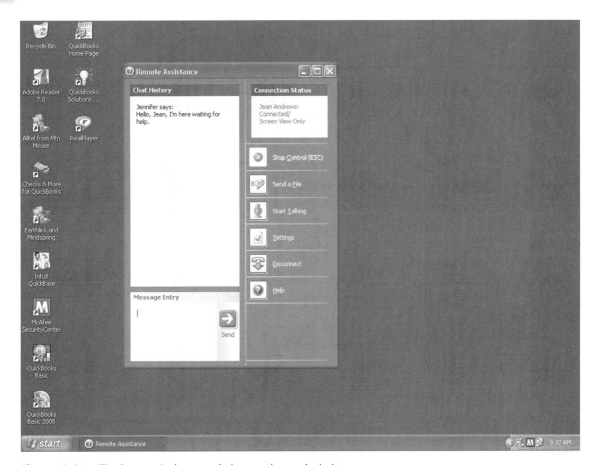

**Figure 13-35** The Remote Assistance window on the user's desktop

**5.** As you work, the user can watch every keystroke and action that you execute on the user's desktop. If the user presses any key, control returns to the user. Either one of you can end the session by clicking **Disconnect**. The invitation can be used more than once until the time limit has expired.

## HOW TO SET UP REMOTE ASSISTANCE FOR FIRST USE

As you have just seen, Remote Assistance is a nifty little tool that can make life easy when it works. It's an especially useful tool in a corporate environment where technical support staff within the company have expected and prepared for Remote Assistance sessions to be used when they support their in-house customers. However, as you're about to see, Remote Assistance is awkward and difficult to use when preparations have not been made in advance and when the user and the technician are connected only by the Internet.

Here is what must happen before Remote Assistance can be used for the first time:

▲ Unless both computers are on the same domain, the technician must have the same user account set up on both computers and this account must have the same password.

A+
220-602
3.4

◢ Remote Assistance must be enabled on the user's computer. To do that, open the System Properties box on the user's computer and select the **Remote** tab (see Figure 13-36). Check **Allow Remote Assistance invitations to be sent from this computer,** and then click **OK.** Some user accounts don't have the privilege of making changes on the System Properties window. If this is the case, the novice user must ask the administrator to enable Remote Assistance on the user's computer.

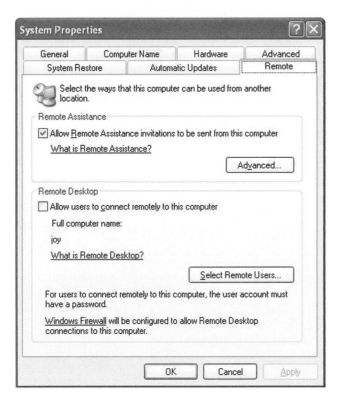

**Figure 13-36**   Remote Assistance must be enabled on the novice user's computer

If you and the user are both on the same local network, you are now ready to create a Remote Assistance session, which should happen with ease. However, if you are connected by way of the Internet, things can get complicated. Here are the concerns:

◢ If the user is behind a hardware or software firewall, the firewall might have to be told to allow a Remote Assistance session. For hardware firewalls, the user must know how to do this, which is different for each device. The user can find the directions in the user manual that came with the firewall and follow these directions.

◢ If you are sitting behind a firewall, you also might have to configure your firewall to allow the Remote Assistance session. How to configure firewalls is covered in Chapter 18.

For a novice user who is already frustrated with a Windows XP problem and is not able to follow directions given by a technician, all this preparation might be too much. You have to judge when Remote Assistance helps and when it just further complicates your situation.

> **✎ Notes**
>
> Several alternatives to Remote Assistance are available. One excellent product is Control-F1 by Blueloop (www.ctrl-f1.co.uk). Using Control-F1, when a technician is in a chat session with a customer somewhere on the Internet, a remote control session can easily be established with a few clicks.

# SUPPORTING HARD DRIVES

Hard drives that are heavily used over time tend to fill up with outdated and unneeded software and data over time. Therefore, they tend to slow down because they are not properly optimized. And inevitably, something is going to go wrong with Windows or the drive itself, and backups will be your only salvation. For all these reasons, a PC support technician needs to know how to perform routine maintenance on a hard drive and show users how to do it, how to configure a hard drive to conserve space, how to keep good backups of user data, and how to recover data when it gets lost or corrupted. All these skills are covered in the following sections of the chapter.

## HARD DRIVE ROUTINE MAINTENANCE TASKS

We now look at three important routine maintenance tasks for hard drives: deleting temporary files, defragging the drive, and scanning it for errors.

### DISK CLEANUP

Temporary or unneeded files accumulate on a hard drive for a variety of reasons. For instance, an installation program might not clean up after itself after it finishes installing an application, and cached Web pages can take up a lot of disk space if you don't have the Internet settings correct. In addition, don't forget about the Recycle Bin; deleted files sit there taking up space until you empty it.

Microsoft says that Windows XP needs at least 318 MB of free hard drive space for normal operation, and the Defrag utility needs at least 15 percent of the hard drive to be free before it can completely defrag a drive. So, it's important to occasionally delete unneeded files. Disk Cleanup (Cleanmgr.exe) is a convenient way to delete temporary files on a hard drive. To access Disk Cleanup under Windows 2000/XP, use one of these two methods:

▲ Enter **Cleanmgr.exe C:** in the Run dialog box and press **Enter**.
▲ Right-click the drive in My Computer or Windows Explorer and select **Properties** from the shortcut menu. The Disk Properties window opens, as shown in Figure 13-37. On the General tab, click **Disk Cleanup**.

Regardless of how you launch the utility, the window in Figure 13-38 opens. From this window, you can select nonessential files to delete in order to save drive space. In addition, Disk Cleanup tells you how much total space you can save and how much space each type of removable file is taking; it also describes each type of file. Included in the list are temporary files created by applications that the applications no longer need.

### DEFRAG AND WINDOWS DISK DEFRAGMENTER

Another problem that might slow down hard drive performance is fragmentation. Recall that a cluster is the smallest unit of space on a hard drive that can hold a file. An OS views a hard drive as a long list of clusters that it can use to hold its data. When several clusters are used to hold a single file, this group of clusters is called a **chain**. **Fragmentation** occurs when a single file is placed in clusters that are not right next to each other.

After many files have been deleted and added to a drive, files become fragmented. On a well-used hard drive, it is possible to have a file stored in clusters at 40 or more locations. Fragmentation is undesirable because when the OS has to access many different locations on the drive to read a file, access time slows down. In addition, if the file becomes corrupted, recovery utilities are less likely to be able to find all the clusters of this file if the file is fragmented rather than located on the drive in one continuous chain.

A+ ESS
3.1
3.2
3.3
3.4

A+
220-602
3.1
3.2
3.4

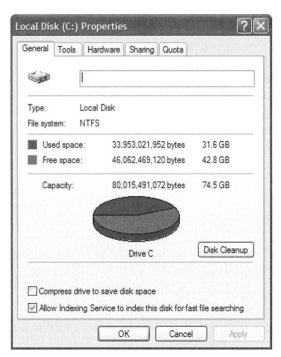

**Figure 13-37**  The Disk Properties window

**Figure 13-38**  Disk Cleanup is a quick-and-easy way to delete temporary files on a hard drive

To reduce fragmentation of the drive, you can **defragment** the hard drive periodically. You should defragment your hard drive at a minimum of every six months, and ideally every month, as part of a good maintenance plan.

Here are the different ways to defrag a drive:

▲ For Windows 2000 or Windows XP, to use Disk Defragmenter, first close all open applications. Then choose **Start, All Programs** (**Programs** for Windows 2000),

**Accessories**, and **System Tools**. Then click **Disk Defragmenter**. From the Disk Defragmenter window (see Figure 13-39), you can select a drive and defragment it.

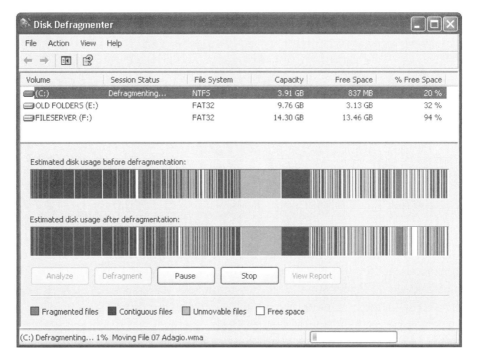

**Figure 13-39** Windows XP defragmenting a volume

- Enter **Dfrg.msc** in the Run dialog box and press **Enter**.
- For Windows XP, recall from earlier in the chapter, the Defrag command (**Defrag.exe**) can be used from a command prompt. Enter Defrag *X*:, where *X*: is the logical drive you want to defrag.

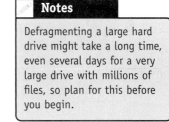

**Notes**

Defragmenting a large hard drive might take a long time, even several days for a very large drive with millions of files, so plan for this before you begin.

Generally, defragmenting a hard drive should be done when the hard drive is healthy; that is, it should be done as part of routine maintenance. If you get an error message when attempting to defrag, try the utilities discussed in the following sections to repair the hard drive and then try to defrag again.

## CHKDSK AND ERROR CHECKING

Recall from earlier in the chapter that you can use the Chkdsk command to repair hard drive errors. The utility is also available from the Windows 2000/XP desktop. Before we see how to use the desktop utility, you might be interested in knowing exactly what the utility is doing.

Recall that a directory or folder on a floppy disk or hard drive contains a list of all the files in that directory or folder. Also recall that for the FAT file system, the FAT contains a long list of cells, one cell for each cluster on the drive. For each file in a directory, the directory entry contains the cluster number for the first cluster used to hold the file. For example, in Figure 13-40, a directory contains four files. File 1 starts in cluster 4 on the drive and uses eight clusters (clusters 4, 5, 6, 7, 22, 23, 24, and 25). In the figure, you can see the directory entry for File 1 contains a 4 that indicates the file begins in cluster 4.

A+ ESS
3.1
3.2
3.3
3.4

A+
220-602
3.1
3.2
3.4

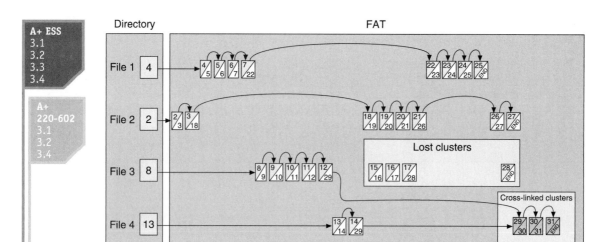

**Figure 13-40**   Lost and cross-linked clusters

To know which other clusters are used for the file, you would have to turn to the FAT because each cell in the FAT contains a pointer to the next cluster used by the file, forming a cluster chain. In Figure 13-40, each box in the FAT represents a cluster on the drive. The top number in the box represents the position of the cell in the FAT and, therefore, the cluster on the drive. For example, for the first box of File 1, the 4 says this box is in the fourth position in the FAT and represents the fourth cluster on the drive. The bottom number in the box is what is actually written in the FAT cell and is a pointer to the next cluster on the drive in the file chain. In the first box of File 1, the bottom number is a 5, indicating the next cluster used by the file is the fifth cluster on the drive. The fifth cell contains a 6, meaning the next cluster used by the file is the sixth cluster on the drive. The sixth cell entry contains a 7. The seventh cluster entry contains a 22 and so forth, until the 25th cell contains an end-of-file marker indicating the file ends with cluster 25. Therefore, the FAT holds the map or chain to all the other clusters in the file.

Occasionally, the chain of entries in the FAT becomes corrupted, resulting either in lost clusters or cross-linked clusters, as shown in Figure 13-40. In the figure, the chain of FAT entries for File 3 has lost track of its clusters and points to a cluster chain that belongs to File 4. Clusters 29 through 31 are called **cross-linked clusters** because more than one chain points to them, and clusters 15 through 17 and 28 are called **lost clusters** or **lost allocation units** because no chain in the FAT points to them. Using the NTFS file system, the same types of errors—cross-linked and lost clusters—can occur inside the master file table (MFT).

Another problem that can occur with hard drives is bad sectors. Bad sectors are caused by a corrupted area on the hard drive that is not able to consistently keep data. If Event Viewer reports many read or write errors to a drive, suspect many sectors are going bad and it's time to replace the drive. Chkdsk cannot actually repair a bad sector, but it might be able to recover the data stored in one.

Using Windows 2000/XP, searching for and repairing file system errors and bad sectors can be done using two different methods. Both methods launch the same utility, Chkdsk.exe, and are described in the following list:

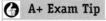 **A+ Exam Tip**

The A+ Essentials exam expects you to know how to check a disk for errors using Windows 2000/XP Chkdsk.

▲ *Error Checking from the Windows desktop.* Open Windows Explorer or My Computer, right-click the drive, and select **Properties** from the shortcut menu.

A+ ESS
3.1
3.2
3.3
3.4

A+
220-602
3.1
3.2
3.4

Click the **Tools** tab, as shown in the left window in Figure 13-41, and then click **Check Now**. The Check Disk dialog box opens, as shown on the right side of Figure 13-41. Check the **Automatically fix file system errors** and **Scan for and attempt recovery of bad sectors** check boxes, and then click **Start**. For the utility to correct errors on the drive, it needs exclusive use of all files on the drive, which Windows calls a locked drive. If files are open, a dialog box opens telling you about the problem and asking your permission to scan the drive the next time Windows starts.

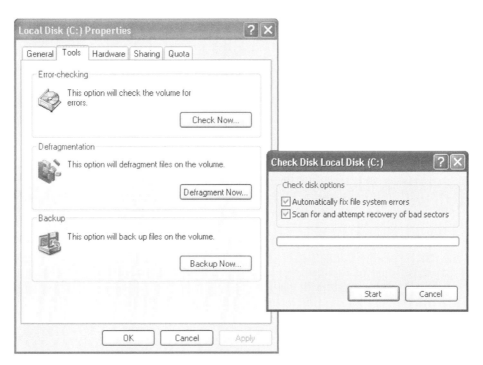

**Figure 13-41** Windows XP repairs hard drive errors under the drive's Properties window using Windows Explorer

▲ *The Windows 2000/XP Chkdsk command.* You learned how to use the Chkdsk command earlier in the chapter. You can use it from a Command Prompt window or from the Recovery Console.

Scanning the entire hard drive for bad sectors can take a long time and must be done when the computer is not in use so that the hard drive can be locked down (that is, have no files open) for the entire process. In other words, start the job and then expect a long wait until it's done.

## CONSERVING HARD DRIVE SPACE

A+
220-602
3.1
3.2
3.4
5.2
6.1

Besides cleaning the hard drive of unneeded files, two other ways to conserve hard drive space are to implement disk, folder, or file compression and to use disk quotas. Both conservation methods are discussed in this section.

### DISK, FOLDER, AND FILE COMPRESSION

Compressing files, folders, or entire volumes reduces the hard drive space required for data and software. As such, using compression can help meet the ever-increasing demand for

more space on hard drives. For instance, software packages requiring 200 to 250 MB of hard drive space were unheard of three or four years ago, but these space requirements are now quite common. Although hard drive sizes have increased as well, we often seek ways to cram still more data onto nearly full hard drives.

**Compression** software works under Windows 2000/XP at the file, folder, or volume level by rewriting data in files in a mathematically coded format that uses less space. Using the NTFS file system in Windows 2000/XP, you can compress a single file or folder or you can compress the entire NTFS volume.

> **Notes**
>
> Windows 2000/XP does not support compression for FAT32 volumes.

When you place a file or folder on a NTFS compressed volume, it will be compressed automatically. When you open a compressed file that is stored on a compressed volume, it will be decompressed automatically and then will be recompressed when you save it back to the compressed volume.

To compress an NTFS volume:

1. Open Windows Explorer or My Computer.

2. Locate and right-click the root folder for the volume you want to compress. For example, to compress drive C, in Windows Explorer, right-click **Local Disk (C:)** and select **Properties** from the shortcut menu. The Properties dialog box opens.

3. Click the **General** tab, as shown in Figure 13-42. This window displays the file system used (NTFS), the capacity of the volume, and the amount of free space. To compress the volume, check the **Compress drive to save disk space** check box, and then click **Apply**.

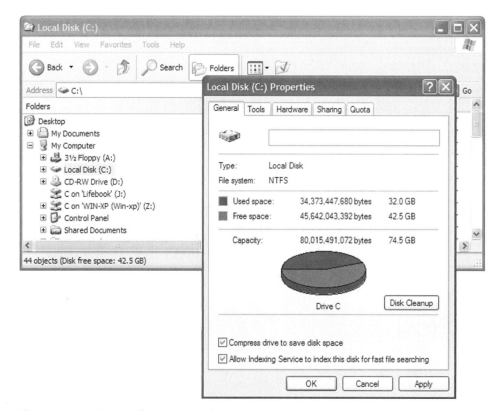

**Figure 13-42** Compressing an NTFS volume

4. The Confirm Attribute Changes dialog box opens. Indicate whether you want to compress only the root folder or the entire volume, and then click **OK** to begin compression.

To compress a single folder or file on a Windows 2000/XP NTFS volume, right-click the folder or file and select **Properties** from the shortcut menu. Click the **General** tab, and then click **Advanced**. In the Advanced Attributes dialog box, check the **Compress contents to save disk space** check box (see Figure 13-43).

> **Notes**
>
> The Disk Properties window for a FAT32 volume under Windows 2000/XP does not display the check box to compress the volume.

**Figure 13-43** Compress a folder using the Advanced Attributes dialog box for the folder

## DISK QUOTAS

To limit how much disk space a user account can access, an administrator can set **disk quotas**. This is important when two or more users are using a single computer and need to share its storage capacity. A disk quota does not specify where a user's files must be located; it just specifies how much total space the user can take up on a volume. The disk quota set applies to all users accounts. You can only set disk quotas if you are using NTFS.

> **Notes**
>
> For a FAT32 volume, files and folders cannot be compressed; as such, the General tab does not have an Advanced button. For these volumes, you can use a third-party file compression utility such as WinZip.

> **Notes**
>
> Windows 2000/XP volume, folder, and file compression can also be done using the Compact command at the command prompt, which executes the program file, Compact.exe.

A+ ESS
3.1
3.2
3.3
3.4

A+
220-602
3.1
3.2
3.4
5.2
6.1

# APPLYING | CONCEPTS

To set disk quotas so that users cannot exceed the specified disk space, do the following:

1. Log on as an administrator, and open **My Computer** or **Windows Explorer**.

2. Find the partition on which you want to set a disk quota. Right-click it and select **Properties** on the shortcut menu.

3. Click the **Quota** tab and the **Enable quota management** check box, as shown in Figure 13-44.

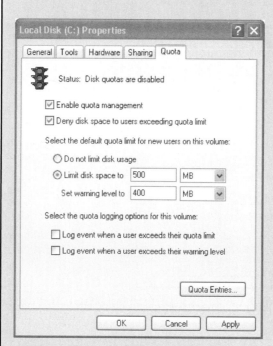

**Figure 13-44** Setting disk quotas

4. To stop a user from using space beyond the quota, check **Deny disk space to users exceeding quota limit**.

5. To set the quota for disk space used, click the **Limit disk space to** radio button, and then enter the value in the two boxes next to it. (In our example, disk space is limited to 500 MB.)

6. In the box next to **Set warning level to**, enter the warning level value (**400 MB** in our example). This warns users when they have used 400 MB of their allotted 500 MB of storage space.

7. So that you can monitor disk drive use and know when users have reached their warning levels, check **Log event when a user exceeds their quota limit** and check **Log event when a user exceeds their warning level**. Later, you can click **Quota Entries** to view these logged entries.

8. Click **OK**. You are prompted to enable disk quotas, as shown in Figure 13-45. Click **OK** to respond to the prompt.

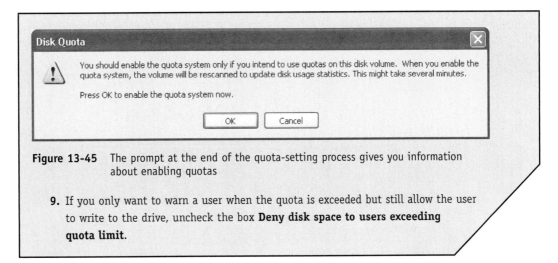

**Figure 13-45** The prompt at the end of the quota-setting process gives you information about enabling quotas

9. If you only want to warn a user when the quota is exceeded but still allow the user to write to the drive, uncheck the box **Deny disk space to users exceeding quota limit**.

## MAKING BACKUPS

A backup is an extra copy of a data or software file that you can use if the original file becomes damaged or destroyed. Losing data due to system failure, a virus, file corruption, or some other problem really makes you appreciate the importance of having backups. In the previous chapter, you learned how to back up system files and even the entire hard drive. This section of the chapter focuses on backing up data files and other user files.

> **Notes**
>
> With data and software, here's a good rule of thumb: If you can't get along without it, back it up.

**APPLYING|CONCEPTS** Dave was well on his way to building a successful career as a PC repair technician. His PC repair shop was doing well and he was excited about his future. But one bad decision changed everything. He was called to repair a server at a small accounting firm. The call was on the weekend when he was normally off, so he was in a hurry to get the job done. He arrived at the accounting firm and saw that the problem was an easy one to fix, so he decided not to do a backup before working on the system. During his repairs, the hard drive crashed and all data on the drive was lost—four million dollars worth! The firm sued, Dave's business license was stripped, and he was ordered to pay the money the company lost. A little extra time to back up the system would have saved his whole future. True story!

Because most of us routinely write data to the hard drive, in this section, we focus on backing up from the hard drive to another media. However, when you store important data on any media such as a flash drive, external hard drive, or floppy disk, always keep a second copy of the data on another media. Never trust important data to only one media.

The following sections cover how to devise a disaster recovery plan, how to make backups, and how to restore data from those backups.

## PLANNING FOR DISASTER RECOVERY

The time to prepare for disaster is before it occurs. If you have not prepared, the damage from a disaster will most likely be greater than if you had made and followed disaster plans. Suppose the hard drive on your PC stopped working and you lost all its data. What would be the impact? Are you prepared for this to happen? Consider these points and tips when making your backup and recovery plans:

▲ Decide on the backup media (tape, CD, DVD, flash drive, another hard drive, or other media). Even though it's easy to do, don't make the mistake of backing up your data to another partition or folder on your same hard drive. When a hard drive crashes, most likely all partitions go down together and you will have lost your data and your backup. Back up to another media and, for extra safety, store it at an off-site location.

▲ Windows 2000/XP offers the Ntbackup.exe program to back up files and folders. However, you can purchase third-party backup software that might be easier to use and offer more features. Also, you can purchase an external hard drive like the one by Kanguru (*www.kanguru.com*) shown in Figure 13-46 that comes with its own backup software. External hard drives use a USB, Firewire, or eSATA port. You can schedule the software to automatically back up to the drive on a regular basis or you can manually create a backup at any time. However, before you decide to use an all-in-one backup system such as this one, be certain you understand the risks of not keeping backups at an off-site location and keeping all your backups on a single media.

**Figure 13-46** This external hard drive by Kanguru uses a USB port and comes bundled with backup software

▲ Because backing up data takes time and backup media is expensive, you can use a selective backup plan where you only back up data that changes often. For example, you might ask users to store all their data in certain folders and then you only maintain current backups of these folders rather than back up an entire hard drive. Also, scheduled backups that run during the night are the least disruptive for users.

▲ Data should be backed up after about every four to ten hours of data entry. This might mean you back up once a day, once a week, or once a month.

▲ So that you'll have the right information when you need to recover data from your backups, always record your regular backups in a log with the following information:
    ▲ Folders or drives backed up
    ▲ Date of the backup
    ▲ Type of backup
    ▲ Label identifying the tape, disk, or other media

If you discover that data has been lost days or weeks ago, you can use this backup log or table to help you recover the data. Keep the records in a notebook. You can

A+ ESS
3.1
3.2
3.3
3.4
6.1
6.2
6.3

A+
220-602
3.1
3.2
3.4

also store the records in a log file (a file where events are logged or recorded) each time you back up. Store the file on a floppy disk or another PC. Figure 13-47 shows one example of a backup log table.

| Folder backed up | Date | Type of backup | Tape label |
|---|---|---|---|
| C:\Payroll | 2006-06-02 | Full | June, First Friday |
| C:\Payroll | 2006-06-05 | Incremental | Monday |
| C:\Payroll | 2006-06-06 | Incremental | Tuesday |
| C:\Payroll | 2006-06-07 | Incremental | Wednesday |
| C:\Payroll | 2006-06-08 | Incremental | Thursday |
| C:\Payroll | 2006-06-09 | Full | June, Second Friday |
| C:\Payroll | 2006-06-12 | Incremental | Monday |

**Figure 13-47**  Keeping backup logs can help you know how to recover data

◢ When you perform a backup for the first time or set up a scheduled backup, verify that you can use the backup tape or disks to successfully recover the data. This is a very important step in preparing to recover lost data. After you create a backup, erase a file on the hard drive, and use the recovery procedures to verify that you can re-create the file from the backup. This verifies that the backup medium works, that the recovery software is effective, and that you know how to use it. After you are convinced that the recovery works, document how to perform it.

---

**Notes**

If you travel a lot and your organization doesn't provide online backup, keeping good backups of data on your notebook computer might be a problem. Several Internet companies have solved this backup-on-the-go problem by providing remote backup services over the Internet. In a hotel room or other remote location, connect to the Internet and back up your data to a Web site's file server. If data is lost, you can easily recover it by connecting to the Internet and logging into your backup service Web site. If security is a concern, be sure you understand the security guarantees of the site. Two online backup services are @Backup (*www.backup.com*) and Remote Backup Systems (*www.remote-backup.com*).

---

## HOW TO BACK UP DATA

To perform a backup using Ntbackup.exe under Windows 2000/XP, follow these steps:

1. Click **Start**, point to **All Programs** (**Programs** for Windows 2000), point to **Accessories**, point to **System Tools**, and then click **Backup**. The Backup Wizard appears. Click **Advanced Mode**.

2. The Backup utility opens. Click the **Backup** tab. Your screen should look like Figure 13-48. If you want to perform a backup immediately, check the drive and subfolders to back up.

3. In the lower-left corner of the Backup Utility window, note the text box labeled Backup media or filename, which specifies where to back up to. To change this location, click the **Browse** button. The Save As dialog box appears. Navigate to the drive and path where you'd like to save the backup file and enter a name for the file. Click **Save**. The new path and name for the backup file appear in the text box.

4. Click the **Start Backup** button in the lower-right corner to perform the backup.

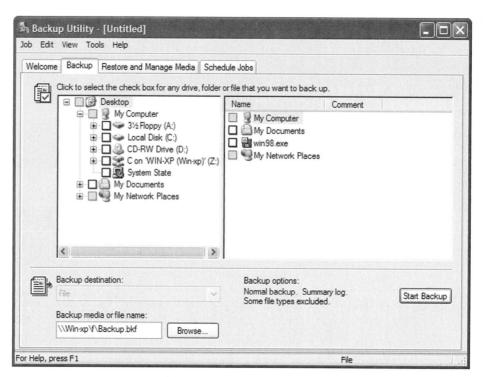

**Figure 13-48**   You can perform an immediate backup from the Backup tab

You can schedule a single backup to be done at a later time or repeated on a schedule until you terminate the schedule. When planning routinely scheduled backups, you have some options so that you don't have to back up everything at each backup. It's a lot less expensive and less time-consuming to only back up what's changed since the last backup. Windows 2000/XP offers these options for scheduled backups:

▲ *Full backup (also called a normal backup).* All files selected for backup are copied to the backup media. Each file is marked as backed up by clearing its archive attribute. Later, if you need to recover data, this full backup is all you need. (After the backup, if a file is changed, its archive attribute is turned on to indicate the file has changed since its last backup.)

▲ *Copy backup.* All files selected for backup are copied to the backup media, but files are not marked as backed up (meaning file archive attributes are not cleared). A Copy backup is useful if you want to make a backup apart from your regularly scheduled backups.

▲ *Incremental backup.* All files that have been created or changed since the last backup are backed up, and all files are marked as backed up (meaning file archive attributes are cleared). Later, if you need to recover data, you'll need the last full backup and all the incremental backups since this last full backup.

▲ *Differential backup.* All files that have been created or changed since the last full or incremental backup are backed up, and files are not marked as backed up. Later, if you need to recover data, you'll need the last full backup and the last differential backup.

▲ *Daily backup.* All files that have been created or changed on this day are backed up. Files are not marked as backed up. Later, if you need to recover data, you'll need the last full backup and all daily backups since this last full backup.

A+ ESS
3.1
3.2
3.3
3.4
6.1
6.2
6.3

A+
220-602
3.1
3.2
3.4

The two best ways to schedule backups are a combination of full backups and incremental backups, or a combination of full backups and differential backups. When using incremental backups, because they are smaller than differential backups, you save time and money when backing up. On the other hand, recovering data is less time-consuming when using differential backups because you only need two backups to perform a full recovery (the last full backup and the last differential backup.)

For a business with heavy data entry, suppose you decide you need to back up every night at 11:55. To implement this backup plan, you might decide to schedule two backups: A full backup each Friday at 11:55 P.M., and a differential backup each Monday, Tuesday, Wednesday, and Thursday at 11:55 P.M. In a project at the end of this chapter, you'll learn how you can reuse tapes on a rotating basis for a backup plan similar to this one.

### Notes

When making your backup plan, for extra protection, take into account that you might want to keep several generations of backups on hand. If you always overwrite the backup with a new backup, you only have one generation of backups. However, sometimes a file gets corrupted or accidentally deleted and you don't discover the problem for several weeks. If you don't keep several generations of backups, you will have no chance of recovering the data. On the other hand, if you back up weekly and keep the last 10 weeks of backups, you can go back and search previous backups to recover the file.

To schedule a backup, do the following:

1. Begin by clicking the **Schedule Jobs** tab, as shown in Figure 13-49. Select a date on which you want to schedule a backup, and then click the **Add Job** button.

2. The Backup Wizard opens. On the first screen, click **Next**. Select **Back up selected files, drives, or network data**, and then click **Next**.

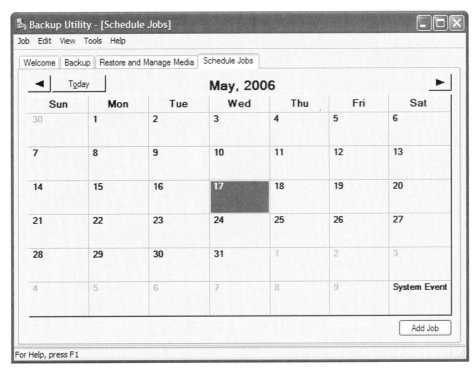

**Figure 13-49** The Schedule Jobs tab of the Windows 2000/XP Backup Utility window

3. On the next screen, select the drives, folders, or files you want to back up, and then click **Next**.

4. Follow the steps through the wizard to choose where you want to save your backup, give a name to the backup, and select the type of backup (Normal, Copy, Incremental, Differential, or Daily). Note that a Normal backup is a full backup.

5. Then you are asked if you want to verify the data after backup and compress the data. Next, you must decide if you want to append the data to an existing backup or replace an existing backup. Your decision largely depends on how much space you have available for backups.

6. When asked if you want to perform the backup now or later, select **Later** and give the backup a name, as shown on the left side of Figure 13-50. Click the **Set Schedule** button.

7. The Schedule Job window appears, as shown on the right side of Figure 13-50. Schedule how often the backup is to occur, and then click **OK**. Notice in the figure, a backup is scheduled for each Monday, Tuesday, Wednesday, and Thursday at 11:55 P.M.

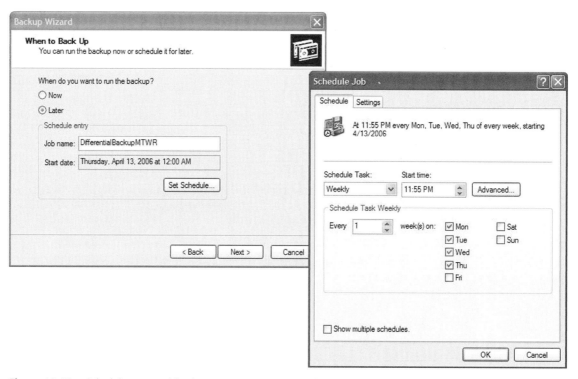

**Figure 13-50**  Schedule repeated backups

8. Click **Next** in the wizard, and follow the remaining instructions to complete the backup. At the end of the process, the wizard gives you an onscreen report summarizing information about the backup.

Besides the folders that contain documents, spreadsheets, databases, and other data files, you also might want to back up these folders:

▲ *E-mail messages and address book.* For Outlook and Outlook Express, back up this folder: C:\Documents and Settings\\*username*\Local Settings\Application Data\Microsoft\Outlook.

▲ *Internet Explorer favorites list.* To back up an IE favorites list, back up this folder: C:\Documents and Settings\\*username*\Favorites.

A+ ESS
3.1
3.2
3.3
3.4
6.1
6.2
6.3

A+
220-602
3.1
3.2
3.4

## RESTORING DATA FROM BACKUPS

To recover files, folders, or the entire drive from backup using the Windows 2000/XP Backup utility, click the **Restore and Manage Media** tab on the Backup Utility window, and then select the backup job to use for the restore. The Backup utility displays the folders and files that were backed up with this job. You can select the ones that you want to restore. When you restore from backup, you'll lose all the data you've entered in restored files since the backup, so be sure to use the most recent backup and then re-enter the data that's missing.

**Notes**

By default, Windows XP Home Edition does not include the Backup utility. To install it manually, go to the \VALUEADD\ MSFT\NTBACKUP folder on your Windows XP setup CD and double-click **Ntbackup.msi**. The installation wizard will complete the installation.

If you are faced with the problem of lost or corrupted data and you don't have a current backup, you still might be able to recover the lost data. Some available options are discussed next.

A+ ESS
1.3
3.3

A+
220-602
3.3

## SOLVING HARD DRIVE PROBLEMS

Although the hard drive itself is a hardware component, problems with hard drives can be caused by software as well. Problems can also be categorized as those that prevent the hard drive from booting and those that prevent data from being accessed. In this section, you will learn about hardware and software problems that prevent data from being accessed. In the next chapter, you'll learn about what to do when you cannot boot from the hard drive.

### START WITH THE END USER

When an end user brings a problem to you, begin the troubleshooting process by interviewing the user. When you interview the user, you might want to include these questions:

- ◢ Can you describe the problem and show me how to reproduce it?
- ◢ Was the computer recently moved?
- ◢ Was any new hardware or software recently installed?
- ◢ Was any software recently reconfigured or upgraded?
- ◢ Did someone else use your computer recently?
- ◢ Does the computer have a history of similar problems?
- ◢ Can you show me how to reproduce the problem?

After you gather this basic information, you can begin diagnosing and addressing the hard drive problems.

### PRIORITIZE WHAT YOU HAVE LEARNED

If a hard drive is not functioning and data is not accessible, setting priorities helps focus your work. For most users, data is the first priority unless they have a recent backup. Software can also be a priority if it is not backed up. Reloading software from the original installation disks or CD can be time-consuming, especially if the configuration is complex or you have written software macros or scripts but did not back them up.

If you have good backups of both data and software, hardware might be your priority. It could be expensive to replace, but downtime can be costly, too. The point is, when trouble arises, determine your main priority and start by focusing on that. If your first priority is solving the problem at hand, as with all computer problems, begin troubleshooting by making an initial determination that the problem is software or hardware related.

A+ ESS
1.3
3.3

A+
220-602
3.3

**Notes**

Know your limitations. After making a reasonable and diligent effort to resolve a problem, getting the problem fixed could become more important than resolving it yourself. There comes a time when you might need to turn the problem over to a more experienced technician.

## USE ALL AVAILABLE RESOURCES

A smart technician is aware of the resources available to help solve a problem. As you are troubleshooting a PC problem, consider the following:

◢ You can use Disk Management to check partitions or Task Manager to look for a process that is a bottleneck for hard drive, memory, or CPU activity. To check for excessive reads and writes to the hard drive, in Task Manager, select the **Processes** tab and click **View, Select Columns**. The Select Columns dialog box appears (see Figure 13-51).

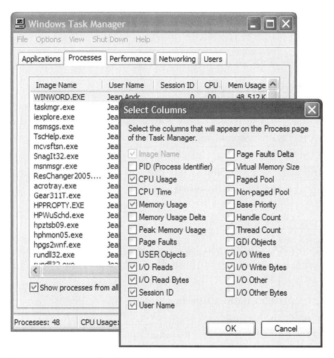

**Figure 13-51** Selecting columns for the Processes tab of Task Manager

Check the four I/O read and write entries and click **OK**. You can then search for applications that are causing excessive reading and writing to the drive, as shown in Figure 13-52.

◢ Documentation often lists error messages and their meanings.

◢ The Internet can also help you diagnose hardware and software problems. Go to the Microsoft Web site for help with Windows or another Web site of a product manufacturer, and search for the FAQs (frequently asked questions) list or bulletin board. It's likely that others have encountered the same problem and posted the question and answer. If you search and cannot find your answer, you can post a new question.

◢ Technical support from the hard drive manufacturer can help you interpret an error message, or it can provide general support in diagnosing a problem. Most technical support is available during working hours by telephone. Check your documentation for telephone numbers. An experienced computer troubleshooter once said, "The people who solve computer problems do it by trying something and making phone calls,

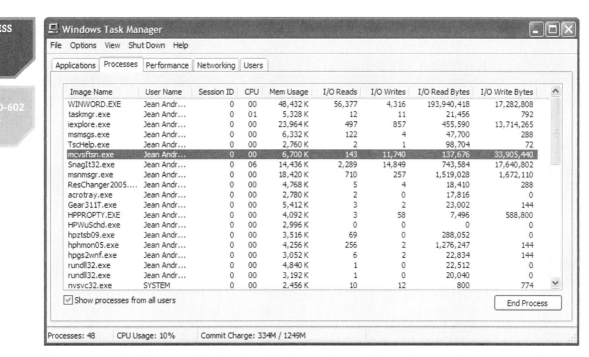

**Figure 13-52** Look for an application that might be causing slow drive performance by excessive reading and writing to the hard drive

trying something else and making more phone calls, and so on, until the problem is solved."

Third-party utility software can be a great help when solving hard drive problems. The following list describes some of those utility programs and tells you what to expect from them when a hard drive fails. Note that these are *not* complete listings of the utility software functions, nor of all available software. See specific software documentation for more details.

▲ *Norton Utilities* by Symantec (*www.symantec.com*) offers several easy-to-use tools to prevent damage to a hard drive, recover data from a damaged hard drive, and improve system performance. Many functions of these tools have been taken over and improved by utilities included with recent versions of Windows. The most commonly used Norton Utilities tools now are the recovery tools. Two examples are Norton Disk Doctor, which automatically repairs many hard drive and floppy disk problems, and UnErase Wizard, which allows you to retrieve accidentally deleted files. When using Norton Utilities, be certain you use the version of the software for the operating system you have installed. Using Norton with the wrong OS can do damage.

▲ *PartitionMagic* by Symantec (*www.symantec.com*) lets you manage partitions on a hard drive more quickly and easily than with Fdisk for Windows 9x/Me or Disk Management for Windows NT/2000/XP. You can create new partitions, change the size of partitions, and move partitions without losing data or moving the data to another hard drive while you work. You can switch file systems without disturbing your data, and you can hide and show partitions to secure your data.

▲ *SpinRite* by Gibson Research (*www.grc.com*) is hard drive utility software that has been around for years. Still a DOS application without a sophisticated GUI interface, SpinRite has been updated to adjust to new drive technologies. It supports FAT32,

A+ ESS
1.3
3.3

A+
220-602
3.3

NTFS, SCSI, Zip drives, and Jaz drives. You can boot your PC from a floppy disk and run SpinRite from a floppy, which means that it doesn't require much system overhead. Because it is written in a language closer to the binary code that the computer understands, it is more likely to detect underlying hard drive problems than software that uses Windows, which can stand as a masking layer between the software and the hard drive. SpinRite analyzes the entire hard drive surface, performing data recovery of corrupted files and file system information. Sometimes, SpinRite can recover data from a failing hard drive when other software fails.

▲ *GetDataBack* by Runtime Software (*www.runtime.org*) can recover data and program files even when Windows cannot recognize the drive. It can read FAT and NTFS file systems and can solve problems with a corrupted partition table, boot record, or root directory.

▲ *Hard drive manufacturer's diagnostic software* is available for download from the Web site of many hard drive manufacturers. For example, Maxtor's diagnostic software is PowerMax (*www.maxtor.com*). Download the software and use it to create a bootable diagnostic floppy disk. You can then boot from the floppy and use it to examine a Maxtor hard drive for errors and, if necessary, low-level format the drive.

> **Notes**
>
> Always check compatibility between utility software and the operating system with which you plan to use it. One place you can check for compatibility is the service and support section of the software manufacturer's Web site.

## HOW TO RECOVER LOST DATA

If a hard drive is giving problems, and you need to recover lost data, don't write anything to the drive until you have copied the data to another media. If the file system is giving errors, it can write to the very area where the lost data is stored. Once the data is overwritten, it is almost impossible to recover it unless you pay for very expensive data recovery services. If a data file is lost, accidentally deleted, or corrupted, but you can still boot to the Windows desktop, do the following to recover the data:

▲ *Try treating a corrupted file as a text file.* If a data file that is used by an application is corrupted, try changing its file extension to .txt and importing the file into the application as a text file. Using this method, if the file header is damaged, you might be able to recover at least part of the file.

▲ *Restore the file from backups.* Do you have a backup of the file? How to restore files from backups is covered earlier in the chapter.

▲ *Check the Recycle Bin.* The file might be there. If you find it, right-click the file and select Restore from the shortcut menu.

▲ *Use commands from a Command Prompt window.* Use the CD command to go to the folder where the file is supposed to be. Then try using the Windows XP Recover command to recover the file. For Windows 2000, try to use the Copy command to copy the file to another media.

▲ *Try data recovery software.* If you are still not able to recover the file, go to the Web site of a data recovery service. Sometimes you can run a utility on the Web site to search for the file and tell you if the software on the site can help you. If the utility says it can recover your file, you can purchase the software to do the job. On the Internet, do a search on "data recovery" for lots of examples.

13

▲ *Consider a data recovery service.* These services are expensive, but might be worth the expense for important data. To find a service, do a Google search on "data recovery." Before engaging a service, be sure to get good recommendations and read some reviews about the service. Before you agree to the service, understand the guarantees and expenses.

If the hard drive will not boot and your first priority is to recover the data, do the following:

▲ Use the Recovery Console to boot the system and copy the data from the hard drive to another media. The Recovery Console is covered in the next chapter.
▲ Following safety procedures discussed in other chapters, carefully remove the hard drive from the computer case. Use a USB to IDE converter to connect the drive to the USB port on a working computer (see Figure 13-53). You can then use Windows Explorer on the working computer to locate and copy the data to the primary hard drive.

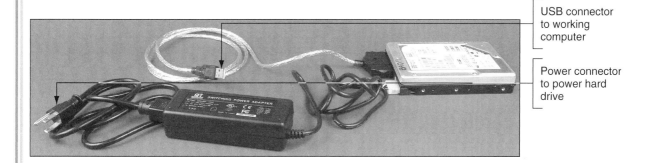

**Figure 13-53**   Connect the hard drive to a working computer using its USB port

▲ If Windows Explorer can't find the data, try using data recovery software to recover the data.
▲ If the hard drive is so damaged that data recovery software doesn't help, try downloading diagnostic software from the hard drive manufacturer's Web site to test the drive and possibly repair it.
▲ Consider a data recovery service. As said earlier, be sure to use a reliable one and understand the expenses and guarantees before you agree to the service.

As you work on a problem, keep notes as to what you've tried and the outcome. The documentation will be useful the next time you face a similar problem.

## >> CHAPTER SUMMARY

▲ Windows 2000/XP requires a valid user account before you can use Windows. The user account identifies the user to Windows. Permissions assigned to a user account control what the user can and cannot do and access in Windows.

▲ Local user accounts apply to a single standalone computer or a single computer in a workgroup, and global user accounts are managed from a domain controller and apply to every computer in the domain.

▲ When using Windows in a domain, global user account information is stored in the SAM, which is part of Active Directory in Windows 2000 Server and Windows Server 2003.

▲ When a user makes changes to the system, the changes are often recorded in the user profile so the next time the user logs on, these changes automatically take effect.

▲ Methods that administrators can use to manage and secure multiple computers and users include roaming user profiles, mandatory user profiles, and group profiles.

▲ Passwords on user accounts are needed to secure computers and their resources. Passwords should not be easy to guess and should be a combination of letters, numbers, and nonalphanumeric characters.

▲ An administrator can create a user account using the Computer Management console or the User Accounts applet in the Control Panel.

▲ Resetting a password under Windows XP causes the OS to lock out the user from using encrypted e-mail or files or using Internet passwords stored on the computer. For that reason, it is a good idea for a user to create a Windows XP forgotten password floppy disk.

▲ In Windows 2000, you can only log on to the system by pressing Ctrl+Alt+Del to open the logon window. In a Windows XP workgroup, you can use the logon window, Welcome screen, or Fast User Switching.

▲ Windows user groups include Administrators, Backup Operators, Power Users, Limited Users, and Guests. In this list, each group has fewer permissions and rights than the previous group.

▲ The Windows XP Files and Settings Transfer Wizard and the User State Migration Tool (USMT) enable a user to make a smooth transition from one computer to another by transferring user files and settings. The first tool is intended to be used by the user in a workgroup, and the second tool is intended to be used by an administrator in a domain.

▲ Commands useful to managing data and hard drives are Help, Dir, Del, Copy, Recovery, Xcopy, MD, CD, RD, Attrib, Chkdsk, Defrag, Edit, and Format.

▲ Windows XP looks to certain folders to find scripts and programs to launch at startup. Group Policy and Scheduled Tasks can be used to set startup scripts.

▲ Remote Assistance can be used for a technician to take control of a user's desktop to solve Windows XP problems.

▲ Show users how to routinely clean up, defrag, and check a hard drive for errors.

▲ Using disk quotas, an administrator can limit the amount of hard drive space a user can use.

▲ File, folder, and volume compression can only be used with the NTFS file system.

▲ For disaster recovery, it is important to create and test a plan that includes keeping records of backups and recovery procedures.

▲ Back up data after about every four to ten hours of data entry. For best security, store the backup media at an off-site location.

▲ When data is lost on a hard drive, don't write anything to the drive if you intend to try to recover the data.

## KEY TERMS

For explanations of key terms, see the Glossary near the end of the book.

Administrator
Backup Operators
batch file
built-in user accounts
chain
compression
cross-linked clusters
defragment
disk quotas
Files and Settings Transfer
    Wizard

forgotten password floppy disk
fragmentation
fragmented files
global user accounts
Group Policy
group profile
Guests
Limited Users
loadstate
local user account
lost allocation units

lost clusters
mandatory user profile
Power Users
Remote Assistance
Remote Desktop
roaming user profiles
scanstate
user account
User State Migration Tool
    (USMT)
wildcard

## REVIEW QUESTIONS

1. How many types of user accounts are possible in Windows 2000/XP?

   a. 1

   b. 2

   c. 3

   d. As many as are needed

2. Which of the following symbols can be used as a wildcard character in a filename when working at the command prompt?

   a. &

   b. #

   c. ?

   d. @

3. Which of the following refers to a new Windows XP feature that allows a user to connect to and use his or her Windows XP computer from anywhere on the Internet?

   a. Remote Assistance

   b. Group Policy

   c. Task Scheduler

   d. Remote Desktop

4. To limit how much disk space a user account can access, an administrator can set which of the following?

   a. User profiles

   b. Group profiles

   c. User access levels

   d. Disk quotas

5. Which of the following must be true to use the Rmdir (RD) command?

   **a.** The directory must not be the current directory.

   **b.** The directory can contain subdirectories as long as each subdirectory is empty.

   **c.** The directory can contain one file.

   **d.** A copy of the directory must be created before using the Rmdir command.

6. True or false? A user group is a predefined set of permissions and rights assigned to user accounts.

7. True or false? In Windows 2000/XP, a power user has the same privileges and access as an administrator.

8. True or false? The Windows XP Files and Settings Transfer Wizard is intended to be used by the user rather than the administrator.

9. True or false? The Attrib command displays or changes the read-only, archive, system, and hidden attributes assigned to files.

10. True or false? Clusters are called lost clusters, or lost allocation units, when a chain in the FAT points to them.

11. When Windows 2000/XP is first installed, it automatically creates two local accounts called the built-in _____ account and the built-in _____ account.

12. When a user moves from one computer to another computer in the workgroup, the _____ follows the user so that he or she does not have to redo settings at each computer.

13. The two commands used by an administrator at the command prompt for the User State Migration Tool (USMT) are_____ and _____.

14. A file written to a disk in noncontiguous clusters is called a(n) _____.

15. Three important routine maintenance tasks for hard drives are: defragging the drive, _____, and scanning it for errors.

# Troubleshooting Windows 2000/XP Startup

In the previous three chapters, you have been learning about supporting and maintaining Windows 2000/XP, its users, and their data. In this chapter, we complete that discussion of Windows 2000/XP by looking at when Windows 2000/XP will not load the Windows desktop or loads the desktop with errors.

When a computer refuses to boot or the Windows desktop refuses to load, it takes a cool head to handle the situation gracefully. What helps more than anything else is to have a good plan so you don't feel so helpless. This chapter is designed to give you just that—a plan with all the necessary details so that you can determine just what has gone wrong and what to do about it. Knowledge is power. When you know what to do, the situation doesn't seem nearly as hopeless.

To begin the chapter, you'll see what happens when Windows 2000/XP starts and loads the Windows desktop. Next, you'll see a survey of all the tools and utilities you can use to solve boot problems. Finally, you'll learn the strategies and step-by-step approaches to solving boot problems with Windows 2000/XP.

# UNDERSTANDING THE WINDOWS 2000/XP BOOT PROCESS

A Windows 2000/XP system has started up when the user has logged on, the Windows desktop is loaded, and the hourglass associated with the pointer has disappeared. To know how to support the boot process, it's not necessary to understand every detail of this process, but it does help to have a general understanding of the more important steps. In this section, you learn what happens during the boot process, what files are needed to boot, and how to change some settings that affect Windows 2000/XP startup.

## WHAT HAPPENS WHEN WINDOWS 2000/XP STARTS UP

Table 14-1 outlines the steps in the boot sequence for Intel-based computers up to the point that the boot loader program, Ntldr, turns control over to the Windows core component program, Ntoskrnl.exe.

| Step Number | Step Performed by | Description of Step |
| --- | --- | --- |
| 1 | Startup BIOS | Startup BIOS runs the POST (power-on self test). |
| 2 | Startup BIOS | Startup BIOS turns to the hard drive to find an OS. It first loads the MBR (Master Boot Record) and runs the master boot program within the MBR. (The master boot program is at the very beginning of the hard drive, before the partition table information.) |
| 3 | MBR program | The MBR program uses partition table information to find the active partition. It then loads the OS boot sector (also called the OS boot record) from the active partition and runs the program in this boot sector. |
| 4 | Boot sector program | This boot sector program launches Ntldr (NT Loader). |
| 5 | Ntldr, the Windows 2000/XP boot strap loader program | Ntldr changes the processor from real mode to 32-bit flat memory mode, in which 32-bit code can be executed. |
| 6 | Ntldr, the Windows 2000/XP boot strap loader program | Ntldr launches the minifile system drivers so files can be read from either a FAT or NTFS file system on the hard drive. |
| 7 | Ntldr, the Windows 2000/XP boot strap loader program | Ntldr reads the Boot.ini file, a hidden text file that contains information about installed OSs on the hard drive. Using this information, Ntldr builds the boot loader menu described in the file. The menu is displayed if Ntldr recognizes a dual boot system or sees a serious problem with the boot (see Figure 14-1). Using the menu, a user can decide which OS to load or accept the default selection by waiting for the preset time to expire. |
| 8 | Ntldr, the Windows 2000/XP boot strap loader program | If the user chooses an OS other than Windows 2000/XP, then Ntldr runs Bootsect.dos and Ntldr is terminated. Bootsect.dos is responsible for loading the other OS. |

Table 14-1 Steps in the Windows 2000/XP boot process for systems with Intel-based processors

A+ ESS
3.1
3.3

A+
220-602
3.3

| Step Number | Step Performed by | Description of Step |
|---|---|---|
| 9 | Ntldr, the Windows 2000/XP boot strap loader program | If the user chooses Windows 2000/XP, then the loader runs Ntdetect.com, a 16-bit real mode program that queries the computer for time and date (taken from CMOS RAM) and surveys hardware (buses, drives, mouse, ports). Ntdetect passes the information back to Ntldr. This information is used later to update the Windows 2000/XP registry concerning the Last Known Good hardware profile used. |
| 10 | Ntldr, the Windows 2000/XP boot strap loader program | Ntldr then loads Ntoskrnl.exe, Hal.dll, and the System hive. Recall that the System hive is a portion of the Windows 2000/XP registry that includes hardware information used to load the proper device drivers for the hardware present. Ntldr then loads these device drivers. |
| 11 | Windows 2000/XP loader (the last step performed by Ntldr) | Ntldr passes control to Ntoskrnl.exe; Ntoskrnl.exe continues to load the Windows desktop and the supporting Windows environment. |

**Table 14-1**  Steps in the Windows 2000/XP boot process for systems with Intel-based processors (continued)

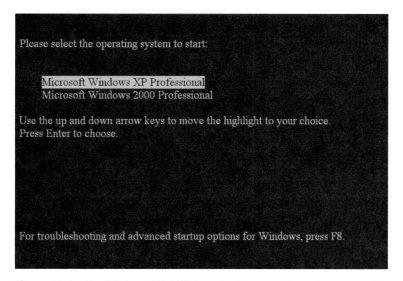

**Figure 14-1**  The Windows 2000/XP boot loader menu allows the user to choose which OS to load

## FILES NEEDED TO START WINDOWS 2000/XP

The files needed to boot Windows 2000/XP successfully are listed in Table 14-2. Several of these system files form the core components of the Windows OS architecture, which you can see diagrammed in Chapter 11 in Figure 11-6.

 **A+ Tip**

The A+ Essentials exam expects you to know about these system files: Boot.ini, Ntldr, Ntdetect.com, and Ntbootdd.sys.

| File | Location and Description |
|------|--------------------------|
| Ntldr | ▲ Located in the root folder of the system partition (usually C:\)<br>▲ Boot strap loader program |
| Boot.ini | ▲ Located in the root folder of the system partition (usually C:\)<br>▲ Text file contains boot parameters |
| Bootsect.dos | ▲ Located in the root folder of the system partition (usually C:\)<br>▲ Used to load another OS in a dual boot environment |
| Ntdetect.com | ▲ Located in the root folder of the system partition (usually C:\)<br>▲ Real-mode program detects hardware present |
| Ntbootdd.sys | ▲ Located in the root folder of the system partition (usually C:\)<br>▲ Required only if a SCSI boot device is used |
| Ntoskrnl.exe | ▲ Located in \*winnt_root*\system32 folder of the boot partition (usually C:\Windows\system32)<br>▲ Core component of the OS executive and kernel services |
| Hal.dll | ▲ Located in \*winnt_root*\system32 folder of the boot partition (usually C:\Windows\system32)<br>▲ Hardware abstraction layer |
| Ntdll.dll | ▲ Located in \*winnt_root*\system32 folder of the boot partition (usually C:\Windows\system32)<br>▲ Intermediating service to executive services; provides many support functions |
| Win32k.sys<br>Kernel32.dll<br>Advapi32.dll<br>User32.dll<br>Gdi32.dll | ▲ Located in \*winnt_root*\system32 folder of the boot partition (usually C:\Windows\system32)<br>▲ Core components of the Win 32 subsystem |
| System | ▲ Located in \*winnt_root*\system32\config folder of the boot partition (usually C:\Windows\system32\config)<br>▲ Registry hive that holds hardware configuration data including which device drivers need loading at startup |
| Device drivers | ▲ Located in \*winnt_root*\system32\drivers folder of the boot partition (usually C:\Windows\system32\drivers)<br>▲ Windows and third-party drivers needed for startup |
| Pagefile.sys | ▲ Located in the root folder of the system partition (usually C:\)<br>▲ Virtual memory swap file |

**Table 14-2**   Files needed to boot Windows 2000/XP successfully

A+ ESS
3.1
3.3

A+
220-602
3.3

## IMPORTANT FOLDERS USED IN THE STARTUP PROCESS

As you can see from Table 14-2, most Windows system files are stored in the C:\Windows\System 32 folder. Here is a list of the key folders used by Windows 2000/XP:

> **Notes**
>
> When repairing a corrupted hard drive, a support person often copies files from one PC to another. However, the Bootsect.dos file contains information from the partition table for a particular hard drive and cannot be copied from another PC.

- ◢ *C:\Windows* – Contains the Windows 2000/XP installation and includes several subfolders.
- ◢ *C:\Windows\System32* – The most important subfolder in C:\Windows, which contains core Windows system files and subfolders.
- ◢ *C:\Windows\System32\config* – Contains the registry hives.
- ◢ *C:\Windows\System32\drivers* – Contains device driver files.
- ◢ *C:\Documents and Settings* – Contains information for each user. Each user account has a subfolder by that name, which contains these important subfolders: My Documents, Desktop, Start Menu.
- ◢ *C:\Program Files* – Contains installed applications.

## THE BOOT.INI FILE

One key file used by Windows 2000/XP startup is Boot.ini. Recall that the Boot.ini file is a hidden text file stored in the root directory of the active partition that Ntldr reads to see what operating systems are available and how to set up the boot. You can view and edit the Boot.ini file, which might be necessary when you are trying to solve a difficult boot problem. Figure 14-2 shows an example of a Boot.ini file for Windows XP. Figure 14-3 shows a similar file for a system that uses a Windows 2000 and Windows XP dual boot.

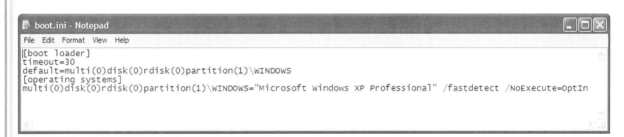

**Figure 14-2**   A sample Windows XP Boot.ini file

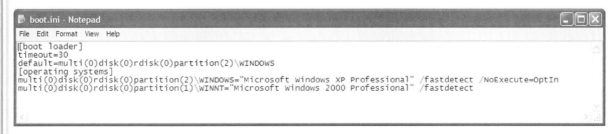

**Figure 14-3**   A sample Boot.ini file on a dual-boot system

A+ ESS
3.1
3.3

A+
220-602
3.3

Before you can view or edit the Boot.ini file using a text editor such as Notepad, you must first change the folder options to view hidden system files. To do so, open **Windows Explorer**, select the root directory, click **Tools** on the menu bar, click **Folder Options**, and then select the **View** tab. Uncheck the option to **Hide protected operating system files**.

There are two main sections in Boot.ini: the [boot loader] section and the [operating systems] section. The [boot loader] section contains the number of seconds the system gives the user to select an operating system before it loads the default operating system; this is called a timeout. In Figure 14-2, the timeout is set to 30 seconds. If the system is set for a dual boot, the path to the default operating system is also listed in the [boot loader] section. In Figure 14-3, you can see the default OS is loaded from the \Windows folder in the second partition.

The [operating systems] section of the Boot.ini file provides a list of operating systems that can be loaded, including the path to the boot partition of each operating system. Here is the meaning of each entry in Figure 14-2:

- *Multi(0).* Use the first hard drive controller.
- *Disk(0).* Use only when booting from a SCSI hard drive.
- *Rdisk(0).* Use the first hard drive.
- *Partition(1).* Use the first partition on the drive.

Switches are sometimes used in the [operating systems] section. In Figure 14-2, the first switch used in this Boot.ini file is /fastdetect, which causes the OS not to attempt to inspect any peripherals connected to a COM port (serial port) at startup.

The second switch is /NoExecute = OptIn. This switch is new with Windows XP Service Pack 2 and is used to configure Data Execution Prevention (DEP). DEP stops a program if it tries to use a protected area of memory, which some viruses attempt to do.

A+ ESS
3.3

## CUSTOMIZING THE WAY WINDOWS 2000/XP STARTS UP

You might want to change the way Windows 2000/XP starts up. In Chapter 13, you learned how to change the way users can log onto the system. In this section, you'll see some other settings you can change to affect what happens when Windows 2000/XP starts up.

It's interesting to know that many of the changes that you learn to make here are implemented in Windows by making a change to the Boot.ini file. Do the following to change Windows startup options:

1. Right-click **My Computer** and select **Properties**. The System Properties dialog box opens. Click the **Advanced** tab, as shown in Figure 14-4.

2. For Windows XP, under Startup and Recovery, click **Settings**. For Windows 2000, click the **Startup and Recovery** button.

3. The Startup and Recovery dialog box opens, as shown in Figure 14-5. Change settings as desired and then click **OK** to save them (or click **Cancel** if you do not want to save them).

Recall that the Boot.ini file can contain the /NoExecute switch to configure Data Execute Prevention (DEP) that stops a program if it oversteps its boundaries in memory. To configure DEP (which changes the /NoExecute switch), select the **Advanced** tab of the Windows XP System Properties window. Then, under Performance, click **Settings**. The Performance Options window opens. Click the **Data Execution Prevention** tab. The default setting is *Turn on DEP for essential Windows programs and services only.*

**Figure 14-4** You can access startup and recovery options from the System Properties dialog box

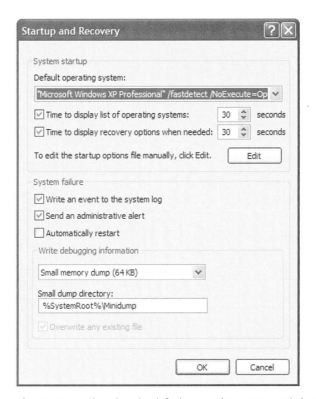

**Figure 14-5** Changing the default operating system and timeout value in the Startup and Recovery dialog box

For added protection, select **Turn on DEP for all programs and services except those I select,** as shown in Figure 14-6. Then, click **Apply** and reboot the system.

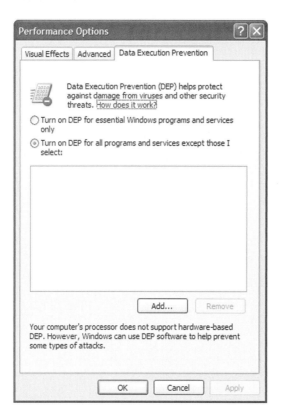

**Figure 14-6**  Configure Windows XP Data Execution Prevention

Later, if DEP stops a program that you know is legitimate, you can go back to this window and add the program to the exceptions list.

## TROUBLESHOOTING TOOLS TO SOLVE STARTUP PROBLEMS

In previous chapters, you learned about several support and maintenance tools for Windows 2000/XP. Some of those tools are useful for solving boot problems. To round out your Windows 2000/XP support skills, you're now ready to learn about some similar tools useful to solve startup problems.

Table 14-3 lists many of the tools that you'll need to solve startup problems. Later in the chapter, you'll learn how to use many of these tools. After you're familiar with the tools, we'll tackle the step-by-step approaches to troubleshooting, and at that time, you'll see how these tools can get you out of a jam when Windows refuses to start.

For more information about any of these tools, search Windows XP Help and Support or Windows 2000 Help. On the Web, you can search the Microsoft Knowledge Base at *support.microsoft.com*, or use the book, *Microsoft Windows XP Professional Resource Kit Documentation*.

> **Notes**
>
> Many technical people use the terms "boot" and "startup" interchangeably. However, in general, the term "boot" refers to the hardware phase of starting up a computer. Microsoft consistently uses the term "startup" to refer to how its operating systems are booted, well, started, I mean.

14

A+ ESS
3.3

A+
220-602
3.1
3.3

| Tool | Available in Windows XP | Available in Windows 2000 | Description |
|------|------------------------|---------------------------|-------------|
| Add or Remove Programs | X | X | ▲ Accessed from the Control Panel.<br>▲ Use it to uninstall, repair, or update software or certain device drivers that are causing a problem. |
| Advanced Options Menu | X | X | ▲ Accessed by pressing the F8 key when Windows first starts to load.<br>▲ Use several options on this menu to help you troubleshoot boot problems. |
| Automated System Recovery (ASR) | X | | ▲ Accessed from the Windows setup CD.<br>▲ Use ASR as a last resort because the logical drive on which Windows is installed is formatted and restored from the most recent backup. All data and applications written to the drive since the last backup are lost. |
| Backup (Ntbackup.exe) | X | X | ▲ Enter Ntbackup.exe in the Run dialog box.<br>▲ Use it to restore the system state, data, and software from previously made backups. |
| Boot logging | X | X | ▲ Press F8 at startup and select from the Advanced Options menu.<br>▲ Log events to the Ntbtlog.txt file to investigate the source of an unknown startup error. |
| Bootcfg (Bootcfg.exe) | X | X | ▲ Enter Bootcfg at a command prompt.<br>▲ Use it to view the contents of the Boot.ini file. |
| Cacls.exe | X | X | ▲ At a command prompt, enter Cacls with parameters.<br>▲ Use it to gain access to a file when permissions to the file are in error or corrupted. The utility can change the access control list (ACL) assigned to a file or group of files to control which users have access to a file. |
| Chkdsk (Chkdsk.exe) | X | X | ▲ At a command prompt, enter Chkdsk with parameters.<br>▲ Use it to check and repair errors on a logical drive. If critical system files are affected by these errors, repairing the drive might solve a startup problem. |
| Cipher.exe | X | X | ▲ At a command prompt, enter Cipher with parameters. |

**Table 14-3** Windows 2000/XP maintenance and troubleshooting tools

| Tool | Available in Windows XP | Available in Windows 2000 | Description |
|---|---|---|---|
| | | | ◢ Log in as an administrator and use this command to decrypt a file that is not available because the user account that encrypted the file is no longer accessible. |
| Compact.exe | X | X | ◢ At a command prompt, enter Compact with parameters. <br> ◢ Use it with an NTFS file system to display and change the compressions applied to files and folders. |
| Computer Management (Compmgmt.msc) | X | X | ◢ Accessed from the Control Panel, or you can enter Compmgmt.msc at a command prompt. <br> ◢ Use it to access several snap-ins to manage and troubleshoot a system. |
| Defrag.exe | X | | ◢ At a command prompt, enter Defrag with parameters. <br> ◢ Use it to defragment a drive to improve drive performance and access time. |
| Device Driver Roll Back | X | X | ◢ Accessed from Device Manager. <br> ◢ Use it to replace a driver with the one that worked before the current driver was installed. |
| Device Manager (Devmgmt.msc) | X | X | ◢ Accessed from the System Properties window. <br> ◢ Use it to solve problems with hardware devices, to update device drivers, and to disable and uninstall a device. |
| Disk Cleanup (Cleanmgr.exe) | X | X | ◢ Accessed from a drive's properties window or by entering Cleanmgr in the Run dialog box. <br> ◢ Use it to delete unused files to make more disk space available. Not enough free hard dive space can cause boot problems. |
| Disk Defragmenter (Dfrg.msc) | X | X | ◢ Accessed from a drive's properties window. <br> ◢ Use it to defragment a logical drive or floppy disk. |
| Disk Management (Diskmgmt.msc) | X | X | ◢ Accessed from the Computer Management console or, at a command prompt, enter Diskmgmt.msc. <br> ◢ Use it to view and change partitions on hard drives and to format drives. |
| Driver Signing and Digital Signatures (Sigverif.exe) | X | X | ◢ At a command prompt, enter Sigverif with parameters. |

**Table 14-3**  Windows 2000/XP maintenance and troubleshooting tools (continued)

| Tool | Available in Windows XP | Available in Windows 2000 | Description |
|------|------------------------|---------------------------|-------------|
| | | | ▲ When a device driver or other software is giving problems, use it to verify that the software has been approved by Microsoft. |
| Error Reporting | X | | ▲ This automated Windows service displays error messages when an application error occurs.<br>▲ Follow directions onscreen to produce an error report and send it to Microsoft. Sometimes the Microsoft Web site responds with suggestions to solve the problem. |
| Event Viewer (Eventvwr.msc) | X | X | ▲ Accessed from the Computer Management console.<br>▲ Check the Event Viewer window for error messages to help you investigate all kinds of hardware, security, and system problems. |
| Expand.exe | X | X | ▲ At a command prompt, enter Expand with parameters.<br>▲ Use it to extract a file from a cabinet file or compressed file. This command is useful from the Recovery Console when you're trying to restore a system file. |
| Group Policy (Gpedit.msc) | X | X | ▲ At a command prompt, enter Gpedit.msc.<br>▲ Use it to display and change policies controlling users and the computer. |
| Last Known Good Configuration | X | X | ▲ Press F8 at startup and select from the Advanced Options menu.<br>▲ Use this tool when Windows won't start normally and you want to revert the system to before a driver or application that is causing problems was installed. |
| Performance Monitor (Perfmon.msc) | X | X | ▲ At a command prompt, enter Perfmon.msc.<br>▲ Use it to view information about performance to help you identify a performance bottleneck. |
| Program Compatibility Wizard | X | | ▲ Accessed by way of a desktop shortcut to a legacy application.<br>▲ Use it to resolve issues that prevent legacy software from working in Windows XP. |

**Table 14-3** Windows 2000/XP maintenance and troubleshooting tools (continued)

A+ ESS
3.3

A+
220-602
3.1
3.3

| Tool | Available in Windows XP | Available in Windows 2000 | Description |
|---|---|---|---|
| Recovery Console | X | X | ◢ Accessed from the Windows setup CD.<br>◢ Boot up this command-driven OS when you cannot boot from the hard drive. Use it to troubleshoot the Windows problem and recover data from the hard drive. |
| Registry Editor (Regedit.exe) | X | X | ◢ At a command prompt, enter Regedit.<br>◢ Use it to view and edit the registry. |
| Runas.exe | X | X | ◢ At a command prompt, enter Runas with parameters.<br>◢ Use it to run a program using different permissions than those assigned to the currently logged-on user. |
| Safe Mode | X | X | ◢ At startup, press F8 and select the option from the Advanced Options menu.<br>◢ Use it when Windows does not start or starts with errors. Safe Mode loads the Windows desktop with a minimum configuration. In this minimized environment, you can solve a problem with a device driver, display setting, or corrupted or malicious applications. |
| SC (Sc.exe) | X | X | ◢ At a command prompt, enter Sc with parameters.<br>◢ Use it to stop or start a service that runs in the background. |
| Services (Services.msc) | X | X | ◢ Enter Services.msc in the Run dialog box.<br>◢ Graphical version of SC. |
| System Configuration Utility (Msconfig.exe) | X | | ◢ Enter Msconfig in the Run dialog box.<br>◢ Troubleshoot the startup process by temporarily disabling startup programs and services. |
| System File Checker (Sfc.exe) | X | X | ◢ At a command prompt, enter Sfc with parameters.<br>◢ Use it to verify the version of all system files when Windows loads. Useful when you suspect system files are corrupted, but you can still access the Windows desktop. |
| System Information (Msinfo32.exe) | X | X | ◢ At a command prompt, enter Msinfo32. |

**Table 14-3**  Windows 2000/XP maintenance and troubleshooting tools (continued)

**14**

A+ ESS
3.3

A+
220-602
3.1
3.3

| Tool | Available in Windows XP | Available in Windows 2000 | Description |
|---|---|---|---|
| | | | ◢ Use it to display information about hardware, applications, and Windows that is useful when troubleshooting. Figure 14-7 shows a view of the System Information window. |
| System Information (Systeminfo.exe) | X | X | ◢ At a command prompt, enter Systeminfo. |
| | | | ◢ A version of System Information to be used from a command-prompt window. Information is listed onscreen as text only. To direct that information to a file, use the command Systeminfo.exe >Myfile.txt. Later the file can be printed and used to document information about the system. |
| System Restore | X | | ◢ Accessed from the Start menu or when loading Safe Mode. |
| | | | ◢ Use it to restore the system to a previously working condition; it restores the registry, some system files, and some application files. |
| Task Killing Utility (Tskill.exe) | X | X | ◢ At a command prompt, enter Tskill with parameters. |
| | | | ◢ Use it to stop or kill a process or program currently running. Useful when managing background services such as an e-mail server or Web server. |
| Task Lister (Tasklist.exe) | X | X | ◢ At a command prompt, enter Tasklist. |
| | | | ◢ Use it to list currently running processes similar to the list provided by Task Manager. |
| Task Manager (Taskman.exe) | X | X | ◢ Right-click the taskbar and select Task Manager. |
| | | | ◢ Use it to list and stop currently running processes. Useful when you need to stop a locked-up application. |
| Windows File Protection | X | X | ◢ Windows background service. |
| | | | ◢ Runs in the background to protect system files and restore overwritten system files as needed. |
| Windows Update (Wupdmgr.exe) | X | X | ◢ Accessed from the Start menu. |
| | | | ◢ Use it to update Windows by downloading the latest patches from the Microsoft Web site. |

**Table 14-3** Windows 2000/XP maintenance and troubleshooting tools (continued)

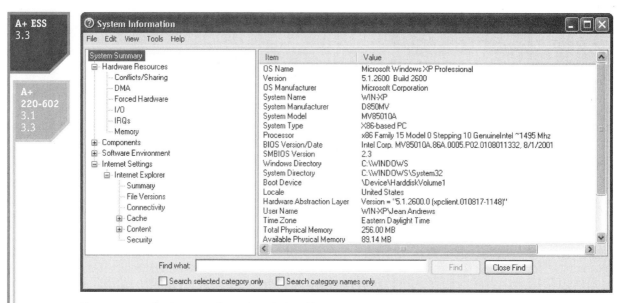

**Figure 14-7** The System Information window displays important information about the system's hardware, software, and environment

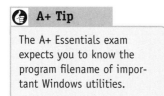

**A+ Tip**

The A+ Essentials exam expects you to know the program filename of important Windows utilities.

by Microsoft Press or *Microsoft Windows 2000 Professional Resource Kit* by Microsoft Press. In addition, to get help about a command-line tool, from a command prompt, enter the Help command followed by the tool name. For example, to get help about Defrag, enter **Help defrag**. For some commands not supported by Help, type the command followed by /?. For example, for help with the Cipher command, enter **Cipher /?**.

Now let's see how to use the options on the Advanced Options Menu and how to use the Recovery Console.

## ADVANCED OPTIONS MENU

As a PC boots and the "Starting Windows" message appears at the bottom of the screen, press the F8 key to display the Windows XP **Advanced Options menu**, which is shown in Figure 14-8, or the Windows 2000 Advanced Options menu, which is shown in Figure 14-9. This menu can be used to diagnose and fix problems when booting Windows 2000/XP. The purpose of each menu option is outlined in the following sections.

**A+ Tip**

The A+ Essentials and A+ 220-602 exams expect you to be able to select the appropriate next step in troubleshooting a failed boot when given a specific scenario. As you study the tools in this section, pay attention to how a tool affects the installed OS, applications, and data. The idea is to fix the problem by using the tool that least affects the OS, applications, and data.

### SAFE MODE

Safe Mode boots the OS with a minimum configuration and can be used to solve problems with a new hardware installation or problems caused by user settings. Safe Mode boots with the mouse, monitor (with basic video), keyboard, and mass storage drivers loaded. It uses the default system services (it does not load any extra

**14**

A+ ESS
3.3

A+
220-602
3.3

```
Windows Advanced Options Menu
Please select an option:

        Safe Mode
        Safe Mode with Networking
        Safe Mode with Command Prompt

        Enable Boot Logging
        Enable VGA Mode
        Last Known Good Configuration (your most recent settings that worked)
        Directory Services Restore Mode (Windows domain controllers only)
        Debugging Mode
        Disable automatic restart on system failure

        Start Windows Normally
        Reboot
        Return to OS Choices Menu


Use the up and down arrow keys to move the highlight to your choice.
```

**Figure 14-8** Press the F8 key at startup to display the Windows XP Advanced Options menu

```
Windows 2000 Advanced Options Menu
Please select an option:

        Safe Mode
        Safe Mode with Networking
        Safe Mode with Command Prompt

        Enable Boot Logging
        Enable VGA Mode
        Last Known Good Configuration
        Directory Services Restore Mode (Windows 2000 domain controllers only)
        Debugging Mode

        Boot Normally

Use ↑ and ↓ to move the highlight to your choice.
Press Enter to choose.
```

**Figure 14-9** The Windows 2000 Advanced Options menu

services) and does not provide network access. It uses a plain video driver (Vga.sys) instead of the video drivers specific to your video card.

When you boot in Safe Mode, you will see "Safe Mode" in all four corners of your screen. In addition, you have a GUI interface in Safe Mode. The screen resolution is 600 x 800 and the desktop wallpaper (background) is black. Figure 14-10 shows Windows XP in Safe Mode. In the figure, you can see the running processes as reported by Task Manager.

After the OS loads in Safe Mode, you can disable any problem device, scan for viruses, use System Restore to restore the system to an earlier restore point, restore the system to a previously saved system state, run diagnostic software, or take other appropriate action to diagnose and solve problems. When you load Windows 2000/XP in Safe Mode, all files used for the load are recorded in the Ntbtlog.txt file. Use this file to identify a service, device driver, or application loaded at startup that is causing a problem.

If you boot into Safe Mode and Windows XP recognizes System Restore has previously been used to create restore points, Windows XP will give you the opportunity to launch the System Restore Wizard (see Figure 14-11). The wizard gives you the opportunity to choose a restore point from those previously saved. Recall that when Windows is restored to a restore point, all Windows settings are returned to the way they were when the restore point was created.

A+ ESS
3.3

A+
220-602
3.3

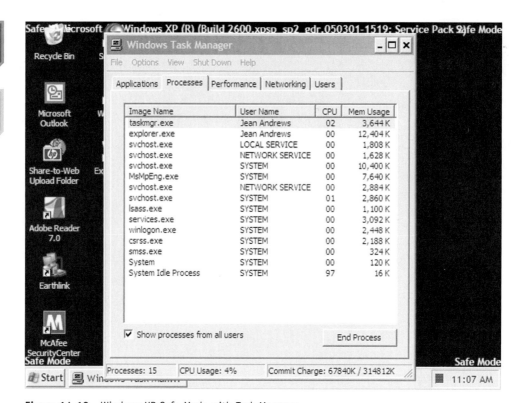

**Figure 14-10** Windows XP Safe Mode with Task Manager

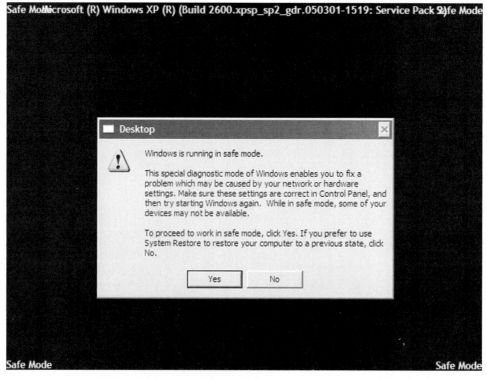

**Figure 14-11** Windows XP gives you the opportunity to launch System Restore before it loads Safe Mode

**14**

## SAFE MODE WITH NETWORKING

Use this option when you are solving a problem with booting and need access to the network to solve the problem. For example, if you have just attempted to install a printer, which causes the OS to hang when it boots, and the printer drivers are downloaded from the network, boot into Safe Mode with Networking. Uninstall the printer and then install it again from the network. Also use this mode when the Windows 2000/XP installation files are available on the network, rather than the Windows 2000/XP setup CD, and you need to access these files.

## SAFE MODE WITH COMMAND PROMPT

If the first Safe Mode option does not load the OS, then try this option. This Safe Mode option does not load a GUI desktop automatically. You would use it to get a command prompt only.

## ENABLE BOOT LOGGING

When you boot with this option, Windows 2000/XP loads normally and you access the regular desktop. However, all files used during the load process are recorded in a file, C:\Windows\Ntbtlog.txt (see Figure 14-12). Thus, you can use this option to see what did and did not load during the boot. For instance, if you have a problem getting a device to work, check Ntbtlog.txt to see what driver files loaded. Boot logging is much more effective if you have a copy of Ntbtlog.txt that was made when everything worked as it should. Then you can compare the good load to the bad load, looking for differences.

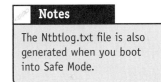

**Notes**

The Ntbtlog.txt file is also generated when you boot into Safe Mode.

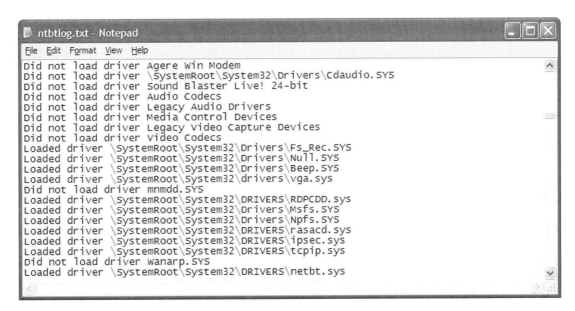

**Figure 14-12** Sample C:\Windows\Ntbtlog.txt file

A+ ESS
3.3

A+
220-602
3.3

> **Notes**
>
> If Windows hangs during the boot, try booting using the option Enable Boot Logging. Then look at the last entry in the Ntbtlog.txt file. This entry might be the name of a device driver causing the system to hang.

## ENABLE VGA MODE

Use this option when the video setting does not allow you to see the screen well enough to fix a bad setting. This can happen when a user creates a desktop with black fonts on a black background, or something similar. Booting in this mode gives you a very plain, standard VGA video. You can then go to the Display settings, correct the problem, and reboot normally. You can also use this option if your video drivers are corrupted and you need to update, rollback, or reinstall your video drivers.

## LAST KNOWN GOOD CONFIGURATION

Each time the system boots completely and the user logs on, the Last Known Good configuration is saved. Windows 2000/XP keeps the Last Known Good configuration in the registry. Use this option if you suspect the system was configured incorrectly. It restores Windows 2000/XP to the settings of the last successful boot, and all system setting changes made after this last successful boot are lost.

> **Notes**
>
> The Last Known Good configuration is saved after the user logs on in normal mode. When booting in Safe Mode, the Last Known Good configuration is not saved. Therefore, if you have a Windows problem you're trying to solve, boot using Safe Mode so that you can log on without overwriting the Last Known Good configuration.

In some situations, the Last Known Good will not help you recover from the problem. If you have booted several times since a problem started, all the saved versions of the Last Known Good reflect the problem.

## DIRECTORY SERVICES RESTORE MODE (WINDOWS DOMAIN CONTROLLERS ONLY)

This option applies only to domain controllers and is used as one step in the process of recovering from a corrupted Active Directory. Recall that Active Directory is the domain database managed by a domain controller that tracks users and resources on the domain. The details of how all this works are beyond the scope of this chapter.

## DEBUGGING MODE

This mode gives you the opportunity to move system boot logs from the failing computer to another computer for evaluation. To use this mode, both computers must be connected to each other by way of the serial port. Then, you can reboot into this mode and Windows 2000/XP on the failing computer will send all the boot information through the serial port and on to the other computer. For more details, see the *Windows XP Professional Resource Kit* or the *Windows 2000 Professional Resource Kit* (Microsoft Press).

## DISABLE AUTOMATIC RESTART ON SYSTEM FAILURE

By default, Windows 2000/XP automatically restarts immediately after it encounters a system failure, which is also called a stop error or a **blue screen of death (BSOD)**. This type of error can be especially troublesome if you're trying to shut down a system and it encounters an error. The error can cause the system to continually reboot rather than shut down. For Windows XP, choose **Disable automatic restart on system failure** to stop the rebooting. (The option is not on the Windows 2000 Advanced Options menu.)

From the Windows 2000/XP desktop, you can modify this same setting using the System Properties window. Click the **Advanced** tab. For Windows XP, under Startup and Recovery, click **Settings**, and, for Windows 2000, click **Startup and Recovery**. On the Startup and Recovery window, uncheck **Automatically restart**, as shown in Figure 14-13. Next time the system encounters a stop error, it will shut down and not automatically restart. You'll learn more about stop errors later in the chapter.

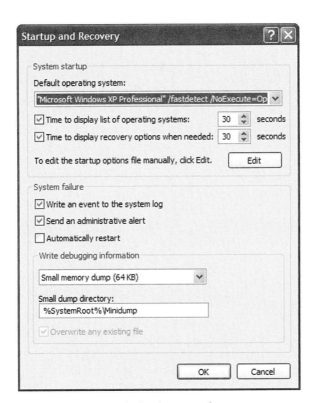

**Figure 14-13**   Control what happens after a stop error

## RECOVERY CONSOLE

The Advanced Options menu can help if the problem is a faulty device driver or system service. However, if the problem goes deeper than that, the next tool to use is the **Recovery Console**. Use it when Windows 2000/XP does not start properly or hangs during the load. It works even when core Windows system files are corrupted. The Recovery Console is a command-driven operating system that does not use a GUI. With it, you can access the FAT16, FAT32, and NTFS file systems.

> **Notes**
>
> Experienced techies remember the days when the Windows 9x/Me startup disk with tried-and-true DOS was the tool to use when Windows would not boot. Today that command-line OS is the Recovery Console. Many Recovery Console commands work and look much like DOS commands.

Using the Recovery Console, you can:

▲ Repair a damaged registry, system files, or file system on the hard drive.

▲ Enable or disable a service or device driver.

▲ Repair the master boot program on the hard drive or the boot sector on the system partition.

◢ Repair a damaged Boot.ini file.

◢ Recover data when the Windows installation is beyond repair.

The Recovery Console is designed so that someone can't maliciously use it to gain unauthorized access. You must enter the Administrator password in order to use the Recovery Console and access an NTFS volume. Unless you first set certain parameters, you are not allowed into all folders, and you cannot copy files from the hard drive to a floppy disk or other removable media. If the registry is so corrupted that the Recovery Console cannot read the password in order to validate it, you are not asked for the password, but you are limited in what you can do at the Recovery Console.

Now let's look at a list of Recovery Console commands, how to access the Recovery Console, how to use it to perform several troubleshooting tasks, and how to install the Recovery Console on the boot loader menu.

## LIST OF RECOVERY CONSOLE COMMANDS

As a summary reference, Table 14-4 lists Recovery Console commands and their descriptions.

| Command | Description | Examples |
| --- | --- | --- |
| Attrib | Changes the attributes of a file or folder, and works the same as the DOS version. | To remove the read-only, hidden, and system attributes from the file:<br><br>`C:\> Attrib -r -h -s filename` |
| Batch | Carries out commands stored in a batch file. | To execute the commands in File1:<br><br>`C:\> Batch File1.bat`<br><br>To execute the commands in File1 and store the results of the commands to File2:<br><br>`C:\> Batch File1.bat File2.txt` |
| Cd | Displays or changes the current folder. It cannot be used to change drives. | To change folders to the C:\Windows\system folder:<br><br>`C:\> Cd C:\windows\system`<br><br>`C:\windows\system>` |
| Chkdsk | Checks a disk and repairs or recovers the data. | To check drive C: and repair it:<br><br>`C:\> Chkdsk C: /r` |
| Cls | Clears the screen. | `C:\> cls` |
| Copy | Copies a single file. Use the command to replace corrupted system files or save data files to another media when the hard drive is failing. | To copy the file File1 on the CD to the hard drive's Winnt folder, naming the file File2:<br><br>`C:\> Copy D:\File1 C:\Winnt\File2` |
| Del | Deletes a file. | To delete File2:<br><br>`C:\Winnt> Del File2` |
| Dir | Lists files and folders. Wildcard characters are allowed. | To list all files with a .exe file extension:<br><br>`C:\> Dir *.exe` |

**Table 14-4** Commands available from the Recovery Console

| Command | Description | Examples |
|---------|-------------|----------|
| Disable | Disables a service or driver. Use it to disable a service or driver that starts and prevents the system from booting properly. After you disable the service, restart the system to see if your problem is solved. | To disable the Event Log service:<br>C:\> **Disable eventlog** |
| Diskpart | Creates and deletes partitions on the hard drive. | Enter the command with no arguments to display a user interface:<br>C:\> **Diskpart** |
| Enable | Displays the status and enables a Windows system service or driver. | To display the status of the Event Log service:<br>C:\> **Enable eventlog** |
| Exit | Quits the Recovery Console and restarts the computer. | C:\> **Exit** |
| Expand | Expands compressed files and extracts files from cabinet files and copies the files to the destination folder. | To extract File1 from the Drivers.cab file:<br>C:\> **Expand D:\i386\Drivers.cab -f:File1**<br>To expand the compressed file, File1.cp_:<br>C:\> **Expand File1.cp_** |
| Fixboot | Rewrites the OS boot sector on the hard drive. If a drive letter is not specified, the system drive is assumed. | To repair the OS boot sector of drive C:<br>C:\> **Fixboot C:** |
| Fixmbr | Rewrites the Master Boot Record boot program. This command is the same as the Windows 9x/Me Fdisk/MBR command. | To repair the Master Boot Record boot program:<br>C:\> **Fixmbr** |
| Format | Formats a logical drive. If no file system is specified, NTFS is assumed. | To format using the NTFS file system:<br>C:\> **Format D:**<br>To format using the FAT32 file system:<br>C:\> **Format D:/fs:FAT32**<br>To format using the FAT16 file system:<br>C:\> **Format D:/fs:FAT** |
| Help | Help utility appears for the given command. | To get help with the Fixboot command:<br>C:\> **Help fixboot** |
| Listsvc | Lists all available services. This command has no parameters. | C:\> **Listsvc** |
| Logon | Allows you to log on to an installation with the Administrator password. Use it to log onto a second installation of Windows in a dual-boot environment. | When logged onto the first Windows installation, use this command to log onto the second installation:<br>C:\> **logon 2**<br>If you don't enter the password correctly after three tries, the system automatically reboots. |

**Table 14-5** Commands available from the Recovery Console (continued)

A+ ESS
3.3

A+
220-602
3.1
3.3

| Command | Description | Examples |
|---------|-------------|----------|
| Map | Lists all drive letters and file system types. | `C:\> Map` |
| Md or Mkdir | Creates a folder. | `C:\> MD C:\TEMP` |
| More or Type | Displays a text file onscreen. | `C:\> Type filename.txt` |
| Rd or Rmdir | Deletes a directory. | `C:\> RD C:\TEMP` |
| Rename or Ren | Renames a file. | `C:\> Rename File1.txt File2.txt` |
| Set | Displays or sets Recovery Console environmental variables. | To turn off the prompt when you are overwriting files:<br>`C:\> Set nocopyprompt=true` |
| Systemroot | Sets the current directory to the directory where Windows 2000/XP is installed. | `C:\> Systemroot`<br>`C:\WINDOWS>` |
| Type | Displays contents of a text file. | `C:\> Type filename.txt` |

**Table 14-5**   Commands available from the Recovery Console (continued)

---

# APPLYING|CONCEPTS   HOW TO ACCESS THE RECOVERY CONSOLE

The Recovery Console software is on the Windows 2000/XP setup CD and the four Windows 2000 setup disks. You can launch the Recovery Console from the CD or four disks, or manually install the Recovery Console on the hard drive and launch it from there.

***How to access the Recovery Console using Windows XP.*** For Windows XP, to use the Recovery Console, insert the Windows XP setup CD in the CD drive and restart the system. When the Windows XP Setup opening menu appears (see Figure 14-14), press **R** to load the Recovery Console.

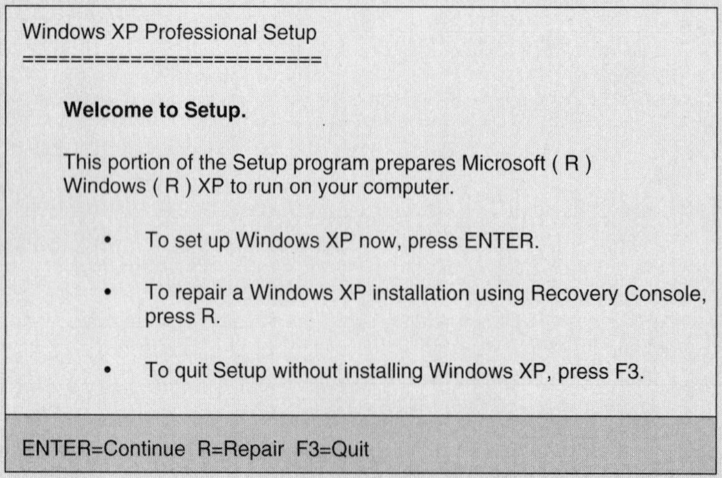

```
Windows XP Professional Setup
============================

  Welcome to Setup.

  This portion of the Setup program prepares Microsoft ( R )
  Windows ( R ) XP to run on your computer.

      •   To set up Windows XP now, press ENTER.

      •   To repair a Windows XP installation using Recovery Console,
          press R.

      •   To quit Setup without installing Windows XP, press F3.

 ENTER=Continue  R=Repair  F3=Quit
```

**Figure 14-14**   Windows XP Setup opening menu

A+ ESS
3.3

A+
220-602
3.1
3.3

***Access the Recovery Console using Windows 2000.*** For Windows 2000, you can boot from the Windows 2000 setup CD or you can boot from the four setup disks. Use the four setup disks if the computer will not boot from a CD drive. If you have not already created the Windows 2000 setup disks, you can go to a working Windows 2000 PC and create the disks by following the directions given in Chapter 11. Follow these steps to load Windows 2000 from the disks or from the setup CD and access the Recovery Console:

1. Insert the first of the four setup disks, and restart the PC. You are directed to insert each of the four disks in turn, and then the Setup screen appears, as shown in Figure 14-15. If you boot from the Windows 2000 setup CD, the same screen appears.

```
Windows 2000 Professional Setup
━━━━━━━━━━━━━━━━━━━━━━━━━━━━━━━━━━━━━━━━━━━━━━

        Welcome to Setup

    This portion of the Setup program prepares Microsoft®
    Windows 2000 ( TM ) to run on your computer

        • To set up Windows 2000 now, press ENTER.
        • To repair a Windows 2000 installation, press R.
        • To quit Setup without installing Windows 2000, press F3.

────────────────────────────────────────────────
ENTER=Continue   R=Repair   F3=Quit
```

**Figure 14-15**   Use this Windows 2000 Setup screen to access the Recovery Console

2. Type **R** to select the "To repair a Windows 2000 installation" option. The Windows 2000 Repair Options window opens (see Figure 14-16). Type **C** to select the Recovery Console.

```
Windows 2000 Professional Setup
━━━━━━━━━━━━━━━━━━━━━━━━━━━━━━━━━━━━━━━━━━━━━━

    Windows 2000 Repair Options:

        • To repair a Windows 2000 installation by using
          the recovery console, press C.

        • To repair a Windows 2000 installation by using
          the emergency repair process, press R.

    If the repair options do not successfully repair your system,
    run Windows 2000 Setup again.

────────────────────────────────────────────────
C=Console   R=Repair   F3=Quit
```

**Figure 14-16**   Windows 2000 offers two repair options

3. Note that as the Recovery Console attempts to load and give you access to the hard drive, it will display one of the following screens depending on the severity of the problem with the drive:

   ◢ If the Recovery Console cannot find the drive, the window in Figure 14-17 appears. Consider the problem hardware related. You might have a totally dead drive.

**Windows XP Professional Setup**

Setup did not find any hard disk drives installed in your computer.

Make sure any hard disk drives are powered on and properly connected to your computer, and that any disk-related hardware configuration is correct. This may involve running a manufacturer-supplied diagnostic or setup program.

Setup cannot continue. To quit Setup, press F3.

F3=Quit

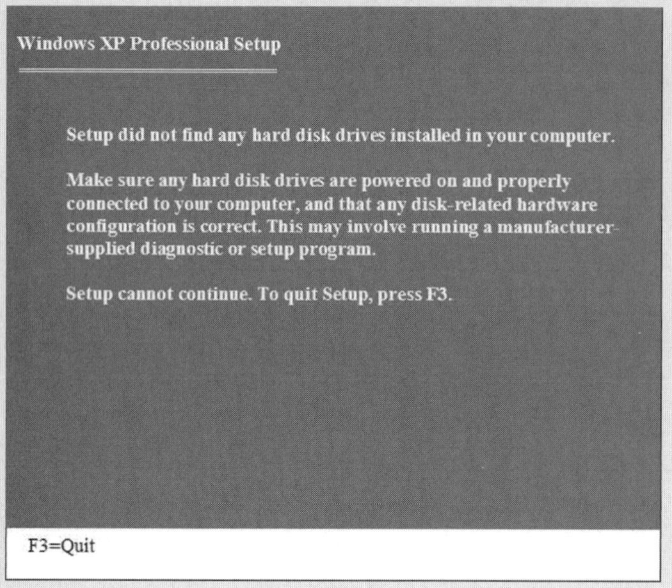

**Figure 14-17**   Windows setup cannot find a hard drive

◢ If the Console can find the hard drive, but cannot read from it, the window in Figure 14-18 appears. Notice in the window the C prompt (C:\>), which seems to indicate that the Recovery Console can access the hard drive, but the message above the C prompt says otherwise. When you try the DIR command, as shown in Figure 14-18, you find out that drive C: is not available. The Fixmbr and Fixboot commands might help.

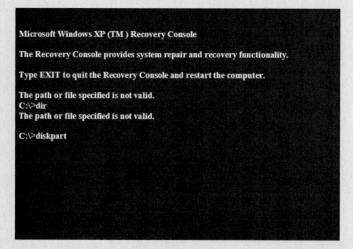

**Figure 14-18**   The Recovery Console cannot read from the hard drive

◢ If the Console is able to read drive C, but Windows is seriously corrupted, the window in Figure 14-19 appears. Use the DIR command to see what files or folders are still on the drive. Is the \Windows folder present? If not, then you might need to reformat the drive and reinstall Windows. But first try to find any important data that is not backed up.

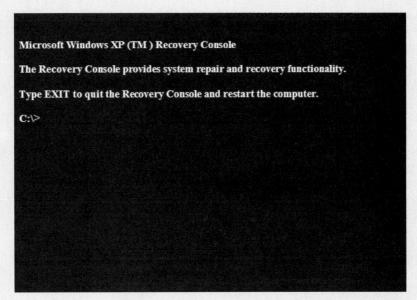

**Microsoft Windows XP (TM) Recovery Console**

**The Recovery Console provides system repair and recovery functionality.**

**Type EXIT to quit the Recovery Console and restart the computer.**

**C:\>**

**Figure 14-19** The Recovery Console can read drive C but cannot find a Windows installation

4. If the Console is able to determine that one or more Windows installations is on the drive, it gives you a choice of with which installation you want to work. If only one installation is showing, as in Figure 14-20, type **1** and press **Enter**. Next, you will be asked for the Administrator password. Enter the password and press **Enter**. The command prompt shows the Windows folder is the current working directory. You can now use the Recovery Console to try to find the problem and fix it. How to do that is coming up.

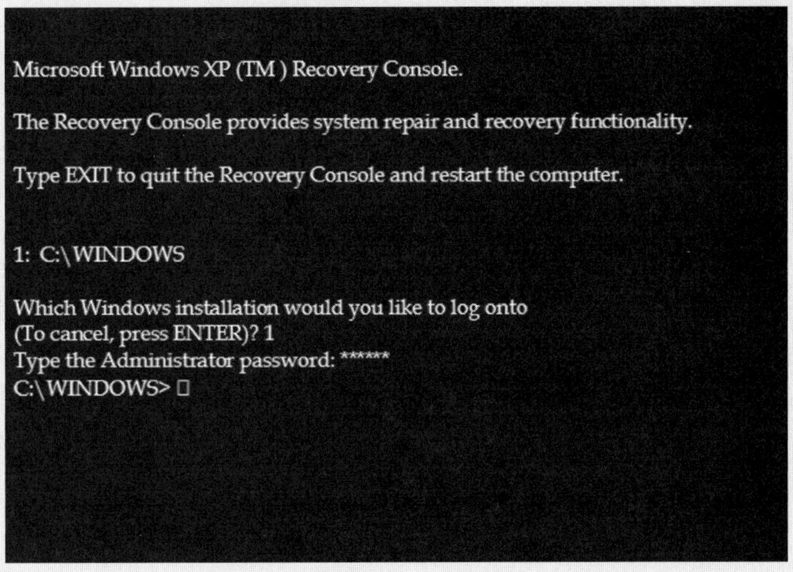

Microsoft Windows XP (TM) Recovery Console.

The Recovery Console provides system repair and recovery functionality.

Type EXIT to quit the Recovery Console and restart the computer.

1: C:\WINDOWS

Which Windows installation would you like to log onto
(To cancel, press ENTER)? 1
Type the Administrator password: ******
C:\WINDOWS> ▯

**Figure 14-20** The Recovery Console has found a Windows installation

5. To exit the Recovery Console, type **Exit** and press Enter. The system will attempt to boot to the Windows desktop.

### Notes

Here are two useful tips to help you when using the Recovery Console: To retrieve the last command, press F3 at the command prompt. To retrieve the command one character at a time, press the F1 key.

## USE THE RECOVERY CONSOLE TO FIX HARD DRIVE PROBLEMS

Here are the commands you can use to examine the hard drive structure for errors and possibly fix them:

▲ *Fixmbr and Fixboot.* The Fixmbr command restores the master boot program in the MBR, and the Fixboot command repairs the OS boot record. As you enter each command, you're looking for clues that might indicate at what point the drive has failed. For example, Figure 14-21 shows the results of using the Fixmbr command, which appears to have worked without errors, but the Fixboot command has actually failed. This tells us that most likely the master boot program is healthy, but drive C is not accessible. After using these commands, if you don't see any errors, exit the Recovery Console and try to boot from the hard drive.

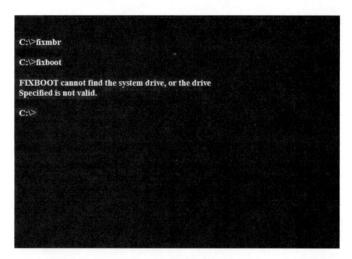

**Figure 14-21** Results of using the Fixmbr and Fixboot commands in the Recovery Console

▲ *Diskpart.* Use the Diskpart command to view, create, and delete partitions on the drive. Type **Diskpart** and press **Enter** and a full screen appears listing the partitions the Console sees on the drive. See Figure 14-22.

▲ *Chkdsk.* Use this command to repair the file system and recover data from bad sectors: **chkdsk C: /r**.

## USE THE RECOVERY CONSOLE TO RESTORE THE REGISTRY

You can use the Recovery Console to restore registry files with those saved at the last time the system state was backed up. Follow the six steps listed in Table 14-5 to restore the registry.

**14**

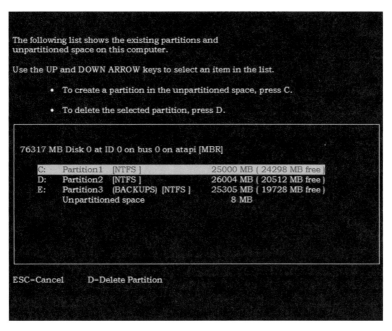

The following list shows the existing partitions and
unpartitioned space on this computer.

Use the UP and DOWN ARROW keys to select an item in the list.

&bull; To create a partition in the unpartitioned space, press C.

&bull; To delete the selected partition, press D.

76317 MB Disk 0 at ID 0 on bus 0 on atapi [MBR]

| | | | |
|---|---|---|---|
| C: | Partition1 | [NTFS ] | 25000 MB ( 24298 MB free ) |
| D: | Partition2 | [NTFS ] | 26004 MB ( 20512 MB free ) |
| E: | Partition3 | (BACKUPS) [NTFS ] | 25305 MB ( 19728 MB free ) |
| | Unpartitioned space | | 8 MB |

ESC=Cancel    D=Delete Partition

**Figure 14-22**  Using the Diskpart screen, you can view, delete, and create partitions

| Step | Command | Description |
|---|---|---|
| 1. | Systemroot | Makes the Windows folder the current folder. |
| 2. | CD System32\Config | Makes the Windows registry folder the current folder. |
| 3. | Ren Default Default.save<br>Ren Sam Sam.save<br>Ren Security Security.save<br>Ren Software Software.save<br>Ren System System.save | Renames the five registry files. |
| 4. | Systemroot | Returns to the Windows folder. |
| 5. | CD repair (for Windows XP)<br>or<br>CD repair\regback<br>(for Windows 2000) | Makes the Windows registry backup folder the current folder. |
| 6. | Copy Default C:\Windows\<br>system32\config<br>Copy Sam C:\Windows\<br>system32\config<br>Copy Security C:\Windows\<br>system32\config<br>Copy Software C:\Windows\<br>system32\config<br>Copy System C:\Windows\<br>system32\config | Copies the five registry files from the backup folder to the registry folder. For hardware problems, first try copying just the System hive and reboot. For software problems, first try copying just the Software hive and then reboot. If you still have problems, try copying all five hives. |

**Table 14-5**  Steps to restore the Windows 2000/XP registry

A+ ESS
3.3

A+
220-602
3.1
3.3

## USE THE RECOVERY CONSOLE TO DISABLE A SERVICE OR DEVICE DRIVER

Sometimes when Windows fails, it first displays a stop error on a blue background (called a BSOD). The stop error might give the name of a service or device driver that caused the problem. If the service or driver is critical to Windows operation, booting into Safe Mode won't help because the service or driver will be attempted in Safe Mode. The solution is to boot the system using the Recovery Console and copy a replacement program file from the Windows 2000/XP setup CD to the hard drive.

In order to know what program file to replace, you'll need to know the name or description of the service or driver causing the problem. If an error message doesn't give you the clue you need, you might try to boot to the Advanced Options Menu (press **F8** while booting) and then select **Enable Boot Logging**. Then compare the Ntbtlog.txt file to one generated on a healthy system. You might be able to find the driver or service that caused the boot to halt.

If you know the service causing the problem, use these commands to list services and disable and enable a service:

▲ *Listsvc*. Enter the command Listsvc to see a list of all services currently installed, which includes device drivers. The list is really long, showing the name of each service, a brief one-line description and its status (disabled, manual, or auto). To find the service giving the problem, you'll have to have more information than what this list shows.

▲ *Disable*. Use the Disable command to disable a service. For example, to disable the service SharedAccess, which is the Windows Firewall service, use this command: **disable sharedaccess**. Before you enter the command, be sure to write down the current startup type that is displayed so you'll know how to enable the service later. For services that are auto-started like this one, the startup type is service_auto_start.

▲ *Enable*. Use the Enable command followed by the name of the service to show the current status of a service. To enable the service, use the startup type in the command line. For example, to reinstate the Firewall service, use this command:

```
enable sharedaccess service_auto-start
```

If you think you've found the service that is causing the problem, disable it and reboot the system. If the problem disappears or the error message changes, you might have found the right service to replace. The next step is to replace the program file with a fresh copy.

## USE THE RECOVERY CONSOLE TO RESTORE SYSTEM FILES

Based on error messages and your research about them, if you think you know which Windows system file is corrupted or missing, you can use the Recovery Console to copy a new set of system files from the Windows setup CD to the hard drive. For example, suppose you get an error message that Ntldr is corrupted or missing. To replace the file, you could execute the commands in Figure 14-23.

Here are other commands to use to restore system files:

▲ *Map*. Displays the current drive letters. This command is useful to find your way around the system, such as when you need to know the drive letter for the CD drive.

▲ *Systemroot*. Use this command to make the Windows directory the default directory (refer to Figure 14-23 for an example of its use).

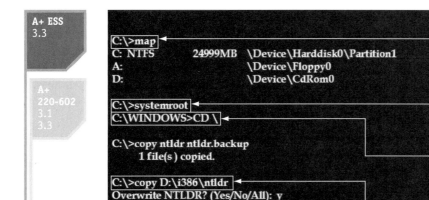

**Figure 14-23** Recovery Console command to repair Ntldr

▲ *CD*. Change directory. For example, to make the root directory the default directory, use **CD \**.

▲ *Delete*. Deletes a file. For example, to delete Ntldr in the Temp directory, use this command: **Delete C:\temp\ntldr**.

▲ *Copy*. To make a backup of the current Ntldr file, use this command:

```
copy ntldr ntldr.backup
```

▲ To copy the Ntldr file from the Windows setup CD to the root directory of the hard drive, use this command:

```
copy D:\i386\ntldr C:\
```

Substitute the drive letter for the CD drive in the command line.

A compressed file uses an underscore as the last character in the file extension; for example, Netapi32.dl_. When you use the Copy command, the file will automatically uncompress. For example, use this command to copy Netapi32.dl_ from the setup CD:

```
copy D:\i386\netapi32.dl_ netapi32.dll
```

▲ *Bootcfg*. This command lets you view and edit the Boot.ini file. Here are useful parameters:

    ▲ **bootcfg /list**         Lists entries in Boot.ini
    ▲ **bootcfg /copy**        Makes a copy of Boot.ini before you rebuild it
    ▲ **bootcfg /rebuild**    Rebuilds the Boot.ini file

▲ *Expand*. When you're looking for a certain file on the Windows 2000/XP setup CD, you'll find cabinet files that hold groups of compressed files (cabinet files have a .cab file extension). Use the Expand command to extract these files. Here are some useful parameters of the Expand command:

    ▲ To list all files in the driver.cab cabinet file:

```
expand D:\i386\driver.cab -f:* /d
```

A+ ESS
3.3

A+
220-602
3.1
3.3

▲ To extract the file Splitter.sys, in the Driver.cab file and copy it from the setup CD to the hard drive, first make the folder where you want the file to go the current folder. Then use the Expand command like this:

```
cd C:\windows\system32\drivers

expand D:\i386\driver.cab /f:splitter.sys
```

You can also use the Expand command to uncompress a compressed file. For example, to expand a file and copy it to the current folder, use this command:

```
expand D:\i386\netapi32.dl_
```

## USE THE RECOVERY CONSOLE TO RECOVER DATA

If your hard drive is corrupted, you still might be able to recover data. The problem with using the Recovery Console to do the job is that, by default, it will not allow you to go into folders other than the system folders or to copy data onto removable media. To do these things, you first need to change some Recovery Console settings. Then you can use the Copy command to copy data from the hard drive to other media.

Here are the commands you'll need to change the settings:

▲ To allow access to all files and folders on all drives:

```
set allowallpaths = true
```

▲ To allow you to copy any file to another media such as a jump drive or floppy disk:

```
set allowremovablemedia = true
```

▲ To allow the use of wildcard characters * and ?:

```
set allowwildcards = true
```

## OPTIONAL INSTALLATION OF THE RECOVERY CONSOLE

Although the Recovery Console can be launched from the Windows setup CD to recover from system failure, you can also install it on your working system so it appears on the OS boot loader menu. You can then use it to address less drastic problems that occur when you can boot from the hard drive.

To install the Recovery Console:

1. Open a command window.

2. Change from the current directory to the \i386 folder on the Windows 2000/XP CD.

3. Enter the command **winnt32 /cmdcons**. The Recovery Console is installed.

4. Restart your computer. Recovery Console should now be shown with the list of available operating systems on the OS boot loader menu.

# STRATEGIES FOR TROUBLESHOOTING WINDOWS 2000/XP STARTUP

**A+ ESS**
**1.3**
**3.3**

**A+**
**220-602**
**3.3**

Now that you know how the Windows 2000/XP boot process works and about the different tools you can use to solve boot problems, you're ready to move on and actually tackle real startup problems that might plague even the best-run and best-maintained computer. In this section of the chapter, you'll learn the general guidelines for troubleshooting, how to respond to startup errors, how to clean up a sluggish startup, and how to restore system files. We'll then wrap up the chapter with some methods to use when you have abandoned all hope of fixing a few Windows errors and are ready to do a major overhaul of the entire Windows installation.

Ready? Let's get started!

## GUIDELINES FOR TROUBLESHOOTING BOOT PROBLEMS

Here are some general guidelines to help you address boot problems:

- Interview the user to find out what has recently changed, what happened just before the problem started, and how to reproduce the problem. Ask what has recently happened. Has new hardware or software been installed? Don't forget to ask about any important data that is not backed up.

- If important data is not backed up, make every effort to copy the data to another media before you try to solve the Windows problem. Don't risk the data without the user's permission. If the system is giving so many errors that you cannot copy data, try booting into Safe Mode. If Safe Mode doesn't load, you can use the Recovery Console to access the data. If Recovery Console cannot access the hard drive, consider the problem related to hardware. The hard drive data cable might be loose, or the drive might be physically damaged.

- Next, determine at what point in the boot the system fails. Decide if you think the problem is hardware or software related.

- If you think the problem is related to hardware, check the simple things first. Turn off the power and restart the system. Check for loose cables, switches that are not on, stuck keys on the keyboard, a wall outlet switch that has been turned off, and similar easy-to-solve problems.

- If an error message is displayed onscreen, start by addressing it. You will learn several ways to address error messages later in the chapter. As you work to correct the problem and restore the system, always keep in mind to use the least drastic solution that will change as little of the system as possible.

- If you think the problem is software related and you cannot boot to the Windows desktop, try booting to the Advanced Options menu (hold down **F8** while Windows loads) and select the **Last Known Good Configuration**. If you want to use this option, it's important to use it early in the troubleshooting process before you accidentally overwrite the last known good.

- If you can load the Windows desktop, but the system is giving many errors or is extremely slow, suspect a virus is present. Run antivirus software to scan the entire hard drive for malicious software. If the antivirus software won't work or is not installed, boot into Safe Mode and install and run the software there. You will learn more about using antivirus software in Chapter 19.

- If the system has recently been changed, such as installing software or hardware, assume the installation is the guilty party until it's proven innocent. Use Device Manager to disable or uninstall the device. If this solves the problem, then try to find updated device drivers for the device. Search the Microsoft Web site for known problems with the device or search the device manufacturer Web site. Try updating or rolling back the device drivers.

▲ If a new application or utility program has just been installed, go to the Add or Remove Programs applet in the Control Panel and uninstall the software. Reboot the system. If the problem goes away, then try reinstalling the software. If the problem comes back, go to the software manufacturer's Web site and download and install any updates or fixes.

▲ The hard drive might be full or the file system corrupted. Use Disk Cleanup to clean up the hard drive, deleting unwanted files. Use Defrag and Chkdsk to optimize and repair the drive. If the system is slow while trying to do this, boot into Safe Mode and do these maintenance tasks from there. How to do these maintenance tasks is covered in Chapter 13.

▲ If you think unknown software is bogging down startup, you can do the following to clean up startup:

1. Boot into Safe Mode. To do that, while Windows is loading, press **F8** and select **Safe Mode with Networking** from the Advanced Options menu.

2. Use up-to-date antivirus software to scan for viruses. If you find a virus, clean it and reboot to see if the problem is solved. Rerun the AV software to make sure it caught everything.

3. Using the Add or Remove Programs applet in the Control Panel, remove any unwanted software. Be sure to stop the software first. If necessary, you can use Task Manager to end a process and then you can uninstall it.

4. Check all folders that contain startup entries and move or delete any startup programs and scripts that might be bogging down the system or causing errors.

5. Use the Windows XP System Configuration utility (Msconfig) to temporarily disable processes that might cause problems.

6. Use the Services Console to permanently disable any services that might be causing a problem. If an error message tells you which service is causing the problem, you can uninstall that software.

▲ If you think Windows system files are missing or corrupted, you can do the following to restore system files:

1. Use the System File Checker utility to recover Windows system files. If SFC won't work, you can restore system files using the Recovery Console.

2. For Windows XP, try using System Restore to return the system to a previously saved restore point. If you can't boot to the normal Windows desktop, boot into Safe Mode and use System Restore from there.

3. If you have a backup of the system state, use Ntbackup to restore the system state using this backup.

▲ If the problem is still not solved, it's time to assume that the Windows installation is corrupted. Here are the tools used to restore a Windows installation:

1. For Windows XP, try using a Windows XP boot disk to find out if the boot files in the root directory of drive C are missing or corrupted. If necessary, you can restore these files using the Recovery Console.

**14**

2. For Windows 2000, use the Emergency Repair Process to restore Windows 2000 to its state immediately after it was installed.

3. For Windows XP, use Automated System Recovery to restore the system to the last ASR backup.

4. Perform an in-place upgrade of Windows 2000/XP.

5. Perform a clean install of Windows 2000/XP.

As you work to solve a Windows problem, keep in mind that many tools are at your disposal. As you decide which tool to use to correct a problem, always use the least drastic solution to make the fewest possible changes to the system. For example, if you know a driver is giving a problem, even though you can use System Restore to restore the system before the driver was installed, doing so is more drastic than simply rolling back the driver. Always choose the method that makes as few changes to the system as possible and still solves the problem.

When you think the problem is solved, be sure to restart the system one last time to make sure all is well. Verify that everything is working and then ask the user to also verify that the problem is solved and all is working. And don't forget the paperwork. As you work, keep notes about the original symptoms, what you're doing, and the outcome. This paperwork will be a great help the next time you're faced with a similar problem.

## RESPOND TO ANY STARTUP ERRORS

Recall that Windows 2000/XP system has successfully started when you can log onto Windows, the Windows desktop is loaded, and the hourglass associated with the pointer has disappeared. If an error message appears before the system startup is completed, the obvious first step is to address the error message. Table 14-6 lists different types of error messages and what to do about them. Most of the errors in the table will cause the system to lock up and the boot to fail.

Now let's see exactly what to do when an error occurs as Windows is loading, when a stop error causes Windows to lock up, when a program is not found, and when a device or service has failed to start.

| Error Message | What It Means and What to Do About It |
|---|---|
| **Errors that occur before the Windows load begins:** | |
| Hard drive not found<br>Fixed disk error<br>Disk boot failure, insert system disk and press enter<br>No boot device available | Startup BIOS cannot find the hard drive. Problems with the hard drive and its subsystem are covered in Chapter 8. |
| Invalid boot disk<br>Inaccessible boot device<br>Invalid partition table<br>Error loading operating system<br>Missing operating system<br>No operating system found<br>Error loading operating system | The program in the MBR displays these messages when it cannot find the active partition on the hard drive or the boot sector on that partition. Use the Diskpart command from the Recovery Console to check the hard drive partition table for errors. Sometimes Fixmbr solves the problem. Third-party recovery software such as PartitionMagic might help. If a setup program came bundled with the hard drive (such as Data Lifeguard from Western Digital or MaxBlast from Maxtor), use it to examine the drive. Check the hard drive manufacturer's Web site for other diagnostic software. |

**Table 14-6** Startup error messages and their meanings

| Error Message | What It Means and What to Do About It |
|---|---|
| Black screen with no error messages | This is likely to be a corrupted MBR, partition table, boot sector, or Ntldr file. Boot the PC using a Windows 2000/XP boot disk and then try the fixmbr and fixboot commands from the Recovery Console. You might have to reinstall Windows. |
| When you first turn on the computer, it continually reboots. | This is most likely a hardware problem. Could be the CPU, motherboard, or RAM. First disconnect or remove all nonessential devices such as USB or FireWire devices. Inside the case, check all connections using safety precautions to protect the system against static electricity as you work. Try reseating RAM. Check for fans that are not working, causing the CPU to quickly overheat. |
| A disk read error occurred Missing NTLDR NTLDR is missing NTLDR is compressed | A disk is probably in the floppy disk drive. Remove the disk and reboot. When booting from the hard drive, these errors occur if Ntldr has been moved, renamed, or deleted, or is corrupted, if the boot sector on the active partition is corrupted, or you have just tried to install an older version of Windows such as Windows 98 on the hard drive. First try replacing Ntldr. Then check Boot.ini settings. |
| When you first turn on a system, it begins the boot process, but then powers down. | The CPU might be quickly overheating. Check for fans not running. Is this a new CPU installation? If so, make sure the cooler assembly on top of the CPU is correctly installed. |
| Stop errors that cause Windows to lock up: | |
| A text error message appears on a blue screen and then the system halts. Some stop errors follow: | Stop errors are usually caused by viruses, errors in the file system, a corrupted hard drive, or a hardware problem. Search the Microsoft Web site for information about an unidentified stop error. |
| Stop 0x00000024 or NTFS_File_System | The NTFS file system is corrupt. Immediately boot into the Recovery Console, and copy important data files that have not been backed up to another media before attempting to recover the system. |
| Stop 0x00000050 or Page_Fault_in_Nonpaged_Area | Most likely RAM is defective. |
| Stop 0x00000077 or Kernel_Stack_Inpage_Error | Bad sectors are on the hard drive, there is a hard drive hardware problem, or RAM is defective. Try running Chkdsk. |
| Stop 0x0000007A or Kernel_Data_Inpage_Error | There is a bad sector on the hard drive where the paging file is stored; there is a virus or defective RAM. Try running Chkdsk. |
| Stop 0x0000007B or Inaccessible_Boot_Device | There is a boot sector virus or failing hardware. Try Fixmbr. |
| While running Windows, a stop error appears and then the system reboots. The reboot happens so fast you can't read the error message. | For Windows XP, boot to the Advanced Options menu and choose Disable automatic restart on system failure. |
| Startup errors that occur because a program is corrupted or not found: | |
| A device has failed to start Service failed to start Program not found | A registry entry or startup folder is referencing a startup program it cannot find. Use Msconfig or the Services Console to find the entry and then replace the missing program. These errors are sometimes caused by uninstall routines that left behind these orphan entries. Depending on the error, the system might or might not halt. |

**Table 14-6**   Startup error messages and their meanings (continued)

# ERRORS THAT OCCUR BEFORE THE WINDOWS LOAD BEGINS

If an error occurs before Windows starts to load, you'll see a screen similar to Figure 14-24. Startup BIOS is still in control at this point. The error in the figure was caused when BIOS could not find a hard drive.

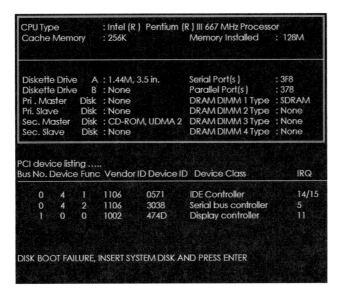

**Figure 14-24** A startup error before the Windows load begins

To successfully boot, a computer needs the bare-bones minimum of hardware and software. If one of these hardware or software components is missing, corrupted, or broken, the boot fails. Also, when you are trying to solve a boot program, you can reduce the hardware and software to a minimum to help you isolate the source of a problem. For example, unplug USB devices, printers, a second monitor, or other peripheral devices. Inside the computer case, you can disconnect data and power connectors to all drives except the hard drive that contains the OS. How to work inside a computer case is covered in Chapter 3.

Here is the list of essential hardware components:

- ▲ CPU, motherboard, memory, keyboard, and video card or onboard video
- ▲ A boot device such as a CD drive with bootable CD, a floppy drive with bootable floppy, or a hard drive with an OS installed
- ▲ A power supply with electrical power

How to troubleshoot hardware problems that cause the boot to fail is covered in other chapters in this book.

## STOP ERRORS

One type of error message is a **stop error**, which is an error so drastic it causes Windows to hang or lock up. Figure 14-25 shows one example of a stop error. Look on the screen for information similar to that marked in the figure. For help with the problem, search the Microsoft support site (*support.microsoft.com*) on the exact text of the error message. This particular stop error in Figure 14-25 was caused by a USB device that had gone bad. When the device was unplugged, the system booted with no problems.

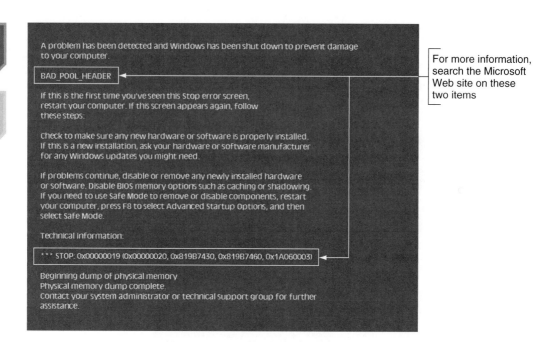

For more information, search the Microsoft Web site on these two items

**Figure 14-25** A BSOD might be caused by hardware or software

## PROGRAM NOT FOUND ERROR

Sometimes when software is uninstalled, the uninstall routine leaves behind an entry in the registry or a startup folder. When the registry entry tries to launch a program and the program has been deleted, an error is displayed. For example, Figure 14-26 shows an error message that appeared on the first boot after antivirus software had found and removed a virus. The antivirus software did not completely remove all parts of the virus, and somewhere in the system, the command to launch 0sis0ijw.dll is still working even though this program has been deleted. One way to find this orphan entry point is to use Msconfig. The Msconfig window in Figure 14-27 is showing us that the DLL is launched from a registry key.

**Figure 14-26** Startup error indicates malware has not been completely removed

The next step is to back up the registry and then use Regedit to find and delete the key, as shown in Figure 14-28.

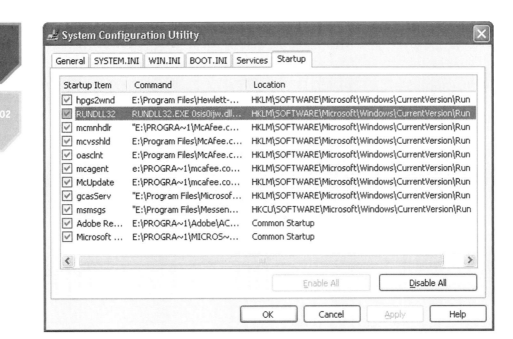

Figure 14-27  Msconfig shows how the DLL is launched during startup

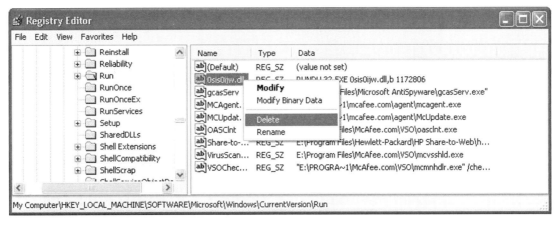

Figure 14-28  Delete orphan registry entry left there by malware

## ERRORS FROM WHEN A DEVICE OR SERVICE HAS FAILED TO START

Error messages might be caused by a device driver, a service, or other software that is missing or corrupted. If the service or device is critical for Windows to run, the startup fails. Otherwise, the error message appears and you can still continue to the Windows desktop.

If you can get to the Windows desktop and the startup error indicates the problem is with a device driver, use Device Manager to update the driver. If that doesn't work, uninstall and reinstall the device. If the error message indicates a service has failed to start, use Msconfig to temporarily disable some or all services until you discover which service is causing the problem. You can then reinstall the application or restore the program from backup or from the Windows 2000/XP setup CD. For Windows services, use System File Checker to restore the system files.

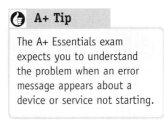

**A+ Tip**

The A+ Essentials exam expects you to understand the problem when an error message appears about a device or service not starting.

If the error causes the system to lock up so that the desktop does not load, try using tools that make the least changes to your system as possible before you use the more drastic tools. First try the Last Known Good Configuration on the Advanced Options menu. If that doesn't work, then try Safe Mode and System Restore. Next, try the Recovery Console to identify the service and replace the system file. If none of these work, then you'll need to consider restoring the Windows installation from backup or reinstalling Windows 2000/XP.

## CLEANING UP STARTUP

When Windows startup is slow or gives errors, one thing you can do is perform a general clean up of the startup processes. For starters, you can check startup folders for startup processes and also look for undesired scheduled tasks, Group Policy startup entries, and installed fonts. Msconfig can help find other startup entries, and the Services Console can be used to disable unneeded services. All these methods are discussed in this section.

### CHECK STARTUP FOLDERS

Certain folders are designated as startup folders for all user accounts or a particular user account. Scripts, programs, or shortcuts to programs can be placed in these startup folders by the user, by an administrator, or by a program without the user's knowledge. For example, Figure 14-29 shows a startup folder with all kinds of services placed there by Windows and other software.

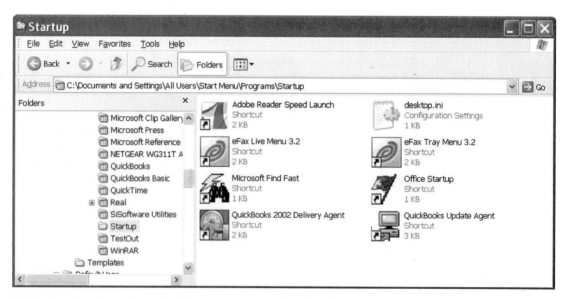

**Figure 14-29**    This startup folder holds several unneeded services that appear in the system tray and take up system resources

To clean up startup, look in each startup folder mentioned in this section. If you find a program or shortcut there that you don't think you want, unless you know it's something you need, move it to a different folder rather than deleting it. Later, if you like, you can return it to the startup folder, or you can start the program manually from the new folder.

A+ ESS
3.2
3.3

A+
220-602
3.2
3.3

> **Notes**
>
> To keep programs kept in startup folders from executing as you start Windows, hold down the Shift key just after you enter your account name and password on the Windows logon screen. Keep holding down the Shift key until the desktop is fully loaded and the hourglass has disappeared. To permanently disable a startup item, remove it from its startup folder.

Your first step is to check these startup folders for any program file or a shortcut that is not needed:

▲ C:\Documents and Settings\*username*\Start Menu\Programs\Startup
▲ C:\Documents and Settings\All Users\Start Menu\Programs\Startup

Your next step is to consider if Windows 2000/XP has been installed as an upgrade from Windows NT. If so, the C:\Winnt\Profiles folder will exist. Programs and shortcuts to programs might be in these folders:

C:\Winnt\Profiles\All Users\Start Menu\Programs\Startup
C:\Winnt\Profiles\*username*\Start Menu\Programs\Startup

## LOOK FOR UNWANTED SCHEDULED TASKS

Tasks scheduled to launch at startup are placed in this folder: C:\Windows\Tasks. The folder might contain a desired task, such as a utility to run a background service to keep software updated. However, it might also contain unwanted or even malicious tasks. When looking for unnecessary programs that slow down startup, be sure to check this folder.

The easiest way to view and change this folder is to open the Scheduled Tasks applet in the Control Panel. When the Scheduled Tasks folder appears, click **View**, **Details**. The left side of Figure 14-30 shows that two tasks are scheduled. One task was placed there by an

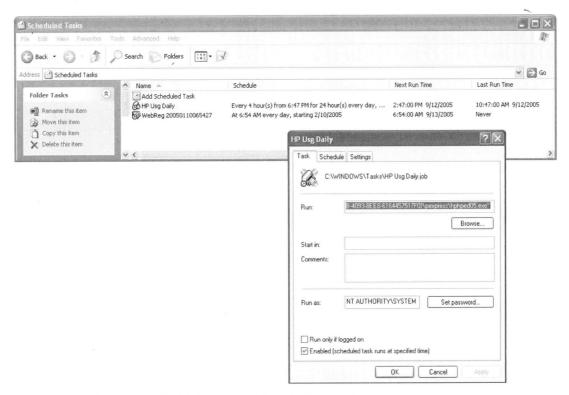

**Figure 14-30** The Scheduled Task folder can contain tasks that launch at startup

A+ ESS
3.2
3.3

A+
220-602
3.2
3.3

HP printer installation program, and another was placed there by an administrator. The right side of the figure shows the details of the HP program task.

> **Notes**
>
> Tasks can be hidden in the Scheduled Tasks folder. To be certain you're viewing all scheduled tasks, unhide them by clicking **Tools**, **Folder Options**. In the Folder Options window, click the **View** tab, select **Show hidden files and folders**, and then uncheck **Hide protected operating system files**.

## CHECK GROUP POLICY FOR UNWANTED STARTUP EVENTS

When an administrator uses Group Policy to cause a script to run, Group Policy places that script in one of the folders in the following list. Also, malicious software is sometimes placed in these same folders. Writers of malicious software pick these folders because many users aren't aware of them and don't know to look here for unwanted programs. When cleaning up a system, be sure to take a look at these folders for unwanted program files:

▲ C:\WINDOWS\System32\GroupPolicy\Machine\Scripts\Startup
▲ C:\WINDOWS\System32\GroupPolicy\Machine\Scripts\Shutdown
▲ C:\WINDOWS\System32\GroupPolicy\User\Scripts\Logon
▲ C:\WINDOWS\System32\GroupPolicy\User\Scripts\Logoff

> **Notes**
>
> Don't forget that we are using C:\Windows as the folder in which Windows is installed. Depending on where the OS is installed, your folder might be different, such as C:\Winnt or E:\Windows.

## CHECK FOR TOO MANY INSTALLED FONTS

Windows comes with a group of fonts that can be used for the Windows desktop and in a variety of other places. Some applications install additional fonts and you can purchase and manually install other fonts. All installed fonts are loaded at startup, so if a system has had many new fonts installed, these can slow down startup. Windows 2000/XP stores all installed fonts in the C:\Windows\Fonts folder. (See Figure 14-31 for a few samples of those fonts). To install or uninstall a font is to simply move the fonts file in or out of this folder.

When Windows starts up for the first time after the Fonts folder has been changed, it rebuilds the fonts table, which means the first reboot after a font change is slowed down. Check the C:\Windows\Fonts folder on your computer. If you see more than 260 files in this folder, new fonts have been installed. You can try moving some files to a different folder to reduce the number of fonts loading at startup.

Actually, you can move all the files out of the Fonts folder and Windows will still work because it doesn't keep the one system font here. But then, your documents will look pretty plain. If you change the Fonts folder, don't forget it'll take the second reboot before you should notice any improvement in startup, because the first reboot must take the time to rebuild the table.

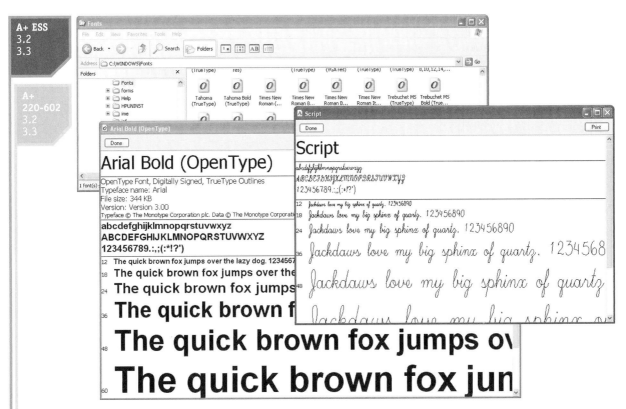

**Figure 14-31** Fonts are kept in the C:\Windows\Fonts folder

## USE WINDOWS XP MSCONFIG TO LIMIT STARTUP EVENTS

Recall from Chapter 12 that the Windows XP System Configuration Utility (Msconfig.exe) can be used to temporarily disable startup services and other programs and help you find the one causing a problem. To use it, enter Msconfig.exe in the Run dialog box. In the Msconfig window, click the **Services** tab to view all services that are set to start (see Figure 14-32).

At the bottom of this window, if you check **Hide All Microsoft Services**, the list of non-Microsoft services is displayed. Check the ones you want to start and uncheck the ones you want to temporarily disable.

Next, select the **Startup** tab showing in Figure 14-33. Listed are all the programs that Windows expects to start during the startup process. You'll be surprised how many there are after you've used a system for some time. Freeware, antivirus software, games, printer drivers, and all sorts of programs put entries in the registry or in startup folders to cause themselves to be launched at startup. Cleaning up this mess can make Windows XP work like new again. Uncheck any program you want to disable at the next startup or click **Disable All** to stop them all. Click **Apply**. Choose **Selective Startup** on the General tab and reboot. If your problem is solved or Windows starts much faster, you can permanently remove the program from startup.

To permanently remove the program from startup, first try to use the program's menus to set the program to not automatically launch at startup or remove the program file or shortcut from the startup folders. If you don't need the program, use the Add or Remove Programs applet to uninstall the program. As a last resort, you can search the registry for the key that is used to start the program. In Figure 14-33, you can see which programs are started because of an entry in a certain key of the registry. Editing the registry is dangerous and should only be done if other methods have failed.

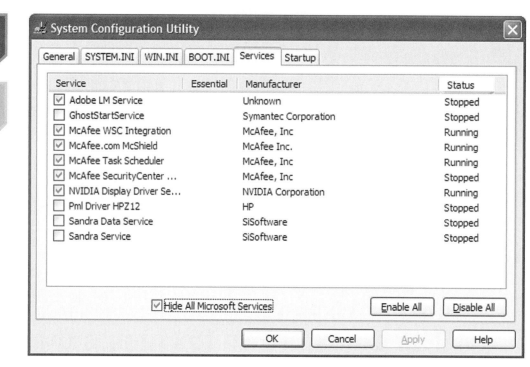

**Figure 14-32** Use the Msconfig Services tab to temporarily control services launched at startup

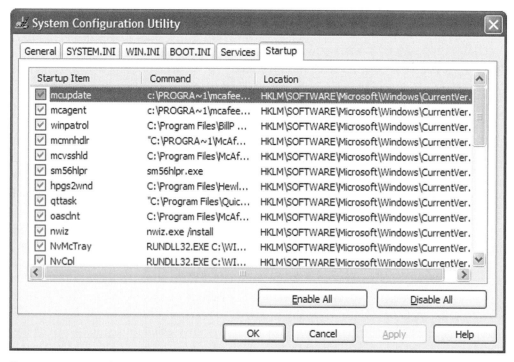

**Figure 14-33** Use the Msconfig Startup tab to control programs launched at startup

**A+ ESS**
3.2
3.3

**A+**
**220-602**
3.2
3.3

Once you have permanently stopped unwanted programs and services from launching at startup and all problems have been resolved, return to the Msconfig window and select **Normal Startup** on the **General** tab.

> **Notes**
>
> If you are not familiar with a startup program, Google the Web on the program filename. If you suspect a Windows system service is causing a problem, you can use Msconfig to disable the service. If this works, then replace the service file with a fresh copy from the Windows setup CD.

## CHECK FOR CORRUPTED OR UNNEEDED SERVICES

Recall that a service is a program that runs in the background to support other programs. Services are managed by the Services console (Services.msc). Use the Services console to see what services have been set to automatically start when Windows loads. To launch the Services console, type **Services.msc** in the Run dialog box and press **Enter**. The Services window opens, as shown on the left side of Figure 14-34.

To learn more about a service, right-click it and select **Properties** from the shortcut menu. In the resulting Properties window, which is shown on the right side of Figure 14-34 for one selected service, you can see the name of the program file and its path.

When investigating a service, try using a good search engine on the Web to search on the name of the service or the name of the program file that launches the service. Either can give you information you need to snoop out unwanted services. If you're not sure you want to keep a certain service, use Msconfig to temporarily disable it at the next boot so you can see what happens.

> **Notes**
>
> Recall from Chapter 12 that you can use Task Manager to investigate processes that are using too much of system resources, including CPU time, memory, and hard drive access.

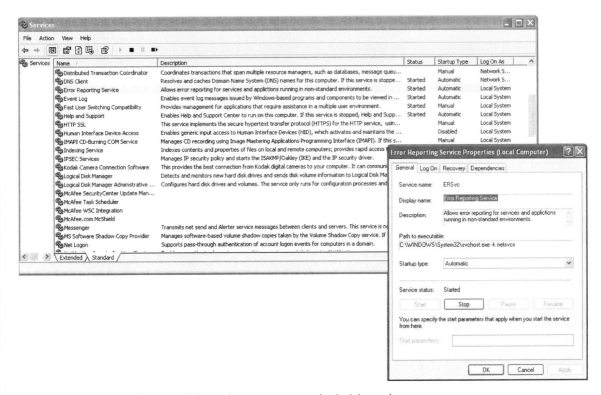

**Figure 14-34** The Services console is used to start, stop, and schedule services

# RESTORE SYSTEM FILES

If Windows startup is so corrupted you cannot identify a single service or program causing the problem, you can take a shotgun approach and just do a general restoration of system files. Tools that can help you do this are System Restore, backups of the system state, System File Checker, the Windows 2000/XP boot disk, and the Recovery Console. In this part of the chapter, we'll look at System Restore, the Windows 2000/XP boot disk, and the Recovery Console.

> **Notes**
>
> When using System Restore and system state backups, you run the risk of undoing *desired* changes to the Windows environment and software installations. Before using one of the fixes in this section, consider what desired changes will be lost when you apply the fix.

## RETURN TO A PREVIOUS WINDOWS XP RESTORE POINT

Recall from Chapter 12 that the Windows XP **System Restore** utility can be used to restore the system state to its condition at the time a restore point was made. Before using System Restore to undo a change, if the change was made to a hardware device, first try Driver Rollback so that as few changes as possible to the system are lost. If Driver Rollback does not work or is not appropriate, then use System Restore to revert the system to the restore point. When selecting a restore point, select a point as close to the present as you can so that as few changes to the system as possible are lost.

If you can't boot to the Windows desktop, try booting into Safe Mode. When you do that, Windows XP asks if you want to go directly to System Restore rather than to Safe Mode. Choose to go directly to System Restore.

> 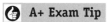 **A+ Exam Tip**
>
> The A+ Essentials exam expects you to know how to boot to a system restore point.

> **Notes**
>
> To roll back the system to a Windows XP restore point using Windows XP requires that you can boot from the hard drive. However, there are other options using third-party utility software. For example, ERD Commander 2003 by Winternals (*www.winternals.com*) is an operating system that can be loaded from CD. Boot from the ERD Commander CD, which loads a GUI interface that looks like Windows XP. Using this Winternals desktop, you can access the registry, event logs, and Disk Management Console and reset a forgotten administrator password. You can also roll back the Windows XP system to a restore point.

## USE THE WINDOWS 2000/XP BOOT DISK TO VERIFY BOOT FILES

A Windows 2000/XP boot disk can be used to boot the system bypassing the boot files stored in the root directory of drive C. If you boot from the disk and the Windows 2000/XP desktop loads successfully, then the problem is associated with damaged sectors or missing or damaged files in the root directory of drive C that are required to boot the OS. These sectors and files include the master boot program, the partition table, the OS boot record, and the boot files, Ntldr file, Ntdetect.com file, Ntbootdd.sys (if it exists), and the Boot.ini file. In addition, the problem can be caused by a boot sector virus. However, a boot disk cannot be used to troubleshoot problems associated with unstable device drivers or any other system files stored in the \Windows folder or its subfolders.

You first create the boot disk by formatting the disk using a working Windows 2000/XP computer and then copying files to the disk. These files can be copied from a Windows

**14**

A+ ESS
3.3

A+
220-602
3.3

2000/XP setup CD, or a Windows 2000/XP computer that is using the same version of Windows XP or Windows 2000 as the problem PC. Do the following to create the disk:

1. Obtain a floppy disk and format it on a Windows 2000/XP computer.

2. Using Explorer, copy Ntldr and Ntdetect.com from the \i386 folder on the Windows 2000/XP setup CD or a Windows 2000/XP computer to the root of the floppy disk.

3. If your computer boots from a SCSI hard drive, then obtain a device driver (*.sys) for your SCSI hard drive, rename it **Ntbootdd.sys,** and copy it to the root of the floppy disk. (If you used an incorrect device driver, then you will receive an error after booting from the floppy disk. The error will mention a "computer disk hardware configuration problem" and that it "could not read from the selected boot disk." If this occurs, contact your computer manufacturer or hard drive manufacturer for the correct version of the SCSI hard drive device driver for your computer.)

4. Look at Boot.ini on the problem computer, and then obtain an identical copy from another known good computer (or create your own) and copy it to the root of the floppy disk.

5. If you can't find a good Boot.ini file to copy, you can use the lines listed below to create a Boot.ini file. These lines work for a Boot.ini file if the problem computer is booting from an IDE hard drive:

```
[boot loader]

timeout=30

default=multi(0)disk(0)rdisk(0)partition(1)\WINDOWS

[operating systems]

multi(0)disk(0)rdisk(0)partition(1)\WINDOWS="Microsoft
Windows XP Professional" /fastdetect
```

6. Write-protect the floppy disk so it cannot become infected with a virus.

7. You have now created the Windows 2000/XP boot disk. Check CMOS setup to make sure the first boot device is set to the floppy disk, and then insert the boot disk and reboot your computer.

 **Tip**

If you are creating your own Boot.ini file, be sure to enter a hard return after the /fastdetect switch in the last line of the file.

**Notes**

To learn more about the Windows XP boot disk, see the Microsoft Knowledge Base Articles 305595 and 314503 at the Microsoft Web site *support.microsoft.com*. To learn more about the Windows 2000 boot disk, see the Microsoft Knowledge Base Article 301680.

If the Windows 2000/XP desktop loads successfully, then do the following to attempt to repair the Windows 2000/XP installation:

1. Load the Recovery Console and use the Fixmbr and Fixboot commands to repair the MBR and the boot sector.

2. Run anti-virus software.

3. Use Disk Management to verify that the hard drive partition table is correct.

4. Defragment your hard drive.

5. Copy Ntldr, Ntdetect.com, and Boot.ini from your floppy disk to the root of the hard drive.

6. If you're using a SCSI hard drive, copy Ntbootdd.sys from your floppy disk to the root of the hard drive.

If the Windows 2000/XP desktop did not load by booting from the boot disk, then the next tool to try is the Recovery Console.

### USE THE RECOVERY CONSOLE TO RESTORE SYSTEM FILES

If you are not able to boot from the hard drive, your next step is to use the Windows 2000/XP setup CD to boot to the Recovery Console using the instructions given earlier in the chapter. Then, try one or more of the following:

- ◢ Get a directory listing of files in the root directory. If you see garbage on the screen instead of a clean directory list, most likely the hard drive file system is corrupted or the hard drive is physically damaged.
- ◢ Use the Chkdsk command to scan the hard drive for errors.
- ◢ Try copying the backup copies of the registry files from the \Windows\repair folder to the \Windows\system32\config folder. Directions are given earlier in the chapter. Reboot to see if the problem is solved.
- ◢ If you have previously identified a key Windows service that is causing the problem, you can locate the file in the \Windows folder and replace it with a fresh copy from the Windows 2000/XP setup CD.
- ◢ To see a list of all services you can disable, use the Listsvc command. Use the Disable and Enable commands to try disabling each service one by one until you find the one causing the problem.

Looking for a failed Windows system file can sometimes be like looking for a needle in a haystack. At some point, you just decide it's time to take more drastic measures and restore the Windows installation to when it was last backed up. That's the subject of the next section.

## RECOVER OR REPAIR THE WINDOWS 2000/XP INSTALLATION

If the Windows installation is so corrupted that none of the previous tools and methods have helped, you need to decide how best to repair the installation. For a notebook computer or a brand name computer such as a Dell or Gateway, the hard drive most likely has a recovery partition that you can use to recover the Windows installation. These computers might also have a recovery CD. For Windows XP, you can use Automated System Recovery, and for Windows 2000, you can use the Emergency Repair Process. You can also perform an in-place upgrade or you can reinstall Windows 2000/XP. All these methods are discussed in this section.

### RECOVERY PARTITIONS AND RECOVERY CDS

In this chapter, we often refer to the Windows 2000/XP setup CD. If you have a notebook computer or a brand name computer such as a Dell, IBM, or Gateway, be sure to use the manufacturer's recovery CD (also called a restore CD) instead of a regular Windows 2000/XP setup CD (see Figure 14-35 for samples of both). This recovery CD has drivers specific to your system and the Windows 2000/XP build might be different from that of an off-the-shelf Windows 2000/XP setup CD. For example, Windows XP Home Edition installed on a notebook computer might have been built with all kinds of changes made to it by the notebook manufacturer making it different from the Windows XP Home Edition that you can buy in a retail store.

**Figure 14-35** Brand name recovery CDs and a Windows XP setup CD

The manufacturer might have also put a hidden partition on the hard drive that can be used to recover the Windows installation. During startup, you'll see a message onscreen such as "Press F2 to recover the system" or "Press F11 to start recovery." When you press the appropriate key, a menu should appear that gives you two options: one repairs the Windows installation, saving user data, and the other reformats drive C and restores your system to the way it was when purchased. First, try to save user data before you attempt the destructive recovery. If neither method works, the hidden partition might be corrupted or the hard drive might be physically damaged.

If the recovery process doesn't work, try to use the recovery CD that came bundled with your computer to repair the installation. If you don't have the recovery CD, you might be able to buy one from the computer manufacturer. For notebook computers, you really must have this recovery CD to reinstall Windows because the device drivers on the CD are specific to your notebook. If you cannot buy a recovery CD, you might be able to download the drivers from the notebook manufacturer's Web site. Download them to another computer and burn them to a CD that you can use on the notebook to install drivers.

## WINDOWS XP AUTOMATED SYSTEM RECOVERY

Recall from Chapter 12 that you can use the Automated System Recovery (ASR) tool to recover a system from the last time you made a full backup of drive C. To restore a system using the ASR backup, begin by booting from the Windows XP setup CD and pressing **F2**

**Notes**

When you use the ASR tool, everything written to drive C since the ASR backup was made will be lost, including software and device drivers, user data, and any changes to the system configuration.

when you see the message, "Press F2 to run the Automated System Recovery process." Then, follow the directions on the screen to restore drive C.

## WINDOWS 2000 EMERGENCY REPAIR PROCESS

The Windows 2000 **Emergency Repair Process** should be used only as a last resort because it restores the system to the state it was in immediately after the Windows 2000 installation. All changes made since the installation are lost. The process uses an Emergency Repair Disk (ERD), which contains information about your current installation. The Windows 2000 ERD points to a folder on the hard drive where the registry was backed up when Windows 2000 was installed. This folder is *%SystemRoot%*\repair, which, in most systems, is C:\Winnt\repair.

**APPLYING CONCEPTS** Using the Windows 2000 ERD to recover from a corrupted registry returns you to the installation version of the registry, and you lose all changes to the registry since that time. Because of the way the ERD works, you do not need to update the disk once you've created it. Before a problem occurs, follow these directions to create the disk:

1. Click **Start**, point to **Programs**, **Accessories**, and **System Tools**, and then click **Backup**. The Backup window appears with the Welcome tab selected (see Figure 14-36). Select **Emergency Repair Disk**.

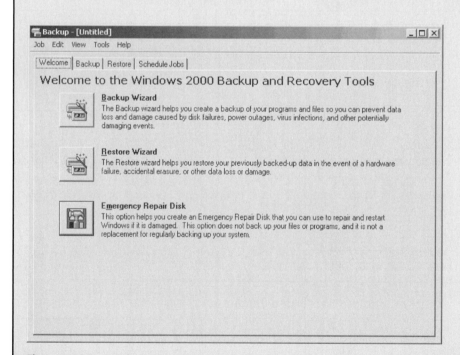

**Figure 14-36** Use the Backup window to back up the registry and create an emergency repair disk

2. The Backup tab and the Emergency Repair Diskette dialog box open. If you check the box shown in Figure 14-37, the system backs up your registry to a folder under the Repair folder, *%SystemRoot%*\repair\RegBack.

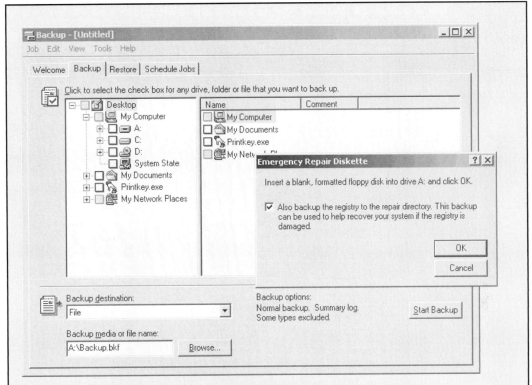

**Figure 14-37** Create an ERD and back up the registry to the hard drive

3. Click **OK** to create the disk. Label the disk "Windows 2000 Emergency Repair Disk," and keep it in a safe place.

If your hard drive fails, you can use the ERD to restore the system, including system files, boot files, and the registry, to its state at the end of the Windows 2000 installation. Follow these steps:

1. Boot the PC from the four Windows 2000 setup disks. The Setup menu appears (refer back to Figure 14-15). Select option **R**.

2. When the Windows 2000 Repair Options window opens (refer back to Figure 14-16), select option **R**.

3. You are instructed to insert the Emergency Repair Disk. Follow the instructions on the screen to repair the installation.

4. If this process does not work, then your next option is to reinstall Windows 2000. If you don't plan to reformat the drive, you need to scan the drive for errors before you reinstall Windows. To do that, you can boot to the Recovery Console and use the Chkdsk command to scan the drive for errors. If you suspect that a virus damaged the file system, also use the Fixmbr command to replace the master boot program in case it has been corrupted by the virus.

### Notes

Sometimes recovering the data on a hard drive is more important than fixing a Windows problem. If Windows is so corrupted it will not boot, but your first priority is to save the data on the drive, consider removing the hard drive and installing it in a working computer as a second drive. You can then copy all data from the drive to the primary drive in the working system. After your data is safe, then reinstall the hard drive in the first computer. At that point, you might want to solve your corrupted Windows problem by formatting the hard drive and reinstalling Windows to get a fresh, clean start.

## IN-PLACE UPGRADE OF WINDOWS 2000/XP

An in-place upgrade installs Windows over the same existing installation. When you do an in-place upgrade of Windows 2000/XP, all installed applications and hardware must be reinstalled, but user data should not be lost.

Do the following to perform an in-place upgrade:

> **🔔 Tip**
>
> There are two ways to reinstall Windows 2000/XP: an in-place upgrade and a clean install. First try the in-place upgrade and if that doesn't work, then try a clean install.

1. Boot the computer from the Windows 2000/XP setup CD.

2. The Welcome to Setup screen appears, as shown back in Figure 14-14 (for Windows XP) or Figure 14-15 (for Windows 2000). Press **Enter** to select the option to set up Windows 2000/XP now.

3. On the next screen, press **F8** to accept the license agreement.

4. On the next screen, shown in Figure 14-38 for Windows XP, verify that the path to your Windows folder (most likely C:\Windows) is selected and then press **R** to repair Windows 2000/XP. Follow the instructions onscreen. During the installation, you'll be asked for the product key, which you'll find printed on the setup CD sleeve or case or stuck to the side of the computer case or bottom of a notebook computer.

5. If the installation gives problems or the original problem is still not solved after you finish the in-place upgrade, then try a clean installation of Windows.

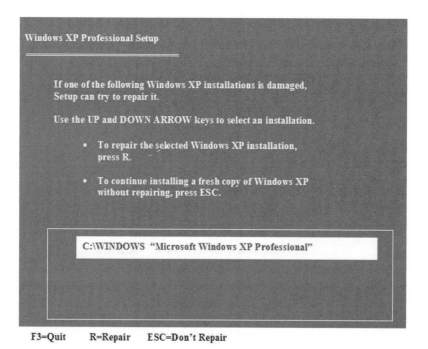

**Figure 14-38**  Windows XP Setup can repair the selected Windows installation

## CLEAN INSTALLATION OF WINDOWS 2000/XP

A clean installation of Windows 2000/XP gives you a fresh start with the OS. First make sure you've copied important data files to a safe place. Then do the following to reinstall Windows 2000/XP:

You need to completely destroy the current Windows 2000/XP installation so that the Windows 2000/XP setup process won't think it is installing Windows as a second OS on the

drive (called a dual boot). One way to do that is to delete the partition used for drive C:. The Windows setup program will then create a new partition. A less drastic way is to delete the C:\Windows folder. Using this last method, data on the drive will be saved. Here is how to use either method:

1. Boot from the Windows 2000/XP setup CD and launch the Recovery Console.

2. If you decide you want to delete only the C:\Windows folder, type **del C:\windows** and then press **Enter**.

3. If you decide you want to totally wipe out the C: partition, type **diskpart** and then press **Enter**. Then select and delete the partition for drive C:.

4. Boot again from the Windows 2000/XP setup CD.

5. The Welcome to Setup screen appears, as shown in Figure 14-39 for Windows XP. Press **Enter** to select the default option to set up Windows XP.

6. Follow the directions onscreen to install the OS. You'll need the product key.

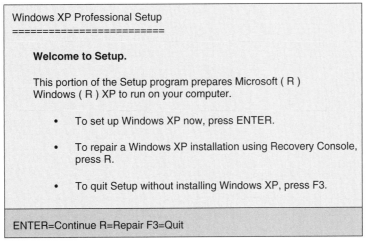

**Figure 14-39** Windows XP Setup opening menu

## >> CHAPTER SUMMARY

▲ The boot process for Windows 2000/XP uses files stored in the root directory of the hard drive and the C:\Windows\system32 folder.

▲ The boot process can be customized with entries in Boot.ini. The Boot.ini file can be edited with a text editor, but it is best to change the file using the System Properties dialog box.

▲ Tools to use to troubleshoot problems with loading Windows 2000/XP are the Advanced Options menu and the Recovery Console.

▲ To access the Advanced Options menu, press F8 when starting Windows 2000/XP.

▲ The Advanced Options menu includes Safe Mode, Safe Mode with networking, Safe Mode with command prompt, enable boot logging, enable VGA mode, Last Known Good configuration, directory services restore mode, debugging mode, and disable automatic restart on system failure. This last option is available only in Windows XP.

▲ The Recovery Console is a command interface with a limited number of commands available to troubleshoot a failing Windows 2000/XP load. The console requires that you enter the Administrator password.

▲ Access the Recovery Console by first booting from the Windows 2000/XP CD, or the four Windows 2000 setup disks or install the console under the boot loader menu and access it from there.

▲ When solving problems with a sluggish or failing Windows 2000/XP startup, you might need to respond to any startup error messages, clean up the startup process, restore system files, and perhaps repair the Windows 2000/XP installation.

▲ Programs can be loaded during Windows startup by storing files in startup folders, using Task Scheduler, Group Policy, or the Services console, or by making entries in the registry. When cleaning up the startup process, be sure to check all these locations and to scan for viruses and other malicious software.

▲ When you cannot load the Windows desktop, tools to use to check for errors with Windows system files and restore these files include System Restore, a boot disk, and the Recovery Console.

▲ The Emergency Repair Process lets you restore the system to its state at the end of the Windows 2000 installation. Don't use it unless all other methods fail, because you will lose all changes made to the system since the installation. The Emergency Repair Process requires the emergency repair disk.

▲ The Windows XP Automated System Recovery (ASR) process creates a backup and an ASR floppy disk that can be used to restore the backup of the volume or logical drive holding Windows XP.

▲ You can use the Windows 2000/XP setup CD to perform an in-place upgrade of Windows.

## >> KEY TERMS

For explanations of key terms, see the Glossary near the end of the book.

| | | |
|---|---|---|
| 32-bit flat memory mode | Boot.ini | Recovery Console |
| Advanced Options menu | Emergency Repair Process | stop error |
| blue screen of death (BSOD) | minifile system | System Restore |

## >> REVIEW QUESTIONS

1. Where is Boot.ini located on a Windows 2000/XP system?

   **a.** The root folder of the system partition (usually C:\)

   **b.** The \winnt_root\system32 folder of the boot partition (usually C:\Windows\system32)

   **c.** The \winnt_root\system32\config folder of the boot partition (usually C:\Windows\system32\config)

   **d.** The \winnt_root\system32\drivers folder of the boot partition (usually C:\Windows\system32\drivers)

2. Which of the following is the virtual memory swap file needed to boot Windows 2000/XP successfully?

   **a.** Hal.dll

   **b.** Kernel32.dll

   **c.** Pagefile.sys

   **d.** System

3. Which of the following statements best describes Safe Mode?

   **a.** It provides network access.

   **b.** It boots the OS with a minimum configuration.

   **c.** It uses video drivers specific to your video card.

   **d.** The GUI interface does not have to display in Safe Mode.

4. Which of the following keys do you press to retrieve the last command one character at a time when using the Recovery Console?

   **a.** F1

   **b.** F2

   **c.** F3

   **d.** F4

5. If you are creating your own Boot.ini file, which of the following must be entered after the /fastdetect switch in the last line of the file?

   **a.** A hard return

   **b.** //

   **c.** \\

   **d.** ..\

6. True or false? Ntdetect.com detects software present.

7. True or false? The Windows 2000 Emergency Repair Process should be used only as a last resort because it restores the system to the state it was in immediately after the Windows 2000 installation.

8. True or false? You can view and edit the Boot.ini file.

9. True or false? By default, the Recovery Console will not allow you to go into folders other than the system folders or to copy data onto removable media when trying to recover data when your hard drive is corrupted.

10. True or false? If a device driver or other software critical for Windows to run is missing or corrupted, the startup enters Safe Mode.

11. Ntldr, the Windows 2000/XP boot strap loader program, changes the processor from real mode to _____ mode.

12. Ntldr launches the _____ drivers so files can be read from either a FAT or NTFS file system.

**13.** There are two main sections in Boot.ini: the _____ section and the _____ section.

**14.** If Windows hangs during the boot, try booting using the option Enable Boot Logging and look at the last entry in the file called _____.

**15.** The system failure that causes Windows 2000/XP to automatically restart is called a(n) _____.

# Windows 9x/Me Commands and Startup Disk

Even though DOS and Windows 9x/Me are no longer supported by Microsoft, there is much to gain in understanding how these legacy OSs work. Just as knowing how to drive a manual-shift car can help you be a better driver when driving an automatic, so can understanding old operating systems help you better support the newer ones. Using DOS and Windows 9x/Me utilities and commands, you can sometimes get a better understanding of how a hardware device works and how an OS interacts with it than you can with the Windows 2000/XP operating system. That's because many times the older the technology, the less complicated it is and the more control you have over it.

Having worked in the computer industry for many years, I can personally tell you that I can see a greater depth of understanding among technicians who support Windows 2000/XP if they have had the benefit of first studying DOS and Windows 9x/Me. In fact, if you are given the opportunity, you might find it helpful to study this chapter and Chapter 16 before you turn your attention to the chapters on Windows 2000/XP (Chapters 11, 12, 13, and 14). Because this chapter is written so that it can be studied before these Windows 2000/XP chapters, you'll find a few short instances where material is duplicated, for example, the commands used at the command prompt to manage files and directories.

In this chapter, you'll learn what happens when DOS and the DOS-core portion of Windows 9x/Me are loaded, how DOS and Windows 9x/Me manage memory, how to use the command line, and how to use the Windows 9x/Me startup disk. You'll then have all the background knowledge you need to begin your study of Windows 9x/Me in the next chapter.

# UNDERSTANDING DOS AND WINDOWS 9X/ME STARTUP

The Windows 9x/Me operating system is built on a DOS core. In this section, you'll learn what first happens during booting when only the MS-DOS core of Windows 9x/Me is loaded, which provides a command prompt for you to enter commands. This command-driven, real-mode OS environment first discussed in Chapter 2 allows you to use commands useful when troubleshooting a system that cannot boot to a Windows desktop.

You can load the MS-DOS core in two ways: from the Windows 9x/Me hard drive or from a Windows 9x/Me startup disk. If the hard drive is healthy enough, it's easier to load from it, but in situations where the hard drive is really messed up, you can boot to a command prompt from a startup floppy disk. You'll learn how to use both methods later in the chapter. Now let's turn our attention to the steps involved in getting the MS-DOS core OS loaded. As you read, refer to Figure 15-1, which outlines the process.

> **Notes**
>
> Windows 9x/Me is fast being outdated by Windows XP. However, the Windows 9x/Me startup disk is still a popular troubleshooting tool and well worth your time to learn how it works. In many situations, you can use it when other more sophisticated tools fail you.

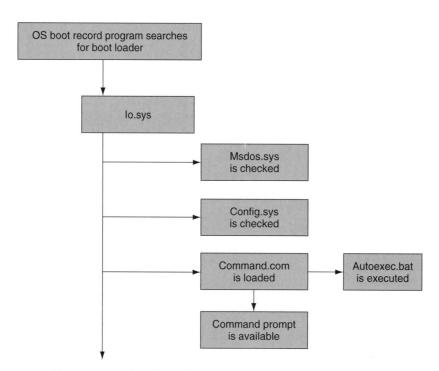

**Figure 15-1** Steps to load the MS-DOS core

## OS BOOT RECORD PROGRAM LOCATES AND EXECUTES IO.SYS

As you learned in Chapter 3, after POST, startup BIOS looks to CMOS RAM to know which storage media to search for an OS. For a hard drive or floppy disk, the little program in the OS boot record is found. This program then searches for the boot loader program. For Windows 9x/Me or MS-DOS, it searches for a hidden file named Io.sys. (A **hidden file** is a file that does not appear in the directory list.) The Io.sys file contains

**15**

the basic I/O software for real mode. Once Io.sys is loaded into memory, the boot record program is no longer needed, and control is turned over to Io.sys.

## MSDOS.SYS IS CHECKED

Io.sys requires that the Msdos.sys file be present. Msdos.sys is a text file that contains some parameters and switches you can set to affect the way the OS boots. You will learn about the contents of Msdos.sys and how to change it to affect the boot process in Chapter 16. Io.sys reads Msdos.sys and uses the settings in it.

## CONFIG.SYS IS CHECKED

Io.sys then looks on the hard drive or floppy for a file named Config.sys. This configuration file contains several commands. Some more important commands are:

▲ How many files it can open at any one time. An example of this command is:

```
Files=99
```

▲ How many file buffers to create. A buffer is a temporary holding area for files. A sample command is:

```
Buffers=40
```

▲ What 16-bit (real mode) device drivers to load. Each device driver requires one command line. The sample command below loads the device driver for a mouse. The name of the driver file is Mouse.sys and should be stored in the root directory of the floppy disk or hard drive.

```
Device=mouse.sys
```

Several 16-bit drivers can be loaded into memory from commands in Config.sys. Io.sys puts these programs in memory wherever it chooses. However, a program can request that it be put in a certain memory location. Know that protected mode (32-bit) drivers are not loaded from Config.sys, but from the registry.

Sometimes Config.sys is used to create a RAM drive. A **RAM drive** is an area of memory that looks and acts like a hard drive, but because it is memory, it is much faster. (Memory is faster than a hard drive mainly because a hard drive has mechanical moving parts and memory is an electronic device with no moving parts.) When booting from the Windows 9x/Me startup disk, DOS creates a RAM drive to hold files after they have been uncompressed. This eliminates the need for hard drive access, and there is no room for the files on the floppy disk. An example of a command in Config.sys to create a RAM drive is:

> **Notes**
>
> Under MS-DOS, a program such as a device driver that stays in memory until the CPU needs it is called a **terminate-and-stay-resident (TSR)** program. The term is seldom used today, except when talking about real-mode programs.

```
device=ramdrive.sys 2048
```

The command tells the OS to create a RAM drive that is 2048K in size.

## COMMAND.COM IS EXECUTED

Next Io.sys looks for another OS file, named Command.com. This file has three parts: more code to manage I/O, programs for internal OS commands such as Copy and Delete, and a short program that looks for the Autoexec.bat file.

> **Notes**
>
> Some OS commands, such as Dir and Copy, are **internal commands**, meaning they are embedded in the Command.com file, and others are **external commands**, meaning they have their own program files. An example of an external command is Format, stored in the file Format.com.

## AUTOEXEC.BAT IS EXECUTED

Command.com looks for Autoexec.bat and, if found, executes it. The filename Autoexec.bat stands for "automatically executed batch file." A **batch file** is a text file that contains a series of commands that are executed in order. Autoexec.bat lists OS commands that execute automatically each time the OS is loaded.

The following commands are examples of commands that might be found in the Autoexec.bat file:

▲ The Path command, shown in the following command line, lists two paths, separated by semicolons. The OS later uses the paths listed in the Path command to locate program files.

```
PATH C:\;C:\Windows;
```

▲ The Set command is used to create and assign a value to an environmental variable. Once the assignment has been made using the Set command, an application can later read and use the value. When an application is installed, the installation program might add a Set command to your Autoexec.bat file. For example, this Set command assigns a value to the variable Mypath:

```
Set Mypath = C:\VERT
```

Later, when the application loads, it can read the value assigned to Mypath, which is C:\VERT, to know where to look to find data it needs.

▲ The Restart command, as shown in the following command line, causes the system to reboot.

```
Restart.com
```

▲ The Temp command lets applications know where to store temporary files. Add the Temp command to Autoexec.bat if applications are putting temporary files in strange locations. An example of a Temp command is:

> **Notes**
>
> By default, DOS stores temporary files in C:\Temp, Windows 9x/Me uses C:\Windows\Temp, Windows 2000 uses C:\Winnt\Temp, and Windows XP uses C:\Windows\Temp.

```
Temp=C:\Temp
```

▲ The Echo command, shown below, turns on and off the displaying of commands and messages. Use it in a batch file to control output to the screen.

```
Echo off
```

Booting into real mode with a command prompt is completed after Autoexec.bat has finished executing. At this point, Command.com is the program in charge, displaying a command prompt and waiting for a command. On the other hand, if a program or menu was executed from Autoexec.bat, it might ask you for a command.

The command prompt indicates the drive that loaded the OS. If the OS files were loaded from a floppy disk, the command prompt is A:\> (called the A prompt). If the OS was loaded from the hard drive, the command prompt is C:\> (the C prompt). The colon following the letter identifies the letter as the name of a drive, and the backslash identifies the directory on the drive as the root or main directory. The > symbol is the prompt symbol that the OS uses to say, "Enter your command here." This drive and root directory are now the default drive and directory, sometimes called the current or working drive or directory.

If you want to load the Windows 9x/Me desktop, use the Win command, which executes the program Win.com. Enter this command at the C prompt:

> **Notes**
>
> Note that commands used at a command prompt are not case sensitive; that is, you can enter *WIN, Win,* or *win.*

```
C:\> WIN
```

## COMMANDS TO MANAGE MEMORY

Memory management under DOS and Windows 9x/Me can seem complicated because of the way the process has evolved over the past 20 years or so. Like an old house that has been added to and remodeled several times, the present-day design is not as efficient as that of a brand-new house. Decisions made by IBM and Microsoft in the early 1980s still significantly affect, and in some cases limit, the way memory is used under Windows 9x/Me. We'll first look at how DOS and Windows 9x/Me divide up the memory address space, and then we'll look at the commands and utilities DOS and Windows 9x/Me use to manage these addresses.

### HOW DOS AND WINDOWS 9X/ME DIVIDE MEMORY

Early CPUs had only 20 lines on the bus available to handle addresses, so the largest memory address the CPU could use was 11111111111111111111 in binary, which is 1,048,575, or 1024K, or 1 MB of memory. This 1 MB of memory was used by DOS and divided up according to the scheme shown in Table 15-1. Then newer CPUs and motherboards were developed with 24 address lines and more, so that memory addresses above 1024K became available. Memory addresses above 1024K are called **extended memory**. And, memory addresses are often expressed using hexadecimal notation.

| Range of Memory Addresses | Range Using Hex Terminology | Type of Memory |
|---|---|---|
| 0 to 640K | 0 to A0000 | Conventional or base memory |
| 640K to 1024K | A0000 to FFFFF | Upper memory (A through F ranges) |
| Above 1024K | 100000 and up | Extended memory |

**Table 15-1**  Division of memory under DOS and Windows 9x/Me

When a PC is first booted, many programs demand memory addresses, including the ROM BIOS programs on the motherboard and some circuit boards, device drivers, the OS, and applications. This process of assigning memory addresses to programs is called memory mapping.

Sometimes older ROM BIOS programs and device drivers expect to be assigned certain memory addresses and will not work otherwise. Windows 9x/Me is committed to maintain backward compatibility with these old programs. This fact is probably the greatest limitation of Windows 9x/Me today.

To get a clear picture of how memory addresses are mapped, look at the memory map shown in Figure 15-2. The first 640K of memory addresses are called **conventional memory**, or base memory. The memory addresses from 640K up to 1024K are called **upper memory**. Memory above 1024K is called extended memory. The first 64K of extended memory is called the **high memory area (HMA)**. Now let's look at each type of memory address.

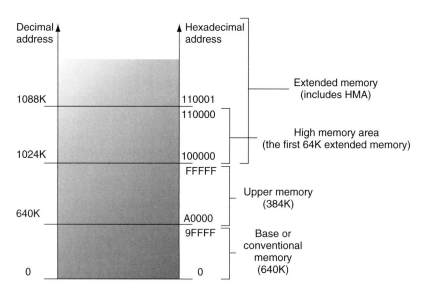

**Figure 15-2** Memory address map (not to scale) showing the starting and ending addresses of conventional, upper, and extended memory, including the high memory area

## CONVENTIONAL MEMORY

In the early 1980s, when IBM and Microsoft were designing the original PCs, they decided to make 640K of memory addresses available to the user, thinking that this was plenty for anything the user would ever want to do. This 640K of addresses was intended to hold the OS, the application software, and the data being processed. At that time, 640K of memory addresses was more than enough to handle all the applications available. Today, 640K of memory addresses is grossly inadequate.

The problem caused by restricting the number of memory addresses available to the user to only 640K could have been solved by simply providing more addresses to the user in future versions of DOS. However, another original design decision ruled this out. The next group of memory addresses is 384K above conventional memory and called upper memory. This group was assigned to utility operations for the system. The system requires memory addresses to communicate with peripherals. The programs (such as BIOS on a video card or on the motherboard) and data are assigned memory addresses in this upper memory area. For example, the video BIOS and its data are placed in the very first part of upper memory, the area from 640K to 768K. All video ROM written for DOS-based computers assumes that these programs and data are stored in this area. Also, many DOS and Windows applications interact directly with video ROM and RAM in this address range.

Programs almost always expect data to be written into memory directly above the addresses for the program itself, an important fact for understanding memory management.

Thus, if a program begins storing its data above its location in conventional memory, eventually it will "hit the ceiling," the beginning of upper memory assigned to video ROM. The major reason that applications have a 640K memory limit is that video ROM begins at 640K. If DOS and Windows 9x/Me allowed applications into these upper memory addresses, all DOS-compatible video ROM would need to be rewritten, and many DOS applications that access these video addresses would not work. The 32-bit device drivers and applications under Windows 9x/Me don't have this problem because they can run from extended memory and turn to the OS to access video.

## UPPER MEMORY

The memory map in Figure 15-2 shows that the memory addresses from 640K up to (but not including) 1024K are called upper memory. This area of memory is used by BIOS and device drivers. In the hexadecimal number system, upper memory begins at A0000 and goes through FFFFF. Because the hex numbers in upper memory begin with A through F, the divisions of upper memory are often referred to as the A range, B range, and so on, up to the F range. Video ROM and RAM are stored in the first part of upper memory, hex A0000 through CFFFF (the A, B, and C areas of memory). Sixteen-bit BIOS programs for other legacy expansion boards are assigned memory addresses in the remaining portions of upper memory. BIOS on the motherboard (the system BIOS) is assigned the top part of upper memory, from F0000 through FFFFF (the F area of upper memory). Upper memory often has unassigned addresses, depending on which boards are present in the system. Managing memory effectively involves gaining access to these unused addresses in upper memory and using them to store device drivers and TSR (terminate-and-stay-resident) programs.

> **Notes**
>
> For more information about how the hexadecimal number system is used with memory addressing, see "The Hexadecimal Number System and Memory Addressing" in the online content.

## EXTENDED MEMORY AND THE HIGH MEMORY AREA

Memory above 1 MB is called extended memory. The first 64K of extended memory is called the high memory area, which exists because a bug in the programming for the older Intel 286 CPU (the first CPU to use extended memory) produced this small pocket of unused memory addresses. Beginning with DOS 5, the OS capitalized on this bug by storing portions of itself in the high memory area, thus freeing some conventional memory where DOS had been stored. This method of storing part of DOS in the high memory area is called "loading DOS high." You will see how to do this later in the chapter.

Extended memory is actually managed by the OS as a device (the device is memory) that is controlled by a device driver. To access extended memory, you need the device driver (called a memory extender) that controls it, and you must use applications that have been written to use extended memory. The amount of extended memory you can have on your computer is limited by the amount of RAM that can be installed on your motherboard and the number of memory addresses the CPU and the memory bus can support.

---

**APPLYING | CONCEPTS**   Using Windows 9x/Me Device Manager, you can see how the first 1 MB of memory addresses are assigned (see Figure 15-3). To view the list on the Device Manager window, select **Computer**, click **Properties**, and then click **Memory**. Notice in the figure that the system BIOS has been assigned memory addresses in the F range of upper memory. This F range is always reserved for motherboard BIOS and is never requested by other programs. When the CPU is first turned on and needs a program in order to know how to boot up, it begins with the instructions stored on the ROM BIOS chip that are assigned to these memory addresses.

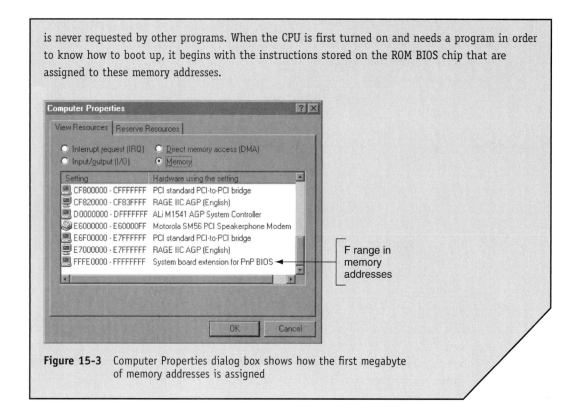

**Figure 15-3** Computer Properties dialog box shows how the first megabyte of memory addresses is assigned

## WINDOWS 9X/ME AND DOS UTILITIES THAT MANAGE MEMORY

The two utilities used by DOS and Windows 9x/Me to manage memory above 640K are Himem.sys and Emm386.exe. **Himem.sys** is the device driver for all memory above 640K. The program file **Emm386.exe** contains the software that loads device drivers and other programs into upper memory. Himem.sys is automatically loaded by Windows 9x/Me during the boot process, but can also be loaded by an entry in Config.sys. Emm386.exe is not loaded automatically by Windows 9x/Me, but you can load it by an entry in Config.sys.

### USING HIMEM.SYS

Himem.sys is considered a device driver because it manages memory as a device. It can be executed by the Device= command in Config.sys. Figure 15-4 shows an example of a very simple Config.sys file on a floppy disk that loads Himem.sys. The Config.sys file is being edited by the Edit.com text editor utility.

To create the file on a floppy disk, at a command prompt, you can use either of these two methods:

◢ Make drive A the default drive and enter this command:

```
A:\> Edit Config.sys
```

◢ Make drive C the default drive and enter this command:

```
C:\> Edit A:Config.sys
```

The second line in the Config.sys file, device=A:\util\mouse.sys, tells DOS to load into memory a device driver from the \Util directory on the floppy disk. This driver allows you to use the mouse while in MS-DOS mode.

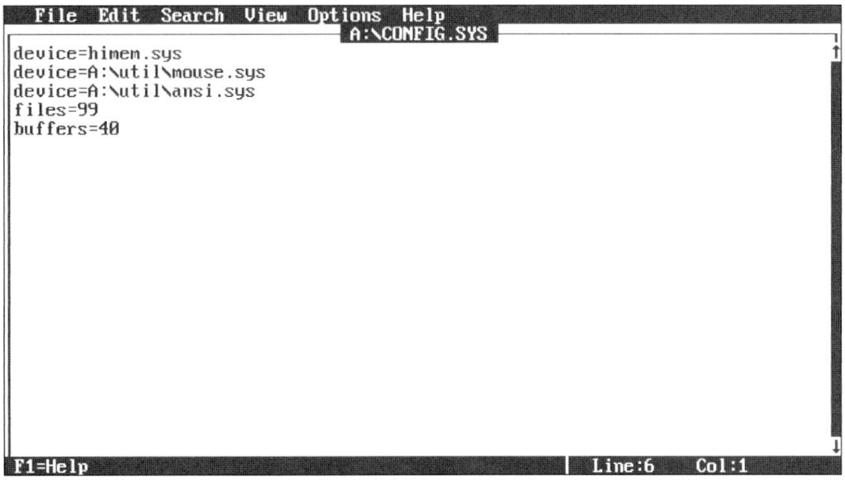

15

```
    File  Edit  Search  View  Options  Help
                        A:\CONFIG.SYS
device=himem.sys                                              ↑
device=A:\util\mouse.sys
device=A:\util\ansi.sys
files=99
buffers=40




















                                                             ↓
F1=Help                                │ Line:6    Col:1
```

**Figure 15-4**  Config.sys set to use memory above 640K

The third line in the Config.sys file, device=A:\util\ansi.sys, tells DOS to load the device driver Ansi.sys into memory. Ansi.sys helps control the keyboard and monitor, providing color on the monitor and an additional set of characters to the ASCII character set. For more information about ASCII and ANSI, see "ASCII Character Set and Ansi.sys" in the online content.

## USING EMM386.EXE

In DOS and Windows 9x/Me, Emm386.exe manages the memory addresses in upper memory. Before we see how to use it, let's begin by examining memory when upper memory addresses are not available. To do that, we use the MEM command, which lets us view how memory is currently allocated. You can use the /C option to get a complete list and include the |MORE option to page the results on your screen. Figure 15-5 was produced using this command:

**MEM /C |MORE**

In Figure 15-5, the first column shows the programs currently loaded in memory. The second column shows the total amount of memory used by each program. The columns labeled Conventional and Upper Memory show the amount of memory being used by each program in each of these categories. This PC is not making use of upper memory for any of its programs. At the bottom of the screen is the total amount of free conventional memory (544,720 bytes) that is available to new programs to be loaded. In this section, we are trying to make this value as high as possible.

```
Modules using memory below 1 MB:

  Name         Total          Conventional        Upper Memory
  ---------    ----------     ----------          ----------
  MSDOS        18,672  (18K)  18,672  (18K)           0   (0K)
  HIMEM         1,168   (1K)   1,168   (1K)           0   (0K)
  DBLBUFF       2,976   (3K)   2,976   (3K)           0   (0K)
  IFSHLP        2,864   (3K)   2,864   (3K)           0   (0K)
  WIN           3,616   (4K)   3,616   (4K)           0   (0K)
  COMMAND       8,416   (8K)   8,416   (8K)           0   (0K)
  SAVE         72,768  (71K)  72,768  (71K)           0   (0K)
  Free        544,720 (532K) 544,720 (532K)          0   (0K)

Memory Summary:

  Type of Memory      Total        Used         Free
  ----------------    ----------   ----------   ----------
  Conventional           655,360      110,640      544,720
  Upper                        0            0            0
  Reserved                     0            0            0
  Extended (XMS)     133,156,864       69,632  133,087,232
  ----------------    ----------   ----------   ----------
-- More --
```

**Figure 15-5**   MEM report with /C option on a PC not using upper memory

## CREATING AND USING UPPER MEMORY BLOCKS

Figure 15-6 shows an example of a Config.sys file that is set to use upper memory addresses. The first line loads the Himem.sys driver. The second line loads the Emm386.exe file. Emm386.exe assigns addresses in upper memory to memory made available by the Himem.sys driver. The NOEMS switch at the end of the command line says to Windows, "Do not create any simulated expanded memory." Expanded memory is an older type of memory above 1 MB that is no longer used by software. The command to load Emm386.exe must appear after the command to load Himem.sys in the Config.sys file.

**Figure 15-6**   Config.sys set to use upper memory

The command DOS=HIGH,UMB serves two purposes. The one command line can be broken into two commands like this:

**DOS=HIGH**

**DOS=UMB**

The DOS=HIGH portion tells the OS to load part of the DOS core into the high memory area ("loading DOS high"). Remember that the high memory area is the first 64K of extended memory. This memory is usually unused unless we choose to store part of DOS in it with this command line. Including this command in Config.sys frees some conventional memory that would have been used by the OS.

The second part of the command, DOS=UMB, creates upper memory blocks. An **upper memory block (UMB)** is a group of consecutive memory addresses in the upper memory area that has had physical memory assigned to it. The OS identifies blocks that are not currently being used by system ROM or expansion boards, and the memory manager makes these blocks available for use. This command, DOS=UMB, enables the OS to access these upper memory blocks. After the UMBs are created, they can be used in these ways:

▲ Devicehigh= command in Config.sys
▲ Loadhigh command in Autoexec.bat
▲ Loadhigh command at the command prompt (explained in the next section)

The fourth line in the Config.sys file in Figure 15-6 uses a UMB. The command Devicehigh=A:\Util\Mouse.sys tells the OS to load the mouse device driver into one of the upper memory blocks created and made available by the previous three lines. This process of loading a program into upper memory addresses is called loading high.

## LOADING DEVICE DRIVERS HIGH

Using the Devicehigh= command in Config.sys, rather than the Device= command, causes the driver to load high. With the Devicehigh= command, the OS stores these drivers in UMBs using the largest UMB first, then the next largest, and so on until all are loaded. Therefore, to make sure there is enough room to hold them all in upper memory, order the Devicehigh= command lines in Config.sys so that the largest drivers are loaded first.

You can determine the amount of memory a device driver allocates for itself and its data by using the MEM command with the /M filename option:

**MEM /M filename**

The filename is the name of the device driver without the file extension.

You can also use a UMB from Autoexec.bat using the Loadhigh (LH) command. For example, to load high Mscdex.exe, a utility to access a CD-ROM drive, use either of the following commands:

**LH Mscdex.exe**

**Loadhigh Mscdex.exe**

In either case, the program is loaded into the largest UMB available and does not use up more precious conventional memory. Note that before the Loadhigh command will work, the program files Himem.sys and Emm386.exe must be available to the OS, and these three lines must be added to Config.sys and executed by booting the computer:

**Device=HIMEM.SYS**

**Device=EMM386.EXE NOEMS**

**DOS=UMB**

If the Himem.sys and Emm386.exe files are not in the root directory of the boot device, you must include the path to the filename in the Device= line, like this:

```
Device=C:\DOS\HIMEM.SYS
```

> **Notes**
>
> When a program is loaded high, two things can go wrong. Either the program might not work from upper memory, causing problems during execution, or there might not be enough room in upper memory for the program and its data. If the program causes the computer to hang when you attempt to run it, or if it simply refuses to work correctly, remove it from upper memory.

Windows 9x/Me, which is mostly a 32-bit OS, "lives" in extended memory together with its device drivers and applications, and uses only base and upper memory for 16-bit components. Managing base and upper memory can get pretty sticky, but the good news is if you are using all 32-bit drivers and applications in a Windows 9x/Me environment, you do not need to be concerned about managing base and upper memory.

## USING THE COMMAND PROMPT

As a PC technician, your tools and skills are not complete until you are comfortable building and using command lines. In this section, you will first learn how to access a command prompt, about file and directory (also called folders) naming conventions, about wildcard characters used in command lines, and how to launch programs from the command prompt. Then you will learn to use several commands to manage files and directories and perform many useful utility tasks when managing an OS, applications, and data. Finally, you'll learn how to create and use batch files. Some of the commands in this section are also found in Chapter 13 where they can also be used in Windows 2000/XP.

### ACCESSING A COMMAND PROMPT

There are several ways to get to a command prompt using Windows 9x/Me and DOS:

▲ To access a command prompt window, sometimes called a **DOS box**, from a Windows 9x/Me desktop, click **Start, Programs,** and **MS-DOS Prompt.** A Command Prompt window opens, as shown in Figure 15-7. Using a command prompt window, you can enter the DOS-like commands discussed in this chapter. To exit the window, type **Exit** at the command prompt.

▲ Click **Start,** click **Run,** and enter **Command.com** in the Run dialog box.

▲ When you boot from the Windows 9x/Me startup disk or any bootable floppy disk, you get a command prompt instead of the Windows desktop. This method does not require access to the hard drive or the Windows desktop to load.

▲ Using Windows 95 or Windows 98 (not Windows Me), click **Start,** click **Shutdown,** and select **Restart in MS-DOS mode** from the Shutdown dialog box. Using this method, you get a command prompt provided by the DOS real-mode core of Windows 95/98.

▲ Using Windows 9x/Me, hold down the **Ctrl** key or the **F8** key while booting, which causes the OS to display a startup menu. From the menu, select **Command prompt only.** This method requires access to the hard drive, but works even when the Windows desktop cannot load.

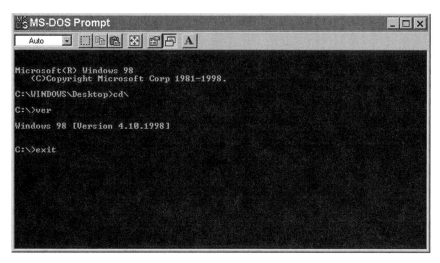

**Figure 15-7** A Command Prompt window can be used to practice the commands given in this section

For convenience, you can add a command prompt icon to your Windows desktop for easy access. To do that, locate the program file (Command.com) in Windows Explorer and, while holding down the Ctrl key, drag the icon to your desktop. Another way to create the shortcut is to click **Start**, point to **Programs**, **Accessories**, and **Command Prompt**. Then, right-click **Command Prompt** and select **Create Shortcut** on the shortcut menu.

| APPLYING CONCEPTS | For practice, try all the preceding methods of accessing a command prompt. Then create a command prompt icon on your desktop. |
| --- | --- |

A command prompt provides information about the current drive and directory. For example, if you booted a Windows 98 PC from a bootable floppy disk into command prompt mode, you would see the A prompt (A:\>). Recall that the A: indicates the current drive. (A drive letter is always followed by a colon.) The backslash indicates the root directory, and the > symbol indicates that you can enter a new command.

To make the hard drive (drive C) the default drive, enter C: at the A prompt. The prompt then changes to indicate the current directory and drive in the root directory of drive C. It looks like this on your screen:

C:\>

## FILE AND DIRECTORY NAMING CONVENTIONS

When working with a command prompt, it is important to understand how to name directories and files, and how to type directory names and filenames in the command line. Under DOS, a filename can contain up to eight characters, a separating period, and a file extension of up to three characters, like this: *filename.ext*. This is called the 8.3 format. Characters can be the letters a through z, the numbers 0 through 9, and the following characters:

_ ^ $ ~ ! # % & - { } ( ) @ ' `

Under MS-DOS, be sure to not use a space, period, *, ?, or \ in a filename or file extension. Acceptable file extensions for program files are .com, .sys, .bat, and .exe. For example, the DOS utility program that displays information about the system is Msd.exe.

Under Windows, directory names and filenames can be as long as 255 characters and can contain spaces. When creating subdirectories under directories, know that the maximum depth of directories you can create is dependent on the length of the directory names. When working from a command prompt and using long directory names or filenames, put double quotation marks around the name, like this: "My long filename.doc".

When using long filenames in Windows 9x/Me, remember that the DOS portion of the system can understand only eight-character filenames with three-character extensions. When the DOS part of the system is operating, it truncates long filenames and assigns new eight-character names. For example, under DOS, the filename Mydocument.doc is displayed with the first seven letters and a tilde (~) character:

```
Mydocum~.doc
```

If you have two documents that would have the same name when truncated in this manner, DOS also adds an identifying number. For example, if you have a document named Mydocument.doc and one named Mydocumentnew.doc, DOS truncates these as:

```
Mydocu~1.doc
```

```
Mydocu~2.doc
```

When you boot using a Windows 9x/Me startup disk or some other MS-DOS disk, be aware of this file-naming convention.

## USING WILDCARD CHARACTERS IN COMMAND LINES

As you work at the command prompt, you can use two **wildcard** characters in a filename to execute a command on a group of files, or in an abbreviated filename if you do not know the entire name. The question mark (?) is a wildcard for one character, and the asterisk (*) is a wildcard for more than one character. For example, if you want to find all files in a directory that start with A and have a three-letter file extension, you would use the following command:

```
dir a*.???
```

## LAUNCHING A PROGRAM USING THE COMMAND PROMPT

In Chapter 2, you learned how to launch a program from the Windows desktop. You can also launch a program from a command prompt window. At the command prompt, when you type a single group of letters with no spaces, the OS assumes that you typed the filename of a program file you want to execute, which is stored in the current directory (the directory showing in your command prompt). The OS attempts to find the program file by that name, copy the file into RAM, and then execute the program.

As an example of launching a program, let's use the program Mem.exe, a program that displays how memory is currently allocated. For Windows 9x/Me, the program file Mem.exe is stored on the hard drive in the C:\Windows\Command folder. Note what happens in

Figure 15-8 when you type the first command shown in the figure, *mem*, at the A: prompt, and then press Enter, like this:

A:\>**mem**

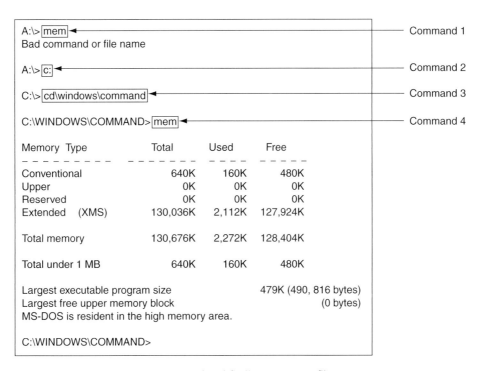

```
A:\> mem ◄──────────────────────────────────── Command 1
Bad command or file name

A:\> c: ◄──────────────────────────────────── Command 2

C:\> cd\windows\command ◄───────────────────── Command 3

C:\WINDOWS\COMMAND> mem ◄───────────────────── Command 4

Memory  Type           Total      Used       Free
- - - - - - - -      - - - - - -  - - - -   - - - -
Conventional            640K       160K       480K
Upper                     0K         0K         0K
Reserved                  0K         0K         0K
Extended    (XMS)    130,036K     2,112K   127,924K

Total memory         130,676K     2,272K   128,404K

Total under 1 MB        640K       160K       480K

Largest executable program size             479K (490, 816 bytes)
Largest free upper memory block                       (0 bytes)
MS-DOS is resident in the high memory area.

C:\WINDOWS\COMMAND>
```

**Figure 15-8** Using the Mem command and finding a program file

The OS says it cannot find the program to execute. It looked only on the floppy disk (drive A) for Mem.com, Mem.exe, or Mem.bat, the three file extensions that the OS recognizes for programs. If the OS finds none of these files in the current directory, it stops looking and displays this error message:

Bad command or file name

Now look at the second command in the figure. To help the OS locate the program file, you must change the default drive to the hard drive by giving this command:

A:\> C:

Notice in Figure 15-8 that the prompt changes to C:\>, indicating that the logical drive C on the hard drive is the default drive. In the third command in the figure, you change the default directory on the hard drive to \Windows\Command using the **CD (change directory) command**, like this:

C:\>CD\windows\command

(Remember that DOS and Windows commands are not case sensitive, so it makes no difference whether you type CD, Cd, or cd.) The prompt now looks like this:

C:\WINDOWS\COMMAND>

You can now enter the mem command again, which is showing as the fourth command in the figure. The OS locates and executes the program file.

## COMMANDS TO MANAGE FILES AND DIRECTORIES

You can use different OS commands to manage files and directories. This section describes a number of commands with some of their more common options. For more information about these and other OS commands, type the command name at a command prompt, type **/?** (slash and question mark) and press **Enter**.

> **Notes**
>
> If you think that you've seen the commands in this section before, you're right! Chapter 13 covers all of the commands that you are expected to know for the A+ exams. However, this book is also designed so that you can cover the Windows 2000/XP chapters (Chapters 11, 12, 13, and 14) before *or* after you cover Chapters 15 and 16 on DOS and Windows 9x/Me. Thus, the duplicated commands are included in this chapter so that you can study this chapter without having first covered Chapter 13, if that's what you choose to do.

Some of the following commands have equivalent Windows tools that are available from the Windows 9x/Me desktop.

### DIR

Use this command to list files and directories. Some examples using parameters, wildcards, and a filename are shown in Table 15-2:

| Sample Command | Effect |
|---|---|
| DIR /P | List one screen at a time. |
| DIR /W | Use wide format, where details are omitted and files and folders are listed in columns on the screen. |
| DIR *.txt | Use a wildcard character, listing all files with a .txt file extension. |
| DIR Myfile.txt | Check that a single file is present. |

**Table 15-2** Examples of the Dir command

### RENAME OR REN

The Rename command renames a file or folder. For example, to change the name of Myfile.txt to Mybackup.txt, use this command:

```
Ren Myfile.txt Mybackup.txt
```

### TYPE

The Type command displays the contents of a text file on your screen. Some examples are shown in Table 15-3.

| Sample Command | Effect |
|---|---|
| Type Myfile.txt | Displays file contents |
| Type My file.txt >PRN | Redirects output to printer |
| Type Myfile.txt |More | Displays output one screen at a time |

**Table 15-3** Examples of the Type command

## DEL OR ERASE

The Del or Erase command erases files or groups of files. If the command does not include drive and directory information, like the following examples, the OS uses the default drive and directory when executing the command.

In the sample command lines that follow, the typed command is in bold and the command prompt is not bold. To erase all files in the A:\DOCS directory, use the following command:

```
C:\> ERASE A:\DOCS\*.*
```

To erase all files in the current default directory, use the following command:

```
A:\DOCS> DEL *.*
```

To erase all files in the current directory that have no file extension, use the following command:

```
A:\DOCS> DEL *.
```

To erase the file named Myfile.txt, use the following command:

```
A:\> DEL MYFILE.TXT
```

## COPY

The Copy command copies a single file or group of files. The original files are not altered. To copy a file from one drive to another and to rename the file, use a command similar to this one:

```
A:\> COPY C:\data\myfile.txt A:\mydata\newfile.txt
```

The drive, path, and filename of the source file immediately follow the Copy command. The drive, path, and filename of the destination file follow the source filename. If you do not specify the filename of the destination file, the OS assigns the file's original name to this copy. If you omit the drive or path of the source or the destination, then the OS uses the current default drive and path.

To copy the file Myfile.txt from the root directory of drive C to drive A, use the following command:

```
C:\> COPY MYFILE.TXT A:
```

Because the command does not include a drive or path before the filename Myfile.txt, the OS assumes that the file is in the default drive and path. Also, because there is no destination filename specified, the file written to drive A will be named Myfile.txt.

To copy all files in the C:\DOCS directory to the floppy disk in drive A, use the following command:

```
C:\>COPY C:\DOCS\*.* A:
```

To make a backup file named System.bak of the System.ini file in the \Windows directory of the hard drive, use the following command:

```
C:\WINDOWS>COPY SYSTEM.INI SYSTEM.BAK
```

If you use the Copy command to duplicate multiple files, the files are assigned the names of the original files. When you duplicate multiple files, the destination portion of the command line cannot include a filename.

> **Notes**
>
> When trying to recover a corrupted file, you can sometimes use the Copy command to copy the file to new media, such as from the hard drive to a floppy disk. During the copying process, if the Copy command reports a bad or missing sector, choose the option to ignore that sector. The copying process then continues to the next sector. The corrupted sector will be lost, but others can likely be recovered.

## XCOPY /C /S /Y /D:

The Xcopy command is more powerful than the Copy command. It follows the same general command-source-destination format as the Copy command, but it offers several more options. For example, you can use the /S parameter with the Xcopy command to copy all files in the directory \DOCS, as well as all subdirectories under \DOCS and their files, to the disk in drive A, like so:

```
C:\>XCOPY C:\DOCS\*.* A: /S
```

To copy all files from the directory C:\DOCS created or modified on March 14, 2006, use the /D switch, as in the following command:

```
C:\>XCOPY C:\DOCS\*.* A: /D:03/14/06
```

Use the /Y parameter to overwrite existing files without prompting, and use the /C parameter to keep copying even when an error occurs.

## DELTREE *[DRIVE:]PATH*

The Deltree command deletes the directory tree beginning with the subdirectory you specify, including all subdirectories and all files in all subdirectories in that tree. Use it with caution! As an example of deleting a directory tree, you can delete the C:\DOCS folder and all its contents by using this command:

```
C:\>DELTREE C:\DOCS
```

## MKDIR *[DRIVE:]PATH* OR MD *[DRIVE:]PATH*

The Mkdir command (abbreviated MD, for make directory) creates a subdirectory under a directory. To create a directory named \GAME on drive C, you can use this command:

```
MKDIR C:\GAME
```

The backslash indicates that the directory is under the root directory. To create a directory named CHESS under the \GAME directory, you can use this command:

```
MKDIR C:\GAME\CHESS
```

The OS requires that the parent directory GAME already exist before it creates the child directory CHESS.

Figure 15-9 shows the result of the Dir command on the directory \GAME. Note the two initial entries in the directory table, the . (dot) and the .. (dot, dot) entries. The Mkdir command creates these two entries when the OS initially sets up the directory. You cannot edit these entries with normal OS commands, and they must remain in the directory for the directory's lifetime. The . entry points to the subdirectory itself, and the .. entry points to the parent directory, in this case, the root directory.

```
C:\>DIR \GAME

 Volume in drive C has no label
 Volume Serial Number is 0F52-09FC
 Directory of C:\GAME

 .            <DIR>      02-18-93    4:50a
 ..           <DIR>      02-18-93    4:50a
 CHESS        <DIR>      02-18-93    4:50a
 NUKE         <DIR>      02-18-93    4:51a
 PENTE        <DIR>      02-18-93    4:52a
 NETRIS       <DIR>      02-18-93    4:54a
 BEYOND       <DIR>      02-18-93    4:54a
        7 file(s)            0 bytes
                    9273344 bytes free

C:\>
```

**Figure 15-9**   Results of the Dir command on the \GAME directory

## CHDIR *[DRIVE:]PATH* OR CD *[DRIVE:]PATH* OR CD..

The Chdir command (abbreviated CD, for change directory) changes the current default directory. Using its easiest form, you simply state the drive and the entire path that you want to be current, like so:

**CD C:\GAME\CHESS**

The command prompt now looks like this:

C:\GAME\CHESS>

To move from a child directory to its parent directory, use the .. variation of the command:

C:\GAME\CHESS> **CD..**

C:\GAME>

Remember that .. always means the parent directory. You can move from a parent directory to one of its child directories simply by stating the name of the child directory:

C:\GAME>**CD CHESS**

C:\GAME\CHESS>

Remember, do not put a backslash in front of the child directory name; doing so tells the OS to go to a directory named CHESS that is directly under the root directory.

## RMDIR *[DRIVE:]PATH* OR RD *[DRIVE:]PATH*

The Rmdir command (abbreviated RD, for remove directory) removes a subdirectory. Before you can use the Rmdir command, three things must be true:

▲ The directory must contain no files.
▲ The directory must contain no subdirectories.
▲ The directory must not be the current directory.

The . and .. entries are present when a directory is ready for removal. For example, to remove the \GAME directory in the preceding example, the CHESS directory must first be removed, like so:

C:\>**RMDIR C:\GAME\CHESS**

Or, if the \GAME directory is the current directory, you can use this command:

C:\GAME>**RD CHESS**

Once you remove the CHESS directory, you can remove the \GAME directory. It's not good to attempt to saw off a branch while you're sitting on it; you must first leave the \GAME directory like this:

C:\GAME>**CD..**

C:\>**RD \GAME**

## ATTRIB

The Attrib command displays or changes the read-only, archive, system, and hidden attributes assigned to files. To display the attributes of the file MYFILE.TXT, you can use this command:

**ATTRIB MYFILE.TXT**

To hide the file, you can use this command:

**ATTRIB +H MYFILE.TXT**

To remove the hidden status of the file, you need only use this command:

**ATTRIB -H MYFILE.TXT**

To make the file a read-only system file, use this command:

**ATTRIB +R +S MYFILE.TXT**

When you put more than one parameter in the Attrib command, the order doesn't matter. This command works the same way as the one above:

**ATTRIB +S +R MYFILE.TXT**

To remove the read-only system status of the file, use this command:

**ATTRIB -R -S MYFILE.TXT**

The archive bit is used to determine if a file has changed since the last backup. To turn on the archive bit, use this command:

**ATTRIB +A MYFILE.TXT**

To turn off the archive bit, use this command:

```
ATTRIB -A MYFILE.TXT
```

### EXTRACT *FILENAME.CAB FILE1.EXT* /D

The Extract command extracts files from a cabinet file such as the Ebd.cab file on the Windows 98 startup disk. To list the files contained in the cabinet file, use this command:

```
EXTRACT EBD.CAB /D
```

To extract the file Debug.exe from the Ebd.cab file, use this command:

```
EXTRACT EBD.CAB DEBUG.EXE
```

To extract all files from the Ebd.cab cabinet file, use this command:

```
EXTRACT EBD.CAB *.*
```

This command is available under Windows 9x/Me. For Windows 2000/XP, use the Expand command, which is available under the Recovery Console.

### EDIT *[PATH][FILENAME]*

The Edit program (Edit.com) is a handy, "quick and dirty" way to edit text files while working at a command prompt. To edit the Autoexec.bat file on a floppy disk, use this command:

```
EDIT A:\AUTOEXEC.BAT
```

If the file does not already exist, Edit creates an empty file. Later, when you exit the Edit editor, changes you made are saved to the newly created file.

If you opened the Autoexec.bat file on the Windows 98 startup disk, your screen should be similar to the one shown in Figure 15-10. (Know that the Autoexec.bat file located on the hard drive will not have much in it because Windows 9x/Me on the hard drive doesn't use it except to support legacy applications and devices.) After you have made changes in this window, you can exit the editor this way: Press the **Alt** key to activate the menus, select the **File** menu, and then choose **Exit**. When asked if you want to save your changes, respond **Yes** to exit the editor and save changes.

If you make a mistake when editing Autoexec.bat or Config.sys, you can cause a boot problem. Before editing these files on your hard drive, always make a rescue disk. If you are editing one of these files on a rescue disk, you can make a backup copy of the file before you edit it or have a second rescue disk ready just in case.

Do not use word-processing software, such as Word or WordPerfect, to edit Autoexec.bat or Config.sys, unless you save the file as a text (ASCII) file. Word-processing applications place control characters in their document files that prevent the OS from interpreting the file correctly.

> **Notes**
>
> When working from a command prompt, you can reboot your computer (Ctrl+Alt+Del) to execute the new Autoexec.bat file, or you can type Autoexec.bat at the command prompt. If the computer stalls during the boot, use another startup disk to reboot. You can also press the F5 key to bypass the startup files during the boot.

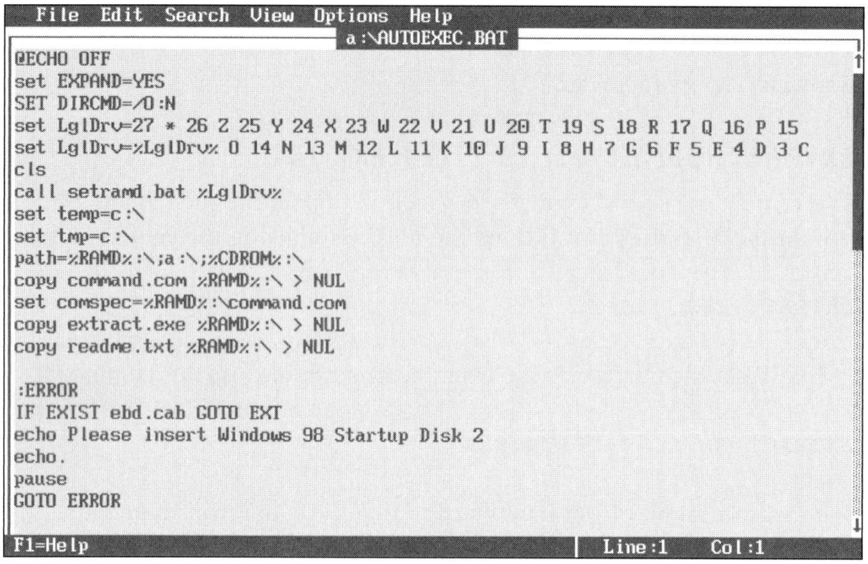

```
   File Edit Search View Options Help
                    a:\AUTOEXEC.BAT
@ECHO OFF
set EXPAND=YES
SET DIRCMD=/O:N
set LglDrv=27 * 26 Z 25 Y 24 X 23 W 22 V 21 U 20 T 19 S 18 R 17 Q 16 P 15
set LglDrv=%LglDrv% O 14 N 13 M 12 L 11 K 10 J 9 I 8 H 7 G 6 F 5 E 4 D 3 C
cls
call setramd.bat %LglDrv%
set temp=c:\
set tmp=c:\
path=%RAMD%:\;a:\;%CDROM%:\
copy command.com %RAMD%:\ > NUL
set comspec=%RAMD%:\command.com
copy extract.exe %RAMD%:\ > NUL
copy readme.txt %RAMD%:\ > NUL


:ERROR
IF EXIST ebd.cab GOTO EXT
echo Please insert Windows 98 Startup Disk 2
echo.
pause
GOTO ERROR

 F1=Help                                         Line:1    Col:1
```

**Figure 15-10** Using the Edit editor to make changes to Autoexec.bat

## COMMANDS TO MANAGE HARD DRIVES AND DISKS

Next, we'll look at some commands used to manage the hard drive and floppy disks. Using the following commands, you can prepare a drive or disk for first use, optimize a drive or disk, repair a damaged file system, and view and edit file system entities.

### CHKDSK *[DRIVE:]* /F /R

Using MS-DOS and Windows 9x/Me, the Chkdsk command fixes file system errors, and the Scandisk command discussed next corrects problems with bad sectors on a drive. Using Windows 2000/XP, both these functions are combined in the one command, Chkdsk; therefore, Windows 2000/XP does not have a Scandisk command.

For all these OSs, used without any parameters, the Chkdsk command reports information about a drive. Use the /F parameter to have Chkdsk fix file system errors it finds, including errors in the FAT or MFT caused by clusters marked as being used but not belonging to a particular file (called lost allocation units) and clusters marked in the FAT or MFT as belonging to more than one file (called cross-linked clusters). To check the hard drive for these types of errors and repair them, use this command:

**CHKDSK C: /F**

To redirect a report of the findings of the Chkdsk command to a file that you can later print, use this command:

**CHKDSK C: >Myfile.txt**

If it finds bad sectors, it attempts to recover the data. The Chkdsk command will not fix anything unless the drive is locked, which means there can be no hard drive activity at the time. Therefore, run Chkdsk with the /F parameters when the drive is not in use.

### SCANDISK *DRIVE:* /A /P

The Scandisk command scans a hard drive for errors and repairs them if possible. Scandisk checks the FAT, long filenames, lost and cross-linked clusters, directory tree structure, bad sectors, and compressed structure, if the drive has been compressed using DriveSpace or

DoubleSpace (these are drive compression utilities). The /A parameter is used to scan all nonremovable local drives. Use this command only to display information without fixing the drive:

**SCANDISK C: /P**

Use this command to display information and fix errors:

**SCANDISK C:**

## DEFRAG *DRIVE*: /S

The Defrag command examines a hard drive or disk for **fragmented files** (files written to a disk in noncontiguous clusters) and rewrites these files to the disk or drive in contiguous clusters. Use this command to optimize a hard drive's performance.

Use the /S:N parameter to sort the files on the disk in alphabetical order by filename.

> **Notes**
>
> In effect, Scandisk C: in Windows 9x/Me is equivalent to Chkdsk C: /R in Windows 2000/XP with one exception. Scandisk can check each sector and, if it finds a sector is not readable, it can mark the sector as bad in the FAT so it won't be used again. Windows 2000/XP Chkdsk only attempts to recover the data from a bad sector but doesn't mark new sectors as bad. Know that neither Scandisk or Chkdsk can actually fix a bad sector.

**DEFRAG C: /S:N**

Use the /S:D parameter to sort the files on the disk by date and time.

**DEFRAG C: /S:D**

## FDISK /STATUS /MBR

The Fdisk command is used to prepare a hard drive for first use. It creates partitions and logical drives on the hard drive, displays partition information, and restores a damaged Master Boot Record. Table 15-4 shows parameters for this command.

| Fdisk Command Parameter | Description |
|---|---|
| FDISK /MBR | Repairs a damaged MBR program stored at the beginning of the hard drive just before the partition table |
| FDISK /Status | Displays partition information for all hard drives in the system |

**Table 15-4** Examples of the Fdisk command

Fdisk works under Windows 9x/Me and is useful when booting from a Windows 9x/Me startup disk to examine the partition table on a malfunctioning hard drive, or to prepare a hard drive for first use. You will learn more about the Fdisk command later in this chapter.

## FORMAT *DRIVE*: /S /V: *VOLUMENAME* /Q /U /AUTOTEST

Recall that the Format command is used to format a disk or a hard drive. For a hard drive using Windows 9x/Me, first run Fdisk to partition the drive and create each logical drive. Then use Format to format each logical drive. Table 15-5 shows parameters for this command.

| Format Command Parameter | Description |
| --- | --- |
| /V | Allows you to enter a volume label only once when formatting several disks. The same volume label is used for all disks. A volume label appears at the top of the directory list to help you identify the disk. |
| /S | Stores the system files on the disk after formatting. Writes the two hidden files and Command.com to the disk, making the disk bootable. Not available under Windows 2000/XP or Windows Me. |
| /Q | Re-creates the root directory and FATs if you want to quickly format a previously formatted disk that is in good condition. /Q does not read or write to any other part of the disk. |

**Table 15-5** Parameters for the Format command

## UNFORMAT

The Unformat command might be able to reverse the effect of an accidental format. To unformat a disk, use this command:

**UNFORMAT C:**

## DEBUG

The Debug program is an editor with few boundaries. Whereas a text editor such as Notepad or WordPad can only edit the contents of a text file, Debug can do so much more. It can view and manipulate the components of a file system on floppy disks and hard drives, including the FAT, directories, boot records, and any other area of the drive or disk. You can also use Debug to view the contents of memory and hexadecimal memory addresses. In fact, its ability to step into any area of a drive, disk, or memory makes it an extremely dangerous tool. To access Debug, enter the command Debug at the command prompt. For an example of using Debug to view contents of memory, see the online content section, "Behind the Scenes with DEBUG."

## COMMANDS TO MANAGE THE OPERATING SYSTEM

Commands that can help you diagnose OS problems and/or repair them include Sys, Scanreg, Ver, and MSD, all discussed next.

### SYS *DRIVE:*

Using Windows 9x/Me, the Sys command copies the Windows 9x/Me system files needed to boot to a disk or hard drive. (The Sys command is not used with Windows 2000/XP.) Use the command if the system files on a drive are corrupt—you can access the drive, but you cannot boot from it. The command to copy system files to the hard drive is:

**SYS C:**

### SCANREG /RESTORE /FIX /BACKUP

The Scanreg command restores or repairs the Windows 98/Me registry. (Scanreg is not available under Windows 2000/XP.) Scanreg uses backups of the registry that Windows 98/Me

Registry Checker automatically makes each day. To restore the registry from a previous backup, use this command:

**SCANREG /RESTORE**

A menu appears asking you which backup to use.

To repair a corrupted registry, use this command:

**SCANREG /FIX**

To create a new backup of the registry, use this command:

**SCANREG /BACKUP**

Don't use this last command if you are having problems with the registry because you might overwrite a good backup of the registry with a corrupted one.

## VER

Use the Ver command to display the version of the operating system in use.

## MICROSOFT DIAGNOSTIC UTILITY (MSD)

DOS and Windows 9x/Me offered the Microsoft Diagnostic Utility (MSD), a utility useful for viewing information about the system, including information about memory, video, ports, device drivers, and system resources.

To load MSD using Windows 9x/Me, click **Start**, click **Run**, enter **MSD.EXE** in the Run dialog box, and then click **OK**. The MSD window appears (see Figure 15-11). Because MSD is a DOS-based 16-bit utility program, it does not always get the full picture of the Windows environment, so beware. Sometimes information on the MSD screen conflicts with information given by Device Manager or System Information. Its most actuate results are given when you execute it from a command prompt provided by the Windows 9x/Me startup disk, which you'll learn to use later in the chapter. You will practice using MSD in a project at the end of this chapter.

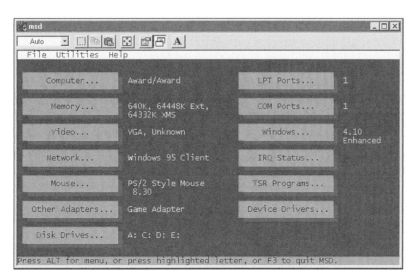

**Figure 15-11** MSD opening screen

## USING BATCH FILES

Recall from earlier in the chapter that Autoexec.bat is a batch file. Batch files can be used in many other ways than just helping with the boot. Suppose, for example, you have a list of OS commands that you want to execute several times. Perhaps you have some data files to distribute to several PCs in your office, but your network is down, so you must walk from one PC to another, repeatedly doing the same job. This kind of task can get real old, real quick. Fortunately, to make life easier, you can store the list of commands in a batch file on disk, and then execute the batch file at each PC. This will save you time and reduce errors.

When using batch files, create the batch file as a text file and give it a .bat file extension. For example, you can store these five OS commands on a disk in a file named MYLOAD.BAT:

```
C:

MD\UTILITY

MD\UTILITY\TOOLS

CD\UTILITY\TOOLS

COPY A:\TOOLS\*.*
```

In the batch file, the first command makes drive C the default drive. Then a new directory and subdirectory on drive C are created. Next, you make the new \Tools directory the default directory and copy files from the floppy disk to it.

From the command prompt, you execute the batch file just as you do other program files, by entering the filename, with or without the file extension:

```
A:\>MYLOAD
```

All commands listed in the file will execute, beginning at the top of the list. Any good book on DOS or DOS Web site provide examples of the very useful ways you can implement batch files, including adding user menus. One excellent site with tons of information about MS-DOS and batch files is by Computer Hope at *www.computerhope.com/msdos.htm*. Also, the Windows XP Help and Support Center has a list of commands you can use in batch files and instructions on how to use these commands.

## *USING THE WINDOWS 9X/ME STARTUP DISK*

A floppy disk with enough software to load an operating system is called a **bootable disk**, or **system disk**. A bootable disk with some utility programs to troubleshoot a failed hard drive is called a **rescue disk, emergency startup disk (ESD),** or **startup disk**. Having a rescue disk available for an emergency is very important, and a PC technician should always have one or more on hand. In this section, you'll learn to create a Windows 9x/Me startup disk and use it to prepare a hard drive or disk for first use and to troubleshoot a failed boot.

## CREATING A WINDOWS 9X/ME STARTUP DISK

A Windows 9x/Me startup disk has everything you need to prepare a new hard drive for use and to troubleshoot a failed hard drive. The disk does not need to be created on the same computer that will use it, although in most cases you should use the same version of

Windows as used by the computer that will be using the disk. Follow these instructions to create a startup disk for Windows 9x/Me:

1. Click **Start** on the taskbar, point to **Settings**, and then click **Control Panel**.

2. In the Control Panel window, double-click the **Add/Remove Programs** icon.

3. Click the **Startup Disk** tab, and then click the **Create Disk** button (see Figure 15-12).

4. Windows might need the Windows CD to create the disk. Insert the CD if it is requested. Windows then creates the startup disk.

5. Write protect the disk so that later when you use it, an infected system cannot put a virus on the disk. Label the disk and keep it in a safe place.

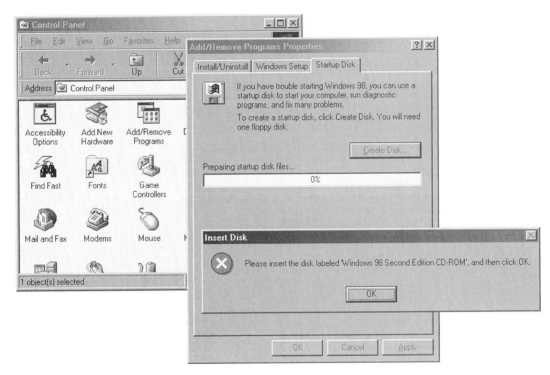

**Figure 15-12** Windows might use the Windows CD to create a startup disk

Windows places many utility programs on the disk that you will learn to use in the next sections. Because there is so much content on the disk, Windows compresses the program files and then stores them all in one large file. This large file is called a **cabinet file**, and is named Ebd.cab. During startup, a RAM drive is created and the contents of the cabinet file are uncompressed and copied to the RAM drive. This RAM drive is necessary because there is not enough space for the cabinet file on the floppy disk, and the startup disk assumes the hard drive might not be accessible. You can also use the Extract command to extract specific files when the RAM drive is not active.

> **Notes**
>
> When Windows 9x/Me creates a startup disk, it copies files to the disk from the \Windows\Command\EBD folder. You can also copy some of these files to a formatted disk to create a startup disk manually.

**APPLYING|CONCEPTS**  Using Windows 9x/Me, create a startup disk and boot from the disk. What messages and questions do you see on the screen when you boot from the disk? If you have access to a Windows 2000 or Windows XP computer, boot it using the Windows 9x/Me startup disk. What messages or questions do you see? Are there any differences?

## USING A STARTUP DISK TO PARTITION AND FORMAT A NEW DRIVE

If you have just installed a new hard drive and you are not ready to install an OS, you can use a Windows 9x/Me startup disk to partition and format the drive. As a hardware technician, you are often called on to install a hard drive and verify that it's in good working order, although you are not expected to install an OS. By partitioning and formatting the drive and then using Scandisk to check each sector, you know all is well. This method also works when you are installing a second hard drive in a system, and this second drive will not hold the OS.

### USE FDISK TO PARTITION A DRIVE

To use Fdisk to partition the drive, do the following:

1. Boot from a startup disk that has the Fdisk.exe utility on it and enter **Fdisk** at the command prompt. The Fdisk opening menu shown in Figure 15-13 appears.

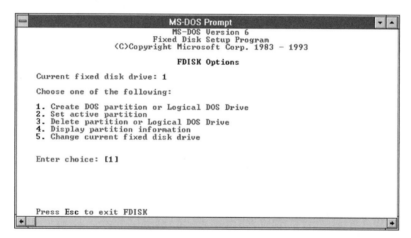

```
┌──────────────────────────── MS-DOS Prompt ────────────────▼─▲─┐
│                         MS-DOS Version 6                        │
│                     Fixed Disk Setup Program                    │
│              (C)Copyright Microsoft Corp. 1983 - 1993           │
│                                                                 │
│                         FDISK Options                           │
│                                                                 │
│   Current fixed disk drive: 1                                   │
│                                                                 │
│   Choose one of the following:                                  │
│                                                                 │
│   1. Create DOS partition or Logical DOS Drive                  │
│   2. Set active partition                                       │
│   3. Delete partition or Logical DOS Drive                      │
│   4. Display partition information                              │
│   5. Change current fixed disk drive                            │
│                                                                 │
│                                                                 │
│   Enter choice: [1]                                             │
│                                                                 │
│                                                                 │
│                                                                 │
│   Press Esc to exit FDISK                                       │
│ ←│                                                          │→  │
└─────────────────────────────────────────────────────────────────┘
```

**Figure 15-13**  Fixed disk setup program (Fdisk) menu

2. Select option **1** to create the first partition. The menu in Figure 15-14 appears.

3. Use option 1 to create the primary DOS partition. If you plan to install Windows 9x, be sure this partition is at least 150 MB, preferably more. Make this first partition the active partition, which is the partition used to boot the OS. Fdisk automatically makes this partition drive C.

4. Next, use either option 1 or 2 to create other DOS partitions using the remainder of the hard drive. If you created an extended partition, use option **3** to create logical drives in the extended partition.

5. When you create logical drives using Fdisk, you need to decide how large you want each drive to be. If you have at least 512 MB available for the drive, a message appears asking, "Do you wish to enable large disk support (Y/N)?" If you respond **Y**, then Fdisk assigns the FAT32 file system to the drive. Otherwise, it uses FAT16.

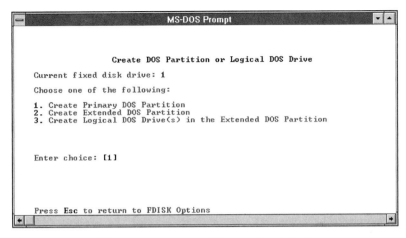

**Figure 15-14** Fdisk menu to create partitions and logical drives

6. When Fdisk is completed, the hard drive has a partition table, an active partition, perhaps other partitions, and logical drives within these partitions, as shown in Figure 15-15.

7. Exit the Fdisk window and reboot the PC before you format the logical drives.

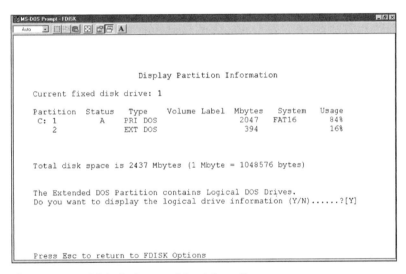

**Figure 15-15** Fdisk displays partition information

## FORMAT EACH LOGICAL DRIVE

Now that the hard drive is partitioned and logical drives are created and assigned drive letters, the next step is to format each logical drive. The three commands used to format logical drives C, D, and E are as follows:

```
Format C:/S
```

```
Format D:
```

```
Format E:
```

In the Format command line, the /S option makes the drive bootable, and the drive letter tells the OS which drive to format. Then, as a last step to verify the drive is in good working order, use Scandisk to check the drive for bad sectors, as shown below.

```
Scandisk C:
```

Remove the floppy disk from the drive and boot the system. The system should boot to the C prompt.

## USING A STARTUP DISK TO TROUBLESHOOT A FAILED BOOT

Suppose you turn on a PC and startup BIOS has successfully performed POST. The next step is to load the OS, but there's an error message onscreen that indicates BIOS cannot access the hard drive or find an OS to load. Table 15-6 lists some error messages that might appear in this situation.

| Error Message | Meaning of the Error Message |
|---|---|
| Invalid drive specification | The BIOS is unable to find a hard drive or a floppy drive that setup tells it to expect. Look for errors in CMOS setup, or use Fdisk to examine the partition table on the hard drive. |
| No boot device available | The hard drive is not formatted, or the format is corrupted, and there is no disk in drive A. Use Fdisk to examine the partition table on the hard drive. |
| Invalid partition table<br>Error loading operating system<br>Missing operating system<br>Invalid boot disk<br>Inaccessible boot device | The Master Boot program at the beginning of the hard drive displays these messages when it cannot find the active partition on the hard drive or the boot record on that partition. Use Fdisk to examine the drive for errors. |
| Non-system disk or disk error<br>Bad or missing Command.com<br>No operating system found<br>Can't find NTLDR | The disk in drive A is not bootable. Remove the disk in drive A and boot from the hard drive. If you still get the error, use Fdisk to examine the partition table on the hard drive. If you can access drive C, look for missing system files on the drive. For Windows 9x or DOS, use the Sys command to restore system files. |
| Not ready reading drive A:<br>Abort, Retry, Fail?<br>General failure reading drive A:<br>Abort, Retry, Fail? | The disk in drive A is missing, is not formatted, or is corrupted. Try another disk or remove the disk to boot from the hard drive. |
| Missing operating system<br>Error loading operating system | The MBR is unable to locate or read the OS boot sector on the active partition, or there is a translation problem on large drives. Boot from a bootable floppy or CD and examine the hard drive file system for corruption. |
| Error in Config.sys line xx | In a Windows 9x/Me environment, an entry in Config.sys is incorrect or is referencing a 16-bit program that is missing or corrupted. |

**Table 15-6** Error messages that appear after the PC has passed POST and before an OS has successfully loaded

> **Notes**
>
> In this chapter, we're assuming you are using Windows 9x/Me. When troubleshooting a failed boot in a Windows 2000/XP environment, you can use the Recovery Console on the Windows 2000/XP setup CD instead of the Windows 9x/Me startup disk. In the Recovery Console, rather than Fdisk, use the Diskpart command to examine the partition table on the hard drive.

In isolating the root cause of these problems, the first question to ask is "Can I boot from another device other than the hard drive?" If so, then you have proven that all essential subsystems except the hard drive subsystem are functioning. In effect, you have isolated the problem to the hard drive. At this point, ask the question, "Can I use commands on the startup disk to read the hard drive?"

Here are commands to try and things to do:

1. Place a Windows 9x/Me startup disk in the floppy drive. Turn off the PC and reboot.

2. When given the opportunity, enter CMOS setup and verify the boot sequence is first drive A and then drive C. Save any changes you made to CMOS and allow the boot to continue. (How to access CMOS setup is covered in Chapter 3 and in a project at the end of this chapter.)

3. The OS loads from the startup disk and a startup menu appears (see Figure 15-16).

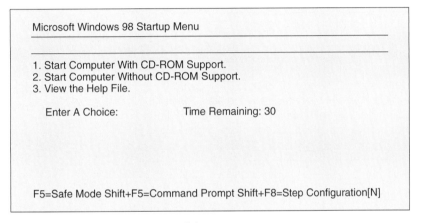

**Figure 15-16**  Windows 98 rescue disk startup menu

4. Select the **Start Computer With CD-ROM Support** option. The OS then examines the system for problems. For a hard drive formatted with the NTFS file system, a message is displayed: "Windows 98 has detected that drive C does not contain a valid FAT or FAT32 partition." It then provides an A prompt where you can enter commands.

5. For a Windows 9x/Me system, type **DIR C:** at the A prompt and then press **Enter**. If this step displays a list of files and folders on the hard drive, then the partition table and file system on the drive are intact. You then know that the problem has to do with the OS boot record, OS hidden files, and command interface files. Try this command to restore these files: **SYS C:**.

6. To examine the partition tables of all installed hard drives, type **Fdisk /status** at the A prompt and press **Enter**. Figure 15-17 shows the results for a system that has two hard drives installed.

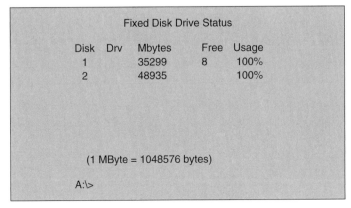

**Figure 15-17**  Results of the Fdisk /status command for a system with one 36 GB hard drive and one 49 GB drive

7. If the partition table is corrupted an error message is displayed. Type the command **Fdisk /MBR** at the A prompt and press **Enter**. If the MBR program on the master boot record is corrupted, this will solve the problem.

> **Notes**
>
> At any time after you have booted from the startup disk, at the A prompt, type **C:** and press **Enter** to get a C prompt. If you successfully get a C prompt, then you can try to load the Windows desktop. To do that, at the C prompt, type **C:\Windows\win** and press **Enter**, which executes Win.com on the hard drive. Win.com and the supporting files needed to load the Windows desktop take up too much room to be stored on a floppy disk, so the only way this last command will work is if the hard drive is accessible and healthy.

> **Notes**
>
> You have just seen how you can use a Windows 98 startup disk to examine the partition table on a Windows 2000/XP system, proving that the boot problem is a Windows problem, and not a hardware problem. However, know that when attempting to solve a Windows problem, always use the disks, CDs, and recovery tools native to the installed OS.

If you still cannot use Fdisk to display the partition information, the problem is with the partition table, the hard drive, its cabling, or its power source. More in-depth troubleshooting of the hard drive is covered in Chapter 8. If you have successfully used Fdisk to display partition information on the drive, then it's time to treat the problem as a Windows problem. How to troubleshoot loading Windows 9x/Me is covered in the next chapter.

# APPLYING|CONCEPTS

Many PC technicians use a Windows 9x/Me startup disk when troubleshooting Windows 2000/XP computers, because the Windows 9x/Me startup disk has a useful set of tools and resources that are not as easily available under Windows 2000/XP. Here are three situations in which you might choose to use a Windows 9x/Me startup disk:

- You are helping someone solve a problem with their Windows 2000/XP system, which refuses to boot. You have your Windows 98 startup disk handy, so you boot from it and get to an A prompt. In order to get to an A prompt successfully, many subsystems in the computer must be functioning, including the motherboard, processor, memory, floppy disk drive, power supply, and video system. In fact, you have just proven that the problem is isolated to the hard drive.

- A Windows XP computer comes to you for repair with a failed hard drive. You install a new hard drive, but you do not have the Windows XP setup CD to install Windows XP on the drive. In this situation, you can use a Windows 9x/Me startup disk to boot the system and create a partition table on the drive. This assures you that the drive is functioning properly even without installing an OS.

- Your Windows 2000 system will not boot, and your term paper is stored on the hard drive! If the hard drive is using the FAT file system, you might be able to use the Windows 98 startup disk to recover the file.

## >> CHAPTER SUMMARY

▲ During the boot, the ROM BIOS startup program searches secondary storage for an OS.

▲ When the OS loads from a hard drive, the BIOS first executes the Master Boot Record (MBR) program, which turns to the partition table to find the OS boot record. The program in the OS boot record attempts to find a boot loader program for the OS, which for Windows 9x/Me, is the program Io.sys.

▲ Io.sys, which uses Msdos.sys, and Command.com, form the core of real-mode Windows 9x/Me. These three files are necessary to boot to a command prompt. Config.sys and Autoexec.bat are not required but are used if they are present. Other files are needed to load the GUI desktop and run GUI applications.

▲ Autoexec.bat and Config.sys are two files that contain commands used to customize the 16-bit portion of the Windows 9x/Me load process.

▲ A RAM drive is an area of memory that looks and acts like a hard drive, only it performs much faster. The Windows 9x/Me startup disk uses a RAM drive to hold program files, assuming the hard drive is not accessible.

▲ Typical commands in the Autoexec.bat file include Path, Set, Restart, Temp, and Echo.

▲ Windows 9x/Me uses Command.com to provide a command prompt window.

▲ DOS and Windows 9x/Me divide memory addresses into conventional (0 to 640K), upper (640K to 1024K), and extended memory (above 1024K).

▲ Conventional memory is used to hold the OS, applications, and data. Upper memory holds BIOS and device drivers. Extended memory can be used only by applications, the OS, and device drivers, if Himem.sys and Emm386.exe are managing it.

▲ The Del or Erase command deletes files or groups of files.

▲ The Copy command copies a single file or group of files. More powerful than the Copy command, the Xcopy command supports copying subdirectories.

▲ Mkdir creates a subdirectory, Chdir changes the current directory, and Rmdir removes a subdirectory.

▲ The Attrib command displays or changes the read-only, archive, system, and hidden attributes assigned to files.

▲ The Fdisk command is used to partition a hard drive and display partition information.

▲ The Format command is used to format floppy disks and logical drives. The /S parameter with the Format command makes a drive bootable. The Unformat command attempts to reverse the effect of an accidental format.

▲ Chkdsk and Scandisk both check drives for errors and repair them. Scandisk does a more thorough scan for Windows 9x/Me and basically replaces Chkdsk.

▲ The Defrag command rewrites files on a hard drive in contiguous clusters to improve hard drive performance.

▲ The Sys command copies the system files needed to boot to a disk or drive.

▲ The Scanreg command restores or repairs the Windows 98/Me registry.

▲ Batch files can be used to execute a group of commands using only a single command.

◢ A floppy disk with enough software to load an operating system is called a bootable disk, or system disk. A bootable disk with some utility programs to troubleshoot a failed hard drive is called a rescue disk, emergency startup disk (ESD), or startup disk.

◢ Create a startup disk in Windows 9x/Me using the Add/Remove Programs applet in the Control Panel.

## >> KEY TERMS

For explanations of key terms, see the Glossary near the end of the book.

| | | |
|---|---|---|
| Autoexec.bat | extended memory | rescue disk |
| batch file | external commands | startup disk |
| bootable disk | fragmented files | system disk |
| CD (change directory) command | hidden file | terminate-and-stay-resident |
| conventional memory | high memory area (HMA) | (TSR) |
| DOS box | Himem.sys | upper memory |
| emergency startup disk (ESD) | internal commands | upper memory block (UMB) |
| Emm386.exe | RAM drive | wildcard |

## >> REVIEW QUESTIONS

1. The first 640K of memory addresses are called which of the following?

   a. Conventional memory

   b. Upper memory

   c. High memory area

   d. Extended memory

2. Which of the following files contains the software that loads device drivers and other programs into upper memory?

   a. Config.sys

   b. Himem.sys

   c. System

   d. Emm386.exe

3. Which of the following statements best describes a RAM drive?

   a. It is a hard drive.

   b. It is an area of memory that looks and acts like a hard drive and is used to eliminate the need for hard drive access.

   c. It is an area of memory that is slower than a hard drive.

   d. It is a drive whose memory is extremely limited.

4. Which of the following commands displays the contents of the file Myfile.txt one screen at a time?

   **a.** Type Myfile.txt

   **b.** Type My file.txt >PRN

   **c.** Type Myfile.txt |More

   **d.** DIR Myfile.txt

5. Pressing which of the following keys will bypass the startup files during the boot?

   **a.** F3

   **b.** F5

   **c.** F7

   **d.** F8

6. True or false? Under DOS, a filename can contain up to ten characters, a separating period, and a file extension of up to three characters.

7. True or false? An upper memory block (UMB) is a group of consecutive memory addresses in the upper memory area that has had physical memory assigned to it.

8. True or false? Under MS-DOS, be sure not to use a space, period, *, ?, or \ in a filename or file extension.

9. True or false? The three file extensions that the OS recognizes for programs are .com, .exe, and .bat.

10. True or false? A bootable disk with some utility programs to troubleshoot a failed hard drive is called a system disk.

11. You can load the MS-DOS core in two ways: from the Windows 9x/Me _____ or from a Windows 9x/Me _____.

12. A file that does not appear in the directory list is called a(n) _____.

13. A(n) _____ file is a text file that contains a series of commands that are executed in order.

14. Internal commands are embedded in the _____ file, whereas external commands have their own _____.

15. Memory addresses above 1024K are called _____.

# Supporting Windows 9x/Me

**A**s a PC support technician, you need to know how to install, use, and troubleshoot the Windows OSs commonly used today. Microsoft considers Windows 9x/Me a legacy OS and no longer supports it. However, it's a great learning tool to prepare you to understand the more sophisticated operating systems such as Windows XP and Windows Vista, and many individual and corporate users still use Windows 9x/Me. This chapter covers how Windows 9x/Me is structured, how it works with various software programs and hardware devices, and how to troubleshoot it.

# WINDOWS 9X/ME ARCHITECTURE

Windows 9x/Me has had several releases, including Windows 95, Windows 95 Service Release 2 (also known as Windows 95 SR2, Windows 95 Rev B, Windows 95B, and

> **Notes**
>
> To learn which version of Windows is installed, right-click the **My Computer** icon and select **Properties** from the shortcut menu. The System Properties window opens. Click the **General** tab.

Windows 95 OSR2), Windows 98, Windows 98 Second Edition (SE), and Windows Me (Millennium Edition). Each of these OSs uses the same basic architecture, and each release improved on previous versions and added new features.

Like other OSs, Windows 9x/Me has a shell and a kernel. Recall from Chapter 2 that the shell is the component of the OS that relates to the user and to applications, and the kernel interacts with hardware. Because the kernel has more power to communicate with hardware devices than the shell, applications operating under the OS cannot get to hardware devices without the shell passing those requests to the kernel. This structure provides for a more stable system.

The two most important parts of the shell are the user component and the GDI. The **user component** manages input from the keyboard and other user devices, output from the user interface, and the **GDI (Graphics Device Interface)**. The GDI is a component of the OS responsible for presenting the graphical interface to the user and providing graphics support to output devices. Table 16-1 lists the purpose of each component.

| Component Name | Main Files Holding the Component | Functions |
|---|---|---|
| Kernel | Kernel32.dll, Krnl386.exe | Handles the basic OS functions, such as managing memory, file I/O, and loading and executing programs |
| User | User32.dll, User.exe | Controls the mouse, keyboard, ports, and desktop, including the position of windows, icons, and dialog boxes |
| GDI | GDI32.dll, GDI.exe | Draws screens, graphics, and lines, and manages printing |

**Table 16-1**   Core components of Windows 9x/Me

## A BRIDGING OF TWO WORLDS

Windows 9x/Me is a compromise OS that bridges the world of 16-bit processing with the world of 32-bit processing. In Figure 16-1, you can see that DOS was a 16-bit OS, used only 16-bit device drivers, and managed base, upper, and extended memory. In contrast, Windows NT/2000/XP is a true 32-bit OS.

Windows 9x/Me is a mix of 16-bit processing and 32-bit processing. In bridging these two worlds, the core components of Windows 9x/Me (kernel, user, and GDI) are compiled as a combination of 16-bit and 32-bit code, and Windows 95/98 accepts both 16-bit and 32-bit drivers. (Windows Me accepts only 32-bit drivers.) In Chapter 15, you learned that it manages memory the same way that DOS does. In this chapter, you'll learn that it uses memory paging and virtual memory as does Windows NT/2000/XP.

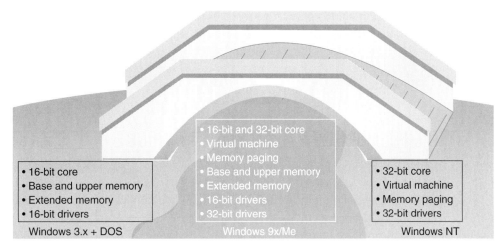

**Figure 16-1** Windows 9x/Me is the bridge from DOS to Windows NT/2000/XP

The Windows 9x/Me core relates to users, software, and hardware by way of several components, as shown in Figure 16-2. The core components (user, GDI, and kernel) stand in the middle between interface tools for the user and applications and the four main components in the figure that manage hardware. These four hardware-related components are as follows:

- The **VMM (Virtual Machine Manager)** is responsible for managing memory, virtual machines, and all the resources needed by each application. Virtual machines are discussed later in the chapter.
- The **IFS (Installable File System)** manager takes care of all disk access.
- The **Configuration Manager** configures all legacy and Plug and Play devices and communicates these configurations to devices.
- The **WDM (Win32 Driver Model)** driver manager, first used with Windows 98, is responsible for managing device drivers.

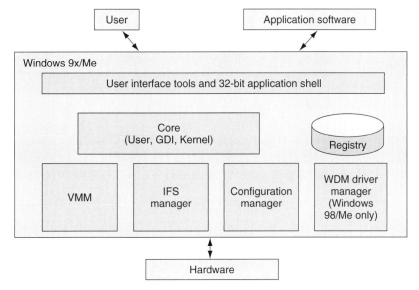

**Figure 16-2** The Windows 9x/Me architecture as it relates to the user, software, and hardware

Configuration data is primarily stored in the Windows 9x/Me registry, a database that also contains the initialization information for applications, a database of hardware and software settings, Windows configuration settings, user parameters, and application settings. In addition, some data is kept in text files called initialization files, which often have an .ini or .inf file extension.

## VIRTUAL MACHINES

You need to understand how the components in Figure 16-2 relate to applications and hardware. Applications call on the OS to access hardware or other software by using an **application programming interface (API) call**. When applications are first loaded by Windows 9x/Me, the methods to access hardware and software are made available to the software through an interface called a **virtual machine (VM)**. An application sees a virtual machine as a set of resources made available to it through these predefined APIs, as shown in Figure 16-3.

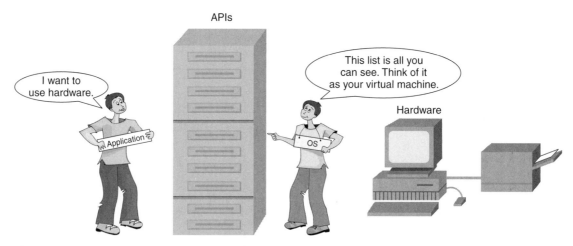

**Figure 16-3**    An application is not allowed direct access to hardware but is allowed access to a list of predefined APIs

An OS can provide a virtual machine to a single application that commands all the resources of that virtual machine, or the OS can assign a virtual machine to be shared by two or more applications. Think of virtual machines as multiple logical machines within one physical machine, similar in concept to several logical drives within one physical drive.

Figure 16-4 shows several virtual machines that Windows 9x/Me can provide. In the figure, the system virtual machine (system VM) is the most important VM under Windows 9x/Me, and is where all OS processes run. It can also support 32-bit and 16-bit Windows applications.

In contrast to Windows applications that expect to share resources, a DOS program expects to directly control the hardware of the entire PC, memory included. If a DOS program were to be run in a VM with other programs running, the DOS program might attempt to use memory addresses not assigned to it, which would cause errors in a multi-tasking environment. Windows 9x/Me solves this problem by providing each DOS program with its own virtual machine. In effect, the DOS program says, "I want all of the memory and all of this and all of that," and Windows 9x/Me says, "OK, here they are,"

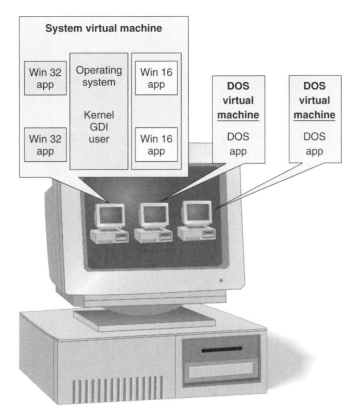

**Figure 16-4** Windows 9x/Me uses the virtual machine concept

and gives the program its own virtual machine, including all the virtual memory addresses it wants from 0 to 4 GB as well as its own virtual hardware! As far as the DOS program is concerned, it can go anywhere and do anything within its own PC. The DOS program does not try to communicate with any other application or to access the data of another program, because it thinks there are no other programs; it controls its entire world, and is the only program in it. That's a virtual machine.

> **Notes**
>
> One important result of running DOS programs in individual virtual machines is that when a DOS program makes an error, the virtual machine it is using hangs, but other programs and the OS are isolated from the problem and, thus, in theory are not affected.

Windows 16-bit applications offer a slightly different challenge to Windows 9x/Me. These programs make some of the same mistakes that DOS programs do and can cause the system to hang. However, they also sometimes expect to access other programs and their data. Fortunately, the 16-bit Windows programs don't expect to control the hardware directly and are content to route their requests to Windows. Because they communicate with hardware through the OS, Windows 9x/Me places these programs within the system virtual machine. In addition, Windows 9x/Me puts these programs together in their own memory space so they can share memory addresses, which means they can also share data.

The result of all 16-bit programs sharing the same memory space also means that when a 16-bit Windows program causes an error called a Windows Protection Error or a **General Protection Fault,** the error can disturb other 16-bit programs, causing them to fail. However, this error does not disturb DOS programs in their own virtual machines or 32-bit programs that don't share their virtual memory addresses.

## VIRTUAL MEMORY

The Windows Virtual Machine Manager (VMM) is responsible for managing virtual memory, which is hard drive space that is made to act like memory. The VMM stores virtual memory in a file called a swap file. The purpose of virtual memory is to increase the amount of memory available. Of course, because a hard drive is much slower than RAM, virtual memory works considerably slower than real memory. The VMM moves 4K segments, called **pages**, in and out of physical RAM, a process called **memory paging**. If RAM is full, the manager takes a page and moves it to the swap file.

If RAM is full much of the time, the VMM might spend excessive time moving pages in and out of RAM. That can cause excessive hard drive use, decrease overall system performance, and even cause the system to lock up or applications to fail. This situation, sometimes called **disk thrashing**, can cause premature hard drive failure. If you are experiencing very slow system response and observe the hard drive is in constant use, suspect excessive memory paging.

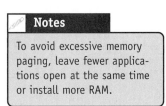

**Notes**

To avoid excessive memory paging, leave fewer applications open at the same time or install more RAM.

You have some control over virtual memory settings. To see what virtual memory settings Windows 9x/Me offers, click **Start**, point to **Settings**, click **Control Panel**, double-click **System**, and then select the **Performance** tab. Click **Virtual Memory** and the Virtual Memory dialog box shown in Figure 16-5 opens. These settings are used to tell Windows how to manage the swap file. Unless you have good reason to do otherwise, select the **Let Windows manage my virtual memory settings** option.

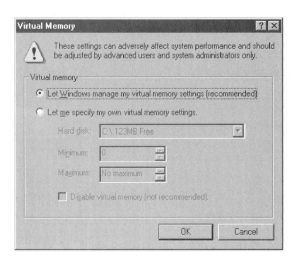

**Figure 16-5** Options for managing virtual memory in Windows 9x/Me

One reason you might want to change a virtual memory setting is to make the file size permanent to prevent Windows from resizing the file, which can slow down performance. To improve performance, first defragment the hard drive so there is plenty of unfragmented space for the file. Then set the maximum and minimum file sizes to the same value, which forces the size not to change. If you have the available hard drive space, set the size to about 2.5 times the amount of RAM.

Notice in Figure 16-5 that you can specify the location of the swap file. The name of the swap file in Windows 9x/Me is **Win386.swp**, and its default location is C:\Windows. You can choose to put the swap file on a compressed drive, but Windows does not compress the swap file itself. You'll learn more about compressed drives later in the chapter.

# INSTALLING WINDOWS 9X/ME, HARDWARE, AND SOFTWARE

In this section, you will learn how to install Windows 9x/Me and how to install hardware and applications with Windows 9x/Me. Because you can't purchase a new license for Windows 9x/Me, you'll never be called on to install Windows 9x/Me on a new computer. However, when a hard drive fails on an older computer, you'll need to install the OS on the replacement drive. Also, if an existing Windows 9x/Me installation gets corrupted, you might need to reinstall the OS.

## INSTALLING WINDOWS 9X/ME

Before installing Windows 9x/Me, verify that your system meets requirements for the OS. Check the following:

▲ Verify that the minimum and recommended hardware requirements for Windows 9x/Me are met. Table 16-2 lists these requirements. For Windows 9x/Me to perform satisfactorily, the PC should meet the recommended requirements.

▲ Windows 95/98 claims that it supports legacy hardware devices, but Windows Me does not. To check whether a particular hardware product has been tested for use with Windows Me, go to *www.microsoft.com/whdc/hcl/default.mspx*.

▲ You also need to check software packages and programs for compatibility. You can do this by checking the documentation or the manufacturer's Web site for each program.

| Description | Windows 95 | Windows 98 | Windows Me |
|---|---|---|---|
| Processor | 486–25 MHz or higher | 486DX–66 MHz (Pentium is recommended) | Pentium 150 MHz |
| RAM | 4 MB (8 MB is recommended) | 16 MB (24 MB is recommended) | 32 MB |
| Free hard drive space | 50 MB | 195 MB (315 MB is recommended) | 320 MB |

**Table 16-2** Minimum and recommended hardware requirements for Windows 9x/Me

Now let's turn our attention to the two types of Windows 9x/Me setup CDs and decisions you must make about the installation before you begin. Then we'll look at the details of installing the OS.

### TWO TYPES OF SETUP CDs

Two kinds of Windows 9x/Me setup CDs exist: Windows 9x/Me for a New PC that can be used to install the OS on a drive that has no previous OS installed, and Windows 9x/Me Upgrade that requires an earlier version of Windows already be installed. When Microsoft was still selling these CDs, the CD for installing Windows on a new PC was significantly more expensive than the upgrade CD.

> **Notes**
>
> Windows Me does not support 16-bit legacy drivers that work under Windows 95/98, so it's important to verify that your hardware devices are compatible with Windows Me.

You have some freedom as to how you can use either CD:

▲ If you begin the installation with a hard drive that has no Windows installed, you can use either the upgrade CD or the CD for a new PC. If you use the upgrade CD, during the installation you must prove you have a Windows setup CD or floppy disk for an earlier version of Windows by providing that CD or floppy when the Setup program asks for it. If you cannot provide the CD or floppy, the upgrade installation terminates. If you use the setup CD for a new PC, that step is skipped during the installation. Using either setup CD, you're performing a new installation of the OS, which is called a **clean install**.

▲ If an older version of Windows is already installed on the hard drive, you can use either the upgrade CD or the CD for a new PC. Using either CD, you can perform an upgrade or you can perform a clean install. However, if you choose to perform a clean install using the upgrade CD, you'll need the setup CD or floppy for the previous version of Windows in hand to use when the Setup program asks for it.

The point is that the two CDs differed in cost, not in how they can be used, with one exception: If you are using the upgrade CD, you must prove you have the right to use it by providing a setup CD or floppy from an older version of Windows, or you must start with an older version of Windows already installed.

## CLEAN INSTALL OR UPGRADE

Two ways you can install Windows are a clean install or an upgrade. Remember you can perform an upgrade or a clean install with either the Windows 9x/Me for a New PC CD or the Windows 9x/Me Upgrade CD. If no previous version of Windows is installed, your only option is a clean install. If Windows is already installed, you can choose between a clean install or an upgrade. Consider these advantages and disadvantages when making your decision:

▲ A clean install ignores any settings in the currently installed OS, including information about installed hardware or software. Therefore, after the clean install, you must reinstall all hardware and applications.

▲ An **upgrade install** carries forward as much information as it can about what the current OS knows concerning installed hardware and software, user preferences, and other settings. If you don't encounter any problems along the way, an upgrade is much faster than a clean install.

▲ If you are having problems with your current operating system and applications, consider doing a clean install rather than an upgrade so that you can get a fresh start. Any unsolved problems with corrupted applications or system settings will not cause you problems in the new installation.

▲ If the old OS is not in good enough shape to boot up successfully, you have no choice: Perform a clean install.

▲ With a clean install, because you're starting over, it's important you verify that you have all the application software installation CDs or floppy disks and then back up all data on the drive. Also take time to verify that the backups are good and that you have all device driver software.

▲ If the PC is on a network, it is possible to install the OS from another computer on the network. However, if you want to do an upgrade, you must begin the upgrade from within the current OS. Therefore, if you are performing an installation across a network, you are forced to do a clean install.

 **Tip**

For an upgrade or a clean install, to speed up the installation, you can copy the files and folders on the Windows 9x/Me setup CD to a folder on your hard drive (see Figure 16-6) and run the Setup program from that folder. Also, having the Windows 9x/Me CD files on your hard drive makes it easier to access the files later when adding Windows components or updating drivers.

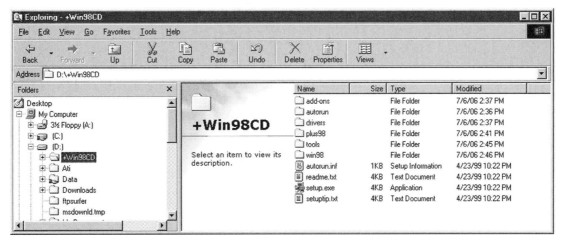

**Figure 16-6** Having Windows set up files stored on the hard drive can make the installation go faster and later be an ongoing convenience

## CHOOSING A FILE SYSTEM

One decision you must make when you install Windows 9x/Me is which file system you will use for the drive that will hold the Windows installation. Your choices are FAT16 and FAT32.

### FAT16

DOS and all versions of Windows support the FAT16 file system, which uses 16 bits for each cluster entry in the FAT. Using 16 bits, the largest possible number is 65,535 (binary 1111 1111 1111 1111). Therefore, it is not possible to have more than 65,535 clusters when using FAT16. Therefore, the number of sectors assigned to each cluster must be large in order to accommodate a large logical drive.

With FAT16, the smallest possible cluster size is four sectors. Each sector is 512 bytes, which means the smallest cluster size is 2,048 bytes. Because an OS writes a file to a drive using one or more clusters, the least amount of space it uses for one file is 2,048 bytes. If a file contains fewer than 2,048 bytes, the remaining bytes in the cluster are wasted. This wasted space is called **slack**. If a drive contains many small files, much space is wasted.

### FAT32

Beginning with Windows 95 OSR2 (OS Release 2), Microsoft offered a FAT that contains 32 bits per FAT entry instead of the older 12-bit or 16-bit FAT entries. Only 28 bits are used to hold a cluster number; the remaining four bits are not used. Because FAT32 has more bits to hold a cluster number, the number of clusters can be larger, which means the size of a cluster can be smaller. Smaller clusters mean the drive is likely to have less slack than when using FAT16. For these reasons, choose FAT32 for your file system unless the same PC will also be running Windows NT, which does not support FAT32.

After you have installed Windows 9x/Me, you can convert a FAT16 volume to FAT32 using Drive Converter. To access the Converter, after Windows is installed, click **Start, Programs, Accessories, System Tools,** and **Drive Converter (FAT32)**. As an alternative, you can use the Run dialog box. For the 16-bit version, enter **cvt.exe,** and for the 32-bit version, enter **cvt1.exe,** and then click **OK.** The Drive Converter Wizard steps you through the process.

## INSTALLING WINDOWS 9X/ME AS A CLEAN INSTALLATION

After you have verified that the system qualifies and decided to perform a clean installation, do the following to prepare your system:

- Enter CMOS setup and verify that the boot sequence is first the floppy disk or CD-ROM, depending on the media that you have for the Windows 9x/Me setup. Also verify that any feature that prevents editing the boot sector of the hard drive is disabled.
- For a new hard drive, recall from Chapter 15 that the drive can be partitioned using Fdisk and formatted using the Format command before an OS is installed. The Windows 9x/Me installation will do this for you, or you can do it before you do the installation.
- If you have important data on your hard drive, copy the data to another medium.
- If you are performing a clean install and Windows is already installed on the drive (such as when the current installation is corrupted and you want to reinstall the OS), you do not need to format the hard drive before you begin the installation, although you should delete all folders on the hard drive used for the OS or applications, including the \Windows folder, files, and subfolders. This forces Setup to perform a clean install and makes certain that no corrupted system files or applications remain, but still keep any data files that might be on the drive.
- If you want, you can also format the hard drive. Do this if you suspect a virus is present. If you suspect a boot sector virus is present, you can use the Fdisk/MBR command (discussed in Chapter 15) to rewrite the master boot sector program.

 **Caution**

Many CMOS setups have an option that can protect against some boot sector viruses. It prevents writing to the boot sector of the hard drive. This feature must be turned off before installing Windows, which must write to the boot sector during installation. Windows 9x/Me does not tell you that you must turn the feature off and start the installation over until about halfway through the installation.

You are now ready to perform the installation. Windows 9x/Me comes on a CD or set of floppy disks (yes, floppy disks are still around). Do one of the following to begin the installation:

- If you are installing Windows 98 or Windows Me from a CD (and your PC can boot from a CD-ROM drive), insert the CD in the drive and reboot.
- If your PC cannot boot from a CD, boot from a floppy disk or hard drive, then insert the CD in the CD-ROM drive, and enter the command **D:\Setup.exe**, substituting the drive letter of your CD-ROM drive for *D* if necessary. The Windows 95 setup CD is not bootable, so you will need a bootable floppy disk to begin the Windows 95 installation.
- If you are installing the OS from floppy disks, you can boot from the hard drive or floppy disk. To boot from the floppy disk, insert the Windows 9x/Me Disk 1, which is bootable, and boot the PC. At the A prompt, enter the command **Setup.exe**. You can also boot from a hard drive; to do so, go to a C prompt, insert the Windows 9x/Me Disk 1 in the floppy disk drive, and then enter the command **A:\Setup** to execute the Setup program on the floppy disk.

However you begin, the Windows 9x/Me setup screen appears. Then, a dialog box opens, as shown in Figure 16-7. Click **Continue** and then follow the directions onscreen.

**Figure 16-7** Exit setup or continue with the Windows installation

## INSTALLING WINDOWS 9X/ME AS AN UPGRADE

It's unlikely you'll ever be called on to upgrade a computer to Windows 9x/Me. However, here's what you need to know just in case the need arises. Before you begin the installation, in addition to the items listed previously, do the following:

- Verify that you have enough space on the hard drive. Delete files in the Recycle Bin and temporary directories.
- Run ScanDisk to check and repair errors on the hard drive. From Windows 95/98, click **Start, Programs, Accessories, System Tools**, and **ScanDisk**, and then scan each logical drive in the system. From a Windows startup disk, enter the command **Scandisk** at the command prompt.
- Run a current version of antivirus software to check for viruses.
- Check Config.sys and Autoexec.bat for potential problems. Verify that any hardware devices using device drivers loaded from these files work under the old OS so that you know your starting point if problems occur under the new OS.
- The Windows 9x/Me upgrade process moves commands in Autoexec.bat that are used to load terminate-and-stay-resident programs (TSRs) required for 16-bit Windows drivers and applications to Winstart.bat. Look for the Winstart.bat file in the root directory after the installation is done. If setup does not find any TSRs to put in the file, it will not be created.
- If TSRs such as QEMM386 (a memory manager by Quarterdeck) are loaded from Config.sys or Autoexec.bat, and problems arise because they run during the installation, disable them. To disable a command line, type **REM** at the beginning of the command line; this turns the line into a remark or comment. Later, after the installation, you can activate these lines again by removing the REMs.
- If you are connected to a network, verify that the connection works. If it does, Windows setup should be able to reestablish the connection correctly at the end of the installation.
- Create a Windows 9x/Me rescue disk for use in the event that the installation fails.
- Decide if you want to use FAT16 or FAT32 for your file system. Remember that you can choose FAT16 and then later convert to FAT32 using the Windows Drive Converter.

▲ If you are installing Windows 98 on a compressed drive, be aware that the registry can reside on any compressed drive, but the swap file can reside on a compressed drive only if the drive is compressed using protected-mode software such as DriveSpace. **DriveSpace** marks the area for the swap file as uncompressible. If your drive is compressed with real-mode compression software, such as DoubleSpace, then know that you cannot put the swap file on this compressed drive. The best practice is to back up the data and then uncompress the drive. You can later compress it using Windows 98 DriveSpace.

▲ Windows Me will not install on a compressed drive, so you must uncompress any portions of your hard drive that are compressed. If you are not sure whether your hard drive is compressed, run ScanDisk, which will tell you.

▲ Uninstall power management tools and disk management tools.

Sometimes Microsoft releases last-minute documentation on the setup CD. Check the Readme.txt file for any setup information provided. Then, after everything is ready for the installation, do the following to get to the setup screen:

1. Start the PC, loading the current operating system.

2. Close all open applications, including any antivirus software that is running. Close any icons that are open in the system tray.

3. Insert the CD in the CD-ROM drive or the floppy disk in the floppy drive. Your CD-ROM drive might be configured to run a CD automatically when it is first inserted. This Autoplay feature causes the Setup opening menu to appear without your entering the Setup command (see Figure 16-8). To disable the feature, hold down the Shift key while inserting the CD.

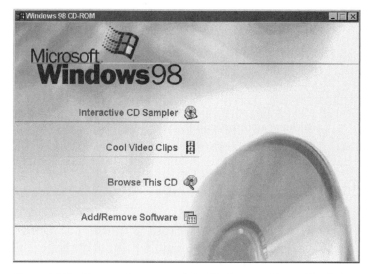

**Figure 16-8** The opening screen of the Windows 98 CD provides links you can use to navigate the CD

4. Open the Run dialog box and enter the command **D:\Setup.exe**, substituting the drive letter for your CD-ROM drive or floppy drive for D if necessary. Click **OK**.

5. Follow the instructions on the setup screen. When you have the opportunity to select the folder to install Windows, select the folder in which the current OS is installed; most likely that is \Windows. If you use the same folder, Setup uses whatever settings it finds there.

## INSTALLATION PROCESS FROM THE SETUP SCREEN FORWARD

After you get to the setup screen, the installation process is the same, no matter whether you are doing an upgrade or a clean install. During the installation, you are asked to choose from four setup options:

> **Notes**
>
> When installing Windows 9x/Me, you have the option of creating the startup disk, as discussed earlier. Be sure to create this disk to help in emergencies.

- ◢ *Typical*. This option installs all components that are usually installed with Windows 9x/Me. Most often, this is the option to choose.
- ◢ *Portable*. Use this option when installing Windows 9x/Me on a notebook computer.
- ◢ *Compact*. Use this option if you are short on hard drive space and want the smallest possible installation. No optional components are installed. After the installation, if you need a component, you can install it by double-clicking the **Add/Remove Programs** applet in the Control Panel.
- ◢ *Custom*. Use this option if you know you need components not normally installed under the Typical installation. You have the opportunity to select any group of components to include in the installation.

During the installation, Setup records information in log files. The primary log file is Setuplog.txt, a hidden text file that Setup uses when recovering from a crash to determine how far it got in the installation. Figure 16-9 shows a portion of Setuplog.txt in which the system ran a virus check on CMOS and began checking drives.

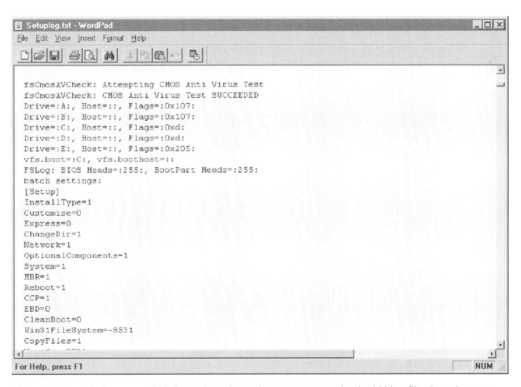

**Figure 16-9**   Windows records information about the setup process in the hidden file, Setuplog.txt

If the system fails to respond during the hardware detection phase, an entry is recorded in Detcrash.log, which is a binary file Setup uses to help recover from a crash caused by a hardware problem. Setup does not use the contents of the hidden Detlog.txt file; it is created only for the benefit of the user. The Detection Log (Detlog.txt) keeps a record of hardware detected, as shown in Figure 16-10.

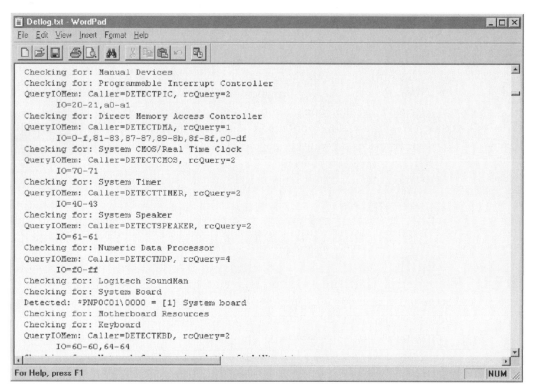

**Figure 16-10**    The hidden Detlog.txt file shows what hardware has been detected

As an example of how a setup crash can still move you forward, suppose Setup sees a network driver installed in Config.sys and, therefore, suspects that a network card is present. It records in Setuplog.txt and Detlog.txt that it is about to look for the card. If it finds the card, it records the success in Detlog.txt. However, if an error occurs while Setup searches for the card, an entry is made in the Detcrash.log file.

If the system crashes while trying to detect the network card and Setup is then restarted, Setup looks at Detcrash.log and Setuplog.txt to determine what it was trying to do at the time of the crash. It then skips that step and goes to the next step, so it doesn't make the same mistake twice. Ultimately, although Setup might crash several times during the installation, progress is still being made. By reading the content of the log files, Setup is able to skip steps that cause a problem and move forward.

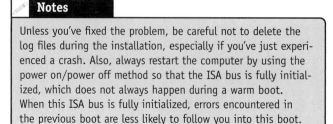

**Notes**

Unless you've fixed the problem, be careful not to delete the log files during the installation, especially if you've just experienced a crash. Also, always restart the computer by using the power on/power off method so that the ISA bus is fully initialized, which does not always happen during a warm boot. When this ISA bus is fully initialized, errors encountered in the previous boot are less likely to follow you into this boot.

In certain situations, you might want to force Setup to begin installation at the beginning instead of looking to Setuplog.txt for the entry point; for example, when you think you might have resolved a problem with hardware and want Setup to attempt to find the hardware again. To do this, delete Setuplog.txt to force a full restart.

After the installation is complete, do the following:

1. Go to the Control Panel and verify that the system date and time are correct. If they are not correct, make the change in CMOS setup.

2. Access the Internet and go to the Microsoft Web site (*windowsupdate.microsoft.com*). Download and install any available **service packs** or **patches**, which are updates and fixes to the OS released by Microsoft.

3. Using the Control Panel, open the **Add/Remove Programs** applet, click the **Windows Setup** tab, and install any additional Windows components.

4. If this is an upgrade installation, open and test the applications you already had installed under Windows 9x/Me. Any problem you have with a particular application might be solved by uninstalling and then reinstalling it, or installing any patches necessary to make it work with the new OS. Check the application manufacturer's Web site for available updates.

## DOWNLOADING AND INSTALLING UPDATES FOR WINDOWS 9X/ME

Microsoft is no longer updating Windows 9x/Me. However, you can download all the previously published updates from the Microsoft Web site, *windowsupdate.microsoft.com*. In Windows 98 and Windows Me, you can access this page by clicking **Windows Update** on the Start menu. The update process examines your system and recommends available updates for you to select, download, and install following directions on the screen (see Figure 16-11). Download all the available updates immediately after you have installed Windows 9x/Me. Because no more updates will be published, you should not have to update this legacy OS again.

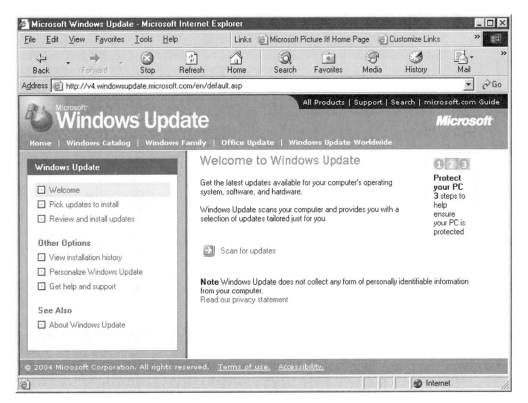

**Figure 16-11** Download Windows updates from the Microsoft Web site

## CONFIGURING THE WINDOWS 9X/ME STARTUP WITH MSDOS.SYS

In Windows 9x/Me, the text file Msdos.sys contains several parameters that affect how the OS boots. You can change some entries in this file to customize the boot process.

The file is a hidden, read-only, system file, so before you can edit it, you must first use the Attrib command at the command prompt to make the file available for editing. (Note that you can change the hidden and read-only attributes using Windows Explorer, but not the system attribute.)

> **☝ Tip**
>
> Make a backup copy of Msdos.sys in case you want to revert to the form it was in before changes were made.

Follow these steps to change the options in Msdos.sys:

1. Go to an OS command prompt.

2. Go to the root directory of your hard drive by entering the following:
   **CD\**

3. Make the file available for editing by entering the following:
   **ATTRIB -R -H -S MSDOS.SYS**

4. Make a backup copy of the file by entering the following:
   **COPY MSDOS.SYS MSDOS.BK**

5. Use Edit.com to edit the file by entering the following:
   **EDIT MSDOS.SYS**

6. Exit the editor, saving your changes. Then return the file to a hidden, read-only, system file by entering the following:
   **ATTRIB +R +H +S MSDOS.SYS**

Table 16-3 lists each entry in the Msdos.sys file and its purpose. You can refer to this table as

| Command-Line Variable Name | Purpose of the Values That Can Be Assigned to the Variable |
|---|---|
| AutoScan | 0 = Computer does not scan hard drive. |
| | 1 = Default. Prompts the user before running ScanDisk on the hard drive when booting up after the computer was not shut down properly. |
| | 2 = Automatically scans without prompting the user. |
| BootMulti | 0 = Default. Boot only to Windows 9x/Me. |
| | 1 = Allows for a dual boot. |
| BootWin | 1 = Default. Boots to Windows 9x/Me. |
| | 0 = Boots to previous version of DOS. |
| BootGUI | 1 = Default. Boots to Windows 9x/Me with the graphical user interface. |
| | 0 = Boots only to the command prompt for DOS 7.0 (the DOS core of Windows 95) or 7.1 (the DOS core of Windows 98). Autoexec.bat and Config.sys will be executed, and you will be in real-mode DOS. |
| BootMenu | 0 = Default. Doesn't display the startup menu. |
| | 1 = Displays the startup menu. |
| BootMenuDefault | 1 through 8 = The value selected on the startup menu by default. (Normally this value should be 1.) |

**Table 16-3** Contents of the Msdos.sys file options section

| Command-Line Variable Name | Purpose of the Values That Can Be Assigned to the Variable |
|---|---|
| BootMenuDelay | *n* = Number of seconds delay before the default value in the startup menu is automatically selected. |
| BootKeys | 1 = Default. The function keys work during the boot process (F4, F5, F6, F8, Shift+F5, Ctrl+F5, Shift+F8).<br><br>0 = Disables the function keys during the boot process. (This option can be used to help secure a workstation.) |
| BootDelay | *n* = Number of seconds the boot process waits (when it displays the message "Starting Windows 95" or "Starting Windows 98") for the user to press F8 to get the startup menu (default is 2 seconds). |
| Logo | 1 = Default. Displays the Windows 9x/Me logo screen.<br><br>0 = Leaves the screen in text mode. |
| Drvspace | 1 = Default. Loads Drvspace.bin, used for disk compression, if it is present.<br><br>0 = Doesn't load Drvspace.bin. |
| DoubleBuffer | 1 = Default. When you have a SCSI drive, enables double buffering for the drive. (See the drive documentation.)<br><br>0 = Doesn't use double buffering for the SCSI drive. |
| Network | 1 = If network components are installed, includes the option "Safe Mode with networking support" in the startup menu.<br><br>0 = Doesn't include the option on the startup menu. (This is normally set to 0 if the PC has no network components installed. The startup menu is renumbered from this point forward in the menu.) |
| BootFailSafe | 1 = Default. Includes Safe Mode in the startup menu.<br><br>0 = Doesn't include Safe Mode in the startup menu. |
| BootWarn | 1 = Default. Displays the warning message when Windows 9x/Me boots into Safe Mode.<br><br>0 = Doesn't display the warning message. |
| LoadTop | 1 = Default. Loads Command.com at the top of conventional memory.<br><br>0 = Doesn't load Command.com at the top of conventional memory. (Use this option when there is a memory conflict with this area of memory.) |

**Table 16-3** Contents of the Msdos.sys file options section (continued)

you read about the different options available when installing and configuring Windows 9x/Me.

Figure 16-12 shows a sample Msdos.sys file. The lines containing Xs at the bottom of the file are used to ensure that the file size is compatible with other programs.

```
[Paths]
WinDir=C:\WIN95
WinBootDir=C:\WIN95
HostWinBootDrv=C

[Options]
BootMulti=1
BootGUI=1
BootMenu=1
Network=0
;
;
;The following lines are required for compatibility with other programs.
;Do not remove them (MSDOS.SYS needs to be >1024 bytes).
;xxxxxxxxxxxxxxxxxxxxxxxxxxxxxxxxxxxxxxxxxxxxxxxxxxxxxxxxxxxxxxa
;xxxxxxxxxxxxxxxxxxxxxxxxxxxxxxxxxxxxxxxxxxxxxxxxxxxxxxxxxxxxxxb
;xxxxxxxxxxxxxxxxxxxxxxxxxxxxxxxxxxxxxxxxxxxxxxxxxxxxxxxxxxxxxxc
;xxxxxxxxxxxxxxxxxxxxxxxxxxxxxxxxxxxxxxxxxxxxxxxxxxxxxxxxxxxxxxd
;xxxxxxxxxxxxxxxxxxxxxxxxxxxxxxxxxxxxxxxxxxxxxxxxxxxxxxxxxxxxxxe
;xxxxxxxxxxxxxxxxxxxxxxxxxxxxxxxxxxxxxxxxxxxxxxxxxxxxxxxxxxxxxxf
;xxxxxxxxxxxxxxxxxxxxxxxxxxxxxxxxxxxxxxxxxxxxxxxxxxxxxxxxxxxxxxg
;xxxxxxxxxxxxxxxxxxxxxxxxxxxxxxxxxxxxxxxxxxxxxxxxxxxxxxxxxxxxxxh
;xxxxxxxxxxxxxxxxxxxxxxxxxxxxxxxxxxxxxxxxxxxxxxxxxxxxxxxxxxxxxxi
;xxxxxxxxxxxxxxxxxxxxxxxxxxxxxxxxxxxxxxxxxxxxxxxxxxxxxxxxxxxxxxj
;xxxxxxxxxxxxxxxxxxxxxxxxxxxxxxxxxxxxxxxxxxxxxxxxxxxxxxxxxxxxxxk
;xxxxxxxxxxxxxxxxxxxxxxxxxxxxxxxxxxxxxxxxxxxxxxxxxxxxxxxxxxxxxxl
;xxxxxxxxxxxxxxxxxxxxxxxxxxxxxxxxxxxxxxxxxxxxxxxxxxxxxxxxxxxxxxm
;xxxxxxxxxxxxxxxxxxxxxxxxxxxxxxxxxxxxxxxxxxxxxxxxxxxxxxxxxxxxxxn
;xxxxxxxxxxxxxxxxxxxxxxxxxxxxxxxxxxxxxxxxxxxxxxxxxxxxxxxxxxxxxxo
;xxxxxxxxxxxxxxxxxxxxxxxxxxxxxxxxxxxxxxxxxxxxxxxxxxxxxxxxxxxxxxp
;xxxxxxxxxxxxxxxxxxxxxxxxxxxxxxxxxxxxxxxxxxxxxxxxxxxxxxxxxxxxxxq
;xxxxxxxxxxxxxxxxxxxxxxxxxxxxxxxxxxxxxxxxxxxxxxxxxxxxxxxxxxxxxxr
;xxxxxxxxxxxxxxxxxxxxxxxxxxxxxxxxxxxxxxxxxxxxxxxxxxxxxxxxxxxxxxs
```

**Figure 16-12** A sample Msdos.sys file

## INSTALLING AND MANAGING HARDWARE WITH WINDOWS 9X/ME

After a hardware device is physically installed in a system, the next step is to install the software necessary to interface with it. This software, called a device driver, is written to interface with a specific device and operating system. Knowing how to install and manage hardware is an essential skill of a PC support technician.

Here are three ways to begin the process of installing a device driver:

▲ When a new device is installed and you power up the PC, Windows recognizes it and immediately launches the Found New Hardware Wizard. If the wizard does not launch automatically, you can start it manually. Go to the Control Panel and double-click the **Add New Hardware** icon, which launches the wizard.

▲ You can run an installation setup program on the floppy disk or CD that came bundled with the device. Look for and run a setup program named Setup.exe or Install.exe.

▲ If you downloaded a driver file from the Internet, double-click the file to launch the setup program.

One step in the Found New Hardware wizard is to select the hardware device from a list of devices (see Figure 16-13). If you click **OK**, Windows uses a Windows driver for the device, or you can click **Have Disk** to use your own drivers. If you have a driver on a floppy disk or CD or you downloaded a driver from the Internet to a folder on your hard drive, click **Have Disk** and point the wizard to the disk, CD, or folder that contains the driver. Sometimes you must select a folder on the disk or CD for the operating system to use. For example, if the disk or CD has three folders named \Win9x, \Win2k, and \Winxp, select the \Win9x folder.

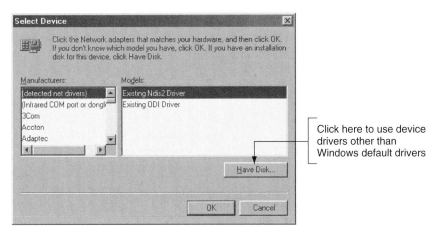

**Figure 16-13** To use device drivers supplied by the device manufacturer, click Have Disk

## VIEWING AND CHANGING CURRENT DEVICE DRIVERS

You can view and change current device drivers from the Control Panel. For example, to view the current video driver in Windows 98, click **Start, Settings, Control Panel**, and then double-click **Display**. Click the **Settings** tab to view the currently installed display driver, as shown in Figure 16-14.

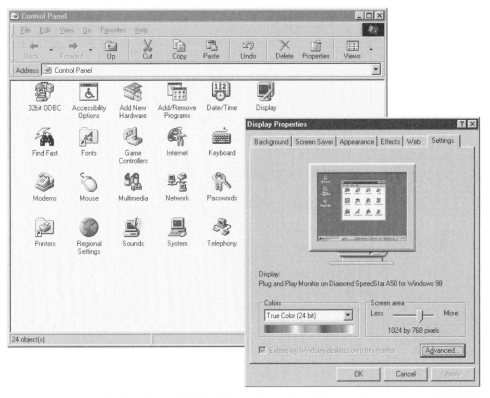

**Figure 16-14** Use the Settings tab of the Display Properties window to view the currently installed display driver

To change the video card driver, click **Advanced**, click the **Adapter** tab, and then click the **Change** button. You see the Windows 98 Update Device Driver Wizard. Click **Next** to see the dialog box in Figure 16-15, which includes options to let Windows 98 search for a new driver from its list of Windows drivers or to display a list of all the drivers in a specific location, so that you can select the driver you want. To provide your own driver, click the second option and then click **Next**. Then click **Have Disk** to provide the new driver from a floppy disk, a CD, or a file downloaded from the Internet.

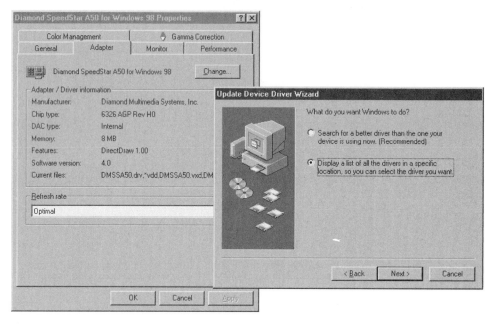

**Figure 16-15**    The Windows 98 Update Device Driver Wizard enables you to install a new device driver for a previously installed device

If the new driver fails, try uninstalling and then reinstalling the device. To uninstall a device, access Device Manager. (Click **Start, Settings, Control Panel**, double-click **System**, and then click **Device Manager**.) Select the device and then click **Remove** (see Figure 16-16). Then reboot the PC and allow the Found New Hardware Wizard to launch.

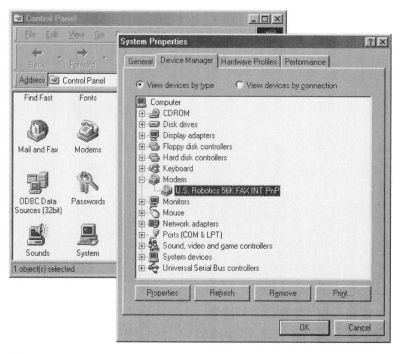

**Figure 16-16**    Use Device Manager to uninstall a device

## PLUG AND PLAY AND HARDWARE INSTALLATIONS

Remember that Plug and Play (PnP) is a set of design specifications for both hardware and software that works to make hardware installations supposedly effortless. For a system to be truly Plug and Play, it must meet these criteria:

▲ The system BIOS must be PnP. (To know if your BIOS is PnP, you can use MSD, a 16-bit command-line diagnostic utility, or you can check the CMOS setup screen.)
▲ All hardware devices and expansion cards must be PnP-compliant. (All PCI expansion cards are PnP.)
▲ The OS must be Windows 9x/Me or another OS that supports PnP.
▲ A 32-bit device driver must be available (from the device manufacturer or Windows).

If all these things are true, hardware installation should be just a matter of installing the new hardware device, turning on the PC, and perhaps providing the 32-bit driver, if it is not included with Windows 9x/Me. During the boot process, Windows 9x/Me surveys the devices and their needs for resources and allocates resources to each device. Windows 9x/Me is free to assign these resources to the devices and avoids assigning the same resource to two devices. For PnP to work, each device in the system must be able to use whatever resources the OS assigns to it.

Although it supports 16-bit device drivers and applications, Windows 95/98 works better using 32-bit drivers and 32-bit applications. If you are using older 16-bit drivers under Windows 95/98, search for 32-bit drivers to replace them. Look on the device manufacturer's Web site or the Microsoft Web site. Windows Me does not support 16-bit drivers, but does support 16-bit applications.

To learn whether a driver is 16-bit or 32-bit, look at how Windows loads it. If the driver is a 32-bit driver written for Windows 9x/Me, it is loaded from the registry. System.ini can contain both 16-bit and 32-bit drivers. If the driver is loaded from Autoexec.bat or Config.sys, it is a 16-bit driver written for DOS. Also look in Device Manager for an exclamation point beside the device, which indicates that the driver has a problem. For instance, this exclamation point might indicate that the driver is a 16-bit driver and, as such, might need updating to a 32-bit driver.

During the Windows 95/98 installation, Windows Setup tries to substitute 32-bit drivers for all 16-bit drivers it finds in use, and, if it can, eliminates the Autoexec.bat and Config.sys files altogether. However, if it can't substitute a 32-bit driver for an older 16-bit driver, it puts (or keeps) the proper lines in the Config.sys file and sets itself up to use the older driver. Because Windows Me does not support 16-bit drivers, it does not allow them to be loaded from Autoexec.bat or Config.sys.

## DISK COMPRESSION IN WINDOWS 95/98

If you run short on hard drive space on a Windows 95/98 system, one thing you can do is compress the drive. Windows 95 and Windows 98 support disk and drive compression (Windows Me does not) using the DriveSpace utility on a FAT16 volume. A compressed volume under Windows 9x is slower to access and somewhat unstable and should not be used if important data is on the volume. Use it with caution!

> **Notes**
>
> Windows 95/98 does not compress FAT32 volumes.

To compress a FAT16 volume in Windows 95/98 using DriveSpace, first back up the data on the volume. Next, click **Start, Programs, Accessories,** and **System Tools.** Then select **DriveSpace** and follow the steps to select and compress the drive. After the drive is compressed, never trust important data to it. Figure 16-17 shows the error message you receive if you attempt to compress a FAT32 drive.

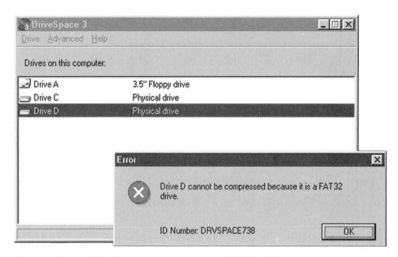

**Figure 16-17** DriveSpace can compress only FAT16 drives

**Notes**

If a Windows 9x/Me utility such as DriveSpace is missing from a menu list, the component might not have been installed when Windows was installed. To install a Windows component after Windows is installed, go to the Control Panel, open **Add/Remove Programs**, and click the **Windows Setup** tab.

## HARD DRIVE PREVENTIVE MAINTENANCE

To keep a hard drive clean, optimized, and error free, you can use these utilities from the Windows 9x/Me desktop:

▲ *Disk Cleanup*. To access Disk Cleanup, right-click the drive in Windows Explorer and select **Properties** from the shortcut menu. The Disk Properties window opens, as shown on the left side of Figure 16-18. On the General tab, click **Disk Cleanup**. From this window, as shown on the right side of Figure 16-18, you can select nonessential files to delete in order to save drive space.

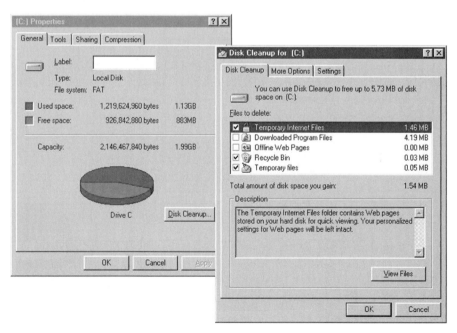

**Figure 16-18** The Disk Properties window provides Disk Cleanup, a quick-and-easy way to delete temporary files on a hard drive

▲ *Disk Defragmenter.* To use Disk Defragmenter, choose **Start, Programs, Accessories, System Tools,** and then **Disk Defragmenter.** Select the drive to defrag and click **OK** (see Figure 16-19). If you want to watch the defragmenting progress as it moves through the FAT, click **Show Details** in the Disk Defragmenter window. Recall from Chapter 15 that you can also defrag a drive using the Defrag command from a command prompt.

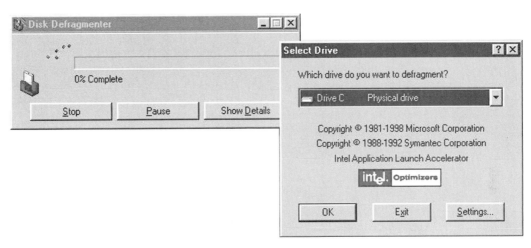

**Figure 16-19**   Windows 98 Disk Defragmenter windows

▲ *ScanDisk.* To use ScanDisk from the Windows 9x/Me desktop, click **Start, Programs, Accessories, System Tools,** and then **ScanDisk.** The ScanDisk utility first asks which drive you want to scan and gives you the choice of a Standard or Thorough scan. The Standard scan checks files and folders for errors. The Thorough scan does all that the Standard scan does and also checks the disk surface for bad sectors. Click **Start** to begin the scan. Figure 16-20 shows the results of a scan. Recall from Chapter 15 that you can also use the Scandisk command from a command prompt.

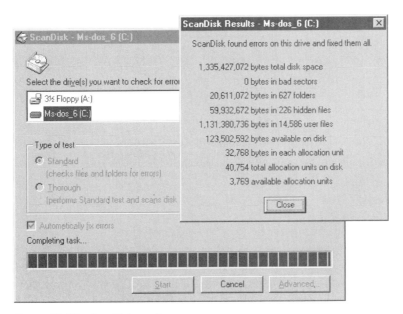

**Figure 16-20**   ScanDisk results

# INSTALLING AND MANAGING SOFTWARE IN WINDOWS 9X/ME

As the bridge between earlier and later versions of Windows, Windows 9x/Me can use both 16-bit and 32-bit software. This section shows you how to install and manage both.

## PREPARING FOR SOFTWARE INSTALLATION

As with installing hardware, you can do several things to prepare your system and to increase the likelihood that installing software on Windows 9x/Me will work without a snag:

▲ *Check available resources.* Check your computer resources to make sure you have (1) enough space on your hard drive, (2) the minimum requirements for memory, and (3) the proper CPU and video monitor. Read the documentation to make sure your system meets the minimum requirements. Remember that you should not completely fill your hard drive with software and data because the operating system needs extra space for temporary files and for the swap file, which changes size depending on how much space is needed.

▲ *Protect the original software.* After the installation is complete, put the original software setup CD or floppy disks in a safe place. If you have the original software handy, reinstalling it will be easier should something go wrong with the installed software.

> **Notes**
>
> For best performance with Windows 9x/Me, allow a minimum of 100 MB of unused hard drive space for working with temporary files used by applications.

▲ *Back up the registry and system configuration files.* Many older software setup programs edit Config.sys, Autoexec.bat, Win.ini, and System.ini files during the installation. Newer software might add its own entries to the Windows registry. Before you begin the installation, make backup copies of all these files so that you can backtrack if you want to. (You will learn more about backing up the registry later in the chapter.)

## INSTALLING SOFTWARE

To install software designed for Windows 9x/Me, access the Control Panel and double-click the **Add/Remove Programs** icon. Insert the software CD in the CD drive or the floppy disk in the floppy disk drive, and then click the **Install** button. If you have downloaded a software file from the Internet, using Windows Explorer, double-click the file. Follow directions on the setup screen. If the CD-ROM drive is set to Autorun, a setup screen might appear automatically as soon as you insert the software installation CD in the drive. For older software, click **Start** and **Run** to display the Run dialog box. Enter the drive and name of the installation program, for example, **A: Install** or **D: Setup**. Either way, the installation program loads and begins executing. If the installation program asks you a question you cannot answer, you can always abandon the installation and try again later.

Most software asks you for a serial number unique to your copy of the software. The number is probably written on the CD or on the first floppy disk, or it might be stamped on the documentation. If necessary, write the serial number on the floppy disk, on the label side of the CD, or on the CD case, so that you have it if you lose the documentation later. Copyright agreements often allow you to install the software on only one computer at a time. This serial number identifies the copy of the software that you have installed on this machine.

After the installation is complete and the software is working, update your backup copies of Autoexec.bat, Config.sys, System.ini, Win.ini, and the registry so that they reflect the changes the application software made to these configuration files.

## TROUBLESHOOTING SOFTWARE INSTALLATIONS

If you have problems installing software in Windows 9x/Me, try the following:

- ◢ If an application locks up when you first open it, try deleting all files and folders under \Windows\Temp. A software installation sometimes leaves files and folders in the Windows temporary directories.
- ◢ Look at the Readme.htm hypertext file in the \Windows directory, which will point you to the Programs.txt file, also in the \Windows directory. If there is a software problem that was known when Windows shipped, information about the problem and what to do about it might be in these text files. You can also check the Web site of the software manufacturer or the Microsoft Web site for help.

## SUPPORTING DOS APPLICATIONS UNDER WINDOWS 9X/ME

Windows 3.x used **PIF** (**program information file**) files to manage the virtual machine environment for DOS applications and provided a PIF editor to alter these files. Each application had its own PIF file that was used to specify the DOS environment that Windows 3.x created for it. If an application had no PIF file, Windows 3.x used the settings in the _Default.pif file in the \Windows\System folder. Windows 9x/Me manages the environment for DOS applications in a slightly different way. The Apps.inf file has a section named [PIF95] that contains a master list of settings to be used for all DOS applications listed in the file.

To customize the settings for any one DOS application, use the Properties feature of the DOS program file, which creates an individual PIF for the program file and serves as the PIF editor. Right-click the program filename, and select **Properties** from the shortcut menu. Windows searches for the program's PIF file and, if none is found, creates one using default values. If Windows 9x/Me was installed over Windows 3.x, then _Default.pif still exists in the \Windows\System directory and default values are read from it. Regardless of where the default values come from, any changes are stored in the PIF for the application. To make changes, from the Properties window of the program file, click the **Program** tab, and then click the **Advanced** button (see Figure 16-21). (Note that the Program tab will not be present for Windows applications. This fact can help you know that Windows recognizes a program to be a DOS program.)

If you select the **Use current MS-DOS configuration** option, Windows executes the contents of Dosstart.bat, which is stored in the Windows folder. **Dosstart.bat** is a type of Autoexec.bat file that executes in two situations: when you select "Restart the computer in MS-DOS mode" from the Shutdown menu, or when you run a program in MS-DOS mode. This file can be used to load real-mode device drivers, but Set commands are not executed.

If you select the **Specify a new MS-DOS configuration** option, you can then change the Autoexec.bat and Config.sys files used for this MS-DOS mode only. For example, if the application runs slowly in DOS mode and does a lot of disk accessing, you can add entries to run real-mode SmartDrive here. SmartDrive is a 16-bit driver used to manage disk caching. It is not normally run under Windows 9x/Me, having been replaced by the faster 32-bit Vcache, which is built into Windows 9x/Me. In this situation of excessive disk accessing, because Windows 9x/Me does not manage disk access in MS-DOS mode, loading SmartDrive from the Advanced Program Settings window is appropriate, because Vcache will not be running.

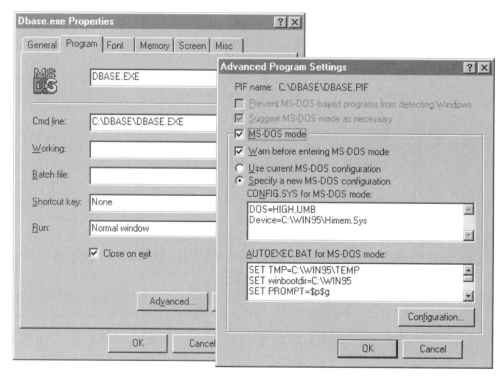

**Figure 16-21** Properties sheets for a DOS application affect the way Windows 9x/Me provides an environment for the application

## BOOTING WINDOWS 9X/ME

In Chapter 15, we discussed how to boot to a command prompt. In this section, we cover the startup process in Windows 9x/Me, including the differences between booting Windows 95 and booting Windows 98/Me. We'll also discuss how an application loads at startup. First, however, let's look at important files that Windows 9x/Me uses when booting.

### FILES USED TO CUSTOMIZE THE STARTUP PROCESS

Windows 9x/Me uses several files to control the startup process. Autoexec.bat and Config.sys are text files that can contain settings for environmental variables and commands to load 16-bit drivers and TSRs. Windows 9x/Me supports Autoexec.bat and Config.sys for backward compatibility with DOS. If Autoexec.bat or Config.sys files are present in the root directory, the command lines in them are executed during the boot, and they are used to customize the loading process.

Just as DOS uses text files to hold information about what is loaded, Windows 3.x also uses text files to hold custom settings that help control the loading process. These files are called **initialization files**, and some entries in them are read and used by Windows 9x/Me. However, most Windows 9x/Me settings are stored in the Windows registry rather than in text files.

You can edit these text files with the Edit.com program from the command prompt or any text editor from within Windows. The Windows System Configuration Editor (**Sysedit**) is a handy Windows text editor designed to be used with these files. To use Sysedit, type **sysedit** in the Run dialog box, and then press **Enter**. These files then automatically appear for editing: Autoexec.bat, Config.sys, **Win.ini**, **System.ini**, and **Protocol.ini** (see Figure 16-22).

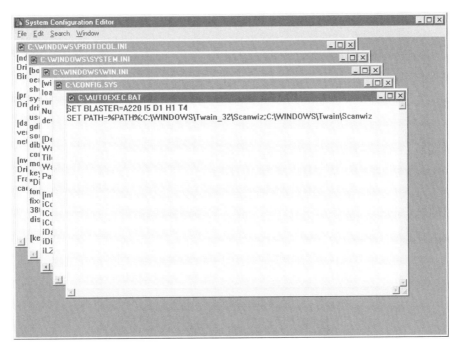

**Figure 16-22** Sysedit can be used to edit Windows system files

Recall that an initialization file, which has a .ini file extension, is used by Windows and application software to store configuration information needed when they are first loaded. An application can have its own .ini files and registry, and can also store its information in the Windows .ini files and the Windows registry. Table 16-4 shows Windows .ini files, which Windows 9x/Me supports for backward compatibility with Windows 3.x.

| Windows Initialization File | General Purpose of the File |
|---|---|
| System.ini | Contains hardware settings and multitasking options; older protected mode (32-bit) drivers loaded from the [386Enh] section can cause problems |
| Progman.ini | Contains information about Program Manager groups |
| Win.ini | Contains information about user settings, including printer, fonts, file associations, and settings made by applications |
| Control.ini | Contains information about the user's desktop, including color selections, wallpaper, and screen saver options |
| Mouse.ini | Contains settings for the mouse |
| Protocol.ini | Contains information about the configuration of the network |

**Table 16-4** Windows .ini files

System.ini and Win.ini are used by both Windows 3.x and Windows 9x/Me. A sample Windows 98 System.ini file is shown in Figure 16-23. The two sections required for the boot process are [boot] and [386Enh]. Windows 3.x kept many more entries in these sections than does Windows 9x/Me, which really uses these files only for backward compatibility with older applications.

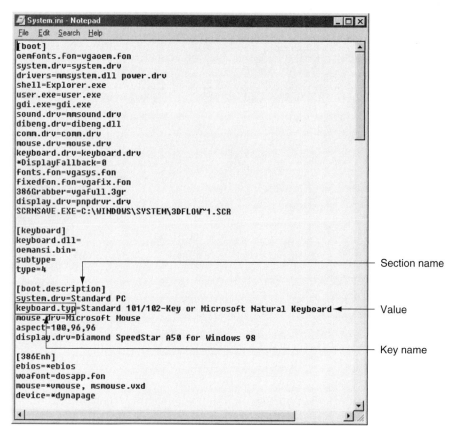

**Figure 16-23**  A sample Windows 98 System.ini file

> **Caution**
>
> Sometimes it is necessary to manually edit an .ini file that belongs to an application, but you should normally not edit System.ini or other Windows 9x/Me initialization files. Incorrect changes to these files might result in Windows not running correctly, and Windows sometimes overwrites these files when changes are made to the file through the Control Panel.

Initialization files are only read when Windows or an application using .ini files starts up. If you change the .ini file for an application, you must restart the software for the change to take effect. If you want the application to ignore a line in the .ini file, you can turn the line into a **comment line** by putting a semicolon or the letters REM at the beginning of the line.

We now turn our attention to the Windows 9x/Me startup process, in which these and other files are used.

## THE WINDOWS 9X/ME STARTUP PROCESS

Windows 9x/Me first loads in real mode and then switches to protected mode. With DOS, the two core real-mode system files responsible for starting up the OS, Io.sys and Msdos.sys, remain in memory, running even after the OS is loaded. With Windows 9x/Me, Io.sys is responsible only for the initial startup process performed in real mode. Then, control is turned over to Vmm32.vxd, which works in protected mode, and Io.sys is terminated. Recall that Windows 9x/Me includes a file named Msdos.sys, but it is only a text file that contains some parameters and switches you can set to affect the way the OS boots.

Startup in Windows 9x/Me is a five-phase process, as shown in Figure 16-24. We will look at each phase in the following sections.

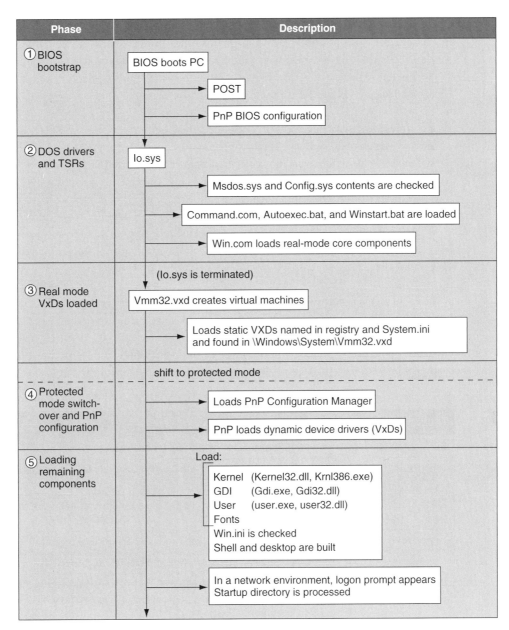

**Figure 16-24** Windows 9x/Me core components and the loading process

## PHASE 1: STARTUP BIOS BOOTSTRAP AND POST

Startup BIOS begins the process by performing POST (power-on self test). Then, BIOS examines the devices on the system and determines which ones are PnP-compliant. BIOS first enables the devices that are not PnP and then tries to make the PnP devices use the leftover resources. It also looks to permanent RAM for information about hardware, and uses that information to help configure PnP devices that have their configuration information recorded there. It saves information that Windows uses later to complete the hardware configuration.

The BIOS then looks for a device (hard drive, floppy disk, CD drive, or other drive) containing the OS. The bootstrap loader program is executed, and it looks for the initial hidden file of Windows 9x/Me (Io.sys). Io.sys is loaded.

## PHASE 2: DOS DRIVERS AND TSRs ARE LOADED

In Phase 2, Io.sys is in control, and it creates a real-mode operating system environment. Io.sys checks the text file Msdos.sys for boot parameters. Then, Io.sys automatically loads the following drivers if they are present: Himem.sys, Ifshlp.sys, Setver.exe, and Drvspace.bin (or Dblspace.bin). Note the following about these files:

- ◢ Himem.sys provides access to extended memory.
- ◢ Sixteen-bit programs use Ifshlp.sys to access the file system.
- ◢ Setver.exe is included for backward compatibility with DOS applications that expect all DOS components to be from the same version. Setver.exe "asks" the DOS application what version of DOS it expects to use and presents DOS components to that application as if they were all from that version, even if they are actually from different versions.
- ◢ Drvspace.bin and Dblspace.bin provide disk compression. One of these two files is loaded only if Io.sys finds Dlbspace.ini or Drvspace.ini in the root directory of the boot drive.

Io.sys also sets several environmental variables to default settings. In DOS, these default settings were loaded from Config.sys. Entries in Io.sys cannot be edited, but an entry in Config.sys overrides the default entry in Io.sys. Therefore, if you want to use settings different from the default, put the command in Config.sys, which is executed at this point in the load. Table 16-5 lists the default Io.sys entries.

| Entry | Description |
|---|---|
| Buffers=30 | The number of file buffers to create |
| DOS=HIGH | The DOS core of Windows 9x/Me is loaded into the high memory area (HMA) |
| Files=60 | The number of files that can be open at one time under 16-bit applications |
| Lastdrive=Z | The last letter that can be assigned to a logical drive |
| Shell=Command.com /P | Loads Command.com and executes Autoexec.bat |
| Stacks=9,256 | The number of frames of instructions that can be held in memory in a queue at one time; used for backward compatibility with older applications |

**Table 16-5**  Entries in Io.sys that once were in Config.sys

Next, Io.sys loads Command.com and follows instructions stored in Autoexec.bat and Winstart.bat. The default assignments made to environmental variables that were stored in Autoexec.bat in DOS are shown in the following list:

- ◢ Tmp=c:\windows\temp
- ◢ Temp=c:\windows\temp
- ◢ Prompt=$p$g
- ◢ Path=c:\windows;c:\windows\command

The Tmp and Temp variables are used by some software to locate where to put their temporary files. You can change any of these variables by making an entry in Autoexec.bat. Next, Io.sys loads Win.com. Then, Win.com loads other real-mode core components.

## PHASE 3: REAL-MODE VxDs ARE LOADED

In Phase 3, Io.sys relinquishes control to the Virtual Machine Manager (VMM) component housed in Vmm32.vxd along with some virtual device drivers. A **virtual device driver (VxD)** creates and manages virtual machines to provide access to hardware for software running in the VM. Under Windows 3.x, these VxDs were loaded from System.ini and had a .386 file extension. Under Windows 9x/Me, if stored in individual files, they have a .vxd file extension. They are called **static VxDs** because after they are loaded into memory, they remain there. (Conversely, **dynamic VxDs** are loaded into and unloaded from memory as needed.)

Vmm32.vxd is built specifically for a particular computer when Windows 9x/Me is installed and contains some VxDs critical for a successful boot. Therefore, each installation of Windows will have a different build of this file. (The VxD drivers now included in Vmm32.vxd were listed in the [386Enh] section of System.ini under Windows 3.x.) Vmm32.vxd terminates Io.sys and, while still in real mode, loads static VxD device drivers as identified in four different locations. They can be embedded in Vmm32.vxd, named in the registry or System.ini, or stored in the .vxd files in the \Windows\System\Vmm32 directory.

If you suspect a problem with a VxD that is part of the Vmm32.vxd file, you can put a new version of the .vxd file in the \Windows\System\Vmm32 directory. If Windows finds a VxD driver there, it uses that driver instead of the one embedded in Vmm32.vxd. Also, VxD drivers are listed in the registry and in System.ini. Normally, the entries are the same, and entries are only listed in System.ini for backward compatibility. However, if an entry in System.ini differs from an entry in the registry, the value in System.ini is used.

## PHASE 4: PROTECTED-MODE SWITCHOVER AND PnP CONFIGURATION

At the beginning of Phase 4, Vmm32.vxd switches to protected mode and loads Configuration Manager. Configuration Manager configures legacy and PnP devices. It uses any information that PnP BIOS might have left for it and loads the 32-bit dynamic device drivers (VxDs) for the PnP devices.

## PHASE 5: LOADING THE REMAINING COMPONENTS

In Phase 5, with Vmm32.vxd still in control, the three core components are loaded, and then fonts and other associated resources are loaded. Win.ini is checked and commands stored there are executed to allow backward compatibility. The shell and user desktop are loaded. If the computer is working in a networked environment, a logon dialog box is displayed, and the user can log on to Windows 9x/Me and the network. Finally, any processes stored in the Startup directory are performed.

## DIFFERENCES BETWEEN THE WINDOWS 95 AND WINDOWS 98/ME BOOT PROCESS

Windows 98 made some minor changes in what happens during startup to speed up the boot process. For instance, Windows 95 waits two seconds, displaying "Starting Windows 95" so that you can press a key to alter the boot process. Windows 98 eliminated this two-second wait and, in its place, allows you to press and hold the Ctrl key as it loads. If you do, you see the startup menu that is also available with Windows 95.

**APPLYING CONCEPTS**   If you want an application to load automatically at startup, you can:

▲ Place a shortcut in the folder C:\Windows\All Users\Startup Menu\Programs\StartUp.

▲ Put the name of the program file in the Load= or Run= line in Win.ini.

▲ Manually edit the registry key HKEY_LOCAL_MACHINE\SOFTWARE\ Microsoft\Windows\CurrentVersion\Run.

Try one of the first two methods yourself.

## TROUBLESHOOTING TOOLS FOR WINDOWS 9X/ME

Now let's look at some support tools that are useful for troubleshooting problems with the OS during or after the boot. Table 16-6 lists tools that monitor and improve system performance, control the OS, and help with troubleshooting. Several of these major tools are covered in detail in this section; in the next section, you will see how to use these tools in troubleshooting situations.

**Notes**

Tools new with Windows Me are System Restore and System File Protection. System Restore automatically backs up the registry and other system files when the system is idle. System File Protection is similar to Windows 2000/XP System File Protection; it prevents system files from being accidentally deleted and prevents application installations from overwriting newer DLL files with older or nonstandard versions.

| Tool | Windows 95 | Windows 98/Me | Description |
|------|-----------|---------------|-------------|
| System Monitor<br>Filename: Sysmon.exe<br>Location: \Windows | | X | Tracks the performance of some important system components. To run, click Start, Programs, Accessories, System Tools, and System Monitor. |
| System Configuration Utility<br>Filename: MsConfig.exe<br>Location: \Windows\ System | | X | Allows you to temporarily modify the system configuration to help with troubleshooting. To run, select System Configuration Utility from the Tools menu of the System Information window or type Msconfig in the Run dialog box. |
| Dr. Watson<br>Filename: Drwatson.exe<br>Location: \Windows | | X | Traps errors in log files created by applications and takes a snapshot of the system to use for troubleshooting. |
| Registry Checker<br>Filename: Scanreg.exe<br>Location: \Windows\ Command | | X | Backs up, verifies, and recovers the registry from the command prompt. To use the Windows version of Registry Checker (Scanregw.exe), select Registry Checker from the Tools menu of the System Information window. |

**Table 16-6**   Windows 9x/Me system performance and troubleshooting tools

| Tool | Windows 95 | Windows 98/Me | Description |
|------|------------|---------------|-------------|
| **Automatic Skip Driver Agent** Filename: Asd.exe Location: \Windows | | X | Automatically skips drivers that prevent Windows from loading and records problems encountered in the log file Asd.log. To run, select **Automatic Skip Driver Agent** from the Tools menu of the System Information window. |
| **Microsoft System Information** Filename: MSInfo32.exe Location: \Program Files\ Common files\Microsoft shared\Msinfo | X | X | Displays system information, including installed hardware and device drivers. To run, click Start, Programs, Accessories, System Tools, and System Information, or type Msinfo32.exe in the Run dialog box. |
| **Hardware Diagnostic tool (Hwinfo.exe)** | | X | Displays the same information as System Information, but in text form. Enter hwinfo/ui in the Run dialog box. |
| **Windows Update** Filename: Iexplore.exe Location: *www.microsoft.com/ windowsupdate* | X | X | Downloads service packs (fixes) for Windows from the Microsoft Web site. |
| **System options in the Control Panel (example: System Properties)** | X | X | Several applets in the Control Panel can be used to monitor and tweak system performance. |
| **System File Checker** Filename: Sfc.exe Location: \Windows\ System | | X | Verifies system files. This tool scans for changed, deleted, or corrupted system files and restores them from the originals on the Windows CD. To run, select System File Checker from the Tools menu of the System Information window. |
| **Microsoft Backup** Filename: Msbackup.exe Location: \Program Files\ Accessories\ Backup | X | X | Backs up files and folders to prevent loss when your hard drive fails. To run, click Start, Programs, Accessories, System Tools, and Backup. |
| **System Recovery** Filename: pcrestor.bat Location: On the Windows 98/Me CD in \Tools\Sysrec | | X | Uses a full system backup created by Microsoft Backup to reinstall Windows and restore the system to its state as of the last backup. |

**Table 16-6**  Windows 9x/Me system performance and troubleshooting tools (continued)

| Tool | Windows 95 | Windows 98/Me | Description |
|------|------------|---------------|-------------|
| Scheduled Task Wizard<br>Filename: Mstask.exe<br>Location: \Windows\System | X | X | Schedules tasks such as MS Backup to run at predetermined times. |
| Version Conflict Manager<br>Filename: Vcmui.exe<br>Location: \Windows | | X | Replaces an older Windows file with a newer file that was saved when Windows or an application was installed. |
| System Configuration Editor<br>Filename: Sysedit.exe<br>Location: \Windows\System | X | X | Text editor to edit files that configure how Windows loads. To run it, enter Sysedit.exe in the Run dialog box. Sysedit automatically opens Protocol.ini, System.ini, Win.ini, Config.sys, and Autoexec.bat for editing. |
| Task Manager<br>Filename: Taskman.exe<br>Location: \Windows | X | X | Runs, switches, and ends applications, and accesses the Shutdown menu. To run it, type Taskman in the Run dialog box. |
| Signature Verification Tool<br>Filename: sigverif.exe<br>Location: \Windows | | X | Checks device drivers for digital signatures given to them by Microsoft, which ensures they have been tested by Microsoft. To run it, use the System Information window. |
| Digital Signature Check | | X | Identifies drivers that have been digitally signed by Microsoft to verify their integrity. To use it, enable this key in the registry: HKEY_LOCAL_MACHINE\Software\Microsoft\Driver Signing. |

**Table 16-6**  Windows 9x/Me system performance and troubleshooting tools (continued)

## SYSTEM MONITOR

System Monitor allows you to monitor how system resources are being used by applications. It can monitor the file system, memory, the kernel, printer sharing services, and network performance data.

---

**APPLYING|CONCEPTS**  System Monitor is not automatically installed in a typical installation. To install it, go to the Control Panel, and select **Add/Remove Programs**. Click **Windows Setup**, and then select **System Tools**. Click the **Details** button, select **System Monitor,** and click **OK**. To run System Monitor, click **Start**, point to **Programs**, **Accessories**, **System Tools**, and then click **System Monitor**.

Figure 16-25 shows System Monitor tracking the kernel and disk cache hits and misses. Under the File menu, you can add and delete items the monitor is tracking. Use System Monitor to help determine if an application is using an inordinate amount of resources or has a memory leak. A memory leak occurs when you exit software and it unloads from memory, but it does not release the memory addresses that it was using for its data back to the OS. Memory leaks can occur when software is corrupted, poorly written, or plagued with a virus. You notice memory leaks when your system gets sluggish after you have launched and exited an application several times before rebooting the system. A reboot releases all memory addresses.

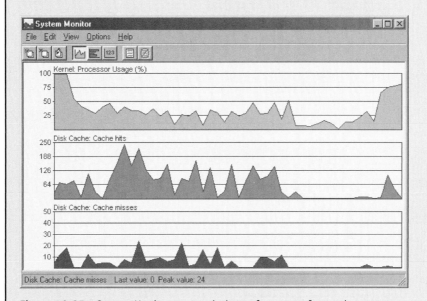

**Figure 16-25**  System Monitor can track the performance of several system resources

## SYSTEM CONFIGURATION UTILITY (MSCONFIG)

Similar to the way Safe Mode works, the System Configuration Utility (Msconfig.exe) reduces the startup process to its essentials. If starting Windows in this condition eliminates the problem you are troubleshooting, you can use this utility to add items back one at a time until the problem occurs; the source of the problem is related to the last item you added. To use the utility, do the following:

1. To access the utility, click **Start**, point to **Programs, Accessories, System Tools**, and then click **System Information**. The Microsoft System Information window opens.

2. From the **Tools** menu, select **System Configuration Utility** (see Figure 16-26). The System Configuration Utility dialog box opens, as shown in Figure 16-27. Another way to access the utility is to type **Msconfig** in the Run dialog box, and then press **Enter**.

3. To diagnose a problem, select **Diagnostic startup–interactively load device drivers and software**, and then click **OK** to restart your computer.

4. If this solves the problem, then the clean start was successful. Next, select **Selective startup** from the dialog box shown in Figure 16-27 and methodically select first one item and then another to restore, until the problem reappears. Begin by restoring all entries in Autoexec.bat and Config.sys, to determine if real-mode drivers and programs loaded from these files are the source of the problem.

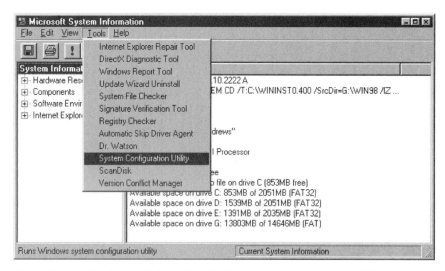

**Figure 16-26**    The System Information window provides access to many Windows support tools

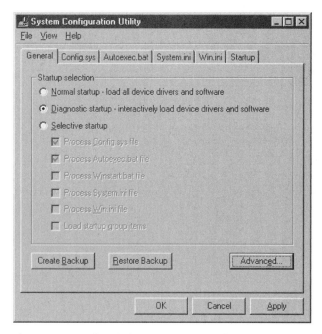

**Figure 16-27**    The Windows 98 System Configuration Utility helps troubleshoot Windows
configuration problems

5. If the problem still occurs, even with the clean boot, then try the following:

▲ If you have not already done so, scan for a virus, using a current version of
antivirus software.
▲ Use Registry Checker to check for corrupted system files.
▲ Use System File Checker to check for corrupted system files.
▲ Check the CMOS setup screen for incorrect settings.

## DR. WATSON

**Dr. Watson** is a troubleshooting tool you can use when you have problems running an
application. Dr. Watson is a Windows utility that can record detailed information about

the system, errors that occur, and the programs that caused them in a log file named \Windows\Drwatson\WatsonXX.wlg, where XX is an incrementing number. Each log file is created as it is needed to record errors. To learn about the benefits of Dr. Watson, start the program (see Figure 16-28), reproduce the application error, and then look at the events logged in the Dr. Watson window under the Diagnosis tab. When you click **View** on the menu bar, you will see the Standard View is selected. To see additional information about the system and programs currently running, select **Advanced View**.

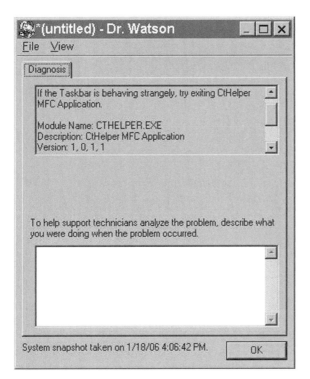

**Figure 16-28**  The Dr. Watson opening window

Information on the Diagnosis tab can be cross-checked to the Microsoft Web site, *support.microsoft.com*, for possible solutions. Also, software developers can sometimes use the information provided by Dr. Watson to help get to the bottom of an application error.

## THE WINDOWS 9X/ME REGISTRY AND REGISTRY CHECKER

In supporting and troubleshooting Windows 9x/Me, you need to understand the role of the registry and .ini files. The registry is a database of configuration information and settings for users, hardware, applications, and the OS. Starting with Windows 9x/Me, the registry takes over the essential functions of .ini files. However, Windows 9x/Me still supports .ini files for compatibility with Windows 3.x and legacy software and hardware devices.

Note that entries that 16-bit Windows applications make in Win.ini and System.ini are not added to the registry because these applications cannot access the registry. Entries made in .ini files by applications that can access the registry are copied into the registry. In this section, we'll examine how the registry is organized, how to recover from a corrupted registry, and how and why you might modify the registry.

> **Notes**
>
> For errors that you cannot reproduce at will, consider having Windows load Dr. Watson each time Windows starts. You can do this by creating a shortcut to Drwatson.exe in the Startup folder.

## HOW THE REGISTRY IS ORGANIZED

The registry organizes information in a hierarchical database with a treelike, top-to-bottom design. The Windows 9x/Me registry allows for keys to cascade to several levels on the tree. Figure 16-29 shows a portion of a Windows 9x/Me registry. Names in the left pane of the window are called **keys**. The values assigned to the selected key are listed in the right pane of the window. Each value has a name such as ScreenSaveTime, and to the right of each name is the **value data** assigned to that name, such as "60."

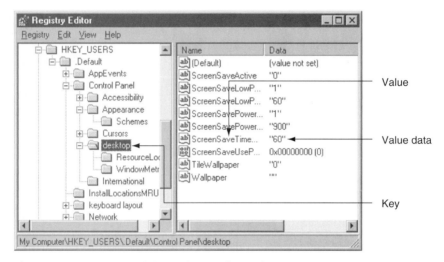

**Figure 16-29**    Structure of the Windows 9x/Me registry

The registry is organized into the six major keys, or branches, as listed in Table 16-7. The Windows 95/98 registry is contained in two files, System.dat and User.dat. Windows Me added a third registry file, Classes.dat. The registry files are located in the Windows directory as hidden, read-only, system files, although the information forms only a single database, which is built in memory each time Windows starts.

| Key | Description |
|-----|-------------|
| HKEY_CLASSES_ROOT | Contains information about file associations and OLE data. (This branch of the tree is a mirror of HKEY_LOCAL_MACHINE\ Software\Classes.) |
| HKEY_USERS | Includes user preferences, including desktop configuration and network connections. |
| HKEY_CURRENT_USER | Contains information about the current user preferences for a multiuser system. If there is only one user of the system, this is a duplicate of HKEY_USERS. |
| HKEY_LOCAL_MACHINE | Contains information about hardware and installed software. |
| HKEY_CURRENT_CONFIG | Contains the same information in HKEY_LOCAL_MACHINE\ Config and has information about printers and display fonts. |
| HKEY_DYN_DATA | Keeps information about Windows performance and Plug and Play information. |

**Table 16-7**    Six major branches, or keys, of the Windows 9x/Me registry

## RECOVERING FROM A CORRUPTED REGISTRY

Windows 95 has a way to recover from a corrupted registry that is different from the method used by Windows 98/Me. These methods are discussed next.

### Windows 95 Backup of the Registry

Windows 95 maintains a backup copy of the two registry files and names the backup files System.da0 and User.da0. Each time Windows 95 boots successfully, it makes a new backup of the two registry files. If Windows 95 has trouble loading and must start in Safe Mode, it does not back up the registry.

If Windows 95 does not find a System.dat file when it starts, it automatically replaces it with the backup System.da0. If both System.dat and User.dat are missing, or if the WinDir= command is missing in Msdos.sys, Windows 95 tells you that the registry files are missing and starts in Safe Mode. It then displays the Registry Problem dialog box. If you see this dialog box, click the **Restore From Backup** and **Restart** buttons to restore the registry files from System.da0 and User.da0. If these files are also missing, the registry cannot easily be restored. You can either restore the files from your own backups or run Windows 95 Setup. There is also another option: Look for the file System.1st in the root directory of the hard drive. This is the System.dat file created when Windows 95 was first installed. In an emergency, you can revert to this file.

### Windows 98/Me Registry Checker

Windows 98/Me offers a utility called the Registry Checker, which is not available with Windows 95. It automatically backs up the registry each day, and by default, it keeps the last five days of backups. In an emergency, you can recover the registry from one of these backups. You can also tell Registry Checker to make an additional backup on demand, for example, when you make changes to the registry and want to back them up before you make new changes. There are two versions of Registry Checker: Scanreg.exe is executed from the command prompt and is a 16-bit real-mode program, and Scanregw.exe is the 32-bit, protected mode, GUI version executed from within Windows.

To access Registry Checker from within Windows, select **Start**, point to **Programs**, **Accessories, System Tools**, and then click **System Information**. The Microsoft System Information window opens. From the menu bar, select **Tools** and then **Registry Checker** (see Figure 16-30). (Alternately, you can click **Start**, click **Run**, and type **Scanregw** in the Run dialog box, and then press **Enter**.) Registry Checker tells you if the registry is corrupted and fixes it, if allowed. You can also create a new backup at this time.

Backups are kept in cabinet files in the \Windows\Sysbckup folder as rb001.cab, rb002.cab, and so on. To revert to one of these backups, you must first be in MS-DOS mode. For Windows Me, boot from a bootable disk. For Windows 98, boot from a bootable disk or boot to an MS-DOS prompt from the Windows 98 startup menu. (Windows Me does not have this option on the startup menu.) From the MS-DOS prompt (not a DOS box within a Windows session), use the commands in Table 16-8 to repair or recover the registry.

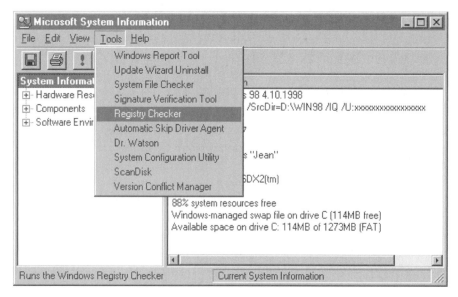

**Figure 16-30** The Registry Checker is available under Programs, Accessories, System Tools, System Information; it is used to back up, restore, and repair the Windows 98/Me registry

| Command | Purpose |
|---------|---------|
| Scanreg /Restore | Restores the registry from a previous backup. A screen appears asking you which backup to use. |
| Scanreg /Fix | Repairs the corrupted registry. If the problem is inherent to the registry itself, this might work. If you want to undo a successful change to the registry, use the Restore option instead. |
| Scanreg /Backup | Creates a new backup of the registry at the DOS prompt. Don't do this if the registry is giving you problems. |
| Scanreg /Opt | Optimizes the registry. ScanReg looks for and deletes information in the registry that is no longer used. This reduces the size of the registry, which might speed up booting. |
| Scanreg /? | Opens the Help feature of ScanReg. |

**Table 16-8** Commands used to repair or recover the Windows 98 or Windows Me registry

## MODIFYING THE REGISTRY

When you make a change in the Control Panel, Device Manager, or many other places in Windows 9x/Me, the registry is modified automatically. This is the only way most users will ever change the registry. However, on rare occasions you might need to edit the registry manually. For example, if a virus infected your registry, you might be instructed to edit the registry by an antivirus technical staff person or by directions downloaded from an antivirus Web site. Following these directions, you might edit a key or delete an entry added by the virus. The first step in editing the registry is to back up the registry. The simplest way to do that is to click **Start**, click **Run**, and type **Scanregw** in the Run dialog box, and then press **Enter**. When the Registry Checker asks if you want to back up the registry, click **Yes**. When you see the "Backup Complete" message, click **OK**.

The next step is to use Regedit.exe, located in the Windows folder. You can use Explorer to locate the file, then double-click it, or you can click **Start**, then **Run**, type **Regedit** in the

Run dialog box, and then press **Enter**. When you do, the window in Figure 16-31 opens. Open one branch of the tree by clicking the + sign to the left of the key, and close the branch by clicking the − sign. To search for an entry in the registry, click the **Edit** menu and then click **Find**.

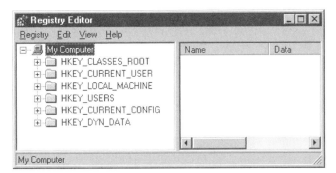

**Figure 16-31**  The six major keys, or branches, of the registry seen in the Registry Editor

## TROUBLESHOOTING WINDOWS 9X/ME

This section covers Windows 9x/Me troubleshooting. It is important for you to know how to troubleshoot problems that occur during a Windows installation, problems that occur during the startup process, and problems that occur during normal Windows operations.

### TROUBLESHOOTING WINDOWS 9X/ME INSTALLATIONS

Table 16-9 lists some problems that might occur while installing Windows 9x/Me and what to do about them.

> **Notes**
>
> For specific error messages that occur during installation and what to do about them, go to the Microsoft Web site *support.microsoft.com* and search for the error message.

| Symptom | Description and Solution |
|---------|--------------------------|
| An error message about BIOS appears during installation. | This is most likely caused by BIOS not allowing changes to the boot sector to protect it from viruses. Disable the feature in CMOS setup. |
| Windows 9x/Me stalls during the first restart after installation. | This is probably caused by legacy hardware that is not configured correctly. Try the following:<br><br>▲ Remark (REM) out all entries in Config.sys and Autoexec.bat.<br><br>▲ Disable the ISA enumerator by commenting out this line in System.ini: Device=ISAPNP.386. |
| During the first restart after installation, an error message appears with information about a bad or missing file. | This is probably caused by an error in Config.sys or Autoexec.bat. Try renaming both files so they are not executed. If this solves the problem, then comment out each line in the file, one at a time, until you know which line caused the problem. |

**Table 16-9**  Some problems and solutions when installing Windows 9x/Me

| Symptom | Description and Solution |
|---------|--------------------------|
| During the first restart after the installation, you get an error message about a missing or damaged VxD file. | This is most likely caused by a missing or corrupted VxD file. Run Windows setup again and select the option to Verify or replace the missing or corrupted VxD (virtual device driver). |
| After upgrading from Windows 95 to Windows 98, the startup screen still says Windows 95. | This can be caused by one of two problems. First, the Io.sys file might not have been updated. If so, use the Sys C: command to replace it. Second, the file Logo.sys might be in the root directory, which overrides the logo screen embedded in Io.sys. Delete or rename the file. |
| "Invalid system disk" error appears during setup. | ◢ Suspect a boot sector virus. Run a current version of antivirus software.<br><br>◢ If this error occurs while installing Windows when disk management software such as DiskPro is running, Windows might have damaged the hard drive MBR. To recover from this problem, see the documentation for the disk management software. |

**Table 16-9** Some problems and solutions when installing Windows 9x/Me (continued)

# TROUBLESHOOTING WINDOWS 9X/ME STARTUP

When Windows 9x/Me does not start up correctly, you can go through these basic steps to troubleshoot it:

1. Check and address any error messages that occur during a normal boot.

2. If you cannot boot to a normal desktop, boot in Safe Mode and begin troubleshooting there. If you can boot to Safe Mode but cannot boot normally, you probably have a driver problem of some kind because the main difference between Safe Mode and normal booting is the drivers that are loaded.

3. If you cannot boot using Safe Mode, the GUI portion of the OS is not functioning. Boot to the command prompt using the startup menu. Use commands at the C prompt for troubleshooting.

4. If the startup menu is not accessible, the MS-DOS core of the OS is not functioning. Boot from an emergency startup disk, and try to access drive C.

5. If you cannot access drive C, then the hard drive is not accessible. Try Fdisk. If Fdisk does not work, treat the problem as a hardware problem.

## ERROR MESSAGES RECEIVED WHILE LOADING WINDOWS 9X/ME

Error messages during startup can be used to help you zero in on the problem and its solution. Table 16-10 shows error messages that Windows 9x/Me might give, and it lists advice about what to do when you see them. Specific errors are covered later in this section. If you get an error not listed in the table, search the Microsoft Web site (*support.microsoft.com*) for the message and what to do about it.

| Error Message or Problem | What to Do |
|---|---|
| MS-DOS compatibility mode | ◢ Windows is using real-mode drivers to access the hard drive rather than the preferred 32-bit drivers. After backing up the Config.sys and System.ini files, remove any references to real-mode drivers for the hard drive in these files.<br><br>◢ The problem might be due to an outdated motherboard BIOS. Consider updating the BIOS. |
| Bad or missing file<br>Real-mode driver missing or damaged | ◢ Verify that Config.sys, Autoexec.bat (root directory of the hard drive), and System.ini (Windows folder) are present and in the right location.<br><br>◢ Check Config.sys and Autoexec.bat for errors using the step-by-step confirmation option from the Windows 9x/Me startup menu. To check System.ini, rename the file so that it will not be used and boot with a bare-bones version of the file.<br><br>◢ Look in the Win.ini file for applications that are attempting to load at startup but have been deleted or uninstalled. Check the Load= or Run= lines. |
| Error in config.sys line xx | There is a problem loading a device driver or with the syntax of a command line. Check the command line for errors. Verify that the driver files are in the right directory. Reinstall the driver files. |
| Cannot open file *.inf | ◢ This error is most likely caused by insufficient memory. Disable any TSRs running in Autoexec.bat.<br><br>◢ Close any applications that are running or remove them from the StartUp folder. |
| Invalid directory | A command issued in the Autoexec.bat file is referencing a working directory that does not exist. Check the Autoexec.bat file for errors. |
| Bad command or file not found | A command in Autoexec.bat cannot be interpreted, or the OS cannot find the program file specified in the command line. Check the spelling of the filename and the path to the program file. |
| Insufficient disk space | Run ScanDisk and Defragmenter. Check free space on the hard drive. |
| Invalid system disk | Suspect a boot sector virus. Run a current version of antivirus software. |
| Bad or missing command.com | Io.sys could be missing or corrupted. Restore the file from a backup or an emergency startup disk. To restore all real-mode files needed to begin loading Windows 9x/Me, do the following: (1) Boot from a Windows 9x/Me emergency startup disk; (2) restore Io.sys, Msdos.sys, Drvspace.bin, and Command.com by executing the command SYS C:, and (3) remove the floppy disk and reboot. |
| Invalid VxD dynamic link call from IFSMGR | This error is caused by a missing or corrupted Msdos.sys file. Restore the file from a backup or from an emergency startup disk. |
| Missing system files | Run the SYS C: command. |

**Table 16-10** Error messages received while loading Windows 9x/Me

| Error Message or Problem | What to Do |
|---|---|
| System registry file missing | System.dat, User.dat, and/or Classes.dat (for Windows Me) is corrupted or missing. For Windows 95, restore them by using either System.da0 or User.da0. For Windows 98/Me, run ScanReg. |
| VxD error returns to command prompt | A VxD file is missing or corrupted. Run Windows Setup from the Windows 9x/Me CD, and choose Verify installed components. |
| Error containing the text "Kernel32.dll" | An error that contains this text probably indicates a corrupted kernel. Try restoring system files. If that doesn't work, reinstall Windows. Note that this error might appear at other times, not just during the boot process. |
| Himem.sys not loaded, missing or corrupt Himem.sys | Himem.sys is corrupted, not in the right directory, or not the right version for the currently loaded OS. Compare Himem.sys in the \Windows folder to the copies in the \Windows\command\ebd folder or on the Windows setup CD. |
| Device not found | Errors are in System.ini, Win.ini, or the registry. Look for references to devices or attempts to load device drivers. Use Device Manager to remove a device or edit System.ini or Win.ini. |
| Device/Service has failed to start | A hardware device or driver necessary to run the device or critical software utility is causing problems. If the device is non-essential, try using Device Manager to remove it. Then reinstall the device. If the device is an essential device, try using System File Checker to restore system files. |

**Table 16-10**   Error messages received while loading Windows 9x/Me (continued)

Windows has several tools you can use to help troubleshoot problems with booting:

▲ Use the System Configuration Utility (Msconfig.exe) to limit what loads during the boot in order to attain the cleanest possible boot.
▲ Use Device Manager to disable a device that you think is causing a problem.
▲ Use Automatic Skip Driver Agent (ASDA) to keep Windows from installing a driver that might be corrupted, including built-in Windows drivers.
▲ Use the Windows 9x/Me startup menu to try Safe Mode, the command prompt, and other troubleshooting options.

## WINDOWS 9X/ME STARTUP MENU OPTIONS

Normally, when you load Windows, the message "Starting Windows" appears and then the OS loads. However, you can force the startup menu to appear rather than the "Starting Windows" message by pressing the F8 key or holding down the Ctrl key during the boot.

The Windows 95/98 startup menu options are listed below. Note that the Windows Me startup menu does not offer options 6 and 7:

1. Normal
2. Logged (\BOOTLOG.TXT)
3. Safe Mode
4. Safe Mode with network support
5. Step-by-step confirmation

6. Command prompt only

7. Safe Mode command prompt only

8. Previous version of MS-DOS

What to expect when you select each menu option is described next. Option 4 appears if the OS is configured for a network, and Option 8 appears if a previous version of DOS was retained during the Windows 9x/Me installation.

### Normal

In Msdos.sys, if BootGUI=1, this option starts Windows 9x/Me. If BootGUI=0, this option boots to the DOS 7.0 or DOS 7.1 prompt (the DOS core of Windows 9x/Me). Either way, the commands in Autoexec.bat and Config.sys are executed.

If a problem appears when you boot in normal mode but does not appear when you boot in Safe Mode, then suspect that Config.sys, Autoexec.bat, System.ini, and Win.ini are the sources of your problem. To eliminate Config.sys or Autoexec.bat as the source of the problem, boot using the Step-by-step confirmation option on the startup menu. To eliminate Win.ini or System.ini as the source of the problem, do the following:

1. Change the name of the System.ini file in the Windows folder to System.sav.

2. Find the System.cb file in the Windows folder, and make a copy of it. Rename the copy System.ini. Don't rename the original System.cb file because you might need it at another time.

3. In the [boot] section of the System.ini file, add this line and then save the file: **drivers=mmsystem.dll**

4. Change the name of the Win.ini file in the Windows folder to Win.sav.

5. Restart your computer.

If this works, the problem was in the Win.ini or System.ini files, and you can reexamine these files in detail to determine the exact source of the problem.

---

**Notes**

If your mouse stops working when you copy the System.cb file and rename it System.ini, add the following lines in the specified sections of the new System.ini file:

```
[boot]

mouse.drv=mouse.drv

[386Enh]

mouse=*vmouse, imsmouse.vxd
```

---

### Logged (\Bootlog.txt)

This option is the same as Normal, except that Windows 9x/Me tracks the load and startup activities and logs them to the Bootlog.txt file. A portion of a sample Bootlog.txt file is shown in Figure 16-32. This file contains information about which components loaded successfully and which did not. The file can be a helpful tool when troubleshooting.

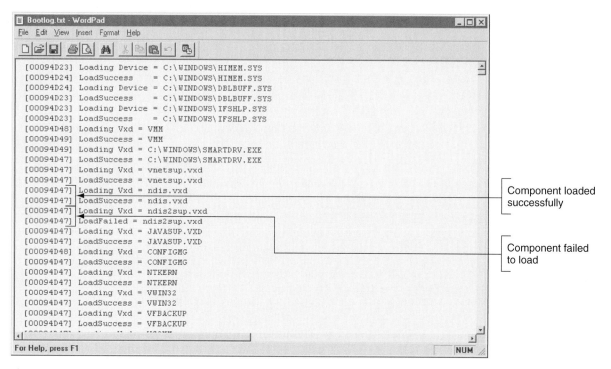

**Figure 16-32** The Bootlog.txt file contains information about successful and unsuccessful boot activities

### Safe Mode (Press the F5 Key While Loading)

When you have problems with the Windows 9x/Me boot process but no error message appears during the boot, you can use Safe Mode to troubleshoot the problems. You can get to Safe Mode either from the startup menu or by pressing the F5 key while Windows is loading. Figure 16-33 shows Windows 98 booted into Safe Mode.

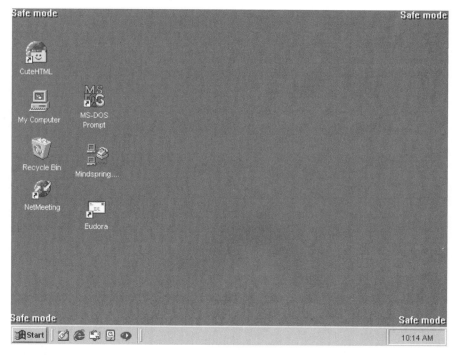

**Figure 16-33** Windows 98 Safe Mode desktop

Safe Mode starts Windows 9x/Me with a minimum default configuration to give you an opportunity to correct an error in the configuration. Safe Mode does not execute entries in the registry that load device drivers and bypasses Config.sys, Autoexec.bat, and the [boot] and [386Enh] sections of System.ini. Therefore, devices such as the CD-ROM drive won't work in Safe Mode. Safe Mode does load basic keyboard and mouse drivers and loads standard VGA display drivers. It sets the display resolution to 640 × 480. Also, when you enter Safe Mode, Windows 98/Me includes support for networks, but Windows 95 does not.

For example, if you selected a video driver that is incompatible with your system, Windows 9x/Me detects the problem when it starts and enters Safe Mode with a standard VGA driver selected. You can then go to Device Manager, select the correct driver, and restart Windows.

From the startup menu, you can choose to enter Safe Mode if you know of a problem you want to correct. For example, if you selected a group of background and foreground colors that makes reading the screens impossible, you can reboot and choose Safe Mode. Safe Mode gives you the standard color scheme along with the VGA mode. You then can go to Display Properties, make the necessary corrections, and reboot.

Sometimes you will use Safe Mode for troubleshooting when you don't know exactly what the problem is. In that situation, after you are in Safe Mode, use the following checklist:

- Use a current version of antivirus software to scan for a virus.
- Sometimes loading in Safe Mode is all that is needed. Try to reboot the PC in normal mode.
- If the Safe Recovery dialog box opens, select the option of Use Safe Recovery. Windows 9x/Me then attempts to recover from previous boot problems. Try to boot again.
- If you were having problems installing a device before the Windows problem started, disable or remove the device in Device Manager. Reboot after disabling each device that you suspect to be a problem.
- If you have just made configuration changes, undo the changes and reboot.
- Look for real-mode drivers or TSRs (programs loaded in Config.sys, Autoexec.bat, or System.ini) that might be causing a problem, and disable them by putting a semicolon or an REM at the beginning of the command line.
- Try to boot again. If the problem is still not solved, restore the registry. For Windows 95, make backups of System.dat and User.dat. Then overwrite them with System.da0 and User.da0. For Windows 98/Me, use ScanReg to restore the registry from backups. (ScanReg was covered earlier in the chapter.)
- Run ScanDisk to repair errors on the hard drive and optimize it. While in Safe Mode, select **Start, Programs, Accessories, System Tools,** and **ScanDisk.** Under Type of Test, click **Thorough** (as shown in Figure 16-34).
- Run the Defragmenter utility to optimize the drive.
- For Windows 98, run System File Checker to verify system files.
- For Windows 98/Me, run Automatic Skip Driver Agent to skip loading any driver that causes a problem. Reboot and examine the Asd.log file for recorded errors.
- For Windows 98/Me, use the System Configuration Utility to reduce the system to essentials and reboot. If the problem goes away, restore one item at a time until the problem returns. Then you can identify the item that is the source of the problem.
- Using Explorer, search for files in system folders that have changed recently. To sort file and folder names by date last modified using Explorer, click the Modified column

heading. To reverse the sort order, hold down the Ctrl key while clicking the Modified column heading. If software or drivers have been installed recently, suspect that they might be the source of the problem.

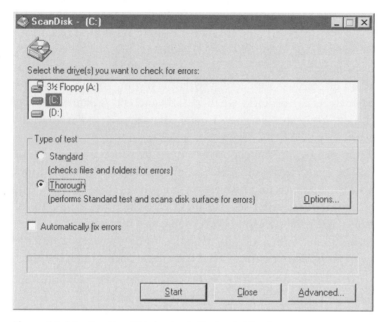

**Figure 16-34** Use ScanDisk to check the hard drive for errors

### Safe Mode with Network Support

This option allows you access to the network when booting into Safe Mode. It is useful if Windows 95 is stored on a network server and you need to download changes to your PC in Safe Mode. This option is not available on the startup menu in Windows 98/Me, which automatically includes network support.

For Windows 95, to eliminate the network connection as a source of a boot problem you are troubleshooting, first boot in Safe Mode without network support and then boot in Safe Mode with network support. If the boot without network support succeeds but the boot with network support gives errors, then suspect that the network drivers might be the source of the problem. For Windows 98/Me, disable the network card in Device Manager to eliminate the network drivers as the source of the problem.

### Step-by-Step Confirmation

This option asks for confirmation before executing each command in Io.sys, Config.sys, and Autoexec.bat. You can accomplish the same thing by pressing Shift+F8 when the message "Starting Windows 95/98" appears.

### Command Prompt Only

This option is not available with Windows Me. Under Windows 95/98, it executes the contents of Autoexec.bat and Config.sys but doesn't start Windows 95/98. You get a DOS prompt instead. Type **WIN** to load Windows 95/98. This command executes the file Win.com. You can use several switches with the WIN command when troubleshooting the OS. Table 16-11 lists these switches.

In a troubleshooting situation, try each switch until you find one that works. You can then identify the source of the problem, and can sometimes put entries in the System.ini file to make the switch a permanent part of the load.

| Command/Switch | Purpose |
|---|---|
| WIN /D:M | Starts Windows in Safe Mode |
| WIN /D:F | Turns off 32-bit disk access; use this option if there appears to be a problem with hard drive access |
| WIN /D:S | Instructs Windows not to use memory address F000:0, which is used by BIOS |
| WIN /D:V | Instructs Windows that the system BIOS should be used to access the hard drive rather than the OS |
| WIN /D:X | Excludes all upper memory addresses from real-mode drivers |

**Table 16-11** Switches used with the WIN command

### Safe Mode Command Prompt Only

This option is not available with Windows Me. Under Windows 95/98, this option does not execute the commands in Autoexec.bat or Config.sys. On the screen, you see only the DOS prompt.

### Previous Version of MS-DOS

This option loads a previous version of DOS if one is present. You can get the same results by pressing the F4 key when the message "Starting Windows 95/98" appears. This option is not available in Windows 98 SE or Windows Me.

## TROUBLESHOOTING WITH THE STARTUP MENU

If you tried using the tools recommended in the previous sections, but have not yet identified the source of the problem, use the following checklist to troubleshoot using the startup menu:

▲ Try a hard boot. A soft boot might not do the trick, because TSRs are not always kicked out of RAM with a soft boot.
▲ If you have not already done so, try Safe Mode next.
▲ Try the Step-by-step confirmation option next. Look for error messages caused by a missing or corrupted driver file. Try not allowing real-mode drivers to load. After the problem command within Autoexec.bat or Config.sys is identified, you can eliminate the command or troubleshoot it. Specific commands in these files and their purposes are covered in Chapter 15.
▲ Use the Logged option next, and examine the Bootlog.txt file that is created to see if it identifies the problem. Try comparing the log file to one created on a working PC to find out what was happening when the error occurred.
▲ Try booting using the Command prompt only option. From the command prompt, run the real-mode version of ScanDisk, which you can find in the \Windows\Command folder, to scan the hard drive for errors. From a command prompt, enter this command: **C:\Windows\Command\Scandisk**. If the Scandisk.exe program on the hard drive is corrupted, use the one on the emergency startup disk.
▲ From the command prompt in Windows 98/Me, type **Scanreg/Fix** and try to reboot.
▲ Next, type **Scanreg/Restore** and select the latest known good backup of the Windows 9x/Me registry. Try to reboot.
▲ From the command prompt, you can use the **WIN** command with the switches listed in Table 16-11. If one of these commands solves the problem, look for real-mode drivers that might be in conflict, eliminating those that you can. Examine Bootlog.txt for errors and try booting from Safe Mode again.

◢ Try booting with the Safe Mode command prompt only. Remember that when you are in Safe Mode, the registry is not executed. If you suspect a corrupted registry, restore it to its last saved version as you learned to do earlier. Then try the WIN command with or without the switches, as necessary.

## USING THE STARTUP DISK FOR TROUBLESHOOTING

If you cannot solve the startup problems by using the troubleshooting utilities within Windows or on the startup menu, use an emergency startup disk to recover from the failed boot. If you do not have an emergency startup disk, create one on another computer and use it to work with the computer that has the problem. How to create this emergency startup disk is covered in Chapter 15.

### Before You Use the Startup Disk

Before using the startup disk, it is a good idea to check it for viruses on a working computer by scanning it with antivirus software. If you find a virus on the emergency startup disk, destroy the disk and use a working computer to create a new one. Chapter 15 gives you some tips and things to try after booting from the disk.

Using the Fdisk command on the disk, you can determine if the partition table on the hard drive is intact. If the partition table is good, the next step is to run the Windows 9x/Me Setup program stored on the Windows setup CD. When given the opportunity, select **Verify installed components**. Setup then restores damaged or missing system files. If you cannot use Fdisk to verify the partition table, you might be faced with a hardware problem or the entire hard drive might need to be repartitioned and Windows reinstalled.

### Accessing the CD-ROM Drive When Booting from a Floppy Disk

Because the Windows setup program and files are normally stored on a CD, your emergency startup disk should include the drivers necessary to access the CD drive. When you are recovering from a failed hard drive, you will not have access to the 32-bit Windows CD-ROM drivers on the hard drive. Windows 98 and later versions of Windows automatically add the real-mode CD-ROM device drivers to their rescue disks, but Windows 95 does not. This section explains how to add this function to a Windows 95 rescue disk.

Two files are required to access a CD-ROM drive while in real mode: the 16-bit device driver provided by the manufacturer of the CD-ROM drive (or a generic real-mode driver that works with the drive) and the 16-bit real-mode OS interface to the driver, Mscdex.exe. The device driver is loaded from Config.sys, and Mscdex.exe is loaded from Autoexec.bat.

For example, suppose your CD-ROM drive comes with a floppy disk that includes the following files:

◢ *Install.exe*. CD-ROM installation program
◢ *Cdtech.sys*. CD-ROM device driver
◢ Instruction files and documentation

To make your Windows 95 rescue disk capable of accessing the CD-ROM drive when you boot from this disk, first you need to copy two files to the root directory of the rescue disk: Mscdex.exe from the C:\Windows\Command folder and Cdtech.sys from the floppy disk bundled with your CD-ROM drive. Then add the following command or a similar one to the Config.sys file (the parameters in the command lines are explained in the following list):

```
DEVICE = A:\CDTECH.SYS /D:MSCD001
```

Put the following command or a similar one in your Autoexec.bat file on the floppy disk:

```
MSCDEX.EXE /D:MSCD001 /L:E /M:10
```

The explanations of these command lines are as follows:

- When the program Mscdex.exe executes, it uses the MSCD001 entry as a tag back to the Config.sys file to learn which device driver is being used to interface with the drive. In this case, it is Cdtech.sys.
- To Mscdex.exe, the drive is named MSCD001 and is being managed by the driver Cdtech.sys.
- Mscdex.exe uses Cdtech.sys as its "go-between" to access the drive.
- Mscdex.exe also assigns a drive letter to the drive. If you want to specify a drive letter, use the /L: option in the command line. In this example, the CD-ROM drive is drive E. If you don't use the /L: option, then the next available drive letter is used.
- The /M: option controls the number of memory buffers.
- If the files referenced in these two commands are stored on the floppy disk in a different directory from the root directory, then include the path to the file in front of the filename.

## TROUBLESHOOTING PROBLEMS AFTER WINDOWS 9X/ME STARTUP

Troubleshooting a PC problem begins with isolating it into one of two categories: problems that prevent the PC from booting and problems that occur after a successful startup. In this section, we look at problems that occur after the boot that might be caused by hardware, applications, or Windows. Begin by asking the user questions such as the following to learn as much as you can:

- When did the problem start?
- Were there any error messages or unusual displays on the screen?
- What programs or software were you using?
- Did you move your computer system recently?
- Has there been a recent thunderstorm or electrical problem?
- Have you made any hardware, software, or configuration changes?
- Has someone else been using your computer recently?
- Can you show me exactly what you did when this problem occurred? (Have the user reproduce the problem and watch each step.)
- Next, ask whether the PC boots properly. If not, then begin troubleshooting the failed boot.

Here are some general tips for troubleshooting hardware:

- Try rebooting the computer. The problem with the device may disappear when Windows redetects it.
- Frequent system lockups and General Protection Faults might indicate corrupted memory modules. Try using memory-testing software to check for intermittent memory errors, which indicate the module needs replacing. An example of memory-testing software is DocMemory by CST, Inc. (*www.docmemory.com*).
- For external devices such as monitors, printers, and scanners, try turning on the device before turning on the computer. If your computer is on and you are rebooting, leave the device on and online.

◢ If a device doesn't work with one application, try it with another. If the problem occurs only with one application, the problem is probably not with the hardware device but with that application.

◢ Check Device Manager for errors it reports about the device. If it reports errors, use the Hardware Troubleshooter in Device Manager to help resolve the problem or go to the Microsoft Web site and search for the error message.

◢ The driver might be corrupted or need updating. Look on the Web for updated device drivers. Search the device manufacturer's Web site or the Microsoft Web site for information about problems with the device and solutions.

◢ Use Device Manager to uninstall the device and then reinstall it. If you uninstall the device and then reboot, Windows should recognize an uninstalled device and automatically launch the Found New Hardware Wizard. If it doesn't launch, then chances are the device is not working or is not PnP.

◢ For PnP devices on expansion cards such as sound cards, modems, and network cards, if you uninstall the device in Device Manager and Windows does not recognize the device when you reboot, the device might not be working. The expansion card needs to be reseated or moved to a different expansion slot. If that doesn't work, the card needs replacing.

◢ If none of these things work, ask yourself what changed since the device last worked. For example, maybe you added another hardware device that conflicts with the one you are using, or maybe you have added software that conflicts with the software that the problem device is using. Try disabling other devices or try uninstalling software that you suspect is causing the problem. Use Automatic Skip Driver Agent to eliminate other devices that might prevent the problem driver from working.

For application software problems, try the following:

◢ Address any error messages that appear when using the software.

◢ If you don't understand the error message, write it down or print it, and then look it up on the Microsoft support Web site or the product manufacturer's Web site. Follow the directions given on the Web sites to solve the problem.

◢ Read the documentation that came with the application and documents on the manufacturer Web site. Perhaps you are using a function incorrectly.

◢ A virus might be the source of the problem. Run current antivirus software.

◢ Consider that data files might be corrupted. Try creating new data files used by the software.

◢ Consider that the hardware the software is using might have a problem. For the hard drive, run ScanDisk and Defrag and check for free disk space. Delete files in the \Windows\Temp folder. For a device other than the hard drive, try using another application to access the device.

◢ Try uninstalling and reinstalling the software. Back up the data first.

◢ Launch Dr. Watson and then try to reproduce the error with the application. Look in the Dr. Watson log files for clues and search the Microsoft Web site.

◢ Perhaps the application depends on OS files that are corrupted. Try restoring Windows system files. Check the Microsoft Web site for Windows 9x/Me service packs that might resolve the problem. Install all Windows service packs. You might have to reinstall Windows.

◢ Ask yourself, "When was the last time the software worked?" What happened differently then? Did you get an error message that seemed insignificant at the time? What has happened to your computer since the software last worked? Have you added more software or changed the hardware configuration?

- A configuration file, which contains software settings, might be corrupted. Look for a file with a file extension of .ini, .inf, or .cfg.

If a shortcut on the Windows desktop does not work or gives errors, try the following:

- Icons on the desktop are created by putting files in the \Windows\Desktop folder. First decide if the icon on the desktop is actually a shortcut. An icon might represent a file stored in the Desktop folder or it might be a shortcut to a file stored anywhere on the drive. If the icon has a small, bent-arrow shortcut symbol on the icon, it is a shortcut. For example, the icon in Figure 16-35 on the right represents the document file MyLetter1.doc stored in the \Windows\Desktop folder, and the icon on the left is a shortcut to the file MyLetter2.doc, which can be stored anywhere on the drive.

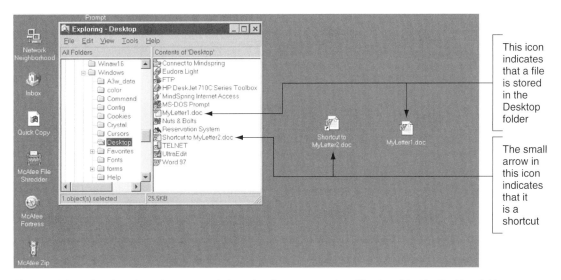

**Figure 16-35** One icon is a shortcut, and the other icon represents a file stored in the Desktop folder

- If the icon is a shortcut, right-click the shortcut and select **Properties** from the drop-down menu. Look for the name and location of the target file for the shortcut. Now search for this file to see if it's still in the same location and named the same.

If the system is performing slowly, try the following:

- The problem might be caused by lack of resources. If your system is running low on memory or has too many applications open, it might not be able to support a device. A corrupted Windows system file or registry can also cause problems with hardware devices. Try verifying system files or restoring the registry from backup.
- Check the hard drive. Run ScanDisk and Defrag. Delete unneeded files and empty the Recycle Bin. Generally clean up the hard drive, making plenty of room for the swap file and temporary files used by applications.
- Suspect a virus. Run a current version of antivirus software. Clean or delete all files that contain viruses. Restore system files.
- Check for applications loaded at startup that use system resources. Close applications not currently in use.
- Look for icons in the **system tray**, the small area on the right side of the taskbar at the bottom of the screen. These icons represent small applets that are loaded at startup and take up system resources. Keep these icons to a minimum.

⊿ Clean up the registry using the Scanreg /opt command.

⊿ Remove extraneous software such as fancy screen savers and desktop wallpaper and photos.

⊿ Verify that Windows is using optimum caching on the hard drive and CD-ROM drive. Go to the System Properties window and click the **Performance** tab. Click **File System**. The File System Properties window opens (see Figure 16-36). On the Hard Disk tab, select Full Read-ahead optimization, and on the CD-ROM tab, select Large cache size.

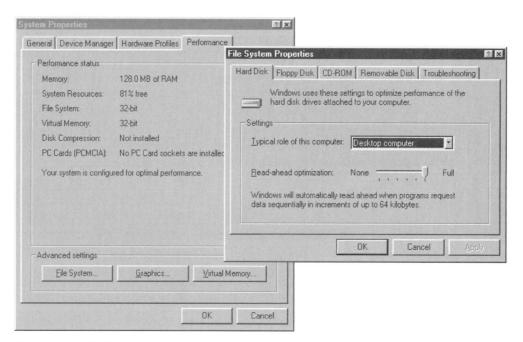

**Figure 16-36**    Verify that the hard drive is set for optimal caching

## ERROR MESSAGES USING WINDOWS 9X/ME

Table 16-12 lists some error messages that might appear when using Windows 9x/Me and what to do about them.

| Error Message | What to Do |
|---|---|
| Bad command or file not found | The OS command just executed cannot be interpreted, or the OS cannot find the program file specified in the command line. Check the spelling of the filename and the path to the file. |
| Insufficient memory | This error happens during or after the boot under Windows when too many applications are open. Close some applications. A reboot might help. |
| Incorrect DOS version | In real-mode DOS, when you execute a DOS external command, the OS looks for a program file with the same name as the command. It finds that this file belongs to a different version of the OS than the one that is now running. Use the Setver command at the command prompt or in Autoexec.bat. |

**Table 16-12**    Error messages when using Windows 9x/Me

## WINDOWS HELP AND THE MICROSOFT WEB SITE

Windows Help might provide useful information when you try to resolve a problem. To access the Troubleshooting tool of Windows Help, click **Start**, click **Help**, and then click **Troubleshooting**. The Help information includes suggestions that can lead you to a solution. For example, in Figure 16-37, the Hardware Troubleshooter suggests that you check to see that the device is not listed twice in Device Manager. If this is the case, you should remove the second occurrence of the device.

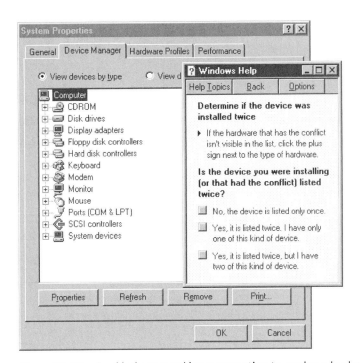

**Figure 16-37** Troubleshooter making a suggestion to resolve a hardware conflict

Also, the Microsoft Web site (*support.microsoft.com*; see Figure 16-38) has lots of information on troubleshooting. Search for the device, an error message, a Windows utility, a symptom, a software application, an update version number, or keywords that lead you to articles about problems and solutions. You can also go to *www.microsoft.com* to browse for links on hardware and software compatibility. Other sources of help are application and device user and installation manuals, training materials, and the Web sites of application and device manufacturers.

**Notes**

For those who are serious about learning to provide professional support for Windows 95 or Windows 98, two good books are *Microsoft Windows 95 Resource Kit* and *Microsoft Windows 98 Resource Kit*, both by Microsoft Press.

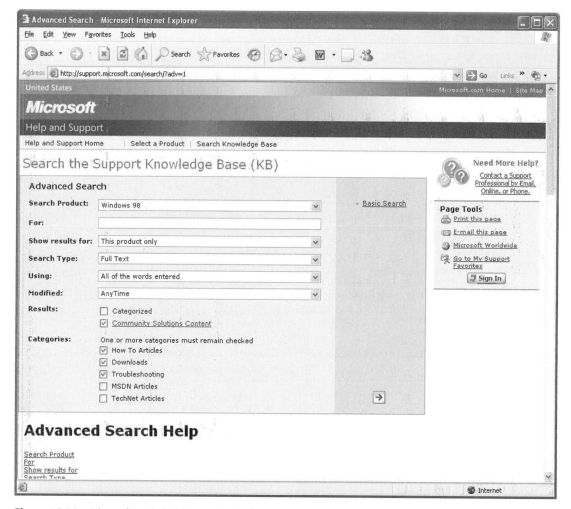

**Figure 16-38** Microsoft Technical Support Web site

## >> CHAPTER SUMMARY

▲ Windows 9x/Me has a shell and kernel; the Windows 9x/Me core consists of the kernel, the user, and the GDI.

▲ Virtual machines (VMs) are multiple logical machines within one physical machine. If an application crashes or produces another type of error within a VM, only that VM is affected, instead of the entire system.

▲ Although Windows 95/98 supports 16-bit drivers, using 32-bit drivers whenever possible is better. Windows Me does not use 16-bit drivers.

▲ If Windows is already installed and you want to do a clean install, delete the \Windows folder or use the setup screen to install the new OS in a different folder.

▲ Before performing a Windows 98/Me upgrade, check hardware and software compatibility, run antivirus software, and back up your system. The Setup Wizard on the Windows 98 CD will guide you through the setup process. After Setup is complete, test installed applications and back up your system again.

▲ When adding new hardware to Windows 9x/Me, use the Add New Hardware Wizard. Select the hardware from a list of devices to use a Windows driver, or click Have Disk to use your own drivers (from a manufacturer's disk or downloaded from the Internet to a folder on your hard drive). Alternately, you can run the Setup program provided by the device manufacturer.

▲ For a Windows 9x/Me system to be truly Plug and Play (PnP), the system BIOS must be PnP, all hardware devices and expansion cards must be PnP-compliant, and a 32-bit device driver must be available for any installed hardware device.

▲ Dosstart.bat is a type of Autoexec.bat file that executes when you restart the computer in MS-DOS mode or when you run a program in MS-DOS mode.

▲ An OS that supports protected mode can create a virtual real mode for a 16-bit application so that the application thinks it is the only program running, has all memory available to it, and accesses data using a 16-bit data path. Windows 9x/Me ordinarily runs a 16-bit DOS application in a virtual DOS machine.

▲ Starting with Windows 9x/Me, the Windows registry takes over the essential functions of .ini files. However, Windows 9x/Me still supports System.ini and Win.ini for backward compatibility with legacy hardware devices and legacy software applications.

▲ The registry is contained in two files, System.dat and User.dat, for Windows 95/98 and in three files, System.dat, User.dat, and Classes.dat, for Windows Me. Windows 95 maintains backups of these files, called System.da0 and User.da0, that you can use when troubleshooting. Windows 98/Me keeps compressed backups of the registry and system files in cabinet files named rb000.cab, rb001.cab, and so forth.

▲ Changes in the Control Panel, Device Manager, and other locations in Windows 9x/Me can change the registry automatically. The Regedit utility is used to edit the registry manually.

▲ The Registry Checker (Scanreg.exe or Scanregw.exe) backs up, verifies, and recovers the registry. It automatically backs up the registry every day and keeps the last five days of backups.

▲ The five phases of the Windows 9x/Me boot process are: (1) BIOS POST and bootstrap; (2) loading the OS real-mode operating environment; (3) loading of real-mode VxDs; (4) protected-mode switchover and PnP configuration; and (5) loading remaining components.

▲ Applications are loaded at startup by a shortcut in the StartUp folder, the name of the program file in the Load= or Run= line in Win.ini, or an entry in the registry.

▲ The System Configuration Utility (Msconfig.exe) allows you to modify the system configuration temporarily to help with troubleshooting. It reduces the startup process to essentials.

▲ The Dr. Watson utility (Drwatson.exe) helps you troubleshoot applications by trapping errors in log files and taking a snapshot of the system.

▲ The System Configuration Editor (Sysedit.exe) is a text editor used to edit system files. When you run Sysedit, it automatically opens Protocol.ini, System.ini, Win.ini, Config.sys, and Autoexec.bat.

▲ Device Manager lists hardware devices installed on a system. For more information about a specific device in Device Manager, click the device and select **Properties**.

▲ When troubleshooting Windows 9x/Me boot problems, first check error messages, then boot in Safe Mode, then boot to the command prompt using the startup menu, and finally try booting from an emergency startup disk.

▲ To force the Windows 9x/Me startup menu to appear, hold down either the Ctrl key or the F8 key during the boot.

▲ You can reach Safe Mode either from the Windows startup menu or by pressing the F5 key while Windows is loading.

▲ Safe Mode starts Windows 9x/Me with a minimum default configuration to give you an opportunity to correct an error in the configuration.

▲ Choosing Command Prompt Only from the startup menu executes the contents of Autoexec.bat and Config.sys but does not start Windows. Instead it brings you to a DOS prompt. Use the WIN command to load Windows 9x/Me.

▲ Use the startup disk to recover from a failed boot when you cannot solve the problem using the startup menu or cannot boot from the hard drive. If you do not have a startup disk or the one you have has a virus, use a working computer to create a new disk.

## >> KEY TERMS

For explanations of key terms, see the Glossary near the end of the book.

| | | |
|---|---|---|
| application programming interface (API) call | IFS (Installable File System) | System.ini |
| clean install | initialization files | system tray |
| comment line | keys | upgrade install |
| Configuration Manager | memory paging | user component |
| disk thrashing | pages | value data |
| Dosstart.bat | patches | virtual device driver (VxD) |
| Dr. Watson | PIF (program information file) | virtual machine (VM) |
| DriveSpace | Protocol.ini | VMM (Virtual Machine Manager) |
| dynamic VxDs | service pack | WDM (Win32 Driver Model) |
| GDI (Graphics Device Interface) | slack | Win.ini |
| General Protection Fault | static VxDs | Win386.swp |
| | Sysedit | |

## >> REVIEW QUESTIONS

1. Which of the following components handles drawing screens, graphics, and lines and manages printing?

   a. GDI

   b. Kernel

   c. User

   d. Virtual Machine Manager

2. Which of the following hardware components is responsible for managing memory, virtual machines, and all the resources needed by each application?

   a. WDM

   b. IFS

   c. Configuration Manager

   d. VMM

3. Which of the following installation setup options is used when installing Windows 9x/Me on a notebook computer?

   a. Typical

   b. Portable

   c. Compact

   d. Custom

4. For best performance with Windows 9x/Me, what is the minimum amount of unused hard drive space that should be available for working with temporary files used by applications?

   a. 28

   b. 64

   c. 100

   d. 127

5. Which of the following Windows initialization files contains information about the configuration of the network?

   a. Win.ini

   b. Protocol.ini

   c. Control.ini

   d. System.ini

6. True or false? In addition to having access to a list of predefined APIs, an application is also allowed direct access to hardware.

7. True or false? Windows Me supports 16-bit legacy drivers that work under Windows 95/98.

8. True or false? CMOS setups that have an option that protects against some boot sector viruses prevent writing to the boot sector of the hard drive. This feature must be turned off before installing Windows.

9. True or false? For a system to be truly Plug and Play, a 32-bit device driver must be available from the device manufacturer or Windows.

10. True or false? Dr. Watson is a Windows utility that can record detailed information about the system, errors that occur, and the programs that caused them in a log file.

11. Applications call on the OS to access hardware or other software by using a(n) _____ call.

12. The process used by the VMM to move 4K segments in and out of physical RAM is called _____.

13. Updates and fixes to the OS released by Microsoft are called _____ or _____.

14. Performing a new installation of the OS is called a(n) _____ install.

15. A(n) _____ VxD (virtual device driver) is loaded into and unloaded from memory as needed.

CHAPTER
**17**

# PCs on a Network

In this chapter, we discuss how to connect PCs in networks and how to access resources on a network. You'll learn about the technologies used to build networks and how Windows supports and manages a network connection, including how computers are identified and addressed on a network. You'll also learn to connect a computer to a network and share its resources with others on the network.

Local networks are often large and complex, and few local networks exist today that are isolated from other networks. In this chapter, you'll learn how switches and routers work to manage large local networks and connect to other networks. You'll also learn how to set up and secure a wireless network. And you'll learn to troubleshoot a network connection. In the next chapter, you'll learn how to connect to the Internet and how to use the resources on it.

# PHYSICAL NETWORK ARCHITECTURES

A+ ESS
5.1

A+
220-602
5.1

In this first part of the chapter, you'll learn about the various types of networking technologies and designs. We'll first look at the different sizes of networks, the different technologies used by networks, and some networking terms. Then, we'll turn our attention to the details of the types of networks you are most likely to encounter as a PC repair technician, which include Ethernet, wireless networks, telephone networks, and the mostly outdated token ring and FDDI networks.

## SIZES OF NETWORKS

A computer network is created when two or more computers can communicate with each other. Networks can be categorized by several methods, including the technology used and the size of the network. When networks are categorized by size or physical area they cover, these are the categories used:

- *PAN.* A **PAN** (**personal area network**) consisting of personal devices at close range such as a cell phone, PDA, and notebook computer in communication. PANs can use wired connections (such as USB or FireWire) or wireless connections (such as Bluetooth or infrared).
- *LAN.* A **LAN** (**local area network**) covers a small local area such as a home, office, or other building or small group of buildings. LANs can use wired (most likely Ethernet) or wireless (most likely 802.11) technologies. A LAN is used for workstations, servers, printers, and other devices to communicate and share resources.
- *MAN.* A **MAN** (**metropolitan area network**) covers a large campus or city. (A small MAN is sometimes called a CAN or campus area network.) Newer technologies used are wireless and Ethernet with fiber-optic cabling. Older technologies used are ATM and FDDI.
- *WAN.* A **WAN** (**wide area network**) covers a large geographical area and is made up of many smaller networks. The best known WAN is the Internet.

## NETWORKING TECHNOLOGIES

Networking technologies have evolved over time based on the type of data the network is intended to support, the data capacity on the network, and how a network is to fit among other networks. When you study the different network technologies, much attention is given to how much data can travel over a given communication system in a given amount of time. This measure of data capacity is called **bandwidth** (or **data throughput** or **line speed**). The greater the bandwidth is, the faster the communication. In analog systems, bandwidth is the difference between the highest and lowest frequency that a device can transmit. Frequencies are measured in cycles per second, or hertz (Hz). In digital systems such as computers and computer networks, bandwidth is a measure of data transmission in bits per second (bps), thousands of bits per second (Kbps), or millions of bits per second (Mbps).

Interconnecting networks (for example, the Internet) are built using technologies that provide varying degrees of bandwidth, each serving a different purpose and following a different set of standards. Generally, the larger the network, the more bandwidth it requires, which dictates which technology is used. Table 17-1 lists bandwidth technologies, their speeds, and their uses. The table is more or less ordered from slowest to fastest bandwidth, although there is some overlap and several factors can affect the actual bandwidth of a particular network.

**17**

| Technology | Maximum Throughput Speeds | Common Uses |
|---|---|---|
| GSM mobile telephone service | 9.6 to 14.4 Kbps | Wireless technology used for mobile phones. |
| Regular telephone (POTS, for plain old telephone service) | Up to 56 Kbps | Home and small business access to an ISP using a modem. |
| Frame Relay | 56 Kbps to 45 Mbps | Businesses that need to communicate internationally or across the country. |
| Fractional T-1 | $n$ times 64 Kbps (where $n$ = number of channels or portions of a T-1 leased) | Companies expecting to grow into a T-1 line, but not yet ready for a T-1. |
| X.25 | 56 Kbps | Outdated technology that provided communication between mainframes and terminals. |
| ISDN | 64 Kbps to 128 Kbps | Mostly outdated small to medium-sized business access to an ISP. |
| IDSL (ISDN Digital Subscriber Line) | 128 Kbps | Home and small business access to an ISP. |
| ADSL (Asymmetric Digital Subscriber Line) | 640 Kbps upstream and up to 24 Mbps downstream | Most bandwidth is from ISP to user. Slower versions of ADSL are called ADSL Lite or DSL Lite. ISP customers pay according to a bandwidth scale. ADSL is a type of broadband technology. (Broadband refers to a networking technology that carries more than one type of signal such as DSL and telephone.) |
| T-1 | 1.544 Mbps | To connect large companies to branch offices or an ISP. E-1, which is used in Europe, is a similar technology. |
| SDSL (Symmetric DSL) | Up to 2.3 Mbps | Equal bandwidths in both directions. |
| Cable modem | 512 Kbps to 5 Mbps | Connects a home or small business to an ISP; is usually purchased with cable television subscription. Cable modem is a type of broadband technology that is used in conjunction with television on the same cable. |
| Token Ring | 4 or 16 Mbps | Outdated technology once used on a LAN. |
| T-3 | 45 Mbps | Large companies that require a lot of bandwidth and transmit extensive amounts of data. |

**Table 17-1** Bandwidth technologies

A+ ESS
5.1

A+
220-602
5.1

| Technology | Maximum Throughput Speeds | Common Uses |
|---|---|---|
| OC-1 | 52 Mbps | Base rate of transmission used by SONET and ATM. Multiples are called Optical Carrier levels (OCx). |
| 802.11b wireless | Up to 11 Mbps | First 802.11 standard that was widely used, but is being replaced by 802.11g. |
| 802.11a wireless | Up to 54 Mbps | Shorter range than 802.11b, but faster. |
| 802.11g wireless | Up to 54 Mbps | Compatible with and replacing 802.11b. |
| VDSL (Very-high-rate DSL) | Up to 200 Mbps | This latest version of DSL can be asymmetric or symmetric DSL. |
| Ethernet | 10, 100, or 1,000 Mbps | Most popular technology for a local network. 1,000-Mbps Ethernet is called Gigabit Ethernet. |
| FDDI | 100 Mbps | Older network backbones. FDDI is being replaced by Gigabit Ethernet. |
| ATM | 25, 45, 155, or 622 Mbps | ATM (Asynchronous Transfer Mode) networks are used for large business networks and LAN backbones. ATM is being replaced by Gigabit Ethernet. |
| OC-3, OC-24, OC-256 | 155 Mbps, 1.23 Gbps, 13 Gbps | Internet backbones; they use optical fiber. |
| Gigabit Ethernet | 1 Gbps | Latest Ethernet standard. |
| 10-gigabit Ethernet | 10 Gbps | Newest Ethernet standard expected to largely replace SONET, OC, and ATM because of its speed, simplicity, and lower cost. |
| OC-768 | 40 Gbps | Currently, this is the fastest OC level. |
| SONET (Synchronous Optical Network) | 52 Mbps to 20 Gbps | Major backbones make use of different OC levels. |

**Table 17-1**    Bandwidth technologies (continued)

> ### Notes
>
> The **Institute of Electrical and Electronics Engineers (IEEE)** creates standards for computer and electronics industries. Of those standards, IEEE 802 applies to networking. For example, IEEE 802.2 describes the standard for Logical Link Control, which defines how networks that use different protocols communicate with each other. For more information on the IEEE 802 standards, see the IEEE Web site, *www.ieee.org*.

A+ ESS
5.1

A+
220-602
5.1

## ADDITIONAL TERMS USED IN NETWORKING

Before we get into the details of network architecture, you need to know a few terms and what they mean:

- A **node**, or **host,** is one device on the network. It can be a workstation, server, printer, or other device.
- A PC makes a direct connection to a network by way of a **network adapter**, which might be a network port embedded on the motherboard or a **network interface card (NIC)**, using a PCI slot, such as the one shown in Figure 17-1. In addition, the adapter might also be an external device connecting to the PC using a USB port, SCSI external port, or serial port. The adapter might provide a port for a network cable or an antenna for a wireless connection. The adapter must match the type and speed of the physical network being used, and the network port must match the type of connectors used on the network. Laptops can make connections to a network through a PC Card NIC, a built-in network port, a wireless connection, or an external device that connects to the laptop by way of a USB port. (You will learn about PC Cards in Chapter 20.)

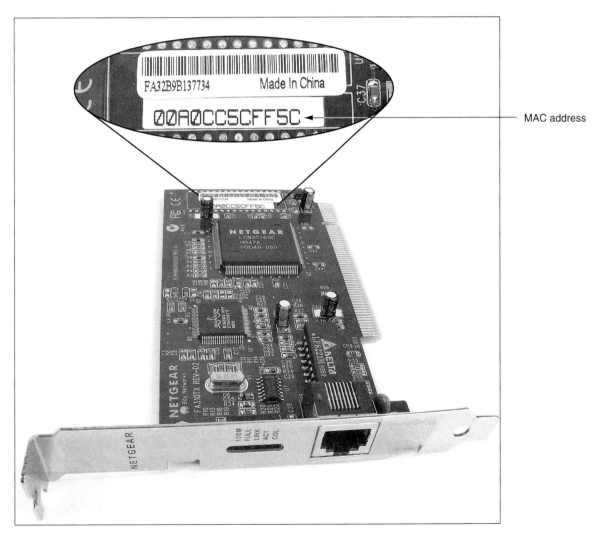

**Figure 17-1**  Ethernet network card showing its MAC address

A+ ESS
5.1

A+
220-602
5.1

▲ Every network adapter (including a network card, onboard wireless, or wireless NIC) has a 48-bit (6-byte) number hard-coded on the card by its manufacturer that is unique for that adapter, and this number is used to identify the adapter on the network. The number is often written in hex and is called the **MAC (Media Access Control) address, hardware address, physical address, adapter address,** or Ethernet address. An example of a MAC address is 00-0C-6E-4E-AB-A5. Part of the MAC address refers to the manufacturer; therefore, no two adapters should have the same MAC address. Most likely the MAC address is written on the card, as shown in Figure 17-1.

▲ Communication on a network follows rules of communication called network protocols. Communication over a network happens in layers. The OS on one PC communicates with the OS on another PC using one set of protocols, and the network card communicates with other hardware devices on the network using another set of networking protocols. Examples of OS protocols are TCP/IP and NetBEUI, and examples of hardware protocols are Ethernet and Token Ring. You'll learn more about these protocols later in the chapter.

▲ Data is transmitted on a network in pieces called **packets, datagrams,** or **frames.** Information about the packet that identifies the type of data, where it came from, and where it's going is placed at the beginning and end of the data. Information at the beginning of the data is called a header, and information at the end of the data is called a trailer. If the data to be sent is large, it is first divided into several packets small enough to travel on the network.

A+ ESS
2.1
5.1

A+
220-602
2.1
5.1
5.3

**⊕ A+ Tip**

The A+ Essentials exam expects you to be familiar with many networking terms. This chapter is full of key terms you need to know for the exam.

# INTRODUCING ETHERNET

**Ethernet** (sometimes abbreviated ENET) is the most popular network architecture used today. The three variations of Ethernet are primarily distinguished from one another by speed: 10-Mbps Ethernet, 100-Mbps or Fast Ethernet, and 1000-Mbps or Gigabit Ethernet. In the following sections, we'll look at the several variations of Ethernet, the ways nodes on an Ethernet network can be connected, and how repeaters perform on a network.

## VARIATIONS OF ETHERNET

Several variations of Ethernet have evolved over the years, which are primarily identified by their speeds and the types of cables and connectors used to wire these networks. Each variation of Ethernet can use more than one cabling method. Table 17-2 compares cable types and Ethernet versions.

As you can see from Table 17-2, the three main types of cabling used by Ethernet are twisted-pair, coaxial, and fiber-optic. Within each category, there are several variations:

▲ *Twisted-pair cable.* Twisted-pair cable is the most popular cabling method for local networks. It comes in two varieties: **unshielded twisted pair (UTP) cable** and **shielded twisted pair (STP) cable.** UTP cable is the most common and least expensive. UTP is rated by category: CAT-3 (Category 3) is less expensive than the more popular CAT-5 cable or enhanced CAT-5 (CAT-5e). CAT-6 has less crosstalk than CAT-5 or CAT-5e. STP uses a covering around the pairs of wires inside the cable that protects it from electromagnetic interference caused by electrical motors, transmitters, or high-tension lines. It costs more than unshielded cable, so it's used only when the situation demands it. Twisted-pair cable has four pairs of twisted wires for a total of eight wires and uses a connector called an

**⊕ A+ Tip**

The A+ Essentials exam expects you to know the details shown in Table 17-2.

**17**

A+ ESS
2.1
5.1

A+
220-602
2.1
5.1
5.3

RJ-45 connector (RJ stands for registered jack) that looks like a large phone jack. Figure 17-2 shows unshielded twisted pair cables and the RJ-45 connector.

| Cable System | Speed | Cables and Connectors | Example of Connectors | Maximum Cable Length |
|---|---|---|---|---|
| 10Base2 (ThinNet) | 10 Mbps | Coaxial uses a BNC connector | | 185 meters or 607 feet |
| 10Base5 (ThickNet) | 10 Mbps | Coaxial uses an AUI 15-pin D-shaped connector | | 500 meters or 1,640 feet |
| 10BaseT, 100BaseT (Twisted-pair), and Gigabit Ethernet | 10, 100, or 1,000 Mbps | UTP or STP uses an RJ-45 connector | | 100 meters or 328 feet |
| 10BaseF, 10BaseFL, 100BaseFL, 100BaseFX, 1000BaseFX, or 1000BaseX (fiber-optic) | 10, 100, or 1,000 Mbps | Fiber-optic cable uses ST or SC connectors (shown to the right) or LC and MT-RJ connectors (not shown) | | 500 meters up to 2 kilometers (6,562 feet) |

**Table 17-2** Variations of Ethernet and Ethernet cabling

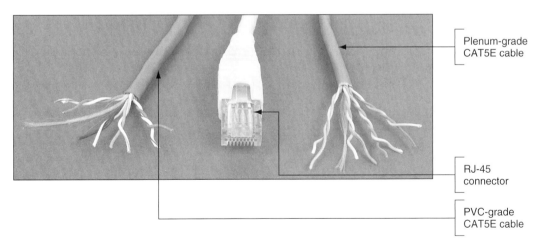

Plenum-grade CAT5E cable

RJ-45 connector

PVC-grade CAT5E cable

**Figure 17-2** The most common networking cable for a local network is UTP cable using an RJ-45 connector

**Notes**

Normally, the plastic covering of a cable is made of PVC (polyvinyl chloride), which is not safe when used inside plenums (areas between the floors of buildings). In these situations, plenum cable covered with Teflon is used because it does not give off toxic fumes when burned. Plenum cable is two or three times more expensive than PVC cable. Figure 17-2 shows plenum cable and PVC cable, both of which are unshielded twisted pair CAT5e cables.

▲ *Coaxial cable*. **Coaxial cable** has a single copper wire down the middle and a braided shield around it (see Figure 17-3). Because it's stiff and difficult to manage, it's not as popular as twisted pair for local networking, although maximum cable lengths for coaxial cable are longer than twisted pair maximum lengths. There are two thicknesses of coaxial cables used for networking: thick and thin. Thick cabling (called RG8 cabling) is used by ThickNet Ethernet, and thin cabling (called RG58 cabling) is used by ThinNet Ethernet. Each type cable uses a different type connector, as shown in Table 17-2. The more popular of the two is thin coaxial cable using a **BNC connector**.

Other important coaxial cables you should know about are RG59, which is used for cable TV and VCR transmission and RG6, which is used for satellite dish signals and video applications requiring greater shielding than RG59.

**Figure 17-3**  Coaxial cable and a BNC connector are used with ThinNet Ethernet

▲ *Fiber optic*. **Fiber-optic** cables transmit signals as pulses of light over glass strands inside protected tubing, as illustrated in Figure 17-4. Fiber-optic cable comes in two types: single-mode (thin, difficult to connect, expensive, and best performing) and multimode (most popular). A single-mode cable uses a single strand of glass fiber and multimode cable uses multiple strands of glass. Both single-mode and multimode fiber-optic cables can be constructed as loose-tube cables for outdoor use or tight-buffered cable for indoor or outdoor use. Loose-tube cables are filled with gel to prevent water from soaking into the cable, and tight-buffered cables are filled with yarn to protect the fiber-optic strands, as shown in Figure 17-4.

Fiber-optic cables can use one of four connectors, all shown in Figure 17-5. The two older types are ST (straight tip) and SC (subscriber connector or standard connector). Two newer types are LC (local connector) and MT-RJ (mechanical transfer registered jack) connectors. Any one of the four connectors can be used with either single-mode or multimode fiber-optic cable.

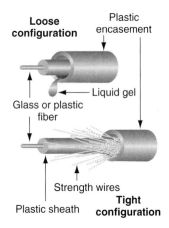

Loose configuration
Plastic encasement
Liquid gel
Glass or plastic fiber
Strength wires
Plastic sheath
**Tight configuration**

**A+ Tip**

The A+ Essentials exam expects you to know about these cable types: Plenum, PVC, UTP, CAT3, CAT5, CAT5e, CAT6, STP, single-mode fiber, multimode fiber, ST, SC, and LC.

**Figure 17-4**  Fiber-optic cables contain a glass core for transmitting light

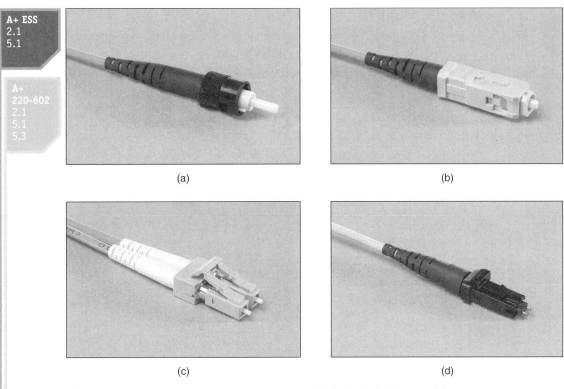

(a)  (b)

(c)  (d)

**Figure 17-5**  Four types of fiber-optic connectors: (a) ST, (b) SC, (c) LC, and (d) MT-RJ

Each version of Ethernet can use more than one cabling method. Here is a brief description of the types of Ethernet identified by the cabling methods they use:

▲ *10-Mbps Ethernet.* The first Ethernet specification was invented by Xerox Corporation in the 1970s, and in 1980 it was enhanced and became known as Ethernet IEEE 802.3. This type of Ethernet operates at 10 Mbps (megabits per second). This speed of Ethernet can use three different cabling methods: **10BaseT** Ethernet uses twisted-pair cabling rated CAT-3 or higher and an RJ-45 connector. **10Base5** Ethernet (sometimes called **ThickNet**) uses thick RG8 coaxial cable with an AUI connector. **10Base2** Ethernet (sometimes called **ThinNet**) uses a thin RG58 coaxial cable with a BNC connector.

▲ *100-Mbps Ethernet or Fast Ethernet.* This improved version of Ethernet (sometimes called **100BaseT** or **Fast Ethernet**) operates at 100 Mbps and uses STP or UTP cabling rated CAT-5 or higher. 100BaseT networks can support slower speeds of 10 Mbps so that devices that run at either 10 Mbps or 100 Mbps can coexist on the same LAN. Two variations of 100BaseT are 100BaseTX and 100BaseFX. The most popular variation is 100BaseTX. 100BaseFX uses fiber-optic cable.

▲ *1000-Mbps Ethernet or Gigabit Ethernet.* This up-and-coming version of Ethernet operates at 1000 Mbps and uses twisted-pair cable and fiber-optic cable. **Gigabit Ethernet** is currently replacing 100BaseT Ethernet as the choice for LAN technology. Because it can use the same cabling and connectors as 100BaseT, a company can upgrade from 100BaseT to Gigabit without great expense.

▲ *10-Gigabit Ethernet.* This version of Ethernet operates at 10 billion bits per second (10 Gbps) and uses fiber cable. It can be used on LANs, WANs, and MANs, and is also a good choice for backbone networks. (A backbone network is a channel whereby local networks can connect to wide area networks.)

## ETHERNET TOPOLOGY

The topology of a network refers to the arrangement or shape used to physically connect devices on a network to one another. Ethernet networks can be configured as either a bus topology or a star topology. Figure 17-6 shows examples of bus and star topologies. A **bus topology** connects each node in a line and has no central connection point. Cables just go from one computer to the next, and then the next. A **star topology** connects all nodes to a centralized hub or switch. PCs on the LAN are like points of a star around the hub or switch in the middle, which connects the nodes on the LAN.

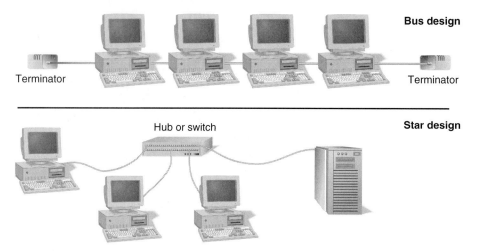

**Figure 17-6** Nodes on an Ethernet network can be connected to one another in a star or bus formation

The star arrangement is more popular because it is easier to maintain than the bus arrangement. In a star topology that uses a hub, the hub passes all data that flows to it to every device connected to it. An Ethernet hub **broadcasts** the data packet to every device, as shown in Figure 17-7.

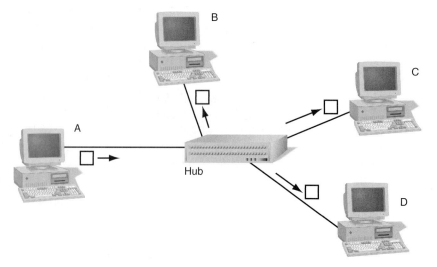

**Figure 17-7** Any data received by a hub is replicated and passed on to every device connected to it

A+ ESS
2.1
5.1

A+
220-602
2.1
5.1
5.3

In Figure 17-7, when computer A sends data to the hub, the hub replicates the data and sends it to every device connected to it. Computers B, C, and D each get a copy of the data. It's up to these computers to decide if the data is intended for them. For this reason, a hub can generate a lot of unnecessary traffic on a LAN, which can result in slow performance when several nodes are connected to the hub.

You can think of a **hub** as just a pass-through and distribution point for every device connected to it, without regard for what kind of data is passing through and where the data might be going. See Figure 17-8.

**Figure 17-8**   A hub is a pass-through device to connect nodes on a network

A **switch** (see Figure 17-9) is smarter and more efficient than a hub and keeps a table of all the devices connected to it. It uses this table to determine which path to use when sending packets. The switch only passes data to the device to which the data is addressed. In the past, because switches were so much more expensive than hubs, most networks used mostly hubs and only used a switch when needed to improve a bottleneck in network performance. Now, because the prices of switches have dramatically decreased and networks built with switches are much faster than those built with hubs, most networks use all switches and no hubs.

**Figure 17-9**   An eight-port switch by Netgear

As network needs grow, you can add a switch or hub so that you can connect more devices to the network. Figure 17-10 shows an example of a network that uses three switches in sequence. The switches themselves form a bus network, but the computers connected to each switch form a star. This network configuration, which uses a logical bus for data delivery but is wired as a physical star, is an example of a **star bus topology**.

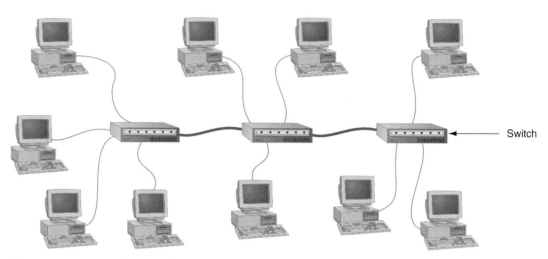

Switch

**Figure 17-10**  A star bus network uses more than one switch

---

# APPLYING|CONCEPTS

## PATCH CABLES, CROSSOVER CABLES, AND CABLE TESTERS

Two types of network cables can be used when building a network: a patch cable and a crossover cable. A **patch cable** (also called a straight-through cable) is used to connect a computer to a hub or switch. A **crossover cable** is used to connect two PCs (when a hub or switch is not used) to make the simplest network of all.

The difference in a patch cable and a crossover cable is the way the read and write lines are wired in the connectors at each end of the cables. A crossover cable has the read and write lines reversed so that one computer reads off the line to which the other computer writes. For older hubs, it was necessary to use a crossover cable to connect a hub to another hub. However, today you can connect a hub or switch to another hub or switch using the more common patch cables because these devices have a special port (called the uplink port) to use for the connection. Also, most switches use auto-uplinking, which means you can connect a switch to a switch using a patch cable on any port.

A patch cable and a crossover cable look identical and have identical connectors. One way to tell them apart is to look for the labeling imprinted on the cables, as shown in Figure 17-11.

If a cable is not labeled, you can use a cable tester to determine the type of cable. A cable tester can have two components. Connect each component to the ends of the cable and turn on the tester. Lights on the tester will show you if the cable is good and what type of cable you have. You'll need to read the user manual that comes with the cable tester to know how to interpret the lights.

17

You can also use cable testers like the one in Figure 17-12 to trace a network cable through a building. Suppose you see several network jacks on walls in a building but you don't know which jacks connect. Install a short cable in each of two jacks and then use the cable tester to test the

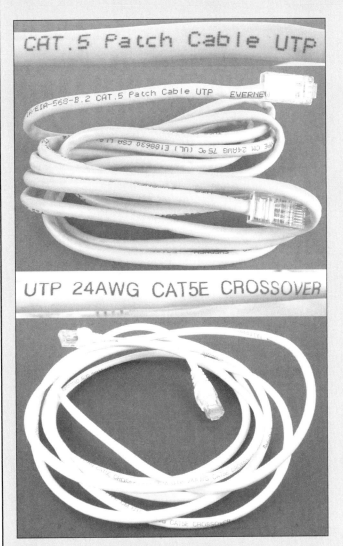

**Figure 17-11**  Patch cables and crossover cables look the same but are labeled differently

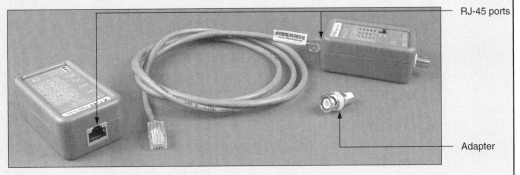

**Figure 17-12**  Use a cable tester pair to determine the type of cable and if the cable is good

A+ ESS
2.1
5.1

A+
220-602
2.1
5.1
5.3

continuity, as shown in Figure 17-13. You might damage a cable tester if you connect it to a live circuit, so before you start connecting the cable tester to wall jacks, be sure that you turn off all devices on the network.

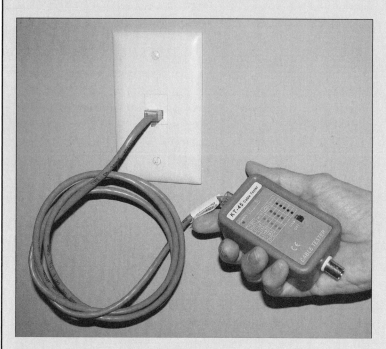

**Figure 17-13**   Use cable testers to trace network cables through a building

**Video**

Ethernet Cables

## REPEATERS

Because signals transmitted over long distances on a network can weaken (in a process called **attenuation**), devices are added to amplify signals in large LANs (see Figure 17-14). For example, if two devices on a 100BaseT Ethernet network are more than 100 meters (328 feet) apart, amplification is required. A **repeater** is a device that amplifies signals on a network. There are two kinds of repeaters. An **amplifier repeater** simply amplifies the incoming signal, noise and all. A **signal-regenerating repeater** reads the signal and then creates an exact duplicate of the original signal before sending it on. Ethernet uses a signal-regenerating repeater. For the typical Ethernet network, a switch or hub acts as a signal-regenerating repeater.

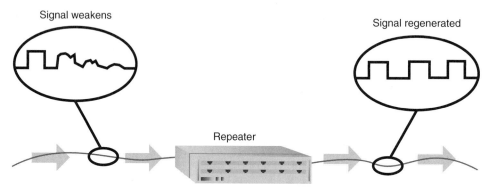

**Figure 17-14**   A repeater on a network restores the clarity of the signal, which degrades over a distance because of attenuation

A+ ESS
2.1
5.1
6.1

A+
220-602
2.1
5.1
6.2
6.3

# WIRELESS NETWORKS

Wireless networks, as the name implies, use radio waves or infrared light instead of cables or wires to connect computers or other devices. A **Wireless LAN (WLAN)** covers a limited geographical area and is popular in places where networking cables are difficult to install, such as outdoors, in public places, and in homes that are not wired for networks. They are also useful in hotel rooms.

 **A+ Tip**

The A+ Essentials exam expects you to be familiar with these wireless technologies: 802.11, infrared, Bluetooth, and cellular.

Three current wireless technologies are 802.11 (also called WiFi), WiMAX, and Bluetooth. Recall from Chapter 9 that an earlier and outdated wireless technology is infrared. Although wireless networks have some obvious advantages in places where running cables would be difficult or overly expensive, wireless networks tend to be slower than wired networks, especially when they are busy. Another problem with wireless networks is security. In this section, you'll learn about the three most popular wireless technologies used primarily to transmit data. In this next section, you'll learn about some wireless telephone networks primarily dedicated to voice communication.

## 802.11 WIRELESS

By far, the most popular technology for desktop and notebook computer wireless connections is IEEE 802.11, first published in 1990. Most new wireless LAN devices operate under the IEEE 802.11g standard, which is backward compatible with the earlier and slower IEEE 802.11b standard. These standards are also called **Wi-Fi (Wireless Fidelity)**.

802.11g and 802.11b use a frequency range of 2.4 GHz in the radio band and have a distance range of about 100 meters. 802.11b/g has the disadvantage that many cordless phones use the 2.4-GHz frequency range and cause network interference. 802.11g runs at 54 Mbps and 802.11b runs at 11Mbps. Apple Computer calls 802.11b **AirPort**, and it calls 802.11g AirPort Extreme.

Another IEEE standard is 802.11a, which works in the 5.0-GHz frequency range and is, therefore, not compatible with 802.11b/g. It has a shorter range from a wireless device to an access point (50 meters compared with 100 meters for 802.11b/g), supports 54 Mbps, and does not encounter interference from cordless phones, microwave ovens, and Bluetooth devices, as does 802.11b/g. Most wireless devices today support all three IEEE standards; look for **802.11a/b/g** on the packages. Another standard is 802.11d, which is designed to run in countries outside the United States where other 802.11 versions do not meet the legal requirements for radio band technologies.

As wireless networks become more and more popular and our wireless devices become more mobile, new IEEE standards are being developed to deal with the new demands on the technology. 802.11k and 802.11r are two standards designed to help manage connections between wireless devices and access points. Normally, if a wireless device senses more than one access point, by default, it connects to the access point with the strongest signal, which can cause an overload on some access points while other access points are idle. The 802.11k standard defines how wireless network traffic can better be distributed over multiple access points covering a wide area so that the access point with the strongest signal is not overloaded. The 802.11r standard defines how a mobile wireless device can easily and quickly transition as it moves out of range of one access point and into the range of another.

Wireless connections using 802.11b/g/a can be made with a variety of devices, four of which are shown in Figure 17-15. Notice in the figure the different types of antennae.

**Video**

Wireless Network Cards

A+ ESS
2.1
5.1
6.1

A+
220-602
2.1
5.1
6.2
6.3

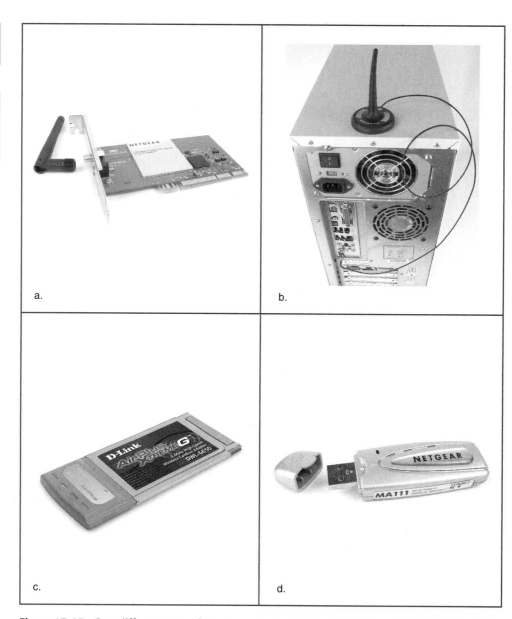

a.

b.

c.

d.

**Figure 17-15** Four different types of wireless network adapters: (a) wireless NIC that fits in a PCI slot; (b) onboard wireless with an antenna that can be moved; (c) PC Card wireless NIC with embedded antenna; and (d) wireless NIC that uses a USB port on a desktop or notebook computer

Wireless devices can communicate directly (such as a PC to a PC, which is called Ad Hoc mode), or they can connect to a LAN by way of a wireless **access point (AP)**, as shown in Figure 17-16. Multiple access points can be positioned so that nodes can access at least one access point from anywhere in the covered area. When devices use an access point, they communicate through the access point instead of communicating directly. Often a wireless access point is doing double duty as a router, a device that connects one network to another (see Figure 17-17). You'll learn more about routers in the next chapter. Also, in a later section of the chapter, you will learn how to install a wireless device in a computer and connect it to a wireless network.

**Video**

Using a Multifunction Router

A+ ESS
2.1
5.1
6.1

A+
220-602
2.1
5.1
6.2
6.3

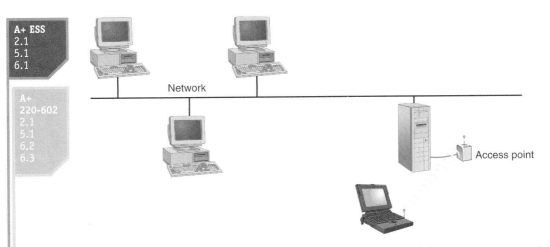

Network

Access point

**Figure 17-16**  Nodes on a wireless LAN connect to a cabled network by way of an access point

Front

Rear

**Figure 17-17**  This multifunction device is a router and also serves as a wireless access point to connect computers wirelessly to the local network

A+ ESS
2.1
5.1
6.1

A+
220-602
2.1
5.1
6.2
6.3

> **Notes**
>
> A LAN is often depicted in a logic diagram as a straight line with devices connecting to it. This method merely shows that devices are connected and is a nondescriptive way of drawing a LAN that might use a bus, ring, or star topology.

## WIMAX OR 802.16 WIRELESS

A newer IEEE wireless standard is WiMAX, which is defined under IEEE 802.16d and 802.16e. WiMAX supports up to 75 Mbps with a range up to 6 miles and uses 2- to 11-GHz frequency. It is used in public hot spots and as a wireless broadband solution for business and residential use. It is often used as a last-mile solution for DSL and cable modem technologies, which means that the DSL or cable connection goes into a central point in an area, and WiMAX is used for the final leg to the consumer.

## BLUETOOTH

**Bluetooth** is a standard for short-range wireless communication and data synchronization between devices. This standard was developed by a group of electronics manufacturers, including Ericsson, IBM, Intel, Nokia, and Toshiba, and it is overseen by the Bluetooth Special Interest Group (*www.bluetooth.com* and *www.bluetooth.org*). Bluetooth, which has a range of only 10 meters, also works in the 2.4-GHz frequency range, transfers data at up to 3 Mbps, is easy to configure, and is considered a viable option for short-range connections. For security, Bluetooth transmissions are encrypted. Examples of Bluetooth connections include connecting a printer to a PC or connecting a notebook computer or PDA to a cell phone so that the PDA or notebook computer can connect to a remote network by way of the cell phone's cellular network. Figure 17-18 shows a cordless Bluetooth headset that you can purchase to use with your mobile phone. The wireless headset clips over your ear and is battery powered.

**Figure 17-18**  This wireless headset accessory for a mobile phone uses Bluetooth wireless between the headset and the phone

# TELEPHONE NETWORKS

As wireless networking technologies and the Internet technologies continue to improve, they are becoming more integrated with telephone and voice communications. In this section, we'll look at different telephone technologies, both wired and wireless, and see how they are integrated with our computer networks.

## PLAIN OLD TELEPHONE SERVICE (POTS)

Almost all wireless and Internet phone systems connect to the regular, wired public phone system, which is called the PSTN (Public Switched Telephone Network) or POTS (plain old telephone service). This system uses a series of switches to create a closed circuit between two telephones; the circuit remains closed and in use as long as the callers are connected. For this reason, charges for calls are made according to the connect time.

## VoIP

VoIP (Voice over Internet Protocol), also called Internet telephone, was once a novelty on the Internet, but not very useful because of all the problems with poor voice quality and dropped connections. However, VoIP has recently come of age and has become a viable residential and business alternative to regular phone service. Using VoIP, voice is converted to digital data for transmission over the Internet and to connect to POTS so that people can make and receive calls to VoIP subscribers as well as those using regular telephone service.

Just as with Ethernet, VoIP uses packets of data to communicate, and these voice packets can travel over the Internet using various paths rather than using a single closed circuit as does the PSTN network. Therefore, charges for VoIP are usually based on data sent rather than connect time.

To use VoIP, you need a broadband Internet connection such as a cable modem or DSL and a subscription to a VoIP provider. Regular analog or digital telephones can be used, which connect to the Internet by way of a network cable just as your computer connects, as shown in Figure 17-19. The digital phone is this figure connects to a network port on a router or to a network wall jack using an RJ-45 connector labeled in the figure. The AC power adapter plugs into a power outlet and provides power to the phone by way of the one cord to the phone. This one cord is doing double duty as a power cord and a network cable. Also, WiFi telephones are beginning to appear on the market that can use a WiFi hot spot to send and receive VoIP wireless data. Because a WiFi phone is a node on a wireless network, it can have an always-up connection to the Internet. Some expect WiFi phones to ultimately replace cell phones, which are discussed next. You'll learn more about VoIP in the next chapter.

A+ ESS
2.1
5.1

A+
220-602
2.1
5.1

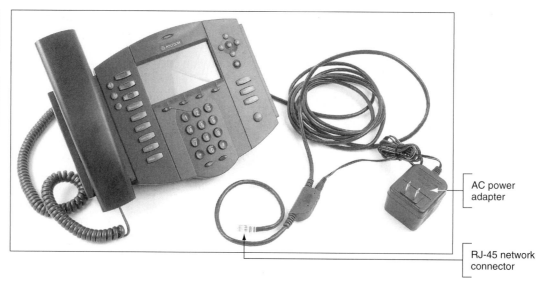

AC power
adapter

RJ-45 network
connector

**Figure 17-19**   This VoIP digital telephone connects to a local network and on to the Internet by way
of a network cable

## CELLULAR WAN

A **cellular network** or **cellular WAN** is a wireless network that is designed to cover a wide area
and is made up of numerous cells, which are sometimes called radio cells (see Figure 17-20).
A cell is a geographical area that offers connectivity and is created by a fixed transceiver and
antenna, also called a **base station**. Each cell can transmit using many different frequencies,
making it possible for many users to be connected at the same time. Also, because each cell is
limited to a small geographical area, one cell does not interfere with the transmissions of
another cell in the same cellular WAN. Access points for WiMAX or 802.11 wireless networks
are sometimes strategically positioned over a wide area to form a cellular WAN.

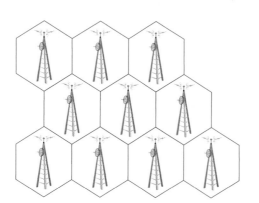

**Figure 17-20**   A cellular WAN is made up of many cells
that provide coverage over a wide area

The most common cellular WAN is
one used to provide mobile phone
service for cell phones, and one technological system to provide this service is
**GSM (Global System for Mobile
Communications)**. GSM is an open standard that uses digital communication of
data, and is accepted and used worldwide. Because of this widespread use, it
is possible for subscribers to use their
GSM mobile phones in over 200 countries around the world. And, because
GSM is digital, it can be used to transmit text messages, video files, and other
digital data. Besides GSM, two other
systems used for mobile phone cellular
WAN transmissions are **CDMA (Code Division Multiple Access)** and **TDMA (Time
Division Multiple Access)**. Most cell phone service providers in the United States use either
CDMA or TDMA for domestic calls. If your cell phone supports the technology, you might
be able to purchase a GSM plan for international calling at a higher rate.

Normally, charges for cell phone service are made according to connect time, similar to
PSTN calling, because cellular calls create a type of closed circuit or channel that is used for

the duration of the call. However, a new communication protocol used with GSM and TDMA is called **General Packet Radio Service (GPRS)**, which sends voice, text, or video data in packets similar to VoIP. Using GPRS, charges for a call are based on packets of data sent rather than connect time. Using GPRS, a cell phone could conceivably have an always-on connection to the Internet similar to a WiFi phone.

All wireless phone systems, including cellular, use **full-duplex** transmission, which means both persons in a conversation can talk or transmit at the same time. This is possible because the cell phones are using one frequency to transmit data and another to receive data. In contrast, walkie-talkies use **half-duplex** transmission, which means transmission works in only one direction at a time because the walkie-talkies are using the same frequency to both send and receive data. Full-duplex and half-duplex transmissions are illustrated in Figure 17-21.

(a) Mobile phone

(b) Walkie-talkie

**Figure 17-21** Full-duplex and half-duplex transmission

Cellular phones sometimes use Bluetooth wireless technology to make the short wireless hop between the phone and a wireless headset. In this case, the phone serves as the base station for the headset. Also, a cellular phone might use Bluetooth to communicate with a notebook computer, as shown in Figure 17-22. The notebook communicates with the nearby cellular phone, which communicates with the cellular WAN to provide Internet access for the notebook.

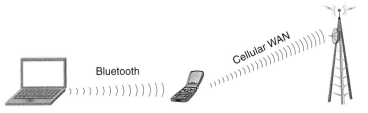

**Figure 17-22** Bluetooth can be used for short transmissions between personal devices such as a cell phone and notebook computer

A+ ESS
2.1
5.1

A+
220-602
2.1
5.1

## SATELLITE PHONE

An alternative to a cellular mobile phone is a satellite phone. A satellite phone communicates directly with satellites orbiting the earth at a low level, which is why a satellite phone is also called an LEO (low earth orbit) phone. The advantages of a satellite phone over a cellular phone are that there are fewer gaps in coverage and these phones can more likely be used around the world. One disadvantage of a satellite phone is that, because it must communicate with a satellite, its antenna must be longer than that used by cellular phones. Also, from personal experience, I can tell you that for best reception, you must be outdoors.

## CORDLESS PHONE

A cordless phone is a wireless telephone that sets in a cradle of a phone base station that connects to a regular house phone line. Cordless phones can be used only within a short range of the base station. They typically use one of these frequency ranges: 900 MHz, 2.4 GHz, or 5.8 GHz. One problem with cordless phones is that a cordless phone operating at 2.4 GHz might interfere with 802.11b/g wireless LANs.

## RADIO PHONE

Another type of wireless phone is a radio phone. Service for a radio phone is provided by the Mobile Telephone Service (MTS) that uses VHF (very high frequency) radio waves. This radio frequency (RF) range is also used by FM radio. Radio phones were once used as car phones, but are mostly outdated, having been replaced by cellular phones. MTS uses high-powered centralized radio towers, and to connect to a tower, a radio phone needs a large transmitter, which means that radio phones tend to be big and bulky. Another disadvantage is that there are a limited number of radio frequencies available for MTS, so not too many people can use these phones at the same time in a given geographical area. Radio phones might still be used in wilderness areas where it is too expensive to install cellular base stations for cellular phones.

## TOKEN RING AND FDDI

**Token Ring** is an older, almost totally outdated LAN technology developed by IBM that transmits data at 4 Mbps or 16 Mbps. Physically, a Token Ring network is arranged in a star topology because each node connects to a centralized device and not to other nodes in the network. However, a token actually travels in a ring on the network. The token is either free or busy, and a node must have the token to communicate. Because it is physically a star and logically a ring, it is sometimes called a **star ring topology**. The centralized device to which the network nodes connect is called a Controlled Access Unit (CAU), a Multistation Access Unit (MSAU or sometimes just MAU), or a Smart Multistation Access Unit (SMAU).

Each workstation contains a Token Ring LAN card (see Figure 17-23) that connects each workstation to an MSAU. Token Ring cables can be either UTP or STP cables that have two twisted pairs, for a total of four wires in the cable. Token Ring connectors can be RJ-45 connectors, but the connector pins are not the same as RJ-45 connectors used on Ethernet. Token Ring can also use another type of connector that has no "male" or "female" version, known as a **Universal Data Connector (UDC)** or an **IBM Data Connector (IDC)**. Because there is no "male" or "female" connector, any connector can connect to any other connector.

**Fiber Distributed Data Interface (FDDI**, pronounced *fiddy*) uses a token that travels in a ring like Token Ring. But with FDDI, data frames travel on the ring without the token, and multiple nodes can have data on the ring at the same time. Nodes on a FDDI network can be connected in a ring using a **ring topology**, meaning that each node is connected to two

**Figure 17-23**   Token Ring network card

other nodes, although most FDDI networks use hubs in a physical star topology. FDDI provides data transfer at 100 Mbps, which is much faster than Token Ring and a little faster than Fast Ethernet, which also runs at about 100 Mbps. It was once used as a network technology for a large LAN in a large company, but more commonly is used as a backbone network to connect several LANs in a large building. Figure 17-24 shows a FDDI network card.

**Figure 17-24**   FDDI network card

So far in the chapter, we've looked at all the different hardware devices and hardware technologies to build networks. Each hardware device on a network such as a NIC, switch, router, or Internet telephone uses a hardware protocol to communicate on the network. For most wired LANs, that protocol is Ethernet. However, in addition to the hardware protocol, there is a layer of network communication at the operating system level. The OS can use one of several communication protocols such as TCP/IP or AppleTalk. For example, a Windows network might use TCP/IP to communicate at the OS level, and the devices on the LAN (NICs and switches) might use Ethernet. The next section looks at the different OS networking protocols, how they work, and how to configure a computer to use them.

# WINDOWS ON A NETWORK

As a system of interlinked computers, a network needs both software and hardware to work. Software includes an operating system installed on each computer on the network, and perhaps an **NOS (network operating system)** such as Windows Server 2003 or Unix to control the entire network and its resources. If the network is small (fewer than 10 computers), it can be a **peer-to-peer network**, in which each computer on the network has the same authority as the other computers.

Recall from Chapter 11 that a Windows peer-to-peer network is called a workgroup. Larger networks use the **client/server** model, in which access to a network is controlled by an NOS using a centralized database. A **client** computer provides a user ID and password to a **server** that validates the data against the security database. In a Windows network, this server is called the domain controller, and the network model is called a domain.

Popular network operating systems are Windows 2003 Server, Novell NetWare, Open Enterprise Server, Unix, and Linux. Windows has client software built in for Windows and Novell NetWare servers. Alternately, for Novell NetWare, you can install Novell client software.

A network can have more than one workgroup or domain in operation, and some computers might not belong to any workgroup or domain. A computer joins a workgroup or domain in order to share resources with other computers and devices in the group or domain. Company policy controls how many workgroups or domains can exist within the company network. This number is based on user needs, security concerns, and administrative overhead required to manage the groups.

> **⊘ A+ Tip**
>
> The A+ Essentials exam expects you to understand the differences between a peer-to-peer network and a client/server network.

## FOUR SUITES OF PROTOCOLS

At the physical network level, Windows supports Ethernet, ATM, Token Ring, and other networking protocols. At the operating system level, Windows supports the four suites of protocols shown in Figure 17-25 and described in the following list. The figure also shows the different ways a computer or other device on the network can be addressed.

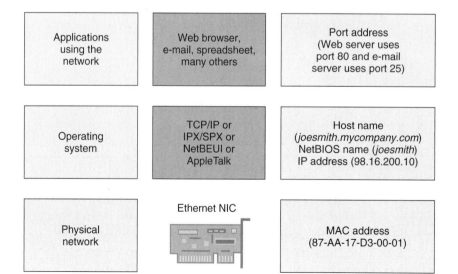

**Figure 17-25** An operating system can use more than one method to address a computer on the network, but at the network level, a MAC address is always used to address a device on the network

Use Figure 17-25 as a reference point throughout this section to understand the way the protocols and addresses relate on the network.

▲ **TCP/IP (Transmission Control Protocol/Internet Protocol)** is the protocol suite used on the Internet and so should be your choice if you want to connect your network to the Internet, with each workstation having Internet access. Novell NetWare, Linux, Unix, and Mac OS also support TCP/IP.

▲ **IPX/SPX (Internetwork Packet Exchange/Sequenced Packet Exchange)** is an NWLink protocol suite designed for use with the Novell NetWare operating system. IPX/SPX is similar to TCP/IP but is not supported on the Internet. **NWLink** is Microsoft's version of the IPX/SPX protocol suite used by Novell NetWare. When a Windows PC is a client on a Novell NetWare network, the Windows PC must be configured to use NWLink, which includes the IPX/SPX protocol.

▲ **NetBEUI (NetBIOS Extended User Interface,** pronounced *net-bouie*) is a proprietary Windows protocol suite used only by Windows computers. NetBEUI supports **NetBIOS (Network Basic Input/Output System)**, a protocol that applications use to communicate with each other. NetBEUI is faster than TCP/IP and easier to configure but does not support routing to other networks, and, therefore, is not supported on the Internet. It should be used only on an isolated network. Windows XP does not automatically install NetBEUI, because Microsoft considers NetBEUI and NetBIOS to both be legacy protocols.

▲ **AppleTalk** is a proprietary networking protocol suite for Macintosh computers by Apple Corporation.

To use one of these protocols on a network, the first step is to physically connect the computer to the network by installing the NIC in the computer and connecting the network cable to the switch, router, or other network device. (For wireless LANs, after installing the NIC, you put the computer within range of an access point.) After the drivers for the NIC are installed, the NIC is automatically associated with an OS networking protocol in a process called binding. **Binding** occurs when an operating system–level protocol such as TCP/IP associates itself with a lower-level hardware protocol such as Ethernet. When the two protocols are bound, communication continues between them until they are unbound, or released.

**A+ Tip**

The A+ Essentials exam expects you to be familiar with these networking protocols: TCP/IP, IPX/SPX, NWLink, and NetBIOS.

You can determine which protocols are installed in Windows by looking at the properties of a network connection. For example, in Windows XP you can right-click **My Network Places** and select **Properties** from the shortcut menu to open the Network Connections window, as shown on the left side of Figure 17-26. Then right-click the **Local Area Connection** icon and select **Properties** from the shortcut menu. The Local Area Connection Properties dialog box opens, as shown on the right side of the figure.

You can see that two of the three available protocols are bound to the NIC because they are checked. In this situation, the PC is using a TCP/IP network, but one network printer uses IPX/SPX and does not support TCP/IP. Because the PC uses that printer, it must have IPX/SPX installed. (A **network printer** is a printer that any user on the network can access using one of those methods: (1) through its own network card and connection to the network, (2) through a connection to a standalone print server, or (3) through a connection to a computer as a local printer, which is shared on the network.)

There is no problem with more than one operating system protocol operating on the network at the same time. Also, if you want to use a protocol and it is not listed, click **Install** in the Local Area Connection Properties window to select the protocol and install it.

A+ ESS
5.1

A+
220-602
5.1

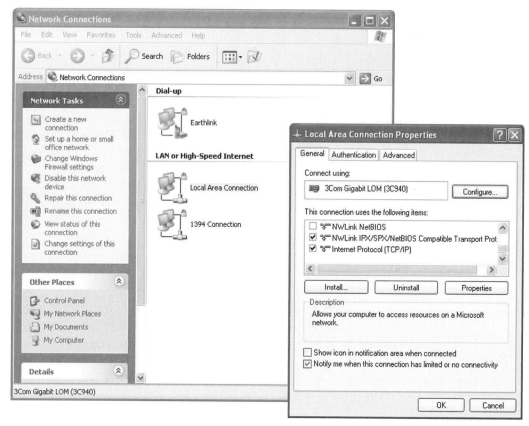

**Figure 17-26** Three Windows XP network protocols are installed and two protocols are bound to this network card

## ADDRESSING ON A NETWORK

Every device on a network has a unique address. Part of learning about a network is learning how a device (such as a computer or a printer) or a program (such as a Web server) is identified on the network. On a network, four methods are used to identify devices and programs:

▲ *Using a MAC address.* As you learned earlier, a MAC address is a unique, 48-bit address permanently embedded in a NIC and identifying a device on a LAN. The MAC address is used only by devices inside the local network, and is not used outside the LAN.

▲ *Using an IP address.* An **IP address** is a 32-bit address consisting of a series of four 8-bit numbers separated by periods. An IP address identifies a computer, printer, or other device on a TCP/IP network such as the Internet or an intranet. (An **intranet** is a private or corporate network that uses TCP/IP.) Because the largest possible 8-bit number is 255, each of the four numbers can be no larger than 255. An example of an IP address is 109.168.0.104. Consider a MAC address a local address and an IP address a long-distance address, as shown in Figure 17-27.

▲ *Using character-based names.* Character-based names include domain names, **host names,** and NetBIOS names used to identify a PC on a network with easy-to-remember letters rather than numbers. (Host names and NetBIOS names are often just called **computer names.**)

**A+ Tip**

The A+ Essentials exam expects you to know each of the methods of identifying devices and programs on a network.

▲ *Using a port address.* A port address is a number that one application uses to address another application installed on a remote computer on the network. Port addresses are covered in the next chapter.

17

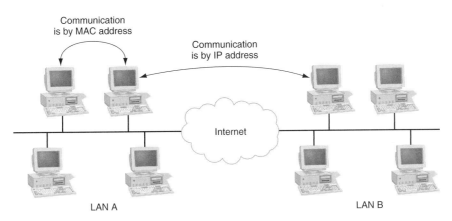

Figure 17-27 Computers on the same LAN use MAC addresses to communicate, but computers on different LANs use IP addresses to communicate over the Internet

# APPLYING|CONCEPTS   EXAMINING YOUR NETWORK CONFIGURATION

If your PC is connected to the Internet or any other TCP/IP network, you can use some Windows utilities to report how the network connection is configured. For Windows 2000/XP, to display the IP address and the MAC addresses of all installed NICs, in a command prompt window, use the command **ipconfig /all**. The screen shown in Figure 17-28 appears.

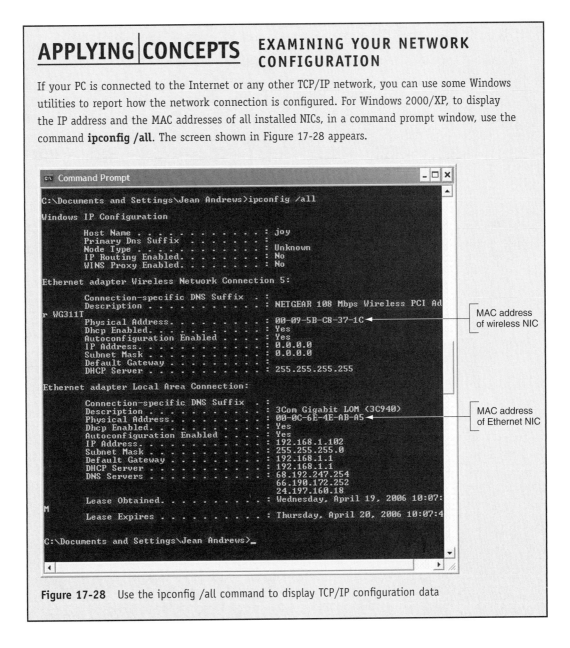

Figure 17-28 Use the ipconfig /all command to display TCP/IP configuration data

A+ ESS
5.1

A+
220-602
5.1

For Windows 9x/Me, use the Winipcfg utility instead of Ipconfig. Enter **winipcfg** in the Run dialog box and press **Enter**. The IP Configuration window opens (see Figure 17-29). Select the NIC in the drop-down list of network devices.

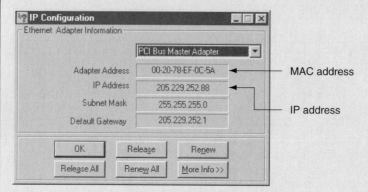

**Figure 17-29**    Use the Windows 9x/Me Winipcfg utility to display a PC's IP address and MAC address

When we use a browser to access a Web site on the Internet, it's interesting to know that we can use an IP address and port number in the place of a domain name. For example, you can access the Microsoft Web site by entering this domain name in your browser address box: *www.microsoft.com*. However, you can also use the IP address and port number instead of the domain name (see Figure 17-30). The IP address (207.46.20.30 in the browser address box) identifies the computer and the port number (80, which follows the IP address and is separated by a colon) identifies the application. The application, service, or program that is responding to requests made to port 80 on this computer is a Web server program that is serving up Web pages. An example of a Web server program is Internet Information Services (IIS) by Microsoft. Also note that if you enter only an IP address in a browser address box without a port number, port 80 is assumed.

**Figure 17-30**    A Web site can be accessed by its IP address and port number

Now let's turn our attention to the details of understanding how IP addresses and computer names are used on a network.

## IP ADDRESSES

All protocols of the TCP/IP suite identify a device on the Internet or an intranet by its IP address. An IP address is 32 bits long, made up of 4 bytes separated by periods, as in this address: 190.180.40.120. The largest possible 8-bit number is 11111111, which is equal to 255 in decimal, so the largest possible IP address in decimal is 255.255.255.255, which in binary is 11111111.11111111.11111111.11111111. Each of the four numbers separated by periods is called an **octet** (for 8 bits) and can be any number from 0 to 255, making a total of 4.3 billion potential IP addresses ($256 \times 256 \times 256 \times 256$). Because of the allocation scheme used to assign these addresses, not all of them are available for use.

The first part of an IP address identifies the network, and the last part identifies the host. It's important to understand how the bits of an IP address are used in order to understand how routing happens over interconnected networks such as the Internet, and how TCP/IP can locate an IP address anywhere on the globe. When data is routed over interconnected networks, the network portion of the IP address is used to locate the right network. After the data arrives at the local network, the host portion of the IP address is used to identify the one computer on the network that is to receive the data. Finally, the IP address of the host must be used to identify its MAC address so the data can travel on the host's LAN to that host. The next section explains this in detail.

## CLASSES OF IP ADDRESSES

When a business, college, or some other organization applies for IP addresses, a range of addresses appropriate to the number of hosts on the organization's networks is assigned. IP addresses that can be used by companies and individuals are divided into three classes: Class A, Class B, and Class C, based on the number of possible IP addresses in each network within each class. IP addresses are assigned to these classes according to the scheme outlined in Table 17-3.

| Class | Network Octets (Blanks in the IP Address Stand for Octets Used to Identify Hosts) | Total Number of Possible Networks or Licenses | Host Octets (Blanks in the IP Address Stand for Octets Used to Identify Networks) | Total Number of Possible IP Addresses in Each Network |
|---|---|---|---|---|
| A | 0.__.__.__ to 126.__.__.__ | 127 | __.0.0.1 to __.255.255.254 | 16 million |
| B | 128.0.__.__ to 191.255.__.__ | 16,000 | __.__.0.1 to __.__.255.254 | 65,000 |
| C | 192.0.0.__ to 223.255.255.__ | 2 million | __.__.__.1 to __.__.__.254 | 254 |

**Table 17-3** Classes of IP addresses

You can determine the class of an IP address and the size or type of company to which an address is licensed by looking at the address. More important, you also can determine what portion of an IP address is dedicated to identifying the network and what portion is used to identify the host on that network.

A+ ESS
5.1

A+
220-602
5.1

Figure 17-31 shows how each class of IP address is divided into the network and host portions. A Class A address uses the first (leftmost) octet for the network address and the remaining octets for host addresses. A Class A license assigns a single number that is used in the first octet of the address, which is the network address. The remaining three octets of the IP address can be used for host addresses that uniquely identify each host on this network. The first octet of a Class A license is a number between 0 and 126. For example, if a company is assigned 87 as its Class A network address, then 87 is used as the first octet for every host on this one network. Examples of IP addresses for hosts on this network are 87.0.0.1, 87.0.0.2, and 87.0.0.3. (The last octet does not use 0 or 255 as a value, so 87.0.0.0 is not valid.) In the example address 87.0.0.1, the 87 is the network portion of the IP address, and 0.0.1 is the host portion. Because three octets can be used for Class A host addresses, one Class A license can have approximately $256 \times 256 \times 254$ host addresses, or about 16 million IP addresses. Only very large corporations with heavy communication needs can get Class A licenses.

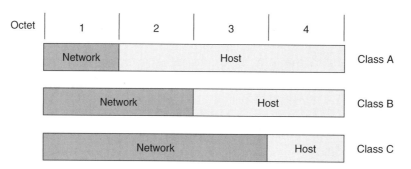

**Figure 17-31**  The network portion and host portion for each class of IP addresses

A Class B address uses the first two octets for the network portion and the last two for the host portion. A Class B license assigns a number for each of the two leftmost octets, leaving the third and fourth octets for host addresses. How many host addresses are there in one Class B license? The number of possible values for two octets is about $256 \times 254$, or about 65,000 host addresses in a single Class B license. (Some IP addresses are reserved, so these numbers are approximations.) The first octet of a Class B license is a number between 128 and 191, which gives about 63 different values for a Class B first octet. The second number can be between 0 and 255, so there are approximately $63 \times 256$, or about 16,000, Class B networks. For example, suppose a company is assigned 135.18 as the network address for its Class B license. The first two octets for all hosts on this network are 135.18, and the company uses the last two octets for host addresses. Examples of IP addresses on this company's Class B network are 135.18.0.1, 135.18.0.2, and 135.18.0.3. In the first example listed, 135.18 is the network portion of the IP address, and 0.1 is the host portion.

A Class C license assigns three octets as the network address. With only one octet used for the host addresses, there can be only 254 host addresses on a Class C network. The first number of a Class C license is between 192 and 223. For example, if a company is assigned a Class C license for its network with a network address of 200.80.15, some IP addresses on the network would be 200.80.15.1, 200.80.15.2, and 200.80.15.3.

Class D and Class E IP addresses are not available for general use. Class D addresses begin with octets 224 through 239 and are used for **multicasting**, in which one host sends messages to multiple hosts, such as when the host transmits a video conference over the Internet. Class E addresses begin with 240 through 254 and are reserved for research.

## SUBNET MASK

A **subnet mask** is a group of four dotted decimal numbers that tells TCP/IP if a computer's IP address is on the same or a different network than another computer. For example, the following are three subnet masks:

▲ *11111111.11111111.11111111.00000000, which can be written as 255.255.255.0.* Using this subnet mask, for computers to be in the same network, the first three octets of their IP addresses must match. For example, if the IP address of a computer is 192.40.18.10, then another IP address of 192.40.18.19 will be in the network, but 192.40.101.12 will not be in the network, because the first three octets don't match. When locating this last IP address, a router managing network traffic knows to expand the search for this IP address beyond the limits of the immediate Class C network.

▲ *11111111.11111111.00000000.00000000, which can be written as 255.255.0.0.* IP addresses that match the first two octets will be in the same Class B network that uses this subnet mask.

▲ *11111111.00000000.00000000.00000000, which can be written as 255.0.0.0.* IP addresses that match the first octet will be in the same Class A network that uses this subnet mask.

Subnet masks that use either all ones or all zeroes in an octet are called **classful subnet masks**. The three subnet masks listed above are classful subnet masks. A **classless subnet mask** can have a mix of zeroes and ones in one octet such as 11111111.11111111.11110000.00000000, which can be written as 255.255.240.0. These types of **classless subnet masks** are used to segment large corporate networks into subnetworks or subnets using a system called Classless Interdomain Routing (CIDR).

For example, suppose a computer in a subnet is assigned the subnet mask of 255.255.240.0 and an IP address of 15.50.212.59. When it wants to communicate with a computer assigned IP address 15.50.235.80, in order to know if these two computers are in the same subnet, a router will determine if the first two octets match and then compares the binary values of the third octet, like this:

```
212 = 11010100

235 = 11101011
```

To be in the same subnet, the first four bits must match, which they don't. Therefore, these two computers are not in the same subnet. However, an IP address that is in the same subnet as 15.50.212.59 is 15.50.220.100, because the first two octets match and the first four bits of the third octet match (comparing 11010100 to 11011100).

Sometimes using CIDR notation, an IP address and subnet mask are written using a shorthand notation like this: 15.50.212.59/20, where the /20 means that the subnet mask is written as 20 ones followed by enough zeroes to complete the full 32 bits.

>  **A+ Tip**
>
> The A+ Essentials exam expects you to be familiar with a classful subnet mask.

## DIFFERENT WAYS OF ASSIGNING IP ADDRESSES

When a small company is assigned a Class C license, it obtains 254 IP addresses for its use. If it has only a few hosts (for example, fewer than 25 on a network), many IP addresses go unused, which is one reason there is a shortage of IP addresses. But suppose that the company grew, now has 300 workstations on the network, and is running out of IP addresses.

There are two approaches to solving this problem: Use private IP addresses or use dynamic IP addressing. Many companies combine both methods. An explanation of each of these solutions follows. Then we'll look at how Network Address Translation is used so that computers assigned private IP addresses can still use the Internet.

### Public, Private, and Reserved IP Addresses

When a company applies for a Class A, B, or C license, it is assigned a group of IP addresses that are different from all other IP addresses and are available for use on the Internet. The IP addresses available to the Internet are called **public IP addresses.**

One thing to consider, however, is that not all of a company's workstations need to have Internet access, even though they might be on the network. So, although each workstation might need an IP address to be part of the TCP/IP network, those not connected to the Internet don't need addresses that are unique and available to the Internet; these workstations can use private IP addresses. **Private IP addresses** are IP addresses used on private intranets that are isolated from the Internet. Because the hosts are isolated from the Internet, no conflicts arise.

In fact, a small company most likely will not apply for a license of public IP addresses at all, but instead rely solely on private IP addresses for its internal network. A company using TCP/IP can make up its own private IP addresses to use on its intranet. IEEE recommends that the following IP addresses be used for private networks:

- ◢ 10.0.0.0 through 10.255.255.255
- ◢ 172.16.0.0 through 172.31.255.255
- ◢ 192.168.0.0 through 192.168.255.255

> **Notes**
>
> IEEE, a nonprofit organization, is responsible for many Internet standards. Standards are proposed to the networking community in the form of an RFC (Request for Comment). RFC 1918 outlines recommendations for private IP addresses. To view an RFC, visit the Web site *www.rfc-editor.org.*

When assigning isolated IP addresses, also keep in mind that a few IP addresses are reserved for special use by TCP/IP and should not be assigned to a device on a network. Table 17-4 lists these reserved IP addresses.

| IP Address | How It Is Used |
|---|---|
| 255.255.255.255 | Broadcast messages |
| 0.0.0.0 | Currently unassigned IP address |
| 127.0.0.1 | Indicates your own workstation |

**Table 17-4** Reserved IP addresses

All IP addresses on a network must be unique for that network. (Figure 17-32 shows the Windows XP error that appears when two computers on the network have been assigned the same IP address.) A network administrator might assign an IP address to a standalone computer (for example, if someone is testing networking software on a PC that is not connected to the network). As long as the network is a private network, the administrator can assign any IP address, although a good administrator avoids using the reserved addresses.

A+ ESS
5.1

A+
220-602
5.1

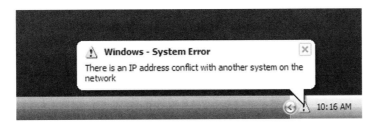

**Figure 17-32**  An error occurs when two networked computers use the same IP address

## Dynamically Assigned IP Addresses

If an administrator must configure each host on a network manually, assigning it a unique IP address, the task of going from PC to PC to make these assignments and keeping up with which address is assigned to which PC can be an administrative nightmare. The solution is to have a server automatically assign an IP address to a workstation each time it comes onto the network. Instead of permanently assigning an IP address (called **static IP addresses**) to a workstation, an IP address (called a **dynamic IP address**) is assigned for the current session only. When the session terminates, the IP address is returned to the list of available addresses.

In most networks, not all workstations are online at all times. Thus, with dynamic IP addressing, fewer IP addresses than the total number of workstations can satisfy the needs of the network. Also, you can use private IP addresses for the range of IP addresses that can be assigned to workstations. When a workstation has an IP address assigned to it, it is said that the workstation is leasing the IP address. **Internet service providers (ISPs)**, organizations through which individuals and businesses connect to the Internet, customarily use dynamic IP addressing for their individual subscribers and static IP addresses for their business subscribers.

The server that manages dynamically assigned IP addresses is called a **DHCP (Dynamic Host Configuration Protocol)** server. Workstations that work with DHCP servers are called DHCP clients. DHCP software resides on both the client and the server to manage the dynamic assignments of IP addresses. DHCP client software is built in to Windows 2000/XP and Windows 9x/Me.

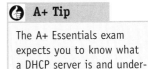

**A+ Tip**

The A+ Essentials exam expects you to know what a DHCP server is and understand how to use static and dynamic IP addressing.

When you configure a DHCP server, you specify the range of IP addresses that can be assigned to clients on the network. Figure 17-33 shows the configuration window for a DHCP server embedded as firmware on a router. (Routers are used to connect networks and are discussed in the next chapter.) To access the configuration window using a Web browser on the network, enter the IP address of the router in the Web browser address box, and then press **Enter**. In the figure, you can see that the router's IP address is 192.168.1.1, and the starting IP address to be assigned to clients is 192.168.1.100. Because the administrator specified that the server can have up to 50 clients, the range of IP addresses is, therefore, 192.168.1.100 to 192.168.1.149. Also shown in the figure is a list of currently assigned IP addresses and the MAC address of the computer that currently leases that IP address.

When a PC first connects to the network, it attempts to lease an address from the DHCP server. If the attempt fails, it uses an **Automatic Private IP Address (APIPA)** in the address range 169.254.x.x. How to configure a Windows workstation to use dynamic or static IP addressing is covered later in the chapter.

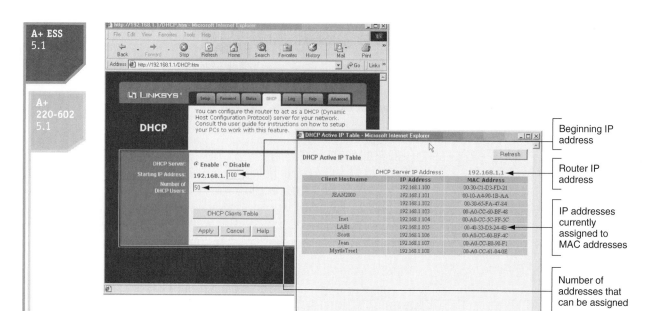

**Figure 17-33** A DHCP server has a range of IP addresses it can assign to clients on the network

## Network Address Translation

If hosts on a network using private IP addresses need to access the Internet, a problem arises because the private IP addresses are not allowed on the Internet. The solution is to use **NAT (Network Address Translation)**, which uses a single public IP address to access the Internet on behalf of all hosts on the network using other IP addresses. Using NAT, a networked computer trying to access the Internet must go through a server, router, or other device that substitutes its own IP address for that of the computer requesting the information. Because the device is standing in proxy for other hosts that want Internet access, it is called a **proxy server**. Figure 17-34 shows how a proxy server stands between the network and the Internet. This proxy server has two network cards installed. One card connects to the LAN, and the other connects to a cable modem and then to the ISP and the Internet.

> **Notes**
>
> Windows 2000/XP, Windows Me, and Windows 98 SE offer a NAT service called Microsoft Internet Connection Sharing (ICS). With it, two or more PCs on a home network can share the same IP address when accessing the Internet. Under ICS, one PC acts as the proxy server for other PCs on the home network.

Because a proxy server stands between a LAN and the Internet, it often does double duty as a firewall. Recall that a firewall is software or hardware that protects a network from illegal entry. Because networks are so often attacked by worms and hackers from the Internet, even a small LAN often has a router or other device between the LAN and the Internet that serves as a proxy server, DHCP server, and firewall. As a firewall, it filters out any unsolicited traffic coming from the Internet. Chapter 19 gives more information about firewalls.

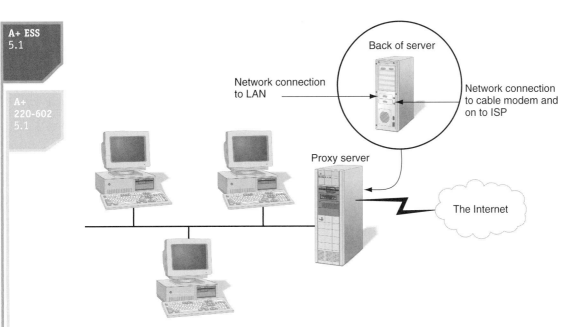

**Figure 17-34** A proxy server stands between a private network and the Internet

## HOST NAMES AND NETBIOS NAMES

Each computer on a TCP/IP network is assigned an IP address, but these numbers are hard to remember. Host names and NetBIOS names use characters rather than numbers to identify computers on a network and are easier to remember and use than IP addresses. In addition, a company might have a **domain name** that can be used to identify the network. An example of a domain name is *amazon.com*. Domain names are covered in the next chapter.

Before TCP/IP became such a popular protocol, Windows assumed that the protocol of choice would be NetBEUI and that all computers on a network would be assigned a NetBIOS name such as *joesmith* or *Workstation12*. These names usually are assigned when the operating system is installed. In contrast, TCP/IP identifies computers by IP addresses, but TCP/IP also allows a computer to be assigned a character-based host name such as *joesmith*. The host name can also have a domain name attached that identifies the network: *joesmith.mycompany.com*. On a TCP/IP network, the NetBIOS name or host name must be associated with an IP address before one computer can find another on the network. This process of associating a character-based name with an IP address is called **name resolution**.

Two name resolution services track relationships between character-based names and IP addresses: **DNS (Domain Name System**, also called **Domain Name Service)** and Microsoft **WINS (Windows Internet Naming Service)**. DNS tracks host names and WINS tracks NetBIOS names. A **DNS server** and a WINS server are computers that can find an IP address for another computer when only the host name and domain name are known, using either the DNS or WINS system. Windows networks sometimes use a combination of DNS and WINS; DNS is the more popular method.

Windows 98 assumes that a computer name is a NetBIOS name, which can have only 15 characters, but Windows 2000 and Windows XP assume that the computer name is a host name that uses the TCP/IP convention for host names. If the name is 15 characters or fewer, it works as a NetBIOS name or a TCP/IP name. If a host name is used, it can be up to 63 characters, including letters, numbers, and hyphens, as long as the computer is not part of a workgroup. If the computer is part of a workgroup, the host

> **🕹 A+ Tip**
>
> The A+ 220-602 exam expects you to be familiar with DNS and WINS services.

name should not exceed 15 characters. Microsoft now considers the default naming convention to be TCP/IP host names rather than NetBIOS names.

## HOW COMPUTERS FIND EACH OTHER ON A LAN

You need to understand how one computer finds another computer on a local network so that you can solve problems when this process of name resolution fails. When an application wants to communicate with another computer on the same TCP/IP LAN, the requesting computer knows the name of the remote computer. Before TCP/IP communication can happen between the two computers, the first computer must discover the IP address of the remote PC. For Windows 98 using NetBIOS names, the computer runs through the following checklist in the order shown to discover the IP address. (A Windows 2000/XP computer using just TCP/IP and not NetBEUI uses DNS to resolve the name, not WINS, and begins at Step 5. If NetBEUI is running on this Windows 2000/XP computer, it tries DNS first, beginning at Step 5, and then turns to NetBEUI in Steps 1 through 4 to resolve the name.)

1. The computer checks the NetBIOS name cache. This cache is information retained in memory from name resolutions made since the last reboot.

2. If the computer has the IP address of a WINS server, it queries the server. A WINS server on the network, such as Windows Server 2003, maintains a database of NetBIOS names and IP addresses.

3. The computer sends a broadcast message to all computers on the LAN asking for the IP address of the computer with the broadcasted NetBIOS name.

4. The computer checks a file named **LMHosts**, which is stored on the local computer. This file, called a host table, contains the NetBIOS names and associated IP addresses of computers on the LAN if someone has taken the time to manually make the entries in the file.

5. If the IP address is still not discovered, the computer assumes that the network is using DNS instead of WINS, so it checks the file named **Hosts** stored on the local computer. The Hosts file is another host table that contains host names and associated IP addresses, and is similar to the information kept by DNS servers.

6. If the computer has the IP address of a DNS server, it queries the DNS server.

Both the LMHosts and Hosts host tables are stored in the \Windows\System32\drivers\etc folder of a Windows 2000/XP computer or in the \Windows folder of a Windows 9x/Me computer. LMHosts serves as a local table of information similar to that maintained by a WINS server for NetBIOS names, and Hosts serves as a local table of information similar to that kept by a DNS server.

If you look in the \Windows\System32\drivers\etc folder of a Windows 2000/XP computer or in the \Windows folder of a Windows 9x/Me computer, you will see a sample of each file named LMHosts.SAM and Hosts.SAM, where the SAM stands for sample. Open each file with Notepad to examine it. Entries in a host table file beginning with the # symbol are comments and are not read by the name resolution process. The sample files contain many commented lines. You can add your entries to the bottom of the file without the # symbol. Then save the file in the same folder as the sample file, naming it Hosts or LMHosts with no file extension. An example of a Hosts file is shown in Figure 17-35. It tells this computer the IP address of the domain name *apache.test.com*. Recall that a domain name is a name of a network. In the example, apache is the host name, and the domain name is test.com. The **fully qualified domain name (FQDN)** is *apache.test.com*, which is often loosely called the domain name.

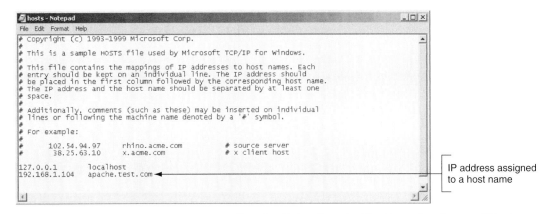

Figure 17-35 An entry in your client Hosts file will tell the client the IP address of an intranet Web site when no DNS service is running on the network

In this example, the computer named *apache.test.com* is used as a Web server for a private network. In order for people on the network to use this domain name, the Hosts file on each PC must have the entry shown in Figure 17-35, and the Web server must have the same IP address at all times. One way to accomplish this is to assign a static IP address to the server. Alternately, if your DHCP server supports this feature, you can configure it to assign the same IP address to your Web server each time if you tell the DHCP server your Web server's MAC address.

Now that you know about the operating system protocols used on a network and how various types of addresses identify computers and devices on the network, let's turn our attention to how to install and configure a NIC and how to configure the OS to access and use resources on a network.

## INSTALLING A NIC AND CONNECTING TO A NETWORK

To connect a PC to a network, you'll need a patch cable and a device for the PC to connect to, such as a switch or router. For most corporate environments, the switch is located in an electrical closet centrally located in the building, and patch cables connect the device to network wall jacks. In this situation, the patch cable connects from the PC to the wall jack.

Installed on the PC, you'll need a network card (NIC), an onboard network port, or a wireless network card or device. When selecting a NIC or wireless device, consider these things:

▲ Match the NIC to the type of bus on the motherboard you plan to use (PCI Express x4, PCI Express x1, or PCI). In most cases, you'll use a PCI slot.
▲ Match the NIC to the speed and type of network to which you are attaching. In most cases, you'll be using a 100BaseT or Gigabit Ethernet network with UTP CAT5e cables using RJ-45 connectors. If the switch uses Gigabit Ethernet, it will also support a 100BaseT NIC, although the network connection will run at the slower rate.
▲ For wireless connections, match the wireless NIC or other device to the type of network technology used by the access point you plan to use. In most cases, that will be 802.11g/b.

**Video**

Setting up a Network with Crossover Cables

A+ ESS
5.2

A+
220-602
5.2
5.3

Installing a network card and connecting the PC to a network involves three general steps: (1) Put the NIC in the PC, and install the NIC's drivers; (2) configure the NIC using Windows, so that it has the appropriate addresses on the network and the correct network protocols; and (3) test the NIC to verify that the PC can access resources on the network. This section discusses these steps to install a wired NIC using Windows 2000/XP and Windows 9x/Me. It also discusses how to install a wireless NIC in a notebook.

## INSTALLING A NIC USING WINDOWS 2000/XP

To install a NIC using Windows 2000/XP, do the following:

> **⊕ A+ Tip**
>
> The A+ Essentials exam expects you to know how to configure a Windows 2000/XP network connection.

1. Read the instructions that come bundled with the NIC. Should you install the NIC first or the drivers first? In these steps, we are installing the NIC first, but always follow specific instructions of the manufacturer.

2. Physically install the network card in the PC.

3. Turn on the PC. The Found New Hardware Wizard launches to begin the process of loading the necessary drivers to use the new device. It is better to use the manufacturer's drivers, not the Windows drivers. If given the opportunity to choose between Windows drivers and the manufacturer drivers on CD, choose the manufacturer drivers. If Windows completes the installation using its own drivers without giving you the opportunity to install the manufacturer's drivers, after the NIC is installed, you can use Device Manager to update the drivers using the manufacturer's drivers.

4. After the Windows desktop loads, verify that the drivers installed successfully. Open **Device Manager**, right-click the card from the list of devices, and click **Properties**. The card's Properties dialog box opens (see Figure 17-36). Look for any conflicts or other errors reported by Device Manager on the General tab and the Resources tab of this dialog box.

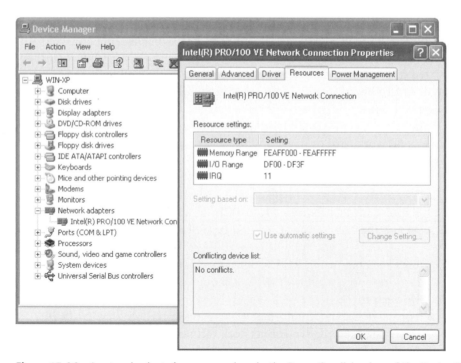

**Figure 17-36**    A network adapter's resources show in the Properties dialog box of the Device Manager window

5. If errors are reported or you want to replace Windows drivers with the manufacturer's drivers, click the **Driver** tab and then click **Update Driver**. Follow the instructions onscreen to use the network card manufacturer's drivers. You'll find other troubleshooting tips for installing NICs later in this chapter.

**Video**
Setting up a Network with Hub and Patch Cables

6. Connect a network patch cable to the NIC port and to the network switch or a wall jack connected to a switch. You are now ready to configure the NIC to access the network.

---

## APPLYING | CONCEPTS

Incidentally, there are three ways to access the network adapter Properties dialog box:

◢ As described earlier, open **Device Manager**, right-click the network adapter, and select **Properties** from the shortcut menu.

◢ From the Control Panel, launch the Windows XP **Network Connections** applet or the Windows 2000 **Network and Dial-up Connections** applet. Right-click the **Local Area Connection** icon and select **Properties** from the shortcut menu. Click **Configure**.

◢ Right-click **My Network Places** and select **Properties** from the shortcut menu. The Windows XP Network Connections applet or Windows 2000 Network and Dial-up Connections applet launches. Right-click the **Local Area Connection** icon and select **Properties** from the shortcut menu. Click **Configure**.

---

## CONFIGURING WINDOWS 2000/XP TO USE A NETWORK

The first step to configure Windows 2000/XP to use a network is to give the computer a name. Remember that if you plan to use NetBEUI as a networking protocol instead of TCP/IP, limit the computer name to 15 characters. For Windows 2000/XP, the protocol is TCP/IP by default. Follow these directions to name a computer:

1. Right-click **My Computer** and select **Properties** from the shortcut menu. The System Properties dialog box opens.

2. For Windows XP, click the **Computer Name** tab, then click the **Change** button. The Computer Name Changes dialog box opens (see Figure 17-37). For Windows 2000, click the **Network Identification** tab, and then click the **Properties** button. The Identification Changes window opens.

3. Enter the Computer name (**win-xp** in the example shown in Figure 17-37). Each computer name must be unique within a workgroup or domain.

4. If the computer is connecting to a workgroup, select **Workgroup** and enter the name of the workgroup (**GOLDEN** in this example). Recall that a workgroup is a group of computers on a network that shares files, folders, and printers. All users in the workgroup must have the same workgroup name entered in this window. If the PC is to join a domain (a network where logging on is controlled by a server), select **Domain** enter the name of the domain here, such as *mycompany.com*. When configuring a PC on a network, always follow the specific directions of the network administrator responsible for the network.

A+ ESS
5.2

A+
220-602
5.2
5.3

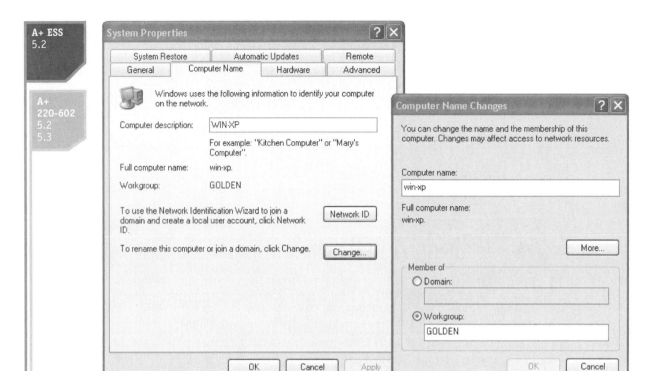

**Figure 17-37**    Windows XP uses the Computer Name Changes dialog box to assign a host name to a computer on a network

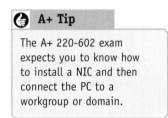

**A+ Tip**

The A+ 220-602 exam expects you to know how to install a NIC and then connect the PC to a workgroup or domain.

5. Click **OK** to exit the Windows XP Computer Name Changes dialog box or the Windows 2000 Identification Changes window, and click **OK** to exit the System Properties dialog box. You will be asked to reboot the computer for changes to take effect.

6. After rebooting a Windows XP system, click **Start, My Network Places,** and then click **View workgroup computers** to view this computer and others on the network. On the Windows 2000 desktop, open **My Network Places**, and double-click **Computers Near Me.** Figure 17-38 shows an example of My Network Places.

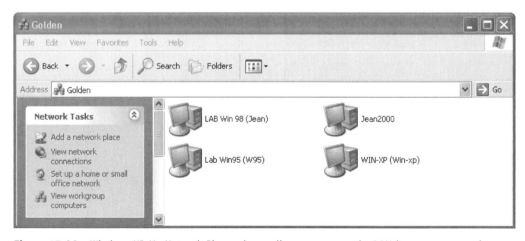

**Figure 17-38**    Windows XP My Network Places shows all computers on the LAN in a common workgroup

A+ ESS
5.2

A+
220-602
5.2
5.3

# CONFIGURING TCP/IP USING WINDOWS 2000/XP

When a network card is installed in Windows 2000/XP, TCP/IP is installed by default. However, if TCP/IP has been uninstalled or gives you problems, you can install it again.

**Notes**

My Network Places for Windows 2000/XP and Network Neighborhood for Windows 9x/Me can be viewed on the desktop and in Windows Explorer. By default, Windows XP puts My Network Places only in Windows Explorer, Windows 2000 puts My Network Places in both places, and Windows 98 puts Network Neighborhood in both places.

Also, Windows makes some assumptions about how TCP/IP is configured, and these settings might not be appropriate for your network. This section addresses all these concerns.

Before you configure TCP/IP, you might need to ask the network administrator the following questions:

1. Will the PC use dynamic or static IP addressing?

2. If static IP addressing is used, what are the IP address, subnet mask, and default gateway for this computer?

3. Do you use DNS? If so, what are the IP addresses of your DNS servers?

4. Is a proxy server used to connect to other networks (including the Internet)? If so, what is the IP address of the proxy server?

In dynamic addressing, the computer asks a DHCP server for its IP address each time it connects to the network. The server also gives the PC its subnet mask and default gateway, so that the computer knows how to communicate with other hosts that are not on its own network. A **gateway** is a computer or other device that allows a computer on one network to communicate with a computer on another network. A **default gateway** is the gateway a computer uses to access another network if it does not have a better option.

**A+ Tip**

The A+ 220-602 exam expects you to be familiar with a gateway, subnet mask, and static and dynamic (or automatic) address assignments.

Most likely, you will be using dynamic IP addressing, and you will obtain the DNS server address automatically. The DHCP server might also act as the proxy server so that computers inside the network can make connections to computers outside the network using the proxy server's public IP address.

To set the TCP/IP properties for a connection, follow these steps:

1. For Windows XP, open the **Network Connections** applet, and for Windows 2000, open the **Network and Dial-up Connections** applet. Right-click the **Local Area Connection** icon, and then select **Properties** from the shortcut menu. See Figure 17-39.

2. Select **Internet Protocol (TCP/IP)** from the list of installed components, and then click the **Properties** button. The Internet Protocol (TCP/IP) Properties dialog box opens, which is also shown in Figure 17-39.

3. For dynamic IP addressing, select **Obtain an IP address automatically**. (This is the most likely choice.) For static IP addressing, select **Use the following IP address**, and enter the IP address, subnet mask, and default gateway.

4. To disable DNS until the DHCP server gives the computer the DNS server address, select **Obtain DNS server address automatically**. (This is the most likely choice.)

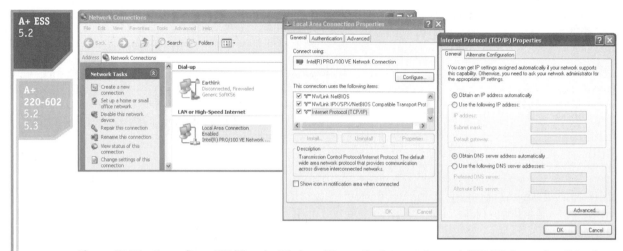

**Figure 17-39**  To configure TCP/IP under Windows XP, use the Internet Protocol (TCP/IP) Properties dialog box

If you have the IP addresses of the DNS servers, click **Use the following DNS server addresses**, and enter the IP addresses. Click **OK** twice to close both windows.

5. Open **My Network Places** and verify that your computer and other computers on the network are visible. If you don't see other computers on the network, reboot the PC.

## CONFIGURING THE NWLINK AND NETBEUI PROTOCOLS

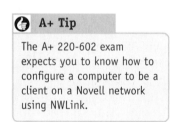

**A+ Tip**

The A+ 220-602 exam expects you to know how to configure a computer to be a client on a Novell network using NWLink.

Instead of or in addition to TCP/IP, a computer might use the NWLink or NetBEUI protocol. These protocols can be used to communicate on a network, but not over the Internet, and a computer can use a combination of TCP/IP, NWLink, and NetBEUI.

A Novell network can use TCP/IP or IPX/SPX. If the network is using IPX/SPX, each Windows computer on the network must be configured to use the NWLink protocol. Do the following to install and use NWLink:

1. NWLink is not normally installed. To install it, right-click the **Local Area Connection** icon in the Network Connections window and select **Properties**. The properties dialog box opens, which lists the installed protocols (refer back to Figure 17-39). If NWLink is not listed, click **Install**. The Select Network Component Type dialog box opens, as shown in Figure 17-40. Select **Protocol** and click **Add**.

2. In the dialog box that opens, also shown in Figure 17-40, select **NWLink IPX/SPX/NetBIOS Compatible Transport Protocol** and click **OK**.

3. You should now see NWLink listed as an installed protocol in the Local Area Connection Properties dialog box (see the left side of Figure 17-41). Make sure that when the NIC used for your network connection is displayed near the top of the properties dialog box, the NWLink IPX/SPX/NetBIOS Compatible Transport Protocol is checked and, therefore, bound to the selected NIC.

4. Check for network connectivity by opening My Network Places and browsing the network. If you have problems with the connection, open the **Local Area Connection Properties** dialog box (see Figure 17-41), select the **NWLink** protocol, and click **Properties**. On the resulting dialog box, shown on the right side of Figure 17-41, verify that **Auto Detect** is selected so that NWLink is able to automatically detect the type of hardware network technology that is present (most likely Ethernet).

A+ ESS
5.2

A+
220-602
5.2
5.3

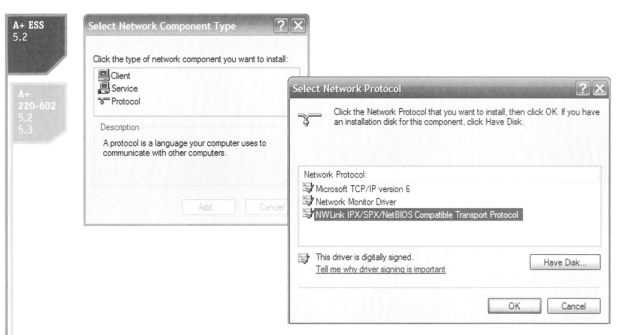

**Figure 17-40** Installing network components

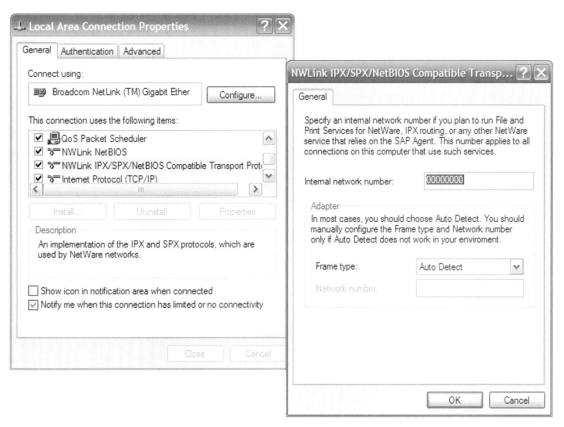

**Figure 17-41** NWLink protocol is installed and bound to the NIC

NetBEUI is used to support legacy applications that require a NetBIOS interface. To connect a Windows 2000 computer to a network using NetBEUI, use the Properties dialog box of the local area connection to install the NetBEUI Protocol, which

automatically binds itself to the NIC providing this local network connection. Then assign a name to the computer. Remember to limit the name to 15 characters. Windows XP does not normally support NetBEUI. However, you can manually install it using the Windows XP Setup CD. For directions, see the Microsoft Knowledge Base Article 301041 at *support.microsoft.com*.

## INSTALLING A NIC USING WINDOWS 9X/ME

After a NIC is physically installed and the PC is turned on, Windows 9x/Me automatically detects the card and guides you through the process of installing drivers. After the installation, verify that the card is installed with no errors by using Device Manager. In Device Manager, the network card should be listed under Network adapters. Right-click the card and select **Properties** to view the card's properties. Last, connect a network patch cable to the NIC port and to the network hub or a wall jack connected to a hub. You are now ready to configure the NIC to access the network.

> **Notes**
>
> The 2006 A+ exams do not cover Windows 9x/Me. However, this book covers Windows 9x/Me because technicians are sometimes called on to support this legacy OS and, at the time this book went to print, the 2003 A+ exams were still live.

### ASSIGNING A COMPUTER NAME

To assign a name to a Windows 9x/Me computer, follow these directions:

1. Access the **Control Panel** and double-click the **Network** icon.

2. Click the **Identification** tab (see Figure 17-42).

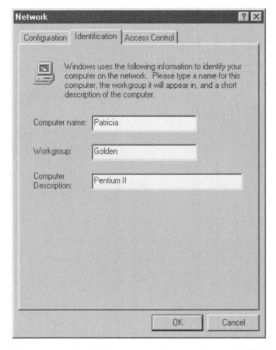

**Figure 17-42** Each computer in a workgroup in Windows 98 must be assigned a name that other users on the network will see in their Network Neighborhood window

3. Enter the computer name (**Patricia** in this example). Enter the name of the workgroup (**Golden** in this example). Each computer name must be unique within the workgroup.

4. Click **OK** to exit the window. You will be asked to reboot the system.

5. After you have rebooted, open **Network Neighborhood** on the Windows desktop. You should be able to see this computer and others on the network. Figure 17-43 shows an example of Network Neighborhood. If you cannot see other computers, you might have to install and configure TCP/IP, as described next.

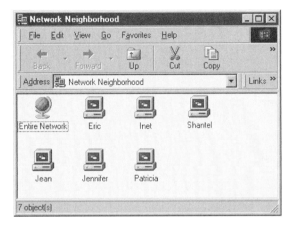

**Figure 17-43** Windows 98 Network Neighborhood shows all computers on the LAN in a common workgroup

## INSTALLING AND CONFIGURING TCP/IP USING WINDOWS 98

If TCP/IP is not already installed, you must install it. For Windows 98, do the following:

1. Access the **Control Panel** and double-click the **Network** icon. The Network window opens.

2. Click **Add** to display the Select Network Component Type window, as shown in Figure 17-44.

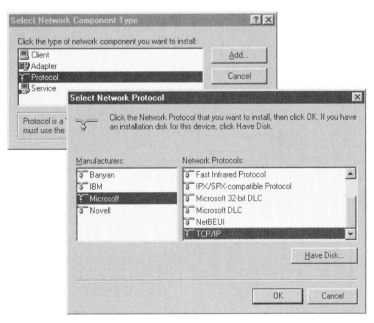

**Figure 17-44** To install TCP/IP in Windows 98, use the Select Network Component Type window

3. Select **Protocol** and click **Add**. The Select Network Protocol window opens. Select **Microsoft** on the left and **TCP/IP** on the right (see Figure 17-44). Click **OK**. The system asks for the Microsoft Windows 98 CD and requests that you reboot the system.

4. When you return to the Network window, notice that TCP/IP is automatically bound to any network cards or modems that it finds installed.

The next step is to configure TCP/IP. Most likely, you will be using dynamic IP addressing, and the DNS service is initially disabled (later the DHCP server will tell the PC to enable it). In Windows 98, do the following to configure TCP/IP that has been bound to a NIC to communicate over a local network:

1. In the Network window, select the item where TCP/IP is bound to the NIC. (On the left side of Figure 17-45, that item is TCP/IP->NETGEAR FA311 Fast Ethernet PCI Adapter.) Then, click **Properties**. The TCP/IP Properties dialog box opens, as shown on the right side of the figure.

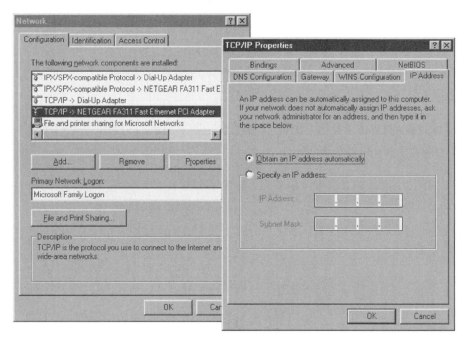

**Figure 17-45**    To configure TCP/IP in Windows 98, select the binding and click Properties to view the TCP/IP Properties dialog box

2. If static IP addressing is used, click **Specify an IP address**, and then enter the IP address and subnet mask supplied by your administrator. If dynamic IP addressing is used (as is usually the case), click **Obtain an IP address automatically**.

3. Click the **DNS Configuration** tab and choose to enable or disable DNS (see Figure 17-46). If you enable DNS, enter the IP addresses of your DNS servers. If your network administrator gave you other specific values for the TCP/IP configuration, you will find the tabs for these settings on this window. But in most cases, the above steps will work for you to configure TCP/IP.

4. When finished, click **OK** to exit the Properties dialog box, and then click **OK** to exit the Network window.

5. On the desktop, verify that you can see your computer and others on the network in Network Neighborhood. If you don't see others on the network, reboot the PC.

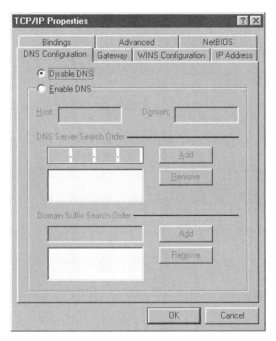

**Figure 17-46** Configure DNS service under TCP/IP for Windows 98

A+ ESS
2.1
3.2
5.2
6.1

A+
220-602
2.3
5.2
6.2
6.3

# INSTALLING A WIRELESS ADAPTER IN A NOTEBOOK

For a notebook computer, a wireless adapter will use a USB port or a PC Card slot. Most new adapters use the USB port, such as the wireless adapter shown in Figure 17-47. The adapter will come with a setup CD and some documentation and maybe an accessory or two.

**Notes**

To use NetBEUI on a Windows 9x/Me network, first verify that NetBEUI is installed or install it as you do TCP/IP. It should automatically bind itself to any network adapters installed. NetBEUI needs no other configuration.

Cradle and extension cable

Drivers and manual on CD

Wireless adapter

**Figure 17-47** This 802.11g wireless adapter by Linksys uses a USB port to connect to a notebook or desktop computer

A+ ESS
2.1
3.2
5.2
6.1

A+
220-602
2.3
5.2
6.2
6.3

Do the following to install the adapter:

1. Read the installation directions that come with the wireless adapter to find out if you install the software first or the adapter first. For the Linksys wireless adapter used in this example, the instructions clearly say to first install the software (see Figure 17-48).

**Figure 17-48**    This label makes it clear you need to install the software before installing the wireless adapter

2. Insert the CD in the CD drive. The opening screen for this adapter is shown in Figure 17-49. Click **Click Here to Start** and follow the directions onscreen to install the device drivers and the utility to configure the wireless connection.

**Figure 17-49**    Install the wireless adapter software

A+ ESS
2.1
3.2
5.2
6.1

A+
220-602
2.3
5.2
6.2
6.3

3. Next, plug the wireless adapter into a USB port. See Figure 17-50. The Found New Hardware bubble appears. See Figure 17-51. Click the bubble to launch the Found New Hardware Wizard. Follow the wizard to install the device.

**Figure 17-50** Plug the wireless USB adapter into the USB port

**Figure 17-51** Windows XP recognizes the presence of a new USB device

When a new device is being installed, Windows might recognize that the drivers were not digitally signed by Microsoft. If this is the case, it displays a dialog box similar to that in Figure 17-52 (for a Netgear wireless adapter). Now you have a decision to make. You can stop the installation and go to the manufacturer's Web site to try to find approved drivers, or you can continue with the installation. For most devices, it is safe to continue the installation using unsigned drivers. To do that, click **Continue Anyway**.

At another point in the installation, the wizard might ask if you want to disable the Windows XP Configuration Manager, which means you are choosing to use the manufacturer's utility to configure the wireless adapter (see Figure 17-53). Unless you have a good reason to do otherwise, click **Yes** to choose to use the manufacturer's utility. This utility will most likely be easier to use and allow you to better manage the wireless NIC than would the Windows XP Network Connections window. (Later, if you change your mind about which utility to use, you might have to uninstall and reinstall the device.)

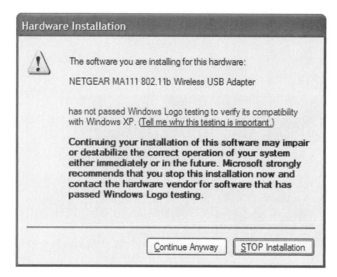

**Figure 17-52** Windows asks you for a decision about using unsigned drivers

**Figure 17-53** During the wireless NIC installation, you are asked which utility you want to use to configure the NIC

After the wireless adapter is installed, the next step is to configure it. Read the adapter's documentation to find out how to use the software. Most likely during installation an icon was added to your system tray. Double-click the icon to open the configuration window. Figure 17-54 shows the configuration window for the Linksys wireless adapter. Click **Manual Setup** to configure the adapter.

Each manufacturer has a different configuration utility, but all utilities should allow you to view information and manage the wireless device using these parameters. Information displayed about the current connection should include:

▲ *The MAC address of the access point device that the adapter is currently using.*
▲ *The current channel the connection is using.* 802.11b/g uses 14 different channels. The United States can use channels 1 through 11. The access point device is configured to use one of these 11 channels.

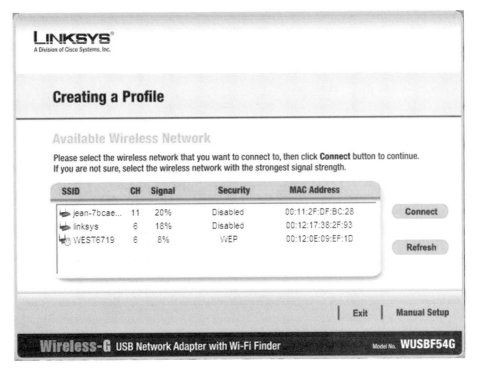

**Figure 17-54** Opening screen to configure a Linksys wireless adapter

▲ *Current transmission rate.* For 802.11b networks, the transmission rate (Tx rate) is about 11 Mbps. For 802.11g, expect about 54 Mbps.

▲ *Throughput, link quality,* and *signal strength.* These values indicate throughput rate and how strong the signal is. For most wireless devices, there is nothing for you to configure to get a connection. If the signal strength is poor, look for a way to scan for a new access point. For the utility shown in Figure 17-54, click the **Refresh** button. If the wireless signal strength is still not good enough, try moving your notebook around a bit.

Configuration changes you can make for a wireless device include:

▲ *Mode or network type.* The mode indicates whether the computer is to communicate through an access point (Infrastructure mode) or directly with another wireless device (Ad Hoc mode).

▲ *SSID.* The SSID (service set identifier) is set to ANY by default, which means the NIC is free to connect to any access point it finds. You can enter the name of an access point to specify that this NIC should connect only to a specific access point. If you don't know the name assigned to a particular access point, ask the network administrator responsible for managing the wireless network. For public hot spots, if you don't know the SSID, try "Hotspot". For some public hot spots, the access point is hidden so you must pay to know its name. Figure 17-55 shows the configuration screen for the Linksys adapter where you can choose the mode and enter an SSID.

▲ *Encryption settings.* Most wireless devices today support one or more standards for encrypted wireless transmission. When you try to connect to a secured network, if the connection is set for encryption, you'll be required to enter a secret passphrase or key to be used for the encryption. This passphrase is a word, such as "ourpassphrase," which generates a digital key used for encryption. Every computer user on the same wireless network must enter the same passphrase or key, which an administrator can change at any time.

A+ ESS
2.1
3.2
5.2
6.1

A+
220-602
2.3
5.2
6.2
6.3

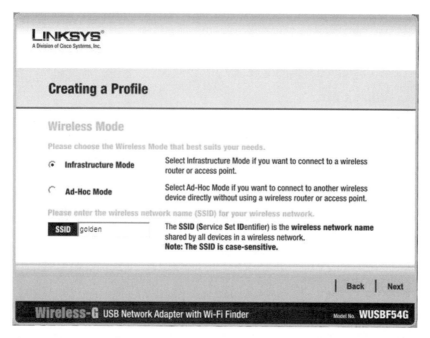

**Figure 17-55** Configure the wireless mode and the SSID of the access point

▲ *Tx rate.* For some adapters, you can specify the transmission rate or leave it at fully automatic so that the adapter is free to use the best transmission rate possible.

▲ *TCP/IP configuration.* Some wireless configuration utilities provide a screen to configure the TCP/IP settings to static or dynamic IP addressing. If your utility does not do that, after you configure the adapter, you'll need to use the Network Connections window to verify the TCP/IP settings. Initially, they'll be set for dynamic IP configuration.

After you have made all configuration changes, you should immediately be able to use your browser. If you can't, then try rebooting the computer. Also, try moving the computer to a better hot spot and click the button to reconnect.

Here are the steps to connect to a public hot spot for a notebook computer that has embedded wireless ability and uses Windows XP network configuration:

1. Turn on your wireless device. For one notebook, that's done by a switch on the keyboard (see Figure 17-56).

**Figure 17-56** Turn on the wireless switch on your notebook

A+ ESS
2.1
3.2
5.2
6.1

A+
220-602
2.3
5.2
6.2
6.3

**2.** Right-click **My Network Places** and select **Properties**. The Network Connections window opens. Right-click the **Wireless Network Connection** icon and select **View Available Wireless Networks** from the shortcut menu. The Wireless Network Connection window opens (see Figure 17-57).

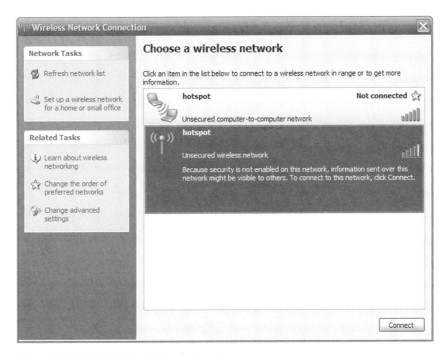

**Figure 17-57** Available wireless hot spots

**3.** Select an unsecured network from those listed and click **Connect**. (Incidentally, if you select a secured network that is protected with an encryption key, to continue, you must enter the key in a dialog box shown in Figure 17-58.)

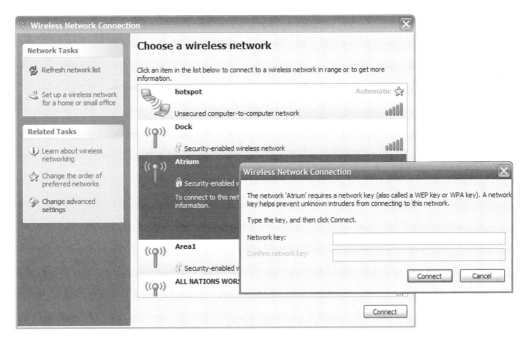

**Figure 17-58** To use a secured wireless network, you must know the encryption key

4. Open your browser to test the connection. For some hot spots, a home page appears and you must enter a code or ticket number to proceed (see Figure 17-59).

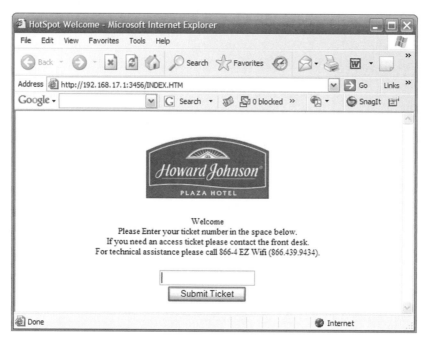

**Figure 17-59** This hot spot requires a ticket number or code to use the wireless network

5. You can see the status of the wireless connection by double-clicking the Wireless Network Connection icon in the Network Connections window or by double-clicking the wireless icon in the system tray. Either way, the status window shown in Figure 17-60 appears.

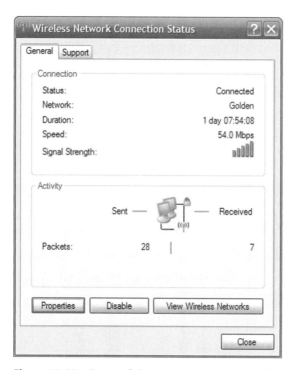

**Figure 17-60** Status of the current wireless connection

A+ ESS
2.1
3.2
5.2
6.1

A+
220-602
2.3
5.2
6.2
6.3

If you have problems connecting, do the following:

1. If you know the SSID of the hot spot, on the Wireless Network Connection window, click **Change advanced settings**. The Wireless Network Connection Properties dialog box opens. Click the **Wireless Networks** tab (see Figure 17-61).

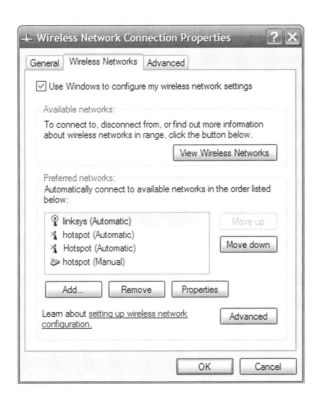

**Figure 17-61**   Manage wireless hot spots using the Wireless Network Connection Properties dialog box

2. Click **Add**. The Wireless network properties window opens (see Figure 17-62). Enter the SSID of the network and make sure that Network Authentication is set to **Open** and Data encryption is set to **Disabled**. Click **OK**. When a dialog box opens to warn you of the dangers of disabling encryption, click **Continue Anyway**. Click **OK** to close the Wireless Network Connection Properties dialog box.

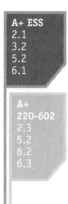

A+ ESS
2.1
3.2
5.2
6.1

A+
220-602
2.3
5.2
6.2
6.3

**Figure 17-62**    Enter the SSID of a hot spot to which you want to connect

3. In the Network Connections window, right-click the **Wireless Network Connection** icon and select **View Available Wireless Networks**. You should now be able to connect to the hot spot.

4. If you still can't connect, it is possible that a private and secured wireless access point has been configured for MAC address filtering in order to control which wireless adapters can use the access point. Check with the network administrator to determine if this is the case; if necessary, give the administrator the adapter's MAC address to be entered into a table of acceptable MAC addresses.

5. To know the MAC address of your wireless adapter, you can look on the back of the adapter itself (see Figure 17-63) or in the adapter documentation. Also, if the adapter is installed on your computer, you can use the command **ipconfig /all** in a command prompt window. By the way, if you're running Windows XP Professional, you can also display your MAC address using the Getmac command.

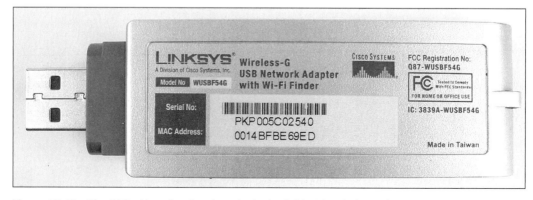

**Figure 17-63**    The MAC address is printed on the back of this USB wireless adapter

17

A+ ESS
2.1
3.2
5.2
6.1

A+
220-602
2.3
5.2
6.2
6.3

> **Notes**
>
> For a desktop computer, know that a wireless NIC uses an internal or external antenna. To install an NIC that uses an external antenna, remove the antenna from the NIC. Turn off the computer, unplug the power cord, open the case, and install the NIC. For an external antenna, screw the antenna on the NIC and raise it to an upright position (see Figure 17-64). Turn on the computer. The computer immediately detects the device and launches the Found New Hardware Wizard. The installation then proceeds the same way as for a wireless NIC installed in a notebook computer.

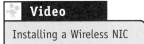

**Video**

Installing a Wireless NIC

**Figure 17-64**  Raise the antenna on a NIC to an upright position

## USING RESOURCES ON THE NETWORK

A+ ESS
3.1
4.1

A+
220-602
5.2

So far in the chapter, you have learned how networks are structured, how to install NICs, and how to set up Windows networking. Let's look next at how to use resources on a network after it's been set up. This section covers how to share folders, files, applications, and even entire hard drives. In Chapter 21, you will learn how to share printers on a network.

### SHARING FILES, FOLDERS, AND APPLICATIONS

If users on a LAN working on a common project need to share applications, files, or printers, then all these users must be assigned to the same workgroup or domain on the LAN. Recall that Windows 2000/XP makes shared resources available by way of My Network Places, and Windows 9x/Me uses Network Neighborhood. Open either applet to see the names of all computers on the network. Figure 17-65 shows My Network Places for Windows XP. Drill down to see shared files, folders, and printers in your workgroup. Using Network Neighborhood or My Network Places, you can copy files from one computer to another, use shared applications installed on one computer from another computer, and share printers.

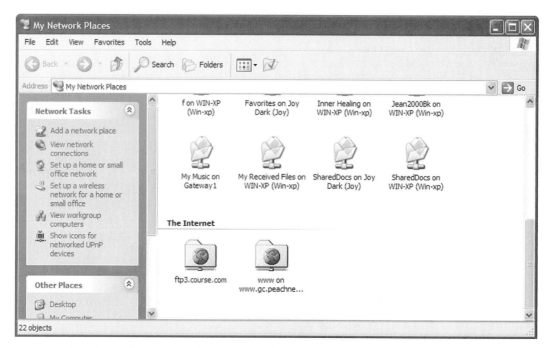

**Figure 17-65** View and access shared resources on the network using My Network Places in Windows XP

Workgroups can be effective when several people work on a common project. For example, if a group of people is building a Web site, sharing resources on the LAN is an effective method of passing Web pages around as they are built. Or one computer on the LAN can be designated as the file server. The user of this computer makes a portion of hard drive space available for the Web site files. All users have access to this one resource, and the Web site files are kept neatly in a single location. When using workgroups, each user is responsible for protecting shared resources by using password protection for read and write privileges to files and folders.

## HOW TO SHARE WINDOWS 2000/XP FILES, FOLDERS, AND APPLICATIONS

Using Windows 2000/XP, do the following to share files, folders, and applications with others on the network:

1. Two Windows components must be installed before you can share resources: Client for Microsoft Networks and File and Printer Sharing. Client for Microsoft Networks is the Windows component that allows you to use resources on the network made available by other computers, and File and Printer Sharing allows you to share resources on your computer with others. To verify these components are installed, open the **Network Connections** window, right-click the **Local Area Connection** icon, and select **Properties** from the shortcut menu. The Local Area Connection Properties dialog box opens. See Figure 17-66.

2. Verify **Client for Microsoft Networks** and **File and Printer Sharing for Microsoft Networks** are both checked. If you don't see these items in the list, click **Install** to install them. When you're done, close all windows.

17

A+ ESS
3.1
4.1

A+
220-602
5.2

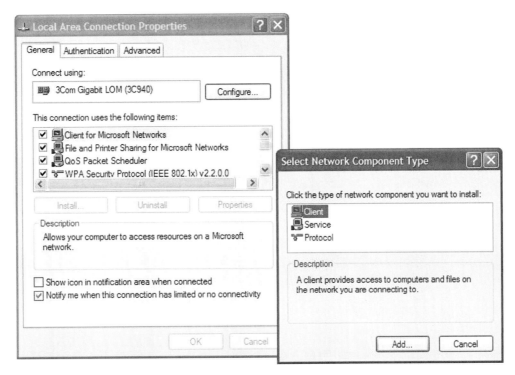

**Figure 17-66** Use the Network Connections applet to install a network client, service, or protocol using Windows XP

3. Using Windows Explorer, select the folder or file you want to share. In this example, we're using a folder named **C:\data**. Right-click the folder name. Select **Sharing and Security** (see Figure 17-67). The Data Properties dialog box opens, as shown in Figure 17-68.

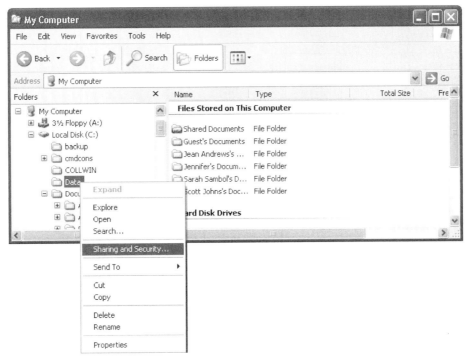

**Figure 17-67** Use Windows Explorer to share a file or folder with others on a network

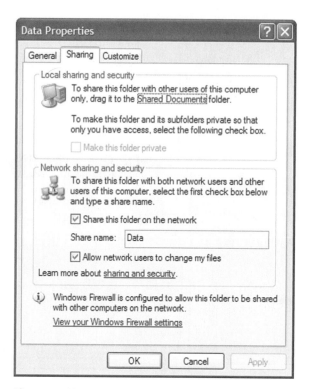

**Figure 17-68** A user on a network can share a folder with others on the network

4. Check **Share this folder on the network**. If you want to allow others to change the contents of the folder, check **Allow network users to change my files**. Click **Apply**, and close the window. Other users on the network can now see the folder when they open My Network Places on their desktop. In Chapter 19, you'll learn how you can configure Windows so that you have more control over how other users are able to access shared resources.

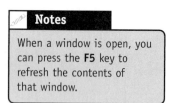

**Notes**

When a window is open, you can press the **F5** key to refresh the contents of that window.

Applications can also be shared with others in the workgroup. If you share a folder that has a program file in it, a user on another PC can double-click the program file in My Network Places and execute it remotely on his or her desktop. This is a handy way for several users to share an application that is installed on a single PC.

## HOW TO SHARE WINDOWS 9X/ME FILES, FOLDERS, AND APPLICATIONS

To share Windows 9x/Me resources, you must first install Client for Microsoft Networks and File and Printer Sharing. Client for Microsoft Networks is the Windows component that allows you to use resources on the network made available by other computers, and File and Printer Sharing allows you to share resources on your computer with others in your workgroup. After these components are installed, the last thing to do is to share the folders, files, or printers that you want others to be able to access. All these steps are covered in this section.

### Installing Windows 9x/Me Components Needed to Share Resources

To install Client for Microsoft Networks and File and Printer Sharing in Windows 98, open the **Network** applet in the Control Panel and click **Add**. Select **Client** and then click **Add**.

The Select Network Client window opens. Select **Microsoft** on the left and **Client for Microsoft Networks** on the right. You might need the Windows 9x/Me CD. Using the same method, install File and Printer Sharing for Microsoft Networks.

After these two components are installed, you must choose to enable File and Print Sharing. In the Network window, click the **File and Print Sharing** button (see Figure 17-69). The File and Print Sharing window opens. Check both options to share both files and printers, and then click **OK**.

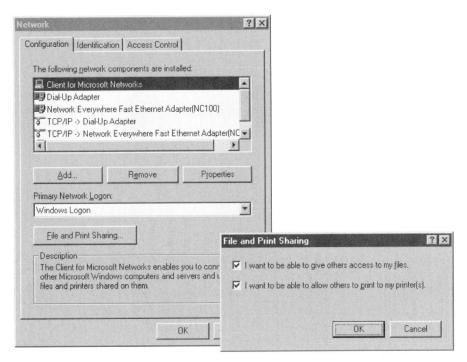

**Figure 17-69** Turn on Windows 98 File and Print Sharing so others on the LAN can access resources on this PC

When they are installed, Client for Microsoft Networks and File and Printer Sharing should automatically bind themselves to the TCP/IP protocol. You can verify this by accessing the TCP/IP Properties dialog box and clicking the **Bindings** tab. On this tab, you can verify that Client for Microsoft Networks and File and Printer Sharing are checked.

## Sharing Files and Folders with the Workgroup

After the computer is configured for File and Print Sharing, do the following to make a folder or file available to others on the LAN:

1. Using Windows Explorer, select the folder or file. In this example, we are using a folder named **C:\data**. Right-click the folder name and select **Sharing** from the shortcut menu. The data Properties dialog box opens, as shown in Figure 17-70.

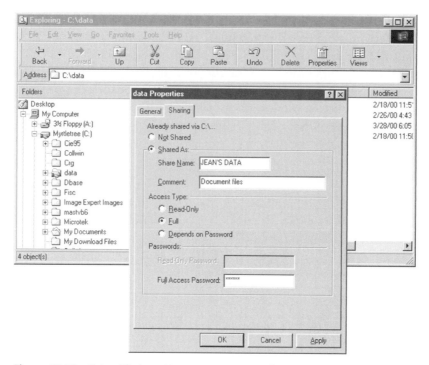

**Figure 17-70**    Using Windows 98, a user on a network can share a folder with others on the network

2. Click the **Shared As** option button. Enter a name for the shared folder. In the figure, the name is JEAN'S DATA. This action makes the folder available to others on the network. They can see the folder when they open My Network Places or Network Neighborhood on their desktop.

3. Click the **Depends on Password** option button in the Access Type section.

4. To allow others the right to make changes to the folder, enter a password under **Full Access Password**. For read-only access, enter a different password. Click **OK** to exit the window.

When using the Depends on Password option, be sure to enter a password in both the Read-Only Password and Full Access Password fields. If you leave a password field empty, then no password is required for a user to have the corresponding read-only or full access to the folder. Distribute the two passwords to people who need to access the folder. You control the access rights (permissions) by selecting which password(s) you give.

## NETWORK DRIVE MAPS

A **network drive map** is one of the most powerful and versatile methods of communicating over a network. A network drive map makes one PC (the client) appear to have a new hard drive, such as drive E, that is really hard drive space on another host computer (the server). This client/server arrangement is managed by a Windows component called the Network File System (NFS), which makes it possible for files on the network to be accessed as easily as if they are stored on the local computer. NFS is a type of distributed file system (DFS), which is a system that shares files on a network. Even if the host computer uses a different OS, such as Unix, the drive map still functions.

Using a network drive map, files and folders on a host computer are available even to network-unaware DOS applications. The path to a file simply uses the remote drive letter instead of a local drive such as drive A or drive C. Also, network drive maps are more reliable than when using My Network Places or Network Neighborhood to access folders on the network.

> **Notes**
>
> A computer that does nothing but provide hard drive storage on a network for other computers is called a file server or a network attached storage (NAS) device. Other computers on the network can access this storage using a network drive map.

To set up a network drive under Windows 2000/XP or Windows 9x/Me, follow these steps:

1. On the host computer, using directions given earlier in the chapter, share the drive or folder on a drive to which you want others to have access.

2. On the remote computer that will use the network drive, connect to the network and access **Windows Explorer**. Click the **Tools** menu and select **Map Network Drive**.

3. The Map Network Drive dialog box opens, as shown in Figure 17-71. Select a drive letter from the drop-down list.

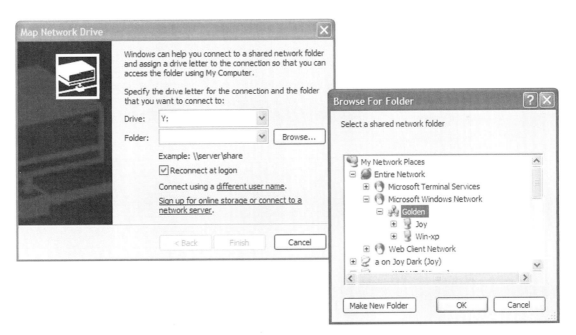

**Figure 17-71**  Mapping a network drive to a host computer

4. Click the **Browse** button and locate the shared folder or drive on the host computer. Click **OK** to close the Browse For Folder dialog box, and click **Finish** to map the drive. The folder on the host computer now appears as one more drive in Explorer on your computer (see Figure 17-72).

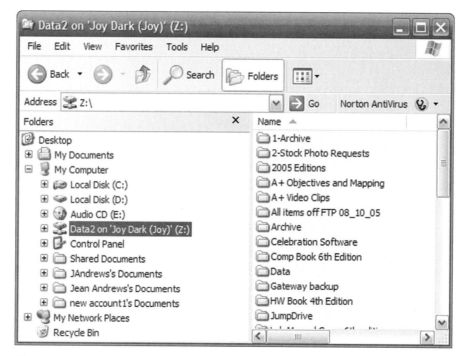

**Figure 17-72**  Contents on the right side of Windows Explorer belong to the host computer; this computer sees the contents as belonging to its drive Z

5. If a network drive does not work, go to My Network Places or Network Neighborhood, and verify that the network connection is good.

> **Notes**
>
> When mapping a network drive, you can type the path to the host computer rather than clicking the Browse button to navigate to the host. To enter the path, in the Map Network Drive dialog box, use two backslashes, followed by the name of the host computer, followed by a backslash and the drive or folder to access on the host computer. For example, to access the Public folder on the computer named Scott, enter **\\Scott\Public** and then click **Finish**.

## WHAT IF YOU DON'T WANT TO SHARE?

If you're concerned about others on your network getting to information on your computer, you can do some things to make sure your PC is secure:

▲ *Disable File and Printer Sharing.* In the Network Connections window, under the Local Area Connection Properties dialog box, uncheck **File and printer sharing for Microsoft Networks**.

▲ *Hide your computer from others looking at My Network Places.* For Windows 2000/XP, in the Control Panel, open the **Administrative Tools** applet and double-click **Service**. Right-click the **Computer Browser** service and select **Properties** from the shortcut menu. Under Startup type, select **Disabled** and click **Apply**. When you restart the PC, it will not be visible in My Network Places over the network.

▲ *Hide a shared folder.* If you want to share a folder, but don't want others to see the shared folder in their My Network Places or Network Neighborhood window, add a $ to the end of the folder name. Others on the network can access the folder only when they know its name. For example, if you name a shared folder MyPrivateFolder$, in order to

A+
220-602
5.2

access the folder, a user must enter \\Computername\MyPrivateFolder$ in the Run dialog box on the remote computer.

▲ *Make your personal folders private.* If you are using the NTFS file system, folders associated with your user account can be made private so that only you can access them. To make a personal folder and all its subfolders private, in Windows Explorer, drill down to a folder that is part of your user profile under the Documents and Settings folder. Right-click the folder and select **Sharing and Security** from the shortcut menu. The folder properties dialog box opens (see Figure 17-73). Check **Make this folder private** and click **Apply**. (It's interesting to see that in Figure 17-68, shown earlier in the chapter, the Make this folder private check box is grayed out because that folder is not part of a user profile in the Documents and Settings folder.) When you make a personal folder private, be sure you have a password associated with your user account. If you don't have a password, anyone can log on as you and gain access to your private folders.

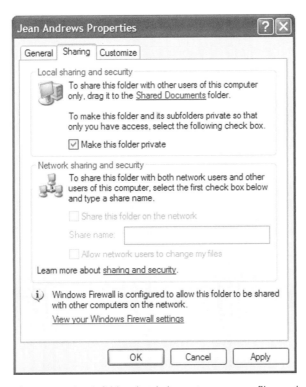

**Figure 17-73**   A folder that belongs to a user profile can be made private

# HOW TO SET UP YOUR OWN WIRELESS NETWORK

A+ ESS
6.1

A+
220-602
6.2
6.3

Setting up your own wireless network involves buying a wireless access point and configuring it and your wireless computers for communication. The key to successful wireless networking is good security. This section first looks at what you need to know about securing a wireless network, then shows how to choose the equipment you'll need and how to set up a wireless network.

## SECURITY ON A WIRELESS LAN

Wireless LANs are so convenient for us at work and at home, but the downside of having a wireless network is that if we don't have the proper security in place, anyone with a wireless computer within range of your access point can use the network—and, if they know how, can intercept and read all the data sent across the network. They might even be able to hack into our computers by using our own wireless network against us. For all these reasons, it's terribly important to secure your wireless network.

Securing a wireless network is generally done in these ways:

- ▲ *Disable SSID broadcasting.* Normally, the name of the access point (called the SSID) is broadcast so that anyone with a wireless computer can see the name and use the network. If you hide the SSID, a computer can see the wireless network, but can't use it unless the SSID is entered in the wireless adapter configuration.

- ▲ *Filter MAC addresses.* A wireless access point can filter the MAC addresses of wireless NICs that are allowed to use the access point. This type of security prevents uninvited guests from using the wireless LAN, but does not prevent others from receiving data in the air.

- ▲ *Data encryption.* Data sent over a wireless connection can be encrypted. The three main methods of encryption for 802.11 wireless networks are **WEP (Wired Equivalent Privacy)**, **WPA (WiFi Protected Access)**, and **WPA2**. With either method, data is encrypted using a firmware program on the wireless device and is only encrypted while the data is wireless; the data is decrypted before placing it on the wired network. With WEP encryption, data is encrypted using either 64-bit or 128-bit encryption keys. (Because the user can configure only 40 bits of the 64 bits, 64-bit WEP encryption is sometimes called 40-bit WEP encryption.) Because the key used for encryption is static (doesn't change), a hacker who spends enough time examining data packets can eventually find enough patterns in the coding to decrypt the code and read WEP-encrypted data. WPA encryption, also called TKIP (Temporal Key Integrity Protocol) encryption, is stronger than WEP and was designed to replace it. With WPA encryption, encryption keys are changed at set intervals. The latest and best wireless encryption standard is WPA2, also called the 802.11i standard or the AES (Advanced Encryption Standard) protocol. As of March 2006, for a wireless device to be WiFi certified, it must support the WPA2 standard, which is included in Windows XP Service Pack 2. When buying wireless devices, be sure the encryption methods used are compatible!

- ▲ *Change firmware default settings.* Default settings are easy to guess. For example, a default password is often set to "password" and the default SSID is often set to the brand name of the device, such as Linksys or Netgear. For added security, be sure to change all default settings so they are not so easy to guess. Change the SSID to keep someone from guessing the SSID when it is not broadcasted. Also, change the default password and username for the configuration utility. You can also disable DHCP and use static IP addressing so others cannot obtain an IP address.

- ▲ *Update firmware.* For added security, keep the firmware on your wireless access point updated with downloads from the device manufacturer.

- ▲ *Use a firewall.* If the access point has firewall capability, be sure to turn it on. In addition, be sure to use a software firewall on every computer using the wireless network. How to manage firewalls is covered in Chapter 19.

- ▲ *Virtual private network (VPN).* A VPN requires a password for entrance and encrypts data over both wired and wireless networks. The basic difference between WEP or WPA encryption and VPN encryption is that VPN encryption applies from the user's PC all the way to the host computer regardless of the type of network used. A VPN uses a technique called tunneling, in which a packet of data is encrypted, as shown in Figure 17-74. The encryption methods used by VPN are stronger than WEP or WPA and are the preferred method when transmitting sensitive data over a wireless connection. How to set up a VPN is beyond the scope of this chapter.

A+ ESS
6.1

A+
220-602
6.2
6.3

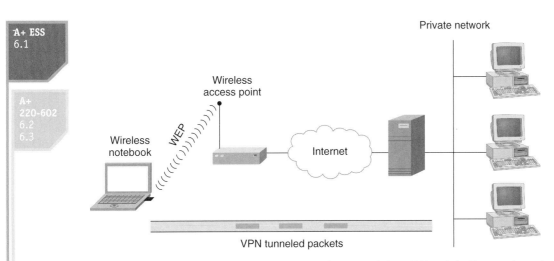

**Figure 17-74** With tunneling, packets can travel over a wireless LAN and the Internet in a virtual private network (VPN), but WEP or WPA applies only to the wireless connection

## CHOOSING A WIRELESS ACCESS POINT

When selecting a wireless access point, look for the ability to use all the security measures listed in the previous section. Also, be sure the access point supports 802.11 b/g. And, as always, before you buy, search the Internet to read hardware reviews about the device. Only buy a device that consistently gets good reviews. If you're also in need of a wireless adapter to use for the computers that will use your wireless networks, for best results, try to find adapters and an access point made by the same manufacturer.

A wireless access point can be a standalone device such as the one in Figure 17-75 by D-Link, which supports 802.11b/g. This particular access point advertises that it can support transfer rates up to 108 Mbps, but be aware that to get this high rate, you must use a compatible D-Link wireless adapter on your notebook or desktop computer. An access point can also serve more than one purpose, such as the Linksys router shown earlier in Figure 17-17.

**Figure 17-75** This wireless access point by D-Link supports 802.11b/g

## CONFIGURE AND TEST YOUR WIRELESS NETWORK

To install a standalone access point, position it centrally located to where you want your hot spot to be and plug it in. It will have a network or USB cable that you can connect to a computer so you can configure the access point. A wireless access point includes firmware.

(You might be able to update or flash the firmware with updates downloaded from the manufacturer's Web site.) The firmware includes a configuration utility. You access this utility by entering the IP address of the access point in a browser on a computer connected to the access point. Any changes you make to the configuration are stored on the access point device.

Run the setup CD that comes with the access point. If you don't have the setup CD, you can open your browser and enter the IP address of the device, which should launch a firmware utility you can use to configure it. All changes you make to the access point configuration will be saved on the device firmware memory.

Go through the following steps to configure the wireless access point:

1. It's very important to change the default password to the administrative utility to configure the access point. Unless you have disabled or secured the wireless access point, anyone outside your building can use your wireless network. If they guess the default password to the access point, they can change the password to hijack your wireless network. Also, your wireless network can be used for criminal activity. When you first install an access point, before you do anything else, change your password.

2. Look for a way to select the channel the access point will use, the ability to change the SSID of the access point, and the ability to disable SSID broadcasting. Figure 17-76 shows these three settings for one Linksys access point. Figure 17-77 shows how a wireless computer sees a wireless access point that is not broadcasting its SSID. This computer would not be able to use this access point until you entered the SSID in the configuration window shown in Figure 17-78.

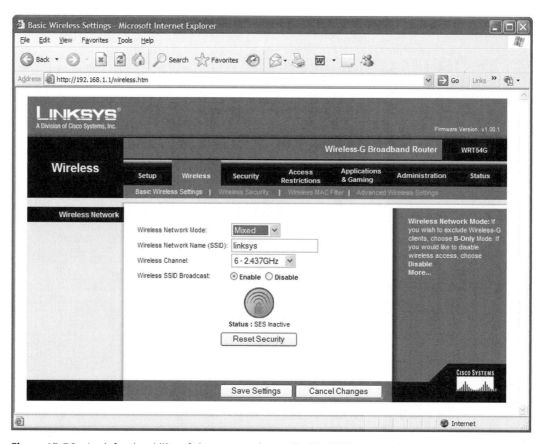

**Figure 17-76** Look for the ability of the access point to disable SSID broadcasting

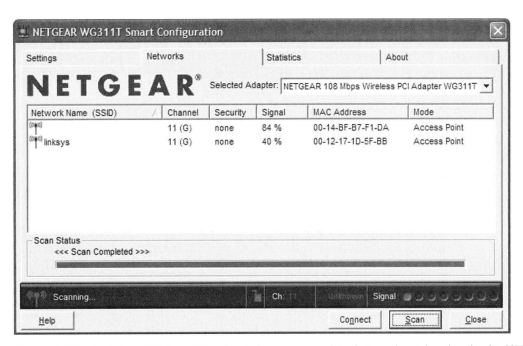

Figure 17-77   A wireless NIC shows it has located two access points, but one is not broadcasting its SSID

Figure 17-78   This wireless adapter configuration screen lets you enter the SSID of a hidden access point and also configure the wireless connection for WEP encryption

3. To configure data encryption on your access point, look for a wireless security screen similar to the one in Figure 17-79 where you can choose between several WPA, WEP, or RADIUS encryption methods. (RADIUS stands for Remote Authentication Dial-In User Service and uses an authentication server to control access.) WPA Personal is the one to choose unless one of your wireless adapters doesn't support it. For example, the wireless adapter configuration screen in Figure 17-78 shows it supports only WEP encryption, so your access point is forced to use that method. Enter the same passphrase for WEP encryption on the access point screen and all your wireless adapter configuration screens.

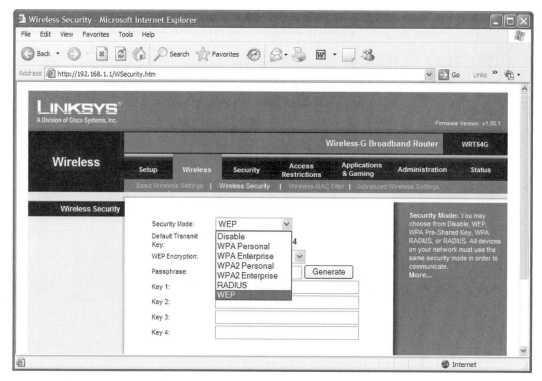

**Figure 17-79** This wireless access point supports several encryption methods

4. Look for MAC filtering on your access point, similar to the screen in Figure 17-80. On this access point, you can enter a table of MAC addresses and decide if this list of MAC addresses is to be used to prevent or permit use of the access point.

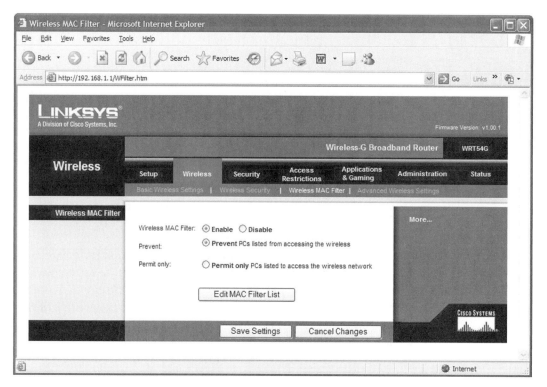

**Figure 17-80** Configure how the access point will filter MAC addresses

**A+ ESS**
**6.1**

**A+**
**220-602**
**6.2**
**6.3**

5. Save all your settings for the access point and test the connection. To test it, on one of your wireless computers, open the configuration window for the wireless adapter and scan for access points. If the scan does not detect your access point, verify the wireless adapter is set to scan all channels or the selected channel of your access point. Try moving your access point or the computer. If you still can't get a connection, remove all security measures and try again. Then restore the security features one at a time until you discover the one causing the problem, or use encryption.

We've just configured your wireless access point to use several security features. Is it really necessary to use them all? Well, not really, but it can't hurt. Encryption is essential to keep others from hacking into your wireless data, and to keep others out of your network, you need to disable SSID broadcasting, filter MAC addresses, or use encryption.

## TROUBLESHOOTING A NETWORK CONNECTION

**A+ ESS**
**1.3**
**5.1**
**5.3**

**A+**
**220-602**
**1.2**
**3.1**
**5.3**

**APPLYING|CONCEPTS**   T.J. has just used a crossover cable to connect his two computers together. My Network Places on both computers refuses to display the other computer. What should T.J. check?

If you have problems connecting to the network, follow the guidelines in this section. First, here are some symptoms that might indicate the NIC is faulty:

▲ You cannot make a connection to the network.
▲ My Network Places or Network Neighborhood does not show any other computers on the network.
▲ You receive an error message while you are installing the NIC drivers.
▲ Device Manager shows a yellow exclamation point or a red X beside the name of the NIC. In the Network Connections window, you see a red X over the network icon.
▲ There are at least two lights on a NIC: One stays on steadily to let you know there is a physical connection (labeled LINK in Figure 17-81), and another blinks to let you know there is activity (labeled ACT in Figure 17-81). If you see no lights, you know there is no physical connection between the NIC and the network. This means there is a problem with the network cable, the card, or the switch, hub, or router to which the PC connects. Similar lights appear on the switch, hub, or router for each network port.

**Figure 17-81**   Lights on the back of a NIC can be used for troubleshooting

◢ The problem might not be caused by the NIC. You can check to see if a network cable is good using a cable tester such as the one shown earlier in Figure 17-12. Electrical interference might be a problem. If you suspect interference, you can install a **ferrite clamp** close to the device end of the cable. The clamp helps to eliminate electromagnetic interference and is shown in Figure 17-82.

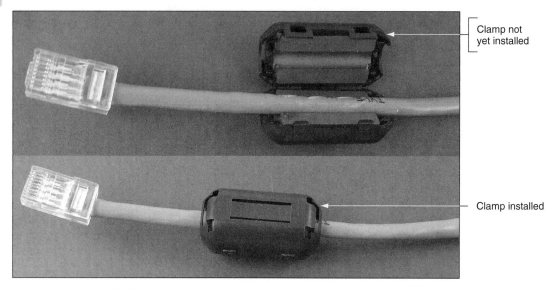

Clamp not
yet installed

Clamp installed

**Figure 17-82**    Install a ferrite clamp on a network cable to protect against electrical interference

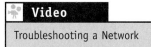

**Video**

Troubleshooting a Network

 **A+ Tip**

The A+ Essentials exam expects you to know how to troubleshoot network problems by using status indictors and activity lights on a NIC. You also need to know how and when to use the Ping and Ipconfig commands.

Sometimes you might have trouble with a network connection due to a TCP/IP problem. Windows TCP/IP includes several diagnostic tools that are useful in troubleshooting problems with TCP/IP. You will learn about several of these in the next chapter. The most useful is **Ping (Packet Internet Groper)**, which tests connectivity and is discussed here. Ping sends a signal to a remote computer. If the remote computer is online and hears the signal, it responds. Ipconfig under Windows 2000/XP and Winipcfg under Windows 9x/Me test the TCP/IP configuration.

Try these things to test TCP/IP configuration and connectivity:

1. For Windows 2000/XP, enter **Ipconfig /all** at the command prompt. For Windows 9x/Me, click **Start**, click **Run**, enter **Winipcfg** in the Run dialog box, and then click **OK**. If the TCP/IP configuration is correct and an IP address is assigned, the IP address, subnet mask, and default gateway appear along with the adapter address. For dynamic IP addressing, if the PC cannot reach the DHCP server, then it assigns itself an IP address. This is called IP autoconfiguration and the IP address is called an Automatic Private IP Address (APIPA). In this situation, the Winipcfg window and the results of the Ipconfig command both show the IP address as the IP Autoconfiguration Address, and the address begins with 169.254. In this case, suspect that the PC is not able to reach the network or the DHCP server is down.

A+ ESS
1.3
5.1
5.3

A+
220-602
1.2
3.1
5.3

2. Try to release the current IP address and lease a new address. To do this for Windows 9x/Me Winipcfg, select the network card, click the **Release** button, and then click the **Renew** button. For Windows 2000/XP, first use the **Ipconfig /release** command, and then use the **Ipconfig /renew** command. Or you can open the Network Connections window, right-click the network connection, and click **Repair** on the shortcut menu (see Figure 17-83).

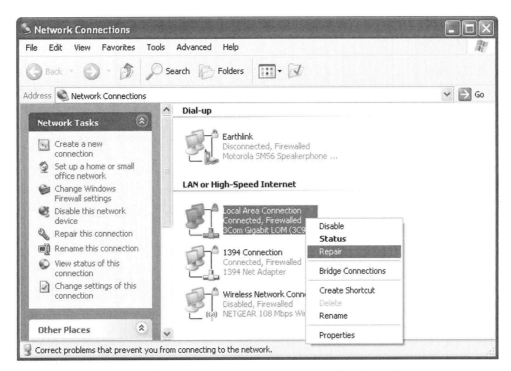

**Figure 17-83** Use the Repair command to release and renew the IP address of a network connection

3. Next, try the loopback address test. At a command prompt, enter the command **Ping 127.0.0.1** (with no period after the final 1). This IP address always refers to your local computer. It should respond with a reply message from your computer. If this works, TCP/IP is likely to be configured correctly. If you get any errors up to this point, then assume that the problem is on your PC. Check the installation and configuration of each component, such as the network card and the TCP/IP protocol suite. Remove and reinstall each component, and watch for error messages, writing them down so that you can recognize or research them later as necessary. Compare the configuration to that of a working PC on the same network.

4. Next, ping the IP address of your default gateway. If it does not respond, the problem might be with the gateway or with the network to the gateway.

5. Now try to ping the host computer you are trying to reach. If it does not respond, the problem might be with the host computer or with the network to the computer.

6. If you have Internet access and substitute a domain name for the IP address in the Ping command, and Ping works, you can conclude that DNS works. If an IP address works, but the domain name does not work, the problem lies with DNS. Try this command: **ping www.course.com**.

7. Determine whether other computers on the network are having trouble with their connections. If the entire network is down, the problem is not isolated to the PC and the NIC you are working on. Check the hub or switch controlling the network.

A+ ESS
1.3
5.1
5.3

A+
220-602
1.2
3.1
5.3

8. Make sure the NIC and its drivers are installed by checking for the NIC in Device Manager. Try uninstalling and reinstalling the NIC drivers.

9. If the drivers still install with errors, try downloading new drivers from the Web site of the network card manufacturer. Also, look on the installation CD that came bundled with the NIC for a setup program. If you find one, uninstall the NIC and run this setup program.

10. Some network cards have diagnostic programs on the installation CD. Try running the program from the CD. Look in the documentation that came with the card for instructions on how to install and run the program.

11. Check the network cable to make sure it is not damaged and that it does not exceed the recommended length for the type of network you are using. If the cable is frayed, twisted, or damaged, replace it. Be sure all network cables are securely attached to the wall or are up and out of harm's way so they will not be tripped over, stepped on, twisted, or otherwise damaged.

12. Connect the network cable to a different port on the hub. If that doesn't help, you might have a problem with the cable or the NIC itself. Uninstall the NIC drivers, replace the NIC, and then install new drivers.

13. Check to see whether you have the most current version of your motherboard BIOS. The motherboard manufacturer should have information on its Web site about whether an upgrade is available.

When a network drive map is not working, first check My Network Places or Network Neighborhood, and verify that you can access other resources on the remote computer. You might need to log on to the remote computer with a valid user ID and password.

**APPLYING│CONCEPTS**  Back to T.J.'s problem connecting his two computers. The problem might be the hardware or software. Begin with the hardware. Are the lights displayed correctly on the NICs? If so, T.J. can assume the hardware is functioning. Next, check the driver installation. Does Device Manager on both computers show no errors or conflicts with each network adapter? Next, check the configuration. In this situation, T.J. should have used static IP addressing. What is the IP address of each PC? Open a command window and try to ping the local computer, and then try to ping the remote computer. Does each computer have a computer name? Try rebooting each computer.

## >> CHAPTER SUMMARY

▲ Networks are categorized in size as a PAN, LAN, MAN, or WAN.

▲ Bandwidth measures how much data can travel over a given communications system in a given amount of time. Common bandwidth technologies for personal or small business networks include Ethernet, WiFi, regular telephone lines, cable modem, ISDN, DSL, and satellite access.

▲ The most popular physical network architecture for LANs is Ethernet.

▲ Ethernet uses a logical bus and can be configured as a star topology, in which all nodes connect to a centralized switch or hub, or a bus topology, which connects nodes in a line and has no central connection point.

◢ An Ethernet hub broadcasts all data that flows through it to every node connected to it. It does not make decisions about where to send packets. Switches keep switching tables of nodes on the network and send packets only to the designated node.

◢ The most popular Ethernet networks are 100BaseT and Gigabit Ethernet, which both use STP or UTP cabling with RJ-45 connectors.

◢ Wireless LANs make connections using radio or infrared technology. A wireless LAN can be used in combination with a wired LAN. The most popular wireless technology for a LAN is 802.11b/g, also called Wi-Fi.

◢ Telephone networks include POTS, VoIP, cellular WAN, satellite phone, and radio phone. Another type of wireless telephone is a cordless phone that communicates with a base station at close range.

◢ A PC connects to a network using a NIC (network interface card) or network adapter, which communicates with NICs on other PCs using a set of hardware protocols (such as Ethernet). The OSs on the two computers use a different set of protocols (such as TCP/IP or NetBEUI) to communicate.

◢ NICs and the device drivers that control them are designed to work with a particular network architecture and are the only PC components that are aware of the type of physical network being used.

◢ The three protocols that Windows supports for network communications are TCP/IP (the protocol suite for the Internet), IPX/SPX (designed for use with Novell NetWare), and NetBEUI (a proprietary Windows protocol for use on networks isolated from the Internet). Only TCP/IP is supported on the Internet.

◢ The four types of addresses on a Windows network are MAC addresses, IP addresses, character-based names (such as NetBIOS names, host names, domain names), and port addresses.

◢ MAC addresses are used only for communication within a local network.

◢ IP addresses identify devices on the Internet and other TCP/IP networks. They consist of four numbers separated by periods. The first part of an IP address identifies the network, and the last identifies the host. The class of an IP address determines how much of the address is used as the network identifier and how much is used for the host identifier.

◢ IP addresses can either be public or private. For private IP addresses to be able to access the Internet, they must go through NAT (Network Address Translation) so that their requests all appear to be coming from a single public IP address for that network.

◢ Character-based names, such as fully qualified domain names, are used as an easy way to remember IP addresses.

◢ The IP address associated with a host name can change. DNS (Domain Name Service) and WINS (Windows Internet Naming Service) track the relationships between host names and IP addresses. DNS is more popular because it works on all platforms.

◢ Windows 2000 and Windows XP assume that a computer name is a host name, which follows the TCP/IP convention and can have up to 63 characters. Windows 98 assumes that a computer name is a NetBIOS name, which can have up to 15 characters.

◢ When installing a NIC, physically install the card, install the device drivers, install the OS networking protocol you intend to use (it might already be installed by default), configure the OS protocol, and give the computer a name.

▲ When configuring TCP/IP, you must know if IP addresses are statically or dynamically assigned.

▲ Before users on a network can view or access resources on a PC, Client for Microsoft Networks and File and Print Sharing must be installed and enabled, and the resources must be shared.

▲ Network drive mapping makes one PC appear to have a new hard drive when that hard drive space is actually on another host computer. Use Windows Explorer to map a network drive.

▲ When setting up a wireless network, configure the wireless access point to secure the network from unauthorized access. Use encryption to keep data from being stolen in transmission.

▲ When troubleshooting a NIC on a PC, check connections in the rest of the network, cabling and ports for the PC, the NIC itself (substituting one known to be working, if necessary), the BIOS, and the device drivers.

▲ Ping is a useful TCP/IP utility to check network connectivity.

▲ Two other useful troubleshooting tools are Ipconfig (Windows 2000 and Windows XP) and Winipcfg (Windows 9x/Me), which test TCP/IP configuration.

## >> KEY TERMS

For explanations of key terms, see the Glossary near the end of the book.

10Base2
10Base5
10BaseT
100BaseT

802.11a/b/g
access point (AP)
adapter address
AirPort
amplifier repeater
attenuation
Automatic Private IP Address (APIPA)
bandwidth
base station
binding
Bluetooth
BNC connector
broadband
broadcast
bus topology
CDMA (Code Division Multiple Access)
cellular network
cellular WAN
classful subnet masks
classless subnet masks
client
client/server
coaxial cable
computer name
crossover cable
data throughput
datagram
default gateway

DHCP (Dynamic Host Configuration Protocol)
DNS (Domain Name System, or Domain Name Service)
DNS server
domain name
dynamic IP address
Ethernet
Fast Ethernet
ferrite clamp
Fiber Distributed Data Interface (FDDI)
fiber optic
frame
full duplex
fully qualified domain name (FQDN)
gateway
General Packet Radio Service (GPRS)
Gigabit Ethernet
GSM (Global System for Mobile Communications)
half duplex
hardware address
host
host name
Hosts (file)
hub
IBM Data Connector (IDC)
Institute of Electrical and Electronics Engineers (IEEE)
Internet service provider (ISP)
intranet

IP address
IPX/SPX (Internetwork Packet Exchange/Sequenced Packet Exchange)
LAN (local area network)
line speed
LMHosts
MAC (Media Access Control) address
MAN (metropolitan area network)
multicasting
name resolution
NAT (Network Address Translation)
NetBEUI (NetBIOS Extended User Interface)
NetBIOS (Network Basic Input/Output System)
network adapter
network drive map
network interface card (NIC)
network operating system (NOS)
network printer
node
NWLink
octet
packet
PAN (personal area network)
patch cable
peer-to-peer network
physical address
Ping (Packet Internet Groper)
private IP address

proxy server
public IP address
repeater
ring topology
RJ-45 connector
server
shielded twisted-pair (STP) cable
signal-regenerating repeater
star bus topology
star ring topology
star topology

static IP address
subnet mask
switch
TCP/IP (Transmission Control
  Protocol/Internet Protocol)
TDMA (Time Division Multiple
  Access)
ThickNet
ThinNet
Token Ring
Universal Data Connector (UDC)

unshielded twisted pair (UTP)
  cable
WAN (wide area network)
WEP (Wired Equivalent
  Privacy)
Wi-Fi (Wireless Fidelity)
WINS (Windows Internet
  Naming Service)
wireless LAN (WLAN)
WPA (WiFi Protected Access)
WPA2 (WiFi Protected Access 2)

## >> REVIEW QUESTIONS

1. Which of the following categories of networks refers to a network that covers a large campus or city?

   a. PAN

   b. MAN

   c. LAN

   d. VAN

2. A twisted-pair cable that uses an RJ-45 connector has how many wires?

   a. 2

   b. 4

   c. 8

   d. 16

3. Which of the following terms refers to the process by which a signal weakens as it travels long distances over a network?

   a. Amplifier repeater

   b. Attenuation

   c. Fade-out

   d. Drop-down

4. Which of the following terms refers to a computer or other device that allows a computer on one network to communicate with a computer on another network?

   a. Gateway

   b. Dynamic address

   c. Static address

   d. Network drive map

5. Which of the following networking protocols is a proprietary Windows protocol suite used only by Windows computers?

   a. TCP/IP

   b. IPX/SPX

   c. AppleTalk

   d. NetBEUI

6. True or false? Multimode fiber-optic cable performs better than single-mode fiber-optic cable.

7. True or false? Half-duplex transmission means both persons in a conversation can talk or transmit at the same time.

8. True or false? Wireless devices can connect to a LAN by way of a wireless access point (AP).

9. True or false? In the client/server network model, each computer on the network has the same authority as the other computers.

10. True or false? Subnet masks that use either all ones or all zeroes in an octet are called classful subnet masks.

11. The measure of data capacity over a given communication system is called _____ or data throughput or line speed.

12. Information about a packet (that identifies the type of data and where it came from) that is placed at the end of the data is called a(n) _____.

13. Ethernet networks can be configured as either a bus topology or a(n) _____ topology.

14. A patch cable, also called a(n) _____ cable, is used to connect a computer to a hub or switch.

15. The process of _____ occurs when an operating system–level protocol such as TCP/IP associates itself with a lower-level hardware protocol such as Ethernet.

# PCs on the Internet

In earlier chapters, you've learned much about how to support computers, applications, and users, and how to connect a PC to a network. This chapter takes the next logical step in effectively using PCs by discussing connections to the Internet using Windows. You will learn how the TCP/IP suite of protocols is used, how to create and troubleshoot broadband and dial-up connections to the Internet, and how to install and use a router to enhance and secure an Internet connection. Then, you'll learn how to support many of the popular applications that use the Internet, such as Web browsers, e-mail clients, FTP software, Internet telephone, and Windows XP Remote Desktop.

# THE TCP/IP SUITE OF PROTOCOLS

In Chapter 17, you learned how to install and configure the hardware and software necessary for networking, and how the operating system uses TCP/IP to make resources on a network available to the user. In this section of the chapter, you'll learn more about how TCP/IP works to support the major Internet applications.

Most applications that use the Internet are **client/server applications**, which means that two computers and two applications are involved. The client application on one computer makes a request for data from the server application on another computer. In this client/server environment, the application serving up data is called the server and the computer on which this server application is installed can also be referred to as the server. In other words, a server is any computer or application serving up data when that data is requested.

The World Wide Web itself is probably the most popular client/server application: The client is called a Web browser because it browses the Web, and the server is called a Web server or a Web host because it hosts a Web site. The requested data is called a Web page, which can have graphics, sound, and video embedded as part of the requested data (see Figure 18-1). Two examples of Web servers are Apache HTTP Server by The Apache Software Foundation (*www.apache.org*) and Internet Information Services (IIS), which is an integrated component of Windows Server 2003.

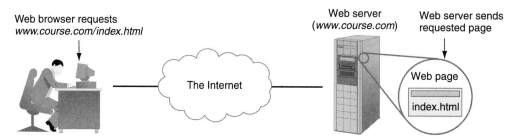

**Figure 18-1** A Web browser (client software) requests a Web page from a Web server (server software); the Web server returns the requested file or files to the client

Client applications such as a Web browser or e-mail client software are installed on computers as any other application is installed. However, because a server application is waiting for a request from another program, it is installed on the computer as a service. Recall from earlier chapters that a service is managed under Windows 2000/XP using the Services console, or it can be managed using a utility program bundled with the server application.

To understand how TCP/IP is used to support client/server applications, let's first look at how a client application addresses a server application. Then, we'll look at the layers of protocols included in TCP/IP to support applications, the OS, and hardware. Finally, in this part of the chapter, we'll look at some utilities you can use when problems arise with TCP/IP communication.

## USING IP AND PORT ADDRESSES TO IDENTIFY SERVICES

A computer on the Internet or an intranet might be running a Web server application, an e-mail server application, and an FTP server application, all at the same time. (You'll learn about FTP later in the chapter.) Recall that each of these server applications is running as a service on that computer.

Having multiple server applications running as individual services on one computer works fine as long as client applications requesting data know how to address a particular service. To understand how these services are addressed, let's start by using an example. Suppose that a computer is running a Web server and an e-mail server. The Web server is Apache HTTP Server and the e-mail server is Ntmail by Gordano LTD (*www.ntmail.co.uk*). The Apache and Ntmail programs are both running as background services on this one computer. How does a Web browser on a client PC say, "I want to speak with the Web server" and an e-mail program say, "I want to speak with the e-mail server," if both programs are running on the same computer using the same IP address? The answer is: they use an identifying number, called a **port, port address,** or **port number,** that has been assigned to each server application when it is started. (Don't confuse these port numbers or addresses with I/O addresses assigned to hardware devices, which were discussed in previous chapters.) Also, keep in mind that not every service running on a computer requires a port number; only those services that are server applications require port numbers.

Each server application "listens" at its assigned port. A network administrator can assign any port number to a server, but there are established port numbers for common servers and protocols. A Web server is normally assigned port 80, and an e-mail server receiving mail is normally assigned port 25, as shown in Figure 18-2. Port assignments are shown at the end of an IP address, following a colon. Using these default port assignments, the Web server would communicate at 138.60.30.5:80, and the e-mail server would communicate at 138.60.30.5:25.

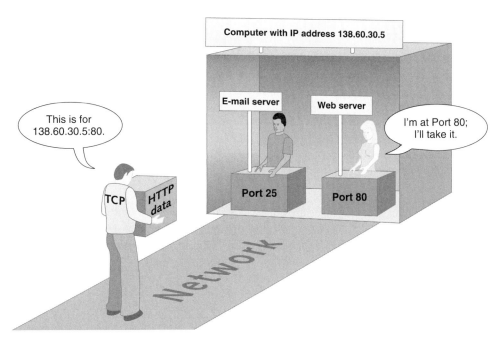

**Figure 18-2** Each server running on a computer is addressed by a unique port number

Unless the administrator has a good reason to do otherwise, he or she will usually use the common port assignments listed in Table 18-1. (One reason not to use the default port assignments is concern about security. You can make a Web site a secret site by using an uncommon port number.) If a Web server is assigned a port number different from the default port number, the Web server can be accessed by entering the server's IP address in the address box of the Web browser, followed by a colon and the port number of the Web server, like this: 138.60.30.5:8080.

| Port | Protocol | Service | Description |
|------|----------|---------|-------------|
| 20 | FTP | FTP | File transfer data |
| 21 | FTP | FTP | File transfer control information |
| 22 | SSH | Secure Shell | Remote control to a networked computer |
| 23 | Telnet | Telnet | Telnet, an application used by Unix computers to control a computer remotely |
| 25 | SMTP | E-mail | Simple Mail Transfer Protocol; used by a client to send e-mail |
| 80 | HTTP | Web server | World Wide Web protocol |
| 109 | POP2 | E-mail | Post Office Protocol, version 2; used by a client to receive e-mail |
| 110 | POP3 | E-mail | Post Office Protocol, version 3; used by a client to receive e-mail |
| 119 | NNTP | News server | News servers that use the Network News Transfer Protocol (NNTP), the protocol used for newsgroups |
| 143 | IMAP | E-mail | Internet Message Access Protocol, a newer protocol used by clients to receive e-mail |
| 443 | HTTPS | Web server | HTTP with added security that includes authentication and encryption |

**Table 18-1** Common TCP/IP port assignments for well-known server applications

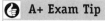

**A+ Exam Tip**

The A+ 220-602 exam expects you to know about these protocols used on the Internet: TCP/IP, SMTP, IMAP, HTTP, HTTPS, SSL, Telnet, FTP, DNS, and VoIP. All these protocols are covered in this chapter.

Notice in Table 18-1 that each service has one or more designated protocols. These protocols are the rules of communication between the client and server components of the applications, and they are each used for different types of communication between the client and server.

Recall from Chapter 17 that at the lowest networking level, the network or hardware protocol controls communication among physical networking devices such as Ethernet NICs and switches. The next layer up is the OS protocol used on the network, such as TCP/IP, AppleTalk, or NetBEUI. Now, on top of the hardware and OS protocols, we add a third level of protocols that control how applications such as those listed in Table 18-1 communicate using the network. That third level consists of the applications protocols.

Figure 18-3 shows how communication happens at the three levels. An application (1) uses an IP address and port number to send its request to the OS (2), which passes the request to the NIC (3), which puts the request on the physical network and on to the NIC on the server (4). On the receiving end, this NIC sends the request to the OS (5), which passes the request to the Web server application (6). The Web server responds by sending data to the OS (5), which passes it down to its NIC (4), which passes it onto the network, and, ultimately, the data is received by the browser. At these different levels, an application has a port address assigned to it, the OS has an IP address assigned, and the NIC has a MAC address.

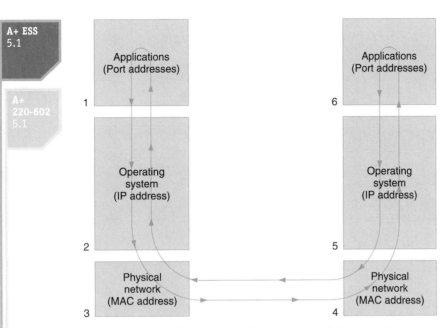

A+ ESS
5.1

A+
220-602
5.1

**Figure 18-3** Applications, operating systems, and the physical network manage communication at all three levels

## TCP/IP PROTOCOL LAYERS

Applications on the Internet all use protocols that are supported by TCP/IP. Figure 18-4 shows these different layers of protocols and how they relate to one another. As you read this section, this figure can serve as your road map to the different protocols.

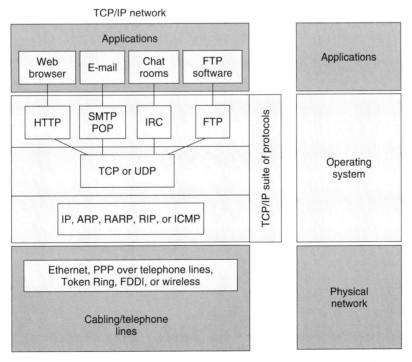

**Figure 18-4** How software, protocols, and technology on a TCP/IP network relate to each other

Several types of protocols operate within the TCP/IP suite. The more significant ones are introduced in this section, from the top layer down. However, you should know that the TCP/IP protocol suite includes more protocols than just those mentioned in this chapter.

## APPLICATION PROTOCOLS

Four of the most common applications that use the Internet are Web browsers, e-mail, chat rooms, and FTP. When one of these applications wants to send data to a counterpart application on another host, it makes an API (application programming interface) call to the operating system, which handles the request. (An API call is a common way for an application to ask an operating system to do something.) The API call causes the OS to generate a request.

For Web browsers, the OS generates an HTTP request. **HTTP (Hypertext Transfer Protocol)** is the protocol used for the World Wide Web and used by Web browsers and Web servers to communicate. In other words, HTTP formats the request, and encrypts and compresses it as necessary. It adds an HTTP header to the beginning of the data that includes the HTTP version being used and how the data is compressed and encrypted, if compression and encryption were done at all. Later, when the response is received from the server, the HTTP component of the OS decrypts and decompresses the data as necessary before passing it on to the browser.

After the response is passed to the browser, a session is established. **Sessions**, which are communication links created between two software programs, are managed by the browser and Web server using HTTP. However, TCP/IP at the OS level can also create a limited type of session.

Later in the chapter, you will learn more about Web and e-mail protocols and how they work.

 **Tip**

Sessions are sometimes called **sockets** because they are established communication links.

## TCP/IP PROTOCOLS USED BY THE OS FOR NETWORK COMMUNICATION

Looking back at Figure 18-4, you can see three layers of protocols between the application protocols and the physical network protocols. These three layers make up the heart of TCP/IP communication. In the figure, TCP or UDP manages communication with the applications protocols above them as well as the protocols shown underneath TCP and UDP, which control communication on the network.

Remember from the previous chapter that all communication on a network happens by way of packets delivered from one location on the network to another. When a Web browser makes a request for data from a Web server, a packet is created and an attempt is made to deliver that packet to the server. In TCP/IP, the protocol that guarantees packet delivery is **TCP (Transmission Control Protocol)**. TCP makes a connection, checks whether the data is received, and resends it if it is not. TCP is, therefore, called a **connection-oriented protocol**. TCP is used by applications such as Web browsers and e-mail. Guaranteed delivery takes longer and is used when it is important to know that the data reached its destination.

On the other hand, **UDP (User Datagram Protocol)** does not guarantee delivery by first connecting and checking whether data is received; thus, UDP is called a **connectionless protocol** or a **best-effort protocol**. UDP is primarily used for broadcasting and other types of transmissions, such as streaming video or sound over the Web, where guaranteed delivery is not as important as fast transmission.

At the next layer, TCP and UDP pass requests to **IP (Internet Protocol)**, which is responsible for breaking up and reassembling data into packets and routing them to their destination.

When IP receives a request from one of these protocols (see Figure 18-5), the request has header information and data and is one long stream of bytes.

**Figure 18-5**   TCP turns to IP to prepare the data for networking

At this point, IP looks at the size of the data and breaks it into individual packets, which can be up to 4K in size. IP adds its own IP header, which includes the IP address of its host (source IP address) and that of the server (destination IP address), and then passes off the packet to the hardware.

If TCP is used to guarantee delivery, TCP uses IP to establish a session between client and server to verify that communication has taken place. When a TCP packet reaches its destination, an acknowledgment is sent back to the source (see Figure 18-6). If the source TCP does not receive the acknowledgment, it resends the data or passes an error message back to the higher-level application protocol. In Figure 18-6, the HTTP data is handled by the TCP protocol, which depends on the IP protocol for transmission. TCP on the receiving end is responsible for acknowledging the delivery.

**Figure 18-6**   TCP guarantees delivery by requesting an acknowledgment

Other protocols that operate in this part of the transmission process include the following:

▲ **ARP (Address Resolution Protocol)** is responsible for locating a host on a local network.
▲ **RARP (Reverse Address Resolution Protocol)** is responsible for discovering the Internet address of a host on a local network.
▲ **ICMP (Internet Control Message Protocol)** is responsible for communicating problems with transmission. For example, if a packet exceeds the number of routers it is permitted to pass through on its way to its destination, which is called a **Time to Live (TTL)** or **hop count**, a router kills the packet and returns an ICMP message to the source, saying that the packet has been killed (see Figure 18-7).

**Figure 18-7**    A router eliminates a packet that has exceeded its TTL

## NETWORK PROTOCOLS USED BY HARDWARE

As you learned in the previous chapter, the most popular hardware protocol for wired networks is Ethernet. Another hardware protocol that you will learn about later in the chapter is PPP, which is used for data communication over phone lines.

## TCP/IP UTILITIES

When TCP/IP is installed as a Windows 2000/XP or Windows 9x/Me component, a group of utility tools is also installed that can be used to troubleshoot problems with TCP/IP. The most commonly used TCP/IP utilities are Ping, Winipcfg, and Ipconfig, which you learned about in the previous chapter. Table 18-2 lists these and other TCP/IP utilities, and lists the purpose for each. The program files are found in the \Windows or \Winnt folder.

| Utility | Description |
|---|---|
| ARP (Arp.exe) | Manages the IP-to-Ethernet address translation tables used to find the MAC address of a host on the network when the IP address is known. |
| Getmac (Getmac.exe) | Displays the NIC's MAC address (Windows XP only). |
| Ipconfig (Ipconfig.exe) | Displays the IP address of the host and other configuration information. (A command used by Unix similar to Ipconfig is config.) |

**Table 18-2**    Utilities installed with TCP/IP on Windows

| Utility | Description |
|---------|-------------|
| | Some parameters are: |
| | ▲ `Ipconfig /all`   Displays all information about the connection |
| | ▲ `Ipconfig /release`   Releases the current IP address |
| | ▲ `Ipconfig /renew`   Requests a new IP address |
| | ▲ `Ipconfig /?`   Displays information about Ipconfig |
| FTP (Ftp.exe) | Transfers files over a network. |
| Nbtstat (Nbtstat.exe) | Displays current information about TCP/IP and NetBEUI when both are being used on the same network. |
| Netstat (Netstat.exe) | Displays information about current TCP/IP connections. |
| NSLookup (Nslookup.exe) | Displays information about domain names and their IP addresses. |
| Ping (Ping.exe) | Verifies that there is a connection on a network between two hosts. |
| Route (Route.exe) | Allows you to manually control network routing tables. |
| Telnet (Telnet.exe) | Allows you to communicate with another computer on the network remotely, entering commands to control the remote computer. |
| Tracert (Tracert.exe) | Traces and displays the route taken from the host to a remote destination; Tracert is one example of a trace-routing utility. |
| Winipcfg (Winipcfg.exe) | A Windows 9x/Me utility to display IP address and other configuration information in a user-friendly window. In the Winipcfg window, use Release and Renew to release the current IP address and request a new one, which can sometimes solve TCP/IP connectivity problems when using a DHCP server. |

**Table 18-2**  Utilities installed with TCP/IP on Windows (continued)

In addition to the utilities that are automatically installed with TCP/IP, another useful utility is the Microsoft SNMP Agent. This utility can be installed after you install TCP/IP; to do so, use the Add or Remove Programs applet in the Control Panel. **SNMP (Simple Network Management Protocol)** provides system management tools for networks. A system administrator can monitor remote connections to computers running Windows clients with SNMP Agent. The administrator will most likely use the utility sparingly because it can be a security risk. For more information about SNMP, see RFC 1157 (*www.rfc-editor.org*).

> **⊕ A+ Exam Tip**
>
> The A+ 220-602 exam expects you to know about the following TCP/IP utilities listed in Table 18-2: Ipconfig.exe, Ping.exe, Tracert.exe, and NSLookup. Know the filename of the utility's program file as well as how and when to use the utility.

**APPLYING|CONCEPTS**   An interesting tool that lets you read information from the Internet name space is NSLookup, which requests information about domain name resolutions from the DNS server's zone data. Zone data is information about domain names and their corresponding IP addresses kept by a DNS server. The NSLookup utility program is included in Windows 2000/XP. For example, to use Windows XP to retrieve what the DNS server knows about the domain name *www.microsoft.com*, follow these directions:

1. Click **Start, Run**. Enter **Cmd** in the Run dialog box and press **Enter**. A command window opens.

2. Enter the command **nslookup www.microsoft.com** and then press **Enter**. Figure 18-8 shows the results. Notice in the figure that the DNS server knows about eight IP addresses assigned to *www.microsoft.com*. It also reports that this information is nonauthoritative, meaning that it is not the authoritative, or final, name server for the *www.microsoft.com* computer name.

**Figure 18-8** The Nslookup command reports information about the Internet name space

The Tracert (trace route) command can be useful when you're trying to resolve a problem reaching a destination host such as an FTP site or Web site. The command sends a series of requests to the destination computer and displays each hop to the destination. For example, to trace the route to the *www.course.com* site, enter this command in a command prompt window:

```
tracert www.course.com
```

The results of this command are shown in Figure 18-9. By default, the command makes 30 requests for up to 30 hops. The final 15 requests in the figure were not needed to show the complete path to the site, causing a "Request timed out" message to appear. Also, the Tracert command depends on ICMP information sent by routers when a packet's hop count has been exceeded. Some routers don't send this information. If a router doesn't respond, the "Request timed out" message appears.

18

A+
220-602
3.1
5.3

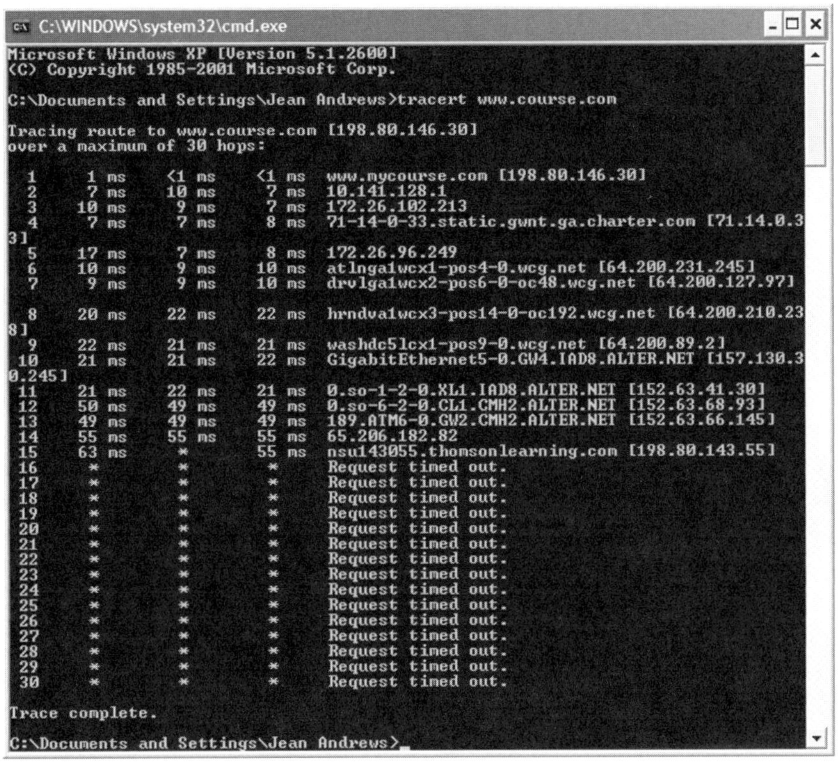

```
C:\WINDOWS\system32\cmd.exe                                          _ □ ×
Microsoft Windows XP [Version 5.1.2600]
(C) Copyright 1985-2001 Microsoft Corp.

C:\Documents and Settings\Jean Andrews>tracert www.course.com

Tracing route to www.course.com [198.80.146.30]
over a maximum of 30 hops:

  1     1 ms    <1 ms    <1 ms  www.mycourse.com [198.80.146.30]
  2     7 ms    10 ms     7 ms  10.141.128.1
  3    10 ms     9 ms     7 ms  172.26.102.213
  4     7 ms     7 ms     8 ms  71-14-0-33.static.gwnt.ga.charter.com [71.14.0.3
3]
  5    17 ms     7 ms     8 ms  172.26.96.249
  6    10 ms     9 ms    10 ms  atlnga1wcx1-pos4-0.wcg.net [64.200.231.245]
  7     9 ms     9 ms    10 ms  drvlga1wcx2-pos6-0-oc48.wcg.net [64.200.127.97]
  8    20 ms    22 ms    22 ms  hrndva1wcx3-pos14-0-oc192.wcg.net [64.200.210.23
8]
  9    22 ms    21 ms    21 ms  washdc5lcx1-pos9-0.wcg.net [64.200.89.2]
 10    21 ms    21 ms    22 ms  GigabitEthernet5-0.GW4.IAD8.ALTER.NET [157.130.3
0.245]
 11    21 ms    22 ms    21 ms  0.so-1-2-0.XL1.IAD8.ALTER.NET [152.63.41.30]
 12    50 ms    49 ms    49 ms  0.so-6-2-0.CL1.CMH2.ALTER.NET [152.63.68.93]
 13    49 ms    49 ms    49 ms  189.ATM6-0.GW2.CMH2.ALTER.NET [152.63.66.145]
 14    55 ms    55 ms    55 ms  65.206.182.82
 15    63 ms     *       55 ms  nsu143055.thomsonlearning.com [198.80.143.55]
 16     *        *        *     Request timed out.
 17     *        *        *     Request timed out.
 18     *        *        *     Request timed out.
 19     *        *        *     Request timed out.
 20     *        *        *     Request timed out.
 21     *        *        *     Request timed out.
 22     *        *        *     Request timed out.
 23     *        *        *     Request timed out.
 24     *        *        *     Request timed out.
 25     *        *        *     Request timed out.
 26     *        *        *     Request timed out.
 27     *        *        *     Request timed out.
 28     *        *        *     Request timed out.
 29     *        *        *     Request timed out.
 30     *        *        *     Request timed out.

Trace complete.

C:\Documents and Settings\Jean Andrews>
```

**Figure 18-9** The Tracert command traces a path to a destination computer

## CONNECTING TO THE INTERNET

A+ ESS
5.1

A+
220-602
5.1
5.3

In this part of the chapter, you'll learn how to connect a single PC to the Internet and then how to share that connection with other computers. Later in the chapter, you'll learn how to use a router to create a more sophisticated and secure Internet connection that can support multiple computers all accessing the Internet.

A single computer or local network connects to the Internet by way of an Internet service provider (ISP) using one of the following bandwidth technologies:

▲ *Regular telephone lines*. Regular telephone lines, the most common and least expensive way to connect to an ISP, require an internal or external modem. As you learned in Chapter 9, a modem converts a PC's digital data (data made up of zeros and ones) to analog data (continuous variations of frequencies) that can be communicated over telephone lines.

▲ *Cable modem*. **Cable modem** communication uses cable lines that already exist in millions of households. Just as with cable TV, cable modems are always connected (always up). Cable modem is an example of broadband media. **Broadband** refers to any type of networking medium that carries more than one type of transmission. With a cable modem, the TV signal to your television and the data signals to your PC share the same cable. Just like a regular modem, a cable modem converts a PC's digital signals to analog when sending them and converts incoming analog data to digital.

▲ *DSL*. **DSL (Digital Subscriber Line)** is a group of broadband technologies that covers a wide range of speeds. DSL uses ordinary copper phone lines and a range of frequencies on the copper wire that are not used by voice, making it possible for you to use the same phone line for voice and DSL at the same time. The voice portion of the phone line requires a dial-up as normal, but the DSL part of the line is always

A+ ESS
5.1

A+
220-602
5.1
5.3

connected or, in some regions, connects as needed. Asymmetric DSL (ADSL) uses one upload speed from the consumer to an ISP and a faster download speed. Symmetric DSL (SDSL) uses equal bandwidths in both directions.

▲ *ISDN.* **ISDN (Integrated Services Digital Network)** is a mostly outdated technology developed in the 1980s that also uses regular phone lines, and is accessed by a dial-up connection. For home use, an ISDN line is fully digital and consists of two channels, or phone circuits, on a single pair of wires called B channels, and a slower channel used for control signals, called a D channel. Each B channel can support speeds up to 64,000 bps. The two lines can be combined so that data effectively travels at 128,000 bps, about three to five times the speed of regular phone lines.

▲ *Satellite access.* People who live in remote areas and want high-speed Internet connections often are limited in their choices. DSL and cable modems might not work where they live, but satellite access is available from pretty much anywhere. Technology is even being developed to use satellites to offer Internet access on commercial airlines. Customers can use their own laptops to connect to the Internet through a connection at their seats to a satellite dish in the airplane. A satellite dish mounted on top of your house or office building communicates with a satellite used by an ISP offering the satellite service.

▲ *Wireless access.* Wireless refers to several technologies and systems that don't use cables for communication, including public radio, cellular phones, one-way paging, satellite, infrared, and private, proprietary radio. Because of its expense and the concern that increasing use of wireless might affect our health, as well as airplane control systems, pacemakers, and other sensitive electronic devices, wireless is not as popular as wired data transmission. Wireless is an important technology for mobile devices and for Internet access in remote locations where other methods are not an option.

> **Notes**
>
> Another bandwidth technology used for Internet access is FiOS by Verizon. FiOS uses fiber-optic cabling from your ISP to your house. You'll learn more about FiOS in a project at the end of this chapter.

In the following sections, you'll learn how to connect to the Internet using cable modem and DSL connections and a standard dial-up connection. You will learn how each type of connection is made as well as some advantages and disadvantages of each. Then, you'll learn how to share Internet connections using Windows. Finally, we'll look at how to use a software firewall to protect a computer from attacks.

> **Tip**
>
> The A+ Essentials and A+ 220-602 exams expect you to know how to connect to the Internet using a dial-up, cable modem, DSL, LAN, ISDN, satellite, and wireless connection. All these connections have many things in common. Skills learned in making one type of connection can be used when making another type.

## CABLE MODEM AND DSL CONNECTIONS

Recall that DSL and cable modem are called broadband technologies because they support the transmission of more than one kind of data at once. These connections can carry voice, data, sound, and video simultaneously. The major differences and similarities between cable modem and DSL are as follows:

▲ Cable modem uses TV cable for transmission and you subscribe to cable modem bundled with your TV cable subscription. On the other hand, DSL uses phone lines for transmission and is bundled with your local phone service.

A+
220-602
5.1
5.3

▲ Cable modem and DSL both can be purchased on a sliding scale depending on the bandwidth you want to buy. Also, both subscriptions offer residential and the more-expensive business plans. Residential plans are likely to use dynamic IP addressing, and business plans are likely to have static IP addressing, increased bandwidth, and better support when problems arise.

▲ With cable modem, you share the TV cable infrastructure with your neighbors, which can result in service becoming degraded if many people in your neighborhood are using cable modem at the same time. I once used cable modem in a neighborhood where I found I needed to avoid Web surfing between 5:00 and 7:00 p.m. when folks were just coming in from work and using the Internet. With DSL, you're using a dedicated phone line, so your neighbors' surfing habits are not important.

▲ With DSL, static over phone lines in your house can be a problem. The DSL company provides filters to install at each phone jack, but still the problem might not be fully solved. Also, your phone line must qualify for DSL; some lines are too dirty (too much static) to support DSL.

▲ Setup of cable modem and DSL works about the same way, using either a cable modem box or a DSL box for the interface between the broadband jack (TV jack or phone jack) and the PC. Figure 18-10 shows the setup for a cable modem connection using a network cable between the cable modem and the PC.

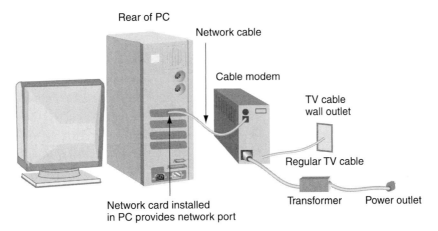

**Figure 18-10** Cable modem connecting to a PC through a network card installed in the PC

▲ With either installation, in most cases, you can have the cable modem or DSL provider do the entire installation for you at an additional cost. A service technician comes to your home, installs all equipment, including a network card if necessary, and configures your PC to use the service.

▲ In most cases, cable modem and DSL use a network port or a USB port on the PC to connect to the cable modem or DSL box.

Generally, when setting up a cable modem or DSL connection to the Internet, the installation goes like this:

1. Connect the PC to the cable modem or DSL box. Connect the cable modem to the TV jack or the DSL box to the phone line. Plug up the power and turn on the broadband device.

2. Configure the TCP/IP settings for the connection to the ISP.

3. Test the connection by using a browser to surf the Web.

A+
220-602
5.1
5.3

Now let's look at the specific details of making a cable modem connection or DSL connection to the Internet.

### INSTALLING A CABLE MODEM

To set up a cable modem installation to the Internet, you'll need the following:

- A computer with an available network or USB port
- A cable modem and a network or USB cable to connect to the PC
- The TCP/IP settings to use to configure TCP/IP provided by the cable modem company. For most installations, you can assume dynamic IP addressing is used. If static IP addressing is used, you'll need to know the IP address, the IP address of one or two DNS servers, the subnet mask, and the IP address of the default gateway (the IP address of a server at the ISP).

Then, follow these instructions to connect a computer to the Internet using cable modem:

1. Select the TV wall jack that will be used to connect your cable modem. You want to use the jack that connects directly to the point where the TV cable comes into your home with no splitters between this jack and the entrance point. Later, if your cable modem connection is constantly going down, you might consider that you've chosen the wrong jack for the connection because an inline splitter can degrade the connection. The cable company that installed the jacks should be able to tell you which jack is best to use for the cable modem (which is one good reason to have a technician come and hook you up for the first time).

2. Using coaxial cable, connect the cable modem to the TV wall jack. Plug in the power cord to the cable modem.

3. When using a network port on your PC, connect one end of the network cable to the network port on the PC and the other end to the network port on the cable modem.

4. You're now ready to configure Windows for the connection. Right-click **My Network Places** and select **Properties** from the shortcut menu. The Network Connections window opens. See Figure 18-11. Click **Create a new connection**.

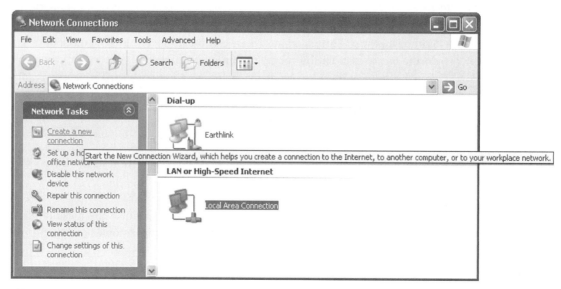

**Figure 18-11** Using Windows XP, launch the New Connection Wizard

A+
220-602
5.1
5.3

5. The New Connection Wizard opens. Click **Next** to skip the welcome screen. On the next screen, select **Connect to the Internet** and click **Next**.

6. On the next screen, select **Set up my connection manually** and click **Next**. On the following screen (see Figure 18-12), select **Connect using a broadband connection that is always on** and then click **Next**. The wizard creates the connection. Click **Finish** to close the wizard.

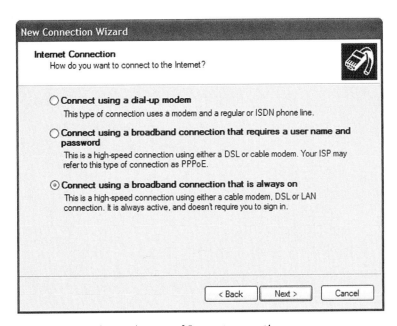

**Figure 18-12** Choose the type of Internet connection

Windows XP makes assumptions about your connection. To view the configuration and make any necessary changes, do the following:

1. In the Network Connections window, right-click the connection icon and select **Properties** from the shortcut menu. The connection's Properties window opens. Click the **General** tab to select it, if necessary, as shown in Figure 18-13.

2. Select **Internet Protocol (TCP/IP)**, if necessary, and click **Properties**. The Internet Protocol (TCP/IP) Properties window opens, as shown in Figure 18-14.

3. Most likely, your ISP is using dynamic IP addressing for your connection, so you will need to select **Obtain an IP address automatically** and **Obtain DNS server address automatically**. If you are using static IP addressing (for example, if you have a business account with your ISP), select **Use the following IP address**, and enter the IP address given to you by the ISP, along with the IP address of the default gateway and the IP addresses of two or more DNS servers. Click **OK** to close the window.

4. On the connection properties window, click the **Advanced** tab and then, under Windows Firewall, click **Settings** and verify the firewall is up. Click **OK** to close the window, and then click **OK** again to close the connection's Properties window.

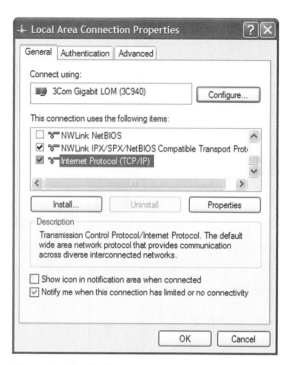

**Figure 18-13**    Configure an Internet connection using the Properties window of the connection icon

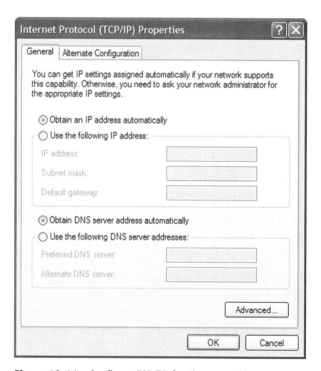

**Figure 18-14**    Configure TCP/IP for the connection

Follow these directions if you are using a USB cable to connect your cable modem to your computer:

1. When using a USB port on your PC, first read the directions that came with your cable modem to find out if you install the software before or after you connect the cable

A+
220-602
5.1
5.3

modem and follow that order. For most installations, you begin with connecting the cable modem.

2. Connect a USB cable to your PC and to the cable modem. Turn on the cable modem and Windows XP will automatically detect it as a new USB device. When the Found New Hardware Wizard launches, insert the USB driver CD that came with your cable modem. The wizard searches for and installs these drivers, as shown in Figure 18-15. Click **Finish** to close the Found New Hardware Wizard. A new connection icon will be added to the Network Connections window. Check the properties of the connection to make sure TCP/IP is configured as you want it.

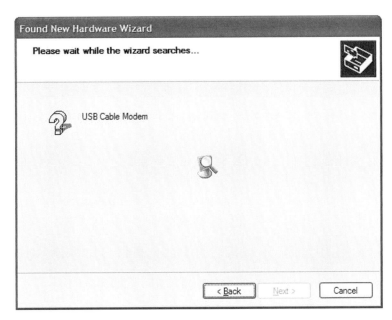

**Figure 18-15** When using a USB cable to connect to the cable modem, the Found New Hardware Wizard will install the cable modem drivers

You are now ready to activate your service and test the connection. Do the following:

1. The cable company must know the MAC address of the cable modem you have installed. If you have received the cable modem from your cable company, they already have the MAC address listed as belonging to you and you can skip this step. If you purchased the cable modem from another source, look for the MAC address somewhere on the back or bottom of the cable modem. Figure 18-16 shows the information on one modem. Contact the cable company and tell them the new MAC address.

2. Test the Internet connection using your Web browser. If you are not connecting, try the following:

   ▲ Open the Network Connections window, right-click the connection and select **Repair** from the shortcut menu. For dynamic IP addressing, this releases and renews the IP address. (For Windows 2000, use **Ipconfig /release** and **Ipconfig /renew** to release and renew the IP address. For Windows 9x/Me, use **Winipcfg** to access the IP Configuration window. Select the network card and click **Release All**. Wait a moment, and then click **Renew**.) Now check for Internet connectivity again.

**Figure 18-16** Look for the MAC address of the cable modem printed on the modem

▲ If this doesn't work, turn off the PC and the cable modem. Wait a full five minutes until all connections have timed out at the cable modem company. Turn on the cable modem and wait for the lights on the front of the modem to settle in. Then turn on the PC. After the PC boots up, again check for connectivity.

▲ Try another cable TV jack in your home.

▲ If this doesn't work, call the cable modem help desk. The technician there can release and restore the connection at that end, which should restore service.

### INSTALLING DSL

DSL service and the older technology, ISDN, are provided by the local telephone company. As with a cable modem, a technician from the phone company can install DSL for you, or they can send you a kit for you to install yourself. If you do the installation yourself, know that it works pretty much the same way as cable modem. Here are the steps that are different:

1. Install a telephone filter on every phone jack in your house that is being used by a telephone, fax machine, or dial-up modem. See Figure 18-17.

2. Connect the DSL modem, as shown in Figure 18-18. If necessary, you can use a Y-splitter on the wall jack (as shown on the left in Figure 18-17) so a telephone can use the same jack. Plug the DSL modem into the DSL port on a filter or directly into a wall jack. (Don't connect the DSL modem to a telephone port on the filter; this setup would prevent DSL from working.) Plug in the power to the DSL modem. Connect a network or USB cable between the DSL modem and the PC.

3. You're now ready to configure the network connection. If your DSL modem came with a setup CD, you can run that setup to step you through the configuration. You can also manually configure the network connection. To do that, using the Network Connections window, click **Create a new connection** and click **Next** to skip the welcome screen. Then click **Connect to the Internet** and click **Next**. Finally, click **Set up my connection manually**.

**Figure 18-17** Filters are needed on every phone jack when DSL is used in your house

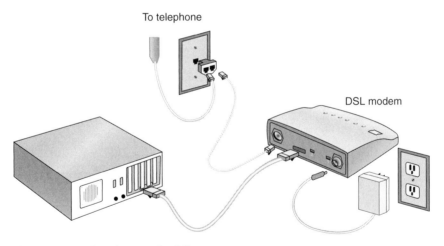

To telephone

DSL modem

**Figure 18-18** Sample setup for DSL

4. On the next screen, shown in Figure 18-12, you have a choice to make, based on the type of DSL subscription you have. If you subscribed to always-up DSL, click **Connect using a broadband connection that is always on**. If you have a DSL subscription that is active only when you log on with a username and password, then click **Connect using a broadband connection that requires a user name and password**. This last type of connection is managed by a protocol called **PPPoE (Point-to-Point Protocol Over Ethernet)**, which is why the connection is sometimes called a PPPoE connection. Follow the wizard through to complete the setup.

**Notes**

If your DSL subscription is not always up and requires you to enter your username and password each time you connect, using a router with autoconnecting ability can be a great help. It can automatically pass the username and password to your DSL provider without your involvement.

# DIAL-UP CONNECTIONS

Dial-up connections are painfully slow, but many times we still need them when traveling and they're good at home when our broadband connection is down or we just plain want to save money. Connecting to a network, such as the Internet, using a modem and regular phone line is called **dial-up networking**.

Dial-up networking works by using **PPP (Point-to-Point Protocol)** to send packets of data over phone lines, and is called a line protocol. (An earlier and outdated line protocol is **Serial Line Internet Protocol (SLIP)**.) The network protocol, TCP/IP, packages the data, making it ready for network traffic, and then PPP adds its own header and trailer to these packets. Figure 18-19a shows how this works. The data is presented to the network protocol, which adds its header information. Then, the packet is presented to the line protocol, PPP, which adds its own header and trailer to the packet and presents it to the modem for delivery over phone lines to a modem on the receiving end.

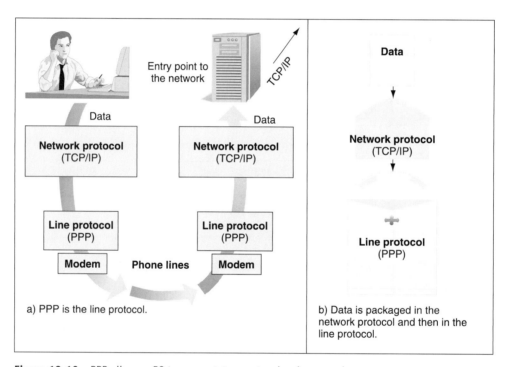

**Figure 18-19**    PPP allows a PC to connect to a network using a modem

The data packet is received by a computer at the ISP. The receiving computer strips off the PPP header and trailer information and sends the packet to the network still packaged in the TCP/IP protocols. In Figure 18-19b, these two protocols act like envelopes. Data is put in a TCP/IP envelope for travel over the network. This envelope is put in a PPP envelope for travel over phone lines. When the phone line segment of the trip is completed, the PPP envelope is discarded.

## CREATING A DIAL-UP CONNECTION USING WINDOWS 2000/XP

To use dial-up networking to connect to the Internet, follow these directions:

1. Install an internal or external dial-up modem. After the modem is installed, you can check Device Manager to make sure Windows recognizes the modem with no errors (see Figure 18-20). How to install a modem is covered in Chapter 9.

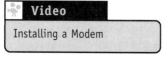

Video

Installing a Modem

18

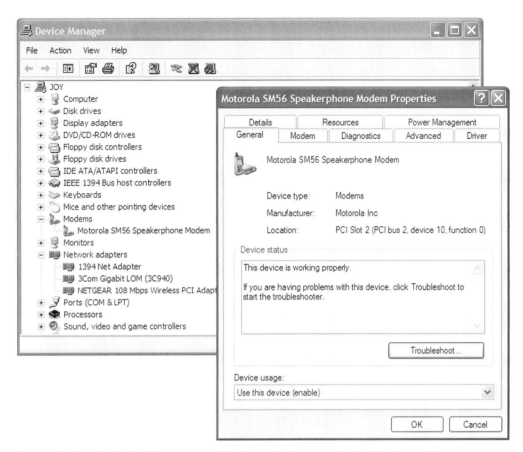

**Figure 18-20** Use Device Manager to verify the modem is recognized by Windows with no errors

2. To launch the New Connection Wizard in Windows XP, right-click **My Network Places** and select **Properties** from the shortcut menu. The Network Connections window opens. Click **Create a new connection**.

3. The New Connection Wizard opens. Click **Next** to skip the welcome screen. On the next screen, select **Connect to the Internet** and click **Next**.

4. On the next screen, select **Set up my connection manually** and click **Next**. On the following screen, select **Connect using a dial-up modem**. Click **Next**.

5. Enter a name to identify the connection, such as the name and city of your ISP. Click **Next**. On the following screen, enter the access phone number of your ISP. Click **Next**.

6. On the next screen (see Figure 18-21), enter your username and password at the ISP. This screen gives options to make the logon automatic and to make this the default connection to the Internet. Make your choices and click **Next**.

7. On the next screen, you can choose to add a shortcut to the connection on the desktop. Make your choice and click **Finish**. A connection icon is added to the Network Connections window; if you selected the option, a shortcut is added to the desktop.

8. To use the connection, double-click the connection icon. The Connect dialog box opens (see Figure 18-22). Click **Dial**. You will hear the modem dial up the ISP and make the connection.

A+
220-602
5.1

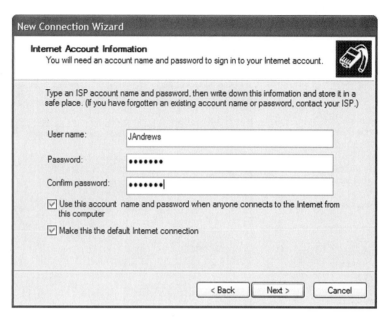

**Figure 18-21** The New Connection Wizard asks how to configure the connection

**Figure 18-22** Make a dial-up connection to your ISP

To view or change the configuration for the dial-up connection, do the following:

> **Notes**
>
> To launch the connection wizard in Windows 2000, right-click **My Network Places** and select **Properties** from the shortcut menu. The Network and Dial-up Connections window opens. Click **Make New Connection**. The wizard launches and steps you through the process to create a connection. The process is similar to that of Windows XP.

**1.** In the Network Connections window, right-click the connection and select **Properties** from the shortcut menu. The connection Properties window opens, as shown in Figure 18-23.

A+
220-602
5.1

**Figure 18-23** Configure an Internet connection using the Properties window of the connection icon

2. Use the tabs on this window to change Windows Firewall settings (Advanced tab), configure TCP/IP (Networking tab), control the way Windows attempts to dial the ISP when the first try fails (Options tab), and change other dialing features.

> **Video**
>
> Troubleshooting a Dial-Up Problem

If the dial-up connection won't work, here are some things you can try:

▲ Is the phone line working? Plug in a regular phone and check for a dial tone. Is the phone cord securely connected to the computer and the wall jack?

▲ Check the Dial-up Networking connection icon for errors. Is the phone number correct? Does the number need to include a 9 to get an outside line? Has a 1 been added in front of the number by mistake? If you need to add a 9, you can put a comma in the field like this "9,4045661200", which causes a slight pause after the 9 is dialed.

▲ Try dialing the number manually from a phone. Do you hear beeps on the other end?

▲ Try another phone number.

▲ When you try to connect, do you hear the number being dialed? If so, the problem is most likely with the phone number, the phone line, or the username and password.

▲ Does the modem work? Check Device Manager for reported errors about the modem. Does the modem work when making a call to another phone number (not your ISP)?

▲ Is TCP/IP configured correctly? Most likely, you need to set it to obtain an IP address automatically.

▲ Reboot your PC and try again.

▲ Using Device Manager, in the modem properties window, click the **Diagnostics** tab, as shown in Figure 18-24. Click **Query Modem** to have Windows attempt to communicate with the modem. If errors appear, assume the problem is related to the modem and not to the dial-up connection. You can also click **View log** to search for possible modem errors.

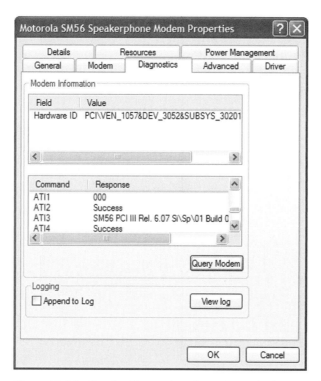

**Figure 18-24** Use the Diagnostics tab on the modem's Properties window to search for modem problems

◢ Try removing and reinstalling the dial-up connection. If that doesn't work, try using Device Manager to uninstall the modem and install it again. (Don't do this unless you have with you the modem drivers on CD or on the hard drive.)

> **Notes**
>
> If you want to disable call waiting while you're connected to the Internet, enter "*70" in front of the phone number (without the double quotes).

> 👍 **A+ Exam Tip**
>
> Even though Windows 9x/Me is not covered on the new 2006 A+ exams, this book is committed to covering both the new exams and the old 2003 exams that are still live at the time this book went to print.

## CREATING A DIAL-UP CONNECTION IN WINDOWS 9X/ME

To use Windows 98 or Windows Me to communicate with a network over phone lines, Dial-Up Networking must be installed as an OS component on your PC using the Add/Remove Programs applet in the Control Panel. (Network and Dial-Up Connections in Windows 2000 and Network Connections in Windows XP are installed by default.)

When Windows 98 installs Dial-Up Networking, it also "installs" a dial-up adapter. In terms of function, think of this dial-up adapter as a virtual network card. Remember that in the previous chapter, you learned how TCP/IP is bound to a network interface card. A dial-up adapter is a modem playing the role of a network card for dial-up networking. After Dial-Up Networking is installed, open the Device Manager to see your "new" dial-up adapter listed under Network adapters, as shown in Figure 18-25. You can also see it listed as an installed network component in the Network window of the Control Panel.

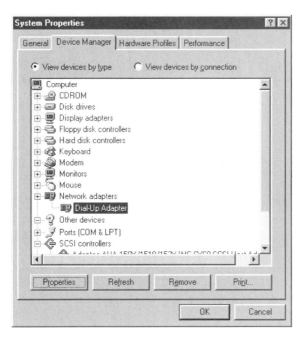

**Figure 18-25** After Dial-Up Networking is installed, a new virtual network device, a dial-up adapter, is listed as an installed hardware device

After you have verified the dial-up adapter is installed, you are now ready to create a Dial-Up Networking connection. To create the connection in Windows 98:

1. After Dial-Up Networking is installed, click **Start,** point to **Programs, Accessories,** and **Communications,** and then click **Dial-Up Networking.** The Dial-Up Networking window opens, as shown on the left side of Figure 18-26.

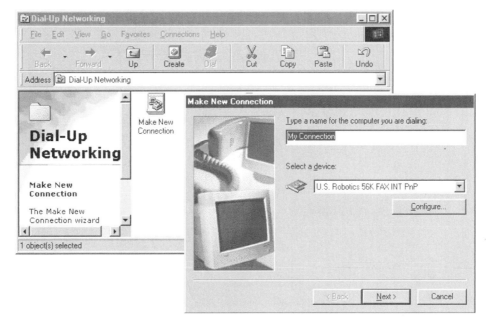

**Figure 18-26** Creating a Windows 98 Dial-Up Networking Connection icon

2. Double-click **Make New Connection**. The Make New Connection Wizard appears, as shown on the right side of Figure 18-26. Click **Next** to move past the first screen.

3. Enter a name for the connection. If your modem is already installed, it appears in the modem list.

4. In the next dialog box, type the phone number to dial, and then click **Next** to continue.

5. Click **Finish** to build the icon. The icon appears in the Dial-Up Networking window.

Next, you will configure the connection. In Windows 98, do the following:

1. Right-click the icon you created for the connection, and select **Properties** from the shortcut menu.

2. Click the **General** tab. Verify that the correct phone number is entered for your ISP.

3. Click the **Server Types** tab. Figure 18-27 shows the resulting dialog box. Verify that these selections are made:

   ◢ Type of Dial-Up Server: **PPP: Internet, Windows NT Server, Windows 98**

   ◢ Advanced Options: Select **Enable software compression** (software compression is most likely enabled, but this option really depends on what the ISP is doing). Also, click **Log on to network**.

   ◢ Allowed Network Protocols: **TCP/IP**

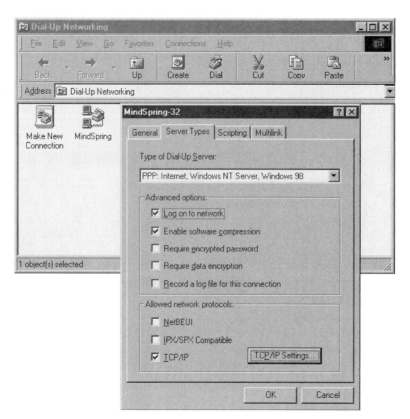

**Figure 18-27** Configuring the server type for a connection to the Internet in Windows 9x/Me

18

4. Click **TCP/IP Settings** to open the TCP/IP Settings dialog box, as shown in Figure 18-28. Most likely, you will need to select:

 ◢ Server assigned IP address

 ◢ Server assigned name server addresses

 ◢ Use IP header compression

 ◢ Use default gateway on remote network

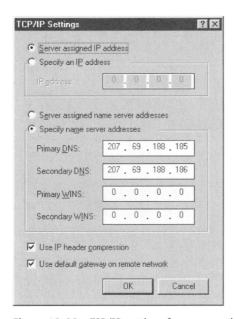

**Figure 18-28**  TCP/IP settings for a connection to the Internet in Windows 9x/Me

5. Click **OK** twice to complete the Dial-Up Networking connection.

6. To connect to your ISP, double-click the icon you created for it, which is now correctly configured. The first time you use the icon, enter the user ID and password to connect to your ISP. Check the option to remember the username and password if you don't want to have to enter them every time, but remember that this selection might not be wise if others who cannot be trusted have access to your PC.

7. Click **Connect**. You should hear the modem making the connection.

---

> **Notes**
>
> When troubleshooting problems with a modem using Windows 9x/Me, you can create a log file showing communication between Windows and the modem. To create the log file, open the **Network** applet in the Control Panel, select **Dial-Up Adapter**, and then click **Properties**. In the Properties window, click the **Advanced** tab. In the Property box, select **Record A Log File**, and in the Value box, select **Yes**. Click **OK**. The file, Ppplog.txt, is created in the Windows folder. The file can get very large, so turn off logging when you don't need it. For tips on how to interpret the file, see the Microsoft Knowledge Base Article 156435, at *support.microsoft.com*.

A+
220-602
5.1

## HIGH-SPEED DIAL-UP

Dial-up connections can be painfully slow when surfing the Web. If your ISP offers the option, you can speed up a dial-up connection to the Internet by using high-speed dial-up, which can

A+
220-602
5.1

almost double the average download times for much Web surfing. Two ISPs that support this feature are NetZero (*www.netzero.net*) and EarthLink (*www.earthlink.net*). Using high-speed dial-up, the phone line connection runs at the regular speed. However, downloading from the Internet is faster because the ISP provides these things to speed up downloading:

▲ *Abbreviated handshake*. When two modems first connect, they go through a handshaking routine to agree on protocols used for the connection. You hear the handshaking routine as a series of hisses and hums when the modems first connect. With high-speed dial-up, this handshaking process is abbreviated so that the initial connection to the ISP happens quickly.

▲ *Data compression*. The ISP uses an acceleration server, as shown in Figure 18-29, to compress data just before it is downloaded to you. Web pages, text, photos, and e-mails are compressed. The degree of compression depends on the type of data.

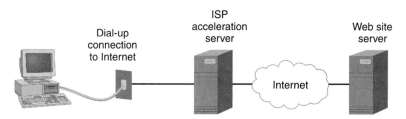

**Figure 18-29** With high-speed dial-up, an acceleration server is used to improve download time

▲ *Filtering*. When your PC requests a Web page, many times that page is filled with unwanted pop-up ads. The acceleration server detects these ads and blocks them before downloading, thus reducing the amount of data to download and increasing the effective download speed.

▲ *Caching*. Recall from earlier chapters that caching is a technique that holds data until it's needed at a later time in order to speed up data access. Caching can happen on the server side (at the ISP) or on the client side (on your PC). These two types of caching are called **server-side caching** and **client-side caching**, as shown in Figure 18-30. When the acceleration server caches data, it holds Web pages that you have already requested in case you ask for them again, so that it doesn't have to go back a second time to the original Web site. With client-side caching, your browser holds in a cache Web pages that you've already seen in case you ask for the same page again. Also, caching software can be smart enough to request only part of the Web page—the part that might have changed—rather than requesting the entire page again. Internet Explorer normally uses caching, but with high-speed dial-up, the high-speed dial-up software you install on your PC when you subscribe to the service enhances IE caching so that it's smarter and works better.

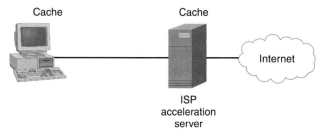

**Figure 18-30** Server-side caching and client-side caching improve download times by reducing the number of requests for data

## SHARING A PERSONAL INTERNET CONNECTION

You have just seen how you can connect a single computer to the Internet using a cable modem, DSL, or dial-up connection. If the computer is networked with other computers, they, too, can access the Internet through this host computer, as illustrated in Figure 18-31. In Figure 18-31a, two computers are connected with a single crossover network cable, and in Figure 18-31b, a hub or switch is used to connect three or more computers in a small network. The host computer is the one that has the direct connection to the Internet.

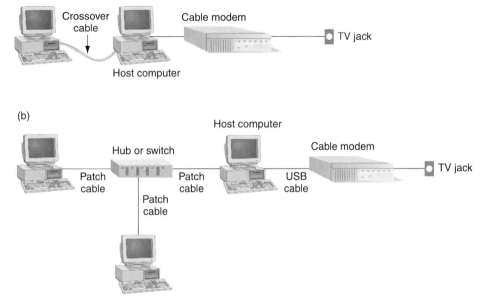

**Figure 18-31**   Two or more networked computers can share a single Internet connection

Windows XP and Windows 98 use **Internet Connection Sharing (ICS)** to manage these types of connections. Using ICS, the host computer uses NAT and acts as the proxy server for the LAN. Windows XP ICS also includes a firewall.

---

**APPLYING | CONCEPTS**   To use Internet Connection Sharing in Windows XP or Windows 98, the computer that has a direct connection to the Internet by way of a phone line, cable modem, or DSL is the host computer. Follow these general directions to configure the LAN for Internet Connection Sharing using Windows XP:

1. Following directions earlier in the chapter, install and configure the hardware (modem, cable modem, or DSL) to connect the host computer to the Internet, and verify that the connection is working so that the host computer can browse the Web.

2. On the host computer, open the Network Connections window in the Windows XP Control Panel, and click the link to **Set up a home or small office network.** The Network Setup Wizard opens. Click **Next** in this window and the next.

3. Select the connection method for your host computer, which is **This computer connects directly to the Internet. The other computers on my network connect to the Internet through this computer.** Click **Next.**

A+
220-602
5.2

4. The wizard looks at your hardware connections (NIC or modem) and selects the one that it sees as a "live" connection. Verify that the wizard selected correctly and then follow the wizard to enter a description for your computer, your computer name, and your workgroup name.

### Notes

To find out how to configure a Macintosh computer to connect to the Internet by way of a Windows computer providing an ICS connection, see the Microsoft Knowledge Base Article 230585 at *support.microsoft.com*.

5. The next screen of the wizard offers you the option of creating a Network Setup Disk (see Figure 18-32). If the other computers are not running Windows XP or Windows 98 and they have floppy disk drives, you'll need to create this disk so they can use the shared Internet connection. (If other computers on your network are running Windows 98 or Windows XP, there is no need to create the disk.) To create the disk, select the option to **Create a Network Setup Disk**, insert a blank floppy disk in the drive, and click **Next**.

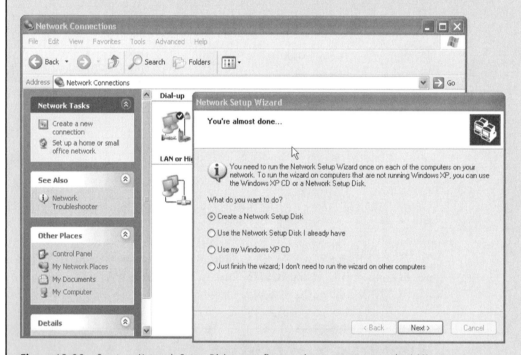

**Figure 18-32**    Create a Network Setup Disk to configure other computers on the LAN

6. The next screen gives you the option to format the disk. If it needs formatting, click **Format Disk**. Otherwise, click **Next**.

7. The wizard tells you that to use the disk, you must insert it into the next computer on the network, and run the program named Netsetup.exe from the disk. Click **Next** and then click **Finish**.

8. For the other computers in your network using Windows XP, open the **Network Connections** window and click the link to **Set up a home or small office network**. Follow the steps of the wizard to make the connection to the Internet. When given the opportunity, select **This computer connects to the Internet through a residential gateway or through another computer on my network**. Test that each computer can browse the Web. If you have problems, verify the TCP/IP configuration is correct. Try rebooting the PC.

**9.** For all other computers, insert the Network Setup Disk in the floppy disk drive. At a command prompt, enter the command **A:Netsetup.exe** and then press **Enter**. After the program is finished, test that the computer can browse the Web. You might have to verify TCP/IP configuration and reboot the PC.

## IMPLEMENTING A SOFTWARE FIREWALL

The Internet is a nasty and dangerous place infested with hackers, viruses, worms, and thieves. Knowing how to protect a single PC or a LAN is an essential skill of a PC support technician. The three most important things you can do to protect a single computer or network are to:

- ◢ Keep Windows updates current so that security patches are installed as soon as they are available.
- ◢ Use a software or hardware firewall.
- ◢ Run antivirus software and keep it current.

In earlier chapters, you learned how to keep Windows updates current. In the next chapter, you'll learn all about using antivirus software. In this section, you'll learn to use a software firewall. Software firewalls are appropriate when you're protecting a single personal computer or a host computer that is sharing an Internet connection with a few other computers. Then, in the later sections of this chapter, you'll learn how to use a hardware firewall.

A hardware or software firewall can function in several ways:

- ◢ Firewalls can filter data packets, examining the destination IP address or source IP address or the type of protocol used (for example, TCP or UDP).
- ◢ Firewalls can filter ports so that outside clients cannot communicate with inside services listening at these ports. Certain ports can be opened, for example, when your network has a Web server and you want Internet users to be able to access it.
- ◢ Firewalls can block certain activity that is initiated from inside the network—such as preventing users behind the firewall from using applications like FTP over the Internet. When evaluating firewall software, look for its ability to control traffic coming from both outside and inside the network.
- ◢ Some firewalls can filter information such as inappropriate Web content for children or employees, and can limit the use of the Internet to certain days or time of day.

Some examples of firewall software are ZoneAlarm (see Figure 18-33) by Zone Labs (*www.zonelabs.com*), Norton Personal Firewall by Symantec (*www.symantec.com*), Check Point Software by Check Point Software Technologies (*www.checkpoint.com*), McAfee Personal Firewall by McAfee (*www.mcafee.com*), Personal Firewall Pro by Sygate (*www.sygate.com*), and Windows XP Firewall.

> ✎ **Notes**
>
> Before Service Pack 2 for Windows XP was released, the firewall software for Windows XP was called Windows XP Internet Connection Firewall (ICF), and if this firewall was turned on, others on the LAN couldn't access resources on the PC. If you have Windows XP, be sure to install Service Pack 2 so that you have the benefit of the upgraded and much improved Windows Firewall.

A+ ESS
6.1

A+
220-602
5.3
6.2
6.3

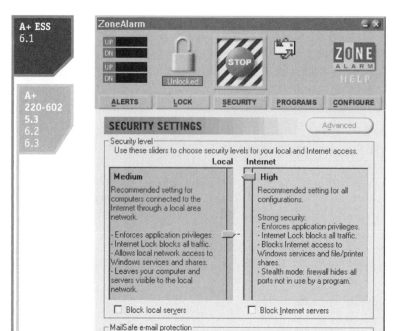

**Figure 18-33**    ZoneAlarm allows you to determine the amount of security the firewall provides

For Windows XP with Service Pack 2 applied, to manage Windows Firewall, open the **Network Connections** window. In the left pane, click **Change Windows Firewall settings**. The Windows Firewall window opens, as shown in Figure 18-34. Verify that **On (recommended)** is selected.

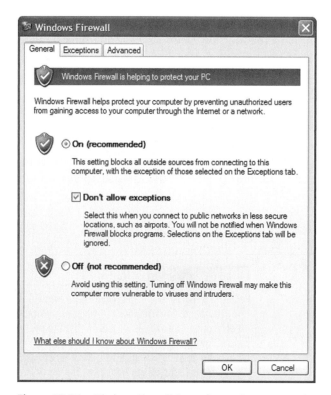

**Figure 18-34**    Windows Firewall is set for maximum protection

If you don't want to allow any communication to be initiated from remote computers, check **Don't allow exceptions**. This is the preferred setting when you're traveling or using public networks or Internet connections. If you are on a local network and need to allow others on the network to access your computer, uncheck **Don't allow exceptions**. Then click the **Exceptions** tab to select the exceptions to allow. For example, if you want to share files and folders on your local network, use the Exceptions tab shown in Figure 18-35, to allow File and Printer Sharing activity. Later in the chapter, you'll see another example of how to use this Exceptions tab to set up Windows XP Remote Desktop.

**Figure 18-35**  Exception communications allowed by Windows Firewall

## USING A ROUTER ON YOUR NETWORK

So far in the chapter, you've seen how one computer can connect to the Internet using a broadband or dial-up connection and also how this host computer can share that connection with others on a LAN. Two major disadvantages of this setup are that the host computer must always be turned on for others on the network to reach the Internet and the fact that security for your network is not as strong as it could be if you use a hardware firewall. Also, access to the Internet for other computers might be slow because of the bottleneck caused by the host computer. Installing a router solves all these problems.

Recall from the previous chapter that a router is a device that manages traffic between two networks. In Figure 18-36, you can see how a router stands between the ISP network and the local network. The router takes the place of the host computer as the gateway to the Internet and also serves as a hardware firewall to protect your network.

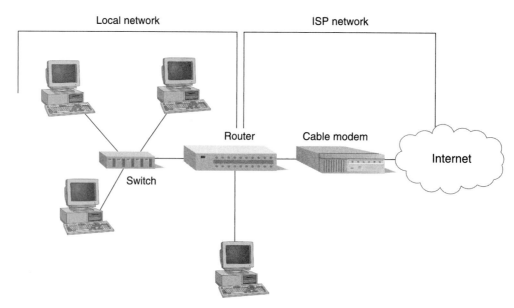

**Figure 18-36**   A router stands between the Internet and a local network

## ADVANTAGES OF USING A ROUTER

The advantages of using a router rather than a host computer are:

▲ The host computer will not be a bottleneck to slow down performance for other computers using the Internet.
▲ Internet access is not dependent on the host computer being up and running.
▲ The router can also serve as a hardware firewall device, which provides better protection than a software firewall. In addition, a router can limit access to the Internet. This added security provided by a router is probably the most important reason to use a router for an Internet connection.
▲ The router can provide additional features—such as a DHCP server, switch, or wireless access point—not available on a host computer.

Three companies that make routers suitable for small networks are D-Link (*www.dlink.com*), Linksys (*www.linksys.com*), and NetGear (*www.netgear.com*). An example of a multifunction router is the Wireless-G Broadband Router by Linksys shown in Figure 18-37, which costs less than $60. It has one port for the broadband modem and four ports for computers on the network. The router is also an 802.11b/g wireless access point having two antennae to amplify the wireless signal and improve its range.

A+
220-602
5.3

**Figure 18-37**  This Linksys router allows computers on a LAN to share a broadband Internet connection and is an access point for computers with wireless adapters

The router shown in Figure 18-37 is typical of many brands and models of routers useful in a small office or small home network to manage the Internet connection. This router is several devices in one:

▲ As a router, it stands between the ISP network and the local network, routing traffic between the two networks.

▲ As a switch, it manages four network ports that can be connected to four computers or to a hub or switch that connects to more than one computer. In the small office setting pictured in Figure 18-38, this router connects to four network jacks that are wired in the walls to four other jacks in the building. Two of these remote jacks have switches connected that accommodate two or more computers.

▲ As a proxy server, all computers on the network route their Internet requests through this proxy server, which stands between the network and the Internet using NAT.

**Figure 18-38**   A router and cable modem are used to provide Internet access for a small network

> **Notes**
>
> Recall that a proxy server adds protection to a network because it stands in proxy for other computers on the network when they want to communicate with computers on the Internet. The proxy server presents its own IP address to the Internet and does not allow outside computers to know the IP addresses of computers inside the network. This substitution of IP addresses is done using the NAT (Network Address Translation) protocol.

- As a DHCP server, all computers can receive their IP address from this server.
- As a wireless access point, a computer can connect to the network using a wireless device. This wireless connection can be secured using four different wireless security features.
- As a firewall, unwanted traffic initiated from the Internet can be blocked.
- As an Internet access restrictive device, the router can be set so that Internet access is limited.

## INSTALLING AND CONFIGURING A ROUTER

To install a router that comes with a setup CD, run the setup program on one of your computers on the network (doesn't matter which one). Follow the instructions on the setup screen to disconnect the cable modem or DSL modem from your host computer and connect it to the router. Next, connect the computers on your network to your router. A computer can connect directly to a network port on the router, or you can connect a switch or hub to the router. Plug in the router and turn it on.

You'll be required to sign in to the utility using a default password. The first thing you want to do is reset this password so others cannot change your router setup.

A+
220-602
5.3

> **⚡ Caution**
>
> Changing the router password is especially important if the router is a wireless router. Unless you have disabled or secured the wireless access point, anyone outside your building can use your wireless network. If they guess the default password to the router, they can change the password to hijack your router. Also, your wireless network can be used for criminal activity. When you first install a router, before you do anything else, change your router password and disable the wireless network until you have time to set up and test the wireless security.

The setup program will then step you through the process of configuring the router. After you've configured the router, you might have to turn the cable modem or DSL modem off and back on so that it correctly syncs up with the router. If you don't get immediate connectivity to the Internet on all PCs, try rebooting each PC.

## CONFIGURING THE ROUTER

Now let's look at how this Linksys router is configured, which is typical of what you might see for several brands and models of small office routers. Firmware on the router (which can be flashed for updates) contains a configuration program that you access using a Web browser from anywhere on the network. In your browser address box, enter the IP address of the router (for our router, it's 192.168.1.1) and press **Enter**. The main Setup window opens, as shown in Figure 18-39. For most situations, the default settings on this and other screens should work without any changes.

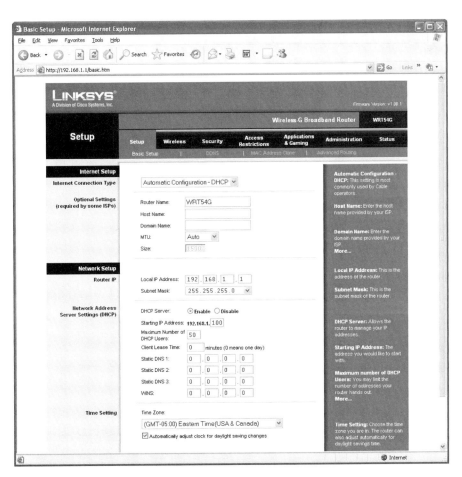

**Figure 18-39** Basic Setup screen used to configure the router

A+
220-602
5.3

Using this Setup screen, under Internet Setup, you can change the host name and domain name if they are given to you by your ISP or leave them blank, which most often is the case. Under Network Setup, you can configure the DHCP server. Notice in the figure that the router can serve up to 50 leased IP addresses beginning with IP address 192.168.1.100. You can also disable the DHCP server if you want to use static IP addressing on your network or you already have another DHCP server on the network.

> **Video**
>
> Using a Hardware Firewall

After the router is configured as a DHCP server, you can configure each PC on your network to use dynamic IP addressing.

## CONFIGURING A HARDWARE FIREWALL

In this section, you'll learn how to configure the Linksys router's firewall abilities to protect the network. You can use this information as a guide to configuring another router because, although the exact steps might vary, the basic principles will be the same.

> **Caution**
>
> Remember that you should always change the password to your router's setup utility. Default passwords for routers are easily obtained on the Web or in the product documentation. This is especially important for wireless routers.

To configure security on the firewall, click the **Security** link (as shown near the top of Figure 18-39). The window shown in Figure 18-40 appears. The most important item on this window is Block Anonymous Internet Requests. Enabling this feature prevents your network from being detected or accessed from others on the Internet without an invitation.

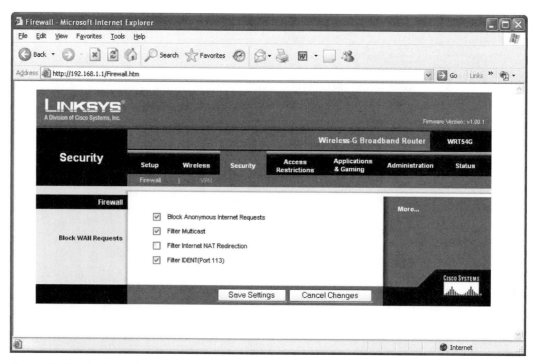

**Figure 18-40**   Configure the router's firewall to prevent others on the Internet from seeing or accessing your network

You can set policies to determine how and when users on your network can access the Internet. To do that, click **Access Restrictions**. The window shown in Figure 18-41 opens, allowing you to set policies about the day and time of Internet access, the services on the Internet that can be used, and the URLs and keywords that are not allowed.

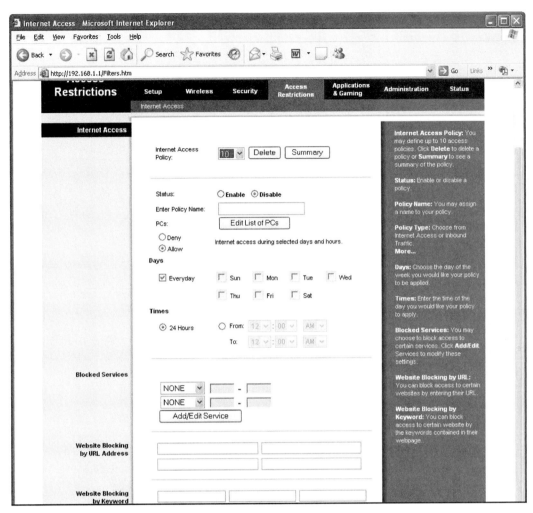

**Figure 18-41** Configure the router's firewall to limit Internet access from within the network

## PORT FILTERING AND PORT FORWARDING

Too much security is not always a good thing. There are legitimate times you want to be able to access computers on your network from somewhere on the Internet or allow others to do so, such as when you're hosting an Internet game or when you're traveling and want to use Remote Desktop to access your home computer. In this section, we'll look at how to drop your shields low enough so that the good guys can get in but the bad guys can't. However, know that when you drop your shields the least bit, you're compromising the security of your network, so be sure to use these methods sparingly. Here are the concepts that can be used; they are illustrated in Figure 18-42:

▲ Port filtering is used to open or close certain ports so they can or cannot be used. Remember that applications are assigned these ports. Therefore, in effect, you are filtering or controlling what applications can or cannot be used across the firewall.

▲ **Port forwarding** means that when the firewall receives a request for communication from the Internet, if the request is for a certain port, that request will be allowed and forwarded to a certain computer on the network. That computer is defined to the router by its IP address.

▲ For port forwarding to work, the local computer that is to receive this communication must have a static IP address.

A+
220-602
5.3

**Figure 18-42**    With port forwarding, a router allows requests initiated outside the network

To demonstrate how to use port filtering and port forwarding to allow limited access to your network from the outside world, suppose you have set up a Web-hosting site on a computer that sits behind your firewalled router. To allow others on the Web to access your site, you would do the following:

1. If your ISP is using dynamic IP addressing, contact the ISP and request a static IP address. Most likely, the ISP will charge extra for this service. Find out the static IP address, which you can give to your friends. Your friends will then enter this IP address in their Web browsers to access your Web site.

2. Configure the router to use static IP addressing. For the Linksys router we're using as our example, the basic setup screen in Figure 18-43 shows how to configure the router for static IP addressing, using the gateway, and DNS server IP addresses and subnet mask provided by the ISP.

3. Next, configure your router to use port forwarding so that it will allow Web browser connections initiated from the Internet to pass through to your computer. Using your router's configuration utility, find the window that allows port forwarding, such as the one shown in Figure 18-44.

4. Enter the port that Web servers use, which, by default, is port 80, and the IP address of your desktop computer. In this example, the IP address chosen is 192.168.1.90. Check **Enable** to allow activity on this port to this computer. Save your changes.

5. Configure the computer that is running your Web server for static IP addressing and assign the IP address 192.168.1.90. Test the connection by using a computer that is somewhere on the Internet to access your Web site.

By the way, if you want your friends to be able to use a domain name rather than an IP address to access your Web site, you'll need to purchase the domain name and register it in the Internet name space to associate it with your static IP address assigned by your ISP. Several Web sites on the Internet let you do both; one site is by Network Solutions at *www.networksolutions.com.*

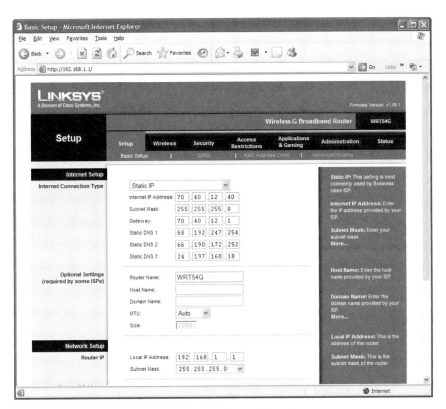

**Figure 18-43** Configure the router for static IP addressing

**Figure 18-44** Using port forwarding, you can program your router to allow activity from the Internet to initiate a session with a computer inside the network on a certain port

A+ ESS
6.1
6.2
6.3

A+
220-602
6.2
6.3

# VIRTUAL PRIVATE NETWORK

Many people travel on their jobs or work from home, and the need is constantly growing for people to access private corporate data from somewhere on the Internet. Also growing are the dangers of private data being exposed in this way. The solution for securing private data traveling over a public network is a virtual private network (VPN) that you first learned about in the previous chapter. Recall that a VPN works by using encrypted data packets between a private network and a computer somewhere on the Internet, as shown in Figure 18-45.

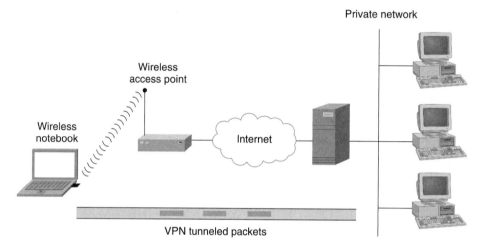

**Figure 18-45** With a VPN, tunneling is used to send encrypted data over wired and wireless networks and the Internet

With a VPN, security is attained using both of these methods:

▲ User accounts and passwords are required for connection to the corporate network. When the remote user sends this information to the authentication server, the data is encrypted. The encryption protocols supported by Windows XP for the user account and password data are EAP (Extensible Authentication Protocol), SPAP (Shiva Password Authentication Protocol), CHAP (Challenge Handshake Authentication Protocol), and MS-CHAP (Microsoft CHAP).

▲ After the user is authenticated, a tunnel is created so that all data sent between the user and the company is strongly encrypted. One of these four tunneling protocols is used: Point-to-Point Tunneling Protocol (PPTP), Layer Two Tunneling Protocol (L2TP), SSL (Secure Sockets Layer), or IPsec (IP security). Of the four, PPTP is the weakest protocol and should not be used if one of the other three is available. The strongest protocol is a combination of L2TP and IPSec, which is called L2TP over IPSec. The two most popular protocols are SSL and IPsec.

To set up a VPN on the corporate side, the network administrator will most likely use a hardware device such as a VPN router to manage the VPN. A router that supports VPN is considerably more expensive than one that does not. To configure the router to support VPN, generally an administrator must:

▲ Select the encryption protocol used to encrypt the user account and password data.
▲ Select the tunneling protocol to use for the VPN.
▲ Configure each tunnel the VPN will support. Each tunnel must be assigned a user account and password, which is kept on the router.

A+ ESS
6.1
6.2
6.3

A+
220-602
6.2
6.3

Figure 18-46 shows a configuration window for a VPN router. The tunneling protocol has been selected to be IPSec. The next step in configuring this VPN is to add one tunnel for each remote user who will use the VPN. So far, no tunnels have been configured.

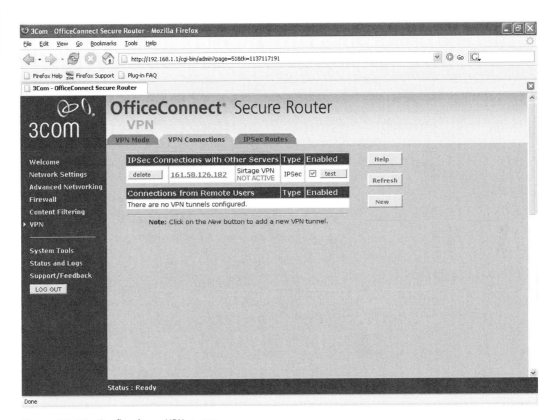

**Figure 18-46**  Configuring a VPN router

On the client end, to configure a VPN using Windows XP, a VPN network connection is created using the Windows XP Network Connections window. Follow these steps:

1. Open the **Network Connections** window and click **Create a new connection**. The New Connection Wizard launches. Click **Next**.

2. On the next screen, select **Connect to the network at my workplace**, and then click **Next**.

3. On the next screen (see Figure 18-47), select **Virtual Private Network connection**, and then click **Next**. Then enter the name of your company and click **Next**.

4. On the next screen, decide whether you want Windows to automatically dial up your ISP when you use the connection, and then click **Next**.

5. Enter the host name or IP address of the VPN (most likely, this is the static IP address that the ISP has assigned to your local network). Click **Next** and then click **Finish**. The VPN icon is added to your Network Connections window.

6. Windows XP automatically uses PPTP encryption. If you want to switch to L2TP over Ipsec (the other allowed protocol), right-click the network connection icon and select **Properties** from the shortcut menu. The properties window appears. Click the **Networking** tab and select **L2TP IPSec VPN** from the drop-down menu under Type of VPN (see Figure 18-48). To view and change the type of protocols allowed to encrypt the user account and password information, click the **Settings** button on the **Security** tab.

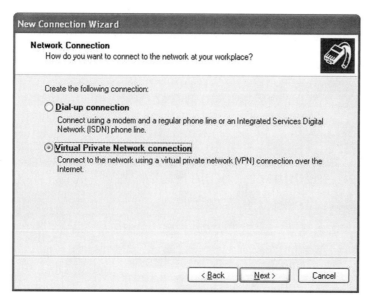

**Figure 18-47**   Use the New Connection Wizard to set up a connection to a VPN

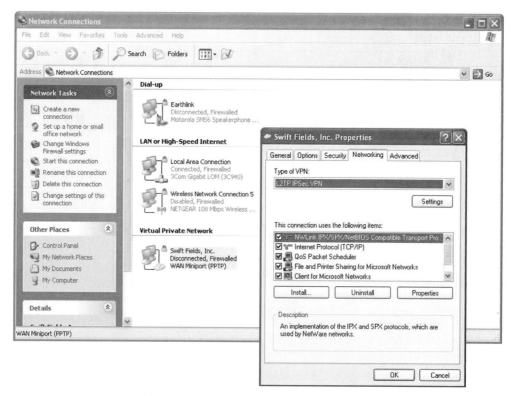

**Figure 18-48**   Properties window of a VPN connection

## SUPPORTING INTERNET CLIENTS

Now that you've learned how to connect to the Internet, let's look at some ways of using it. Earlier in the chapter in Table 18-1, you saw a list of application services that use the Internet. In this section, you will learn how to support some of the most common Internet clients: Web browsers, e-mail, FTP, VoIP, and Windows XP Remote Desktop.

A+
220-602
5.1
5.2

## SUPPORTING WEB BROWSERS

A Web browser is a software application on a user's PC that is used to request Web pages from a Web server on the Internet or an intranet. A Web page is a text file with an .htm or .html file extension. It can include text coded in **HTML (Hypertext Markup Language)** that can be interpreted by a Web browser to display formatted text, graphics, and video, as well as play sounds. If the HTML code on the Web page points to other files used to build the page, such as a sound file or a photograph file, these files are also downloaded to the browser. In this section, you will learn about the addresses that Web browsers use to locate resources on a Web server, how to configure a browser, and how to solve problems with browsers. You'll also learn about using secure Web sites.

> **Notes**
>
> The HTTP protocol is used by browsers and Web servers for communication. The HTML language is used to build and interpret Web pages.

### HOW A URL IS STRUCTURED

Earlier in the chapter you saw that a Web browser requests a Web page by sending an IP address followed by an optional port number. This works well on an intranet, but on the Internet, a more user-friendly address is preferred. That user-friendly address is a **URL (Uniform Resource Locator)**, which is an address for a Web page or other resource on the Internet. Figure 18-49 shows the structure of a URL.

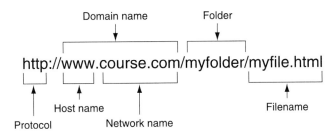

**Figure 18-49** A URL contains the protocol used, the host name of the Web server, the network name, and the path and filename of the requested file

The first part of the URL shown in Figure 18-49 indicates the protocol, which in this case is HTTP. The protocol part of the URL specifies the rules, or protocol, the Web server should use when transmitting the page to the browser. A Web server is sometimes called an HTTP server.

Recall from Chapter 17 that a host name identifies a server or another computer within a network. In this last example, the host name is *www* (a Web server), and *course.com* is the name of the Course Technology network, sometimes called the domain name. A name that contains not only the network name (in this case, *course.com*) but also the host on that network is called a fully qualified domain name (FQDN), as you learned in Chapter 17. In this case, the FQDN is *www.course.com*. The Web page requested is located in the folder *myfolder* on the *www* server, and the file within that folder is named *myfile.html*. The FQDN must be resolved to an IP address before the request can happen.

The final segment, or suffix, of a domain name is called the **top-level domain** (*.com* in our example) and tells you something about the organization or individual who owns the name. Some domain names in the United States end in the suffixes listed in Table 18-3. There are other endings as well, including codes for countries, such as .uk for the United Kingdom. With the growth of the Internet, there has been a shortage of available domain names; because of this shortage, additional suffixes are being created.

A+
220-602
5.1
5.2

| Domain Suffix | Description |
|---|---|
| .air | Aviation industry |
| .biz | Businesses |
| .com | Commercial institutions |
| .coop | Business cooperatives |
| .edu | Educational institutions |
| .gov | Government institutions |
| .info | General use |
| .int | Organizations established by international treaties between governments |
| .mil | U.S. military |
| .museum | Museums |
| .name | Individuals |
| .net | Internet providers or networks |
| .org | Nonprofit organizations |
| .pro | Professionals |

**Table 18-3**  Suffixes used to identify top-level domain names

Domain names stand for IP addresses and provide an easy way to remember them, but domain names and IP addresses are not necessarily permanently related. A host computer can have a certain domain name, can be connected to one network and assigned a certain IP address, and then can be moved to another network and assigned a different IP address. The domain name can stay with the host while it connects to either network. It is up to a name resolution service, such as DNS or WINS, to track the relationship between a domain name and the current IP address of the host computer.

## CONFIGURING A BROWSER

Many browsers are available for downloading from the Internet. The most popular browsers are Internet Explorer by Microsoft (*www.microsoft.com*), Firefox by Mozilla (*www.mozilla.com*), and Netscape Navigator by Netscape (*browser.netscape.com*). By far, the most popular browser is Internet Explorer because it comes installed as a part of Windows.

 **A+ Exam Tip**

The A+ 220-602 exam expects you to know how to install and configure browsers, to enable and disable script support, and to configure proxy and other security settings. You will get practice installing a browser in a project at the end of this chapter.

Depending on user needs, performance, and security requirements, some Internet Explorer settings you might need to change are listed next.

Keep in mind that a few of these changes are for features that are available only if you have Internet Explorer version 6 or later.

▲ *Configure the pop-up blocker.* Internet Explorer version 6 and later has a pop-up blocker. To control Pop-up Blocker, open Internet Explorer, click **Tools**, and point to **Pop-up Blocker**, as shown in Figure 18-50. The first item in the menu in Figure 18-50 toggles between turning Pop-up Blocker on and off. To change settings, click **Pop-up**

**Blocker Settings.** From the Pop-up Blocker Settings window that opens, you can create a list of Web sites that are allowed to present pop-ups and control how Pop-up Blocker informs you when it blocks a pop-up.

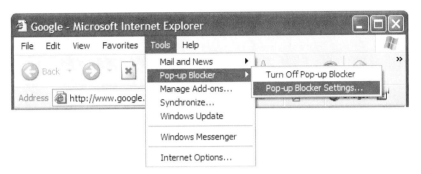

**Figure 18-50** Internet Explorer Pop-up Blocker can be turned on or off, and you can adjust its settings

> **Notes**
>
> If Pop-up Blocker is turned on, you might have a problem when you try to download something from a Web site. Sometimes the download routine tries to open a Security Warning window to start the download, and your pop-up blocker suppresses this window and causes an error. To solve the problem, you can temporarily turn off Pop-up Blocker before you begin the download or you can allow the Security Warning window to appear by clicking the pop-up block message and selecting **Download File**, as shown in Figure 18-51.

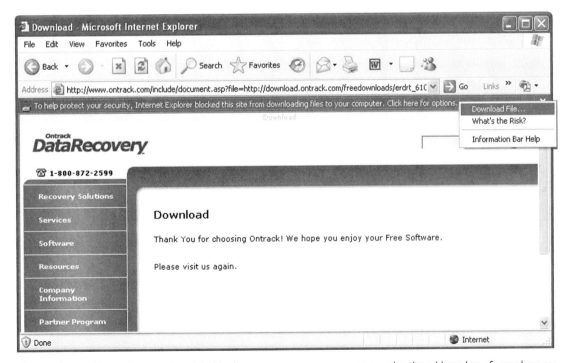

**Figure 18-51** If your browser is set to block pop-ups, a message appears under the address bar of your browser

◢ *Manage IE add-ons.* Add-ons to Internet Explorer are small programs that are installed within IE to enhance the browser. Examples include an animated mouse pointer and various extra toolbars. An add-on can make your browser do what you

A+
220-602
5.1
5.2

don't want it to do, such as displaying a toolbar you don't need, and sometimes malicious software hides as an add-on. Add-on programs are controlled from the Tools menu. To see a list of add-ons already installed, click **Tools**, and then click **Manage Add-ons**. The Manage Add-ons window opens (see Figure 18-52). You can toggle between a list of currently loaded add-ons and previously used add-ons. And you can update, disable, and enable add-ons. Also notice in the figure that you can see the DLL file that provides the add-on. To permanently get rid of an add-on, search for and delete that file.

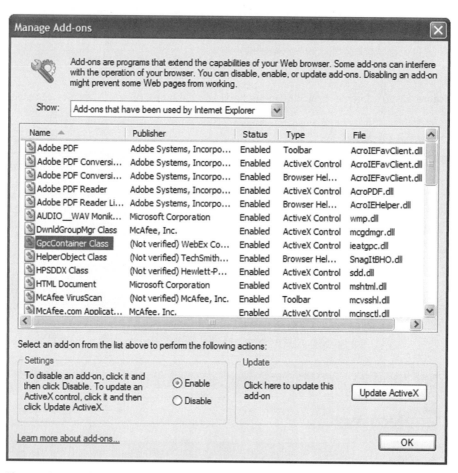

**Figure 18-52**    Disable and enable Internet Explorer add-ons

▲ *Set Internet Explorer security levels.* Internet Explorer offers several security options. To set them, click **Internet Options** on the Tools menu, and then click the **Security** tab (see Figure 18-53). Using the sliding bar on the left side of this window, you can choose the security level. (If the sliding bar is not visible, click the **Default Level** button to display the bar.) The Medium level is about right for most computers. If you click the Custom Level button, you can see exactly what is being monitored and controlled by this security level and change what you want. These settings apply to ActiveX plug-ins, downloads, Java plug-ins, scripts, and other miscellaneous settings and add-on programs. Adware or spyware can make changes to these security settings without your knowledge. These settings are not password protected, so they will not help if you are trying to secure the browser from what other users of this computer can do.

18

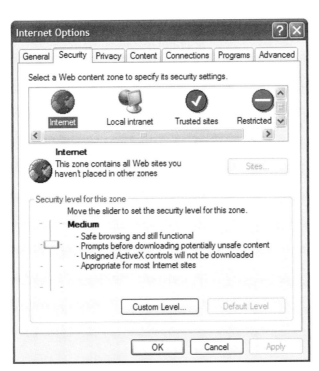

**Figure 18-53** Set the security level of Internet Explorer using the Internet Options window

▲ *Control how and if scripts are executed.* Scripts are small programs embedded inside a Web page that control how the Web page functions. To enable and disable scripts or to cause a prompt to appear before a script is executed, click the **Security** tab (if necessary), and then click **Custom Level**. The Security Settings dialog box opens. Scroll down to the Scripting section (see Figure 18-54).

**Figure 18-54** Enable and disable scripts on the Security tab of the Internet Options window

A+
220-602
5.1
5.2

▲ *Configure ActiveX controls.* An ActiveX control is a small add-on program that can be downloaded by a Web site to your computer (sometimes without your knowledge). Using the Security tab, you can enable and disable ActiveX controls and control how they are used. ActiveX controls are considered a security risk because Microsoft designed these controls to have access to core Windows components. Writers of malicious software sometimes use ActiveX controls.

▲ *Control proxy settings.* Under the **Connections** tab of the Internet Options window, you can control proxy settings for an Internet connection, giving the browser the IP address of the proxy server to use. However, if you only have one proxy server on your LAN, the browser should find the server without your having to give it an IP address. (On the other hand, if this computer is part of a large network that has more than one proxy server, the network administrator might give you the IP address of the one proxy server this computer is to use.) If you connect to the Internet through a local network, click **LAN Settings** and verify that **Automatically detect settings** is checked (see Figure 18-55). If your browser says it is working offline when you know it has an Internet connection or your PC tries to make a dial-up connection when you don't want it to, one thing you can do is check the windows shown in the figure for errors.

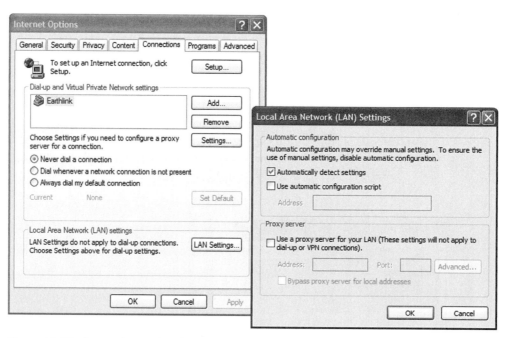

**Figure 18-55** Connection settings for Internet Explorer

> **Notes**
>
> Three ways to access the Internet Options window are: (1) Use the **Internet Options** applet in the Control Panel; (2) from Internet Explorer, click **Tools** on the menu bar and then click **Internet Options**; and (3) right-click the **Internet Explorer** icon on your desktop or Start menu and select **Properties** from the shortcut menu.

A+
220-602
3.2
5.2

## SOLVING INTERNET EXPLORER PROBLEMS

If Internet Explorer gives errors or is slow, use the tools described in earlier chapters, such as Defrag, ScanDisk, and System Information, to make sure that you have enough free hard drive space, that the hard drive is clean, and that the virtual memory settings

A+
220-602
3.2
5.2

are optimized. Also, reduce the number of applications running and close any unneeded background tasks. After doing these things, if the browser is still slow or still gives errors, follow these steps:

1. *Clean out the cache that IE uses to hold temporary files.* Internet Explorer must search the entire cache each time it accesses a Web page. If the cache is too big, performance is affected. To clean out the cache, open the **Internet Options** window shown in Figure 18-56. Click **Delete Files** under the Temporary Internet files heading to clean out the IE cache. The Delete Files dialog box opens, asking you to confirm the deletion. Click **OK**. Click **Clear History** under the History heading to clean out the shortcuts cache. The Internet Options dialog box opens, asking you to confirm the deletions. Click **OK**. If this cache gets too big, performance slows down. Also, if you reduce the number of days that Internet Explorer keeps pages in the history folder, performance might improve because there will be less material for Internet Explorer to search. For example, change the number of days to keep pages in history from the default value of 20 to 7.

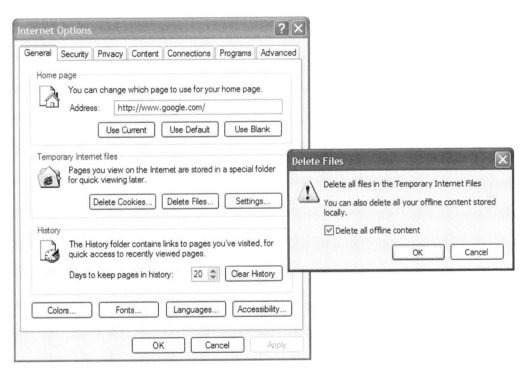

**Figure 18-56** Use the Internet Options window to control the Internet Explorer environment

2. *Suppress downloading images.* Slow browser performance can be caused by a slow Internet connection. In this case, one thing you can do is to suppress the downloading of images. Image files can be large and account for most of the downloaded data from Web sites. To suppress images, sound, animation, and video on the Internet Options window, click the **Advanced** tab. Scroll

> **Notes**
>
> Because other users might use the IE cache to trace your browsing habits, you might want to permanently eliminate the cache. To do that, in the Internet Properties window, click the **Advanced** tab (see Figure 18-57). Scroll down through the list of settings to the **Security** items. Check **Empty Temporary Internet Files folder when browser is closed** and click **Apply**.

**Notes**

To display an individual video or picture when you have cleared the related check boxes, right-click the icon with which it has been replaced on the Web page.

down to the multimedia section of the check box list, and clear the check box or boxes for the feature or features that you do not want to display (**Show pictures, Play animations in web pages, Play videos in web pages,** or **Play sounds in web pages**).

3. *Repair a corrupted Internet Explorer cache.* If problems still persist, they might be caused by a corrupted IE cache. The easiest way to solve this problem is to delete the entire IE cache folder for the user account that has the problem. The next time the user logs on, the folder will be rebuilt. To delete the folder, first make sure you're logged on to the system using a different account that has administrative privileges. The folder you want to delete is C:\Documents and Settings\\*user name*\Local Settings\Temporary Internet Files. You will not be able to delete the folder if this user is logged on.

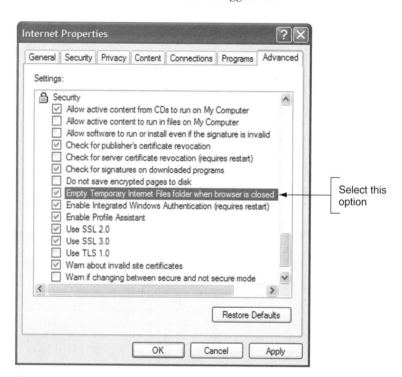

**Figure 18-57**   Empty the IE cache each time you close Internet Explorer

4. *Run antivirus software.* Unwanted pop-up ads or toolbars and other errors might be caused by malicious software, which can attack Internet Explorer as adware, spyware, browser hijackers, and viruses. Make sure your antivirus software is current and then scan your entire hard drive for viruses. You might also consider using anti-adware software such as Windows Defender by Microsoft (*www.microsoft.com*), Ad-Aware by Lavasoft (*www.lavasoftusa.com*), or SpyBot Search & Destroy by PepiMK Software (*www.safer-networking.org*). These products sometimes find malicious software attacking IE that antivirus software does not find. You'll learn more about ridding your system of malicious software in Chapter 19.

**Notes**

Because of the way Internet Explorer is closely integrated with Windows, it is easier for writers of malicious software to attack Windows through IE than through other browsers. Therefore, if you use a different browser such as Firefox by Mozilla, you might evade attacks targeting IE.

5. *Update Internet Explorer.* Internet Explorer 6 is included in Windows XP Service Pack 2, and normal Windows updates include updates for IE as well as other system components. To get the latest Windows XP updates, including those for IE, connect to the Internet and then click **Start**, point to **All Programs**, and click **Windows Updates**. The Web site shown in Figure 18-58 appears. Click **Express** and follow the directions onscreen to get the updates. You might have to perform the update process more than once to get them all. If your problem is not solved, move on to the next step.

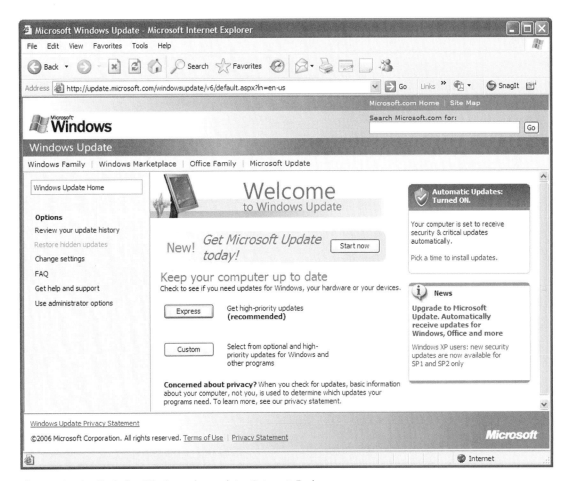

**Figure 18-58**  Updating Windows also updates Internet Explorer

6. *Use the Windows XP System File Checker (Sfc.exe) to verify Windows system files.* To use the utility to scan all Windows 2000/XP system files and verify them, first close all applications and then enter the command **sfc /scannow** in the Run dialog box. Click **OK**. The Windows File Protection window opens, as shown in Figure 18-59. Have your Windows setup CD handy in case it is needed during the scan, also shown in Figure 18-59. If you have problems running the utility, try the command **sfc /scanonce**, which scans files immediately after the next reboot. If your problem is still not solved after a reboot, move on to the next step.

7. *Remove and reinstall Internet Explorer 6.* For a Windows XP system, know that Internet Explorer 6 came with Windows XP Service Pack 2. Therefore, if you remove SP2, you also remove Internet Explorer 6. Beware, however, that you'll change other Windows components and settings other than IE when you do this. To remove Service Pack 2, open the Add or Remove Programs applet in Control

A+
220-602
3.2
5.2

Panel. Check the check box **Show updates,** as shown in Figure 18-60. Scroll down through the list of Windows updates and select **Windows XP Service Pack 2**. Click **Remove**. Follow the directions onscreen and reboot your computer when done. To reinstall SP2, first download the service pack at this Microsoft Web page: *www.microsoft.com/athome/security/protect/windowsxp/default.mspx*. If you have problems removing or installing the service pack, see the Microsoft Knowledge Base Article 875350 for additional help.

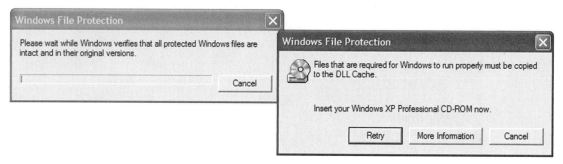

**Figure 18-59**   System File Checker might need the Windows setup CD

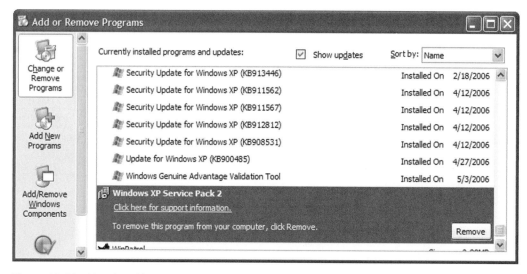

**Figure 18-60**   Use the Add or Remove Programs applet to uninstall Service Pack 2

At this point, if Internet Explorer is still not working, most likely you have a more serious problem than just IE and you need to refresh your entire Windows installation. Several methods and tools to do this are covered in Chapter 14 for Windows 2000/XP and in Chapter 16 for Windows 9x/Me.

**Notes**

If you cannot solve a problem with Internet Explorer without making considerable changes to your Windows installation, you might consider abandoning IE and installing another browser such as Firefox by Mozilla (*www.mozilla.com*). If you can't use your computer to access the Web site to download the installation file, go to another computer and download the file and burn it to a CD. Then use the CD to install the browser.

## USING SECURED WEB CONNECTIONS

When banking or doing some other private business on the Web, you might have noticed https in the address box of your browser, such as

A+
220-602
5.1

**18**

A+
220-602
5.1

*https://onlineservices.wachovia.com.* **HTTPS (HTTP secure)** can mean HTTP over SSL or HTTP over TLS and tells you that the secure protocol being used is SSL or TLS. SSL and TLS can be used to secure several application protocols including HTTP, FTP, e-mail, and newsgroups. When SSL or TLS is used, all data communicated between the client and server is encrypted and the initial connection between the server and the client can be authenticated. However, know that only the communication over the Internet is secure. After the data reaches the server, SSL and TLS protocols don't apply. The purpose of these security protocols is to prevent others on the Internet from eavesdropping on data in transit or change that data. (This last type of intrusion is called a man-in-the-middle attack.) Here is some additional information about SSL and TLS:

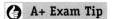

> ✪ **A+ Exam Tip**
>
> The A+ 220-602 exam expects you to know about HTTPS and SSL.

- ◢ **SSL (Secure Sockets Layer)** is the de facto standard developed by Netscape and used by all browsers; it uses an encryption system that uses a digital certificate. Public keys are secret codes used to encrypt and later decrypt the data, and are exchanged before data is sent (see Figure 18-61). A **digital certificate**, also called a **digital ID** or **digital signature**, is a code assigned to you by a certificate authority such as VeriSign (*www.verisign.com*) that uniquely identifies you on the Internet and includes a public key. Recall from Chapter 12 that Microsoft uses digital certificates to validate or digitally sign device drivers certified by Microsoft.

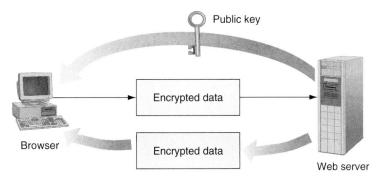

**Figure 18-61**  Using secure HTTP, a Web server and browser encrypt data using a public key before the data is transmitted

- ◢ **TLS (Transport Layer Security)** is an improved version of SSL. There are only slight differences between TLS and SSL, although the protocols are not interchangeable. Both client and server applications must support either SSL or TLS to create a secure connection, and all current browsers support both protocols.

To know if a connection to a Web site is secured, look for https in the browser address box and a lock icon at the bottom of the browser window, as shown in Figure 18-62.

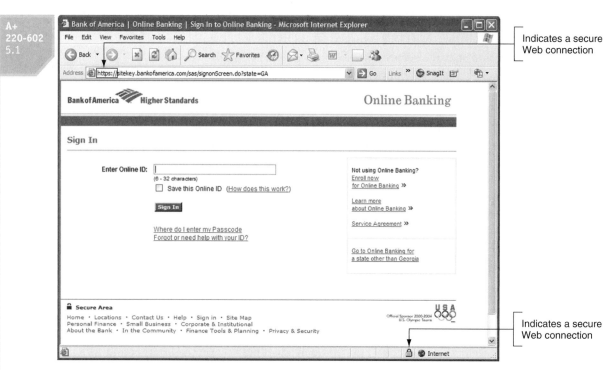

Indicates a secure Web connection

Indicates a secure Web connection

**Figure 18-62** A secured connection from browser to Web server

## SUPPORTING E-MAIL

E-mail is a client/server application used to send text messages to individuals and groups. When you send an e-mail message, it travels from your computer to your e-mail server. Your e-mail server sends the message to the recipient's e-mail server. The recipient's e-mail server sends it to the recipient's PC, but not until the recipient asks that it be sent by logging in and downloading e-mail. Different parts of the process are controlled by different protocols.

Figure 18-63 shows the journey made by an e-mail message as well as the protocols that control the different parts of the journey. The sender's PC and e-mail server both use **SMTP (Simple Mail Transfer Protocol)** to send an e-mail message to its destination. An improved version of SMTP is **SMTP AUTH (SMTP Authentication)**. This protocol is used to authenticate a user to an e-mail server when the e-mail client first tries to connect to the e-mail server to send e-mail. Using SMTP AUTH, an extra dialogue between the client and server happens before the client can fully connect that proves the client is authorized to use the service. After authentication, the client can then send e-mail to the e-mail server.

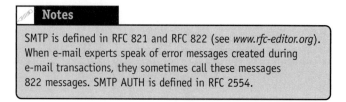

**Notes**

SMTP is defined in RFC 821 and RFC 822 (see *www.rfc-editor.org*). When e-mail experts speak of error messages created during e-mail transactions, they sometimes call these messages 822 messages. SMTP AUTH is defined in RFC 2554.

After the message arrives at the destination e-mail server, it remains there until the recipient requests delivery. The recipient's e-mail server uses one of two protocols to deliver the message: **POP (Post Office Protocol)** or **IMAP4 (Internet Message Access Protocol, version 4)**, which is a newer e-mail protocol. The current version of POP is version 3, often abbreviated as POP3. IMAP is slowly replacing POP for receiving e-mail.

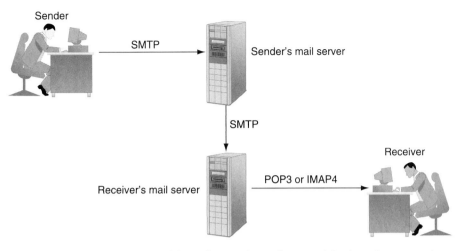

**Figure 18-63** The SMTP protocol is used to send e-mail to a recipient's mail server, and the POP3 or IMAP4 protocol is used to download e-mail to the client

E-mail client software communicates with an e-mail server when it sends and receives e-mail. Two common e-mail clients are Eudora and Microsoft Outlook Express. Figure 18-63 shows a user with one e-mail server on his side of the transmission (there is a second e-mail server on the receiver's side of the transmission). However, it's possible to have two e-mail servers on the sender's side of the transmission; one would be for sending e-mail and the other for receiving e-mail. Figure 18-64 shows this arrangement.

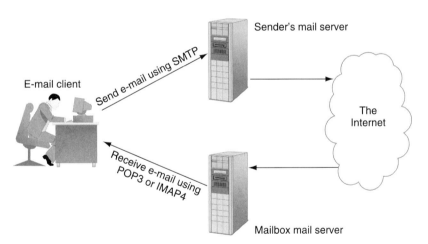

**Figure 18-64** An e-mail client can use one server to send e-mail and another to receive e-mail

The e-mail server that takes care of sending e-mail messages (using the SMTP protocol) is often referred to as the SMTP server. The e-mail server from which you collect messages sent to you is often referred to as the POP server, because it uses the POP protocol.

When you configure your e-mail client software for the first time, you need to enter the addresses of your e-mail servers. If you are connecting to e-mail via an Internet service provider, the ISP can tell you these addresses. For example, if your ISP is *MyISP.net*, you might have an outgoing mail server address of *smtp.myISP.net*, *smtpauth.myISP.net*, or *mail.myISP.net* and an incoming mail server address of *pop3.myISP.net* or *pop.myISP.net*.

In most e-mail client software, you enter the addresses of your POP or IMAP server and your SMTP server in a dialog box when setting up the program, along with your e-mail address you will use when sending e-mail. Look for menus or icons labeled Options, Preferences, Configuration, Setup, or similar names. Figure 18-65 shows a setup window in Microsoft Outlook where the outgoing mail server is named smtpauth.earthlink.net (using the SMTP AUTH protocol) and the incoming mail server is pop.earthlink.net (using the POP3 protocol).

**Figure 18-65**   Servers used for incoming and outgoing e-mail

After you enter the addresses, the software saves this and other configuration information in an initialization file, the Windows registry, or some other location. When you first connect to an e-mail server, the e-mail client can pass the account name and password to the server to access the account.

## SUPPORTING FTP

A common task of communications software is file transfer, which is the passing of files from one computer to another. For file transfer to work, the software on both ends must use the same protocol. The most popular way to transfer files over the Internet is to use the **File Transfer Protocol (FTP)**, which can transfer files between two computers using the same or different operating systems.

Many software vendors use FTP sites for downloading software to their customers. When you click a link on a Web site to download a file, if the protocol in your browser address box changes from http to ftp, then you are using FTP for the download. The FTP server application is most likely running on a Windows Server 2003 or Unix server. These servers are called FTP servers or FTP sites. A commercial FTP site might provide only the ability to download a file to your PC, but some FTP sites also give you the ability to copy, delete, and rename files; make and remove directories; and view details about files and directories, provided the user has the appropriate permissions on the FTP site.

**18**

A+
220-602
5.1

Most communications applications provide an FTP utility that has a unique look and feel, but the basics of file transfer are the same from one utility to another. If you don't have graphical FTP software installed on your PC, you can use FTP commands from a command prompt.

## FTP FROM A COMMAND PROMPT

FTP can be initiated at a Windows 2000/XP, Windows 9x/Me, or DOS command prompt, if a connection to a network or the Internet is established. Table 18-4 shows a sample set of FTP commands entered at the command prompt.

| Command Entered at the Command Prompt | Description |
| --- | --- |
| FTP | Execute the FTP program, ftp.exe. |
| OPEN 110.87.170.34 | Open a session with a remote computer having the given IP address. |
| LOGIN: XXXXXX | The host computer provides a prompt to enter a user ID for the computer being accessed. |
| PASSWORD: XXXXXX | The host computer requests the password for that ID. Logon is then completed by the host computer. |
| CD /DATA | Change directory to the /DATA directory. |
| GET YOURFILE.DAT | Copy the file YOURFILE.DAT (or whatever file you want) from the remote computer to your computer. |
| PUT MYFILE.DAT | Copy the file MYFILE.DAT (or whatever file you want) from your computer to the remote computer. |
| BYE | Disconnect the FTP session. |

Table 18-4  A sample FTP session from a command prompt

## FILE TRANSFER USING FTP SOFTWARE

FTP client software can be downloaded from the Internet or directly from your ISP. In addition, any browser can be used as an FTP client. The following steps show you how to use FTP client software:

1. Start the FTP utility software. In this example, we are using CuteFTP by Globalscape (*www.globalscape.com*). The FTP utility screen that appears is similar to the one in Figure 18-66.

2. On the menu, click **File** and then click **Connect** to log on to an FTP site. A Site Properties dialog box opens, similar to the one in Figure 18-66.

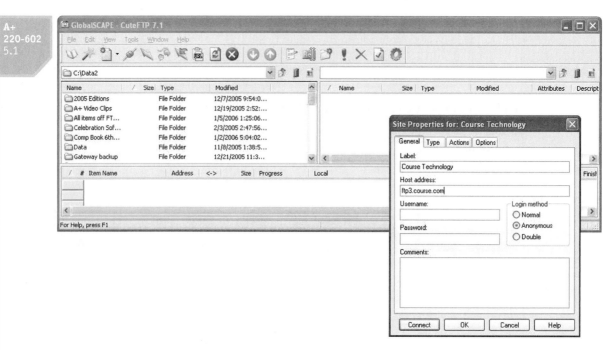

**Figure 18-66** A typical FTP utility

3. Enter the Label (**Course Technology** in our example), Host address (**ftp3.course.com**), Username and Password, and then click **OK**.

4. The connection is made and your ID and password are passed to the host. After you have been authenticated by the host computer, a screen similar to that in Figure 18-67 appears.

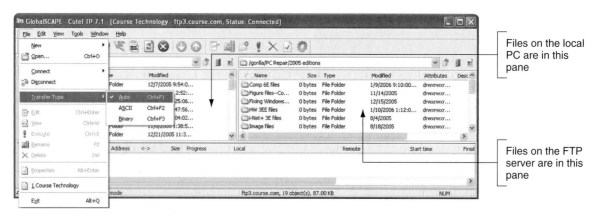

**Figure 18-67** An FTP utility screen showing local and remote files

5. The files on the left belong to you, and the files on the right belong to the remote host computer. You can drag and drop files either to or from the other computer. Notice in Figure 18-67 the choices you have when you click File, Transfer on the menu bar: Auto, ASCII, or Binary. These choices refer to the format to be used to transfer the files. Text files are written in ASCII code; therefore, use ASCII for text files, and use Binary for all others. If you are not sure which to use, choose **Auto**.

6. When the transfer of files is complete, click **File, Exit** to leave the utility.

**18**

A+
220-602
5.1

Many Web pages provide a link on the page offering you the ability to download a file. Click the link to download the file. This file is probably not being downloaded from the Web server, but from an FTP server. When you click the filename on the Web page, the program controlling the page executes FTP commands to the FTP server to download the file to you. If you receive an error, you can sometimes solve the problem by going directly to the company's FTP server and using an FTP utility (such as the one in the previous procedure) to download the file, or even see a list of other files that you might also like to download.

A Web browser such as Internet Explorer can also serve as an FTP client. To have it serve as an FTP client, enter the URL of the FTP server in the address box (for example, **ftp3.course.com**) and then press **Enter**. The browser changes menu options to become an FTP client. For example, the Login As command is added to the File menu. To log on to the FTP server in Internet Explorer, click **File** on the menu bar, and then click **Login As**. The Log On As dialog box opens for you to enter a user ID and password. Files and folders on the FTP server then display in the browser, as shown in Figure 18-68. You can drag files back and forth between the FTP server and your PC using this Internet Explorer FTP window and Windows Explorer opened on your desktop.

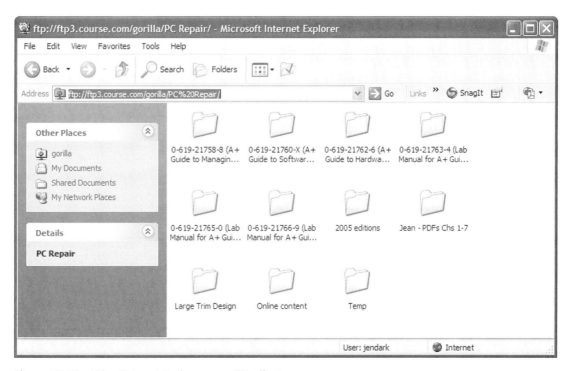

**Figure 18-68** Using Internet Explorer as an FTP client

A+ ESS
5.1

A+
220-602
5.1
5.3

## SUPPORTING VoIP

VoIP is a protocol that is used by Internet or intranet telephone networks to provide voice communication over a network. Using a VoIP service, you plug a digital telephone, such as the one shown in Figure 18-69, into a network port on a local network that is connected to the Internet and use that phone to make a phone call to anywhere on the planet. Notice in the figure the power cord and network cable share a common cable and connector to the phone. You can also use a regular analog phone as an Internet phone if you use an Analog Telephone Adapter (ATA), such as the one shown in Figure 18-70. Plug the phone into the ATA, which uses a network cable to connect to the network. Just as with mobile phones, the digital phone or ATA is programmed for a particular phone number.

A+ ESS
5.1

A+
220-602
5.1
5.3

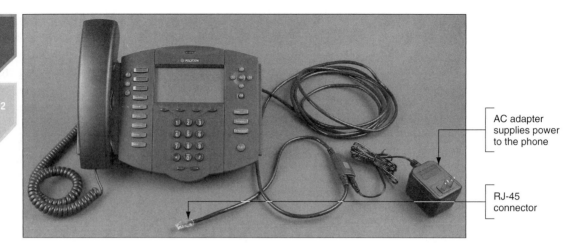

AC adapter
supplies power
to the phone

RJ-45
connector

**Figure 18-69** This digital telephone has a network port to connect to a network

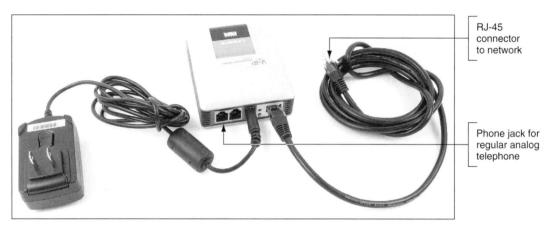

RJ-45
connector
to network

Phone jack for
regular analog
telephone

**Figure 18-70** Use this ATA to turn an analog telephone into an Internet phone

# APPLYING|CONCEPTS

**Quality of Service (QoS)** refers to the success of communication over the Internet. Communication is degraded on the Internet when packets are dropped, delayed, delivered out of order, or corrupted. In order for VoIP to have the high quality it needs to compete with regular POTS voice communication, QoS on the Internet must be high. VoIP gave problems for many years with dropped lines, echos, delays, static, and jittered communication. ("Jitter" is the term used to describe a voice conversation that is mingled with varying degrees of delays.) However, more recently, many of these problems are for the most part solved to make VoIP a viable option for personal and business use. Recently, my daughter, Jill West, was responsible for selecting a telephone system for a small business. I asked her to describe the success and woes of having chosen a VoIP solution. Here is her story:

*We planned our company so that we all can work from our home offices and live in several regions of the country, yet we compete in a market where we must present a unified front. More and more businesses are built this way these days, and, thankfully, technology is adapting.*

*When we first began investigating phone systems, we tried to patchwork together various telco (local telephone company) services, but with dismal results. Then we began researching several VoIP providers, from the industry flagship Vonage (www.vonage.com), to smaller and lesser-known companies. With a little searching, we found a company that provides the services important to us. Here are a few features:*

▲ *We were able to buy the digital phones and ATA adapters from this company that configured and tested them for us before shipping and then taught us how to use them.*

A+ ESS
5.1

A+
220-602
5.1
5.3

▲ We were able to port our existing toll-free number to our new VoIP account.

▲ We are able to transfer live calls from one team member to another with three- or four-digit dialing and no long-distance charges for the transferred calls, even with our team spread over several states.

▲ We have an integrated voice-mail system using a Web portal. One window of our portal is shown in Figure 18-71.

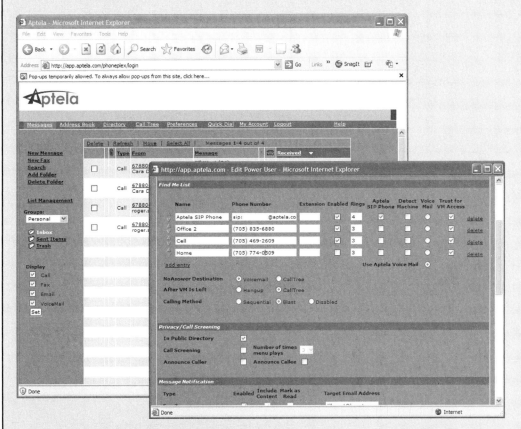

**Figure 18-71** This Web portal is used to manage a VoIP service

▲ We can easily set up conference calls with the entire team.

▲ A single auto-attendant handles all incoming calls, or we can direct incoming calls to any number and still use the auto-attendant as a convenient backup.

▲ The company provided professional voice talent to record our auto-attendant message and other call-tree menu options.

▲ We have unlimited long distance, even for our high-volume salespeople.

▲ We can add or remove users as our company's payroll changes with no extensive implementation charges or technical difficulties.

▲ Each of our users can program various phone numbers into their account, such as cell phone, home phone, or home-office phone numbers. They can then tell the system at which phone to direct their individual incoming calls. Each call can be sent sequentially through the list of numbers, or "blast" all numbers simultaneously.

▲ Voice-mail messages and faxes can all be forwarded to our various e-mail accounts, and even the message itself is attached for immediate review.

▲ When we travel, we can take the service with us. I can pack my IP phone or ATA and plug it up wherever I am if I have high-speed Internet access. Even without the phone or adapter, I can still use a computer to access my Web portal and make calls from the portal Web site.

A+ ESS
5.1

A+
220-602
5.1
5.3

*With all this, it seems there would be no drawbacks. But all is not well in paradise. We've had a few issues with dropped calls or annoying delays while talking. Sometimes we have to hang up and call the person back. Occasionally, the signal will phase out briefly, where one party can hear the other, but not vice versa. And, if your ISP drops your service for any reason, even just a temporary outage, you're pretty much without a phone. However, incoming calls are still directed through the auto-attendant, and messages are saved there until you again have access.*

*Overall, even with these drawbacks, VoIP was the right choice for our company. We're pleased with the features and are willing to tolerate the growing pains as technology catches up with our needs.*

When setting up a VoIP system, know that each digital phone or ATA must be programmed with a phone number from the VoIP provider. Each device is also programmed to use dynamic IP addressing and must be assigned an IP address just like any other device on the network, which means your network must be using a DHCP server such as that provided by a multipurpose router. Plug up the devices to the network and then configure the VoIP service using the Web site of the VoIP provider.

 **A+ Tip**

The A+ 220-602 exam expects you to know how to eliminate electrical interference from a network.

Because electrical interference can be a problem with VoIP phones, each network cable connected to a VoIP phone needs a **ferrite clamp** attached. You first learned about a ferrite clamp (see Figure 18-72) in Chapter 17. Attach the clamp on the cable near the phone port. This clamp helps to eliminate electromagnetic interference. Some cables come with preinstalled clamps, and you can also buy ferrite clamps to attach to other cables.

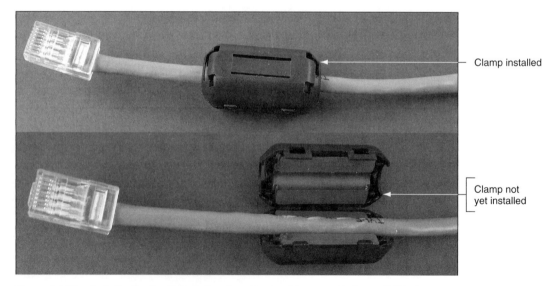

Clamp installed

Clamp not yet installed

**Figure 18-72** Install a ferrite clamp on each network cable connected to a VoIP phone

A+
220-602
3.1
3.3

## SUPPORTING REMOTE DESKTOP

Windows XP Professional Remote Desktop gives a user access to his or her Windows XP desktop from anywhere on the Internet. As a software developer, I find Remote Desktop extremely useful when I work from a remote location (my home office) and need to access a corporate network to support software on that network. Using the Internet, I can access a file server on

18

these secured networks to make my software changes. It's easy to use and relatively safe for the corporate network. To use Remote Desktop, the computer you want to remotely access (the server) must be running Windows XP Professional, but the computer you're using to access it (the client) can be running Windows XP Home Edition or Windows XP Professional.

In this section, you'll first see how Remote Desktop can be used, and then you'll see how to set it up for first use.

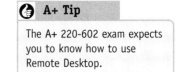
**A+ Tip**

The A+ 220-602 exam expects you to know how to use Remote Desktop.

**Notes**

Many third-party applications besides Windows XP Remote Desktop exist that also allow you to remotely connect to another computer so that you can see and use the remote computer's desktop. One excellent product I've used for years is PC Anywhere by Symantec (*www.symantec.com*).

## HOW TO USE REMOTE DESKTOP

To use Remote Desktop to connect to and use the desktop of your home or office computer, do the following from any Windows XP computer connected to the Internet:

1. Click **Start**, point to **All Programs**, point to **Accessories**, point to **Communications**, and then click **Remote Desktop Connection**. The Remote Desktop Connection window opens. Click **Options** and the window expands to full view, as shown in Figure 18-73.

**Figure 18-73**   Enter the IP address of the remote computer to which you want to connect

2. Enter the IP address of the Windows XP computer to which you want to connect and enter your user account name and password on the remote computer.

3. If you plan to transfer files from one computer to the other, click the **Local Resources** tab shown in Figure 18-74 and check **Disk drives**. If you want to print from the remote computer, also check **Printers**. Click **Connect** to make the connection.

A+
220-602
3.1
3.3

**Figure 18-74** Allow files and printers to be shared using the Remote Desktop connection

4. The desktop of the remote computer appears, as shown in Figure 18-75. When you click the desktop, you can work with the remote computer just as if you were sitting in front of it, except response time is slower. To move files back and forth between computers, use Windows Explorer on the remote computer. Files on your local computer will appear under My Network Places in Windows Explorer on the remote computer. To close the connection to the remote computer, simply close the desktop window.

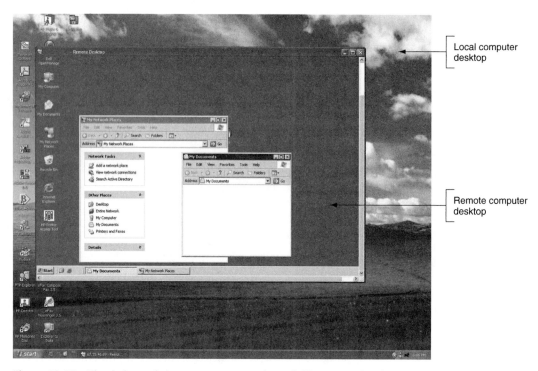

Local computer desktop

Remote computer desktop

**Figure 18-75** The desktop of the remote computer is available on your local computer

**18**

A+
220-602
3.1
3.3

## HOW TO PREPARE REMOTE DESKTOP FOR FIRST USE

To prepare a Windows XP Professional computer to be used as a Remote Desktop server so that you can access it from the Internet, you need to configure the computer for static IP addressing and also configure Remote Desktop for service. Here are the steps needed:

1. As described earlier in the chapter, you'll need a static IP address assigned to you by your ISP. If your computer is connected directly to your ISP, assign this IP address to your computer. If you are using a router on your network, configure the router for static IP addressing and assign it the IP address from the ISP. Then configure your computer for static IP addressing and assign it a private IP address (for example, 192.168.1.90).

2. If you are using a router on your network, configure the router for port forwarding and allow incoming traffic on port 3389. Forward that traffic to the IP address of your desktop computer. Figure 18-76 shows a setup screen for one router configured for these settings.

**Figure 18-76** To set up a network for supporting a Remote Desktop server, configure your router for port forwarding on port 3389

3. Use your browser to verify you have Internet access before you continue to the next steps. If you have a problem, first try repairing your connection and then try rebooting your PC.

A+
220-602
3.1
3.3

You are now ready to configure Remote Desktop on your Windows XP Professional home or office computer. Do the following:

1. Right-click **My Computer** and click **Properties** to open the **System Properties** window, as shown in Figure 18-77. Click the **Remote** tab and check **Allow users to connect remotely to this computer**. Click **Select Remote Users**. In the dialog box that opens, also shown in Figure 18-77, add the users of this computer who will be using Remote Desktop. Users who have administrative privileges will be allowed to use Remote Desktop by default, but other users need to be added. Click **OK** twice to exit both windows.

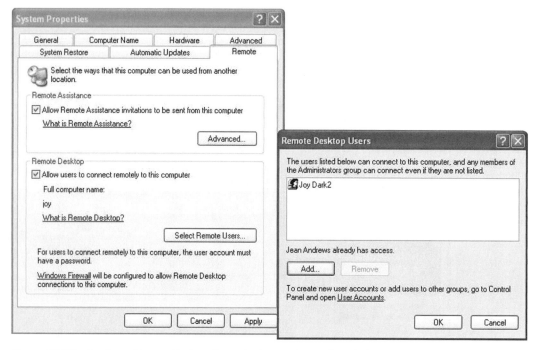

**Figure 18-77** Configure Remote Desktop from the System Properties window

2. Verify that Windows Firewall is set to allow Remote Desktop activity to this computer. To do that, open the **Network Connections** window and click **Change Windows Firewall settings**. The Windows Firewall window opens. On the **General** tab, verify that Windows Firewall is turned on and that **Don't allow exceptions** is *not* selected. Then click the **Exceptions** tab and verify that **Remote Desktop** is checked so that Remote Desktop incoming activity is allowed.

> **Notes**
>
> Even though Windows XP normally allows more than one user to be logged on at the same time, this is not the case with Remote Desktop. When a Remote Desktop session is opened, all local users are logged off.

3. You are now ready to test Remote Desktop using your local network. Try to use Remote Desktop from another computer somewhere on your local network. Verify you have Remote Desktop working on your local network before you move on to the next step of testing the Remote Desktop connection from the Internet.

Is your desktop computer now as safe as it was before you programmed the router? Actually, no, so take this into account when you decide to use Remote Desktop. In a project at the end of this chapter, you'll learn how you can take further steps to protect the security of your computer when using Remote Desktop.

18

## >> CHAPTER SUMMARY

▲ Ports are used to address particular software or services running on a computer. Common port assignments are port 80 for HTTP (Web browser requests), port 25 for SMTP (sending e-mail), port 110 for POP3 (receiving e-mail), and port 20 for FTP.

▲ Communication using TCP/IP involves communication at the application level, the OS level, and the hardware level.

▲ TCP guarantees that a packet reaches its destination and so is called a connection-oriented protocol. UDP does not guarantee delivery and so is called a connectionless or best-effort protocol.

▲ IP is responsible for breaking data into packets and passing them from TCP or UDP to the hardware.

▲ Some TCP/IP utilities useful in solving networking problems are Ipconfig, Winipcfg, Tracert, Nslookup, Ping, and Nbtstat.

▲ DSL and cable modem are broadband Internet connections that use a converter box, which can connect to a USB port or network port on a PC. In addition, a router is sometimes placed between the converter box and a single PC or local network.

▲ When a PC is connected directly to the Internet, the PC can share the Internet connection. Windows XP and Windows 98 use Internet Connection Sharing (ICS) to manage the connection on the host computer, or you can use a router that stands between the converter box and the network.

▲ Use a firewall on the host computer or router to protect the network from unsolicited activity from the Internet.

▲ A router can be configured to use port forwarding so that certain applications, such as a Web server, on a computer on the network can be accessed from the Internet.

▲ A virtual private network (VPN) can be used to authenticate a user and encrypt data when a user connects to a private network from somewhere on the Internet.

▲ A URL consists of a protocol, a host name, a network or domain name, and a top-level domain extension. Common top-level domains include .com for commercial institutions, .gov for divisions of government, and .org for nonprofit organizations.

▲ E-mail uses SMTP or SMTP AUTH to send messages and POP3 to receive messages. POP3 is being replaced by IMAP. Your ISP will provide you with information on the server types and addresses that it uses to send and receive e-mail.

▲ FTP is used to transfer files from one computer to another, regardless of whether the computers are using the same operating system. Both computers must have an FTP utility installed. It can be executed from user-friendly GUI software or from a command prompt.

▲ VoIP can be used to provide Internet phone service.

▲ Windows XP Remote Desktop is used to make a home or office computer's Windows XP Professional desktop available to the user anywhere on the Internet.

## >> *KEY TERMS*

For explanations of key terms, see the Glossary near the end of the book.

ARP (Address Resolution
  Protocol)
best-effort protocol
broadband
cable modem
client/server application
client-side caching
connectionless protocol
connection-oriented protocol
dial-up networking
digital certificate
digital ID
digital signature
DSL (Digital Subscriber Line)
File Transfer Protocol (FTP)
hop count
HTML (Hypertext Markup
  Language)
HTTP (Hypertext Transfer
  Protocol)
HTTPS (HTTP secure)

ICMP (Internet Control Message
  Protocol)
IMAP4 (Internet Message Access
  Protocol, version 4)
Internet Connection Sharing (ICS)
IP (Internet Protocol)
ISDN (Integrated Services Digital
  Network)
Network News Transfer Protocol
  (NNTP)
POP (Post Office Protocol)
port
port address
port forwarding
port number
PPP (Point-to-Point Protocol)
PPPoE (Point-to-Point Protocol
  over Ethernet)
Quality of Service (QoS)
RARP (Reverse Address
  Resolution Protocol)

Serial Line Internet Protocol
  (SLIP)
server-side caching
session
SMTP (Simple Mail Transfer
  Protocol)
SMTP AUTH (SMTP
  Authentication)
SNMP (Simple Network
  Management Protocol)
socket
SSL (Secure Sockets Layer)
TCP (Transmission Control
  Protocol)
Time to Live (TTL)
TLS (Transport Layer Security)
top-level domain
UDP (User Datagram Protocol)
URL (Uniform Resource
  Locator)

## >> *REVIEW QUESTIONS*

1. Which of the following protocols guarantees packet delivery?

   a. TCP

   b. UDP

   c. IP

   d. HTTP

2. Which of the following utilities verifies that there is a connection on a network between two hosts?

   a. FTP

   b. NSLookup

   c. Ping

   d. ARP

3. Which of the following concepts is used to open or close certain ports so they can or cannot be used?

   a. Using Internet Connection Sharing (ICS)

   b. Using port filtering

   c. Using a router

   d. Using port forwarding

4. Which of the following is an example of a top-level domain?

   a. *course.com*

   b. *www.course.com*

   c. *.com*

   d. *www*

5. Which of the following protocols is responsible for breaking up and reassembling data into packets and routing them to their destination?

   a. RARP

   b. ICMP

   c. TCP

   d. IP

6. True or false? Every service running on a computer requires a port number, even if the service is not a server application.

7. True or false? Domain names and IP addresses are permanently related.

8. True or false? Caching can happen on the server side (at the ISP) or on the client side (on your PC).

9. True or false? Although there are only slight differences between Transport Layer Security (TLS) and Secure Sockets Layer (SSL), these two protocols are not interchangeable.

10. True or false? If you use Windows, using a browser other than IE (such as Firefox by Mozilla) might help you evade malicious software attacks.

11. A(n) _____ or _____ is a communication link created between two software programs that is managed by the browser and Web server using HTTP.

12. The number of routers that a packet is permitted to pass through on its way to its destination is called a(n) _____ or a(n) _____.

13. Any type of networking medium that carries more than one type of transmission is called _____.

14. If you want to disable call waiting while you're connected to the Internet, enter _____ in front of the phone number.

15. To eliminate electromagnetic interference from a network, use a(n) _____.

# Securing Your PC and LAN

In today's computing environment, we all need to know how to keep our shields up. Security is an important concern for PC support technicians and many of the chapters of this book have addressed security concerns as appropriate within the content of each chapter. This chapter focuses on the tools and methods you need to know to protect a computer and a small network, and it summarizes several security tools and methods mentioned in other chapters. As you read this chapter, keep in mind that knowledge won't help much unless you use it. As a user or PC support technician, be sure to apply what you're about to learn!

Even with the best of security, occasionally a virus, worm, or some other type of malicious software gets into a computer. In these situations, it helps to understand how they work and how they hide. In this chapter, you'll learn about malicious software and then learn the step-by-step attack plan to get rid of it.

# SECURING YOUR DESKTOP OR NOTEBOOK COMPUTER

A+ ESS
6.1
6.2

A+
220-602
6.1
6.2
6.3

Even though a desktop computer sits behind a firewall in a secured network, you still need to protect the system and its data from attacks within and from attacks that get into your network through security loopholes. In addition, when traveling with a notebook computer, security is especially important because your notebook is more exposed than when you're working in a more secured environment.

Here are the methods of securing a computer:

- ◢ Control access to a system by using strong authentication techniques.
- ◢ Limit use of the administrator accounts.
- ◢ Always use a personal firewall.
- ◢ Set AV software to run in the background and keep it current.
- ◢ Keep Windows updates current.
- ◢ Set Microsoft Internet Explorer for optimum security.
- ◢ Use alternate third-party client software.
- ◢ When supporting public Windows XP computers, use Microsoft Shared Computer Toolkit.
- ◢ Secure important files and folders.
- ◢ Physically protect your equipment.
- ◢ Beware of social engineering situations trying to lure you into compromising your security.
- ◢ Keep good backups of user data.
- ◢ Back up system files when you make major changes to your system.
- ◢ Make use of event logging and incident reporting.
- ◢ Destroy trash that might contain sensitive data.
- ◢ Perform monthly security maintenance chores.

All these techniques to secure a computer are covered in this part of the chapter. Later in the chapter, you'll learn about securing a wired or wireless network.

## APPLYING | CONCEPTS

Three of the items listed earlier are so important to keep a secure system that Microsoft added the Windows Security Center to Windows XP Service Pack 2 to track these items. To open the Security Center, you can click its icon (looks like a shield) in the system tray or open the Security Center applet in Control Panel. Either way, the Windows Security Center window opens, as shown in Figure 19-1.

**Notes**

If a Windows XP computer is configured to belong to a domain instead of a workgroup, all security is managed by the network administrator for the entire network. In this situation, the Windows Security Center does not alert you to problems with security or allow you, as the user, to adjust security settings.

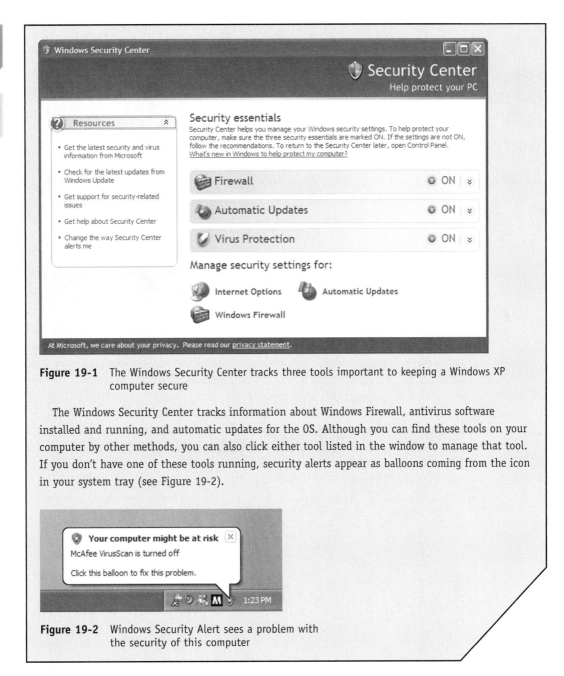

**Figure 19-1** The Windows Security Center tracks three tools important to keeping a Windows XP computer secure

The Windows Security Center tracks information about Windows Firewall, antivirus software installed and running, and automatic updates for the OS. Although you can find these tools on your computer by other methods, you can also click either tool listed in the window to manage that tool. If you don't have one of these tools running, security alerts appear as balloons coming from the icon in your system tray (see Figure 19-2).

**Figure 19-2** Windows Security Alert sees a problem with the security of this computer

Now let's turn our attention to all the different ways you can secure a computer.

## ACCESS CONTROL

Controlling access to a computer, file, folder, or network is done by using a combination of authentication and authorization techniques. First, let's look at a definition of these two key words:

▲ **Authentication** proves that an individual is who he says he is and is accomplished by a variety of techniques, including a username, password, personal identification number (PIN), smart card, or biometric data (for example, a fingerprint or iris scan). After an individual is authenticated, the individual is allowed access. (In practice, even though an individual is most often a person, sometimes an individual is a computer program or process.)

A+ ESS
1.1
6.1
6.2

A+
220-602
6.1
6.2
6.3

◢ **Authorization** determines what an individual can do in the system after he or she is authenticated. The privileges and rights the individual has are assigned to the identity of the individual. As you learned in Chapter 13, for Windows, these privileges and rights are assigned to a user account.

You can lock down a computer by using power-on passwords and Windows passwords. In addition, you need passwords to protect your online accounts that you access through Web sites. Also, many applications give you the option to set a password on the data files associated with the application. Passwords need to be strong passwords, which means they are not easy to guess.

To help you know how to control access to a computer and resources on that computer, let's look at how passwords can be used outside Windows and how to create strong passwords. Then, we'll turn our attention to how access control is accomplished inside Windows. Later in the chapter, you'll learn how to control access to networks.

## POWER-ON PASSWORDS AND OTHER BIOS SECURITY

Power-on passwords are assigned in CMOS setup to prevent unauthorized access to the computer and/or to the CMOS setup utility. Power-on passwords are set and configured in CMOS setup using a security screen. Most likely, you'll find the screen under the boot menu options. For one BIOS, this security screen looks like that in Figure 19-3, where you can set a supervisor password and a user password. In addition, you can configure how the user password works. Also notice in Figure 19-3 that you can enable or disable boot sector virus protection so that a virus is less likely to be able to change the boot sectors of the hard drive.

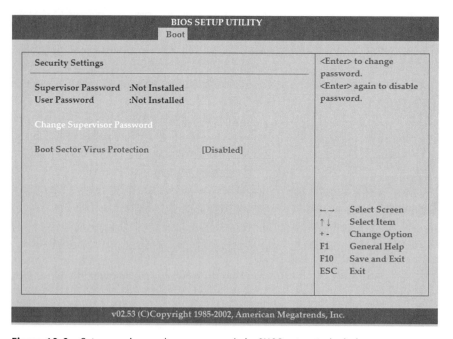

**Figure 19-3** Set supervisor and user passwords in CMOS setup to lock down a computer

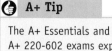 **A+ Tip**

The A+ Essentials and A+ 220-602 exams expect you to know how to secure a workstation from unauthorized use.

After you enter a supervisor password, the security screen changes to that shown in Figure 19-4 where you can now set a user password and decide how that password will be used. The choices under User Access Level are **Full Access** (the user can access the CMOS setup utility and make any changes), **No Access** (the user cannot access the CMOS setup utility), **Limited** (the user can access

**19**

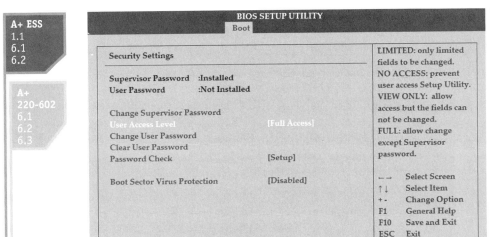

| BIOS SETUP UTILITY |
| Boot |

Security Settings

Supervisor Password    :Installed
User Password          :Not Installed

Change Supervisor Password
User Access Level                    [Full Access]
Change User Password
Clear User Password
Password Check                       [Setup]

Boot Sector Virus Protection         [Disabled]

LIMITED: only limited
fields to be changed.
NO ACCESS: prevent
user access Setup Utility.
VIEW ONLY: allow
access but the fields can
not be changed.
FULL: allow change
except Supervisor
password.

←→    Select Screen
↑↓    Select Item
+-    Change Option
F1    General Help
F10   Save and Exit
ESC   Exit

v02.53 (C)Copyright 1985-2002, American Megatrends, Inc.

**Figure 19-4** Change the way a user password functions to protect the computer

A+ ESS
1.1
6.1
6.2

A+
220-602
6.1
6.2
6.3

**Video**

Configuring a
Motherboard

CMOS setup and make a few changes such as date
and time), and **View Only** (the user can access CMOS
setup, but cannot make changes).

For added security, you can change the Password Check
entry from Setup (the user must enter the password to enter
CMOS setup) to Always (the user must enter the password
to boot the system). If you use this last option, you can
totally lock down the computer from unauthorized access.

**Notes**

For added protection, configure
the CMOS setup utility so that a
user cannot boot from a removable device such as a CD, USB
device, or floppy disk.

**Caution**

Recall from Chapter 6 that these supervisor and user passwords to the computer can be reset by setting a
jumper on the motherboard to clear all CMOS setup customized settings and return CMOS setup to default
settings. To keep someone from using this technique to access the computer, you can use a computer case
with a lockable side panel and install a lock on the case (see Figure 19-5). If you are concerned that the
computer case might be stolen, you can also install a lock and cable to securely tie the case to a table or
other fixture.

**Figure 19-5** This computer case allows you to use a lock and
key to keep intruders from opening the case

## HOW TO CREATE STRONG PASSWORDS AND PROTECT THEM

Recall from Chapter 9 that a fingerprint reader or other biometric device can be used in the place of a password to access your Windows user account and online accounts. However, these biometric solutions are not as secure as a strong password, which should be used to access corporate networks or protect sensitive data, such as financial information. A strong password meets all of the following criteria:

- ◢ Use eight or more characters (14 characters or longer is better).
- ◢ If your system allows it, a passphrase rather than a password is easier to remember and harder to guess. A **passphrase** is made of several words with spaces allowed.
- ◢ Combine uppercase and lowercase letters, numbers, and symbols.
- ◢ Use at least one symbol in the second through sixth position of your password.
- ◢ Don't use consecutive letters or numbers, such as "abcdefg" or "12345."
- ◢ Don't use adjacent keys on your keyboard, such as "qwerty."
- ◢ Don't use your logon name in the password.
- ◢ Don't use words in any language.
- ◢ Don't use the same password for more than one system.
- ◢ Don't store your passwords on a computer.

> **Notes**
>
> Microsoft offers a password checker at *www.microsoft.com/athome/security/privacy/password_checker.mspx*. Go to this link and enter your password on the window shown in Figure 19-6 for Microsoft to rate the strength of your password.

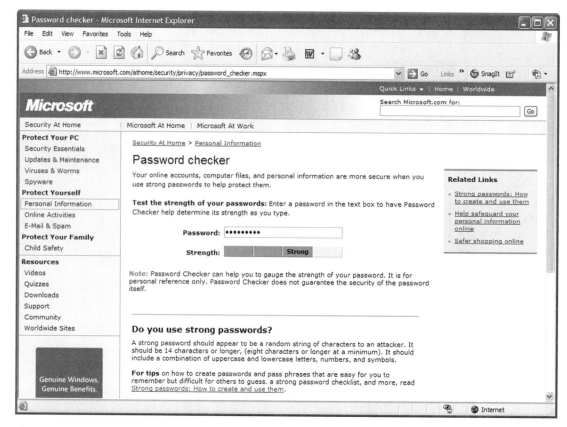

**Figure 19-6** Microsoft password checker window

A+ ESS
6.1
6.2

A+
220-602
6.1
6.2
6.3

A+
220-602
5.2
6.1
6.2
6.3

For Windows XP, in some situations, a blank password might be more secure than an easy-to-guess password such as "1234." That's because you cannot log on to a Windows XP computer from a remote computer unless the user account has a password. A criminal might be able to guess an easy password and log on remotely. For this reason, if your computer is always sitting in a protected room such as your home office, you might choose to use no password. However, for notebook computers that are not always protected in public places, always use a password. It's too easy for a criminal to log on to your Windows notebook if you use a blank password.

If you write your password down, keep it in as safe a place as you would the data you are protecting. Don't send your passwords over e-mail or chat. Change your passwords regularly, and don't type your password on a public computer. For example, computers in hotel lobbies or Internet cafes should only be used for Web browsing—not for logging on to your e-mail account or online banking account. These computers might be running keystroke-logging software put there by criminals to record each keystroke. Several years ago, while on vacation, I entered credit card information on a computer in a hotel lobby in a foreign country. Months later, I was still protesting $2 or $3 charges to my credit card from that country. Trust me. Don't do it—I speak from experience.

## ACCESS CONTROL USING WINDOWS

Using Windows, controlling access to a computer or the resources on that computer is accomplished with user accounts and passwords. A password is used to authenticate a user, and the rights and permissions assigned a user account authorize what a user can or cannot do. For best security, recall from Chapter 13 that each user account that is set up on a Windows 2000/XP computer needs a password. As an administrator, when you first create an account, you can specify that the user is allowed to change the password at any time. And, as an administrator, you can reset a password if a user forgets it. Also, for added security, as you learned to do in Chapter 13, configure the Windows XP logon screen so that user accounts, including the powerful Administrator account, are not displayed on a Welcome screen. Using this method, a user must press Ctrl+Alt+Del to see the logon dialog box.

In Chapter 13, you also learned that you can share a file or folder with users in your workgroup. Remember that a limited or guest account cannot normally access files belonging to another account. Using the tools in Chapter 13, when you shared a file or folder, you had no control over which user or user group was allowed access to the shared file or folder. Using more advanced security techniques, you can control which user account or account group can access a shared file or folder. Follow these steps to configure which users are allowed access to certain files and folders:

1. Log on as an administrator to do all the following tasks.

2. To disable simple file sharing so that you have more control over file and folder access and can monitor that access, open the **Folder Options** applet in Control Panel and click the **View** tab of the Folder Options window (see Figure 19-7).

3. Scroll down to the bottom of the **Advanced settings** list, uncheck **Use simple file sharing (Recommended)** and click **Apply**. Close the window.

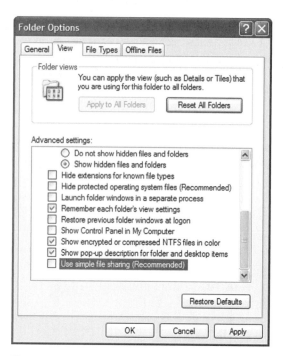

**Figure 19-7** Turn off simple file sharing so that you have more control over access to files and folders

4. In Explorer, right-click a folder and select **Properties** from the shortcut menu. In our example, we're using the folder C:\Budget. Click the **Sharing** tab, shown in Figure 19-8. Notice the Sharing tab is now more complex than it was when simple sharing was enabled. (Also notice the new Security tab on the Properties window.)

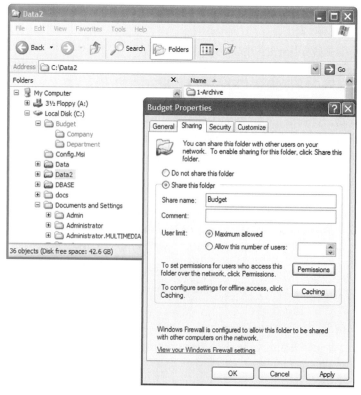

**Figure 19-8** The Sharing tab for a folder when simple sharing is disabled

A+ ESS
6.1
6.2

A+
220-602
5.2
6.1
6.2
6.3

5. To share the folder, select **Share this folder**. To control who can access the folder, click **Permissions**. The Permissions dialog box opens, similar to the one shown in Figure 19-9.

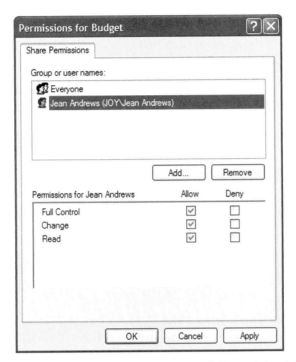

**Figure 19-9** Control who can access a folder and the rights given that user or user group

6. By default, share permissions are assigned to everyone. To remove permissions from everyone, select **Everyone** and click **Remove**. To add permission to a particular user or user group, click **Add** and enter the name of the user or user group and click **OK**. To control the permissions for a user, select the user and then select the permissions in the bottom pane of the dialog box. In Figure 19-9, full control has been given to the selected user. Click **Apply** twice when you're done.

7. When a user logged on to this computer or a remote computer on the network tries to access this folder or file, Windows authenticates the user account and password. If the user account and password don't match, a dialog box appears asking for an authorized user account and password. (Figure 19-10 shows the dialog box to access the \Data2 folder on a remote computer.) If the user doesn't enter the expected information, an error occurs (see Figure 19-11).

In addition to the method just discussed, at a command prompt, you can use the Cacls command to control how user accounts can access files and folders. Suppose, for example, an administrator wants to give permission for a user account, JSmith, to have access to a file, Myfile.txt. Figure 19-12 shows the use of five Cacls commands that can be used. The first, third, and fifth commands display access information for the Myfile.txt file (Cacls Myfile.txt). The second command grants read-only access for the user JSmith. (In the command line, the /E parameter says to edit the list and the /G parameter says to grant permission to the following user. The :R parameter says the permission is read-only.) The fourth command revokes JSmith's access permission. To use the command, you do not have to turn off simple file sharing.

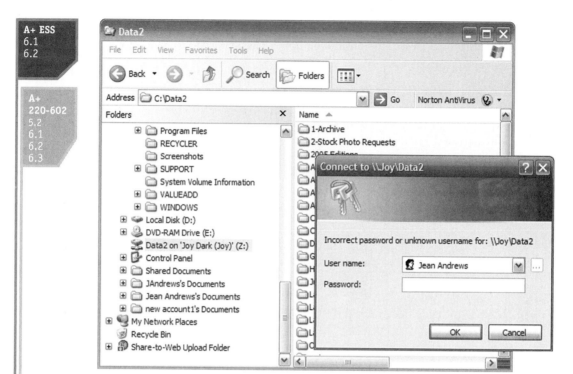

**Figure 19-10** User account and password is authenticated to a remote folder

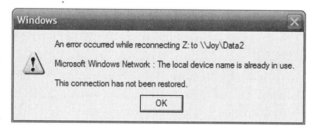

**Figure 19-11** Access is denied to a remote folder

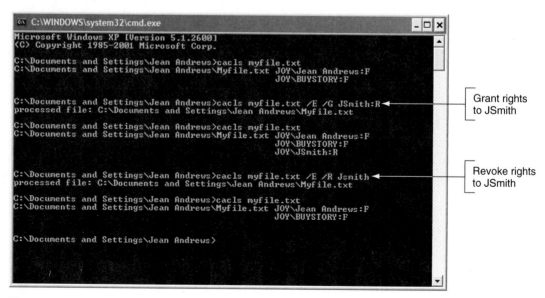

**Figure 19-12** Use the Cacls command to change user permissions for files and folders

**A+ ESS**
6.1
6.2

**A+ 220-602**
6.1
6.2
6.3

# LIMIT USE OF THE ADMINISTRATOR ACCOUNT

Another thing you can do to secure your computer is to limit the use of the more powerful Administrator account. Recall that just after you complete a Windows XP installation or you buy a new computer with the OS already installed, you have two accounts, the Administrator account and the Guest account. You can't do much with the Guest account, so few people want to use it. Most of us find it convenient to log on each time as the Administrator, so we can install hardware and software and change any setting.

The problem is that a malware program might be at work while we're logged on and it will then most likely be running under our account with more privileges and the ability to do more damage than if we had been logged on under a less powerful account. For that reason, it's a good idea to create a Limited User account to use for your every-day normal computer activities. Then only use the Administrator account when you need to do maintenance or installation chores that require the power of the Administrator account.

To help you remember to limit the use of the Administrator account, change the desktop wallpaper and color scheme for this one account to something that stands out at a glance, such as that in Figure 19-13. Also, be sure to change the password of the Administrator account on a regular basis and use a strong password for this account.

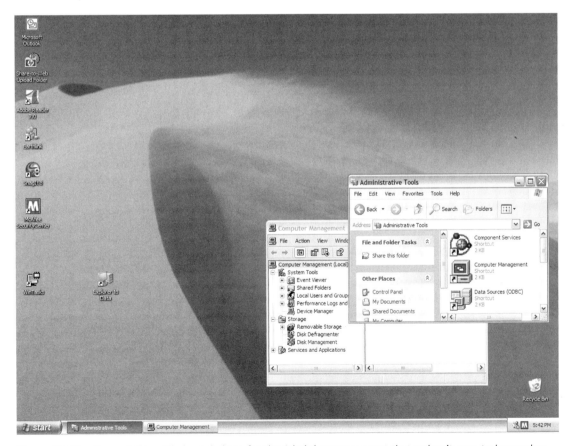

**Figure 19-13** Use a striking Windows desktop for the Administrator account that makes it easy to know when you're logged on as the administrator

A+ ESS
6.1
6.2

A+
220-602
6.2
6.3

# USE A PERSONAL FIREWALL

Never connect your computer to an unprotected network without using a firewall. Recall that a firewall is software or hardware that prevents worms or hackers from getting into your system. In the last chapter, you saw how to configure a software firewall using Windows Firewall and a hardware firewall using a multipurpose router on a small network.

Here I go again telling you to not do what I did: Once while traveling, I used my Windows 2000 notebook to dial up my ISP before I remembered to turn on my McAfee firewall software. It was up no more than 10 minutes before I turned on the firewall, but in that time I received a nasty worm that infected my e-mail software. It sent out dozens of e-mail messages to Navy military addresses in that short time.

As you learned in the last chapter, for Windows XP with Service Pack 2 applied, you can use Windows Firewall as a personal firewall (see Figure 19-14). In that chapter, you learned to turn on Windows Firewall and configure it so that certain activity such as Remote Desktop and File and Printer Sharing can still be initiated from other computers on the network.

> **Notes**
>
> Even with Windows Firewall, Microsoft still recommends that you use a hardware firewall to protect your system from attack. Software firewalls are better than no firewall at all, but a hardware firewall offers greater protection.

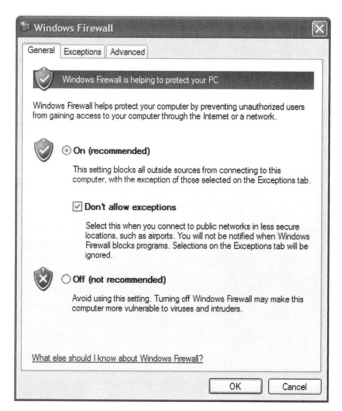

**Figure 19-14**   Use Windows Firewall to protect a Windows XP computer

# USE AV SOFTWARE

As a defensive and offensive measure to protect against malicious software, install and run **antivirus (AV) software** and keep it current. Configure the AV software so that it automatically downloads updates to the software and runs in the background. To be effective, AV software must be kept current and must be turned on. Set the AV software to automatically scan e-mail attachments.

AV software can only detect viruses identical or similar to those it has been programmed to search for and recognize. AV software detects a known virus by looking for distinguishing characteristics called **virus signatures**, which is why AV software cannot detect a virus it does not know. Therefore, it's important to have AV software regularly download updates to it. Figure 19-15 shows McAfee VirusScan software set to automatically stay current.

**Figure 19-15** Set your AV software to stay current automatically

Table 19-1 lists popular antivirus software and Web sites that also provide information about viruses.

| Antivirus Software | Web Site |
|---|---|
| AVG Anti-Virus by Grisoft | www.grisoft.com |
| Computer Associates | www.ca.com |
| F-Secure Antivirus by F-Secure Corp. | www.f-secure.com |
| eSafe by Aladdin Knowledge Systems, Ltd. | www.esafe.com |
| F-Prot by FRISK Software International | www.f-prot.com |
| McAfee VirusScan by McAfee Associates, Inc. | www.mcafee.com |
| NeaTSuite by Trend Micro (for networks) | www.trendmicro.com |
| Norman by Norman Data Defense Systems, Inc. (complicated to use, but highly effective) | www.norman.com |
| Norton AntiVirus by Symantec, Inc. | www.symantec.com |
| Panda Software | www.pandasoftware.com |
| PC-cillin by Trend Micro (for home use) | www.trendmicro.com |

**Table 19-1** Antivirus software and information

When selecting AV software, find out if it can:

- Automatically download new software upgrades and virus definitions from the Internet so that your software is continually aware of new viruses.
- Automatically execute at startup.
- Detect macros in a word-processing document as it is loaded by the word processor.
- Automatically monitor files being downloaded from the Internet, including e-mail attachments and attachments sent during a chat session, such as when using AOL Instant Messenger.
- Send virus alerts to your e-mail address to inform you of a dangerous virus and the need to update your antivirus software.
- Scan both automatically and manually for viruses.

Because AV software does not always stop adware or spyware, it's also a good idea to run anti-adware software in the background. The distinction between adware and spyware is slight and sometimes a malicious software program is displaying pop-up ads and also spying on you. There are tons of removal software products available on the Web, but I recommend the three in the following list. They all can catch adware, spyware, cookies, browser hijackers, dialers, keyloggers, and Trojans, which you'll learn about later in this chapter.

- Ad-Aware by Lavasoft (*www.lavasoft.com*) is one of the most popular and successful adware and spyware removal products. It can be downloaded without support for free.
- Spybot Search and Destroy by Patrick M. Kolla (*www.safer-networking.org*). This product does an excellent job of removing malicious software.
- Windows Defender by Microsoft (*www.microsoft.com*) is an up-and-coming product that, even in its current beta stage, does a great job removing malware.

## KEEP WINDOWS UPDATES CURRENT

Although Unix, Linux, and the Apple Mac OS sometimes get viruses, Windows is plagued the most by far for two reasons. First, Windows is the most popular OS for desktop and notebook computers. Being the most popular also makes it the most targeted by authors of

A+ ESS
6.1
6.2

malware. Second, Windows is designed with highly integrated components and many user-level entry points into those components. After a program has penetrated a Windows user-mode process, it is possible to infect more than one component. Security holes are being found all the time, and Microsoft is constantly releasing patches to keep up. But you have to download and install those patches before they'll help you.

Recall from Chapter 11 that you can keep Windows updates current by using the Web site *windowsupdate.microsoft.com*. The easiest way to start the process is to click **Start, All Programs, Windows Update**. Recall that you can also set Windows XP to update in the background automatically without your involvement. To do that, right-click **My Computer**, select **Properties** on the shortcut menu, and then click the **Automatic Updates** tab. On this window, shown in Figure 19-16, select **Automatic (recommended)**. Figure 19-17 shows a balloon that is letting you know that it restarted during the night to install updates.

The only reason you might not want to keep this feature set to Automatic is if you don't use an always-up Internet connection and don't want to be bothered with the time spent downloading updates when you first connect to the Internet.

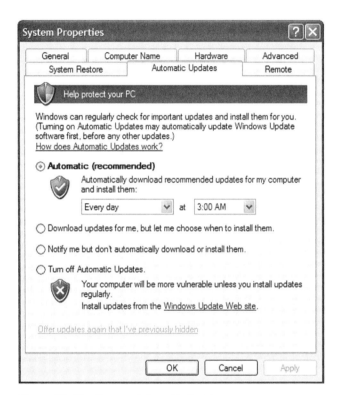

**Figure 19-16** Turn on Automatic Updates

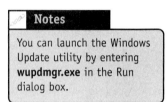

**Notes**

You can launch the Windows Update utility by entering **wupdmgr.exe** in the Run dialog box.

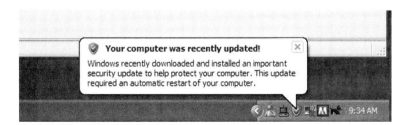

**Figure 19-17** Automatic Updates might restart your computer to complete the process of installing Windows updates

## SET INTERNET EXPLORER FOR OPTIMUM SECURITY

In the last chapter, you learned about the security features of Internet Explorer, which include the pop-up blocker, the ability to manage add-ons, the ability to block scripts and disable scripts embedded in Web pages, and the ability to set the general security level. Figure 19-18 shows the Internet Properties window where many of these options are configured. For most Web browsing, set the security level to Medium, as shown in the figure.

**Figure 19-18**   Control security settings for Internet Explorer

## USE ALTERNATE CLIENT SOFTWARE

Using alternate client software, including browsers and e-mail clients, can give you an added layer of protection from malicious software that targets Microsoft products.

### BROWSER SOFTWARE

Internet Explorer gets attacked by malware more than any other browser product for these reasons:

- ◢ Internet Explorer is by far the most popular browser, and, therefore, writers of malware know they are more likely to get more hits than when they write malware for less-popular browsers.
- ◢ Internet Explorer is written to more closely integrate with Windows components than other browsers. When malware penetrates Internet Explorer, it can then get to other Windows components that are inherently tied to IE.
- ◢ Internet Explorer is written to use ActiveX controls. An ActiveX control is a small program that can be downloaded by a Web site to your computer (sometimes without your knowledge). Microsoft invented ActiveX controls so that Web sites could use some nifty multimedia features. However, ActiveX controls allow Web pages to execute program code on your machine—and there's no way for you to know ahead of time whether that code is harmless or a malicious attack on your computer. For these reasons, you might consider using a different browser than Internet Explorer. One excellent browser is Firefox by Mozilla (*www.mozilla.com*). It's free and easy to use. See Figure 19-19.

A+ ESS
6.1
6.2

**Figure 19-19** Firefox by Mozilla is not as vulnerable to malware as is Internet Explorer

If you do decide to stay with Internet Explorer, be sure to take advantage of its security features.

### E-MAIL CLIENTS

Microsoft Outlook and Outlook Express are probably the most popular e-mail clients. That means they're also the most often attacked. They also support ActiveX controls and are closely integrated with Windows components, making your system more vulnerable to malware. To help stay out of the line of fire, you can use alternate e-mail clients. Personally, I use Eudora by Qualcomm (*www.eudora.com*). Mozilla offers Thunderbird, which others have told me is also a great product.

> **Notes**
>
> You might want to also consider using an alternate e-mail address. When you have to give an e-mail address to companies that you suspect might sell your address to spammers, use a second e-mail address that you don't use for normal e-mailing.

A+
220-602
6.1
6.2
6.3

## CONSIDER USING MICROSOFT SHARED COMPUTER TOOLKIT FOR WINDOWS XP

If you are responsible for Windows XP computers used in a public place such as classrooms, labs, hotel lobbies, Internet cafes, and so forth, you might want to consider installing and running Microsoft Shared Computer Toolkit for Windows XP. Basically, this software locks down the drive on which Windows is installed so that a user cannot permanently change Windows configuration, installed software or hardware, user settings, or user data. A user can make

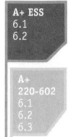

some changes to the drive, but when the system reboots, all these changes are undone and the system returns to its state when you enabled the toolkit. One feature of the tool is Windows Disk Protection, which prevents changes to the drive on which Windows is installed.

To learn more about the toolkit, go to the Microsoft Web site at *www.microsoft.com* and search for "Microsoft Shared Computer Toolkit for Windows XP." The toolkit can be downloaded for free to computers that are running a genuine Windows XP license (see Figure 19-20).

**Figure 19-20**   Microsoft Shared Computer Toolkit for Windows XP can secure a Windows installation on a computer used in public places

If you decide to use this tool, first get your drive in tip-top shape with everything just the way you want it. Then configure and enable the toolkit. You can configure it so that Windows updates can be installed when users are not working on the computer. Routinely, at least monthly, you need to check the computer to make sure any updates to applications are downloaded and installed.

## HIDE AND ENCRYPT FILES AND FOLDERS

In Chapter 17, you learned that you can do the following to protect files and folders from unauthorized access:

▲ Disable file and printer sharing so that others on the network cannot access resources on your computer.
▲ Hide your computer from others on the network.

A+ ESS
6.1
6.2

A+
220-602
3.1
6.2
6.3

◢ Hide a shared folder so that others must know the name of the folder to access it.
◢ Make your personal folders private.

Another way you can protect files and folders is to use the Windows 2000/XP **Encrypted File System (EFS)**, which works only when using the Windows 2000/XP NTFS file system. (Windows XP Home Edition does not provide encryption.)

**Encryption** puts data into code that must be translated before it can be accessed, and can be applied to either a folder or file. If a folder is marked for encryption, every file created in the folder or copied to the folder will be encrypted. At the file level, each file must be encrypted individually. Encrypting at the folder level is considered a best practice because it provides greater security: Any file placed in an encrypted folder is automatically encrypted so you don't have to remember to encrypt it. An encrypted file remains encrypted if you move it from an encrypted folder to an unencrypted folder on the same or another NTFS logical drive. A user does not have to go through a complex process of encryption to use EFS; from a user's perspective, it's just a matter of placing a file in a folder marked for encryption.

Now let's look at how to encrypt a file or folder, share an encrypted file, decrypt a file or folder, and use the Cipher command.

## HOW TO ENCRYPT A FILE OR FOLDER

To encrypt a file or folder on an NTFS drive, do the following:

1. Right-click the folder or file you want to encrypt and select **Properties** from the shortcut menu. The Properties window for that file or folder opens, as shown on the left side of Figure 19-21.

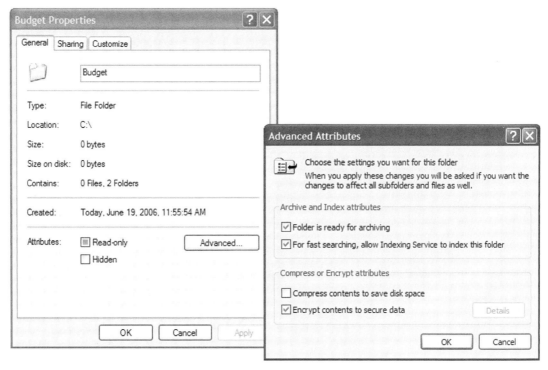

**Figure 19-21**  Encrypt a file or folder using the Properties window

2. Click the **Advanced** button. The Advanced Attributes dialog box opens, as shown on the right side of Figure 19-21.

3. To encrypt the folder or file, check **Encrypt contents to secure data** and click **OK**. On the Properties window, click **Apply**. The dialog box shown in Figure 19-22 opens, asking you if you want the encryption to apply to subfolders. Make your choice and click **OK**.

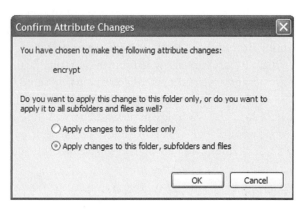

**Figure 19-22**   Encryption can apply to subfolders or just to the one folder

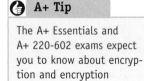

**A+ Tip**

The A+ Essentials and A+ 220-602 exams expect you to know about encryption and encryption technologies.

Encrypted files or folders are displayed in Explorer in green. For a standalone computer that is not part of a Windows domain, the EFS encrypting process generates a self-signed digital certificate to be used for the encryption. This certificate contains both the private key and public key needed to decrypt the file or folder. If some other user on this same computer who is not an administrator or any user on the network attempts to access the encrypted file or folder, an "Access Denied" message appears.

**Notes**

When you open an encrypted file with an application, Windows decrypts the file for the application to use. While the application is working on the file, data written to the virtual memory file, Pagefile.sys, might contain decrypted data from your file. If your computer goes into hibernation while the file is open, a criminal might later be able to read the data in the Pagefile.sys file by booting the system from another OS. For this reason, disable hibernation while working on encrypted files. Also, for added protection, configure Windows to clean out Pagefile.sys at shutdown. To do that, use Group Policy. In Group Policy, drill down to **Computer Configuration, Windows Settings, Security Settings, Local Policies**, and **Security Options**, as shown in Figure 19-23. Double-click **Shutdown: Clear virtual memory pagefile**, and enable the feature.

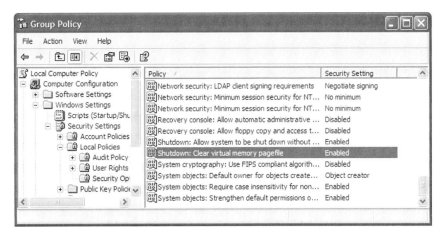

**Figure 19-23** Use Group Policy to configure Windows to clear Pagefile.sys at shutdown

## HOW TO SHARE AN ENCRYPTED FILE

You cannot share encrypted folders, but you can share encrypted files. In order to give another user on this same computer access to an encrypted file, you need to export your certificate and then the other user can import that certificate to be used to access the encrypted file. Here are the steps involved:

1. To export the certificate, on the file's properties window, click the **Advanced** button. The Advanced Attributes dialog box opens. Click **Details**. The Encryption Details dialog box opens, showing the users and recovery agents who can access the file, as shown on the left side of Figure 19-24. Click **Add**. The Select User dialog box opens, also shown in Figure 19-24.

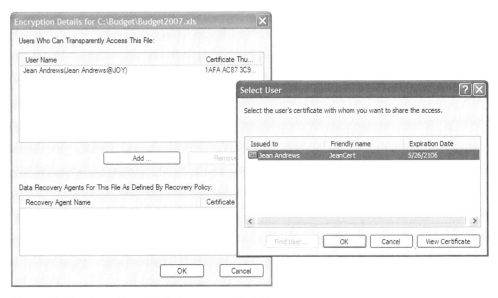

**Figure 19-24** Encryption details for an encrypted file

2. Click **View Certificate**. The Certificate dialog box opens (see Figure 19-25). Notice on this dialog box that Windows does not recognize the certificate to be trusted. That's because the certificate was issued by EFS rather than obtained from a trusted certification authority (CA). A CA is an organization such as VeriSign (*www.verisign.com*) that issues digital certificates.

**Figure 19-25** The Certificate dialog box shows information about the certificate used for encryption

3. Click the **Details** tab, as shown on the left side of Figure 19-26. Then click **Copy to File**. The Certificate Export Wizard launches, as shown on the right side of Figure 19-26. Follow the wizard to export the certificate. The wizard will give you the opportunity to name the file and decide in what folder it will be stored. Also, the wizard will ask you if you want to export the private key portion of the certificate, which you don't need to do. When the wizard completes, the file is created with a .pfx file extension.

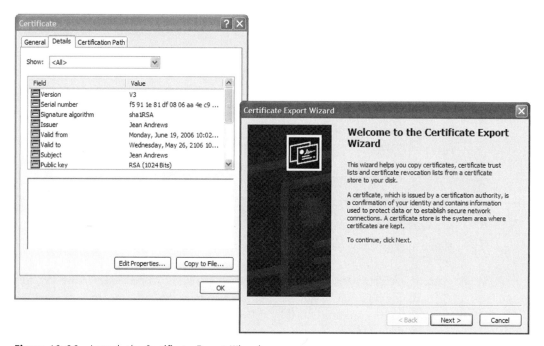

**Figure 19-26** Launch the Certificate Export Wizard

A+ ESS
6.1
6.2

A+
220-602
3.1
6.2
6.3

4. Have the user who is to have access to the encrypted file log on to the system and import the certificate. To import the certificate, the user needs to locate the .pfx file in Explorer and double-click the file. The user can then access the encrypted file.

5. For added security, after all users who need access to the file have imported the certificate, delete the .pfx file.

The method just described to share an encrypted file might not work when you are part of a Windows domain. When you encrypt a file or folder on a Windows domain, the domain administrator might have set up the domain so that trusted certificates are used for the encryption. To know how to share an encrypted file on a Windows domain, check with your network administrator.

## HOW TO DECRYPT A FILE OR FOLDER

To ensure that a file can be accessed if a user is not available or forgets the password to log on to the system, an administrator for the OS can decrypt a file. In this case, the administrator is called a data recovery agent (DRA).

Here are three ways to decrypt a file or folder:

▲ From the file's Properties dialog box, click the **Advanced** button. In the Advanced Attributes dialog box, uncheck **Encrypt contents to secure data**.

▲ Encryption is removed automatically when you move a file or folder to a FAT logical drive (volume) because the FAT file system does not support encryption. Figure 19-27 shows the message you see when an encrypted file is about to be moved to a jump drive.

▲ Use the Cipher command, which is discussed next.

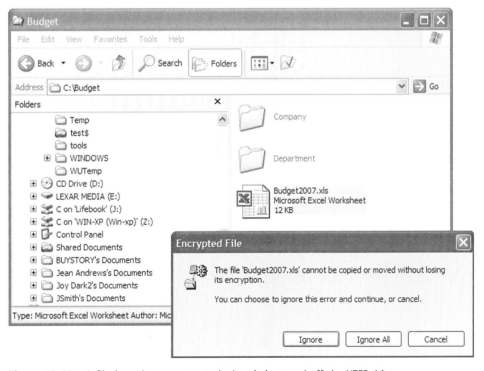

**Figure 19-27** A file is no longer encrypted when it is moved off the NTFS drive

A+ ESS
6.1
6.2

A+
220-602
3.1
6.2
6.3

## HOW TO USE THE CIPHER COMMAND

If you are encrypting a large number of files or folders from a command prompt or using a batch file, you can use the Cipher command:

CIPHER [/E, /D] [/S:*DIR*] [*PATHNAME*[. . .]]

Note the following about this command:

▲ /E encrypts the specified files or folders.
▲ /D decrypts the specified files or folders.
▲ /S:*DIR* applies the action to the specified folder (directory) and all its subfolders.
▲ *PATHNAME* is the path to and the name of the file or folder that is to be encrypted or decrypted.

For example, at the command prompt, to decrypt all files in the C:\Public folder, use this command:

```
CIPHER /D C:\Public\*.*
```

## PHYSICALLY PROTECT YOUR EQUIPMENT

It's only common sense, but worth mentioning anyway. There are some things you can do to physically protect your computer equipment. Here is a list of do's and don'ts. You can probably add your own tips to the list:

▲ *Don't move or jar your computer when it's turned on.* Before you move the computer case even a foot or so, power it down. Don't put the computer case under your desk where it might get bumped or kicked. Although modern hard drives are sealed and much less resistant to vibration than earlier drives, it's still possible to crash a drive by banging into it while it's reading or writing data.

▲ *Don't smoke around your computer.* Tar from cigarettes can accumulate on fans, causing them to jam and the system to overheat. For older hard drives that are not adequately sealed, smoke particles can get inside and crash a drive.

▲ *Don't leave the PC turned off for weeks or months at a time.* My daughter once left her PC turned off for an entire summer. At the beginning of the new school term, the PC would not boot. We discovered that the boot record at the beginning of the hard drive had become corrupted. PCs, like old cars, can give problems after long spans of inactivity.

▲ *High humidity can be dangerous for hard drives.* I once worked in a basement with PCs, and hard drives failed much too often. After we installed dehumidifiers, the hard drives became more reliable.

▲ *In CMOS setup, disable the ability to write to the boot sector of the hard drive.* This alone can keep boot viruses at bay. However, before you upgrade your OS, such as when you upgrade Windows XP to Windows Vista, be sure to enable writing to the boot sector, which the OS setup will want to do.

▲ *If your data is really private, keep it under lock and key.* You can use all kinds of security methods to encrypt, password protect, and hide data, but if it really is that important, one obvious thing you can do is store the data on a removable storage device such as a flash drive and, when you're not using the data, put the flash drive in a fireproof safe. And, of course, keep two copies. Sounds simple, but it works.

▲ *Keep magnets away from your computer.* Don't work inside the computer case with magnetized screwdrivers or sit magnets on top of the computer case.

▲ *Lock down the computer case.* As mentioned earlier in the chapter, some computer cases allow you to add a lock so that you can physically prevent others from opening the case. Besides this lock, you can also use a lock and chain to physically tie the case to a desk or other permanent fixture so someone can't walk away with it. As an added precaution, physically mark the case so it can be identified if it is later stolen. You embed an ID plate into the case or engrave your ID information into it. Record serial numbers and model numbers in a safe place separate from the equipment.

## BEWARE OF SOCIAL ENGINEERING

Generally speaking, the weakest link in setting up security in a computer environment is people. That's because people can often be tricked into giving out private information. Even with all the news and hype about identify theft and criminal Web sites, it's amazing how well these techniques still work. Many users naively download a funny screen saver, open an e-mail attachment, or enter credit card information into a Web site, without regard to security. In the computer arena, **social engineering** is the practice of tricking people into giving out private information or allowing unsafe programs into the network or computer. A good support technician is aware of the criminal practices used and is able to teach users how to recognize this mischief and avoid it. Most of the danger you need to be aware of comes over the Internet. Here are three common ways criminals might use the Internet to lure users into taking their bait:

▲ **Phishing** (sounds like "fishing") is a type of identity theft where the sender of an e-mail message scams you into responding with personal data about yourself. The scam artist baits you by asking you to verify personal data on your bank account, ISP account, credit card account, or something of that nature. Often you are tricked into clicking a link in the e-mail message, which takes you to an official-looking site complete with company or bank logos where you are asked to enter your user ID and password to enter the site.

▲ Scam artists use **scam e-mail** to lure you into their scheme. One scam e-mail I recently received was supposedly from the secretary of a Russian oil tycoon who was being held in jail with his millions of dollars of assets frozen. If I would respond to the e-mail and get involved, I was promised a 12 percent commission to help recover the funds.

▲ A **virus hoax** or e-mail hoax is e-mail that does damage by tempting you to forward it to everyone in your e-mail address book with the intent of clogging up e-mail systems or to delete a critical Windows system file by convincing you the file is malicious. Also, some e-mail scam artists promise to send you money if you'll circulate their e-mail message to thousands of people. I recently received one that was supposedly promising money from Microsoft for "testing" the strength of the Internet e-mail system. Beware! Always check Web sites that track virus hoaxes before pressing that Send button!

 **A+ Tip**

The A+ 220-602 exam expects you to be aware of social engineering situations that might compromise security.

Let's take a look at how to use the Internet responsibly, how to smoke out an e-mail hoax, and how to deal with suspicious scripts.

### RESPONSIBLE INTERNET HABITS

In this section, we'll look at some best practices that, for the most part, simply equate to using good judgment when using the Internet to keep you out of harm's way.

**19**

Here is a list of what I'll call the Six Commandments for using the Internet:

1. *You shall not open e-mail attachments without scanning them for viruses first.* In fact, if you don't know the person who sent you the attachment, save yourself a lot of trouble and just delete it without opening it.

2. *You shall not click links inside e-mail messages.* These links might contain a malicious script. To keep the script from running, copy and paste the link to your browser address bar instead.

3. *You shall not forward an e-mail message without first checking to see if that warning is a hoax.* Save us all the time of having to delete the thing from our Inbox.

4. *You shall always check out a Web site before you download anything from it.* Freeware isn't so free if you end up with an infected computer. Only download from trusted sites.

5. *You shall never give your private information to just any ole Web site.* Use a search engine and search for information about a site before you trust it with your identity.

6. *You shall never trust an e-mail message asking you to verify your private data on a Web site with which you do business.* If you receive an e-mail that looks like it came from your bank, your PayPal account, or your utility company, don't click those links in that message. If you think it might be legitimate, open your browser, type in the link to the business's Web site, and check out the request.

## HOW TO DEBUNK AN E-MAIL HOAX

An e-mail hoax is itself a pest because it overloads network traffic when naive users pass it on. Figure 19-28 shows an example of a virus hoax e-mail message I received.

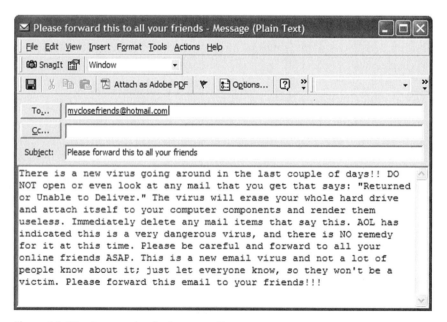

**Figure 19-28**   An example of a hoax e-mail message

Viruses grow more powerful every day, but this message is just absurd. It is unlikely that a virus can render computer components useless. No virus has been known to do actual physical damage to hardware, although viruses can make a PC useless by destroying programs or data, and a few viruses have been able to attack system BIOS code on the motherboard.

What's most important is not to be gullible and take the bait by forwarding the message to someone else. The potential damage a hoax like this can do is to overload an e-mail system with useless traffic, which is the real intent of the hoax. When I received this e-mail, over a hundred names were on the distribution list, sent by a friend who was innocently trying to help us all out.

Here are some Web sites that specialize in debunking virus hoaxes:

▲ *hoaxbusters.ciac.org* by Computer Incident Advisory Capability
▲ *www.hoaxinfo.com* by Jeff Richards
▲ *www.hoaxkill.com* by Oxcart Software
▲ *www.snopes.com* by Urban Legends
▲ *www.viruslist.com* by Kaspersky Lab
▲ *www.vmyths.com* by Rhode Island Soft Systems, Inc.

When you get a hoax, if you know the person who sent it to you, do us all a favor and send that person some of these links!

## PROTECT AGAINST MALICIOUS E-MAIL SCRIPTS

One popular Trojan technique to spread a virus or worm is to put a malicious script in the body of an e-mail message or in an e-mail attachment. The e-mail is written with the intent of luring you to open the attachment or click a link in the e-mail text. For example, you receive spam in your e-mail, open it, and click the link "Remove me" to supposedly get removed from the spam list. However, by doing so, you spread a virus or worm, or install adware onto your PC.

To counteract this approach to spreading malicious software, let's take a look at how scripts work. Then we'll look at how you can protect yourself from malicious ones.

### How Scripts Work

Scripts can be written in several scripting languages, such as VBScript or Jscript, and are executed in Windows using the Windows Scripting Host (WSH) utility, Wscript.exe. A script is stored in a file with a script file extension—the extension depends on the scripting language used to write the script. The scripting languages and file extensions that Windows recognizes by default are Jscript (.js file extension), Jscript Encoded (.jse), VBScript Encoded (.vbe), VBScript (.vbs), and Windows Script (.wsf). You can add other file extensions to this list.

The program that is used to handle a particular file type or file extension is determined by the Windows default settings. For instance, Windows does know how to handle a .txt file before any application is installed, because Notepad (the executable is Notepad.exe) is part of Windows, which is the program that is launched to open a .txt file.

On the other hand, file extensions that are not part of the Windows default settings can be added to the list of known file extensions when a new application is installed on a computer. For example, Windows will not know how to handle a .doc file until Microsoft Word has been installed. After Word is installed, when you double-click a .doc file, the Word executable, Winword.exe, is launched and then opens the document file.

### How Scripts Are Spread

Now, let's use all this information to help protect a system against malicious scripts. Many times, a link that reads something like this one appears in an e-mail message from someone you don't know: "Click *www.symantec.com* to read about the latest virus attack." The link is not the URL to the Symantec Web site, but rather points to *www.symantec.com.vbs*,

A+ ESS
6.1
6.2

which is a script embedded in the e-mail message. When you click the link, the script with the .vbs file extension is executed by Wscript.exe and malicious software is spread to your computer.

Another malicious technique is to attach a file to an e-mail message. The filename is displayed, looking something like this: CoolPic.jpg. But because extensions of known file types are normally hidden, you are not aware that the real filename is CoolPic.jpg.vbs. When you click, thinking you're about to view a photo, you are executing a malicious script.

### How to Help Protect Against Malicious Scripts

So, how do you protect yourself? Here is what you can do:

▲ Set Windows so that script file extensions display by default. If that e-mail attachment had appeared as CoolPic.jpg.vbs, you probably would not have opened it.

▲ Set Windows to not execute scripts, but rather to open them in a Notepad window. After you've examined a script, you can decide if you want to execute it.

Now let's see how to use both options. To display file extensions of scripts, do the following:

1. Using Windows Explorer or the Start menu, open **My Computer**. Click **Tools, Folder Options**. The Folder Options window opens. Click the **File Types** tab, as shown in Figure 19-29. Listed under *Registered file types* are all the file types that Windows knows how to handle.

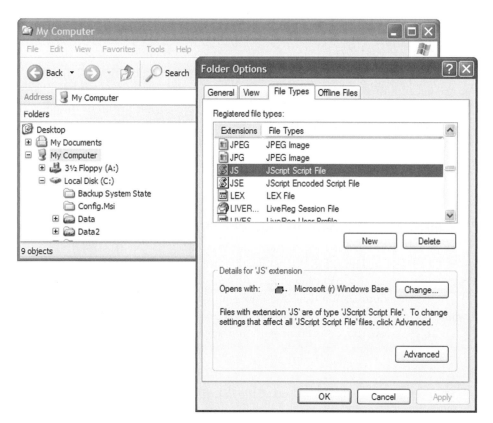

**Figure 19-29** The File Types tab of the Folder Options window lists all the file types that Windows recognizes

**A+ ESS**
**6.1**
**6.2**

2. Select **JS** in the Extensions column and click **Advanced**. The Edit File Type window opens, as shown in Figure 19-30. Check the **Always show extension** check box. Click **OK**.

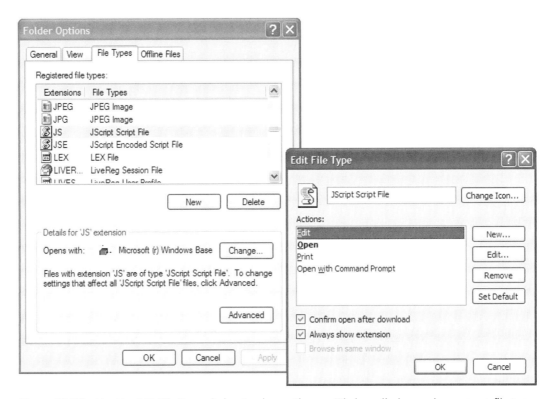

**Figure 19-30**   Use the Edit File Type window to change the way Windows displays and manages a file type

3. Do the same for the other script file types: JSE, VBE, VBS, and WSF. Click **Close** to close the Folder Options window.

A more drastic measure to protect yourself is to set Windows so that unknown scripts will not be executed. To do that, change the action that Windows takes each time you double-click a script file. Looking back at Figure 19-30, select **Edit** in the list of Actions (not the Edit button), click **Set Default**, and then click **OK**. The next time you double-click a script, it will be opened by Notepad for editing. Doing so will give you the opportunity to examine the script before it's executed. However, to actually execute the script, you have to manually use Wscript.exe to run it by entering this command at a command prompt (where Myscript.vbs is the name of the script):

```
Wscript.exe Myscript.vbs
```

## KEEP GOOD BACKUPS OF USER DATA

One of the more important chores of securing a computer is to prepare in advance for disaster to strike. One of the most important things you can do to prepare for disaster is to make good backups of user data. You learned how to make backups in Chapter 13, so we won't repeat that information here.

## BACK UP SYSTEM FILES

Recall that in Chapter 12, you learned how to use Ntbackup.exe to back up the System State and registry before we edited the registry. You need to back up the System State after you have made major changes to the system, such as when you install a new hard drive or software application. If others in your organization have permission to install hardware or applications, you might need to explain to them the importance of backing up the System State. At the least, you can make it a routine part of your monthly maintenance tasks.

## MAKE USE OF EVENT LOGGING AND INCIDENT REPORTING

As a part of managing the security of a computer or network, your organization might make you accountable to report incidents of unusual or atypical events. Incidents that you might be expected to report can include an attempt at breaking in to a secured computer or network, the security has been broken, an accident has occurred, property has been lost or damaged, a hazard has been reported, an alarm has been activated, unauthorized changes to a system or its data were made, or other such events. Reasons for incident reporting include the need for others to respond to an incident, the need to know about a weak security loophole that can be plugged, the need to be aware of trends in problems over the entire organization, and legal concerns.

For large networks, a computerized incident reporting tool is most likely already in place and your responsibility might be to learn how to use it, to know your user account and password to the system, and to make sure you report all incidents in a timely manner. On the other hand, old-fashioned paper reporting might be used. Either way, the incident-reporting forms will most likely include your name, job title, contact information, and full description of the incident. The description might include the system or systems affected, the people involved, the resulting damage, and if the problem is resolved or still active. Also included might be your recommendations or actions to resolve the problem.

You can use several monitoring tools to log events that can help you know if a computer or its security has been compromised. Several of these are discussed next.

### MONITORING WINDOWS 2000/XP LOGON EVENTS

One event you might be expected to monitor is logging on to a local computer. Logging on to a domain is monitored at the domain level, but you can track logging on to a standalone computer or a computer in a workgroup by using Event Viewer. (Windows XP Home Edition does not support this feature.) You can track successful and/or failed attempts at logging on. For most situations, it is only required that you track failures. To set Event Viewer to track failures when people are attempting to log on to the system, do the following:

1. Log on to the system as an administrator. In Group Policy, drill down to **Computer Configuration, Windows Settings, Security Settings, Local Policies**, and **Audit Policy**, as shown in Figure 19-31.

2. Double-click **Audit account logon events**. The Audit logon events Properties dialog box opens, also shown in Figure 19-31. Check **Failure** and click **Apply**. Do the same for **Audit logon events** and then close the Group Policy window.

A+ ESS
3.3
6.1
6.2

A+
220-602
3.1
3.3
6.1
6.2

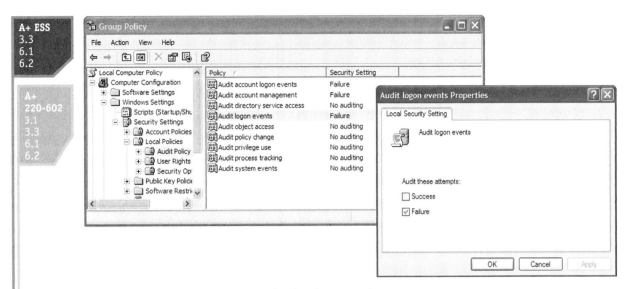

**Figure 19-31**   Set Windows XP to monitor logging on to the system

3. To see the events that are logged, open **Event Viewer** and select **Security** in the left pane (see Figure 19-32).

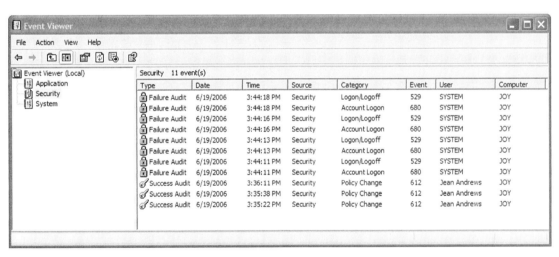

**Figure 19-32**   Event Viewer monitoring failures at logging on to Windows XP

4. Recall from earlier chapters that you can change the maximum allowed size of the log file. Besides changing the size of the Security log file, for added security, you can set the system to halt when the Security log file is full. To do that, right-click **Security** and select **Properties**. The Security Properties window opens (see Figure 19-33).

5. Select **Do not overwrite events (clear log manually)** and click **OK**. Close Event Viewer.

6. The next step is to edit the registry to tell the system to halt when the log file size is exceeded. First open the Registry Editor and navigate to this key:

   **HKLM\SYSTEM\CurrentControlSet\Control\Lsa.**

7. To back up the key, right-click it and select **Export** from the shortcut menu; save the key to your desktop.

A+ ESS
3.3
6.1
6.2

A+
220-602
3.1
3.3
6.1
6.2

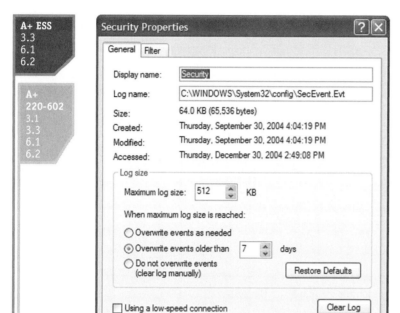

**Figure 19-33** Control the Security log file settings

8. In the right pane, double-click the name **CrashOnAuditFail**. The Edit DWORD Value dialog box opens. Assign **1** to its value and click **OK**. Close the Registry Editor.

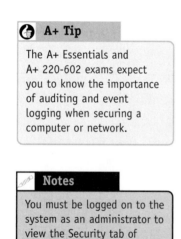

**A+ Tip**

The A+ Essentials and A+ 220-602 exams expect you to know the importance of auditing and event logging when securing a computer or network.

**Notes**

You must be logged on to the system as an administrator to view the Security tab of Event Viewer.

If the size of the Security log file is exceeded, you must restart the system, log on to the system as an administrator, open Event Viewer, save the log file, and then clear the log file. And, if you want the system to halt the next time the log file is full, you must use the Registry Editor and reset the CrashOnAuditFail value to 1.

## MONITORING CHANGES TO FILES AND FOLDERS

Earlier in the chapter, you learned how to disable simple file sharing so that you can control which user accounts have access to a file or folder. After simple file sharing is disabled, you can also monitor access to a file or folder. Do the following:

1. To set the Group Policy to audit an object, open the **Group Policy** window. Then click **Computer Configuration, Windows Settings, Security Settings, Local Policies,** and **Audit Policy,** and then double-click **Audit object access** (see Figure 19-34). Check **Failure** and click **Apply**. Close the Group Policy windows.

2. Open the Properties window of the file or folder you want to monitor or audit and click the **Security** tab. Then click **Advanced**. The Advanced Security Settings window for the file or folder opens. Click the **Auditing** tab.

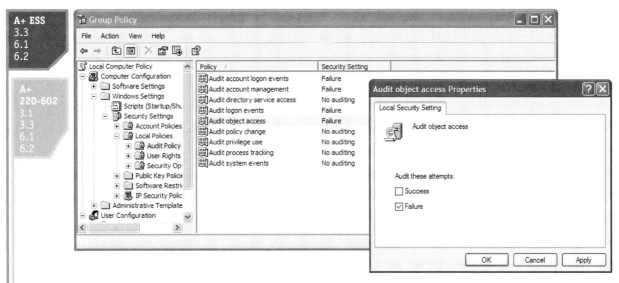

**Figure 19-34** Set the Group Policy to audit an object

3. You can now add users that you want to monitor and decide what activity to monitor. To add a user, click **Add**. When you're done, click **Apply** to close the window and apply your changes. Figure 19-35 shows that all activity by the user BUYSTORY on the folder C:\Budget will be monitored. Close all windows when you're done.

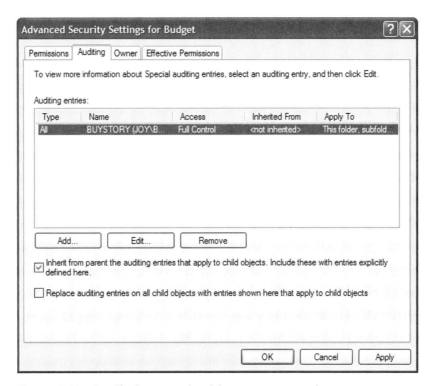

**Figure 19-35** Specify the user and activity you want to monitor

4. To view the logged activity, open **Event Viewer** and double-click **Security**. Figure 19-36 shows the results when someone logged on using the Buystory account attempted to open the Budget folder for which they did not have permission to access.

A+ ESS
3.3
6.1
6.2

A+
220-602
3.1
3.3
6.1
6.2

**Figure 19-36** Event Viewer shows object access events have been logged

**Notes**

When simple file sharing is disabled, on the Properties window of a file or folder, you can use the Security tab to change the owner of the file or folder. If you are having a problem decrypting an encrypted file that belongs to another user, try changing the owner of the file. On the Security tab, click **Advanced**, and then click the **Owner** tab (see Figure 19-37).

**Figure 19-37** Change the owner of a file or folder

## MONITORING CHANGES TO STARTUP

You can install some third-party monitoring tools to monitor the startup processes and let you know when installation software attempts to add something to your startup routines. Three good products are Autoruns by Sysinternals (*www.sysinternals.com*), WinPatrol by BillP Studios (*www.winpatrol.com*), and Startup Control Panel by Mike Lin (*www.mlin.net*). Figure 19-38 shows a window that displays when WinPatrol detected a startup process that was about to be added to a system.

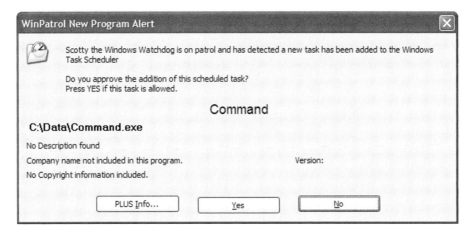

**Figure 19-38** WinPatrol is asking permission to allow a startup process to be added

## MONITORING NETWORK ACTIVITY

You can use Windows Firewall to monitor and log network activity. On the Windows Firewall window, click the **Advanced** tab, as shown on the left side of Figure 19-39. Under Security Logging, click **Settings**. The Log Settings window opens, as shown on the right side of Figure 19-39. Select what you want to log (dropped packets and/or successful connections) and click **OK**. Also notice the path and name of the log file: C:\Windows\pfirewall.log. A packet is a segment of data sent over a network connection and a dropped packet is a packet that could not be successfully delivered. Log dropped packets when you're trying to solve a connection problem and log successful connections when you want to monitor network activity.

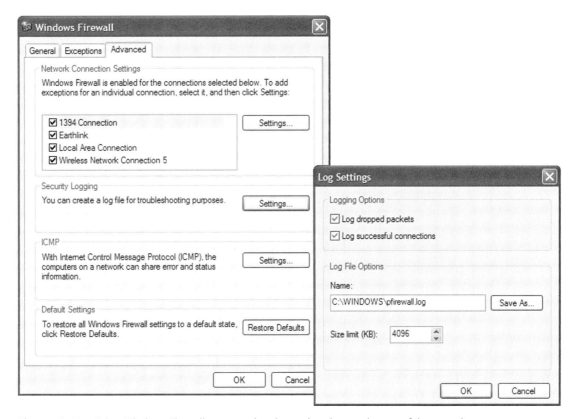

**Figure 19-39** Using Windows Firewall, you can log dropped packets and successful connections

## DESTROY THE TRASH

Criminals can find out a lot about you by going through your trash. For computer equipment and hard copies, be sure to do the following to make sure important information is not exposed:

- ▲ Destroy all storage media before you throw it out. Break CDs and DVDs and physically do damage to old hard drives before you put them in the trash. For a hard drive, you can use a hammer and nail and drive the nail all the way through all disks inside the hard drive housing.
- ▲ Shred or otherwise destroy hard copies that contain sensitive data.
- ▲ **Data migration** is moving data from one application to another application or from one storage media to another, and most often involves a change in the way the data is formatted. For example, if accounts receivables for a small organization have been kept in Excel spreadsheets, and are now being moved into an Access database, that data must be migrated from Excel to Access. As the data is moved, keep in mind that sensitive data still needs to be encrypted and user access controlled. Then, after the migration is complete, be sure to destroy old data storage media that is no longer used.
- ▲ When retiring a computer system or when a user is no longer actively using a certain desktop or notebook computer, remnants of data and other sensitive information can accidentally be left on the system for criminals to find. The surest way to make certain that these data remnants are totally erased is to totally erase everything on the hard drive. The best way to totally erase everything on a hard drive is to use a **zero-fill utility** provided by a hard drive manufacturer. These utilities fill every sector on the drive with zeroes. For example, for Seagate (*www.seagate.com*) hard drives, download the DiscWizard Starter Edition diagnostic software, create a bootable floppy disk using the utility, and boot from the disk. Then select **Utilities Zero Fill Drive (Full)** from the startup menu, which fully erases all data on the drive. You can then repartition and reformat the drive to use it again.

## PERFORM A MONTHLY SECURITY MAINTENANCE ROUTINE

Make it a habit to check every computer for which you are responsible each month. You can use the following checklist. However, know that routine maintenance tends to evolve over time based on an organization's past problems that might need special attention. Start with this list and then add to it as the need arises:

1. Change the administrator password. (Use a strong password.)

2. Check that Windows Automatic Updates is turned on and working. For applications that users routinely rely on, you might also download and install any critical updates.

3. Check that AV software is installed and current. If you are running anti-adware software, also verify that it is running and current.

4. Visually check the equipment to make sure the case has not been tampered with. Is the lock secure?

5. Check Event Viewer. Take a look at the Security list, looking for failed attempts to access the system.

6. Verify that user backups of data are being done and current backups of data and the System State exist.

7. If you are running Windows Disk Protection, discussed earlier in the chapter, you need to save any changes to disk that are required to update installed software.

19

# SECURING YOUR WIRED OR WIRELESS NETWORK

Unsecured networks are like leaving your front door open when you go to work in the morning or signing every check in your checkbook and then leaving it lying around in a coffee shop. Don't even think about it! If you're responsible for a home or small office network, take security seriously. In this section, you'll see how to use a router to secure a small network, how to secure a wireless network, and about authentication techniques used for larger networks.

## USE A ROUTER TO SECURE A SOHO NETWORK

For most networks for a small office or home office (SOHO), the device you'll want for security is a router that can be used to secure a wired network or provide a secured wireless network. Routers don't cost that much nowadays, and the investment is well worth it. In Chapters 17 and 18, you learned how to configure a hardware firewall built in to a multi-purpose router and how to set up and secure a wireless network. To refresh your memory of that information, recall that a router can be used to limit communication from outside or inside the network in these ways:

▲ *Limit communication from outside the network.* Turn on the router's firewall so that anonymous communication initiated from outside the network is not allowed in.

▲ *Limit communication from within the network.* Access to the Internet can be limited to certain PCs on the network and certain times of day or days of the week. Also, certain services (such as gaming) can be blocked. Certain Web sites can be blocked (by entering the URL of the Web site in a list of blocked sites), and Web sites can be blocked by keywords contained in the Web pages. Figure 19-40 shows the setup screen for one router that allows you to limit Internet access.

▲ *Secure a wireless access point.* In Chapter 17, you learned that you can secure a wireless access point by renaming the SSID and disabling SSID broadcasting, filtering MAC addressing, encrypting data, using a firewall, and keeping the firmware updated.

▲ *Implement a virtual private network (VPN).* Some high-end routers can create a virtual private network whereby users logged on to the network from a remote location on the Internet can have a private encrypted session with the corporate network using a technique called tunneling.

As part of your routine maintenance chores to secure a network, you can keep the router firmware up to date with the latest downloads to help make sure the router firewall is as secure as possible. Go to the Web site of the router manufacturer and download the firmware updates to a file on your hard drive. Then, using the router's setup utility, perform the upgrade. The Firmware Upgrade window for one router is shown in Figure 19-41.

A+ ESS
1.4
6.2

A+
220-602
6.2

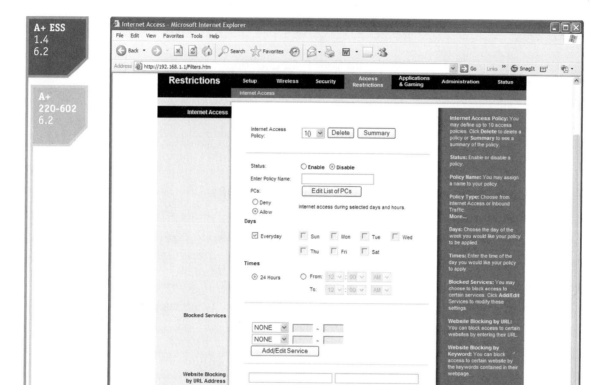

**Figure 19-40** A router can be used to block Internet access

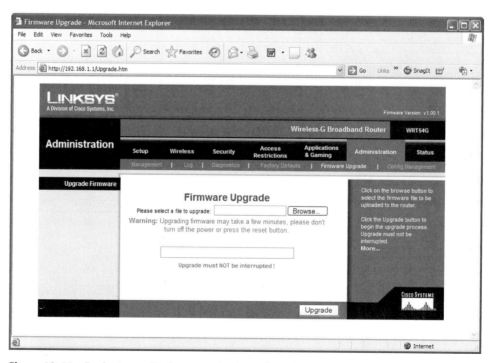

**Figure 19-41** For best security, keep your hardware firewall firmware updated

A+ ESS
1.1
6.1
6.2

# AUTHENTICATION TECHNOLOGIES FOR LARGER NETWORKS

Large corporate networks require more security than that provided by a multipurpose router or wireless access point. How to secure a large network is beyond the scope of this book. However, as a PC support technician, you might be called on to support the devices and techniques that are used to authenticate users when they first try to connect to a large network. In this part of the chapter, you'll learn how user accounts and passwords are encrypted as this information is sent over the network when authenticating the user. You'll also learn how smart cards and biometric data can be used to authenticate users.

## ENCRYPTED USER ACCOUNTS AND PASSWORDS

When logging on to a network, such as that managed by Windows Server 2003, the user account and password must be passed over the network in order to be authenticated by the domain controller. If someone intercepts that information, the network security can be compromised. For this reason, user accounts and passwords are encrypted at the entry point to the network and decrypted just before they are validated. The protocols used to encrypt account names and passwords are called authentication protocols. The two most popular protocols are **CHAP (Challenge Handshake Authentication Protocol)** and **Kerberos**. Kerberos is the default protocol used by Windows 2000/XP.

## SMART CARDS

Besides a user account and strong password, a network might require more security to control access. Generally, the best validation to prove you are who you say you are requires a two-factor authentication: You prove you have something in your possession and you prove you know something. For example, a user can enter a user ID and password and also prove he has a token in hand. This token can take on many forms. The most popular type of token is a **smart card**, which is any small device that contains authentication information that can be keyed into a logon window by a user or can be read by a **smart card reader** when the device is inserted in the reader. (You also need to know that some people don't consider a card to be a smart card unless it has an embedded microprocessor.)

> **⊖ A+ Tip**
>
> The A+ Essentials exam expects you to know about using smart cards and biometric devices for hardware and software security.

Here are some variations of smart cards:

▲ One type of smart card is a **key fob**, so called because it fits conveniently on a keychain. RSA Security (*www.rsasecurity.com*), a leader in authentication technologies, makes several types of smart cards, called SecurIDs. One SecurID key fob by RSA Security is shown in Figure 19-42. The number on the key fob changes every 60 seconds. When a user logs on to the network, she must enter the number on the key fob, which is synchronized with the network authentication service. Entering the number proves that the user has the smart card in hand.

**Figure 19-42** A smart card such as this SecurID key fob is used to authenticate a user gaining access to a secured network

A+ ESS
1.1
6.1
6.2

◢ Other smart cards that look like a credit card also have an embedded microchip that displays a number every few seconds for a user to enter during the authentication process. The advantage of using smart cards that display a number to key in is that no special equipment needs to be installed on the computer. The disadvantage is that the smart card can only validate that the person has the token in hand but can provide no additional data about the user.

◢ Other smart cards have magnetic strips that can be read by a smart card reader that has a slot for the card (see Figure 19-43). Because these cards don't contain a microchip, they are sometimes called memory cards, and are sometimes used to gain entrance into a building. They can also be read by a smart card reader such as the one shown in Figure 19-44 that connects to a PC using a USB port. Used in this way, they are part of the authentication process into a network. The magnetic strip can contain information about the user to indicate their permissions on the system. Not only does the smart card validate the person has a token, but can also be used to control other functions on the network. The major disadvantage of this type of smart card is that each computer used for authentication must have one of these smart card reader machines installed. Also, in the industry, because a card with a magnetic strip does not contain a microchip, some in the industry don't consider it to fit into the category of a smart card, but rather simply call it a magnetic strip card.

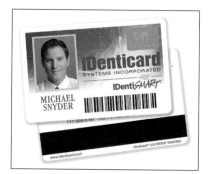

**Figure 19-43**   A smart card with a magnetic strip can be used inside or outside a computer network

**Figure 19-44**   This smart card reader by Athena Smartcard Solutions (*www.athena-scs.com*) uses a USB connection

◢ Another type of smart card plugs directly into a USB port such as the one in Figure 19-45 by Aladdin (*www.aladdin.com*). The device is read by software installed

A+ ESS
1.1
6.1
6.2

on the computer and most likely contains one or more digital certificates that a user needs to authenticate into the private network and do business on the network. Digital certificates are transported over the Internet and verified using **PKI (Public-key Infrastructure)** standards. These smart cards are designed to encrypt any data sent over the Internet to the corporate network, such as that used by a VPN. In fact, many VPN solutions are based on a VPN router at the corporate office and a smart card token at the user end of the VPN tunnel. The advantage of this type of smart card is that it can contain sensitive data that can be read by a remote computer, but the computer does not need any special equipment to read the card. Remember that it's best to use two-factor authentication. Even though a user's password could be stored on this type of smart card, for added security, the user should still be expected to enter a password to gain access to the system.

**Figure 19-45** This eToken by Aladdin can contain digital certificates so that a user can do business over a VPN

## BIOMETRIC DATA

As part of the authentication process, rather than proving a person is in possession of a token, some systems are set to use biometric data to validate the person's physical body. Biometric data can include a fingerprint or an iris scan. How to install a fingerprint reader or other biometric input device is covered in Chapter 9. Recall from Chapter 9 that these devices are not considered the stronger authentication techniques.

## _DEALING WITH MALICIOUS SOFTWARE_

A+ ESS
3.3
6.1
6.2

A+
220-602
3.1

Even with the best of security, occasionally a virus, worm, or other type of malicious software penetrates a system. **Malicious software**, also called **malware** or a computer **infestation**, is any unwanted program that means you harm and is transmitted to your computer without your knowledge. The best-known malicious software is a virus, which is malicious software that can replicate itself by attaching itself to other programs. However, many types of malicious software have evolved over the past few years and there is considerable overlap in what they do, how they spread, and how to get rid of them.

A+ ESS
3.3
6.1
6.2

A+
220-602
3.1

This part of the chapter covers all about dealing with malicious software. A PC support technician needs to know how to recognize that a system is infected, to understand how malicious software works, and to know how to clean up the mess.

## YOU'VE GOT MALWARE

Here are some warnings that suggest malicious software is at work:

- Pop-up ads plague you when surfing the Web.
- Generally, the system works much slower than it used to. Programs take longer than normal to load.
- The number and length of disk accesses seem excessive for simple tasks. The number of bad sectors on the hard drive continues to increase.
- The access lights on the hard drive and floppy drive turn on when there should be no activity on the devices. (However, sometimes Windows XP performs routine maintenance on the drive when the system has been inactive for a while.)
- Strange or bizarre error messages appear. Programs that once worked now give errors.
- Less memory than usual is available, or there is a noticeable reduction in disk space.
- Strange graphics appear on your computer monitor, or the computer makes strange noises.
- The system cannot recognize the CD-ROM drive, although it worked earlier.
- In Windows Explorer, filenames now have weird characters or their file sizes seem excessively large. Executable files have changed size or file extensions change without reason. Files mysteriously disappear or appear.
- Files constantly become corrupted.
- The OS begins to boot, but hangs before getting a Windows desktop.
- Your antivirus software displays one or more messages.
- You receive e-mail messages telling you that you have sent someone an infected message.
- Task Manager shows unfamiliar processes running.
- When you try to use your browser to access the Internet, strange things happen and you can't surf the Web. Your Internet Explorer home page has changed and you see new toolbars you didn't ask for.
- A message appears that a downloaded document contains macros, or an application asks whether it should run macros in a document. (It is best to disable macros if you cannot verify that they are from a trusted source and that they are free of viruses or worms.)

> **Notes**
>
> Malicious software is designed to do varying degrees of damage to data and software, although it does not damage PC hardware. However, when boot sector information is destroyed on a hard drive, the hard drive can appear to be physically damaged.

A+ ESS
3.3
6.1
6.2

A+
220-602
3.1

# HERE'S THE NASTY LIST

You need to know your enemy! Different categories of malicious software are listed next and are described in a bit more detail in this section:

⬧ A **virus** is a program that replicates by attaching itself to other programs. The infected program must be executed for a virus to run. The program might be an application, a macro in a document, a Windows 2000/XP system file, or the boot sector programs. The damage a virus does ranges from minor, such as displaying bugs crawling around on a screen, to major, such as erasing everything written on a hard drive. Figure 19-46 shows the results of a harmless virus that simply displays garbage on the screen. The best way to protect against viruses is to always run antivirus (AV) software in the background.

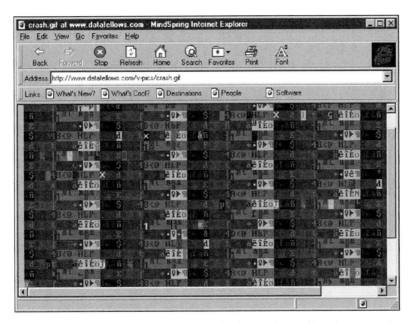

**Figure 19-46** The crash virus appears to be destructive, making the screen show only garbage, but does no damage to hard drive data

⬧ **Adware** produces all those unwanted pop-up ads. Adware is secretly installed on your computer when you download and install shareware or freeware, including screen savers, desktop wallpaper, music, cartoons, news, and weather alerts. Then, it displays pop-up ads based on your browsing habits. Sometimes when you try to uninstall adware, it deletes whatever it was you downloaded that you really wanted to keep. And sometimes adware is also spying on you and collecting private information.

⬧ **Spam** is junk e-mail that you don't want, that you didn't ask for, and that gets in your way.

⬧ **Spyware** is software that installs itself on your computer to spy on you, and collects personal information about you that it transmits over the Internet to Web-hosting sites that intend to use your personal data for harm. Spyware comes to you by way of e-mail attachments, downloaded freeware or shareware, instant messaging programs, or when you click a link on a malicious Web site.

⬧ A **worm** is a program that copies itself throughout a network or the Internet without a host program. A worm creates problems by overloading the network as it replicates. Worms cause damage by their presence rather than by performing a specific damaging act, as a virus does. A worm overloads memory or hard drive space by replicating repeatedly. When a worm (for example, Sasser or W32.Sobig.F@mm) is loose on the Internet, it can cause damage such as sending mass e-mailings. The best way to protect against worms is to use antivirus software and a firewall.

▲ A **browser hijacker**, also called a home page hijacker, does mischief by changing your home page and other browser settings. Brower hijackers can set unwanted bookmarks, redirect your browser to a porn site when you key in a wrong URL, produce pop-up ads, and direct your browser to Web sites that offer pay-per-view pornography.

▲ A **dialer** is software installed on your PC that disconnects your phone line from your ISP and dials up an expensive pay-per-minute phone number without your knowledge. The damage a dialer does is the expensive phone bill.

▲ A **keylogger** tracks all your keystrokes, including passwords, chat room sessions, e-mail messages, documents, online purchases, and anything else you type on your PC. All this text is logged to a text file and transmitted over the Internet without your knowledge. A keylogger is a type of spyware.

▲ A **logic bomb** is dormant code added to software and triggered at a predetermined time or by a predetermined event. For instance, an employee might put code in a program to destroy important files if his name is ever removed from the payroll file.

▲ A **Trojan horse** does not need a host program to work; rather, it substitutes itself for a legitimate program. In most cases, a user launches it thinking she is launching a legitimate program. Figure 19-47 shows a pop-up that appears when you're surfing the Web. Click OK and you've just introduced a Trojan into your system. A Trojan is likely to introduce one or more viruses into the system. These Trojans are called downloaders.

**Figure 19-47** Clicking OK on a pop-up window might invite a Trojan into your system

Last year, I got fooled with a Trojan when I got an e-mail message near the actual date of my birthday from someone named Emilia, whom I thought I knew. Without thinking, I clicked the link in the e-mail message to "View my birthday card to you." Figure 19-48 shows what happened when I clicked.

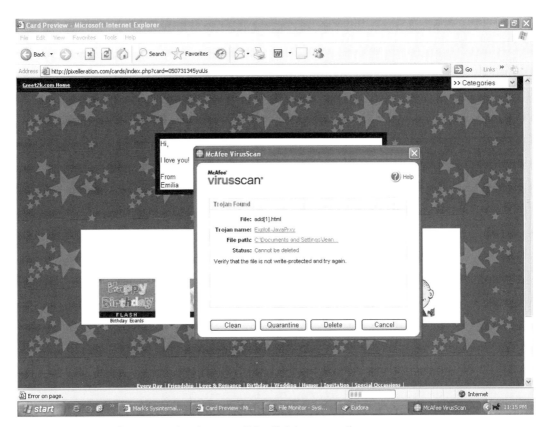

**Figure 19-48** A Trojan can get in when you click a link in an e-mail message

## HOW A VIRUS WORKS

A virus attacks your system and hides in several different ways. Consider the following:

◢ A **boot sector virus** hides in the boot sector program of a hard drive or floppy disk or in the master boot program in the Master Boot Record (MBR).

◢ A **file virus** hides in an executable (.exe, .com, or .sys) program or in a word-processing document that contains a macro.

◢ A **multipartite virus** is a combination of a boot sector virus and a file virus and can hide in either.

◢ A **macro** is a small program contained in a document that can be automatically executed either when the document is first loaded or later by pressing a key combination. For example, a word-processing macro might automatically read the system date and copy it into a document when you open the document.

◢ Viruses that hide in macros of document files are called macro viruses. **Macro viruses** are the most common viruses spread by e-mail, hiding in macros of attached document files.

◢ A **script virus** is a virus that hides in a script, which might execute when you click a link on a Web page or in an HTML e-mail message, or when you attempt to open an e-mail attachment.

## HOW MALWARE REPLICATES AND HIDES

A virus or other malware can use various techniques to load itself in memory and replicate itself. Also, malware attempts to hide from antivirus (AV) software by changing its distinguishing characteristics (its signature) and by attempting to mask its presence. Here are some techniques used by malware to start itself and prevent detection:

- ▲ A virus can search a hard drive for a file with an .exe extension and then create another file with the same filename but with a .com file extension. The virus then stores itself there. When the user launches the program, the OS first looks for the program name with the .com file extension. It then finds and executes the virus. The virus is loaded into memory and loads the program with the .exe extension. The user appears to have launched the desired program. The virus is then free to do damage or spread itself to other programs.
- ▲ Because AV software can detect a virus by noting the difference between a program's file size before the virus infects it and after the virus is present, the virus alters OS information to mask the size of the file in which it hides.
- ▲ The virus monitors when files are opened or closed. When it sees that the file in which it is hiding is about to be opened, it temporarily removes itself or substitutes a copy of the file that does not include the virus. The virus keeps a copy of this uninfected file on the hard drive just for this purpose. A virus that does this or changes the attributes of its host program is called a **stealth virus**.
- ▲ As a virus replicates, it changes its characteristics. This type of virus is called a **polymorphic virus**.
- ▲ Some viruses can continually transform themselves so they will not be detected by AV software that is looking for a particular characteristic. A virus that uses this technique is called an **encrypting virus**.
- ▲ The virus creates more than one process; each process is watching the other. If one process gets closed, it will be started up again by one of the other processes. (This method of preventing detection is also used by spyware.) Figure 19-49 shows a Task Manager window of an infected system. Look carefully at the two processes, both named pludpm.exe. On this system, when you try to stop one process, the other starts it back up.

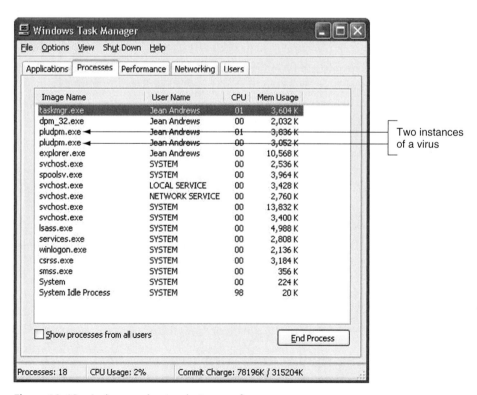

**Figure 19-49** A virus running two instances of a process

A+ ESS
3.3
6.1
6.2

A+
220-602
3.1

◢ Entries are often made in obscure places in the registry that allow the software to start when you start up Windows or launch Internet Explorer. (This method is used by several types of malware.)

◢ One type of malware, called a **rootkit**, loads itself before the OS boot is complete. Because it is already loaded when the AV software loads, it is sometimes overlooked by AV software. In addition, a rootkit hijacks internal Windows components so that it masks information Windows provides to user-mode utilities such as Task Manager, Explorer, the Registry Editor, and AV software—this helps it remain undetected.

## STEP-BY-STEP ATTACK PLAN

A+
220-602
3.1
3.3

This section is a step-by-step attack plan to clean up an infected system. We'll first use AV software and anti-adware software to do a general cleanup. But sometimes a system is so infected that normal measures of dealing with the problem are not going to help. So, to help you in these types of situations, we'll dig deeper to use some more complex tools and methods to smoke out any lurking processes that elude normal methods of de-infesting a system. When you're cleaning a system, as with solving any computer problem, be sure to keep good notes as you work. Document what you did and the outcome. These notes will be useful the next time you're faced with a similar problem.

### RUN AV SOFTWARE

The first step to cleaning up an infected system is to run AV software. However, if you find yourself dealing with a highly infected system that does not have AV software already installed, you might not be able to download and install the software. Here are steps to use in this situation when AV software is not installed:

> **Notes**
>
> It's handy to have AV software on CD, but recognize that this AV software won't have the latest updates and will need these updates downloaded from the Internet before it will catch new viruses.

1. Purchase the AV software on CD (see Figure 19-50).

2. Disconnect from the Internet so you won't open yourself up for more mischief.

**Figure 19-50** AV software on CD means you don't need Internet access to install the software

A+ ESS
3.3
6.1
6.2

A+
220-602
3.1
3.3

**Notes**

If viruses are launched even after you boot in Safe Mode and you cannot get the AV software to work, try searching for suspicious entries in the subkeys under HKLM\System\ CurrentControlSet\Control\SafeBoot. Subkeys under this key control what is launched when you boot into Safe Mode. Also, if you are unable to boot into Safe Mode, system files might be infected. Chapter 14 covers how to deal with boot problems.

3. Boot into Safe Mode. To do that, press **F8** when Windows begins to load. The Windows XP Advanced Options menu appears. Choose **Safe Mode with Networking** and press **Enter**.

4. Insert the AV software CD. Most likely, the AV main menu will be displayed automatically, as shown in Figure 19-51. Choose to install the software.

**Figure 19-51**  Boot into Safe Mode and then install the AV software

5. When given the opportunity, enter the information to register the AV software so that you will be allowed to download updates. At this point, you won't be connected to the Internet to complete the registration, but at least the software is poised to register you later when the connection works (see Figure 19-52).

**Figure 19-52**  Choose to register your AV software so you can download updates

6. During the installation, when given the opportunity, choose to scan the system for viruses (see Figure 19-53). Set the software to scan all drives and all type files and to look for all types of malware.

**Figure 19-53** Choose to scan for viruses

7. Figure 19-54 shows the results of a McAfee scan that detected a bunch of adware, spyware, Trojans, and potentially unwanted programs (PUPs).

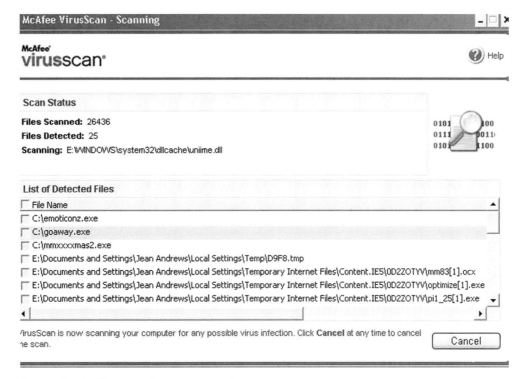

**Figure 19-54** Virus scan detects unwanted programs

8. Sometimes, AV software detects a program that you know you have downloaded and want to keep, but the AV software recognizes it as potentially harmful. This type of software is sometimes called **grayware** or a PUP (potentially unwanted program). When the AV software displays the list of detected files, unless you recognize something you want to keep, I suggest you tell the AV software to delete them all.

9. Reboot into Safe Mode with Networking, connect to the Internet, and allow your AV software to get any current updates from the AV software Web site. Figure 19-55 shows that happening for McAfee VirusScan software. If the software requests you reboot the system for the installation to complete, be sure to reboot into Safe Mode with Networking.

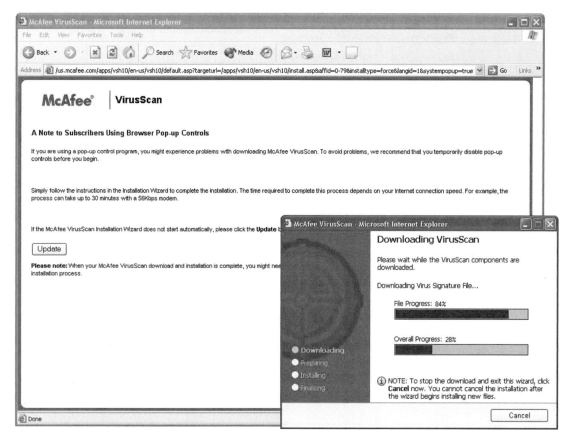

**Figure 19-55** McAfee VirusScan getting updates from the McAfee Web site

10. After the updating is finished, scan the system again. Most likely, some new malware will be discovered for you to delete. For example, when I cleaned up an infected system using the McAfee CD version of the software, it found 34 viruses, Trojans, and adware. After all McAfee updates were applied, it found an additional 54 viruses, Trojans, adware, worms, and spyware. Keep repeating the scan until you get a clean scan. Reboot between scans and take notes of any program files the software is not able to delete.

11. Now it's time to see where you stand. If you use an always-up connection to the Internet, unplug your network cable. Reboot the system to the normal Windows 2000/XP desktop and check Task Manager. Do you see any weird processes, see pop-ups when you open your browser, or get strange messages like the one in Figure 19-56 asking permission to connect to the Internet? If so, you still have malware.

A+ ESS
3.3
6.1
6.2

A+
220-602
3.1
3.3

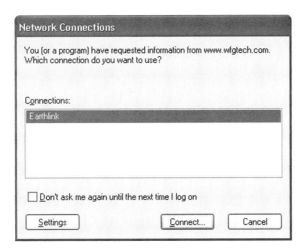

**Figure 19-56** Evidence that malware is still infecting the system

It might be more fun to begin manually removing each program yourself, but it's probably quicker and more thorough to use anti-adware software next. I suggest you resist the temptation to poke around looking for the malware and move on to the next step.

## RUN ADWARE OR SPYWARE REMOVAL SOFTWARE

Almost all AV software products today also search for adware and spyware. However, software specifically dedicated to removing this type of malware generally does a better job of it than does AV software. The next step in the removal process is to use anti-adware or anti-spyware software. Figure 19-57 shows what Windows Defender discovered on one computer.

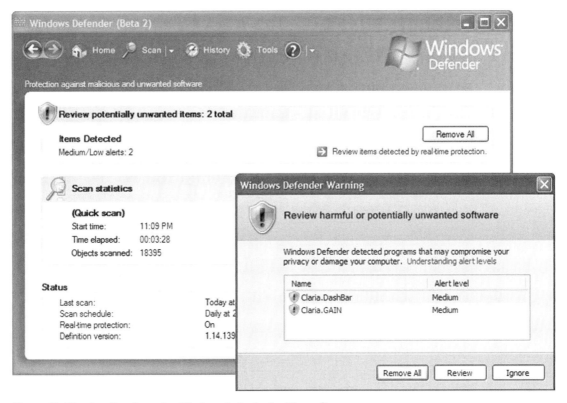

**Figure 19-57** Results of running Windows Defender by Microsoft

To completely clean your system, you might have to run a removal product more than once or use several different products. For example, what Ad-Aware doesn't find, Windows Defender does, but what Windows Defender doesn't find, Ad-Aware finds. To be sure, run two products.

## SEARCH OUT AND DESTROY WHAT'S LEFT

Next, you'll need to clean up anything the AV or anti-adware software left behind. Sometimes AV software tells you it is not able to delete a file or it deletes an infected file, but leaves behind an orphan entry in the registry or startup folders. If the AV software tells you it was not able to delete or clean a file, first check the AV software Web site for any instructions you might find to manually clean things up. In this section, you'll learn about general things you can do to clean up what might be left behind.

### Respond to Any Startup Errors

On the first boot after AV software has found and removed malware, you might find some startup errors caused by incomplete removal of the malware. One example of such an error is shown in Figure 19-58. Somewhere in the system, the command to launch 0sis0ijw.dll is still working even though this DLL has been deleted. One way to find this orphan entry point is to use Msconfig. Figure 19-59 shows the Msconfig window showing us that the DLL is launched from a registry key.

**Figure 19-58** Startup error indicates malware has not been completely removed

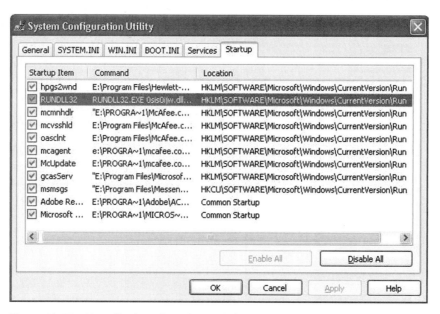

**Figure 19-59** Msconfig shows how the DLL is launched during startup

19

A+ ESS
3.3
6.1
6.2

A+
220-602
3.1
3.3

The next step is to back up the registry and then use Regedit to find and delete the key (see Figure 19-60).

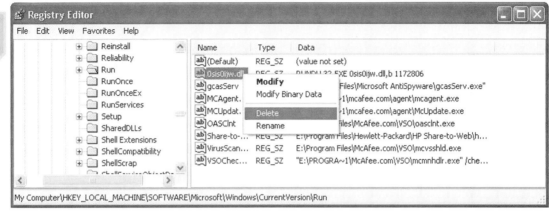

**Figure 19-60** Delete orphan registry entry left there by malware

## Delete Malicious Files

For each program file the AV software told you it could not delete, try to delete the program file yourself using Windows Explorer. For peace of mind, don't forget to empty the Recycle Bin when you're done. You might need to open a command prompt window and remove the hidden or system attributes on a file so that you can delete it. Figure 19-61 shows how this is done for the file C:\INT0094.exe. Table 19-2 explains each command used.

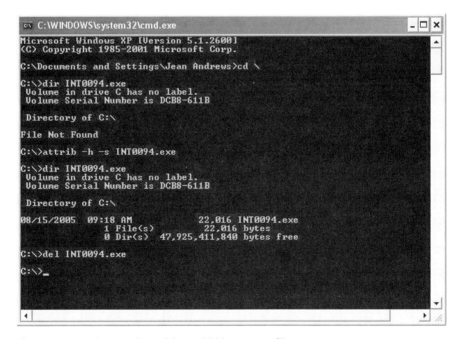

**Figure 19-61** Commands to delete a hidden system file

A+ ESS
3.3
6.1
6.2

A+
220-602
3.1
3.3

| Command | Explanation |
|---------|-------------|
| cd \ | Make the root directory of drive C the current directory |
| dir INT0094.exe | The file does not appear in the directory because it is hidden |
| attrib –h –s INT0094.exe | Remove the hidden and system attributes of the file |
| dir INT0094.exe | The Dir command now displays the file |
| del INT0094.exe | Delete the file |

**Table 19-2**  Commands to delete a hidden system file

To get rid of other malware files, you might need to delete all Internet Explorer temporary Internet files. To do that, open the **Properties** window for drive C and click **Disk Cleanup** on the General tab. Then, from the Disk Cleanup window shown in Figure 19-62, make sure **Temporary Internet Files** is checked and click **OK**. (Alternatively, you can click **Delete Files** on the General tab of the Internet Options window.)

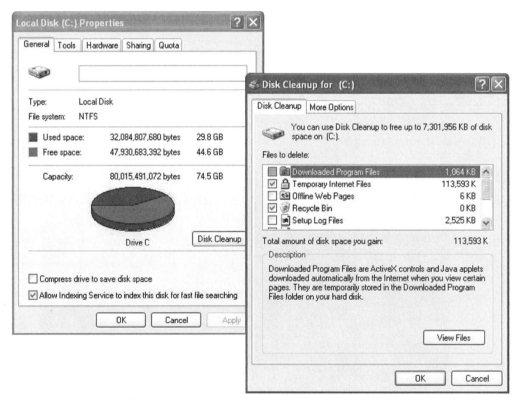

**Figure 19-62**  Delete all temporary Internet files

## Purge Restore Points

Some malware hides its program files in the data storage area of the Windows XP System Restore utility. Windows does not always allow AV software to look in this storage area when it is scanning for malware. To get rid of that malware, you must turn off System Restore, reboot your system, and turn System Restore back on. How to do that was covered in earlier chapters. Turning off System Restore causes the data storage area to be purged. You'll get rid of any malware there, but you'll also lose all your restore points.

If your AV software is running in the background and reports it has found a virus in the C:\System Volume Information\_Restore folder, it means malware is in a System Restore

point (see Figure 19-63). If you see a message similar to the one in Figure 19-63 or your AV software scan feature found lots of malware in other places on the drive, the best idea is to purge all restore points. Don't do this if, for some reason, you desperately need to keep a restore point you've previously made.

**Figure 19-63** Malware found in a restore point

## Clean the Registry

Sometimes AV software deletes a program file but does not delete the registry entries that launch the program at startup. In the last chapter, you learned how to search registry keys for startup processes. To get the job done more quickly, you can use Autoruns by Sysinternals to help you search for these registry entries. Figure 19-64 shows a screen shot where Autoruns is displaying a registry key used to launch the Pludpm.exe malware program. AV software had already found and deleted this program file, but it left the registry key untouched.

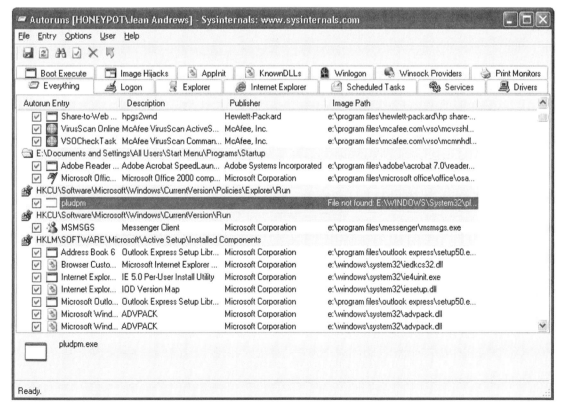

**Figure 19-64** Autoruns finds orphan registry entries left there by AV software

A+ ESS
3.3
6.1
6.2

A+
220-602
3.1
3.3

Scan the Autoruns window looking for suspicious entries. Research any entries that you think might be used by malware. To get rid of these keys, back up the registry and then use Regedit to delete unwanted keys.

### Root Out Rootkits

A rootkit is a program that uses unusually complex methods to hide itself on a system, and many spyware and adware programs are also rootkits. The term rootkit applies to a kit or set of tools used originally on Unix computers. In Unix, the lowest and most powerful level of Unix accounts is called the root account; therefore, this kit of tools was intended to keep a program working at this root level without interruption.

Rootkits can prevent Task Manager from displaying the running rootkit process, or might cause Task Manager to display a different name for this process. The program file-name might not be displayed in Windows Explorer, the rootkit's registry keys might be hidden from the Registry Editor, or the Registry Editor might display incorrect information. All this hiding is accomplished in one of two ways, depending on whether the rootkit is running in user mode or kernel mode (see Figure 19-65). A rootkit running in user mode intercepts the API calls between the time when the API retrieves the data and when it is displayed in a window. A rootkit running in kernel mode actually interferes with the Windows kernel and substitutes its own information in place of the raw data read by the Windows kernel.

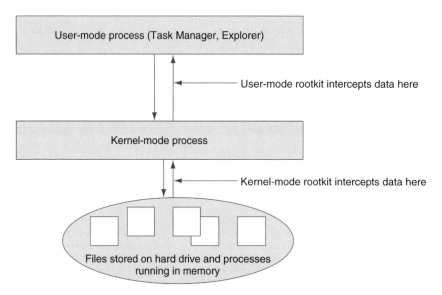

**Figure 19-65** A rootkit can run in user mode or kernel mode

Because most AV software, to one degree or another, relies on Windows tools and components to work, the rootkit is not detected if the Windows tools themselves are infected. Rootkits are also programmed to hide from specific programs designed to find and remove them. Generally, anti-rootkit software works using these two methods:

- ▲ The software looks for running processes that don't match up with the underlying program filename.
- ▲ The software compares files, registry entries, and processes provided by the OS to the lists it generates from the raw data. If the two lists differ, a rootkit is suspected.

19

A+ ESS
3.3
6.1
6.2

A+
220-602
3.1
3.3

Two good anti-rootkit programs are:

▲ RootkitRevealer by Sysinternals (*www.sysinternals.com*)
▲ BackLight by F-Secure (*www.f-secure.com*)

After you have used other available methods to remove malware and you still believe you're not clean, you might want to download and run one of these products. Close all open applications and don't use the computer for any other task while the anti-rootkit software is running. If you change a file or the registry changes while the software is running, it might report a false positive because the list taken with the OS and without the OS might differ simply because you changed something between the times the two lists were taken. Figure 19-66 shows RootkitRevealer scanning for rootkits.

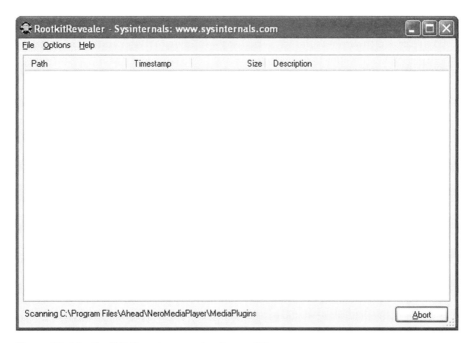

**Figure 19-66**   Rootkit Revealer scanning for rootkits

For best results when scanning for rootkits, run the anti-rootkit software from another computer so that the software is not dependent on the OS that might be infected. For example, you can share drive C on the network and then, from another computer on the network, run the anti-rootkit software and instruct it to scan drive C on the remote computer.

If the software detects a discrepancy that might indicate a rootkit is installed, you'll need to go to the Sysinternals or F-Secure Web site or do a general Web search to find information about the potential rootkit and instructions for removing it. Follow the instructions to manually remove the program and all its remnants. Sometimes the removal is so complicated, you might decide it makes more sense to just start over and reinstall Windows.

If you have tried all the techniques and products just described and still have malware, I'm sorry to say the next suggestion I have to offer is to restore the entire system from backups. If you don't have a current backup, as a last resort, you can back up your data, completely erase your hard drive, reinstall Windows and all your applications, and then restore your data.

## >> CHAPTER SUMMARY

▲ Part of securing a Windows 2000/XP desktop or notebook computer includes securing the logon process, setting power-on passwords, using strong passwords, and limiting the use of the administrator account.

▲ All computers need to run a personal firewall such as Windows Firewall under Windows XP with SP2 applied.

▲ For AV software or anti-adware software to be effective, it must be kept current and always be running in the background.

▲ Keeping Windows updates current is necessary to plug up any security holes as they become known.

▲ Internet Explorer can be set for better security by controlling the way scripts are used.

▲ Because Internet Explorer and Outlook or Outlook Express are closely integrated with Windows components and are the most-popular browser and e-mail clients, they are more susceptible to malicious software than other client applications. Using less-popular clients such as Firefox by Mozilla (a browser) or Eudora by Qualcomm (an e-mail client) might mean you are less likely to be attacked.

▲ Practice and teach responsible Web surfing, such as never opening an e-mail attachment from unknown senders and never downloading from Web sites you have not carefully checked out.

▲ Microsoft Shared Computer Toolkit can be used to lock down a public personal computer.

▲ Files and folders can be hidden and made private, and data within these files and folders can be encrypted using the Windows Encrypted File System (EFS).

▲ Physically protect the equipment for which you are responsible. You can buy locks and chains to tie the equipment down and keep others from opening the computer case.

▲ Social engineering techniques used by criminals include phishing, scamming, and virus hoaxes.

▲ To make it less likely you'll launch a malicious script on your computer, set Windows to display file extensions of scripts.

▲ You can configure Windows so that the file extensions of scripts are displayed within the e-mail program so that users are less likely to be tricked by a script masquerading as a picture or Web link.

▲ To secure a system, maintain good backups of user data and System State files.

▲ Monitor and log events concerning logon failures, access to files and folders, changes to startup, and network activity. When atypical events happen, record those events using the incident-reporting tools recommended by your organization.

▲ Don't throw away or recycle storage media without first destroying all data on the media.

▲ Maintain a monthly routine to check your security implementations to make sure all is working as it should and make any changes as appropriate.

▲ A small network can be secured using a router. For larger networks, a user can be authenticated on a network using encrypted user accounts and passwords, a token such as a smart card, and/or biometric data.

▲ Malicious software includes viruses, adware, spam, spyware, worms, browser hijackers, dialers, keyloggers, logic bombs, and Trojan horses.

▲ To clean a system of malicious software, run AV software and anti-adware software, respond to any startup errors, delete files, purge restore points, and remove orphan entries in the registry or other startup location.

## >> KEY TERMS

For explanations of key terms, see the Glossary near the end of the book.

adware
antivirus (AV) software
authentication
authorization
boot sector virus
browser hijacker
CHAP (Challenge Handshake
   Authentication Protocol)
data migration
dialer
Encrypted File System (EFS)
encrypting virus
encryption
file virus
grayware

infestation
Kerberos
key fob
keylogger
logic bomb
macro
macro virus
malicious software
malware
multipartite virus
passphrase
phishing
PKI (Public-key Infrastructure)
polymorphic virus
rootkit

scam e-mail
script virus
smart card
smart card reader
social engineering
spam
spyware
stealth virus
Trojan horse
virus
virus hoax
virus signature
worm
zero-fill utility

## >> REVIEW QUESTIONS

1. Which color is used to indicate that a file or folder has been encrypted in Explorer?

   a. Green

   b. Blue

   c. Red

   d. Purple

2. Which of the following approaches is a type of identity theft where the sender of an e-mail message scams you into responding with personal data about yourself?

   a. Scripts

   b. Virus hoax

   c. Phishing

   d. Decryption

3. Which of the following is an authentication protocol used to encrypt account names and passwords?

   a. Smart card

   b. Kerberos

   c. Key fob

   d. Public-key Infrastructure

4. Malicious software is also called which of the following?

   **a.** Pop up

   **b.** Boot sector destroyer

   **c.** Computer infestation

   **d.** .exe extension

5. Which of the following types of malicious software is dormant code added to software and triggered at a predetermined time or by a predetermined event?

   **a.** Adware

   **b.** Polymorphic virus

   **c.** Spyware

   **d.** Logic bomb

6. True or false? You can share encrypted folders as well as encrypted files.

7. True or false? Viruses have been known to do actual physical damage to hardware.

8. True or false? Prior to allowing a user access to a computer system, authentication is needed to prove that the individual is who he says he is.

9. True or false? You must be logged on to the system as an administrator to view the Security tab of Event Viewer.

10. True or false? Encrypting at the folder level is considered a best practice because it provides greater security.

11. AV software detects a known virus by looking for distinguishing characteristics called _____.

12. The _____ command can be used to encrypt or decrypt a large number of files or folders.

13. The practice of tricking people into giving out private information or allowing unsafe programs into the network or computer is called _____.

14. Moving data from one application to another application or from one storage media to another is called _____.

15. The best way to totally erase everything on a hard drive is to use a(n) _____ utility provided by a hard drive manufacturer.

# CHAPTER 20

# Notebooks, Tablet PCs, and PDAs

So far in this book, you've learned how computers work, explored some of the devices used to work with them, examined operating systems, and discovered how to connect a PC to a network. Most devices and software you've learned about relate to desktop computers, which are stationary and cannot be moved easily. However, recent statistics show that more than half of personal computers purchased today are notebook computers, and almost 30 percent of personal computers in use today are notebooks. As notebooks become more and more popular, PC service technicians will need to know how to support them. In this chapter, you'll learn about supporting, upgrading, and troubleshooting notebooks. You'll also learn about other portable devices, including tablet PCs and personal digital assistants (PDAs).

## *SUPPORTING NOTEBOOKS*

A **notebook** or **laptop computer** is a computer designed to be portable (see Figure 20-1). Notebooks use the same technology as PCs but with modifications to use less power, consume less space, and operate on the move.

**Figure 20-1**  A notebook is a computer designed for portability

In many situations, the task of troubleshooting, upgrading, and maintaining a notebook computer requires the same skills, knowledge, and procedures as when servicing a desktop computer. However, you should take some special considerations into account when purchasing, caring for, supporting, upgrading, and troubleshooting notebooks. When you think of all the new notebooks sold this past year or so, learning about notebooks and how to support them can position you for some great career opportunities supporting notebooks!

Now let's turn our attention to some useful tips when selecting and purchasing a notebook and the special considerations when servicing them. Then you'll learn how to care for notebooks and how to connect peripheral equipment to them.

### TIPS FOR BUYING A NOTEBOOK

A PC repair technician is often called on to help customers select and buy computer and networking products. Listed below are some special considerations you need to keep in mind when selecting a notebook computer:

▲ The main advantage a notebook has over a desktop is portability. A notebook computer generally costs about twice as much as a comparable desktop system, when comparing speed, computing power, and features. Notebooks are generally slower than desktops because of slower processors, motherboards, hard drives, and video systems. Notebooks generally cannot be upgraded as easily as a desktop and the upgrades cost more. In addition, notebooks tend to drop in value over three or four years faster than do desktops. For all these reasons, if the computer is to remain at one location, buy a desktop rather than a notebook.

▲ Most people buy a desktop expecting to be able to upgrade it over the course of its lifetime. Not so with notebooks. It is unlikely that you will be able to upgrade the processor, motherboard, or video, although you can upgrade memory or add a new Mini PCI card. In general, buy a notebook without expecting to upgrade internal components.

▲ Because added features cost more on a notebook than a desktop and add to the weight of the notebook, don't buy these extra features unless you really need them.

▲ Servicing your own notebook when internal components break might not be possible because you might not be able to purchase the parts or obtain the instructions for disassembling the notebook. Therefore, it's probably a good idea to pay for the extended warranty on a notebook that will last the three or four years that the notebook still has value. After about four years, any notebook is most likely not going to be worth more than $400. At that time, you can buy a new one.

▲ Selecting the brand of notebook is your most important decision when selecting a notebook. As with any buying decision, do your research. Read online reviews of notebooks and their manufacturer. Pay special attention to how satisfied customers are with the service when the notebook breaks.

▲ Keep these key points about notebook components in mind:

  ▲ Buy the fastest processor that you can afford. Mobile processors are built to conserve power and take up less space. Chapter 5 discusses mobile processors in detail.

  ▲ For the LCD panel, active matrix is better than dual scan. Also consider the resolution, backlighting, and size. For more information on selecting an LCD panel, see Chapter 9.

  ▲ Buy as much memory as you plan to use later. Sometimes, to upgrade memory on a notebook, you must replace a module that has low RAM with one that has more RAM, which can make upgrading memory more expensive.

  ▲ The best type of battery to buy is a lithium battery.

  ▲ Also consider the weight and size of the notebook, keyboard, pointing device, optical drives, and other features.

## SPECIAL CONSIDERATIONS WHEN SERVICING NOTEBOOKS

Notebooks and their replacement parts cost more than desktop PCs with similar features because their components are designed to be more compact and stand up to travel. They use thin LCD panels instead of CRT monitors for display, compact hard drives, and small memory modules and CPUs that require less power than regular components. Whereas a desktop computer is often assembled from parts made by a variety of manufacturers, notebook computers are almost always sold by a vendor that either manufactured the notebook or had it manufactured as a consolidated system. Factors to consider that generally apply more to notebook computers than desktop computers are the original equipment manufacturer's warranty, the service manuals and diagnostic software provided by the OEM, and the customized installation of the OS that is unique to notebooks.

### WARRANTY CONCERNS

Most manufacturers or retailers of notebooks offer at least a one-year warranty and the option to purchase an extended warranty. Therefore, when problems arise while the notebook is under warranty, you are dealing with a single manufacturer or retailer to get support or parts. After the notebook is out of warranty, this manufacturer or retailer can still be your one-stop shop for support and parts.

The warranty often applies to all components in the system, but it can be voided if someone other than an authorized service center services the notebook. Therefore, you as a service technician must be very careful not to void a warranty that the customer has purchased. Warranties can be voided by opening the case, removing part labels, installing other-vendor parts, upgrading the OS, or disassembling the system unless directly instructed to do so by the service center help desk personnel.

Before you begin servicing a notebook, to avoid problems with a warranty, always ask the customer, "Is the notebook under warranty?" If the notebook is under warranty, look at the documentation to find out how to get technical support. Options are phone numbers, chat rooms on the Web, and e-mail. Use the most appropriate option. Before you contact technical support, have the notebook model and serial number ready (see Figure 20-2). You'll also need the name, phone number, and address of the person or company that made the purchase.

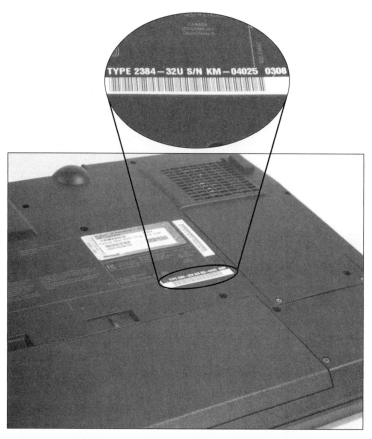

TYPE 2384—32U S/N KM—04025  0308

**Figure 20-2** The model and serial number stamped on the bottom of a notebook are used to identify the notebook to service desk personnel

Based on the type of warranty purchased by the notebook's owner, the manufacturer might send an on-site service technician, ask you to ship or take the notebook to an authorized service center, or help you solve the problem over the phone. Table 20-1 lists manufacturers of notebooks and tablet PCs. Tablet PCs are discussed later in the chapter.

| Manufacturer | Web Site |
|---|---|
| Acer America | *global.acer.com* |
| Apple Computer | *www.apple.com* |
| Compaq and HP | *www.hp.com* |
| Dell Computer | *www.dell.com* |
| eMachines by Gateway | *www.emachines.com* |
| Fujitsu/Fuji | *www.fujitsu.com* |
| Gateway | *www.gateway.com* |
| Lenovo (formally IBM Thinkpads) | *www.lenovo.com* |
| MPC Computers | *www.mpccorp.com* |
| NEC | *www.nec.com* |
| PC Notebook | *www.pcnotebook.com* |
| Sony (VAIO) | *www.sonystyle.com* |
| Toshiba America | *www.csd.toshiba.com* |
| WinBook | *www.winbook.com* |

**Table 20-1**  Notebook and tablet PC manufacturers

## SERVICE MANUALS AND OTHER SOURCES OF INFORMATION

Desktop computer cases tend to be similar to one another, and components in desktop systems tend to be interchangeable among manufacturers. Not so with notebooks. Notebook manufacturers tend to take great liberty in creating their own unique computer cases, buses, cables, connectors, drives, circuit boards, fans, and even screws, all of which are likely to be proprietary in design.

Every notebook model has a unique case. Components are installed in unique ways and opening the case for each notebook model is done differently. Because of these differences, servicing notebooks can be very complicated and time consuming. For example, a hard drive on one notebook is accessed by popping open a side panel and sliding the drive out of its bay. However, to access the hard drive on another model notebook, you must remove the keyboard, video card, memory modules, internal antennae, and even the LCD panel. If you are not familiar with a particular notebook model, you can do damage to the case as you pry and push trying to open it. Trial and error is likely to damage a case. Even though you might successfully replace a broken component, the damaged case can result in an unhappy customer.

Fortunately, a notebook service manual can save you much time and effort—if you can locate one (see Figure 20-3). Two notebook manufacturers, Lenovo (formally IBM) and Dell, provide their service manuals online free of charge. In addition, Compaq offers detailed information on its Web site to help you service its notebooks (see Figure 20-4). For all notebook manufacturers, check the FAQ pages of their Web sites for help in tasks such as opening a case without damaging it and locating and replacing a component.

Sometimes, you can find service manuals on the Web. One useful and very interesting Web site that contains service manuals for several different brands of notebooks as well as service manuals for lots of other electronic devices is *www.eserviceinfo.com*. It is published out of Bulgaria. Some of these service manuals are presented as files with an .rar file extension. An RAR file is a compressed file similar to a Zip file, except a very large file can be broken into two or more RAR files. You can download a trial version of the software to manage RAR files from RARLAB at *www.rarlab.com*.

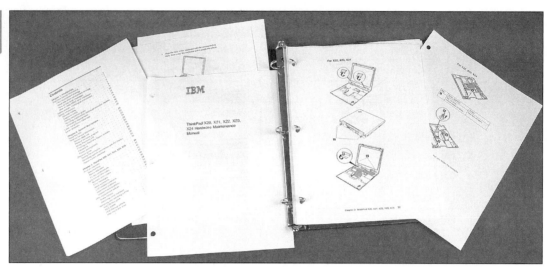

**Figure 20-3** A notebook service manual tells you how to use diagnostic tools, troubleshoot a notebook, and replace components

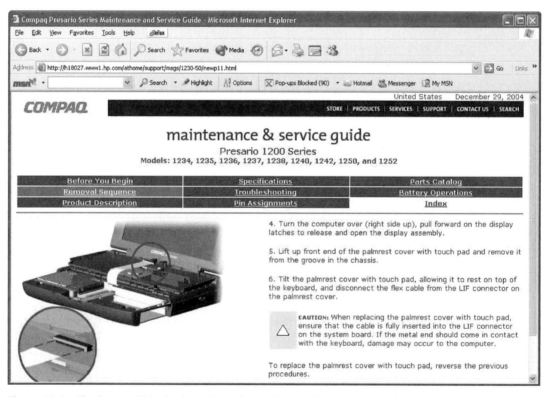

**Figure 20-4** The Compaq Web site (*www.hp.com*) provides detailed instructions for troubleshooting and replacing components

Of course, don't forget about the user manuals. They might contain directions for upgrading and replacing components that do not require disassembling the case, such as how to upgrade memory. User manuals also include troubleshooting tips and procedures and possibly descriptions of CMOS settings. In addition, you can use a Web search engine (for example,

**Notes**

Just as with desktop computers, you might be able to solve a problem with an unstable system or a motherboard component by flashing BIOS. Be sure to download BIOS updates only from the motherboard manufacturer Web site.

A+ ESS
1.4
2.4

Google at *www.google.com*) to search on the computer model and component that is giving you the problem.

## DIAGNOSTIC TOOLS PROVIDED BY MANUFACTURERS

Most notebook manufacturers provide diagnostic software that can help you test components to determine which component needs replacing. As one of the first steps when servicing a notebook, check the user manual, service manual, or manufacturer Web site to determine if diagnostic software exists and how to obtain it and use it. Use the software to pinpoint the problem component, which can then be replaced.

> **Notes**
>
> When you purchase a replacement part for a notebook from the notebook's manufacturer, most often the manufacturer also sends you detailed instructions for exchanging the part.

For older notebooks, the software is usually contained on a floppy disk and run from the disk. This test disk might come with the notebook or can be purchased from the manufacturer as a separate item. Check the manufacturer Web site for test software that can be downloaded for a particular model notebook. For newer notebooks, the software is stored on CDs bundled with the notebook or on the hard drive and accessed by pressing certain keys during the boot process.

One example of diagnostic software is PC-Doctor, which is used by several Lenovo and IBM ThinkPad models. The test software is stored on a floppy disk, CD, or hard drive. If stored on a floppy disk or CD, you can boot from the device to run the tests. If the software is stored on the hard drive, you can run it from the Windows Start menu or by pressing a function key at startup before Windows loads. Either way, PC-Doctor can run tests on the keyboard, video, speakers, mouse, joystick, floppy disk drive, CD drive, DVD drive, wireless LAN, motherboard, processor, serial and parallel ports, hard drive, Zip drive, and memory. To learn how to use the software, see the notebook's service manual or user manual.

A+ ESS
1.4
2.4
3.2
3.3

A+
220-602
3.3

## THE OEM OPERATING SYSTEM BUILD

Notebook computers are sold with an operating system preinstalled at the factory. The OS installation is tailored by the manufacturer to satisfy the specific needs of the notebook. In this situation, the manufacturer is called the OEM (original equipment manufacturer) and the customized installation of the OS is called the operating system build or OS build. Drivers installed are also specific to proprietary devices installed in the notebook. Diagnostic software is often written specifically for a notebook and its installed OS. For all these reasons, use caution when deciding to upgrade to a new OS and know that, if you have problems with a device, in most circumstances, you must turn to the OEM for solutions and updates for device drivers. Now let's look at some OS features designed with notebooks in mind, tools helpful when notebook OS problems arise, and special considerations to be aware of when upgrading notebook operating systems.

### Windows Notebook Features

Windows 2000/XP and Windows 98 include several features that can be useful when supporting notebooks:

- *Channel aggregation.* This OS feature allows you to use two modem connections at the same time to speed up data throughput when connected over phone lines. To use the feature, you must have two phone lines and two modem cards that are physically designed to connect two phone lines at the same time.
- *Power management.* Some power-management features include automatically powering down a PC Card when it is not in use, support for multiple battery packs, and individual power profiles. Power profiles are described later in this chapter.
- *Support for PC Cards.* This support includes many Windows drivers for PC Card devices.

▲ *Windows 9x/Me Briefcase.* When returning from a trip with a notebook, you might want to update your desktop PC with all e-mail documents and other files created or updated during the trip. To do this, use Windows 9x/Me Briefcase, a system folder used to synchronize files between two computers. Briefcase automatically updates files on the original computer to the most recent version. You can use a null modem cable, disk, or network for the file transfer.

▲ *Windows 2000/XP Offline Files and Folders.* Offline Files and Folders replaces Windows 9x/Me Briefcase and stores shared network files and folders in a cache on the notebook hard drive so that you can use them offline. When you reconnect to the network, Offline Files and Folders synchronizes the files in the cache with those on the network.

▲ *Folder redirection under Windows 2000/XP.* **Folder redirection** lets you point to an alternate location on a network for a folder. This feature can make the location of a folder transparent to the user. For example, a user's My Documents folder is normally located on the local computer's logical drive C. Using folder redirection, an administrator can put this My Documents folder on a file server. Having this folder on a shared file server has two important benefits:

   ▲ Regardless of which computer a user logs on to, her My Documents folder is available.
   ▲ A company routinely backs up data on a shared file server so backing up the user's data happens without her having to do anything.

   When using folder redirection with Offline Files and Folders, a user can access her My Documents folder even when the notebook is not attached to the company network.

▲ *Hardware profiles under Windows 2000/XP.* **Hardware profiles** let you specify which devices are to be loaded on startup for a particular user or set of circumstances. For example, you might set two different hardware profiles for a notebook computer, one for when it is on the road and one for when it is at home connected to a home network.

## The Recovery CDs and Recovery Partitions

Most notebook computers come with one or more support CDs provided by the manufacturer. This CD might or might not contain an installable version of the OS preinstalled on the notebook. If you need to install the OS again, such as when you are replacing a faulty hard drive, you might have to request that the notebook manufacturer provide you with a recovery CD for the OS installation (see Figure 20-5).

**Figure 20-5** The Recovery CD is an important tool needed to recover from a failed notebook hard drive

A+ ESS
1.4
2.4
3.2
3.3

A+
220-602
3.3

Some notebooks come with the utilities and system files needed to install a new copy of the OS stored on the hard drive in a separate partition. This partition might or might not be hidden. Figure 20-6 shows the Disk Management information for a hard drive on one notebook that has a 3.95-GB recovery partition that is not hidden. The files stored on this partition are protected from access when using Windows Explorer, as shown in Figure 20-7.

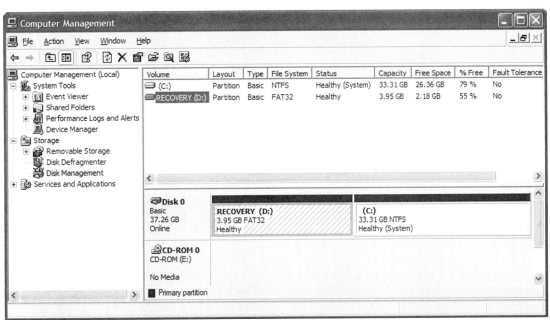

**Figure 20-6** This notebook hard drive has a recovery partition that can be used to recover the system

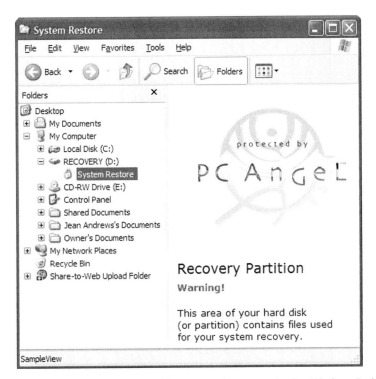

**Figure 20-7** A recovery partition cannot be accessed using Windows Explorer

A+ ESS
1.4
2.4
3.2
3.3

A+
220-602
3.3

To know how to access the recovery tools stored on a recovery partition, see the user reference manual. Most likely, you'll see a message at the beginning of the boot, such as "Press ESC for diagnostics," or "Press F12 to recover the system." When you press the key, a menu appears giving you options to diagnose the problem, to repair the current OS installation, or to completely rebuild the entire hard drive to its state when the notebook was first purchased. Of course, this won't work if your hard drive is broken and/or the recovery partition is damaged. In this situation, you're dependent on the OS recovery CD and other support CDs to build the new hard drive after it is installed.

The support CDs that come bundled with a notebook should definitely contain all the device drivers you need for the currently installed OS and might contain device drivers for another OS. For example, if Windows 98 is installed on a system, one of the support CDs most likely contains device drivers for Windows 98 and Windows 2000. The CDs might also include setup programs for the applications that come preinstalled on the notebook.

> **Notes**
>
> When you first purchase a notebook, make sure you have a recovery CD containing the installed OS so you can recover from a failed hard drive. If one doesn't come bundled with the notebook, purchase it from the notebook manufacturer. (The price should be less than $20.) Do this before problems arise. If the notebook is more than three years old, the manufacturer might no longer provide the CD.

## Operating System Upgrades

For desktop systems, upgrading the operating system is usually a good thing to do if the desktop system has the power and hard drive space to support the new OS. Not so with notebooks. Unless a specific need to upgrade arises, the operating system preinstalled on the notebook should last the life of the notebook.

As an example of a specific reason to upgrade, consider a situation in which a notebook holds private data and you need to provide the best possible security on the notebook. In this situation, it might be appropriate to upgrade from Windows 98 to Windows XP. However, Windows 2000 might be the appropriate second choice if the notebook manufacturer has a Windows 2000 build for this particular model notebook, but does not have a Windows XP build for it.

If at all possible, always upgrade the OS using an OS build purchased from the notebook manufacturer complete with supporting device drivers specific to your notebook. In addition, carefully follow their specific instructions for the installation.

If you decide to upgrade the OS using an off-the-shelf version of Windows 2000 or Windows XP, first determine that all components in the system are compatible with the upgrade. Be certain to have available all the device drivers you need for the new OS before you upgrade. Download the drivers from the notebook manufacturer's Web site and store them in a folder on the hard drive. After you upgrade the OS, install the drivers from this folder. The notebook manufacturer might also suggest you first flash the BIOS before you perform the upgrade. And, if applications came preinstalled on the notebook, find out if you have the applications' setup CDs and if they will install under the new OS.

An interesting situation occurred when I attempted to upgrade a notebook computer from Windows 98 to Windows 2000. This situation demonstrates the importance of having the notebook manufacturer's correct device drivers for the OS. The support CD that came with the notebook claimed to have on it device drivers for the internal modem and network cards for both OSs. I performed the OS upgrade and then attempted to use this support CD to install the Windows 2000 modem and network drivers. They would not install. I discovered the drivers on the CD were not the correct drivers for this system. However, without the modem or network ports working, I could not connect to the Internet to download good drivers.

A+ ESS
1.4
2.4
3.2
3.3

A+
220-602
3.3

A+ ESS
1.4
2.4
7.1

A+
220-602
1.2
1.3
7.1

The solution was to download the drivers onto another computer and burn a CD with the drivers. Then, I used that CD on the notebook to install the drivers.

## CARING FOR NOTEBOOKS

Notebook computers tend to not last as long as desktop computers because they are portable and, therefore, subjected to more wear and tear. Also, notebooks are more susceptible to worms and viruses than desktop systems, because you are more likely to use them on a public network such as when you sit down at a coffee shop hot spot to work. A notebook's user manual gives specific instructions on how to care for the notebook. Generally, however, follow these guidelines:

- ◢ LCD panels on notebooks are fragile and can be damaged fairly easily. Take precautions against damaging a notebook's LCD panel. Don't touch it with sharp objects like a ballpoint pen.
- ◢ Don't connect the notebook to a phone line during an electrical storm.
- ◢ Run antivirus software and always keep the software current.
- ◢ Never, ever connect to the Internet using a public wireless connection or ISP without first turning on a software firewall.
- ◢ Only use battery packs recommended by the notebook manufacturer. Keep the battery pack away from moisture or heat, and don't attempt to take the pack apart. When it no longer works, dispose of it correctly. Chapter 3 covers how to dispose of batteries. Best practices to prolong the life of your battery are discussed in the next section of this chapter.
- ◢ Use an administrator password to protect the system from unauthorized entry, especially if you are connected to a public network.
- ◢ Don't tightly pack the notebook in a suitcase because the LCD panel might get damaged. Use a good-quality carrying case and make it a habit of always transporting the notebook in the carrying case. Don't place heavy objects on top of the notebook case.
- ◢ Don't pick up or hold the notebook by the display panel. Pick it up and hold it by the bottom. Keep the lid closed when the notebook is not in use.
- ◢ Don't move the notebook while the hard drive is being accessed (the drive indicator light is on). Wait until the light goes off.
- ◢ Don't put the notebook close to an appliance such as a TV, large audio speakers, or refrigerator that generates a strong magnetic field, and don't place your cell phone on a notebook while the phone is in use.
- ◢ As with any computer, keep the OS current with the latest Windows updates.
- ◢ Keep your notebook at a controlled temperature. For example, never leave it in a car overnight when it is cold, and don't leave it in a car during the day when it's hot. Don't expose your notebook to direct sunlight for an extended time.
- ◢ Don't leave the notebook in a dusty or smoke-filled area. Don't use it in a wet area such as near a swimming pool or in the bathtub. Don't use it at the beach where sand can get in it.
- ◢ Don't power it up and down unnecessarily.
- ◢ Protect the notebook from overheating by not running it when it's still inside the case, resting on a pillow, or partially covered with a blanket or anything else that would prevent proper air circulation around it.
- ◢ Don't connect a modem in a notebook to a private branch exchange (PBX) or other digital telephone service such as that used in some hotels because these private telephone systems often carry too much voltage on the phone line, which can damage the modem.

▲ If a notebook has just come indoors from the cold, don't turn it on until it reaches room temperature. In some cases, condensation on the hard drive platters can cause problems. Some manufacturers recommend that when you receive a new notebook shipped to you during the winter, you should leave it in its shipping carton for several hours before you open the carton to prevent subjecting the notebook to a temperature shock.

▲ Protect a notebook against ESD. If you have just come in from the cold on a low-humidity day when there is the possibility that you are carrying ESD, don't touch the notebook until you have grounded yourself.

▲ Before placing a notebook in a carrying case for travel, remove any CDs, DVDs, or PC Cards and put them in protective covers. Verify that the system is powered down and not in suspend or standby mode.

A well-used notebook, especially one that is used in dusty or dirty areas, needs cleaning occasionally. Here are some cleaning tips:

▲ It is not necessary to disassemble a notebook for routine cleaning. In fact, you can clean the LCD panel, battery connections, keyboard, touch pad, or even memory contacts as needed without opening the notebook case.

▲ Clean the LCD panel with a soft dry cloth. If the panel is very dirty, you can dampen the cloth with water. Even though some books advise using a mixture of isopropyl alcohol and water to clean an LCD panel, notebook manufacturers say not to.

▲ Use a can of compressed air meant to be used around computer equipment to blow dust and small particles out of the keyboard, track ball, and touch pad. Turn the notebook at an angle and direct the air into the sides of the keyboard. Then use a soft, damp cloth to clean key caps and touch pad.

▲ Use compressed air to blow out all air vents on the notebook to make sure they are clean and unobstructed.

▲ If keys are sticking, remove the keyboard so you can better spray under the key with compressed air. If you can remove the key cap, remove it and clean the key contact area with contact cleaner. One example of a contact cleaner you can use for this purpose is Stabilant 22 (*www.stabilant.com*). Reinstall the keyboard and test it. If the key still sticks, replace the keyboard.

▲ Remove the battery and clean the battery connections with a contact cleaner.

## SECURING A NOTEBOOK AND ITS DATA

Because a notebook computer is smaller and lighter than a desktop system and is carried out into public places, it is more susceptible to being stolen. In addition, many times the most valuable thing in the notebook is the data. For these reasons, it is important for a PC support technician to know about ways to protect the notebook and its data.

### Security Devices

According to the Safeware Insurance Group, the owner of a notebook computer has a 1 in 14 chance of it being stolen. Some commonsense rules can help protect your notebook. When traveling, always know where your notebook is. If you're standing at an airport counter, tuck your notebook case securely between your ankles. When flying, never check in your notebook as baggage, and don't store it in airplane overhead bins; keep it at your feet. Never leave a notebook in an unlocked car or hotel room and, when you're using it, always log off the

A+ ESS
6.1
6.3

A+
220-602
6.3

network before you walk away from it. When leaving work, lock your notebook in a secure place or use a notebook cable lock to secure it to your desk. Figure 20-8 shows a cable lock system. Most notebooks have a security slot on the case to connect the cable lock.

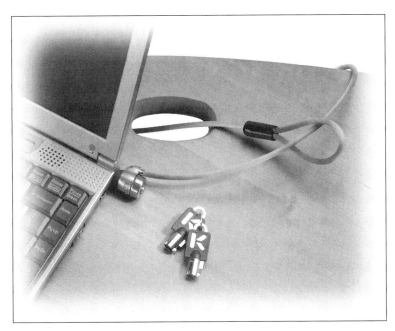

**Figure 20-8** Use a cable lock system to secure a notebook computer to a desk to help prevent it from being stolen

Another security device you can use is a theft-prevention plate that includes a label identifying the notebook, which is permanently engraved into your notebook case. The identifying numbers or bar code identify you, the owner, and can also clearly establish to police that the notebook has been stolen. Two sources of theft-prevention plates and cable locks are Computer Security Products, Inc. (*www.computersecurity.com*) and Flexguard Security System (*www.flexguard.com*).

### Power-On and Hard Drive Passwords

Recall from Chapter 19 that you can set a supervisor password and a user password (also called a power-on password). These passwords can be configured so they are required to boot the system, view CMOS setup, or make changes to setup. In addition, some notebooks give you the option of setting a hard drive password, which is written on the hard drive. Data on the hard drive cannot be changed without entering this password. The advantage of using a hard drive password over a power-on password or Windows password is that if the hard drive is removed and installed in another notebook, it still protects the hard drive's data. Just as with the power-on password, the hard drive password is requested by the system when it is powering up.

To know if your notebook supports these three types of power-on passwords, look on the CMOS setup screens. Figure 20-9 shows one notebook CMOS screen that shows the options to set four passwords (supervisor password, user password, and a hard drive password for each of two hard drives in the system). To set a hard drive password or the user password, you must first set a supervisor password. After that is set, to set a hard drive password, on the Security menu, select Hard Disk Security. The submenu in Figure 20-10 shows where you can choose to set a password for either or both hard drives.

> **Video**
> Configuring a Motherboard

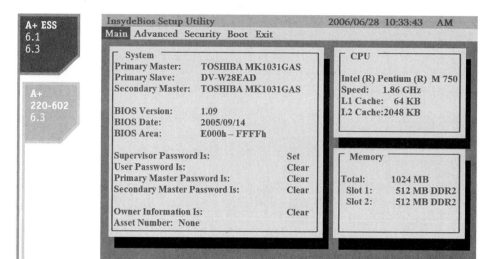

**Figure 20-9** The CMOS setup main menu shows support for four power-on passwords

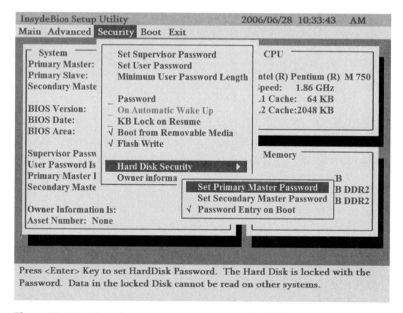

**Figure 20-10** The submenu shows how to set a hard drive password that will be written on the drive

## Data Backups

As discussed earlier in the book, if you can't get along without the data, back it up. Don't trust your hard drive with data you can't do without; back it up to another media. How to back up user data is covered in Chapter 13.

One problem with backups on notebook computers is that standard backup techniques often rely on company file servers, CD burners, or other media that are not always available when traveling with your notebook. If you need to back up data or have access to this backed-up data while traveling, one solution is an online backup service such as @Backup (*www.backup.com*) or Computer Security Products, Inc. (*www.computersecurity.com*). Also, some high-end notebooks have two hard drives. For these systems, you can back up data from one hard drive to the other, although, if your notebook is stolen, so is your backup.

A+ ESS
2.1
2.2

A+
220-602
1.3
2.2

## POWER MANAGEMENT

A notebook can be powered in several ways, including an AC adapter (which uses regular house current to power the notebook), a DC adapter (which uses DC power such as that provided by automobile cigarette lighters), and a battery pack. Some AC adapters are capable of auto-switching from 110 V to 220 V AC power, in contrast to fixed-input AC adapters that can handle only one type of AC voltage.

Types of batteries include the older and mostly outdated Ni-Cad (nickel-cadmium) battery, the longer-life NiMH (nickel-metal-hydride) battery, and the current Lithium Ion battery, which is more efficient than earlier batteries. A future battery solution is a fuel cell battery, technically called a Direct Methanol Fuel Cell (DMFC) battery. A DMFC initially provides up to five hours of battery life, and future versions will provide up to 10 hours of battery life. A notebook user might need one or more batteries and a DC adapter for travel and an AC adapter at home and for recharging the batteries.

Here are some general dos and don'ts for switching power sources and protecting the battery and notebook, which apply to most notebooks. See a notebook's user manual for specific instructions.

> **Notes**
>
> If you're using the AC adapter to power your notebook when the power goes out, the installed battery serves as a built-in UPS. The battery immediately takes over as your uninterruptible power supply.

▲ If you need to use the notebook for extended periods away from an electrical outlet, you can use extra battery packs. When the notebook signals that power is low, remove the old battery and replace it with a charged one. To remove a battery, generally, you release a latch and then remove the battery, as shown in Figure 20-11.

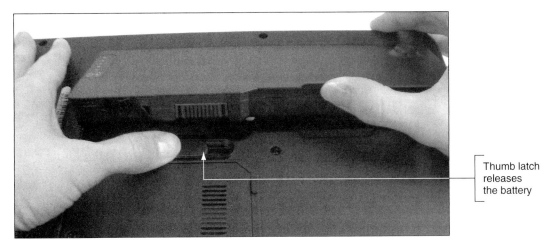

Thumb latch releases the battery

**Figure 20-11**   Release a latch to remove the battery from a notebook

▲ For some notebook batteries, don't recharge the battery pack until all the power is used. Recharging too soon can shorten the battery life. For other batteries, it doesn't matter how often you recharge them. Check your user manual to learn how and when to recharge your battery.

▲ For some older batteries, when you're recharging the battery, don't use it until it's fully recharged. Also, some manufacturers of older batteries recommend that you don't leave the battery in the notebook while the notebook is turned on and connected to an electrical outlet.

A+ ESS
2.1
2.2

A+
220-602
1.3
2.1

▲ If you're not using the notebook for a long time (more than a month), remove the battery from the notebook and store the notebook and battery in a cool, dry place. Leaving a battery in a notebook for extended periods when it is not used can damage the battery.

▲ Use power-management features of your OS, which are covered later in this chapter. Also, to make a battery charge last longer while working with your notebook, you can dim the LCD panel and remove any PC Cards you're not using.

▲ CD and DVD drives use a lot of power. Therefore, whenever possible, connect the notebook to an electrical outlet to play a movie on DVD or burn a CD.

▲ Use standby or hibernate mode whenever you are not using the notebook.

▲ While working with your notebook and using the battery, if you get a message that the battery is low, you can immediately plug in the AC or DC adapter without first powering down your notebook.

 **A+ Tip**

The A+ Essentials and A+ 220-602 exams expect you to know how notebooks get their power and about conserving power to prolong battery life.

▲ To conserve power when the battery is running, a notebook sometimes reduces LCD panel brightness. For example, when you unplug the AC adapter on one notebook, a message appears (see Figure 20-12) telling you brightness has been reduced. To save even more power, lower the brightness even more.

▲ A notebook has an internal surge protector. However, for extra protection, you might want to use a power strip for added surge protection.

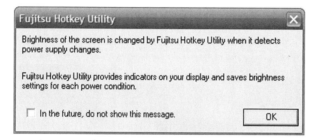

**Figure 20-12** Reduce LCD panel brightness to conserve power when running the battery

A notebook ACPI-compliant BIOS supports features to help manage power consumption, which were all discussed in Chapter 4. The goal is to minimize power consumption to increase the time before a battery pack needs recharging. Using CMOS setup, you can disable and enable some power-management features, and configuring power management is best done in Windows. Instructions are given next for Windows 2000/XP, but Windows 9x/Me works about the same way.

To access the Power Management dialog box using Windows 2000/XP, open the **Control Panel**, and double-click the **Power Options** applet (in Windows 9x/Me, the applet is named Power Management). Figure 20-13 shows the Power Options Properties dialog box for one Windows XP notebook. (A different brand of notebook might have different tabs in its Properties dialog box.) Notice there is one set of power-management options for when an AC or DC adapter is plugged in and when the battery is running. Use this dialog box to create, delete, and modify multiple power-management schemes to customize how Windows 2000/XP manages power consumption.

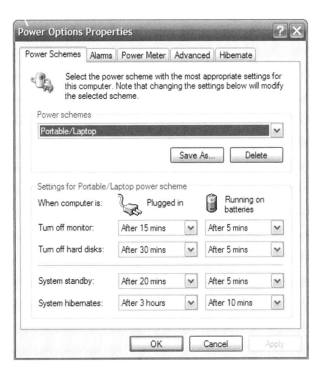

**Figure 20-13** The Power Options Properties dialog box of Windows 2000/XP allows you to create and manage multiple power schemes

For example, one power-saving feature of Windows 2000/XP and Windows 9x/Me puts a notebook into hibernation, as discussed in Chapter 4. Before you direct a notebook to hibernate, make sure you know the keystrokes or buttons required to restore the system to an active state without turning off the computer. For many computers, pressing the power button or a function key wakes up a system from hibernation.

If the notebook supports hibernating, you can configure Windows 2000/XP to cause the notebook to hibernate after a set period of time, when you press the power button, or when you close the lid of the notebook. Do the following:

> **Notes**
>
> The disadvantage of using hibernation is that it takes longer for the computer to go into suspend mode and resume from suspend mode. This extra time is required because, if hibernation is enabled, the computer saves everything in memory to the hard drive before suspending.

1. In the Power Options Properties dialog box, click the **Hibernate** tab (see Figure 20-14), and verify that hibernate support is enabled. If there is no Hibernate tab, your notebook does not support hibernating.

2. Click the **Advanced** tab, as shown in Figure 20-15. With the options on this tab, you can control what happens when you press the power button or close the lid of the notebook.

3. Click the **When I close the lid of my portable computer** list arrow and select **Hibernate**. (Other choices are Standby, Power Off, and None.)

**Figure 20-14** Verify that hibernate support is enabled

**Figure 20-15** The Advanced tab of the Power Options Properties dialog box allows you to control the behavior of the power button and what happens when you close the lid of your notebook

4. You can also control what happens when you press the power button. You can see your choices in Figure 20-16. When you're done, click **Apply** and then click **OK** to close the Power Options dialog box and save your changes.

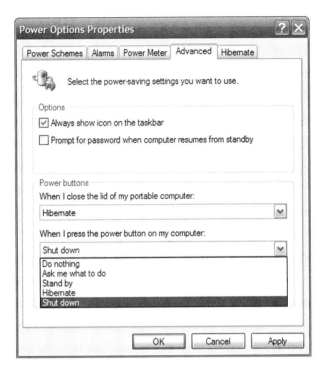

**Figure 20-16** Choices of action when you press the power button of your notebook

Using Windows 2000/XP, you can monitor and manage batteries on notebooks that are ACPI- and APM-enabled. You can access the battery meter directly by adding the battery status icon to the taskbar. Follow these steps:

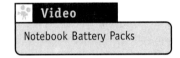

1. From the **Start** menu, open the **Control Panel**.

2. Double-click **Power Options** to open the Power Options Properties dialog box.

3. Click the **Advanced** tab.

4. Click the **Always show icon on the taskbar** check box (refer to Figure 20-16), and then click **OK**.

Note that the Power Options Properties dialog box also offers the Alarms tab on which you can set alarms to alert you when battery power is low or critical.

## PORT REPLICATORS AND DOCKING STATIONS

Some notebooks have a connector on the bottom of the notebook to connect to a port replicator, such as the one shown in Figure 20-17, or a docking station, shown in Figure 20-18. A **port replicator** provides a means to connect a notebook to a power outlet and provides additional ports to allow a notebook to easily connect to a full-sized monitor, keyboard, and other peripheral devices. A **docking station** provides the same functions as a port replicator, but also adds secondary storage, such as an extra hard drive, a floppy drive, or a DVD drive.

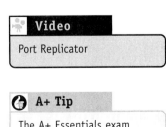

**Video**

**Notebook Battery Packs**

**Video**

**Port Replicator**

👍 **A+ Tip**

The A+ Essentials exam expects you to know the difference between a port replicator and a docking station.

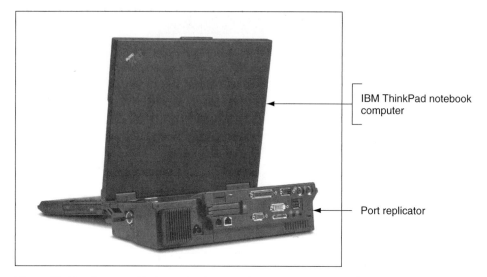

**Figure 20-17** A port replicator makes it convenient to connect a notebook computer to resources and peripherals at your office

**Figure 20-18** An IBM ThinkPad dock, an example of a docking station

If a notebook has a docking station, you can set up one hardware profile to use the docking station and another when you are on the road and don't have access to it. To create a hardware profile in Windows 2000/XP for a mobile user:

1. Open the **System Properties** window and click the **Hardware** tab.

2. Click the **Hardware Profiles** button at the bottom of the Hardware tab. The Hardware Profiles dialog box opens (Figure 20-19).

3. Select a profile from the list of available hardware profiles and then click the **Copy** button.

4. Type a new name for the profile, and then click **OK**.

5. Under *When Windows starts*, select either the option for Windows 2000/XP to wait for you to select a hardware profile or the option for Windows 2000/XP to start with the first profile listed if you don't select one in the specified number of seconds. Close all open windows.

6. Restart the computer and, when prompted, select the new hardware profile.

7. Open the **System Properties** dialog box. Click the **Hardware** tab, click **Device Manager**, and then double-click the icon for a device that you want enabled or disabled in the new profile. For example, you might set one profile to access a second hard drive that is installed on the docking station, which is not available when traveling.

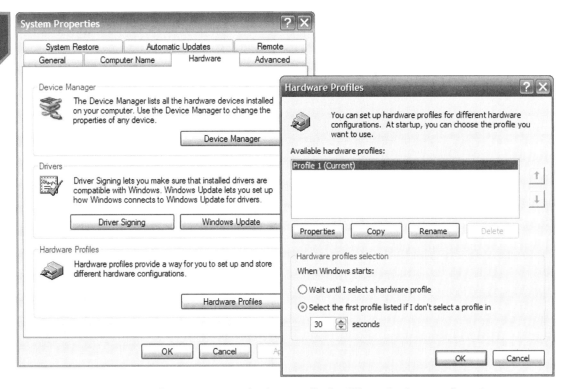

**Figure 20-19** Windows XP allows you to set a hardware profile for different hardware configurations

8. Click the **General** tab in the Properties dialog box for the device. In the area for Device usage, select the option to enable or disable the device for the current profile or for all hardware profiles. Close all open dialog boxes.

## CONNECTING PERIPHERAL DEVICES TO NOTEBOOKS

A notebook provides ports on its back or sides (see Figure 20-20), which are used for connecting peripherals.

In addition to the ports labeled in Figure 20-20, a notebook might have these slots, switches, and ports, several of which are discussed in the following subsections:

▲ PC Card or CardBus slot with lock switch and eject button
▲ ExpressCard slot with slot protective cover
▲ USB and FireWire ports
▲ Network port (RJ-45) and modem port (RJ-11)
▲ Headphone jack and microphone jack
▲ Volume control
▲ Secure Digital (SD) or CompactFlash Card slot
▲ Wireless antenna on/off switch (for onboard wireless, the antenna is inside the notebook case)
▲ 15-pin VGA video port
▲ Audio input and video input jacks if the notebook has an embedded TV tuner
▲ Airflow vents
▲ Power jack for DC or AC power adapter
▲ Security lock for installing a chain and lock
▲ Older notebooks might have a parallel port, serial port, PS/2 port, or infrared port

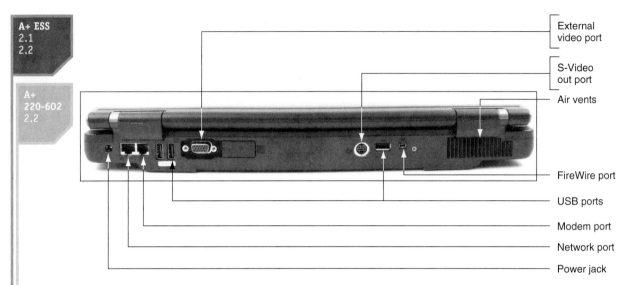

**Figure 20-20** Ports on the back of a notebook

Before we get into the discussion of ports used primarily on notebooks, keep in mind that USB ports have become a popular way of adding devices to all types of computers, including notebooks. For example, if the notebook does not have an RJ-45 port for an Ethernet connection, you can buy a device that plugs into the USB port and provides the Ethernet port. Another example shown in Figure 20-21 involves a wireless mouse and keypad that use a receiver connected to a USB port. Installing this mouse and keypad on a Windows 2000/XP notebook is very simple. You plug the receiver into the port. Windows displays a message that it has located the device, and the mouse and keypad are ready to use. This ease of installation is quickly making USB the preferred method of connecting peripheral devices.

**Figure 20-21** This wireless mouse and keypad use a receiver that connects to a USB port

## PC CARD, CARDBUS, AND EXPRESSCARD SLOTS

Notebook computers typically have one or more I/O card slots, which can accommodate one or more standards of I/O cards. These card standards have evolved over the years and

A+ ESS
2.1
2.2

A+
220-602
2.2

have been designed and supported by the PCMCIA (Personal Computer Memory Card International Association). PCMCIA standards include one or more variations of PC Card, CardBus, and ExpressCard.

### PC Card and CardBus

A **PC Card** is about the size of a credit card, but thicker, and inserts into a **PC Card slot**. Originally, PC Cards were called **PCMCIA (Personal Computer Memory Card International Association) Cards** and the first of these cards were used to add memory to a notebook. For example, Figure 20-22 shows a modem PC Card being inserted into a PC Card slot. The card provides a phone line port for the telephone line to the modem, as shown in Figure 20-23.

**Figure 20-22**  Many peripheral devices are added to a notebook using a PC Card slot; here, a modem PC Card is inserted in a PC Card slot

**Figure 20-23**  Connect the phone line to the modem PC Card

Some docking station PCs also have a PC Card slot, so that the device you use with your notebook can also be attached to the docking station. PC Card slots are considered standard equipment on notebooks, although the trend is moving from using PC Card slots toward using USB ports to connect peripheral equipment to a notebook. PC Card slots are used by many devices, including modems, network cards for wired or wireless networks, sound

A+ ESS
2.1
2.2

A+
220-602
2.2

> 👍 **A+ Exam Tip**
>
> The A+ Essentials exam expects you to know about PCMCIA Type I, II, and III, CardBus, and ExpressCard slots and cards.

cards, SCSI host adapters, IEEE 1394 controllers, USB controllers, flash memory adapters, TV tuners, and hard disks.

The PCMCIA organization has developed four standards for these slots. The latest PCMCIA specification that can use the PC Card slot is **CardBus**, which improves I/O speed, increases the bus width to 32 bits, and supports lower-voltage PC Cards while maintaining backward compatibility with earlier standards. Three standards for **PCMCIA slots** pertain to size and are named Type I, Type II, and Type III. Generally, the thicker the PC Card, the higher the standard. A thick hard drive card might need a Type III slot, but a thin modem card might only need a Type II slot. Type I cards can be up to 3.3-mm thick and are primarily used for adding RAM to a notebook PC. Type II cards can be up to 5.5-mm thick and are often used as modem cards. Type III cards can be up to 10.5-mm thick, large enough to accommodate a portable disk drive. When buying a notebook PC, look for Type I, Type II, and Type III PC Card slots. Often, two slots are included, and a slot might support more than one type. Also, the motherboard bus used by the PC Card slot to communicate with the processor can be a 16-bit or 32-bit PCMCIA I/O bus. For improved performance, look for 32-bit CardBus slots.

Some PC Cards have dongles or pigtails such as the network PC Card shown in Figure 20-24. The RJ-45 connection is at the end of a dongle so that the thick RJ-45 connection does not have to fit flat against the PC Card. Other PC Cards are thick at the end so that the ports can be embedded directly on the card, such as the TV tuner PC Card shown in Figure 20-25.

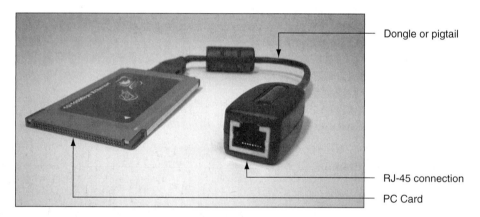

Dongle or pigtail

RJ-45 connection

PC Card

**Figure 20-24**  This PC Card serves as a NIC for an Ethernet 100BaseT network

**Figure 20-25**  This TV tuner card connects to a notebook by way of a PCMCIA CardBus slot

A+ ESS
2.1
2.2

A+
220-602
2.2

PC Cards are often used to provide proprietary ports or adapters that are not available on the notebook, such as those used for flash memory devices, including Secure Digital (SD) card, CompactFlash card, or Microdrive CF, all discussed in Chapter 10. One example is the PC Card shown in Figure 20-26 that contains a slot for a CompactFlash memory card.

**Figure 20-26**   The PC card contains an adapter for a CompactFlash memory card

The underlying technology for a PC Card slot is 16-bit ISA or 32-bit PCI. Before CardBus, all PC Card slots used the 16-bit ISA interface between the card slot and the processor. The CardBus technology uses 32-bit PCI for the interface standard. PCMCIA has announced that it no longer will present any new developments for the PC Card, because it is now promoting the ExpressCard slot as the replacement slot for the PC Card slot.

## ExpressCard

The latest PCMCIA standard is **ExpressCard**, which was designed to use the same type of interface used by the PCI Express or USB 2.0 standard. Currently, two sizes of ExpressCards exist: ExpressCard/34 is 34-mm wide and ExpressCard/54 is 54-mm wide. Both of these types of cards are 75-mm long and 5-mm high. Figure 20-27 compares a CardBus PC Card to each of the two ExpressCard cards. An ExpressCard/34 card can fit into an ExpressCard/54 slot, but not vice versa.

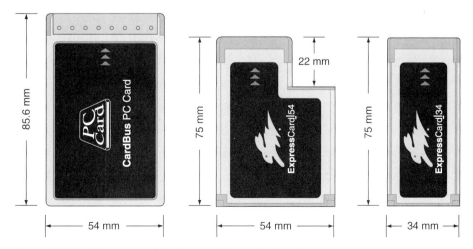

**Figure 20-27**   Dimensions of CardBus and ExpressCard cards

Just as PCI Express slots are not backward compatible with PCI slots on a desktop computer, ExpressCard slots are not backward compatible with PC Card slots on a notebook. Some notebooks will have both types of slots, such as the notebook in Figure 20-28. An ExpressCard slot is fully hot-pluggable, hot-swappable, and supports autoconfiguration, just as does a USB port. PCMCIA is also promoting the ExpressCard slot as an option for desktop computers, rather than using PCI or PCI Express slots for expansion cards.

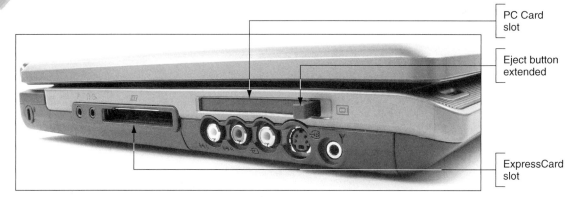

PC Card slot

Eject button extended

ExpressCard slot

**Figure 20-28** This notebook has one PC Card and one ExpressCard slot

One example of an ExpressCard/34 card is the Gigabit Ethernet card shown in Figure 20-29. Figure 20-30 shows an ExpressCard/54 card that provides two eSATA ports for external SATA drives.

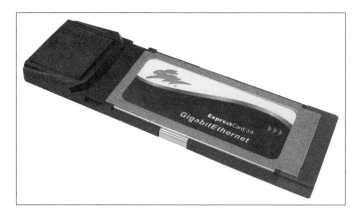

**Figure 20-29** This ExpressCard/34 card supports Gigabit Ethernet

**Figure 20-30** This ExpressCard/54 card supports two eSATA drives

20

## USING PC CARD AND EXPRESSCARD SLOTS

A+ ESS
2.1
2.2

A+
220-602
2.2

The operating system must provide two services for a PC Card, ExpressCard, or another type of proprietary card: a socket service and a card service. The socket service establishes communication between the card and the notebook when the card is first inserted, and then disconnects communication when the card is removed. The card service provides the device driver to interface with the card after the socket is created.

To remove a device that is not hot-swappable, you must first power down the notebook. Hot-swapping allows you to remove one card and insert another without powering down. PC Cards and ExpressCards can be hot-swapped, but you must stop and then unplug one card before inserting another. For example, if you currently use a wireless network card in the PC Card slot of a Windows XP notebook and want to switch to a TV tuner card, first turn off the wireless network card, remove the network card, and then insert the TV tuner card and connect the TV cable to the card. Follow these directions to remove a card from a PC Card or ExpressCard slot:

1. For Windows XP, the easiest way to stop a card is to use the Unplug or Eject Hardware icon in the system tray, shown in Figure 20-31. Click the icon and the Safely Remove Hardware dialog box on the left side of Figure 20-32 opens.

Icon used to stop a device

**Figure 20-31**  Use this icon in the Windows XP system tray to stop a hot-pluggable device before removing it

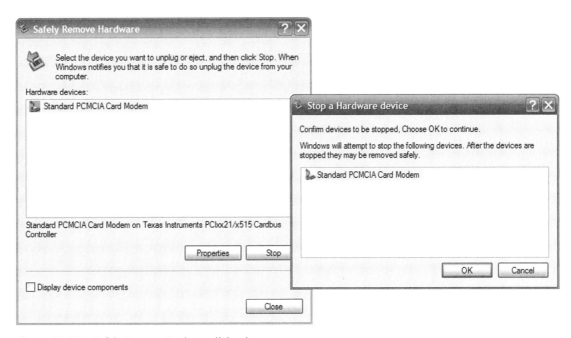

**Figure 20-32**  Safely Remove Hardware dialog box

2. Click **Stop**. The Stop a Hardware device dialog box opens, as shown on the right side of Figure 20-32. Click **OK** to continue. The bubble shown in Figure 20-33 appears telling you that you can now remove the device. If Windows tells you it cannot stop the device, you must shut down your computer before removing the card.

**Figure 20-33** The stopped device can now be removed

**A+ Exam Tip**

The A+ Essentials exam expects you to know how to remove a hot-swappable and non-hot-swappable device from a notebook.

**Notes**

A bug in Windows XP causes the system to hang if you remove a PC Card while the system is in sleep mode or is hibernating. To solve the problem, download the latest service pack for Windows XP.

After you have stopped the card, press the eject button beside the PC Card slot, which causes the button to pop out. You can then press the button again to eject the card. For an ExpressCard, push on the card, which causes it to pop out of the slot. Then, you can remove the card.

For Windows 2000, to stop a PC Card, use the Add/Remove Hardware icon in the Control Panel. The Add/Remove Hardware Wizard starts; click **Next**, and click **Uninstall/Unplug a device** in the next dialog box. Click **Next**, and then click **Unplug/Eject a device** in the next dialog box. A list of devices appears. Sometimes, only one item will be in the list, as shown in Figure 20-34. Select the device and click **Next**. The final window tells you that you can safely unplug the device and gives you the option to display an Unplug/Eject icon in the taskbar when the device is used again. For Windows 9x/Me, use the PC Card icon in the Control Panel to stop a card.

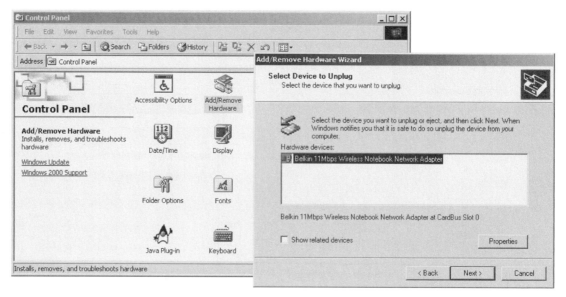

**Figure 20-34** Before removing a PC Card from a Windows 2000 notebook, stop the card (open the socket)

The first time you insert a PC Card or ExpressCard in a notebook, the Found New Hardware Wizard starts (see Figure 20-35) and guides you through the installation steps in which you can use the drivers provided by the hardware manufacturer or use Windows drivers. The next time you insert the card in the notebook, the card is detected and starts without help.

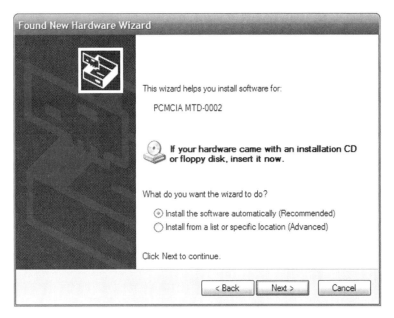

**Figure 20-35** The Found New Hardware Wizard launches the first time you insert a PC Card or ExpressCard in the I/O slot

If you are having problems getting a notebook to recognize a PC Card or ExpressCard, try the following:

> ⚠ **Caution**
>
> Inserting a card in a PC Card or ExpressCard slot while the notebook is shutting down or booting up can cause damage to the card and/or to the notebook.

◢ Don't insert a card in a slot if the card is damaged or is wet. Doing so can damage the slot.

◢ Make sure the system is on and not in hibernation or standby mode when you insert the card.

◢ When you first insert a card and the notebook does not recognize it, the slot might be disabled in CMOS setup. Reboot the notebook and enter the CMOS setup program. Look for the feature to enable or disable a PC Card or ExpressCard slot on the Power Management screen or an Advanced Settings screen.

◢ In Device Manager, verify the PCMCIA or PC Card controller is functioning correctly with no errors. You can update the controller drivers; be sure to use drivers provided by the notebook manufacturer. Check the driver CD that came bundled with the notebook.

◢ A program, such as antivirus software, might be interfering with the Card Services program. Try disabling any software not certified for your OS by Microsoft.

◢ Try installing the card's drivers before you insert the card. Look for a setup program on the manufacturer's CD bundled with the card.

Here are some additional tips when using an ExpressCard slot:

◢ When using an ExpressCard/54 slot, insert an ExpressCard/34 card in the left side of the slot. Push a card firmly into the slot until you feel it snap into the connector.

◢ When you're not using an ExpressCard slot, to protect the slot, insert the protective cover into the slot (see Figure 20-36).

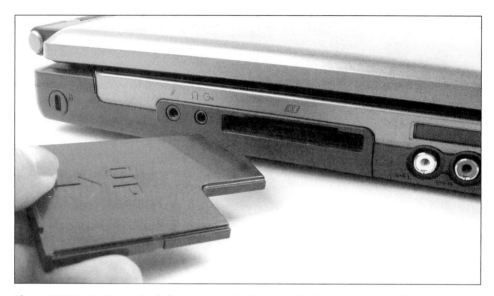

**Figure 20-36** An ExpressCard slot uses a protective cover in the slot to protect it

## USING WIRELESS DEVICES WITH NOTEBOOKS

A notebook might have the ability to support a cellular WAN connection such as WiFi or a personal area network (PAN) connection such as Bluetooth or infrared. In Chapter 17, you learned how to set up and secure a WiFi connection, and infrared connections are covered in Chapter 9.

Because supporting WiFi connections on a notebook is such an important subject, let's briefly review some information you learned in Chapter 17. Recall that a wireless notebook can be configured to connect in ad hoc mode (to another computer) or in infrastructure mode (to a wireless access point). And, if a notebook has an internal wireless NIC, most likely the NIC is configured using Windows tools. To change wireless settings, use the Network Connections window. For example, to decide between using ad hoc mode or infrastructure mode, right-click the **Wireless Network Connection** icon in the Network Connections window and click **Properties** from the shortcut menu. In the properties dialog box, click the **Wireless Networks** tab, as shown on the left side of Figure 20-37. Click **Advanced** and then make your mode selection, as shown on the right side of Figure 20-37. Most likely, the first selection is the correct one because it allows you to connect using either mode. Click **Close** and **OK** to close both boxes.

To make the wireless connection, turn on the wireless switch on your notebook. Most likely, this is all that is necessary for the connection to be made unless you need to enter a passphrase to a secured network. If you have a problem connecting, double-click the wireless icon in the Network Connections window. A list of wireless networks appears. You can refresh the list by clicking **Refresh network list** (see Figure 20-38). Select a network and click **Connect**. If the network is secured, you'll be asked to enter a passphrase to use the network. To change networks, select the network you are connected to and click **Disconnect**, as shown in Figure 20-38. You can then connect to a different network.

| Notes |
| --- |
| By default, a wired or wireless network connection is set for dynamic ID addressing, which is the right choice for most public and corporate networks. However, you can configure a notebook for dynamic IP addressing, and assign a static IP address to be used when a DHCP server is not available. After you have configured the notebook for dynamic IP addressing, on the **Internet Protocol (TCP/IP) Properties** dialog box, click the **Alternate Configuration** tab and assign a static IP address, subnet mask, and DNS servers. |

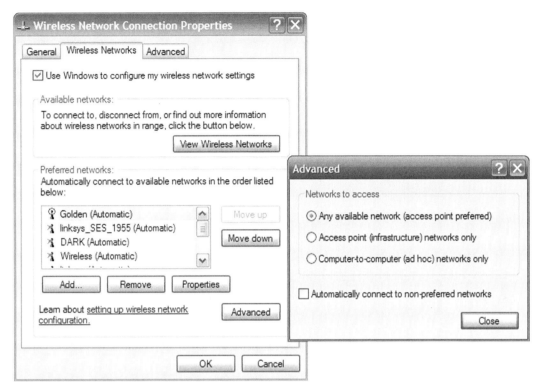

**Figure 20-37** Use the Wireless Network Connection Properties dialog box to configure a wireless NIC installed in a notebook

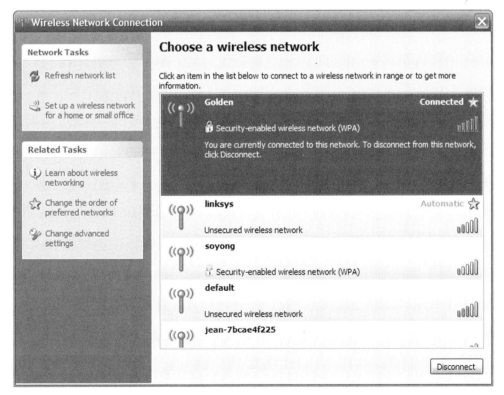

**Figure 20-38** Select a wireless network from those in range

After the connection is made, a bubble appears identifying the network (see Figure 20-39). Notice in Figure 20-39 that this network connection is unsecured. Be careful to not transmit private data over an unsecured network and to keep your Windows Firewall fully enabled. For more information about wireless networks and wireless security, see Chapters 17 and 19.

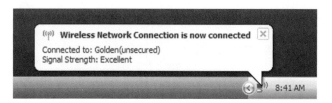

**Figure 20-39** Windows XP reports the wireless connection

If your notebook supports a Bluetooth connection used to connect to a printer, mouse, headset, camera, cell phone, or connect a PDA to the notebook, you need to read the documentation for configuring the Bluetooth connection that came with the notebook. If you don't have that documentation, download it from the notebook manufacturer Web site. You'll need it because Bluetooth setups differ from one notebook to another. Following the directions for your notebook, turn on Bluetooth. After Bluetooth is turned on, you should be able to make a connection with your Bluetooth device when it is set close to the notebook.

If you are having problems getting the Bluetooth connection to work, try the following:

▲ Make sure the wireless switch is turned on (for some notebooks, this switch turns on and off both the WiFi and Bluetooth signal).

▲ Verify that Windows sees Bluetooth enabled. You might do this by using an applet in the Control Panel or by using a program on the Start menu. For example, one Toshiba notebook has a Radio Control applet in the Control Panel and another notebook uses Bluetooth Manager software in the Start menu. For many notebooks, you should see an icon in the system tray showing the status of Bluetooth.

▲ Be sure you have downloaded all Windows updates. (Windows XP Service Pack 2 is required for Bluetooth.)

▲ Look in Device Manager to make sure the Bluetooth component is recognized with no errors. For some notebooks, even though the component is an internal device, it is seen in Device Manager as a USB device.

▲ You can also try uninstalling and reinstalling the Bluetooth drivers that come bundled on CD with your notebook.

▲ You can also try uninstalling and reinstalling the drivers for your Bluetooth device. For example, if you are trying to connect to a printer using a Bluetooth wireless connection, try first turning on Bluetooth and then uninstalling and reinstalling the printer. During the printer installation, select the Bluetooth connection for the printer port, which might be called Bluetooth COM or something similar.

For more ideas for solving a Bluetooth problem, try the Web site of the notebook manufacturer or the Web site of the device you are trying to connect to your notebook using Bluetooth.

If your notebook doesn't have Bluetooth capability and you'd like to add it, you can buy a USB Bluetooth adapter like the one shown in Figure 20-40. After you have installed the drivers and the adapter, you can use it to wirelessly connect to any Bluetooth-enabled device.

A+ ESS
2.1
2.2
5.1

A+
220-602
2.1
5.2

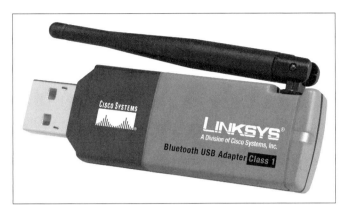

**Figure 20-40** Use a USB Bluetooth adapter to add Bluetooth capability to a notebook

# REPLACING AND UPGRADING INTERNAL PARTS

A+ ESS
2.3

A+
220-602
1.2

Sometimes it is necessary to open a notebook case so that you can upgrade memory, exchange a hard drive, or replace a broken component such as the LCD panel. Most notebooks sold today are designed so that you can easily get memory modules or drives to upgrade or exchange them. However, replacing a broken LCD panel can be a complex process, taking most of your day. In this section, we'll first look at the alternatives you need to consider before you decide to take on complex repair projects, and then we'll look at how to upgrade memory, exchange a drive, and perform other complex repair projects, including exchanging an LCD panel.

## THREE APPROACHES TO DEALING WITH A BROKEN INTERNAL DEVICE

When a component on a notebook needs replacing or upgrading, first you need to consider the warranty and how much time the repair will take. Before you decide to upgrade or repair an internal component, take into consideration these three alternatives:

▲ *Return the notebook to the manufacturer or another service center for repair.* If the notebook is under warranty, you need to return it to the manufacturer to do any serious repair work such as fixing a broken LCD panel. However, for simple repair and upgrade tasks, such as upgrading memory or exchanging a hard drive, most likely you can do these simple jobs by yourself without concern for voiding a warranty. If you're not sure about the possibility of voiding the warranty, check with the manufacturer before you begin working on the notebook. If the notebook is not under warranty and you don't have the experience or time to fix a broken component, find out how much the manufacturer will charge to do the job. Also, consider using a generic notebook repair service. Know that some notebook manufacturers refuse to sell internal components for their notebooks except to authorized service centers. In this case, you have no option but to use the service center for repairs.

▲ *Substitute an external component for an internal component.* As you'll see later in the chapter, replacing components on notebooks can be time consuming and require a lot of patience and know-how. If the notebook is not under warranty, sometimes, it's wiser to simply avoid opening the case and working inside it. Instead, you could simply use CMOS setup to disable an internal component and then use an external device in its place. For example, if a keyboard fails, you can use a wireless keyboard with an access point connected to the USB port. Also, if an internal modem fails, the simplest solution might be to disable the internal modem and replace it with a PC Card modem card.

▲ *Replace the internal device.* Before deciding to replace an internal device that is not easy to get to, such as an LCD panel, first find out if you can get the documentation necessary to know how to open the notebook case and exchange the component. How to find this documentation was discussed earlier in the chapter. Without the instructions or a lot of experience servicing notebooks, the project could be very frustrating and result in a notebook useful only as a paperweight.

> **Notes**
>
> Before making the decision to replace an internal part, ask the question, "Can an external device or PC Card substitute?" Many customers appreciate these solutions, because most often they are much less labor-intensive and less costly.

Now let's turn our attention to how to substitute an external device for an internal one and then how to prepare to work inside a notebook computer case.

## SUBSTITUTE AN INTERNAL DEVICE WITH AN EXTERNAL DEVICE

To substitute an internal device with an external device, first go into CMOS setup and disable the internal device. For most notebooks, you enter CMOS setup when the notebook is booting. Table 20-2 lists how to access CMOS setup for different notebook computers.

| Notebook Model | To Run CMOS Setup |
| --- | --- |
| Dell, Gateway, Fujitsu, Sony, Acer, and most other notebooks | During booting, press F2 when the logo appears. |
| Lenovo or IBM ThinkPad models series 240, 390, 570, iSeries 1200, 1300, 1400, 1500, 172x, A20, A21, A22, A30, A31, R30, R31, R32, S30, S31, T20, T21, T22, T23, T30, X20, X21, X23, X24, X30, X31 | Press F1 when the ThinkPad logo appears during the boot. |
| Lenovo or IBM ThinkPad R40, R40e, T40 | During startup, press the Access IBM button. Then select Start setup utility. |
| IBM ThinkPad 510, 300350500 | Put the system in MS-DOS mode (not a DOS box under Windows) and then press Ctrl+Alt+F3 at a DOS prompt. |
| IBM ThinkPad 310, 315310E | Press F2 when the ThinkPad logo appears during booting. |
| IBM ThinkPad 365C, CS365CD, CSD365, ED | Put the system in MS-DOS mode (not a DOS box under Windows) and then press Ctrl+Alt+F11 at a DOS prompt. |
| IBM ThinkPad 365X, 365XD | During booting, press and hold down the F1 key until the Setup screen appears. |
| IBM ThinkPad 360, 355, 380, 385, 560, 600, 701x, 76x, 770 | During booting, press and hold down the F1 key until the Setup screen appears. Also, for the 701 notebook, you can access CMOS setup at any time by pressing the Fn and F1 keys. |
| IBM ThinkPad 700x, 720x | During booting, press Ctrl+Alt+Ins right after the memory count. |

**Table 20-2**  How to access CMOS setup for different notebooks

| Notebook Model | To Run CMOS Setup |
|---|---|
| IBM ThinkPad 710T, 730T | During booting, press and hold down the suspend/resume switch. |
| Toshiba Satellite models 16xx, 17xx, 30xx, 100x, 19xx, 1000, 1200, 1100x | Turn the system off. Press the power button and then press and hold down F2 until the CMOS Setup screen appears. |
| Toshiba Satellite models 500x, 510x, 520x | A CMOS setup program is not included in the motherboard ROM. To access setup, after Windows is loaded, open the Control Panel and double-click the HWSetup program. |
| Toshiba all Libretto, all Portege, and other Satellite models not listed earlier | Three ways to access setup:<br><br>◢ In Windows, double-click HWSetup in the Control Panel.<br><br>◢ Power off and on the system. During the boot, when you see the message to press F1, press it.<br><br>◢ In MS-DOS mode (not a DOS box inside Windows), run the TSETUP program, which can be downloaded from the Toshiba Web site. |
| Compaq Presario models | During booting, press F2 when the logo screen appears. |
| Compaq Evo models | During booting, when the message "F10 = ROM Based Setup" appears, press F10. |
| Compaq Prosignia models | During booting, while the cursor is blinking, press F10. |

**Table 20-2** How to access CMOS setup for different notebooks (continued)

After you have disabled the internal device, install the external peripheral device as described earlier in the chapter.

## PREPARATION FOR SERVICING A NOTEBOOK

Before attempting to replace or upgrade a component installed in a notebook, always do the following:

◢ If the computer is working, have the user back up any important data stored on the notebook.

◢ Ground yourself by using an antistatic ground strap. If no ground strap is available, periodically touch the port to discharge any static electricity on your body.

◢ Turn off any attached devices such as a printer and then shut down the notebook.

◢ Disconnect the AC adapter from the computer and from the electrical outlet.

◢ If the notebook is attached to a port replicator or docking station, release it to undock the computer.

◢ Remove the battery pack.

◢ Remove any PC Cards, CDs, or DVDs.

 **Caution**

It is very important to unplug the AC adapter and remove the battery pack before working inside a notebook case. If the battery is still in the notebook, power provided by the battery could damage components as you work on them.

You are now ready to follow specific instructions for your particular notebook model to replace or upgrade an internal component. Some components can easily be accessed by either removing a panel to expose the component or by removing a screw or two and then sliding the component out the side of the case. When a component can be accessed this easily, most users can do the job if given detailed instructions. However, some components, such as the LCD panel or motherboard, are not so easily accessed. To get to these components requires opening the case and disassembling the notebook.

## UPGRADING MEMORY

When deciding how much memory a notebook should have, several factors need to be taken into consideration:

- ◢ For most situations, the more memory the better. If memory is low, upgrading memory can make a dramatic improvement in performance.
- ◢ If a notebook has special features such as video-editing software or a TV tuner, you'll need additional memory to support these features. See the notebook user manual for recommendations about the amount of memory needed.
- ◢ A notebook might have dedicated video memory or the video system might use regular RAM for video data. Using regular RAM for video is called **video sharing** or **shared memory**. Video sharing can take from 1 MB to 8 MB of RAM for video depending on the screen resolution you are using. Shared memory reduces the amount of memory available for other tasks, which might mean you need to install more RAM. Using shared memory means that the system can cost less, produce less heat, weigh less, use less power, and help extend battery life.

 **A+ Tip**

The A+ 220-602 exam expects you to know how sharing memory with video affects decisions made when upgrading memory.

In this section, you'll learn about the different types of memory modules used with notebook computers and how to upgrade memory.

### TYPES OF MEMORY USED IN NOTEBOOKS

Notebooks use several types of memory, including SO-DIMMs (small outline DIMMs), SO-RIMMs (small outline RIMMs), credit card memory, and proprietary memory modules. Table 20-3 lists SO-DIMMs and SO-RIMMs. All of these memory modules are smaller than regular SIMMs, DIMMs, or RIMMs.

| Memory Module Description | Sample Memory Module |
| --- | --- |
| 2.66" 200-pin SO-DIMM contains DDR2 SDRAM. One notch is near the side of the module. | |
| 2.66" 200-pin SO-DIMM contains DDR SDRAM. One notch near the side of the module is slightly offset from the notch on a DDR2 SDRAM module. | |

**Table 20-3** Memory modules used in notebook computers

A+ ESS
1.1
2.1

A+
220-602
2.2

| Memory Module Description | Sample Memory Module |
|---|---|
| 2.66" 144-pin SO-DIMM contains SDRAM. One notch is slightly offset from the center of the module. | 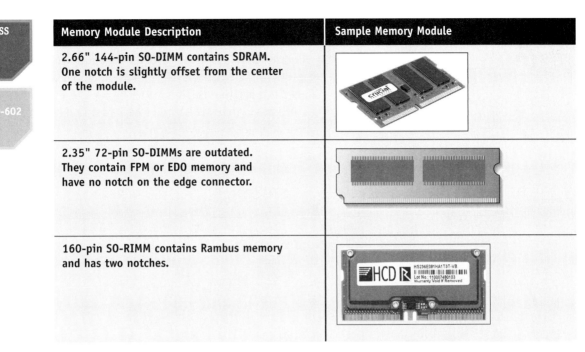 |
| 2.35" 72-pin SO-DIMMs are outdated. They contain FPM or EDO memory and have no notch on the edge connector. | |
| 160-pin SO-RIMM contains Rambus memory and has two notches. | |

**Table 20-3**   Memory modules used in notebook computers (continued)

In addition, some older notebooks use **credit card memory** or proprietary memory modules, both installed in slots inside the notebook case. Figure 20-41 shows credit card memory, proprietary memory, and SO-DIMMs for comparison.

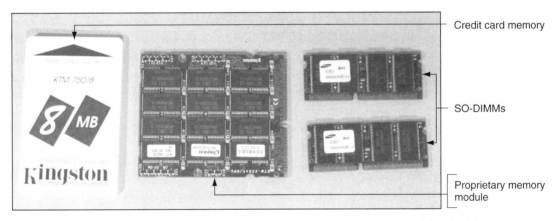

**Figure 20-41**   Older notebooks used credit card memory and proprietary memory modules, both larger than the current SO-DIMM modules

**SO-DIMMs** (small outline DIMMs, pronounced "sew-dims") come in several types. 72-pin SO-DIMMs, which support 32-bit data transfers, use FPM or EDO (which you learned about in Chapter 7), and could be used as single modules in 386 or 486 machines but must be used in pairs in Pentium machines. 144-pin SO-DIMMs, which support 64-bit data transfers, use EDO and SDRAM and can be used as single modules in Pentium machines. 200-pin SO-DIMMs are 2.625 inches wide and contain DDR SDRAM or DDR2 SDRAM. They have a single notch near the edge of one side of the module. A DDR SO-DIMM uses 2.5 volts of power, and a DDR2 SO-DIMM uses 1.8 volts. The notch of a DDR2 SO-DIMM is slightly offset from the DDR SO-DIMM's notch. Another type of memory for notebooks is the 160-pin **SO-RIMM (small outline RIMM)**, which uses a 64-bit data path and the Rambus technology discussed in Chapter 7.

Subnotebooks sometimes use **MicroDIMMs** that are smaller than SO-DIMMs and have a 64-bit data path. A MicroDIMM that contains SDRAM has 144 pins. A MicroDIMM that contains DDR SDRAM has 172 pins and uses 2.5 volts of power, and a MicroDIMM that contains DDR2 SDRAM has 214 pins and uses 1.8 volts. Figure 20-42 shows a 214-pin MicroDIMM being installed in a memory socket on a subnotebook computer.

Video

Upgrading Memory on a Notebook

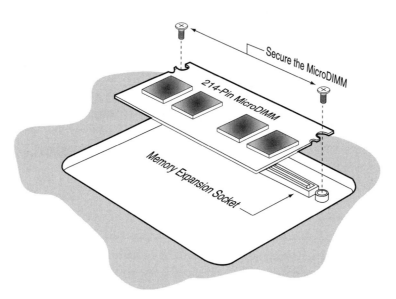

**Figure 20-42** Installing a MicroDIMM in a subnotebook computer

## HOW TO UPGRADE MEMORY ON A NOTEBOOK

Before upgrading memory, make sure you are not voiding your warranty. Search for the best buy, but make sure you use memory modules made by or authorized by your notebook's manufacturer and designed for the exact model of your notebook. Installing generic memory might save money but might also void the notebook's warranty.

Upgrading memory on a notebook works about the same way as with upgrading memory on a desktop: Decide how much memory you can upgrade, purchase the memory, and install it. As with a desktop computer, be sure to match the type of memory to the type the notebook supports.

Most notebooks are designed for easier access to memory. For example, for the notebook shown in Figure 20-43, to replace a memory module, turn the notebook upside down. Remove the screws and the panel cover to expose the modules. Always check the notebook user guide for specific directions.

A+ ESS
2.1

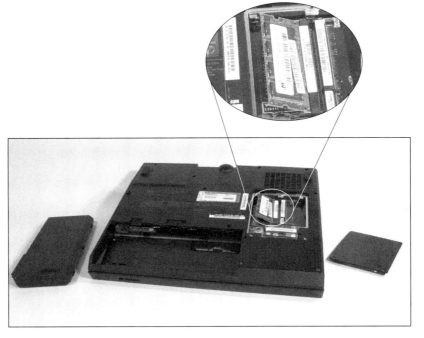

**Figure 20-43** To access memory modules, remove a panel cover on the bottom of the notebook

# APPLYING|CONCEPTS

Older notebooks often make it much more difficult to upgrade memory. In this example, reaching the memory slots requires first removing the keyboard. Do the following:

1. Turn off the notebook and remove the battery pack and all cables.

2. Lift the keyboard brace, as shown in Figure 20-44. (Your notebook might have a different way to enter the system, such as from the bottom of the case.)

**Figure 20-44** Lift the keyboard brace

3. Turn the keyboard over and toward the front of the notebook (see Figure 20-45). The keyboard is still connected to the notebook by the ribbon cable.

Ribbon cable connecting keyboard to notebook

**Figure 20-45** Turn the keyboard over toward the front of the notebook to expose the memory module socket

4. Lift the plastic sheet covering the memory module socket.

5. Insert the SO-DIMM module into the socket. See Figure 20-46. The socket braces should snap into place on each side of the module when the module is in position.

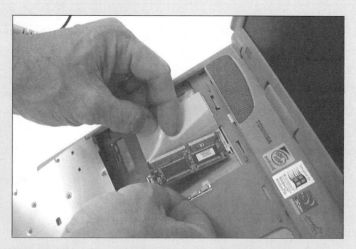

**Figure 20-46** Install the SO-DIMM into the memory socket

6. Replace the keyboard and keyboard brace. (If you entered from the bottom, you might be replacing a cover on the bottom of the case in this step.)

7. Power up the notebook so that it can detect the new memory.

## REPLACING A HARD DRIVE

When purchasing and installing an internal hard drive, floppy drive, CD/CD-RW drive, DVD/DVD-RW drive, or removable drive, see the notebook manufacturer's documentation about specific sizes and connectors that will fit the notebook. Also be aware of voiding a warranty if you don't follow the notebook manufacturer's directions. When purchasing a hard drive, know that hard drives for notebooks often use proprietary form factors and

A+ ESS
1.2
2.1

connectors, which means you must purchase a drive from the notebook manufacturer or at least buy one that uses the same connector and form factor. Here is what you need to know when shopping for a notebook hard drive:

▲ A desktop hard drive is 3.5 inches wide and a notebook drive is 2.5 inches wide. Figure 20-47 shows a comparison of the two sizes. Because the form factor of a notebook drive is more compact, it costs more than a desktop drive holding the same amount of data. (Notebook drives generally run at 4200 RPM or 5400 RPM, compared to 5400 RPM or 7200 RPM for desktop drives.)

Hard drive for a desktop computer

Hard drive for a notebook

**Figure 20-47**  Hard drives for notebooks are smaller than hard drives for desktop computers

▲ Most notebook hard drives sold today use a universal 40-pin connector for an IDE notebook. A few notebook manufacturers are making serial ATA hard drives for their notebooks. Check your notebook manual to know which to buy.

▲ For IDE drives, some notebooks use an adapter to interface between a proprietary connector on their hard drives and the 40-pin connector on the notebook motherboards. You'll need to remove the old drive and see how it's connected to know if an adapter is used. If you find an adapter, most likely, you can then connect the adapter to the new drive.

Before deciding to replace a hard drive, consider these issues:

▲ If the old drive has crashed, you'll need the recovery CD and notebook drivers CDs to reinstall Windows and the drivers. Make sure you have all these CDs before you start.

▲ If you are upgrading from a low-capacity drive to a higher-capacity drive, you need to consider how you will transfer data from the old drive to the new one. One way to do that is to use a USB to IDE converter that you first learned about in Chapter 8 (refer back to Figure 8-56). Using this converter, both drives can be up and working on the notebook at the same time so you can copy files. For less than $10, you can also purchase an even more convenient notebook hard drive enclosure case. Using one of these cases, you can slide the drive into the case and plug the case into the notebook's USB port.

To replace a hard drive, older notebook computers required that you disassemble the notebook. With newer notebooks, you can easily replace a drive. For example, to remove the IBM ThinkPad X20 hard drive, first power down the system and remove the battery

A+ ESS
1.2
2.1

pack. Then remove a coin screw that holds the drive in place (see Figure 20-48). Pull the drive out of its bay, and replace it with a new drive. Next, replace the screw and power up the system.

When the system boots up, if CMOS setup is set to autodetect hard drives, BIOS recognizes the new drive and searches for an operating system. If the drive is new, boot from the Windows recovery CD that came from the notebook manufacturer and install the OS.

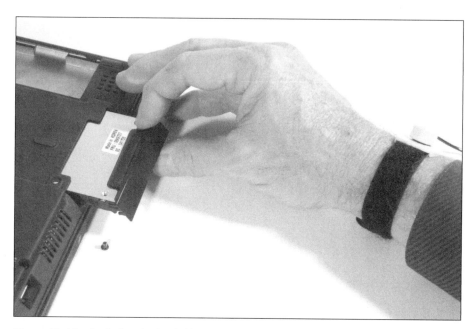

**Figure 20-48** Replacing the hard drive in an IBM ThinkPad X20

Let's look at one more example. To replace the hard drive for the notebook shown in Figure 20-49, first remove the floppy disk drive to reveal the hard drive under it. Remove the screws holding the hard drive in place, remove the drive, and replace it with a drive designed to fit this particular cavity.

> **Notes**
>
> In other chapters, it is possible to give general directions on PC repair that apply to all kinds of brands, models, and systems. Not so with notebooks. Learning to repair notebooks involves learning unique ways to assemble, disassemble, and repair notebook components for specific brands and models of notebooks.

A+ ESS
1.2
2.1

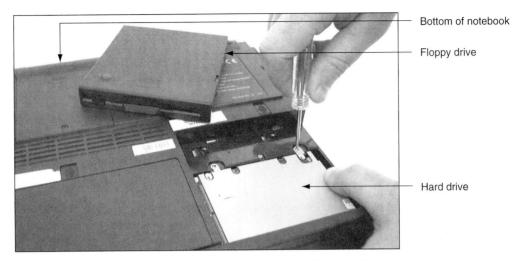

Bottom of notebook

Floppy drive

Hard drive

**Figure 20-49** First remove the floppy drive to reveal the hard drive cavity

A+
220-602
2.1

## REPLACING THE LCD PANEL

Because the LCD panel is so fragile, it is one component that is likely to be broken when a notebook is not handled properly. If the LCD panel is dim or black when the notebook is running, first try to use the video port on the notebook to connect it to an external monitor. After you connect the monitor, use a function key to toggle between the LCD panel, the external monitor, and both the panel and monitor. If the external monitor works, but the LCD panel does not work, then most likely the problem is with the LCD panel assembly.

If the LCD display is entirely black, most likely you'll have to replace the entire LCD assembly. However, if the screen is dim, but you can make out that some display is present, the problem might be the video inverter card, which is the interface between the LCD panel and the motherboard (see Figure 20-50). Check with the notebook manufacturer to confirm that it makes sense to first try replacing just the relatively inexpensive inverter card before you replace the more expensive entire LCD panel assembly. If the entire assembly needs replacing, the cost of the assembly might exceed the value of the notebook.

**Figure 20-50** An IBM ThinkPad video inverter card

Let's first look at the special tools and procedures for disassembling a notebook and then we'll look at how to replace components in the LCD panel assembly.

A+ ESS
1.2
7.1
7.2

A+
220-602
1.2

## DISASSEMBLING A NOTEBOOK

Working on notebooks requires special tools and extra patience. Just as when you are working with desktop systems, before opening the case of a notebook or touching sensitive components, you should always use a ground strap to protect the system against ESD. You can attach the alligator clip end of the ground strap to an unpainted metallic surface on the notebook. This surface could be, for instance, a port on the back of the notebook (see Figure 20-51). If a ground strap is not available, first dissipate any ESD between you and the notebook by touching a metallic unpainted part of the notebook, such as a port on the back before you touch a component inside the case.

A+ ESS
1.2
7.1
7.2

A+
220-602
1.2

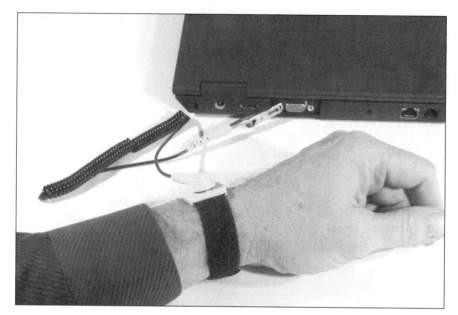

**Figure 20-51**  To protect the system against ESD, attach the alligator clip of a ground strap to an I/O port on the back of the notebook

Screws and nuts on a notebook are smaller than a desktop system and require smaller tools. You will need the following tools to disassemble a notebook, although you can get by without several of them. See Figure 20-52 for a display of some of these tools:

- ◢ Antistatic ground strap
- ◢ Small flat-head screwdriver
- ◢ Number 1 Phillips-head screwdriver
- ◢ Dental pick (useful for prying without damaging plastic cases, connectors, and screw covers such as the one in Figure 20-53)
- ◢ Torx screwdriver set, particularly size T5
- ◢ Something such as a pill box to keep screws and small parts organized
- ◢ Notebook for note taking or digital camera (optional)
- ◢ Flashlight (optional)
- ◢ Three-prong extractor to pick up tiny screws (optional)

**Figure 20-52**  Tools for disassembling a notebook computer

**Figure 20-53** Use a small screwdriver or dental pick to pry up the plastic cover hiding a screw

Notebooks contain many small screws of various sizes and lengths. When reassembling, put screws back where they came from so that when you reassemble the system, you won't use screws that are too long and that can protrude into a sensitive component and damage it. As you remove a screw, store or label it so you know where it goes when reassembling. One way to do that is to place screws in a pill box with each cell labeled. Another way is to place screws on a soft padded work surface and use white labeling tape to label each set of screws. A third way to organize screws is to put them on notebook paper and write beside them where the screw belongs (see Figure 20-54). Whatever method you use, work methodically to keep screws and components organized so you know what goes where when reassembling.

**Figure 20-54** Using a notepad can help you organize screws so you know which screw goes where when reassembling

As you disassemble the computer, if you are not following directions from a service manual, keep notes as you work to help you reassemble later. Draw diagrams and label things carefully. Include in your drawings cable orientations and screw locations. You might consider using a digital camera. Take photos as you work and use the photos to guide you through the reassembly process.

When disassembling a notebook, consider the following tips:

◢ Take your time. Patience is needed to keep from scratching or marring plastic screw covers, hinges, and the case.

◢ As you work, don't force anything. If you find yourself forcing something, you're likely to break it.

◢ Always wear a ground strap or use other protection against ESD.

◢ When removing cables, know that sometimes cable connectors are ZIF connectors. To disconnect a cable from a ZIF connector, first pull up on the connector and then remove the cable, as shown in Figure 20-55. Figure 20-56 shows a notebook using three ZIF connectors that hold the three keyboard cables in place.

◢ Again, use a dental pick or very small screwdriver to pry up the plastic cover hiding a screw.

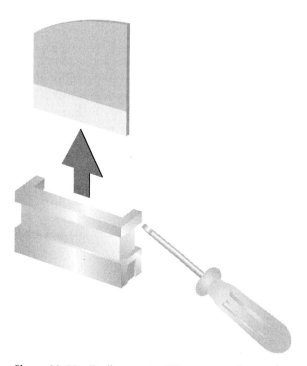

**Figure 20-55**  To disconnect a ZIF connector, first push up on the connector, release the latch, and then remove the cable

A+ ESS
1.2

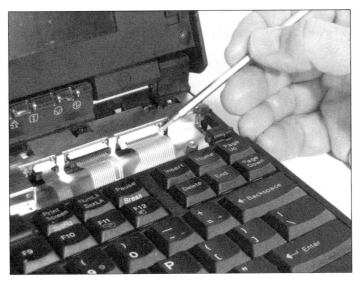

**Figure 20-56** Three ZIF connectors hold the three keyboard cables in place

## HOW TO REPLACE AN LCD PANEL ASSEMBLY

Sometimes, a notebook LCD panel including the entire cover and hinges are considered a single field replaceable unit, and sometimes components within the LCD assembly are considered an FRU. For example, the field replaceable units for the display panel in Figure 20-57 are the LCD front bezel, the hinges, the LCD panel, the inverter card, the LCD interface cables, the LCD USB cover, and the rear cover. Some high-end notebooks contain a video card that has embedded video memory. This video card might also need replacing. In most cases, you would replace only the LCD panel and perhaps the inverter card.

The following are some general directions to replace an LCD panel:

1. Remove the battery pack.

2. For many notebooks, to remove the LCD top cover, you must first remove the keyboard. A keyboard is sometimes removed by first removing screws on the bottom or top of the case and then prying up the keyboard using the edge of a blank key, as shown in Figure 20-58.

3. Sometimes, you must also remove screws in the back of the notebook to release the hinge assembly.

4. Remove the hinge covers; be careful not to break these plastic covers.

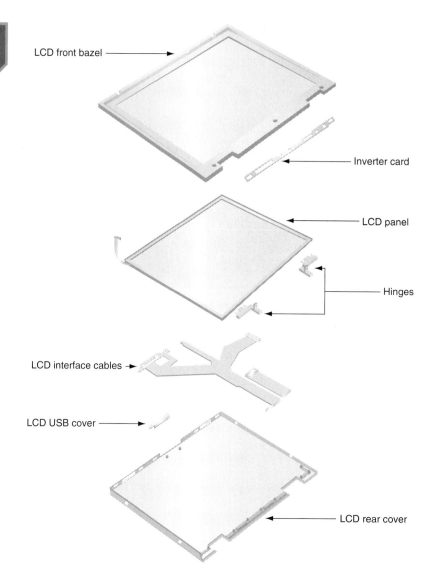

LCD front bazel

Inverter card

LCD panel

Hinges

LCD interface cables

LCD USB cover

LCD rear cover

**Figure 20-57** Components in an LCD assembly

**Figure 20-58** Pry up the keyboard using the edge of a screwdriver on the right of the keyboard

**5.** After you remove the hinge screws, you should then be able to lift the cover off the notebook case (see Figure 20-59).

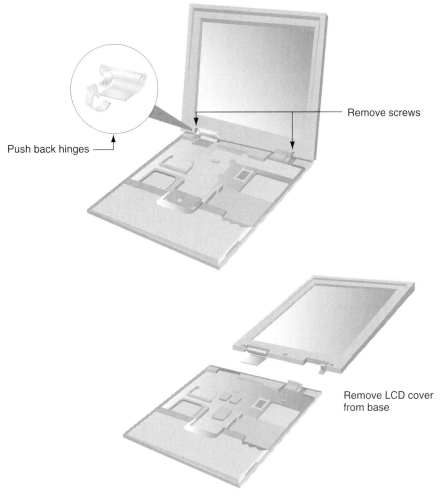

Push back hinges

Remove screws

Remove LCD cover from base

**Figure 20-59** Remove the top LCD cover by first removing hinge screws and disconnecting the hinges; then lift off the cover

**6.** The LCD panel might connect to the notebook case by way of wires running through the hinge assembly, cables, or a pin connector. Cables might be connected to the motherboard using ZIF connectors. As you remove the LCD top cover, be careful to watch for how the panel is connected. Don't pull on wires or cables as you remove the cover, but first carefully disconnect them.

**7.** Next, remove screws that hold the top cover and LCD panel together. Sometimes, these screws are covered with black plastic circles. First use a dental pick or small screwdriver to pick off these covers. You should then be able to remove the front bezel and separate the rear cover from the LCD panel.

**8.** For notebooks that provide a USB connection on the top cover, the cable system might be complex. Carefully remove all connections (see Figure 20-60).

A+ ESS
1.2

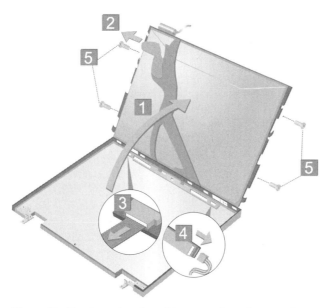

**Figure 20-60** Removing the cable system from the rear of an LCD panel

A+ ESS
1.2
2.1
2.3

## REPLACING A MINI PCI CARD

A notebook does not contain the normal PCI Express, PCI, and ISA expansion slots found in desktop systems. Until recently, most internal cards, such as wired and wireless network adapters, SCSI host adapters, IEEE 1394 controllers, and USB controllers, used proprietary slots designed and supported by the notebook manufacturer. Recently, however, the industry has turned toward a standard method of connecting an internal card to a notebook using the **Mini PCI** specifications, which are based on the PCI industry standard for desktop computer expansion cards, but applied to a much smaller form factor for notebook expansion cards.

The standards include three types of cards—Type I, II, and III—that define how the internal card provides a port on the notebook and how the card connects to the motherboard. Type I and II cards connect to the motherboard using a 100-pin stacking connector, and Type III cards use a 124-pin stacking connector, are smaller than the Type I and II cards, and are expected to be the most popular. Figure 20-61 shows an example of a Mini-PCI card that you install inside a notebook to provide wireless WiFi connectivity.

**Figure 20-61** This Cisco 802.11b wireless internal adapter is a Type III Mini-PCI card made by IBM

Figure 20-62 shows how to remove a Mini PCI wireless network card in a Dell notebook. First, you must remove the hinged cover and the keyboard. Then disconnect the cable to the wireless antenna from the card. Next, pull outward on the securing tabs that hold the card in place. The card will pop up slightly. Lift it out of the cavity.

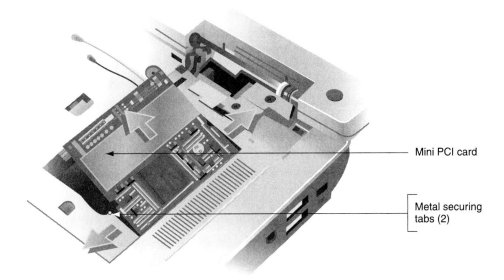

Mini PCI card

Metal securing tabs (2)

**Figure 20-62** Remove a Mini PCI card

To replace the card, align the card in the cavity and press it down until it pops in place. Then reconnect the wireless antenna cable, as shown in Figure 20-63. Replace the keyboard and hinged cover.

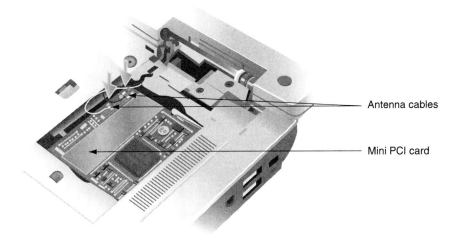

Antenna cables

Mini PCI card

**Figure 20-63** Install a Mini PCI card

## OTHER FIELD REPLACEABLE UNITS FOR NOTEBOOKS

Besides memory, hard drives, LCD panels, and Mini PCI cards, other field replaceable units (FRUs) for notebooks might be the motherboard, the CPU, the keyboard, the PC Card socket assembly, the optical drive (CD or DVD drive), the floppy drive, a sound card, a

A+ ESS
1.2
2.1
2.3

pointing device, the AC adapter, the battery pack, and the DC controller. Parts either made or approved by the notebook manufacturer must be used to replace all these parts. The **DC controller** is a card inside the notebook that converts voltage to CPU core voltage. The DC controller can support battery mode, AC adapter mode, and various sleep modes, and must be specifically rated for the notebook's processor. For more information about disassembling a notebook, see Appendix D.

## TROUBLESHOOTING NOTEBOOKS

A+ ESS
1.3
2.3

A+
220-602
1.2
2.3

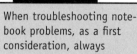

> 📎 **Notes**
>
> When troubleshooting notebook problems, as a first consideration, always remember to protect the user's data and to find out what warranty the notebook might be covered by.

> 🎥 **Video**
>
> Troubleshooting Notebooks

This section contains some general troubleshooting steps to follow when solving problems with notebooks. Problems with software and hardware are covered. As when solving any computer problem, begin by interviewing the user and, if appropriate, backing up any important data. Be sure to keep notes as you go and document what you did and the outcome.

### PROBLEMS WITH THE POWER SYSTEM

Here are some guidelines when troubleshooting problems with the power system:

▲ Check the power light. For many notebooks, a blinking light indicates the notebook has power and is in standby mode. If the power light is steady, the system has power. If the light is off, press the power button.

▲ The battery charge might be depleted. Connect the AC adapter.

▲ The AC adapter might not be solidly connected at both ends. Also check the connectors at the adapter unit, as shown in Figure 20-64.

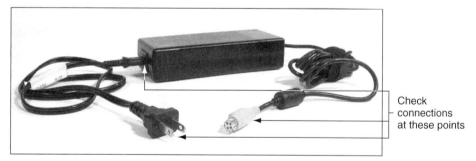

Check connections at these points

**Figure 20-64**  When troubleshooting an AC adapter, check connections at all points

▲ Eliminate power strips or other devices that might cause problems. Connect the AC adapter directly to an electrical outlet.

▲ Note that the memory modules might be defective or loose. Try reseating them.

▲ Too many peripherals might be drawing the system down. Try unplugging all unnecessary devices.

A+ ESS
1.3
2.3

A+
220-602
1.2
2.3

▲ If the system fails only when the AC adapter is connected, it might be defective. Try a new AC adapter, or, if you have a multimeter, use it to verify the voltage output of the adapter. Do the following for an adapter with a single center pin connector:

   ▲ Unplug the AC adapter from the computer, but leave it plugged into the electrical outlet.

   ▲ Using a multimeter set to measure voltage in the 1 to 20 V DC range, place the red probe of the multimeter in the center of the DC connector that would normally plug into the DC outlet on the notebook. Place the black probe on the outside cylinder of the DC connector (see Figure 20-65).

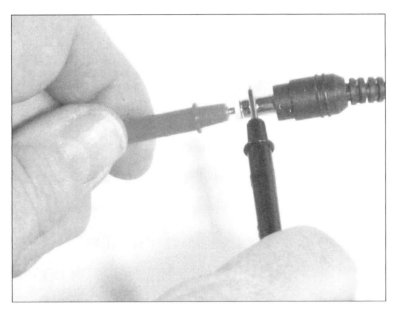

**Figure 20-65** To use a multimeter to test this AC adapter, place the red probe (which, in the image, is in the person's left hand) in the center connector and the black probe on the outside

▲ The voltage range should be plus or minus five percent of the accepted voltage. For example, if a notebook is designed to use 16V, the voltage should measure somewhere between 15.2 and 16.8V DC.

▲ If you boot the notebook and discover CMOS setup has lost configuration information or the date and time are wrong, most likely the small battery inside the case that powers CMOS RAM needs replacing. Notebook manufacturers sometimes call this battery the backup battery or reserve battery. Notebook service manuals will provide instructions to exchange the battery. If you don't have a service manual, and you order the battery from the notebook manufacturer, most likely they will send you the battery along with detailed instructions on how to install it. Before you decide to replace the battery, if you have a multimeter, look on the battery for the voltage output and use the multimeter to determine if the voltage is correct. If not, replace the battery. If backup batteries need replacing often, replace the motherboard.

> **Video**
>
> Troubleshooting a Boot
> Problem 1

▲ Sometimes the backup battery is easy to get to, and sometimes it isn't. Figure 20-66 shows an example of one IBM ThinkPad in which the backup battery is easily accessed by removing a plate on the bottom of the notebook.

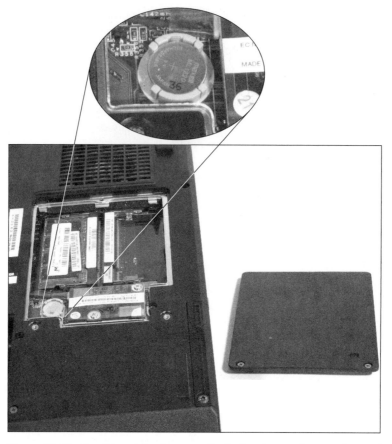

**Figure 20-66** For this notebook, access the backup battery by removing a plate on the bottom of the notebook

---

**Notes**

A backup battery is often a lithium battery, which can explode if not treated correctly. Dispose of a used battery by taking it to a recycle center or following other county regulations for disposing of hazardous waste.

---

**A+ Tip**

The A+ Essentials and A+ 220-602 exams expect you to know how to diagnose and troubleshoot problems with notebook computers.

---

▲ If suspend mode or standby mode does not work, the problem might be a faulty battery, DC controller, or motherboard. Eliminate the battery as the problem by trying suspend mode or standby mode while connected to an electrical outlet. If the problem still persists, first replace the DC controller and then replace the motherboard.

▲ Some notebooks can hold suspend mode for a short time while you exchange a battery pack or install an AC adapter after the battery pack is discharged. These systems use a standby battery. If the standby battery does not work, first try replacing the standby battery, then the DC controller. If this doesn't work and the situation merits having the standby battery function, replace the motherboard.

## PROBLEMS WITH VIDEO

Problems with the video system can be caused by display settings, the power system, or a faulty LCD panel or inverter board. Use Table 20-4 as a starting point to troubleshoot video.

A+ ESS
1.3
2.3

A+
220-602
1.2
2.3

| Problem | What to Do |
|---|---|
| Display is blank | ▲ The problem might be caused by lack of power. Check the power light. Check the battery. Try another electrical outlet. Check the AC adapter. Check the power properties for incorrect settings.<br><br>▲ Does the LCD panel have a cutoff switch that is turned off?<br><br>▲ Perhaps display settings are turned down so low you cannot see the screen. Try using buttons on the keyboard to adjust brightness and contrast. See the user manual to learn how.<br><br>▲ There might be a loose connection. Try reseating the LCD connector inside the notebook.<br><br>▲ The LCD panel or inverter board might be broken. Try connecting a regular monitor to the system using the video port on the back of the notebook. Use a function key to toggle between the monitor and the LCD panel. If the monitor works, consider replacing the LCD assembly. Is the system under warranty?<br><br>▲ The LCD panel might be set too dim, so it's hard to read. Try adjusting the brightness and contrast level. |
| Display is hard to read | ▲ Consider electrical devices that might give interference, such as a powerful speaker system, stereo systems, fans, or halogen or fluorescent lights.<br><br>▲ Is the notebook in direct sunlight? Try eliminating glare.<br><br>▲ Try restoring the refresh rate, resolution, and other Windows display settings to default values. |
| Bright dots, dark dots, bright or dark vertical or horizontal lines, discoloration, dents, or bubbles appear on the LCD panel | ▲ All these symptoms indicate a damaged LCD panel. A few defective dots on an LCD panel (for example, fewer than 11 dots) is considered a cosmetic problem, and notebook manufacturers generally will not replace the LCD panel under warranty. If the problems are disruptive, replace the LCD panel. |
| Screen flickers | ▲ Most likely, display settings need adjusting and the LCD panel is not the problem. |
| LCD contrast and brightness cannot be adjusted | ▲ Try reseating the LCD connector inside the notebook.<br><br>▲ Replace the LCD assembly. |
| LCD panel is unreadable, characters are missing, or incorrect characters appear | ▲ Try reseating the LCD connector inside the notebook.<br><br>▲ Replace the LCD assembly. |

**Table 20-4** Problems with video and what to do about them

If you must replace the LCD panel or inverter board, be certain you purchase the same LCD assembly installed in the notebook. Variations in LCD panels are: some are monochrome; some are color; some have contrast and brightness adjustments; and some don't. In most cases, putting a different LCD assembly in a notebook other than the one it is designed to support will not work.

A+ ESS
1.3
2.3

A+
220-602
1.2
2.3

## A NOTEBOOK GETS WET

To prevent a shock, if a notebook gets wet and is connected to an electrical outlet, turn off the electricity at the circuit breaker before touching the notebook or any cables connected to it. Then do the following:

- ▲ Turn off the computer and disconnect the AC adapter from the computer and from the electrical outlet.
- ▲ Turn off any attached devices such as a printer and disconnect them from the power source.
- ▲ Ground yourself by touching a metal unpainted part of the notebook such as a serial or parallel port on the back of the notebook.
- ▲ Remove any PC Cards or removable drives.
- ▲ Remove the battery pack.
- ▲ Remove the hard drive and memory modules.
- ▲ Open the notebook up and set it across two bricks or books so that air can circulate around it.
- ▲ Allow the notebook and all components to dry for at least 24 hours at room temperature. Don't use a hair dryer or fan to speed up the drying. Don't reassemble the components until you are sure all are dry. Then reinstall the hard drive and memory modules. Connect the notebook to the AC adapter and turn it on. Verify that the notebook is working and then install the battery pack, removable drives, and PC Cards. If the notebook does not work correctly, begin troubleshooting the system that is not working.

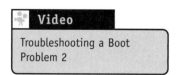

**Video**

Troubleshooting a Boot Problem 2

## THE NOTEBOOK IS DROPPED

If the notebook is dropped, do the following:

- ▲ If the system is still running, save your work and close any open files or applications. Shut down the computer.
- ▲ Disconnect the AC adapter from the notebook and from the electrical outlet.
- ▲ Turn off and disconnect any external devices such as a printer and remove the battery pack.
- ▲ Reinstall the battery pack or the AC adapter and turn on the notebook.
- ▲ If the notebook does not work, begin troubleshooting the system that is not working.

## PROTECTING AND RETRIEVING DATA

**Video**

Recovering Data on a Laptop

Sometimes, the most important component in a notebook computer is the user data. If data is not backed up but the hard drive is not physically damaged, before you begin servicing the system, you can download the data to a hard drive in a desktop system. After the data is safe on another computer, the user can relax and you can focus on getting the notebook working. Follow these steps:

1. Obtain a notebook IDE adapter kit such as the one purchased from PC Cables (*www.pccables.com*, see Figure 20-67), used to install a notebook hard drive in a desktop system.

A+ ESS
1.3
2.3

A+
220-602
1.2
2.3

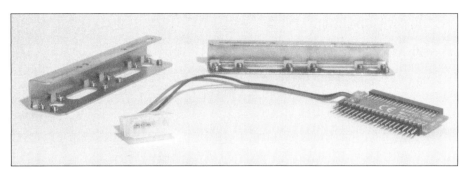

**Figure 20-67** Use an IDE adapter kit to install a notebook hard drive into a desktop system

2. Remove the notebook hard drive from the notebook and connect the adapter to the drive. You can either set the drive on top of the PC case to make the connection or you can use the braces that come with the adapter kit to install the drive in a drive bay in the desktop. Just to copy data from the drive, it's really only necessary to set the drive on top of the desktop case.

3. Copy the data onto a hard drive in the desktop system.

4. If appropriate, you can then put the notebook hard drive back in the notebook to help you troubleshoot the system.

If you must replace the notebook hard drive, you can use the converter kit to install the drive in the desktop system and copy the data from the desktop system onto the new drive, before or after you have installed the OS on the drive.

## MORE ERRORS AND WHAT TO DO ABOUT THEM

Table 20-5 contains a list of common and not-so-common error messages and what to do about them. In addition to this list, error messages given throughout the book that apply to desktop systems also might apply to notebooks. If you receive an error message that is not in the list or you are not familiar with, first check the Web site of the notebook manufacturer or the notebook service manual. Search on the error message to find out what to do. If this doesn't give results, do a general Web search using a search engine.

> **Notes**
>
> Newsgroups can be an interesting source of information when repairing notebooks. Check out the Yahoo newsgroup "laptoprepair" at *groups.yahoo.com/group/Laptop_Repair/*.

A+ ESS
1.3
2.3

A+
220-602
1.2
2.3

| Error Message | What to Do |
| --- | --- |
| Operating system not found | ▲ Remove any bootable devices, such as a floppy disk or CD, and try a reboot. |
| | ▲ Suspect damaged system files on the hard drive. For Windows 2000/XP, try booting to the Advanced Options menu by pressing F8 during the boot. |
| | ▲ Try booting from a support CD or rescue disk for the OS and examine the hard drive for errors. |
| | ▲ Go to CMOS setup and verify that the hard drive is correctly identified. |
| | ▲ Reseat the hard drive. |
| | ▲ Troubleshoot the operating system installed on the hard drive. |
| | ▲ Flash BIOS and then reinstall the operating system. |
| | ▲ Replace the motherboard. |
| Error reading PC Card | ▲ Try reseating the card and rebooting. |
| | ▲ Reinstall the drivers for the PC Card. |
| Keyboard controller error | ▲ Try reseating the internal keyboard cable. |
| | ▲ Try an external keyboard, disabling the internal keyboard. |
| | ▲ Replace the keyboard. |
| Certain keys on the keyboard don't work | ▲ Is the NumLock key set correctly? |
| | ▲ An application might not be configured correctly. Try a different application. |
| One beep and the LCD panel is blank | ▲ Reseat the LCD connectors. |
| | ▲ Replace the LCD panel. |
| | ▲ Replace the motherboard. |
| Wireless connectivity is not working or is weak | ▲ Move the notebook to a better hot spot. |
| | ▲ Is the wireless switch turned on? |
| | ▲ The internal antenna might be loose. Check with the notebook manufacturer for a solution. |
| Touchpad or touch screen does not work | ▲ Are you using the correct type of digital pen? Try rebooting the notebook. |
| | ▲ Check Device Manager for errors. |
| | ▲ Try updating device drivers and flashing BIOS. |
| Intermittent problems | ▲ Intermittent problems might or might not have to do with hardware. Run diagnostic software. If a hardware component fails the diagnostic test, replace it. Then rerun the test. |
| | ▲ Keep detailed records of what happened just before intermittent problems occur. Watch for patterns that might uncover the source of the problem. |
| The system does not detect a PC Card or ExpressCard | ▲ Try a different card. |
| | ▲ Reinstall the PCMCIA drivers. |
| | ▲ Consider using a USB port for external devices rather than depending on the PC Card or ExpressCard slot. |
| | ▲ Replace the PCMCIA assembly. |
| | ▲ Replace the motherboard. |

**Table 20-5**   Error messages and what to do about them

A+ ESS
1.3
2.3

A+
220-602
1.2
2.3

## ONLINE RESOURCES FOR TROUBLESHOOTING NOTEBOOKS

Except for the differences discussed in this section, notebooks work identically to desktop PCs, and the troubleshooting guidelines in previous chapters also apply to notebooks. When troubleshooting notebooks, be especially conscious of warranty issues; know what you can do within the guidelines of the warranty. The documentation that comes with a notebook is much more comprehensive than what comes with a PC and most often contains troubleshooting guidelines for the notebook. Remember that the loaded OS and the hardware configuration are specific to the notebook, so you can rely on the notebook's manufacturer for support more than you can for a desktop PC. Support CDs that come bundled with a notebook include device drivers for all embedded devices. You can also download additional or updated drivers from the notebook manufacturer's Web site.

## *SURVEYING TABLET PCs*

A tablet PC is a type of notebook computer that is designed for users who require a more graphical, user-friendly interface and need more portability than a full-size notebook allows. A tablet PC is a cross between a notebook computer and a pad and pencil. It costs about the same or more than a notebook, but is smaller, more portable, and provides many of the same features of a notebook, plus it lets you use a digital pen or stylus to write handwritten text on the LCD panel, which also serves as a touch screen. See Figure 20-68.

**Figure 20-68** Tablet PC

Tablet PCs come in these forms:

▲ A convertible tablet PC looks like a regular clamshell notebook with LCD monitor and keyboard. To convert to a slate-top tablet PC, rotate the LCD panel 180 degrees and lay the back of the LCD panel flat against the bottom of the notebook. See Figure 20-69.

**Figure 20-69** Acer TMC 110 tablet PC

▲ A slate model tablet PC such as the one shown in Figure 20-68 is slimmer and lighter than a notebook. It can easily dock to a desktop so you can use a regular monitor, mouse, and keyboard.

▲ A tablet PC with a docking station offers some interesting variations such as a grab-and-go docking station that lets you dock or undock your tablet PC without having to power down. (Microsoft calls this feature surprise hot docking.) Another type of docking station has dual-monitor support, which uses a regular monitor for some open applications, while others are shown on the tablet PC's LCD panel.

Using a digital pen, a user can write on the LCD panel/touch screen pad, comfortably resting her hand on it because the pad only picks up data written by the digital pen. Handwriting-recognition software interprets handwriting and can import it into Word documents, Excel spreadsheets, PowerPoint presentations, and other application files. Tablet PCs use Microsoft Windows XP Tablet PC Edition, which is Windows XP Professional with additional features included, such as voice-recognition and handwriting-recognition software. Features of a tablet PC include the following:

▲ A functioning Windows XP computer with the power of a full-sized notebook
▲ Onscreen writing ability for handwritten notes and drawings
▲ Voice-recognition and handwriting-recognition software that can import interpreted text into Word documents, Excel spreadsheets, and other application files
▲ Ability to record handwritten notes on top of other files, such as a handwritten note written on a PowerPoint presentation or photograph (see Figure 20-70)
▲ Built-in support for wireless, wired, and dial-up networking
▲ AC power adapter and rechargeable battery
▲ Windows XP Tablet PC Edition
▲ PC Card, USB ports, and VGA port for peripheral devices
▲ Hardware keyboard or onscreen software keyboard
▲ Accessories might include extra batteries, portfolio-style case, additional flash memory, screen protector, extra digital pens, or wireless keyboard

**Figure 20-70**  Handwritten note on a tablet PC document

Because a tablet PC uses Windows XP Tablet PC Edition operating system, which is an extension of Windows XP Professional, an application written for Windows XP Professional should have no problem working on a tablet PC. Also, many industries have software written specifically for the tablet PC, including real estate, legal, architecture, and medicine. An example of an application written specifically for a tablet PC is OmniForm Filler Solution for the Tablet PC by ScanSoft (*www.scansoft.com*) that uses the handwriting-recognition abilities built into Windows XP Tablet PC Edition to provide the ability to check boxes and radio buttons, select from drop-down lists, and add digital photographs or drawings to forms.

---

## APPLYING|CONCEPTS

As a PC support technician, many times you are called on to help people make good purchasing decisions. Choosing among a notebook, tablet PC, and PDA is most often a function of a user's lifestyle and job description. Here is a good example of a user finding just the right product to fit her needs:

Lacey is a successful real estate agent in a resort town on the Atlantic coast. She has many clients who live in distant cities and often works with these clients in long-distance relationships. Lacey tried to use a notebook computer, but found it awkward to carry a notebook when viewing real estate and working out of her car. She got frustrated with her notebook and sold it at an online auction Web site. Next, she tried using a PDA to track her clients and real estate listings, but the small screen also frustrated her. Then she came across an ad for a tablet PC and bought one. During the first week she owned the tablet PC, she was looking for a beach house for a client who lived in Oklahoma. She found just the right property, but it needed a lot of renovation. She took pictures with her digital camera and uploaded them to her tablet PC. Then she wrote several handwritten notes across each photograph pointing out problems that needed correcting and her ideas for renovation. She e-mailed the entire proposal to her client and made the sale!

Now Lacey has imported into her tablet PC all the forms necessary for a client to list or make an offer on a property. Clients can fill out these forms by hand on her tablet PC while on-site, and Lacey can later convert them to typed text before printing the forms for the client's signature. Lacey also says she can informally take notes at a client meeting on her tablet PC without the raised LCD panel of her old notebook computer standing stiffly between her and her client. She likes being able to appear professional, yet casual and friendly at the same time.

## SURVEYING PDAs

Notebooks and tablet PCs provide portability or flexibility, but even the smallest can be cumbersome in some situations, especially for simple tasks such as checking addresses, viewing stock prices, or recording and receiving short messages. **PDAs (personal digital assistants)**, sometimes called personal PCs or handheld PCs, provide greater ease of use for such situations. Figure 20-71 shows a typical PDA.

**Figure 20-71** Garmin iQue M5 Color Pocket PC PDA and GPS

**Notes**

The GPS (Global Positioning System) is a group of 24 orbiting satellites. A GPS receiver can use signals received from three or more satellites to calculate its position and then use preinstalled software to give directions to a destination.

A PDA, such as a Palm Pilot, Pocket PC, BlackBerry, or Symbian, is a small, handheld computer with its own operating system and applications. A PDA connects to your desktop computer by way of Bluetooth wireless or a USB or serial port and is powered using an AC adapter or battery. Some PDAs come with more than one wireless technology such as Bluetooth (to sync with a notebook), a GPS receiver (to find your position and give directions to a destination), cellular WAN (to serve double duty as a cell phone), and WiFi. A PDA in combination with a cell phone is called a smart phone.

A PDA uses either a grayscale or color LCD panel, and can sometimes benefit from additional memory. Other PDA hardware includes a stylus used to operate the PDA by touching the screen. You tap the screen with the stylus to open applications or make menu selections. You can also hold down the stylus to scroll through menu options. For quick access to commonly used applications such as a calendar or an address book, most PDAs provide application buttons below the screen that you can press to open the application. A PDA might use an AC/DC adapter that can plug into the PDA itself or into the universal cradle. Some PDAs have optional accessories such as the fold-out keyboard shown in Figure 20-72.

— PDA snaps in here

**Figure 20-72**  This fold-out keyboard attaches to a PDA

When purchasing a PDA, first decide how you will use it, and then match the features of the PDA to its intended purpose. Following are the main questions to consider when purchasing a PDA. The next sections cover several of these items.

▲ What applications come with the PDA, and what applications can be added later?
▲ How easy is the PDA to use, and how thorough is its documentation?
▲ How easy is it to keep the PDA synchronized with your desktop computer or notebook, and will your organization approve the type of PDA synchronization?
▲ What support is available on the manufacturer's Web site? What software for the PDA can be downloaded from this site? What is the cost of that software?
▲ What type of batteries does the PDA use, and what is the battery life?
▲ Can the PDA use e-mail and the Web, and what extra hardware and software is required to do that? How much will this service cost?
▲ What additional devices can be purchased to make the PDA more versatile and easier to use?
▲ What operating system does the PDA use? How easy is the OS to use?
▲ What is the warranty? Does the warranty cover such things as dropping the PDA or damaging the LCD panel by pressing too hard on it?
▲ What is the price of the PDA, and what is the price of additional years of warranty?

## BATTERY LIFE ON A PDA

Battery life on a PDA varies by model, and short battery life is one of the largest complaints made about PDAs. Some PDAs use rechargeable batteries, and others do not. If your PDA's battery runs down all the way and discharges, you lose all the data and applications on the PDA! Many manufacturers suggest that you get in the habit of setting your PDA in its cradle whenever you are not carrying it, and that you never trust it with data or downloaded software for more than a few hours. It is a good idea to have a cradle and adapter wherever you use your PDA; you might want to keep one at your home, another at your office, and another in your briefcase.

## APPLICATIONS ON A PDA

You can use a PDA to store addresses and phone numbers, manage a calendar, run word-processing software, send and receive e-mail, access Web sites, play music, find directions using a GPS receiver, and exchange information with a desktop computer. Some PDAs also serve double duty as a cell phone. A PDA can come with all application software preinstalled or require the user to download applications at additional cost. Some PDAs support only the preinstalled applications and cannot download others. Some PDAs allow you to download e-mail or Web site content from a desktop computer or a notebook, and others can access the Internet directly by way of a modem or wireless connection. Not all Web sites are designed to be accessed by a PDA, and the Web content a PDA can read is more limited than the content a desktop or notebook computer can read.

## CONNECTING A PDA TO A PC

Typically, a PDA comes with a universal cradle that has an attached cable to connect to a desktop computer or notebook by way of a USB or serial port, or a PDA might use an infrared or Bluetooth wireless connection. For example, the ASUS MyPal shown in Figure 20-71 supports the Bluetooth standard introduced in Chapter 17.

The process by which the PDA and the PC "talk" to each other through the universal cradle, cable, or wireless connection is called **synchronization**. This process enables you to back up information on your PDA to the PC, work with PDA files on the PC, and download applications to the PDA that you downloaded from the Web using the PC.

> **Notes**
>
> Special software, such as ActiveSync by Microsoft, might be needed to synchronize a PDA and the other computer attached via the cable. You need to install this software before connecting the PDA to the PC. Follow the instructions in the PDA documentation and on the CD included with it to install the software.

To set up communication between a PDA and a PC, do the following:

▲ Read the PDA documentation about how to synchronize it with the PC and install on the PC the synchronization software that came bundled with the PDA. If the synchronization software must first be launched, launch it.

▲ For cable connections, connect the PDA to the PC by way of a USB cable or serial cable that most likely also came bundled with the PDA.

▲ For wireless connections, if the PDA and PC both use the same wireless standard (for example, Bluetooth, infrared, or WiFi), verify they are both set to the same standards, channel, and encryption methods. Also, both PDA and PC wireless abilities must be enabled and switches turned on.

▲ The PDA and PC should immediately synchronize. Data entered on one device should be reflected on the other.

If the PDA and PC have problems communicating, check out and try the following:

▲ Is the USB or serial cable plugged in at both ends?

▲ For a USB connection, verify the USB controller is working in Device Manager with no conflicts.

- Is the USB or serial port enabled in CMOS setup?
- Is the wireless switch turned on? Is wireless software enabled, and does Device Manager correctly recognize the wireless component?
- Is the PDA turned on?
- Check the PDA documentation for other things to do and try.
- Uninstall and reinstall the PDA software on the PC.
- Check the Web site of the PDA manufacturer for problems and solutions.

## PDA MANUFACTURERS AND OPERATING SYSTEMS

Listed below are several operating systems for PDAs, together with the percentage of the market share they had in 2005, as reported by Gartner, Inc. When selecting a PDA, generally, you first decide what applications you intend to use on the PDA and then select the operating system that supports these applications. After you have decided on the applications and the OS, you're ready to select the PDA. Only one OS is installed on a PDA and generally it is not upgraded for the life of the PDA. Here is a list of operating systems used on PDAs:

- *Windows Mobile*. Windows Mobile by Microsoft (*www.microsoft.com*) with 49 percent of the market and increasing. Earlier handheld OSs by Microsoft are Pocket PC and Windows CE. A PDA that uses Windows Mobile is likely to be called a Pocket PC.
- *BlackBerry*. BlackBerry by Research in Motion (*www.rim.com*) with 25 percent of the market and increasing.
- *Palm OS*. Palm OS by Access Co (*www.access-us-inc.com*) with 15 percent of the market and decreasing.
- *Symbian OS*. Symbian OS by Symbian (*www.symbian.com*) with 6 percent of the market and increasing.

These operating systems support both smart phones and PDAs. The principle differences between the OSs are the hardware and applications they support. Windows Mobile is considered the more versatile OS that can better be used to download and run applications similar to those supported by Windows, such as Microsoft Word or Excel. The other OSs are generally tied to the hardware manufacturers of PDAs and smart phones. Table 20-6 lists some manufacturers of PDAs.

> **Notes**
>
> Hewlett-Packard sponsors a forum to promote open source software (programming code is made public and no royalties are paid) to use the Linux operating system on handheld computers. For more information, see *www.handhelds.org*.

| Manufacturer | Web Site |
| --- | --- |
| ASUS | *www.asus.com* |
| Casio | *www.casio.com* |
| Compaq | *www.hp.com* |
| Hewlett-Packard | *www.hp.com* |
| Palm (was PalmOne) | *www.palm.com* |
| Sony | *www.sonystyle.com* |
| Samsung | *www.samsung.com* |

**Table 20-6** Manufacturers of PDAs

## >> CHAPTER SUMMARY

▲ Notebook computers are designed for travel. They use the same technology as desktop computers, with modifications for space, portability, and power conservation. A notebook generally costs more than a desktop with the same specifications.

▲ When supporting notebooks, pay careful attention to what the warranty allows you to change on the computer.

▲ The notebook manufacturer service manual, diagnostic software, and Windows Recovery CD are useful when disassembling, troubleshooting, and repairing a notebook.

▲ A notebook uses a customized installation of the Windows OS, customized by the notebook manufacturer. For most situations, the OS does not need upgrading for the life of the notebook unless you need to use features of a new OS. To perform an upgrade, obtain a customized version of the new OS from the notebook manufacturer.

▲ Windows features useful on notebooks include Multilink Channel Aggregation, power management, PC Card support, Windows 9x/Me Briefcase, and Windows 2000/XP Offline Files, folder redirection, and hardware profiles.

▲ A notebook can be powered by its battery pack or by an AC or DC adapter connected to a power source.

▲ PC Cards are a popular way to add peripheral devices to notebooks. Types of PC Cards that vary in thickness are Types I, II, and III. CardBus cards can be used in PC Card slots. The latest I/O cards are ExpressCard/34 and ExpressCard/54, which are not backward compatible with the PC Card slots.

▲ When an internal component needs replacing, consider the possibility of disabling the component and using an external peripheral device in its place.

▲ Current notebooks use SO-DIMMs and SO-RIMMs for memory. SO-DIMMs can have 72 pins, 144 pins, or 200 pins and SO-RIMMs have 160 pins.

▲ When upgrading components on a notebook, including memory, use components that are the same brand as the notebook, or use only components recommended by the notebook's manufacturer.

▲ Notebook settings and procedures vary more widely from model to model than those of desktop computers. Check the manufacturer's documentation and Web site for information specific to your notebook model.

▲ A tablet PC is a notebook computer with a touch screen that can input handwritten notes, interpreting them as text.

▲ A tablet PC can be a convertible model or a slate model and can come with a docking station that supports surprise hot docking.

▲ Input on a tablet PC can be by handwriting, voice, keyboard, or an onscreen keyboard.

▲ A PDA provides even more portability than a notebook computer or tablet PC for applications such as address books and calendars. PDAs are designed to provide handheld computing power and can interface with a desktop or notebook computer to transfer files and applications.

▲ PDAs synchronize with PCs through a USB, serial, or wireless port. For wireless, check that the PC and PDA support the same wireless standard.

## >> KEY TERMS

For explanations of key terms, see the Glossary near the end of the book.

CardBus
credit card memory
DC controller
docking station
ExpressCard
folder redirection
hardware profiles
laptop computer
MicroDIMM

Mini PCI
notebook
PC Card
PC Card slot
PCMCIA (Personal Computer
    Memory Card International
    Association) Card
PCMCIA slot
PDA (personal digital assistant)

port replicator
shared memory
SO-DIMM (small outline
    DIMM)
SO-RIMM (small outline
    RIMM)
synchronization
video sharing

## >> REVIEW QUESTIONS

1. Which of the following is true about notebook computers?

   a. The price of a notebook computer is about the same as a comparable desktop system.

   b. The speed of notebooks is about the same as a desktop.

   c. The main advantage a notebook has over a desktop is portability.

   d. It is easy to upgrade notebooks.

2. Which of the following features allows you to use two modem connections at the same time to speed up data throughput when connected over phone lines?

   a. Channel aggregation

   b. Power management

   c. Windows 9x/Me Briefcase

   d. Support for PC Cards

3. Which of the following types of PCMCIA slots has the highest standard and can accommodate a portable disk drive?

   a. Type I.

   b. Type II.

   c. Type III.

   d. All types have the same standard.

4. Which of the following needs to be considered before making the decision to upgrade or repair an internal component?

   a. Ground yourself by using an antistatic ground strap.

   b. Return the notebook to the manufacturer or another service center for repair.

   c. Unplug the AC adapter and remove the battery pack before working inside a notebook case.

   d. If the notebook is attached to a port replicator or docking station, release it to undock the computer.

5. Which of the following refers to a card inside the notebook that converts voltage to CPU core voltage?

   **a.** PC Card socket assembly

   **b.** AC adapter

   **c.** Optical drive

   **d.** DC controller

6. True or false? A notebook warranty often applies to all components in the system and can be voided if someone other than an authorized service center services the notebook.

7. True or false? A supervisor password or a user password (also called a power-on password) will protect the hard drive's data if the hard drive is removed and installed in another notebook.

8. True or false? A port replicator provides a means to connect a notebook to a power outlet and provides additional ports to allow a notebook to easily connect to a full-sized monitor, keyboard, and other peripheral devices.

9. True or false? The process by which the PDA and the PC "talk" to each other through the universal cradle, cable, or wireless connection is called synchronization.

10. True or false? A bug in Windows XP causes the system to hang if you remove a PC Card while the system is in sleep mode or is hibernating.

11. Making the location of a folder transparent to the user by pointing to an alternate location on a network (for the folder) is called _____.

12. Use _____ to specify which devices are to be loaded on startup for a particular user or set of circumstances.

13. A(n) _____ provides the same functions as a port replicator, but also adds secondary storage, such as an extra hard drive, a floppy drive, or a DVD drive.

14. Removing one PC Card or ExpressCard and inserting another without powering down is called _____.

15. Using regular RAM for video is called _____ or shared memory.

# Supporting Printers and Scanners

**T**his chapter discusses the most popular types of printers, how they work, and how to support them. You'll also learn about supporting scanners. As you work through the chapter, you'll learn how to install a printer and scanner and how to share a printer with others on a network. Then, you'll learn about maintaining printers and scanners and troubleshooting printer and scanner problems.

# HOW PRINTERS AND SCANNERS WORK

A+ ESS
4.1

A+
220-602
4.1

Local printers and scanners connect directly to a computer by way of a USB port, parallel port, serial port, wireless connection (Bluetooth, infrared, or WiFi), IEEE 1394 (FireWire) port, SCSI port, PC Card, or ExpressCard connection, or a computer can access a network printer by way of the network. Some printers support more than one method. Printers can also be combined with fax machines, copiers, and scanners in the same machine. Most often, printers and scanners are powered by AC power or by using an AC adapter that converts power to DC. In addition, some printers are battery powered.

Printers can have a variety of options, including extra paper trays to hold different sizes of paper, special paper feeders or transparency feeders, staplers, collators, and sorters. Printers can print in color or black and white, and printers can print on one side of the page or automatically print on both sides (called duplex printing). Besides these features, printers are rated by the time it takes for the first page to print (warm-up time), the resolution (for example, 1200 × 1200 dpi), the maximum pages printed per month so as not to void the warranty (called the maximum duty cycle), the printing speed (for example, 35 PPM or 35 pages per minute), and the technology the printer uses to format a page before it is printed (choices are PCL, PostScript, and GDI).

 **A+ Tip**

The A+ Essentials exam expects you to know that printers and scanners can connect using these interfaces: parallel, network, USB, SCSI, serial, IEEE 1394 (FireWire), and wireless (Bluetooth, 802.11, and infrared).

**Notes**

If you can afford it, the best practice is to purchase one machine for one purpose instead of bundling many functions into a single machine. For example, if you need a scanner and a printer, purchase a good printer and a good scanner rather than a combo machine. Routine maintenance and troubleshooting are easier and less expensive on single-purpose machines, although the initial cost is higher.

There are two major categories of printers: impact printers and nonimpact printers. An impact printer creates a printed page by using some mechanism that touches or hits the paper. An example of an impact printer is a dot matrix printer. A nonimpact printer does not use a mechanism to touch the page. Examples of nonimpact printers are laser, ink-jet (ink dispersion), solid ink, dye sublimation, and thermal printers. In the following sections, we'll look at the different types of printers for desktop computing. Then we'll look at how a scanner works.

## LASER PRINTERS

A **laser printer** is a type of electrophotographic printer that can range from a small, personal desktop model to a large, network printer capable of handling and printing large volumes continuously. Figure 21-1 shows an example of a typical laser printer for a desktop computer system.

 **A+ Exam Tip**

The A+ Essentials exam expects you to be familiar with these types of printers: laser, ink-jet, solid ink, thermal, and impact.

Laser printers require the interaction of mechanical, electrical, and optical technologies to work. Understanding how they work will help you support and service them. You'll also learn how to protect yourself and the printer while you work on it.

**Figure 21-1** A desktop laser printer

Laser printers work by placing toner on an electrically charged rotating drum and then depositing the toner on paper as the paper moves through the system at the same speed the drum is turning. Figure 21-2 shows the six steps of laser printing. The first four use the printer components that undergo the most wear. These components are contained within the removable cartridge to increase the printer's life. The last two steps are performed outside the cartridge.

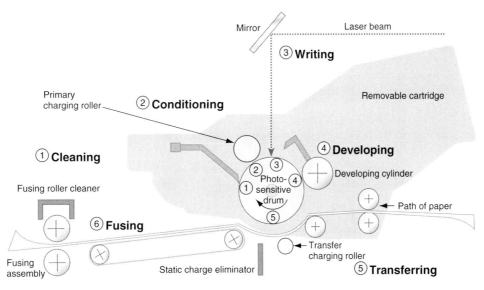

**Figure 21-2** The six progressive steps of laser printing

Note that Figure 21-2 shows only a cross-section of the drum, mechanisms, and paper. Remember that the drum is as wide as a sheet of paper. The mirror, blades, and rollers in the drawing are also as wide as paper. Also know that toner responds to a charge and moves from one surface to another if the second surface has a more positive charge than the first.

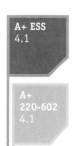

**A+ Tip**

The A+ Essentials exam expects you to know the six steps in the printing process for a laser printer.

As you read about and visualize the process, first note the location of the removable cartridge in the drawing, the photosensitive drum inside the cartridge turning in a clockwise direction, and the path of the paper, which moves from right to left.

The six steps of laser printing are described next.

### STEP 1: CLEANING

In the cleaning step, shown in Figure 21-3, the drum is cleaned of any residual toner and electrical charge. First, a sweeper strip cleans the drum of any residual toner, which is swept away by a sweeping blade. A cleaning blade completes the physical cleaning of the drum. Next, the drum is cleaned of any electrical charge by erase lamps in the hinged top cover of the printer. The lamps light the surface of the drum to neutralize any electrical charge left on it.

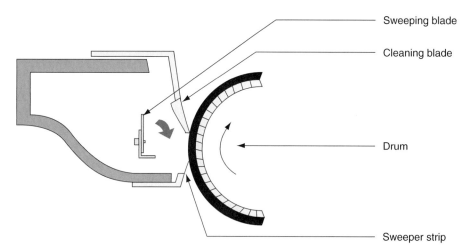

Sweeping blade

Cleaning blade

Drum

Sweeper strip

**Figure 21-3** The cleaning step cleans the drum of toner and electrical charge

### STEP 2: CONDITIONING

In the conditioning step, the drum is conditioned to contain a high electrical charge. A uniform electrical charge of –600 V is put on the surface of the drum. The charge is put there by a primary charging roller or primary corona, which is charged by a high-voltage power supply assembly. The primary charging roller in Figure 21-2 is inside the toner cartridge and regulates the charge on the drum, ensuring that it is a uniform –600 V.

### STEP 3: WRITING

In the writing step, a laser beam discharges a lower charge only to places where toner should go. The uniform charge applied in Step 2 is discharged only where you want the printer to print. This is done by controlling mirrors to reflect laser beams onto the drum in a pattern that re-creates the image desired. This is the first step in which data from the computer must be transmitted to the printer. Figure 21-4 shows the process. Data from the PC is received by the formatter (1) and passed on to the DC controller (2), which controls the laser unit (3). The laser beam is initiated and directed toward the octagonal mirror called the **scanning mirror**. The scanning mirror (4) is turned by the scanning motor in a clockwise direction. There are eight mirrors on the eight sides of the scanning mirror. As the mirror turns, the laser beam is directed in a sweeping motion that can cover the entire length of the drum. The laser beam is reflected off the scanning mirror, focused by the focusing lens (5), and sent on to the mirror (6), which is also shown in Figure 21-2. The mirror deflects the laser beam to a slit in the removable cartridge and onto the drum (7).

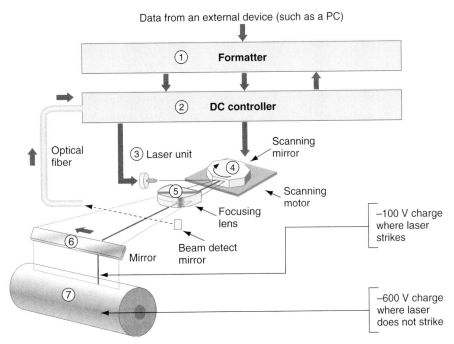

**Figure 21-4** The writing step, done by an invisible laser beam, mirrors, and motors, causes a discharge on the drum where the images will be

The speed of the motor turning the drum and the speed of the scanning motor turning the scanning mirror are synchronized so that the laser beam completes one pass, or scanline, across the drum and returns to the beginning of the drum (right side of the drum in Figure 21-4) to begin a new pass, until it completes the correct number of passes for each inch of the drum circumference. For example, for a 1200 dots per inch (dpi) printer, the beam makes 1200 passes for every one inch of the drum circumference. The laser beam is turned on and off continually as it makes a single pass down the length of the drum, so that dots are written along the drum on every pass. For a 1200-dpi printer, 1200 dots are written along the drum for every inch of linear pass. The 1200 dots per inch down this single pass, combined with 1200 passes per inch of drum circumference, accomplish the resolution of 1200 × 1200 dots per square inch of many desktop laser printers.

> **Notes**
>
> A laser printer can produce better-quality printouts than a dot matrix printer, even when printing at the same dpi, because it can vary the size of the dots it prints, creating a sharp, clear image. Hewlett-Packard (HP) calls this technology of varying the size of dots **REt (Resolution Enhancement technology)**.

In a laser printer, where the laser beam strikes the surface of the drum, the drum discharges from its conditioned charge of –600 V down to –100 V where toner will be placed on the drum. Toner does not stick to the highly charged areas of the drum.

Just as the scanning laser beam is synchronized to the rotating drum, the data output is synchronized to the scanning beam. Before the beam begins moving across the scanline of the drum, the **beam detect mirror** detects the laser beam by reflecting it to an optical fiber. The light travels along the optical fiber to the DC controller, where it is converted to an electrical signal that synchronizes the data output. The signal is also used to diagnose problems with the laser or scanning motor.

The laser beam has written an image to the drum surface as a –100 V charge. The –100 V charge on this image area will be used in the developing stage to transmit toner to the drum surface.

## STEP 4: DEVELOPING

Figure 21-5 shows the developing step, in which toner is placed on the drum where the charge has been reduced. Toner is applied by the developing cylinder to the discharged (–100 V) areas of the drum. Toner transfers from the cylinder to the drum as the two rotate very close together. The cylinder is coated with a layer of toner, made of black resin bonded to iron, which is similar to the toner used in photocopy machines. The toner is held on the cylinder surface by its attraction to a magnet inside the cylinder. (A toner cavity keeps the cylinder supplied with toner.) A **control blade** prevents too much toner from sticking to the cylinder surface. The toner on the cylinder surface takes on a negative charge (between –200 V and –500 V) because the surface is connected to a DC power supply, called the DC bias.

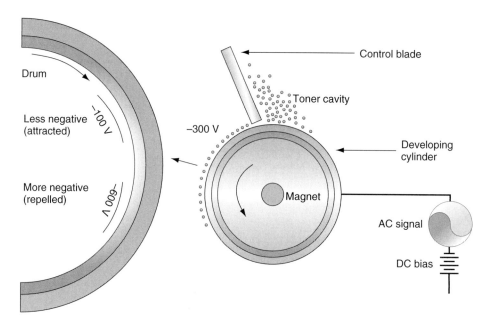

**Figure 21-5** In the developing step, charged toner is deposited onto the drum surface

The negatively charged toner is more negative than the –100 V on the drum surface but less negative than the –600 V surface. This means that the toner is attracted to the –100 V area of the drum surface (the –100 V area is positive relative to the toner). The toner is repelled from the –600 V part of the drum surface, which is negative relative to the toner. The result is that toner sticks to the drum where the laser beam has hit and is repelled from the area where the laser beam has not hit.

You can adjust printer density manually at the printer or through software controlling the printer. When you adjust print density with laser printers, you are adjusting the DC bias charge on the developing cylinder, which controls the amount of toner attracted to the cylinder; this, in turn, results in a change in print density.

## STEP 5: TRANSFERRING

In the transferring step (shown in Figure 21-2), a strong electrical charge draws the toner off the drum onto the paper. This is the first step that takes place outside the cartridge. The transfer charging roller, or transfer corona, produces a positive charge on the paper that pulls the toner from the drum onto the paper when it passes between the transfer charging roller and the drum. The static charge eliminator (refer again to Figure 21-2) weakens the positive charge on the paper and the negative charge on the drum so that the paper does not adhere to the drum, which it would otherwise do because of the difference in charge between the two. The stiffness of the paper and the small radius of the drum also help the paper move away from the drum and toward the fusing assembly. Very thin paper can wrap around the drum, which is why printer manuals usually instruct you to use only paper designated for laser printers.

## STEP 6: FUSING

The fusing step uses heat and pressure to fuse the toner to the paper. Up to this point, the toner is merely sitting on the paper. The fusing rollers apply heat to the paper, which causes the toner to melt, and the rollers apply pressure to bond the melted toner into the paper. The temperature of the rollers is monitored by the printer. If the temperature exceeds an allowed maximum value (410 degrees F for some printers), the printer shuts down.

The previous steps describe how a black-and-white printer works. Color laser printers work in a similar way, but the writing process repeats four times, one for each toner color of cyan, magenta, yellow, and black. Then, the paper passes to the fusing stage, when the fuser bonds all toner to the paper and aids in blending the four tones to form specific colors.

## INK-JET PRINTERS

Ink-jet printers use a type of ink-dispersion printing and don't normally provide the high-quality resolution of laser printers, but are popular because they are small and can print color inexpensively. Most ink-jet printers today give photo-quality results, especially when used with photo-quality paper.

Earlier ink-jet printers used 300 × 300 dpi, but ink-jet printers today can use up to 4800 × 1200 dpi. Increasing the dpi has drawbacks. It increases the amount of data sent to the printer for a single page, and all those dots of ink can produce a wet page. An improved technology that gives photo-quality results mixes different colors of ink to produce a new color that then makes a single dot. Hewlett-Packard calls this PhotoREt II color technology. HP mixes as many as 16 drops of ink to produce a single dot of color on the page.

Ink-jet printers tend to smudge on inexpensive paper, and they are slower than laser printers. If a printed page later gets damp, the ink can run and get quite messy. The quality of the paper used with ink-jet printers significantly affects the quality of printed output. You should use only paper that is designed for an ink-jet printer, and you should use a high-grade paper to get the best results. Figure 21-6 shows one example of an ink-jet printer.

An ink-jet printer uses a print head that moves across the paper, creating one line of text with each pass. The printer puts ink on the paper using a matrix of small dots. Different types of ink-jet printers form their droplets of ink in different ways. Printer manufacturers use several technologies, but the most popular is the bubble-jet. Bubble-jet printers use tubes of ink that have tiny resistors near the end of each tube. These resistors heat up and cause the ink to boil. Then, a tiny air bubble of ionized ink (ink with an electrical charge) is ejected onto the paper. A typical bubble-jet print head has 64 or 128 tiny nozzles, all of which can fire a droplet simultaneously. (High-end printers can have as many as 3,000 nozzles.) Plates carrying a magnetic charge direct the path of ink onto the paper to form shapes.

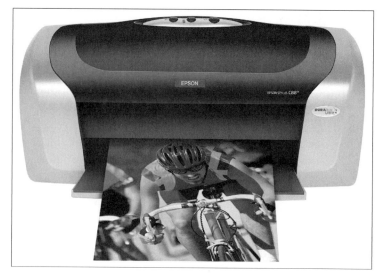

**Figure 21-6** An example of an ink-jet printer

Ink-jet printers include one or more ink cartridges. When purchasing an ink-jet printer, look for the kind that uses two or four separate cartridges. One cartridge is used for black ink. In addition, some color printers use one cartridge for three-color printing (colors are yellow, blue, and red, better known as yellow, cyan, and magenta, sometimes written as CcMmY). Other less-expensive printers use three separate color cartridges. Some low-end ink-jet printers use a single three-color cartridge and don't have a black ink cartridge. These printers must combine all colors of ink to produce a dull black. Having a separate cartridge for black ink means that it prints true black and, more important, does not use the more expensive colored ink. To save money, you should be able to replace an empty cartridge without having to replace all cartridges.

Figure 21-7 shows two ink cartridges. The black cartridge is on the left and the three-color cartridge is on the right. The print head assemblage moves across the page as it prints. When not in use, the assemblage sits in the far-right position shown in the figure, which is called the home position. This position helps protect the ink in the cartridges from drying out.

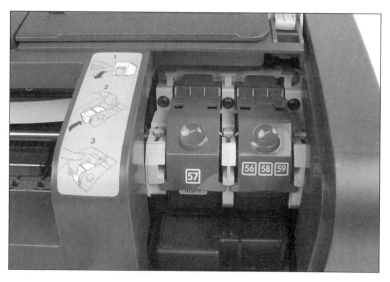

**Figure 21-7** The ink cartridges of an ink-jet printer

A+ ESS
4.1

A+
220-602
4.1

## DOT MATRIX PRINTERS

Dot matrix printers are almost nonexistent now because they have been replaced with ink-jet or laser printers. The two reasons you still see some around are: (1) they are impact printers and can print multicopy documents, which some businesses still find useful: and (2) they last forever. A dot matrix printer has a print head that moves across the width of the paper, using pins to print a matrix of dots on the page. The pins shoot against a cloth ribbon, which hits the paper, depositing the ink. The ribbon provides both the ink for printing and the lubrication for the pinheads.

Occasionally, you should replace the ribbon of a dot matrix printer. If the print head fails, check on the cost of replacing the head versus the cost of buying a new printer. Sometimes, the cost of the head is so high, it's best to just buy a new printer. Overheating can damage a print head (see Figure 21-8), so keep it as cool as possible to make it last longer. Keep the printer in a cool, well-ventilated area, and don't use it to print more than 50 to 75 pages without allowing the head to cool down.

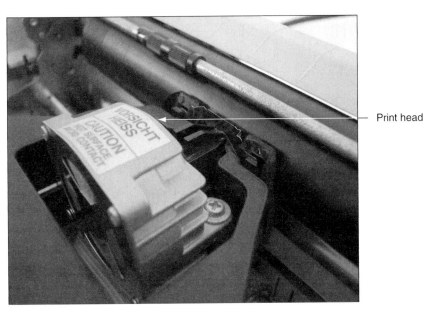

Print head

**Figure 21-8**  Keep the print head of a dot matrix printer as cool as possible so that it will last longer

## THERMAL PRINTERS AND SOLID INK PRINTERS

Two similar and relatively new technologies are thermal printers and solid ink printers. Both are nonimpact printers that use heat to produce printed output. **Thermal printers** use wax-based ink that is heated by heat pins that melt the ink onto paper. The print head containing these heat pins is as wide as the paper. The internal logic of the printer determines which pins get heated to produce the printed image. Thermal printers are popular in retail applications for printing bar codes and price tags. A thermal printer can burn dots onto special paper, as done by older fax machines (called direct thermal printing), or the printer can use a ribbon that contains the wax-based ink (called thermal wax transfer printing).

One variation of thermal printing uses thermal dye sublimation technology to print identification cards and access cards. A **dye-sublimation printer** uses solid dyes embedded on different transparent films. As the print head passes over each color film, it heats up, causing the dye to vaporize onto the glossy surface of the paper. Because the dye is vaporized onto the paper rather than jetted at it, the results are more photo-lab quality than with ink-jet printing.

**Solid ink printers** such as the Xerox Phaser 8550 shown in Figure 21-9 use ink stored in solid blocks, which Xerox calls color sticks. The sticks or blocks are easy to handle and several can be inserted in the printer to be used as needed, avoiding the problem of running out of ink in the middle of a large print job. The solid ink is melted into the print head, which spans the width of the paper. The head jets the liquid ink onto the paper as it passes by on a drum. The design is simple, print quality is excellent, and solid ink printers are easy to set up and maintain. The greatest disadvantage to solid ink printing is the time it takes for the print head to heat up to begin a print job, which is about 15 minutes. For this reason, some solid ink printers anticipate that a print job might be coming based on previous use of the printer, and automatically heat up.

**Figure 21-9**    Phaser 8550 solid ink printer by Xerox

Table 21-1 lists some printer manufacturers.

| Printer Manufacturer | Web Site |
|---|---|
| Brother | www.brother.com |
| Canon | usa.canon.com |
| Hewlett-Packard | www.hp.com |
| IBM | www.ibm.com |
| Lexmark | www.lexmark.com |
| Okidata | www.okidata.com |
| SATO | www.satoamerica.com |
| Seiko Epson | www.epson.com |
| Tally Genicom | www.tallygenicom.com |
| Xerox | www.xerox.com |

**Table 21-1**    Printer manufacturers

## INTRODUCING SCANNERS

A **scanner** is a device that allows a computer to convert a picture, drawing, bar code, or other image into digital data that can be input into the computer as a file. Some scanners have embedded optical character recognition (OCR) software that can interpret written text so that the text scanned in can be input into a word-processing program such as Microsoft Word.

Basically, there are three types of scanners:

- ◢ A flat-bed scanner has a glass bed on which you place a sheet of paper. Then, the scanning head moves across the glass, scanning the page. Figure 21-10 shows an example of a flat-bed scanner. One advantage of using a flat-bed scanner over a sheet-fed scanner is that you can scan pages in books and additional types of media other than single sheets of paper.

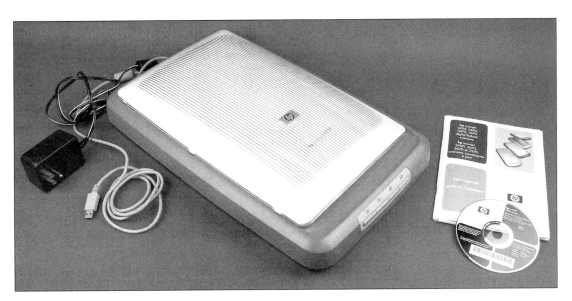

**Figure 21-10**   The HP Scanjet 3970 is a type of flat-bed scanner

- ◢ A sheet-fed scanner pulls a sheet of paper through the scanner mechanism similar to the way a fax machine works. In fact, a fax machine is actually a sheet-fed scanner in combination with a modem. Some high-end scanners are a combination sheet-fed and flat-bed scanner such as the one shown in Figure 21-11.
- ◢ A portable or handheld scanner can be a bar-code scanner or a sheet-fed scanner. You learned about bar-code scanners in Chapter 9. Figure 21-12 shows one example of a portable sheet-fed scanner that is designed to scan receipts and business cards and is useful for a traveling (and well-organized) businessperson.

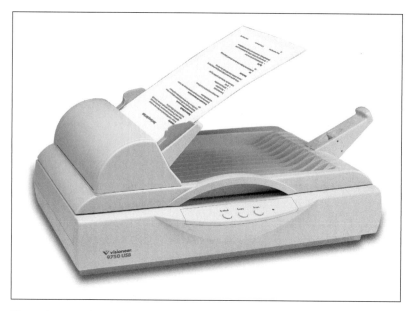

**Figure 21-11** A combination flat-bed and sheet-fed scanner by Visioneer (*www.visioneer.com*)

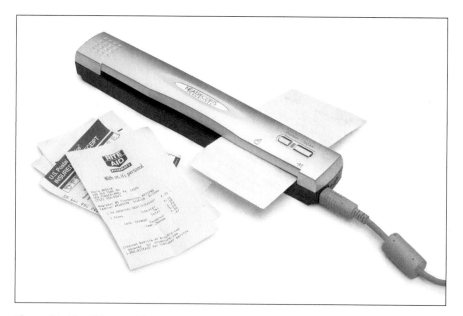

**Figure 21-12** This portable scanner is a type of sheet-fed scanner useful for travelers to input receipts and business cards into a database

Besides the type of scanner, other features to look for when shopping for a scanner include:

▲ *Scanning speed.* How fast the scanner can scan is especially important if the scanner is to be used for high-volume input. Also, for high volume input, some sheet-fed scanners are stack loading, which means that you can put in a stack of paper and let it scan the entire stack as does a copier or fax machine.

▲ *Scanner resolution.* An example of scanner resolution is 400 dpi (dots per inch).

▲ *Scanning mode.* The scanning mode might be color, black and white, or grayscale. The best scanners work in all three modes.

▲ *Preview mode.* Most flat-bed scanners have a preview mode so that you can scan in a preview of the page and then select that portion of the page you want to include in the final scan.

▲ *Bundled software.* Examples of bundled software are OCR software and image-editing software.

▲ *Maximum document size.* The maximum document size might be $8\frac{1}{2} \times 11$ or larger.

▲ *File formats.* The file formats that the image can be saved into might be JPEG, TIFF, PDF, GIF, HTML, and others.

▲ *Connection to PC.* The type of connection to the PC a scanner uses might be a USB, FireWire, or SCSI connection. Some older scanners use a serial or parallel port connection.

A flat-bed scanner works by using a motor that moves the scanning head across the paper laid on the glass bed of the scanner, as shown in Figure 21-13. A type of fluorescent lamp is used to provide light under the glass that shines on the page. Reflected light is diverted by a series of mirrors into a lens. The lens focuses the light onto a series of diodes that converts the light into electrical current. At the heart of a scanner is this array of diodes called a CCD (charge-coupled device) array that senses light and converts it to electricity. The varying amounts of current are then digitized and sent to the PC where it is translated into a graphics file. If OCR software is involved, this software on the PC converts the graphics file into a text file.

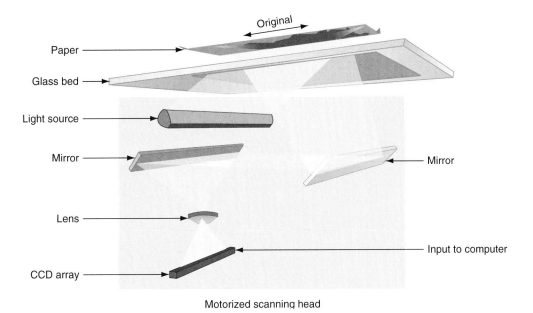

**Figure 21-13** How a flat-bed scanner works

Also, for some less-expensive scanners, the light source and CCD array are replaced by a series of light-emitting diodes (LEDs) that produce the light, and a contact image sensor (CIS) converts the reflected light to electricity. Therefore, the two major technologies used by scanners are CCD (higher quality) and CIS (lower quality).

# INSTALLING AND SHARING A PRINTER

A+ ESS
3.1
3.2
4.2

A+
220-602
4.2

When a printer is connected to a port on a computer, the computer can share the printer with others on the network. There are also network printers with Ethernet ports that can connect the printer directly to the network.

Each computer on a network that uses the printer must have printer drivers installed so the OS on each computer can communicate with the printer and provide the interface between applications it supports and the printer. This section covers how to install a local printer and how to share that printer with others on the network.

> **Notes**
>
> As you go through this part of the chapter, remember that a printer connected to a computer by way of a port on the computer is called a **local printer**, and a printer accessed by way of a network is called a **network printer**. A computer can have several printers installed. Of these, Windows designates one printer to be the **default printer**, which is the one Windows prints to unless another is selected.

> **A+ Exam Tip**
>
> The A+ Essentials and A+ 220-602 exams expect you to know how to install a local and network printer.

## INSTALLING A LOCAL PRINTER

Installing a local printer begins differently depending on the type of port you are using. For hot-pluggable ports such as a FireWire, USB, PC Card, ExpressCard, or wireless connection, you need to first install the software before connecting the printer. Remember that when using a hot-pluggable port, you don't need to power down a computer before plugging in or unplugging a hot-pluggable device. Follow these steps to install a local printer using a hot-pluggable port:

1. Log onto the system as an administrator. Begin the installation by running the setup program that came on the CD bundled with the printer before you install the printer. If you don't have the CD, download the printer drivers from the printer manufacturer Web site and then execute that downloaded program. The setup program installs the drivers. For one HP printer, the setup program shows its progress in a window shown in Figure 21-14. Follow the directions onscreen to complete the printer installation.

2. At one point in the setup, you will be told to connect the printer (see Figure 21-15). Connect the printer to the port. For this printer, a USB port is used. For wireless printers, verify that the software for the wireless connection on your PC is installed and the wireless connection is enabled. For infrared wireless printers, place the printer in line of sight of the infrared port on the PC. (Most wireless printers have a status light that stays lit when a wireless connection is active.) Turn on the printer.

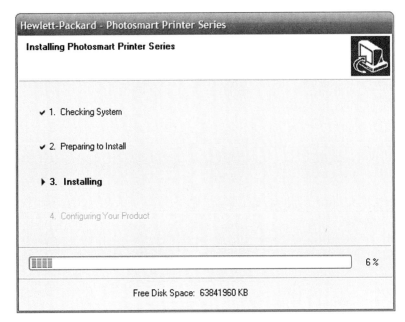

**Figure 21-14** The printer setup program installs the drivers

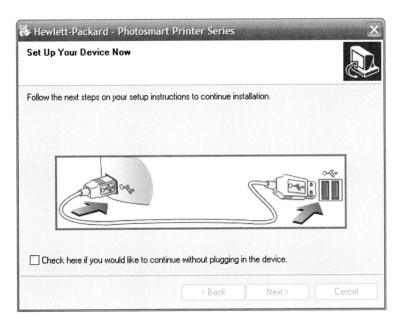

**Figure 21-15** The printer setup program tells you when to connect the printer

3. The setup program detects the printer and tells you so, as shown in Figure 21-16. If Windows launches the Found New Hardware Wizard, it should close quickly. If not, cancel the wizard.

4. The setup program asks if you want this printer to be the default printer (see Figure 21-17). Click Yes or No to make your selection. The setup program finishes the installation.

5. You can now test the printer. For Windows XP, open the Printers and Faxes window by clicking **Start, Control Panel,** and **Printers and Faxes** (in Classic view) or **Printers and Other Hardware** (in Category view). The Printers and Faxes window opens

A+ ESS
3.1
3.2
4.2

A+
220-602
4.2

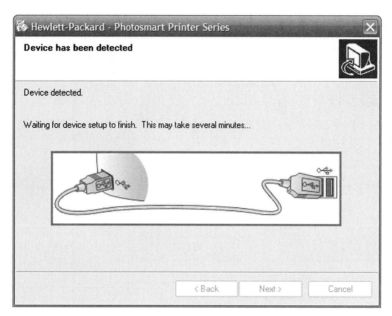

**Figure 21-16** The printer setup program detects the printer

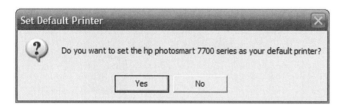

**Figure 21-17** During the printer setup, you are asked if this printer will be the default printer

(see the left side of Figure 21-18). For Windows 2000 and Windows 98, click **Start, Settings,** and **Printers** to open the Printers window. Right-click the printer and select **Properties** from the shortcut menu. Click the **General** tab and then click the **Print Test Page** button, as shown on the right side of Figure 21-18.

6. Show the user how to use the printer and any add-ons. These add-ons include feeders, sorters, and staplers. In addition, show the user how to install paper and envelopes in the various paper trays. Let the user know whom to contact if printer problems arise. You might also consider providing a means for the user to record problems with the printer that don't require immediate attention. For example, you can hang a clipboard and paper close to the printer for the user to write questions that you can address at a later time.

Here are the directions to install a local printer using an older port, such as a SCSI, serial, or parallel port, that is not hot-pluggable:

1. Plug in the printer to the port and turn on the printer. Now, you must decide how you want to install the drivers. You can use the setup program from the printer manufacturer or use the Windows installation process. First try using the setup program that came on the printer's setup CD or downloaded from the manufacturer's Web site. If you have problems with the installation, you can then try the Windows approach.

2. To use the manufacturer's installation program, launch the printer setup program from the printer setup CD or downloaded from the manufacturer's Web site and follow the directions onscreen to install the printer.

21

A+ ESS
3.1
3.2
4.2

A+
220-602
4.2

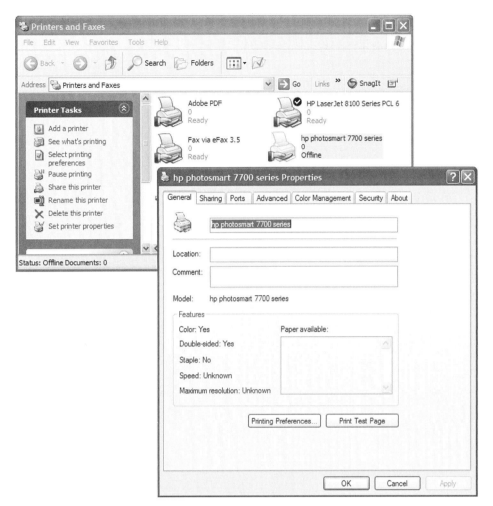

**Figure 21-18** To verify a printer installation, always print a test page as the last step in the installation

3. Alternatively, you can use the Windows installation process to install the printer drivers. For Windows XP, open the Printers and Faxes window, or for Windows 2000 and Windows 98, open the Printers window. Click **Add a Printer**. The Add Printer Wizard launches, shown in Figure 21-19. Follow the directions onscreen to install the printer drivers.

4. To test the printer after it is installed, in the Printers and Faxes window or the Printers window, right-click the printer and select **Properties** from the shortcut menu. Click **Print Test Page**.

> **Notes**
>
> For Windows XP, by default, the Printers and Faxes window shows on the Start menu. If it is missing and you want to add it, right-click **Start** and select **Properties**. The Taskbar and Start Menu Properties dialog box opens. On the Start Menu tab, click **Customize** (see Figure 21-20). In the Customize Start Menu dialog box, click the **Advanced** tab. Check **Printers and Faxes**. Click **OK** to close the Customize Start Menu dialog box. Then click **Apply** and **OK** to apply your changes and close the Taskbar and Start Menu Properties dialog box.

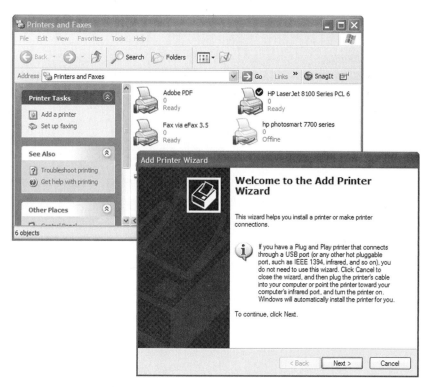

**Figure 21-19** Use the Add Printer Wizard to install a printer

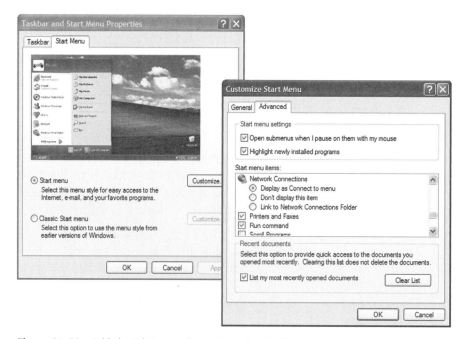

**Figure 21-20** Add the Printers and Faxes item to the Start menu

## SHARING A PRINTER WITH OTHERS IN A WORKGROUP

To share a local printer using Windows, File and Printer Sharing must be installed, and to use a shared printer on a remote PC, Client for Microsoft Networks must be installed. In most cases, it is easiest to simply install both components on all computers on the network. How to install the components under Windows 2000/XP and Windows 98 was covered in Chapter 17.

**21**

A+ ESS
3.1
4.2

A+
220-602
4.2

To share a local printer connected to a Windows 2000/XP workstation, do the following:

1. Open the Printers and Faxes window or Printers window. Right-click the printer you want to share, and select **Sharing** from the shortcut menu. The printer's Properties dialog box opens, as shown in Figure 21-21 for Windows XP; the dialog box in Windows 2000 is similar. Select **Share this printer** and enter a name for the printer.

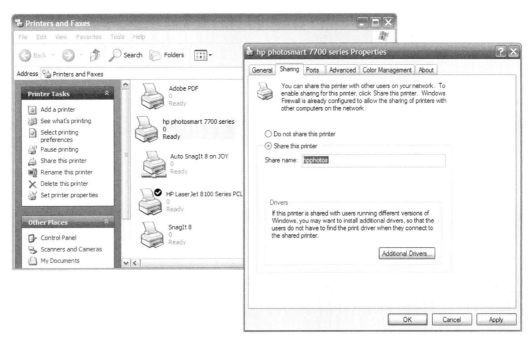

**Figure 21-21** Sharing a printer on a Windows XP PC

2. If you want to make drivers for the printer available to remote users who are using an operating system other than the OS being used, click **Additional Drivers**.

3. The Additional Drivers window opens, as shown in Figure 21-22. Select the OS. In the figure, Windows 2000, XP, 95, 98, and Me are selected so that users of these OSs will have the printer drivers they need. Click **OK** twice to close both windows. You might be asked for the Windows installation CD or other access to the installation files. A shared printer shows a hand icon under it in the Printers and Faxes window, and the printer is listed in My Network Places or Network Neighborhood of other PCs on the network.

You can share a printer on a Windows 9x/Me computer in the same way as for Windows 2000/XP, except the Additional Drivers option is not available.

## USING A SHARED PRINTER

Recall that for a remote PC to use a shared network printer, the drivers for that printer must be installed on the remote PC. There are two approaches to installing shared network printer drivers on a remote PC. You can perform the installation using the drivers on CD (either the Windows CD or printer manufacturer's CD), or you can perform the installation using the printer drivers on the host PC. The installations work about the same way for Windows 2000/XP and Windows 98. The Windows XP installation is shown here, but differences for Windows 2000 and Windows 98 are noted.

**Figure 21-22** Make drivers for other operating systems available for the shared printer

To use a shared printer on the network by installing the manufacturer's printer drivers from CD, do the following using Windows XP:

1. Open the Printers and Faxes window and click **Add a printer**. The Add Printer Wizard opens. Click **Next**.

2. In response to the question, "Select the option that describes the printer you want to use:" select **a network printer, or a printer attached to another computer**. Click **Next**. The Specify a Printer page of the Add Printer Wizard opens, as shown in Figure 21-23.

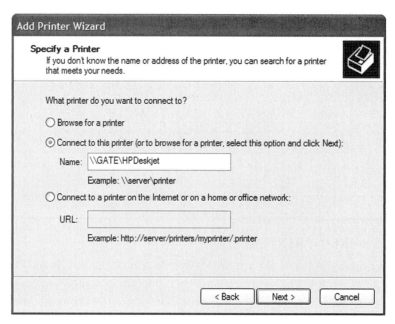

**Figure 21-23** To use a network printer under Windows XP, enter the host computer name followed by the printer name, or have Windows XP browse the network for shared printers

3. Enter the host computer name and printer name. Begin with two backslashes and separate the computer name from the printer name with a backslash. Or, you can click **Browse**, search the list of shared printers on the network, and select the printer to install. (If your network is using static IP addressing and you know the IP address of the host PC, you can enter the IP address instead of the host name in this step.) Click **Next**.

4. Windows XP searches for Windows XP drivers on the host computer for this printer. If it finds them (meaning that the host computer is a Windows XP machine), the wizard skips to Step 6. If it doesn't find the drivers (the host computer is not a Windows XP machine), a message asks if you want to search for the proper driver. Click **OK**.

5. Click **Have Disk** to use the manufacturer's drivers, or to use Windows drivers, select the printer manufacturer and then the printer model from the list of supported printers. Click **OK** when you finish.

6. In response to the question, "Do you want to use this printer as the default printer?" answer **Yes** if you want Windows to send documents to this printer until you select a different one. Click **Next**. Click **Finish** to complete the wizard.

7. The printer icon appears in the Printers and Faxes window. To test the printer installation, right-click the icon and select **Properties** from the shortcut menu. Click the **General** tab and then click **Print Test Page**.

Here are some additional things to know about installing a network printer using the Windows 98 Add Printer Wizard:

- When the wizard asks, "Do you print from MS-DOS-based programs?" answer Yes if you have any intention of ever doing so.
- The wizard gives you the opportunity to name the printer. You might include the location of the printer, such as 3rd Floor Laser or John's Laser.
- Sometimes, a DOS-based program has problems printing to a network printer. You can choose to associate the network printer with a printer port such as LPT1 to satisfy the DOS application. Click **Capture Printer Port**, and then select the port from the drop-down menu in the Capture Printer Port dialog box (see Figure 21-24).

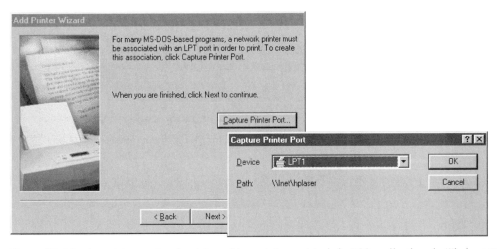

**Figure 21-24** Associate a network printer with a printer port to help DOS applications in Windows 98

▲ The Windows 98 Add Printer Wizard gives you the opportunity to print a test page on the last window of the wizard. It's always a good idea to print this test page to verify that the printer is accessible.

▲ Know that the Windows 98 Add Printer Wizard does not attempt to use the printer drivers on the host PC, but always installs local Windows 9x/Me drivers or uses the manufacturer's CD.

Another way to install a shared printer is to first use My Network Places or Network Neighborhood to locate the printer on the network. This method is faster because the remote PCs can use the printer drivers on the host PC. Do the following:

1. On a remote PC that uses Windows 2000/XP, open **My Network Places** and find the printer. Right-click the printer and select **Connect** from the shortcut menu. See Figure 21-25. (For Windows 9x/Me, open **Network Neighborhood** and find the printer. Right-click the printer and select **Install** from the shortcut menu.)

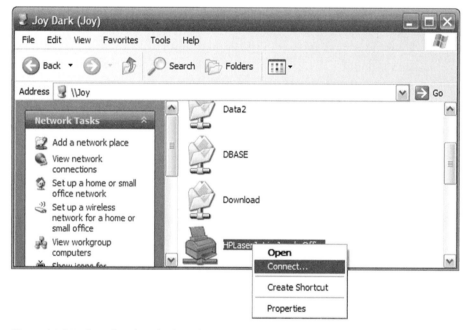

**Figure 21-25**   Install a shared printer in Windows XP using My Network Places

2. If the host computer is using the same OS as you are, or if you have a Windows 2000/XP host computer and the additional drivers for your OS have been installed, you can use those drivers for the installation. If Windows cannot find the right drivers, it sends you an error message and gives you the opportunity to install the drivers from your Windows CD or the printer manufacturer's CD.

 **Notes**

When installing a shared printer on a Windows 9x/Me PC where the host computer is also a Windows 9x/Me PC, you must first share the \Windows folder on the host PC so the remote PC can access the printer drivers. This is a security risk, so remove the share status on this important folder as soon as all remote PCs have the printer installed.

**21**

## OTHER METHODS OF SHARING PRINTERS OVER A NETWORK

A+ ESS
3.1
4.2

A+
220-602
4.2

The three ways to make a printer available on a network are listed here:

- ◢ A regular printer can be attached to a PC using a port on the PC, and then that PC can share the printer with the network. (This method was described in the last section.)
- ◢ A network printer with embedded logic to manage network communication can be connected directly to a network with its own NIC.
- ◢ A dedicated device or computer called a print server can control several printers connected to a network. For example, HP has software called HP JetDirect, designed to support HP printers in this manner. For more information, see the HP Web site, *www.hp.com*.

If printers are available on the network using one of the last two methods, follow the printer manufacturer's directions to install the printer on each PC. If you don't have these directions, do the following:

1. Download the printer drivers from the printer manufacturer's Web site and decompress the downloaded file, if necessary.

2. Open the Printers and Faxes or Printers window and start the wizard to add a new printer. Select the option to install a local printer but do not ask Windows to automatically detect the printer.

3. On the next window shown in Figure 21-26, choose **Create a new port**. From the list of port types, select **Standard TCP/IP Port**. Click **Next** twice.

**Figure 21-26** Configure a local printer to use a standard TCP/IP port

4. On the next window shown in Figure 21-27, you need to identify the printer on the network. If you know the IP address of the printer, enter it in the first box on this window and click **Next**. Some network printers have assigned printer names or the printer might have an assigned port name. To know how your network printer is configured, see the network printer's configuration window. How to access this window is discussed later in the chapter.

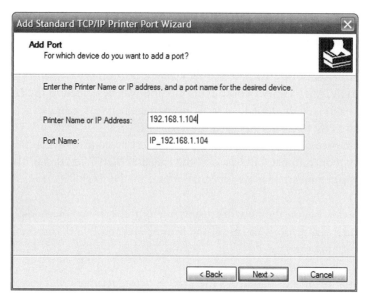

**Figure 21-27** Enter the printer name or IP address to identify the printer on the network

 **Notes**

To know the IP address of a network printer, look in the printer documentation. Or you can press a key on the front panel of the printer to instruct it to print setup information about the printer, which should include its IP address. To know which keys to press to print the setup report, see the printer documentation.

5. On the next window (see Figure 21-28), click **Have Disk** so you can point to and use the downloaded driver files that will then be used to complete the printer installation.

6. When asked if you want this printer to be the default printer, make your selection. You'll also be given the opportunity to choose to share the printer. When asked if you want to print a test page, select **Yes**. Click **Finish** to close the wizard.

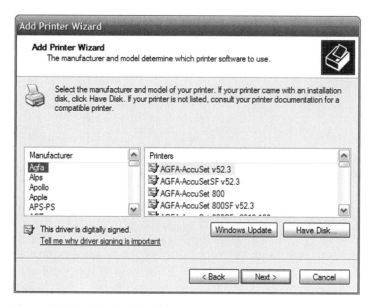

**Figure 21-28** Select printer drivers

**21**

A+ ESS
3.1
4.2

A+
220-602
4.2

> **Notes**
>
> Because a network printer has no OS installed, the printer's NIC contains all the firmware needed to communicate over the network. For a PC, some of this software is part of Windows, including the network protocols TCP/IP and IPX/SPX. A network printer's NIC firmware usually supports TCP/IP and IPX/SPX. The network printer documentation will tell you which protocols are supported. One of these protocols must be installed on a PC using the printer.

One shortcut you might take to speed up the process of installing a printer connected directly to the network is to install the printer on one PC and then share it on the network. Then, you can install the printer on the other PCs by using My Network Places for Windows 2000/XP or Network Neighborhood for Windows 98, following the directions given earlier. Find the printer, right-click it, and then select **Connect** (for Windows 2000/XP) or **Install** (for Windows 9x/Me) from the shortcut menu. The disadvantage of using this method is that the computer sharing the printer must be turned on when other computers on the network want to use the printer.

## MAINTAINING PRINTERS AND SCANNERS

A+ ESS
3.3
4.2

A+
220-602
3.3
4.2

Printers and scanners generally last for years if they are properly used and maintained. To get the most out of a printer or scanner, it's important to follow the manufacturer's directions when using the device and to perform the necessary routine maintenance. For example, the life of a printer can be shortened if you allow the printer to overheat, don't use approved paper, or don't install consumable maintenance kits when they are required.

When supporting printers using Windows, it is helpful to know about the protocols used by printers for communication between Windows and the printer, so we will begin our discussion of maintaining printers here. Then, we'll turn our attention to managing printers, including the routine maintenance that printers need. Finally, you'll learn how to install and support a scanner.

### PRINTER LANGUAGES

Years ago, all printers were dot matrix printers that could only print simple text using only a single font. Communication between the OS and the printer was simple. Today's printers can produce beautiful colored graphics and text using a variety of fonts and symbols, and communication between the OS and a printer can get pretty complicated.

The languages or methods the OS and printer use for communication and building a page before it prints are listed in the following. The method used depends on what the printer is designed to support and the printer drivers installed. If the printer has sophisticated firmware, it might be able to support more than one method. In this case, the installed printer drivers determine which methods can be used:

▲ *The printer uses PostScript commands to build the page.* For Windows 2000/XP or Windows 9x/Me using a PostScript printer, the commands and data needed to build a page to print are sent to the printer using the PostScript language. The printer firmware then interprets these commands and draws and formats the page in the printer memory before it is printed. **PostScript** is a language used to communicate how a page is to print and was developed by Adobe Systems. PostScript is popular with desktop publishing, the typesetting industry, and the Macintosh OS.

A+ ESS
3.3
4.2

A+
220-602
3.3
4.2

▲ *The printer uses PCL commands to build the page.* For Windows 2000/XP, a printer language that competes with PostScript is **PCL (Printer Control Language)**. PCL was developed by Hewlett-Packard but is considered a de facto standard in the printing industry. Many printer manufacturers use PCL.

▲ *The Windows GDI builds the page and then sends it to the printer.* For Windows 2000/XP or Windows 9x/Me, a less-sophisticated method of communicating to a printer is to use the **GDI (Graphics Device Interface)** component of Windows. GDI draws and formats the page and then sends the almost-ready-to-print page to the printer in bitmap form. Because Windows, rather than the printer, does most of the work of building the page, a GDI printer needs less firmware and memory, and, therefore, generally costs less than a PCL or PostScript printer. The downside of using the GDI method is that Windows performance can suffer when printing a lot of complicated pages. Most low-end ink-jet and laser printers are GDI printers. If the printer specifications don't say PCL or PostScript, you can assume it's a GDI printer. Many high-end printers support more than one protocol and can handle GDI, PCL, or PostScript printing.

▲ *Raw data is printed with little-to-no formatting.* Text data that contains no embedded control characters is sent to the printer as is, and the printer can print it without any processing. The data is called raw data. Dot matrix printers that can only print simple text receive and print raw data.

Normally, when Windows receives a print job from an application, it places the job in a queue and prints from the queue, so that the application is released from the printing process as soon as possible. Several print jobs can accumulate in the queue, which you can view in the Printers and Faxes or Printers window. This process is called **spooling**. (The word spool is an acronym for *si*multaneous *p*eripheral *o*perations *onl*ine.) Most printing from Windows uses spooling.

If the printer port, printer cable, and printer all support bidirectional communication, the printer can communicate with Windows. For example, Windows XP can ask the printer how much printer memory is available and what fonts are installed. The printer can send messages to the OS, such as an out-of-paper or paper-jam message.

## USING WINDOWS TO MANAGE PRINTERS

From the Printers and Faxes window (for Windows XP) or the Printers window (for Windows 2000 and Windows 9x/Me), you can delete printers, change the Windows default printer, purge print jobs to troubleshoot failed printing, and perform other printer maintenance tasks. For example, to manage the print jobs for a printer, double-click the printer in the Printers and Faxes window. The printer window opens, and is similar to the one in Figure 21-29. From this window, you can see the status and order of the print jobs. If the printer reports a problem with printing, it will be displayed as the status for the first job in the print queue. To cancel a single print job, right-click the job and select **Cancel** from the shortcut menu, as shown in Figure 21-29. To cancel all print jobs, click **Printer** on the menu and select **Cancel All Documents**. (For Windows 9x/Me, click **Purge Print Documents**.)

 **Notes**

> When you use the Windows 2000/XP default settings, user accounts in the Everyone group are assigned the Print permission level, which means users can send documents to a printer. They cannot manage the print queue or change printer settings. Users in the Administrator and Power User groups are assigned the Manage Printers permission level, which means they have complete control over a printer, including printer settings and the print queue. A third permission level, Manage Documents, can be assigned to a user so that the user can manage the print queue while not being allowed to change printer settings.

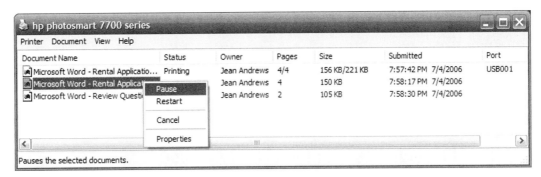

**Figure 21-29** Manage print jobs using the printer window

The Printers and Faxes or Printers window can also be used to manage printer settings and options. For example, a printer that supports automatically printing on both sides of the paper (called duplex printing) needs to be configured in Windows to use this feature. On the printer's Properties window, click the **Configure** tab, shown in Figure 21-30. On this window, to enable duplexing, check **Duplexing Unit**. (Also notice the Mopier Enabled option on this window, which is the ability to print and collate multiple copies of a single print job.) To apply your changes, click **Apply** and then click **OK** to close the window. Now, when a user attempts to print from an application, the Print window gives the option to print on both sides of the paper. For example, when a user attempts to print a Word document, the Print window shown in Figure 21-31 appears. To print on both sides of the paper, the user can click **Properties** and then check **Print on Both Sides** in the window on the right side of Figure 21-31.

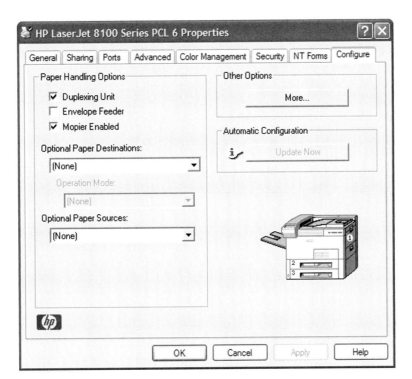

**Figure 21-30** Configure printer options and settings using the printer's Properties window

A+ ESS
3.3
4.2

A+
220-602
3.3
4.2

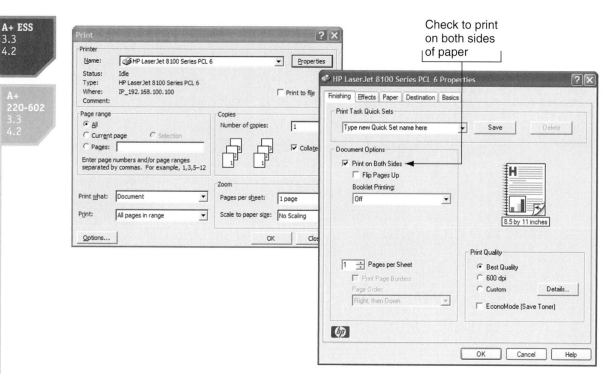

**Figure 21-31** Printing on both sides of the paper

A printer might be able to accommodate different types of input trays and feeders for various envelopes, oversized paper, colored paper, transparencies, and other media. In addition, you can install on the printer staplers, sorters, stackers, binders, and output trays so that the printer can sort output by user (called mailboxes). After you have physically installed one of these devices, use the printer properties window to enable it. For example, suppose you have installed a 3,000-sheet stapler and stacker unit on the printer whose properties window is shown in Figure 21-30. To enable this equipment, in the drop-down list of Optional Paper Destinations, select **HP 3000-Sheet Stapler/Stacker** and click **Apply** (see Figure 21-32). Compare the picture of the printer in Figure 21-30 to the picture in Figure 21-32 where the equipment is enabled and drawn into the printer picture. After the equipment is enabled, when a user prints, the equipment is listed as an option in the Print window.

After this new equipment is installed or you have enabled a printer feature, users might see additional options available when they are printing. For example, when a user prints using Microsoft Word, the Print dialog box opens for the user to make selections for the print job. When the user clicks **Properties**, the printer properties dialog box opens. When the user clicks the **Paper** tab, she can then select the source tray for the print job, as shown in Figure 21-33.

21

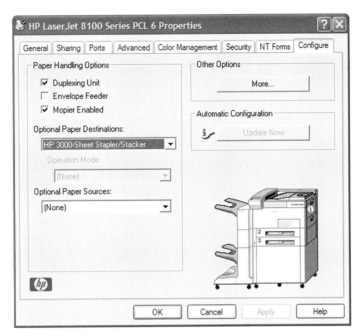

Figure 21-32 Optional printer equipment has been installed by Windows

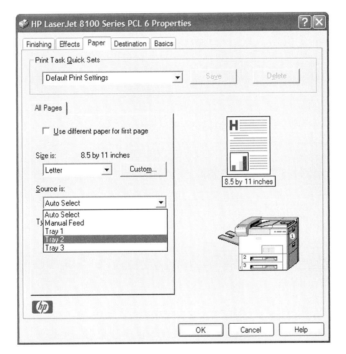

Figure 21-33 Select the source tray for print jobs

Some printers give you the option to install additional memory to hold fonts and print job buffers or a hard drive can be installed in some printers to give additional printer storage space. See the printer reference manual to find out how to install more memory or an internal hard drive. Most likely, you will use a screwdriver to remove a cover plate on the printer to expose a cavity where memory or a drive can be installed. After this equipment is installed, you must enable and configure it using the printer properties window. For example, for the HP 8100 printer properties window shown in Figure 21-30, when you click **More** under Other Options, the More Configuration Options dialog box opens, as shown in Figure 21-34. Using this dialog box, you can enable and configure the amount of additional printer memory or the size of a hard drive that you have just installed.

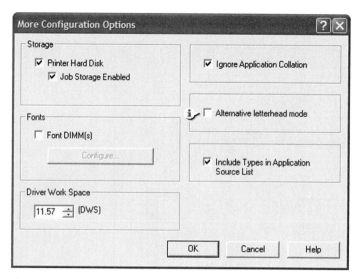

**Figure 21-34** Enable and configure newly installed printer memory and hard drive

If a printer is giving you problems or you want to upgrade the printer drivers to add new functionality, search the printer manufacturer's Web site for the latest drivers for your printer and operating system. Download the drivers to a folder on the hard drive, such as C:\Downloads\Printer, and then double-click the driver file to extract files and launch the installation program to update the printer drivers.

## ROUTINE PRINTER MAINTENANCE

Routine printer maintenance procedures vary widely from manufacturer to manufacturer and printer to printer. For each printer you support, research the printer documentation or the manufacturer's Web site for specific maintenance procedures and how often you should perform them for each printer you support. In the following sections, you'll learn about printer consumables, printer maintenance kits, cleaning printers, online help for printers, and updating printer firmware.

### PRINTER CONSUMABLES

Make sure consumables for the printer are on hand. These consumables can include paper, ink ribbons, color sticks, toner cartridges, and ink cartridges. Know how to exchange these consumables and also know how to recognize when they need exchanging. Each printer's requirements are different, so you'll need to study the printer documentation to find out what your printer requires. Buy the products in advance of when you think you'll need them. Nothing is more frustrating to a user than to have a printer not working because the support technician responsible for the printer forgot to order extra toner cartridges.

Figure 21-35 shows an ink cartridge being installed in one ink-jet printer. To replace a cartridge, turn on the printer and open the front cover. The printer releases the cartridges. You can then open the latch on top of the cartridge and remove it. Install the new cartridge as shown in the figure.

When a cartridge is not in use, put it in the cradle on the left side of the printer to protect it from drying out, as shown in Figure 21-36.

**21**

A+ ESS
1.4

A+
220-602
1.2
4.3
4.4

**Figure 21-35** Installing an ink cartridge in an ink-jet printer

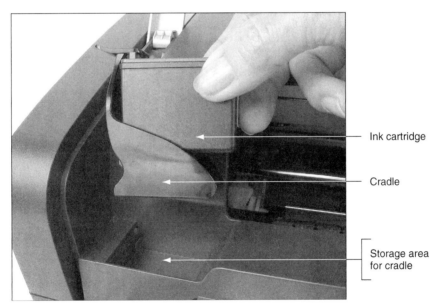

Ink cartridge

Cradle

Storage area
for cradle

**Figure 21-36** Use the protective cradle to keep an ink cartridge from drying out
when it is not installed in the printer

## PRINTER MAINTENANCE KITS

Manufacturers of high-end printers provide **printer maintenance kits**, which include specific
printer components, step-by-step instructions for performing maintenance, and any special tools
or equipment you need to do maintenance. For example, the maintenance plan for the HP
Color LaserJet 4600 printer says to replace the transfer roller
assembly after printing 120,000 pages and replace the fusing
assembly after 150,000 pages. The plan also says the black
ink cartridge should last for about 9,000 pages and the color
ink cartridge for about 8,000 pages. HP sells the image transfer kit, the image fuser kit, and the ink cartridges designed for
this printer.

 **A+ Tip**

The A+ 220-602 exam expects
you to know about the importance of resetting the page
count after installing a
printer maintenance kit.

A+ ESS
1.4

A+
220-602
1.2
4.3
4.4

> **👍 A+ Tip**
>
> The A+ Essentials exam expects you to know that printers use certain consumables and require routine preventive maintenance.

To find out how many pages a printer has printed so that you know if you need to do the maintenance, you need to have the printer give you the page count since the last maintenance. You can tell the printer to display the information or print a status report by using buttons on the front of the printer (see Figure 21-37) or you can use utility software from a computer connected to the printer. See the printer documentation to know how to get this report.

After you have performed the maintenance, be sure to reset the page count so it will be accurate to tell you when you need to do the next routine maintenance. Keep a written record of the maintenance and other service done. If a printer gives problems, one of the first things you can do is check this service documentation to find out if maintenance is due. You can also check for a history of prior problems and how they were resolved.

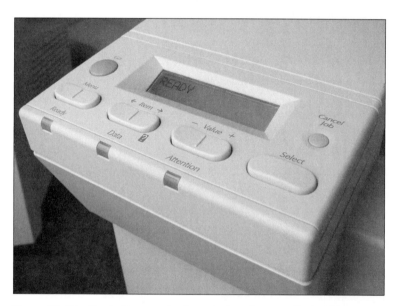

**Figure 21-37** Use buttons on the front of the printer to display the page count

## CLEANING A PRINTER

A printer gets dirty inside and outside as stray toner, ink, dust, and bits of paper accumulate. As part of routine printer maintenance, you need to regularly clean the printer. How often depends on how much the printer is used and the work environment. Some manufacturers suggest a heavily used printer be cleaned weekly, and others suggest you clean it whenever you exchange the toner or ink cartridges.

Clean the outside of the printer with a damp cloth. Don't use ammonia-based cleaners. Clean the inside of the printer with a dry cloth and remove dust, bits of paper, and stray toner. Picking up stray toner can be a problem. Don't try to blow it out with compressed air because you don't want the toner in the air. Also, don't use an antistatic vacuum cleaner. You can, however, use a vacuum cleaner designed to pick up toner, called a toner-certified vacuum cleaner. This type of vacuum does not allow the toner that it picks up to touch any conductive surface. Some printer manufacturers also suggest you use an **extension magnet brush**. The long-handled brush is made of nylon fibers that are charged with static electricity and easily attract the toner like a magnet. For a laser printer, wipe the rollers from side to side with a dry cloth to remove loose dirt and toner. Don't touch the soft

> **📝 Notes**
>
> If you get toner on your clothes, dust it off and clean your clothes with cold water. Hot water will set the toner.

black roller (the transfer roller), or you might affect the print quality. You can find specific instructions for cleaning a printer on the printer Web site.

For some ink-jet printers, you can use software to clean the ink-jet nozzles or align the cartridges, which can help improve print quality when colors appear streaked or out of alignment. How to access these tools differs from one printer to another. For some printers, a Services tab is added to the printer properties window. Other printer installations might put utility programs in the Start menu. Here is one example of how to clean and calibrate an ink-jet printer that adds a tab to the Printing Preferences window:

1. Open the Printers and Faxes or the Printers window. Right-click the **ink-jet printer** icon, and select **Properties** from the shortcut menu.

2. On the General tab, click **Printing Preferences**. The Printing Preferences window opens. Click the **Services** tab and then click **Service this device,** as shown on the left side of Figure 21-38. The Toolbox window for the printer is displayed, as shown on the right side of the figure.

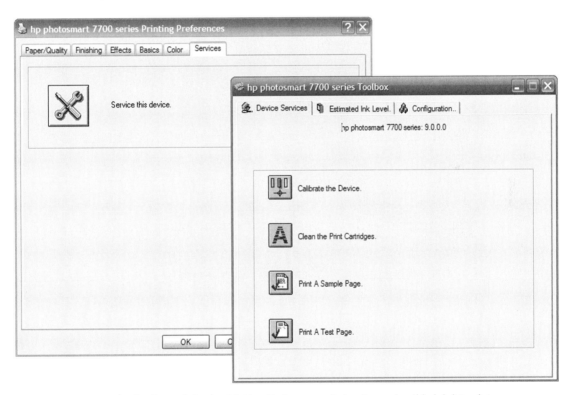

**Figure 21-38**  Use the Services tab in the Printing Preferences window to service this ink-jet printer

3. To calibrate the printer, click **Calibrate the Device.** In the next window, click **Calibrate.** As the printer calibrates itself, a page prints. The page contains a test pattern. If the test pattern does not look straight and smooth, first try to calibrate the printer a second time. If it still does not produce a smooth test pattern, you might have to replace the ink cartridges.

4. To have the printer automatically clean the ink nozzles, click **Clean the Print Cartridges** in the Toolbox window shown in Figure 21-38.

5. A test page prints. If the page prints sharply with no missing dots or lines, you are finished. If the page does not print correctly, perform the auto-clean again.

6. You might need to perform the auto-clean procedure six or seven times to clean the nozzles completely.

A+ ESS
1.4

A+
220-602
1.2
4.3
4.4

If the printer still does not print with the quality printing you expect, you can try to manually clean the cartridge nozzles. Check the printer manufacturer Web site for directions. For most ink-jet printers, you are directed to use clean, distilled water and cotton swabs to clean the face of the ink cartridge, being careful not to touch the nozzle plate. To prevent the ink-jet nozzles from drying out, don't leave the ink cartridges out of their cradle for longer than 30 minutes. Here are some general directions:

1. Following manufacturer directions, remove the ink-jet cartridges from the printer and lay them on their sides on a paper towel.

2. Dip a cotton swab in distilled water (not tap water) and squeeze out any excess water.

3. Hold an ink cartridge so that the nozzle plate faces up and use the swab to wipe clean the area around the nozzle plate, as shown in Figure 21-39. Do not clean the plate itself.

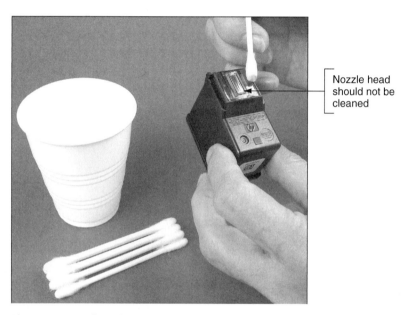

Nozzle head should not be cleaned

**Figure 21-39**   Clean the area around the nozzle plate with a damp cotton swab

4. Hold the cartridge up to the light and make sure that no dust, dirt, ink, or cotton fibers are left around the face of the nozzle plate. Make sure the area is clean.

5. Clean all the ink cartridges the same way and replace the cartridges in the printer.

6. Print a test page. If print quality is still poor, try repeating the automatic nozzle cleaning process using the printer Properties window described earlier.

7. If you still have problems, you need to replace the ink cartridges.

## ONLINE SUPPORT FOR PRINTERS

The printer manufacturer's Web site is an important resource when supporting printers. Here are some things to look for:

▲ *Online documentation.* Expect the printer manufacturer's Web site to include documentation on installing, configuring, troubleshooting, using, upgrading, and maintaining the printer. Also look for information on printer parts and warranty, compatibility information, specifications and features of your printer, a way to register your printer,

A+ ESS
1.4

A+
220-602
1.2
4.3
4.4

and how to recycle or dispose of a printer. You might also be able to download your printer manual in PDF format.

▲ *A knowledge base of common problems and what to do about them.* Some Web sites also offer a newsgroup service or discussion group where you can communicate with others responsible for supporting a particular printer. Also look for a way to e-mail for technical support.

▲ *Updated device drivers.* Sometimes, you can solve printer problems by downloading and installing the latest drivers. Also, a manufacturer makes new features and options available through these drivers. Be sure you download files for the correct printer and OS.

▲ *Catalog of options and upgrades for purchase.* Look for memory upgrades, optional trays, feeders, sorters, staplers, printer stands, and other equipment to upgrade your printer. Expect to find the parts as well as how to install and maintain them.

▲ *Replacement parts.* When a printer part breaks, buy only parts made by or approved by the printer manufacturer. Manufacturers also sell consumable supplies such as toner and ink cartridges.

▲ *Printer maintenance kits.* The best practice is to buy everything you need for routine maintenance either from the printer manufacturer or an approved vendor. If you buy from a nonapproved vendor, you risk damaging the printer or shortening its lifespan.

▲ *Additional software.* Look for software to use with your printer, such as software to produce greeting cards or edit photographs.

▲ *Firmware updates.* Some high-end printers have firmware that can be flashed to solve problems and add features. Be careful to verify that you download the correct update for your printer.

## UPDATING PRINTER FIRMWARE

Now let's look at one example of how to upgrade the firmware on one network printer. The printer we are using is an HP 8100 DN printer. Follow these directions:

1. To know how to access the firmware utility on the printer, see the printer documentation. For this network printer, you enter its IP address in a browser address box from any computer on the network. Recall that this is the same method used to access the firmware utility for a router, which is the method typically used for any network device. The opening window of the utility opens, as shown in Figure 21-40. On this window, you can see the MAC address of the printer, the firmware version installed, the IP address, and other basic information.

2. Click **Administration** and then click the **Configuration** tab, as shown in Figure 21-41. Notice in this window you can configure the printer for static or dynamic IP addressing, which is labeled in the figure as TCP Configuration Type. If you are addressing the printer by its IP address, choose **Manual** so that the IP address doesn't change.

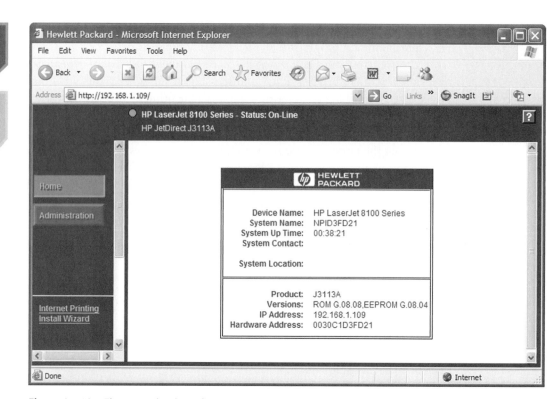

**Figure 21-40** The network printer firmware is accessed on the network using a browser

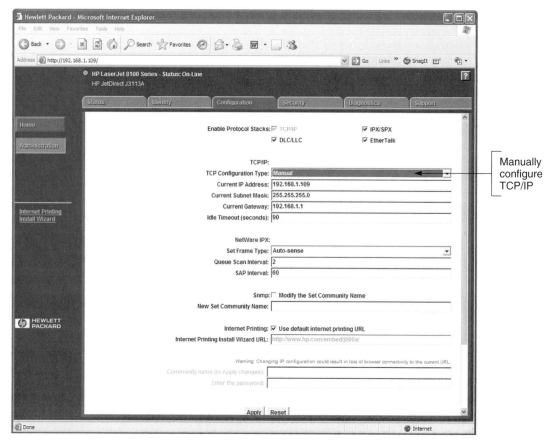

**Figure 21-41** Configure a network printer for static IP addressing

3. To check for firmware upgrades, click the **Support** tab, which provides a connection to the HP Web site. Search the site for the printer downloads. Figure 21-42 shows the correct page for this printer. At the bottom of this page, click **Cross operating system (BIOS, Firmware, Diagnostics, etc.)**.

4. Follow the onscreen directions to download and install any available updates you select.

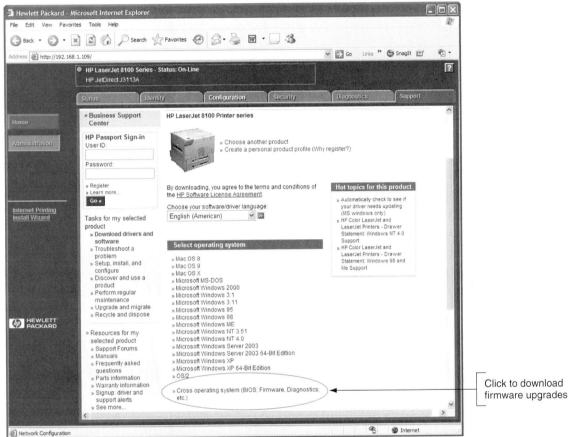

**Figure 21-42** Locate any firmware updates for the printer on the HP Web site

## SUPPORTING SCANNERS

In this part of the chapter, you'll learn how to install a scanner and about the routine maintenance a scanner might need.

### HOW TO INSTALL A SCANNER

The most common type of connector for a scanner intended to be used with a desktop system is a USB port, which means the scanner is hot-pluggable. Here are general directions for installing a scanner:

1. Read the manufacturer setup instructions and follow them in detail rather than using the general directions here. For USB scanners or other scanners that are hot-pluggable, most likely you'll be told to first run the setup CD before connecting the scanner.

2. Log on to the Windows 2000/XP system as an administrator.

3. Launch the setup program on the scanner setup CD and follow the onscreen instructions to install device drivers and other software. Figure 21-43 shows the main menu of one installation program for an HP scanner.

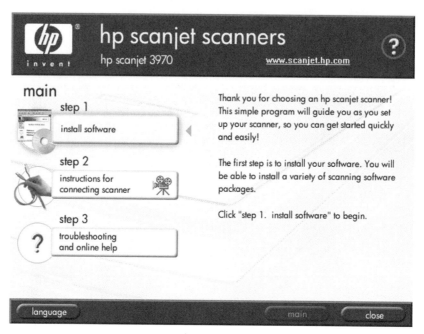

**Figure 21-43**   Main menu of a scanner setup program

4. Connect the scanner, plug it up, and turn it on.

5. Test the scanner by scanning a document or picture and saving it to a file. To scan an item, you can use the software that came bundled with the scanner or you can press a button on the front of the scanner. Generally, you have more control over scanning when you use the software rather than the buttons. For example, for one scanner, you launch the scanner software that displays a menu shown in Figure 21-44. To scan a picture, place the picture face down on the glass surface of the scanner and click **Scan Picture**.

**Figure 21-44**   Scanner software main menu

6. The next window shows a preview of the scanned image (see Figure 21-45). Adjust the area of the page you want to scan and select your output type. Then click **Accept**. The scanner rescans and saves the image to a file. You can select the file format on the next window.

**Figure 21-45** Make adjustments before the final scan is made

For older scanners that use a serial or parallel port, first power down your PC and connect the scanner. Then restart your PC. The Found New Hardware Wizard should launch and you can then install the software. For some products, the scanner installation instructions might tell you to first install the scanner drivers from the setup CD before connecting the scanner.

For SCSI scanners, be sure to set the SCSI ID for the scanner as one SCSI device on the chain. Figure 21-46 shows the dial where you set the SCSI ID on one scanner.

**Notes**

Remember that you should not unplug or plug in a USB device into a USB port without first powering down or unplugging the device, turning off the device, or disconnecting it from its power source.

A+ ESS
4.2

A+
220-602
4.3
4.4

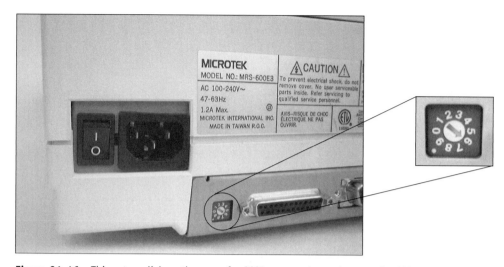

**Figure 21-46** This rotary dial on the rear of a SCSI scanner is used to set the SCSI ID, which is now set to 6

A+ ESS
1.4

## SCANNER ROUTINE MAINTENANCE

Most scanners come bundled with utility software that you can use to adjust scanner settings. Look for ways to change the scanner resolution, output type (colors, black and white, or grayscale), destination folder for files, file format, automatic cropping, percentage scaling for slides and negatives, and image quality in a saved file. Figure 21-47 shows one settings window for an HP scanner. If you're not sure which setting gives the best results, first try restoring all default settings. Perhaps a user has made a setting that is causing odd scanning results. Restoring default settings might solve the problem.

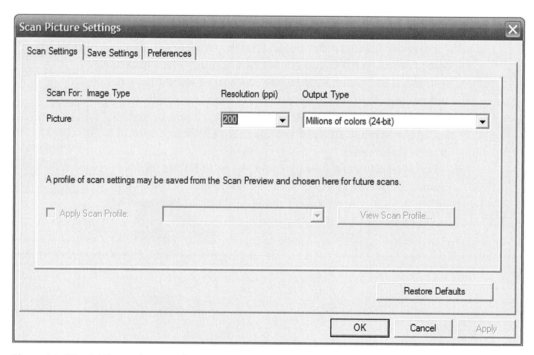

**Figure 21-47** Setting preferences for a scanner

A+ ESS
1.4

A+
220-602
4.3
4.4

Besides changing settings, to find out about other routine maintenance chores for a scanner, read the scanner documentation. For flat-bed scanners, you can clean the glass window with a soft dry cloth or you can use mild glass cleaner. First unplug the scanner. Don't use acetone or isopropyl alcohol on the glass because these chemicals can leave streaks. Before you're done, make sure the glass is dry. If the underside of the glass needs cleaning, see the Web site of the scanner manufacturer for specific instructions to remove the glass to clean it.

Some scanners have a built-in device to scan negatives and slides such as the one shown in Figure 21-48. This device is underneath the scanner lid. Just as with the glass-scanning window, you can also clean this surface with a soft dry cloth or use mild glass cleaner.

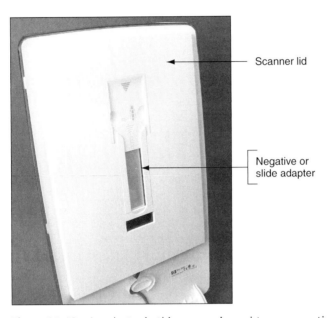

Scanner lid

Negative or
slide adapter

**Figure 21-48**  An adapter in this scanner is used to scan negatives and slides

## TROUBLESHOOTING PRINTERS AND SCANNERS

A+ ESS
1.3
3.3
4.3

A+
220-602
1.2
3.3
4.3
4.4

This section first discusses general printer troubleshooting and then explains how to troubleshoot problems specific to each of the three major types of printers. Then you'll see how to troubleshoot problems with scanners.

In these sections, you'll learn some general and specific troubleshooting tips. If you exhaust this list and still have a problem, turn to the manufacturer's Web site for additional information and support.

**APPLYING CONCEPTS**  Jill is the PC support technician responsible for supporting 10 users, their peer-to-peer network, printers, and computers. Everything was working fine when Jill left work one evening, but the next morning three users meet her at the door, complaining that they cannot print to the network printer and that important work must be printed by noon. What do you think are the first three things Jill should check?

As with all computer problems, begin troubleshooting by interviewing the user, finding out what works and doesn't work, and making an initial determination of the problem. When you think the problem is solved, ask the user to check things out to make sure he is

A+ ESS
1.3
3.3
4.3

A+
220-602
1.2
3.3
4.3
4.4

satisfied with your work. And, after the problem is solved, be sure to document the symptoms of the problem and what you did to solve it.

## PRINTER DOES NOT PRINT

When a printer does not print, the problem can be caused by the printer, the PC hardware or OS, the application using the printer, the printer cable, or the network. Follow the steps in Figure 21-49 to isolate the problem.

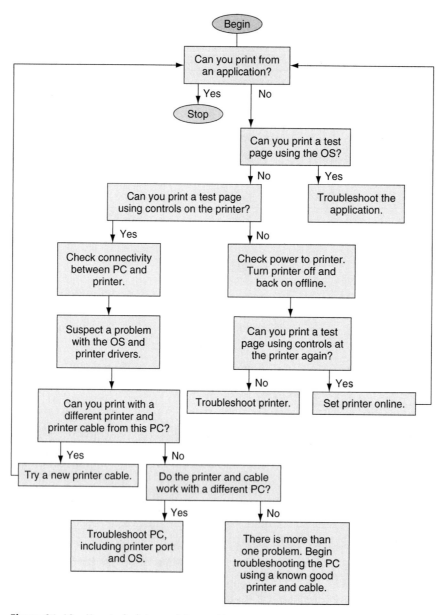

**Figure 21-49** How to isolate a printer problem

As you can see in the figure, the problem can be isolated to one of the following areas:

◢ The printer itself
◢ Connectivity between the PC and its local printer

A+ ESS
1.3
3.3
4.3

A+
220-602
1.2
3.3
4.3
4.4

◢ Connectivity between the PC and a network printer
◢ The OS and printer drivers
◢ The application attempting to use the printer

The following sections address printer problems caused by all of these categories, starting with hardware.

## PROBLEMS WITH THE PRINTER ITSELF

To eliminate the printer as the problem, first check that the printer is on, and then print a self-test page. For directions to print a self-test page, see the printer's user guide. For example, you might need to hold down a button or buttons on the printer's front panel. If this test page prints correctly, then the printer works correctly.

A printer test page generally prints some text, some graphics, and some information about the printer, such as the printer resolution and how much memory is installed. Verify that the information on the test page is correct. For example, if you know that the printer should have 2 MB of on-board printer memory, but the test only reports 1 MB, then there is a problem with memory. If the information reported is not correct and the printer allows you to upgrade firmware on the printer, try doing that next.

If the self-test page does not print or prints incorrectly (for example, it has missing dots or smudged streaks through the page), then troubleshoot the printer until it prints correctly. Does the printer have paper? Is the paper installed correctly? Is there a paper jam? Is the paper damp or wrinkled, causing it to refuse to feed? Are the printer cover and rear access doors properly closed and locked? Try resetting the printer. For a laser printer, check that a toner cartridge is installed. For an ink-jet printer, check that ink cartridges are installed. Has the protective tape been removed from the print cartridge? Check that power is getting to the printer. Try another power source. Check the user guide for the printer and the printer Web site for troubleshooting suggestions. For a laser printer, replace the toner cartridge. For ink-jet printers, replace the ink cartridge. Check the service documentation and printer page count to find out if routine maintenance is due or if the printer has a history of similar problems. Other things to try to troubleshoot problems with laser, ink-jet, and dot matrix printers are covered later in the chapter.

If none of these steps works, you might need to take the printer to a certified repair shop. Before you do, though, try contacting the manufacturer. The printer documentation can be very helpful and most often contains a phone number for technical support.

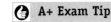

**A+ Exam Tip**

The A+ Essentials exam expects you to know the importance of printing a test page when solving printer problems. You also need to know about using diagnostic tools available on the Web.

## PROBLEMS WITH A LOCAL PRINTER CABLE OR PORT

If the printer self-test worked, but the OS printer test did not work, check for connectivity problems between the printer and the PC. For a local printer connected directly to a PC, the problem might be with the printer cable or the port the printer is using. Do the following:

◢ Check that the cable is firmly connected at both ends. For some parallel ports, you can use a screwdriver to securely anchor the cable to the parallel port with two screws on each side of the port. If you suspect the cable is bad, you can use a multimeter to check the cable.

◢ A business might use an older switch box (sometimes called a T-switch) to share one printer between two computers. A printer cable connects to the printer port of each computer. The two cables connect to the switch box. A third cable connects from the switch box to the printer. A switch on the front of the box controls which computer has access to the printer. Switch boxes were built with older dot matrix printers in mind. Some

A+ ESS
1.3
3.3
4.3

A+
220-602
1.2
3.3
4.3
4.4

switch boxes are not recommended for ink-jet or laser printers that use a bidirectional parallel cable, and can even damage a printer. For these printers, remove the switch box.

▲ Try a different cable. Use a shorter cable. (Parallel cables longer than 10 feet can sometimes cause problems.) Verify that a parallel cable is IEEE 1284-compliant.

▲ Try printing using the same printer and printer cable but a different PC.

▲ Enter Device Manager and verify the port the printer is using is enabled and working properly. Try another device on the same port to verify the problem is not with the port.

▲ Enter CMOS setup of the PC and check how the port is configured. Is it enabled? For a parallel port, is the port set to ECP or bidirectional? Recall that an ECP parallel port requires the use of a DMA channel. Try setting the port to bidirectional.

▲ If you have access to a port tester device, test the port.

## PROBLEMS WITH CONNECTIVITY FOR A NETWORK PRINTER

If the self-test page prints but the OS test page does not print and the printer is a network printer, the problem might be with connectivity between the PC on the network and the network printer. Try the following:

▲ Is the printer online?

▲ Turn the printer off and back on. Try rebooting the PC.

▲ If the printer is installed directly to one computer and shared with other computers on the network, check that you can print a test page from the computer that has the printer attached to it locally. Right-click the printer you want to test, and choose **Properties** from the shortcut menu. Click the **Print Test Page** button to send a test page to the printer.

▲ If you cannot print from the local printer, solve the problem there before attempting to print over the network.

▲ Verify that the correct default printer is selected.

▲ Return to the remote computer, and verify that you can access the computer to which the printer is attached. Go to Network Neighborhood or My Network Places, and attempt to open shared folders on the printer's computer. Perhaps you have not entered a correct user ID and password to access this computer; if so, you will be unable to use the computer's resources.

▲ Using the Printers and Faxes window, delete the printer, and then use Windows 2000/XP My Network Places or Windows 9x/Me Network Neighborhood to reconnect the printer.

▲ Is the correct network printer selected on the remote PC?

▲ Can you print to another network printer? If so, there might be a problem with the printer. Look at the printer's configuration.

▲ Is enough hard drive space available on the remote PC?

▲ For printers connected directly to the network, try pinging the printer. Try using another network port, and try using another network cable for the printer.

▲ Run diagnostic software provided by the printer manufacturer.

▲ If a PC cannot communicate with a network printer connected directly to the network, try installing a second network protocol that the network printer supports, such as IPX/SPX. If this works, then suspect that the firmware on the NIC is having a problem with TCP/IP. Try flashing the network printer's firmware.

## PROBLEMS PRINTING FROM WINDOWS

If a self-test page works and you have already stepped through checking the printer connectivity, but you still cannot print a test page from Windows, try the following:

▲ The print spool might be stalled. Try deleting all print jobs in the printer's queue. Double-click the printer icon in the Printers and Faxes or Printers window. Select **Printer** on the

**21**

menu bar, and then select **Cancel All Documents** (for Windows 2000/XP) or **Purge Print Documents** (for Windows 9x/Me). (It might take a moment for the print jobs to disappear.)

◢ Verify that the correct default printer is selected.

◢ Verify that the printer is online. See the printer documentation for information on how to determine the status from the Control Panel of the printer.

◢ If you still cannot print, reboot the PC. Verify that the printer cable or cable connections are solid.

◢ Try removing and reinstalling the printer driver. To uninstall the printer driver, right-click the printer icon in the Printers and Faxes or Printers window, and select **Delete**. Then reinstall the printer.

◢ Check the Web site of the printer manufacturer for an updated printer driver. Download and install the correct driver.

◢ Check Event Viewer for recorded events surrounding the printer or the port it is using. To access the log, in the Control Panel, open the **Administrative Tools** applet and select **Event Viewer**. Then click **System**. For example, Figure 21-50 shows a recorded event about a print job.

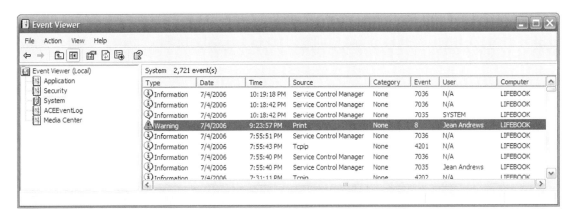

**Figure 21-50** Check Event Viewer for recorded errors about the printer or its port

◢ In the printer's Properties dialog box, select the **Ports** tab (see Figure 21-51) and uncheck **Enable bidirectional support** for this printer. The PC and printer might have a problem with bidirectional communication.

◢ Verify printer properties. Try lowering the resolution.

◢ Try disabling printer spooling. On the printer's Properties dialog box, select the **Advanced** tab and then select **Print directly to the printer** (see Figure 21-52). Click **Apply**. Spooling holds print jobs in a queue for printing, so if spooling is disabled, printing from an application can be slower.

◢ If you have trouble printing from an application, you can also bypass spooling in the application by selecting the option to print to a file. Then drag that file to the icon representing your printer in the Printers and Faxes window.

◢ Verify that enough hard drive space is available for the OS to create temporary print files.

◢ Use Chkdsk, Error-checking (Windows 2000/XP), or ScanDisk (Windows 9x/Me) to verify that the hard drive does not have errors. Use Defragmenter to optimize the hard drive.

◢ Boot Windows into Safe Mode and attempt to print. If this step works, there might be a conflict between the printer driver and another driver or application.

◢ Check the printer documentation for troubleshooting steps to solve printer problems. Look for diagnostic software that you can download from the printer manufacturer Web site or diagnostic routines you can run from the printer menu.

A+ ESS
1.3
3.3
4.3

A+
220-602
1.2
3.3
4.3
4.4

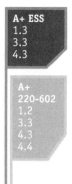

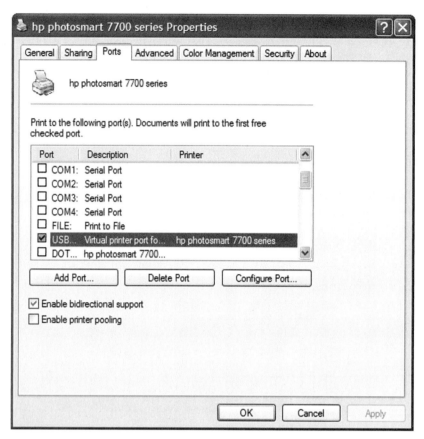

**Figure 21-51** On this tab, you can enable and disable bidirectional support for a printer

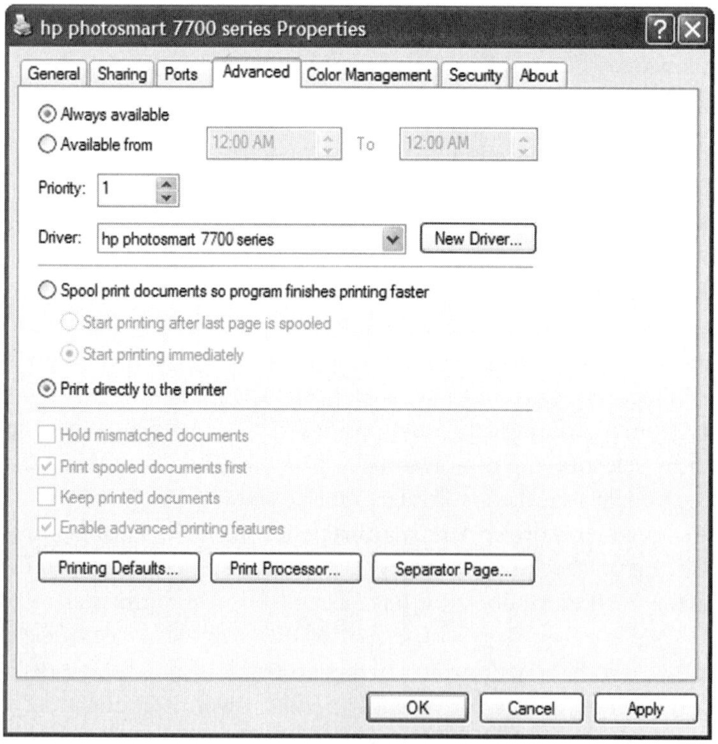

**Figure 21-52** Disable printer spooling

## PROBLEMS PRINTING FROM APPLICATIONS

If you can print a Windows test page, but you cannot print from an application, try the following:

- ◢ Verify that the correct printer is selected in the Print Setup dialog box.
- ◢ Try printing a different application file.
- ◢ Delete any files in the print spool. From the Printers and Faxes or Printers window, double-click the printer icon. Click **Printer** on the menu bar of the window that opens, and then click **Cancel All Documents** or **Purge Print Documents**.
- ◢ Reboot the PC. Immediately enter Notepad or WordPad, type some text, and print.
- ◢ Reopen the application giving the print error and attempt to print again.
- ◢ Try creating data in a new file and printing it. Keep the data simple.
- ◢ Try printing from another application.
- ◢ If you can print from other applications, consider reinstalling the problem application.
- ◢ Close any applications that are not being used.
- ◢ Add more memory to the printer.
- ◢ Remove and reinstall the printer drivers.
- ◢ For DOS applications, you might need to exit the application before printing will work. Verify that the printer is configured to handle DOS printing.

## PROBLEMS WITH LASER PRINTERS

This section covers some problems that can occur with laser printers. For more specific guidelines for your printer model, refer to the printer documentation or the manufacturer's Web site.

### POOR PRINT QUALITY OR A TONER LOW MESSAGE IS DISPLAYED

Poor print quality, including faded, smeared, wavy, speckled, or streaked printouts, often indicates that the toner is low. All major mechanical printer components that normally create problems are conveniently contained within the replaceable toner cartridge. In most cases, the solution to poor-quality printing is to replace this cartridge. Follow these general guidelines:

- ◢ If you suspect the printer is overheated, unplug it and allow it to cool.
- ◢ The toner cartridge might be low on toner or might not be installed correctly. Remove the toner cartridge and gently rock it from side to side to redistribute the toner. Replace the cartridge. To avoid flying toner, don't shake the cartridge too hard.
- ◢ If this doesn't solve the problem, try replacing the toner cartridge immediately.
- ◢ EconoMode (a mode that uses less toner) might be on; turn it off.
- ◢ The printer might need cleaning. Some printers have a cleaning utility program that you can run from the printer menu or from software downloaded to the PC. On some laser printers, you can clean the mirror. Check the user guide for directions.
- ◢ A single sheet of paper might be defective. Try new paper.
- ◢ The paper quality might not be high enough. Try a different brand of paper. Only use paper recommended for use with a laser printer. Also, some types of paper can receive print only on one side.
- ◢ Clean the inside of the printer with a dry, lint-free cloth. Don't touch the transfer roller, which is the soft, spongy black roller.
- ◢ If the transfer roller is dirty, the problem will probably correct itself after several sheets print. If not, take the printer to an authorized service center.

> **Notes**
>
> Extreme humidity can cause the toner to clump in the cartridge and give a Toner Low message. If this is a consistent problem in your location, you might want to invest in a dehumidifier for the room where your printer is located.

A+ ESS
4.3

A+
220-602
1.2
4.3
4.4

▲ Does the printer require routine maintenance? Check the Web site of the printer manufacturer for how often to perform the maintenance and to purchase the required printer maintenance kit.

## PRINTER STAYS IN WARM-UP MODE

The "warming up" message on the front panel of the printer (refer back to Figure 21-37) should turn off as soon as the printer establishes communication with the PC. If this doesn't happen, try the following:

1. Turn off the printer and disconnect the cable to the computer.

2. Turn on the printer. If it now displays a Ready message, the problem is communication between the printer and computer.

3. Verify that the cable is connected to the correct port.

4. Verify that data to the installed printer is being sent to the correct port. For example, open the Properties dialog box of the installed printer and click the Ports tab, as shown earlier in Figure 21-51.

5. Try rebooting the PC.

6. Consider the network connecting the printer and PC is down. Try printing from another PC.

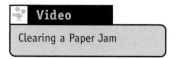

## A PAPER JAM OCCURS OR PAPER OUT MESSAGE APPEARS

If paper is jammed inside the printer, follow the directions in the printer documentation to remove the paper. Don't jerk the paper from the printer mechanism, but pull evenly on the paper, with care. Here are some guidelines:

▲ Check for jammed paper from both the input tray and the output bin. Check both sides.
▲ If there is no jammed paper, then remove the tray and check the metal plate at the bottom of the tray. Can it move up and down freely? If not, replace the tray.
▲ When you insert the tray in the printer, does the printer lift the plate as the tray is inserted? If not, the lift mechanism might need repair.
▲ Damp paper can cause paper jams. Be sure to only use dry paper in a printer.

## ONE OR MORE WHITE STREAKS APPEAR IN THE PRINT

Do the following:

▲ Remove the toner cartridge, shake it from side to side to redistribute the toner supply, and replace the cartridge.
▲ Streaking is usually caused by a dirty developer unit or corona wire. The developer unit is contained in the toner cartridge. Replace the cartridge or check the printer documentation for directions on how to remove and clean the developer unit. Allow the corona wire to cool and clean it with a lint-free swab.

## PRINT APPEARS SPECKLED

For this problem, do the following:

▲ Try replacing the cartridge. If the problem persists, the power supply assembly might be damaged.
▲ Replace the laser drum.

> **Notes**
>
> If loose toner comes out with your printout, the fuser is not reaching the proper temperature. Professional service is required.

## PRINTED IMAGES ARE DISTORTED

If printed images are distorted and there is no paper jam, foreign material inside the printer might be interfering with the mechanical components. Check for debris that might be interfering with the printer operation. If the page has a gray background or gray print, the photoreceptor drum is worn out and needs to be replaced.

## PRINTING IS SLOW

Laser printers are rated by two speed properties: the time it takes to print the first page (measured in seconds) and the print speed (measured in pages per minute). Try the following if the printer is slow:

▲ Space is needed on the hard drive to manage print jobs. Clean up the drive. Install a larger drive if necessary.
▲ Add more memory to the printer. See the printer manual for directions.
▲ Lower the printer resolution and the print quality (which lowers the REt settings).
▲ Verify that the hard drive has enough space.
▲ Upgrade the computer's memory or the CPU.

## A PORTION OF THE PAGE DOES NOT PRINT

For some laser printers, an error occurs if the printer does not have enough memory to hold the entire page. For other printers, only a part of the page prints. Some might signal this problem by flashing a light or displaying an error message on their display panels. (Some HP LaserJet printers have a Control Panel and send an error message for low memory, "20 Mem Overflow.") The solution is to install more memory or to print only simple pages with few graphics. Print a self-test page to verify how much memory is installed. Check the user guide to determine how much memory the printer can support and what kind of memory to buy.

## PROBLEMS WITH INK-JET PRINTERS

This section covers some problems that can occur with ink-jet printers. For more specific guidelines for your printer, refer to the printer documentation or the manufacturer's Web site.

## PRINT QUALITY IS POOR

Is the correct paper for ink-jet printers being used? The quality of paper determines the final print quality, especially with ink-jet printers. In general, the better the quality of the paper used with an ink-jet printer, the better the print quality. Do not use less than 20-LB paper in any type of printer, unless the printer documentation specifically says that a lower weight is satisfactory. Here are some more things to check:

▲ Is the ink supply low, or is there a partially clogged nozzle?
▲ Remove and reinstall the cartridge.

▲ Follow the printer's documentation to clean each nozzle.

▲ In the Printer Setup dialog box, click the Media/Quality tab, then change the Print Quality selection. Try different settings with sample prints.

▲ Is the print head too close to or too far from the paper?

▲ There is a little sponge in some printers near the carriage rest that can become clogged with ink. It should be removed and cleaned.

▲ If you are printing transparencies, try changing the fill pattern in your application.

## PRINTING IS INTERMITTENT OR ABSENT

For these problems, do the following:

▲ Make sure the correct printer driver is installed.

▲ Is the ink supply low?

▲ Are nozzles clogged?

▲ Replace the ink cartridges or replenish the ink supply.

▲ Sometimes, leaving the printer on for a while will heat up the ink nozzles and unclog them.

Video
Replacing Ink Cartridges

## LINES OR DOTS ARE MISSING FROM THE PRINTED PAGE

The ink nozzles on an ink-jet cartridge occasionally dry out, especially when the printer sits unused for a long time. Symptoms are missing lines or dots on the printed page. Follow directions given earlier in the chapter for cleaning ink-jet nozzles.

## INK STREAKS APPEAR ON THE PRINTED PAGE

Sometimes, dust or dirt gets down into the print head assemblage, causing streaks or lines on the printed page. Follow the manufacturer's directions to clean the ink-jet nozzles.

## PAPER IS JAMMED

Ink-jet printers have a door in the back of the printer that you can open to gently remove jammed paper, as shown in Figure 21-53. Don't try to pull the paper out from the front of the printer because doing so can tear the paper, leaving pieces inside the printer.

**Figure 21-53**   Open the door on the back of an ink-jet printer to remove jammed paper

A+ ESS
4.3

A+
220-602
1.2
4.3
4.4

## PROBLEMS WITH DOT MATRIX PRINTERS

This section covers some problems that can occur with dot matrix printers. Again, for more specific guidelines for your printer, see the printer documentation or the manufacturer's Web site.

### PRINT QUALITY IS POOR

For poor print quality, do the following:

▲ Begin with the ribbon. Does it advance normally while the carriage moves back and forth? If not, replace the ribbon.

▲ If the new ribbon still does not advance properly, check the printer's advance mechanism.

▲ Adjust the print head spacing. Look for a lever adjustment you can use to change the distance between the print head and plate.

▲ Check the print head for dirt. Make sure it's not hot before you touch it. If debris has built up, wipe each wire with a cotton swab dipped in alcohol or contact cleaner.

### PRINT HEAD MOVES BACK AND FORTH BUT NOTHING PRINTS

Do the following:

▲ Check the ribbon. Is it installed correctly between the plate and print head?

▲ Does the ribbon advance properly? Is it jammed? If the ribbon is dried out, it needs to be replaced.

---

**APPLYING CONCEPTS** Now back to Jill and her company's network printer problem. Generally, Jill should focus on finding out what works and what doesn't work, always remembering to check the simple things first. Jill should first go to the printer and check that the printer is online and has no error messages, such as a Paper Out message. Then, Jill should ask, "Can anyone print to this printer?" To find out, she should go to the closest PC and try to print a Windows test page. If the test page prints, she should next go to one of the three PCs that do not print and begin troubleshooting that PC's connection to the network. If the test page did not print at the closest PC, the problem is still not necessarily the printer. To eliminate the printer as the problem, the next step is to print a self-test page at the printer. If that self-test page prints, then Jill should check other PCs on the network. Is the entire network down? Can one PC see another PC on the network? Perhaps part of the network is down (maybe because of a switch or hub serving one part of the network).

---

## TROUBLESHOOTING SCANNERS

Here are some troubleshooting tips if Windows cannot find an installed scanner or the scanner refuses to scan:

▲ Try turning off the scanner or unplugging it from its power source and then turning it back on.

▲ Try disconnecting the USB cable and then reconnecting it. If you are using a USB hub, remove the hub and connect the scanner directly to the PC.

▲ Try rebooting your computer.

▲ Is there enough free hard drive space? If necessary, clean up the hard drive.

A+ ESS
4.3

A+
220-602
1.2
4.3
4.4

▲ Many scanners have a repair utility and troubleshooting software that installs when the setup program runs. For example, looking back at Figure 21-43, to get help, click **troubleshooting and online help.** The resulting instructions give you suggestions of things to check. It also tells you that a repair utility is available from the Add or Remove Programs applet in the Control Panel. In the Control Panel, open the applet and select the scanner. Click **Change.** The installation wizard launches and gives you the opportunity to repair or remove the software (see Figure 21-54).

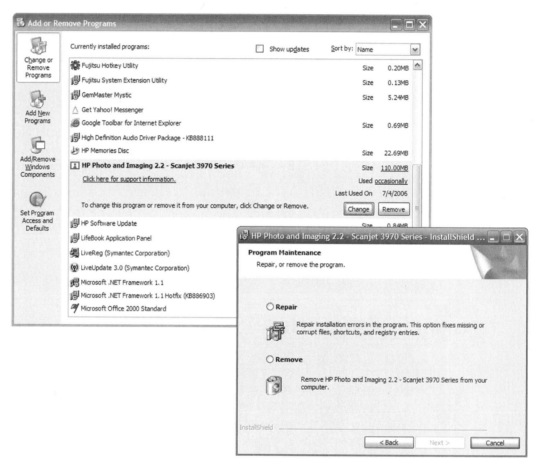

**Figure 21-54** When a scanner gives problems, you can repair or remove the software

▲ Check the Web site of the scanner manufacturer for troubleshooting guidelines and other help. You might be able to post a question to a newsgroup on the site or start a chat session with technical support. Figure 21-55 shows help given at the HP site for one flat-bed scanner. Notice the two links to chat with an online technician and to e-mail technical support. Also notice the link to download drivers. Try downloading and installing new drivers for the scanner.

▲ Try uninstalling and reinstalling the scanner software. To uninstall the software, use the Add or Remove Programs applet in the Control Panel.

▲ Install the scanner on another computer to determine if the problem is with the computer or the scanner.

**Figure 21-55**  Online help for a scanner

A+ ESS
4.3

A+
220-602
1.2
4.3
4.4

## >> CHAPTER SUMMARY

▲ The two most popular types of printers are laser and ink-jet. Other types of printers are solid ink, dye sublimation, thermal printers, and dot matrix. Laser printers produce the highest quality, followed by ink-jet printers. Dot matrix printers have the advantage of being able to print multicopy documents.

▲ The six steps that a laser printer performs to print are cleaning, conditioning, writing, developing, transferring, and fusing. The first four steps take place inside the removable toner cartridge.

▲ Ink-jet printers print by shooting ionized ink at a sheet of paper.

▲ The nozzles of an ink-jet printer tend to clog or dry out, especially when the printer remains unused. The nozzles can be cleaned automatically by means of printer software or buttons on the front panel of the printer.

▲ Dot matrix printers print by projecting pins from the print head against an inked ribbon that deposits ink on the paper.

▲ Three types of scanners are flat-bed, sheet-fed, and portable scanners.

▲ A printer is installed as a local printer connected directly to a computer, a network printer that works as a device on the network, or a network printer connected to a print server. A local printer can be shared so that others can use it as a resource on the network.

▲ Printers can process print jobs using PostScript, PCL (Printer Control Language), or GDI input. In addition, printers can receive raw data that can be printed with no processing.

▲ Windows manages and configures a printer using the Windows XP Printers and Faxes window or the Windows 2000 or Windows 9x/Me Printers window.

▲ Routine maintenance and cleaning help a printer or scanner to last longer and work better.

▲ When troubleshooting printers, first isolate the problem. Narrow the source to the printer, cable, PC hardware, operating system including the device driver, application software, or network. Test pages printed directly at the printer or within Windows can help narrow down the source of the problem.

## >> KEY TERMS

For explanations of key terms, see the Glossary near the end of the book.

| | | |
|---|---|---|
| beam detect mirror | ink-jet printer | REt (Resolution Enhancement |
| control blade | laser printer | technology) |
| default printer | local printer | scanner |
| dye-sublimation printer | network printer | scanning mirror |
| extension magnet brush | PCL (Printer Control Language) | solid ink printer |
| GDI (Graphics Device | PostScript | spooling |
| Interface) | printer maintenance kit | thermal printer |

## >> REVIEW QUESTIONS

1. Which of the following is an example of an impact printer?

   **a.** Laser printer

   **b.** Ink-jet printer

   **c.** Dot matrix printer

   **d.** Thermal printer

2. Which of the following steps in laser printing refers to a strong electrical charge drawing the toner off the drum onto the paper?

   **a.** Conditioning

   **b.** Writing

   **c.** Transferring

   **d.** Fusing

3. Which of the following prevents too much toner from sticking to the cylinder surface?

   **a.** Scanning mirror

   **b.** Control blade

   **c.** Beam detect mirror

   **d.** Developing cylinder

4. During conditioning, how much electrical charge is uniformly put on the surface of the drum?

   **a.** −100 V

   **b.** −200 V

   **c.** −400 V

   **d.** −600 V

5. Which of the following refers to a scanner that has a scanning head that moves across the glass, scanning the page?

   **a.** Flat-bed

   **b.** Sheet-fed

   **c.** Portable

   **d.** Optical character recognition software

6. True or false? If loose toner comes out with your printout, the fuser is exceeding the proper temperature.

7. True or false? Thermal printers use solid dyes embedded on different transparent films.

8. True or false? Printer Control Language is a printer language that competes with PostScript.

9. True or false? A scanner's scanning mode might be color, black and white, or grayscale.

10. True or false? You can press a key on the front panel of the printer to instruct it to print setup information about the printer, which should include its IP address.

11. Automatically printing on both sides of a sheet of paper is called _____ printing.

12. Printers are rated by the time it takes for the first page to print, called _____ time.

13. HP calls varying the size of the dots printed by a printer REt or _____ technology.

14. Solid ink printers use ink stored in solid blocks, which Xerox calls _____.

15. When Windows receives a print job from an application, it places the job in a queue and prints from the queue so that the application is released from the printing process as soon as possible. This process is called _____.

# The Professional PC Technician

**A**s a professional PC technician, you can manage your career by
staying abreast of new technology, using every available resource
to do your job well, and striving for top professional certifications.
In addition, you should maintain excellent customer relationships and
know how to communicate well and behave with professionalism.
As you know, PC technicians provide service to customers over the
phone or online, in person on-site, and sometimes in a shop where
they have little customer contact. Although each setting poses specific
challenges, almost all the recommendations in this chapter apply
across the board.

> **Notes**
>
> If you meet someone who doesn't have a smile, give them yours.

## JOB ROLES AND RESPONSIBILITIES

As a PC troubleshooter, you might have to solve a problem on your own PC or for someone else. As a PC technician, you might fulfill four different job functions:

▲ *PC support technician.* A PC support technician works on-site, closely interacting with users, and is responsible for ongoing PC maintenance. Of the four technician types listed here, a PC support technician is the only one responsible for the PC before trouble occurs, and, therefore, is able to prepare for a problem by keeping good records and maintaining backups (or teaching users how to do so). Some job titles that fall into this category include enterprise technician, IT administrator, PC technician, support technician, and PC support specialist.

▲ *PC service technician.* A PC service technician goes to a customer site in response to a service call and, if possible, repairs a PC on-site. PC service technicians are usually not responsible for ongoing PC maintenance but usually do interact with users. Other job titles might include field technician or field service technician.

▲ *Bench technician.* A bench technician works in a lab environment, might not interact with users of the PCs being repaired, and is not permanently responsible for them. Bench technicians probably don't work at the site where the PC is kept. They might be able to interview the user to get information about the problem, or they might simply receive a PC to repair without being able to talk to the user. A bench technician is sometimes called a depot technician.

▲ *Help-desk technician.* A help-desk technician provides telephone or online support. Help-desk technicians, who do not have physical access to the PC, are at the greatest disadvantage of the four types of technicians. They can interact with users only over the phone and must obviously use different tools and approaches than technicians at the PC. Other job titles in this category include remote support technician and call center technician.

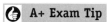 **A+ Exam Tip**

Presently, there are three A+ advanced exams: A+ 220-602 certifies a person to be a PC support technician or PC service technician, A+ 220-603 certifies a person to be a help-desk technician, and A+ 220-604 certifies a person to be a bench technician. For certification, you must also pass the A+ Essentials exam.

This chapter emphasizes the job of the on-site PC support technician. However, the special needs and perspectives of the service technician, bench technician, and help-desk technician are also addressed. Now let's look at the need to be certified, and then we'll look at the recordkeeping and information tools needed by a technician. Then, we'll turn our attention to what customers want and expect from PC support technicians beyond their technical know-how.

## CERTIFICATIONS AND PROFESSIONAL ORGANIZATIONS

Many people work as PC technicians without any formal classroom training or certification. However, by having certification or an advanced technical degree, you prove to yourself, your customers, and your employers that you are prepared to do the work and are committed to being educated in your chosen profession. Certification and advanced degrees serve as recognized proof of competence and achievement, improve your job opportunities, create a higher level of customer confidence, and often qualify you for other training or degrees.

The most significant certifying organization for PC technicians is the Computing Technology Industry Association (CompTIA, pronounced "comp-TEE-a"). CompTIA sponsors the A+ Certification Program and manages the exams. The CompTIA home page for A+ Certification is *http://certification.comptia.org/a* and is shown in Figure 22-1. Follow the *Download exam objectives* link on this page to get the list of objectives for the exams. To become certified, all individuals must pass the A+ Essentials exam that covers content on hardware, operating systems, security, and soft skills (skills involving relationships with people). Passing the A+ Essentials exam validates entry-level skills in any PC repair job.

**Figure 22-1** CompTIA A+ Certification Web page

In addition to passing the A+ Essentials exam, you must also pass one of the following advanced exams:

- A+ 220-602, which grants you the IT Technician designation
- A+ 220-603, which grants you the Remote Support Technician designation
- A+ 220-604, which grants you the Depot Technician designation

**A+ Certification** has industry recognition, so it should be your first choice for certification as a PC technician. CompTIA has more than 13,000 members from every major company that manufactures, distributes, or publishes computer-related products and services. For more information about CompTIA and A+ Certification, see the CompTIA Web site at *www.comptia.org*.

Other certifications are more vendor specific. For example, Microsoft, Novell, and Cisco offer certifications to use and support their products. These are excellent choices for additional certifications when your career plan is to focus on these products.

In addition to becoming certified and seeking advanced degrees, the professional PC technician should also stay abreast of new technology. Helpful resources include on-the-job training, books, magazines, the Internet, trade shows, interaction with colleagues, seminars, and workshops. One popular trade show is Interop by CMP Media (*www.interop.com*), where you can view the latest technology, hear industry leaders speak, and network with vast numbers of organizations and people.

## RECORDKEEPING AND INFORMATION TOOLS

If you work for a service organization, it will probably have most of the tools you need to do your job, including forms, online recordkeeping, procedures, and manuals. In some cases, help-desk support personnel might have software to help them do their jobs, such as programs that support the remote control of customers' PCs (such as Control-F1 by Blueloop and Windows XP Remote Assistance, which you learned about in Chapter 13), an online help utility, or a problem-solving tool developed specifically for their help desk.

Several types of resources, records, and information tools can help you support PCs, such as the following:

- ◢ The specific software or hardware you support must be available to you to test, observe, and study and to use to re-create a customer's problem whenever possible.
- ◢ You need a copy of the same documentation the user sees and should be familiar with that documentation.
- ◢ Hardware and software products generally have more **technical documentation** than just a user manual. A company should make this technical documentation available to you when you support its product.
- ◢ Online help targeted to field technicians and help-desk technicians is often available for a product. This online help will probably include a search engine that searches by topics, words, error messages, and the like.
- ◢ **Expert systems** software is designed and written to help solve problems. It uses databases of known facts and rules to simulate human experts' reasoning and decision making. Expert systems for PC technicians work by posing questions about a problem to be answered by the technician or the customer. The response to each question triggers another question from the software, until the expert system arrives at a possible solution or solutions. Many expert systems are "intelligent," meaning the system will record your input and use it in subsequent sessions to select more questions to ask and approaches to try.
- ◢ **Call tracking** can be done online or on paper. Most organizations have a call-tracking system that tracks: (1) the date, time, and length of help-desk or on-site calls; (2) causes of and solutions to problems already addressed; (3) who did what and when; and (4) how each call was officially resolved. Call-tracking software or documents can also help to escalate calls when necessary and track the escalation.

## WHAT CUSTOMERS WANT: BEYOND TECHNICAL KNOW-HOW

Probably the most significant indication that a PC technician is doing a good job is that customers are consistently satisfied. You should provide excellent service and treat customers as you would want to be treated in a similar situation. One of the most important ways to achieve customer satisfaction is to do your best by being prepared, both technically and non-technically. Being prepared includes knowing what customers want, what they don't like, and what they expect from a PC technician.

Your customers can be "internal" (you both work for the same company, in which case you might consider the customer your colleague) or "external" (your customers come to you or your company for service). Customers can be highly technical or technically naive,

A+ ESS
8.1
8.2

A+
220-602
8.1
8.2

represent a large company or simply own a home PC, be prompt or slow at paying their bills, want only the best (and be willing to pay for it) or be searching for bargain service, be friendly and easy to work with or demanding and condescending. In each situation, the key to success is always the same: Don't allow circumstances or personalities to affect your commitment to excellence.

The following traits distinguish one competent technician from another in the eyes of the customer:

▲ *Have a positive and helpful attitude.* This helps establish good customer relationships. You communicate your attitude in your tone of voice, the words you choose, how you use eye contact, your facial expressions, how you dress, and in many other subjective and subtle ways. Generally, your attitudes toward your customers stem from how you see people, how you see yourself, and how you see your job.

▲ *Own the problem.* Taking ownership of the customer's problem builds trust and loyalty because the customer knows you can be counted on.

▲ *Be dependable.* Customers appreciate those who do as they say. If you promise to be back at 10:00 the next morning, be back at 10:00 the next morning. If you cannot keep your appointment, never ignore your promise. Call, apologize, let the customer know what happened, and reschedule your appointment.

▲ *Be customer-focused.* When you're working with or talking to a customer, focus on him or her. Make it your job to satisfy this person, not just your organization, your boss, your bank account, or the customer's boss. For example, when talking with a customer, be a good communicator and learn to listen carefully to what he or she is saying without interrupting.

▲ *Be credible.* Convey confidence to your customers. Being credible means being technically competent and knowing how to do your job well, but credible technicians also know when the job is beyond their expertise and when to ask for help.

▲ *Maintain integrity and honesty.* Don't try to hide your mistakes from your customer or your boss. Everyone makes mistakes, but don't compound them by a lack of integrity. Accept responsibility and do what you can to correct the error.

▲ *Know the law with respect to your work.* For instance, observe the laws concerning the use of software. Don't use or install pirated software.

▲ *Act professionally.* Customers want a technician to look and behave professionally. Dress appropriately for the environment. Consider yourself a guest at the customer's site. If a customer is angry, allow the customer to vent, keeping your own professional distance. (You do, however, have the right to expect a customer not to talk to you in an abusive way.)

▲ *Perform your work in a professional manner.* Troubleshoot the problem in a systematic way that portrays confidence and credibility. Get the job done and do it with excellence. Fill out the paperwork accurately and on time.

> **Notes**
> 
> Your customers might never remember what you said or what you did, but they will always remember how you made them feel.

## SUPPORT CALLS: PROVIDING GOOD SERVICE

Customers want good service. Even though each customer is different and might expect different results, the following characteristics constitute good service in the eyes of most customers:

▲ The technician responds and completes the work within a reasonable time.
▲ For on-site visits, the technician is prepared for the service call.
▲ The work is done right the first time.

A+ ESS
8.1
8.2

A+
220-602
8.1
8.2

◢ The price for the work is reasonable and competitive.

◢ The technician exhibits good interpersonal skills.

◢ If the work extends beyond a brief on-site visit or phone call, the technician keeps the customer informed about the progress of the work.

In the following sections of the chapter, you'll learn how to plan a good service call that is sure to satisfy your customers, how to make a good service call, and how to provide phone support. Because you won't be able to solve every problem you face, you'll also learn how to support customers when you can't fix their problems.

## PLANNING FOR GOOD SERVICE

Whether you support customers and their computers on the phone or online, on-site, or in a shop, you need a plan to follow when you approach a service call. This section surveys the entire service situation, from the first contact with the customer to closing the call. Follow these general guidelines when supporting computers and their users:

◢ Almost every support project starts with a phone call or an Internet chat session. Follow company policies to obtain the specific information you should take when answering an initial call.

◢ Don't assume that an on-site visit is necessary until you have asked questions to identify the problem and asked the caller to check and try some simple things while on the phone with you. For example, the customer can check cable connections, power, and monitor settings and can look for POST error messages.

◢ Be familiar with your company's customer service policies. You might need to refer questions about warranties, licenses, documentation, or procedures to other support personnel or customer relations personnel. Your organization might not want you to answer some questions, such as questions about upcoming releases of software or new products or questions about your personal or company experience with supporting particular hardware or software.

◢ After reviewing your company's service policies, begin troubleshooting. Take notes, and then interview the customer about the problem so that you understand it thoroughly. Have the customer reproduce the problem, and carefully note each step taken and its results. This process gives you clues about the problem and about the customer's technical proficiency, which helps you know how to communicate with the customer.

◢ Search for answers. If the answers to specific questions or problems are not evident, become a researcher. Learn to use online documentation, expert systems, and other resources your company provides.

◢ Use your troubleshooting skills. Isolate the problem. Check for user errors. What works and what doesn't work? What has changed since the system last worked? Reduce the system to its essentials. Check the simple things first. Use the troubleshooting guidelines throughout this book to help you think of approaches to test and try.

◢ If you have given the problem your best, but still haven't solved it, ask for help. You learn when to ask for help from experience. After you have made a reasonable effort to help, and it seems clear you are unlikely to be successful, don't waste a customer's time.

◢ When you think you've solved the problem, allow the customer to decide when the service is finished to his or her satisfaction. Generally, the customer ends the call or chat session, not the technician.

◢ After a call, create a written record to build your own knowledge base. Record the initial symptoms of the problem, the source of the problem you actually discovered, how you made that discovery, and how the problem was finally solved. File your documentation according to symptoms or according to solutions.

A+ ESS
1.3
3.3
8.1
8.2

A+
220-602
8.1
8.2

# MAKING AN ON-SITE SERVICE CALL

When a technician makes an on-site service call, customers expect him or her to have both technical and interpersonal skills. Prepare for a service call by reviewing information given you by whoever took the call. Know the problem you are going to address, the urgency of the situation, and what computer, software, and hardware need servicing. Arrive with a complete set of equipment appropriate to the visit, which might include a tool kit, flashlight, multimeter, grounding strap and mat, and bootable CDs.

## INTERACTING WITH THE CUSTOMER

Set a realistic time for the appointment (one that you can expect to keep) and arrive on time. When you arrive at the customer's site, greet the customer in a friendly manner. Use Mr. or Ms. and last names rather than first names when addressing the customer, unless you are certain the customer expects you to use first names. The first thing you should do is listen; save the paperwork for later.

As you work, be as unobtrusive as possible. Don't make a big mess. Keep your tools and papers out of the customer's way. Don't use the phone or sit in the customer's desk chair without permission. If the customer needs to work while you are present, do whatever is necessary to accommodate that.

Ask the user questions to learn as much as you can about the problem. Refer to Chapter 3 for several sample questions, the most important being, "Can you show me how to reproduce the problem?" What procedure was taking place at the time? What had just happened? What recent changes did the user make? When did the computer last work? What has happened in the meantime? What error messages did the user see? Ask the user to listen while you repeat the problem to make sure you understand it correctly. Re-create the circumstances that existed when the computer stopped in as much detail as you can. Make no assumptions. All users make simple mistakes and then overlook them. And before you begin work, be sure to ask the very important question, "Does the system hold important data that is not backed up?"

**A+ Tip**

The A+ Essentials and A+ 220-602 exams expect you to know how to communicate with a user and how to respond when the user is angry.

Use diplomacy and good manners when you work with a user to solve a problem. For example, if you suspect that the user dropped the PC, don't ask, "Did you drop the PC?" Put the question in a less accusatory manner: "Could the PC have been dropped?" If the user is sitting in front of the PC, don't assume you can take over the keyboard or mouse without permission. Also, if the user is present, ask permission before you make a software or hardware change, even if the user has just given you permission to interact with the PC.

When working at a user's desk, consider yourself a guest and follow these general guidelines:

- Don't take over the mouse or keyboard from the user without permission.
- Ask permission again before you use the printer or other equipment.
- Don't use the phone without permission.
- Don't pile your belongings and tools on top of the user's papers, books, and so forth.
- Accept personal inconvenience to accommodate the user's urgent business needs. For example, if the user gets an important call while you are working, delay your work until the call is over.

A+ ESS
1.3
3.3
8.1
8.2

A+
220-602
8.1
8.2

Whether or not you are at the user's desk, you should follow these guidelines for good communication with the user:

- When you ask the user to describe the problem, be a good listener. Don't interrupt. If you don't understand exactly what the user is telling you, ask him or her to repeat it or ask good questions.
- When talking, use clear, concise, and direct statements.
- Don't talk down to or patronize the user. Don't make the user feel he or she is inferior.
- If the problem is simple to solve, don't make the user feel he or she has wasted your time. The user should always be made to feel that the problem is important to you.
- Don't use techie language or acronyms the user might not understand.
- Don't take drastic action, such as formatting the hard drive, before you ask the user about important data that might not be backed up.
- Provide users with alternatives where appropriate before making decisions for them.
- Protect the confidentiality of data on the PC, such as business financial information.
- Don't disparage the user's choice of computer hardware or software. Don't be judgmental or insulting.
- Don't be rude and answer your cell phone while the customer is speaking with you. Avoid unnecessary interruptions.
- If you make a mistake or must pass the problem on to someone with more expertise, be honest.

In some PC support situations, it is appropriate to consider yourself a support to the user as well as to the PC. Your goals can include educating the user as well as repairing the computer. If you want users to learn something from a problem they caused, explain how to fix the problem and walk them through the process if necessary. Don't fix the problem yourself unless they ask you to. It takes a little longer to train the user, but it is more productive in the end because the user learns more and is less likely to repeat the mistake.

## WHEN THE CUSTOMER IS INVOLVED WITH SOLVING THE PROBLEM

If the problem is caused by hardware or software, keep the customer informed as you work. Explain the problem and what you must do to fix it, giving as many details as the customer wants. When a customer must make a choice, state the options in a way that does not unfairly favor the solution that makes the most money for you as the technician or for your company.

## AFTER THE PROBLEM IS SOLVED

After you have solved the problem:

- Allow the customer enough time to be fully satisfied that all is working before you close the call. Does the printer work? Print a test page. Does the network connection work? Can the customer log on to the network and access data on it?
- If you backed up data before working on the problem and then restored the data from backups, ask the user to verify that the data is fully restored.
- If you changed anything on the PC after you booted it, reboot one more time to make sure you have not caused a problem with the boot.
- Review the service call with the customer. Summarize the instructions and explanations you have given during the call. This is an appropriate time to fill out your paperwork and explain to the customer what you have written.

A+ ESS
1.3
3.3
8.1
8.2

A+
220-602
8.1
8.2

A+ ESS
8.1
8.2

◢ Explain preventive maintenance to the customer (such as deleting temporary files from the hard drive or cleaning the mouse). Most customers don't have preventive maintenance contracts for their PCs and appreciate the time you take to show them how they can take better care of their computers.

## PHONE SUPPORT

When someone calls asking for support, you must control the call, especially at the beginning. Follow these steps at the beginning of a service call:

◢ Identify yourself and your organization. (Follow the guidelines of your employer on what to say.)

◢ Ask for and write down the name and phone number of the caller. Ask for spelling if necessary. If your help desk supports businesses, get the name of the business the caller represents.

◢ Your company might require that you obtain a licensing or warranty number to determine whether the customer is entitled to receive your support free of charge or that you obtain a credit card number, if the customer is paying for the call. Get whatever information you need at this point to determine that you should be the one to provide service, before you start to address the problem.

◢ Open up the conversation for the caller to describe the problem.

Phone support requires more interaction with customers than any other type of PC support. To give clear instructions, you must be able to visualize what the customer sees at his or her PC. Patience is required if the customer must be told each key to press or command button to click. Help-desk support requires excellent communication skills, good phone manners, and lots of patience. As your help-desk skills improve, you will learn to think through the process as though you were sitting in front of the PC yourself. Drawing diagrams and taking notes as you talk can be very helpful.

If you spend many hours on the phone at a help desk, use a headset similar to the one shown in Figure 22-2 instead of a regular phone to reduce strain on your ears and neck. (Investing in a high-quality headset will be worth the money.)

**Figure 22-2** Help-desk technicians can benefit from a hands-free headset

A+ ESS
8.1
8.2

A+
220-602
8.1
8.2

If your call is accidentally disconnected, call back immediately. Don't eat or drink while on the phone. If you must put callers on hold, tell them how long it will be before you get back to them. Don't complain about your job, your company, or other companies or products to your customers. A little small talk is okay and is sometimes beneficial in easing a tense situation, but keep it upbeat and positive. As with on-site service calls, let the user make sure all is working before you close the phone call. If you end the call too soon and the problem is not completely resolved, the customer can be frustrated, especially if it is difficult to contact you again.

## WHEN THE CUSTOMER IS NOT KNOWLEDGEABLE

A help-desk call is the most difficult situation to handle when a customer is not knowledgeable about how to use a computer. When on-site, you can put a PC in good repair without depending on a customer to help you, but when you are trying to solve a problem over the phone, with a customer as your only eyes, ears, and hands, a computer-illiterate user can present a challenge. Here are some tips for handling this situation:

- Don't use computer jargon while talking. For example, instead of saying, "Open Windows Explorer," say, "Using your mouse, right-click the Start button and select Explore from the menu."
- Don't ask the customer to do something that might destroy settings or files without first having the customer back them up carefully. If you think the customer can't handle your request, ask for some on-site help.
- Frequently ask the customer what the screen displays to help you track the keystrokes and action.
- Follow along at your own PC. It's easier to direct the customer, keystroke by keystroke, if you are doing the same things.
- Give the customer plenty of opportunity to ask questions.
- Compliment the customer whenever you can to help the customer gain confidence.
- If you determine that the customer cannot help you solve the problem without a lot of coaching, you might need to tactfully request that the caller have someone with more experience call you.

> **Notes**
>
> When solving computer problems in an organization other than your own, check with technical support instead of working only with the PC user. The user might not be aware of policies that have been set on the PC to prevent changes to the OS, hardware, or applications.

### WHEN THE CUSTOMER IS OVERLY CONFIDENT

Sometimes customers are proud of their computer knowledge. Such customers might want to give advice, take charge of a call, withhold information they think you don't need to know, or execute commands at the computer without letting you know, so you don't have enough information to follow along. A situation like this must be handled with tact and respect for the customer. Here are a few tips:

- When you can, compliment the customer's knowledge, experience, or insight.
- Show respect for the customer's knowledge. For example, you can ask the customer's advice. Say something like, "What do you think the problem is?" (However, don't ask this question of customers who are not confident because they most likely don't have the answer and might lose confidence in you.)
- Slow the conversation down. You can say, "Please slow down. You're moving too fast for me to follow. Help me understand."

A+ ESS
8.1
8.2

A+
220-602
8.1
8.2

▲ Don't back off from using problem-solving skills. You must still have the customer check the simple things, but direct the conversation with tact. For example, you can say, "I know you've probably already gone over these simple things, but could we just do them again together?"

▲ Be careful not to accuse the customer of making a mistake.

▲ Use technical language in a way that conveys you expect the customer to understand you.

## WHEN THE CUSTOMER COMPLAINS

When you are on-site or on the phone, a customer might complain to you about your organization, products, or service or the service and product of another company. Consider the complaint to be helpful feedback that can lead to a better product or service and better customer relationships. Here are a few suggestions on how to handle complaints and customer anger:

▲ Be an active listener, and let customers know they are not being ignored. Look for the underlying problem. Don't take the complaint or the anger personally.

▲ Give the customer a little time to vent, and apologize when you can. Then start the conversation from the beginning, asking questions, taking notes, and solving problems. Unless you must have the information for problem solving, don't spend a lot of time finding out exactly whom the customer dealt with and what happened to upset the customer.

▲ Don't be defensive. It's better to leave the customer with the impression that you and your company are listening and willing to admit mistakes. No matter how much anger is expressed, resist the temptation to argue or become defensive.

▲ Know how your employer wants you to handle a situation where you are verbally abused. If this type of language is happening, you might say something like this in a very calm tone of voice: "I'm sorry, but my employer does not require me to accept this kind of talk."

▲ If the customer is complaining about a product or service that is not from your company, don't start off by saying, "That's not our problem." Instead, listen to the customer complain. Don't appear as though you don't care.

▲ If the complaint is against you or your product, identify the underlying problem if you can. Ask questions and take notes. Then pass these notes on to people in your organization who need to know.

▲ Sometimes simply making progress or reducing the problem to a manageable state reduces the customer's anxiety. As you are talking to a customer, summarize what you have both agreed on or observed so far in the conversation.

▲ Point out ways that you think communication could be improved. For example, you might say, "I'm sorry, but I'm having trouble understanding what you want. Could you please slow down, and let's take this one step at a time."

## WHEN THE CUSTOMER DOESN'T WANT TO END A PHONE CALL

Some customers like to talk and don't want to end a phone call. In this situation, when you have finished the work and are ready to hang up, you can ease the caller into the end of the call. Ask if anything needs more explanation. Briefly summarize the main points of the call, and then say something like, "That about does it. Call if you need more help." Be silent about new issues. Answer only with yes or no. Don't take the bait by engaging in a new topic. Don't get frustrated. As a last resort, you can say, "I'm sorry, but I must go now."

A+ ESS
8.1
8.2

A+
220-602
8.1
8.2

## WHEN YOU CAN'T SOLVE THE PROBLEM

You are not going to solve every computer problem you encounter. Knowing how to **escalate** a problem to those higher in the support chain is one of the first things you should learn on a new job. When escalation involves the customer, generally follow these guidelines:

▲ Before you escalate, first ask knowledgeable coworkers for suggestions for solving the problem, which might save you and your customer the time and effort it takes to escalate it.

▲ Know your company's policy for escalation. What documents do you fill out? Who gets them? Do you remain the responsible "support" party, or does the person now addressing the problem become the new contact? Are you expected to keep in touch with the customer and the problem, or are you totally out of the picture?

▲ Document the escalation. It's very important to include the detailed steps necessary to reproduce the problem, which can save the next support person lots of time.

▲ Pass the problem on according to the proper channels of your organization. This might mean a phone call, an online entry in a database, or an e-mail message.

▲ Tell the customer you are passing the problem on to someone who is more experienced and has access to more extensive resources. In most cases, the person who receives the escalation will immediately contact the customer and assume responsibility for the problem. However, you should follow through, at least to confirm that the new person and the customer have made contact.

▲ If you check back with the customer only to find out that the other support person has not called or followed through to the customer's satisfaction, don't lay blame or point fingers. Just do whatever you can to help within your company guidelines. Your call to the customer will go a long way toward helping the situation.

## *PROTECTING SOFTWARE COPYRIGHTS*

As a computer support technician, you will be faced with the legal issues and practices surrounding the distribution of software. When someone purchases software from a software vendor, that person has only purchased a **license** for the software, which is the right to use it. The buyer does not legally *own* the software and, therefore, does not have the right to distribute it. The right to copy the work, called a **copyright**, belongs to the creator of the work or others to whom the creator transfers this right.

As a PC technician, you will be called upon to install, upgrade, and customize software. You need to know your responsibilities in upholding the law, especially as it applies to software copyrights. Copyrights are intended to legally protect the intellectual property rights of organizations or individuals to creative works, which include books, images, and software. While the originator of a creative work is the original owner of a copyright, the copyright can be transferred from one entity to another.

### FEDERAL COPYRIGHT ACT OF 1976

The Federal Copyright Act of 1976 was designed in part to protect software copyrights by requiring that only legally obtained copies of software be used; the law also allows for one backup copy of software to be made. Making unauthorized copies of original software violates the Federal Copyright Act of 1976 and is called software piracy or, more officially, software copyright infringement. Making a copy of software and then selling it or giving it away is a violation of the law. Because it is so easy to do, and because so many people do it, many people don't realize that it's illegal. Normally, only the person who violated the copyright law is liable for infringement; however, in some cases, an employer or supervisor is also held responsible, even when the copies were made without the employer's knowledge. The Business Software Alliance (*www.bsa.org*) is a membership organization of software manufacturers and vendors, which has estimated that 26 percent of the business software in the United States is obtained illegally.

By purchasing a **site license**, a company can obtain the right to use multiple copies of software, which is a popular way for companies to provide software to employees. With this type of license, companies can distribute software to PCs from network servers or execute software directly off the server. Read the licensing agreement of any software to determine the terms of distribution.

## INDUSTRY ASSOCIATIONS

One of two associations committed to the prevention of software piracy is the Software Information Industry Association, a nonprofit organization that educates the public and enforces copyright laws. Its Web address is *www.siia.net*, and its antipiracy hotline is 1-800-388-7478. The other organization, the Business Software Alliance, manages the BSA Anti-Piracy Hotline at 1-888-NOPIRACY. The BSA can also be reached at its e-mail address: *software@bsa.org*. Its Web site is *www.bsa.org*. These associations are made up of hundreds of software manufacturers and publishers in North and Latin America, Europe, and Asia. They promote software raids on large and small companies; in the United States, they receive the cooperation of the U.S. government to prosecute offenders.

Vendors might sometimes sell counterfeit software by installing unauthorized software on computers for sale. This practice is called **hard-disk loading**. Vendors have even been known to counterfeit disk labels and Certificates of Authenticity. Warning signs that software purchased from vendors is pirated include:

- ◢ No end-user license is included.
- ◢ There is no mail-in product registration card.
- ◢ Software is installed on a new PC, but documentation and original disks are not included in the package.
- ◢ Documentation is photocopied, or discs have handwritten labels.

## WHAT ARE YOUR RESPONSIBILITIES UNDER THE LAW?

The Federal Copyright Act of 1976 protects the exclusive rights of copyright holders. It gives legal users of software the right to make one backup copy. Other rights are based on what the copyright holder allows. In 1990, the U.S. Congress passed the Software Rental Amendment Act, which prevents renting, leasing, lending, or sharing software without the express written permission of the copyright holder. In 1992, Congress instituted criminal penalties for software copyright infringement, which include imprisonment for up to five years and/or fines up to $250,000 for the unlawful reproduction or distribution of 10 or more copies of software.

Your first responsibility as an individual user is to use only software that has been purchased or licensed for your use. When you install software, one step in the installation is to agree to the end-user licensing agreement (EULA). Print and file this agreement as a record of the licensing requirements you have agreed to follow.

As an employee of a company that has a site license to use multiple copies of the software, your responsibility is to comply with the site license agreement. It is also your responsibility to purchase only legitimate software. Purchasers of counterfeit or copied software face the risk of corrupted files, virus-infected disks, inadequate documentation, and lack of technical support and upgrades as well as the legal penalties for using pirated software.

## >> CHAPTER SUMMARY

▲ Four key job roles of a PC repair technician include PC support technician, PC service technician, bench technician, and help-desk technician.

▲ A+ Certification by CompTIA is the most significant and most recognized certification for PC repair technicians.

▲ Staying abreast of new technology can be done by attending trade shows, reading trade magazines, researching the Internet, and attending seminars and workshops.

▲ Customers want more than just technical know-how. They want a positive and helpful attitude, respect, good communication, ownership of their problem, dependability, credibility, and professionalism.

▲ The buyer of software does not legally own the software or have the right to distribute it. According to the Federal Copyright Act of 1976, you have the right to make one backup copy of software.

## >> KEY TERMS

A+ Certification
call tracking
copyright

escalate
expert systems
hard-disk loading

license
site license
technical documentation

## >> REVIEW QUESTIONS

1. Which of the following PC technician job functions is the only one responsible for the PC before trouble occurs?

   **a.** PC support technician

   **b.** PC service technician

   **c.** Bench technician

   **d.** Help-desk technician

2. Which of the following PC technician job functions only interacts with customers and users over the phone?

   **a.** PC support technician

   **b.** PC service technician

   **c.** Bench technician

   **d.** Help-desk technician

3. Which of the following certification exams grants you the Remote Support Technician designation?

   **a.** A+ Essentials exam

   **b.** A+ 220-602 exam

   **c.** A+ 220-603 exam

   **d.** A+ 220-604 exam

4. Which of the following is probably the most significant indication that a PC technician is doing a good job?

   a. You are in and out of a customer site quickly.

   b. Customers are consistently satisfied.

   c. You have a smile on your face even when the job is not going well.

   d. You make sure to record everything about the customer visit.

5. When an individual purchases software from a software vendor, that person has only purchased which of the following?

   a. The copyright

   b. A site license

   c. The right to ongoing, free upgrades

   d. A license for the software

6. True or false? To become certified, all individuals must pass the A+ Essentials exam.

7. True or false? Hardware and software products typically do not have additional technical documentation and tend to rely on just the user manual.

8. True or false? Your internal customers work for the same company that you do.

9. True or false? The practice of selling counterfeit software by installing unauthorized software on computers for sale is called hard-disk pirating.

10. True or false? Purchasing a site license gives a company the right to use multiple copies of software.

11. The most significant certifying organization for PC technicians is the _____.

12. Software that is designed and written to help solve problems by using databases of known facts and rules to simulate human experts' reasoning and decision making is called _____ software.

13. Most organizations have a(n) _____ system in which the date, time, and length of help-desk or on-site calls are recorded.

14. The process of transferring a customer problem (that you have been unable to solve) to someone higher in the support chain is called _____.

15. Presently, there are _____ A+ advanced exams.

# How an OS Uses System Resources

**A** system resource is a tool used by either hardware or software to communicate with the other. When BIOS or a driver wants to send data to a device (such as when you save a file to the hard drive), or when a device needs attention (such as when you press a key on the keyboard), the device or software uses system resources to communicate. When you install a hardware device under DOS or Windows 9x/Me, it is sometimes necessary to configure which system resources a device will use. Therefore, for these operating systems, a technician needs a general understanding about system resources discussed in this appendix.

There are four types of system resources: interrupt request numbers (IRQs), memory addresses, I/O addresses, and direct memory access (DMA) channels. Table A-1 lists these system resources used by software and hardware, and defines each.

As you can see in Table A-1, all four resources are used for communication between hardware and software. Hardware devices signal the CPU for attention using an IRQ. Software addresses a device by one of its I/O addresses. Software looks at memory as a hardware device and addresses it with memory addresses, and DMA channels pass data back and forth between a hardware device and memory.

All four system resources depend on certain lines on a bus on the motherboard (see Figure A-1). A bus such as the system bus has three components: the data bus carries data, the address bus communicates addresses (both memory addresses and I/O addresses), and the control bus controls communication. (IRQs and DMA channels are controlled by this portion of the bus.)

| System Resource | Definition |
|---|---|
| IRQ | A line of a motherboard bus that a hardware device can use to signal the CPU that the device needs attention. Some lines have a higher priority for attention than others. Each IRQ line is assigned a number (0 to 15) to identify it. |
| Memory addresses | Numbers assigned to physical memory located either in RAM or ROM chips. Software can access this memory by using these addresses. Memory addresses are communicated on the address bus. |
| I/O addresses | Numbers assigned to hardware devices that software uses to send a command to a device. Each device "listens" for these numbers and responds to the ones assigned to it. I/O addresses are communicated on the address bus. |
| DMA channel | A number designating a channel on which the device can pass data to memory without involving the CPU. Think of a DMA channel as a shortcut for data moving to and from the device and memory. |

**Table A-1**   System resources used by software and hardware

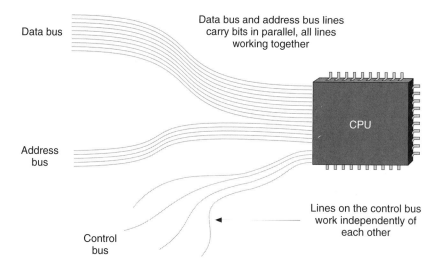

**Figure A-1**   A bus consists of a data bus, an address bus, and a control bus

Let's turn our attention to a more detailed description of the four resources and how they work.

## INTERRUPT REQUEST NUMBER (IRQ)

When a hardware device needs the CPU to do something—for instance, when the keyboard needs the CPU to process a keystroke after a key has been pressed—the device needs a way to get the CPU's attention, and the CPU must know what to do once it turns its attention to the device. Getting the CPU's attention is known as a hardware interrupt, and the device creates a hardware interrupt by placing voltage on the designated interrupt request (IRQ) line assigned to the device. This voltage on the line serves as a signal to the CPU that the device has a request that needs processing. Often, a hardware device that needs attention from the CPU is referred to as "needing servicing." Interrupts initiate many processes that the CPU carries out, and these processes are said to be "interrupt-driven."

Table A-2 lists common uses for the sixteen available IRQs. The respective I/O addresses, which are listed in the second column of the table, are discussed in the third section of this appendix.

| IRQ | I/O Address | Device |
|---|---|---|
| 0 | 0040–005F | System timer |
| 1 | 0060–006F | Keyboard controller |
| 2 | 00A0–00AF | Access to IRQs above 7 |
| 3 | 02F8–02FF | COM2 (covered in Chapter 9) |
| 3 | 02E8–02EF | COM4 (covered in Chapter 9) |
| 4 | 03F8–03FF | COM1 (covered in Chapter 9) |
| 4 | 03E8–03EF | COM3 (covered in Chapter 9) |
| 5 | 0278–027F | Sound card or parallel port LPT2 (covered in Chapter 9) |
| 6 | 03F0–03F7 | Floppy drive controller |
| 7 | 0378–037F | Printer parallel port LPT1 (covered in Chapter 9) |
| 8 | 0070–007F | Real-time clock |
| 9–10 | N/A | Available |
| 11 | N/A | SCSI or available |
| 12 | 0238–023F | Motherboard mouse |
| 13 | 00F8–00FF | Math coprocessor |
| 14 | 01F0–01F7 | IDE hard drive (covered in Chapter 8) |
| 15 | 0170–017F | Secondary IDE hard drive or available (covered in Chapter 8) |

**Table A-2**   IRQs and I/O addresses for devices

In Table A-2, notice the COM and LPT assignments. Recall from Chapter 9 that a COM or LPT assignment is an agreed-on grouping of I/O addresses and an IRQ value. In the industry, it is agreed that when a device is configured to use COM1, it is using I/O addresses 03F8 through 03FF and IRQ 4. When all device and motherboard manufacturers agree to this and other COM and LPT assignments, it is less likely that devices will attempt to use conflicting resources, and it makes it easier to configure a device.

COM1 and COM2 are predetermined assignments that can be made to serial devices such as modems, and LPT1 and LPT2 are predetermined assignments that can be made to parallel devices such as printers. For example, a modem is built so that you can choose between using COM1 or COM2 for its resource assignments, rather than having to specify a particular IRQ or range of I/O addresses.

On motherboards, part of the chipset called the interrupt controller manages the IRQs for the CPU. The CPU actually doesn't know which IRQ is "up" because the interrupt controller manages that. If more than one IRQ is up at the same time, the interrupt controller selects the IRQ that has the lowest value to process first. For example, if a user presses a key on the keyboard at the same time that she moves the mouse configured to use COM1, the keystroke is processed before the mouse action, because the keyboard is using IRQ 1 and the mouse on COM1 is using IRQ 4. In other words, the interrupt controller is sort of the doorman to the CPU's apartment building. All devices wait outside the door while the interrupt controller decides who should be "let in" first, according to the IRQ value each holds in his hand.

The interrupt controller on early motherboards was designed to handle only eight different IRQs. To accommodate the need for more devices, a second group of IRQs was later added (IRQs 8 through 15), and a second interrupt controller was added to manage these new IRQs. This second controller did not have access to the CPU, so it had to communicate with the CPU through the first controller (see Figure A-2). To signal the first controller, the second controller used one of the first controller's IRQ values (IRQ 2). These last eight IRQs plug into the system using IRQ 2. Because of this, the IRQ priority level became: 0, 1, (8, 9, 10, 11, 12, 13, 14, 15), 3, 4, 5, 6, 7.

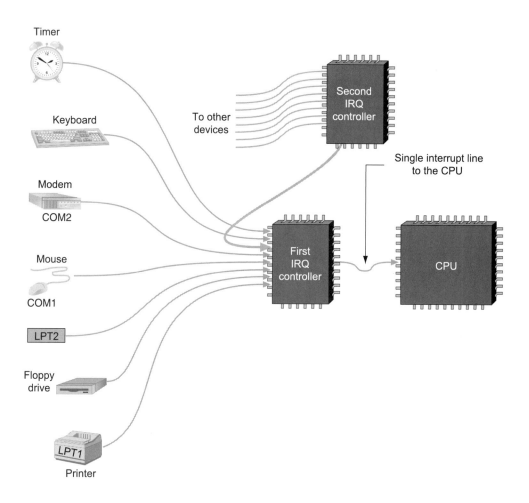

**Figure A-2** The second IRQ controller uses IRQ 2 to signal the first IRQ controller

# APPLYING|CONCEPTS

To see how the IRQs are assigned on your computer, you can use Device Manager for Windows 2000/XP and Windows 9x/Me. (For DOS, use a utility called MSD.) For Windows XP, click **Start**, right-click **My Computer**, and select **Properties** on the shortcut menu. For Windows 2000, right-click **My Computer** on the desktop and select **Properties** on the shortcut menu. The System Properties dialog box opens, as shown in Figure A-3. Click the **Hardware** tab and then click the **Device Manager** button. On the menu, click **View**, and then click **Resources by Type**, if necessary. Click the plus sign next to Interrupt request (IRQ) to open the list of assigned IRQs. Notice in the figure that IRQ 9 is being shared by three devices, and IRQ 11 is being shared by two.

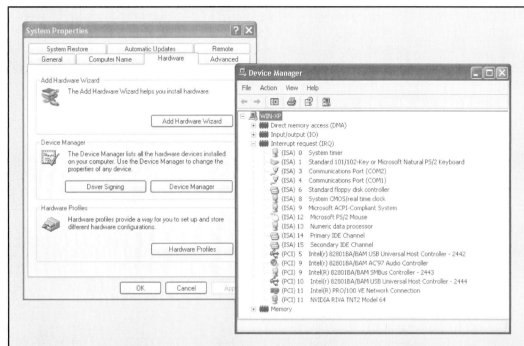

**Figure A-3**   Use Device Manager to see how your system is using IRQs and other system resources

To see current assignments in Windows 9x/Me, click **Start**, point to **Settings**, click **Control Panel**, and double-click **System**. Click the **Device Manager** tab, select **Computer,** and then click **Properties.** Figure A-4 shows the Computer Properties dialog box. Notice that IRQ 2 is assigned to the programmable interrupt controller because it is being used to manage IRQs 8 through 15.

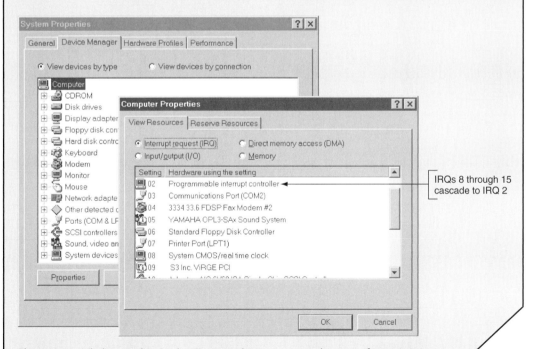

**Figure A-4**   Windows 9x/Me Device Manager shows current assignments for system resources

When using interrupts, the hardware device or the software does the work of getting the CPU's attention. However, the flow of "attention getting" can go the other way as well. This other way is called polling. With polling, software that was written for a specific hardware device constantly runs and occasionally asks the CPU to check this hardware device to see if it needs service. Not very many devices use polling as the method of communication; most hardware devices use interrupts. A joystick is one example of a device that does use polling. Software written to manage a joystick has the CPU check the joystick periodically to see if the device has data to communicate, which is why a joystick does not need an IRQ to work.

**Notes**

Sharing IRQs is not possible with ISA devices on the ISA bus. However, newer buses are designed to allow more than one device to share an IRQ.

## MEMORY ADDRESSES

An operating system relates to memory as a long list of cells that it can use to hold data and instructions, somewhat like a one-dimensional spreadsheet. Each memory location or cell is assigned a number beginning with zero. These number assignments are made when the OS is first loaded and are called **memory addresses**.

Think of a memory address as a seat number in a theater (see Figure A-5). Each seat is assigned a number regardless of whether someone is sitting in it. The person sitting in a seat can be data or instructions, and the OS does not refer to the person by name, but only by the seat number. For example, the OS might say, "I want to print the data in memory addresses 500 through 650."

**Figure A-5**   Memory addresses are assigned to each location in memory, and these locations can store data or instructions

These addresses are most often displayed on the screen as hexadecimal (base 16 or hex) numbers in segment: offset form (for example, C800:5, which in hex is C8005 and in decimal is 819,205).

**Notes**

Windows offers a calculator that can quickly convert numbers in binary, digital, and hexadecimal. Enter a number in one number system, and then click another number system to make the conversion. To access the calculator in Windows 2000/XP or Windows 9x/Me, click **Start, Programs** (**All Programs** in Windows XP), **Accessories**, and then **Calculator**. To view the version of the calculator that can convert number systems, click **View, Scientific**.

## I/O ADDRESSES

Another system resource made available to hardware devices is the input/output address, which is also known as an I/O address, a port address, or a port. I/O addresses are numbers the CPU can use to access hardware devices, in much the same way it uses memory addresses to access physical memory. Each device needs a range of I/O addresses so that the CPU can communicate more than one type of command to it.

The address bus on the motherboard sometimes carries memory addresses and sometimes carries I/O addresses. If the address bus has been set to carry I/O addresses, then each device "listens" to this bus (see Figure A-6). If a device (such as a hard drive, floppy drive, or keyboard) hears an address that belongs to it, then it responds; otherwise, it ignores the request for information. In short, the CPU "knows" a hardware device as a group of I/O addresses. If it wants to know the status of a printer or a CD drive, for example, it places a particular I/O address on the address bus on the motherboard.

Because IBM made many address assignments when it manufactured the first PC in the late 1970s, common devices such as a hard drive, a floppy drive, or a keyboard use a range of predetermined I/O addresses that never change. Their BIOS is simply programmed to use these standard addresses and standard IRQs. Legacy devices (devices that use older technologies) were designed to use more than one group of addresses and IRQs, depending on how jumpers or DIP switches were set on the device. Newer devices, called Plug and Play devices, can use any I/O addresses or IRQ assigned to them during startup.

> **Notes**
>
> Refer back to Table A-2 for a listing of a few common assignments for I/O addresses. Because these addresses are usually written as hex numbers, you sometimes see them written with 0x first, such as 0x0040, or with the h last, like this: 0040h.

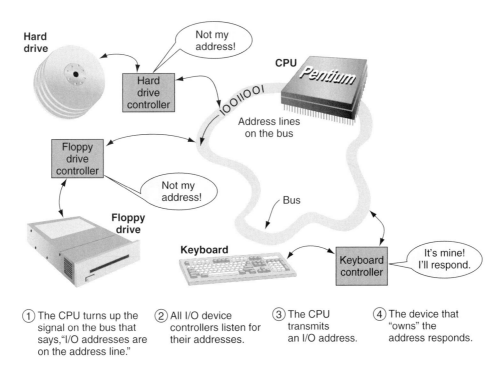

① The CPU turns up the signal on the bus that says, "I/O addresses are on the address line."

② All I/O device controllers listen for their addresses.

③ The CPU transmits an I/O address.

④ The device that "owns" the address responds.

**Figure A-6**   I/O address lines on a bus work much like people sitting in a waiting room waiting for their number to be called; all devices "hear" the addresses, but only one responds

## DMA CHANNELS

Another system resource used by hardware and software is a direct memory access (DMA) channel, a shortcut method that lets an I/O device send data directly to memory. This bypasses the CPU and improves performance.

A chip on the motherboard contains the DMA logic and manages the process. Earlier computers had four DMA channels numbered 0, 1, 2, and 3. Later, channels 5, 6, and 7 were added. DMA channel 4 is used as IRQ 2 was used, as the entry point for the higher DMA channels to connect to the lower channels. This allows the higher channels a way to connect to the DMA controller on the motherboard and on to the CPU. In Figure A-7, you can see that DMA channel 4 is used to point to or cascade into the lower DMA channels.

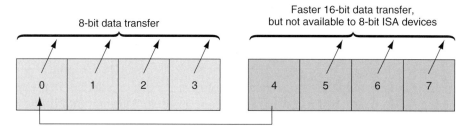

**Figure A-7**   DMA channel 4 is not available for I/O use because it is used to cascade into the lower-four DMA channels

Some devices, such as a printer, are designed to use DMA channels, and others, such as the mouse, are not. Those that use the channels might be able to use only a certain channel, say channel 3, and no other. Alternately, the BIOS might have the option of changing a DMA channel number to avoid conflicts with other devices. Conflicts occur when more than one device uses the same channel. DMA channels are not as popular as they once were, because their design makes them slower than newer methods such as a faster I/O bus. However, slower devices such as floppy drives, sound cards, and tape drives might still use DMA channels.

# APPENDIX B

# Electricity and Multimeters

This appendix gives you a general introduction to what electricity is and how it is measured. In addition, you will learn how to use a multimeter to measure the voltage output of a power supply. Knowing the basics of electricity and how it works with your equipment will make you a stronger PC support technician. In addition, a multimeter can be a handy little tool to help you identify an unknown cable, test continuity in a fuse or other device, or test the voltage output of a notebook AC adapter or PC power supply.

# ELECTRICITY: A BASIC INTRODUCTION

Electricity is energy and water is matter, but the two have enough in common to make some comparisons, as shown in Figure B-1. The water system shown in the top part of the figure is closed; that is, the amount of water in the system remains the same because no water enters and no water leaves the system. The electrical system in the lower part of the figure is closed as well.

Just as water flows down because of the force of gravity, electricity flows from negative to positive because of the force of like charges repelling one another. The water pump produces water pressure in the system by lifting the water, and a battery produces electrical pressure in the system by creating a buildup of negative charges (in the form of electrons) in one location, which are driven to move. This difference in charge, which is similar to water pressure in a water system, is called potential difference. Water seeks a place of rest, moving from a high to a low elevation, and electrons seek a place of rest by moving from a negatively charged location (sometimes called "hot") to a positively charged location (sometimes called "ground"). In the figure, as water flows through the closed system, the water wheel harnesses some of its force and converts it to a form of energy, motion. Also in the figure, as the electrons flow in the closed electrical system called a circuit, the light bulb harnesses some of the force of the moving electrons and converts it to another form of energy, light. When the water returns to the pool, water pressure

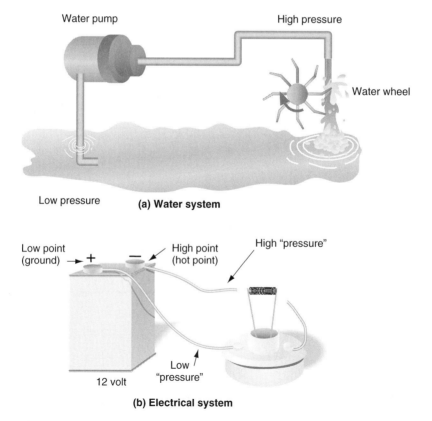

**Figure B-1**   Two closed systems: (a) water system with pump, wheel, and pool; (b) electrical system with battery and light bulb

decreases and the water is at rest. When the electrons arrive at the positive side of the battery, electrical potential difference decreases, and the system is at rest.

Electrical energy has properties that you can measure in various ways. Table B-1 defines four properties of electricity, how they can be measured, and some examples of each. These properties are explained in detail later in this appendix.

> **Notes**
>
> Electron flow goes from the hot point, or negative terminal, to the ground, or positive terminal. Because early theories of electricity assumed that electricity flowed from positive to negative, most electronics books show the current flowing from positive to negative. This theory is called conventional current flow; if it were used in Figure B-1, the figure would show reversed positive and negative symbols.

| Unit | Definition and Measurement | Computer Example |
|---|---|---|
| **Volt (measures potential difference)** | Abbreviated as V (for example, 110 V). Volts are measured by finding the potential difference between the electrical charges on either side of an electrical device in an electrical system. | An AT power supply provides four separate voltages: +12 V, −12 V, +5 V, and −5 V. An ATX or BTX power supply provides these voltages and +3.3 V as well. |
| **Amp or ampere (measures electrical current)** | Abbreviated as A (for example, 1.5 A). Amps are measured by placing an ammeter in the flow of current and measuring that current. | A 17-inch monitor requires less than 2 A to operate. A small laser printer uses about 2 A. A CD-ROM drive uses about 1 A. |
| **Ohm (measures resistance)** | Abbreviated with the symbol $\Omega$ (for example, 20 $\Omega$). Devices are rated according to how much resistance to electrical current they offer. The ohm rating of a resistor or other electrical device is often written somewhere on the device. The resistance of a device is measured when the device is not connected to an electrical system. | Current can flow in typical computer cables and wires with a resistance of near zero $\Omega$. |
| **Watt (measures power)** | Abbreviated W (for example, 20 W). Watts are calculated by multiplying volts by amps. | A computer power supply is rated at 200 to 600 W. |

**Table B-1**   Measures of electricity

## VOLTAGE

Consider how to measure the water pressure in Figure B-1. If you measure the pressure of the water directly above the water wheel and then measure the pressure just as the water lands in the pool, you find that the water pressure above the wheel is greater than the water pressure below it.

Now consider the electrical system. If you measure the electrical charge on one side of the light bulb and compare it with the electrical charge on the other side of the bulb, you see a difference in charge. The potential difference in charge creates an electrical force called voltage, which drives the electrons through the system between two points. Voltage is measured in units called volts (V).

In Figure B-2, the leads of a voltmeter, a device for measuring electrical voltage, are placed on either side of a light bulb that consumes some electrical power. The potential difference between the two points on either side of the device is the voltage in the closed system. Voltage is measured when the power is on.

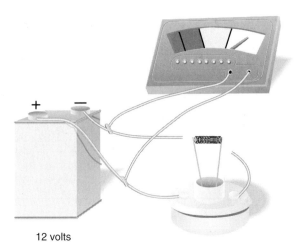

12 volts

**Figure B-2** A voltmeter measuring the voltage across a bulb and a battery

## AMPS

The volume of electrons (or electricity) flowing through an electrical system is called current. Look back at Figure B-1. The volume or amount of water flowing through the water system does not change, although the water pressure changes at different points in the system. To measure that volume, you pick one point in the system and measure the volume of water passing through that point over a period of time. The electrical system is similar. If you measure the number of electrons, or electrical current, at any point in this system, you find the same value as at any other point, because the current is constant throughout the system. (This assumes that the entire closed water or electrical system has only a single pipe or a single wire.)

Electrical current is measured in amperes (A), abbreviated amps. Figure B-3 shows an ammeter, a device that measures electrical current in amps. You place the ammeter in the path of the electrical flow so that the electrons must flow through the ammeter. The measurement, which you take with the power on, might not be completely accurate because the ammeter can influence the circuit. Nonetheless, the measurement still provides useful information.

Because the current flows through an ammeter, check the rating of the ammeter before measuring amps to make sure it can handle the flow of electricity. More flow than the ammeter is designed to handle can blow the meter's fuse.

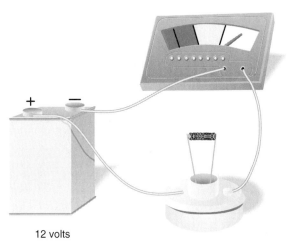

12 volts

**Figure B-3** Battery and bulb circuit with ammeter in line

Refer again to the water system in Figure B-1. To increase the volume of water flowing through the system, you increase the difference in water pressure between the low and high points (which is called the pressure differential). As the pressure differential increases, the water flow (or current) increases, and as the water pressure differential decreases, the water flow (or current) decreases. In other words, there is a direct relationship between pressure differential and current. An electrical system works the same way. As the electrical potential difference (or voltage) increases, the electrical current increases; as the voltage decreases, the current decreases. There is a direct relationship between voltage and current.

## OHMS

Suppose you are working your water pump to full capacity. If you still want to increase the overall power of your water system—so the wheel turns faster to produce more mechanical energy—you could decrease the resistance to water flow, allowing more water to flow to push the wheel faster. You might use a larger pipe or a lighter water wheel, or, if the system has a partially open water valve, you could open the valve more; these alternatives all would lower resistance to water flow. As resistance decreases, current increases. As resistance increases (smaller pipes, heavier wheel, partially closed valve), current decreases.

Similarly, resistance in an electrical system is a property that opposes the flow of electricity. As electrical resistance increases, the flow of electrons decreases. As resistance decreases, the electricity increases. (A condition of low resistance that allows current to flow in a completed circuit is called continuity.) When too much electricity flows through a wire, it creates heat energy (similar to friction) in the wire. This heat energy can cause the wire to melt or burn, which can result in an electrical fire, just as too much water current can cause a pipe to burst. Reducing the size of a wire reduces the amount of electricity that can safely flow through it. Electrical resistance is measured in ohms ($\Omega$).

Resistors are devices used in electrical circuits to resist the flow of electricity. These devices control the flow of electricity in a circuit, much as partially closed valves control the flow of water.

Voltage and current have a direct relationship. This means that when voltage increases, current increases. Resistance has an inverse relationship with current and a direct relationship with voltage. This means that as resistance increases, current decreases if voltage remains constant, such as when you use a dimmer switch to dim a light. As a general rule, the more voltage you expect in an electrical system, in order for current to remain constant, the more resistance you must add in the form of a larger-capacity resistor. This last statement is known as Ohm's Law. A similar statement defines the relationship among the units of measure: volts, amps, and ohms. One volt drives a current of one amp through a resistance of one ohm.

## WATTAGE

Wattage is the total amount of power needed to operate an electrical device. When thinking of the water system, you recognize that the amount of water power used to turn the water wheel is not just a measure of the water pressure that forces current through the system. The amount of power also depends on the amount of water available to flow. For a given water pressure, you have more power with more water flow and less power with less water flow. A lot of power results when you have a lot of pressure and a lot of current.

As with the water system, electrical power increases as both voltage and current increase. Wattage, measured in watts (W), is calculated by multiplying volts by amps in a system ($W = V \times A$). For example, 120 volts times 5 amps is 600 watts. Note that while volts and amps are measured to determine their value, watts are calculated from those values.

## MEASURING THE VOLTAGE OF A POWER SUPPLY

If you suspect a problem with a power supply, the simplest and preferred solution is to replace it with a new one. However, in some situations, you might want to measure the voltage output first. You will learn how to do so in this part of the appendix.

> **Notes**
>
> When a power supply works properly, voltages all fall within an acceptable range (plus or minus 10 percent). However, be aware that even if measured voltage falls within the appropriate range, a power supply can still cause problems. This is because problems with power supplies can be intermittent—in other words, they come and go. Therefore, if the voltages are correct, you should still suspect the power supply is the problem when certain symptoms are present. To learn for certain whether the power supply is the problem, replace it with a unit you know is good.

### USING A MULTIMETER

A voltmeter measures the difference in electrical potential between two points, in volts, and an ammeter measures electrical current in amps. A multimeter, as shown in Figure B-4, can make a variety of measurements, depending on the dial or function switch setting.

Multimeters are sometimes small, portable, battery-powered units. Larger ones are designed to sit on a countertop and are powered by a wall outlet. A multimeter can provide either a digital or an analog display. A digital display shows the readings as digits on an LCD (liquid crystal display) panel. A digital multimeter is sometimes called a DMM (digital

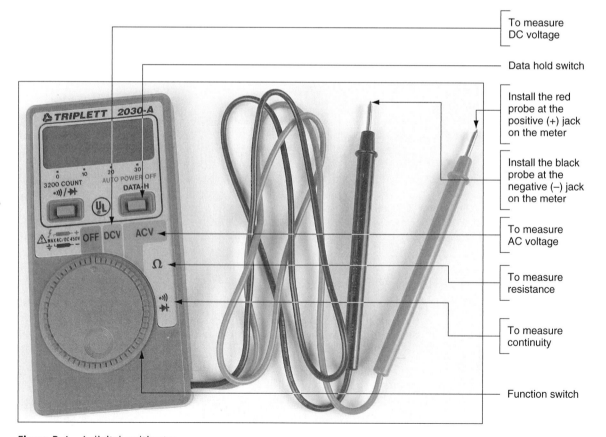

**Figure B-4** A digital multimeter

multimeter) or a DVM (digital voltage meter). An analog display shows the readings as a needle moving across a scale of values.

Before you begin to use a multimeter, you must tell it three things: (1) what you want it to measure (voltage, current, or resistance); (2) whether the current is AC or DC; and (3) what range of values it should expect. If you are measuring the voltage output from a wall outlet (110–120 V), the range should be much higher than when you are measuring the voltage output of a computer power supply (3–12 V). Setting the range high assures you that the meter can handle a large input without pegging the needle (exceeding the highest value the meter is designed to measure) or damaging the meter. However, if you set the range too high, you might not see the voltage register at all. Set the range low enough to ensure that the measure is as accurate as you need but not lower than the expected voltage. When you set the range too low on some digital multimeters, the meter reads "OL" on the display.

For example, to measure the voltage of house current, if you expect the voltage to be 115 volts, set the voltage range from 0 to somewhere between 120 and 130 volts. You want the high end of the range to be slightly higher than the expected voltage. To protect themselves, most meters do not allow a very large voltage or current into the meter when the range is set low. Some multimeters are autorange meters, which sense the quantity of input and set the range accordingly.

> **Notes**
>
> Less expensive multimeters commonly measure voltage, resistance, and continuity, but not amps.

## HOW TO MEASURE VOLTAGE

To measure voltage, place the other end of the black probe at the ground point and the other end of the red probe at the hot point, without disconnecting anything in the circuit and with the power on. For example, to measure voltage using the multimeter in Figure B-4, turn the function switch dial to DCV for DC voltage measurement. This meter is autoranging, so that's all that needs to be set. With the power on, place the two probes in position and read the voltage from the LCD panel. The DATA-H (data hold) switch allows you to freeze the displayed reading.

> **Caution**
>
> When using a multimeter to measure voltage, current, or resistance, be careful not to touch a chip with the probes.

## HOW TO MEASURE CURRENT

In most troubleshooting situations, you will measure voltage, not current. However, you should still know how to measure current. To measure current in amps, the multimeter itself must be part of the circuit. Disconnect the circuit at some point so that you can connect the multimeter in line to find a measure in amps. Note that not all multimeters can measure amps.

## HOW TO MEASURE CONTINUITY

You can also use a multimeter to measure continuity. If there is little or no resistance (less than 20 ohms gives continuity in a PC) in a wire or a closed connection between two points, the path for electricity between the two points is unhindered or "continuous." This measurement is taken with no electricity present in the circuit.

For example, if you want to know that pin 2 on one end of a serial cable is connected to pin 3 on the other end of the cable, set the multimeter to measure continuity, and work without connecting the cable to anything. Put one probe on pin 2 at one end of the cable and the other probe on pin 3 at the other end. If the two pins connect, the multimeter shows a reading on the LCD panel, or a buzzer sounds (see the multimeter documentation).

In this situation, you might find that the probe is too large to extend into the pinhole of the female connection of the cable. A straightened small paper clip works well here to extend the probe. However, be very careful not to use a paper clip that is too thick and might widen the size of the pinhole, because this can later prevent the pinhole from making a good connection.

One way to determine if a fuse is good is to measure continuity. Set a multimeter to measure continuity, and place its probes on each end of the fuse. If the fuse has continuity, then it is good. If the multimeter has no continuity setting, set it to measure resistance. If the reading in ohms is approximately zero, there is no resistance and the fuse is good. If the reading is infinity, resistance is infinite; the fuse is blown and should not be used.

## HOW TO MEASURE THE VOLTAGE OF A POWER SUPPLY

To determine whether a power supply is working properly, measure the voltage of each circuit the power supply supports. To do so, first open the computer case and identify all power cords coming from the power supply. Look for the cords from the power supply to the motherboard and other power cords to the drives (see Figure B-5).

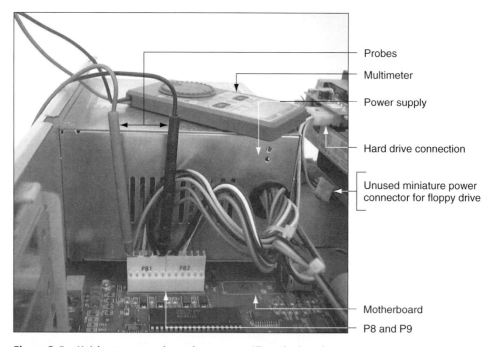

**Figure B-5**  Multimeter measuring voltage on an AT motherboard

The computer must be turned on to test the power supply output. Be very careful not to touch any chips or disturb any circuit boards as you work. The voltage output from the power supply is no more than 14 volts, not enough to seriously hurt you if you accidentally touch a hot probe. However, you can damage the computer if you are not careful.

You can hurt yourself if you accidentally create a short circuit from the power supply to ground through the probe. If you touch the probe to the hot circuit and to ground, you divert current from the computer circuit and through the probe to ground. This short might be enough to cause a spark or to melt the probe, which can happen if you allow the two probes to touch while one of them is attached to the hot circuit and the other is attached to ground. Make sure the probes only touch one metal object, preferably only a single power pin on a connector, or you could cause a short.

Because of the danger of touching a hot probe to a ground probe, you might prefer not to put the black probe into a ground lead too close to the hot probe. Instead, when the directions say to place the black probe on a lead very close to the hot probe, you can use a black wire lead on an unused power supply connection meant for a hard drive. The idea is that the black probe should always be placed on a ground or black lead.

All ground leads are considered at ground, no matter what number they are assigned. Therefore, you can consider all black leads to be equal. For an AT motherboard, the ground leads for P8 and P9 are the four black center leads 5, 6, 7, and 8. For an ATX motherboard, the ground leads are seven black leads in center positions on the ATX P1 power connector. The ground leads for a hard drive power connection are the two black center leads, 2 and 3.

The following sections first discuss how to measure the power output for AT, ATX, and BTX motherboards and then discuss the procedure for a secondary storage device.

## MEASURING VOLTAGE OUTPUT TO AN AT MOTHERBOARD

1. Remove the cover of the computer. The voltage range for each connection is often written on the top of the power supply. The two power connections to the motherboard are often labeled P8 and P9. Figure B-6 shows a close-up of the two connections, P8 and P9, coming from the power supply to the motherboard. Each connection has six leads, for a total of 12 leads. Of these 12, four are ground connections and lead 1 is a "power good" pin, used to indicate that the motherboard is receiving power. Table B-2 lists the purposes of these 12 leads.

2. Set the multimeter to measure voltage in a range of 20 volts, and set the AC/DC switch to DC. Insert the black probe into the negative (–) jack and the red probe into the positive (+) jack of the meter.

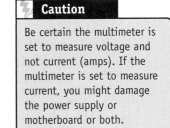

**Caution**

Be certain the multimeter is set to measure voltage and not current (amps). If the multimeter is set to measure current, you might damage the power supply or motherboard or both.

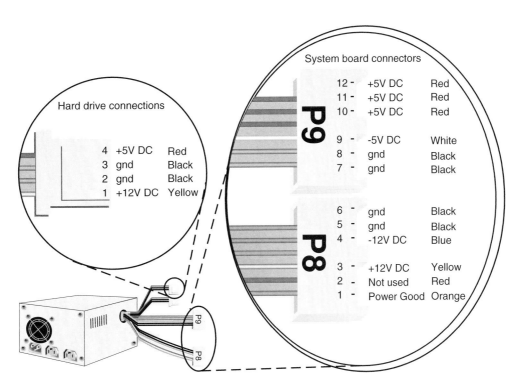

**Figure B-6**   AT power supply connections

| Connection | Lead | Description | Acceptable Range |
|---|---|---|---|
| P8 | 1 | "Power Good" | |
| | 2 | Not used or +5 volts | +4.4 to +5.2 volts |
| | 3 | +12 volts | +10.8 to +13.2 volts |
| | 4 | –12 volts | –10.8 to –13.2 volts |
| | 5 | Black ground | |
| | 6 | Black ground | |
| P9 | 7 | Black ground | |
| | 8 | Black ground | |
| | 9 | –5 volts | –4.5 to –5.5 volts |
| | 10 | +5 volts | +4.5 to +5.5 volts |
| | 11 | +5 volts | +4.5 to +5.5 volts |
| | 12 | +5 volts | +4.5 to +5.5 volts |

**Table B-2**  Twelve leads to the AT motherboard from the AT power supply

3. Turn on the multimeter and turn on the computer.

4. To measure the +12-volt circuit and all four ground leads:

   a. Place the red probe on lead 3. The probe is shaped like a needle. (Alligator clips don't work too well here.) Insert the needle down into the lead housing as far as you can. Place the black probe on lead 5. The acceptable range is +10.8 to +13.2 volts.

   b. Place the red probe on lead 3, and place the black probe on lead 6. The acceptable range is +10.8 to +13.2 volts.

   c. Place the red probe on lead 3, and place the black probe on lead 7. The acceptable range is +10.8 to +13.2 volts.

   d. Place the red probe on lead 3, and place the black probe on lead 8. The acceptable range is +10.8 to +13.2 volts.

5. To measure the –12-volt circuit, place the red probe on lead 4, and place the black probe on any ground lead or on the computer case, which is also grounded. The acceptable range is –10.8 to –13.2 volts.

6. To measure the –5-volt circuit, place the red probe on lead 9, and place the black probe on any ground. The acceptable range is –4.5 to –5.5 volts.

7. To measure the three +5-volt circuits:

   a. Place the red probe on lead 10, and place the black probe on any ground. The acceptable range is +4.5 to +5.5 volts.

   b. Place the red probe on lead 11, and place the black probe on any ground. The acceptable range is +4.5 to +5.5 volts.

   c. Place the red probe on lead 12, and place the black probe on any ground. The acceptable range is +4.5 to +5.5 volts.

8. Turn off the PC and replace the cover.

## MEASURING VOLTAGE OUTPUT TO AN ATX MOTHERBOARD

To measure the output to the ATX motherboard, follow the procedure just described for the AT motherboard. Recall that the ATX board uses 3.3, 5, and 12 volts coming from the power supply. Figure B-7 shows the power output of each pin on the connector. Looking at Figure B-7, you can see the distinguishing shape of each side of the connector. Notice the different hole shapes (square or rounded) on each side of the connector, ensuring that the plug from the power supply is oriented correctly in the connector. Also notice the notch on the connector and on the pinout diagram on the right side of the figure. This notch helps orient you as you read the pinouts. You can also use the color of the wires coming from the power supply to each pin on the P1 connector to help orient the connector. Table B-3 lists the leads to the motherboard and their acceptable voltage ranges.

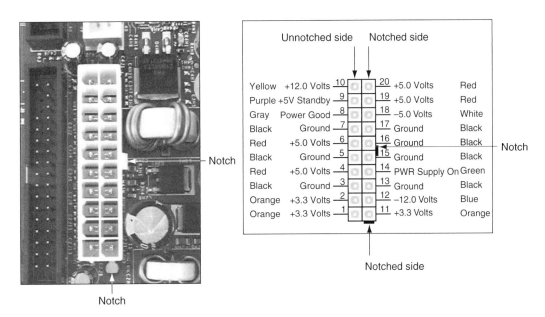

**Figure B-7**   Power connection on an ATX motherboard

| Unnotched Side | | | Notched Side | | |
|---|---|---|---|---|---|
| Lead | Description | Acceptable Range (Volts) | Lead | Description | Acceptable Range (Volts) |
| 1 | +3.3 volts | +3.1 to +3.5 V | 11 | +3.3 volts | +3.1 to +3.5 V |
| 2 | +3.3 volts | +3.1 to +3.5 V | 12 | −12 volts | −10.8 to −13.2 V |
| 3 | Black ground | | 13 | Black ground | |
| 4 | +5 volts | +4.5 to +5.5 V | 14 | Power supply on | |
| 5 | Black ground | | 15 | Black ground | |
| 6 | +5 volts | +4.5 to +5.5 V | 16 | Black ground | |
| 7 | Black ground | | 17 | Black ground | |
| 8 | Power Good | | 18 | −5 volts | −4.5 to −5.5 V |
| 9 | +5 volts standby | +4.5 to +5.5 V | 19 | +5 volts | +4.5 to +5.5 V |
| 10 | +12 volts | +10.8 to +13.2 V | 20 | +5 volts | +4.5 to +5.5 V |

**Table B-3**   Twenty leads to the ATX motherboard from the ATX power supply

> **Notes**
>
> Dell ATX power supplies and motherboards made after 1998 might not use the standard P1 pinouts for ATX, although the power connectors look the same. For this reason, never use a Dell power supply with a non-Dell motherboard, or a Dell motherboard with a non-Dell power supply, without first verifying that the power connector pinouts match; otherwise, you might destroy the power supply, the motherboard, or both. End PC Noise (*www.endpcnoise.com*) sells a pinout converter to convert the P1 connector of a Dell power supply or motherboard to standard ATX. Also, PC Power and Cooling (*www.pcpowerandcooling.com*) makes power supplies modified to work with a Dell motherboard.

## MEASURING VOLTAGE OUTPUT TO AN ENHANCED ATX OR BTX MOTHERBOARD

An Enhanced ATX (ATX version 2.2) or BTX motherboard has a 24-pin P1 power connector, which is diagrammed in Figure B-8. The purposes for the pins for this power connector are listed in Table B-4. These motherboards and power supplies are designed so that the power supply monitors the range of voltages provided to the motherboard and halts the motherboard if voltages are inadequate. Therefore, measuring voltages for these systems is usually not necessary.

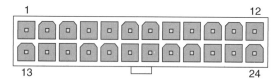

**Figure B-8**   Enhanced ATX or BTX 24-pin power connector on the motherboard

| Unnotched Side | | | Notched Side | | |
|---|---|---|---|---|---|
| Lead | Description | Acceptable Range (Volts) | Lead | Description | Acceptable Range (Volts) |
| 1 | +3.3 volts | 3.2 to 3.5 V | 13 | +3.3 volts | 3.2 to 3.5 V |
| 2 | +3.3 volts | 3.2 to 3.5 V | 14 | −12 volts | −10.8 to −13.2 V |
| 3 | COM | | 15 | COM | |
| 4 | +5 volts | 4.75 to 5.25 V | 16 | PS ON | Power supply is on |
| 5 | COM | | 17 | COM | |
| 6 | +5 volts | 4.75 to 5.25 V | 18 | COM | |
| 7 | COM | | 19 | COM | |
| 8 | Power OK | All voltages are in acceptable ranges | 20 | NC | |
| 9 | +5 volts | Standby voltage is always on | 21 | +5 volts | 4.75 to 5.25 V |
| 10 | +12 volts | 11.4 to 12.6 V | 22 | +5 volts | 4.75 to 5.25 V |
| 11 | +12 volts | 11.4 to 12.6 V | 23 | +5 volts | 4.75 to 5.25 V |
| 12 | +3.3 volts | 3.2 to 3.5 V | 24 | COM | |

**Table B-4**   Twenty-four leads to the Enhanced ATX or BTX motherboard from the power supply

## TESTING THE POWER OUTPUT TO A FLOPPY OR HARD DRIVE

The power cords to the hard drive, CD-ROM drive, floppy drive, and other drives all supply the same voltage: one +5-volt circuit and one +12-volt circuit. These connectors use four leads; the two outside connections are hot, and the two inside connections are ground (see Figure B-6). The power connection to a 3.5-inch floppy disk drive is usually a miniature connection, slightly smaller than other drive connections, but still with four pins. Follow these steps to measure the voltage to any drive:

1. With the drive plugged in, turn on the computer.

2. Set the multimeter to measure voltage, as described earlier.

3. Place the red probe on lead 1, shown in the drive connection callout in Figure B-6, and place the black probe on lead 2 or 3 (ground). The acceptable range is +10.8 to +13.2 volts.

4. Place the red probe on lead 4, and place the black probe on lead 2 or 3 (ground). The acceptable range is +4.5 to +5.5 volts.

You may choose to alter the method you use to ground the black probe. In Step 4, the red probe and black probe are very close to each other. You may choose to keep them farther apart by placing the black probe in a ground lead of an unused hard drive connection.

## PRACTICING MEASURING THE OUTPUT OF YOUR POWER SUPPLY

To practice, measure the power output to your motherboard and to the hard drive. As you do so, fill in the following charts as appropriate. Note that the "red" and "black" designations in the column headers refer to the color of the physical probes.

### AT MOTHERBOARD

| Red Lead | Black Lead | Voltage Measure |
|----------|------------|-----------------|
| 3 | 5 | |
| 3 | 6 | |
| 3 | 7 | |
| 3 | 8 | |
| 4 | Ground | |
| 9 | Ground | |
| 10 | Ground | |
| 11 | Ground | |
| 12 | Ground | |

## ATX MOTHERBOARD

| Red Lead | Black Lead | Voltage Measure |
|----------|------------|-----------------|
| 10 | 7 | |
| 10 | 5 | |
| 10 | 3 | |
| 10 | 17 | |
| 10 | 16 | |
| 10 | 15 | |
| 10 | 13 | |
| 9 | Ground | |
| 6 | Ground | |
| 4 | Ground | |
| 2 | Ground | |
| 1 | Ground | |
| 20 | Ground | |
| 19 | Ground | |
| 18 | Ground | |
| 12 | Ground | |
| 11 | Ground | |

## HARD DRIVE

| Red Lead | Black Lead | Voltage Measure |
|----------|------------|-----------------|
| 1 | 3 | |
| 4 | 2 | |

# Supporting SCSI and Legacy Devices

**I**n Chapter 8, you were introduced to SCSI, an interface standard used by hard drives, CD and DVD drives, scanners, printers, and other devices. Because devices that use a SCSI interface are more expensive and more difficult to install than devices that use other interfaces, they are mostly used in corporate settings and are seldom seen in the small office or used on home PCs. SCSI is slowly being replaced by SATA, FireWire, and USB interfaces. However, because you may find yourself working with SCSI on older systems, the first half of this appendix discusses how SCSI technology works, as well as advantages and disadvantages of SCSI.

In Chapter 9, you learned how to install various external and internal devices using motherboard ports such as a USB port, serial port, or parallel port, and also using AGP, PCI, and PCI Express expansion slots. However, occasionally, as a PC repair technician, you'll be called on to install devices in the older ISA expansions slots. In addition, when supporting Windows 95 or Windows 98, you might have to use legacy 16-bit drivers for an ISA card or an external device that uses a serial or parallel port. The second half of this appendix covers supporting these older ISA cards and 16-bit drivers under Windows 95/98.

## *ALL ABOUT SCSI*

The two general categories of all SCSI standards used on PCs have to do with the width in bits of the SCSI data bus, either 8 bits (**narrow SCSI**) or 16 bits (**wide SCSI**). In almost every case, if the SCSI standard is 16 bits, then the word *wide* is in the name for the standard. In most cases, the word *narrow* is not mentioned in names for 8-bit standards. Narrow SCSI uses a cable with a 50-pin connector (also called an A cable), and wide SCSI uses a cable with a 68-pin connector (also called a P cable).

> **Notes**
>
> The wide SCSI specification allows for a data path of 32 bits, although this is not broadly implemented in PCs. When you see a SCSI device referred to as wide, you can generally assume 16 bits.

### SIGNALING METHODS USED ON SCSI CABLES

A SCSI cable can be built in two different ways, depending on the method by which the electrical signal is placed on the cable: single-ended and differential. Both types of cables send a signal on a pair of twisted wires. In **single-ended (SE) cables**, one of the wires carries voltage and the other is a ground; in **differential cables**, both wires carry voltage and the signal is calculated to be the difference between the two voltages (see Figure C-1).

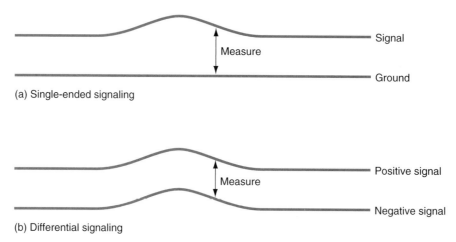

**Figure C-1** A SCSI pair of wires can carry a signal using (a) ground and a signal, or (b) a positive and negative signal, but differential signaling is less likely to be affected by noise on the line

A single-ended cable is less expensive than a differential cable, but the maximum cable length cannot be as long because data integrity is not as great. With differential cabling, signal accuracy is better; noise on the line and electromagnetic interference are less likely to affect signaling because the reading is the difference between the two signals rather than the amplitude of one signal. Differential signaling also sends an extra verifying signal for each bit, providing greater reliability and reducing the chance of data errors.

When differential signaling was first introduced, the difference in voltage between the two wires was high (called **High Voltage Differential**, or **HVD**). This required a large amount of power and circuitry and made it impossible to mix differential and single-ended devices on a system without burning out the hardware. HVD became obsolete with the introduction of the SCSI-3 standard. The introduction of **Low Voltage Differential** (**LVD**) signaling and termination made it possible to develop less expensive, low-voltage interfaces on the device, host adapter, cables, and terminators. As its name implies, LVD signaling uses lower voltages on the two-wire pair. It provides for cable lengths up to 12 meters (about 39.4 feet) and is required with Ultra SCSI standards. There is a type of LVD signaling called LVD/SE multimode that can work with SE devices and cables. If an LVD/SE device is used on a bus with SE devices, it uses the SE signaling method, which is slower and cannot accommodate longer cable lengths. Table C-1 lists and describes the four types of cables.

| SCSI Cable | Maximum Length (meters and feet) | Maximum Speed | Transfer Rate | Description |
|---|---|---|---|---|
| Single-ended (SE) | 3 M (10 ft.) for wide or 6 M (20 ft.) for narrow SCSI | 20 MHz | 40 Mbps | One wire in the pair is ground. |
| High voltage differential (HVD) | 25 M (82 ft.) | 20 or 40 MHz | 40 Mbps | Both wires in the pair have high voltage. |
| Low voltage differential (LVD) | 12 M (40 ft.) for 15 devices or 25 M (80 ft.) for 7 devices | 320 MHz | 80 Mbps | Both wires in the pair have low voltage. |
| LVD/SE multimode | | | | If one SE device is on the bus, the smaller length and speed apply. |

**Table C-1**   SCSI cables

Cables for both narrow SCSI and wide SCSI can be either single-ended or differential. Single-ended, HVD, and LVD cables look the same, so you must make sure that you use the correct cable. It's important to know that you cannot look at a cable, the cable connector, or the connector on a device and know what type of signaling it uses. Connecting an HVD device to a SCSI bus using SE or LVD devices could burn the SE or LVD devices with the high voltage from the HVD device. Look at the device documentation to

> **Notes**
>
> Never use an HVD device on a bus with SE or LVD devices, because the high voltage put on the cable by the HVD device can destroy the low-voltage devices.

learn what type of signaling a device uses, or look for a symbol on the device that indicates the signaling method. Figure C-2 shows the different symbols used on devices and cables to show what kind of signaling they use.

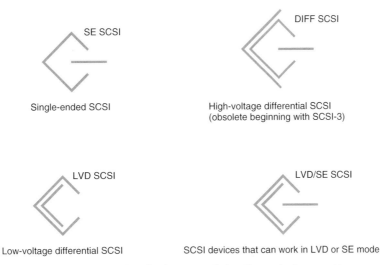

SE SCSI

Single-ended SCSI

DIFF SCSI

High-voltage differential SCSI
(obsolete beginning with SCSI-3)

LVD SCSI

Low-voltage differential SCSI

LVD/SE SCSI

SCSI devices that can work in LVD or SE mode

**Figure C-2**   These symbols tell what type of signaling a device or cable uses

Adapters are available for mixing single-ended and differential devices and cables, but using them is not recommended. Mixing single-ended and differential signaling types is not a good idea because of the different ways they transmit data. Even with adapters, incompatible connections between single-ended and differential signals can damage both the host adapter and the devices connected to it. An exception to this principle is LVD/SE devices designed to work with either LVD or SE and revert to SE mode whenever the two are connected. Even then, however, know that the device is running at a slower speed than it could run if connected to an all-LVD signaling system, and that all cables in the system must meet the shorter SE standard lengths.

## CONNECTORS USED WITH SCSI CABLES

The connector type or the number of pins on a SCSI cable connector are not affected by the signaling method used. Within each signaling method, the number of pins can vary. Figure C-3 shows just a few of the many types of SCSI connectors. Although there are two main types of SCSI connectors, 50-pin (A cable) and 68-pin (P cable), there are other, less common types as well, such as the 80-pin SCA (Single Connector Attachment) connector used with some hot-swapping drives. Only 80-pin connectors supply power to the device in the connector; other devices require separate power connections. A SCSI bus can support more than one type of connector, and you can use connector adapters in order to plug a cable with one type of connector into a port using another type of connector.

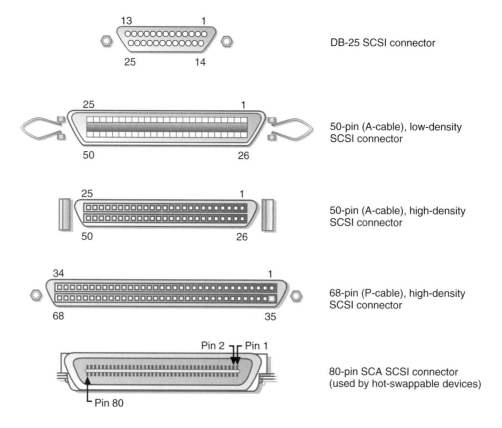

**Figure C-3** The most popular SCSI connectors are 50-pin, A cable connectors for narrow SCSI and 68-pin, P cable connectors for wide SCSI

For each type of connector, there can be variations in shape and pin density. Different companies and device manufacturers can make different connector types. For example, in an attempt to trim the size of the connector, a 25-pin SCSI connector was designed for narrow SCSI. The problem was that this connector looked like a parallel port connector. Never plug a SCSI connector into a parallel port or vice versa; you can damage equipment, because the signals work completely differently.

The good news in all this variety is that adapters are generally available to connect one type of connector to another, meaning that you can mix wide and narrow SCSI devices that use different connector variations. If you have any wide devices on your system at all, the cable from the host adapter must have a 68-pin connector, and you will need to use converters to attach 50-pin narrow devices.

Most recent SCSI devices and buses use D-shaped 50-pin or 68-pin connectors that cannot be plugged in incorrectly. Older 50-pin connectors did not have this shape and could be oriented incorrectly. To line up a 50-pin connector to an internal SCSI device, look for a red or blue stripe on one side of the cable; this stripe lines up with pin 1 on the connector. Look also for a tab on one edge of the connector and a corresponding notch where you are to insert it.

The SCSI bus inside a computer is a ribbon or round cable, and the device connectors for internal devices are plugs at different positions on the cable. Having multiple connectors on the SCSI bus (see Figure C-4) enables you to connect multiple internal devices easily. One end of the bus attaches to the host adapter, and for best results, you should always plug a device into the last connector on the cable.

**Figure C-4**   Internal SCSI cables can be ribbon cables or round cables and can support several devices. This 68-pin ribbon cable by Adaptec supports single-ended and LVD connections.

For external SCSI chains, there are two connectors on each device; both can send or receive information. That means it doesn't matter which connector on one device is linked to which connector on the next. A cable goes from the host adapter to a connector on the first device, and then another cable goes from the second connector on the first device to a connector on the second device, and so on. The last connector on the last device must be filled with a terminator, unless that device provides software termination. External SCSI chains work like some Christmas lights: if one goes out, they all go out. Therefore, when connecting devices in an external SCSI chain, you should make sure to snap in the retaining clips or wires to complete the connection.

## TERMINATION

**Termination** prevents an echo effect from electrical noise and reflected data at the end of the SCSI daisy chain, which can cause interference with data transmission. Each end of a SCSI chain must be terminated, and there are several ways to do that:

▲ The host adapter can have a switch setting that activates or deactivates a terminating resistor on the card, depending on whether or not the adapter is at one end of the chain.

▲ A device can have either a single SCSI connection requiring that the device be placed at the end of the chain, or the device can have two connections. When a device has two connections, the second connection can be used to connect another device or to terminate the chain by placing an external terminator on the connection. This external terminator serves as the terminating resistor.

▲ The device at the end of the chain can also be terminated by a resistor physically mounted on that device in a specially designated socket.

▲ Some devices have built-in terminators (internal terminators) that you can turn on or off with a jumper setting on the device.

▲ Termination can be controlled by software. Sometimes this software uses automatic termination that does not require your intervention.

Termination is needed at the end of both internal and external SCSI chains. If the host adapter is at the end of the SCSI chain, it must be terminated. Only when you have both internal and external devices attached to a host adapter do you remove termination from the host adapter.

There are several types of terminators:

▲ **Passive terminators,** the least reliable type, are used with SCSI-1 devices that operate at low speed and at short distances. They use simple resistors only and are rarely used today, because they are not sufficient for today's faster SCSI devices and longer cabling distances. Passive termination should only be used with narrow SCSI.

▲ **Active terminators** include voltage regulators in addition to the simple resistors used with passive termination. Most of today's single-ended SCSI cables use active termination, which was recommended with SCSI-2. Active termination is used with wide SCSI and is required with fast SCSI. It also works better over longer distances than passive termination.

▲ **Forced perfect terminators (FPTs)** are a more advanced version of active terminators and include a mechanism to force signal termination to the correct voltage, eliminating most signal echoes and interference. FPTs are more expensive and more reliable than passive and active terminators.

Passive terminators, active terminators, and FPTs are all used with single-ended SCSI cables. Differential cables use either HVD or LVD terminators.

## SCSI-1, SCSI-2, AND SCSI-3

Recall that the three major versions of SCSI are SCSI-1, SCSI-2, and SCSI-3, commonly known as Regular SCSI, Fast SCSI, and Ultra SCSI. SCSI-1 was the original version of the SCSI standard. It covered the design of wiring on the SCSI bus but did not include a common command set. Therefore, there were still a lot of incompatibilities between SCSI-1 devices. With SCSI-1, only an 8-bit data bus was used, and there could be only seven devices besides the host adapter.

SCSI-2 improved the standard by developing a common command set so that devices could communicate with each other more easily. It also introduced wide SCSI, which expanded the width of the data bus to 16 bits and the number of possible devices to 15. SCSI-2 also made parity checking of the data bus mandatory.

SCSI-3, which has grown to be a set of standards rather than a single standard, supports both parallel and serial data transmission, supports FireWire connections, and increases the possible rate of data transfer to 320 MB/sec and higher. The **SPI (SCSI Parallel Interface)** standard is part of SCSI-3 and specifies how SCSI devices are connected. There have been three versions of SPI; the latest is Ultra 320 SCSI. SCSI-3 uses an 8-, 16-, or 32-bit data bus and supports up to 32 devices on a system.

Because SCSI standards vary, when you buy a new SCSI device, you must be sure that it is compatible with the SCSI bus you already have, taking into consideration that some SCSI standards are backward-compatible. If the new SCSI device is not compatible, you cannot use the same SCSI bus, and you must buy a new host adapter to build a second SCSI bus system, increasing the overall cost of adding the new device.

Table C-2 summarizes characteristics of the different SCSI standards. Other names used in the industry for these standards are also listed in the table. Note that both Fast SCSI (SCSI-2) and Ultra SCSI (SCSI-3) have narrow and wide versions.

| Standard Name | Standard Number | Bus Width (Narrow = 8 bits, Wide = 16 bits) | Transfer Rate (MB/sec) | Maximum Number of Devices |
|---|---|---|---|---|
| Regular SCSI | SCSI-1 | Narrow | 5 | 8 |
| Fast SCSI or Fast Narrow | SCSI-2 | Narrow | 10 | 8 |
| Fast Wide SCSI or Wide SCSI | SCSI-2 | Wide | 20 | 16 |
| Ultra SCSI, Ultra Narrow, or Fast-20 SCSI | SCSI-3 | Narrow | 20 | 8 |
| Wide Ultra SCSI or Fast Wide 20 | SCSI-3 | Wide | 40 | 16 |
| Ultra2 SCSI or SPI-2 | SCSI-3 | Narrow | 40 | 8 |
| Wide Ultra2 SCSI | SCSI-3 | Wide | 80 | 16 |
| Ultra3 SCSI or SPI-3 | SCSI-3 | Narrow | 80 | 8 |
| Wide Ultra3 SCSI or Ultra 160 SCSI | SCSI-3 | Wide | 160 | 16 |
| Ultra 320 SCSI (Ultra4 SCSI or SPI-4) | SCSI-3 | Wide | 320* | 16 |

*SPI-4 is expected to soon be rated at 640 MBps and then 1280 MBps.

**Table C-2**   Summary of SCSI standards

> ### Notes
>
> The latest SCSI standard, serial SCSI, also called serial attached SCSI (SAS), allows for more than 15 devices on a single SCSI chain, uses smaller, longer, round cables, and uses smaller hard drive form factors that can support larger capacities. Serial SCSI is compatible with serial ATA drives in the same system, and claims to be more reliable and better performing than serial ATA. For more information on serial SCSI, see the SCSI Trade Association's Web site at *www.serialattachedscsi.com*.

Table C-3 summarizes cable specifications for the SCSI standards listed in Table C-2. Note that 8-bit narrow SCSI uses a 50-pin cable and 16-bit wide SCSI uses a 68-pin cable.

| SCSI Standard Name | Maximum Length of Single-Ended Cable (Meters) | Maximum Length of Differential Cable (Meters) | Cable Type |
|---|---|---|---|
| Regular SCSI | 6 | 25 | 50-pin |
| Fast SCSI or Fast Narrow | 3 | 25 | 50-pin |
| Fast Wide SCSI or Wide SCSI | 3 | 25 | 68-pin |
| Ultra SCSI, Ultra Narrow, or Fast-20 SCSI | 1.5 | 25 | 50-pin |
| Wide Ultra SCSI or Fast Wide 20 | 1.5 | 25 | 68-pin |
| Ultra2 SCSI or SPI-2 | | 12 LVD | 50-pin |
| Wide Ultra2 SCSI | | | 68-pin |
| Ultra3 SCSI or SPI-3 | | 12 LVD | 50-pin |
| Wide Ultra3 SCSI or Ultra 160 SCSI | | 12 LVD | 68-pin |
| Ultra 320 SCSI (Ultra4 SCSI or SPI-4) | | 12 LVD | 68-pin |

**Table C-3**   SCSI standard cable specifications

## USING ISA EXPANSION SLOTS

Using legacy ISA expansion slots is a little more difficult than using PCI slots because the configuration is not as automated. The ISA bus itself does not manage system resources, as does the PCI bus controller. It is up to the ISA device to request system resources at startup. If the ISA device does not support Plug and Play (PnP), you select the I/O address, DMA channel, and IRQ by setting jumpers or DIP switches on the card. If the ISA device is PnP-compliant, then at startup, PnP allocates the required resources to the device. After the device and its drivers are installed, look at Device Manager to find out what resources it is using.

 **A+ Tip**

To discover if a device is PnP-compliant, look for "Ready for Windows" on the box or read the documentation.

When adding a legacy ISA expansion card to a system, the most difficult problems you are likely to encounter are resource conflicts between two legacy devices or problems using legacy device drivers. For example, suppose you install a legacy network card in a system, and the card does not work and the modem card has stopped working. Most likely you have a resource conflict. The tool to use for help in resolving hardware conflicts in Windows is Device Manager.

Follow this general approach when installing a legacy device:

> **Notes**
>
> Device Manager is not infallible because it depends on what the OS knows about resources being used, and sometimes a legacy device does not tell the OS what it is using.

1. Recall that Windows 95 and 98 allow legacy 16-bit drivers, but Windows Me and Windows 2000/XP do not. For Windows Me or Windows 2000/XP, search the manufacturer's Web site for 32-bit drivers. If you cannot find them, the device will not work in this system.
2. Know the system resources already in use. See the documentation for devices already installed, use Device Manager, or try both. It's important to keep a notebook dedicated to your PC, in which you keep records of each device and its present settings, as well as any changes you make to your system.
3. Know what resources the device will need (see the documentation). Install the device using resources that are not already used by your system. If the device is set to use a resource already in use, read the documentation to see if you can set a jumper or DIP switch to use an alternate resource. For example, Figure C-5 shows a diagram of a modem card pictured in Figure C-6. The card has a bank of DIP switches on the back of the card and a bank of jumpers on the card itself. By using combinations of these DIP switches and jumpers, you can configure this modem to use a specific set of IRQ and I/O addresses.

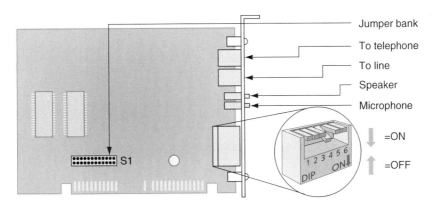

**Figure C-5**   Diagram of a modem card

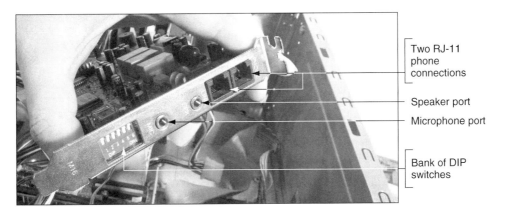

**Figure C-6**   Ports and DIP switches on the back of an internal legacy modem

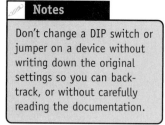

**Notes**

Don't change a DIP switch or jumper on a device without writing down the original settings so you can backtrack, or without carefully reading the documentation.

4. If a card does not work after you install it, try reseating the card in the slot or using a different slot.
5. If the device still does not work or another device stops working, suspect a resource conflict. If you do have a conflict, use Device Manager, CMOS setup, and documentation for the motherboard and devices to first identify and then resolve the conflict. To find out what resources your system is using for Windows 9x/Me, follow Step 6.

6. Click **Start**, point to Settings, click **Control Panel, System**, and then click **Device Manager**. Click **Computer** and then **Properties**. Select the **View Resources** tab. The window in Figure C-7 is displayed. From it, you can view current assignments for IRQs, I/O addresses, DMA channels, and upper memory addresses.

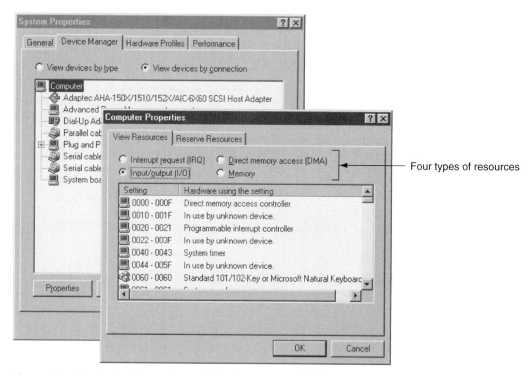

**Figure C-7** Use Device Manager to see I/O addresses currently in use

After you have found the conflicting resource, try the following to resolve the conflict:

1. If the device is a legacy ISA device, physically set the device's jumpers or DIP switches to use a different resource.
2. If a legacy device can only use one IRQ, use CMOS setup to reserve that IRQ for the device.
3. If your BIOS supports PCI bus IRQ steering, enable the feature. That alone might solve the problem. In Device Manager, go to the device's Properties dialog box, click the **IRQ Steering** tab, and check **Use IRQ Steering**. Windows 9x/Me is then allowed to assign the IRQ based on what it knows about IRQs currently being used.
4. Using PCI bus IRQ steering, tell Windows 98 to use a different IRQ for a PCI device. To do that, use the Properties dialog box for the device in Device Manager.
5. Move the device to a different slot. Use the slot closest to the CPU, if you can.

6. Disable PCI bus IRQ steering.

7. Suspect that the documentation for the device is wrong, that the device is faulty, or that there is a problem with the motherboard or the OS. Try a new device in this system, or try this device in another working system.

Sometimes the problem might be that an ISA card can use only a certain IRQ, but that IRQ is not available. When ISA slots and PCI slots exist on the same motherboard, know that the PCI controller is managing the IRQ assignments. These IRQs are the ones left over after legacy ISA bus devices claim their IRQs. However, sometimes BIOS gives the PCI bus controller an IRQ that a legacy ISA device needs, which can prevent either device from working. You can counteract this conflict by going into CMOS setup, where you can specify which IRQ to assign to a PCI slot. You can also tell setup that a particular IRQ is reserved for a legacy device, and thereby prevent the PCI bus from using it, as shown in Figure C-8.

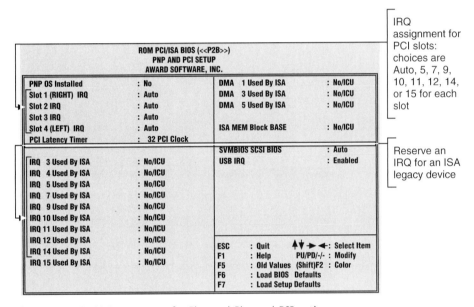

Figure C-8   CMOS Setup screen for Plug and Play and PCI options

## USING LEGACY DRIVERS

Windows 9x/Me contains 32-bit drivers for hundreds of hardware devices, and even more are provided by the device manufacturers. However, some older legacy devices, including ISA cards and external devices that use serial or parallel ports, do not have 32-bit drivers. In this situation, for Windows 95/98, you are forced to use a 16-bit, real-mode device driver. These 16-bit drivers are loaded by entries in the Config.sys, Autoexec.bat, or System.ini file and probably use upper memory addresses.

If you decide to install 16-bit drivers, be sure to back up these files before you begin the installation. Then run a setup program on the floppy disk or CD provided with the device. Next, use the Run dialog box or double-click the program filename in Explorer. The setup program copies the driver files to the hard drive and adds the DEVICE= command to Config.sys. In addition, it might make entries in Autoexec.bat, or, for drivers written for Windows 3.x, it might make entries in System.ini. After you have verified that the device is working, note the changes made to Autoexec.bat, Config.sys, and System.ini. You might want to keep a record of the commands the setup program put in these files, in case you need it for future troubleshooting.

If you have problems with installing or running a legacy driver, do the following:

1. Make every effort to locate a 32-bit driver for the device. Check the Microsoft Web site at *support.microsoft.com*, and check the device manufacturer's Web site. Use a search engine to search the Web for shareware drivers.
2. If you cannot find 32-bit drivers, create an empty copy of Autoexec.bat and Config.sys on your hard drive. Boot up into MS-DOS mode and run the 16-bit setup program from the command prompt. Look at the entries it puts into Autoexec.bat and Config.sys and copy these command lines into your original versions of Autoexec.bat and Config.sys.

# Disassembling a Notebook

If you enjoy putting together a thousand-piece jigsaw puzzle, you'll probably enjoy working on notebook computers. With desktop systems, replacing a component is not a time-consuming task, but with notebooks, the job could take several hours. This appendix gives you some tips and procedures to help make your work easier.

If you take the time to carefully examine the notebook's case before attempting to open it, you will probably find markings provided by the manufacturer to assist you in locating components that are commonly upgraded. If you have a service manual, your work will be much easier than without one. However, after a little practice, you'll see that notebook assemblies have some things in common and disassembling one gets easier with experience.

The best way to learn to disassemble a notebook is to practice on an old one that you can afford to break. Find an old Dell or IBM ThinkPad for which you can download the service manual from the Dell (*www.dell.com*) or IBM Web sites (*www.ibm.com* or *www.lenovo.com*). Then carefully and patiently follow the disassembly instructions and then reassemble it. When done, you can congratulate yourself and move on to newer notebooks. One advantage of starting out this way is that the older notebooks are often more difficult to disassemble than the newer ones. By starting with an older one, you learn skills that will make disassembling a new notebook much easier. One caution is worth repeating: Always make sure the notebook you are disassembling is not under warranty. You don't want to void that warranty.

When disassembling a notebook, consider the following tips, which are also covered in Chapter 20:

▲ Take your time. Patience is needed to keep from scratching or marring plastic screw covers, hinges, and the case.

▲ As you work, don't force anything. If you find yourself forcing something, you're likely to break it.

▲ Always wear a ground strap or use other protection against ESD.

▲ When removing cables, know that sometimes cable connectors are ZIF connectors. To disconnect a cable from a ZIF connector, first lift up the sides of the connector, which releases the cable from the connector, and then remove the cable.

▲ Use a dental pick or very small screwdriver to pry up the plastic cover hiding a screw. Screws around the LCD panel and keyboard are often hidden beneath plastic circles pasted on top of the screw. This plastic can easily be damaged or lost.

## DISASSEMBLING AN OLDER THINKPAD

As a general rule, the older the notebook is, the more difficult it will be to disassemble, and the ThinkPad is no exception. Fortunately, though, the older IBM ThinkPad 755c notebook, which uses a 486 processor, uses some disassembly procedures that are typical to several older notebooks. Generally, follow these steps to disassemble the notebook:

1. The easy-to-get-to drives and battery pack are hidden under the keyboard. Release the spring latches on both sides of the keyboard and raise it. You can then use a ribbon or handle connected to the battery, hard drive, and floppy drive to remove each (see Figure D-1).

**Figure D-1**   Raise the keyboard as a lid, which exposes drives and the battery inside the case

2. To remove the keyboard, pry up the black plastic covers near the keyboard hinges, and remove the screws under these covers, which allows you to then remove the keyboard hinges. Next, remove the plastic cover at the top of the keyboard, which exposes the three cable connectors for the keyboard (see Figure D-2). Disconnect these three ZIF connectors by first using a small screwdriver or dental pick to raise the sides of the connector, which releases pressure on the cable. Then remove the cable.

3. This notebook uses a DRAM credit card memory module. The module is removed by sliding it out of its motherboard slot (see Figure D-3).

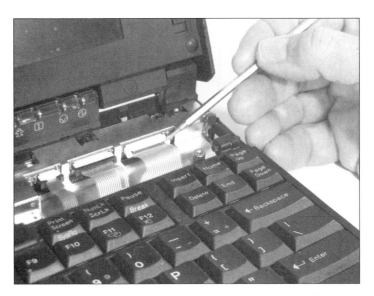

**Figure D-2**    Three ZIF connectors hold the three keyboard cables in place

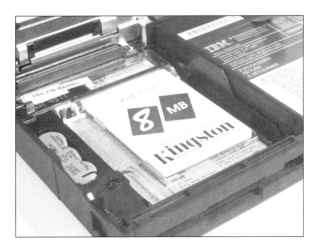

**Figure D-3**    Remove the DRAM memory module

4. To remove the modem card, audio card, or DC controller card, you must first remove a speaker shield located just under the top half of the keyboard (see Figure D-4). The shield is secured with 10 screws. Remove the screws and then the shield. Take care to record where each screw goes because they are not all the same size.

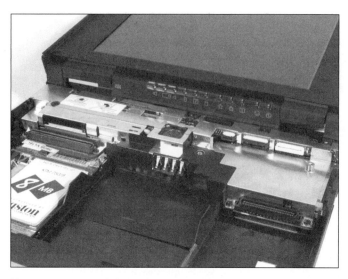

**Figure D-4**    A speaker shield separates the keyboard from the audio card underneath

5. The audio card is now exposed. Lift it up, gently disconnecting it from its slot on the motherboard (see Figure D-5). Then disconnect the audio cable.

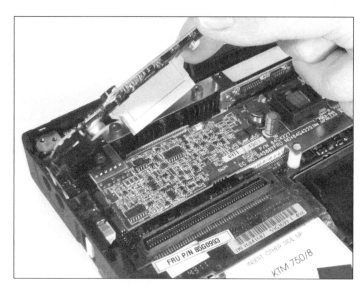

**Figure D-5**    Remove the audio card and then disconnect the audio cable

6. If you need to remove the DC controller, first remove the LCD panel assembly, which is rather tedious because the LCD panel is connected to the motherboard by several small wires and cables. After they are removed, the DC controller is exposed and can be removed by first removing two screws and a bracket that hold it in place.

7. Next, the backup and standby batteries can be removed and then the motherboard. (These batteries are covered in the next section.) The motherboard comes out of the case with the rear panel assembly still connected (see Figure D-6). The PCMCIA slot assembly is then exposed and can be removed.

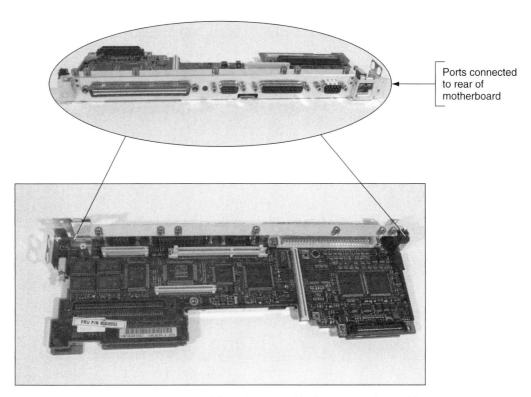

Ports connected
to rear of
motherboard

**Figure D-6**    The motherboard is removed from the case with the rear panel assembly
connected, which can then be removed

This notebook is one of the more difficult to disassemble. Figure D-7 shows all parts
ready to be reassembled in reverse order.

> **Notes**
>
> After assembling a notebook, before powering it up, turn the notebook upside down a couple of times
> and listen for any rattles that might indicate a loose screw, spring, or other small part. If you hear any
> rattles, disassemble the notebook and correct the problem.

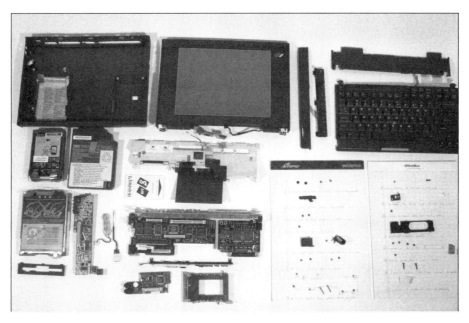

**Figure D-7**    Notebook parts disassembled

## DISASSEMBLING A NEWER DELL NOTEBOOK

In this next example, we'll disassemble a Pentium II notebook, the Dell Latitude CPi. This notebook is more typical of newer notebooks because there are not so many small brackets and screws.

**Notes**

If you plan to disassemble a Dell Latitude computer, download the entire service manual from the Dell Web site so that you will have the complete details of the procedures. In this appendix, to conserve space, some details have been omitted.

1. Back up data, turn the system off, and remove the battery pack. Put on a ground strap to protect the system against ESD.

2. Remove the hard drive by turning the computer over and removing two screws on the bottom near the hard drive door. Then pull the drive out of the case (see Figure D-8).

3. Another easy-to-get-to component is the memory card. First remove the plate on the bottom of the computer. Then gently push the two clips outward on each side of the memory card. Rotate it up and out of the slot (see Figure D-9).

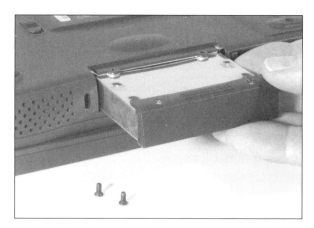

**Figure D-8**   Remove the hard drive by first removing two screws that hold the drive in place

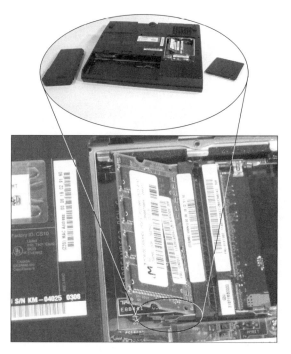

**Figure D-9**   Remove the memory module card by first releasing clips on both sides of the card

4. You can now open the case. Figure D-10 shows the order of components to be removed. First, on the bottom of the computer, remove six screws that hold the keyboard to the case.

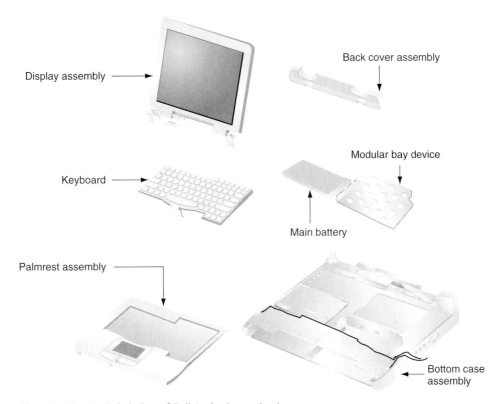

Display assembly

Back cover assembly

Modular bay device

Keyboard

Main battery

Palmrest assembly

Bottom case assembly

**Figure D-10**  Exploded view of Dell Latitude notebook

5. Next, push the latches on the palm rest assembly outward to release the assembly from the keyboard.

6. Insert a small screwdriver under the edge of the blank key on the right edge of the keyboard and push up on the keyboard (see Figure D-11). Lift the keyboard up and out.

**Figure D-11**  Pry up the keyboard using a screwdriver on the right of the keyboard

7. The rear assembly is removed next. To do that, remove the 12 screws on each side of a port and on the right and left sides of the back cover. The back cover can then be removed (see Figure D-12).

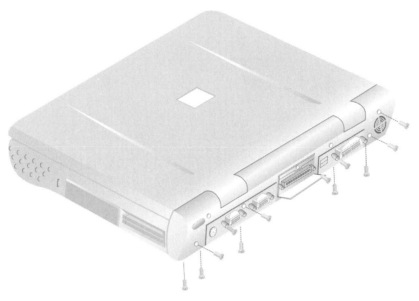

**Figure D-12**   Twelve screws hold the back cover in place

8. The palm rest assembly is removed next by first disconnecting the touch pad cable from the ZIF connector, removing six screws that hold the assembly in place, and then removing the assembly itself.

9. The display assembly is removed next. Its components are shown in Figure D-13. First remove the grounding screw from the LCD interface cable and disconnect the interface cable from the connector on the motherboard. Close the display.

10. Remove the four hinge screws, two on each side, and lift the display assembly from the case.

11. To disassemble the LCD panel assembly, first remove the four screws along the top of the assembly and the two screws on the bottom (refer to Figure D-13). Be certain to keep track of which screw goes where; they are not all the same size.

12. Separate the front bezel from the LCD panel by first prying them apart slightly. You can then see hidden snaps holding them together. Release the hidden snaps and remove the bezel.

> ⚡ **Caution**
>
> As you work, be careful not to put pressure on the LCD panel. If it breaks, and fluid gets on your skin or in your eyes, run water over your skin or eyes for at least 15 minutes.

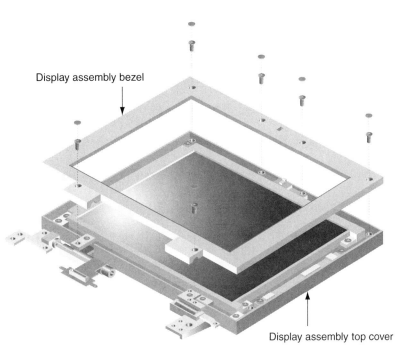

**Figure D-13**   Exploded LCD panel assembly

13. Next, remove the audio card (see Figure D-14). To do that, remove the screw holding the speaker shield in place and then remove the shield. Then disconnect the audio wires and microphone wires from the audio board, and lift the audio board from the case.

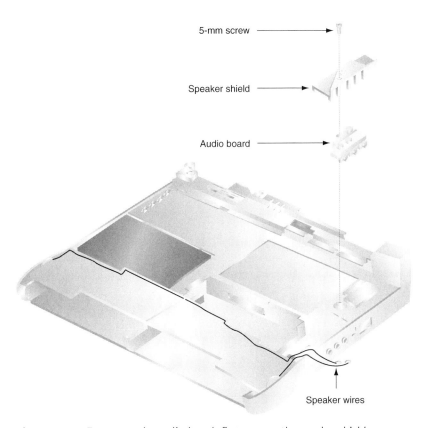

**Figure D-14**   To remove the audio board, first remove the speaker shield

14. The motherboard is removed next (see Figure D-15). First remove the two screws holding the thermal cooling assembly in place, and then remove the assembly, which is on top of the processor. Remove the airflow duct.

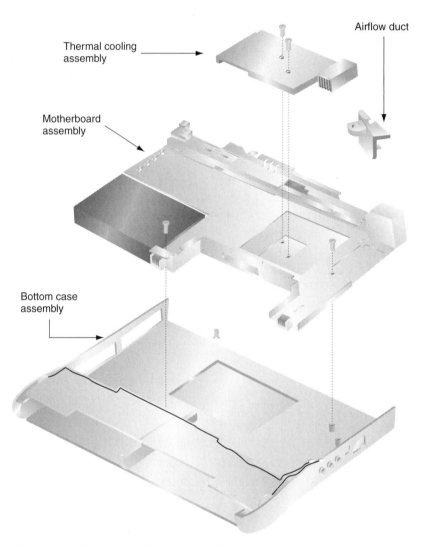

Thermal cooling assembly

Airflow duct

Motherboard assembly

Bottom case assembly

**Figure D-15** Exploded motherboard assembly

15. Remove the left rear foot on the base of the computer, and then remove the two screws holding the motherboard in place. Lift it out of the case.

# Introducing Linux

**U**nix is a popular OS used to control networks and to support applications used on the Internet. A variation of Unix is Linux (pronounced "Lih-nucks"), an OS created by Linus Torvalds when he was a student at the University of Helsinki in Finland. Basic versions of this OS are available for free, and all the underlying programming instructions (called source code) are also freely distributed.

Like Unix, Linux is distributed by several different companies, whose versions of Linux are sometimes called distributions. Popular distributions of Linux are shown in Table E-1. Linux can be used both as a server platform and a desktop platform, but its greatest popularity has come in the server market. Hardware requirements for Linux vary widely, depending on the distribution and version installed.

### Notes

For more information on Linux, see *www.linux.org* as well as the Web sites of the different Linux distributors.

| Name | Comments | Web Site |
|------|----------|----------|
| Red Hat Linux | The most widely used distribution in the world, from Red Hat Software. | *www.redhat.com* |
| OpenLinux | Produced by The SCO Group (formerly Caldera International). Aimed at business users. | *www.sco.com* |
| UnitedLinux | A Linux distribution created by multiple Linux vendors as a common base product on which numerous Linux applications can be designed to run. | *www.unitedlinux.com* |
| TurboLinux | Focused on providing high-end, specialized server software to businesses. | *www.turbolinux.com* |
| Mandrake | Built on Red Hat Linux with many additional packages. Popular at retail outlets. | *www.mandrakelinux.com* |
| Stampede | A distribution optimized for speed. | *www.stampede.org* |
| Debian | A noncommercial Linux distribution targeted specifically to free software enthusiasts. Debian does not have a company behind it. It is created and maintained by developers of free software. | *www.debian.org* |
| SuSE | The leading German distribution. Increasingly popular in the United States. | *www.novell.com/linux/suse* |
| Yellow Dog Linux | A version of Linux for Macintosh computers, written for the PowerPC processor. | *www.yellowdoglinux.com* |

**Table E-1**   Popular Linux distributions

Some of the advantages and disadvantages of Linux are:

▲ Linux rarely crashes.
▲ Basic versions can be downloaded and installed free of charge.
▲ Linux distributions that include technical support and software packages are available at a lower cost than other operating systems.
▲ Linux has strong features for handling network connections.
▲ Source code is available to users, enabling customization of the development environment.
▲ Linux on an inexpensive PC is an excellent training tool for learning Unix.
▲ Linux can be difficult to install, particularly for users who are not familiar with Unix commands.
▲ Most distributions of Linux run from a command line, which can be difficult for casual users to operate.
▲ Documentation can be spotty.
▲ Optimizing a Linux system can take a significant investment of time and research.
▲ Not as many desktop applications are available for Linux as for Windows, though a Windows-like office suite (Star Office) can be installed.

Network services such as a Web server or e-mail server often are provided by a computer running the Linux operating system. Linux is well suited to support various types of servers. Because Linux is very reliable and does not require a lot of computing power, it is sometimes used as a desktop OS, although it is not as popular for this purpose because it is not easy to use.

As a PC support technician, you should know a little about Linux, including a few basic commands, which are covered in this appendix. You will learn about root and user accounts, file structure, some common commands, and how to use the vi editor. Finally, we'll discuss window managers.

The material in this section is meant as a general introduction to the OS. The organization of files and folders, the desktop's appearance, and the way each command works might be slightly different with the distribution and version of Linux you are using.

## ROOT ACCOUNT AND USER ACCOUNTS

Recall that an operating system is composed of a kernel, which interacts with the hardware and other software, and a shell, which interacts with the user and the kernel. Linux is a Unix-like operating system, and can use more than one shell, just as with other versions of Unix. The default shell for Linux is the Bash shell. The name stands for "Bourne Again Shell" and takes the best features from two previous shells, the Bourne and the Korn shells.

For a Linux or Unix server, the system administrator is the person who installs updates to the OS (called patches), manages backup processes, supports the installation of software and hardware, sets up user accounts, resets passwords, and generally supports users. The system administrator has root privileges, which means that he or she can access all the functions of the OS; the principal user account is called the root account. The administrator protects the password to the root account because this password gives full access to the system. When logged on, the administrator is logged on as the user root. You can use the *who* command to show a list of all users currently logged on to the system. In the following example, typing *who* shows that three users are currently logged on: the root user, James, and Susan.

```
who

root tty1 Oct 12 07:56

james tty1 Oct 12 08:35

susan tty1 Oct 12 10:05
```

**Notes**

The Linux command prompt for the root user is different from the command prompt for ordinary users. The root command prompt is #, and other users have the $ command prompt.

## DIRECTORY AND FILE LAYOUT

The main directory in Unix and Linux is the root directory and is indicated with a forward slash. (In Unix and Linux, directories in a path are separated with forward slashes, in contrast to the backward slashes used by DOS and Windows.) Use the *ls* command, which is similar to the DOS Dir command, to list the contents of the root directory. The command (*ls -l /*) and its results are shown in Figure E-1.

Notice that the *-l* parameter is added to the command, which displays the results using the long format, and that there are spaces included before and after the parameters of the command. Also notice in the figure the format used to display the directory contents. The *d* at the beginning of each entry indicates that the entry is a directory, not a file. The other letters in this first column have to do with the read and write privileges assigned to the directory and the right to execute programs in the directory. The name of the directory is in the last column. The rights assigned the directory can apply to the owner of the directory, to other users, or to an entire group of users.

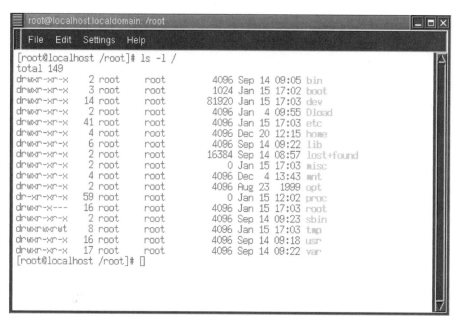

**Figure E-1**   A directory listing using the ls command

Table E-2 lists directories that are created in the root directory during a typical Linux installation. The actual list of directories for a Linux computer that you work with might be a little different, because the directories created in the root directory depend on what programs have been installed.

| Directory | Description |
|---|---|
| /bin | Contains programs and commands necessary to boot the system and perform other system tasks not reserved for the administrator, such as shutdown and reboot. |
| /boot | Consists of components needed for the boot process, such as boot loaders. |
| /dev | Holds device names, which consist of the type of device and a number identifying the device. Actual device drivers are located in the /lib/modules /[kernel version]/ directory. |
| /etc | Contains system configuration data, including configuration files and settings and their subdirectories. These files are used for tasks such as configuring a user account, changing system settings, and configuring a domain name resolution service. |
| /home | Contains user data. Every user on the system has a directory in the /home directory, such as /home/jean or /home/scott, and when a user logs on, that directory becomes the current working directory. |
| /lib | Stores common libraries used by applications so that more than one application can use the same library at one time. An example is the library of C programming code, without which only the kernel of the Linux system could run. |
| /lost+found | Stores data that is lost when files are truncated or when an attempt to fix system errors is unsuccessful. |
| /opt | Contains installations of third-party applications such as Web browsers that do not come with the Linux OS distribution. |
| /root | The home directory for the root user; contains only files specific to the root user. Do not confuse this directory with the root directory, which contains all the directories listed in this table. |

**Table E-2**   Directories in a typical Linux root directory

| Directory | Description |
|-----------|-------------|
| /sbin | Stores commands required for system administration. |
| /tmp | Stores temporary files, such as the ones that applications use during installation and operation. |
| /usr | Constitutes the major section of the Linux file system and contains read-only data. |
| /var | Holds variable data such as e-mail, news, print spools, and administrative files. |

**Table E-2**   Directories in a typical Linux root directory (continued)

## LINUX COMMANDS

This section describes some basic Linux and Unix commands, together with simple examples of how some are used. As you read along, be aware that all commands entered in Linux or Unix are case sensitive, meaning that uppercase and lowercase matter. Table E-3 shows some common commands for Linux and Unix. This is not meant to be a comprehensive list of commands, but simply a list you might find useful in working with files, directories, network connections, and system configuration. In the rest of the section, you will learn how to use a few common commands. For all of these procedures, assume that you are in your home directory (which would be /home/<yourname>/).

| Command | Description |
|---------|-------------|
| cat | Lets you view the contents of a file. Many Linux commands can use the redirection symbol > to redirect the output of the command. For example, use the redirection symbol with the cat command to copy a file:<br><br>`cat /etc/shells > newfile`<br><br>The contents of the shells file are written to newfile. |
| cd | Changes the directory. For example, `cd/etc` changes the directory to /etc. |
| chmod | This command changes the attributes assigned to a file and is similar to the DOS Attrib command. For example, to grant read permission to the file myfile:<br><br>`chmod+r myfile` |
| clear | Clears the screen. This command is useful when the screen has become cluttered with commands and data that you no longer need to view. |
| cp | Used to copy a file:<br><br>`cp <source> <destination>` |
| date | Entered alone, this command displays the current system date setting. Entered in the format date `<mmddhhmmyy>`, this command sets the system date. For example, to set the date to Dec 25, 2006 at 11:59 in the evening:<br><br>`date 1225235906` |
| echo | Displays information on the screen. For example, to display which shell is currently being used, enter this command:<br><br>`echo $SHELL` |
| fdisk | Creates or makes changes to a hard drive partition table:<br><br>`fdisk <hard drive>` |

**Table E-3**   Some common Linux and Unix commands

| Command | Description |
|---------|-------------|
| grep | Searches for a specific pattern in a file or in multiple files:<br>`grep <pattern> <file>` |
| hostname | Displays a server's FQDN:<br>`hostname` |
| ifconfig | Used to troubleshoot problems with network connections under TCP/IP. This command can disable and enable network cards and release and renew the IP addresses assigned to these cards. For example, to show all configuration information:<br>`ifconfig -a`<br>To release the given IP address for a TCP/IP connection named eth0 (the first Ethernet connection of the system):<br>`ifconfig eth0 -168.92.1.1` |
| kill | Kills a process instead of waiting for the process to terminate:<br>`kill <process ID>` |
| ls | The ls command is similar to the DOS Dir command, which displays a list of directories and files. For example, to list all files in the /etc directory, using the long parameter for a complete listing:<br>`ls -l /etc` |
| man | Displays the online help manual, called man pages. For example, to get information about the echo command:<br>`man echo`<br>The manual program displays information about the command. To exit the manual program, type q. |
| mkdir | This command makes a new directory:<br>`mkdir <directory>` |
| \|more | Appended to a command to display the results of the command on the screen one page at a time. For example, to page the ls command:<br>`ls \|more` |
| mv | Moves a file or renames it, if the source and destination are the same directory:<br>`mv <source> <destination>` |
| netstat | Shows statistics and status information for network connections and routing tables:<br>`netstat` |
| nslookup | Queries domain name servers to look up domain names:<br>`nslookup` |
| ping | Used to test network connections by sending a request packet to a host. If a connection is successful, the host will return a response packet:<br>`ping <host>` |
| ps | Displays the process table so that you can identify process IDs for currently running processes (once you know the process ID, you can use the kill command to terminate a process):<br>`ps` |

**Table E-3**   Some common Linux and Unix commands  (continued)

| Command | Description |
|---------|-------------|
| pwd | Shows the name of the present working directory:<br><br>`pwd` |
| reboot | Reboots the system:<br><br>`reboot` |
| rm | Removes the file or files that are specified:<br><br>`rm <file>` |
| rmdir | This command removes a directory:<br><br>`rmdir <directory>` |
| route | Entered alone, this command shows the current configuration of the IP routing table. Entered in the following format, it configures the IP routing table:<br><br>`route[options]` |
| traceroute | Shows the route of IP packets; used for debugging connections on a network:<br><br>`traceroute <host>` |
| useradd | Adds a user to a system:<br><br>`useradd [option] <user>` |
| userdel | Removes a user from a system:<br><br>`userdel <user>` |
| vi | Launches a full-screen editor that can be used to edit a file:<br><br>`vi <file>` |
| whatis | Displays a brief overview of a command. For example, to get quick information about the echo command:<br><br>`whatis echo` |
| who | Displays a list of users currently logged in:<br><br>`who` |

**Table E-3**  Some common Linux and Unix commands  (continued)

## EDITING COMMANDS

When you add options and file or directory names to a command, it can get quite long, and if you make a mistake while typing the command, you will want to edit it. Also, once the command has been entered, you can retrieve it, edit it, and press Enter to reissue the command. Some shells allow you to use the arrow, Backspace, Insert, and Delete keys to edit command lines, but other shells do not. Instead, you need to use the following keystrokes to edit a command line:

- Alt+D to delete a word
- Ctrl+K to delete from the current position to the end of the line
- Ctrl+A to move the cursor to the beginning of the command line
- Alt+B to move the cursor left one word
- Alt+F to move the cursor right one word

Follow these steps to edit a command line:

1. Type **who is this** but *do not* press Enter.

2. To move one word to the left, press **Alt+B** so that your cursor is positioned on the word "is."

3. To delete the word "is," press **Alt+D**.

4. To delete the portion of the command line that follows the current cursor position, press **Ctrl+K**.

5. To move the cursor to the beginning of the command line, press **Ctrl+A**.

## VIEWING THE SHELLS FILE

The shells file in the /etc directory contains a list of available shells to use on a Linux system. Each shell incorporates slightly different support for programming and scripting languages. In addition, different Linux shells may use keystrokes other than the ones you just learned in supporting command-line editing; the keystrokes in the procedure in the last section work in Bash, the default Linux shell. To determine whether you are using the Bash shell, type **echo $shell** and press **Enter**. If you see the output /bin/bash, you are using the Bash shell. If you are not using the Bash shell, type **bash** and press **Enter** to change to the Bash shell.

To view a list of available shells:

1. Type **cat /etc/shells**, and then press **Enter**.

2. A list of available shells appears. This list might include the entries /bin/bash, /bin/bsh, /bin/csh, /bin/sh, /bin/tcsh, and /bin/zsh. Notice that all these shells are stored in the /bin directory. Type **clear**, and then press **Enter** to clear the screen.

3. Type **cat –n /etc/shells**, and then press **Enter**. Notice that this time, the same list of shells is displayed with a number before each line because you used the –n option. (See Figure E-2.) Notice in the figure that the current user is root.

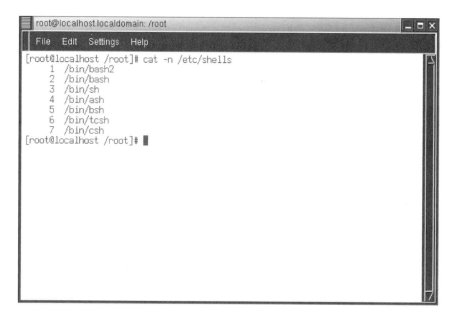

**Figure E-2**   Use the Cat command to display a list of shells

## REDIRECTING OUTPUT

When you entered the command cat /etc/shells in the preceding procedure, the list of available shells, which is the output of that command, was sent to the screen. What if you wanted to save that list? You would use the **redirection symbol**, which is the greater-than (>) sign, to direct the output to a file, perhaps with the name available_shells. To do so, use these steps:

1. Go to the root directory by typing **cd /** and pressing **Enter**.

2. Type **cat /etc/shells > available_shells**, and then press **Enter**.

3. Notice that no command output appears on the screen, because the output has been saved to the new file available_shells (the file is created when the command is entered). To view the contents of the file, type **cat available_shells**, and then press **Enter**. The file is created in the current directory, which is the root directory.

## CREATING A DIRECTORY

It is not a good idea to store data files in the root directory, so let's create a directory to which to move the new file available_shells:

1. Type **mkdir myfiles**, and then press **Enter**. This creates a directory named myfiles under the current directory, which is root.

2. Type **cd myfiles** to change from the current directory to the new directory.

3. Type **mv /available_shells .** and then press **Enter**. (Don't overlook the space and the period at the end of the command line; type them, too.) This moves the file from the root directory to the current directory, which is /myfiles. The source directory is the root and the destination directory is /myfiles. The period in a command line means the current directory.

4. Type **ls** to see the contents of the myfiles directory. The available_shells file is listed. (See Figure E-3.)

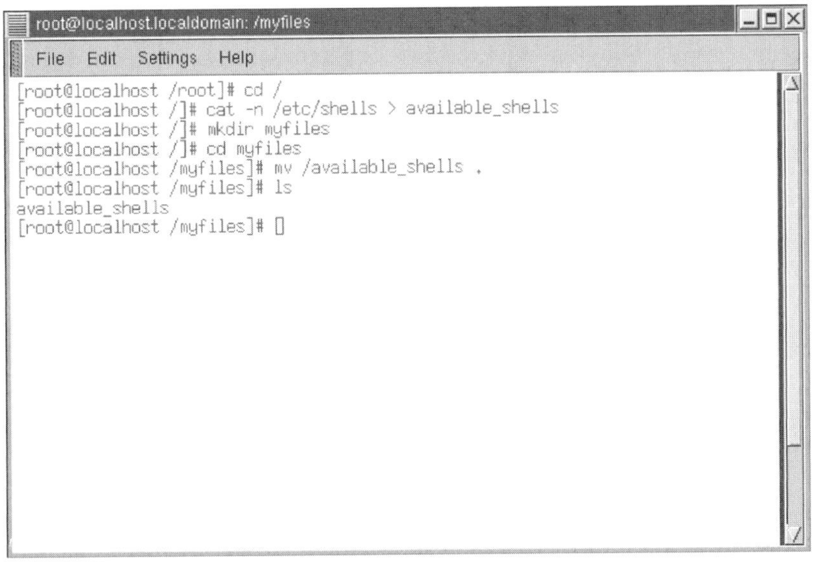

```
root@localhost.localdomain: /myfiles                        _ □ ×

 File   Edit   Settings   Help

[root@localhost /root]# cd /
[root@localhost /]# cat -n /etc/shells > available_shells
[root@localhost /]# mkdir myfiles
[root@localhost /]# cd myfiles
[root@localhost /myfiles]# mv /available_shells .
[root@localhost /myfiles]# ls
available_shells
[root@localhost /myfiles]# []
```

**Figure E-3**   Creating and moving files to a directory

## USING THE VI EDITOR

You were introduced to the vi command in Table E-3 earlier in the appendix. This command launches the vi editor, which got its name because it is a visual editor; at one time, vi was the most popular Unix text editor. It is still used with shells that don't allow the use of the arrow, Delete, or Backspace keys. You can use the editor in insert mode, in which you can enter text, or command mode, which allows you to enter commands to perform editing tasks to move through the file. In this section, you will learn how to create and use commands on a text file in the vi editor. All of these commands are case sensitive.

Let's create and work with a file called mymemo.

1. To open the vi editor and create a file at the same time, type the command followed by the filename, as follows: **vi mymemo**, and then press **Enter**. The vi editor screen is shown in Figure E-4.

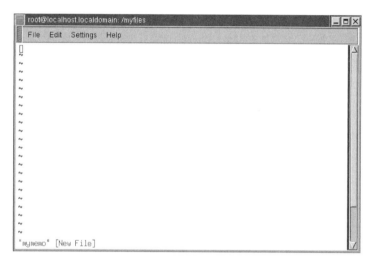

**Figure E-4**   The vi text editor

2. When you first open the vi editor, you are in command mode, which means that anything you type will be interpreted as a command by the vi editor. Type **i** to switch to insert mode. You will not see the command on the screen, and you do not need to press Enter to execute it. The command automatically switches you to insert mode. When you are in insert mode, the word INSERT is shown at the bottom of the screen.

3. Type the first two sentences of Step 2 as the text for your memo. If your shell supports it, practice using the arrow keys to move the cursor through the text, up, down, left, and right, one character at a time. If arrow keys are not supported, you can use keystrokes to move the cursor; these keystrokes are listed in Table E-4.

4. To switch back to command mode, press the **Esc** key. Now you are ready to enter commands to manipulate your text. Type **H** to move the cursor to the upper-left corner of the screen. You must use an uppercase H, because all these commands are case sensitive.

5. Type **W** repeatedly until you reach the beginning of the word "first."

6. Type **dw** to delete the word "first." To delete one character at a time, you would use x; to delete an entire line, you would use dd.

7. To save the file and exit the vi editor, type **:x** and press **Enter**. This will save the file and close the editor.

Table E-4 lists the vi editor commands to move the cursor. There are many more commands to manipulate text, set options, cancel, or temporarily leave a vi editor session. For a more complete list of vi editor commands, see a reference dedicated to Linux.

| Command | Alternate | Description |
|---------|-----------|-------------|
| Ctrl+B | Pg up | Back one screen |
| Ctrl+F | Pg down | Forward one screen |
| Ctrl+U | — | Up half a screen |
| Ctrl+D | — | Down half a screen |
| k | Up arrow | Up one line |
| j | Down arrow | Down one line |
| h | Left arrow | Left one character |
| l | Right arrow | Right one character |
| W | — | Forward one word |
| B | — | Back one word |
| 0 (zero) | — | Beginning of the current line |
| $ | — | End of current line |
| NG | — | Line specified by number *n* |
| H | — | Upper-left corner of screen |
| L | — | Last line on the screen |

**Table E-4**  vi editor commands

## WINDOW MANAGERS

Because many users prefer a Windows-style desktop, several applications have been written to provide a GUI for Unix and Linux. These GUIs are called window managers. One popular desktop environment application is GNU Network Object Model Environment (GNOME). GNOME (pronounced "guh-nome") provides a desktop that looks and feels like Windows 98, but is free software designed to use a Linux kernel. The major components of a GNOME window are shown in Figure E-5. For more information about GNOME, see the organization's Web site at *www.gnome.org*. Another popular Linux window manager is the KDE Desktop (*www.kde.org*).

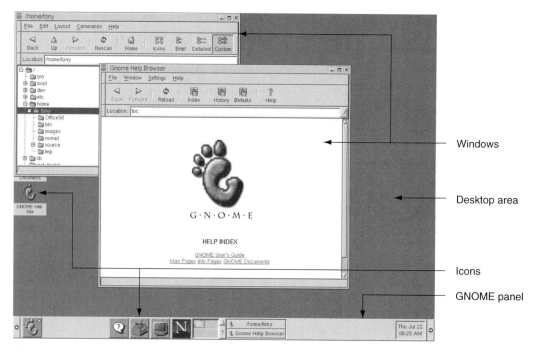

**Figure E-5**   GNOME is popular desktop environment software used on Linux systems

# Introducing the Mac OS

Mac OS X is the latest version of the proprietary OS for Apple Macintosh computers. This appendix covers the basic file and folder organization and startup process for the Mac OS. It is not intended to qualify you to support Macs, but rather to give you a passing familiarity with them, so that you will recognize some of the main features of the OS and know where to go for more information.

## STARTING UP A MAC

When the Mac starts up, you see a graphical record of some of the events occurring in the startup process, such as the loading of the desktop and system applets, including the Finder window (which is used to explore the Mac system). Most of the startup process, however, is hidden from the user. Here are the main steps in the process:

1. The self-test, which is controlled from ROM, is conducted.
2. PRAM (parameter RAM) settings are retrieved.
3. The System folder is located.
4. The Mac OS ROM file is loaded.
5. The smiling Mac icon and welcome screen are displayed.
6. Enablers are loaded.
7. Disk First Aid runs if the Mac was not shut down properly.
8. Other System folder contents are located.
9. The Mac desktop is displayed.
10. Finder and startup programs are loaded.

Each of these steps is described in more detail here, and major differences between Mac OS X and Mac OS 9 are noted.

▲ *The self-test is controlled from ROM.* When you press the power button on a Mac and power is sent to the motherboard, the ROM signals the Mac to perform a self-test. Components tested include the hard drive, the processor, ports, controllers, and expansion cards. The self-test ensures that they are operating correctly. Once this is confirmed, the Mac tests its RAM and halts the startup process if major damage or incorrect installations of RAM modules are detected. Minor damage to RAM might not be detected during the startup test of RAM but might show up in system malfunctions later.

▲ *PRAM settings are retrieved.* In the Mac, PRAM, or parameter RAM, stores configuration information for the Mac OS. After tests of components and RAM are completed, the Mac looks at the PRAM for settings that tell the system which drive is presently designated as the bootable drive (the startup disk). If it looks in that drive and does not find the Mac OS, it keeps looking in drives until it finds a bootable drive. If it cannot find one, the system displays a flashing question mark and pauses the startup process.

▲ *The System folder is located.* After the Mac locates a bootable disk, it looks for an active System folder, which is the folder that the system designates as the one from which the Mac OS is to be loaded. A System folder is required for a disk to be bootable. In Mac OS 9, the System folder is named System Folder, and in Mac OS X, the System folder is named System. See Figure F-1.

▲ *The Mac OS ROM file is loaded.* The first item that the Mac loads into memory from the System folder is the Mac OS ROM file, which contains commands required for interaction with hardware and the lower levels of the Mac OS. Before the iMac, these commands were stored in ROM on the motherboard in the Mac.

▲ *The smiling Mac icon and welcome screen are displayed.* When the smiling Mac icon is displayed, the system is loading the OS into RAM, beginning with the System file containing the libraries and commands that make up the core of the OS.

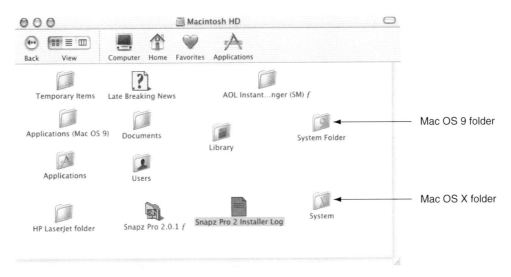

**Figure F-1**   Mac OS 9 is stored in the System Folder, but Mac OS X uses System

▲ *The system loads enablers for hardware components.* If Mac hardware is put on the market before the instructions to control it are included with the OS, an enabler file will be included with it that will enable it to function with the version of Mac OS being used on the computer. The enabler files are loaded after the System file. Generally, each revision of the Mac OS incorporates information included in enabler files that were necessary with the previous version.

▲ *Disk First Aid runs if the* system *was not shut down properly.* If the system is not shut down properly, the next time the computer starts up, the system will run Disk First Aid, a Mac disk utility, to search for and repair any problems that it finds with the hard drive. Disk First Aid runs after the System file and any enabler files are loaded.

▲ *Other contents of the System folder are located.* In Mac OS 9, in addition to the System file and enabler files, the System folder also contains the Control Panels and Extensions folders (see Figure F-2). The Control Panels folder controls system settings such as time and date, speaker volume, and the configuration of the Finder window and the desktop. The Extensions folder contains add-ons to provide new features to a Mac, as well as shared libraries and icons. These no longer exist in Mac OS X; their functions are incorporated into a single Library folder, which is shown in Figure F-3.

▲ *The Mac desktop is displayed.* The Mac desktop is displayed after the necessary contents of the System folder have been loaded. All the required components of the Mac OS have been loaded at this point.

▲ *The Finder window and startup programs are loaded.* After the Mac OS is completely loaded, the Finder window launches so that the user can access programs and files. The Finder itself is an application that is loaded automatically during the startup process, not a part of the OS. When the Finder window has been loaded, the system loads items in the Startup Items folder, which contains items that the user wants to open immediately upon startup. In Mac OS 9, it also opens the Launcher, which provides easy access to commonly used folders, programs, and files, if the Launcher Control Panel has been installed.

**Figure F-2**  In OS 9, the Control Panels and Extensions folders are used to contain OS and applications utilities

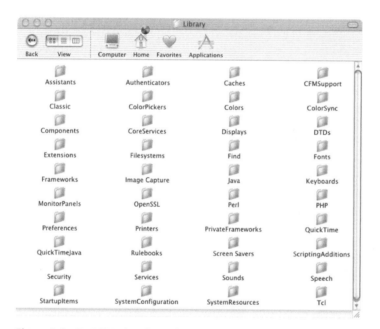

**Figure F-3**  In OS X, the Library folder replaces the Control Panels and Extensions folders of OS 9

## USING A MAC

Now that you've had an overview of the Mac OS startup process, let's look at some major features of the Mac interface and learn some important procedures and hints for using the Mac. In this section, you'll learn about the Finder window, the Apple menu, and procedures to help you work with files and applications in a Mac environment.

### THE MAC DESKTOP

The Mac OS X desktop, with its major components labeled, is shown in Figure F-4. The Finder application is open and active. Because it is the currently active application, the menu bar for the Finder window is displayed at the top of the screen. The menu bar provides pull-down menus that contain options for working with applications, files, and the interface.

A new feature in the Mac OS X user interface is the **dock** that appears at the bottom of the desktop. It contains icons that provide access to frequently used applications. When you click the minus button to minimize a window, an icon representing that window appears in the dock. To open an application from its icon in the dock, just click it once. The icons in the dock that represent open applications have a small triangle underneath them. The Mac OS X desktop also includes shortcut icons that are usually located on the right side of the screen and provide quick access to files, folders, and programs.

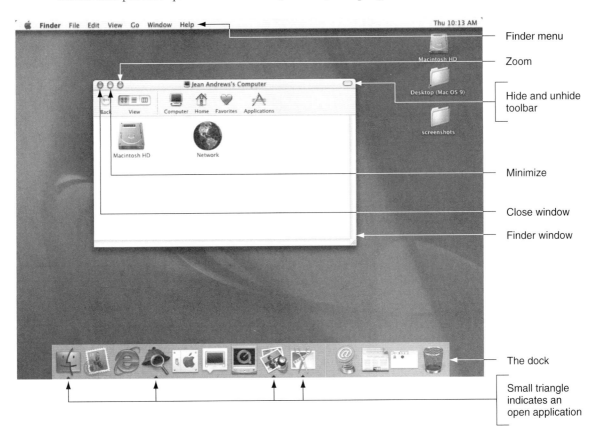

**Figure F-4**  The Mac OS X desktop with a Finder Window showing

The Mac OS X interface has been redesigned, and it does not use its own interface to run applications that were written for OS 9. Instead, it stores the Mac OS 9 applications in a separate folder and launches the OS 9 interface, which it calls the classic interface, whenever a user wants to use one of those applications. In this way, a user can still use older Mac applications with the newer Mac interface. In Figure F-4 you can see the icon on the right side of the screen to launch the Desktop (Mac OS 9) classic interface.

## USING THE FINDER

The Mac's Finder window functions something like Explorer or My Computer in Windows, enabling the user to navigate and access the Mac's files and applications. The Finder window at the computer level, which is the top level of the Mac OS X's hierarchical file structure, shows an icon for the computer's hard drive as well as a Network icon to provide access to any other workstations to which the computer is connected. The Finder window and other windows contain a toolbar that appears at the top of the window and contains buttons that function much like the buttons in a Web browser, such as Back, Home, and Favorites. The Home button on the Mac OS X window toolbar takes the user back to the computer level.

If you use a folder frequently, such as the Documents folder, you can keep it open all the time without having it in your way. In Mac OS 9, drag it down to the bottom of the screen until it becomes a tab on the title bar. In Mac OS X, drag it down to the dock, and it will become an icon on the dock.

Besides allowing you to access programs, files, and folders, the Finder window provides you with a way to organize and manage them. For instance, to create a new folder, locate the folder in which you want to create the new folder using the Finder. When you've reached the desired folder, go to the File menu and click **New Folder.** The new folder will appear with its name highlighted. Type its new name and press the **Return** key to rename the folder.

It is easier to locate a file or folder in the Finder window if you know exactly where it is, especially if there are several levels of folders inside each other. If you don't know the location of the file or folder you want to find, use the Sherlock utility to search for it. By default, the dock in Mac OS X contains an icon for Sherlock; it looks like a hat and a magnifying glass. The search screen for Sherlock is shown in Figure F-5. Type the name of the file, folder, or text you want to find, click the check box next to the location you want to search, and then click the green magnifying glass button to begin the search. In the figure, you are searching the hard drive for a file that is named Myfile.

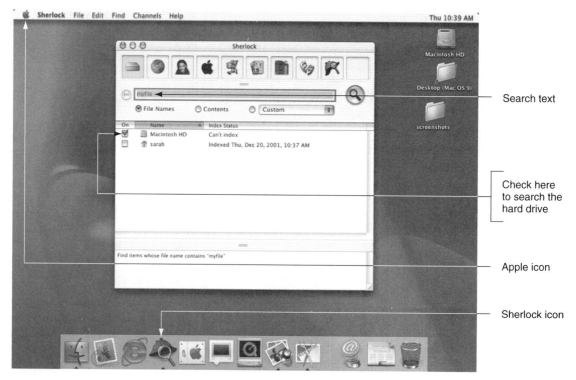

**Figure F-5**  Use Sherlock to search for files and folders

When you don't need a file or folder any more, just drag its icon to the Trash Can until the Trash Can is highlighted, and release the mouse button. Note that this is the only way you can delete icons from the Finder window. When an item is moved to the Trash Can, you can still recover it by double-clicking the Trash Can and locating the item. Items are not actually removed from the system until you chose File, Empty Trash from the menu.

## USING THE APPLE MENU

The menu at the top of the Mac OS screen changes with each application that is active except for the Apple icon, which is always shown at the far left of the menu bar. The Apple menu, which opens when you click the Apple icon, and is similar to the Microsoft Windows Start menu, is present and is constantly accessible no matter what folder, window, or application you are using. It contains accessories to help you manage system tasks as well as programs such as media players, a calculator, search programs, and word-processing programs. The Mac OS X Apple menu is shown in Figure F-6.

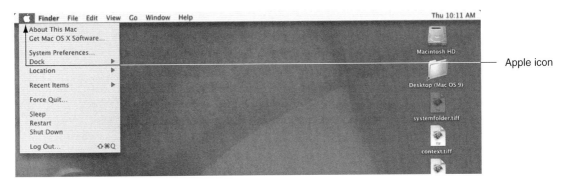

**Figure F-6**   The Apple menu is always available no matter what application is active

System Preferences on the Apple menu contains options for customizing the Mac interface. Click **Apple** and then click **System Preferences** to open the System Preferences window, shown in Figure F-7. Control Panels, which you learned about earlier in this appendix, are also accessible from the Apple menu in OS 9. In Mac OS 9, you can customize the Apple menu to contain anything you want by adding items to or removing items from the Apple folder, which is located in the System folder. You can create up to five levels of submenus under the Apple menu. In Mac OS X, the Apple menu is no longer customizable.

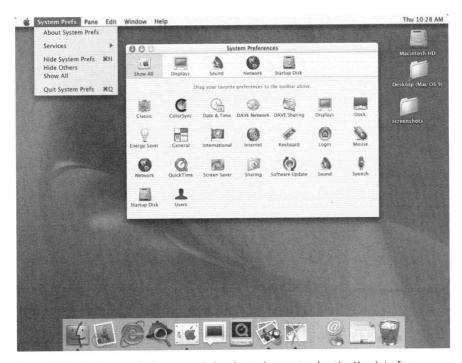

**Figure F-7**   The System Preferences window is used to customize the Mac interface

In Mac OS 9, there are three submenus on the Apple menu, called Recent Applications, Recent Documents, and Recent Servers. To customize these submenus, from the Apple menu, select **Control Panels, Apple Menu Options**. From this Control Panel, you can select whether to use recent menus and how many items to include on them. In Mac OS X, the Recent Items submenu on the Apple menu (shown in Figure F-8) gives you access to recently accessed documents and applications.

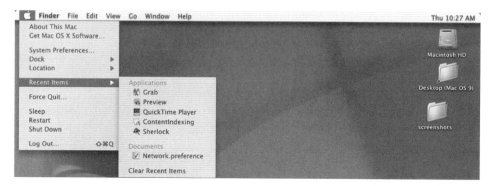

**Figure F-8**   Using Mac OS X, the Recent Items menu under the Apple menu lists recently accessed documents and applications

## LAUNCHING AN APPLICATION

There are four ways to execute applications on the Mac:

- ▲ Double-click the icon for the application from the Finder window or another window or from the desktop.
- ▲ Choose the application from the Recent Applications submenu on the Apple menu.
- ▲ Double-click the icon of a file associated with that application, such as a text file saved from the Notepad application.
- ▲ Drag to the application's icon the icon of a document that you want to open with it.

The first two methods have already been discussed. The last option works well if you want to open a document with an application other than the one in which it was originally saved.

As you work with applications on the Mac, you may find that you want to have more than one application open at a time. In Mac OS 9, the Applications menu, which you can access from the upper-right corner of your screen, allows you to switch between open applications easily. The menu will show the icon and name of the currently active application. To access other open applications, click the menu and choose the name of the application you want to access. Recall that in Mac OS X, open applications are shown as icons in the dock with a small triangle under them.

## *SUPPORTING HARDWARE*

In addition to working with files and applications, you will also need to know how to support hardware in a Mac system, such as monitors and hard drives, and including changing settings for video, understanding the file system used on the hard drive, and using system maintenance tools. Again, this section will not give you all you need to know to work with Mac hardware; it is simply intended to show you some important tools for working with the system. For more information specific to working with Mac hardware, study books devoted specifically to the Mac, documentation and manuals that come with your system or with specific components, and the Apple Computer, Inc. Web site (*www.apple.com*).

## ADJUSTING DISPLAY SETTINGS

To change display settings such as color depth and resolution, double-click the **Displays** icon under System Preferences. The Displays window appears, as seen in Figure F-9. You can change the following settings in the Displays window:

▲ *Resolution.* The resolution of a display affects how many pixels are shown on-screen. A resolution of $1024 \times 768$ means that there are 1,024 columns of pixels and 768 rows of pixels. When you change the resolution of your monitor, remember that the size of the items on the screen will change; the more pixels there are, the smaller items will be. This can be good if you want to see more items and space on your screen at one time, but it can be a drawback if you have vision problems. Two advantages to an $800 \times 600$ resolution are that it will produce a view close to what you will actually see in a printed document and that many Web pages are designed to be viewed at this resolution. A Web page optimized at $800 \times 600$ will look cramped at a lower resolution such as $640 \times 480$.

▲ *Contrast and brightness.* The sliders on the bottom of the Display tab of the Displays window enable you to control how much contrast there is between colors on your screen and how bright the overall display is. It is not a good idea to set a monitor to the highest brightness setting, because this can burn out the monitor prematurely.

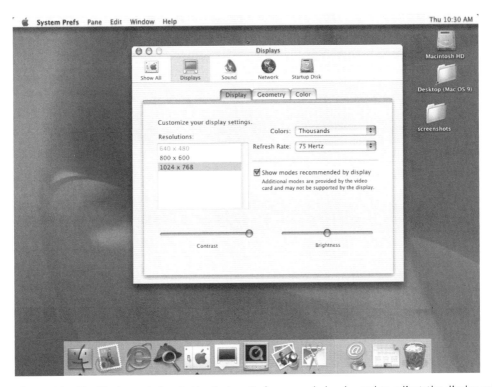

**Figure F-9**   The Displays window in the System Preferences window is used to adjust the display settings

▲ *Color depth*. Click the **Color** tab on the Displays window to view and change the settings for depth of color. The Color Depth box allows you to change how many colors can be shown on the screen: either 256, thousands, or millions. More colors mean a more realistic and more detailed picture. Sometimes a picture was created using a certain setting and will not be displayed correctly in a different setting. If a picture appears blurred or too gray, change the color depth until it appears correctly.

▲ *Display geometry*. Click the **Geometry** tab in the Displays window to reach options for changing the shape of the display on the screen. On most monitors, the display area is actually slightly smaller than the screen size, and you may see some black space around the display area. Use the Geometry settings to change the height, width, position, and shape of the display area.

## SUPPORTING THE HARD DRIVE

As with other OSs, the Mac OS supports IDE and SCSI drive technologies and, for hard drives, there is a choice of file systems to use.

### DRIVE TECHNOLOGIES: IDE AND SCSI

Recall from earlier chapters that IDE drives follow an interface standard that allows for up to four PATA drives in a system or up to six PATA and SATA drives. SCSI drives are generally faster than IDE drives, and there can be up to 15 SCSI devices on a system. It is possible to mix IDE and SCSI devices on a system.

> **Notes**
>
> The terms *IDE* and *SCSI* refer not only to hard drives but also to other devices such as CD-ROM drives, Zip drives, and DVD drives.

In the mid-1990s, IDE became the main technology for connecting internal devices in a Mac, partially because it is less expensive than SCSI and is more widely used in the computer industry. However, because it is faster and can support more devices, SCSI can be a better choice for complex multimedia and graphics work. If you have a Mac that uses IDE technology and want to convert to SCSI, you can purchase a SCSI host adapter for that purpose. Choose a drive technology according to your needs, your budget, and what technology your system supports.

### FILE SYSTEMS ON THE MAC

Recall that a file system is the overall structure that an OS uses to name, store, and organize files on a disk. The two main choices for a file system on a Mac hard drive are HFS (Hierarchical File System), also called Mac OS Standard Format, and HFS+, also called the Mac OS Extended Format. HFS was the format used for Mac disks before 1998, when drives larger than 1 GB started to become more common. HFS limited the number of allocation units on a disk to 65,536; how big each allocation unit was depended on the total size of the drive. These allocation units are called allocation blocks or simply blocks, and are similar to the Microsoft Windows file system's clusters; they are sets of hard drive sectors where the Mac's file system stores files. Files smaller than the size of a block still take up an entire block, which can cause a significant amount of space to be wasted; this wasted space is called slack.

> **Notes**
>
> In Mac OS 9, the File Exchange Control Panel is a component that can be installed to allow the Mac to use Microsoft Windows FAT16 and FAT32 partitions. Macs can read some NTFS or Linux/Unix file systems using utilities specially designed for that purpose. Mac OS X includes the ability to mount FAT drives but does not include a utility to format them as Mac OS 9 did.

In 1998, with the release of Mac OS 8.1, HFS was updated to HFS+, which allows for smaller blocks and can format drives up to 2048 GB. Any drive larger than 1 GB should be formatted with HFS+. Hard drives or removable media disks (such as floppy disks) smaller than 1 GB should be formatted with HFS, as should any hard drive that you plan to use with a Mac running Mac OS 8.1 or earlier.

The formatting of a hard drive with a file system creates blocks. It also creates a directory structure that allows the OS to access the drive. Some important elements of the directory structure are listed here.

◢ Boot blocks are the first two allocation blocks on the hard drive. They are initially empty, but once a System folder is installed on a computer, the boot blocks contain the location of the System folder so that the system can find and load the OS. You can correct damage to the boot blocks or replace erased boot blocks by installing a new System folder.

◢ Right after the boot blocks comes the volume information block, which holds information about the drive, including its format, name, number of files and folders, and allocation block size. This information must be present for a Mac to be able to access a drive. Because of the importance of the volume information block, a copy of it is stored in the next-to-last allocation block on the drive.

◢ A map of the allocation blocks on a hard drive is contained in the volume bit map, which uses a 1 to indicate that a block is storing files and a 0 to indicate that it is empty and is available for use. Damage to or corruption of the volume bit map does not prevent the Mac from being able to access the drive. However, when the Mac cannot determine from the volume bit map which allocation blocks are used, it might write new information to blocks that are full, overwriting the existing information. Regular disk maintenance (including use of the tools described in the next section) can help guard against this problem.

◢ The catalog tree is a database of the folders and files on a Mac hard drive, including information such as filenames and extensions, the application used to open a file, the creator of the file or folder, and the date the file or folder was created.

◢ The extents tree contains information about where the allocation blocks are located for files that take up more than one allocation block. When a file is larger than one allocation block, it is broken up into pieces called extents. One extent is stored in one allocation block. If a large proportion of the space on a hard drive is being used, the extents that make up a file might not be stored next to each other. The catalog tree and the extents tree work together and are both necessary for the Mac to be able to access data stored on the hard drive. They are the closest thing in the Mac to the FAT and the root directory in Windows.

## DRIVE MAINTENANCE TOOLS

In Mac OS X, the Utilities folder (shown in Figure F-10) contains various system tools, including Disk Utility (shown in Figure F-11).

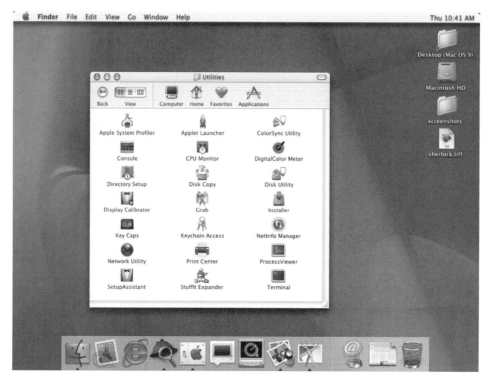

**Figure F-10** The Max OS X Utilities folder contains several utilities, including those used to manage a hard drive

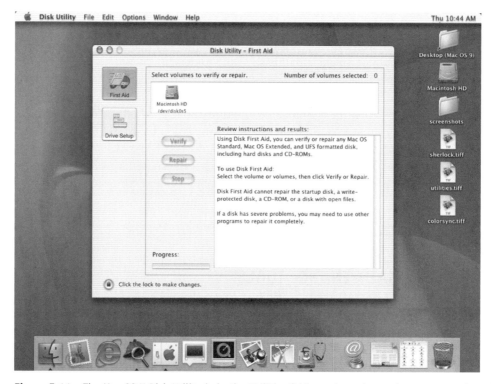

**Figure F-11** The Mac OS X Disk Utility is in the Utilities folder and can be used to set up and repair a hard drive

## DRIVE SETUP

The Drive Setup function can be used to format a hard drive when it is initially installed or to reformat a damaged hard drive. Remember that reformatting a drive erases all data and programs on it because the format process creates new allocation blocks and directory structures. When you format a drive, you can choose whether or not to create partitions on it. Partitioning a drive is not required, but can be done to divide the drive into one or more logical drives. Drive Setup can format most IDE and SCSI drives.

To use Drive Setup, on the Disk Utility window, click **Drive Setup,** select the disk you want to partition, and then click **Partition**. When you repartition a drive, all data on the current partitions is erased, and you cannot partition a drive that is currently used as the startup drive.

## DISK FIRST AID

Disk First Aid is a disk repair tool that checks for errors on the hard drive and runs automatically on reboot when a Mac is not shut down properly. You can also run this tool manually as a preventive maintenance measure or as an attempt to address poor hard drive performance. Disk First Aid is part of the free Apple utility Disk Utility and is less powerful than third-party disk repair utilities such as Norton Disk Doctor, which is part of Norton Utilities, or Alsoft's Disk Warrior (*www.alsoft.com*). There are some problems that these utilities can repair that Disk First Aid can only detect.

# Supporting Windows
# NT Workstation

**W**indows NT Workstation is a retired and pretty much dead operating system. However, at the time this book went to print, the CompTIA 2003 A+ exams were still alive, and the 2003 A+ Operating System Technologies exam does have coverage on Windows NT Workstation. The coverage of Windows NT is not extensive, but you should know about installing it and supporting the boot process. In this appendix, you'll learn the different ways to install Windows NT, and then we'll look at how to troubleshoot the Windows NT boot process.

## INSTALLING WINDOWS NT AS THE ONLY OS

Windows NT comes with three disks that contain a simplified version of Windows NT, enough to boot a PC. If the hard drive does not contain an OS, the installation begins by booting from these three disks. After Windows NT is loaded from these three disks, it can access the CD-ROM drive, and installation continues from the CD. The program on the CD executed at that point is Winnt.exe, a 16-bit program. A faster version of Winnt.exe on the CD named Winnt32.exe, a 32-bit program, can be used instead of Winnt.exe in certain situations. Winnt32.exe can be run only after Windows NT has already been installed for the first time; it is used to upgrade from an older NT version to a newer version or to reinstall a corrupted version. It must be executed from within Windows NT.

The three startup disks can later be used to boot the PC if files on the hard drive become corrupted. You can also create a new set of bootable disks.

The Windows NT installation files are stored in the \i386 directory on the CD-ROM drive. If you have enough hard drive space, you can copy the contents of the \i386 directory and its subdirectories to the hard drive and install from there, which is faster because access to the hard drive is faster than access to the CD-ROM drive. If the computer is connected to a network, the contents of the \i386 directory can be copied to a network server, and the Winnt.exe program can be executed from the server to install Windows NT on the PC, if certain conditions exist. (Installations from servers are not covered in this appendix.) To perform an upgrade to Windows NT, boot the OS and execute the Winnt.exe program on the Windows NT CD.

## TROUBLESHOOTING THE WINDOWS NT BOOT PROCESS

In this section, you will learn how to troubleshoot the Windows NT boot process and about some diagnostic tools that you can use for maintenance and troubleshooting. Many general troubleshooting tips you learned in earlier chapters apply to Windows NT as well. However, many troubleshooting tools, such as Safe Mode and Device Manager, which are available for Windows 2000/XP, don't exist under Windows NT.

> **Notes**
>
> As Windows NT/2000/XP is booting, if it thinks there is a problem you should know about or the system is set for a dual boot, a boot loader menu appears and gives you options such as which OS you want to load or how you want to handle a problem.

---

**APPLYING|CONCEPTS**    To recover from a failed Windows NT boot:

1. If the Windows NT boot loader menu appears, use the Last Known Good configuration to return to the last registry values that allowed for a successful boot. Any configuration changes since the last good boot will be lost.

2. If you cannot boot from the hard drive, boot using the three boot disks that came with the OS. If you don't have these three disks, you can create them on a working PC. Check for corrupted boot and system files that you can replace. (How to create the three boot disks is covered later in this section.)

3. Boot from the three disks, and select the option "To repair a damaged Windows NT version 4.0 installation."

4. Try reinstalling Windows NT in the same folder it currently uses. Tell the Setup program this is an upgrade.

5. As a last resort, if you are using the NTFS file system and you must recover data on the hard drive, move the hard drive to another system that runs Windows NT and install the drive as a secondary drive. You might then be able to recover the data.

## LAST KNOWN GOOD CONFIGURATION

Just as with Windows 2000/XP, each time Windows NT boots and the first logon is made with no errors, the OS saves a copy of the hardware configuration from the registry, which is called the Last Known Good configuration. (All hardware configuration sets stored in the registry, including the Last Known Good, are called control sets.) If an error occurs the next time the PC boots, it can use the Last Known Good configuration.

If Windows NT detects the possibility of a problem, it adds the Last Known Good option to the Windows NT boot loader menu. You can select this Last Known Good option to revert to the control set used for the last good boot. For example, if you install a new device driver, restart Windows NT, and find that the system hangs, you can use the Last Known Good option to revert to the previous configuration.

> **Notes**
>
> The key in the registry that contains the Last Known Good configuration is HKEY_LOCAL_MACHINE\ HARDWARE.

Because the configuration information is not saved to the Last Known Good control set until after the logon, don't attempt to log on if you have trouble with the boot. Doing so causes the Last Known Good to be replaced by the current control set, which might have errors. For example, if you install a new video driver, restart Windows, and find the screen very difficult to read, don't log on. Instead, press the reset button to reboot the PC. When given the choice, select Last Known Good from the boot loader menu.

To prevent hard drive corruption, if you have problems booting Windows NT, wait for all disk activity to stop before pressing the reset button or turning off the PC, especially if you are using the FAT file system.

If you accidentally disable a critical device, Windows NT decides to revert to the Last Known Good for you. You are not provided with a menu choice.

Reverting to the Last Known Good causes the loss of any changes made to the hardware configuration since the Last Known Good was saved. Therefore, it is wise to make one hardware configuration change at a time and reboot after each change. That way, if problems during booting are encountered, only the most recent change is lost. When installing several hardware devices, install them one at a time, rebooting each time.

> **Caution**
>
> If you have problems booting in Windows NT, don't log on. If you do, you will overwrite your previous Last Known Good.

## WINDOWS NT BOOT DISKS

Windows NT requires three disks to hold enough of Windows NT to boot the OS. If the original three disks to boot Windows NT become corrupted or are lost, you can make extra copies using Winnt32.exe if you are running Windows NT, or using Winnt.exe if you are running another OS, such as

DOS or Windows 9x. You do not have to be working on the PC where you intend to use the disks in order to make them, because the disks don't contain unique information for a specific PC.

## CREATING WINDOWS NT BOOT DISKS

Do the following to create boot disks using Windows NT:

1. Click **Start,** click **Run,** and then enter one of the following commands in the Run dialog box. Substitute the letter of your CD drive for E in the command line, if necessary:

   ```
   E:\i386\winnt32.exe /ox
   ```

   ```
   E:\i386\winnt.exe /ox
   ```

   The /OX parameters cause the program to create only the set of three disks, without performing a complete installation. In Figure G-1, you can see the command line from within Windows NT used to create the disks when drive E contains the Windows NT installation CD.

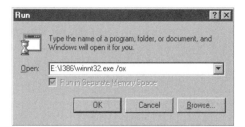

**Figure G-1**   Using Winnt32.exe to create a set of boot disks

2. The program asks for the location of the installation files. In this example, you would enter E:\i386. You are then prompted to insert three disks. The program creates the disks beginning with disk 3, then 2, then 1.

Windows NT does not have a Safe Mode, so if the PC later cannot boot Windows NT from the hard drive, these three disks can be used to load Windows NT, which loads using a generic VGA mode. After Windows NT is loaded, use a fourth disk—the Emergency Repair Disk (ERD)—to restore critical system files to their state at the time the last update was made to the ERD.

## THE WINDOWS NT EMERGENCY REPAIR DISK

The Emergency Repair Disk (ERD) contains information unique to your OS and hard drive. You are given the opportunity to create the disk during installation. Always create this disk, because it is your record of critical information about your system that can be used to fix a problem with the OS.

The ERD enables restoration on your hard drive of the Windows registry, which contains all the configuration information for Windows. In addition, the disk includes information used to build a command window to run DOS-like commands. The files on the ERD are listed in Table G-1. Files stored on the ERD are also written to the hard drive during the installation. Using Explorer, you can see the files listed in the \*winnt_root*\repair folder.

> **Notes**
>
> In Microsoft documentation, \*winnt_root*\ is the folder in which Windows NT is installed, which most likely is C:\Winnt\.

| File | Description |
| --- | --- |
| Setup.log | A read-only, hidden system file used to verify the files installed on a system |
| System._ | A compressed file containing part of the registry |
| Sam._ | A compressed file containing some of the security part of the registry |
| Security._ | A compressed file containing some of the security part of the registry |
| Software._ | A compressed file containing software information in the registry |
| Default._ | A compressed file containing part of the registry |
| Config.nt | The Windows NT version of Config.sys used in creating a command window |
| Autoexec.nt | The Windows NT version of Autoexec.bat |
| Ntuser.da_ | A compressed file containing information about authorized users of the system |

**Table G-1**  Files on the Windows NT Emergency Repair Disk

After the installation, you can create a new ERD or update the current one by using the Rdisk.exe utility in the \*winnt_root*\system32 folder. You should update the disk any time you make any major changes to the system, for example, when you install hardware or software. To use the Rdisk.exe utility, click **Start**, then **Run**, and then either click **Browse** or enter the path to the utility. Add the /S option so that the utility also backs up the registry to the hard drive.

If Windows NT is stored on drive D, the command line is:

```
D:\Winnt\System32\rdisk.exe /s
```

First, files are updated in the D:\Winnt\Repair directory; then you are given the opportunity to create a new ERD.

## USING THE BOOT DISKS AND THE ERD TO RECOVER FROM A FAILED BOOT

In the case of a hard drive failure, you can boot from the three boot disks that come with the Windows NT CD or that you made using either Winnt.exe or Winnt32.exe. The Windows NT programs on these disks might also request that you provide the ERD. Insert the first boot disk, and reboot. You will be

> **Notes**
>
> Windows NT does not have a Device Manager. When installing and troubleshooting hardware, look for individual icons in the Control Panel to manage hardware devices. For a detailed report of the system configuration, use the WinMSD command. At a command prompt enter **Winmsd /a /f**. The command creates the report in the current directory.

prompted to insert disk 2, followed by disk 3. The Setup menu in Figure G-2 then appears. Select the option to repair a damaged installation by pressing R, and follow directions on the screen.

```
Windows NT Workstation Setup

Welcome to Setup.
The Setup program for the Microsoft(R) Windows NT(TM) OS version 4.0
prepares Windows NT to run on your computer.

        *To learn more about Windows NT Setup before continuing, press F1
        *To set up Windows NT now, press ENTER
        *To repair a damaged Windows NT version 4.0 installation, press R
        *To quit Setup without installing Windows NT, press F3
```

**Figure G-2**    Windows NT Workstation Setup menu

# CompTIA A+ Acronyms

**C**ompTIA provides a list of acronyms which you need to know before you sit for the A+ exams. You can download the list from the CompTIA Web site at *www.comptia.org*. The list is included here for your convenience. However, CompTIA occasionally updates the list, so be sure to check the CompTIA Web site for the latest version.

| Acronym | Spelled Out |
| --- | --- |
| AC | alternating current |
| ACPI | advanced configuration and power interface |
| ACT | activity |
| ADSL | asymmetrical digital subscriber line |
| AGP | accelerated graphics port |
| AMD | advanced micro devices |
| AMR | audio modem riser |
| APIPA | automatic private Internet protocol addressing |
| ARP | address resolution protocol |
| ASR | automated system recovery |
| AT | advanced technology |
| ATA | advanced technology attachment |
| ATAPI | advanced technology attachment packet interface |
| ATM | asynchronous transfer mode |
| ATX | advanced technology extended |
| BIOS | basic input/output system |
| BNC | Bayonet-Neill-Concelman or British navel connector |
| BRI | basic rate interface |
| BTX | balanced technology extended |
| CD | compact disc |
| CD-ROM | compact disc-read-only memory |
| CD-RW | compact disc-rewritable |
| CDFS | compact disc file system |
| CGA | color/graphics adapter |
| CMOS | complementary metal-oxide semiconductor |
| COM1 | communication port 1 |
| CPU | central processing unit |
| CRIMM | continuity-Rambus inline memory module |
| CRT | cathode-ray tube |
| DB-25 | serial communications D-shell connector, 25 pins |
| DC | direct current |
| DDR | double data-rate |
| DDR RAM | double data-rate random access memory |
| DDR SDRAM | double data-rate symmetric dynamic random access memory |
| DFS | distributed file system |
| DHCP | dynamic host configuration protocol |
| DIMM | dual inline memory module |
| DIN | Deutsche Industrie Norm |
| DIP | dual inline package |

| Acronym | Spelled Out |
|---------|-------------|
| DMA | direct memory access |
| DNS | domain name service or domain name server |
| DOS | disk operating system |
| DB-9 | 9-pin D shell connector |
| DRAM | dynamic random access memory |
| DSL | digital subscriber line |
| DVD | digital video disc |
| DVD-R | digital video disc-recordable |
| DVD-RAM | digital versatile disc-random access memory |
| DVD-ROM | digital video disc-read only memory |
| DVD-RW | digital video disc-rewritable |
| DVI | digital visual interface |
| ECC | error correction code |
| ECP | extended capabilities port |
| EDO SDRAM | extended data out symmetric dynamic random access memory |
| EEPROM | electrically erasable programmable read-only memory |
| EFS | encrypting file system |
| EGA | enhanced graphics adapter |
| EIDE | enhanced integrated drive electronics |
| EISA | extended industry standard architecture |
| EMI | electromagnetic interference |
| ENET | Ethernet |
| EPP | enhanced parallel port |
| ERD | emergency repair disk |
| ESD | electrostatic discharge |
| ESDI | enhanced small device interface |
| EVGA | extended video graphics adapter/array |
| EVDO | evolution data optimized or evolution data only |
| FAT | file allocation table |
| FAT12 | 12-bit file allocation table |
| FAT16 | 16-bit file allocation table |
| FAT32 | 32-bit file allocation table |
| FCC | Federal Communications Commission |
| FDD | floppy disk drive |
| FERPA | Family Educational Rights and Privacy Act |
| FPM | fast page-mode |
| FPM SDRAM | fast page-mode symmetric dynamic random access memory |
| FRU | field replaceable unit |
| FTP | file transfer protocol |

| Acronym | Spelled Out |
|---------|-------------|
| GB | gigabyte |
| GDI | graphics device interface |
| GHz | gigahertz |
| GRPS | general radio packet system |
| GSM | global system manager or graphics size modification or graphics screen manager |
| GUI | graphical user interface |
| HCL | hardware compatibility list |
| HDD | hard disk drive |
| HDMi | high definition media interface |
| HPFS | high performance file system |
| HTML | hypertext markup language |
| HTTP | hypertext transfer protocol |
| HTTPS | hypertext transfer protocol over secure sockets layer |
| I/O | input/output |
| ICMP | Internet control message protocol |
| ICS | Internet connection sharing |
| IDE | integrated drive electronics |
| IEEE | Institute of Electrical and Electronics Engineers |
| IIS | Internet information server |
| IMAP | Internet mail access protocol |
| IP | Internet protocol |
| IPSEC | Internet protocol security |
| IPX | internetwork packet exchange |
| IPX/SPX | internetwork packet exchange/sequenced packet exchange |
| IR | infrared |
| IrDA | Infrared Data Association |
| IRQ | interrupt request |
| ISA | industry standard architecture |
| ISDN | integrated services digital network |
| ISO | Industry Standards Organization |
| ISP | Internet service provider |
| KB | kilobyte |
| LAN | local area network |
| LAT | local area transport |
| LCD | liquid crystal display |
| LED | light emitting diode |
| LPT | line printer terminal |
| LPT1 | line printer terminal 1 |
| LPX | low profile extended |

| Acronym | Spelled Out |
|---------|-------------|
| LVD | low voltage differential |
| MAC | media access control |
| MAN | metropolitan area network |
| Mb | megabit |
| MB | megabyte |
| MBR | master boot record |
| MCA | micro channel architecture |
| MHz | megahertz |
| MicroDIMM | micro dual inline memory module |
| MIDI | musical instrument digital interface |
| MLI | multiple link interface |
| MMC | Microsoft management console |
| MMX | multimedia extensions |
| MP3 | Moving Picture Experts Group Layer 3 Audio |
| MPEG | Moving Picture Experts Group |
| MSDS | material safety data sheet |
| MUI | multilingual user interface |
| NAS | network-attached storage |
| NAT | network address translation |
| NetBEUI | networked basic input/output system extended user interface |
| NetBIOS | networked basic input/output system |
| NFS | network file system |
| NIC | network interface card |
| NLI | not logged in or natural language interface |
| NLX | new low-profile extended |
| NNTP | network news transfer protocol |
| NTFS | new technology file system |
| NTLDR | new technology loader |
| OEM | original equipment manufacturer |
| OS | operating system |
| OSR | original equipment manufacturer service release |
| PAN | personal area network |
| PATA | parallel advanced technology attachment |
| PCI | peripheral component interconnect |
| PCIX | peripheral component interconnect extended |
| PCL | printer control language |
| PCMCIA | Personal Computer Memory Card International Association |
| PDA | personal digital assistant |
| PGA | pin grid array |

| Acronym | Spelled Out |
|---------|-------------|
| PGA2 | pin grid array 2 |
| PIN | personal identification number |
| PnP | plug and play |
| POP | post office protocol |
| POP3 | post office protocol 3 |
| POST | power-on self test |
| PPP | point-to-point protocol |
| PPTP | point-to-point tunneling protocol |
| PRI | primary rate interface |
| PROM | programmable read-only memory |
| PS/2 | personal system/2 connector |
| PSTN | public switched telephone network |
| PVC | permanent virtual circuit |
| QoS | quality of service |
| RAID | redundant array of independent disks |
| RAM | random access memory |
| RAMBUS | trademarked term |
| RAS | remote access service |
| RDRAM | Rambus dynamic random access memory |
| RF | radio frequency |
| RGB | red green blue |
| RIMM | Rambus inline memory module |
| RIP | routing information protocol |
| RIS | remote installation service |
| RISC | reduced instruction set computer |
| RJ | registered jack |
| RJ-11 | registered jack function 11 |
| RJ-45 | registered jack-45 |
| ROM | read only memory |
| RS-232 | recommended standard 232 |
| RTC | real-time clock |
| SAN | storage area network |
| SATA | serial advanced technology attachment |
| SCSI | small computer system interface |
| SCSI ID | small computer system interface identifier |
| SD card | secure digital card |
| SDRAM | symmetric dynamic random access memory |
| SEC | single edge connector |
| SFC | system file checker |

| Acronym | Spelled Out |
|---------|-------------|
| SGRAM | synchronous graphics random access memory |
| SIMM | single inline memory module |
| SLI | scalable link interface or system level integration or scanline interleave mode |
| SMB | server message block |
| SMTP | simple mail transport protocol |
| SNMP | simple network management protocol |
| SoDIMM | small outline dual inline memory module |
| SOHO | small office/home office |
| SP | service pack |
| SP1 | service pack 1 |
| SP2 | service pack 2 |
| SPDIF | Sony-Philips digital interface format |
| SPGA | staggered pin grid array |
| SPX | sequenced package exchange |
| SRAM | static random access memory |
| SSH | secure shell |
| SSID | service set identifier |
| SSL | secure sockets layer |
| ST | straight tip |
| STP | shielded twisted pair |
| SVGA | super video graphics array |
| SXGA | super extended graphics array |
| TB | terabyte |
| TCP/IP | transmission control protocol/Internet protocol |
| TFTP | trivial file transfer protocol |
| UART | universal asynchronous receiver transmitter |
| UDF | user-defined functions or universal disk format or universal data format |
| UDMA | ultra direct memory access |
| UDP | user datagram protocol |
| UFS | universal file system |
| UPS | uninterruptible power supply |
| URL | uniform resource locator |
| USB | universal serial bus |
| UTP | unshielded twisted pair |
| UXGA | ultra extended graphics array |
| VESA | Video Electronics Standards Association |
| VFAT | virtual file allocation table |
| VGA | video graphics array |
| VoIP | voice over Internet protocol |

| Acronym | Spelled Out |
|---------|-------------|
| VPN | virtual private network |
| VRAM | video random access memory |
| WAN | wide area network |
| WAP | wireless application protocol |
| WEP | wired equivalent privacy |
| WIFI | wireless fidelity |
| WINS | Windows Internet name service |
| WLAN | wireless local area network |
| WPA | wireless protected access |
| WUXGA | wide ultra extended graphics array |
| XGA | extended graphics array |
| XPR | is an AIX command-line utility |
| ZIF | zero-insertion-force |
| ZIP | zigzag inline package |

# Answers to Chapter Review Questions

## CHAPTER 1

1. c
2. a
3. a
4. c
5. b
6. True
7. False
8. False
9. False
10. True
11. bit
12. port
13. resolution
14. peripheral device
15. BIOS (basic input/output system)

## CHAPTER 2

1. d
2. b
3. a
4. c
5. d
6. True
7. False
8. False
9. False
10. True

11. distributions
12. X Windows
13. protected
14. Device drivers
15. virtual memory

## CHAPTER 3

1. a
2. d
3. c
4. c
5. b
6. True
7. True
8. False
9. True
10. True
11. substances
12. ground bracelet
13. cold boot
14. operating system
15. power-on self test

## CHAPTER 4

1. a
2. c
3. d
4. b
5. d
6. True
7. True
8. False
9. False
10. True
11. chassis
12. Enhanced ATX
13. active, passive
14. subnotebooks
15. power supply

## CHAPTER 5

1. c
2. b
3. d
4. a
5. b
6. True
7. True
8. False
9. True
10. False
11. processor frequency
12. dual-core
13. Level 3 (L3)
14. processor package
15. input/output (I/O) unit, control unit, arithmetic logic unit(s)

## CHAPTER 6

1. c
2. d
3. a
4. b
5. c
6. False
7. True
8. False
9. True
10. True
11. embedded, on-board
12. CMOS setup
13. wait state
14. 8-bit, 4.77
15. expansion

## CHAPTER 7

1. b
2. a
3. b
4. c
5. d

6. False
7. True
8. True
9. True
10. False
11. unbuffered
12. bank
13. parity
14. 9
15. ROM (read-only memory) and RAM (random access memory)

## CHAPTER 8

1. b
2. d
3. d
4. c
5. a
6. True
7. True
8. True
9. False
10. False
11. sector, cluster
12. actuator
13. cylinder
14. terminating resistor
15. formatting

## CHAPTER 9

1. b
2. a
3. c
4. d
5. a
6. True
7. True
8. True
9. False
10. False

11. foil contact, metal contact

12. wheel, optical

13. chip creep

14. active matrix

15. DTE (Data Terminal Equipment), DCE (Data Communications Equipment)

## CHAPTER 10

1. c
2. b
3. a
4. a
5. d
6. True
7. True
8. True
9. False
10. False
11. CDFS (Compact Disc File System) or UDF (Universal Disk Format)
12. fault tolerance
13. TWAIN
14. spanned
15. solid state device (SSD) or solid state disk

## CHAPTER 11

1. b
2. c
3. d
4. d
5. a
6. True
7. False
8. True
9. True
10. False
11. Setuplog.txt
12. boot sector virus
13. domain
14. extended
15. directory or the security accounts manager (SAM) database

## CHAPTER 12

1. b
2. c
3. d
4. d
5. a
6. True
7. False
8. True
9. True
10. False
11. digital signatures
12. hardware profile
13. Two of: create partitions, create volumes on dynamic disks, convert a basic disk to a dynamic disk, or format logical drives
14. Sigverif.exe
15. snap-ins

## CHAPTER 13

1. b
2. c
3. d
4. d
5. a
6. True
7. False
8. True
9. True
10. False
11. administrator, guest
12. roaming profile
13. scanstate and loadstate
14. fragmented file
15. deleting temporary files

## CHAPTER 14

1. a
2. c
3. b
4. a

5. a
6. False
7. True
8. True
9. True
10. False
11. 32-bit flat memory
12. minifile system
13. boot loader, operating systems
14. Ntbtlog.txt
15. stop error or a blue screen of death (BSOD)

## CHAPTER 15

1. a
2. d
3. b
4. c
5. b
6. False
7. True
8. True
9. True
10. False
11. hard drive, startup disk
12. hidden file
13. batch
14. Command.com, program files
15. extended memory

## CHAPTER 16

1. a
2. d
3. b
4. c
5. b
6. False
7. False
8. True
9. True
10. True

11. application programming interface (API)
12. memory paging
13. service packs, patches
14. clean
15. dynamic

## CHAPTER 17

1. b
2. c
3. b
4. a
5. d
6. False
7. False
8. True
9. False
10. True
11. bandwidth
12. trailer
13. star
14. straight-through
15. binding

## CHAPTER 18

1. a
2. c
3. b
4. c
5. d
6. False
7. False
8. True
9. True
10. True
11. session, socket
12. Time to Live (TTL), hop count
13. broadband
14. *70
15. ferrite clamp

## CHAPTER 19

1. a
2. c
3. b
4. c
5. d
6. False
7. False
8. True
9. True
10. True
11. virus signatures
12. CIPHER
13. social engineering
14. data migration
15. zero-fill

## CHAPTER 20

1. c
2. a
3. c
4. b
5. d
6. True
7. False
8. True
9. True
10. True
11. folder redirection
12. hardware profiles
13. docking station
14. hot-swapping
15. video sharing

## CHAPTER 21

1. c
2. c
3. b
4. d
5. a

6. False

7. False

8. True

9. True

10. True

11. duplex

12. warm-up

13. Resolution Enhancement technology

14. color sticks

15. spooling

## CHAPTER 22

1. a

2. d

3. c

4. b

5. d

6. True

7. False

8. True

9. False

10. True

11. Computing Technology Industry Association or CompTIA

12. expert systems

13. call-tracking

14. escalation

15. 3 or three

# GLOSSARY

This glossary defines the key terms listed at the end of each chapter and other terms related to managing and maintaining a personal computer.

**3-D RAM**   Special video RAM designed to improve 3-D graphics simulation.

**10Base2**   An Ethernet standard that operates at 10 Mbps and uses small coaxial cable up to 200 meters long. Also called ThinNet.

**10Base5**   An Ethernet standard that operates at 10 Mbps and uses thick coaxial cable up to 500 meters long. Also called ThickNet.

**32-bit flat memory mode**   A protected processing mode used by Windows NT/2000/XP to process programs written in 32-bit code early in the boot process.

**80 conductor IDE cable**   An IDE cable that has 40 pins but uses 80 wires, 40 of which are ground wires designed to reduce crosstalk on the cable. The cable is used by ATA/100 and ATA/133 IDE drives.

**100BaseT**   An Ethernet standard that operates at 100 Mbps and uses STP cabling. Also called Fast Ethernet. Variations of 100BaseT are 100BaseTX and 100BaseFX.

**802.11a/b/g**   *See* IEEE 802.11a/b/g.

**A+ Certification**   A certification awarded by CompTIA (The Computer Technology Industry Association) that measures a PC technician's knowledge and skills.

**access point (AP)**   A device connected to a LAN that provides wireless communication so that computers, printers, and other wireless devices can communicate with devices on the LAN.

**ACPI (Advanced Configuration and Power Interface)**   Specification developed by Intel, Compaq, Phoenix, Microsoft, and Toshiba to control power on notebooks and other devices. Windows 98 and Windows 2000/XP support ACPI.

**active backplane**   A type of backplane system in which there is some circuitry, including bus connectors, buffers, and driver circuits, on the backplane.

**Active Directory**   A Windows 2000 Server and Windows Server 2003 directory database and service that allows for a single point of administration for all shared resources on a network, including files, peripheral devices, databases, Web sites, users, and services.

**active matrix**   A type of video display that amplifies the signal at every intersection in the grid of electrodes, which enhances the pixel quality over that of a dual-scan passive matrix display.

**active partition**   The primary partition on the hard drive that boots the OS. Windows NT/2000/XP calls the active partition the system partition.

**active terminator**   A type of terminator for single-ended SCSI cables that includes voltage regulators in addition to the simple resistors used with passive termination.

**adapter address**   *See* MAC address.

**adapter card**   A small circuit board inserted in an expansion slot and used to communicate between the system bus and a peripheral device. Also called an interface card.

**administrator account**   In Windows NT/ 2000/XP, an account that grants to the administrator(s) rights and permissions to all hardware and software resources, such as the right to add, delete, and change accounts and to change hardware configurations.

**Advanced Options menu**   A Windows 2000/XP menu that appears when you press F8 when Windows starts. The menu can be used to troubleshoot problems when loading Windows 2000/XP.

**Advanced SCSI Programming Interface (ASPI)**   A popular device driver that enables operating systems to communicate with a SCSI host adapter. (The "A" originally stood for Adaptec.)

**Advanced Transfer Cache (ATC)**   A type of L2 cache contained within the Pentium processor housing that is embedded on the same core processor die as the CPU itself.

**adware**   Software installed on a computer that produces pop-up ads using your browser; the ads are often based on your browsing habits.

**AirPort**   The term Apple computers use to describe the IEEE 802.11b standard.

**alternating current (AC)**   Current that cycles back and forth rather than traveling in only one direction. In the United States, the AC voltage from a standard wall outlet is normally between

110 and 115 V. In Europe, the standard AC voltage from a wall outlet is 220 V.

**ammeter**   A meter that measures electrical current in amps.

**ampere or amp (A)**   A unit of measurement for electrical current. One volt across a resistance of one ohm will produce a flow of one amp.

**amplifier repeater**   A repeater that does not distinguish between noise and signal; it amplifies both.

**ANSI (American National Standards Institute)**   A nonprofit organization dedicated to creating trade and communications standards.

**answer file**   A text file that contains information that Windows NT/2000/XP requires to do an unattended installation.

**antivirus (AV) software**   Utility programs that prevent infection or scan a system to detect and remove viruses. McAfee Associates' VirusScan and Norton AntiVirus are two popular AV packages.

**application program interface (API) call**   A request from software to the OS to access hardware or other software using a previously defined procedure that both the software and the OS understand.

**ARP (Address Resolution Protocol)**   A protocol that TCP/IP uses to translate IP addresses into physical network addresses (MAC addresses).

**ASCII (American Standard Code for Information Interchange)**   A popular standard for writing letters and other characters in binary code. Originally, ASCII characters were seven bits, so there were 127 possible values. ASCII has been expanded to an 8-bit version, allowing 128 additional values.

**asynchronous SRAM**   Static RAM that does not work in step with the CPU clock and is, therefore, slower than synchronous SRAM.

**AT**   A form factor, generally no longer produced, in which the motherboard requires a full-size case. Because of their dimensions and configuration, AT systems are difficult to install, service, and upgrade. Also called full AT.

**AT command set**   A set of commands that a PC uses to control a modem and that a user can enter to troubleshoot the modem.

**ATAPI (Advanced Technology Attachment Packet Interface)**   An interface standard, part of the IDE/ATA standards, that allows tape drives, CD-ROM drives, and other drives to be treated like an IDE hard drive by the system.

**attenuation**   Signal degeneration over distance. Attenuation is solved on a network by adding repeaters to the network.

**ATX**   The most common form factor for PC systems presently in use, originally introduced by Intel in 1995. ATX motherboards and cases make better use of space and resources than did the AT form factor.

**ATX12 V power supply**   A power supply that provides a 12 V power cord with a 4-pin connector to be used by the auxiliary 4-pin power connector on motherboards used to provide extra power for processors.

**audio/modem riser (AMR)**   A specification for a small slot on a motherboard to accommodate an audio or modem riser card. A controller on the motherboard contains some of the logic for the audio or modem functionality.

**authentication**   The process of proving an individual is who they say they are before they are allowed access to a computer, file, folder, or network. The process might use a password, PIN, smart card, or biometric data.

**authorization**   Controlling what an individual can or cannot do with resources on a computer network. Using Windows, authorization is granted by the rights and permissions assigned to user accounts.

**autodetection**   A feature of system BIOS and hard drives that automatically identifies and configures a new drive in CMOS setup.

**Autoexec.bat**   A startup text file once used by DOS and used by Windows to provide backward-compatibility. It executes commands automatically during the boot process and is used to create a 16-bit environment.

**Automated System Recovery (ASR)**   The Windows XP process that allows you to restore an entire hard drive volume or logical drive to its state at the time the backup of the volume was made.

**Automatic Private IP Address (APIPA)**   An IP address in the address range 169.254.x.x, used by a computer when it cannot successfully lease an IP address from a DHCP server.

**autorange meter**   A multimeter that senses the quantity of input and sets the range accordingly.

**Baby AT**   An improved and more flexible version of the AT form factor. Baby AT was the industry standard from approximately 1993 to 1997 and can fit into some ATX cases.

**back side bus**   The bus between the CPU and the L2 cache inside the CPU housing.

**backplane system**   A form factor in which there is no true motherboard. Instead, motherboard components are included on an adapter card plugged into a slot on a board called the backplane.

**backup**   An extra copy of a file, used in the event that the original becomes damaged or destroyed.

**backup domain controller (BDC)**   In Windows NT, a computer on a network that holds a read-only copy of the SAM (security accounts manager) database.

**Backup Operator**   A Windows 2000/XP user account that can back up and restore any files on the system regardless of its having access to these files.

**bandwidth**   In relation to analog communication, the range of frequencies that a communications channel or cable can carry. In general use, the term refers to the volume of data that can travel on a bus or over a cable stated in bits per second (bps), kilobits per second (Kbps), or megabits per second (Mbps). Also called data throughput or line speed.

**bank**   An area on the motherboard that contains slots for memory modules (typically labeled bank 0, 1, 2, and 3).

**baseline**   The level of performance expected from a system, which can be compared to current measurements to determine what needs upgrading or tuning.

**basic disk**   A way to partition a hard drive, used by DOS and all versions of Windows, that stores information about the drive in a partition table at the beginning of the drive. Compare to dynamic disk.

**batch file**   A text file containing a series of OS commands. Autoexec.bat is a batch file.

**baud rate**   A measure of line speed between two devices such as a computer and a printer or a modem. This speed is measured in the number of times a signal changes in one second. *See also* bits per second (bps).

**beam detect mirror**   Detects the initial presence of a laser printer's laser beam by reflecting the beam to an optical fiber.

**best-effort protocol**   *See* connectionless protocol.

**binary number system**   The number system used by computers; it has only two numbers, 0 and 1, called binary digits, or bits.

**binding**   The process by which a protocol is associated with a network card or a modem card.

**BIOS (basic input/output system)**   Firmware that can control much of a computer's input/output functions, such as communication with the floppy drive and the monitor. Also called ROM BIOS.

**bit (binary digit)**   A 0 or 1 used by the binary number system.

**bits per second (bps)**   A measure of data transmission speed. For example, a common modem speed is 56,000 bps, or 56 Kbps.

**block mode**   A method of data transfer between hard drive and memory that allows multiple data transfers on a single software interrupt.

**blue screen**   A Windows NT/2000/XP error that displays against a blue screen and causes the system to halt. Also called a stop error.

**Bluetooth**   A standard for wireless communication and data synchronization between devices, developed by a group of electronics manufacturers and overseen by the Bluetooth Special Interest Group. Bluetooth uses the same frequency range as 802.11b, but does not have as wide a range.

**BNC connector**   A connector used with thin coaxial cable. Some BNC connectors are T-shaped and called T-connectors. One end of the T connects to the NIC, and the two other ends can connect to cables or end a bus formation with a terminator.

**boot loader menu**   A startup menu that gives the user the choice of which operating system to load such as Windows 98 or Windows XP which are both installed on the same system, creating a dual boot.

**boot partition**   The hard drive partition where the Windows NT/2000/XP OS is stored. The system partition and the boot partition may be different partitions.

**boot record**   The first sector of a floppy disk or logical drive in a partition; it contains information about the disk or logical drive. On a hard drive, if the boot record is in the active partition, then it is used to boot the OS. Also called boot sector.

**boot sector**   *See* boot record.

**boot sector virus**   An infectious program that can replace the boot program with a modified, infected version, often causing boot and data retrieval problems.

**Boot.ini**   A Windows NT/2000/XP hidden text file that contains information needed to start the boot and build the boot loader menu.

**bootable disk**   For DOS and Windows, a floppy disk that can upload the OS files necessary for computer startup. For DOS or Windows 9x/Me, it must contain the files Io.sys, Msdos.sys, and Command.com.

**bootstrap loader**   A small program at the end of the boot record that can be used to boot an OS from the disk or logical drive.

**bridge**   A device used to connect two or more network segments. It can make decisions about allowing a packet to pass based on the packet's destination MAC address.

**bridging protocol**   *See* line protocol.

**Briefcase**   A system folder in Windows 9x/Me that is used to synchronize files between two computers.

**broadband** A transmission technique that carries more than one type of transmission on the same medium, such as cable modem or DSL.

**broadcast** Process by which a message is sent from a single host to all hosts on the network, without regard to the kind of data being sent or the destination of the data.

**brouter** A device that functions as both a bridge and a router. A brouter acts as a router when handling packets using routable protocols such as TCP/IP and IPX/SPX. It acts as a bridge when handling packets using nonroutable protocols such as NetBEUI.

**brownouts** Temporary reductions in voltage, which can sometimes cause data loss. *Also called* sags.

**browser hijacker** A malicious program that infects your Web browser and can change your home page or browser settings. It can also redirect your browser to unwanted sites, produce pop-up ads, and set unwanted bookmarks. Also called a home page hijacker.

**BTX (Balanced Technology Extended)** The latest form factor expected to replace ATX. It has higher quality fans, is designed for better airflow, and has improved structural support for the motherboard.

**buffer** A temporary memory area where data is kept before being written to a hard drive or sent to a printer, thus reducing the number of writes to the devices.

**built-in user account** An administrator account and a guest account that are set up when Windows NT/2000/XP is first installed.

**burst EDO (BEDO)** A refined version of EDO memory that significantly improved access time over EDO. BEDO was not widely used because Intel chose not to support it. BEDO memory is stored on 168-pin DIMM modules.

**burst SRAM** Memory that is more expensive and slightly faster than pipelined burst SRAM. Data is sent in a two-step process; the data address is sent, and then the data itself is sent without interruption.

**bus** The paths, or lines, on the motherboard on which data, instructions, and electrical power move from component to component.

**bus mouse** A mouse that plugs into a bus adapter card and has a round, 9-pin mini-DIN connector.

**bus riser** *See* riser card.

**bus speed** The speed, or frequency, at which the data on the motherboard is written and read.

**bus topology** A LAN architecture in which all the devices are connected to a bus, or one communication line. Bus topology does not have a central connection point.

**byte** A collection of eight bits that can represent a single character.

**cabinet file** A file with a .cab extension that contains one or more compressed files and is often used to distribute software on disk. The Extract command is used to extract files from the cabinet file.

**cable modem** A technology that uses cable TV lines for data transmission requiring a modem at each end. From the modem, a network cable connects to an NIC in the user's PC, or a USB cable connects to a USB port.

**call tracking** A system that tracks the dates, times, and transactions of help-desk or on-site PC support calls, including the problem presented, the issues addressed, who did what, and when and how each call was resolved.

**CAM (Common Access Method)** A standard adapter driver used by SCSI.

**capacitor** An electronic device that can maintain an electrical charge for a period of time and is used to smooth out the flow of electrical current. Capacitors are often found in computer power supplies.

**CardBus** A PCMCIA specification that improved on the earlier PC Card standards. It improves I/O speed, increases the bus width to 32 bits, and supports lower-voltage PC Cards, while maintaining backward compatibility with earlier standards.

**cards** Adapter boards or interface cards placed into expansion slots to expand the functions of a computer, allowing it to communicate with external devices such as monitors or speakers.

**carrier** A signal used to activate a phone line to confirm a continuous frequency; used to indicate that two computers are ready to receive or transmit data via modems.

**CAS Latency (CL)** A feature of memory that reflects the number of clock cycles that pass while data is written to memory.

**CAU (Controlled-Access Unit)** *See* MAU.

**CCITT (Comité Consultatif International Télégraphique et Téléphonique)** An international organization that was responsible for developing standards for international communications. This organization has been incorporated into the ITU. *See also* ITU.

**CD (change directory) command** A command given at the command prompt that changes the default directory, for example CD \Windows.

**CDFS (Compact Disc File System)** The 32-bit file system for CD discs and some CD-R and CD-RW discs that replaced the older 16-bit mscdex file system used by DOS. *See also* Universal Disk Format (UDF).

**CDMA (code-division multiple access)**  A protocol standard used by cellular WANs and cell phones

**CD-R (CD-recordable)**  A CD drive that can record or write data to a CD. The drive may or may not be multisession, but the data cannot be erased once it is written.

**CD-RW (CD-rewritable)**  A CD drive that can record or write data to a CD. The data can be erased and overwritten. The drive may or may not be multisession.

**central processing unit (CPU)**  Also called a microprocessor or processor. The heart and brain of the computer, which receives data input, processes information, and executes instructions.

**chain**  A group of clusters used to hold a single file.

**CHAP (Challenge Handshake Authentication Protocol)**  A protocol used to encrypt account names and passwords that are sent to a network controller for validation.

**checksum**  A method of checking transmitted data for errors, whereby the digits are added and their sum compared to an expected sum.

**child directory**  *See* subdirectory.

**child, parent, grandparent backup method**  A plan for backing up and reusing tapes or removable disks by rotating them each day (child), week (parent), and month (grandparent).

**chip creep**  A condition in which chips loosen because of thermal changes.

**chipset**  A group of chips on the motherboard that controls the timing and flow of data and instructions to and from the CPU.

**CHS (cylinder, head, sector) mode**  An outdated method by which BIOS reads from and writes to hard drives by addressing the correct cylinder, head, and sector. Also called normal mode.

**circuit board**  A computer component, such as the main motherboard or an adapter board, that has electronic circuits and chips.

**CISC (complex instruction set computing)**  Earlier CPU type of instruction set.

**clamping voltage**  The maximum voltage allowed through a surge suppressor, such as 175 or 330 volts.

**clean install**  Installing an OS on a new hard drive or on a hard drive that has a previous OS installed, but without carrying forward any settings kept by the old OS, including information about hardware, software, or user preferences. A fresh installation.

**client/server**  A computer concept whereby one computer (the client) requests information from another computer (the server).

**client/server application**  An application that has two components. The client software requests data from the server software on the same or another computer.

**client-side caching**  A technique used by browsers (clients) to speed up download times by caching Web pages previously requested in case they are requested again.

**clock speed**  The speed, or frequency, expressed in MHz, that controls activity on the motherboard and is generated by a crystal or oscillator located somewhere on the motherboard.

**clone**  A computer that is a no-name Intel- and Microsoft-compatible PC.

**cluster**  One or more sectors that constitute the smallest unit of space on a disk for storing data (also referred to as a file allocation unit). Files are written to a disk as groups of whole clusters.

**CMOS (complementary metal-oxide semiconductor)**  The technology used to manufacture microchips. CMOS chips require less electricity, hold data longer after the electricity is turned off, are slower, and produce less heat than earlier technologies. The configuration, or setup, chip is a CMOS chip.

**CMOS configuration chip**  A chip on the motherboard that contains a very small amount of memory, or RAM   enough to hold configuration, or setup, information about the computer The chip is powered by a battery when the PC is turned off. Also called CMOS setup chip or CMOS RAM chip.

**CMOS setup**  (1) The CMOS configuration chip. (2) The program in system BIOS that can change the values in CMOS RAM.

**CMOS setup chip**  *See* CMOS configuration chip.

**COAST (cache on a stick)**  Memory modules that hold memory used as a memory cache. *See also* memory cache.

**coaxial cable**  Networking cable used with 10-Mbps Ethernet ThinNet or ThickNet.

**cold boot**  *See* hard boot.

**combo card**  An outdated Ethernet card that contains more than one transceiver, each with a different port on the back of the card, to accommodate different cabling media.

**Command.com**  Along with Msdos.sys and Io.sys, one of the three files that are the core components of the real-mode portion of Windows 9x/Me. Command.com provides a command prompt and interprets commands.

**comment**   A line or part of a line in a program that is intended as a remark or comment and is ignored when the program runs. A semicolon or an REM is often used to mark a line as a comment.

**communication and networking riser (CNR)**   A specification for a small expansion slot on a motherboard that accommodates a small audio, modem, or network riser card.

**compact case**   A type of case used in low-end desktop systems. Compact cases, also called low-profile or slimline cases, follow either the NLX, LPX, or Mini LPX form factor. They are likely to have fewer drive bays, but they generally still provide for some expansion.

**Compact.exe**   Windows 2000/XP command and program to compress or uncompress a volume, folder, or file.

**Compatibility Mode utility**   A Windows XP utility that provides an application with the older Microsoft OS environment it was designed to operate in.

**compressed drive**   A drive whose format has been reorganized to store more data. A Windows 9x compressed drive is really not a drive at all; it's actually a type of file, typically with a host drive called H.

**compression**   To store data in a file, folder, or logical drive using a coding format that reduces the size of files to save space on a drive or shorten transport time when sending a file over the Internet or network.

**computer name**   Character-based host name or NetBIOS name assigned to a computer.

**Config.sys**   A text file used by DOS and supported by Windows 9x/Me that lists device drivers to be loaded at startup. It can also set system variables to be used by DOS and Windows.

**Configuration Manager**   A component of Windows Plug and Play that controls the configuration process of all devices and communicates these configurations to the devices.

**connectionless protocol**   A protocol such as UDP that does not require a connection before sending a packet and does not guarantee delivery. An example of a UDP transmission is streaming video over the Web. Also called a best-effort protocol.

**connection-oriented protocol**   In networking, a protocol that confirms that a good connection has been made before transmitting data to the other end. An example of a connection-oriented protocol is TCP.

**console**   A window in which one or more Windows 2000/XP utility programs have been installed. The window is created using Microsoft Management Console, and installed utilities are called snap-ins.

**constant angular velocity (CAV)**   A technology used by hard drives and newer CD-ROM drives whereby the disk rotates at a constant speed.

**constant linear velocity (CLV)**   A CD-ROM format in which the spacing of data is consistent on the CD, but the speed of the disc varies depending on whether the data being read is near the center or the edge of the disc.

**continuity**   A continuous, unbroken path for the flow of electricity. A continuity test can determine whether or not internal wiring is still intact, or whether a fuse is good or bad.

**control blade**   A laser printer component that prevents too much toner from sticking to the cylinder surface.

**conventional memory**   DOS and Windows 9x/Me memory addresses between 0 and 640 K. Also called base memory.

**cooler**   A combination cooling fan and heat sink mounted on the top or side of a processor to keep it cool.

**copyright**   An individual's right to copy his/her own work. No one else, other than the copyright owner, is legally allowed to do so without permission.

**CRC (cyclical redundancy check)**   A process in which calculations are performed on bytes of data before and after they are transmitted to check for corruption during transmission.

**credit card memory**   A type of memory used on older notebooks that could upgrade existing memory by way of a specialized memory slot.

**C-RIMM (Continuity RIMM)**   A placeholder RIMM module that provides continuity so that every RIMM slot is filled.

**cross-linked clusters**   Errors caused when more than one file points to a cluster, and the files appear to share the same disk space, according to the file allocation table.

**crossover cable**   A cable used to connect two PCs into the simplest network possible. Also used to connect two hubs.

**CVF (compressed volume file)**   The Windows 9x/Me file on the host drive of a compressed drive that holds all compressed data.

**data bus**   The lines on the system bus that the CPU uses to send and receive data.

**data cartridge**   A type of tape medium typically used for backups. Full-sized data cartridges are $4 \times 6 \times 2\frac{5}{8}$ inches in size. A minicartridge is only $3\frac{1}{4} \times 2\frac{1}{2} \times 2\frac{3}{5}$ inches in size.

**data line protector**   A surge protector designed to work with the telephone line to a modem.

**data migration** Moving data from one application to another application or from one storage media to another, and most often involves a change in the way the data is formatted.

**data path** The number of bits transported into and out of the processor.

**data path size** The number of lines on a bus that can hold data, for example, 8, 16, 32, and 64 lines, which can accommodate 8, 16, 32, and 64 bits at a time.

**data throughput** *See* bandwidth.

**datagram** *See* packet.

**DC controller** A card inside a notebook that converts voltage to CPU voltage. Some notebook manufacturers consider the card to be an FRU.

**DCE (Data Communications Equipment)** The hardware, usually a dial-up modem, that provides the connection between a data terminal and a communications line. *See also* DTE.

**DDR SDRAM** *See* Double Data Rate SDRAM.

**DDR2 SDRAM** A version of SDRAM that is faster than DDR and uses less power.

**default gateway** The gateway a computer on a network will use to access another network unless it knows to specifically use another gateway for quicker access to that network.

**default printer** The printer Windows prints to unless another printer is selected.

**Defrag.exe** Windows program and command to defragment a logical drive.

**defragment** To "optimize" or rewrite a file to a disk in one contiguous chain of clusters, thus speeding up data retrieval.

**demodulation** The process by which digital data that has been converted to analog data is converted back to digital data. *See also* modulation.

**desktop** The initial screen that is displayed when an OS has a GUI interface loaded.

**device driver** A program stored on the hard drive that tells the computer how to communicate with an input/output device such as a printer or modem.

**DHCP (Dynamic Host Configuration Protocol) server** A service that assigns dynamic IP addresses to computers on a network when they first access the network.

**diagnostic cards** Adapter cards designed to discover and report computer errors and conflicts at POST time (before the computer boots up), often by displaying a number on the card.

**diagnostic software** Utility programs that help troubleshoot computer systems. Some Windows

diagnostic utilities are CHKDSK and SCANDISK. PC-Technician is an example of a third-party diagnostic program.

**dialer** Malicious software installed on your PC that disconnects your phone line from your ISP and dials up an expensive pay-per-minute phone number without your knowledge.

**dial-up networking** A Windows 9x/Me and Windows NT/2000/XP utility that uses a modem and telephone line to connect to a network.

**differential backup** Backup method that backs up only files that have changed or have been created since the last full backup. When recovering data, only two backups are needed: the full backup and the last differential backup.

**differential cable** A SCSI cable in which a signal is carried on two wires, each carrying voltage, and the signal is the difference between the two. Differential signaling provides for error checking and greater data integrity. Compare to single-ended cable.

**digital certificate** A code used to authenticate the source of a file or document or to identify and authenticate a person or organization sending data over the Internet. The code is assigned by a certificate authority such as VeriSign and includes a public key for encryption. Also called *digital ID* or *digital signature*.

**digital ID** *See* digital certificate.

**digital signature** *See* digital certificate.

**DIMM (dual inline memory module)** A miniature circuit board installed on a motherboard to hold memory. DIMMs can hold up to 2 GB of RAM on a single module.

**diode** An electronic device that allows electricity to flow in only one direction. Used in a rectifier circuit.

**DIP (dual inline package) switch** A switch on a circuit board or other device that can be set on or off to hold configuration or setup information.

**direct current (DC)** Current that travels in only one direction (the type of electricity provided by batteries). Computer power supplies transform AC to low DC.

**Direct Rambus DRAM** A memory technology by Rambus and Intel that uses a narrow network-type system bus. Memory is stored on a RIMM module. Also called RDRAM or Direct RDRAM.

**Direct RDRAM** *See* Direct Rambus DRAM.

**directory table** An OS table that contains file information such as the name, size, time and date of last modification, and cluster number of the file's beginning location.

**discrete L2 cache**   A type of L2 cache contained within the Pentium processor housing, but on a different die, with a cache bus between the processor and the cache.

**disk cache**   A method whereby recently retrieved data and adjacent data are read into memory in advance, anticipating the next CPU request.

**disk cloning**   *See* drive imaging.

**disk compression**   Compressing data on a hard drive to allow more data to be written to the drive.

**disk imaging**   *See* drive imaging.

**Disk Management**   A Windows 2000/XP utility used to display, create, and format partitions on basic disks and volumes on dynamic disks.

**disk quota**   A limit placed on the amount of disk space that is available to users. Requires a Windows 2000/XP NTFS volume.

**disk thrashing**   A condition that results when the hard drive is excessively used for virtual memory because RAM is full. It dramatically slows down processing and can cause premature hard drive failure.

**Display Power Management Signaling (DPMS)**   Energy Star standard specifications that allow for the video card and monitor to go into sleep mode simultaneously. *See also* Energy Star.

**distribution server**   A file server holding Windows setup files used to install Windows on computers networked to the server.

**DMA (direct memory access) channel**   A number identifying a channel whereby a device can pass data to memory without involving the CPU. Think of a DMA channel as a shortcut for data moving to/from the device and memory.

**DMA transfer mode**   A transfer mode used by devices, including the hard drive, to transfer data to memory without involving the CPU.

**DNS (domain name service or domain name system)**   A distributed pool of information (called the name space) that keeps track of assigned domain names and their corresponding IP addresses, and the system that allows a host to locate information in the pool. Compare to WINS.

**DNS server**   A computer that can find an IP address for another computer when only the domain name is known.

**docking station**   A device that receives a notebook computer and provides additional secondary storage and easy connection to peripheral devices.

**domain**   In Windows NT/2000/XP, a logical group of networked computers, such as those on a college campus, that share a centralized directory database

of user account information and security for the entire domain.

**domain controller**   A Windows NT/2000 or Windows Server 2003 computer which holds and controls a database of (1) user accounts, (2) group accounts, and (3) computer accounts used to manage access to the network.

**domain name**   A unique, text-based name that identifies a network.

**DOS box**   A command window.

**Dosstart.bat**   A type of Autoexec.bat file that is executed by Windows 9x/Me in two situations: when you select Restart the computer in MS-DOS mode from the shutdown menu, or you run a program in MS-DOS mode.

**dot pitch**   The distance between the dots that the electronic beam hits on a monitor screen.

**Double Data Rate SDRAM (DDR SDRAM)**   A type of memory technology used on DIMMs that runs at twice the speed of the system clock.

**doze time**   The time before an Energy Star or "Green" system will reduce 80 percent of its activity.

**Dr. Watson**   A Windows utility that can record detailed information about the system, errors that occur, and the programs that caused them in a log file. Windows 9x/Me names the log file \Windows\ Drwatson\WatsonXX.wlg, where XX is an incrementing number. Windows 2000 names the file \Documents and Settings\user\Documents\ DrWatson\Drwtsn32.log. Windows XP calls the file Drwatson.log.

**drive imaging**   Making an exact image of a hard-drive, including partition information, boot sectors, operating system installation, and application software to replicate the hard drive on another system or recover from a hard drive crash. Also called *disk cloning* and *disk imaging*.

**DriveSpace**   A Windows 9x/Me utility that compresses files so that they take up less space on a disk drive, creating a single large file on the disk to hold all the compressed files.

**drop height**   The height from which a manufacturer states that its device, such as a hard drive, can be dropped without making the device unusable.

**DSL (Digital Subscriber Line)**   A telephone line that carries digital data from end to end, and can be leased from the telephone company for individual use. Some DSL lines are rated at 5 Mbps, about 50 times faster than regular telephone lines.

**DTE (Data Terminal Equipment)**   Both the computer and a remote terminal or other computer to which it is attached. *See also* DCE.

**dual boot** The ability to boot using either of two different OSs, such as Windows 98 and Windows XP.

**dual channel** A motherboard feature that improves memory performance by providing two 64-bit channels between memory and the chipset. DDR and DDR2 memory can use dual channels.

**dual-core processing** Two processors contained in the same processor housing that share the interface with the chipset and memory.

**dual-scan passive matrix** A type of video display that is less expensive than an active-matrix display and does not provide as high-quality an image. With dual-scan display, two columns of electrodes are activated at the same time.

**dual-voltage CPU** A CPU that requires two different voltages: one for internal processing and the other for I/O processing.

**dump file** A file that contains information captured from memory at the time a stop error occurred.

**DVD (digital video disc or digital versatile disk)** A faster, larger CD format that can read older CDs, store over 8 GB of data, and hold full-length motion picture videos.

**dye-sublimation printer** A type of printer with photo-lab-quality results that uses transparent dyed film. The film is heated, which causes the dye to vaporize onto glossy paper.

**dynamic disk** A way to partition one or more hard drives, introduced with Windows 2000, in which information about the drive is stored in a database at the end of the drive. Compare to basic disk.

**dynamic IP address** An assigned IP address that is used for the current session only. When the session is terminated, the IP address is returned to the list of available addresses.

**dynamic RAM (DRAM)** The most common type of system memory, it requires refreshing every few milliseconds.

**dynamic volume** A volume type used with dynamic disks for which you can change the size of the volume after you have created it.

**dynamic VxD** A VxD that is loaded and unloaded from memory as needed.

**ECC (error-correcting code)** A chipset feature on a motherboard that checks the integrity of data stored on DIMMs or RIMMs and can correct single-bit errors in a byte. More advanced ECC schemas can detect, but not correct, double-bit errors in a byte.

**ECHS (extended CHS) mode** *See* large mode.

**ECP (Extended Capabilities Port)** A bidirectional parallel port mode that uses a DMA channel to speed up data flow.

**EDO (extended data out)** A type of outdated RAM that was faster than conventional RAM because it eliminated the delay before it issued the next memory address.

**EEPROM (electrically erasable programmable ROM)** A type of chip in which higher voltage may be applied to one of the pins to erase its previous memory before a new instruction set is electronically written.

**EIDE (Enhanced IDE)** A standard for managing the interface between secondary storage devices and a computer system. A system can support up to six serial ATA and parallel ATA IDE devices or up to four parallel ATA IDE devices such as hard drives, CD-ROM drives, and DVD drives.

**electromagnetic interference (EMI)** A magnetic field produced as a side effect from the flow of electricity. EMI can cause corrupted data in data lines that are not properly shielded.

**electrostatic discharge (ESD)** Another name for static electricity, which can damage chips and destroy motherboards, even though it might not be felt or seen with the naked eye.

**Emergency Repair Disk (ERD)** A Windows NT record of critical information about your system that can be used to fix a problem with the OS. The ERD enables restoration of the Windows NT registry on your hard drive.

**Emergency Repair Process** A Windows 2000 process that restores the OS to its state at the completion of a successful installation.

**emergency startup disk (ESD)** *See* rescue disk.

**Emm386.exe** A DOS and Windows 9x/Me utility that provides access to upper memory for 16-bit device drivers and other software.

**Encrypted File System (EFS)** A way to use a key to encode a file or folder on an NTFS volume to protect sensitive data. Because it is an integrated system service, EFS is transparent to users and applications and is difficult to attack.

**encrypting virus** A type of virus that transforms itself into a nonreplicating program to avoid detection. It transforms itself back into a replicating program to spread.

**encryption** The process of putting readable data into an encoded form that can only be decoded (or decrypted) through use of a key.

**Energy Star** "Green" systems that satisfy the EPA requirements to decrease the overall consumption of electricity. *See also* Green Standards.

**enhanced BIOS**   A system BIOS that has been written to accommodate large-capacity drives (over 504 MB, usually in the gigabyte range).

**EPIC (explicitly parallel instruction computing)**   The CPU architecture used by the Intel Itanium chip that bundles programming instructions with instructions on how to use multiprocessing abilities to do two instructions in parallel.

**EPP (Enhanced Parallel Port)**   A parallel port that allows data to flow in both directions (bidirectional port) and is faster than original parallel ports on PCs that allowed communication only in one direction.

**EPROM (erasable programmable ROM)**   A type of chip with a special window that allows the current memory contents to be erased with special ultraviolet light so that the chip can be reprogrammed.

**error correction**   The ability of a modem to identify transmission errors and then automatically request another transmission.

**escalate**   When a technician passes a customer's problem to higher organizational levels because he or she cannot solve the problem.

**Ethernet**   The most popular LAN architecture that can run at 10 Mbps (ThinNet or ThickNet), 100 Mbps (Fast Ethernet), or 1 Gbps (Gigabit Ethernet).

**Execution Trace Cache**   A type of Level 1 cache used by some CPUs to hold decoded operations waiting to be executed.

**executive services**   In Windows NT/2000/XP, a group of components running in kernel mode that interfaces between the subsystems in user mode and the HAL.

**expansion bus**   A bus that does not run in sync with the system clock.

**expansion card**   A circuit board inserted into a slot on the motherboard to enhance the capability of the computer.

**expansion slot**   A narrow slot on the motherboard where an expansion card can be inserted. Expansion slots connect to a bus on the motherboard.

**expert systems**   Software that uses a database of known facts and rules to simulate a human expert's reasoning and decision-making processes.

**ExpressCard**   The latest PCMCIA standard for notebook I/O cards that uses the PCI Express and USB 2.0 data transfer standards. Two types of Express-Cards are ExpressCard/34 (34 mm wide) and ExpressCard/54 (54 mm wide).

**extended memory**   Memory above 1024 K used in a DOS or Windows 9x/Me system.

**extended partition**   The only partition on a hard drive that can contain more than one logical drive.

**extension magnet brush**   A long-handled brush made of nylon fibers that are charged with static electricity to pick up stray toner inside a printer.

**external cache**   Static cache memory, stored on the motherboard or inside the CPU housing, that is not part of the CPU (also called L2 or L3 cache).

**external command**   Commands that have their own program files.

**faceplate**   A metal or plastic plate that comes with the computer case and fits over the empty drive bays or slots for expansion cards to create a well-fitted enclosure around them.

**Fast Ethernet**   *See* 100BaseT.

**FAT (file allocation table)**   A table on a hard drive or floppy disk that tracks the clusters used to contain a file.

**FAT12**   The 12-bit wide, one-column file allocation table for a floppy disk, containing information about how each cluster or file allocation unit on the disk is currently used.

**fault tolerance**   The degree to which a system can tolerate failures. Adding redundant components, such as disk mirroring or disk duplexing, is a way to build in fault tolerance.

**Fiber Distributed Data Interface (FDDI)**   A ring-based network that does not require a centralized hub and can transfer data at a rate of 100 Mbps.

**field replaceable unit (FRU)**   A component in a computer or device that can be replaced with a new component without sending the computer or device back to the manufacturer. Examples: power supply, DIMM, motherboard, floppy disk drive.

**file allocation unit**   *See* cluster.

**file extension**   A three-character portion of the name of a file that is used to identify the file type. In command lines, the file extension follows the filename and is separated from it by a period. For example, Msd.exe, where exe is the file extension.

**file system**   The overall structure that an OS uses to name, store, and organize files on a disk. Examples of file systems are FAT32 and NTFS.

**file virus**   A virus that inserts virus code into an executable program file and can spread whenever that program is executed.

**filename**   The first part of the name assigned to a file. In DOS, the filename can be no more than eight characters long and is followed by the file extension. In Windows, a filename can be up to 255 characters.

**firewall**    Hardware or software that protects a computer or network from unauthorized access.

**FireWire**    *See* IEEE 1394.

**firmware**    Software that is permanently stored in a chip. The BIOS on a motherboard is an example of firmware.

**flash ROM**    ROM that can be reprogrammed or changed without replacing chips.

**flat panel monitor**    A desktop monitor that uses an LCD panel.

**FlexATX**    A version of the ATX form factor that allows for maximum flexibility in the size and shape of cases and motherboards. FlexATX is ideal for custom systems.

**floppy disk drive (FDD)**    A drive that can hold either a $5\frac{1}{4}$ inch or $3\frac{1}{2}$ floppy disk.

**flow control**    When using modems, a method of controlling the flow of data to adjust for problems with data transmission. Xon/Xoff is an example of a flow control protocol.

**folder**    *See* subdirectory.

**folder redirection**    A Windows XP feature that allows a user to point to a folder that can be on the local PC or somewhere on the network, and its location can be transparent to the user.

**forced perfect terminator (FPT)**    A type of SCSI active terminator that includes a mechanism to force signal termination to the correct voltage, eliminating most signal echoes and interference.

**forgotten password floppy disk**    A Windows XP disk created to be used in the event the user forgets the user account password to the system.

**form factor**    A set of specifications on the size, shape, and configuration of a computer hardware component such as a case, power supply, or motherboard.

**formatting**    Preparing a hard drive volume or floppy disk for use by placing tracks and sectors on its surface to store information (for example, FORMAT A:).

**FPM (fast page mode)**    An outdated memory mode used before the introduction of EDO memory. FPM improved on earlier memory types by sending the row address just once for many accesses to memory near that row.

**fragmentation**    The distribution of data files on a hard drive or floppy disk such that they are stored in noncontiguous clusters.

**fragmented file**    A file that has been written to different portions of the disk so that it is not in contiguous clusters.

**frame**    The header and trailer information added to data to form a data packet to be sent over a network.

**front side bus (FSB)**    *See* system bus.

**FTP (File Transfer Protocol)**    The protocol used to transfer files over a TCP/IP network such that the file does not need to be converted to ASCII format before transferring it.

**full AT**    *See* AT.

**full backup**    A complete backup, whereby all of the files on the hard drive are backed up each time the backup procedure is performed. It is the safest backup method, but it takes the most time.

**full-duplex**    Communication that happens in two directions at the same time.

**fully qualified domain name (FQDN)**    A host name and a domain name such as *jsmith.amazon.com*. Sometimes loosely referred to as a domain name.

**gateway**    A computer or other device that connects networks.

**GDI (Graphics Device Interface)**    A core Windows component responsible for building graphics data to display or print. A GDI printer relies on Windows to construct a page to print and then receives the constructed page as bitmap data.

**General Packet Radio Service (GPRS)**    A protocol standard that can be used by GSM or TDMA on a cellular WAN to send voice, text, or video data in packets similar to VoIP.

**General Protection Fault (GPF)**    A Windows error that occurs when a program attempts to access a memory address that is not available or is no longer assigned to it.

**Gigabit Ethernet**    The next generation of Ethernet. Gigabit Ethernet supports rates of data transfer up to 1 gigabit per second but is not yet widely used.

**gigahertz (GHz)**    One thousand MHz, or one billion cycles per second.

**global user account**    Sometimes called a domain user account, the account is used at the domain level, created by an administrator, and stored in the SAM (security accounts manager) database on a Windows 2000 or Windows 2003 domain controller.

**graphics accelerator**    A type of video card that has an on-board processor that can substantially increase speed and boost graphical and video performance.

**graphics DDR (G-DDR), graphics DDR2, graphics DDR3** Types of DDR, DDR2, and DDR3 memory specifically designed to be used in graphics cards.

**grayware** A program that AV software recognizes to be potentially harmful or potentially unwanted.

**Green Standards** A computer or device that conforms to these standards can go into sleep or doze mode when not in use, thus saving energy and helping the environment. Devices that carry the Green Star or Energy Star comply with these standards.

**ground bracelet** A strap you wear around your wrist that is attached to the computer case, ground mat, or another ground so that ESD is discharged from your body before you touch sensitive components inside a computer. Also called static strap, ground strap, ESD bracelet.

**group profile** A group of user profiles. All profiles in the group can be changed by changing the group profile.

**GSM (Global System for Mobile communication)** An open standard for cellular WANs and cell phones that uses digital communication of data and is accepted and used worldwide.

**guard tone** A tone that an answering modem sends when it first answers the phone, to tell the calling modem that a modem is on the other end of the line.

**Guest user** A user who has limited permissions on a system and cannot make changes to it. Guest user accounts are intended for one-time or infrequent users of a workstation.

**HAL (hardware abstraction layer)** The low-level part of Windows NT/2000/XP, written specifically for each CPU technology, so that only the HAL must change when platform components change.

**half life** The time it takes for a medium storing data to weaken to half of its strength. Magnetic media, including traditional hard drives and floppy disks, have a half-life of five to seven years.

**half-duplex** Communication between two devices whereby transmission takes place in only one direction at a time.

**handshaking** When two modems begin to communicate, the initial agreement made as to how to send and receive data.

**hard boot** Restart the computer by turning off the power or by pressing the Reset button. Also called a cold boot.

**hard copy** Output from a printer to paper.

**hard drive** The main secondary storage device of a PC, a small case that contains magnetic coated platters that rotate at high speed.

**hard drive controller** The firmware that controls access to a hard drive contained on a circuit board mounted on or inside the hard drive housing. Older hard drives used firmware on a controller card that connected to the drive by way of two cables, one for data and one for control.

**hard drive standby time** The amount of time before a hard drive will shut down to conserve energy.

**hard-disk loading** The illegal practice of installing unauthorized software on computers for sale. Hard-disk loading can typically be identified by the absence of original software disks in the original system's shipment.

**hardware** The physical components that constitute the computer system, such as the monitor, the keyboard, the motherboard, and the printer.

**hardware address** *See* MAC address.

**hardware cache** A disk cache that is contained in RAM chips built right on the disk controller. Also called a buffer.

**hardware interrupt** An event caused by a hardware device signaling the CPU that it requires service.

**hardware profile** A set of hardware configuration information that Windows keeps in the registry. Windows can maintain more than one hardware profile for the same PC.

**HCL (hardware compatibility list)** The list of all computers and peripheral devices that have been tested and are officially supported by Windows NT/2000/XP (see *www.microsoft.com/whdc/hcl/default.mspx*).

**head** The top or bottom surface of one platter on a hard drive. Each platter has two heads.

**heat sink** A piece of metal, with cooling fins, that can be attached to or mounted on an integrated chip (such as the CPU) to dissipate heat.

**hertz (Hz)** Unit of measurement for frequency, calculated in terms of vibrations, or cycles per second. For example, for 16-bit stereo sound, a frequency of 44,000 Hz is used. *See also* megahertz.

**hexadecimal notation (hex)** A numbering system that uses 16 digits, the numerals 0–9, and the letters A–F. Hexadecimal notation is often used to display memory addresses.

**hibernation** A notebook OS feature that conserves power by using a small trickle of electricity. Before the notebook begins to hibernate, everything currently stored in memory is saved to the hard drive. When the notebook is brought out of hibernation, open applications and their data are returned to the state before hibernation.

**hidden file** A file that is not displayed in a directory list. Whether to hide or display a file is one of the file's attributes kept by the OS.

**high memory area (HMA)** In DOS or Windows 9x/Me, the first 64K of extended memory.

**High Voltage Differential (HVD)** A type of SCSI differential signaling requiring more expensive hardware to handle the higher voltage. HVD became obsolete with the introduction of SCSI-3.

**high-level formatting** Formatting performed by means of the DOS or Windows Format program (for example, FORMAT C:/S creates the boot record, FAT, and root directory on drive C and makes the drive bootable). Also called OS formatting.

**Himem.sys** The DOS and Windows 9x/Me memory manager extension that allowed access to memory addresses above 1 MB.

**hive** Physical segment of the Windows NT/ 2000/XP registry that is stored in a file.

**hop count** *See* time to live (TTL).

**host** Any computer or other device on a network that has been assigned an IP address. Also called node.

**host adapter** The circuit board that controls a SCSI bus supporting as many as seven or fifteen separate devices. The host adapter controls communication between the SCSI bus and the PC.

**host bus** *See* memory bus or system bus.

**host drive** Using Windows 9x, typically drive H on a compressed drive. *See* compressed drive.

**host name** A name that identifies a computer, printer, or other device on a network.

**hot-pluggable** *See* hot-swappable.

**hot-swappable** A device that can be plugged into a computer while it is turned on and the computer will sense the device and configure it without rebooting, or the device can be removed without an OS error. Also called hot-pluggable.

**HTML (HyperText Markup Language)** A markup language used for hypertext documents on the World Wide Web. This language uses tags to format the document, create hyperlinks, and mark locations for graphics.

**HTTP (HyperText Transfer Protocol)** The communications protocol used by the World Wide Web.

**HTTPS (HTTP secure)** A version of the HTTP protocol that includes data encryption for security.

**hub** A network device or box that provides a central location to connect cables.

**hypertext** Text that contains links to remote points in the document or to other files, documents, or graphics. Hypertext is created using HTML and is commonly distributed from Web sites.

**i.Link** *See* IEEE 1394.

**I/O addresses** Numbers that are used by devices and the CPU to manage communication between them. Also called ports or port addresses.

**I/O controller card** An older card that can contain serial, parallel, and game ports and floppy drive and IDE connectors.

**IBM Data Connector** *See* IDC.

**IBM-compatible PC** A computer that uses an Intel (or compatible) processor and can run DOS and Windows.

**ICMP (Internet Control Message Protocol)** Part of the IP layer that is used to transmit error messages and other control messages to hosts and routers.

**IDC (IBM Data Connector)** A connector used with STP cable on a Token Ring network. Also called a *UDC (Universal Data Connector)*.

**IDE (Integrated Drive Electronics or Integrated Device Electronics)** A hard drive whose disk controller is integrated into the drive, eliminating the need for a controller cable and thus increasing speed, as well as reducing price. *See also* EIDE.

**IEEE 1284** A standard for parallel ports and cables developed by the Institute for Electrical and Electronics Engineers and supported by many hardware manufacturers.

**IEEE 1394** Standards for an expansion bus that can also be configured to work as a local bus. It is expected to replace the SCSI bus, providing an easy method to install and configure fast I/O devices. Also called FireWire and i.Link.

**IEEE 1394.3** A standard, developed by the 1394 Trade Association, that is designed for peer-to-peer data transmission and allows imaging devices to send images and photos directly to printers without involving a computer.

**IEEE 802.11a/b/g** IEEE specifications for wireless communication and data synchronization. Also known as Wi-Fi. Apple Computer's versions of 802.11b/g are called AirPort and AirPort Extreme.

**IFS (Installable File System)** The Windows 9x/Me component that configures all devices and communicates these configurations to the device drivers.

**IMAP4 (Internet Message Access Protocol version 4)** Version 4 of the IMAP protocol, which is an e-mail protocol that has more functionality than its predecessor, POP. IMAP can archive messages in folders on the e-mail server and can allow the user to choose not to download attachments to messages.

**incremental backup**  A time-saving backup method that only backs up files changed or newly created since the last full or incremental backup. Multiple incremental backups might be required when recovering lost data.

**infestation**  Any unwanted program that is transmitted to a computer without the user's knowledge and that is designed to do varying degrees of damage to data and software. There are a number of different types of infestations, including viruses, Trojan horses, worms, and logic bombs. *See also* malicious software.

**information (.inf) file**  Text file with an .inf file extension, such as Msbatch.inf, that contains information about a hardware or software installation.

**infrared transceiver**  A wireless transceiver that uses infrared technology to support some wireless devices such as keyboards, mice, and printers. A motherboard might have an embedded infrared transceiver, or the transceiver might plug into a USB or serial port. The technology is defined by the Infrared Data Association (IrDA). Also called an *IrDA transceiver* or *infrared port*.

**initialization files**  Configuration information files for Windows. System.ini is one of the most important Windows 9x/Me initialization files.

**ink-jet printer**  A type of ink dispersion printer that uses cartridges of ink. The ink is heated to a boiling point and then ejected onto the paper through tiny nozzles.

**Institute of Electrical and Electronics Engineers (IEEE)**  A nonprofit organization that develops standards for the computer and electronics industries.

**instruction set**  The set of instructions, on the CPU chip, that the computer can perform directly (such as ADD and MOVE).

**intelligent UPS**  A UPS connected to a computer by way of a USB or serial cable so that software on the computer can monitor and control the UPS. Also called *smart UPS*.

**interlaced**  A type of display in which the electronic beam of a monitor draws every other line with each pass, which lessens the overall effect of a lower refresh rate.

**internal bus**  The bus inside the CPU that is used for communication between the CPU's internal components.

**internal cache**  Memory cache that is faster than external cache, and is contained inside CPU chips (also referred to as primary, Level 1, or L1 cache).

**internal command**  Commands that are embedded in the Command.com file.

**Internet Connection Firewall (ICF)**  Windows XP software designed to protect a PC from unauthorized access from the Internet. Windows XP Service Pack 2 improved on ICF and renamed it Windows Firewall.

**Internet Connection Sharing (ICS)**  A Windows 98 and Windows XP utility that uses NAT and acts as a proxy server to manage two or more computers connected to the Internet.

**Internet service provider (ISP)**  A commercial group that provides Internet access for a monthly fee. AOL, EarthLink, and CompuServe are large ISPs.

**intranet**  A private network that uses the TCP/IP protocols.

**Io.sys**  Along with Msdos.sys and Command.com, one of the three files that are the core components of the real mode portion of Windows 9x/Me. It is the first program file of the OS.

**IP (Internet Protocol)**  The rules of communication in the TCP/IP stack that control segmenting data into packets, routing those packets across networks, and then reassembling the packets once they reach their destination.

**IP address**  A 32-bit address consisting of four numbers separated by periods, used to uniquely identify a device on a network that uses TCP/IP protocols. The first numbers identify the network; the last numbers identify a host. An example of an IP address is 206.96.103.114.

**IPX/SPX (Internetwork Packet Exchange/Sequenced Packet Exchange)**  A networking protocol suite first used by Novell NetWare, and which corresponds to the TCP/IP protocols.

**IrDA transceiver**  *See* infrared transceiver.

**IRQ (interrupt request) line**  A line on a bus that is assigned to a device and is used to signal the CPU for servicing. These lines are assigned a reference number (for example, the normal IRQ for a printer is IRQ 7).

**ISA (Industry Standard Architecture) slot**  An older slot on the motherboard used for slower I/O devices, which can support an 8-bit or a 16-bit data path. ISA slots are mostly replaced by PCI slots.

**ISDN (Integrated Services Digital Network)**  A digital telephone line that can carry data at about five times the speed of regular telephone lines. Two channels (telephone numbers) share a single pair of wires.

**isochronous data transfer**  A method used by IEEE 1394 to transfer data continuously without breaks.

**ITU (International Telecommunications Union)**  The international organization responsible for

**developing** international standards of communication. Formerly CCITT.

**joule** A measure of work or energy. One joule of energy produces one watt of power for one second.

**JPEG (Joint Photographic Experts Group)** A graphical compression scheme that allows the user to control the amount of data that is averaged and sacrificed as file size is reduced. It is a common Internet file format. Most JPEG files have a .jpg extension.

**jumper** Two wires that stick up side by side on the motherboard and are used to hold configuration information. The jumper is considered closed if a cover is over the wires, and open if the cover is missing.

**Kerberos** A protocol used to encrypt account names and passwords that are sent to a network controller for validation. Kerberos is the default protocol used by Windows 2000/XP.

**kernel** The portion of an OS that is responsible for interacting with the hardware.

**kernel mode** A Windows NT/2000/XP "privileged" processing mode that has access to hardware components.

**key** (1) In encryption, a secret number or code used to encode and decode data. (2) In Windows, a section name of the Windows registry.

**key fob** A device, such as a type of smart card, that can fit conveniently on a key chain.

**keyboard** A common input device through which data and instructions may be typed into computer memory.

**keylogger** A type of spyware that tracks your keystrokes, including passwords, chat room sessions, e-mail messages, documents, online purchases, and anything else you type on your PC. Text is logged to a text file and transmitted over the Internet without your knowledge.

**LAN (local area network)** A computer network that covers only a small area, usually within one building.

**land grid array (LGA)** A feature of a CPU socket whereby pads, called lands, are used to make contact in uniform rows over the socket. Compare to *pin grid array (PGA)*.

**lands** Microscopic flat areas on the surface of a CD or DVD that separate pits. Lands and pits are used to represent data on the disk.

**laptop computer** *See* notebook.

**large mode** A mode of addressing information on hard drives that range from 504 MB to 8.4 GB, addressing information on a hard drive by translating cylinder, head, and sector information in

order to break the 528-MB hard drive barrier. Also called ECHS mode.

**large-capacity drive** A hard drive larger than 504 MB.

**laser printer** A type of printer that uses a laser beam to control how toner is placed on the page and then uses heat to fuse the toner to the page.

**Last Known Good configuration** In Windows NT/2000/XP, registry settings and device drivers that were in effect when the computer last booted successfully. These settings can be restored during the startup process to recover from errors during the last boot.

**LBA (logical block addressing) mode** A mode of addressing information on hard drives in which the BIOS and operating system view the drive as one long linear list of LBAs or addressable sectors, permitting drives to be larger than 8.4 GB (LBA 0 is cylinder 0, head 0, and sector 1).

**Level 1 (L1) cache** *See* internal cache.

**Level 2 (L2) cache** *See* external cache.

**Level 3 (L3) cache** *See* external cache.

**license** Permission for an individual to use a product or service. A manufacturer's method of maintaining ownership, while granting permission for use to others.

**Limited user** Windows XP user accounts known as Users in Windows NT/2000, which have read-write access only on their own folders, read-only access to most system folders, and no access to other users' data.

**line conditioner** A device that regulates, or conditions, power, providing continuous voltage during brownouts and spikes.

**line protocol** A protocol used to send data packets destined for a network over telephone lines. PPP and SLIP are examples of line protocols.

**line speed** *See* bandwidth.

**line-interactive UPS** A variation of a standby UPS that shortens switching time by always keeping the inverter that converts AC to DC working, so that there is no charge-up time for the inverter.

**LMHosts** A text file located in the Windows folder that contains NetBIOS names and their associated IP addresses. This file is used for name resolution for a NetBEUI network.

**local bus** A bus that operates at a speed synchronized with the CPU frequency. The system bus is a local bus.

**local I/O bus** A local bus that provides I/O devices with fast access to the CPU. The PCI bus is a local I/O bus.

**local printer**   A printer connected to a computer by way of a port on the computer. Compare to network printer.

**local profile**   User profile that is stored on a local computer and cannot be accessed from another computer on the network.

**local user account**   A user account that applies only to a local computer and cannot be used to access resources from other computers on the network.

**logic bomb**   A type of malicious software that is dormant code added to software and triggered at a predetermined time or by a predetermined event.

**logical drive**   A portion or all of a hard drive partition that is treated by the operating system as though it were a physical drive. Each logical drive is assigned a drive letter, such as drive C, and contains a file system. Also called a volume.

**logical geometry**   The number of heads, tracks, and sectors that the BIOS on the hard drive controller presents to the system BIOS and the OS. The logical geometry does not consist of the same values as the physical geometry, although calculations of drive capacity yield the same results. The use of communicating logical geometry is outdated.

**Logical Unit Number (LUN)**   A number assigned to a logical device (such as a tray in a CD changer) that is part of a physical SCSI device, which is assigned a SCSI ID.

**long mode**   A CPU processing mode that processes 64 bits at a time. The AMD Athlon 64 and the Intel Itaninum CPUs use this mode.

**lost allocation units**   *See* lost clusters.

**lost clusters**   File fragments that, according to the file allocation table, contain data that does not belong to any file. The command CHKDSK/F can free these fragments. Also called lost allocation units.

**low insertion force (LIF) socket**   A socket that requires the installer to manually apply an even force over the microchip when inserting the chip into the socket.

**Low Voltage Differential (LVD)**   A type of differential signaling that uses lower voltage than does HVD, is less expensive, and can be compatible with single-ended signaling on the same SCSI bus.

**low-level formatting**   A process (usually performed at the factory) that electronically creates the hard drive tracks and sectors and tests for bad spots on the disk surface.

**low-profile case**   *See* compact case.

**LPX**   A form factor in which expansion cards are mounted on a riser card that plugs into a motherboard. The expansion cards in LPX systems are mounted parallel to the motherboard, rather than perpendicular to it as in AT and ATX systems.

**MAC (Media Access Control) address**   A 48-bit hardware address unique to each NIC card and assigned by the manufacturer. The address is often printed on the adapter as hexadecimal numbers. An example is 00 00 0C 08 2F 35. Also called a physical address, an adapter address, or a hardware address.

**macro**   A small sequence of commands, contained within a document, that can be automatically executed when the document is loaded, or executed later by using a predetermined keystroke.

**macro virus**   A virus that can hide in the macros of a document file.

**main board**   *See* motherboard.

**malicious software**   Any unwanted program that is transmitted to a computer without the user's knowledge and that is designed to do varying degrees of damage to data and software. Types of infestations include viruses, Trojan horses, worms, adware, spyware, keyloggers, browser hijackers, dialers, and downloaders. Also called malware or an infestation.

**malware**   *See* malicious software.

**mandatory user profile**   A roaming user profile that applies to all users in a user group, and individual users cannot change that profile.

**Master Boot Record (MBR)**   The first sector on a hard drive, which contains the partition table and a program the BIOS uses to boot an OS from the drive.

**master file table (MFT)**   The database used by the NTFS file system to track the contents of a logical drive.

**material safety data sheet (MSDS)**   A document that explains how to properly handle substances such as chemical solvents; it includes information such as physical data, toxicity, health effects, first aid, storage, disposal, and spill procedures.

**megahertz (MHz)**   One million Hz, or one million cycles per second. *See also* hertz (Hz).

**memory**   Physical microchips that can hold data and programming, located on the motherboard or expansion cards.

**memory address**   A number assigned to each byte in memory. The CPU can use memory addresses to track where information is stored in RAM. Memory addresses are usually displayed as hexadecimal numbers in segment/offset form.

**memory bus**   *See* system bus.

**memory cache**   A small amount of faster RAM that stores recently retrieved data, in anticipation of what the CPU will request next, thus speeding up access. *See also* system bus.

**memory dump** The contents of memory saved to a file at the time an event halted the system. Support technicians can analyze the dump file to help understand the source of the problem.

**memory extender** For DOS and Windows 9x/Me, a device driver named Himem.sys that manages RAM, giving access to memory addresses above 1 MB.

**memory paging** In Windows, swapping blocks of RAM memory to an area of the hard drive to serve as virtual memory when RAM is low.

**memory-resident virus** A virus that can stay lurking in memory even after its host program is terminated.

**microATX** A version of the ATX form factor. MicroATX addresses some new technologies that were developed after the original introduction of ATX.

**microcode** A programming instruction that can be executed by a CPU without breaking the instruction down into simpler instructions. Typically, a single command line in a Visual Basic or C++ program must be broken down into numerous microcode commands.

**MicroDIMM** A type of memory module used on sub-notebooks that has 144 pins and uses a 64-bit data path.

**microprocessor** *See* central processing unit (CPU).

**Microsoft Management Console (MMC)** A utility to build customized consoles. These consoles can be saved to a file with an .msc file extension.

**Mini PCI** The PCI industry standard for desktop computer expansion cards, applied to a much smaller form factor for notebook expansion cards.

**Mini-ATX** A smaller ATX board that can be used with regular ATX cases and power supplies.

**minicartridge** A tape drive cartridge that is only $3\frac{1}{4} \times 2\frac{1}{2} \times \frac{3}{5}$ inches. It is small enough to allow two drives to fit into a standard $5\frac{1}{2}$-inch drive bay of a PC case.

**minifile system** In Windows NT/2000/XP, a simplified file system that is started so that Ntldr (NT Loader) can read files from any file system the OS supports.

**Mini-LPX** A smaller version of the LPX motherboard.

**mixed mode** A Windows 2000 mode for domain controllers used when there is at least one Windows NT domain controller on the network.

**MMX (Multimedia Extensions)** Multimedia instructions built into Intel processors to add functionality such as better processing of multimedia, SIMD support, and increased cache.

**modem** From MOdulate/DEModulate. A device that modulates digital data from a computer to an analog format that can be sent over telephone lines, then demodulates it back into digital form.

**modem eliminator** *See* null modem cable.

**modem riser card** A small modem card that uses an AMR or CNR slot. Part of the modem logic is contained in a controller on the motherboard.

**modem speed** The speed at which a modem can transmit data along a phone line, measured in bits per second (bps). Also called line speed.

**modulation** Converting binary or digital data into an analog signal that can be sent over standard telephone lines.

**monitor** The most commonly used output device for displaying text and graphics on a computer.

**motherboard** The main board in the computer, also called the system board. The CPU, ROM chips, SIMMs, DIMMs, RIMMs, and interface cards are plugged into the motherboard.

**motherboard bus** *See* system bus.

**motherboard mouse** *See* PS/2-compatible mouse.

**mouse** A pointing and input device that allows the user to move a cursor around a screen and select items with the click of a button.

**MP3** A method to compress audio files that uses MPEG level 1. It can reduce sound files as low as a 1:24 ratio without losing much sound quality.

**MPEG (Moving Pictures Experts Group)** A processing-intensive standard for data compression for motion pictures that tracks movement from one frame to the next and only stores the data that has changed.

**Msdos.sys** In Windows 9x/Me, a text file that contains settings used by Io.sys during booting. In DOS, the Msdos.sys file was a program file that contained part of the DOS core.

**MultiBank DRAM (MDRAM)** A type of video memory that is faster than VRAM and WRAM, but can be more economical because it can be installed on a video card in smaller increments.

**multicasting** A process in which a message is sent by one host to multiple hosts, such as when a video conference is broadcast to several hosts on the Internet.

**multimeter** A device used to measure the various components of an electrical circuit. The most common measurements are voltage, current, and resistance.

**multipartite virus** A combination of a boot sector virus and a file virus. It can hide in either type of program.

**multiplier** The factor by which the bus speed or frequency is multiplied to get the CPU clock speed.

**multi-processor platform**   A system that contains more than one processor. The motherboard has more than one processor socket and the processors must be rated to work in this multi-processor environment.

**multiscan monitor**   A monitor that can work within a range of frequencies and thus can work with different standards and video cards. It offers a variety of refresh rates.

**multisession**   A feature that allows data to be read from or written to a CD during more than one session. This is important if the disk was only partially filled during the first write.

**Multistation Access Unit (MSAU or MAU)**   A centralized hub used in Token Ring networks to connect stations. Also called CAU.

**multitasking**   Doing more than one thing at a time. A true multitasking system requires two or more CPUs, each processing a different thread at the same time. Compare to cooperative multitasking and preemptive multitasking.

**multithreading**   The ability to pass more than one function (thread) to the OS kernel at the same time, such as when one thread is performing a print job while another reads a file.

**name resolution**   The process of associating a NetBIOS name or host name to an IP address.

**narrow SCSI**   One of the two main SCSI specifications. Narrow SCSI has an 8-bit data bus. The word "narrow" is not usually included in the names of narrow SCSI devices.

**NAT (Network Address Translation)**   A process that converts private IP addresses on a LAN to the proxy server's IP address before a data packet is sent over the Internet.

**native mode**   A Windows 2000 mode used by domain controllers when there are no Windows NT domain controllers present on the network.

**NetBEUI (NetBIOS Extended User Interface)**   A fast, proprietary Microsoft networking protocol used only by Windows-based systems, and limited to LANs because it does not support routing.

**NetBIOS (Network Basic Input/Output System)**   An API protocol used by some applications to communicate over a NetBEUI network. NetBIOS has largely been replaced by Windows Sockets over a TCP/IP network.

**network adapter**   *See* network interface card.

**network drive map**   Mounting a drive to a computer, such as drive E, that is actually hard drive space on another host computer on the network.

**network interface card (NIC)**   An expansion card that plugs into a computer's motherboard and provides a port on the back of the card to connect a PC to a network. Also called a network adapter.

**network operating system (NOS)**   An operating system that resides on the controlling computer in the network. The NOS controls what software, data, and devices a user on the network can access. Examples of an NOS are Novell NetWare and Windows Server 2003.

**network printer**   A printer that any user on the network can access, through its own network card and connection to the network, through a connection to a standalone print server, or through a connection to a computer as a local printer, which is shared on the network.

**NLX**   A low-end form factor that is similar to LPX but provides greater support for current and emerging processor technologies. NLX was designed for flexibility and efficiency of space.

**NNTP (Network News Transfer Protocol)**   The protocol used by newsgroup server and client software.

**node**   *See* host

**noise**   An extraneous, unwanted signal, often over an analog phone line, that can cause communication interference or transmission errors. Possible sources are fluorescent lighting, radios, TVs, lightning, or bad wiring.

**noninterlaced**   A type of display in which the electronic beam of a monitor draws every line on the screen with each pass.

**non-memory-resident virus**   A virus that is terminated when the host program is closed. Compare to memory-resident virus.

**nonparity memory**   Eight-bit memory without error checking. A SIMM part number with a 32 in it ($4 \times 8$ bits) is nonparity.

**nonvolatile**   Refers to a kind of RAM that is stable and can hold data as long as electricity is powering the memory.

**normal mode**   *See* CHS mode.

**North Bridge**   That portion of the chipset hub that connects faster I/O buses (for example, AGP bus) to the system bus. Compare to South Bridge.

**notebook**   A portable computer that is designed for travel and mobility. Notebooks use the same technology as desktop PCs, with modifications for conserving voltage, taking up less space, and operating while on the move. Also called a laptop computer.

**NTFS (NT file system)**   The file system for the Windows NT/2000/XP operating systems. NTFS cannot be accessed by other operating systems such as DOS. It provides increased reliability and security in comparison to other methods of organizing and accessing files. There are several versions of NTFS that might or might not be compatible.

**Ntldr (NT Loader)** In Windows NT/2000/XP, the OS loader used on Intel systems.

**NTVDM (NT virtual DOS machine)** An emulated environment in which a 16-bit DOS application resides within Windows NT/2000/XP with its own memory space or WOW (Win16 on Win32).

**null modem cable** A cable that allows two data terminal equipment (DTE) devices to communicate in which the transmit and receive wires are cross-connected and no modems are necessary.

**NWLink** Microsoft's version of the IPX/SPX protocol suite used by Novell NetWare operating systems.

**octet** Term for each of the four 8-bit numbers that make up an IP address. For example, the IP address 206.96.103.114 has four octets.

**ohm (Ω)** The standard unit of measurement for electrical resistance. Resistors are rated in ohms.

**on-board ports** Ports that are directly on the motherboard, such as a built-in keyboard port or on-board serial port.

**operating system (OS)** Software that controls a computer. An OS controls how system resources are used and provides a user interface, a way of managing hardware and software, and ways to work with files.

**operating system formatting** *See* high-level formatting.

**overclocking** Running a processor at a higher frequency than is recommended by the manufacturer, which can result in an unstable system, but is a popular thing to do when a computer is used for gaming.

**P1 connector** Power connection on an ATX or BTX motherboard.

**P8 connector** One of two power connectors on an AT motherboard.

**P9 connector** One of two power connectors on an AT motherboard.

**packet** Segment of network data that also includes header, destination address, and trailer information that is sent as a unit. Also called data packet or datagram.

**page fault** An OS interrupt that occurs when the OS is forced to access the hard drive to satisfy the demands for virtual memory.

**page file** *See* swap file.

**Pagefile.sys** The Windows NT/2000/XP swap file.

**page-in** The process in which the memory manager goes to the hard drive to return the data from a swap file to RAM.

**page-out** The process in which, when RAM is full, the memory manager takes a page and moves it to the swap file.

**pages** 4K segments in which Windows NT/2000/XP allocates memory.

**parallel ATA (PATA)** An older IDE cabling method that uses a 40-pin flat data cable or an 80-conductor cable and a 40-pin IDE connector. *See also* serial ATA.

**parallel port** A female 25-pin port on a computer that can transmit data in parallel, 8 bits at a time, and is usually used with a printer. The names for parallel ports are LPT1 and LPT2.

**parity** An error-checking scheme in which a ninth, or "parity," bit is added. The value of the parity bit is set to either 0 or 1 to provide an even number of ones for even parity and an odd number of ones for odd parity.

**parity error** An error that occurs when the number of 1s in the byte is not in agreement with the expected number.

**parity memory** Nine-bit memory in which the ninth bit is used for error checking. A SIMM part number with a 36 in it (4 × 9 bits) is parity. Older PCs almost always use parity chips.

**partition** A division of a hard drive that can be used to hold logical drives.

**partition table** A table at the beginning of the hard drive that contains information about each partition on the drive. The partition table is contained in the Master Boot Record.

**passive backplane** A type of backplane system in which the backplane contains no circuitry at all. All circuitry in a passive backplane system is contained on a mothercard plugged into a backplane.

**passive terminator** A type of terminator for single-ended SCSI cables. Simple resistors are used to provide termination of a signal. Passive termination is not reliable over long distances and should only be used with narrow SCSI.

**passphrase** A type of password that can contain a phrase where spaces are allowed. A passphrase is stronger than a one-word password.

**patch** An update to software that corrects an error, adds a feature, or addresses security issues. Also called an update or service pack.

**patch cable** A network cable that is used to connect a PC to a hub, switch, or router.

**path** (1) A drive and list of directories pointing to a file such as C:\Windows\command. (2) The OS command to provide a list of paths to the system for finding program files to execute.

**PC Card**   A credit-card-sized adapter card that can be slid into a slot in the side of many notebook computers and is used by modems, network cards, and other devices. Also called PCMCIA Card.

**PC Card slot**   An expansion slot on a notebook computer, into which a PC Card is inserted. Also called a PCMCIA Card slot.

**PCI (Peripheral Component Interconnect) bus**   A bus common on Pentium computers that runs at speeds of up to 33 MHz or 66 MHz, with a 32-bit-wide or 64-bit-wide data path. PCI-X, released in September 1999, enables PCI to run at 133 MHz. For some chipsets, it serves as the middle layer between the memory bus and expansion buses.

**PCL (Printer Control Language)**   A printer language developed by Hewlett-Packard that communicates to a printer how to print a page.

**PCMCIA (Personal Computer Memory Card International Association) Card**   *See* PC Card.

**PCMCIA Card slot**   *See* PC Card slot.

**PDA (Personal Digital Assistant)**   A small, handheld computer that has its own operating system and applications.

**peer-to-peer network**   A network of computers that are all equals, or peers. Each computer has the same amount of authority, and each can act as a server to the other computers.

**peripheral devices**   Devices that communicate with the CPU but are not located directly on the motherboard, such as the monitor, floppy drive, printer, and mouse.

**phishing**   (1) A type of identity theft where a person is baited into giving personal data to a Web site that appears to be the Web site of a reputable company with which the person has an account. (2) Sending an e-mail message with the intent of getting the user to reveal private information that can be used for identify theft.

**physical address**   *See* MAC address.

**physical geometry**   The actual layout of heads, tracks, and sectors on a hard drive. Compare to logical geometry.

**PIF (program information file)**   A file used by Windows to describe the environment for a DOS program to use.

**pin grid array (PGA)**   A feature of a CPU socket whereby the pins are aligned in uniform rows around the socket.

**Ping (Packet Internet Groper)**   A Windows and Unix command used to troubleshoot network connections. It verifies that the host can communicate with another host on the network.

**pinout**   A description of how each pin on a bus, connection, plug, slot, or socket is used.

**PIO (Programmed I/O) transfer mode**   A transfer mode that uses the CPU to transfer data from the hard drive to memory. PIO mode is slower than DMA mode.

**pipelined burst SRAM**   A less expensive SRAM that uses more clock cycles per transfer than non-pipelined burst but does not significantly slow down the process.

**pits**   Recessed areas on the surface of a CD or DVD, separating lands, or flat areas. Lands and pits are used to represent data on a disc.

**pixel**   A small spot on a fine horizontal scan line. Pixels are illuminated to create an image on the monitor.

**PKI (public key infrastructure)**   The standards used to encrypt, transport, and validate digital certificates over the Internet.

**Plug and Play (PnP)**   A standard designed to make the installation of new hardware devices easier by automatically configuring devices to eliminate system resource conflicts (such as IRQ or I/O address conflicts). PnP is supported by Windows 9x/Me, Windows 2000, and Windows XP.

**polling**   A process by which the CPU checks the status of connected devices to determine if they are ready to send or receive data.

**polymorphic virus**   A type of virus that changes its distinguishing characteristics as it replicates itself. Mutating in this way makes it more difficult for AV software to recognize the presence of the virus.

**POP (Post Office Protocol)**   The protocol that an e-mail server and client use when the client requests the downloading of e-mail messages. The most recent version is POP3. POP is being replaced by IMAP.

**port**   (1) As applied to services running on a computer, a number assigned to a process on a computer so that the process can be found by TCP/IP. Also called a port address or port number. (2) Another name for an I/O address. *See also* I/O address. (3) A physical connector, usually at the back of a computer, that allows a cable from a peripheral device, such as a printer, mouse, or modem, to be attached.

**port address**   *See* I/O address.

**port forwarding**   A technique that allows a computer on the Internet to reach a computer on a private network using a certain port when the private network is protected by a router using NAT as a proxy server. Port forwarding is also called tunneling.

**port number**   *See* port.

**port replicator**  A device designed to connect to a notebook computer to make it easy to connect the notebook to peripheral devices.

**port settings**  The configuration parameters of communications devices such as COM1, COM2, or LPT1, including IRQ settings.

**port speed**  The communication speed between a DTE (computer) and a DCE (modem). As a general rule, the port speed should be at least four times as fast as the modem speed.

**POST (power-on self test)**  A self-diagnostic program used to perform a simple test of the CPU, RAM, and various I/O devices. The POST is performed by startup BIOS when the computer is first turned on, and is stored in ROM-BIOS.

**PostScript**  A printer language developed by Adobe Systems which tells a printer how to print a page.

**power conditioner**  A line conditioner that regulates, or conditions, power, providing continuous voltage during brownouts.

**power scheme**  A feature of Windows XP support for notebooks that allows the user to create groups of power settings for specific sets of conditions.

**power supply**  A box inside the computer case that supplies power to the motherboard and other installed devices. Power supplies provide 3.3, 5, and 12 volts DC.

**power-on password**  A password that a computer uses to control access during the boot process.

**PPP (Point-to-Point Protocol)**  A protocol that governs the methods for communicating via modems and dial-up telephone lines. The Windows Dial-up Networking utility uses PPP.

**PPPoE (Point-to-Point Protocol over Ethernet)**  The protocol that describes how a PC is to interact with a broadband converter box, such as cable modem, when the two are connected by an Ethernet cable, connected to a NIC in a PC.

**preemptive multitasking**  A type of pseudo-multitasking whereby the CPU allows an application a specified period of time and then preempts the processing to give time to another application.

**primary cache**  *See* internal cache.

**primary domain controller (PDC)**  In a Windows NT network, the computer that controls the directory database of user accounts, group accounts, and computer accounts on a domain. *See also* backup domain controller.

**primary partition**  A hard disk partition that can contain only one logical drive.

**primary storage**  Temporary storage on the motherboard used by the CPU to process data and instructions. Memory is considered primary storage.

**printer**  A peripheral output device that produces printed output to paper. Different types include dot matrix, ink-jet, and laser printers.

**printer maintenance kit**  A kit purchased from a printer manufacturer that contains the parts, tools, and instructions needed to perform routine printer maintenance.

**private IP address**  An IP address that is used on a private TCP/IP network that is isolated from the Internet.

**process**  An executing instance of a program together with the program resources. There can be more than one process running for a program at the same time. One process for a program happens each time the program is loaded into memory or executed.

**processor**  *See* central processing unit (CPU).

**processor speed**  The speed, or frequency, at which the CPU operates. Usually expressed in GHz.

**product activation**  The process that Microsoft uses to prevent software piracy. For example, once Windows XP is activated for a particular computer, it cannot be legally installed on another computer.

**program**  A set of step-by-step instructions to a computer. Some are burned directly into chips, while others are stored as program files. Programs are written in languages such as BASIC and C++.

**program file**  A file that contains instructions designed to be executed by the CPU.

**protected mode**  An operating mode that supports preemptive multitasking, the OS manages memory and other hardware devices, and programs can use a 32-bit data path. Also called 32-bit mode.

**protocol**  A set of rules and standards that two entities use for communication.

**Protocol.ini**  A Windows initialization file that contains network configuration information.

**proxy server**  A server that acts as an intermediary between another computer and the Internet. The proxy server substitutes its own IP address for the IP address of the computer on the network making a request, so that all traffic over the Internet appears to be coming from only the IP address of the proxy server.

**PS/2-compatible mouse**  A mouse that plugs into a round mouse PS/2 port on the motherboard. Sometimes called a motherboard mouse.

**public IP address**  An IP address available to the Internet.

**QIC (Quarter-Inch Committee or quarter-inch cartridge)** A name of a standardized method used to write data to tape. These backup files have a .qic extension.

**Quality of Service (QoS)** A measure of the success of communication over the Internet. Communication is degraded on the Internet when packets are dropped, delayed, delivered out of order, or corrupted. VoIP requires a high QoS.

**RAID (redundant array of inexpensive disks or redundant array of independent disks)** Several methods of configuring multiple hard drives to store data to increase logical volume size and improve performance, or to ensure that if one hard drive fails, the data is still available from another hard drive.

**RAM (random access memory)** Memory modules on the motherboard containing microchips used to temporarily hold data and programs while the CPU processes both. Information in RAM is lost when the PC is turned off.

**RAM drive** An area of memory that is treated as though it were a hard drive, but works much faster than a hard drive. The Windows 9x/Me startup disk uses a RAM drive. Compare to virtual memory.

**RARP (Reverse Address Resolution Protocol)** A protocol used to translate the unique hardware NIC addresses (MAC addresses) into IP addresses (the reverse of ARP).

**RDRAM** *See* Direct Rambus DRAM.

**read/write head** A sealed, magnetic coil device that moves across the surface of a disk either reading data from or writing data to the disk.

**real mode** A single-tasking operating mode whereby a program can use 1024 K of memory addresses, has direct access to RAM, and uses a 16-bit data path. Using a memory extender (Himem.sys) a program in real mode can access memory above 1024 K. Also called 16-bit mode.

**Recovery Console** A Windows 2000/XP command interface utility and OS that can be used to solve problems when Windows cannot load from the hard drive.

**rectifier** An electrical device that converts AC to DC. A PC power supply contains a rectifier.

**refresh** The process of periodically rewriting data, such as on dynamic RAM.

**refresh rate** As applied to monitors, the number of times in one second an electronic beam can fill the screen with lines from top to bottom. Also called vertical scan rate.

**registry** A database that Windows uses to store hardware and software configuration information, user preferences, and setup information.

**re-marked chips** Chips that have been used and returned to the factory, marked again, and resold. The surface of the chips may be dull or scratched.

**Remote Assistance** A Windows XP feature that allows a support technician at a remote location to have full access to the Windows XP desktop.

**repeater** A device that amplifies signals on a network so they can be transmitted further down the line.

**rescue disk** A floppy disk that can be used to start up a computer when the hard drive fails to boot. Also called emergency startup disk (ESD) or startup disk.

**resistance** The degree to which a device opposes or resists the flow of electricity. As the electrical resistance increases, the current decreases. *See also* ohm and resistor.

**resistor** An electronic device that resists or opposes the flow of electricity. A resistor can be used to reduce the amount of electricity being supplied to an electronic component.

**resolution** The number of pixels on a monitor screen that are addressable by software (example: $1024 \times 768$ pixels).

**restore point** A snapshot of the Windows Me/XP system state, usually made before installation of new hardware or applications.

**REt (Resolution Enhancement technology)** The term used by Hewlett-Packard to describe the way a laser printer varies the size of the dots used to create an image. This technology partly accounts for the sharp, clear image created by a laser printer.

**RIMM** A type of memory module developed by Rambus, Inc.

**ring topology** A network topology in which the nodes in a network form a ring. Each node is connected only to two other nodes, and a centralized hub is not required.

**RISC (Reduced Instruction Set Computing) chips** Chips that incorporate only the most frequently used instructions, so that the computer operates faster (for example, the PowerPC uses RISC chips).

**riser card** A card that plugs into a motherboard and allows for expansion cards to be mounted parallel to the motherboard. Expansion cards are plugged into slots on the riser card.

**RJ-11** A phone line connection found on modems, telephones, and house phone outlets.

**RJ-45 connector** A connector used with twisted-pair cable that connects the cable to the NIC.

**roaming user profile** A user profile for a roaming user. Roaming user profiles are stored on a server so that the user can access the profile from anywhere on the network.

**ROM (read-only memory)** Chips that contain programming code and cannot be erased.

**ROM BIOS** *See* BIOS.

**root directory** The main directory created when a hard drive or disk is first formatted. In Linux, it's indicated by a forward slash. In DOS and Windows, it's indicated by a backward slash.

**rootkit** A type of malicious software that loads itself before the OS boot is complete and can hijack internal Windows components so that it masks information Windows provides to user-mode utilities such as Windows Explorer or Task Manager.

**routable protocol** A protocol that can be routed to interconnected networks on the basis of a network address. TCP/IP is a routable protocol, but NetBEUI is not.

**router** A device that connects networks and makes decisions as to the best routes to use when forwarding packets.

**sags** *See* brownouts.

**sampling rate** The rate of samples taken of an analog signal over a period of time, usually expressed as samples per second, or hertz.

**SBAC (SCSI bus adapter chip)** The SCSI chip within a device housing that controls data transfer over the SCSI bus.

**SCAM (SCSI Configuration AutoMatically)** A method of configuring SCSI device settings that follows the Plug and Play standard. SCAM makes installation of SCSI devices much easier, provided that the devices are SCAM-compliant.

**scam e-mail** E-mail sent by a scam artist intended to lure you into a scheme.

**scanner** A device that allows a computer to convert a picture, drawing, barcode, or other image into digital data that can be input into the computer.

**scanning mirror** A component of a laser printer consisting of an octagonal mirror that can be directed in a sweeping motion to cover the entire length of a laser printer drum.

**script virus** A type of virus that hides in a script which might execute when you click a link on a Web page or in an HTML e-mail message, or when you attempt to open an e-mail attachment.

**SCSI (Small Computer System Interface)** A fast interface between a host adapter and the CPU that can daisy chain as many as 7 or 15 devices on a single bus.

**SCSI ID** A number from 0 to 15 assigned to each SCSI device attached to the daisy chain.

**SDRAM II** *See* Double Data Rate SDRAM (DDR SDRAM).

**secondary storage** Storage that is remote to the CPU and permanently holds data, even when the PC is turned off, such as a hard drive.

**sector** On a disk surface one segment of a track, which almost always contains 512 bytes of data.

**security accounts manager (SAM)** A portion of the Windows NT/2000/XP registry that manages the account database that contains accounts, policies, and other pertinent information about local accounts.

**sequential access** A method of data access used by tape drives, whereby data is written or read sequentially from the beginning to the end of the tape or until the desired data is found.

**serial ATA (SATA)** An ATAPI cabling method that uses a narrower and more reliable cable than the 80-conductor cable. *See also* parallel ATA.

**serial ATA cable** An IDE cable that is narrower and has fewer pins than the parallel IDE 80-conductor cable.

**serial mouse** A mouse that uses a serial port and has a female 9-pin DB-9 connector.

**serial port** A male 9-pin or 25-pin port on a computer system used by slower I/O devices such as a mouse or modem. Data travels serially, one bit at a time, through the port. Serial ports are sometimes configured as COM1, COM2, COM3, or COM4.

**server-side caching** A technique used by servers on the Internet to speed up download times by caching Web pages previously requested in case they are requested again.

**service** A program that runs in the background to support or serve Windows or an application.

**service pack** *See* patch.

**session** An established communication link between two software programs. On the Internet, a session is created by TCP.

**SFC (System File Checker)** A Windows tool that checks to make sure Windows is using the correct versions of system files.

**SGRAM (synchronous graphics RAM)** Memory designed especially for video card processing that can synchronize itself with the CPU bus clock.

**shadow RAM or shadowing ROM** ROM programming code copied into RAM to speed up the system operation, because of the faster access speed of RAM.

**shared memory** When the video system does not have dedicated video memory, but is using regular RAM instead. A system with shared memory generally costs less than having dedicated video memory. Also called *video sharing*.

**shell** The portion of an OS that relates to the user and to applications.

**shielded twisted-pair (STP) cable** A cable that is made of one or more twisted pairs of wires and is surrounded by a metal shield.

**shortcut** An icon on the desktop that points to a program that can be executed or to a file or folder.

**signal-regenerating repeater** A repeater that is able to distinguish between noise and signal. It reads the signal and retransmits it without the accompanying noise.

**Sigverif.exe** A Windows 2000/XP utility that allows you to search for digital signatures.

**SIMD (single instruction, multiple data)** A process that allows the CPU to execute a single instruction simultaneously on multiple pieces of data, rather than by repetitive looping.

**SIMM (single inline memory module)** A miniature circuit board used in older computers to hold RAM. SIMMs hold 8, 16, 32, or 64 MB on a single module.

**simple volume** A type of dynamic volume used on a single hard drive that corresponds to a primary partition on a basic disk.

**single-ended (SE) cable** A type of SCSI cable in which two wires are used to carry a signal, one of which carries the signal itself; the other is a ground for the signal.

**single-voltage CPU** A CPU that requires one voltage for both internal and I/O operations.

**site license** A license that allows a company to install multiple copies of software, or to allow multiple employees to execute the software from a file server.

**slack** Wasted space on a hard drive caused by not using all available space at the end of clusters.

**sleep mode** A mode used in many "Green" systems that allows them to be configured through CMOS to suspend the monitor or even the drive, if the keyboard and/or CPU have been inactive for a set number of minutes. *See also* Green Standards.

**slimline case** *See* compact case.

**SLIP (Serial Line Internet Protocol)** A line protocol used by regular telephone lines that has largely been replaced by PPP.

**smart card** Any small device that contains authentication information that can be keyed into a logon window or read by a reader to authenticate a user on a network.

**smart card reader** A device that can read a smart card used to authenticate a person onto a network.

**Smart Multistation Access Unit (SMAU)** *See* MAU.

**smart UPS** *See* intelligent UPS.

**SMARTDrive** A hard drive cache program that came with Windows 3.x and DOS and can be executed as a TSR from the Autoexec.bat file (for example, Device = Smartdrv.sys 2048).

**SMTP (Simple Mail Transfer Protocol)** The protocol used by e-mail clients and servers to send e-mail messages over the Internet. *See also* POP and IMAP.

**SMTP AUTH (SMTP Authentication)** A protocol that is used to authenticate or prove that a client who attempts to use an email server to send email is authorized to use the server. The protocol is based on the Simple Authentication and Security Layer (SASL) protocol.

**snap-ins** A Windows utility that can be installed in a console window by Microsoft Management Console.

**SNMP (Simple Network Management Protocol)** A protocol used to monitor and manage network traffic on a workstation. SNMP works with TCP/IP and IPX/SPX networks.

**social engineering** The practice of tricking people into giving out private information or allowing unsafe programs into the network or computer.

**socket** *See* session.

**SO-DIMM (small outline DIMM)** A type of memory module used in notebook computers that uses DIMM technology and can have either 72 pins or 144 pins.

**soft boot** To restart a PC without turning off the power, for example, in Windows XP, by clicking Start, Turn Off Computer, and Restart. Also called warm boot.

**soft power** *See* soft switch.

**soft switch** A feature on an ATX or BTX system that allows an OS to power down the system and allows for activity such as a keystroke or network activity to power up the system. Also called soft power.

**software** Computer programs, or instructions to perform a specific task. Software may be BIOS, OSs, or applications software such as a word-processing or spreadsheet program.

**software cache** Cache controlled by software whereby the cache is stored in RAM.

**solid ink printer** A type of printer that uses sticks or blocks of solid ink. The ink is melted and then jetted onto the paper as the paper passes by on a drum.

**solid state device (SSD)**   A storage device that uses memory chips to store data instead of spinning disks (such as those used by hard drives and CD drives). Examples of solid state devices are jump drives (also called key drives or thumb drives), flash memory cards, and solid state disks used as hard drives in notebook computers designed for the most rugged uses. Also called solid state disk (SSD).

**solid state disk (SSD)**   *See* solid state device.

**SO-RIMM (small outline RIMM)**   A 160-pin memory module used in notebooks that uses Rambus technology.

**South Bridge**   That portion of the chipset hub that connects slower I/O buses (for example, an ISA bus) to the system bus. Compare to North Bridge.

**spacers**   *See* standoffs.

**spam**   Junk e-mail you don't ask for, don't want, and that gets in your way.

**spanned volume**   A type of dynamic volume used on two or more hard drives that fills up the space allotted on one physical disk before moving to the next.

**SPI (SCSI Parallel Interface)**   The part of the SCSI-3 standard that specifies how SCSI devices are connected.

**spikes**   Temporary surges in voltage, which can damage electrical components. Also called swells.

**spooling**   Placing print jobs in a print queue so that an application can be released from the printing process before printing is completed. Spooling is an acronym for simultaneous peripheral operations online.

**spyware**   Malicious software that installs itself on your computer to spy on you. It collects personal information about you that it transmits over the Internet to Web-hosting sites that intend to use your personal data for harm.

**SSE (Streaming SIMD Extension)**   A technology used by the Intel Pentium III and later CPUs and designed to improve performance of multimedia software.

**SSL (secure socket layer)**   A secure protocol developed by Netscape that uses a digital certificate including a public key to encrypt and decrypt data.

**staggered pin grid array (SPGA)**   A feature of a CPU socket whereby the pins are staggered over the socket to squeeze more pins into a small space.

**standby time**   The time before a "Green" system will reduce 92 percent of its activity. *See also* Green Standards.

**standoffs**   Round plastic or metal pegs that separate the motherboard from the case, so that components on the back of the motherboard do not touch the case.

**star bus topology**   A LAN that uses a logical bus design, but with all devices connected to a central hub, making a physical star.

**star ring topology**   A topology that is physically arranged in a star formation but is logically a ring because of the way information travels on it. Token Ring is the primary example.

**star topology**   A LAN in which all the devices are connected to a central hub.

**start bits**   Bits that are used to signal the approach of data.

**startup BIOS**   Part of system BIOS that is responsible for controlling the PC when it is first turned on. Startup BIOS gives control over to the OS once it is loaded.

**startup disk**   *See* rescue disk.

**startup password**   *See* power-on password.

**stateless**   Term for a device or process that manages data or some activity without regard to all the details of the data or activity.

**static electricity**   *See* ESD.

**static IP address**   An IP address permanently assigned to a workstation.

**static RAM (SRAM)**   RAM chips that retain information without the need for refreshing, as long as the computer's power is on. They are more expensive than traditional DRAM.

**static VxD**   A VxD that is loaded into memory at startup and remains there for the entire OS session.

**stealth virus**   A virus that actively conceals itself by temporarily removing itself from an infected file that is about to be examined, and then hiding a copy of itself elsewhere on the drive.

**stop error**   An error severe enough to cause the operating system to stop all processes.

**streaming audio**   Downloading audio data from the Internet in a continuous stream of data without first downloading an entire audio file.

**striped volume**   A type of dynamic volume used for two or more hard drives that writes to the disks evenly rather than filling up allotted space on one and then moving on to the next. Compare to spanned volume.

**subdirectory**   A directory or folder contained in another directory or folder. Also called a child directory or folder.

**subnet mask**   A subnet mask is a group of four numbers (dotted decimal numbers) that tell TCP/IP if a remote computer is on the same or a different network.

**subsystems**   The different modules into which the Windows NT/2000/XP user mode is divided.

**surge suppressor or surge protector**   A device or power strip designed to protect electronic equipment from power surges and spikes.

**Surround Sound**   A sound compression standard that supports six separate sound channels using six speakers known as Front Left and Right, Front Center, Rear Left and Right, and Subwoofer. Surround Sound 7.1 supports two additional rear or side speakers. Also known Dolby AC-3, Dolby Digital Surround, or Dolby Surround Sound.

**suspend time**   The time before a "Green" system will reduce 99 percent of its activity. After this time, the system needs a warm-up time so that the CPU, monitor, and hard drive can reach full activity.

**swap file**   A file on the hard drive that is used by the OS for virtual memory. Also called a page file.

**swells**   *See* spikes.

**switch**   A device used to segment a network. It can decide which network segment is to receive a packet, on the basis of the packet's destination MAC address.

**synchronization**   The process by which files and programs are transferred between PDAs and PCs.

**synchronous DRAM (SDRAM)**   A type of memory stored on DIMMs that runs in sync with the system clock, running at the same speed as the motherboard.

**synchronous SRAM**   SRAM that is faster and more expensive than asynchronous SRAM. It requires a clock signal to validate its control signals, enabling the cache to run in step with the CPU.

**SyncLink DRAM (SLDRAM)**   A type of DRAM developed by a consortium of 12 DRAM manufacturers. It improved on regular SDRAM but is now obsolete.

**Sysedit**   The Windows 9x/Me System Configuration Editor, a text editor generally used to edit system files.

**system BIOS**   BIOS located on the motherboard.

**system board**   *See* motherboard.

**system bus**   The bus between the CPU and memory on the motherboard. The bus frequency in documentation is called the system speed, such as 400 MHz. Also called the memory bus, front side bus, local bus, or host bus.

**system clock**   A line on a bus that is dedicated to timing the activities of components connected to it. The system clock provides a continuous pulse that other devices use to time themselves.

**system disk**   Windows terminology for a bootable disk.

**system partition**   The active partition of the hard drive containing the boot record and the specific files required to load Windows NT/2000/XP.

**system resource**   A channel, line, or address on the motherboard that can be used by the CPU or a device for communication. The four system resources are IRQ, I/O address, DMA channel, and memory address.

**System Restore**   A Windows Me/XP utility, similar to the ScanReg tool in earlier versions of Windows, that is used to restore the system to a restore point. Unlike ScanReg, System Restore cannot be executed from a command prompt.

**system state data**   In Windows 2000/XP, files that are necessary for a successful load of the operating system.

**System Tray**   An area to the right of the taskbar that holds the icons for running services; these services include the volume control and network connectivity.

**System.ini**   A text configuration file used by Windows 3.x and supported by Windows 9x/Me for backward-compatibility.

**TAPI (Telephony Application Programming Interface)**   A standard developed by Intel and Microsoft that can be used by 32-bit Windows communications programs for communicating over phone lines.

**taskbar**   A bar normally located at the bottom of the Windows desktop, displaying information about open programs and providing quick access to others.

**TCP (Transmission Control Protocol)**   Part of the TCP/IP protocol suite. TCP guarantees delivery of data for application protocols and establishes a session before it begins transmitting data.

**TCP/IP (Transmission Control Protocol/Internet Protocol)**   The suite of protocols that supports communication on the Internet. TCP is responsible for error checking, and IP is responsible for routing.

**TDMA (time-division multiple access)**   A protocol standard used by cellular WANs and cell phones.

**technical documentation**   The technical reference manuals, included with software packages and peripherals, that provide directions for installation, usage, and troubleshooting. The information extends beyond that given in user manuals.

**telephony**   A term describing the technology of converting sound to signals that can travel over telephone lines.

**terminating resistor**   The resistor added at the end of a SCSI chain to dampen the voltage at the end of the chain.

**termination**   A process necessary to prevent an echo effect of power at the end of a SCSI chain, resulting in interference with the data transmission.

**thermal printer**  A type of line printer that uses wax-based ink, which is heated by heat pins that melt the ink onto paper.

**ThickNet**  *See* 10Base5 Ethernet.

**ThinNet**  *See* 10Base2 Ethernet.

**thread**  Each process that the CPU is aware of; a single task that is part of a longer task or program.

**TIFF (Tagged Image File Format)**  A bitmapped file format used to hold photographs, graphics, and screen captures. TIFF files can be rather large, and have a .tif file extension.

**time to live (TTL)**  Number of routers a network packet can pass through on its way to its destination before it is dropped. Also called hop count.

**TLS (Transport Layer Security)**  A protocol used to secure data sent over the Internet. It is an improved version of SSL.

**token ring**  An older LAN technology developed by IBM that transmits data at 4 Mbps or 16 Mbps.

**top-level domain**  The highest level of domain names, indicated by a suffix that tells something about the host. For example, .com is for commercial use and .edu is for educational institutions.

**touch screen**  An input device that uses a monitor or LCD panel as a backdrop for user options. Touch screens can be embedded in a monitor or LCD panel or installed as an add-on device.

**tower case**  The largest type of personal computer case. Tower cases stand vertically and can be as high as two feet tall. They have more drive bays and are a good choice for computer users who anticipate making significant upgrades.

**trace**  A wire on a circuit board that connects two components or devices.

**track**  One of many concentric circles on the surface of a hard drive or floppy disk.

**training**  *See* handshaking.

**transceiver**  The component on a NIC that is responsible for signal conversion. Combines the words transmitter and receiver.

**transformer**  A device that changes the ratio of current to voltage. A computer power supply is basically a transformer and a rectifier.

**transistor**  An electronic device that can regulate electricity and act as a logical gate or switch for an electrical signal.

**translation**  A technique used by system BIOS and hard drive controller BIOS to break the 504-MB hard drive barrier, whereby a different set of drive parameters are communicated to the OS and other software than that used by the hard drive controller BIOS.

**Travan standards**  A popular and improved group of standards for tape drives based on the QIC standards and developed by 3M.

**triad**  Three dots of color that make up one composite dot on a CRT screen.

**Trojan horse**  A type of infestation that hides or disguises itself as a useful program, yet is designed to cause damage when executed.

**TSR (terminate-and-stay-resident)**  A program that is loaded into memory and remains dormant until called on, such as a screen saver or a memory-resident antivirus program.

**UART (universal asynchronous receiver-transmitter) chip**  A chip that controls serial ports. It sets protocol and converts parallel data bits received from the system bus into serial bits.

**UDC (Universal Data Connector)**  *See* IDC (IBM Data Connector).

**UDP (User Datagram Protocol)**  A connectionless protocol that does not require a connection to send a packet and does not guarantee that the packet arrives at its destination. UDP is faster than TCP because TCP takes the time to make a connection and guarantee delivery.

**unattended installation**  A Windows NT/ 2000/XP installation that is done by storing the answers to installation questions in a text file or script that Windows NT/2000/XP calls an answer file so that the answers do not have to be typed in during the installation.

**Universal Disk Format (UDF) file system**  A file system for optical media used by all DVD discs and some CD-R and CD-RW discs.

**unshielded twisted-pair (UTP) cable**  A cable that is made of one or more twisted pairs of wires and is not surrounded by shielding.

**upgrade install**  The installation of an OS on a hard drive that already has an OS installed in such a way that settings kept by the old OS are carried forward into the upgrade, including information about hardware, software, and user preferences.

**upper memory**  In DOS and Windows 9x/Me, the memory addresses from 640 K up to 1024 K, originally reserved for BIOS, device drivers, and TSRs.

**upper memory block (UMB)**  In DOS and Windows 9x/Me, a group of consecutive memory addresses in RAM from 640 K to 1 MB that can be used by 16-bit device drivers and TSRs.

**UPS (uninterruptible power supply)**   A device designed to provide a backup power supply during a power failure. Basically, a UPS is a battery backup system with an ultrafast sensing device.

**URL (Uniform Resource Locator)**   An address for a resource on the Internet. A URL can contain the protocol used by the resource, the name of the computer and its network, and the path and name of a file on the computer.

**USB host controller**   Manages the USB bus. If the motherboard contains on-board USB ports, the USB host controller is part of the chipset. The USB controller uses only a single set of resources for all devices on the bus.

**USB (universal serial bus) port**   A type of port designed to make installation and configuration of I/O devices easy, providing room for as many as 127 devices daisy-chained together.

**user account**   The information, stored in the SAM database, that defines a Windows NT/ 2000/XP user, including username, password, memberships, and rights.

**user component**   A Windows 9x/Me component that controls the mouse, keyboard, ports, and desktop.

**user mode**   In Windows NT/2000/XP, a mode that provides an interface between an application and the OS, and only has access to hardware resources through the code running in kernel mode.

**user profile**   A personal profile about a user that enables the user's desktop settings and other operating parameters to be retained from one session to another.

**User State Migration Tool (USMT)**   A Windows XP utility that helps you migrate user files and preferences from one computer to another to help a user make a smooth transition from one computer to another.

**V.92**   The latest standard for data transmission over phone lines that can attain a speed of 56 Kbps.

**value data**   In Windows, the name and value of a setting in the registry.

**VCACHE**   A built-in Windows 9x/Me 32-bit software cache that doesn't take up conventional memory space or upper memory space as SMARTDrive did.

**VESA (Video Electronics Standards Association) VL bus**   An outdated local bus used on 80486 computers for connecting 32-bit adapters directly to the local processor bus.

**VFAT (virtual file allocation table)**   A variation of the original DOS 16-bit FAT that allows for long filenames and 32-bit disk access.

**video card**   An interface card installed in the computer to control visual output on a monitor. Also called display adapter.

**video sharing**   See shared memory.

**virtual device driver (VxD or VDD)**   A Windows device driver that may or may not have direct access to a device. It might depend on a Windows component to communicate with the device itself.

**virtual machine**   One or more logical machines created within one physical machine by Windows, allowing applications to make serious errors within one logical machine without disturbing other programs and parts of the system.

**virtual memory**   A method whereby the OS uses the hard drive as though it were RAM. Compare to RAM drive.

**virtual real mode**   An operating mode that works similarly to real mode and is provided by a 32-bit OS for a 16-bit program to work.

**virus**   A program that often has an incubation period, is infectious, and is intended to cause damage. A virus program might destroy data and programs or damage a disk drive's boot sector.

**virus hoax**   E-mail that does damage by tempting you to forward it to everyone in your e-mail address book with the intent of clogging up e-mail systems or by persuading you to delete a critical Windows system file by convincing you the file is malicious.

**virus signature**   A set of distinguishing characteristics of a virus used by antivirus software to identify the virus.

**VMM (Virtual Machine Manager)**   A Windows 9x/Me program that controls virtual machines and the resources they use including memory. The VMM manages the page table used to access memory.

**volatile**   Refers to a kind of RAM that is temporary, cannot hold data very long, and must be frequently refreshed.

**volt (V)**   A measure of potential difference in an electrical circuit. A computer ATX power supply usually provides five separate voltages: +12 V, –12 V, +5 V, –5 V, and +3.3 V.

**voltage**   Electrical differential that causes current to flow, measured in volts. See also volt.

**voltage regulator module (VRM)**   A device embedded or installed on the motherboard that regulates voltage to the processor.

**voltmeter**   A device for measuring electrical AC or DC voltage.

**volume**   See logical drive.

**VRAM (video RAM)** RAM on video cards that holds the data that is being passed from the computer to the monitor and can be accessed by two devices simultaneously. Higher resolutions often require more video memory.

**VxD** *See* virtual device driver.

**wait state** A clock tick in which nothing happens, used to ensure that the microprocessor isn't getting ahead of slower components. A 0-wait state is preferable to a 1-wait state. Too many wait states can slow down a system.

**WAN (wide area network)** A network or group of networks that span a large geographical area.

**warm boot** *See* soft boot.

**watt (W)** The unit used to measure power. A typical computer may use a power supply that provides 200 W.

**wattage** Electrical power measured in watts.

**WDM (Win32 Driver Model)** The only Windows 9x/Me Plug and Play component that is found in Windows 98 but not Windows 95. WDM is the component responsible for managing device drivers that work under a driver model new to Windows 98.

**WEP (Wired Equivalent Privacy)** A data encryption method used on wireless networks that uses either 64-bit or 128-bit encryption keys that are static keys, meaning the key does not change while the wireless network is in use.

**WFP (Windows File Protection)** A Windows 2000/XP tool that protects system files from modification.

**wide SCSI** One of the two main SCSI specifications. Wide SCSI has a 16-bit data bus. *See also* narrow SCSI.

**Wi-Fi** *See* IEEE 802.11b.

**wildcard** A * or ? character used in a command line that represents a character or group of characters in a filename or extension.

**Win.ini** The Windows initialization file that contains program configuration information needed for running the Windows operating environment. Its functions were replaced by the registry beginning with Windows 9x/Me, which still supports it for backward compatibility with Windows 3.x.

**Win16 on Win32 (WOW)** A group of programs provided by Windows NT/2000/XP to create a virtual DOS environment that emulates a 16-bit Windows environment, protecting the rest of the OS from 16-bit applications.

**Win386.swp** The name of the Windows 9x/Me swap file. Its default location is C:\Windows.

**WINS (Windows Internet Naming Service)** A Microsoft resolution service with a distributed database that tracks relationships between NetBIOS names and IP addresses. Compare to DNS.

**WinSock (Windows Sockets)** A part of the TCP/IP utility software that manages API calls from applications to other computers on a TCP/IP network.

**wireless LAN (WLAN)** A type of LAN that does not use wires or cables to create connections, but instead transmits data over radio or infrared waves.

**word size** The number of bits that can be processed by a CPU at one time.

**workgroup** In Windows, a logical group of computers and users in which administration, resources, and security are distributed throughout the network, without centralized management or security.

**worm** An infestation designed to copy itself repeatedly to memory, on drive space or on a network, until little memory or disk space remains.

**WPA (WiFi Protected Access)** A data encryption method for wireless networks that use the TKIP (Temporal Key Integrity Protocol) encryption method and the encryption keys are changed at set intervals while the wireless LAN is in use.

**WPA2 (WiFi Protected Access 2)** A data encryption standard compliant with the IEEE802.11i standard that uses the AES (Advanced Encryption Standard) protocol. WPA2 is currently the strongest wireless encryption standard.

**WRAM (window RAM)** Dual ported video RAM that is faster and less expensive than VRAM. It has its own internal bus on the chip, with a data path that is 256 bits wide.

**zero insertion force (ZIF) socket** A socket that uses a small lever to apply even force when you install the microchip into the socket.

**zero-fill utility** A utility provided by a hard drive manufacturer that fills every sector on the drive with zeroes.

**zone bit recording** A method of storing data on a hard drive whereby the drive can have more sectors per track near the outside of the platter.

# INDEX

## License Agreement/Notice of Limited Warranty

**By opening the sealed disc container in this book, you agree to the following terms and conditions. If, upon reading the following license agreement and notice of limited warranty, you cannot agree to the terms and conditions set forth, return the unused book with unopened disc to the place where you purchased it for a refund.**

### License:

The enclosed software is copyrighted by the copyright holder(s) indicated on the software disc. You are licensed to copy the software onto a single computer for use by a single user and to a backup disc. You may not reproduce, make copies, or distribute copies or rent or lease the software in whole or in part, except with written permission of the copyright holder(s). You may transfer the enclosed disc only together with this license, and only if you destroy all other copies of the software and the transferee agrees to the terms of the license. You may not decompile, reverse assemble, or reverse engineer the software.

### Notice of Limited Warranty:

The enclosed disc is warranted by Thomson Course Technology PTR to be free of physical defects in materials and workmanship for a period of sixty (60) days from end user's purchase of the book/disc combination. During the sixty-day term of the limited warranty, Thomson Course Technology PTR will provide a replacement disc upon the return of a defective disc.

### Limited Liability:

THE SOLE REMEDY FOR BREACH OF THIS LIMITED WARRANTY SHALL CONSIST ENTIRELY OF REPLACEMENT OF THE DEFECTIVE DISC. IN NO EVENT SHALL THOMSON COURSE TECHNOLOGY PTR OR THE AUTHOR BE LIABLE FOR ANY OTHER DAMAGES, INCLUDING LOSS OR CORRUPTION OF DATA, CHANGES IN THE FUNCTIONAL CHARACTERISTICS OF THE HARDWARE OR OPERATING SYSTEM, DELETERIOUS INTERACTION WITH OTHER SOFTWARE, OR ANY OTHER SPECIAL, INCIDENTAL, OR CONSEQUENTIAL DAMAGES THAT MAY ARISE, EVEN IF THOMSON COURSE TECHNOLOGY PTR AND/OR THE AUTHOR HAS PREVIOUSLY BEEN NOTIFIED THAT THE POSSIBILITY OF SUCH DAMAGES EXISTS.

### Disclaimer of Warranties:

THOMSON COURSE TECHNOLOGY PTR AND THE AUTHOR SPECIFICALLY DISCLAIM ANY AND ALL OTHER WARRANTIES, EITHER EXPRESS OR IMPLIED, INCLUDING WARRANTIES OF MERCHANTABILITY, SUITABILITY TO A PARTICULAR TASK OR PURPOSE, OR FREEDOM FROM ERRORS. SOME STATES DO NOT ALLOW FOR EXCLUSION OF IMPLIED WARRANTIES OR LIMITATION OF INCIDENTAL OR CONSEQUENTIAL DAMAGES, SO THESE LIMITATIONS MIGHT NOT APPLY TO YOU.

### Other:

This Agreement is governed by the laws of the State of Massachusetts without regard to choice of law principles. The United Convention of Contracts for the International Sale of Goods is specifically disclaimed. This Agreement constitutes the entire agreement between you and Thomson Course Technology PTR regarding use of the software.